NORTH CAROLINA
REAL ESTATE MANUAL

Patrick K. Hetrick

Patricia A. Moylan

Larry A. Outlaw

NORTH CAROLINA REAL ESTATE COMMISSION

NORTH CAROLINA REAL ESTATE MANUAL

In Memoriam
This edition is dedicated
to former principal author,
Larry A. Outlaw
1944 - 2015

ISBN 978-0-9864465-1-1

Initial Printing August, 2017

Printed in the United States by: West Publishing Corp
610 Opperman Drive
Eagan, Minnesota 55123

TABLE OF CONTENTS

PREFACE

ABOUT THIS MANUAL

The *North Carolina Real Estate Manual* is published by the North Carolina Real Estate Commission, an independent state regulatory licensing agency. This *Manual* addresses the basics of North Carolina real estate law and real estate brokerage practice. It is intended to serve both as the textbook for the real estate broker postlicensing courses and as a reference book for real estate licensees, as well as real estate attorneys, instructors, or anyone else interested in real estate law and brokerage practice.

All rights to this publication belong to the North Carolina Real Estate Commission, which self-publishes the *Manual* to make it available to licensees, postlicensing course students, and the public at a reasonable cost. Revenues from *Manual* sales are used to defray the cost of development, publication, distribution, and continuing revisions. For decades, the Commission has engaged the services of author Patrick K. Hetrick on a consulting basis. Larry A. Outlaw was also a principal author, contributing enormously to these materials during his thirty-five year tenure as the Commission's Director of Education and Licensing, retiring in 2014.

The *Manual* evolved from the Commission's text *North Carolina Real Estate for Brokers and Salesmen*, Fourth Edition, by Patrick K. Hetrick and Larry A. Outlaw (Prentice Hall, Inc., 1994), that was replaced in 2000 by the first edition of the *Manual*. The original text of the former book was initially prepared for the Commission by Dr. James A. Webster, Jr. of the Wake Forest University School of Law and published in 1974. After Dr. Webster's death in 1974, subsequent editions were produced for the Commission by Messrs. Hetrick and Outlaw.

The authors have attempted to eliminate as much as reasonably possible the use of masculine personal pronouns in deference to the many women who are in the real estate business. Unfortunately, the English language has not yet developed a set of gender neutral personal pronouns, and the traditional use of masculine personal pronouns has been retained in some instances to prevent making the language of the text extremely cumbersome.

The authors are privileged to have been entrusted with the important task of preparing this valuable text and reference manual and we hope that readers will find it informative and useful.

THE REAL ESTATE COMMISSION

The North Carolina Real Estate Commission is an independent state governmental agency responsible for the licensing and regulation of real estate brokers, that is licensed persons and business entities who assist others in the sale, purchase, lease or exchange of real estate for compensation.

The offices of the Commission are located at 1313 Navaho Drive, Raleigh, North Carolina. The mailing address, telephone number and web site are shown below.

North Carolina Real Estate Commission
P.O. Box 17100
Raleigh, North Carolina 27619-7100
Telephone: (919) 875-3700
Web site: *www.ncrec.gov*

The Commission operates under the direction of nine Commission members who are appointed as follows: seven by the Governor; one by the General Assembly upon the recommendation of the Speaker of the State House of Representatives; and one by the General Assembly upon the recommendation of the President *Pro Tempore* of the State Senate. The Commission's daily operations are conducted by a staff employed by the Commission. The members of the Commission and the Commission's Executive Director at the time this edition is published are listed below.

Commission Members

Robert J. Ramseur, Jr., Raleigh, Chairman
Anna Gregory Wagoner, Winston-Salem, Vice Chair
George Bell, Winston-Salem
L. S. "Cindy" Chandler, Charlotte
Leonard H. "Tony" Craver, Jr., Durham
Judy F. Greenhill, Hickory
Thomas R. Lawing, Jr. Charlotte
James Sherrill, Fayetteville
Patrice Willetts, Wilmington

Executive Director

Miriam J. Baer

THE AUTHORS

Patrick K. Hetrick, B.S., J.D.

Patrick K. Hetrick is a retired professor emeritus at the Norman Adrian Wiggins School of Law, Campbell University, where he served as dean and taught real estate law for nearly four decades. He is a *magna cum laude* graduate of the Marquette University School of Law, where he also was on the law faculty and was Associate University Legal Counsel before moving to North Carolina. Professor Hetrick's public service and professional activities have been numerous. He is a member of the American College of Real Estate Lawyers, has served on the North Carolina General Statutes Commission, and on numerous committees of the North Carolina Bar Association and the American Bar Association.He has taught well over one hundred continuing legal education programs. Recognized as a leading authority on North Carolina real property law, Professor Hetrick was for years the co-revising author of a two-volume treatise for attorneys, *Webster's Real Estate Law in North Carolina,* (Sixth Edition, 2011, LexisNexis Group). Professor Hetrick has been a principal author of the *North Carolina Real Estate Manual,* as he was for its predecessor publication, *North Carolina Real Estate for Brokers and Salesmen.*

Larry A. Outlaw, B.A., J.D.

Larry A. Outlaw was Director of Education and Licensing for the North Carolina Real Estate Commission from 1979 until his retirement in February 2014. A graduate of Davidson College and the University of North Carolina School of Law, he was a licensed real estate broker and a licensed attorney in North Carolina. Mr. Outlaw was responsible for the administration of education, examination, and licensing programs for the Commission. He served on numerous committees of the Association of Real Estate License Law Officials and the Real Estate Educators Association, and was president of the latter organization in 1990-91. Mr. Outlaw also was co-author of this *Manual's* predecessor publication, *North Carolina Real Estate for Brokers and Salesmen.*

Patricia A. Moylan, B.A., J.D.

Patricia A. Moylan has served as the Legal Education Officer for the North Carolina Real Estate Commission since joining the Commission staff in 1999. Ms. Moylan is an honors graduate of the University of North Carolina and earned her law degree from the University of Toledo College of Law. She was actively engaged in the practice of law for two decades in North Carolina and Ohio prior to joining the Commission staff. Included among Ms. Moylan's duties at the Commission is responsibility for co-authoring this *Manual,* developing, coordinating, and teaching the Commission's *Broker-in-Charge Course,* and assisting in developing other educational materials, such as the annual mandatory General *Update* course.

ACKNOWLEDGMENTS

The North Carolina Real Estate Commission wishes to acknowledge the persons below for their contributions to the *North Carolina Real Estate Manual* and to express its appreciation for sharing their insights and knowledge.

Garth K. Dunklin, B.A. J.D., CCIM

Mr. Dunklin first drafted the chapter on "Commercial Real Estate Brokerage" for the *Manual* in 2000. Mr. Dunklin is a graduate of the University of North Carolina at Chapel Hill (Morehead Scholar, Phi Beta Kappa) and the University of North Carolina at Chapel Hill School of Law. He is a practicing real estate attorney and a licensed commercial real estate broker in Charlotte. Mr. Dunklin holds the prestigious CCIM designation and is a North Carolina State Bar Board Certified Specialist in Real Property Law-Residential, Business, Commercial and Industrial Transactions.

Robert L. Forshaw B.A .

Mr. Forshaw, the Commission's Publications Officer, has again devoted many hours to preparing the *Manual* for publication. His hard work, patience, and cooperation are greatly appreciated by the authors. He is primarily responsible for managing the Real Estate Commission's publications and for editing the award-winning *Real Estate Bulletin*.

Everett "Vic" Knight, B.S.

Mr. Knight contributed substantially to the significant revisions to the chapter on "Real Estate Valuation" in the 2013-2014 edition of the *Manual* and graciously reviewed and commented upon updates to that chapter for this edition. Mr. Knight, a graduate of North Carolina State University, is a certified real estate appraiser and owner of Chapel Hill Appraisals and Consultants. He has extensive experience as a real estate broker in sales and property management and previously served as Vice Chairman and Chairman of the North Carolina Real Estate Commission. For decades, Mr. Knight has actively served the local, state, and national REALTOR® organizations as well as serving as chair of NAR's Appraisal Committee and on the Board of Trustees of the Appraisal Foundation.

North Carolina Association of REALTORS®
North Carolina Bar Association

These associations graciously consented to the reproduction in this *Manual* of many of their contract and related forms for illustrative purposes and the North Carolina Real Estate Commission sincerely appreciates their cooperation in this matter.

1 | PROPERTY OWNERSHIP

Real estate brokers must understand basic real property law. This chapter discusses basic legal concepts of property, the difference between real and personal property, estates in real property, and different forms of real property ownership. Real estate brokers must apply this knowledge daily when working with consumers.

THE CONCEPT OF PROPERTY

Collectively, "property" is a legal concept defining the rights and interests a person has in things. **Property** is often referred to as a **"bundle of legal rights"** or a *bundle of sticks.*[1] Each stick in the bundle represents a different legal right. Property rights can include the exclusive ability to own, possess, use, or dispose of things. Property also includes nonphysical legal rights and interests, such as an easement right-of-way or the right to certain profits from land.

REAL PROPERTY

The history of property law extends back hundreds of years, and historical terminology still infiltrates property law. Older documents referred to "lands, tenements, and hereditaments," but today the terms "real property," "real estate," and "realty" are used interchangeably.

Real property includes (1) the soil, (2) things growing naturally on the soil, (3) minerals and water beneath the surface of the soil, (4) airspace above the soil (so far as it may be reasonably necessary for use or enjoyment of the surface), and (5) things that have been affixed to the soil (such as houses, buildings, barns, or fences) with the legal intent of becoming a permanent addition or improvement on the land.[2]

Rights of Real Property Owners

A real property owner not only owns the physical land, but also enjoys "rights" by virtue of ownership. These rights include:

- *Right to Exclusive Possession and Use.* An owner has the exclusive right to occupy and use their property in any manner permitted by law. This right of possession and use is sometimes called the "right of enjoyment." An owner who leases property temporarily transfers the right to possess the property to the lessee/tenant. If a proposed use of the property is prohibited by zoning regulations or private restrictions, then that use is illegal.

- *Right to Profits.* An owner has the right to any profits derived from the use of the property unless those rights have been transferred to another party.

- *Right to Transfer Ownership or Interests.* An owner can (1) transfer ownership of property by deed (sale or gift) or devise the property by will, (2) rent or lease property, or (3) transfer, temporarily or permanently, other "interests" or "rights" in the property. For example, an owner might convey an easement right-of-way or mineral rights to the property.

- *Right to Mortgage the Property.* The owner has the right to mortgage the property as security for the payment of a debt.

Appurtenances

In addition to basic real property rights, an owner is entitled to "appurtenances" or "appurtenant rights." *An **appurtenance** is a right, privilege, or interest that passes as an incident of real property ownership.* Appurtenances are often said to "run with the land," and transfer documents generally provide for the transfer of the property "with all rights appurtenant thereto." Examples of appurtenances or appurtenant rights include those below.

A. Subsurface Rights

Land ownership includes owning any minerals or water beneath the surface. A landowner may use water from underground rivers or reservoirs under their property and may also remove minerals, oil, and gas from the subsurface. Once removed, minerals become personal property. Mining rights for subsurface minerals, oil, and gas can be conveyed separately from full ownership of the land. Conversely, full ownership of the surface rights can be conveyed with the grantor reserving subsurface mineral rights.

B. Air Rights

Land ownership includes the airspace above the land. Ownership of such airspace is protected only to the extent of actual or potential use of that airspace. Modern law allows public use of airspace for transportation purposes. A landowner can obtain legal relief from aircraft flights over their land only when flights repeatedly and materially interfere with the landowner's possession, use, and enjoyment of the property.

C. Right to Lateral Support

Landowners also have the right of **lateral support** – that is, the right to have the sides of their land naturally supported by the lands of adjacent owners. Neighboring landowners may not use their lands in a way that causes an adjacent landowner's property to sink.

D. Right to Subjacent Support

Like lateral support, landowners may require **subjacent support.** Where one party owns the land's surface and another owns (or has the right to use or mine) the subsurface, the surface owner has the right to have the land supported from below.

E. Water Rights

Land ownership may also entail the right to use adjacent bodies of water. The extent of this right depends on the nature of the body of water. Bodies of water in North Carolina are classified either as **navigable** or **nonnavigable waterways**. Navigable waterways can be traveled by a vessel. North Carolina law very broadly defines the term "navigable waters" to include all of the ocean and sound waters, every major river, most major creeks, and most lakes.

Where land borders on a **navigable** body of water, ownership of the land under the water belongs to the state of North Carolina under the *public trust doctrine,* not to the bordering owner. Only the banks of navigable waters are private property, and special rules apply to littoral property, discussed shortly.

Nonnavigable waterways are bodies of water that vessels generally cannot travel and include smaller creeks, ponds, and man-made lakes. If the banks of a nonnavigable stream are owned by different persons (such as opposing sides of the stream), each owner normally owns to the middle of the waterway. Under current North Carolina law, nonnavigable waterways are extremely rare.

Riparian Rights

Riparian land is land that borders a body of water that typically does not have tides, such as rivers, streams, and lakes. **Riparian rights** traditionally include water access, fishing and swimming rights, and, subject to state and federal law, the right to build piers and other water structures. North Carolina owners of riparian land bordering nonnavigable bodies of water can use the water up to the center of the water/waterway. Landowners bordering navigable waterways, such as rivers, have rights of possession and use only to the banks of the river. In North Carolina, the public maintains a right of travel along navigable waterways, which are considered public highways.

Riparian rights can never harm other owners of riparian land or impede or alter the flow of the body of water. A prospective purchaser with questions about the nature and extent of riparian rights should consult an attorney.[3]

Littoral Rights

Rights of real property owners bordering the ocean or other tidal waters are known as littoral rights. **Littoral rights** entitle the owner to use the tidal body, but ownership ends at the average high-water mark. The strip of land between the high- and low-tide lines, known as the "foreshore" area, is owned by the State of North Carolina under the "public trust" doctrine. A littoral owner of land bordering the ocean has rights to use the foreshore so long as the use complies with applicable laws, regulations, and rights of the public. Although the public has rights to use the foreshore and ocean itself, they are not entitled to cross the private property of littoral owners without first obtaining a license or easement for ocean access. Beach renourishment projects are common in North Carolina and can impact the property rights of littoral owners. A consumer considering the purchase of littoral property on a renourished beach should be encouraged to consult an attorney.

Shifting Boundaries

Forces of nature can change riparian land boundaries. To understand how this occurs, you must understand the following terms.

- **Accretion** is an increase in the amount of riparian land caused by natural forces (usually water flows or tides) *gradually* depositing soil onto the riparian land formerly covered by water, thereby expanding the boundary of the riparian land.

- **Reliction** is similar to accretion in that there is a *gradual* increase in the riparian land, but the increase is caused by the *permanent* gradual *recession* of a body of water.

- **Erosion** is the *gradual* loss or depletion of riparian land by the action of water (including tidal flows). Thus, erosion is the opposite of accretion.

- **Avulsion** is the *sudden* gain **or** loss of riparian land caused by powerful natural forces like floods or hurricanes.

PERSONAL PROPERTY

Simply defined, **personal property** is all property that is not real property. Personal property's primary characteristic is movability. Classification as real property or personal property determines what laws apply. For instance, personal property is governed in large part by the **Uniform Commercial Code (UCC)**, a uniform act dealing with the sale, financing, and leasing of personal property.[4] In contrast, the law of real property is based on centuries of English common law combined with modern statutes and regulations dealing with real property as opposed to personal property.

The line between real and personal property is sometimes blurred with certain objects that appear to fit into both categories. Real estate law has special categories and tests, including the law of "fixtures," to determine whether an item is personal or real property.

FRUITS OF THE SOIL

For example, plants may be classified as either real or personal property. Often called "fruits of the soil," property law classifies plants as either "fructus naturales" or "fructus industriales." *Fructus naturales* are uncultivated plants, crops, and perennial plantings, such as trees, grasses, and bushes. So long as fructus naturales remain planted, they transfer with the land as part of the real property. Only when fructus naturales are severed from the land do they become personal property.

In contrast, *fructus industriales*, or "fruits of industry," are products or benefits produced by the labor or industry of a person, rather than nature. Also known as **emblements**, *cultivated* crops and vegetable products are examples of fructus industriales and are generally considered personal property.[5] A broker representing a seller or purchaser of a farm with growing crops should clarify the legal status of crops that will not be harvested prior to closing.

FIXTURES

A *fixture* is a thing or object that was originally personal property but is now attached to real property in a more or less permanent manner. Legally, the object becomes part of the real property and belongs to the owner of the real property to which it is attached. For instance, bricks, stone, or lumber are initially personal property, but when used to construct a building, they become part of the real property. A fixture automatically transfers with the property unless agreed otherwise.[6]

However, not every attachment of personal property to the land or the buildings thereon become real property. The question frequently arises in real estate transactions: Is a particular item attached to the land a fixture and thus it passes with the land? What if a seller removes an item that the buyer thought should transfer with the real property? Common misunderstandings include swing sets, storage sheds, grain storage bins, fireplace screens and utensils, satellite dishes, automatic garage door openers, garden fountains and decorative statues, or almost any item that can be carried away. If the item taken is "personal property," the seller may take it unless it is expressly included in the sales contract. If, however, the item is a "fixture," it will automatically transfer with the real property unless it is *specifically excluded* from transfer in the sales contract.

The parties' intentions concerning items that will or will not transfer with the real property should be clearly set out in writing. Another way to avoid misunderstandings is to have the seller remove items they want to retain before showing the property to prospective purchasers. Fortunately, the standard residential offer to purchase and contract form lists property that will automatically transfer with the real property as fixtures, unless the parties specifically identify items that will not convey because the seller is removing them. There is no presumption that any personal property will automatically transfer with the real property.

Fixture Test

To determine whether something is a fixture, you apply a four-part legal test, known as the "total circumstances test." All four parts of the test must be met, although generally the intention prong receives the greatest weight and importance. If all four factors are satisfied, the attached item will be a fixture. The factors are:

- Intention of the annexor/attacher
- Character of the attachment
- Adaptability of item to use of the land
- Relationship of the annexor to the real property

1. Intention of the annexor. The ultimate question to ask when determining if an item is a fixture is: *Did the person attaching the item to the land intend to make a permanent annexation?* If the owner of the real property attaches personal property to the land with the intent that it be permanent, the item becomes a fixture and part of the real property to which it is attached. It will automatically transfer with the real property, unless the sales contract provides otherwise. *Express intentions will control,* **even if the item is a fixture under the total circumstances test.**

> *Example:* Sam Seller and Bob Buyer enter into a valid contract to convey Sam's residence to Bob. The contract contains the following provision: "The solar collector panels on the roof of the garage are not included with this property and shall be removed by Seller prior to the real estate closing. Seller agrees to repair any roof shingles damaged by such removal." Even though solar panels attached to a roof would normally be treated as fixtures, Seller's express intention to the contrary was communicated and agreed to by Buyer. For purposes of this real estate sale, the solar panels will be treated as personal property.

The intention that the law requires is objective, not subjective; intention will be determined from surrounding circumstances, not from unexpressed thoughts going through the mind of the person who attached the item.

> *Example:* Mary's husband gives her a reproduction of an antique corner cabinet as an anniversary gift that she vows to keep forever. The cabinet is bolted into the dining room walls, and molding that matches the ceiling molding is nailed to the top of the corner cabinet and painted to match the other wall molding. Two years later, Mary and her husband contract to sell the house. The contract does not mention the corner cabinet. The sellers remove the corner cabinet prior to closing and, upon discovery, the new purchaser is outraged. Based on the circumstances at the time the purchaser saw the property and made the offer, the purchaser

could justifiably conclude the cabinet was a fixture. If Mary and her husband wanted to take the corner cabinet with them, they should have expressly excluded it in the sales contract or removed it prior to listing the property for sale.

2. Relationship of the annexor. The relationship of the party attaching (annexing) personal property to the real property is important. The more interest the annexing party has in the real property, the more likely the attached item will be a fixture. Typically, attachment of personal property by a real property **owner** makes the attached item part of the real property, and the attached item will pass as part of the real property in any transfer unless specifically excluded in the transfer document.

> *Example:* A residential property owner purchases a storage shed, lays a cement foundation in his back yard, and bolts the shed to the foundation. Later, the owner sells the residential property to a buyer; the sales contract says nothing about the shed. After the closing, the buyer is shocked to discover that the seller has removed the storage shed, leaving only the foundation in the yard. Even if the shed is easily removable, it is a fixture that should have transferred automatically to the buyer, unless expressly excluded in the sales contract.

Because an owner has a *permanent* interest in real property, an owner's annexation of personal property is presumed to be for the permanent improvement of the real property. However, when the annexor only has a *temporary* interest in the real property, such as a tenant renting residential property, the attachment of personal property by the tenant is **not** presumed to be for the permanent benefit of the real property. To the contrary, attachment of personal property *by a tenant* is presumed to be for the tenant's temporary benefit during his tenancy.

> *Example:* A tenant under a two-year lease of residential property attaches a storage shed to a cement foundation. At the end of the lease, the tenant removes the storage shed and cement foundation. The shed did not become a fixture, because the tenant had the right to occupy the property during the lease term but never had any ownership interest in the real property.

3. Method of annexation. This part of the *total circumstances test* focuses on how the item was annexed to the real property. Was the method of attachment more or less permanent?

> *Example:* A buyer agrees to purchase a historic farm house on five acres of land. The land is bounded by an old split-rail fence built of rails resting upon one another in a zigzag fashion. The contract does not mention the fence. Even though the fence is resting on but not physically attached to the land, the method of attachment is more or less permanent, and it would be a fixture under the total circumstances test.

4. Adaptation to real estate. This factor looks at whether the item was customized to fit specifically with the use and purpose of the real property.

> *Example:* A homeowner cuts a hole in the family room wall and installs a large window air conditioning unit in the opening. While the unit is not attached to the wall in any substantial way and could be easily removed, the special adaptability of the unit to the use of the home and the custom-made opening indicates that it is a fixture. (If the window unit is simply placed in an open window, it would remain personal property.)

Trade Fixtures

Trade fixtures are items of personal property attached to real property by a tenant for use in the tenant's trade or business. Trade fixtures are treated completely differently than the law of fixtures discussed above. *When a tenant attaches a "trade fixture" to leased property to use in a trade or business, the tenant may remove the trade fixture any time prior to lease termination, as long as its removal does not materially injure the leased property.*[7] Common examples of trade fixtures are: shelving and display racks, outdoor advertising signs, machinery and equipment, specialized equipment in a restaurant or bar, and storage tanks.

> *Example:* A tenant rents commercial space for a five-year term to operate a bookstore. The tenant installs bookshelves and counters bolted to the floor and walls. Prior to lease termination, the tenant removes all installed items and returns the leased space to its original condition. Because they are trade fixtures, the tenant has the right to remove them.

The general presumption is that trade fixtures may be removed unless the lease expressly prohibits removal. A prospective tenant should carefully review proposed lease terms prior to agreeing to lease property.

Agricultural Fixtures

Agricultural fixtures are items placed on real property by tenant farmers for agricultural purposes. While common law held that agricultural fixtures became part of the real property and could not be removed at the end of the lease term, the modern trend is to treat agricultural fixtures the same as trade fixtures.[8] Prospective agricultural tenants should carefully review proposed lease terms prior to agreeing to lease and should address the right of removal.

Security Interests in Fixtures under the UCC

The North Carolina Uniform Commercial Code (UCC) has numerous provisions concerning fixtures. Under the UCC, an item attached to real estate may nonetheless be treated as personal property by a creditor.

> *Example:* A homeowner purchased a $6,000 heat pump on credit and gave the creditor a security interest in the heat pump. One year later, the homeowner sells the home to a buyer, but there is still $4,500 owed on the heat pump. Subsequently, the former homeowner stops making payments on the heat pump. The creditor has a right to remove the heat pump by following proper procedures under the UCC.

A security interest is a creditor's right to take property pledged as collateral to secure a borrower's promise to repay a debt. Under the UCC, an item that appears to be part of the real estate will be treated as personal property under some circumstances. By complying with the UCC, a creditor may remove what otherwise is a fixture if a borrower defaults in repaying the debt, even though the item is attached to the real property.[9] Legal questions about security interests and their priorities in specific situations should be referred to an attorney. Why does a real estate broker need to be aware of this potential issue? A homeowner who sells a home that includes a fixture with an outstanding security interest places the new homeowner at risk. Real estate brokers must realize that a fixture purchased on credit and pledged as security for the debt remains personal property until the debt is paid in full.[10] A title search by an attorney should reveal any outstanding security interests.

IMPROVEMENTS

An "**improvement**" is an addition to or a change in condition of land that amounts to more than mere repairs or replacement and is intended to enhance the land's value, beauty, or utility or to adapt it for new or additional purposes.[11] An improvement may be further categorized as an "improvement on land" or an "improvement to land," depending on context. Common examples of *"improvements **on** land"* are permanent structures such as buildings, walls, fences, and paved driveways. Examples of *"improvements **to** land"* include grading, drainage ditches, utility connections, sidewalks, curbs, and gutters. An improvement does **not** include additions or alterations that are merely "repairs" or "replacement."

Brokers will also encounter the terms "**improved land**" or "**improved lot**." These terms can have two meanings, namely: 1) land on which "improvements" such as buildings have been constructed, or 2) land which has been prepared ("improved") for further development by grading, draining, installing utility connections, or similar actions. Brokers encountering these terms must determine the appropriate meaning in each situation.

MANUFACTURED HOMES

The term "**manufactured home**" is defined for some purposes by North Carolina statute.[12] N.C. Gen. Stat. §143-143.9(6) defines "manufactured home" as:

> A structure, transportable in one or more sections, which, in the traveling mode, is eight feet or more in width or is 40 feet or more in length, or when erected on site, is 320 or more square feet, and which is built on a permanent chassis and designed to be used as a dwelling with or without a permanent foundation when connected to the required utilities, and includes the plumbing, heating, air conditioning and electrical systems contained therein.

Manufactured homes (sometimes called mobile homes) *can be classified as* <u>either</u> *real property or personal property.* A manufactured home becomes real property when the moving hitch, wheels, and axles are removed, and it has been placed on a permanent foundation on land owned by the manufactured home's owner. If these statutory requirements are *not* met, a manufactured home is categorized as "tangible personal property"[13] and is listed and taxed as other kinds of personal property.[14]

Once a manufactured home previously titled under the motor vehicle laws meets the statutory definition of "real property," the owner must submit an affidavit to the Division of Motor Vehicles (Form MVR-46G) stating that the moving hitch, wheels, and axles of the manufactured home have been removed; that it has been placed upon a permanent foundation; and that it is now considered real property.[15] Once the title has been canceled by DMV, the affidavit must be recorded in the register of deeds office of the county where the real property is located.[16] Once recorded, the manufactured home exists as an "improvement" on real property for purposes of the recording act, real estate conveyancing rules, and mortgages and lien laws.[17]

ESTATES IN REAL PROPERTY

The amount and kind of interest an owner holds in real property is known as an "estate in land." Estates in real property are divided into two main categories: **freehold estates** and **nonfreehold estates**.

Freehold Estates	**Nonfreehold Estates (Leases)**
• Estates of Inheritance at Will	• Estate for Years
• Defeasible Fee States	• Estate at Will
• Defeasible Fee Estates	• Estate from Period to Period
• Estate for the Life of Another	• Estate at Sufferance
• Estates <u>Not</u> of Inheritance	
• Conventional Life States	
• Marital Life Estates	

FREEHOLD ESTATES

*Any interest in real property that lasts for at least a lifetime is classified as a **freehold estate**.* Freehold estates are divided into **estates of inheritance** or **estates not of inheritance**. Estates of inheritance may continue beyond the life of the owner and transfer under the owner's will or by intestate succession (if the owner dies without a will). Estates not of inheritance extend only for the term of the holder's life.

Estates of Inheritance

Most *"estates of inheritance"* are *"fee estates"* and are inheritable by the owner's heirs as specified by will or law. A brief description of these estates follows.

Fee Simple Absolute Estate

The **fee simple absolute estate** (often referred to as a " fee simple") is the ultimate form of land ownership. It is by far the most desired and common form of real property ownership in the United States. Fee simple absolute estates are potentially infinite in duration. An owner has the unconditional power to transfer ownership to whomever they wish during the owner's life or under the owner's will or by intestate succession at death. Fee simple absolute owners may use the property however they wish, as long as the use is permitted under applicable governmental restrictions, private restrictions, and the rights of others.[18]

Historically, to create a fee simple absolute, the conveyance language included the words "and his/her heirs." However, in North Carolina and many states, a fee simple absolute is presumed to be created in the grantee, regardless of whether "heirs" language is included. Thus, a fee simple absolute owner may transfer his interest by deed to: 1) "Mildred Smith," or 2) "Mildred Smith and her heirs," and Mildred will receive a fee simple interest under either deed.

Defeasible Fee Simple Estates

Estates of inheritance can also be created with conditions or limitations on the owner's title. These estates are inferior to the fee simple absolute because the owner's estate may terminate if the condition does or does not occur. Thus, these estates are referred to as fee simple defeasible estates or "*defeasible fees.*" The most common defeasible fees are the *fee simple determinable* and the *fee simple subject to a condition subsequent.* While different, both estates are terminable/revocable by the grantor (or the grantor's heirs) if the specified condition does or does not occur.

In a *fee simple determinable*, the grantor conveys property to Y "for so long as" some limiting event does or does not occur. As long as the condition does not happen, the grantee has an inheritable estate and is the owner. The grantor, however, holds an interest in the property because *if the condition or limitation does or does not occur, then the property reverts automatically to the grantor or the grantor's estate.* The grantor's interest in a fee simple determinable is called a "*possibility of reverter*," because title to the property may revert back to the grantor.

> *Example:* A grantor deeds land to a school district "for so long as the school district maintains a public elementary school on the parcel and, if it ceases to do so, this estate shall end immediately." The district has a fee simple determinable estate. If at some point the district does not maintain a public elementary school on the parcel, then title to the land reverts back to the grantor or his/her heirs.

A *fee simple subject to a condition subsequent* is created by the grantor through language that limits a grantee's use of or activities on the land.

> *Example:* A grantor deeds land to a grantee and adds: "But if the grantee ever ceases to use the land for agricultural purposes, then the grantor has the right to re-enter the land and terminate the grantee's estate."

How do these two defeasible fees differ? The chief difference is that a fee simple determinable terminates *automatically* upon the happening of the limiting event and title reverts to the grantor or his/her heirs, while a fee simple subject to condition subsequent terminates only if the grantor (or the grantor's heirs, if the grantor is deceased) takes action to regain possession and terminate the grantee's estate. The grantor's interest in a fee simple subject to a condition subsequent is called a **right of re-entry** or **power of termination.** Often, legal action to regain possession will be necessary.[19]

Estate for the Life of Another ("Pur Autre Vie")

Most estates of inheritance are fee estates. A rarely encountered exception is an estate known as an *estate for the life of another* (or a life estate *pur autre vie,* i.e., literally "for the life of another" in French). The duration of a life estate *pur autre vie* is <u>not</u> based on the life of the person who holds the estate, but instead it lasts as long as a named third party lives, referred to as "the measuring life." To create such a life estate, the grantor would convey the property "to A for the life of B." A, the life tenant, only has the right to use and possess the property while B, the measuring life, is alive; at B's death, A, if still living, must vacate the property and it would pass to whomever the grantor named as grantee after A. Estates for the life of another are rarely encountered in modern brokerage practice, but if it arises, brokers should recommend that the consumer seek legal advice.

Estates NOT of Inheritance (Life Estates)

All freehold estates that are not inheritable are **life estates**. A life estate is an estate for the duration of the life or lives of one or more persons. The holder of a life estate is called the "life tenant." Life estates may be "conventional" life estates created by an intentional act or "marital" life estates created by law.

Conventional Life Estate[20]

The most common life estate is the **conventional life estate** created by express transfer of land ("To A for life") granting A ownership for the duration of A's own life. If the conveyance fails to specify who takes title after termination of the life estate, a **reversion** of the property to the grantor occurs. If the grantor specifies to whom the real property will go upon the death of the life tenant, that person holds a future interest, called a **remainder**, and will take title and possession after the life tenant's death. Because life estates are valuable tools in estate planning, they may be encountered occasionally by a broker, who should recommend that the parties consult an attorney, if they have any questions.

Marital Life Estate

In North Carolina, **marital life estates** arise by law when a married person owning real property solely in his or her name (without the spouse having a title interest) dies survived by a spouse. The statute gives the surviving spouse *the option to take a life estate of one-third in value of all the real estate the deceased spouse owned during the marriage (even if not owned at death)* instead of anything the spouse would otherwise receive by inheritance from the deceased spouse. However, the untitled spouse may not assert a marital interest claim as to real property for which the untitled spouse joined in signing the conveyance document. The reason that untitled spouses should always sign the conveyance deed is to extinguish this marital life estate.

NONFREEHOLD ESTATES (LANDLORD & TENANT)

Nonfreehold estates, or **leasehold estates**, include *estates for years, periodic estates or tenancies* (from year to year, month to month, week to week,), *estates at will*, and *estates at sufferance*. Nonfreehold estates held by a tenant under residential landlord and tenant law are discussed in detail in Chapter 16.

OWNERSHIP OF REAL PROPERTY

Just as there are different estates in real property, there are also different forms of property ownership that brokers must understand. This section examines the different ways title to real property may be held by one or more persons.

Ownership in Severalty

A sole owner of real property owns the property in **severalty.** The term "severalty" is the legal term for "sole ownership," or simply ownership by one person alone without any other person being joined or connected with him/her in interest.

Concurrent Ownership[21]

Real property can be owned by two or more people simultaneously. This is called **concurrent ownership**, also commonly referred to as "co-ownership" or "cotenancy."

> *Example:* An owner of a farm dies leaving the farm to both his son and daughter. The son and daughter jointly own the entire farm, rather than separate and distinct parts of the farm. They are *concurrent* owners.

There are three types of concurrent ownership in North Carolina: **tenancy in common, joint tenancy,** and **tenancy by the entirety.** Hybrid forms of co-ownership in use today include **condominium ownership** (actually a combination of concurrent ownership with ownership in severalty), **townhouse ownership, cooperative ownership,** and **time share ownership.** These forms of concurrent ownership are briefly discussed in this section.

Tenancy in Common

The most common type of concurrent ownership in North Carolina is the **tenancy in common.** *A tenancy in common exists when two or more persons own undivided interests in the same land.* The co-owners are referred to as "tenants in common."

> *Example:* Dad conveys land to his two sons, Fred and Ned. Fred and Ned own the land as tenants in common, each having a 50% undivided interest in the whole.

Each tenant in common owns a separate but undivided interest in the land and each has an equal right to possession and use of the land. Tenants in common are not required to have equal shares and interests. One tenant could own a 95 percent undivided interest and the other a 5 percent undivided interest. A tenant in common may transfer his or her undivided property interest by any means (deed, sale, will, etc.) to any person at any time, without the consent of the other cotenants. This right to transfer may be restricted by terms of the deed or other agreement among the cotenants.

Additionally, there is *no right of survivorship* in a tenancy in common. Whenever a cotenant dies, his or her interest will pass according to the terms of a will or state intestacy laws, if no will exists. The deceased cotenant's interest will ***not*** automatically pass to the surviving cotenants.

> *Example:* Assume from the previous example where Fred and Ned are tenants in common that Fred sells one-half of his undivided interest to Marvin Jones, and Ned deeds his entire undivided interest to his five adult children: Chris, Susan, Mary, Frank, and Cheryl. The status of concurrent ownership of the former Smith farm is now as follows:
>
> | | |
> |---|---|
> | Fred = 25% undivided interest | Chris = 10% undivided interest |
> | Jones = 25% undivided interest | Susan = 10% undivided interest |
> | | Mary = 10% undivided interest |
> | | Frank = 10% undivided interest |
> | | Cheryl = 10% undivided interest |

Tenants in common hold undivided interests in land, and no cotenant can exclude another cotenant from possessing the property. Tenants in common also cannot claim portions of the property for their exclusive use. Each cotenant must pay taxes based on his or her interest. Each cotenant also has the right to force a partition of the land. A partition will terminate the tenancy in common either by dividing the property into separate parcels among the cotenants or by dividing proceeds from a partition sale among the cotenants based on their respective interests.[22]

Joint Tenancy

The significant difference between a joint tenancy and a tenancy in common is that joint tenants have a "right of survivorship," meaning that when one joint tenant dies, his/her share automatically passes to the surviving joint tenant or tenants without reference to any deed, will, or intestacy laws.

Example: A sister and brother purchase a beach cottage, taking title as joint tenants with the right of survivorship. The brother later dies. His undivided interest in the beach cottage *automatically* passes to and vests in his sister as the surviving joint tenant.

However, a joint tenancy may be destroyed by the unilateral action of any joint tenant while alive. Any joint tenant may choose to sell his/her interest in the property without the consent of the other joint tenants. Where there are only two joint tenants, the joint tenancy will be converted into a tenancy in common without survivorship if one of the two joint tenants transfers his/her interest to another person.

Example: Same facts as the preceding example except that the brother conveys his interest in the beach cottage to a nephew by warranty deed. Post transfer, the brother has no ownership interest in the beach cottage, and the sister and nephew each own an undivided 50% interest as *tenants in common* with no right of survivorship.

In many states, a joint tenancy may be created by transferring property to two or more named grantees "as joint tenants" without any additional language. However, **to create a joint tenancy in North Carolina, a deed or will must specifically state that the grantees take title "as joint tenants with right of survivorship."** If the magic words "with right of survivorship" are omitted and the *deed is merely to the grantees as "joint tenants," then only a tenancy in common is created under North Carolina law with no survivorship feature.*

The law in some jurisdictions requires joint tenants to hold equal undivided interests in the property. If two joint tenants own property in those jurisdictions, their undivided interests must be 50/50, three joint tenants must own 1/3 each, and so on. North Carolina once had this requirement but *eliminated* it in 2009 by revising the joint tenancy statute to allow joint tenants to hold *unequal ownership interests.*[23]

Example: Parents deed property to their daughter and son as joint tenants with right of survivorship, specifying that the son has a 25% undivided interest and the daughter has a 75% undivided interest. Because North Carolina law permits joint tenants to hold unequal interests, a valid joint tenancy has been created under North Carolina law.

If three or more joint tenants hold unequal shares and one of them dies, the share of the deceased joint tenant is divided among the surviving joint tenants according to their percentage interest and not equally.

Example: Oswald Owner deeds property "to Ann Able, Carol Cook, and Robert Cook, as joint tenants with right of survivorship, Ann to hold a 20% undivided interest, Carol to hold a 60% undivided interest, and Robert to hold a 20% undivided interest." If Ann dies, Carol and Robert remain joint tenants with right of survivorship. Based on their pro rata interests, Robert would receive 1/4 (20/80) and Carol would receive 3/4 (60/80) of Ann's 20%. Thus, Robert's final undivided interest in the property is 25% and Carol's is 75%.

Joint tenancy with right of survivorship interests are *presumed* to be equal *unless* the conveyance specifies an unequal ownership. Each joint tenant, like tenants in common, has a right to use and possess the property and may force a "partition" of the land. A partition terminates the joint tenancy and either divides the property itself among the joint tenants or divides the proceeds of a partition sale.

Tenancy by the Entirety

A ***tenancy by the entirety*** *is a form of concurrent ownership that is **only possible between legally married spouses.*** North Carolina law presumes that any conveyance by deed or will to a legally married couple creates a tenancy by the entirety unless the conveyance expressly states otherwise.[24]

> *Example:* An owner of real property conveys it "to Mary Smith and Bill Smith" as grantees. At the time of the conveyance, Mary and Bill are legally married. Under North Carolina law, <u>a tenancy by the entirety is created</u> even though that term is not included in the deed, nor does the deed identify Mary and Bill as being married.

A well-drafted deed will include the "tenancy by the entirety" term and the fact that Mary and Bill are married, but a tenancy by the entirety nevertheless is created by the simple language in the example above.

While tenancy by the entirety is the preferred and most common form of ownership for married couples in North Carolina, a married couple is not required under North Carolina law to hold property as tenants by the entirety. They may choose to own property either as tenants in common or as joint tenants with right of survivorship, but the conveyance or will must clearly state the alternate form of concurrent ownership to defeat the presumption of tenancy by the entirety.

Further, married persons are not required to own real property jointly; rather, each may acquire and hold real property individually, but the nontitled spouse will have a marital interest in the property as discussed under "Marital Life Estates," unless the nontitled spouse also signs a conveyance document. Understand as well that the subsequent marriage of parties does not convert property already owned into a tenancy by the entirety.

> *Example:* While engaged to marry, Tom and Nancy purchase a home in Asheville. They are both named as grantees on the deed. They marry one month later. Their marriage does not convert ownership of the home into a tenancy by the entirety because they were not legally married at the time they took title.

If Tom and Nancy want to own the property as tenants by the entirety, they must consult an attorney to prepare a deed in which they formally transfer the property from themselves as tenants in common or joint tenants to themselves as tenants by the entirety now that they are legally married.

An entirety tenancy differs from a tenancy in common or joint tenancy in several respects including that *neither* spouse can individually sever the concurrent ownership. A spouse is unable to individually transfer his or her interest or eliminate the other spouse's right of survivorship. Neither spouse may seek partition of the property so long as the entirety tenancy exists. Both spouses must consent to convey or transfer any interest in the property.

By law, each spouse enjoys an equal right to the control, use, possession, and income of a tenancy by the entirety. An entirety tenancy is *terminated* only by one of the following methods: 1) agreement of *both* spouses, 2) entry of a valid divorce decree terminating the marital relationship (which *automatically* converts the property into a tenancy in common), or 3) death of one or both spouses.

COMMON INTEREST COMMUNITY OWNERSHIP

The term "common interest community" encompasses several categories of property ownership including:

- Condominium Unit Ownership
- Townhouse Ownership
- Cooperative Ownership
- Planned Community Ownership

A "common interest community" is a real estate development in which the owners of individual lots or units have a legal obligation to financially support the upkeep of common areas and other community costs of operation such as liability insurance, management fees, and legal fees. Members of common interest communities pay dues and, if authorized, special assessments. Common interest communities are managed by groups of property or unit owners known as Home Owner Associations (HOAs) or Property Owner Associations (POAs) that are governed by traditional real property documents as well as entire chapters of the General Statutes.[25] While a majority of common interest communities are residential, mixed-use and commercial common interest communities are becoming commonplace.

Condominium Ownership

Condominiums, or condos, are a very popular form of real estate ownership in North Carolina today. The word "condominium" literally means "joint dominion" or "joint ownership." Only parts of condominium property are held jointly, and the remaining portions of the property are owned by individuals.[26]

Most North Carolina condominiums are governed by the **North Carolina Condominium Act**, Chapter 47C of the General Statutes. That Act covers important matters concerning the creation, management, and sale of condominiums. Of particular importance are the Act's consumer protection provisions discussed later in this section.

Characteristics of a Condominium

Condominium refers to property ownership where *a person owns a particular unit in a multi-unit structure or development but also shares ownership of the common areas as a tenant in common with all other unit owners. Common areas include the building(s), amenities, and land that make up the complex.* The boundaries of each individually owned unit are defined by the declaration creating the condominium and typically include the airspace within the unit but not the exterior walls. A unit may also include additional space such as a balcony, patio, or storage area. Even though a unit may be on an upper floor and not physically attached to land, legally it is still considered to be "real estate."

Ownership of all other non-unit areas, or common elements/areas, is shared by all unit owners. *The unit owners hold an undivided interest as tenants in common in the common areas subject to statutory guidelines.* The *common areas* include:

1. *all* parts of the building *other than* the units, including the basement, foundation, main walls, ceilings, floors, roof, halls, stairs, elevators, lobbies, etc.;
2. *all* installations for central services such as electricity, gas, water, heating, air conditioning, etc.;
3. the land under the buildings and *all* parking areas; and
4. community facilities intended for common use, such as a swimming pool, clubhouse, park, playground, greenway, garden, tennis court, etc.

Condominium ownership is not limited to residential properties but may also be used for business, commercial, or industrial properties. *A condominium unit owner's interest is similar to the interest of any other freehold estate in real property, and a condominium unit can be owned by two or more persons as concurrent owners.* A unit owner may sell or convey their interest as they please.

A condominium unit owner pays real property taxes as does any other property owner. Each unit and its percentage of undivided interest in the common areas is considered a "parcel" for tax purposes. Condominium property is managed through a *unit owners' association.* Each unit owner is automatically a voting member of the unit owners' association that is responsible for managing the common areas and has duties, powers, and obligations under the Condominium Act. Alternately, a property management company may be hired to handle these duties. Unit owners pay dues monthly, quarterly, or annually to the association to cover management and maintenance expenses. These fees may be increased as specified by both the Condominium Act and governing documents of the development. The association may also have the power to levy special assessments on unit owners for special projects and improvements.

Creation of a Condominium

The North Carolina Condominium Act sets the requirements to create a condominium. A condominium developer prepares a *declaration* describing the condominium in detail and records the declaration in the county register of deeds office. Under state law, the declaration must contain any "covenants, conditions, or restrictions" relating to the use of the property or to any rights reserved by the developer. Any listed covenants or restrictions will "run with the land," meaning that any transfer of a unit, whether from the developer or future unit owners, will be subject to such covenants, conditions, and restrictions. A developer must also record a detailed *plat* or *plan* providing a precise physical description of the condominium and other statutory information. Additionally, *bylaws* must be prepared for the internal management of the condominium development by the unit owners.

Consumer Protection Provisions in Condominium Act

The North Carolina Condominium Act includes certain consumer protection provisions for purchasers of units **created on or after October 1, 1986**. The major provisions and their impact on real estate brokers are discussed briefly below. Note: a developer must provide a public offering statement and allow a seven-day cancellation period not only when the purchaser is buying a condo unit physically located in North Carolina but also when the buyer is purchasing a condo unit located outside of North Carolina, if the buyer signed the purchase contract in North Carolina.

Public Offering Statement. Condominium developers must provide prospective purchasers of a new unit a copy of a public offering statement before a purchase contract is finalized. The public offering statement must contain information required by law about the condominium, including the purchaser's right to cancel the contract.

Purchaser's Right to Cancel. A buyer purchasing a new unit from a developer has an absolute right to cancel the purchase contract for any reason within seven (7) calendar days of signing the contract. A purchaser cannot be penalized for cancelling the contract within that seven day period and is entitled to a refund of any monies deposited. No conveyance of a unit pursuant to a purchase contract can be completed until the buyer's cancellation period has expired.

Resale Certificate. When a **unit owner** of a condominium resells the unit, the owner must provide a resale certificate to a prospective purchaser before conveying the unit. This certificate describes common expense assessments and any other fees payable by unit owners. Unlike a unit purchased from a developer, a purchaser does not have a cancellation right by law in a resale conveyance.

Warranties. Condominium purchasers are protected by the law of implied warranties. Unless specifically disclaimed, the seller of a condominium unit warrants that the premises are free from defects, constructed in a workmanlike manner, and usable for the purpose sold.

Townhouse Ownership

Townhouses are another popular form of property ownership. A townhouse development consists of a group of single family homes connected to another home by a common wall or walls. Each townhouse is individually owned. The entire group of townhouse unit owners may also be members of a homeowner association. If a townhouse development contains common areas, the association owns and maintains the common areas for the benefit of all.

Townhouses typically exhibit a "row house style" of architecture with a group or row of *two- to three-story units that are attached by common walls*. A townhouse development may also be part of a common interest community.

Unlike condominium ownership, *townhouse ownership includes a deed to the tract of land on which the townhouse is located*. The property boundaries typically include one or more common walls shared with an adjoining unit or units and may include a limited amount of yard space or an outside patio. In other cases, the homeowner's association will hold title to all land/space outside of the townhouse unit itself.

Rules on the use and maintenance of townhouse common areas are set forth in restrictive covenants that run with the land and bind all individual townhouse owners. These covenants specify the common-area rights of individual owners, provide for regular payment of fees to the homeowners' association, and authorize periodic assessments against townhouse owners as needed.

Townhouses and Condominiums Distinguished

At first glance, the typical townhouse development and condominium development may seem similar. Subtle legal differences, however, place the two developments into different categories.

1) A townhouse unit owner owns the unit in severalty, i.e., the physical structure (subject to the existence of party walls) and the plot of land upon which the unit rests. A condominium unit owner individually owns only the enclosed space within the condominium unit.

2) The common areas of townhouse developments in North Carolina are owned by the homeowners' association, whereas the common areas of a condominium development are owned by all the condominium unit owners as tenants in common.

3) Contemporary townhouse developments most likely are subject to the statutory requirements of the Planned Community Act. Developments created prior to 1999 are subject to certain retroactive provisions of that Act. There are fewer consumer protections available to purchasers and owners of townhouse units than there are for condominium purchasers and owners.

Although most residential townhouse developments must comply with the Planned Community Act, they need not comply with the stricter, consumer-oriented Condominium Act. Note, too, that the townhouse form of ownership is not possible where the units are stacked *vertically*, because townhouse ownership includes ownership of the underlying land on which the unit is situated. Obviously, this is not possible with vertically stacked units, which must be condominium units in North Carolina.

Cooperative Ownership

Cooperative ownership has not been exceedingly popular or common in North Carolina. It consists of a multiunit development, often an apartment building, that is collectively owned. A purchaser becomes a member of the "cooperative" and receives stock certificates representing part ownership of the entire building in combination with a lease to a specific unit. The lease of one of the units in the building or project is termed a "proprietary lease."[27]

Time-share Ownership

Another type of property especially popular in vacation and resort areas is a **time-share ownership**. A **time-share** is a *guaranteed use of a unit of real property for a stated period of time over a period of years.*[28]

Planned Unit Development

Although a **Planned Unit Development (PUD)** is actually a method of real estate *development*, not a category of *ownership*, it is closely related to the hybrid forms of property ownership discussed above, especially townhouse ownership.

In a PUD, a tract of land is developed according to a plan that differs from a typical residential subdivision. Buildings are not confined to traditional lot lines but are instead clustered together with space available for parks, recreational facilities, and similar amenities. PUDs may include a variety of land ownership forms and uses: clusters of single-family houses, townhouses, and even a mixture of residential and business uses. Clusters of single-family homes with townhouse traits, such as common walls, are very popular in PUDs, as this method creates more open space than the usual one-home-per-lot allowed in traditional subdivisions.

Much like a townhouse owner, the purchaser of a residence in a PUD usually receives a deed to the housing unit itself and becomes a member of an association that owns the open spaces and common facilities. Most planned unit developments will fit the definition of "planned community" under the Planned Community Act and will be subject to the provisions of that Act.

OWNERSHIP BY A BUSINESS ENTITY

In addition to the various ways an individual may take title to real estate, an individual may also join others, form a business entity, and take title to land in the name of that entity. Some business entities have a legal identity separate from the individual members or owners and are legally distinct from their individual owners. The following websites provide information on the advantages and disadvantages of various types of entities:
- NC Secretary of State, Corporations Division: www.secretary.state.nc.us/corporations
- Business Link of NC, sponsored by the NC Department of Commerce: www.blnc.gov

Corporation

A corporation is a separate legal entity capable of owning and conveying real estate in its own name. Chapter 55 of the North Carolina General Statutes is the North Carolina Business Corporations Act. The day-to-day operation of a corporation is governed by its articles of incorporation and bylaws, subject to compliance with state law. Corporations are owned by people or entities that purchase shares of stock in the corporation. Corporate stock certificates are the personal property of each shareholder. Corporate entities continue to exist beyond the death of any shareholder. Generally, corporate real estate debt is the corporation's responsibility, not an individual shareholder's. This insulates the individual from personal liability and makes corporate stock more attractive. However, lending institutions often require shareholders in smaller corporations to agree to be personally liable for debt repayment if the corporation fails to pay.

In North Carolina, a conveyance of land owned by a corporation will be valid if it is executed by the president or vice president and is *in the ordinary course of the corporation's business.* If *not in the ordinary course of the corporation's business,* the corporation may not sell, exchange, or lease all or substantially all of its property without proper authorization by its board of directors and approval by its shareholders pursuant to state law.

Limited Liability Company (LLC)

Chapter 57D of the North Carolina General Statutes deals with limited liability companies (LLCs). The LLC is a hybrid of both corporations and partnerships. An LLC has the flexibility of a traditional partnership and the limitations on owner liability found in the corporate form of ownership. There are also tax advantages to the LLC entity that are beyond the scope of this chapter.

Powers of a LLC are established in an operating agreement and generally include the same powers as an individual or a domestic corporation to do all things necessary or convenient to carry out its business. Limited liability companies are comprised of members, economic interest owners, and managers, all defined in G.S. §57D-1-03. Of the three, however, it is the managers who have the legal authority to enter into contracts and create obligations on the LLC's behalf.

Partnership

Traditionally, partnerships were classified into two major subcategories: *general* and *limited.* However, a third subcategory, the *limited liability partnership (LLP),* is now recognized. Both limited liability partnerships and limited liability company entities are rapidly replacing traditional general partnerships.

General Partnership

North Carolina has adopted the Uniform Partnership Act that defines a general partnership as *an association of two or more persons to carry on as co-owners of a business for profit.*[29] Courts elaborate by stating that, to make a partnership, two or more persons should combine their property, labor, or skill in a common business or venture. The parties should function under an agreement to share profits and losses in equal or specified proportions. Each partner also becomes an agent of the others in matters relating to the partnership's scope of business. A general partnership does not register with the NC Secretary of State, Corporations Division.

Title to partnership property can be held in the name of the partnership, some or all of the individual partners, or by a third person in trust for the partnership.

Limited Liability Partnership

A limited liability partnership is created when a general partnership registers as a limited liability partnership with the Secretary of State.[30] Technically, a new entity has not been created; instead, the general partnership continues to exist with new characteristics.[31]

Like the limited liability company, the limited liability partnership is an attractive choice for small businesses because it protects the partners from some forms of liability not protected under the traditional general partnership.[32] As with general partnerships, any partner may execute a contract, conveyance, or lease on behalf of the limited liability partnership.

Limited Partnership

North Carolina has also adopted the Revised Uniform Limited Partnership Act. It defines a limited partnership as "a partnership formed by two or more persons ... having as members one or more general partners and one or more limited partners."[33] **General** partners have the legal authority to control and operate the business, while the "silent" **limited** partners provide investment capital by purchasing their limited partnership interests. From the limited partner perspective there are a number of advantages, including limited liability for partnership debts, tax benefits, and the opportunity to earn profits without the responsibility of day-to-day business conduct. The general partner manages the real estate investments and earns a fee or profit as compensation for their knowledge and services.

REIT

A Real Estate Investment Trust (REIT) is a company that invests in real estate. It is established in strict compliance with federal tax laws. It is a type of security owned by a large number of people with transferable shares of beneficial interests. Title to real estate is held by the trustees, who are responsible for the daily conduct of business. A number of investor tax advantages can result from a REIT. A REIT also affords investors a means of investing in real estate that is managed by others.

Endnotes

1.   In a very important decision dealing with real property law, the United States Supreme Court in *United States v. Craft*, 535 U.S. 274, (2002), defines property in part as "a bundle of sticks - a collection of individual rights which, in certain combinations, constitute property."

2.   Hetrick & McLaughlin, *Webster's Real Estate Law in North Carolina*, 6th ed. (LexisNexis), §1.07, pp. 1–16.

3.   For a summary of riparian and littoral rights, see *Newcomb v. County of Carteret*, 207 N.C. App. 527, 701 S.E.2d 325 (2010). See also Hetrick & McLaughlin, *Webster's Real Estate Law in North Carolina*, 6th ed. (LexisNexis) §16.03-16.14, pp. 16-1–16-36.

4.   The North Carolina Uniform Commercial Code (UCC) is located at Chapter 25 of the North Carolina General Statutes. The articles of the UCC deal with sales, leases, negotiable instruments, bank deposits and collections, funds transfers, letters of credit, documents of title, investment securities, and secured transactions.

5.   John W. Reilly, <u>The Language of Real Estate</u> with (Marie S. Spodek ed., 7th ed. 2013).

6.   Hetrick & McLaughlin, *Webster's Real Estate Law in North Carolina*, 6th ed. (LexisNexis), §2.01.

7.   Hetrick & McLaughlin, *Webster's Real Estate Law in North Carolina*, 6th ed. (LexisNexis), §2.04[3][f], pp. 2-12–2-16.

8.   Hetrick & McLaughlin, *Webster's Real Estate Law in North Carolina*, 6th ed. (LexisNexis), §2.04[3][f], pp. 2-16–2-17.

9.   N.C.Gen.Stat. §25-9-102(a)(40). See also comment 6 to this statute, stating that a "fixture filing" is "a filing for record in the real property records and indexed therein, so that it will be found in a real-property

title search."

10. N.C.Gen.Stat. §25-9-334(e)(1).

11. Black's Law Dictionary, 7th ed. (1999), p. 761.

12. Manufactured homes are federally regulated by HUD. See 24 CFR 3280, providing design and construction requirements. For additional information, see www.hud.gov (HUD Office of Manufactured Housing Programs), and www.ncdoi.com/OSFM (North Carolina Department of Insurance, Office of State Fire Marshall).

13. N.C. Gen. Stat. §105-273(13); §143-143.9(6). Manufactured homes that have not been converted to real property remain personal property and must be listed in the name of the owner as shown on the certificate of title. N.C. Gen. Stat. §105-306(a). See, for example, *Patterson v. City of Gastonia*, 220 N.C. App. 233, 725 SE2d 82; *disc. rev. denied* 366 N.C. 406, 759 SE2d 82 (2012) (loss of mobile homes that remained personal property cannot support a claim for inverse condemnation); *Singletary v. P & A Investments, Inc.*, 190 N.C. App. 432 712 S.E.2d 681 (2011) (mobile home was personal property and "good" under the Uniform Commercial Code)

14. See Chapter 3, infra, Property Taxation and Assessment. For up-to-date materials and resources on all aspects of the listing, assessment, and appraisal of real and personal property in North Carolina, see the webpage for the School of Government, University of North Carolina at Chapel Hill: http://www.sog.unc.edu/. The authors highly recommend the following comprehensive treatment of the subject: Shea, Riggsbee, Denning, *A Guide To The Listing, Assessment, and Taxation of Property in North Carolina* (2009), published by the UNC School of Government.

15. N.C. Gen. Stat. §20-109.2. Subsection (c) of this statute concludes with a requirement that the owner or secured party file the affidavit returned from DMV with the Register of Deeds office in the county where the real property is located.

16. N.C. Gen. Stat. §47-20.6(a).

17. N.C. Gen. Stat. §47-20.6(b), which reads: "After the affidavit is recorded, the manufactured home becomes an improvement to real property. Any lien on the manufactured home shall be perfected and given priority in the manner provided for a lien on real property." See also, N.C. Gen. Stat. §47-20.7, titled "Declaration of intent to affix manufactured home; transfer of real property with manufactured home attached."

18. Hetrick & McLaughlin, *Webster's Real Estate Law in North Carolina*, 6th ed. (LexisNexis), §§4.01-4.03, pp. 4-1–4-6; §4.06-4.12 pp 4-9–4-16.26.

19. For an example of a fee simple with a condition subsequent, see *County of Moore v. Humane Society of Moore County, Inc,* 157 N.C. App. 293, 578 S.E.2d 682 (2003) involving a conveyance made by a county upon the condition that "in the event property ... ever ceases to be used as an animal shelter for lost, stray, or homeless animals, then in such event The County shall have the right to immediately re-enter upon said premises and take and hold possession of said premises without let or hindrance ...."

20. The "rights and obligations of life tenants" is a complex topic involving both case law and statutory provisions. This treatment of the topic is intended as a cursory introduction. An attorney experienced in real estate matters should be consulted for advice regarding any specific question relating to life estates. With the exception of life estates contained in trusts as estate planning tools, creating life estates in real property should be avoided whenever possible, as they have a long history of legal disputes between the life tenant and the remaindermen.

21. The law of concurrent ownership is a complex topic that is based in part upon case law and statutory provisions. This treatment of the topic is merely a cursory introduction. An attorney experienced in real estate matters should be consulted for complete advice regarding any specific question relating to the rights and obligations of concurrent owners. See Hetrick & McLaughlin, *Webster's Real Estate Law in North Carolina*, 6th ed. (LexisNexis), Chapter 7, "Concurrent Ownership," for comprehensive coverage of this area of law.

22. The law and procedure for partition can be found at Chapter 46 of the North Carolina General Statutes.

23. N.C. Gen. Stat. § 41-2.

24. N.C. Gen. Stat. §39-13.6. See also *Boone v. Rogers*, 210 N.C. App. 269, 708 S.E.2d 103 (2011).

25. See the North Carolina Planned Community Act, Chapter 47F, and North Carolina Condominium Act, Chapter 47C of the General Statutes. (Condominiums created in North Carolina prior to October 1, 1986 are governed by the **Unit Ownership Act** (Chapter 47A of the General Statutes). See also, the Restatement (Third) of Property: Servitudes, § 6.2, "Common-Interest-Community Definitions. "

26. North Carolina Comment 2 to N.C. Gen. Stat. §47F-1-101 reads in part: "It is understood and intended that any development which incorporates or permits horizontal boundaries or division between the physical portions of the planned community designated for separate ownership or occupancy will be created under and governed by the North Carolina Condominium Act and not [the Planned Community Act]." See Hetrick & McLaughlin, *Webster's Real Estate Law in North Carolina*, 6th ed. (LexisNexis), Chapter 30, "North Carolina Condominium Act," for comprehensive coverage of this subject.

27. One of the few North Carolina appellate decisions dealing with a cooperative form of ownership is *Sanders v. Tropicana*, 31 N.C. App. 276, 229 S.E.2d 304 (1976), holding that the board of directors of a cooperative apartment could not unreasonably withhold consent to the transfer by a tenant-shareholder of his lease and stock subscription.

28. N.C. Gen. Stat. §93A-42(a) revised as of January 1, 2012, reads: "A time-share which in whole or in part burdens or pertains to real property in this State is deemed to be an interest in real estate and shall be governed by the law of this State relating to real estate." Subparagraph (b) of the same statute allows time-share deeds pertaining to real property in North Carolina to be recorded but expressly notes that: "An instrument concerning a time-share which burdens or pertains to no real property located in this State shall not be recorded in the office of the register of deeds in any county in this State."

29. Article 2 of Chapter 59 of the N.C. General Statutes is the Uniform Partnership Act.

30. N.C. Gen. Stat. §59-84.2(a).

31. A general partnership could opt instead to convert to a limited liability company form, but that would mean going through the legal formation of a new business entity.

32. In a general partnership, each partner is jointly and separately liable for the wrongful acts and debts of the partnership. Partners in a limited liability partnership are not personally liable for certain debts and obligations of the limited liability partnership and other partners.

33. Article 5 of Chapter 59 of the N.C. General Statutes is the Revised Uniform Limited Partnership Act.

2 | ENCUMBRANCES & NONPOSSESSERY INTERESTS

NONPOSSESSORY INTERESTS

A nonpossessory interest in land gives the holder a right to use or restrict the use of another's land, but it is less than ownership of the land itself. For example, an *easement* is a nonpossessory interest in land recognized by law, but it does *not* provide the easement holder with *title* to the land subject to the easement or any estate in that land. Even if the easement holder is granted exclusive use of the easement, the owner of the land continues to enjoy all ownership rights and may use the property in any manner not inconsistent with the easement. Restrictive or protective covenants are another example of nonpossessory interests in the land of another. If A sells land to B restricting that land for residential use only, A has a nonpossessory interest in the land conveyed to B, who has full possessory ownership subject to the residential use only restrictions.

ENCUMBRANCES

An **encumbrance** is a burden, claim, or charge on real property that may affect the quality of title as well as the value and/or use of the property. *Encumbrances come in many forms and include liens, restrictive covenants, easements, and encroachments.*[1] The existence of an encumbrance can affect the buyer's obligation to purchase in a real estate transaction.

> *Example:* A seller and buyer enter into a contract to purchase the seller's land. In the contract, the seller promises to deliver marketable title at closing with no exceptions. A title search reveals that part of the land is subject to a neighbor's right-of-way easement over the land. Title to the land is unmarketable and the contract may be terminated at the buyer's option, even if the due diligence period has expired.

Some encumbrances can be satisfied by at closing by paying the indebtedness in full to the encumbrance holder. For example, a seller's outstanding mortgage is an encumbrance that can be eliminated at closing by paying the outstanding balance to the seller's lender with part of the sale proceeds. Encumbrances that are not removed or satisfied at closing remain attached to and burden the property.

Example: A seller and buyer enter into a purchase contract for the seller's land. The seller promises to deliver marketable title. It is a cash sale and to save money, the buyer decides not to have a title search and does not purchase a title insurance policy. Public records reveal that a creditor has a judgment lien against the seller in that county in the amount of $25,000. Title to the land passes to the buyer with the $25,000 judgment lien still attached. Although the buyer may have a legal remedy against the seller, the creditor may force a sale of the property to satisfy the judgment lien if the creditor is not paid.

A full warranty deed contains a series of covenants of title, including a "covenant against encumbrances." Under that covenant, a grantor promises a grantee that no encumbrances exist on the land other than those specifically excepted in the deed. Title insurance policies typically exclude encumbrances from coverage. An attorney's title opinion will list encumbrances discoverable from a public records search. Because they may have an adverse effect on land value or use, the existence of encumbrances on property being transferred is of utmost importance to all parties involved in the transaction. A broker should have a working knowledge of encumbrances, including the following:

- **Liens**, both **specific** and **general**
- **Lis Pendens**
- **Encroachments**
- **Restrictive Covenants**
- **Easements**

LIENS

A *lien* is an encumbrance created by contractual agreement or operation of law that constitutes a "charge" upon property. It is a right granted to creditors to have sums due them satisfied by a sale of property belonging to the debtor. By use of a lien, a creditor imposes a charge or claim against real property as security for the payment of an obligation. The property secures the underlying obligation to pay money. Liens are classified as *general* or *specific*.

Specific Liens

Deeds of Trust (Mortgages)

*A **deed of trust** (or mortgage) is the most common lien on real property. A deed of trust creates a lien against the specific parcel of property that is the subject of the deed of trust.* A deed of trust or mortgage creates a specific lien on a parcel of real property that serves as security for repayment of a loan. If the balance owed on the loan is not paid, the lender or creditor holding the deed of trust or mortgage can force a foreclosure sale of the property. Technically, there are legal distinctions between a deed of trust and a mortgage. These distinctions and other characteristics of deeds of trust and mortgages are discussed in Chapter 12.

Real Estate Tax and Assessment Liens

General Statute §105-355 states that **real estate taxes** *levied by a county or municipality constitute a specific lien on the real property involved until paid.* A **levy** is the amount of money to be raised or collected for taxes by a governmental unit against property. The tax lien attaches to the parcel of real property on the date the property is to be listed (January 1).[2] A lien on real property for unpaid property taxes remains an encumbrance on the land for ten years from the date the taxes became due

(September 1). *If the tax lien is not paid in full prior to a transfer in ownership, then the tax lien transfers with the property and can be enforced against a subsequent owner of the property.*

> *Example:* Smith owned a residence in Raleigh, North Carolina. He forgot to pay the property taxes in 2015. In 2017, with the 2015 property taxes still unpaid, Smith sells the residence to Jones. The real property is still subject to the tax lien, and Jones must either pay Smith's delinquent taxes or risk having the property sold at a tax foreclosure sale. (A thorough title search should have revealed the unpaid tax bill, which should have been paid in full at closing from the sale proceeds.)

For various reasons, tax liens are given a ***special priority*** by law over other liens. Thus *as a general rule, a real property tax lien takes precedence over all other encumbrances, whether the other encumbrances come into existence prior or subsequent to the levy of taxes.* In addition to levying real estate taxes, local governments are authorized by law to make special improvements (e.g., curbs, gutters, or sidewalks) and to assess the adjacent benefited real estate for these improvements. Real property abutting an improvement is subject to liens for these ***special assessments***. As with tax liens, *the lien for special assessments is given special priority over most other types of encumbrances, but city and county real property tax liens take priority over special assessment liens.*

Mechanic's Liens

A **"mechanic's lien"** is a lien on real property for funds owed to contractors and subcontractors who have made an improvement to that property. Although centuries old, the term "mechanics lien" continues to be used and has been significantly expanded to provide lien rights to a variety of contractors, subcontractors, suppliers, and "design professionals" who provide labor, materials, design or surveying services, or furnish rental equipment to "improve" real property pursuant to an express or implied contract with the owner.[3] If these service providers who improve the property are not paid, they have a right to file a claim of lien against the owner's interest in the improved real property. The term "improve" is an extensive one defined in N.C. Gen. Stat. §44A-7(3) as:

> … to build, effect, alter, repair, or demolish any improvement upon, connected with, or on or beneath the surface of any real property, or to excavate, clear, grade, fill, or landscape any real property, or to construct driveways and private roadways, or to furnish materials, including trees and shrubbery, for any of such purposes, or to perform any labor upon such improvements, and shall also mean and include any design or other professional or skilled services furnished by architects, engineers, land surveyors, and landscape architects registered under [applicable Chapters of] the General Statutes, and rental of equipment directly utilized on the real property in making the improvement.[4]

Historically, a person who provides labor or materials to improve an owner's real property, but who was not paid, could file a claim of lien against the real property *within 120 days* ***after the last day*** *of furnishing labor, materials, or services, but the lien related back to and was* ***effective from the first day*** *of furnishing labor, materials, or services.* This procedure created major problems in that mechanic's liens could remain undiscoverable in a search of the public land records because a lien claim could be filed after the fact yet relate back to a date several months earlier. To further complicate matters, the possibility that this lien might arise was known only to the owner and the persons who provided the labor, materials, design or surveying services, or rental equipment for the improvements.

Example: A homeowner hires a contractor to remodel the kitchen for $25,000. The contractor begins the remodeling project on March 1 and completes it on July 14. On September 15, the owner sells the house to a purchaser, while still owing $15,000 on the remodeling project. On October 1 (within 120 days of July 14) the contractor files a "claim of lien on real property" with the Clerk of Court in the county where the property is located. The lien claim securing the $15,000 still due the contractor relates back to March 1, the date the contractor commenced the remodeling project. Even though there was nothing in the public record as of the date of the real estate closing to alert the buyer or closing attorney to the possibility of this lien, the buyer's title to the property is encumbered by and subject to the contractor's mechanic's lien.

Effective April 1, 2013, the General Assembly revised the mechanic's lien statutes to create a new procedure involving a "lien agent." Under current law, real property owners must designate a lien agent whenever the cost of an improvement project is **$30,000 or more**, whether commercial or residential. The lone exception is that an owner is not required to designate a lien agent for improvements or additions to an *existing* single-family residential dwelling *occupied by the owner as a residence.* Thus, in the above example, the property owner would not be required to designate a lien agent or the lien agent process of obtaining a lien.

When an owner must designate a lien agent, the law imposes the following obligations:

- A lien agent must be a title insurance company or agency that has registered with the North Carolina Department of Insurance to serve as a lien agent.
- The real property owner must designate a lien agent at the time the original building permit is issued, or if no permit is required, then no later than the time the owner first contracts with any person to improve the property.[5]
- The statutes specify information the owner must provide to and about the lien agent, including that the owner "conspicuously and continuously" post the lien agent's contact information on the property until the completion of all construction or improvements.
- To perfect a claim of lien on the real property, potential lien claimants (service providers) must serve a "Notice to Lien Agent" upon the designated agent *no later than fifteen days after* first furnishing labor, materials, or services to the project but are permitted to give the required Notice to Lien Agent before providing any services, labor, or materials.[6]
- A lien claimant's failure to timely notify the lien agent may result in the mechanic's lien being subordinate to a bona fide purchaser's previously recorded mortgage or deed of trust, subject to a few named exceptions.[7]
- The statutory Notice to Lien Agent is not filed with any court. An unpaid service provider still must perfect its claim by following the traditional procedure of filing a formal Claim of Lien with the clerk of superior court of the county where the property is located within 120 days from last furnishing materials or services and seek to enforce its claim within 180 days from the last date services or materials were furnished.
- The lien claimant must also serve a copy of the Claim of Lien on the record owner of the property.[8]

At least under the current mechanic's lien statutes, there now is someone other than the owner and service provider who will know about potential claims, namely, the designated lien agent. Prospective purchasers, lenders, closing attorneys, title insurance companies, and other interested persons may contact the lien agent at any time during or after the project to learn who provided what services to assess whether any potential liens may attach retroactively to the property. The relation-back doctrine and prior laws and procedure remain largely intact,[9] subject to compliance by both property owners and lien claimants with the new lien agent requirements.

Liens of Homeowners' Associations

Planned community homeowners' associations and condominium owners' associations have the legal authority to obtain a lien for the nonpayment of past-due assessments. The lien may cover other charges such as late fees, attorneys' fees, interest,[10] or fines imposed on a property owner for violating a restrictive covenant. After required legal notices are given to a property owner, the association can file a claim of lien with the clerk of superior court in the county where the community is located.[11] Once filed, the existence of the lien is discoverable by an attorney searching title.

Once properly filed, the lien takes priority over all liens and encumbrances, except liens for property taxes and other government liens.[12] Association liens are superior to all other liens and encumbrances recorded after the claim of lien is filed and are not subject to prior mortgages and encumbrances filed or recorded prior to the date the lien claim was filed. In a worst-case scenario, the association has the power to enforce the lien by filing a foreclosure action against the delinquent owner's property.

Federal Environmental Liens

Under federal law, an owner of real property can be liable for all or part of the costs for cleaning up environmentally contaminated property. The owner's real property may be subject to a federal "Superfund Lien" to secure the clean-up cost.[13]

Commercial Broker Liens

Commercial real estate brokers are authorized by statute to obtain a lien against an owner's property when the broker's client has not been paid the broker's commission or fee.[14] The lien is available to real estate brokers licensed in North Carolina, including nonresident brokers who hold a North Carolina Limited Non-Resident Commercial License. However the lien is only available to *listing brokers/firms* who have a written agency agreement with the property owner to sell or lease the owner's *commercial* real estate, and it applies only to the parcel of commercial real estate that is the subject of the brokerage services agreement, not to any other real property the person or entity may own. The details of this lien law are discussed in greater depth in Chapter 19, "Commercial Real Estate Brokerage."

General Liens

A **general** lien is a lien that applies to any real or personal property owned by the debtor. The most common general liens are discussed below.

Judgment Liens

*A money judgment becomes a lien on **all** real property owned or subsequently acquired by the judgment debtor in each county where the judgment has been properly docketed.* A judgment is "docketed" when it is entered and indexed in a judgment book in the office of the Clerk of Superior Court. A judgment lien generally is valid for ten years from the date the original judgment is entered.[15] A thorough title search will always include a search of the judgment indices under the sellers name in the county where the property is located.

Example: In 2015, a debtor defaulted on a used-car loan after the uninsured car was stolen. The creditor sued, obtained a judgment against the debtor in the amount of $10,000, and properly docketed (filed) the judgment in Yadkin County. While the debtor owned no real property at that time, in 2017, the debtor received a gift of a tract of land in Yadkin County from a relative. The judgment lien filed in 2015 automatically and immediately attaches to this subsequently acquired real property.

Personal Property Tax Liens

While unpaid real estate taxes are a *specific lien* on the particular parcel of real property, unpaid *personal property taxes* are a *general lien* on **all** real property of the taxpayer located within the taxing unit (county and/or city).[16] Like the real estate tax lien, the personal property tax lien attaches on the date the property is to be listed (January 1) and is valid for ten years from the date the unpaid taxes become due (September 1).

State Tax Liens

The real property of a taxpayer delinquent in the payment of *state income taxes* will become subject to a tax lien at the time a certificate of tax liability or a judgment by the North Carolina Commissioner of Revenue is docketed in the office of the clerk of superior court of the county where the real property is located.[17] Similarly, there is a lien against decedent's real property for the benefit of the State of North Carolina for unpaid *estate taxes*.[18] This lien does not have to be docketed and affects land passing to the heirs and devisees of the decedent. The life of both liens is ten years. In the case of the state income tax lien, the ten-year period runs from the date of docketing. The estate tax lien is valid for ten years from the date of death.

Federal Tax Liens

The federal government is entitled to a lien upon the real property of a taxpayer who is delinquent in payment of *federal income taxes*. This tax lien is filed in the office of the clerk of superior court in the county in which the taxpayer's real estate is located. Certificates of release, discharge, or subordination of the federal tax lien are also filed in the clerk's office.[19]

Lien Priority

As a general rule, North Carolina statutes determine lien priority on a "pure race" concept, meaning that recording alone usually decides priority; even actual notice of a pre-existing *unrecorded* lien or encumbrance usually does not affect lien priority unless fraud is involved.

> *Example:* On June 3, Smith grants X Bank a deed of trust on Smith's home to secure the payment of a loan obligation to X Bank, which fails to promptly record the deed of trust. On July 20, Smith executes a deed of trust to Jones to secure a loan. Jones knows about the earlier deed of trust to X Bank, but he promptly records his deed of trust on July 21. Assuming no fraud, the priority between these two competing deeds of trust is determined by the order of recordation, not execution. Therefore, Jones' deed of trust has first priority and X Bank's deed of trust, once recorded, will have second priority. Absent fraud, Jones' actual knowledge of the pre-existing deed of trust held by X Bank is irrelevant in North Carolina.

Thus, while the order of recording usually determines priority, there are several *exceptions* to this, including, but not limited to, the following:

- Real property tax and special assessment liens are accorded a special priority status over virtually all other types of liens.
- A purchase money deed of trust and a future advances deed of trust are given special priority in certain situations.
- If more than one judgment is rendered during the same term of court and docketed within ten days after the term of court terminates, then all such judgments have equal priority among each other, even though one was rendered prior to the others.
- Priority can be altered by private agreement. For example, the holder of a first lien can contractually agree to make it "subordinate to" (junior to) other liens.

The relative priority of competing liens and encumbrances can be an extremely complex legal tangle. Brokers should advise parties to consult an attorney with expertise in this area whenever a priorities problem exists in a property transaction.

LIS PENDENS (NOTICE OF PENDING LITIGATION)

*A **lis pendens** is a recorded notice informing all interested parties that a legal action has been commenced that affects in some way the title to a certain parcel of real estate.*[20] It operates as a claim or encumbrance against real property because a person receiving the property under a subsequent conveyance or encumbrance will be bound by the outcome of the pending lawsuit insofar as it affects the property subject to the *lis pendens.*

Example: Smith owns land over which her neighbor claims an easement. Her neighbor files a lawsuit against Smith seeking to have a court declare that an easement exists. The neighbor also properly files a *lis pendens* (notice of pending litigation) on Smith's parcel. One year later, while the legal action is still pending, Smith sells the property to Davis. Davis takes title to Smith's property subject to the outcome of the legal action concerning the easement. If the neighbor wins the lawsuit, Davis's ownership of the parcel will be subject to the neighbor's easement.

Even if a notice of *lis pendens* has not been recorded, persons dealing with the real property who have actual notice of pending litigation affecting title to that property take ownership subject to the outcome of the litigation.[21]

ENCROACHMENTS

Every tract of land has defined legal boundaries. An ***encroachment*** occurs when a property owner makes an improvement on his or her lot that extends over the property boundary line onto a neighboring property or when a neighboring property owner makes an improvement on her lot that extends over the homeowner's property line.

Example: A homeowner fenced his back yard. Instead of ordering a survey first, he estimated where the fence should go based on old survey stakes at the rear of his lot. He installed a wood privacy fence with fence posts imbedded in cement foundations in the ground. Unfortunately, the fence encroached on his neighbor's yard by six inches to two feet.

Whether the fence encroachment is by a few inches or several feet or includes a portion of a structure, the net effect is that title to *both parcels* is unmarketable. The homeowner's encroaching lot has a title marketability issue because the homeowner doesn't have title to all of the land upon which the fence located. The neighbor, who now owns an encroached-upon lot, has a marketability of title issue because she does not have use of her entire tract and may have to sue the homeowner to have the encroachment removed or obtain other legal relief.

In addition to causing title marketability issues, encroachments can go well beyond a few feet and can result in litigation and significant practical problems. In a 2006 North Carolina legal dispute, lot owners moved a home onto what they believed to be their lot without first obtaining a survey. In fact, the home encroached 22 feet onto the neighbor's lot. Six years later, the neighbor sold his lot, but the purchaser did not order a survey until three years after the closing and then sued the encroaching owners. The owners of the encroaching property were ordered to move their home entirely onto their lot within 180 days, an expensive result that could easily have been avoided had they ordered a survey of their lot prior to constructing the home.[22] Common examples of encroachments include:

1) buildings and outbuildings, including overhanging eaves;
2) fences;
3) driveways and walkways.

Lessons from the above encroachment examples should be obvious. A purchaser of land should be advised to obtain an up-to-date survey prior to purchasing. All owners planning improvements to their property should order a survey to determine the property boundaries and then plan the location of the building, driveway, fence, or other improvement.

Please see the illustration at the end of Chapter 4 for an example of an encroachment.

RESTRICTIVE COVENANTS

Restrictive covenants are *private deed restrictions* that limit the use of real property. They are set forth in a Declaration of Restrictions and Covenants recorded in the Register of Deed's office. Modern restrictive covenants are extensive in scope and may dictate permitted property uses, setback and sideline requirements, minimum square footage, and architectural design. Lots in modern property developments are both benefited and burdened by restrictive covenants. Because compliance with the covenants is not optional, all lots are considered "burdened," and restrictive covenants are considered an encumbrance on title. Each owner's lot is also benefited by the restrictive covenants because each has the legal right to require other lot owners in the development to comply with all covenants. This subject is covered in detail in Chapter 7.

EASEMENTS

An *easement* is a nonpossessory "right" to use or enjoy the land of another in some limited way not amounting to full ownership. It may exist for a limited period of time or be of unlimited duration. Easements are classified as *appurtenant* or *in gross*. In a nutshell, *appurtenant easements are created for the benefit of other lands, while easements in gross benefit a person or legal entity.*

Appurtenant Easements

An *appurtenant easement* is a right to use one tract of land for the benefit of another tract of land.[23] A common example is a *right of way* across one tract of land that provides access to a second tract of land. *An appurtenant easement always involves* **two tracts of land owned by two different owners**. Frequently, the two tracts will be adjoining tracts.

The land benefited from the easement is called "**dominant land**" (or "dominant tract" or "dominant estate"), while the land that is subject to and burdened by the easement is called "**servient land**" (or "servient tract" or "servient estate"). *An appurtenant easement legally attaches to the title of* **both** *the dominant estate and servient estate and will transfer automatically with* **both** *tracts.* When a dominant land is transferred, the benefit of any appurtenant easement passes with the land. Likewise, when servient land is transferred, the new owner takes subject to the burden of the easement.

> *Example:* A, the owner of Lot 10, grants to B, the owner of adjoining Lot 11, a right-of-way easement across Lot 10 for the benefit of Lot 11 (see illustration below). The easement is recorded. B has an easement over A's property. Lot 11 is the "dominant estate," and Lot 10 is the "servient estate." The easement is "appurtenant" to Lot 11 and an "encumbrance" to Lot 10. If B transfers Lot 11, the benefit of the easement transfers with it. If A transfers Lot 10, the burden of the easement transfers with it.

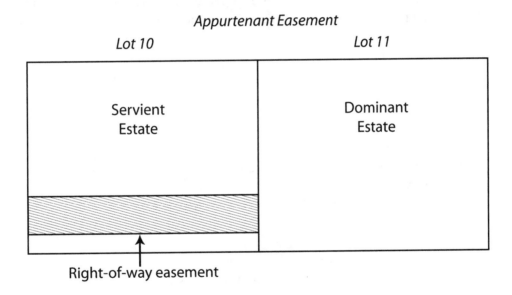

Appurtenant Easement

Lot 10   Lot 11

Servient Estate

Dominant Estate

Right-of-way easement

An appurtenant easement cannot be used to benefit non-dominant land. Assume in the above example that B subsequently purchases Lot 12, a lot adjacent to Lot 11. The right-of-way appurtenant easement cannot be used for the benefit of Lot 12 because Lot 12 was not part of the dominant estate when the easement was created.

Easements in Gross

An **easement in gross** *is a right of a person or other legal entity to use the land of another* and should be in writing since it affects an interest in real property. With an easement in gross, only one tract of land is involved, and this tract is the *servient estate*. There is *no dominant estate*. Is an easement in gross transferable by the benefited person? The common law of property treats easements in gross as mere "personal rights" not assignable by the easement holder and terminating with the death of the easement holder. However, *so long as the easement exists, it is an "encumbrance" on the servient lands and transfers with such lands.*

Example: A, the owner of an oceanfront beach cottage, grants B (who may or may not own land in the area) a *purely personal* easement right to cross A's lot in order to get to the ocean; the easement is in writing and recorded. The easement does not refer to any land owned by B, so there is no dominant estate. A's land is a servient estate, and B has a purely personal, nonassignable, uninheritable easement in gross that will burden A's lot until B dies or releases the right.

North Carolina law permits the assignability of commercial easements in gross for public policy reasons and based on the express terms of the easement in gross. Public utility easements, for example, are considered "in gross" and yet transferable by the company holding the benefit of the easement. Easements of economic benefit are likewise transferable. Any question about the transferability of the benefit of an easement in gross should be referred to an attorney with expertise in real estate law.

Often, public utility easements give the utility sweeping rights to control the easement area and restrict the landowner (the servient estate owner) from many uses. For example, in a 2006 case, the easement gave the power company the right to keep the easement area clear of all structures, trees, fire hazards, and other objects of any nature. The court held that the easement right precluded the owner of the servient estate, a shopping center, from placing a sign in the easement area.[24]

Creation of Easements

In addition to the appurtenant and in gross classification, easements are also classified by the method of creation as either *express, implied,* or arising by *operation of law.* These methods of easement creation are summarized below and then discussed.

  I.   **Express Easements**
       • Easements by Express Grant or Reservation
       • Party Wall Agreements
       • Easements by Dedication

 II.   **Implied Easements**
       • Easements of Necessity
       • Easements Implied from Prior Use (Quasi-Easements)
       • Easements Implied from Reference to a Map or Plat

III.   **Easements Arising by Operation of Law**
       • Statutory Cartway Proceedings
       • Easements by Condemnation (Eminent Domain)
       • Easements by Prescription

Express and Implied Easements Distinguished

An **express easement** is created by a written document that specifically grants or reserves the easement and complies with the Statute of Frauds. The formal writing must adequately describe the easement and the dominant and servient estates. In contrast, an **implied easement** arises although no document granting an easement exists. Implied easements arise as a matter of public policy based on the probable intent of the parties.

Express Easements

Easements by Express Grant or Reservation. An express easement is one created by *express grant in a deed*. When conveying a part of his or her land, the grantor may also expressly grant an easement to the grantee to make some use of land retained by the grantor.

> *Example:* A person owns five acres of land adjacent to a state park on the west boundary. The owner conveys two acres on the eastern boundary of his property that do not have convenient access to the park to a grantee. In the deed, the grantor also grants a pedestrian easement over a defined part of the grantor's retained land to provide the grantee with convenient access to the park. An easement by express grant benefitting the grantee has been created.

Alternately, where a grantor sells one tract of land, but retains another adjacent tract, the grantor in the conveyance deed may "reserve" or "except" an easement for the grantor's benefit over the tract of land conveyed to the grantee.

> *Example:* In the above example, assume instead that the grantor conveys all of the five acres of land except for part of the land that borders on the east boundary and does not have convenient access to the state park. In the deed, the grantor also reserves a pedestrian easement over a defined part of the remaining five acres conveyed to the grantee to provide the grantor with convenient access to the park. The grantor has reserved an express easement.

Easements may be granted in a document other than a deed. *Since an easement is an "interest" in real property, an easement created by express grant or reservation must be **in writing** to comply with the Statute of Frauds.* The writing that creates an easement by express grant or reservation must describe with reasonable certainty the easement created, as well as the dominant and servient tracts of land involved. Any attempt to create an easement by oral grant is void because the Statute of Frauds requires the grant to be in writing. Additionally, any easement created by express written grant must be *recorded* in the public land records in order to be valid against subsequent purchasers of the servient land or lien creditors of the servient owner.

> *Example:* A farmer grants an express easement to cross part of the farm to a neighbor. The neighbor does not record the document granting the easement. Several years later, when the neighbor still has not recorded the easement document, the farmer conveys the farm to a purchaser who promptly records the deed. The purchaser owns the farm free and clear of the neighbor's easement. This is true in North Carolina even if the purchaser had actual knowledge of the easement.

Party Wall Agreements. While rare in modern building construction, older buildings in urban areas were often constructed with common walls, necessitating party wall agreements. Such agreements are contracts between adjoining property owners calling for the construction and joint use of a wall between two buildings for the support of both. Party wall arrangements may take a number of legal forms. One method provides that the property line runs through the center of the wall with each adjoining owner owning one-half of the wall subject to "cross-easements."

Easements by Dedication. An easement may be created by "dedication." *Dedication is a form of transfer, either formal or informal, whereby a property owner grants easement rights to the public.* Most easements by dedication are express grants; however, some dedications are informal and implied.[25] For instance, where a grantor conveys land and describes the parcel being conveyed by reference to a plat showing a street providing access to the property, the grantor is "equitably estopped" to deny the easement for the street to a purchaser. The purchaser has an easement over the street irrespective of whether the streets are accepted by the governing board of a town or city in which the land is located. Dedications are express when the owner of land indicates an unequivocal intention to make a dedication of an easement to the public, and the public accepts the offer of dedication in some recognized legal manner. Acceptance of offers of dedication of private roads by local governments is now a rare occurrence.

Implied Easements

Easements created by implication are more complicated and less common than expressly created easements. Often, these easements are implied in law when land granted cannot be reasonably used or beneficially enjoyed by the grantee unless an easement is inferred. Following are some examples of easements created by implication.

Easements by Necessity. Where a grantor conveys a tract of land entirely surrounded by land retained by the grantor (or land retained by the grantor and other surrounding property owners), and the conveyed tract has no legal access to a public road, the law implies an *"easement by necessity"* for the grantee to pass over the grantor's retained land to access a public road.

> *Example:* X owns a large farm and conveys to Y a five-acre parcel in the middle of the farm. There is no legal access from the five-acre tract to a public road, and the deed from X to Y contains no language regarding the creation of any express easement rights. Y has an easement by necessity implied by law across X's remaining lands in order to gain access to a public road. A court will impose an easement by necessity, regardless of whether X actually intended to grant one.[26]

An implied easement may **not** *be acquired against the lands of persons other than the grantor (or the grantor's successors).* Thus, if a grantor conveys land that is entirely landlocked by lands of persons other than the grantor, the grantee will not have any right to an implied easement of necessity over the others' lands to provide the grantee access to a public road.

What if the grantor landlocks himself by conveying all lands surrounding a tract retained by the grantor? Under the common law rule, the grantor is not entitled to an easement of necessity and thus may have no legal access to the retained tract. North Carolina may be moving away from the traditional rule;[27] if the issue arises, a party should seek legal advice from an attorney specializing in real property law.

Easements Implied from Prior Use (Quasi-Easements). Easements implied from prior use occur when the owner of land is using one part to benefit another part. Because the entire parcel is owned by one person, no true easement can exist. *You cannot have an easement over your own land.* However, under property law, one part (the "quasi-servient" land) is being used to benefit another part (the "quasi-dominant land"). If the owner of the land subsequently divides it into two or more parcels and sells part of the land, an easement by implication may arise by operation of law if the following legal requirements are proved by the party claiming the easement.
1. There is a conveyance of part of the grantor's land;
2. The grantor retains part of the land;

3. Prior use of the land was such that, if the two tracts had been separate, one tract would have been serving the other through an appurtenant easement;
4. The prior usage must be "reasonably necessary;" and
5. The prior usage must be "apparent" or "visible."[28]

Example: X owns a 160-acre parcel of farmland with a house located in the middle of the parcel and connected to Highway 421 by a graded driveway. At the western boundary of the parcel is a dirt road that eventually also connects with Highway 421. X splits the land into two parcels, selling the house and 100 acres to Y. X retains a 60-acre parcel fronting on Highway 421. (See illustration.) If the driveway is reasonably necessary for the enjoyment by Y of the 100-acre parcel, Y will have acquired an implied easement over it. (Note that Y's parcel is not landlocked, so an easement of necessity is not applicable.)[29]

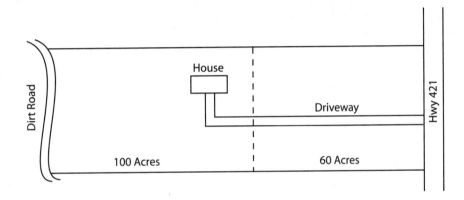

Because disputes and litigation involving claims of an implied easement are common, a broker should never presume the existence of an easement and should advise prospective purchasers to seek legal counsel.

Easements Implied from Reference to a Plat or Map. When a property owner sells lots with reference to a map or plat showing streets or alleys, an easement may be implied for the benefit of lot purchasers, even though no express easement was ever created in the deed conveying the parcel. One theory behind implying an easement under these circumstances is that purchasers have expended money and relied on the representation that streets or alleys would be placed on the land as indicated on the map or plat. Sometimes courts discuss this in terms of *"estoppel;"* i.e., the seller is "estopped" to deny the existence of easements over these streets and alleys.

Easements Arising by Operation of Law
Statutory Cartway. In *limited instances*, North Carolina law allows an owner of landlocked property to acquire an easement, known as a **cartway**, over another's land. The General Statutes state that if an owner's land has no reasonable access to a public road, the owner may acquire a "cartway" over another's land *if* the cartway is necessary to cultivate land; cut or remove timber; work quarries, mines, or minerals; operate industrial or manufacturing plants; or for private cemeteries. The owner of the land over which the cartway runs is entitled to be paid by the person receiving the cartway.[30]

Easements by Condemnation (Eminent Domain). The state and its agencies, municipal corporations, and various public service corporations possess the power of eminent domain and may condemn and take easement rights in lands for public roads, streets, rights-of-way, and other necessary public purposes by following statutory procedures and paying "just compensation" to the property owner.

Easements by Prescription. "*Prescription*" is *the acquisition of a legal right by long continued use.* An easement can be obtained by prescription after adverse use over a specified length of time. In North Carolina, an "open, continuous, adverse use" of an identifiable part of another's land for **twenty years** creates an easement by prescription in the user for the uses made during the statutory period.[31] To obtain an easement by prescription, all legal prerequisites must be met. The burden of proof is on the party seeking to establish a prescriptive easement. In summary form, a claimant must prove the following:

1) Use that is adverse, hostile, or under a claim of right. A use that begins with the permission or consent of the owner cannot form the basis of an easement by prescription.

2) Use that is visible, open, and notorious. The property owner must have the ability to discover that another person is using a portion of the owner's land.

3) Use that is continuous and uninterrupted for the twenty-year statutory period. The use must be sufficiently regular to put the property owner on notice that someone is using the owner's property without any permission to do so.

Example: X owns land adjoining the Cape Fear River. Y owns land adjacent to X's parcel but separated from the river by X's land. Over twenty years ago, Y began regularly using a footpath across X's land to get to the river. Y's open use of this path continued until recently, when X placed a fence across the path and told Y to keep off X's land. Assuming that Y has met all of the legal prerequisites listed above, Y has acquired an easement by prescription over X's land. X has waited too long to object to Y's use and may not now block the easement path.

If in the above example, Y had asked X in advance whether Y could use a footpath and X had agreed, then Y's use of the footpath began with X's permission. Y's permissive use will never ripen into a prescriptive easement, and X can revoke permission at any time, regardless of how long Y uses the footpath. Legal advice should be sought if there is any question as to whether an easement by prescription may exist.

Scope, Extent and Location of Easements

The scope, extent, and location of an easement depend upon the method by which the easement was created. Where the easement has been *expressly created*, these matters are determined first by the terms of the written document granting the easement. Where the written terms are incomplete or unclear, a court may consider the circumstances surrounding the creation of the easement to infer what reasonable use was intended by the parties. The scope and extent of *implied easements* and *prescriptive easements* will depend in large part on *prior use* of the road or path. Brokers should be aware of four basic rules related to the scope, extent, and location of easements.

1) An easement cannot be expanded to serve nondominant (unbenefited) land.
2) Once fixed in location, an easement cannot be relocated by the owner of the servient estate without the permission of the owner of the dominant estate.
3) An easement with a defined width cannot be expanded without the permission of the owner of the servient estate.
4) Once an easement has been established, the easement holder (dominant estate) is prohibited from changing or greatly increasing the use so as to increase the burden on the servient estate.

Termination of Easements

Easements may be terminated in a number of ways. Whether an easement has been terminated is a legal matter; neither a broker nor a party should assume that an easement has been terminated without legal documentation or certification by an attorney with expertise in real property law. Examples of when an easement is terminated include the following:

- *Cessation of Purpose.* If an easement has been created for a particular purpose, and the purpose ceases or has been fulfilled, the easement likewise ceases. For example, an easement granted to a timber company to cross land to harvest timber from a neighboring tract will cease once all the timber has been removed.

- *Easement for a Limited Time Period.* While some easements are of unlimited duration, others are created for only a specified period of time and then terminate automatically.

- *Release of Easement.* The holder of the easement (usually the owner of the dominant tract) can expressly release and thereby extinguish the easement.

- *Extinguishment by Merger.* If the owner of the dominant estate acquires the servient estate, or vice versa, or a third party acquires both parcels, the easement is extinguished because an owner cannot have an easement over his or her own land.

- *Abandonment.* An easement may be terminated if the holder of the easement legally abandons it. Clear evidence of abandonment must exist.

- *Adverse Use by Servient Owner.* An easement may be terminated because of adverse use by the servient owner for the prescriptive period (twenty years in North Carolina). For example, if A has an easement to use a footpath across B's land and B erects a fence that blocks that footpath for twenty years, B's adverse use has terminated A's easement.[32]

- *Failure to Record.* Expressly created easements are extinguished by a failure to record the document granting the easement. This occurs when the servient estate is conveyed to a subsequent purchaser.

Only easements created by express grant are required to be recorded to protect the easement owner against subsequent purchasers of the burdened land (servient estate). Easements arising by implication, necessity, prior use, estoppel, and prescriptive use are outside the scope of the recordation statutes and will **not** be extinguished by a failure to record.

Endnotes

1. Title to land may also be subject to an outstanding lease. A lease is not considered an "encumbrance" or "nonpossessory interest" because it is a possessory nonfreehold estate in land.

2. N.C.Gen.Stat. § 105-285.

3. N.C. Gen. Stat. §44A-8.2.

4. N.C. Gen. Stat. §44A-7(4) defines "improvement" as: "All or any part of any building, structure, erection, alteration, demolition, excavation, clearing, grading, filling, or landscaping, including trees and shrubbery, driveways and private roadways, on real property." See also *Waters Edge Builders v. Longa*, 214 N.C. App. 350, 715 S.E.2d 193 (2011).

5. N.C. Gen. Stat. §44A-11.1(a).

6. N.C. Gen. Stat. §§44A-11.1 and 44A-11.2.

7. Potential lien claimants who fail to deliver a "Notice To Lien Agent" pursuant to N.C. Gen. Stat. §44A-11.2 may nonetheless have lien rights on the real property under circumstances set forth in the same statute, but the mechanic's lien generally will be subordinate to a previously recorded mortgage or deed of trust, subject to a few exceptions. The delivery of the required Notice to the lien agent *does not* satisfy the separate service or filing requirements applicable to the requirements for a notice for a lien upon funds (Part 2 of Article 2 of Chapter 44A of the General Statutes). The key provisions regarding the relative priority of lien rights are found in N.C. Gen. Stat. §44A-11.2(k) and (l) and will require interpretation by an attorney with expertise in this area.

8. N.C. Gen. Stat. §44A-11(a) as revised by Session Law 2012-175, House Bill 1052, effective January 1, 2013. This session law added new definitions to the mechanic's lien law and new requirements for perfecting a mechanic's lien on real property. It also added technical and substantive changes to the lien on funds portion of the mechanic's lien law which is not addressed in this text.

9. See *Wachovia Bank National Association v. Superior Construction Corp.*, 213 N.C. App. 341 718 S.E.2d 160 (2011) summarizing the relation-back doctrine.

10. N.C.Gen.Stat. §§47F-3-102(11); §47C-3-102(11).

11. N.C.Gen.Stat. §47F-3-116(a);§47C-3-116(a).

12. N.C.Gen.Stat. §47F-3-116(d); §47C-3-116(d).

13. The primary federal law affecting real property environmental contamination is the Comprehensive Environmental Response Compensation and Liability Act ("CERCLA" or "SUPERFUND"), and amendments thereto that will be discussed in the chapter on land use controls.

14. N.C.Gen.Stat. chapter 44A, Part 4, "Commercial Real Estate Broker Lien Act."

15. N.C. Gen. Stat. §§1-233, 1-234. See N.C. Gen. Stat. §7A-193 for the same procedure in district courts.

16. See N.C. Gen. Stat. §§105-355, 105-356.

17. See N.C. Gen. Stat. §105-242(c).

18. See N.C. Gen. Stat. §105-32.6.

19. See the Uniform Federal Lien Registration Act, Article 11A of Chapter 68 of the North Carolina General Statutes.

20. See N.C. Gen. Stat. §1-116. See also *Deans v. Mansfield*, 210N.C. App.222 , 707 S.E.2d 658 (2011).

21. *Hill v. Memorial Park*, 304 N.C. 159, 282 S.E.2d 779 (1981).

22. *Cornelius v. Corry*, 179 N.C.App. 863, 635 S.E.2d 537 (2006) (unpublished); See also *Williams v. South & South Rentals, Inc.*, 82 N.C. App. 378, 346 S.E.2d 665 (1986); *Bishop v. Reinhold*, 66 N.C. App. 379, 311 S.E.2d 298 (1984); *Terry v. Jim Walter Homes*, 8 N.C. App. 637, 175 S.E.2d 354 (1970).

23. For cases involving easements, see *Woodring v. Swieter:* 180 N.C.App. 362, 637 S.E.2d 269 (2006); *ZA. Sneeden's Sons, Inc. v. ZP No. 116, L.L.C.*, 190 N.C.App. 90, 660 S.E.2d 204 (2008).

24. *Duke Energy Corporation v. Malcolm*, 178 N.C.App. 62, 630 S.E.2d 639, aff'd *per curiam*, 361 N.C. 111, 637 S.E.2d 538 (2006).

25. *Kraft v. Town of Mt. Olive*, 183 N.C.App. 415, 645 S.E.2d 132 (2007).

26. Example based on *Pritchard v. Scott*, 254 N.C. 277, 118 S.E.2d 890 (1961).

27. *Cieszko v. Clark*, 92 N.C.App. 290, 374 S.E.2d 456 (1988).

28. See, for example, *Cash v. Craver*, 62 N.C. App. 257, 302 S.E.2d 819 (1983).

29. Example based on *Spruill v. Nixon*, 238 N.C. 523, 78 S.E.2d 323 (1953).

30. N.C.Gen.Stat. §§136-68 & 136-69.

31. See, for example, *West v. Slick*, 313 N.C. 33, 326 S.E.2d 601 (1985); *Potts v. Burnette*, 301 N.C. 663, 273 S.E.2d 285 (1981); *Caldwell v. Branch,* 181 N.C.App. 107, 638 S.E.2d 552 (2007).

32. See, for example, *Phillips and Jordan Investment Corporation v. Greun Madainn, Inc.*, 189 N.C. App. 787, 661 S.E.2d 56 (2008).

3 | PROPERTY TAXATION AND ASSESSMENT

Real property taxes and assessments are issues in virtually all real estate transactions. Every well-drafted contract to convey real estate has language detailing the proration of *ad valorem* real property taxes. As noted in Chapter 2, taxes and assessments are encumbrances on real property and will be a cloud on the title. Brokers will routinely encounter taxation considerations in residential or commercial sales or leasing and must understand the basics of assessment, listing, and collection of *ad valorem* property taxes and the fundamentals of special assessments.[1]

AD VALOREM PROPERTY TAX

An "*ad valorem* property tax" is a tax levied on property literally "according to its value." Unless specifically exempted by statute, all real and personal property in North Carolina is subject to *ad valorem* property taxation whether the property is owned by a resident or nonresident of this State.[2] The public policy behind this tax is to provide counties and municipalities with the revenues they need to operate and to treat all property owners equally so that the tax burden will be shared. One source has summarized the property tax system as follows:

> Both real and personal property are subject to taxation in North Carolina. Real property includes land, buildings, and permanent fixtures, as well as rights and privileges pertaining to land, such as mineral or forestry rights. Personal property includes all other property, both tangible and intangible, that is not permanently affixed to land, although most types of intangible personal property are exempt from property taxation in North Carolina.[3]

Authority to Tax

The North Carolina Constitution, Article V, Section 2, addresses the "Power of Taxation." It reads: "The power of taxation shall be exercised in a just and equitable manner, for public purposes only, and shall never be surrendered, suspended or contracted away." The North Carolina General Assembly has the exclusive power to levy taxes and to establish the method and procedure for the discovery, listing, and assessing of property for taxation. While the General Assembly regulates *ad valorem* taxation within constitutional guidelines, *it is the county government that actually administers and collects the tax.* Cities and towns are also authorized by statute to exact an *ad valorem* tax on property.

North Carolina Machinery Act

Comprehensive legislation known as the **Machinery Act** governs the topic of *ad valorem* property taxation in North Carolina.[4] The Machinery Act describes property subject to and exempt from taxation, standards for appraisal and assessment, matters concerning the listing of property, duties of tax officials, review and appeal procedures, levy of taxes, collection of taxes, and tax liens and their foreclosure. Some highlights of the Machinery Act are discussed below.

Determining the Tax Rate

Each year, counties and municipalities determine the amount of their budget that must be funded through *ad valorem* property tax revenues and arrive at a **tax rate** as part of their budgetary process.[5] The tax rate is derived by dividing the revenue needed from the *ad valorem* property tax by the total assessed value of property in the taxing unit, whether county or city.[6] The tax rate must be established no later than July 1, the first day of each new fiscal year.

Tax Rate: Per One Hundred Dollars of Assessed Value

In North Carolina, the tax rate is calculated in terms of a dollar amount per one hundred dollars ($100) of assessed value.

Example 1: A county's tax rate is $0.75 per one hundred dollars of assessed value. A property owner's home has an assessed value of $300,000. The amount of real property tax is calculated as follows:

$$\$300,000 \div 100 = 3,000 \text{ "one hundreds"}$$
$$3,000 \times .75 = \$2,250 \text{ tax}$$

Example 2: An owner's lot has an assessed value of $90,000. The county's tax rate is $1.50 per one hundred dollars of assessed value. The *ad valorem* tax amount is calculated as follows:

$$\$90,000 \div 100 = 900 \text{ "one hundreds"};$$
$$900 \times \$1.50 = \$1,350 \text{ tax}$$

In the example below, the tax rate is applied to both the real and personal property of an owner

Example 3: An owner's real property has an assessed value of $246,580 and the owner's personal property has an assessed value of $27,830. The county tax rate is $0.89 per $100 of assessed value. The amount of tax owed is calculated as follows:

$$\$246,580 + \$27,830 = \$274,410 \text{ (total assessed value)}$$
$$\$274,410 \div 100 = 2744.10 \text{ "one hundreds;"} \quad 2744.10 \times \$.89 = \$2442.25 \text{ tax}$$

In some states, a "mill" is used to express the tax rate. *A "mill" is 1/1000 of a dollar* or 1/10 of one cent ($.001). A *mill rate* is described in terms of "mills per dollar" of assessed value. While North Carolina brokers should be familiar with the term, how to calculate the tax rate under that method is omitted, since it is not used in North Carolina.

PROPERTY SUBJECT TO TAXATION

All real and personal property within North Carolina is subject to taxation unless exempted by legislative or constitutional authority. For example, federal, state and local government property is exempt from taxation and exemptions exist for nonprofit, religious, educational, and charitable organizations. Tax exemptions and preferential tax treatment provisions also exist for other kinds of property including various categories of historic property, burial property, continuing care retirement homes, homeowner association property, low-income housing, protected natural areas, nonprofit water and sewer associations, solar energy systems, and standing timber.[7]

LISTING PROPERTY FOR TAXATION

An expert on North Carolina *ad valorem* property tax distinguishes "listing" from "appraising" as follows:

> Unfortunately, tax officials as well as property owners confuse listing and appraising; what are actually two separate processes are often treated and thought of as a single process. The listing process is equivalent to making an inventory of items of property; the appraisal process is the separate and distinct means by which value is assigned listed items.[8]

Permanent County Real Property Listing System

Real property must be listed annually in the name of the owner unless the board of county commissioners has adopted a permanent listing system.[9] Since all North Carolina counties have adopted a permanent listing system, annual listing of all real property owned is no longer necessary, but an owner must still provide an annual update reporting improvements made to the real estate and separate rights created.[10] The duty to list and pay taxes on interests in real property may extend beyond property held in fee simple. *All taxable* **real property**[11] *must be listed in the county in which it is situated.*

Personal Property Listing

The listing rules for personal property are more complicated than those for real property, due in part to the mobile nature of personal property. *As a general rule,* **personal property**[12] *must be listed in the county of the owner's residence.* The residence of a corporation or other business entity is where its principal place of business in North Carolina is located. Where there is no principal office in North Carolina, personal property is taxable at the place in North Carolina where it is located.[13]

Location of Listing

The Machinery Act requires that property subject to *ad valorem* taxation in any city or town must be listed during the prescribed period with the city or town, but instead of having a listing procedure separate from the county, the city or town is authorized to use the applicable county tax records. For most property, the city or town by law must accept the appraisals and assessments fixed by the authorities of the county in which the city or town is located. Special rules apply where the city or town is situated in more than one county.

APPRAISAL AND ASSESSMENT[14]

An important principle of property taxation is that all taxes be assessed and levied uniformly within the county or municipality.[15] Understanding the following terms is helpful when discussing the valuation of property for *ad valorem* tax purposes.

- **Appraisal** has two meanings: (1) An opinion or conclusion as to the value of property; and (2) the *process* of developing and communicating an opinion of value, also referred to as "**appraising**."

- **Assessment** is the *process* of determining property value for the purpose of *ad valorem* taxation.

- **Market value** is "the price estimated in terms of money at which the property would change hands between a willing and financially able buyer and willing seller, neither under any compulsion to buy or sell and both having reasonable knowledge of all the uses to which the property is adapted and for which it is capable of being used."[16]

- **Assessed value** is the value of property established for *ad valorem* tax purposes, often referred to as the "**tax value**."

General Statute 105-283 states that "… [A]ll property, real and personal, shall as far as practicable be appraised or valued at its true value in money" and defines "true value" as meaning "market value," as defined above. Thus, *"assessed value" (tax value) by law is supposed to equal "market value,"* at least at the time the assessed value is established. In reality, the assessed value frequently is less than true market value because of the techniques used to derive assessed value and the fact that the value usually is assessed only every eight years.

Assessment at Present Use Value

Subject to detailed statutory requirements, agricultural, horticultural, forestland, and wildlife conservation land can qualify for taxation on the basis of the present-use value of the property, but "[t]he statutory scheme is undoubtedly the most complicated of any in the Machinery Act."[17]

Indeed, the statutory scheme is complicated, detailed, and often subject to amendments and revisions by the General Assembly. Therefore, it is important that any person interested in qualifying real property for present-use value taxation obtain expert legal advice.[18]

The Assessment Process

"Assessment" is a specialized form of "appraising." County tax assessors use the same basic appraisal principles and concepts that appraisers follow when performing appraisals for other purposes, but the techniques employed are very different. Obviously, the time and detail devoted to appraising a single property for lending purposes cannot be duplicated by tax assessors who periodically must value thousands of land parcels within a county within a few months. Consequently, tax assessors routinely employ what is called "mass appraisal" techniques to derive assessed values for all parcels of land in the county. While the value for a particular property usually approximates market value as of the date the assessment is performed, it usually is less accurate than the value derived through a detailed appraisal of the property using conventional appraisal methods. The assessed value becomes increasingly less accurate as more time passes.

General Statute 105-317 provides guidelines and requirements for the assessment process. For example, it requires an appraiser to consider the advantages and disadvantages regarding location, zoning, quality of soil, and other listed factors. When determining the value of a building or improvement, the same statute requires the appraiser

> … to consider at least its location; type of construction; age; replacement cost; cost; adaptability for residence, commercial, industrial, or other uses; past income; probable future income; and any other factors that may affect its value.

Real Property: Eight-Year and Four-Year General Reappraisals

Under state law, real property must be reappraised in each county on a staggered schedule every eight years, although the board of county commissioners may adopt a resolution establishing a more frequent reappraisal cycle for that county, *e.g.*, every four years.[19]

Between general reappraisals, the tax assessor may increase or decrease the appraised value of real property to recognize changes in the property's value resulting from: 1) the correction of a clerical, mathematical, or appraisal error; 2) a conservation or preservation agreement; 3) a physical change to the land or improvements thereon; or, 4) a change in the legally permitted use of the property. A tax assessor is prohibited from changing the real property valuation between general reappraisals because of depreciation, economic factors affecting the county in general, or betterments, such as repainting or landscaping.[20]

Personal Property

Personal property is listed and appraised *annually* for taxation purposes. Personal property not used to produce income or for a business purpose may be exempt as "non-business property." The legal definition of "*nonbusiness property*" specifically *includes* "… *household furnishings, clothing, pets, lawn tools, and lawn equipment* …" but excludes "… motor vehicles, mobile homes, aircraft, watercraft, or engines for watercraft …" that must be listed and are subject to personal property taxes.[21] The Machinery Act requires that the value and ownership of personal property be determined as of January 1.[22] A fiscal year can be used for valuation purposes when the value of inventories and other goods and materials is held and used in connection with the business enterprise of a taxpayer whose fiscal year closes at a date other than December 31.

Appeals of Tax Valuations

The Machinery Act establishes a system for the formal appeal and review of tax listings and valuations.[23] Every county has a board of equalization and review to hear appeals by property owners regarding the tax valuation of their properties. A State Property Tax Commission serves as a board of equalization and review for the state and hears appeals from county board decisions. As a practical matter, the formal review and appeal procedure frequently can be circumvented by going directly to the county tax supervisor and presenting evidence that the property valuation is erroneous or unreasonable.

Officially, *ad valorem* tax assessments are presumed by law to be correct and the burden is on the taxpayer to prove that an assessment is incorrect. The taxpayer must show that an arbitrary or illegal method of valuation was used by the county tax supervisor and that the assessment *substantially* exceeded the true value of the property. If the taxpayer rebuts the presumption of correctness, the burden then shifts back to the county to show that the valuation is reasonable.[24]

TIMETABLE FOR LISTING, TAX LIEN, AND TAX COLLECTION

As previously noted, all North Carolina counties have adopted a permanent listing system for real property, thereby relieving the owner of the duty to annually list all real property owned; however the owner must provide an annual update concerning improvements made to the real estate and separate rights created. All personal property subject to *ad valorem* taxation must be listed annually.[25] Key dates are as follows:

- The fiscal year for counties and municipalities in North Carolina begins on July 1 and ends on June 30.

- Property must be listed between the first business day of January and the end of January (subject to any extensions that may be granted).

- Taxes (tax bills) for the upcoming fiscal year are issued between July 1 and September 1 of each year and are legally due on the first day of September, but often are paid between September 1 and early January of the next year because there is no interest penalty until January.

  Example: A typical cycle for the listing and payment of taxes by a North Carolina real property owner can be summarized as follows:
  • *January 1, 2017.* A tax lien attaches to the owner's real property even though the taxes are not due until later in the year.[26]
  • *June or July of 2017.* Taxes are levied by the county.
  • *September 1, 2017.* Taxes for the 2017 fiscal year (July 1, 2017 to June 30, 2018) are due, although taxes can be paid up until January 5, 2018 without an interest penalty.[27]
  • *December 30, 2017.* The property owner pays the 2017 *ad valorem* property taxes so the property tax can be deducted on federal and state income tax returns. Since payment was made prior to January 5, 2018, there is no interest or penalty.
  • *January 1, 2018.* The property tax cycle starts over again with a tax lien attaching to the owner's property for the 2018 property tax, even though the tax is not due until later that year.

The overwhelming custom or practice when closing residential real estate sales transactions in North Carolina is to prorate real property *ad valorem* taxes on a *calendar* year basis. The fact that the tax is levied to fund governmental operations for a fiscal year that does not coincide with the calendar year does not alter the calendar year method of proration.

PROPERTY TAX LIEN

The Machinery Act states:
> … regardless of the time at which liability for a tax for a given fiscal year may arise or the exact amount thereof be determined, the *lien* for taxes levied on a parcel of *real property* shall attach to the *parcel* taxed on the date as of which property is to be listed under G.S. 105-285 (January 1), and the *lien* for taxes levied on *personal property* shall attach to all ***real property*** of the taxpayer in the taxing unit on the same date.[28]
> (Emphasis added.)

The statute further states that "taxes levied on real and personal property (including penalties, interest, and costs allowed by law) shall be a lien on personal property from and after levy or attachment and garnishment of the personal property."

Thus, a city or county taxing unit acquires a continuing lien against a taxpayer's real property until the principal amount of the taxes plus any interest, penalties, and applicable costs are paid. ***A lien against real property attaches to the property itself and transfers with it.*** If a previous owner fails to pay the real property taxes when due and subsequently sells the property, the new owner, who is not personally liable for the back taxes, may have to pay the accrued taxes, interest, and costs to prevent the county from initiating a tax foreclosure sale. An attorney handling the real estate closing should discover the unpaid taxes in a title search and would require their payment or an escrow of funds to pay them as a prerequisite to closing.

TAX LIEN SUMMARY

- The tax lien on real property attaches as of the first day of the listing period, even though the tax is not due until later in the year.

- The lien for taxes levied on a parcel of **real property** is a **specific lien** on that parcel.

- The lien for taxes levied on **personal property** is a **general lien** on all ***real property*** owned by the taxpayer in the taxing unit.

- A lien for taxes levied on both real and personal property becomes effective against the taxpayer's *personal property* only after legal action has been initiated to seize or attach that property.

While the tax lien attaches to the real property as of January 1, it does not become actionable until the following January, and then only if the taxes have not been paid. Understand, however, that *the tax lien attaches to the real property itself and is enforceable against the property no matter who owns it.*

SPECIAL PRIORITY OF TAX LIENS

Tax liens imposed on real property for the nonpayment of *ad valorem* real or personal property taxes enjoy an almost absolute position of priority compared to other liens or claims against the real property. The relevant statute reads, in part:

> ... the lien ... shall be superior to all other liens, assessments, charges, rights, and claims of any and every kind in and to the real property to which the lien for taxes attaches regardless of the claimant and *regardless of whether acquired prior or subsequent to the attachment of the lien for taxes.*[29]
> (Emphasis added.)

An example can best illustrate the special priority.

Example: A buyer purchased land in North Carolina in 2014. She borrowed $350,000 from a bank to purchase the property and executed a deed of trust to the bank to secure repayment of the debt. In 2016, she failed to pay her real property tax bill. The lien for nonpayment of the 2016 property tax has priority over the earlier 2014 deed of trust held by the bank. When the property is sold, whether voluntarily or by foreclosure, the county will be paid all the back taxes, interest, penalties, and costs *before* the bank receives any monies.

Thus, contrary to the general rule that lien priority is determined by recording date, liens recorded *prior* to the attachment of a tax lien on real property are junior to a property tax lien. The priority has limited exceptions. For example, a state income tax lien *recorded* prior to the effective date of an *ad valorem* property tax lien takes priority.[30] *Ad valorem* property tax liens of any taxing unit stand on equal footing.[31]

Finally, it should be clear that events happening *after* the attachment of a property tax lien do not matter. General Statute 105-356(a)(3) states:

> The priority of the lien for taxes shall not be affected by transfer of title to the real property after the lien has attached, nor shall it be affected by the death, receivership, or bankruptcy of the owner of the real property to which the lien attaches.

SPECIAL ASSESSMENTS

Property taxes are assessed to defray the ordinary expenses of government, whereas a **special assessment** *is an individual charge against certain real property that is benefited by a local improvement such as a sidewalk or street.* North Carolina's local governmental units (i.e., counties, cities, and sanitary districts) often engage in "public works" projects that enhance the usefulness and value of privately owned real estate. The construction of sidewalks, sewer lines, streets, and drainage systems are typical examples of such works. While all public works projects must be in the "public interest," private property owners who receive a direct benefit from a project may be required to pay for all or a portion of the costs of constructing it.

By Counties

The North Carolina General Statutes authorize a *county* to make *special assessments* against benefitted property within the county to pay for the cost of all or part of specified public works improvements or projects.[32] Special assessments are authorized for:

- constructing, reconstructing, extending, or otherwise building or improving water systems and sewage collection and disposal systems;

- acquiring, constructing, reconstructing, extending, renovating, enlarging, maintaining, operating, or otherwise building and improving beach erosion control or flood and hurricane protection works, watershed improvement projects, drainage projects, and water resources development projects;

- constructing, reconstructing, paving, widening, installing curbs and gutters, and otherwise building and improving streets; and,

- providing street lights and street lighting in a residential subdivision.[33]

Basis for Determining Amount of Special Assessment

The criteria for determining the amount of the special assessment include each or a combination of the following:
- real property abutting the project at an equal rate per foot of frontage;
- street frontage of the lots served at an equal rate per foot of frontage;
- area of land served/benefitted by the project at an equal rate per unit of area; or,
- value of land benefitted by the project.[34]

The county board of commissioners may establish exemptions from assessments for water or sewer projects for corner lots when water or sewer lines are installed along both sides of the lots.[35]

Procedures for Imposing Special Assessments

Before a county board of commissioners may finance all or part of a proposed project by special assessments, it must first do the following:

- adopt a *preliminary assessment resolution* with required information about the project.

- issue notice of and hold a *public hearing*.

- adopt a ***final*** *assessment resolution* after public hearing directing that the public improvement project be undertaken in whole or in part.

- determine the costs of the project or improvement and issue a *preliminary assessment roll* containing: a brief description of each land parcel assessed, the basis of the assessment, the amount assessed against each parcel, the terms of payment, and the name of each property owner.

- issue proper notice to the public and hold a second public hearing to confirm the preliminary assessment roll.

- deliver, once confirmed, a copy of the assessment roll to the county tax collector for collection in the same manner as property taxes.[36]

Assessments Held in Abeyance

Each owner of assessed property must pay the assessment in full within thirty days after published notice of confirmation of the assessment roll, unless the board of commissioners allows the assessment to be paid in installments.[37] General Statute §153A-201 states:

> …The assessment resolution may provide that assessments made…shall be held in abeyance without interest for any benefitted property assessed. Water or sewer assessments may be held in abeyance until improvements on the assessed property are connected to the water or sewer system for which the assessment was made, or until a date certain not more than 10 years from the date of confirmation of the assessment roll, whichever event occurs first.

Beach erosion control and flood and hurricane protection assessments may also be held in abeyance.

By Cities or Towns

A city or town may make special assessments against benefitted property within its corporate limits for many of the same projects and improvements as counties.[38] The procedure for authorizing the special assessment and determining the amount and method of assessment is similar to the county procedure. As with county special assessments, city and town assessments for water and sewer may be held in abeyance. A city or town may also impose an *availability charge* for water or sewer services that are available to property owners who choose not to connect to the system, but the charge must be reasonable.[39]

Appeal of Amount of Assessment

A property owner dissatisfied with the amount of the special assessment must work quickly to preserve legal rights. The property owner only has **ten days** after confirmation of the special assessment roll to file a notice of appeal to the appropriate court and must serve on the county, city, or town a statement of the facts upon which the assessment appeal is based within **twenty days** after confirmation of the assessment roll. The appeal is then tried in court.[40]

Special Assessment Liens

Like a property tax lien, *a special assessment lien is a **specific lien** against the real property assessed and the lien transfers with the property.* In terms of **lien priority**, a special assessment lien is *inferior* to all prior or subsequent liens for state, local, and federal taxes, but is *superior* to all other liens.[41] Because unpaid special assessments transfer with the property to a new owner, any thorough title search will include a check for outstanding special assessments, especially since property owners frequently are allowed to spread the payments over a period of years.

Endnotes

1. A comprehensive treatment of the subject may be found in Shea, Riggsbee, Denning, *A Guide To The Listing, Assessment, and Taxation of Property in North Carolina* (2009), published by the UNC School of Government. (Hereafter referred to as Shea Riggsbee Denning, *Listing, Assessment, and Taxation of Property*.) Helpful websites include the North Carolina Department of Revenue at www.dornc.com which has a summary of types of property to be taxed, listing requirements, tax bill calculations, and contact information for each county, and UNC's School of Government website at www.sog.unc.edu. Official county websites also provide property tax information and allow online property tax searches and bill payment.

2. NC Gen. Stat. §105-274 titled "Property Subject to Taxation."

3. Shea, Riggsbee, Denning, *Listing, Assessment, and Taxation of Property*, p. 3.3. N.C.Gen.Stat. §105-274(a).

4. N.C. Gen. Stat. §105-271 *et. seq.* The full title of the Machinery Act is: "Listing, Appraisal, and Assessment of Property and Collection of Taxes on Property." N.C. Gen. Stat. §105-271 states: "This Subchapter may be cited as the Machinery Act."

5. For an excellent resource on county property tax rates, see the North Carolina Association of County Commissioners webpage at *http://www.ncacc.org/taxrate.htm*. The webpage contains a report of the tax rate in every North Carolina county, a recent history of county tax rates, and reports on trends in rate increases. See also the North Carolina Department of Revenue webpage, *http://www.dornc.com/publications/propertyrates.html*, for a report titled "Property Tax Rates and Latest Year of Revaluation for North Carolina Counties and Cities."

6. "Taxing unit" means a county or municipality authorized to levy *ad valorem* property taxes. N.C. Gen. Stat. §105-273(16). See also, Shea, Riggsbee, Denning, *Listing, Assessment, and Taxation of Property* §2.3, "Setting the Tax Rate," pp. 27 - 31.

7.　For a comprehensive outline of real and personal property tax exemptions, present-use categories, and exclusions from taxation, see Shea, Riggsbee, Denning, *Listing, Assessment, and Taxation of Property*, Appendix, pp. 237 - 273.　For each category, the Appendix summarizes the statutory authority, qualifying property, qualified owner, qualifying use, application procedure, and relief granted.

8.　Lewis, *The Property Tax in North Carolina, An Introduction*, p.14.

9.　N.C. Gen. Stat. §§105-302(a) and 105-303(b).

10.　N.C.Gen.Stat. §105-303(b)(2) refers to N.C.Gen.Stat. §105-309(c)(3)-(5) that require a short description of any buildings or improvements belonging to the property owner, any improvements exceeding $100 that have occurred since the last revaluation, and any buildings, improvements or separate rights on or in the real property owned by others. "Separate rights" include "… mineral, quarry, timber, waterpower, or other rights therein …."

11.　"Real property" is defined at N.C. Gen. Stat. §105-273(13) as follows:

> "Real property," "real estate," and "land" mean not only the land itself, but also buildings, structures, improvements, and permanent fixtures thereon, and all rights and privileges belonging or in any wise appertaining thereto.　These terms also mean a manufactured home as defined in G.S. §143-143.9(6) if it is a multi-section residential structure (consisting of two or more sections), has the moving hitch, wheels, and axles removed, and is placed upon a permanent enclosed foundation on land owned by the owner of the manufactured home.

12.　"Personal property" is comprehensively defined as "intangible" and "tangible" at N.C. Gen. Stat. §105-273(8) and (14). See also the definition of "inventories" at N.C. Gen. Stat. §105-273(8a). Guidelines for counties to provide for electronic listing of personal property were revised effective June 23, 2011. See Session Law 2011-238 repealing portions of the previous law and replacing it with N.C.Gen. Stat. § 105-310.1.

13.　N.C.Gen.Stat. §105-304(c)(2).　See also *In re Appeal of Amusements of Rochester, Inc.,* 201 N.C. App. 419, 689 S.E.2d 451 (N.C. App. 2009) in which the Court held that a New York corporation's principal place of business in North Carolina was Pender County where for six months each year the corporation stored and repaired carnival equipment used along the East Coast.

14.　A complete list of key terms and definitions relevant to the *ad valorem* taxation process is found in N.C. Gen. Stat. §105-273. For an excellent primer on the revaluation and assessment process in North Carolina, see Shea Riggsbee Denning, "A Citizens' Guide to the Revaluation and Assessment of Property by North Carolina Counties," UNC School of Government Property Tax Bulletin No. 144, March 2008. (Available on the School of Government bookstore website: http://shopping.netsuite.com/sogstore.)

15.　N.C.Gen.Stat. §105-284(a). As with all tax legislation, specific exceptions exist. Some categories of property, such as historic properties, receive special tax treatment as a special class of property.　See, for example, N.C.Gen.Stat. §105-278(b).

16.   N.C. Gen. Stat. §105-283.

17.   Shea, Riggsbee, Denning, *Listing, Assessment, and Taxation of Property* § 7.3, "Assessment at Present-Use Value," pp. 200- 201. See *www.dornc.com/downloads/av4.pdf* for the North Carolina General Statutes pertaining to present-use value.

18.   The statutes defining and classifying these types of properties and the requirements to apply a present-use value are found primarily at N.C.Gen.Stat. §105-277.2 to §105-277.7 and §105-277.15. Article 12 of Chapter 105 addresses all property subject to taxation.

19.   N.C.Gen.Stat. §105-286(a) & (a)(3). For an excellent summary of the real property tax appraisal process, see Shea, Riggsbee, Denning, *Listing, Assessment, and Taxation of Property* §4.1, pp. 92 - 98.

20.   N.C.Gen.Stat. §105-287(a) and (b).

21.   N.C.Gen.Stat. §105-275(16).

22.   N.C. Gen. Stat. §105-285. See also endnote 31 below.

23.   N.C. Gen. Stat. §§105-288, 105-322, 105-325.

24.   *In re Amp, Inc.*, 287 N.C. 547, 215 S.E.2d 752 (1975). See, for example, the case of *In Re Appeal of Bermuda Run Property Owners*, 145 N.C. App. 672, 551 S.E.2d 541 (2001), where the Court of Appeals reaffirmed that the correctness of tax assessments, the good faith of tax assessors, and the validity of their actions is presumed, that *ad valorem* tax assessments are presumed to be correct, and that the taxpayer has the burden of showing an erroneous assessment. See also, *In Re Appeal of Winston-Salem Joint Venture*, 144 N.C. App. 706, 551 S.E.2d 450 (2001) where the Court of Appeals reaffirmed the presumption of correctness.

       For additional cases dealing with tax appeals, see *In re Morgan*, 362 N.C. 339, 661 S.E.2d 733 (2008) reversing the Court of Appeals, 186 N.C.App. 567, 652 S.E.2d 655 (2007); *In re Murray*, 179 N.C.App. 780, 635 S.E.2d 477 (2006) (involving a taxpayer's manufactured home); *In re Tillman*, 187 N.C.App. 739, 653 S.E.2d 911 (2007); *In re Battle*, 166 N.C. App. 240, 601 S.E.2d 253 (2004); *In re Weaver Investment Company*, 165 N.C. App. 198, 598 S.E.2d 591 (2004).

25.   N.C. Gen. Stat. §105-285 is titled: "Date as of which property is to be listed and appraised." Subsection (a) of this statute requires the annual listing, subsection (b) sets forth the general rule as to personal property, and subsection (d) deals with real property.

       As noted earlier, N.C.Gen.Stat. §105-302(a) requires real property owners to annually list real property titled in the owner's name *unless* the board of county commissioners has adopted a permanent listing system pursuant to N.C.Gen.Stat. §105-303(b) which all counties have done. Thus, owners no longer must list their real property annually, but they must provide an annual update regarding improvements made to the real estate and separate rights created. See endnote 10 as to "separate rights."

26.   N.C. Gen. Stat. §105-355(a).

27.   N.C. Gen. Stat. §105-360.

28. N.C. Gen. Stat. §105-355(a) & (b).

29. N.C. Gen. Stat. §105-356(a)(1).

30. *County of Carteret v. Long*, 349 N.C. 285, 507 S.E.2d 39 (1998).

31. N.C. Gen. Stat. §105-356(a)(2).

32. See Article 9 of Chapter 153A of the North Carolina General Statutes, G.S. §153A-185 to 153A-206.

33. N.C. Gen. Stat. §153A-185.

34. N.C. Gen. Stat. §153A-186, titled "Bases for making assessments."

35. N.C. Gen. Stat. §153A-187. The statute provides in part: "A schedule may not allow exemption of more than seventy-five percent (75%) of the frontage of any side of a corner lot, or 150 feet, whichever is greater."

36. The procedure summarized here is authorized under N.C. Gen. Stat. §§153A-190 to 153A-195.

37. N.C. Gen. Stat. §§153A-196 and 153A-199.

38. See Article 10 of Chapter 160A of the General Statutes, G.S. §§160A-216 to 160A-238.

39. N.C.Gen.Stat. §160A-317.

40. N.C. Gen. Stat. §153A-197 for counties; N.C. Gen. Stat. §160A-230 for cities and towns. See, for example, *Parker v. New Hanover County*, 173 N.C.App. 644, 619 S.E.2d 868 (2005), involving a special assessment by a county for the relocation of an inlet to prevent beach erosion. See also *Ricks v. Town of Selma*, 99 N.C. App. 82, 392 S.E.2d 437 (1990) regarding availability charges for a newly extended sewage system that included a mobile home park in which many residents had septic systems.

41. N.C. Gen. Stat. §153A-200(c) for counties; N.C. Gen. Stat. §160A-233(c) for cities and towns. *Town of Cary v. Stallings*, 97 N.C. App. 484, 389 S.E.2d 143 (1990). In addition to special assessments by governmental units, special assessments can be levied by many homeowner and unit owner associations under the Planned Community act and Condominium Act. For cases involving the levying of special assessments by homeowner associations, see *Page v. Bald Head Association*, 170 N.C. App. 151, 611 S.E.2d 463 (2005); *cf. Midsouth Golf, LLC v. Fairfield Harbourside Condominium Ass'n, Inc.*, 187 N.C.App. 22, 652 S.E.2d 378 (2007); *Parker v. Figure "8" Beach Homeowners' Association*, 170 N.C. App. 145, 611 S.E.2d 874 (2005).

4 | PROPERTY DESCRIPTION

Real estate sales contracts, leases, and deeds must contain an adequate description of the subject property to be valid.[1] The absence of a legally adequate description may invalidate title to a parcel of real estate. North Carolina courts have stated the following legal standard on many occasions:

> ...It [the contract or conveyance] must contain a description of the land, the subject matter of the contract, either certain in itself or capable of being reduced to certainty by reference to something extrinsic about which the contract refers. If the description is sufficiently definite for the court, with the aid of extrinsic evidence, to apply the description to the exact property intended to be sold, it is enough.[2]

ADEQUACY OF DESCRIPTIONS

A **patent ambiguity** in the property description will invalidate the parties' agreement. It occurs when the language in the property description is so poorly drafted that the location of the parcel cannot be determined. A description with a patent ambiguity refers either to no outside facts or to facts too ambiguous to adequately identify a property. If the description is too vague and lacks external references, outside evidence may *not* be admitted in a lawsuit to assist in identifying the parcel involved.[3]

A **latent ambiguity** occurs when the description is not sufficient in itself to identify the property, but it refers to something extrinsic by which the land might be identified. A description with a latent ambiguity is valid if the precise parcel can be identified by use of the extrinsic reference.[4]

Patent and latent ambiguities often result from imprecise and incomplete drafting of property descriptions by laypersons.

Example: Able conveys to Baker property described in the deed only as "the Able homeplace in Lillington, North Carolina containing a house and about three acres of land." Extrinsic evidence could be introduced as to the existence of a parcel of land known as "the Able homeplace." Because the description, while inadequate, refers to specific extrinsic facts, it contains a **latent ambiguity**. The conveyance will be valid if one parcel known as "the Able homeplace" can be located that fits this description.

Example: Cook contracts to convey to Davis "my red house on Market Street in Brevard, N.C." This is a **latent ambiguity**. If outside evidence shows that Cook owns only one red house on Market Street, the description will be adequate and the contract to convey valid.

Example: A seller and buyer execute a contract to convey "land owned by the seller to be determined at a future date." This is a **patent ambiguity**, and the contract is unenforceable. At best, it is a nonbinding "agreement to agree" on a precise parcel at a future date.

When preparing real estate sales contracts or leases, a broker should never gamble on how much less than a full legal description will pass muster as meeting the "bare minimum" required by North Carolina law. *The best way to avoid problems is to duplicate the legal description from an existing deed or other evidence of title on any long-term lease or contract to convey.* As a practical matter, street addresses are often used in short-term residential leases and sometimes in listing contracts when the legal description is not available. This practice is adequate to create a binding listing contract or lease, so long as the address is accurate and clearly identifies the subject property.

A licensed surveyor or engineer should be hired when a legal description is needed for a parcel carved out of a larger parcel. Any doubt about the validity of an existing description should be referred to an experienced real estate attorney.

METHODS OF DESCRIBING REAL ESTATE

Various methods of describing real estate are listed below and then discussed separately.
- Metes and Bounds
- Rectangular (Governement) Survey System
- Reference to Plat or Map
- Reference to Publicly Recorded Documents
- Informal Reference

Metes and Bounds

A **metes and bounds** description is one that begins at some known point, called the *point of beginning,* and then describes the outside boundaries of a parcel through a series of *calls* between landmarks or monuments. The direction and distance of each call are stated. A metes and bounds description must meet two basic elements: (1) it must start at a known and readily identifiable point so that it can be duplicated with some degree of certainty by later surveyors; and (2) it must "close." This means that no gap in the boundary exists and that the last call ends at the point of beginning.

To understand how to read a metes and bounds description, a number of points must be understood. First, metes and bounds descriptions have *directions* given in terms of *deviation from north and south.*

It might be helpful to view the compass as containing the following quadrants:

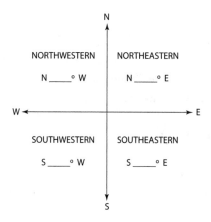

Any line in the direction of the southeastern quadrant will be described in terms of how many degrees east it is of due south, expressed as South a certain number of degrees East (S __° E). Any line in the direction of the southwestern quadrant will be described in terms of how many degrees west it is of due south, expressed as South a certain number of degrees West (S __° W). Similarly any line in the direction of the northeastern quadrant will be described as how many degrees east it is of due north, (N __° E), and any line in the direction of the northwestern quadrant will be described as how many degrees west it is of due north, (N __° W). See the directions shown on the following surveyor's compass:

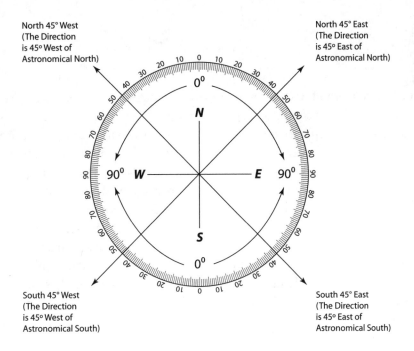

The directions can be further refined by use of *minutes* and *seconds*. **Each degree consists of 60 minutes, and each minute consists of 60 seconds.** Thus a direction may be expressed as N 83°30'30"E (North 83 degrees, 30 minutes, 30 seconds east, or about 83 degrees east of astronomical north).

Metes and bounds descriptions also refer to the following terms: *monument* (both natural and artificial), *course,* and *distance.* A **monument** is simply any item on the ground – a tree, a fence, a river, an iron stake, a cement marker – that serves as a point of reference to a person who is trying to locate the property lines. *Artificial monuments* are those made by man. *Natural monuments* are products of nature. A **course** is the direction of a line. A **distance**, logically, is the length of a line.

An example of a correct metes and bounds description with a corresponding diagram illustrating the description follows.

Example: A parcel of land along State Road 1350, commencing at the southern line of the highway right of way of said road at an iron stake that is the northwest corner of the Taylor Stewart farm, then South 29° East 250 feet along the Taylor Stewart line to a notched pine tree; then South 83° 30' West 248.25 feet to an iron stake; then North 54° 30' West 109.50 feet to an iron stake; then North 28° 30' East 172 feet to the southern line of the right of way of State Road 1350; then North 81° East 156.25 feet along the southern line of the right of way of said road to the point of beginning.

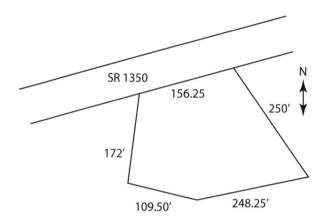

The most accurate method of describing property by metes and bounds is to give the directions in terms of deviation from north and south. It is not unusual, however, for calls in old metes and bounds descriptions to refer to relatively temporary objects or matters not necessarily known to a surveyor or attorney trying to locate the boundaries one or two hundred years after the description was drafted. For example, one North Carolina description refers "to the place where the old mare used to stand in the pasture." An old Connecticut description instructs you to pace "... just 18 rods more from the stump of the big hemlock tree where Phil Blake killed the bear ...." The fact that many of these old descriptions are crude and informal does not necessarily make them invalid. If a surveyor can locate the original boundaries, the description is sufficient.

North Carolina courts generally have applied a common sense approach to resolving technical problems and minor ambiguities associated with inadequately drafted metes and bounds descriptions. For example, where a final call in a description is to the point of beginning but the distance in the call falls short of that point, the courts have held that the call obviously was meant to run to that point and the inaccurate statement of distance is disregarded.[5] In construing any legal description, *the goal of the court is to ascertain the intent of the parties.*

Software programs and cell phone apps are available that can convert a metes and bounds description into a plat drawing, calculate square footage or acreage, and enter measurements.[6] While these software programs provide a convenient method of informally drawing a plat, a licensed surveyor or professional engineer should always be consulted when a new property description is needed and a survey required. Parties' attempts to draft metes and bounds descriptions or produce and rely upon unofficial surveys often lead to legal problems.

Government (Rectangular) Survey System

In 1785, Congress adopted the Rectangular or Government Survey System to use as a reliable method for describing enormous tracts of land the federal government had acquired in the Western Territories and wanted to sell to generate revenue. This system is still used today in many states other than the original thirteen colonies that opted to use the British metes and bounds system previously described.

Under the Rectangular or Government Survey System, now overseen by the federal Bureau of Land Management, the division of land into tracts is based from an "initial point" that is the intersection of the principal meridian (the north-south line) and the baseline (the east-west line). Land is divided into 24 square-mile districts composed of quadrants of 6 square-miles each called "townships" that are further subdivided into 1 square-mile tracts called "sections." While licensees rarely will encounter this system in North Carolina, they should be familiar with the basic principles. Details about this system may be found in most real estate principles texts and on the Internet.[7]

Reference to Recorded Plat

The most common method of describing small parcels of land is by **reference to a recorded plat** (map) of a subdivision. The plat is a surveyed description of all lot locations with designating numbers of each lot and block.[8] The subdivision itself is given a name and the plat is then recorded at the office of the Register of Deeds. North Carolina statutes set forth minimum requirements and standards for land plats presented to the Register of Deeds for recording. One of the central statutes dealing with these requirements and standards provides, in part:

> ... A plat, when certified ... and presented for recording, shall be recorded in the plat book or plat file and when so recorded shall be duly indexed. Reference in any instrument hereafter executed to the record of any plat herein authorized shall have the same effect as if the description of the lands as indicated on the record of the plat were set out in the instrument.[9]

Once the plat is recorded, any given lot within the subdivision may be described by reference to lot number, block number (if necessary), and recorded plat, *e.g.,* "Lot 5, Block 2 of Happy Hills Subdivision, as recorded in Book of Maps 1240, Page 35 in the Register of Deeds, Harnett County, North Carolina."

Reference to the book and page number of the recorded subdivision plat is helpful and recommended but not mandatory for the description to be legally valid. A description reading "Lot 5, Block 2 of Happy Hills Subdivision in Harnett County" is a legally sufficient description *so long as* there is a duly created and recorded Happy Hills Subdivision in that county. A danger with this type of description is when a contract to convey describes the lot by reference to a plat, but the plat is neither recorded nor available when the validity of the legal description is disputed. The contract may be invalid for inadequacy of a description that referred to an unavailable or nonexistent plat.

*If a property being sold is shown on a recorded plat, then reference to the **recorded** plat (i.e., book and page number) is the best method to describe the real property when preparing a sales contract.*

Reference to Publicly Recorded Documents

Real property is commonly described by **reference to publicly recorded documents**; that is, by including in a contract or deed a reference to the legal description contained in some recorded document affecting the subject property.

> *Example:* Smith contracts to convey to Jones "a tract containing 310 acres, more or less, known as the 'Ned Nickle place,' as more fully described in a deed from Ned Nickle to Sam Smith dated April 10,1980 recorded in Book 520, page 130, Office of the Register of Deeds of Lee County, N.C."

The above description is completely valid if the deed referred to exists. The deed from Smith to Jones will be interpreted as if it contains the full legal description set out in the deed from Nickle to Smith. This is a perfectly acceptable method to use when preparing a sales contract; however, care must be taken to *ensure the reference is accurate.*

In many counties, real property is indexed and described in the public records based on a parcel identifier number (PIN). Each parcel of land is assigned a unique parcel identifier number[10] and any tract can be described simply by referring to the PIN, e.g., Able contracts to convey to Baker "a lot in Orange County, North Carolina, Parcel Identifier Number 12345." While this description is valid, a cautious person will double check the accuracy of the PIN.

Informal Reference

While the method of describing property by **informal reference** may ultimately lead to practical and legal problems, any reference that is clear enough to enable a surveyor to locate the precise parcel of land involved is legally sufficient. A contract to convey may sometimes describe the property only by street number. This can lead to problems at times, if, for example, the seller owns more than one lot at that location.

> *Example:* Jones agrees to sell Baker his residence at 324 North Cedar Street in Raleigh, North Carolina. Next to the Jones house is another lot that Jones landscaped and Baker thought was part of the transaction. Before the closing, Baker drives by the property and notices a "for sale" sign on the adjacent lot. When he calls Jones, he is told that the lot is at 326 North Cedar Street and is not part of the contract. The informality of the description saved time in the beginning, but may lead to a misunderstanding and possible legal problems in the long run.

Street numbers are, of course, commonly used in relatively short-term rental agreements where the consequences of error or misunderstanding are not nearly as significant as they are when long-term or highly valuable property interests are transferred. They are also common in listing contracts.

PROPERTY SURVEY

A *survey* is the determination of the boundaries of a tract of land by a licensed surveyor or civil engineer. The professional land surveyor or professional engineer[11] then drafts a map or plat of the property. If title insurance is ordered, the surveyor will also complete a certificate or report disclosing certain information about the property and the improvements located on it. The North Carolina Board of Professional Engineers and Land Surveyors has established "Standards for Surveys."[12] One of these standards provides:

> ... Any and all visible or determined encroachments or easements on the property being surveyed shall be accurately located and clearly indicated. With respect to recorded easements, the surveyor shall, at a minimum, examine the most recent deeds and recorded plats adjacent to the subject property as well as all deeds and plats recorded after the date of the deed or plat upon which the survey is being based.[13]

Land surveying techniques now utilize advanced computer technologies that yield land description and other property reports with unprecedented accuracy. Surveyors and professional engineers undergo extensive training and regularly use global positioning satellite systems and other technologies. Sophisticated computer programs and Internet resources are available for use in data collection, analysis, plotting, imaging, and generating boundary descriptions that will remain accurate even if physical markers and boundaries on the ground eventually disappear.

The specialized role of the professional land surveyor (or professional engineer) should be emphasized. He or she is an expert on the latest techniques and standards for property description and measurement. The surveyor investigates and reports boundaries and other information, but does not draw conclusions concerning legal title matters or property ownership. A survey is a very important report that should be reviewed by a real estate attorney.

A real estate broker should never offer an opinion as to whether the boundaries of a parcel are correct, whether improvements are properly located on the tract, where easements are located on the property, or similar matters. Instead, the parties should be referred to a licensed surveyor or civil engineer.

Some of the more important information revealed by a survey is summarized below and then briefly discussed.

INFORMATION CONTAINED IN A SURVEY

- Boundaries of a parcel or lot.
- Location of buildings, fences, and other improvements.
- Location of utility easements and right of way easements.
- Location of water bordering, located on, or running through the property.
- Acreage and/or Square Footage.
- Access.
- Correct Parcel or Lot.

Boundaries

A survey will show the precise boundaries of a tract, including each corner and the various "calls." It is not uncommon for monuments to disappear and boundary lines to become indistinct over the years. A real estate purchaser is well advised to have the tract surveyed prior to closing and to have the surveyor clearly mark each corner. The surveyor will also compute the area of the tract so the purchaser can verify the amount of land being purchased. By having a survey performed prior to closing, the purchaser may be able to resolve any existing disputes about boundaries before concluding the transaction. (A seller who has a recent survey might consider making the information available to prospective purchasers.)

Location of Buildings and Improvements

A survey will reveal whether improvements have been located in compliance with setback requirements in restrictive covenants and zoning laws. For example, if all houses must be at least 40 feet back from the front lot line and the survey shows that the house is only 35 feet back, the survey has revealed a relatively serious problem. A survey will reveal whether the owner who constructed a garage based on an "estimate" of where the lot line was succeeded, or whether the garage encroaches on a neighbor's property. Surveys also will reveal whether fences have been properly located and whether neighboring property owners have constructed their buildings or other improvements so they do not encroach on the parcel being surveyed.

Property owners run the risk of inadvertently encroaching on adjacent property if they fail to obtain a survey in advance of placing improvements on property. In a 2008 North Carolina Court of Appeals decision, a property owner constructed a house on a lot without a survey. The house later was sold on two separate occasions to grantees who did not obtain a survey. Ten years after the third owners purchased the property, they had it surveyed. The survey revealed that the driveway and some landscaping encroached onto an adjacent tract of land owned by another person. These mistakes resulted in litigation and an unsuccessful appeal by the owners to the Court of Appeals, all of which could have been avoided had the original owner had a survey prior to constructing the driveway or landscaping.[14]

Location of Easements

A survey will reveal the location of easements on the property. Where property has one boundary along a railroad right-of-way, a survey will show the actual boundary of that right-of-way — a boundary that could be several hundred feet closer than the actual tracks. Similarly, a public utility power line easement can be significantly wider than the actual location of the poles or towers. A survey should also reveal any private right-of-way easements crossing the property.

Location of Water

A survey will show any creeks, rivers, lakes, ponds, or other bodies of water located on or bordering the surveyed property and whether the boundary of the property actually extends to the body of water giving the property riparian rights.

Acreage

A survey will reveal the actual acreage or square footage of the property. This can be significant when the parcel is to contain a certain number of acres or square footage and the purchase or lease price is based on a stated amount per acre or area. It can also be significant where a public ordinance or private restriction sets forth a minimum lot size requirement.

Access

"Legal access" is a requirement in most real estate sales transactions. A survey will disclose the location of the parcel with respect to public roads and rights-of-way. It will also reveal the location of driveways across other parcels of land where the parcel is not adjacent to a public road.

Correct Parcel or Lot

In rare but troublesome instances, houses have been constructed on the wrong lot or parcel. Sometimes in a new subdivision, a purchaser will have pointed out one undeveloped lot with a certain view and accidentally executes a contract containing the wrong lot description. A survey should reveal this serious error

Lenders' Requirements, Title Insurance Coverage, and Surveys

Surveys may be required in real estate transfers involving mortgage financing due to lenders' closing instructions, title insurance requirements (which at times can be waived), or both. (Title insurance and survey issues are discussed in Chapter 6.)

The illustration on the following page is part of a survey of a lot with a single family residence on it. The survey reveals that the dwelling on the adjoining lot encroaches on the surveyed lot by .70' to .89'. Put simply, the owners of the adjoining lot built over their lot line, and the driveway on the adjoining lot encroaches slightly onto the surveyed lot. These encroachments are defects in the titles to both lots. In the event of a sale or refinancing of either property, they are problems that need to be corrected. Fortunately, the existing owners of the adjoining lots worked things out; the owner of Lot 2 conveyed the small area of encroachment by the neighbor's home to the owner of Lot 3. In addition, the parties worked out a license (permission) from the owner of Lot 2 for the owner of Lot 3 to continue the slight driveway encroachment. This license is revocable at any time.

In short, the survey revealed two title defects and the common sense of good neighbors prevented a court battle and legal fees over this problem. The owners of Lot 3 should have had a survey performed prior to constructing their home and driveway which would have prevented their inadvertent encroachments on their neighbor's property.

Illustration

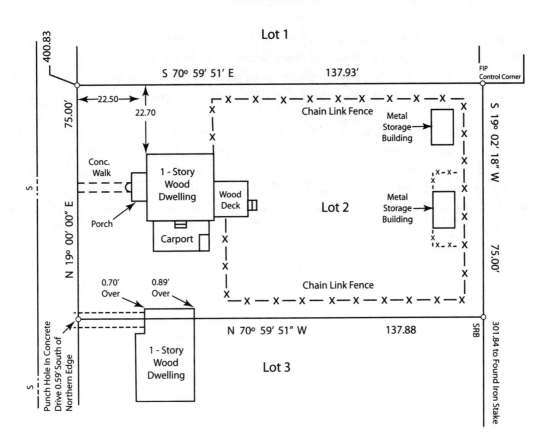

Endnotes

1. *Overton v. Boyce*, 289 N.C. 291, 221 S.E.2d 347 (1976) and numerous other North Carolina Supreme Court decisions recite this rule, *i.e.* adequate description of property.

2. See, for example, *Harris v. Woodard*, 130 N.C. 580, 41 S.E. 790 (1902).

3. *Lane v. Coe*, 262 N.C. 8, 136 S.E.2d 269 (1964); *Taylor v. Bailey*, 34 N.C. App. 290, 237 S.E.2d 918 (1977). The distinction between "patent" and "latent" ambiguities in legal descriptions persists. See, for example, *Wolfe v. Villines*, 169 N.C. App. 483, 610 S.E.2d 754 (2005), a case where the court ultimately found that a latent ambiguity existed.

4. *Kidd v. Early*, 289 N.C. 343, 222 S.E.2d 392 (1976). For more recent cases reaffirming the traditional definitions of *latent* and *patent* ambiguities, see *King v. King*, 146 N.C. App. 442, 552 S.E.2d 262 (2001), *Rawls & Assoc. v. Hurst*, 144 N.C. App. 286, 550 S.E.2d 219 (2001) where there was a latent ambiguity in a contract to convey; and *Lancaster v. Maple Street Homeowners Association, Inc*, 156 N.C. App. 429, 577 S.E.2d 365 (2003) holding that a poorly drafted deed description nonetheless was not patently ambiguous. See also Hetrick & McLaughlin, *Webster's Real Estate Law in North Carolina*, 6th ed. (LexisNexis) § 9.09, pp. 9-36 – 9-40.

5. See, for example, *Sugg v. Town of Greenville*, 169 N.C. 606, 86 S.E.2d 695 (1915); *Cowles v. Reavis*, 109 N.C. 417, 13 S.E. 930 (1891).

6. *See, for example,* Metes and Bounds Pro, by Sandy Knoll Software, LLC, https://itunes.apple.com/ us/metes-and-bounds-pro/id; Metes and Bounds, Sandy Knoll Software, http://download.cnet.com/ Metes-and-Bounds/3000-2064 . (Reference to these products is not an endorsement of them by either the North Carolina Real Estate Commission or the co-authors of this Manual.)

7. For a description of this system, see Cunningham, Stoebuck & Whitman, *The Law of Property*, §11.2 (West Publishing Co. 1993).

8. See, for example, *Parrish v. Hayworth*, 138 N.C. App. 637, 532 S.E.2d 202 (2000), where the Court of Appeals notes: "A map or plat, referred to in a deed, becomes part of the deed, as if it were written therein." [Quoting from *Stines v. Willyng, Inc.*, 81 N.C.App. 98, 344 S.E.2d 546 (1986).]

9. N.C. Gen. Stat. §47-30(g). Statutes dealing with governmental approval of plats and the regulation of subdivisions are located in Chapter 153A of the North Carolina General Statutes. See, for example, N.C. Gen. Stat. §§153A-330 through 153A-335.

10. N.C. Gen. Stat. §161-22.2, titled "Parcel identifier number indexes."

11. For the regulation of professional land surveyors and engineers, see Chapter 89C of the North Carolina General Statutes, "Engineering and Land Surveying." The term "professional land surveyor" is defined at N.C. Gen. Stat. §89C-3(9), and "professional engineer" is defined at N.C. Gen. Stat. §89C-3(8). The term "land surveying" is defined at N.C. Gen. Stat. §89C-3(7).

12. See 21 NCAC 56.1602, "Surveying Procedures."

13. 21 NCAC 56.1602(b) and (c).

14. *Jones v. Miles*, 189 N.C.App. 289, 658 S.E.2d 23 (2008)

5 | TRANSFER OF TITLE TO REAL PROPERTY

METHODS OF TRANSFERRING TITLE

Real estate brokers must understand how title to real property is transferred, both voluntarily and involuntarily, although the primary focus here will be the various deeds used most frequently for voluntary transfers of title. Title to real property may be transferred in the following ways:

- descent
- will
- survivorship
- foreclosure
- adverse possession
- escheat to the state
- eminent domain (condemnation)
- deed

Transfer by Descent (Intestate Succession)

If an owner of property dies without a will, that owner has died "intestate." Statutes dealing with "intestate succession," sometimes called "descent and distribution," specify who is entitled to the deceased owner's real and personal property.[1] Intestate succession is highly technical and requires legal advice.

Transfer by Will

A person who disposes of property upon death by will (or "last will and testament") has died "testate." Historically, the transfer of real property by will was termed a devise while the transfer of personal property was known as a bequest. That distinction in terminology may well linger in everyday practice, but the modern trend—as evidenced by amendments to the law of wills in North Carolina—eliminates the distinction and refers to either transfer as a "**devise**."[2] The subject of wills is governed by Chapter 31 of the North Carolina General Statutes. An attorney should always be consulted concerning the transfer of property by will.

Surviving Spouse's Statutory Right to Life Estate

N.C. Gen. Stat. §29-30 can affect the marketability of title.[3] It allows a surviving spouse to elect to take a life estate in one-third the value of all real estate owned by the deceased spouse during the marriage. This is the true even if the real property was titled solely in the name of the deceased spouse. This statute replaced common law concepts of dower (a life estate for a widow) and curtesy (a life estate for a widower) with the marital life estate discussed in Chapter 1. The election to take a one-third life estate under the statute is rarely exercised because the surviving spouse either must elect not to take his or her intestate share or must dissent from the will of the deceased spouse. Occasionally the election is made due to statutory protection from creditors' claims.

However, if the nontitled spouse signed any deed, deed of trust, or contract to convey real estate owned by the other spouse, she or he waived any rights under this statute. Thus, *it is critical that both spouses sign any listing contract, contract to convey, deed, or other conveyance even if the real property is titled only in the name of one spouse, so long as the owner-spouse is legally married at the time of the transfer.*

Transfer by Survivorship

Property held as tenants by the entirety or joint tenants with right of survivorship does not pass by last will and testament or by intestate succession. Property with a survivorship feature transfers to the surviving co-owners ***immediately and automatically by operation of law***. There is no need to rely on estate or probate law to determine who receives the deceased owner's interest in the real property as that share vests at death in the surviving co-owners. Property owned as tenants in common has no survivorship feature and thus is subject to distribution by intestate succession or by last will and testament upon the death of a co-owner.

Transfer by Involuntary Alienation

Involuntary alienation occurs when title to real property is transferred against the wishes and without the consent of the owner. Examples of involuntary alienation include the following:

- **Foreclosure Sales.** Sale by **foreclosure** under a deed of trust is the most common example of involuntary alienation.[4] Other examples include tax foreclosure sales for nonpayment of taxes[5] or foreclosure sales for nonpayment of an assessment or fine due a planned community or condominium.

- **Execution Sales (Sheriff's Sales).** A sheriff's execution sale to satisfy a judgment against a debtor is another method of involuntary alienation.[6]

- **Adverse Possession.** Involuntary alienation may also occur through **adverse possession**, where a person acquires title by occupying and possessing real property of another for a statutory period. If the occupant maintains adverse possession of the land for the requisite time period, the occupant acquires "title by adverse possession." A new or "original" title is created in the adverse possessor, and the title of the record owner is extinguished. Adverse possession is discussed later in this chapter.

- **Escheat.** When a person dies without a will leaving absolutely no heirs, that person's property will **escheat** to the State of North Carolina.[7] Once the property escheats to the state, a deed from the state that complies with statutory requirements is necessary for further transfers of the property.

- **Eminent Domain (Condemnation).** The federal and state governments, as well as some government agencies and public utilities, can compel a property owner to transfer property to the government if the property is needed for a public purpose. This power to take citizens' property is known as *eminent domain* or *condemnation*. The property owner must be paid "just compensation" for the property by the condemning authority.

The most common purposes for taking all or part of a parcel of land by eminent domain include highway construction, sewer and water line easements, and easements for power transmission lines. Subject to very limited exceptions, the affected property owner has no choice in transferring the property to the condemning agency; rather, the most frequent legal controversy is whether the amount of money offered by the condemning agency constitutes "just compensation" for the property interest taken.

Transfer by Voluntary Alienation (Deeds)

Most land is voluntarily transferred by a deed executed pursuant to a contract, agreement, or gift. The property owner conveying the property is called the ***grantor***, and the person or entity receiving the property is called the ***grantee***. Real estate brokers must be familiar with deeds commonly used in real estate conveyances.

DEEDS

A familiar saying in property law is that a deed must be "signed, sealed, and delivered" to be effective. The North Carolina Supreme Court has defined a deed as "... *an instrument in writing, signed, sealed, and delivered by the grantor, whereby an interest in realty is transferred from the grantor to the grantee.*" However, as will be discussed shortly, a "seal" is no longer required to create a valid deed under North Carolina law.[8]

All deeds should be prepared by an attorney. While certain forms are included in this text to enhance an understanding of deeds, *a broker should **never** prepare any deed or other legal document for others.* Anyone who prepares or aids in the preparation of a deed, mortgage, or deed of trust for any other person or entity is engaged in the "practice of law." Persons who are not licensed attorneys are prohibited from "practicing law" and may be prosecuted.[9] A real estate licensee who performs any legal service for others also violates License Law and may be subject to disciplinary action by the Real Estate Commission.

Essential Elements of a Valid Deed

To create a legally valid deed, several essential elements must exist. These elements are summarized below and are then briefly explained.

Checklist of Essential Deed Elements
- In Writing
- Competent and Identified Parties
- Adequate Property Description
- Operative Words of Conveyance
- Grantor's Signature
- Legal Delivery and Acceptance

In Writing

The Statute of Frauds, General Statute §22-2, requires that a deed *must be in writing*. While the majority of modern deeds are on printed, approved forms, there is no legal requirement that any particular form be used as long as the essential elements of a deed are present. Computer-generated forms designed by attorneys are also in common use.

Competent and Identified Grantor and Grantee

*The grantor must be competent to convey, and the grantee must be capable of receiving the grant of the property. Any person who is competent to make a valid contract is competent to be a **grantor***. A deed made after a person has been judicially declared mentally incompetent is absolutely void.[10] A deed from a minor (in North Carolina, a person younger than eighteen years of age) is voidable *by that minor* upon reaching the age of majority.[11] Therefore, no one should facilitate a real estate transaction with such persons or take a deed from any grantor who is a minor or mentally incompetent.

Even if a grantor is mentally competent, a deed may be set aside where undue influence has been exerted. Undue influence is the improper influence over the mind and will of another to such an extent that the grantor does not act freely in signing the deed but signs it because of a third person who is exerting excessive influence.

While a grantee need not have contractual capacity to receive a grant of land by deed, every grantee must be a person in being, either a natural person or an artificial person such as a corporation or partnership, capable of taking title at the time the deed is executed.[12] A dead person cannot be a grantee.[13] Both parties, the grantor and grantee, must be properly identified, especially the grantee, who must be ascertainable.

Adequate Property Description

As noted on the checklist, *the property conveyed must be adequately described.* There are thousands of court decisions concerning the legal adequacy of property descriptions. Property descriptions are discussed in Chapter 4.

Operative Words of Conveyance

The deed must contain language demonstrating that the grantor actually grants and presently transfers the property. In legal jargon, this requirement is known as *"operative words of conveyance."* All standard form deeds comply with this requirement; it is the "homemade" document that must be carefully examined for the presence of this element.[14]

Grantor's Signature

The deed must be signed by the grantor. The signing requirement, found in the Statute of Frauds (General Statute §22-2), requires a signing "by the party to be charged therewith or by some other person by him thereto lawfully authorized." Assuming compliance with the law of agency and other applicable laws, a person can be authorized as the grantor's agent to sign a deed on behalf of the grantor. However, *real estate brokers* serve as agents in a completely different capacity and *do not have the authority to execute deeds on behalf of grantors.* Of course, if the property is owned by more than one person, all co-owners must sign as grantors to convey full ownership of the entire parcel. Recall, too, that if any grantors are married, then the spouses must sign the deed to waive his or her marital life estate, even if the property is inherited by or titled in the other spouse's name only.

Legal Delivery and Acceptance

A deed must be properly delivered to be effective. It must be delivered to the grantee or to someone on behalf of the grantee with the intention by the grantor to pass title.[15] A rarely controversial requirement for a valid transfer by deed is *acceptance* by the grantee. Acceptance of delivery of a deed is presumed because deeds usually benefit grantees,[16] but a proposed grantee can refuse to accept a deed by specifically rejecting delivery.

Example: An owner of an old, abandoned, country gasoline station executes and records a deed transferring the property as a gift to his nephew without the nephew's knowledge. The deed is valid in all respects, but the nephew refuses to accept it because he fears possible environmental issues caused by leaking underground storage tanks. The deed is invalid because of a lack of acceptance, and title remains in the owner. (It would be wise for the nephew to record a document of his refusal to accept the deed in the Register of Deeds office.)

*A **recorded** deed is presumed to have been legally delivered and accepted as of the date of the deed, but these presumptions are rebuttable.*[17] Unlike a will that can be revised or revoked by a competent person at any time prior to death, a validly delivered deed can neither be reformed nor revoked by the grantor except in very rare and limited circumstances.[18]

Legally Nonessential Elements

Only the foregoing six essential elements are required to create a valid deed, but there are other items, called nonessential elements, that typically are included in professionally drafted deeds for practical reasons and as a matter of preventive law. Defective or invalid deeds result most commonly from inadequate drafting by laypersons. The following legally nonessential elements are commonly found in deeds.

Date

A deed does not have to be dated to be valid, but the date is important from a practical standpoint because a legal presumption exists that the deed was delivered on the date that it bears. Since a deed is effective as of proper delivery, the date of the deed can be a significant fact in some legal disputes. For this reason, a deed should always be dated.

Acknowledgement & Recording

Acknowledging and recording are related. *A deed does **not** have to be acknowledged to be valid, but a deed cannot be recorded unless it is properly acknowledged.*[19] Although recordation does not affect validity between the original parties, *recordation is absolutely essential to protect the grantee against the claims of lien creditors and purchasers for value from the original grantor.*

Recitation of Consideration

A deed need not recite the amount of consideration paid or the fact that consideration has been paid to be valid. In practice, the actual purchase price is rarely stated in the deed; instead, a nominal amount is recited, such as "$10.00 and other good and valuable consideration." A recitation of a nominal amount of consideration is included to indicate that the deed is not a deed of gift.

Witnesses

A deed does not have to be witnessed and, absent unusual circumstances, there is no practical reason to have it witnessed.

Seal

Originally, all deeds needed to be "sealed" to be valid. The classic rule that a deed must be "signed, sealed, and delivered" is well-known to all. In 1999, the General Assembly abolished the seal requirement.[20] While the seal no longer is technically necessary for the execution of a valid deed, it is likely that standard deed forms will continue to contain the word "seal" after the grantor's signature in spite of the elimination of the seal requirement. Documents under seal continue to enjoy certain legal advantages, including a longer statute of limitations protecting the rights of the parties to the conveyance. *Note that this change in the law does not affect a notary public's seal, which is still required.*

Signature of Grantee

The signature of a grantee is not required for a deed to be valid. Almost all deeds are signed by the grantor or grantors only.

TYPES AND CLASSIFICATIONS OF DEEDS

Deeds may be categorized in a number of ways. One primary classification is "private" deeds and "official" deeds. Official deeds are those executed pursuant to court or legal proceedings, such as trustees' deeds and tax deeds, and may require an attorney's legal opinion regarding their validity. The bulk of day-to-day property transactions are by individuals and business entities using private deeds.

Deeds are also classified by the type of title warranty given by the grantor. In North Carolina, the deeds that brokers deal with almost exclusively are **general warranty deeds, special warranty deeds,** and **quitclaim deeds** (also called nonwarranty deeds). The primary difference between warranty and quitclaim deeds is the presence or absence of title warranties. In a **general warranty deed**, the grantor conveys the property and warrants that the title being transferred is good. If title is impaired because of a title defect that existed prior to the transfer and was not excepted from the warranty, the grantee has a legal claim against the grantor. In a **special warranty deed**, the grantor warrants that the grantor has done nothing to impair title during the grantor's ownership period. In contrast, the grantor makes no promises as to title in a **quitclaim deed or nonwarranty deed**, saying in essence to the grantee: "Whatever interest I may have in this property, I hereby transfer to you." If title turns out to be defective, the grantee has no legal recourse against the grantor under the deed. A point that is often overlooked, however, is that a quitclaim deed is just as effective as a warranty deed to transfer title. That is, if the grantor has good title, the quitclaim deed will transfer it as completely as the warranty deed. It is the lack of any warranties that makes the quitclaim deed less desirable from a grantee's standpoint.

The **general warranty deed**, **special warranty deed**, and **quitclaim deed** (nonwarranty deed) are the most commonly used deeds in North Carolina, and a broker must be familiar with each. The difference in the title warranty among the three is readily apparent upon reading the language at the top of the second page of each deed.

General Warranty Deed

In a general warranty deed, the grantor makes a series of legally binding promises (known as "covenants") to the grantee and the grantee's heirs and assigns that the grantor will warrant and defend the title conveyed against the claims and demands of *all persons whomsoever since the beginning of time.*

In North Carolina, the usual covenants of title in warranty deeds are (1) the covenant of seisin and right to convey; (2) the covenant against encumbrances and (3) the covenant of warranty and quiet enjoyment. An example of a **General Warranty Deed** is reprinted at the end of this chapter.

1)   **The Covenant of Seisin and the Right to Convey.** A covenant that the grantor possesses the estate and has the right to convey it in quality and quantity that the deed purports to convey.[21]

2) **Covenant against Encumbrances**. A covenant that there are no outstanding encumbrances against the property that would affect the title conveyed, and that if any encumbrances predating the conveyance emerge, the grantor agrees to protect and save the grantee harmless. A covenant against encumbrances is a guarantee by the grantor that there are no liens, attachments, taxes, assessments, servitudes, or other claims against the property that impair title or require financial expenditures to remove.[22]

3) **Covenant of Warranty and Quiet Enjoyment**. A covenant by which the grantor assures or guarantees that there are no outstanding paramount interests in the real property existing at the time the property is conveyed and that the grantor will protect and defend the grantee's title against persons claiming by, through, or under the grantor or prior grantors.[23] The covenant of warranty and quiet enjoyment guarantees to the grantee that she or he will never be evicted by a person who has a title superior to the title the grantee received from the grantor.

Special Warranty Deed

Unlike a general warranty deed, where the grantor covenants to warrant and defend the title conveyed against *any* prior claims and demands *of any person since the beginning of time*, the grantor in a **special warranty deed** only warrants title *as against those persons claiming by, through, or under the grantor*. In other words, a grantor using a special warranty deed in essence says that he or she has not done anything *since acquiring title* to create a defect and will only warrant and defend title against defects arising since he or she took title but not against all persons since the beginning of time.

Example: Jones purchases real property from Smith in 2010 and conveys the property to the Browns in 2015 using a special warranty deed. In 2017, the Browns learn that Smith granted an easement to a power company in 2008. Even though this easement is a title defect, the Browns have no recourse against Jones, because Jones conveyed the property by a special warranty deed and the defect arose before Jones took title to the property.

The *special* warranty deed is commonly used in North Carolina by banks conveying foreclosed property to a purchaser. In the overwhelming majority of other real property conveyances, most purchasers of real property and title insurance companies insist on a *general* warranty deed.

Quitclaim (Nonwarranty) Deed

A grantor who uses a **quitclaim or nonwarranty deed** conveys whatever interest the grantor has in the real estate, if any. The grantor makes absolutely no warranties or promises as to the *quality* of title.[24] The warranty paragraph that appears in the general or special warranty deeds is absent in the quitclaim deed. Quitclaim deeds are often used as deeds of release or correction.

Example: A title search reveals that the wife of a past grantor may still have an interest in the property because she did not sign a past deed in the chain of title. One way to eliminate this defect is to have the wife execute a quitclaim deed to the present owner of the property "quitclaiming" any interest she may have in the property.

Quitclaim deeds are sometimes used when the grantor is not sure of the status of title or when the grantor simply wants no potential liability under the title covenants in a warranty deed.

> *Example:* The family homestead has been in the Smith family for four generations, and Smith now wants to transfer it to his son. Smith may execute a quitclaim deed under these circumstances. (A deed titled "deed of gift" may also be used. If the deed of gift contains no warranties, it is, in effect, a quitclaim deed.)

Special Purpose Deeds

Specialized deeds are used in specific fact situations, court proceedings, or matters requiring a deed from a person acting in an official capacity. The validity of these deeds may depend on specialized statutes and rules of law. Brokers should recognize when a transaction may involve a special purpose deed but should never offer an opinion concerning the deed's validity or interpretation as those issues involve questions of law. The list of special-purpose deeds below is not all-encompassing, and most will only be briefly discussed.

Examples of North Carolina Special-Purpose Deeds

- Deed of Gift
- Correction Deed
- Deed of Release
- Deed in Lieu of Foreclosure
- Timber Deed
- Mineral Deed
- Partition Deed
- Official Capacity Special-Purpose Deeds

Deed of Gift

A deed of gift is a conveyance for no consideration or for only a token consideration. Its status as a deed of gift is important because North Carolina law requires that a deed of gift be recorded within two years from the time of its making or it is ***void***.[25]

> *Example:* A mother decides to give her oceanfront lot at Topsail Beach to her son. She executes and delivers a valid deed of gift to him on September 15, 2015. The son, however, doesn't record the deed until October 10, 2017. Mother now owns the beach lot. The deed of gift to her son became absolutely void because he failed to record it within two years. Mother is free to transfer the property to anyone. If she still wants her son to have the property, she must execute a new deed to him.[26]

The regular recording act, known as the "Conner Act,"[27] applies to all deeds, including deeds of gift. The Conner Act is covered in Chapter 6, "Title Assurance," but special rules applicable to deeds of gift are briefly noted here. In addition to the "two-year" recordation requirement, the following two recording priority rules apply in North Carolina and other states:

> 1. *A prior donee who records first takes priority over a subsequent purchaser of the same property from the same grantor.*

Example 1: A father gives land to his daughter by deed of gift on December 5, 2017, and the *daughter records the deed on that same date.* The father then becomes upset with his daughter and conveys the land to a buyer for $50,000 on December 20, 2017. The buyer records his deed that same date. The buyer owns no interest in the land. The prior valid deed of gift to the daughter was recorded first, and the buyer, a subsequent grantee of the same land, is charged with record notice that the land had already been conveyed to the daughter.

2. *A prior purchaser for value who fails to record first takes priority over a subsequent donee of the same property from the same grantor.*

Example 2: A seller conveys land to a buyer for $50,000 on December 5, 2017, but the buyer does not record the deed until December 15, 2017. A few days after conveying the land to the buyer, the seller conveys the same land to his son by deed of gift and tells the son to "hurry up" and record the deed of gift. The son records the deed of gift on December 8, 2017, one week before the buyer's deed is recorded. Even though the son's deed was the first to be recorded and normally would have priority, the son does *not* own any interest in the land.

The rationale behind the outcome in Example 2 should be apparent. To allow a subsequent donee to defeat a prior purchaser for value would encourage fraud. Thus the rule that *a deed of gift will not be given priority over a prior unrecorded* **purchase** *deed* is practical and promotes public policy.[28]

Correction Deed

A correction deed is often used by a title examiner to remedy some defect in a previous conveyance, such as to correct a minor defect in a legal description in an earlier conveyance. Errors in dates, names, and manner of execution of a deed are also corrected by using this deed.

Deed of Release

A deed of release is most frequently used to release a portion of a parcel of property from a deed of trust or some general lien or encumbrance on the property. A deed of release discharging a deed of trust must comply with a number of legal requirements to be effective.

Deed in Lieu of Foreclosure

A borrower (mortgagor) in default on a mortgage debt who wants to avoid going through a foreclosure and possible deficiency judgment may, with the consent of the mortgage lender, convey the borrower's interest in the property directly to the lender. The deed is given directly to the lender "in lieu of" (instead of) foreclosure. The courts carefully scrutinize this type of transfer because of the potential for undue pressure to be applied on the borrower.

Timber Deed

A timber deed conveys an interest in all standing timber on a specified tract of land and is subject to the usual rules applicable to all deeds, *i.e.,* the six essential elements.

Mineral Deed

As mentioned in Chapter 1, title to real property traditionally includes title to the surface, certain rights to useable space above the surface, and rights to the subsurface, including mineral rights. When these subsurface mineral rights are severed from surface ownership, a mineral deed is often used.

General mineral rights or the right to exploit and remove specified minerals or substances may be conveyed by deed without conveying the surface land itself.

Partition Deed

Partition involves the division of jointly owned real estate into separate individual parcels or shares for each co-owner, thereby dissolving the joint tenancy or tenancy-in-common. Partition may be accomplished by the co-owners voluntarily agreeing to divide the original parcel between or among them or, failing agreement, by court proceedings. When a voluntary partition occurs, partition deeds are executed and exchanged by all of the co-owners setting forth which subdivided parcel of land each person shall separately own thenceforth. If the co-owners cannot agree on a division of the jointly held property, then any one of them may file a partition action against the others in the judicial district in which the property is located, asking the court to partition (divide) the property among the joint owners. The Court may divide the property "in kind" such that each co-owner receives a subparcel from the original tract, with all subparcels being of equal value although not necessarily equal size, or, if the original tract cannot be divided "in kind," then the Court may order the property to be sold and apportion the net sale proceeds among the joint owners according to their respective interests.[29]

Official Capacity Special-Purpose Deeds

"Official capacity special-purpose deeds" are deeds executed by a person acting in an official capacity rather than as a private individual. This category of deeds includes: sheriff's deeds, tax deeds, guardian's deeds, executor or administrator's deeds, commissioner's deeds and trustee's deeds. Most of these official capacity special-purpose deeds are beyond the scope of these materials and trigger the need for expert legal advice concerning interpretation and validity; however, a brief explanation of trustee's deeds is warranted.

Trustee's Deed

A number of different forms of trustee's deeds exist in North Carolina. A trustee may hold real property in trust for the benefit of another and may sell the property if the trust instrument grants the trustee that authority. A trustee under a deed of trust may transfer title to the property following foreclosure on the deed of trust. This latter type of trustee's deed must comply with the deed of trust statutes found in Chapter 45 of the North Carolina General Statutes. A trustee in bankruptcy may execute a deed conveying the bankrupt person's real property following procedures specified under bankruptcy laws.

EXCISE TAX

Every person conveying an interest in real estate located in North Carolina for consideration (money or other things or services of value) must pay an "excise tax" on each instrument by which any interest in real property is conveyed to a grantee. The term "person" is broadly defined to include "an individual, a fiduciary, a firm, an association, a partnership, a limited liability company, a corporation, a unit of government, or another group acting as a unit."[30] However, transfers by a governmental unit are specifically exempted from paying any excise tax.[31] Years ago, excise tax "stamps" in the form of actual stamps (or the equivalent affixed by meter or other device) were affixed to documents by the register of deeds. Because of the stamp requirement, some commonly referred to the excise tax as "revenue stamps."

While the excise tax remains the same, *the statutes no longer require excise tax stamps*, and all references to "stamps" have been deleted. General Statute §105-228.30(a) states:

> An excise tax is levied on each instrument by which any interest in real property is conveyed to another person. The tax rate is one dollar ($1.00) on each five hundred dollars ($500.00) or fractional part thereof of the consideration or value of the interest conveyed. The transferor must pay the tax to the register of deeds of the county in which the real estate is located before recording the instrument of conveyance. If the instrument transfers a parcel of real estate lying in two or more counties, however, the tax must be paid to the register of deeds of the county in which the greater part of the real estate with respect to value lies.

The excise tax on instruments imposed by this Article applies to timber deeds and contracts for the sale of standing timber to the same extent as if the deeds and contracts conveyed an interest in real property.

To calculate the amount of excise tax to be paid in connection with a particular real estate transfer, divide the sale price by $500 (and multiply the result by $1.00, if you wish).

Example: Sale price is $179,500. 179,500 ÷ 500 = 359
359 x $1.00 = $359.00. The excise tax is $359.00.

If the sale price is *not* an exact multiple of $500 (*e.g.* $179,700, $280,200), round the sale price to the next highest $500 and then perform the calculations as above.

Example: Sale price is $280,200; round to the next highest $500 is $280,500.
280,500 ÷ 500 = 561. 561 x $1.00 = $561.00. The excise tax is $561.00

The excise tax applies to all "of the consideration or value of the interest conveyed." This is an important point. If the purchaser assumes the seller's existing mortgage loan or takes the property subject to the seller's existing mortgage loan, then the amount of the seller's loan is included in the consideration and is subject to the tax.

Example: The sale price of a farm is $250,000. As part of the transfer, the purchaser assumes the seller's existing mortgage loan with an outstanding principal balance of $137,513.53. The assumption does not affect excise tax liability. The total consideration for the farm is the $250,000 sale price. The fact that part of the purchase price is paid by the purchaser's assumption of the seller's mortgage loan is irrelevant. Thus, the excise tax due is $500. [250,000/500 = 500.]

Likewise, if a seller takes a purchase money mortgage as all or part of the purchase price, the amount of the mortgage loan is subject to excise tax.

Example: A seller agrees to sell a beach cottage to a buyer for $237,500, with $37,500 payable in cash at closing and the remaining $200,000 to be paid over a 15-year period. The buyer signs a promissory note to the seller for the $200,000 balance and executes a purchase money deed of trust to secure payment. The amount of the purchase money deed of trust is not exempt from excise tax, which is calculated on the total sale price of $237,500, resulting in an excise tax of $475.00. [$237,500 ÷ 500 = 475; 475 x $1.00 = $475.00.]

The excise tax is payable by the transferor (grantor) to the register of deeds when the deed or other instrument of conveyance is presented for recordation. In essence, it is a tax on the revenue the seller receives from the sale. The person who presents an instrument to be recorded must report to the register of deeds the amount of the tax due. The register of deeds must first collect the tax and mark the amount of tax paid on the instrument **before** the instrument may be recorded.[32]

By statute,[33] excise tax does **not** apply to any of the following transfers of an interest in real property: (1) by operation of law; (2) by lease for a term of years; (3) by or pursuant to the provisions of a will; (4) by intestacy; (5) by gift; (6) if no consideration in property or money is due or paid by the transferee to the transferor; (7) by merger, conversion, or consolidation; or, (8) by an instrument securing indebtedness (e.g. a deed of trust). The register of deeds or an attorney should be consulted if a real estate broker has any questions about property transfers exempt from excise tax.

Recording Fees

The excise tax paid by the seller should not be confused with the separate and distinct recording fees that typically are paid by the buyer to record the deed and deed of trust. These recording fees are to cover the governmental cost of maintaining a public record system. While recording fees are always subject to change, as of spring 2017, fees to record a deed of trust or mortgage were $64 for the first 35 pages and $4 per additional page, and for all other instruments, including deeds, $26 for 15 pages or less, plus $4 per additional page. The amount of recording fees is uniform statewide and may be found on any county register of deeds website, where you can also search numerous property and other records.

ADVERSE POSSESSION

Adverse possession is one method by which property is involuntarily transferred. ***Adverse possession** is a way of acquiring title to another's real property by occupying and possessing it for a period of time specified by statute.* It is unusual, but not unheard of, for entire tracts of land to be acquired by adverse possession. More commonly, the doctrine serves a useful public purpose by settling boundary disputes between neighbors.

There are two kinds of adverse possession: 1) **regular** and 2) **under color of title**. A r*egular adverse possession* claim exists when there is no document giving the claimant a right to be on the land. A claim *"under color of title"* means that the claimant thinks he or she has a valid title to the real property under a deed, will, or court order, but in reality, the deed, will, or court order does not pass title to that person because of some defect. Thus, the person does *not* have valid legal title but only "color of title."

While relatively rare in modern property law, *a broker should be able to recognize potential adverse possession situations upon investigating and discovering facts about the possession and use of a property by one who is not the owner of record.*

> *Example:* A broker is contacted by a prospective client who wants to sell 5 acres of land. The client explains that, while he has no deed to the property, both he and his father have farmed the land for over 25 years without any objection from the owner of record. While a potential adverse possession fact situation may exist, the client must first prove to a court that he and his

father have met all requirements to obtain title by adverse possession. Until then, the client's "title" to the land is clearly unmarketable. The broker should advise the person to consult an attorney and should not list the property until the title issue is settled.

Requirements to Establish Valid Claim

Not every possession of land by one other than the owner will ripen into title for the possessor. Each of the following elements must be proved in every case. There must be: 1) an *actual possession* of the real property claimed; 2) the possession must be *hostile to the true owner;* 3) the possession must be *open and notorious;* 4) the possession must be *continuous and uninterrupted for the statutory period;* and 5) the possession must be with *an intent to claim title to the land occupied* (although a mistaken belief as to the location of a boundary does not negate the required intent).[34]

1. **Actual Possession.** A person claiming land under the doctrine of adverse possession must actually occupy and possess the land. A mere intent to occupy and claim the land is not sufficient. Making an ordinary use of the land, such as farming it or harvesting timber on a regular basis, are examples of the kind of possession that the law requires.

2. **Hostile to the True Owner.** Mere possession alone does not amount to adverse possession. Possessing land with the permission of the true owner will never result in a valid claim of title under the adverse possession theory, although the term "hostile" is somewhat misleading. What really is required is that the person has the intent to actually claim the land contrary to the true owner's rights and not just occupy it in subordination to the true owner.[35]

3. **Open and Notorious.** The possession must not be secret or hidden. It must be visible enough that the true owner is put on notice that another is apparently occupying and claiming the land.

4. **Continuous and Uninterrupted Possession for the Statutory Period.** *Regular adverse possession must be continuously maintained for a period of* **twenty years;** *if it is under color of title, possession must be continuously maintained for a period of* **seven years.**[36]

5. **Intent to Claim Title to Land Occupied.** The intent to claim title to another's land can be satisfied in one of two ways: (1) the person claiming by adverse possession takes possession knowing the title belongs to another but intending to wrongfully become the owner; or (2) the possessor takes possession under a mistaken belief that title belongs to him or her.

Note that the elements required to prove adverse possession are similar to those necessary to prove a prescriptive easement (discussed in Chapter 2) *except* for the "intent to claim title" element which is not required for a prescriptive easement. It is this critical element that, if satisfied, yields *title, i.e.,* ownership, to an adverse possessor, while one claiming a prescriptive easement receives only the right to use, but not possess, the property. Understand as well that until title by adverse possession is confirmed in a legal proceeding, whatever interest the adverse possessor has in the property will be unmarketable.

Property That Cannot Be Acquired By Adverse Possession

Real property owned by the United States government cannot be acquired by adverse possession.[37] Title to specified real property held by the State of North Carolina, including all "public trust" property, cannot be acquired by adverse possession. Public trust rights are rights held in trust by the State for the use and benefit of the people of the State in common and include park lands and "the right to navigate, swim, hunt, fish, and enjoy all recreational activities in the watercourses of the State and the right to freely use and enjoy the State's ocean and estuarine beaches and public access to the beaches."[38] In the few instances when an adverse possession claim may be allowed against the State, it is subject to longer statutory periods: thirty years instead of twenty years for regular adverse possession, and twenty-one years instead of seven years for adverse possession under color of title.[39]

Endnotes

1.   See Chapter 29 ("Intestate Succession") of the North Carolina General Statutes.

2.   Session Law 2011-284. See N.C. Gen. Stat. §12-3(14).

3.   The statute is a lengthy and detailed one. Legal advice should be sought in any title transaction involving a surviving spouse's right to a life estate.

4.   Some might argue that the debtor agreed to the possibility of foreclosure when signing the mortgage or deed of trust, but in a practical sense, foreclosure is treated here as "involuntary."

5.   N.C. Gen. Stat. §105-374.

6.   N.C. Gen. Stat. §§1-339.68; 1-339.47.

7.   N.C. Gen. Stat. §116B-2.

8.   N.C. Gen. Stat. §39-6.5, titled "Elimination of seal."

9.   N.C. Gen. Stat. §84-2.1 and §84.4 are the unauthorized practice of law statutes, and G.S. §93A-6(a)(11) is the License Law under which real estate licensees may be disciplined for undertaking to perform a legal service.

10.   See, for example, *Davis v. Davis*, 223 N.C. 36, 25 S.E.2d 181 (1943); *Sprinkle v. Wellborn*, 140 N.C. 163, 52 S.E. 666 (1905); *Tomlins v. Cranford*, 227 N.C. 323, 42 S.E.2d 100 (1947).

11.   *Weeks v. Wilkins*, 139 N.C. 215, 51 S.E. 909 (1905). A minor may not disaffirm a contract, including a deed, which was made for "necessaries." *Personnel Corp. v. Rogers*, 276 N.C. 279, 172 S.E.2d 19 (1970).

12.   See, for example, *Byrd v. Patterson*, 229 N.C. 156, 48 S.E.2d 45 (1948); *Heath v. Heath*, 114 N.C. 547, 19 S.E. 155 (1894).

13.   *Thompson v. John L. Roper Lumber Co.*, 168 N.C. 226, 84 S.E. 289 (1915).

14.   *New Home Building Supply Co. v. Nations*, 259 N.C. 681, 131 S.E.2d 425 (1963).

15.   *Williams v. North Carolina State Bd. of Education*, 284 N.C. 588, 201 S.E.2d 889 (1974).

16.   *Ballard v. Ballard*, 230 N.C. 629, 55 S.E.2d 316 (1949).

17.   *Williams v. North Carolina State Bd. of Education*, 284 N.C. 588, 201 S.E.2d 889 (1974).

18.   In *Willis v. Willis*, 365 N.C. 454, 722 S.E.2d 505 (2012), a widow executed a last will and testament but subsequent thereto, executed a warranty deed conveying real property to one of her two sons and reserving a life estate to herself. The grantee son died before his mother, at which point the mother wanted to give the real property to her surviving son. Had she devised the property to her son in her will, she could have changed the terms of the will, but once she conveyed the property to her son by *deed*, she could not later change her mind and rescind the deed. The Supreme Court held that a unilateral mistake by the grantor as to the law will not support reformation of a deed. Thus, the deceased son's wife owned the property subject to the widow's life estate.

19.   Chapter 10B of the North Carolina General Statutes deals with requirements for the proper notarizing of documents. See, for example, N.C. Gen. Stat. §10B-37, setting forth notary seal requirements.

20.   N.C. Gen. Stat. §39-6.5.

21.   *Smith v. People's Bank & Trust Co.*, 254 N.C. 588, 119 S.E.2d 623 (1961).

22.   *Thompson v. Avery County*, 216 N.C. 405, 5 S.E.2d 146 (1939).

23.   *Cover v. McAden*, 183 N.C. 641, 112 S.E. 817 (1922); *Shuford v. Phillips*, 235 N.C. 387, 70 S.E.2d 193 (1952).

24.   *Hayes v. Ricard*, 245 N.C. 687, 97 S.E.2d 105 (1957).

25.   N.C. Gen. Stat. §47-26.

26.   For examples of North Carolina deed of gift cases, see *Booth v. Hairston*, 195 N.C. 8, 141 S.E. 480 (1928); *Ferguson v. Ferguson*, 225 N.C. 375, 35 S.E.2d 231 (1945).

27.   N.C. Gen. Stat. §47-18.

28.   *King v. McRackan*, 168 N.C. 621, 84 S.E. 1027 (1915).

29.   See, generally, Chapter 46 of the North Carolina General Statutes for the law and procedures regarding partition actions

30.   For complete details on recording fees for the register of deeds, see N.C. Gen. Stat. §161-10(a)(1), (a)(1a) and (a)(16), as well as N.C. Gen. Stat. §161-11.6 as to deeds (but not deeds of trust). N.C. Gen. Stat. §161-10(a)(3) and (a)(4) set forth the recording fees for plats and right-of-way plans respectively. Most registers of deeds also post these filing fees on their websites.

31.   N.C. Gen. Stat. §105-228.28.

32.   N.C. Gen. Stat. §105-228.32.

33.   N.C. Gen. Stat. §105-228.29.

34.   The leading North Carolina court decision on adverse possession is *Walls v. Grohman*, 315 N.C. 239, 337 S.E.2d 556 (1985). For a more recent case discussing both regular adverse possession and adverse possession under color of title, see *Merrick v. Peterson*, 143 N.C. App. 656, 548 S.E.2d 171 (2001). The court summarizes the law of adverse possession, in part, as follows:

> To acquire title to land by adverse possession, the claimant must show actual, open, hostile, exclusive, and continuous possession of the land claimed for the prescriptive period (seven years or twenty years) under known and visible lines and boundaries. *Curd v. Winecoff,* 88 N.C. App. 720, 364 S.E.2d 730 (1988); N.C. Gen. Stat. §1-38 (1999); N.C. Gen. Stat. §1-40 (1999). Successive adverse users in privity with prior adverse users can tack successive adverse possessions of land so as to aggregate the prescriptive period (twenty years or seven years). *Dickinson v. Pake*, 284 N.C. 576, 201 S.E.2d 897 (1974). Under the legal principle of tacking, it is permissible to tie the possession of an ancestor to that of an heir when there is no hiatus or interruption in the possession. *Paper Company v. Jacobs*, 258 N.C. 439, 128 S.E.2d 818 (1963).

See also Hetrick & McLaughlin, *Webster's Real Estate Law in North Carolina*, 6th ed. (LexisNexis), Chapter 14, "Adverse Possession," for comprehensive coverage of this topic.

35.   For recent decisions on the hostility requirement, see *Jones v. Miles,* 189 N.C. App. 289, 658 S.E.2d 23 (2008); *Pegg v. Jones*, 187 N.C. App. 355, 653 S.E. 2d 229 (2007).

36.   For a recent decision discussing adverse possession under color of title, see *White v. Farabee*, 212 N.C. App.126, 713 S.E.2d 4 (2011).

37.   Quiet Title Act of 1972, 29 U.S.C. §2409a.

38.   N.C. Gen. Stat. §1-45.1 (1994) (title to real property held by the State and subject to public trust rights may not be acquired by adverse possession). *Friends of Hatteras Island Nat'l. Historic Maritime Forest Land Trust for Preservation, Inc. v. Coastal Resources Commission*, 117 N.C. App. 556, 452 S.E.2d 337 (1995).

39.   N.C. Gen. Stat. §1-35.

NORTH CAROLINA GENERAL WARRANTY DEED

Excise Tax: _____

Parcel Identifier No._____ Verified by _____ County on the ____ day of_____, 20____
By:_____

Mail/Box to:_____

This instrument was prepared by:_____

Brief description for the Index:_____

THIS DEED made this _____ day of _____, 20___, by and between

GRANTOR	GRANTEE

Enter in appropriate block for each Grantor and Grantee: name, mailing address, and, if appropriate, character of entity, e.g. corporation or partnership.

The designation Grantor and Grantee as used herein shall include said parties, their heirs, successors, and assigns, and shall include singular, plural, masculine, feminine or neuter as required by context.

WITNESSETH, that the Grantor, for a valuable consideration paid by the Grantee, the receipt of which is hereby acknowledged, has and by these presents does grant, bargain, sell and convey unto the Grantee in fee simple, all that certain lot, parcel of land or condominium unit situated in the City of _____, _____ Township, _____ County, North Carolina and more particularly described as follows:

The property hereinabove described was acquired by Grantor by instrument recorded in Book _____ page _____.

All or a portion of the property herein conveyed ___ includes or ___ does not include the primary residence of a Grantor.

A map showing the above described property is recorded in Plat Book _____ page _____.

1

NC Bar Association Form No. 3 © 1976, Revised © 1/1/2010, 2013
Printed by Agreement with the NC Bar Association

This standard form has been approved by:
North Carolina Bar Association – NC Bar Form No. 3

Figure 5-1

TO HAVE AND TO HOLD the aforesaid lot or parcel of land and all privileges and appurtenances thereto belonging to the Grantee in fee simple.

And the Grantor covenants with the Grantee, that Grantor is seized of the premises in fee simple, has the right to convey the same in fee simple, that title is marketable and free and clear of all encumbrances, and that Grantor will warrant and defend the title against the lawful claims of all persons whomsoever, other than the following exceptions:

IN WITNESS WHEREOF, the Grantor has duly executed the foregoing as of the day and year first above written.

_____   _____ (SEAL)
(Entity Name)   Print/Type Name:_____

By:_____

Print/Type Name & Title:_____   _____ (SEAL)
           Print/Type Name:_____

By:_____   _____ (SEAL)
Print/Type Name & Title:_____   Print/Type Name:_____

By:_____   _____ (SEAL)
Print/Type Name & Title:_____   Print/Type Name:_____

State of _____ - County or City of _____
    I, the undersigned Notary Public of the County or City of _____ and State aforesaid, certify that _____
_____ personally appeared before me this day and acknowledged the due execution of the foregoing instrument for the purposes therein expressed. Witness my hand and Notarial stamp or seal this _____ day of _____, 20___.

My Commission Expires:_____   _____
(Affix Seal)   _____Notary Public
                 Notary's Printed or Typed Name

State of _____ - County or City of _____
    I, the undersigned Notary Public of the County or City of _____ and State aforesaid, certify that _____
_____ personally appeared before me this day and acknowledged the due execution of the foregoing instrument for the purposes therein expressed. Witness my hand and Notarial stamp or seal this _____ day of _____, 20___.

My Commission Expires:_____   _____
(Affix Seal)   _____Notary Public
                 Notary's Printed or Typed Name

State of _____ - County or City of _____
    I, the undersigned Notary Public of the County or City of _____ and State aforesaid, certify that _____
_____ personally came before me this day and acknowledged that _he is the
_____ of _____, a North Carolina or _____ corporation/limited liability company/general partnership/limited partnership (strike through the inapplicable), and that by authority duly given and as the act of such entity, __he signed the foregoing instrument in its name on its behalf as its act and deed. Witness my hand and Notarial stamp or seal, this _____ day of _____, 20___.

My Commission Expires:_____   _____
(Affix Seal)   _____Notary Public
                 Notary's Printed or Typed Name

NC Bar Association Form No. 3 © 1976, Revised © 1/1/2010, 2013   This standard form has been approved by:
Printed by Agreement with the NC Bar Association   North Carolina Bar Association – NC Bar Form No. 3

Figure 5-1

6 | TITLE ASSURANCE

Brokers must have a basic understanding of title assurance. **Title assurance** is a shorthand term for: (1) the process to determine if an owner has title to the property; (2) whether title is marketable; and (3) statutes designed to protect title and enhance its marketability.[1] The following title assurance topics are discussed in this chapter.

- Title Examination
- Title Insurance
- Title Recordation
- Covenants of Title in Deeds
- Various Laws Affecting Land Titles

TITLE SEARCH INTRODUCTORY POINTS

Real estate brokers must know four introductory points.
1) Brokers are prohibited from offering an opinion on real estate titles.
2) Providing a title opinion is the practice of law and requires an active law license.
3) Brokers should always recommend a title search by an attorney.
4) Purchasers generally choose their closing attorney.

Brokers should understand the purpose of a title examination and what a title examiner does when "searching" a title. In North Carolina, title examinations must be performed by a licensed attorney or their closely supervised paralegal assistants. Under state law, the preparation of deeds, mortgages, or opinions concerning title to real property is "the practice of law."[2] A real estate broker engaging in these activities is practicing law without a license, a ground for disciplinary action by the Real Estate Commission.

A title examination seeks to determine the status of title to real property that is the subject of a sales contract and/or security for a loan. Before consummating the transaction, a purchaser needs clear assurance that the seller is conveying marketable title to the property. Likewise, a lending institution that finances part of the purchase price and takes a security interest in the property by mortgage or deed of trust will insist on evidence of marketable title to confirm that its lien will be a first lien against the property. The lender will also require a lender's policy of title insurance.

Online Real Estate Record Data Bases

Traditionally, the status of title to real property was determined by thoroughly searching the real estate records in the office of the register of deeds, the clerk of superior court, and other government agencies. The need to make a trip to the appropriate government records office is now diminished by the availability of online register of deeds databases. The North Carolina Association of Register of Deeds website provides an excellent starting point.[3] It contains quick links to helpful information, including the following:

- E-Recording Counties
- Recording Standards
- Recording Fees
- Recording Links

In many North Carolina counties, real estate records are available in searchable online databases.[4] Although online databases in land title and other public records facilitate a search of those records, brokers should *never* attempt to provide an opinion as to the status of title or the significance of legal documents located online or elsewhere.

Basic Steps in Title Examination

Whether a traditional title search in the public offices or an online computer search method is used, an attorney will perform the following tasks when conducting a title examination:

1. Obtain preliminary information, such as names of current owners, date they acquired title, and a copy of the last title insurance policy or opinion.
2. Verify the legal description and, if applicable, the parcel identifier number (PIN).
3. Run the chain of title.
4. Check for title defects.
5. Prepare an opinion of title.

The goal of any title examination is to run a property's *chain of title*. A "*chain of title*" is a history of all conveyances of a parcel of land, and each property transfer is a *link* in the chain. To piece together a chain of title, link by link back in time, records in the offices of the register of deeds and clerk of superior court are reviewed. Once a chain of title is established, the title examiner checks for title defects that may have occurred while each person in the chain owned the property.

Theoretically, a complete title search could extend back to the original grant of land from the State (or king) containing the parcel in question; however, such extensive title searches are rare, difficult, and usually unnecessary. The vast majority of title problems will be discovered in a search of the preceding 30-60 years. Title examiners are aided in their search by statutory provisions that extinguish many "ancient" defects in title. Curative statutes and marketable title statutes (summarized later) eliminate title defects under specified conditions. In practice, how far back a title search goes is determined by the title insurance company that will issue the title policy. In addition, many title companies in North Carolina customarily allow a title searcher to tack onto or update an existing title insurance policy.

Example: An attorney is preparing for a real estate closing on November 15, 2017. The title company has authorized the attorney to tack onto an existing title insurance policy it issued to the current owner in 2010 when he purchased the property. In essence, "tacking" allows the title searcher to rely on the accuracy of the prior policy and only update that policy by looking for liens and encumbrances that have attached to the property since the current owner took title in 2010, rather than conduct a traditional 30-60 year search. Again, the title insurance company generally will instruct the closing attorney how far back in time to search.

Land Records Indexing System

Records of title to real property would be virtually unusable without a practical indexing system to locate the recorded documents affecting a specific parcel of land. All register of deeds offices operate under some index system. Most have converted to an online index system based on the ***grantor and grantee index system***, while some counties use a ***parcel identifier number index system*** (PIN system). *The grantor and grantee index system is searched by the surnames of the persons who acquired an interest in the land rather than referencing the parcel itself.* ("Grantor" means the person who conveyed an interest in the property, and the "grantee" is the person or entity who received that interest.)

The grantor index lists the surnames or business names of all grantors in alphabetical order with all common surnames listed together. Certain additional information is provided in the columns after the name of each grantor listed. This information includes:

1) the name of the grantee;
2) the type of instrument recorded;
3) the book and page number where the instrument is recorded in the register of deeds office;
4) an abbreviated description of the property; and
5) a column where cancellations of deeds of trust can be noted.

The grantee index is a mirror image of the grantor index, except that the index is arranged alphabetically based on the grantee's surname and the first item of information in the columns is the name of the grantor. A title examiner's initial question is: "Where did the present owner obtain title?" The title examiner searches under the name of the current owner, then under the previous owner, and then the owner before that, and so on until the names of past owners over a period of years are obtained. The title searcher examines the full deed or other document of title at each link in the chain to verify that it is in proper form and valid to transfer title. The original documents are in books in the office of the register of deeds, but most documents can now be viewed online and obtained electronically.

In contrast to the grantor/grantee index system, *the parcel identifier number index system, a form of "tract index" system, is based on the identity of the parcel itself.*[5] In counties that have adopted this system, a search by parcel identifier number (PIN) should reveal every transaction recorded in the register of deed's office dealing with the property since the tract system was put in place. As to title transactions that took place prior to the effective date of the tract index system, resort must be made to the traditional grantor and grantee index system.

ATTORNEY'S OPINION ON TITLE

The attorney who searches the title provides a title opinion or report most frequently to the title insurance company, since most transactions involve title insurance. If no title insurance is involved, the title opinion is provided to the purchaser. While numerous formats exist, all title opinions will contain the following components:

- a description of the public records that have been searched and the time period covered
- names of the present owners of the property and a legal description of the property
- matters not covered by the title search
- specific and general exceptions to title

A preliminary title opinion will be performed in advance of the real estate closing. If title defects were discovered, they are listed in this preliminary report and must be satisfied or resolved prior to or at the closing. For example, a common "defect" is the seller's deed of trust securing the seller's mortgage loan. Unless the purchaser is assuming the mortgage, mortgage loans must be paid at closing to discharge the deed of trust. Other matters, such as unpaid taxes, junior mortgages, and judgment liens may be revealed by the preliminary title report and must be satisfied and released at or before the closing date.

Limitations on an Attorney's Title Opinion

While an attorney's title opinion is a very important step toward assuring good title, it is merely a report of the attorney's opinion regarding the status of title—it is not title insurance, and it does not guarantee that title is good. An attorney searching a title is only responsible for title defects that can be discovered by searching the public records. An attorney's title opinion may have a number of exceptions due to title defects that may not be revealed by a search of the public records.

> *Example:* In 2014, a niece forged her aunt's name on a deed conveying land to the niece and recorded the deed. The public land records will not reveal to a title searcher that the deed was forged and thus void. The title searcher is not responsible for this title defect, because it cannot be discovered from the public records. Title insurance, on the other hand, insures against a forged deed.

> *Example:* A farmer contracts to sell her farm to a buyer. Part of the farm, however, is being claimed by a neighbor under the doctrine of adverse possession. Unless a lawsuit has been filed, the public records will not reveal the adverse possession claim to a title searcher, but title insurance would insure against the unfiled adverse possession claim.

Public records may not disclose other defects such as a missing heir, an incompetent grantor, ancient property rights, prescriptive easements, and errors in recording. On rare occasions, an attorney searching title may mistakenly conclude that title is good by inadvertently overlooking some defect in title. To avoid these risks, a grantee should purchase title insurance to shift the risk of loss due to defects in title to the title insurance company.

TITLE INSURANCE

Because buyers too often are simply told that title insurance is required without any explanation of its purpose or value, a real estate broker should explain to a buyer the following introductory points:
1. What title insurance is and why it is important.
2. Why a lender will require title insurance as a condition of making a mortgage loan.
3. Why a prudent purchaser will order an owner's title policy.
4. Purchasers have a choice in selecting a title insurance company.

Title insurance is a unique form of insurance. Unlike most insurance policies that covers events in the future, title insurance protects against title defects occurring prior to the grantee acquiring title. The policy is based on and guarantees the accuracy of the title search, excepting from coverage those matters disclosed in the attorney's title opinion. It indemnifies the insured for damages caused by title defects created prior to the effective date of the policy. It does not cover title defects created after the effective date of the policy.

Title insurance is a policy protecting the insured (either the owner or the lender or both) against actual damage caused by a defective title to real estate. The policy is a contract of indemnity and not a guarantee against claims that might disturb one's possession of the property. Once a loss has occurred or it appears that a loss will occur unless the title company steps in to defend, the company will take the necessary action to clear the title or compensate the insured for loss up to the face amount of the policy. The title company generally must also pay the costs and expenses in defending or clearing any title defect covered under the policy.

Unlike other forms of insurance, title insurance does not protect the insured against the occurrence of future events adverse to title. For example, fire insurance insures from the effective date of the policy against the occurrence of a fire in the future. Title insurance insures from the effective date (usually the closing) *backward in time* and insures that no *past event or factor* will result in a future loss relating to the title of the insured. A title insurance policy, like an attorney's opinion of title, reports on the status of title as of the date of the policy and reveals existing defects or adverse claims to the title disclosed in the policy as "Exceptions."

A title company promises to indemnify the insured against loss or damage resulting from the title not being as described in the policy. *Existing defects disclosed in the policy are not covered by the insurance.* For example, in most contemporary residential transactions, the title policy will except (exclude) "easements and covenants of record" from coverage. This is necessary because both easements and covenants are encumbrances on title that exist in most residential land transactions. However, title insurance often will cover title defects that a search of the public records will not reveal. Consider the following examples.

> *Example:* A buyer purchasing a lot orders an owner's title insurance policy. The title policy reports that the seller owns the property in fee simple absolute but lists the following exception: "Property is subject to a right-of-way easement on the east 30 feet of the lot. A copy of this easement is attached." While the easement constitutes an encumbrance on title, the buyer cannot file a claim under the title policy after closing because this defect was specifically excluded from coverage.

> *Example:* After a title policy is issued on July 12, 2017, it is later discovered that a 2010 deed to the seller was forged and is void. Title insurance will indemnify the buyer, because this title defect existed prior to the effective date of the policy, was not excepted in any way by the policy, and was not discoverable from a public records search.

> *Example:* After a title policy is issued on July 12, 2017, it is discovered that a 1990 deed to the seller from two heirs who believed that they had inherited the property is defective because a third heir at law, who had been presumed dead, is alive and now claims an interest in the property. Title insurance will indemnify the buyer because this title defect existed prior to the effective date of the policy.

> *Example:* A title insurance policy erroneously omitted the existence of a private right-of-way easement over the property. Title insurance will indemnify the insured because of the title report's inaccuracy.

Example: A title insurance policy issued on June 15, 2017 erroneously failed to discover a past recorded mortgage or a filed judgment lien. Title insurance will indemnify the insured because of the inaccuracy of the title report.

TYPES OF POLICIES

Title insurance policies and endorsements are issued by North Carolina title insurance companies using forms approved by the American Land Title Association (ALTA), a voluntary national association of title insurance underwriters. Title insurance is issued in three major forms:
1) lender's policy (or mortgagee's policy)
2) owner's policy
3) leasehold policy

Lender's (Mortgagee's) Policy

This policy insures the security interest of the lender (mortgagee) in the property. It protects the lender against any defects in the title and against prior liens on the property. The title insurance company's liability is limited to the outstanding balance on the mortgage loan and thus diminishes over time. A lender's policy affords little or no protection for the owner, as the only insured under a lender's policy is the lender and only the lender's interest is protected.

A mortgagee's or lender's title insurance policy is required in almost all property transactions involving financing because the secondary mortgage market[6] relies on and requires title insurance when mortgage indebtedness is acquired as an investment from banks and other lenders, because title insurance policies are nationally standardized.

A mortgage lender cannot require that a purchaser use any specific title insurance company or limit a purchaser's choice of title insurers. The closing attorney may properly recommend a title insurer, but purchasers should be informed that, as the consumer, they have a choice. Typically, however, a title insurance company may decline to issue a policy based on a title opinion from an attorney who is not on the company's list of approved attorneys.

Owner's Policy

An owner's policy is issued in an amount equal to the purchase price of the property and the title insurance company remains liable for this amount so long as the grantee or his/her heirs retain an interest in the property. The policy insures the owner for any loss sustained by reason of a defect or defects in the title to the property that are not excepted and existed prior to the grantee acquiring title.

Traditionally, a lender's policy of title insurance could be ordered while a purchaser chose not to order an owner's policy. Currently, however, most purchasers are automatically protected by what is called a "simultaneous issue rate." A lender's policy of title insurance is included with the owner's policy at no additional cost when the two policies are ordered at the same time. Even if there is no mortgage financing, *a real estate broker still should strongly recommend that the purchaser order an owner's title insurance policy.*

Leasehold Policy

Many commercial tenants sign long-term leases and invest substantial sums of money in property improvements to adapt the property for their planned use. These tenants often obtain a "leasehold" title insurance policy protecting their investment from a defective title in the owner (lessor).

POLICY COVERAGE

A title insurance policy protects the insured against almost any claim arising against the title to the insured property not otherwise excepted. Sources of covered claims may include:

- errors or omissions in the title report
- the discovery of undisclosed or missing heirs
- forged or fraudulent deeds
- improper delivery of deeds
- lack of mental capacity of a grantor
- unrecorded easements arising by operation of law

A buyer may think that the warranties in a general warranty deed are sufficient and that title insurance merely duplicates these warranties, but this is misguided. Without title insurance, if a defect later surfaces, a buyer's only recourse is against the grantor under the deed warranties, but the grantee may not be able to recover against the grantor if the grantor cannot be found, is deceased, or is insolvent.

Special Note on Title Insurance and Survey Coverage

Faced with many transaction costs when purchasing real estate, a prospective purchaser may ask a broker "Is a property survey really necessary?" The purchaser may have been told that the mortgage lender is not requiring a survey. For a number of reasons, *a broker should not tell a purchaser that a survey is unnecessary.* Consider the following:

- Title companies often provide more coverage to lenders even without a survey, but this coverage does not benefit the purchaser.
- An owner's title insurance policy does not cover matters a survey would reveal. In fact, most owner title insurance policies contain a standard exception for matters that would have been shown on a survey.
- Whether a purchaser should have a survey raises legal issues best answered by the closing attorney.

Example: A purchaser of a home plans to close on August 3, 2017. After signing the purchase contract, the buyer is informed that the seller had a survey done ten years earlier when the seller purchased the property. The lender tells the buyer that it is not requiring a current survey as a condition for the mortgage loan. After closing, the buyer discovers that a neighbor's garage built seven years earlier encroaches on the buyer's property by two feet. The buyer also learns that the seller had recently added a screened-in porch to the home that violates setback requirements in the subdivision covenants. The owner's title insurance policy does *not* indemnify the buyer for these title defects because they would have been revealed by a survey.

Title Policy Duration

Under an owner's title insurance policy, *the owner is permanently protected as to all matters not excepted from coverage.* Not only does the policy protect the owner for the period he or she owns the property, it remains in effect after the owner sells the property. A mortgagee (lender) is fully protected under a lender's policy of title insurance for *as long as the loan remains outstanding.* Once the loan is paid off, coverage under the lender's policy automatically ends because the lender no longer has an interest in the property.

Cost of Title Insurance

The cost of title insurance differs from other forms of insurance because *title insurance involves the payment of a one-time premium.* The amount of this one-time premium is calculated based on rates filed with the N.C. Department of Insurance and depends on a number of factors, including the amount of the purchase price of the property; whether the company is giving a discount, such as a reissue rate; and the nature of the title coverage. Many title insurance companies display their current insurance rates and have a program to calculate the rate on their websites.

As noted earlier, both an owner's policy and a lender's policy may be obtained for a single premium based on the cost of the owner's policy if the two policies are issued simultaneously. In transactions involving financing, the lender will require title insurance, and a prudent buyer will always order an owner's policy. *In North Carolina, the buyer customarily pays the total cost of title insurance.*

Title Report Basis for Title Insurance Policy

Title insurance in North Carolina is issued only on the basis of an opinion of title prepared by the examining attorney and provided to the title insurance company. The attorney must be "approved" by the title insurance company but is prohibited by law from being an employee or agent of the title insurance company.[7]

TITLE RECORDATION

The two chief methods of title assurance discussed above, title examination and title insurance, are based on a comprehensive system of recordation of all conveyances of real property and other instruments affecting real property that are authorized to be recorded. The status of title to property can be difficult to ascertain. If a person wishes to sell real estate, how can you verify that he or she owns a marketable fee simple title? Without a central location where all conveyances of real estate are officially copied and indexed, there would be no reliable source of information as to property ownership. "Recordation" is simply the placing of deeds, leases, deeds of trust, easements, plats, and other important documents affecting title to real property in the public records. Documents affecting real estate must be *recorded in the office of the register of deeds in the county where the property is situated.*

THE CONNER ACT

To insure the accuracy of the public land records and to protect persons who rely on these records, the North Carolina recording act, known as the Conner Act, places a potentially serious penalty on a grantee who does not promptly record. ("Registration" is another term for "recording" in North Carolina.) The first subsection of the Conner Act states:

§ 47-18. Conveyances, contracts to convey, options and leases of land.

(a) No (i) conveyance of land; or (ii) contract to convey; or (iii) option to convey; or (iv) lease of land for more than three years shall be valid to pass any property interest as against lien creditors or purchasers for a valuable consideration from the donor, bargainer, or lessor but from the time of registration thereof in the county where the land lies, or if the land is located in more than one county, then in each county where any portion of the land lies to be effective as to the land in that county.[8]

The crux of the Conner Act is that *if a grantee fails to promptly record a conveyance, it will be considered absolutely void with respect to purchasers for value from or lien creditors of the same grantor who record their conveyance or docket their liens prior to recordation by the first grantee.*[9] North Carolina's Conner Act is categorized as a "pure race" statute. This means that the person who "wins the race" to the office of the register of deeds will prevail, even if that person knew about the earlier, but unrecorded, document. A few examples will illustrate the extreme importance of prompt recordation.

> *Example:* Able owned the Happy Acre lot located in North Carolina and conveyed it by warranty deed to Baker on March 11. Baker paid $30,000 for the lot but foolishly neglected to record the deed. Subsequently, Able fell upon hard times and conveyed the same lot to Cook by warranty deed for $35,000 on July 10, and Cook recorded the same day. The result under the Conner Act is that Cook, the subsequent purchaser for value from the same grantor, owns Happy Acre. Baker lost his interest in Happy Acre as of the date that Cook recorded his deed. Baker's failure to record promptly has caused him to be divested of legal title. Baker may have a legal claim against Able for money damages for selling the same property twice, but as a practical matter, Baker may not be able to collect on any judgment rendered against Able if Able has no assets.

What if Baker finally records his deed on July 10, but *after* Cook has recorded his deed? It is too late and the conclusions above do not change; even if Baker were to record *one minute* after Cook, the result would be the same. However, if Baker records his deed at any time *prior* to Cook, Baker would protect and preserve his ownership interest in Happy Acre, and Cook would have a legal claim against Able.

Fortunately, the result in the above example is now extremely rare. All real estate transactions involving mortgage financing are recorded immediately. It is the cash sale without bank financing when a purchaser sometimes fails to promptly record. Even in that event, most sellers are honest and do not convey the same land twice. However, third-party creditors can cause substantial problems for a purchaser who fails to promptly record.

> *Example:* A seller conveys land to a purchaser who delays in recording the deed. Several days later, a judgment creditor of the seller files a judgment lien. The judgment lien attaches to the land, because the public land records continue to show that the seller is the record owner. If the seller fails to pay the amount owed, the creditor has the right to execute on the judgment and have the sheriff sell the land.

A purchaser's failure to promptly record is a serious matter. It creates the possibility that a purchaser's title may become inferior to:
- a subsequent purchaser for value from the same grantor who records first;
- a judgment lien creditor who files a judgment first;
- a mortgagee of the seller who records first.

Failure to record does not, however, affect the validity of a conveyance or other document transferring an interest in land as between the parties to the instrument.[10]

Example: A man conveys his farm to a buyer by warranty deed for $310,000. The buyer does not record the deed nor does the buyer have a mortgage loan. Two years later, the buyer still has not recorded the deed. The deed is completely valid between the man and the buyer. Recordation is not necessary for the validity of a deed between the grantor and grantee. Recordation should be promptly done, however, to protect the buyer from *subsequent* purchasers for value or lien creditors of the man, because the public land records continue to show the man, not the buyer, as owner.

The reasoning behind the results in these examples is *to protect innocent third parties subsequently dealing with the property who have no way of discovering from the public records* that the grantor does *not*, in fact, own the property he purports to convey or pledge in exchange for the valuable consideration paid by the innocent party. This is particularly true because the lack of public record notice arises from the first grantee's failure to protect his or her own interest by promptly recording.

DOCUMENTS REQUIRED TO BE RECORDED

Because a conveyance that must be recorded to be protected under the Conner Act is considered *void* as to subsequent conveyances and liens placed in the public records first, it is important to know what documents must be recorded. As a general rule, **any document affecting title to real property should be recorded**. A review of the *Conner Act* and court interpretations of that Act result the following list:

Documents that Must Be Recorded for Protection under the Conner Act
- Deeds
- Deeds of trust and mortgages
- Leases for terms exceeding three years
- Easements
- Restrictive covenants
- Assignment of certain property interests
- Contracts to convey
- Option contracts
- Installment land contracts
- Rights of first refusal

Residential Contracts are Rarely Recorded

The Conner Act clearly states that a "contract to convey" is not valid to pass any property interest "as against lien creditors or purchasers for a valuable consideration," except from the time the contract is registered. Despite the law, *the overwhelming majority of residential purchase contracts in North Carolina are **not** recorded,* even though the purchaser could lose all rights to the real property under the unrecorded contract. Multiple contracts to convey the same property are rare. Additionally, in most residential sales transactions, the interim period between contract formation and closing is usually brief, often 30 to 60 days.

While custom may be to not record purchase contracts of relatively short duration, a real estate broker should never recommend that a buyer not record the purchase contract if the buyer asks about recording; instead, the broker should tell the buyer to seek legal advice from a real estate attorney about the merits of recording the contract and the dangers of nonrecordation.

*It is **essential** that all* **option contracts, rights of first refusal, and installment land contracts *be recorded*** to protect the rights of the optionee, holder of the right of first refusal, or vendee against the possible rights of third parties.[11] There often is a substantial period of time under these contracts before title is conveyed to the purchaser, or the option period or right of first refusal expires. Purchasers or long-term tenants of commercial property may want to record the purchase contract or lease contract, particularly if the lease includes a right of first refusal, or some memorandum of the contract to protect their interests during the due diligence period or lease term.

Recordation of "Memorandum of Contract"

State law allows a *memorandum* of a real estate sales contract, option contract, or lease contract to be recorded, rather than record the entire contract itself. The memorandum must include the following:

1) the names of the parties;
2) a description of the property that is the subject of the transaction;
3) the contract expiration date; and
4) "reference sufficient to identify the complete agreement" between the parties.

The applicable statutes have sample forms for a memorandum of lease, for an option to purchase contract, and for a purchase contract.[12] A memorandum that complies with the applicable statute and is properly recorded constitutes record notice.[13] What if a title search reveals a recorded memorandum, but the stated contract expiration date has passed? How does a title examiner learn whether the parties are still obligated under that contract? The same statute sets forth a detailed "60-day rule."[14] A real estate broker should not offer any opinion regarding the validity of a recorded memorandum and instead should recommend that any consumer consult a real estate attorney if there are any questions about the continuing validity of a memorandum of contract.

REQUIREMENTS FOR RECORDATION

A document must be in proper form and must be properly *acknowledged* to be recorded. The acknowledgment appears below the signature lines on the document. See the General Warranty Deed at the end of Chapter 5 for an example of an acknowledgment. *The purpose of an acknowledgment is to insure the authenticity of the signatures on the instrument by having the person appear before a public official, most often a notary public, and either sign the document in the official's presence or acknowledge or declare to that official that the person signed the instrument.* Consult an attorney if an acknowledgment appears irregular or defective, as numerous curative statutes exist to "cure" or legitimize acknowledgments having certain deficiencies.

State law prescribes recording standards for documents submitted to the register of deeds for recordation.[15] With one very limited exception,[16] all instruments presented to the register of deeds for recordation must meet various formatting requirements, including margins, page size, font size and color, and the type of instrument being recorded. The best resource to review these requirements is on the website of a county register of deeds.

The register of deeds must still record an instrument that does not meet the formatting standards but may charge an extra fee for "nonstandard documents" in addition to the normal recording fee.[17] *All major approved forms related to real estate practice and conveyancing comply with the statutory standards.*

RECORDATION PROCEDURES

Recordation itself is an easy process, so long as an instrument is in proper form. The instrument is delivered to the register of deeds office in the county where the property is located, recording fees and any excise tax are paid, and the original instrument is left to be copied or microfilmed. The register of deeds places a copy of each recorded document in a book in chronological order of receipt. All documents are promptly indexed in a temporary index book and then in the permanent grantor and grantee index books.[18] After recording, the original document is mailed to the owner or other designated person by the register of deeds. North Carolina now authorizes both electronic recordation and electronic notarization.

UNIFORM REAL PROPERTY ELECTRONIC RECORDING ACT (URPERA)

In 2005, North Carolina enacted the Uniform Real Property Electronic Recording Act (URPERA).[19] This cutting-edge legislation authorized the secretary of state to adopt erecording standards coupled with an adequate information security system to ensure that electronic documents are accurate, authentic, adequately preserved, and resistant to tampering. URPERA defines key terms and officially validates electronic records.

URPERA facilitates electronic commerce (e-commerce) by authorizing totally electronic real property transactions, including a completely electronic mortgage system where deeds of trust can be electronically originated, executed, and recorded. E-recording is a necessary component of the e-commerce movement made possible by two other state laws, namely, the North Carolina Electronic Commerce Act and the 2000 North Carolina Uniform Electronic Transactions Act (NCUETA), discussed in a later chapter.

ELECTRONIC NOTARIZATION

As a necessary supplement to e-commerce legislation, the General Assembly enacted the Electronic Notarization Act setting forth procedures for electronic notary acts that was implemented by "E-Notary Permanent Administrative Rules" duly approved by the North Carolina Department of the Secretary of State.[20] Together, the Act and Administrative Rules specify the details and guidelines to effectively transition the notarization process into the e-commerce age.

Under the Act, a notary must register his or her capability to notarize electronically with the secretary of state.[21] In addition to the normal prerequisites to become a notary, to become an *electronic* notary, a person must complete a special course of instruction approved by the secretary of state and pass the course examination.[22] Electronic notarization is prohibited under certain circumstances.[23]

COVENANTS OF TITLE IN DEEDS

Another method of title assurance is the use of covenants of title in deeds whereby the grantor indemnifies the grantee against a total or partial failure of title. Covenants of title in deeds enable a grantee to sue the grantor for damages if a covenant is breached, but covenants of title are not as reliable or effective as title insurance coverage. The reader is referred to Chapter 5 for a fuller discussion of the various covenants, including the covenants:

1) of seisin and the right to convey title;
2) against encumbrances; and
3) of warranty and quiet enjoyment.

LAWS ENHANCING THE MARKETABILITY OF TITLE

Marketable Title Act

The Marketable Title Act (Chapter 47B of the General Statutes) attempts to enhance the marketability of title to real property by extinguishing old claims to or defects in title that originated 30 or more years ago. The crux of the Act is that if a person claims title to real property under a recorded chain of title of at least 30 years and no other claimant has recorded a notice of any claim affecting the property during the 30-year period, then all conflicting claims based on any title transaction that predated the 30-year chain of title are extinguished.[24]

The Act is complex and contains more than a dozen exceptions.[25] Any question about an "old" property issue should be referred to an experienced real estate attorney. The fact that the problem occurred more than three decades ago does not mean it has been cured by the passage of time.

Statutes of Limitation and Statutes of Repose

Statutes of limitation are laws that establish a specific time period within which a legal action must be brought. If the legal action is not commenced within the time prescribed, the once valid legal claim will be time barred and can no longer be enforced in a judicial proceeding. For example, North Carolina has a three-year statute of limitations applicable to certain kinds of fraud under General Statute 1-52, but the three-year period starts to run *upon discovery by the injured party of the facts constituting the fraud or when the fraud should have been discovered by the exercise of due diligence.*[26]

In some statutes of limitation, the time period starts to run from an *event*, not discovery. These types of statutes or similar provisions are often referred to as statutes of repose. For example, North Carolina has a statute of repose that precludes any claim for damages pertaining to *improvements to real property* from being initiated more than six years from the specific last act or omission of the defendant or substantial completion of the improvement, *whichever is later.*[27] Under statutes of repose, the time period starts to run from the happening of an event, regardless of whether the injured party has discovered the defect or injury.

Curative Statutes

Curative statutes assist in the title assurance process by "curing" defects that exist in conveyances by eliminating technical title defects and holding the document to be validly recorded . Curative statutes include those declaring past defects in deed acknowledgments to be cured, such as where the notary public lacked authority or had an expired commission.[28]

Torrens System of Land Registration

North Carolina has a separate statutory system of land registration known as the Torrens System found in Chapter 43 of the General Statutes. The Torrens System will never be encountered in a residential home sales transaction. The idea for the Torrens System was borrowed from a system of registering title to ships. The end result of a successful Torrens registration is a governmental representation that a certain person owns title to specified property.

Land is registered in the Torrens System by commencing a special proceeding in superior court in which the person claiming title must prove that he or she has good title. If the claimant is successful, an **owner's certificate of title** is issued. *Every owner of land registered under the Torrens System holds the land free from any and all adverse claims, rights, or encumbrances not noted in the certificate of title.* Further, no person can acquire title to nor any right or interest in Torrens-registered land contrary to the rights of the registered owner by prescription or adverse possession, as the latter does not apply to Torrens-registered land.

Although rarely used, a broker might encounter the Torrens System of land registration in North Carolina. Owners of large tracts of land in some parts of the state may use Torrens registration precisely because of the protection the Torrens Act affords against adverse claims arising by prescriptive easements or adverse possession. Legal advice should be sought if a broker encounters a client dealing with land registered under the Torrens system.

Endnotes

1. For a comprehensive discussion of title assurance, see Hetrick & McLaughlin, *Webster's Real Estate Law in North Carolina, 6th ed.* (LexisNexis), Chapter 17, "Priorities; Recordation"; Chapter 21, "Title Examination Generally"; Chapter 22, "The Chain of Title"; Chapter 23, "Examination of Sources of Title"; Chapter 24, "Objections To Title"; Chapter 25, "Marketable Title Act; Perpetuities Reform; Related Legislation"; Chapter 26, "Opinion of Title"; and Chapter 27, "Title Insurance."

2. N.C. Gen. Stat. §84-2.1.

3. http://www.ncard.us.

4. See, for example, http://wakegov.com/realestate for Wake County and http://harnett.org/deeds or http://rod.harnett.org for Harnett County.

5. See N.C. Gen. Stat. §161-22.2, authorizing and describing parcel identifier number indexing.

6. The "secondary mortgage market" is a descriptive term for a national market in which individual mortgages are combined into pools and then sold to investors. Three entities are primarily involved in this market: The Federal National Mortgage Association (Fannie Mae), the Federal Home Loan Mortgage Corporation (Freddie Mac), and the Government Mortgage Association (Ginnie Mae).

7. N.C. Gen. Stat. §58-26-1(a).

8. See also N.C. Gen. Stat. §47-20 dealing with the recording of deeds of trust and similar instruments, and N.C. Gen. Stat. §47-27 dealing with deeds of easements. Pursuant to N.C. Gen. Stat. §47-26, deeds of gift must be recorded within two years or they are absolutely void, even as between the parties.

9. *Bourne v. Lay & Co.*, 264 N.C. 33, 140 S.E.2d 769 (1965); *Simmons v. Quick Stop Food Mart, Inc.*, 307 N.C. 33, 296 S.E.2d 275 (1982).

10. *Patterson v. Bryant*, 216 N.C. 550, 5 S.E.2d 849 (1939); *Glass v. Shoe Co.*, 212 N.C. 70, 192 S.E.2d 899 (1937).

11. *Chapel Hill Cinemas, Inc. v. Robbins*, 143 N.C. App. 571, 547 S.E.2d 462, reversed on other grounds, 354 N.C. 349, 554 S.E.2d 644 (2001). In this case, the lessee/tenant of a theater building failed to record the lease that gave the lessee a right of first refusal (a right to purchase the building in the event the lessor ever decided to sell). The lessor ignored the lessee's right and sold the property to a third person,

who promptly recorded the deed and, therefore, took free and clear ownership of the lease and its right of first refusal. While the lessee won in an action for damages against the lessor, the lessee still lost all rights under the unrecorded lease and right of first refusal.

12. N.C. Gen. Stat. §47-118, "Forms of registration of lease"; N.C. Gen. Stat. §47-119, "Form of memorandum for option to purchase real estate"; and N.C. Gen. Stat. §47-119.1, "Form of memorandum for contract to purchase real estate."

13. N.C. Gen. Stat. §47-120, "Memorandum as notice," begins with: "Such memorandum of a lease, an option to purchase real estate, or a contract to convey real estate … when executed, acknowledged, delivered, and registered as required by law, shall be as good and sufficient notice and have the same force and effect as if the written lease, option to purchase real estate, or contract to convey had been registered in its entirety."

14. After its opening sentence quoted above, N.C. Gen. Stat. §47-120 describes the "60-day rule" as follows:

> … However, it shall be conclusively presumed that the conditions of any contract to purchase that is the subject of a recorded memorandum under this section have been complied with or have expired and are no longer enforceable as against creditors or purchasers for valuable consideration who have recorded their interests after the memorandum from and after the expiration of 60 days from whichever of the following events occurs first:
>
> (1) The closing date stated in the memorandum, or any recorded extension or renewal of the memorandum, signed by the parties and acknowledged before an officer authorized to take acknowledgments.
>
> (2) The date when the conditions of the contract to convey, including payment of the last installment of earnest money or balance of purchase price (other than a purchase money note or deed of trust), and delivery of the deed from the seller to buyer were required by the terms of the recorded memorandum to have been performed, or the date of any recorded extension or renewal thereof signed by the parties and acknowledged before an officer authorized to take acknowledgments.

15. N.C. Gen. Stat. §161-14(b). The standards for recordation are effective for all documents recorded on or after July 1, 2002. The term "instruments" covers most real estate contracts, deeds, mortgages, and other documents. It is defined at N.C. Gen. Stat. §161-14(d).

16. Instruments that comply with another statute, N.C. Gen. Stat. §25-9-521 (specifying the proper form for a Uniform Commercial Code financing statement) are also acceptable. N.C. Gen. Stat. §161-14(b).

17. N.C. Gen. Stat. §161-14(b)(5).

18. N.C. Gen. Stat. §161-14(a) reads, in part:

> After the register of deeds has determined that all statutory and locally adopted prerequisites for recording have been met, the register of deeds shall immediately register all written instruments presented to him for registration.

When an instrument is presented for registration, the register of deeds shall endorse upon it the day and hour on which it was presented. This endorsement forms a part of the registration of the instrument. All instruments shall be registered in the precise order in which they were presented for registration. Immediately after endorsing the day and hour of presentation upon an instrument, the register of deeds shall index and cross-index it in its proper sequence. The register of deeds shall then proceed to register it on the day that it is presented unless a temporary index has been established.

19. N.C. Gen. Stat. Chapter 47, Article 1A, §§47-16.1 to 47-16.7.

20. The 2000 North Carolina Uniform Electronic Transactions Act (NCUETA) had recognized the ability of officials authorized to perform notarial acts to use electronic signatures. The 2005 Electronic Notarization Act is found in N.C. Gen. Stat. Chapter 10B, Article 2, §§10B-100 to 10B-146, and the administrative rules are found at 18 NCAC 07C .0101–.0604, titled "Electronic Notary Standards."

21. All of the requirements for registration as an electronic notary are set forth at N.C. Gen. Stat. §§10B-106, 10B-107, and 10B-108.

22. N.C. Gen. Stat. §10B-107, titled "Course of Instruction" states:
   (a) Before performing electronic notarial acts, a notary shall take a course of instruction of least three hours approved by the Secretary and pass an examination of this course, which shall be in addition to the educational requirements provided in Article 1 of this Chapter.
   (b) The content of the course and the basis for the examination shall be notarial laws, procedures, technology, and ethics as they pertain to electronic notarization. (2005-391, s. 4.)

23. N.C. Gen. Stat. §10B-116, titled "Prohibitions." This statute provides that an electronic notarization shall not be performed if the signer of the electronic document is not in the presence of the electronic notary at the time of notarization and is not personally known to the notary or properly identified under the provisions of the Act (or for any of the traditional statutory reasons set forth at N.C. Gen. Stat. §10B-20).

24. See N.C. Gen. Stat. §47B-2, titled "Marketable record title to estate in real property; 30-year unbroken chain of title of record; effect of marketable title." For a recent case discussing the Marketable Title Act as it applies to a town's interest in an alley, see *Kraft v. Town of Mt. Olive*, 183 N.C. App. 415, 645 S.E.2d 132 (2007).

25. N.C. Gen. Stat. §47B-3 sets forth 13 exceptions.

26. See, for example, *Carlisle v. Keith*, 169 N.C. App. 674, 614 S.E.2d 542 (2005).

27. See G.S. §1-50(a)(5). *Wood v. BD&A Construction LLC, et.al.*, 166 N.C. App. 216, 601 S.E.2d 311 (2004); *Mary Mitchell v. Mitchell's Formal Wear, Inc., Lewis Construction, Inc. & Crabtree Valley Mall*, 168 N.C. App. 212, 606 S.E.2d 704 (2005).

28. Samples of curative statutes may be found in Chapter 47, Article 4, of the General Statutes.

7 | LAND USE REGULATION

This chapter introduces **public land use regulation** and the numerous ways in which local, state, and federal governments regulate land development and use to protect the public interest.[1] Because public land use regulation is primarily a function of local government, this chapter emphasizes the zoning and planning ordinances adopted by cities and counties.

Private land use regulation is the control of land development and use by private parties. It includes covenants and restrictions on land and other privately created rules and regulations affecting land use. Most contemporary private land use restrictions are created by real property developers. A majority of residential development is accomplished by creating a "common interest community."

Importance to Real Estate Brokers

Real estate brokers must develop a working knowledge of public and private land use regulation. All real property is restricted by public land use regulation, and most developed real property is also subject to private land use regulation. A working knowledge includes the ability to advise and answer questions concerning the possible uses of real property. Any use limitation on real property is a material fact. Real estate brokers hold themselves out as possessing special skills, understanding, and information with respect to the listing, sale, and transfer of real property, and competent brokers understand the various land use restrictions that may apply to a property. *Brokers should advise prospective buyers or tenants to verify that their proposed land use is permissible and should direct them to the city or county planning department for information on land use restrictions.* A broker must not give false information, either intentionally or negligently, about land use restrictions. To do so may result in a legal dispute and subject the broker to disciplinary action by the Real Estate Commission.

> *Example:* An owner listed a vacant building previously used as a computer repair shop with a broker. A prospective buyer looked at the property and asked the broker if a manufacturing company could operate in the building. Without investigating, the broker answered affirmatively, and the buyer signed an offer to purchase the building that was accepted by the owner. Prior to closing, the prospective buyer discovered that the property was zoned "commercial," a zoning classification that excluded manufacturing uses. A lawsuit by the prospective buyer to rescind the contract may be successful in light of the broker's misrepresentation. In addition, the broker could be sued for damages and also disciplined by the N.C. Real Estate Commission.

Once a broker becomes aware of a client's special needs or plans for a property, the broker must inform the client that land use restrictions may exist that may affect the buyer's decision to purchase. A broker should have a general awareness of the procedures to change an existing land use restriction, as some prospects are interested in buying listed real estate only if public land use restrictions can be modified. Minimally, the prospect should be directed to contact the appropriate county or city planning department for information and to seek legal advice from an attorney with expertise in zoning and planning.

PUBLIC LAND USE CONTROLS

ZONING

"Zoning" consists of dividing land into districts or zones and specifying permitted and prohibited land uses in each zone. The original zoning ordinances were relatively simple, dividing a municipality into only three zones—residential, commercial, and industrial. Modern zoning ordinances are much more sophisticated and complex, regulating not only uses but the placement and height of buildings on land through so-called "bulk" and "density" controls. Land development and use is now extensively regulated by government in myriad ways, and zoning and planning is in a continual state of revision and expansion, reflecting the complexity of an ever-changing society.[2]

Unified Development Ordinances (UDOs)
Unified Development Ordinances (UDOs) represent the current generation of public zoning and land use controls and guidelines. Many North Carolina cities have enacted a UDO. A UDO combines multiple ordinances, regulations, and standards relating to and regulating land development into one coordinated, comprehensive document. For example, the City of Raleigh has adopted a Unified Development Ordinance to "…preserve, protect, and promote the public health, safety, and general welfare of residents and businesses in the City…." This 481-page document may be found on the city's website and contains the following chapters:

1) Introductory Provisions
2) Residential Districts
3) Mixed-Use Districts
4) Special Districts
5) Overlay Districts
6) Use Regulations
7) General Development Standards
8) Subdivision & Site Plan Standards
9) Natural Resource Protection
10) Administration
11) Building and Housing Code
12) Definitions

In spite of its daunting length, the Raleigh UDO is user friendly and provides a helpful and clear resource for almost any question involving land use, zoning, and development.[3]

Early versus Modern Zoning
Early zoning ordinances were basic documents primarily designed to keep commercial and industrial uses away from residential zones. As the Raleigh UDO illustrates, modern zoning ordinances are more complex in terms of permitted uses in each zoning district. Although there are clear prohibited and permitted uses in each zoning district, **limited uses, conditional uses,** and **special uses** may be allowed in some districts. In the Raleigh UDO, for example, **mixed-use districts and conditional-use districts** detail the specifics of permitted uses.[4]

Authority for Governmental Zoning and Land Use Control

The fundamental purpose of public zoning and land-use control is to regulate the development and use of land for the public welfare. The legal basis for governmental authority to zone is the exercise of the *police power* of the State of North Carolina, namely, the power to restrict the use of private property to promote the public health, safety, morals, or welfare. The United States Supreme Court, in *Euclid* v. *Ambler Realty Company*[5], upheld the validity of zoning ordinances, stating, "The ordinance now under review and all similar laws and regulations must find their justification in some aspect of the police power, asserted for the public welfare."

The original zoning power of the State of North Carolina is vested in the General Assembly, which in turn has delegated zoning power to municipalities and counties, subject to statutory standards and parameters. Without enabling legislation from the General Assembly, a municipality or county has no inherent power to zone its territory. The power to enact zoning laws is found in Chapter 160A of the North Carolina General Statutes as to municipalities and in Chapter 153A as to counties.[6] The purposes of zoning and public land use planning and guidelines by which municipalities and counties may zone are set forth in these statutes as further interpreted by court decisions. In a nutshell, zoning and public land use planning ordinances and regulations must:

1. be enacted as part of a comprehensive plan.
2. address "public purposes," including promoting the public health, safety, and general welfare.
3. encourage the most appropriate use of land throughout the municipality or county.

All North Carolina city zoning ordinances comply with the comprehensive plan requirement. The City of Ashville's Code of Ordinances, for example, includes the following summary:

> It is the intent of the City of Asheville to administer this chapter in accordance with the city's current, adopted comprehensive plan. This plan sets forth the goals and policies which serve as the basic policy guide for development in the City of Asheville and its extraterritorial jurisdiction. These goals and policies may be amended from time to time to meet the changing requirements of the city and its extraterritorial jurisdiction.[7]

The North Carolina Court of Appeals[8] has held that a separate written master plan is not necessary as long as there exists a plan that zones an entire city rather than only a specified portion arbitrarily selected.

Official zoning maps are part of a comprehensive plan. Most municipal websites have an official zoning map that is updated with revisions to zoning regulations and boundaries.[9] Some maps may have an interactive feature.

A zoning ordinance is not a contract between government and property owners. There is no guarantee that boundaries of a zone will remain the same or that restrictions imposed on a given parcel of land will not change. For example, the City of Raleigh continued the process of rezoning and remapping most of the city during 2015 and 2016, demonstrating the importance of keeping up-to-date on current zoning and planning regulations.

> *Example:* A university town enacted a zoning amendment to curb overoccupancy of rental homes by students in a residential neighborhood. The amendment permitted no more than four cars to be parked on any residential lot and applied to both owner-occupied and rental properties. The amendment allowed enforcement of the four-car rule against the owners of rental properties, rather than the student-tenants. The Court of Appeals held that the duly enacted zoning amendment was within the town's zoning authority and was constitutional.[10]

Zoning reclassifications can significantly increase or decrease property values. However, even if the reclassification substantially decreases a property's value, that fact alone is not sufficient to make a zoning ordinance invalid.[11]

Zoning ordinances are presumptively valid. Courts are extremely reluctant to interfere with zoning and planning ordinances and decisions. A presumption of validity places a heavy burden upon a party legally challenging an ordinance.[12] Courts intervene, however, when the power to zone is abused. Two primary limitations on local governmental zoning and planning authority are:

1) Municipalities and counties must comply with statutory requirements of notice and public hearing before adopting or amending zoning and planning ordinances.

2) Constitutional limitations on the zoning and planning power forbid arbitrary and unduly discriminatory interference with property rights.

Extraterritorial Jurisdiction—Zoning and Planning Regulations

Cities have a legitimate need to regulate development in areas adjacent to but just beyond a city's corporate limits. For this public policy reason, cities are granted **extraterritorial jurisdiction** for zoning and planning purposes. The extraterritorial power to zone and plan is governed by General Statute §160A-360. Depending on the population of a city, extraterritorial jurisdiction extends one to three miles beyond the corporate limits. Statutory prerequisites exist before a city can exercise these powers.[13] *Brokers must be aware that city zoning and regulations may extend beyond the city's borders.*

ZONING AND PLANNING ADMINISTRATION

Modern zoning ordinances contain detailed provisions concerning administration of zoning ordinances. A separate chapter in most zoning codes deals with administration, including review bodies, review procedures, and enforcement. For example, Chapter 10 of the Raleigh UDO addresses review procedures and enforcement; Section 10.1 lists the following review bodies and specifies the composition, authority, and procedural rules for each.

- City Council
- Planning Commission
- Board of Adjustment
- Historic Development Commission
- Appearance Commission
- Open Meeting Requirements
- Planning and Development Officer
- Summary of review authority

Zoning ordinances are administered primarily by a city or county planning department. The director of planning or a member of the planning department is the primary contact for information about local zoning and planning restrictions.

A **board of adjustment** exists to hear and grant or deny requests for "variances" to a zoning ordinance and to determine whether a "special-" or "conditional-use permit" is justified in particular situations.

ZONING AND PLANNING CONCEPTS AND TERMS

Key zoning and planning concepts and terms include:
- Mixed-use districts
- Overlay districts
- Historic preservation zoning
- Special uses and special-use permits
- Conditional-use zoning
- Nonconforming uses
- Zoning amendments (rezoning)
- Variances
- Illegal contract zoning
- Illegal uses
- Aesthetic zoning
- Spot zoning

Mixed-Use Districts

Unlike the earliest zoning ordinances that specified separate uses for each district, modern zoning includes mixed-use districts. A **mixed-use district** allows a combination of uses subject to specific regulations.

> *Example:* A 20-story building in a mixed-use district permits retail business on the ground floor, offices on the second and third floors, and apartments on the remaining floors. The Raleigh UDO defines a mixed-use building as "a multistory building constructed to accommodate retail on the ground floor and uses in addition to retail on the upper floors."[14]

Mixed-use districts are not limited to a single high-rise building. They may include a number of buildings with residential, retail, service, and commercial uses; or office, housing, and residential uses; or light manufacturing uses combined with commercial and housing uses. A variety of mixed-use districts provides flexibility in modern zoning and planning and accommodates current trends in land development. For example, the Raleigh UDO lists seven mixed-use districts:[15]
- Residential mixed use
- Office park
- Office mixed use
- Neighborhood mixed use
- Commercial mixed use
- Downtown mixed use
- Industrial mixed use

Overlay Districts

*An **overlay district** is one that superimposes a certain zoning use over the existing traditional zoning map.* The term "overlay" gets its name because a zoning map was traditionally modified by placing a coded plastic "overlay" that altered permitted uses in all or part of the underlying zones. Computer technology now allows the same function to be performed electronically. Common contemporary examples of overlay districts include watershed districts, historic preservation districts, and neighborhood conservation districts.[16] A watershed overlay district limits the amount of impervious surface, requires buffer zones, and regulates land use for the purpose of protecting the integrity of drinking water. Historic overlay districts add regulations protecting a neighborhood of special historic, architectural, or cultural significance.

Historic Preservation Zoning

A common overlay district in zoning ordinances is one for historic preservation because public policy strongly supports the preservation of historically significant structures. In a 1979 decision, *A-S-P Associates v. City of Raleigh*,[17] the North Carolina Supreme Court upheld the validity of historic preservation zoning. In that case, the City of Raleigh created a historic preservation district to preserve a 19th-century 20-block area known as Oakwood. The City Council created an "overlay" district, i.e., all zoning regulations applicable to the area in effect prior to passage of the historic district ordinance remained in effect. Compliance with the historic overlay requirements was *in addition* to the pre-existing zoning regulations. In a comprehensive discussion of historic zoning, the N.C. Supreme Court held that *it is a proper exercise of the police power to control the exterior appearance of buildings to preserve North Carolina's legacy of historically significant structures.*

Properties in historic districts and individual historic properties must obtain a "certificate of appropriateness" before the historic property can be materially altered, restored, moved, or demolished. ***No exterior portion of historic properties can be erected, altered, restored, moved, or demolished until after a certificate of appropriateness has been submitted to and approved by the historic district commission***. There are certain advantages to owning historic properties that should not be overlooked. Rehabilitating such structures may entitle the owner to special tax incentives.

Special Uses and Special-Use Permits

Zoning ordinances specify uses allowed as a matter of right and list other special uses allowed only after a ***special-use permit*** application has been approved. The Raleigh UDO, for example, defines "special uses" as those "that may be appropriate in a particular zoning district but because of the increased potential for incompatibility with adjacent uses require individual review by the Board of Adjustment."[18] Raleigh's land use regulations identify special uses requiring a permit and the application and approval process.[19]

A property owner who wants to use his property for a purpose not permitted as of right in a zoning district must first apply for and obtain a special-use permit. The permit is issued only if specific prerequisites are met.[20]

> *Example:* A corporation purchased a lot in a residentially zoned district, planning to construct and operate a day care center and preschool on the lot to serve 50 children. The zoning ordinance permits a day care center and preschool of this size only as a special use. The corporation must first apply for a special-use permit. If all special-use requirements are satisfied in the application process, the corporation's application for a special-use permit to operate the center should be approved.[21]

> *Example:* A charitable organization plans to construct and operate a rest home in a residentially zoned district. The charity must first apply and qualify for a special-use permit.

> *Example:* Two partners purchase and restore a house built in 1791, planning to use it as a bed & breakfast. After the restoration is completed, the house is designated as a historic landmark and is listed on the National Register of Historic Places. The house is located in a single-family

residential district that is also a historic overlay district. A bed-and-breakfast is allowed under the ordinance as a special use and will be approved only if the special-use permit requirements are met, which hopefully the buyers investigated prior to closing on the purchase.[22]

Conditional-Use Zoning

The term *conditional use* is sometimes used interchangeably with *special use*. While the two terms have much in common, most codes distinguish the two. In North Carolina, the term "*conditional use*" is most often associated with zoning districts in which the development and use of property must comply with specific conditions and standards. The North Carolina Supreme Court has summarized conditional use as follows:

> Conditional zoning is an outgrowth of the need for compromise between the interests of the developer seeking appropriate zoning changes for his tract and the neighboring landowner whose property interest would suffer if the most intensive use permitted by the new classification were instituted. In an attempt to reconcile these conflicting pressures, the municipality will authorize the proposed change but minimize the adverse effects by imposing conditions.[23]

For example, in the Raleigh Unified Development Ordinance, a list of "General-Use Zoning Districts" also appears in a separate category titled "Conditional-Use Zoning Districts." Section 1.3.2 of that ordinance provides:

> The following conditional-use zoning districts are established and applied to property as set forth on the Official Zoning Map. Each conditional-use district (bearing the designated CU on the Official Zoning Map) corresponds to a general-use district. All zoning requirements that apply to the general-use district are also applicable to the corresponding conditional-use district unless adopted conditions are more restrictive.

Nonconforming Uses

The term "**nonconforming use**" applies when a zoning ordinance is enacted or amended after property already has been developed or is being used in a manner permitted under the previous zoning ordinance. To accommodate the reasonable expectations of property owners and avoid possible invalidation of an ordinance as unlawful, zoning ordinances allow nonconforming uses to continue as before, subject to guidelines in the ordinance. The following are common changes in amendments to zoning ordinances that result in nonconforming uses:

- Lot area, width, or frontage standards
- Setback or height standards of existing structures
- Development features, such as off-street parking, landscaping, or buffer areas
- Impervious surface coverage
- Location and size of signs

Subject to specific conditions in a zoning ordinance, a landowner can continue a nonconforming use as a matter of right. This right to continued use does not depend on either a showing of hardship or on any discretion by the director of planning or the board of adjustment. Most zoning ordinances have detailed guidelines concerning the continuation of a nonconforming use.

Nonconforming uses are not favored by the law.[24] Therefore, most zoning ordinances limit the enlargement and expansion of nonconforming uses, prohibit resumption of the nonconforming use after it has been discontinued for a specified period of time, prohibit change to other nonconforming uses, and address whether a property may be rebuilt if destroyed and under what conditions.

Example: An owner of a gasoline station that is a nonconforming use in an area that has been rezoned single-family residential retires, closes the station, and lists it for sale. Two years later, a prospective buyer becomes interested in the property. Under most zoning ordinances, the right to operate the gasoline station as a nonconforming use in a residential zone may have terminated because of nonuse. In this event, the property can only be used for single-family residential purposes since that is the current zoning classification.

For example, Section 10.3.2 of the Raleigh UDO reads in part: "When a nonconforming use of land or a nonconforming use of part of all of a structure is discontinued, vacated, or abandoned for a period of 365 consecutive days or more, the use shall not be reestablished or resumed." If a nonconforming-use structure is significantly damaged or destroyed, restoration may not be permitted or may be permitted subject to compliance with existing zoning regulations. Detailed provisions and guidelines exist in modern zoning ordinances and must be consulted by any prospective buyer or renter of a property with a nonconforming use or other nonconformity.

Zoning Amendments (Rezoning)

If a property owner is prevented by existing zoning from making a particular use of land, he or she may petition to amend the zoning ordinance to allow the desired use. Sometimes a prospective buyer will sign an offer to purchase agreement with the condition that the land must be "rezoned" to fit the buyer's intended use. A party seeking a zoning amendment will not have an easy task. Amendments typically are not approved unless a significant error existed in the original ordinance or unless substantial change has occurred in the community since adoption of the original ordinance. That said, ordinances can be amended, supplemented, changed, modified, or repealed.

Generally, interested persons must file a petition to the legislative body through its planning agency, requesting an amendment to the ordinance. The petition is published in a public newspaper for a specified period of time with a notice that a public hearing will be held. Sometimes ordinances direct that a legible public notice be placed on the land for a certain period of time announcing that an amendment to the zoning ordinance is being requested. At the expiration of a set period after the petition and the notice requirements have been met, a public hearing is held by the legislative body to determine if the amendment to the ordinance will be made. As to municipal zoning ordinances, in North Carolina, if persons owning 20 percent of the land area in the immediate district to be rezoned protest the amendment, then the amendment will not be effective unless three-fourths of the legislative body approves it.[25] Cities have developed helpful websites to assist citizens in obtaining information concerning zoning matters.[26]

Variances

A variance is another zoning procedure designed to meet a prospective buyer's plans for use of land where existing zoning precludes that use.[27] If a variance is granted, a land owner will be allowed to deviate from the terms of the ordinance where strict and literal application causes undue hardship or serious practical difficulty. A board of adjustment cannot vary a zoning ordinance at will. Courts have worked out a number of requirements to justify allowing particular landowners to use their land in a way not authorized by the terms of the zoning ordinance. To be entitled to a variance, a landowner must demonstrate that:

1. The zoning regulation creates a special and peculiar hardship to his particular property. (If the hardship affects all property in the zone in the same way, the hardship is not special or peculiar to his particular property and no variance will be granted.)
2. The term "hardship" is narrowly defined to mean that if the landowner complies with the provisions of the ordinance, then no reasonable use of or reasonable return from the property is possible.
3. The hardship must not be a result of the landowner's own actions.
4. A granted variance must not change the essential character of the zone.

A variance does not necessarily mean a major change in classification or use. It can involve a minor modification of a setback or height requirement, the waiver of a parking space formula, or a change in some other detail or regulation relating to use of the property.

Example: Dooley, an experienced real estate developer, purchased a large vacant warehouse and sought to convert it into a 12-unit apartment building, a use that the zoning classification would allow if he could comply with an onsite parking requirement of two parking spaces. Because the warehouse physically occupies much of the land, Dooley only can create 12 parking spaces instead of the required 24. Dooley may be entitled to a variance of the onsite parking requirement under these circumstances.

Illegal Contract Zoning

In rare instances, a zoning decision by a local zoning authority may constitute what was originally termed "illegal contract zoning." A leading expert on zoning law summarizes the practice, in part, as follows:

> Two early 1970s cases from Raleigh invalidating rezonings that allowed multifamily development in single-family residential neighborhoods established a basic principle for review of rezonings in North Carolina: a rezoning that is based on a single project rather than on all permissible uses in the new zoning district is invalid. These early cases termed this practice contract zoning. The court has since dropped this characterization but retained the result—the practice remains illegal in North Carolina...[28]

Illegal Uses

An ***illegal use*** *is a use established* ***after*** *enactment of a zoning ordinance that violates the zoning ordinance.* If a building or structure is erected or if land is used in violation of a zoning ordinance, the municipality or other zoning authority will initiate a legal action to prevent the unlawful use of the property. A person who buys property that is being used in violation of a zoning ordinance has no right to continue that use, no matter how long it has existed.

Aesthetic Zoning

A zoning provision based solely on aesthetic considerations is legally permissible according to a 1982 North Carolina Supreme Court decision holding that a county ordinance that required owners of junkyards to screen the property from public view was constitutional.[29] The Court, adopting guidelines previously set forth in historic zoning cases, held that the possible diminution in value of an individual's property because of an aesthetic zoning ordinance must be balanced against the corresponding gain to the general public.

Spot Zoning

"Spot zoning" has been defined by the North Carolina Supreme Court as:

> A zoning ordinance or amendment that singles out and reclassifies a relatively small tract owned by a single person and surrounded by a much larger area uniformly zoned, so as to impose upon the small tract greater restrictions than those imposed upon the larger area, or so as to relieve the small tract from restrictions to which the rest of the area is subjected, is called "spot zoning."[30]

In other jurisdictions, the term "spot zoning" refers to a practice that is always illegal. In such jurisdictions, if "spot zoning" is found to occur, the practice is automatically invalid.[31] North Carolina falls within a smaller group of jurisdictions that view the term "spot zoning" as descriptive of a fact situation but not automatically an illegal practice. Thus, spot zoning is not automatically invalid in North Carolina but if it lacks a reasonable basis, then it will be void.

URBAN AND REGIONAL PLANNING

To assure the orderly and systematic development of land use, urban and regional land use plans exist. Zoning is one major tool to assist the planner. A broker interested in long-range planning and extensive information regarding land use in his/her area will want to become familiar with the local land use plan.[32]

Development Standards

Comprehensive lot and building standards regulate land development in each zoning district. Categories of standards include maximum density per acre; minimum lot width and frontage; minimum front, side, rear, and corner setbacks; maximum building height; and maximum impervious coverage of lots. All developments must comply with minimum lot and building standards, although special standards may apply to some, including cluster and open space residential developments.[33]

Cluster and Open Space Subdivision Development

As mentioned, modern UDOs include subdivision, lot, and building standards. Two special forms of subdivision design, **cluster development** and **open space development**, are common. These development models encourage design that provides greater protection of open space and natural resources. Purposes of cluster development and open space development include:

- Creating more open space and preserving more natural resources than conventional subdivision design
- Using compact and less costly networks of roads and utilities
- Reducing storm water runoff
- Preserving an area's character
- Creating open space and recreational amenities for residents
- Preserving natural, environmentally sensitive, and historic resources

As the names suggest, cluster and open space development require that a specified part of each subdivision be set aside and permanently preserved as open space. The distinction between the two has been summarized as follows:

> The primary difference between cluster developments and open space developments is the amount of open space that must be preserved. Cluster developments are required to set aside a modest amount of open space, while open space developments are required to set aside a far greater amount.[34]

SUBDIVISION APPROVAL

Every subdivision of land affects the environment and thus the health, safety, and welfare of both future subdivision residents and members of the general public. *State law authorizes counties and municipalities to regulate the subdivision of lands within their borders.*[35] Almost every area of the state is therefore subject to either county or municipal subdivision regulations.

Subject to some exceptions, property owners who convey part of their land to another may be subject to subdivision regulations and must have at least preliminary approval of the subdivision by the county or municipality *before* selling lots. Brokers must understand that merely having a survey of the new lots prepared by a surveyor or engineer does *not* mean the subdivision has been officially *approved* by the proper government authorities.

Brokers Should Verify Subdivision Approval

Before a real estate broker accepts a listing for a subdivided lot or lots, the broker should request to see, and preferably have, a copy of the final approved and recorded subdivision plat. If there is no final recorded plat, the broker should meet with the seller and the seller's attorney to assure that offering the property for sale or lease can be accomplished in accordance with applicable law. The lack of proper subdivision approval can lead to serious consequences for buyers, the seller-developer, and any real estate broker involved in the sale of lots in an unapproved subdivision. Problems often come to a head when the lot buyer tries to obtain a building permit or a permit to place a septic system on the property.

Definition of Subdivision

For the purpose of subdivision approval ordinances, a "**subdivision**" is defined by General Statute 153A-335 as "*all divisions of a tract or parcel of land into two or more lots, building sites, or other divisions … for the purpose of sale or building development (whether immediate or future) and includes all division of land involving the dedication of a new street or a change in existing streets.*" Certain combinations and recombinations of land and the division of land into parcels more than 10 acres each (if no street right-of-way dedication is involved) are not within the definition of "subdivision" for purposes of subdivision approval laws. The same statute also excludes from the definition of a subdivision "the division of a tract in single ownership the entire area of which is no greater than two acres into not more than three lots, if no street right-of-way dedication is involved and if the resultant lots are equal to or exceed the standards of the county as shown by its subdivision regulations."

Criminal Penalty for Selling Lots in an Unapproved Subdivision

In a county or municipality with a subdivision ordinance, no subdivided plat of land can be filed with the register of deeds until final approval has been obtained from both the applicable planning board and the county commissioners or city council. Approval by the appropriate city or county board will be noted on the plat map that will then be accepted for recording by the register of deeds. Since January 1, 2006, owners and developers or their brokers may offer lots for sale or lease and enter into contracts once *preliminary* plat approval has been obtained *as long as* the contracts comply with state law.[36] The contract must:

1. *include a copy of the preliminary plat as an attachment* and obligate the owner to *deliver a copy of the final recorded plat to the buyer prior to closing and conveyance*;

2. "plainly and conspicuously" notify the buyer or lessee that the final plat has not been recorded, that no governmental body incurs any obligation to the buyer/lessee regarding final plat approval, that changes between the preliminary and final plats are possible, and that *the buyer/lessee may terminate the contract without breach "... if the final recorded plat differs in any material respect from the preliminary plat;"*

3. not require the buyer/lessee to close earlier than five days after the seller/lessor delivers a copy of the final recorded plat to the buyer/lessee *if there are no material differences between the preliminary and final plats*; and

4. *Allow the buyer/lessee to terminate the contract within* (or does not require buyer/lessee to close sooner than) *15 days following delivery of the final recorded plat if there are material differences between the final and preliminary plat*, in which case the buyer/lessee is entitled to a refund of all earnest monies or prepaid purchase monies.

Subdivision Streets Disclosure Laws

If a developer or grantor of lots in a subdivision created on or after October 1, 1975, intends to dedicate the subdivision's streets to **public** use, the developer must build streets that comply with North Carolina Department of Transportation standards. Prior to selling or conveying a lot, the developer also is required to supply the prospective buyer with a **disclosure statement** providing information about the street on which the property being sold fronts.[37] *The disclosure statement must fully disclose whether the street will be "public" or "private."* If the street is dedicated **public**, the developer or seller must certify to prospective buyers that the street has been approved by the Division of Highways and that the street has been or will be constructed in accordance with state standards. Disclosure of additional information about subdivision streets also is required, depending on the nature and location of the streets involved.

Who is responsible for maintaining the roads providing ingress and egress to a property is a material fact that brokers must disclose. Information as to whether subdivision streets are public or private is particularly important to prospective buyers, because street maintenance costs can be extremely high. If the streets will be private, then state law[38] further requires the developer/seller to include in the disclosure statement an explanation of the consequences and maintenance responsibilities of the private street, to "fully and accurately disclose the party or parties upon whom responsibility for construction and maintenance of such street or streets shall rest ...," and to disclose that the street may not be constructed to minimum NCDOT standards sufficient to allow the State to assume maintenance responsibilities. It is critically important that brokers understand that *the fact that streets are dedicated as "public" on the plat* **does not mean that a governmental entity has accepted responsibility for maintaining those streets.**

Brokers should at least ask the owner who is responsible for maintaining the streets that provide access to any given property and to disclose that information to both prospective buyers and to lenders, particularly where there is no governmental maintenance responsibility. Real estate brokers should be very careful not to make unverified representations about the public or private maintenance of streets, regardless of the subdivision's age. *Do not assume that public designation equates to gov-*

ernmental acceptance of maintenance and repair responsibilities. A real estate broker's duty to discover and disclose is heightened when there are signs, such as the condition of the roads, which would lead a reasonable broker to question whether there is public maintenance. Where streets are designated as private, there should be some agreement for maintenance by someone, whether that is the original developer, the adjacent property owners, or an owners' association as a whole.

BUILDING CODES

The General Assembly created a State Building Code Council empowered to adopt a North Carolina State Building Code in accordance with statutory guidelines.[39] State laws detail **statewide building codes** that specify various requirements regarding the construction of buildings to promote safety, such as requirements relating to fireproof construction, boiler construction and maintenance, electrical installations, mechanical devices, heating, plumbing, sanitation, drainage, sewers, ventilation, means of exit, illumination of exits, size and location of rooms, and many other matters.

These building codes not only dictate minimum standards for new construction but also apply to owners or purchasers of older structures who intend to renovate or remodel; the remodeling or renovations must meet the current building code standards.

HIGHWAY ACCESS CONTROLS

Land may lie on a public highway or street to which access has been restricted or forbidden by the state or a municipality.[40] A prospective buyer's plans to make a use requiring access to the highway or street may be thwarted because such access has been cut off at some previous time. *"Access" to an existing street or highway is a part of the "property" of the owner who owns land abutting the street or highway, and access may be the most important aspect of a particular tract.* Under the laws of condemnation or eminent domain, the governmental unit that cuts off an owner's access must compensate the property owner at the time of the taking; however, if a former owner was *previously* compensated or the statute of limitations has run on any action to recover damages from the state or municipality for the "taking" or closing of access to a particular road or street, then any claim is extinguished.

Access to a public road or street is important to the use of real property. Anyone buying real property on a public highway or street should be careful to determine whether the right of access to such highway or street has been restricted or controlled in any way and to what extent.

FEDERAL REGULATION OF INTERSTATE LAND SALES

The **Interstate Land Sales Full Disclosure Act**[41] was enacted to prevent fraudulent and misleading practices by developers in the interstate sale of subdivision lots. When it was enacted by Congress in 1968, mail order and telephone fraud in the interstate sale of subdivision lots, especially in retirement and recreational developments, was a serious problem. To enable buyers to make an informed decision, the Act requires full disclosure of important information to lot buyers prior to any decision to purchase. The Act applies to the sale or lease of subdivision lots in *interstate commerce*, i.e., offers to sell or lease property located in one state to residents of other states.

Real estate brokers should be aware of the existence but not the details of the Act. The Act has myriad exemptions, including the sale of lots in a subdivision containing fewer than 25 lots. A real estate law attorney should be consulted concerning the many exemptions to the Interstate Land Sales Full Disclosure Act, which are found at 17 U.S.C. §1702.

ENVIRONMENTAL ISSUES AND DUE DILIGENCE

Federal and state environmental laws have a major impact on existing and proposed land use. Comprehensive and often overlapping federal and state environmental legislation addresses subjects such as beneficial land use, the conservation of natural resources, clean air, the disposal of hazardous substances, leaking underground storage tanks, sedimentation control, and lead paint and asbestos hazards.

Environmental Site Assessments (ESAs)

Although the substance and requirements of these various laws go well beyond what a real estate broker must know, a broker should be aware of the need for an environmental inspection prior to the purchase or leasing of commercial, industrial, office, and other nonresidential property. ESAs are conducted by environmental experts who investigate the property to assess environmental issues based on technical standards. The assessment includes a history of past use of the property, an inspection of public records that might reveal environmental issues, and an evaluation of suitability for the current or proposed use.

An ESA is highly advisable for a purchaser of suspect land, since real property owners in North Carolina generally are not compelled to disclose potential environmental problems or a history of environmental problems on the property being transferred, in part because North Carolina is a *caveat emptor* state. Both the **Comprehensive Environmental Response, Compensation, and Liability Act (CERCLA)** and state law require owners, operators, and "responsible parties" to notify the Inactive Hazardous Waste Sites Branch of the NC Division of Waste Management within 90 days of discovering any inactive hazardous substance or waste disposal site.

If a broker is aware of a prior use that may have caused environmental issues, the broker must disclose that prior use to all parties, including lenders. Disclosure should include the existence of underground storage tanks in which hazardous substances have been stored, any history of hazardous waste disposal or the storage of hazardous substances on the property, and other environmental danger signals, such as the existence of a former sanitary landfill on the property. Hopefully, an expert conducting an ESA would discover these prior uses through his/her research.

Environmental issues can complicate any real estate transaction, whether residential or commercial, because of the owner/purchaser's potential liability to clean up any contamination even if they did not cause it. A real estate broker who knows or has reasonable cause to believe that a prior use may have had adverse environmental effects on the property must disclose what s/he knows and should strongly recommend that any prospective buyer or lessee fully use their due diligence to conduct any and all inspections, investigations, or inquiries they wish. Brokers need not fully understand the multitude of environmental laws and regulations, but they are expected to be familiar with the general requirements of federal and state environmental laws and regulations.

ENVIRONMENTAL LAWS AND REGULATIONS

National Environmental Policy Act

The **National Environmental Policy Act (NEPA)**[42] mandates that all federal agencies fully weigh the environmental effects of federal programs. NEPA requires federal agencies to prepare environmental impact statements describing in detail the effect of proposed projects on the environment. North Carolina requires **environmental impact statements** of state agencies for certain projects under the North Carolina Environmental Policy Act.[43]

CERCLA

Congress enacted the **Comprehensive Environmental Response, Compensation, and Liability Act (CERCLA)**[44] in 1980 to address the liability, compensation, cleanup, and emergency response to hazardous substances released into the environment. *CERCLA authorizes both the federal and state governments to institute actions for the containment, cleanup, and removal of **hazardous wastes** on property.* At the federal level, CERCLA is enforced by the Environmental Protection Agency (EPA). The North Carolina Department of Environmental Quality (DEQ) enforces CERCLA at the state level. CERCLA authorizes actions for damages, including actions by private parties, to recover the necessary costs of an environmental cleanup.

The federal government might fund a cleanup with what is known as "Superfund" money. The "Superfund" is a fund financed jointly by industry and the federal government. North Carolina also has a "Superfund" program, and a list of reported waste sites may be found on the NC DEQ's Division of Waste Management website.[45] If government funds the cleanup, it will seek to recover the cost from the "responsible parties" for the environmental damage.

CERCLA is important to all parties who sell, purchase, lease, and finance real estate because it imposes liability for the cost of correcting and cleaning up the environmental damage not only on the polluting party but also, in many instances, on the current owner or operator of a property who may not have been the polluting party. For this reason, real estate brokers should be alert for possible environmental damage to property they are listing, selling, or leasing.

CERCLA's purpose is cleaning up hazardous waste on contaminated land. It provides a remedy for federal, state, and local governments and private parties to clean up a site. CERCLA and related environmental laws reinforce the preventive necessity of exercising due diligence before purchasing or leasing real property.

> *Example:* A developer wanted to purchase a five-acre vacant lot to construct an office building and entered into a 12-month option to purchase the lot. During due diligence, the developer hired an expert to investigate the environmental condition of the land. Research by the expert revealed that the lot was once part of a larger site on which a company for many years had treated telephone poles and railroad ties with creosote oil that through the years had seeped into the ground, contaminating the lot. Not surprisingly, the developer chose not to exercise the option to purchase.

Amendments to CERCLA offer a defense to innocent landowners who conscientiously perform due diligence, undertaking all appropriate inquiries,[46] but who had no actual or constructive knowledge of the hazardous substance. Landowners who purchased without exercising due diligence remain liable with prior owners for site clean-up even though they did not cause the hazardous substance pollution.

> *Example:* An investor finds a lot located in a commercial zone near a busy intersection that had been vacant for decades. The seller knew that an ancestor had operated an electronic transformer repair company on the lot, but the seller never mentioned this to his listing broker or to the investor. The investor was in such a rush to get title to this bargain lot that he did not perform any due diligence investigation of the property. Several years after the real estate closing, the investor discovers that the lot is contaminated with PCP (polychlorinated biphenyl) from the earlier operation of the electronic transformer repair company. The investor is jointly

and severally liable for cleaning up the lot along with prior owners. Too often, however, these other parties are bankrupt, deceased, or a company no longer in existence.

Example: A real estate broker familiar with a rural area recalls that an old abandoned paint factory that operated throughout World War II is located only one block away from a one-acre parcel of land that is for sale and zoned for multifamily residential purposes. Prospective buyers must be informed of the possibility of adverse environmental consequences, such as lead contamination of the groundwater. Environmental damage can be a devastating problem for a buyer who may have to expend substantial sums on cleanup costs.

Resource Conservation and Recovery Act

The Resource Conservation and Recovery Act (RCRA)[47] creates what is sometimes called a "cradle to grave" program dealing with the treatment, storage, and disposal of hazardous waste. Guidelines exist for the collection, transportation, separation, recovery, and disposal of hazardous waste.

Clean Air Act

The federal **Clean Air Act**[48] deals with the problem of **air pollution** and provides federal regulatory air standards.

N.C. Coastal Area Management Act

Property development in the coastal areas of North Carolina is subject to the **North Carolina Coastal Area Management Act**[49] (**CAMA**) and state regulations. Among other things, CAMA requires that a permit be obtained prior to engaging in any "development" of an *"area of environmental concern."* Coastal wetlands and marshlands are areas of environmental concern. The term *"development"* is a broad one, encompassing *construction, excavation, dredging, filling, dumping, bulkheading, or the clearing or altering of land as part of construction.*[50]

The North Carolina Supreme Court has described the purpose of CAMA, in part, as follows: "... to protect, preserve, manage, and provide for the orderly development of one of North Carolina's most valuable resources, the coastal estuarine system ...," which is "unique, fragile, and irreplaceable."[51] In that case, a property owner who constructed an enlarged bulkhead and retaining wall was ordered to remove everything and restore the site to its pre-violation condition at the owner's expense. *Property owners who disregard CAMA may find themselves with serious legal problems and a court order requiring them to pay the cost of repairing the damage done to the estuarine system.*

The Commission expects real estate brokers who work in coastal areas subject to CAMA to be aware of the potential impact of this law and regulations implementing it. Developer clients and prospective buyers planning to "develop" a property should routinely be advised to inquire and assure that any proposed development is permitted under CAMA and to consult an attorney, both to investigate and incorporate the planned use of the property as a condition in any offer to purchase.

N.C. Mountain Ridge Protection Act

North Carolina was the first state in the nation to enact comprehensive legislation regulating construction on protected mountain ridges.[52] This legislation was enacted in reaction to the construction of a 10-story condominium project at the summit of Little Sugar Mountain in Avery County.[53] General Statute §113A-208 allows any county or city to adopt and enforce "... an ordinance that regulates the construction of tall buildings or structures on protected mountain ridges ...."

Waterway Vegetation Buffer Zones

To minimize the adverse effects of pollution, North Carolina administrative regulations and some zoning ordinances require a buffer zone of undisturbed vegetation along some river basins and coastal waterways. The undisturbed vegetation zone runs from 30 to 50 feet from the water's edge, depending upon the location and nature of the waterway.[54] Zoning and land use ordinances in certain areas require more extensive buffer zones.

Brokers dealing with land in the Neuse River Basin or in coastal areas should familiarize themselves with environmental regulations and ordinances having a direct impact on land development. Coastal areas are governed by the North Carolina Coastal Resources Commission. In a federal court decision involving a buyer of timber rights that included land in an environmental buffer zone created by an ordinance of the Town of Garner, a timber company made a claim against a title insurance company because the timber on 179 out of more than 700 acres was within a waterway buffer zone and could not be harvested.[55] A town ordinance created a buffer zone of 500 feet from the center of Swift Creek, or the 100-year floodplain plus 50 feet. The timber company estimated its loss by valuing the timber that could not be harvested at $374,769.

Scenic Corridor Zones

Land may be located in what is known as a "scenic corridor zone." If a scenic corridor zoning ordinance does not deprive a landowner of all economically beneficial or productive use of the property, it does not amount to an unconstitutional taking. In one North Carolina Court of Appeals decision, property within a scenic corridor zone adjoining Interstate 40 could not be used as a vehicle storage lot. The Court found that this ordinance was constitutional and did not deprive the landowners of all economically beneficial or productive use of their property.[56]

N. C. Leaking Petroleum Underground Storage Tank Cleanup Act

The North Carolina Leaking Petroleum Underground Storage Tank Cleanup Act regulates the unauthorized discharge of oil or other hazardous chemicals and substances from underground petroleum storage tanks.[57] Under this environmental law, the owner of polluted property may have the heavy burden of cleanup costs even though the owner had nothing to do with the discharge of the hazardous substance. Leaking underground storage tanks are a common environmental issue.[58]

Example: An investor purchased a commercial lot not knowing that a former owner had operated a small country gasoline station on the property. The building was demolished and the lot graded when the former owner died a decade earlier, but the underground storage tank with fuel was never removed. After purchasing the property without conducting an environmental assessment, the investor discovered the underground tank and that it had been slowly leaking for years. The investor is now liable for substantial environmental cleanup costs. (Past owners who caused the problem are also liable, but they may be deceased, unable to be found, or insolvent.)

Commercial USTs have been regulated at the federal level since 1974 following the enactment of the Resource Conservation and Recovery Act (RCRA). Unfortunately, discovering whether a *noncommercial underground fuel storage tank* was ever installed on a property may not be easy. It does not appear that there have ever been any regulatory or permitting requirements for **noncommercial** USTs at either the federal or state level. Even today, a property owner apparently can install a noncommercial UST without notifying any authority or obtaining any permit.

A current owner may not know if a prior owner installed a UST, particularly where the present heat source is nonfuel. As part of the discovery process, a reasonable prudent broker should consider factors such as:

- the age of the structure,
- its location when built (e.g., urban, suburban, rural),
- previous uses of the property,
- the presence of radiators in the dwelling,
- pipes sticking out of the ground, and
- how long the current owner has owned the property.

A structure built decades ago in what was then a rural environment that has always been used for residential purposes raises the question: what was the original heat source? What inquiries might a reasonable prudent broker make to discover whether an underground storage tank could be on the property? The broker might contact NCDEQ's UST Division and ask whether they have any records of any USTs being removed from the property.

Any broker who knows that there is or was a UST on the property *must **disclose** its presence to all prospective purchasers or tenants,* and if acting as a buyer agent, should **strongly encourage** the buyer to hire an expert to inspect the tank and conduct a soil contamination test to determine whether the buyer is purchasing a major liability.

Property owner liability for USTs has become even more important since the General Assembly passed legislation in September 2015 that *eliminated a state trust fund administered by the Underground Storage Tank Section of the NC Department of Environmental Quality that helped defray remediation expenses related to noncommercial USTs.* (Session Law 2015-241.) Owners who first learned of a problem with a noncommercial UST after July 1, 2015, are not eligible for any state reimbursement funds nor is there any federal program for noncommercial USTs. If, however, an owner discovers that a **commercial UST** was installed sometime earlier on his/her property, the owner *may be eligible for contribution from federal funds* administered by the NCDEQ, UST Section.

N.C. Sediment Pollution Control Act

The North Carolina Sediment Pollution Control Act[59] deals with the problem of sedimentation of state waters. *"Sedimentation" occurs from the erosion or depositing of soil or other materials into waters caused by activities such as land development, manufacturing, farming, and mining.* The environmental problem with sedimentation is its adverse impact on the waters of the state, including the fish and plants located in them.

Any person engaging in an activity that disturbs land by altering the natural vegetation or topography in a way that creates sedimentation is subject to the Act. Land-disturbing activities are regulated by the North Carolina Department of Environmental Quality.

> *Example:* A new shopping center is under construction. The Sediment Pollution Control Act and state regulations require that the construction include both a sedimentation and erosion control plan and devices. A natural buffer zone between the project and nearby waters also must be maintained. Numerous other sedimentation and erosion controls may be required.

Solar Collectors on Homes

Zoning laws may be unenforceable because they contravene public policy. For example, a zoning ordinance that violates federal or state fair housing legislation is void.[60] In 2007, the General Assembly enacted legislation prohibiting zoning ordinances, covenants, or other restrictions that prohibit or have the effect of prohibiting the installation of solar collectors on homes.[61]

Clean Water Acts

The federal and state **Clean Water Acts**[62] make the depositing of dredged or fill materials into wetlands and other waters of the United States or North Carolina illegal unless a permit is obtained in advance. "**Wetlands**" *are areas periodically inundated or saturated to the extent that they can or do support vegetation adapted to aquatic conditions.* The federal dredge and fill permit program is administered by the U.S. Army Corps of Engineers, and the Environmental Protection Agency is also involved. The *North Carolina Dredge and Fill Act*[63] requires that a permit— issued by the Coastal Resources Commission—be obtained before any dredging or filling is done in North Carolina waters or marshlands.

Wastewater Systems

Directly related to environmental health is the treatment and disposal of wastewater, which is governed both by statute and administrative rules.[64] The rules state that "any person owning or controlling a residence, place of business, or place of public assembly containing water-using fixtures connected to a water-supply source shall discharge all wastewater directly to an approved wastewater system permitted for that specific use."[65] "Residence" includes a private home, dwelling unit in a multiple family structure, hotel, motel, summer camp, labor work camp, manufactured home, institution, or any other place where people reside.[66] Wastewater includes water from sinks, showers, or washing machine drains (often referred to as "grey water"), sewage (sometimes called "black water"), and industrial process wastewater.

All wastewater must be treated either through a septic system or sewage treatment plant. Despite state law, some properties still employ "straight-piping" where wastewater is discharged directly into streams or onto land. ***This is illegal.*** *A straight-pipe system is a material fact that brokers must disclose to all parties involved in the transaction.*[67]

Laws Regarding Lead Poisoning and Asbestos

North Carolina law requires the State Commission for Health Services to adopt rules for the prevention and control of lead poisoning in children, including rules for the abatement of lead poisoning hazards in dwellings, schools, and day care facilities. Congress has also legislated in this area. The **Lead-Based Paint Poisoning Prevention Act**, passed in 1971, is aimed at eliminating the presence of lead-based paint in housing connected with HUD-assisted projects.[68] (The mandatory lead-based paint disclosure requirements under federal law for pre-1978 housing are discussed in Chapter 8.)

In addition, North Carolina has enacted laws concerning the abatement of environmental hazards caused by **asbestos**, which is still present in many older buildings.[69]

FLOOD HAZARD AREA REGULATIONS & INSURANCE

Real estate located in designated *"flood hazard areas"* is subject to special federal laws and regulations.[70] Flood hazard areas are designated on maps issued by the Federal Emergency Management Agency. *Flood insurance is required in all flood hazard areas under the National Flood Insurance Program if a federally related mortgage loan is being made on improved property or property on which improvements will be made.* Federally related loans would include FHA loans, VA loans, and most loans sold in the secondary mortgage market. Altogether, this accounts for a vast majority of all mortgage loans. Flood insurance can be obtained from a property insurance broker. Land use within flood hazard areas is subject to special regulations and restrictions in terms of the location, elevation, and type of improvements that can be placed on the property.

> *Example:* A couple purchased a vacant lot on the Cape Fear River. The property is located in a flood hazard area. When the couple builds their home, they must construct it in accordance with flood plain regulations that will dictate how close the home can be to the river and the elevation of finished floors. If they will need conventional financing, the couple must also obtain a standard flood insurance policy pursuant to the National Flood Insurance Program.

GOVERNMENT OWNERSHIP

Government ownership is yet another method of public land use control. The federal government owns extensive tracts of land throughout the country, with a total area of hundreds of millions of acres. A detailed and complex series of federal laws and regulations governs land use in these areas. State and local governments may control land development and use through full ownership of land or by the acquisition of certain rights in land, such as easements. Public parks, roads and highways, libraries, museums, and other governmental buildings are some examples of land use for the benefit of the public.

PRIVATE LAND USE CONTROLS

The concept of private land use restrictions can be confusing because multiple terms may be used interchangeably to refer to the same concept. Simply defined, a **covenant** is *an enforceable private promise that defines how land may and may not be used.* It may be called any of the following terms: covenant, restrictive covenant, equitable servitude, protective covenant, conditions and restrictions (CC&Rs), or restrictions. *In modern usage, these terms all refer to a special type of private promise affecting land.* This text will use "covenant" as an all-inclusive term.

Historical Overview

Under the English common law and during the formative years of this nation, if a person owned a home, there was nothing to prevent a neighbor from constructing a slaughterhouse, factory, or making some other offensive use of nearby property. A legal remedy called *"nuisance"* was developed to prevent a person from using real property in a manner dangerous to the health and well-being of others, but that remedy was and remains expensive, time-consuming, and inadequate to prevent common land use abuses. Additionally, public policy under both the common law and modern law favors the free use of land.

The Development of Covenants

Because early land development often was haphazard with little rational forethought, and because early zoning laws were very simple and incomplete, landowners began using a private method of land use control known originally as the law of **covenants.** Once courts recognized this right of private land use control, it became common.

Originally, covenants were very basic promises affecting land use, with a grantor often placing restrictions on land use in the deed to a grantee.

Example: An owner decided to sell half of his large lot to a buyer. Because the owner did not want the buyer to use the conveyed land for any commercial or industrial purpose, the owner included a clause in the deed requiring that the land always be used for single-family residential purposes only. If properly worded, both the buyer and subsequent owners will be bound by the deed covenant.

Property owners may still create binding covenants by specifying the permissible and prohibited uses in every deed to each grantee. However, the much more common practice today is for a developer to prepare a detailed document specifying all permitted and prohibited uses for all lots within that subdivision. This document, often called a "declaration of covenants," is recorded in the register of deeds office and assigned a book and page number. All subsequent deeds from the developer to buyers state that the property transferred is subject to recorded covenants, citing the book and page number and registrar's office where recorded. The use and extent of private land use restrictions has increased exponentially since the mid-1900s.

The Creation of Common-Interest Communities

The current generation of private land use restrictions centers on the development of a "common-interest community." A **common-interest community** is a real estate development in which the owners of individual lots or units have a legal obligation to financially support the upkeep of common areas and other community operating costs such as liability insurance, management fees, and legal fees. There are two legal categories of common interest communities: 1) planned communities and 2) condominium developments. Members of common-interest communities pay annual dues and, if authorized, special assessments. Common-interest communities are managed by associations of persons owning property within the community, referred to as property owner associations (POA) or home owner associations (HOAs). These associations are privately created and operate pursuant to the association's bylaws in conformity with state law.[71] The majority of common-interest communities are still residential, but the number of mixed-use and commercial common-interest communities is increasing. Condominiums, townhomes, cooperative ownership, and other common interest communities are discussed in Chapter 1.

Common Covenant Declarations

Modern planned community covenants deal with myriad topics, including covenants that:
- establish the property owners association and define its authority.
- address the voting rights of each property owner.
- define common expenses and annual and special assessments.[72]
- specify the architecture and minimum requirements of structures. (Often, covenants will require approval of construction plans by an architectural review committee.)
- restrict the uses that can be made of property. (The most common restriction is the single-family residential restriction,[73] although planned communities can and often do have mixed uses in different areas.)
- specify the consequences of property owners violating covenants.
- make the entire set of covenants binding on successors and assigns of the original lot owner (covenantee).
- state the period of time during which the covenants will be in effect (for example, 25 years) with a provision for renewal by a vote of a specified percentage of the property owners.
- establish standards for maintenance of homes, units, and lots by each owner.

Covenants "Run with the Land"

Once restrictions are created in the deed to each lot owner, either by listing all restrictions or by referring to a master declaration of covenants duly recorded in the register of deeds office, *the restrictive covenants "run with the land" and are binding on all subsequent purchasers of land in the particular subdivision.*[74] No subsequent purchaser or lot owner in the subdivision can use the land for any purpose that violates the restrictions. *Any person who later acquires the land takes with legal "notice" that the land is subject to covenants that may impose conditions or limitations on the land's use.* If the declaration of covenants has been recorded in the proper office, the covenants "run with the land," and subsequent purchasers will take the land subject to the restricted uses imposed by the covenants, *even if the purchaser did not know that the property was subject to covenants.*

> *Example:* Twenty years ago, a developer created a residential subdivision and recorded a "declaration of protective covenants" containing numerous restrictions on land use. Purchasers quickly bought lots, constructed homes, and used their property in compliance with the covenants. When the original owners sell their homes, the successor owners will own the property subject to the original covenants. This is true even if the successor owners did not know about the covenants prior to closing. The covenants automatically "run with the land" and transfer with the land, both burdening and benefitting each lot no matter who owns it.

Thus, if duly recorded covenants permit the land to be used only for residential purposes, a purchaser may not use it to construct a service station or for some other commercial purpose. The discovery of covenants restricting permissible land uses is one compelling reason for having a thorough title search prior to purchasing property. The title search should reveal the existence of any recorded covenants as well as any other encumbrances of record.

Enforcement of Private Covenants

Any owner subject to covenants may enforce the restrictions on use against other owners, and in some instances, persons who are not parties to the deed may enforce covenants. Covenants are deemed to be created for the benefit of every lot in the subdivision, simultaneously burdening and benefiting each lot. As a result, the right to enforce such restrictions usually is not confined to immediate purchasers from the original grantor who created the covenants. Rather, any owner of a lot in the subdivision covered by the general plan may enforce such restrictions against any subdivision lot owner who violates them.

If a covenant is violated, then anyone entitled to enforce it may file a legal action in court seeking an injunction (court order) to compel compliance with the covenant. In certain cases, the court may also award the complainant monetary damages. A court may even order that a building or a portion of it be removed if it has been built in violation of a covenant. While not generally applicable, some land use restrictions may include forfeiture conditions whereby a person's estate in land is forfeited and terminated upon the happening of certain conditions.

Although covenants are said to have a perpetual duration and "run with the land" forever, there may be several reasons why a covenant terminates or becomes unenforceable. Modern covenants frequently have a built-in time limit of several decades and expire after the initial term unless a stated percentage of the property owners vote to retain the covenants. Covenants may also become unenforceable because of waiver or acquiescence to prior violations or a radical change of circumstances within the development. Some ancient restrictions in North Carolina may have been eliminated by the Marketable Title Act. Covenants also may be unenforceable because they contravene public policy as discussed below.

Private Covenants and Public Policy

Since covenants are *private* enforceable promises restricting land use, they can be more restrictive than public zoning ordinances, which must derive from a legitimate exercise of the police power.

Example: A zoning ordinance specifies that land in a certain district may be used for either single- or multifamily residential use and certain commercial/retail uses, including fast-food restaurants. A developer creates a subdivision with covenants stating that only single-family homes of a certain size and design may be constructed on each subdivision lot. Several years later, a lot owner announces plans to construct a fast-food restaurant on his property as permitted under the zoning ordinance. Any other lot owner may apply to a court for an injunction prohibiting the proposed use. A private covenant may validly limit use of property to less than all of the uses permitted under the applicable zoning ordinance.

However, private covenants that contravene public policy are void and unenforceable. What constitutes "public policy" evolves over time through both court decisions and legislative changes. For example, the current "green" movement in home construction and energy conservation has influenced a change in public policy making some covenants and restrictions void that originally were valid.

Example: A declaration of covenants in a residential subdivision developed 30 years ago prohibits all solar collectors on homes. A buyer purchases a home in the subdivision with full notice of the prohibited use and petitions the homeowners association to allow installation of solar panels in a manner that will screen the panels from view from the front of the house. The owner is entitled to install the solar panels despite the covenant expressly prohibiting them. Even though the covenant was perfectly valid when imposed, North Carolina law was changed later to declare covenants "void" that prohibit solar collector panels.

Under General Statute 22B-20, the law mentioned above, a covenant or restriction that regulates the location or screening of solar panels is not prohibited as long as the restriction "does not have the effect of preventing the reasonable use of a solar collector for a residential property." Conversely, there may be situations where obligations imposed by restrictive covenants may not be satisfied due to superseding local, state or federal laws.

Example: A covenant in a coastal subdivision developed in the 1950s requires that the owners association maintain a canal to a sufficient depth to allow boats access to a nearby navigable creek. The covenant requires an annual dredging of the canal if necessary to preserve navigability. In 2011, the canal requires significant dredging because of erosion and storm damage. The owners association is prohibited by state and federal law from any canal-dredging activities without obtaining a permit in advance. That permit may or may not be granted, and, if granted, will be subject to specific environmental requirements.[75]

Summary of Brokers' Duty to Disclose

Under normal circumstances, a real estate broker *with no actual knowledge of a land use issue or problem in a given transaction* may assume that a consumer's intended use of ***residential property*** will be consistent with any zoning requirements or recorded covenants governing the property's use. A broker certainly is not expected to conduct any title search or search the public records for restrictive covenants, nor is a broker expected to interpret covenants or advise buyers on whether a particular land use is permissible. These tasks are legal in nature.

Even so, a real estate broker does have certain duties under License Law to disclose zoning ordinances or covenants restricting the use of property to consumers.

1. When a real estate broker working with a consumer is aware, or reasonably should be aware, that a property is subject to zoning and/or covenants, the broker should advise the consumer that:
   a) the property may be subject to ordinances or covenants that could affect the consumer's use and enjoyment of the property;
   b) property owners in the subdivision may be subject to owners' association dues and assessments; and
   c) the consumer should obtain a copy of any covenants and any owners' association governing documents and should carefully review those documents prior to signing any offer to purchase or lease.
2. Any time a broker working with a consumer becomes aware that the consumer's intended or desired use of a property may be a potential problem under either the zoning ordinances or covenants governing the property, the broker must disclose the possible conflict or limitation to the consumer and recommend that the consumer investigate. This duty under License Law arises when a consumer expresses a concern over a land use issue, if not earlier.

A broker who either willfully or negligently makes an incorrect statement about permitted land uses under zoning ordinances or covenants violates the License Law by misrepresenting a material fact. A broker who attempts to advise a consumer about land use restrictions must: 1) do so accurately and be certain his/her statement is correct, and 2) be careful not to cross the line into the unauthorized practice of law. A broker should not offer an opinion unless the point in question is very clear and unambiguous. If there is *any question at all* about the proper interpretation of a zoning or covenant provision, or if there is any chance that the ordinances or covenants may have been modified, then the broker should recommend that the consumer consult an attorney.

Making consumers aware that ordinances or covenants may exist prior to preparing an offer to purchase or lease, explaining the purpose of such covenants, and encouraging further inquiry by buyers or tenants yields not only more satisfied parties but helps avoid potential problems at closing and enables parties to avoid inadvertent violations of ordinances or covenants after they take possession of the property.

NORTH CAROLINA PLANNED COMMUNITY ACT

The traditional law of property includes strict and confusing rules that often made effective enforcement of covenants a difficult task. Further, covenants requiring a property owner to pay annual dues or assessments, known as "*affirmative assessment covenants*," have been treated with general disfavor by North Carolina courts unless they are very carefully drafted.[76] owner associations often were at a disadvantage when attempting to enforce covenants against a violating property owner. In response to these shortcomings, a sweeping set of statutes, known as the "Planned Community Act,"[77] were enacted. The North Carolina Planned Community Act significantly expands the authority of owner associations and makes the enforcement of covenants and restrictions significantly easier where a development fits the definition of a "planned community."[78] Prospective purchasers of a property within a "planned community" should:

1. be informed of the nature of planned community governance and the significant powers of the owner association;[79]
2. receive an explanation that annual and special assessments may be made by the owners' association; and
3. be informed of the enforcement and collection remedies allowed by law, including a denial of some planned community privileges, a lien on the owner's land, and the awarding of attorney fees to the owner association.[80]

Because this Act grants significant powers to owner associations, state law was revised as of January 1, 2012, to amend the Residential Property Disclosure Statement to include disclosures regarding owners' associations. While the disclosure statement must be provided by most sellers of one-to-four family dwellings, it does not compel an owner to disclose whether the property is subject to regulation by an owners' association, because it retains the "no representation" option as discussed in Chapter 8.

An alternative is Form 2A12-T, jointly approved by the North Carolina Bar Association and the North Carolina REALTORS® and titled "Owners' Association Disclosure and Condominium Resale Statement Addendum," that may be used in sales of new construction or vacant land, or resales of condominium units. Unit owners' associations, like owner associations, are granted significant powers under the law, and consumers should understand that owning a unit in a condominium development will obligate the owner to pay dues, fees, and assessments. The addendum discloses the following information to prospective purchasers:

- The name of the owners' association and contact information
- The name, address, and telephone number of the president of the owners' association or the association manager
- The owners' association website (if any)

Additionally, the seller checks from the list below the various services and amenities paid by the owners' association from regular assessments (dues) paid by each property owner.

Master Insurance Policy Including All Units	Street Lights
Real Property Taxes on the Common Areas	Water
Common-Area Casualty/Liability Insurance	Sewer
Private Road Maintenance	Management Fees
Exterior Building Maintenance	Parking Area Maintenance
Exterior Yard/Landscaping Maintenance	Common Areas Maintenance
Storm Water Management/Drainage Ponds, Culvert	Cable
Pest Treatment/Extermination	Internet Services
Legal/Accounting	Trash Removal
Recreational Amenities (specify): _____	Gate and/or Security

Governing documents and helpful information related to a planned community or condominium development often is readily available on a development's master association website. The planned community's website typically provides valuable information to prospective purchasers and current residents alike. Websites often are organized into categories, including a "documents" section which may contain electronic copies of legal documents such as the planned community covenants, bylaws, and articles of incorporation. Covenants, community association bylaws, and rules and regulations are detailed and extensive. It is not unusual for the combined documents to run 50 to 100 pages.

Additionally, a planned community website may also include architectural guidelines, architectural review board procedures, and a form required before an exterior modification of a home can be made. Some websites include access to an online newsletter and calendar of events that may give a prospective purchaser a sense of the community.

CONSERVATION AND PRESERVATION AGREEMENTS

In response to a growing concern about disappearing farmland, natural areas, and historic buildings, the General Assembly enacted legislation allowing the creation of ***conservation agreements*** and ***preservation agreements*** designed to preserve and protect these valuable resources and parts of our heritage. The "Conservation and Historic Preservation Agreements Act" is located at Article 4 of Chapter 121 of the North Carolina General Statutes. While these land use agreements are facilitated by a number of enabling statutes, they are in essence private and voluntary agreements between landowners and government agencies or nonprofit organizations. For this reason, they are included within the category of private land use controls.

The term *conservation agreement* is defined, in part as "a right, whether or not stated in the form of a restriction, reservation, easement, covenant, or condition ... executed by or on behalf of the owner of land or improvement thereon ..."[81] Often, the document by which the landowner voluntarily restricts the land will be called a "conservation easement."

When the preservation of farmland is involved, it is often called an *agricultural conservation easement.* Under General Statute §106-744, a county has the authority to purchase agricultural conservation easements over qualifying farmland from an owner who voluntarily wishes to participate. Although stated to be perpetual in duration, a county may agree to reconvey the easement to the owner of the land after 20 years if the landowner can demonstrate that commercial agricultural is no longer practicable on the land in question.

A *preservation agreement,* often called a *historic preservation agreement,* involves restrictions on land to preserve a historically or archeologically significant structure or site. This agreement usually will prohibit the alteration of historic structures and uses not historically appropriate to the structure.[82]

Endnotes

1. Numerous University of North Carolina-Chapel Hill School of Government publications provide an excellent resource on legal and practical issues related to public land use controls. David Owens, the leading North Carolina expert in this area, authors and co-authors a series of publications, including the following: *Planning Legislation in North Carolina* (2008 ed.); *Introduction to Zoning* (3rd ed. 2007); *Land Use Law in North Carolina* (2nd ed 2011.); "Zoning Amendments in North Carolina" (Special Series No. 24, Feb. 2008); "North Carolina Experience With Municipal Extraterritorial Planning Jurisdiction" (Special Series No. 20, Jan. 2006). See also, David Owens and Nathan Brascome, "An Inventory of Local Government Land Use Ordinances in North Carolina" (Special Series No. 21, May 2006); David Owens and Andrew Stevenson, "An Overview of Zoning Districts, Design Standards, and Traditional Neighborhood Design in North Carolina Zoning Ordinances" (Special Series No. 23, Oct. 2007). These publications can be found at http://shopping.netsuite.com. This is the School of Government's publications website. Some of the publications can be downloaded free of charge.

2.   See, for example, *Fort v. County of Cumberland*, __ N.C.App. __, 721 S.E.2d 350 (2012), involving a typical contemporary zoning ordinance that lists permissible commercial uses in an A1 Agricultural District, in addition to a list of permitted and conditional uses possible within the same district.

3.   http://www.raleighnc.gov/content/extra/Books/PlanDev/UnifiedDevelopmentOrdinance/ Throughout this chapter, references are made to the Raleigh UDO for purposes of consistency and convenience. Many other North Carolina cities also have excellent UDOs, and the reader is encouraged to refer to the webpage of his or her home city.

4.   See, for example, Chapter 6, "Use Regulations," of the Raleigh Unified Development Code.

5.   *Euclid v. Amber Realty Company*, 272 U.S. 365, 47 S.Ct. 114, 71 L.Ed. 303 (1926); see also *Elizabeth City v. Aydlett*, 201 N.C. 602, 161 S.E.2d 78 (1931).

6.   N.C. Gen. Stat. §§160A-381 to 160A-392 (municipal); N.C. Gen. Stat. §§153A-340 to 153A-348 (county).

7.   Asheville, North Carolina, Code of Ordinances, Chapter 7, Development, Article IV., Comprehensive Plan. https://www.municode.com/library/nc/asheville/codes. Chapter 7, Development , Article II., Official Map, Rules of Construction, and Definitions.

8.   *Alfred v. City of Raleigh,* 7 N.C. App. 602, 173 S.E.2d 533 (1970), *rev'd on other grounds*, 277 N.C. 530, 178 S.E.2d 432 (1971). See, also, N.C. Gen. Stat. §§153A-341 and 160A-383. For a case finding that a zoning ordinance was not in conformity with the comprehensive plan, see *Godfrey v. Union Cty. Bd. of Commissioners*, 61 N.C. App. 100, 300 S.E.2d 273 (1983).

9.   See, for example, Wake County Unified Development Ordinance (2015), Article 1.2, "Zoning Map"

10. *Patmore v. Town of Chapel Hill*, 233 N.C.App.133, 757 S.E.2d 302 (2014). Contrast with *Lanvale Properties, LLC. v. County of Cabarrus*, 366 N.C. 142, 731 S.E.2d 800 (2012), where a Cabarrus County "adequate public facilities ordinance" was struck down by the courts, holding that the ordinance was not a zoning ordinance, because it didn't address permitted and prohibited land uses. Rather, it was a fee developers were to pay to subsidize new school construction to gain approval of new residential subdivisions.

11. *Zopfi v. City of Wilmington*, 273 N.C. 430, 160 S.E.2d 325 (1968).

12. *Grace Baptist Church v. City of Oxford*, 320 N.C. 439, 358 S.E.2d 372 (1987). One who attacks the validity of a zoning ordinance by asserting that it has no rational relation to a police power objective has the burden of proving invalidity.

13. N.C.Gen.Stat. §160A-360, Territorial Jurisdiction; See, also, UNC School of Government summary by David W. Owens, titled "Extraterritorial Jurisdiction for Planning and Development Regulation," May, 2014,

14. Raleigh Unified Development Ordinance, Sec. 1.4. "Building Types."

15. Raleigh Unified Development Ordinance, Chapter 3, "Mixed-Use Districts."

16. Raleigh Unified Development Ordinance, Chapter 5, "Overlay Districts."

17. *A-S-P Assoc. v. City of Raleigh,* 298 N.C. 207, 258 S.E.2d 444 (1979). For a sampling of state statutes dealing with historic preservation, *see* N.C.G.S. Chapter 160A, Article 19, Part 3C, "Historic Districts and Landmarks." *See also,* Chapter 105, Article 3D, "Historic Rehabilitation Tax Credits." North Carolina's tax credit program is coordinated with the federal income tax credits for historic rehabilitation contained in Section 47 of the Internal Revenue Code (26 U.S.C. § 47).

18. Raleigh Unified Development Ordinance, Sec. 10.2.9, "Special Use Permit.

19. Raleigh Unified Development Ordinance, Sec.6.1. For decisions involving a special use permit, see *Harding v. Board of Adjustment of Davie County,* 170 N.C. App. 392, 612 S.E.2d 431 (2005) (grant of a special use permit for a go-cart track); *Ward v. Inscoe,* 166 N.C. App. 586, 603 S.E.2d 393 (2004) (holding in part that substantial evidence existed to justify the granting of a special-use permit).

20. Raleigh Unified Development Ordinance, Sec. 10.2.9.E.

21. Compare and contrast ordinances in some cities allowing an in-home day care center serving a limited number of persons. Some zoning ordinances refer to this as a "limited use." See, for example, Raleigh Unified Development Ordinance, Sec. 6.4.1.B. "Day Care, Home," limited enrollment to eight persons. *Cf.* Sec. 6.4.1.C., "Day Care Center."

22. Raleigh Unified Development Ordinance, Sec. 6.4.6, "Overnight Lodging."

23. *Chrismon v. Guilford County,* 322 N.C. 611 (1988).

24. *JCL Investments Inc. v. Guilford Cty. Bd. of Adjustment,* 133 N.C. App. 426, 515 S.E.2d 715 (1999); *CG&T Corp. v. Bd. of Adjustment of Wilmington,* 105 N.C. App. 32, 411 S.E.2d 655 (1992); *Forsyth Co. v. Shelton,* 74 N.C. App. 674, 329 S.E.2d 730 (1985); *Williams v. Town of Spencer,* 129 N.C. App. 828, 500 S.E.2d 473 (1998).

25. N.C. Gen. Stat. §§160A-364 and 160A-385. David Owens, "Zoning Amendments in North Carolina" (UNC-CH School of Government, Special Series No. 24, Feb. 2008).

26. See, for example, Charlotte Code, Chapter 6, Amendments. Section 6.101 of the Code provides: "The purpose of this Chapter is to provide a means for amending the text of these regulations and the classification of any parcel of land identified on the Official Zoning Maps. The purpose is not to relieve particular hardships, nor to confer special privileges or rights on any person, but only to make adjustments (i) necessary in light of changed conditions or changes in public policy, or (ii) likely to achieve the purposes of these regulations."

27. For Court of Appeals cases involving variances, see *Robertson v. Zoning Bd. Of Adjustment*, 167 N.C. App. 531, 605 S.E.2d 723 (2004) (holding in part that the city zoning board of adjustment's denial of a request for a variance did not violate the property owners' due process rights); *In the matter of The Granting of a Variance by the Town of Franklin*, 131 N.C. App. 846, 508 S.E.2d 841 (1998); *Crist v. City of Jacksonville*, 131 N.C. App. 404, 507 S.E.2d 899 (1998).

28. http://www.sog.unc.edu/organizations/planning/keyissues/contr.htm for article, "Key Legal Issues – Contract Zoning," May 1998 by David W. Owens. For a decision in which the Court of Appeals held that the City of Charlotte had not engaged in illegal contract zoning, see *Massey v. City of Charlotte*, 145 N.C. App. 345, 550 S.E.2d 838 (2001); *Kerik v. Davidson County*, 2001 WL 880509.

29. *State v. Jones*, 305 N.C. 520, 290 S.E.2d 675 (1982). See also, *CMH Mfg. Co. v. Catawba County*, 994 F. Supp. 697 (W.D.N.C. 1998).

30. *Chrismon v. Guilford County*, 322 N.C. 611, 370 S.E.2d 579 (1988), citing *Blades v. City of Raleigh*, 280 N.C. 531, 187 S.E.2d 35 (1972). See *Friends of Mt. Vernon Springs, Inc. v. Tawil of Siler City*, 190 N.C. App. 633, 660 S.E.2d 657 (2008), where the Court of Appeals noted that the tract of land in question was approximately 1,076 acres and was not "a relatively small tract" as contemplated by the leading cases on point, and that the zoning activity did not constitute spot zoning.

31. *Chrismon v. Guilford County*, 322 N.C. 611, 618, 370 S.E.2d 579, 583 (1988), citing a number of zoning treatises.

32. See *Everhart & Assoc., Inc. v. Dept. of Environment, Health And Natural Resources*, 127 N.C. App. 693, 493 S.E.2d 66 (1997) where a denial of a development permit was found to be consistent with a county land use plan.

33. See, for example, Wake County Unified Development Ordinance (2015), Article 5, "Lot and Building Standards."

34. See, for example, Wake County Unified Development Ordinance (2015), Section 5-12, "Cluster and Open Space Development."

35. Subdivision enabling legislation for counties can be found at Chapter 153A, Article 18, Part 2 of the North Carolina General Statutes, N.C. Gen. Stat. §153A-330 *et seq.*

36. See N.C. Gen. Stat. §153A-334, titled, "Penalties for transferring lots in unapproved subdivisions." The county is also authorized by this statute to bring an action for an injunction to prevent the transfer of lots in an unapproved subdivision and to require the landowner to comply with the subdivision laws and regulations. See N.C. Gen. Stat. §160A-375 for corollary provision for cities.

37. N.C. Gen. Stat. §136-102.6 sets forth requirements for this disclosure. The developer/seller is to prepare and sign the disclosure and also signs an acknowledgment of receipt of the streets disclosure statement.

38.   N.C. Gen. Stat. §136-102.6. "Private" and "public" streets are treated differently by the statute. All new or changed streets designated as "public" must comply with minimum right-of-way and construction standards established by the board of transportation. Any street designated as "public" automatically is presumed to constitute an offer of dedication to public use. See also provisions in the North Carolina Administrative Code, including 19A NCAC 2C.0103 ("Addition of Roads to the Secondary Road System"), 19A NCAC 2C.0202 ("Application Requirements"), and 19A NCAC 2C.0203 ("Requirements/Addition of Subdivision Roads to the System"). The North Carolina Department of Transportation publishes a volume titled, "Subdivision Roads," restating information from the Administrative Code concerning minimum design and construction criteria for subdivision streets. This free publication may be obtained from the Secondary Roads Department, Division of Highways in Raleigh, or from division and district highway offices throughout the state.

39.   N.C. Gen. Stat. §143-136 and §143-138.

40.   For a sampling of cases involving restricted access, see *North Carolina State Highway Commission v. Nuckles,* 271 N.C. 1, 155 S.E.2d 772 (1967); *Southern Furniture Co. of Conover, Inc. v. Dept. of Transportation,* 133 N.C. App. 400, 516 S.E.2d 383 (1999).

41.   The Interstate Land Sales Full Disclosure Act is found at 15 U.S.C. §1701 *et seq.*

42.   42 U.S.C. §§4321-4327.

43.   N.C. Gen. Stat. §113A-1 *et seq.*

44.   42 U.S.C. §9601 *et seq.*

45.   N.C. Gen. Stat. §§130A-310.20 – 310.22. NCDEQ's website has a wealth of information, including guidance documents for reporting hazardous substances or waste sites as well as a list of all reported sites in North Carolina by county. See guidance documents at: https://deq.nc.gov/about/divisions/waste-management/waste-management-permit-guidance/inactive-hazardous-sites-guidance-documents. The list of Inactive Hazardous Sites and Pollutant-Only Sites by county with site name and address are at: https://ncdenr.s3.amazonaws.com/s3fs-public/Waste%20Management/DWM/SF/IHS/Reports/rpt-countyforweb042817.pdf.

46.   40 CFR § 312.20. See also American Society for Testing and Materials (ASTM) E1527-13, "Standard Practice For Environmental Site Assessments: Phase I Environmental Site Assessment Process (2013) http://www.astm.org/Standards/E1527.htm.

47.   42 U.S.C. §§6901-6991.

48.   42 U.S.C. §§7401-7642.

49.   N.C. Gen. Stat. §133A-100 *et seq.*

50.   N.C. Gen. Stat. §113A-103(5)a.

51. *State ex rel. Cobey v. Simpson,* 333 N.C. 81, 423 S.E.2d 759 (1991). The owner's actions also violated the North Carolina Dredge and Fill Act, N.C.G.S. §113-229.

52. See N.C. Gen. Stat. Chapter 113A, Article 14, titled "Mountain Ridge Protection."

53. For an excellent article discussing the background and specifics of passage of the statute, see Milton S. Heath, Jr., *The North Carolina Mountain Ridge Protection Act,* 63 N.C.L. Rev. 183 (1984).

54. See, for example, N.C. Gen. Stat. §§143-214.20 and 143-214.21, dealing with the "Riparian Buffer Protection Program." The reader is cautioned to seek legal advice concerning any question related to waterway buffer zones and their effect on land use.

55. *Haw River Land & Timber Co., Inc. v. Lawyers Title Insurance Corp.,* 152 F.3d 275 (4th Cir. 1998).

56. *JCL Investments, Inc. v. Guilford County Bd. of Adjustment,* 133 N.C. App. 426, 515 S.E.2d 715 (1999).

57. N.C. Gen. Stat. §143-215.94A *et seq.* Federal law deals with legal issues related to underground storage tanks in the Resource Conservation and Recovery Act ("RCRA"), 42 U.S.C. §6991 *et seq.*

58. See the United States Environmental Protection Agency (EPA) Home Page, Underground Storage Tanks (USTs). www2.epa.gov/ust/cleaning-underground-storage-tank-ust-releases (2015); N.C. Division of Waste Management, Underground Storage Tank Section, portal.ncdenr.org/web/wm/ust.

59. N.C. Gen. Stat. §113A-50 *et seq.; Cox v. North Carolina,* 81 N.C. App. 612, 344 S.E.2d 808 (1986); *In re Appeal,* 324 N.C. 373, 379 S.E.2d 30 (1989). See, for example, approved rules of the Department of Environment and Natural Resources related to storm water runoff in coastal counties, 15A NCAC 2H.1005, titled "Storm Water Requirements: Coastal Counties." *Applewood Properties LLC v. New South Properties,* LLC, __S.E.2d __, 2012 WL 924859.

60. See Chapter 18, *infra,* Fair Housing and Laws Against Discrimination.

61. N.C.Gen.Stat. §160A-201, dealing with city ordinances; and §153A-144, dealing with county ordinances. Both statutes became effective October 1, 2007. These statutes contain a number of qualifications and exceptions concerning the location of solar collectors. (*See, also,* the discussion of private covenants that prohibit solar collectors and N.C.Gen.Stat. §22B-20 later in this chapter.

62. 33 U.S.C. §1344; N.C. Gen. Stat. §143-214.1. For a landmark United States Supreme Court decision dealing with this area, see *Rapanos v. United States,* 126 S. Ct. 2208, 165 L.Ed.2d 159 (2006), a case in which the Supreme Court narrowed the judicial interpretation of the term "navigable waters" under the Clean Water Act.

63. N.C. Gen. Stat. §113-229.

64. See N.C. Gen. Stat. §130A-333 to §130A-343.1 and 15A NCAC 18A.1937. See, also, *Cambridge Southport, LLC v. Southeast Brunswick Sanitary District*, __ N.C. App. __, 721 S.E.2d 736 (2012) discussing the "Permit Extension Act of 2009" and holding that a successor developer was not required to reapply for wastewater service capacity.

65. 15A NCAC 18A. 1937(a).

66. N.C. Gen. Stat. §130A-334(10).

67. See "*Straight-talk on straight-piping*," Vol. 31, No. 2, Real Estate Bulletin, Summer, 2000, p. 1, by Janet B. Thoren, Deputy Legal Counsel, North Carolina Real Estate Commission, and "*Impact of wastewater treatment regulations on real estate licensees*," Vol. 31, No. 3 Real Estate Bulletin, Fall, 2000, p. 6, by Blackwell M. Brogden, Jr., Chief Deputy Legal Counsel, North Carolina Real Estate Commission.

68. N.C. Gen. Stat. §130A-131.5; 42 U.S.C. §§4821-4826.

69. See N.C.G.S. Chapter 130A, Article 19 titled, "Asbestos Hazard Management."

70. See the "National Flood Insurance" chapter in the United States Code, 42 U.S.C. §4001 *et seq.*

71. See the North Carolina Planned Community Act, Chapter 47F, and North Carolina Condominium Act, Chapter 47C of the General Statutes. Condominiums created in North Carolina prior to October 1, 1986, are governed by the Unit Ownership Act (Chapter 47A of the General Statutes). See also, the Restatement (Third) of Property: Servitudes, §6.2, "Common-Interest-Community Definitions."

72. The leading North Carolina Supreme Court decision on affirmative obligations to pay fees is *Southeastern Jurisdictional Administrative Council, Inc. v. Emerson*, 363 N.C. 749, 688 S.E.2d 692 (2009).

73. See *Winding Ridge Homeowners Assoc., Inc. v. Joffe*, 362 N.C. 225, 657 S.E.2d 356 (2008), reversing the Court of Appeals decision and agreeing with the reasoning in the dissent (that a limitation on the type of structure is not necessarily a limitation on the type of occupancy permitted); *Danaher v. Joffe*, 184 N.C. App. 642, 646 S.E.2d 783 (2007).

74. The leading North Carolina Supreme Court decision (and a leading decision throughout the nation) on the running of covenants with the land is *Runyon v. Paley*, 331 N.C. 293, 416 S.E.2d 177 (1992).

75. See, for example, *www.nccoastalmanagement.nte/handbook.*

76. For the traditional treatment of affirmative assessment covenants, see *Allen v. Sea Gate Ass'n, Inc.*, 119 N.C. App. 761, 460 S.E.2d 197 (1995).

77. The North Carolina Planned Community Act is located at Chapter 47F of the General Statutes. The Act contains numerous statutes providing a detailed and comprehensive regulation of and authorization for planned communities. See Hetrick, *Of "Private Governments" and the Regulation of Neighborhoods: The North Carolina Planned Community Act*, 22 Campbell Law Review 1 (Fall, 1999).

78.　The term "planned community" is defined at N.C. Gen. Stat. §47F-1-103 as meaning "real estate with respect to which any person, by virtue of that person's ownership of a lot, is expressly obligated by a declaration to pay real property taxes, insurance premiums, or other expenses to maintain, improve, or benefit other lots or other real estate described in the declaration." Specific statutory exemptions exist, including developments of 20 lots or less, condominiums, and nonresidential communities.

79.　N.C. Gen. Stat. §47F-3-102 sets forth 17 powers provided by statute to a homeowner association.

80.　See N.C. Gen. Stat. §§47F-3-102, 47F-3-107, 47F-3-107.1, 47F-3-115.

81.　N.C. Gen. Stat. §121-35(1).

82.　N.C. Gen. Stat. §121-35(3).

8 | RELATIONSHIPS IN BROKERAGE PRACTICE

In North Carolina, the relationship between a real estate broker and a consumer is governed primarily by the **common law of agency**—legal principles developed centuries ago that still regulate the principal-agent/master-servant relationship. North Carolina Real Estate License Law and Commission rules supplement and expand upon the fundamentals of agency by requiring, for example, that all agency agreements be in writing. All brokers must understand these fundamental principles to effectively and competently interact and work with or for consumers.

Contract law principles generally govern business interactions between real estate brokers, particularly regarding compensation agreements. A real estate broker who affiliates with a company should have a written employment agreement with the company (even if treated as an independent contractor for tax purposes) but is also known as an *"affiliated agent."* Thus, that relationship is subject to both contract law and agency law.

Laws and Regulations Governing Brokerage Relationships

- Common Law of Agency
- Contract Law
- Real Estate License Law (Chapter 93A, NC General Statutes)
- NC Real Estate Commission Rules (Chapter 58, Title 21 NCAC)

This chapter explains how these various laws and rules impact a real estate broker's business relationships, conduct, and obligations. After a brief introduction to common-law agency principles, we will review:

- agency options companies have in real estate brokerage sales transactions;
- the legal duties agents and principals owe <u>to each other</u> under the law of agency and North Carolina Real Estate License Law and Commission rules;
- the legal duties agents and principals owe <u>to third parties</u> under agency and Real Estate License Law, including *disclosure of material facts* and seller disclosure obligations under the North Carolina Residential Property Disclosure Act and federal and state lead-based paint disclosure regulations; and
- a broker's agency disclosure obligations and use of the *Working with Real Estate Agents* mandatory brochure in all sales transactions.

Real estate brokerage contracts (agency agreements) and broker practices when working with sellers and buyers are covered in Chapter 9. **NOTE:** The term *"broker"* will be used to refer to *either an individual agent or to the firm or to both,* as the context dictates.

INTRODUCTION TO THE COMMON LAW OF AGENCY

There are *always* at least two parties in any agency relationship: the ***principal*** and the ***agent***. *An agency relationship is created when one person (the "Principal") authorizes another person (the "Agent") to handle certain matters on behalf of the principal.* It harkens back to the day when the king and earls (the masters) could not personally oversee their fiefdoms and employed trusted servants (agents) to supervise specific operations.

Basic Terms

Agency: The relationship that exists when one person is authorized to act for and on behalf of another.

Principal: The person who authorizes another (the agent) to act on the principal's behalf within specified parameters and to whom the agent owes certain legal duties.

Agent: The person acting for and on behalf of the principal within the bounds of the authority granted and who owes fiduciary (legal) duties to the principal.

Subagent: Literally the agent of an agent, a person designated or employed *by an agent* to perform all or part of the agent's assigned tasks or services on behalf of the agent's principal. A subagent stands in the shoes of the agent and owes the same fiduciary duties to the principal as the agent.

Agent's Fiduciary Duties

A "fiduciary" is a person who acts for another in a relationship of trust and who is obligated to act in the other's best interests, placing the other's interests before any self-interest. Persons considered fiduciaries include guardians, executors, attorneys, and real estate brokers when acting as an agent. Under the common law of agency, an agent owes certain fiduciary duties to the principal, including obligations to be **loyal** to the principal and preserve personal, confidential information about the principal, to operate in **good faith** to promote the principal's interests, and to **disclose all facts** to the principal that may influence the principal's decision. An agent's fiduciary obligations to the principal preclude the agent from taking advantage of the principal in any manner during the course of the agency relationship.

*Agency law also requires that a real estate broker, like any other agent, exercise a high degree of **skill, care, and diligence** in the conduct of the agent's duties.* The level of skill, care, and diligence required of a real estate broker is determined by standards set forth in the North Carolina General Statutes, North Carolina Real Estate Commission rules, court decisions, and the professional standards prevailing in the community where the broker works.

An agent will be responsible to the principal for any loss resulting from the agent's failure to fulfill his/her fiduciary duties. An agent must also fully and truthfully disclose to the principal all facts and information known to the agent or discoverable by the agent with reasonable diligence that may affect the principal's decision, and the principal has a right to rely on the agent's statements.[1]

Classification Based on Scope of Authority

Under the common law of agency, the scope or extent of the authority granted to the agent by the principal determines whether the agent is classified as a 1) special, 2) general, or 3) universal agent. While a broker won't see these terms in any agency agreement, they continue to be used to define the extent of the authority conveyed by the principal to the agent. *The vast majority of real estate sales transactions typically authorize special agency, whereas property management agreements may authorize a general agency.* Each classification is defined below.

Special Agency: A *special* agent is *only authorized to perform one or more specific acts on behalf of the principal in accordance with the principal's instructions.* Most sales transactions involve special agency, as the agent is hired to help the buyer find or the seller sell a particular piece of property, and that is all.

General Agency: A *general* agent is *authorized to perform a range of acts, within specified parameters or limitations,* on behalf of the principal. Some property management agency agreements may grant a general agency, authorizing the agent to not only find a tenant but also to collect the periodic rent, respond to repair and maintenance requests, authorize certain repairs, pay certain monthly property expenses on the owner/principal's behalf, etc.

Universal Agency: A *universal* agent is *authorized to transact all of the principal's business of every kind.* A principal may only have one universal agent at a time, i.e., one person authorized to handle all of the principal's business and personal matters. Real estate brokerage practice rarely, if ever, involves a universal agency.

Creation of Agency Relationships

Under the *common law of agency,* agency relationships could be created by an *express agreement,* whether oral or in writing, or by an *implied agreement* based on the actions and conduct of the parties. The most common methods of creating agency relationships in real estate brokerage transactions are listed and briefly described below. **In each situation the consumer— whether the owner, buyer, or tenant—is the principal, and the broker or brokerage company is the agent.** A more in-depth discussion of agency contracts used in real estate sales transactions is found in Chapter 9; property management contracts are addressed in Chapter 17; and tenant representation agreements in commercial transactions are covered in Chapter 19.

<u>**Common Agency Agreements in Real Estate Brokerage**</u>

Listing Agreement: A listing agreement is a written agreement in which a property owner hires a broker to assist the owner in marketing the owner's property and in locating a ready, willing, and able buyer to purchase the property at a price and terms acceptable to the owner.

Property Management Agreement: A property management agreement is a written agreement in which a property owner hires a broker to manage property, find tenants, collect rents, maintain the property, enforce rules, evict tenants, and such other services as are expressly delegated to the agent. If the broker is hired solely to locate a tenant without any additional management services, then the owner and broker typically enter into an ***Agreement to Procure Tenant*** rather than a full-service property management agreement.

Buyer Agency Agreement: A buyer agency agreement is an express agreement in which a prospective purchaser hires a broker to locate a home or other property for the buyer at a price and upon terms acceptable to the buyer.

Tenant Representation Agreement: A tenant representation agreement is an express agreement wherein a prospective tenant hires a broker to locate a suitable property for the tenant to lease. These agreements more frequently are encountered in commercial rather than residential transactions, as residential tenants often are unrepresented.

As mentioned, the common law of agency permits an agency relationship to be implied from the parties' actions. In an implied agency, the parties never *expressly* agree to act as principal and agent, yet the way they interact with each other evidences a silent or implied intent to act as principal and agent. *This should never happen in a real estate brokerage transaction as the Commission's rule requires all agency agreements to be **express from the outset** (and **in writing** if representing an owner).* Nonetheless, if not careful, a broker may unintentionally create an implied agency with a consumer based on the broker's conduct.

This frequently was the case prior to the advent of buyer agency in the 1990s, when the default presumption was that all brokers represented the seller, even if not affiliated with the listing company. Yet the broker showing the unrepresented buyer numerous properties, as the agent of a seller the broker had never met, frequently would begin giving advice or counsel or acting as if the buyer was the broker's principal rather than the seller, creating an implied agency relationship with the buyer contrary to the broker's fiduciary duties.

Who Pays the Agent Does Not Control the Agency Relationship

Agency relationships in brokerage transactions must be based on an express agreement between the parties where the consumer affirmatively hires a brokerage company to represent the consumer's interest. Who pays the broker does not necessarily determine who the broker represents; it is merely one factor to consider. For example, a buyer agency agreement may obligate the buyer to pay the broker, but the broker may agree to first seek compensation from the seller or listing company from the sale proceeds. Even if the listing company or seller pays the buyer agent, it in no way negates the buyer agency agreement nor converts the buyer agent into a seller's agent.

Types of Agent Authority

In addition to being classified as either a special agent, general agent, or universal agent, the principal and agent should clearly specify and agree upon the scope/limits of the agent's authority to avoid the agent overstepping the limits of the authority delegated by the principal. Legal theory recognizes three sources of an agent's authority:

1. express authority
2. implied authority
3. apparent authority

Express Authority: The authority specifically granted in the agency agreement that concerns what services the consumer-principal desires from and authorizes the agent to provide. Express authority is synonymous with actual authority. To avoid misunderstandings or the agent exceeding the authority granted, the parties should have a very clear mutual understanding of what each party—principal and agent—will or will not do.

Implied Authority: The opposite of "express," implied authority rests on custom and practices, rather than on an oral or written grant of authority from the principal to the agent. Custom may define or limit an agent's authority. For example, an "Exclusive Right to Sell" listing agreement does not authorize the listing broker to actually sell the owner's property nor is such authority implied by custom. However, custom might imply the authority of a property manager to sign leases that bind the owner, even if such authority is not expressly granted in the written property management agreement, so long as the agreement does not specifically withhold that authority.

Apparent Authority: Apparent authority is a more complex concept. Typically, it refers to situations where the principal is aware that his/her agent is going beyond the limits of the authority granted by the express agency agreement or implied by custom in the agent's dealings with a third party, who reasonably believes the agent has authority to act in a particular manner, *and the principal does nothing* to stop the agent or inform the third party. Because the third party reasonably believes that the agent has this (apparent) authority, the principal may be legally bound by the agent's actions, even though the actions exceeded the agent's actual authority.

Independent Brokers versus Broker-Associates

Provisional brokers must be affiliated with a real estate company under the supervision of a broker-in-charge to legally engage in brokerage activities. A broker who has removed provisional status may choose to provide brokerage services independently, either as a sole proprietor or an entity/firm, or affiliate with a real estate company. If the broker practices independently, then the consumer enters into an agency agreement with the broker's company and has only one agent, unless the broker has other agents affiliated with the broker's company.

However, many brokers choose to affiliate with a real estate firm or company and conduct business under the company's umbrella. The individual licensees are called associated or affiliated *agents*, and the company is the principal to whom the individual agents owe the same fiduciary obligations as they do to consumer-clients. Licensees must understand that the consumer legally is doing business with the *firm;* **the agency agreement is between the firm as agent and the consumer** (*seller, buyer, landlord, or tenant*) **as principal**, *not the individual affiliated agents.*

A broker affiliated with a real estate firm is an agent of the firm under the common law of agency. This is true regardless of whether the individual broker is paid as an "employee" or an "independent contractor" for income tax purposes. As agents of the firm, *all individual brokers affiliated with the firm automatically become agents of any principal-client of the firm upon the signing of the agency agreement between the firm and the principal.* For example, when a listing agreement for the sale of property is executed for a real estate firm by a broker affiliated with the firm, all brokers affiliated with the firm automatically become agents of the property owner (seller). *Technically, the firm is the agent of the seller, and each affiliated broker is a subagent of the seller.* The agent-subagent distinction is a legal distinction having little practical effect, since both an agent and subagent owe the principal the same duties.

AGENCY RELATIONSHIPS IN REAL ESTATE SALES

Note: While the remainder of this chapter focuses on agency law and practice in real estate sales, the agency law principles apply equally to both sales and lease or rental transactions.

AGENCY OPTIONS FOR REAL ESTATE FIRMS

For most of the 20th century, the prevailing custom in real estate brokerage was that all real estate brokers represented the seller, even if the broker was not affiliated with the company that held the listing. The listing company and its affiliated brokers were the agents of the seller, and nonaffiliated brokers acted as subagents of the listing company, thus also representing the seller's interests. Under this custom, buyers legally had no representation, yet brokers working with these buyer-customers as seller subagents often tended to view the buyer as their client. Such advocacy for the buyer-customer, rather than the seller-client, violated the nonaffiliated brokers' fiduciary duties to the seller and caused them to unwittingly engage in undisclosed dual agency. This practice changed in the early 1990s when most states began recognizing not only buyer agency but dual agency.

Real estate brokers and real estate consumers may now choose to work together in a number of different ways. Their choice of the type of agency relationship that will apply to their dealings is important because it determines the level of service the broker will provide and the relative duties the broker owes to the various parties to a transaction. A broker's duties to a principal are considerably greater than the broker's duties to other parties to the transaction.

Brokers have three basic options for their company policy on agency relationships: (1) seller agency only; (2) buyer agency only; (3) both seller and buyer agency, with dual agency for "in-house" sales.

Seller Agency Only

A real estate firm may choose to practice seller agency only, meaning that the company only acts as a seller's agent in the listing and sale of properties. When a firm practices seller agency only, all licensees affiliated with the firm are agents of the seller. Some firms in less populous markets may still represent sellers only and not offer buyer representation in residential sales. In most markets, firms cannot be competitive unless they offer buyer agency because most prospective buyers prefer to work with an agent who is obligated to promote their best interests, rather than the best interests of the seller.

Recognizing buyers' preference for representation, it is still customary in the brokerage industry for the listing company to offer cooperation and compensation to brokers affiliated with other companies acting as buyer agents, since the listing company cannot act in that capacity. Whether the listing company allows brokers affiliated with other companies to act as seller subagents when showing the company's listings to prospective buyers depends on company policy. The listing company should clearly disclose who it will offer to compensate to its owner-principal and obtain the principal's consent to share with a buyer agent or seller subagent or both in the listing agreement.

Brokers affiliated with the listing firm may work with unrepresented buyers as seller's agents when showing the company's listings, but cannot advise or counsel the buyer and must remember that their loyalty and fiduciary duties are to their seller-clients, not the buyer-customers to whom they are showing property. A broker must avoid any conduct that might lead a buyer to believe that the broker is representing the buyer, as that could result in undisclosed dual agency.

Buyer Agency Only

The second agency option a real estate firm might choose is to practice buyer agency only. A firm choosing this option generally will not list property for sale and will represent only buyers. Once an affiliated broker enters into an express buyer agency agreement with a prospective buyer on behalf of the company, all licensees affiliated with that company become agents of the buyer and owe their fiduciary duties to the buyer. A buyer agent focuses on promoting the buyer's best interests in locating and purchasing property. A firm representing only buyers must cooperate with other firms that list properties to satisfy their buyer-clients' needs, since the firm itself has no listings. Those who practice buyer agency only believe this option enables their firm to more effectively represent the interests of buyer-clients. *Caution: Brokers selling their own property may not represent or offer to represent a buyer due to the obvious conflict of interest.*

Representing Sellers and Buyers with Dual Agency for "In-House" Sales

The third agency relationship option, and the one chosen by a substantial majority of real estate firms, is to represent both sellers and buyers as clients. These firms enter into listing agreements with property owners and buyer-agency agreements with prospective buyers.

When a firm's buyer-client is only being shown properties that are listed with *other* firms, the relationship with that buyer-client is the same as a firm practicing buyer agency *only* and its buyer-client. Similarly, when a seller-client's listed property is only being shown to prospective buyers who are not buyer-clients of the listing firm, the relationship with that seller-client is the same as a firm practicing seller agency *only* and its seller-client.

However, when a buyer-client of the firm becomes interested in a property that is listed with the firm — that is, when a potential "in-house" sale situation arises — different agency issues arise as the company attempts to serve two masters (principals) with opposing interests. Because the firm represents both the seller and the buyer, the firm becomes a "dual agent."

Introduction to Dual Agency

The practice of dual agency in "in-house" sale transactions places the firm and its affiliated brokers in the difficult position of having the same fiduciary duties to parties with conflicting interests. Because dual agency may influence the degree to which the brokers can fulfill their fiduciary obligations owed equally to both clients, brokers must obtain advance express consent from all principals before acting as dual agents.

Unintentional, Undisclosed Dual Agency

Undisclosed dual agency is prohibited by both case law and the North Carolina Real Estate License Law, both of which require agents representing principals with adverse interests to obtain the "informed consent" of both principals. As previously mentioned, the problem with unintended dual agency typically arises where agents acting as sellers' subagents create by their conduct an implied agency relationship with buyers and acts in the buyers' interest, to the detriment of sellers. In such situations, the courts consistently have been tough on agents who worked with buyers and favored the buyers' interest when the agents legally had the obligation to work in the sellers' interest. The best way to guard against these situations is for brokers to clearly understand who they represent and to inform other participants in the real estate transaction of their agency status, as required by Real Estate Commission rules.

Intentional, Disclosed Dual Agency

License Law has long required a broker who undertakes to represent a party with an interest adverse to the broker's principal to both disclose the representation and obtain the principal's consent to represent another principal in the transaction. Not only must *all* principals consent to dual agency, agency case law holds that *the principal's consent must be "informed consent."* Informed consent requires an affirmative answer to both of the following questions.

Were both principals (seller and prospective purchaser) provided with a clear explanation of dual agency and the consequences of having the broker operate as agent for both parties? After being adequately informed, did the principals consent to the dual agency arrangement?

As will be discussed in greater detail in Chapter 9, Commission Rule 58A.0104(d) requires that all principals' consent to dual agency be in writing; this consent typically is obtained at the time the seller or buyer enters into a listing agreement or buyer agency agreement. Not only must the broker have the informed consent of both principals, the broker must deal fairly and in good faith with both and must disclose to each principal any facts the broker knows or should reasonably know that might influence the principal's judgment in the transaction (unless the principal has indicated prior knowledge of these facts or does not wish to be made aware of them). A dual agent must treat both principals equally, not favoring one over the other, and must not do anything to advance the interests of one principal at the expense of the other principal. A dual agent is fully accountable to both principals and must exercise skill, care, and diligence in performing services to both principals.

Through its rules, the Real Estate Commission has provided some additional guidance on practicing dual agency, especially a type of dual agency referred to as "Designated Agency." The NC REALTORS® has also developed agency contract forms that address dual agency and attempt to modify the fiduciary agency duties owed to both principals.

AGENCY RELATIONSHIPS WHEN BROKERS/FIRMS COOPERATE

Although brokers and firms sometimes procure buyers themselves for property they have listed for sale, more often the buyer is procured by a broker affiliated with a different firm. *It is customary in the real estate brokerage industry for a company to list a property for sale and to cooperate with other brokers/firms in the sale of such property.* The most common method of advertising is through a local "multiple listing service" (MLS) or cooperative listing service (discussed in Chapter 9). Even if no MLS or cooperative listing service functions in a particular area, it remains common for listing firms to cooperate with and compensate other real estate firms who produce the buyer.

Extensive advertising and cooperation by the listing firm with other firms is virtually always in the seller's best interest. Thus, listing firms generally will be expected to cooperate with other firms in fulfilling their duty under agency law to exercise their best efforts to accomplish the seller's goals. When two firms are cooperating in a real estate sale through a multiple listing service or otherwise, two different agency arrangements are possible. *The cooperating or selling broker who procures the buyer may be operating as either 1) the agent of the buyer or 2) the subagent of the seller.*

The listing agreement between the seller and listing company typically addresses whether the listing firm is authorized to cooperate and share its brokerage fee with other firms acting as buyer agents and/or seller subagents. If the listing firm intends to restrict its offer of compensation to only certain brokers who procure a ready, willing, and able buyer, such restrictions must be disclosed to the owner prior to signing a listing agreement, since most likely a seller wants the listing firm to cooperate with any other firm who can produce a buyer on terms satisfactory to the seller.

Cooperating Broker/Firm as Buyer's Agent

In most real estate sales transactions today, the company working with the buyer acts as the agent of the buyer and not the seller. The consumer enters into an express buyer-agency agreement with the company, thereby creating the principal-agent relationship and making all the company's affiliated brokers agents of the buyer. A buyer agent's goal is to locate a property for the buyer at the best possible price and under terms most advantageous to the buyer. Most buyers prefer representation and having an advisor/advocate instead of working with a broker who is a seller's agent or subagent.

North Carolina Real Estate Commission rules require a broker to orally disclose buyer agent status to the seller or seller's agent upon initial contact. Such contact typically occurs when the buyer's agent contacts the listing firm to request an appointment to show the buyer a property listed by the listing firm.

Compensation. Seller's agents and subagents almost always are paid by the seller, directly or indirectly, from the sale proceeds. A cooperating firm acting as a buyer agent may be compensated by the buyer, by the seller indirectly through the listing firm that agrees to share, or by both. Most commonly, a buyer agent agrees to first seek compensation from the listing firm (that is, to share the listing firm's brokerage fee), but if the listing firm refuses to share, the buyer must compensate the buyer agent if a purchase is made. *All compensation issues should be clearly addressed in the buyer-agency agreement. Additionally, any questions about a listing company's willingness to compensate a cooperating buyer agent should be resolved between the buyer agent and the listing broker prior to the buyer making any offer.*

Cooperating Broker/Firm as Seller's Subagent

As the popularity of buyer agency has grown, some listing firms are reluctant to cooperate with other firms that propose to work with buyers as a seller's subagent. The concern often expressed is that as the *principal* of the cooperating firm that acts as a seller's subagent, the *listing firm* may be increasing its potential liability for the wrongful acts of licensees affiliated with the cooperating firm. (Under the same theory, the *seller* might be answerable for the acts of a seller's subagent.) Such a result is certainly possible, since a principal can be liable for certain wrongful acts of the principal's agent (or subagent) that were performed within the scope of the agent's authority.

Whatever the reason, *any listing firm that does NOT intend to cooperate with firms that want to act as a seller's subagent must have the seller's permission to restrict its cooperation.* Without the seller's permission, a listing broker may be remiss in fulfilling its agency duties to the seller if the listing company refuses to allow other brokers who want to cooperate as a seller's subagent in selling the client's property. The listing agreement should address whether the listing company may share the compensation paid by its seller-client with a company that procures a buyer and is acting as either a buyer agent and/or a seller subagent or both.

Compensation. When a real estate firm proposes to work with a prospective buyer as a seller's subagent, the firm procuring the buyer will want the listing firm to split its brokerage fee from the seller upon the transaction closing. Where cooperation between real estate firms is through an MLS or cooperative listing service, a fee-sharing agreement generally is not necessary in each transaction, since the MLS listing usually states to whom the listing firm is offering compensation (buyer agent, seller subagent, or both) in the event of a sale to a buyer procured by the cooperating firm. If a selling agent is not a member of the cooperative listing service or there is no service, then the firm working with a prospective buyer should contact the listing company to learn whether the listing firm will share its compensation *prior to showing the buyer* any property listed by such firm.

If the listing company does not authorize seller subagency, then brokers from other firms technically may only show that company's listings when acting as buyer agents. If seller subagency is offered and a cooperating broker initially shows the property to a prospective buyer acting as seller subagent, could the cooperating broker switch from being a seller's subagent to a buyer's agent at the buyer's request later in the transaction? It *may* be permissible for a broker to make such a switch if the broker has not acquired any confidential information about the seller and the listing company, as principal of the seller subagent, consents to the switch. *It is never appropriate for a broker to switch from being a seller's subagent to being a buyer's agent after the broker has received confidential information about the seller unless the seller expressly consents to the switch. In any event, such switching is strongly discouraged.*

Certainly, no broker should adopt a policy of routinely beginning to work with buyers as seller's subagents and solicit the buyer to enter into a buyer-agency agreement at a later point in the transaction. This situation arises with less frequency in current brokerage practice as many listing companies choose not to authorize seller subagency, making the point somewhat moot.

LEGAL DUTIES OF REAL ESTATE AGENTS AND PRINCIPALS

In any real estate agency relationship, the principal and the agent have certain inherent legal duties and liabilities. A real estate broker owes specific duties to principals (whether the principal is seller, buyer, lessor, or lessee) as well as to third parties with whom the broker deals on behalf of the principal. The principal also owes certain duties to the agent. Both agent and principal may face potential liability in the event duties are breached. Additionally, a party to a real estate transaction — particularly a seller — has certain duties under the common law. This section examines in depth the legal duties owed by the various parties involved in a real estate transaction and the liabilities and consequences that may result from a breach of these duties.

IMPORTANT NOTES

- This section focuses on the duties and liabilities of brokers in sales transactions in an effort to avoid making a complex subject even more difficult. However, the legal principles apply equally to real estate leasing or rental transactions. To understand an agent's duties in leasing or rental transactions, simply substitute "landlord" or "lessor" for "seller," and "tenant" or "lessee" for "buyer."
- To make the text and examples less confusing, the authors frequently use the terms "broker" and "agent" throughout the remainder of the chapter. While the materials do not expressly refer to real estate *firms*, a firm has the same duties to consumers as individual real estate brokers through whom the firm fulfills its contractual obligations under the agency agreement. A firm may be civilly liable for an affiliated broker's conduct because the firm is the broker-agent's *principal* within the relationship of the individual and the company. Thus, when the materials state that an individual "broker" or "agent" has a particular duty, understood that any employing firm of the broker or agent has the same duty.
- A real estate company that employs brokers whose licenses are on "provisional" and the provisional broker's broker-in-charge may also be held accountable for the provisional broker's conduct by the North Carolina Real Estate Commission under License Law and Real Estate Commission rules.

Before exploring an agent's duties to his/her principal and third parties under the common law of agency, a brief discussion of "**material fact**" is warranted, as that term appears frequently in the remainder of this text. ***The duty to discover and disclose material facts is imposed by License Law and thus applies only to real estate brokers.*** *It does not apply to sellers, buyers, lessors, or lessees unless they also hold a current North Carolina real estate license.*

"MATERIAL FACTS"

Part of the difficulty real estate brokers may experience in grasping the concept of *"material fact"* is that there is no precise definition. The term was intended to apply broadly to multiple factors that could impact real property. A given fact may be considered "material" and require disclosure in one context but not in another. In its broadest sense, a "material fact" may be *any fact that is important or relevant to the issue at hand.* The Real Estate Commission has provided guidelines in its educational materials over the years regarding what facts the Commission generally will consider to be "material" in most real estate transactions. These guidelines are discussed below.

Material Facts That Must Be Disclosed to Both Principals and Third Persons

General Statute §93A-6(a)(1) imposes upon real estate brokers the duty to discover and disclose material facts. The Commission considers "material facts" to include at least the following categories, regardless of whom an agent represents in the transaction. The *License Law* duty to disclose material facts is completely consistent with agency common-law duties regarding information that an agent must disclose to the *principal.* It goes beyond the common-law obligations, however, by requiring *disclosure of material facts to **all persons** with whom the broker deals if the broker is or should be aware of such facts, regardless of whom a broker represents in a transaction.*

1. **Facts about the property itself.** This category includes any significant property defects or abnormalities, such as a structural defect, a malfunctioning system, a leaking roof, or a drainage or flooding problem.

2. **Facts that relate directly to the property.** These are typically external factors that affect the use, desirability, or value of a property, such as a pending zoning change, the existence of restrictive covenants, plans to widen an adjacent street, or plans to build a shopping center on an adjacent property.

3. **Facts directly affecting the principal's ability to complete the transaction.** This category includes any fact that might adversely affect the ability of a principal (seller or buyer) to consummate the transaction. Examples include a buyer's inability to qualify for a loan; a buyer's inability to close on a home purchase without first selling a currently owned home; or a seller's inability to convey clear title due to the commencement of a foreclosure proceeding (posting of a notice of sale) against the seller. [**Note:** The fact that a seller is behind in mortgage payments is not a material fact until the foreclosure process has officially been started by posting a notice of foreclosure sale.]

4. **Facts that are known to be of special importance to a party.** There are many facts relating in some way to a property that normally would not be considered "material," but because a broker knows they are of special interest or importance to a party, they become material facts that the broker must discover and disclose.

For example, the fact that a residential property may not be used for a home business due to zoning or restrictive covenants normally would not be a material fact that a broker must specifically discover and disclose. However, if a broker working with a buyer knows that the buyer wants to operate a business from the home, then the issue of whether that is a permissible use becomes a material fact. The broker should caution the prospective buyer to investigate before making an offer on the house. If the broker knows that any business use is prohibited, the broker must disclose that to the buyer, regardless of whether the broker is acting as a seller agent or buyer agent.

Any fact falling within any of the preceding four categories must be disclosed by a broker not only to the parties to the transaction but to any interested third parties as well, regardless of the broker's agency role within the transaction. A broker's duty to affirmatively "discover and disclose" material facts will be discussed later in this chapter under "Negligent Omission."

Additional Facts That Must Be Disclosed to an Agent's PRINCIPAL

Under agency law, *an agent must disclose to the principal **any information** that may affect the principal's rights and interests or influence the principal's decision in the transaction.* The Real Estate Commission adopts this broader definition of relevant information that an agent must communicate to the principal, even if the information does not rise to the level of "material fact" as defined above. Examples of relevant information a broker-agent must share only with his/her principal are discussed below.

- **A third party's willingness to agree to a price or terms different from those previously stated.**

Examples: 1) A buyer-customer's willingness to pay more than the amount stated in the buyer's offer must be disclosed by a seller's agent or subagent to the seller-principal. 2) A seller's willingness to accept an offer for less than the list price must be disclosed by a buyer's agent to the buyer-principal.

- **A third party's motivation for engaging in the transaction.**

Examples: 1) A buyer-agent who learns that a third-party seller must sell quickly due to a job change must disclose that information to his/her buyer-principal. 2) A seller's agent or subagent who learns that a third-party buyer has a special need to acquire the seller's property must disclose that to the seller-principal. The same is true if a seller's agent learns that a negotiating buyer intends to purchase and immediately resell the property to another party at a substantially higher price, or if a seller's agent learns that an adjoining property owner has a special interest in acquiring the listed property.

- **Any other information that might affect the principal's rights and interests or influence the principal's decision in a transaction.**

Example: **Broker as a Source of Buyer's Funds.** Sara Seller listed her beach cottage with Bob Broker. Terri Tucker offered to purchase the property for $160,000, tendering $15,000 as a down payment. Terri arranged for $100,000 financing from a conventional lending institution, and Sara Seller agreed to take back a purchase money second mortgage in the amount of $45,000. Unbeknownst to Sara, her listing agent Bob Broker had loaned the $15,000 down payment to Terri. Bob Broker received an $8,000 commission when the transaction closed. Terri Tucker soon went into default on her payments to Sara under the second mortgage. If Sara Seller sues Bob Broker, she is entitled to recover the $8,000 she paid as a commission. The broker breached his duty to disclose to his principal all material facts and breached his duty of loyalty by assisting an adverse party without the seller's knowledge. In addition to recouping the commission, the seller also might be able to rescind the sale, if she so elects.[2]

Example: **Existence of Offers or Potential Offers.** Sam Smith agreed to purchase a house from Joe Jones that was listed with Brenda Broker, the seller's agent. Smith then listed his own house for sale with Brenda Broker. Broker and Smith agreed that if Smith's home was not sold by the date of closing on the Jones home, then Broker would purchase Smith's home to give Smith sufficient funds to close on the Jones home. Although Broker received an offer to purchase Smith's home just prior to the closing date for the Jones home, Broker did not communicate the offer to Smith. Smith then executed a deed conveying his house to Broker, enabling Smith to close on the Jones house. Broker's failure to divulge the offer to purchase to Smith is a clear violation of a broker's agency duties to the principal. The transfer of property to the broker can be rescinded due to the broker's failure to disclose all relevant facts surrounding the transaction.[3]

State Law and Disclosure of Certain "Material" Facts

A broker's duty to disclose certain facts that may seem "material" is excused by state law in two instances and fair housing laws in a third situation explained below.

1. **Death or Serious Illness of Previous Property Occupant.** General Statute 39-50 states: "In offering real property for sale it shall not be deemed a material fact that the real property was occupied previously by a person who died or had a serious illness while occupying the property …" The statute adds, however, that a false statement about past occupancy is not permissible. Since by law the information is not "material," a broker or seller may decline to answer a question about the death or illness of a previous occupant. However, *if a seller or broker chooses to answer a prospective buyer's question about such matters, they must answer honestly and cannot lie.* [**Caution:** If a buyer's question deals with whether a current or former occupant suffers from AIDS/HIV, the broker and seller should be very careful that their answers do not violate state and federal fair housing laws. (See "AIDS/HIV of Current or Former Property Occupant" below.)]

2. **Convicted Sex Offender Occupying, Having Occupied, or Residing Near a Property.** The same North Carolina statutes[4] that address whether the death or serious illness of a previous occupant is a material fact contains a similar provision relating to convicted sex offenders. The statutes state that when offering property for sale, rent, or lease "… it shall not be deemed a material fact … that a person convicted of any crime for which registration is required by Article 27A of Chapter 14 of the General Statutes [statutes establishing North Carolina's registration programs for sex offenders and sexually violent predators] occupies, occupied, or resides near the property; provided, however, that no seller [or landlord or lessor] may knowingly make a false statement regarding such fact." Since the statute states that this information is not a material fact, brokers are *not required* to volunteer to a prospective buyer or tenant information that a registered sex offender occupies, has occupied, or resides near a property being offered for sale or rent. If asked about sex offenders in a neighborhood, brokers may either decline to answer or answer truthfully to the best of their knowledge. Brokers may also provide a prospective buyer or tenant with information on how to access the county sheriff's registry or the statewide registry at *http://sbi.jus.state.nc.us/sor.*

3. **AIDS/HIV Status of Current or Former Occupant.** Other laws apply to situations where a current or previous occupant suffers from Acquired Immune Deficiency Syndrome (AIDS) or Human Immunodeficiency Virus (HIV). Under federal and state fair housing laws, a person with AIDS/HIV is considered to be legally handicapped and is protected from discrimination in housing transactions. If a real estate broker is asked by a prospective purchaser (or tenant) whether a current or previous occupant has/had AIDS/HIV, it should be treated as an impermissible question. The response should be that it is a violation of fair housing laws for the broker to answer the question.

Having defined and discussed the concept of material facts and the few exceptions provided by other state laws, we now return to a discussion of an agent's fiduciary duties to the principal under agency law.

AGENT'S DUTIES TO PRINCIPAL — AGENCY LAW

The basic legal source of duties owed by an agent to a principal is the law of agency, augmented by other laws including contract law, North Carolina Real Estate License Law, North Carolina Real Estate Commission Rules, and other federal and state laws. Real estate brokers should understand that *virtually any breach of duties imposed by agency law will also violate one or more provisions of the Real Estate License Law or Commission rules.* An agent's general duties to his/her principal under agency law are listed below and then discussed.

- Loyalty and Obedience
- Skill, Care, and Diligence
- Disclosure of Information
- Accounting

Loyalty and Obedience

When a principal employs a real estate broker as an agent, that principal is entitled to receive absolute loyalty and obedience from the agent. The agent must comply with all *lawful* instructions of the principal that are consistent with the terms of the agency agreement. Note the emphasis in the preceding sentence on the word "lawful." Agency law does not expect an agent to obey a principal's instructions to perform an unlawful or illegal act.

The faith and confidence principals place in their agents imposes upon the agents the duty to exert themselves with reasonable diligence in the principals' behalf and to obtain for their principals the most advantageous bargain possible under the circumstances. *The broker's duty to represent the principal's best interests is paramount to the interests of all others, including the broker's own interests.* An agent must be very careful to avoid any situation that might compromise the agent's loyalty to the principal.

Self-Dealing by Agent

An agent's duty of loyalty to the principal means that the agent should be free from any pressures or temptations that may distract the agent from putting his principal's interests above the agent's interests. Brokers must assiduously avoid any appearance of "self-dealing." If a broker has a personal interest in a transaction and such interest might affect the broker's loyalty or obedience to the principal, the broker must either withdraw as an agent in the transaction or disclose the personal interest to the principal and proceed *only with the principal's informed consent.*

Example: A broker with whom an owner has listed certain property engages in conduct that favors one of the prospective purchasers over the others to indirectly advance the broker's future business prospects with that purchaser. Specifically, the broker discourages offers from other purchasers and incorrectly informs the seller that they are better off with the purchaser the broker favors. The broker has breached his/her duty of good faith and undivided loyalty to the seller-principal.

Agents should not deal on their own behalf, either directly or through a "strawman," in a manner that might harm the principal's interest unless the agent has the principal's informed consent. Brokers employed to list property must not sell to themselves or to any entity or organization in which the broker has any substantial interest without fully disclosing that interest to the principal. *A broker is forbidden from making a secret profit from any transaction in which the broker is acting as an agent.*

> *Example:* A broker sells property listed with him to a corporation owned by his wife, son, and other family members. The corporation was formed specifically for this real estate transaction. The broker fails to disclose these facts to the seller-principal at the time of sale. The broker has breached his duty of loyalty to the seller-principal in this transaction and is liable to the principal for both the commission paid to him and any profits made by the corporation.[5]

If an agent engages in self-dealing, either for personal benefit or for the benefit of a relative, partner, business associate, or other person where there would be a temptation to favor that person, *without the express knowledge and informed consent of the principal, the transaction is voidable at the option of the principal.* The principal may rescind any resulting contract and may recover any property with which the principal parted, including any fees paid to the agent. To win a lawsuit, the principal need only prove that the broker violated the duty of loyalty and obedience — *no proof of actual harm to the principal would be required.* This rule is designed to close the door to temptation and keep the agent's attention focused only on fidelity to the principal and advancing the principal's interests and goals.

If an agent wants to negotiate with the principal on the agent's own behalf, the principal must have full knowledge of all facts concerning the agent's personal interest and must acquiesce in the transaction. The Commission's agency rule also addresses what must occur before an affiliated broker or the company may make an offer on any of the company's listings, which will be discussed in Chapter 9.

Agent Representing Adverse Interests

An agent must not represent any interest adverse to those of his/her principal without the full knowledge and informed consent of all principals. To represent an adverse party without full disclosure to and informed consent of all principals invites any number of unfavorable consequences including:

1. The agent will have breached agency duties to the principal and may be liable for damages;
2. The contract negotiated by the agent for the parties may be voidable;
3. The agent will not be entitled to a commission or any form of compensation for the transaction; and
4. The broker will have violated General Statute §93A-6(a)(4) that prohibits brokers from "acting for more than one party in a transaction without the knowledge of all parties for whom he or she acts."

The principal does not need to prove that the broker is guilty of fraud or that any actual harm to the parties resulted from the broker's violation of agency duties. *An agent who attempts to act for both sides in a transaction without full disclosure and informed consent by all the principals assumes a role that is not permitted under the law of agency.* Agency law strongly disapproves of an agent representing adverse or conflicting interests in the same transaction without full disclosure and informed consent of all principals. Thus, contracts entered into under these situations may be voidable, regardless of whether there is intentional wrongdoing on the part of the broker and even though the principal suffers no actual injury or damage.

Example: A prospective buyer hires a broker to act only as a buyer agent to look for a certain type of investment property. While acting as a buyer agent, the broker obtains a listing on the very type of investment property his buyer seeks. The broker is the seller's agent for this particular investment property, which in and of itself is permissible, and the listing agreement does not authorize dual agency. Without disclosing to either party his agency relationship with each party, the broker negotiates a sale of the property from his seller-principal to his buyer-principal. Even without any fraudulent intent or unfair dealing, the broker has breached his duties of good faith and undivided loyalty to each principal involved. While the parties may not seek to rescind the transaction if it was at arm's length and both are satisfied, they could refuse to pay the broker a commission and the broker could be subject to disciplinary action by the Real Estate Commission.

Affiliated brokers of a real estate company hired to list a property may only work with unrepresented buyers interested in that listing as seller agents, unless the listing agreement authorizes dual agency and the buyer consents to both buyer agency and dual agency. Likewise, if a real estate company is hired as a buyer agent to locate a property, no affiliated broker may show or negotiate the purchase of a property listed with the company to that buyer client without disclosing the proposed dual agency relationship to both seller and buyer and obtaining the informed written consent of both.

Skill, Care, and Diligence

Brokers hold themselves out as being specially qualified by reason of experience, ability, and knowledge to competently represent principal in real estate transactions. As a general rule, *a broker must exercise that degree of reasonable skill and care ordinarily possessed and used by other brokers engaged in similar undertakings.* An agent must exert reasonable diligence on the principal's behalf and strive to obtain the most advantageous bargain possible under the circumstances. A broker must exercise that degree of skill, care, and diligence that a reasonably prudent real estate broker would exercise under similar circumstances.[6]

Agents who do not perform with the required degree of skill, care, and diligence, or are guilty of negligence or misconduct, not only are liable to the principal for any damages the principal may sustain, but may also forfeit any claim to compensation. The broker-agent will be liable to the principal for all damages that are a direct or "proximate" consequence of the negligence. Failure to exercise skill, care, and diligence not only is a breach of duties under agency law, but probably violates License Law as well, discussed shortly.

A Few Examples of Services Expected from an Agent

The subject of services sellers or buyers may expect from a real estate broker with whom they have an agency relationship is addressed in more depth in Chapter 9; however, a few examples are listed here for illustrative purposes.

Provide Reliable Information on Matters Relevant to the Transaction. Brokers are expected to be knowledgeable about a broad range of real estate matters taught in their prelicensing, postlicensing, and continuing education programs, as well as facts and issues that affect the interests of their principals and information sources to access when questions arise. In other words, brokers should not only have a broad personal knowledge of real estate matters, but also should know where to go to get the information they or their clients need.

Provide Competent Advice on a Property's Probable Selling Price. A broker's client, whether seller or buyer, generally has the right to rely upon the broker to provide a reasonable estimate of the approximate selling price of a property without the client having to employ a real estate appraiser. (An agent should not, however, attempt such an estimate if the broker cannot competently perform a comparative market analysis and thereby determine a reliable estimate.)

Discover Pertinent Facts Related to a Property. Brokers are expected to take reasonable steps to discover all pertinent facts about a property that are necessary to serve their client's interest. Listing agents, for example, are expected to accurately gather all information about a listed property necessary to effectively market the property and to comply with disclosure requirements to prospective buyers. Buyer's agents are likewise expected to assist buyer-clients in obtaining any information related to a property that is of particular interest to the buyer-clients.

Effectively Advertise a Listed Property. A listing broker must advertise and promote the listed property in the manner that is customary in the area where the property is located.

Advise about Offers. A broker is expected to competently advise his/her principal, whether seller or buyer, as to the desirability of offers received and negotiating strategies.

Assist with Contract Preparation. A buyer agent is expected to provide the buyer-client with an appropriate sales contract form and to assist the buyer in completing the form. Similarly, a seller's agent is expected to assist a seller-client with preparing a contract acceptance or counteroffer using appropriate contract forms.

Other Points to Remember

It is important for real estate brokers to realize that *the value of a property has no effect on an agent's duties to a seller or buyer client.* Brokers owe exactly the same duties to a principal involved in the sale or purchase of a $50,000 property as they do to a principal involved in the sale or purchase of a $1,000,000 property. Even though the broker's commission on the sale of the $1,000,000 property will be many times the amount received upon sale of the $50,000 property, the broker is obligated to use the same degree of skill, care, and diligence in both transactions.

It should be emphasized that *the broker's duties do not end with the signing of a sales contract.* The broker is expected to provide numerous services until the sales transaction is properly closed and has a duty to assist as necessary in consummating the transaction. For example, where the buyer is not represented by a buyer's agent, the seller's agent may be expected to assist the buyer in locating satisfactory financing to enable the buyer to complete the purchase. *It is considered part of a seller's agent's duties for the broker to assist the buyer (as well as the seller) in taking whatever steps are necessary to promote the successful conclusion of the transaction.* Providing these services to the buyer indirectly serves the best interest of the seller-principal (not to mention the interest of the broker) by facilitating the closing to accomplish the actual sale of the property.

Finally, *when a sale involves cooperating agents, it is the responsibility of both brokers to cooperate in all matters necessary to facilitate the closing of the transaction.* This is true regardless of whether the brokers are with the same firm or with different firms, or whether the buyer is represented by one broker and the seller is represented by another broker.

Disclosure of Information

Under the common law of agency, an agent is obligated to act with the utmost good faith toward the principal and to fully disclose to the principal any and all information that might influence the principal's decision while simultaneously protecting the principal's personal information. Thus, a real estate broker must fully and promptly disclose to the principal not only "material facts," but all facts that may affect the principal's rights and interests or influence the principal's decisions in the transaction.

Duty of Agent to Protect Principal's Personal Information

In addition to the agent's affirmative duty to disclose all material facts and relevant information to the principal pertaining to the transaction for which the agent is employed, *the fiduciary relationship between principal and agent imposes a duty on the agent NOT to disclose certain personal information about the client-principal to third persons without the consent of the principal.* This obligation arises by virtue of the agent's duty of loyalty and obedience to the principal.

An agent who, without authority from the principal, discloses to a third party information about the principal's personal or business matters thereby improving the bargaining position of the third party has violated the agent's duty of loyalty that includes preserving and protecting the principal's confidential information. Thus, broker-agents must not share any personal information about their principals that may adversely affect a principal's bargaining position with third parties without the principal's consent.

Personal Information about Seller-Clients. Personal information about a seller-principal may include comments concerning the need to sell due to ill health, or a job transfer, or marital separation, or an urgent need for money, all of which comments violate a seller-agent's duty of loyalty and obedience to the seller-principal if the disclosure is made without the seller's permission. While not common, occasionally sellers are so anxious to sell their property that they will not object to the listing broker disclosing their need for a quick sale and may even authorize the broker to disclose this fact when advertising the property. In fact, statements such as "motivated seller," or "bring all offers," or "seller needs quick sale" are sometimes found in real property advertisements; these statement are acceptable so long as the listing broker first obtained the seller's permission before including such phrases in the advertising. Obviously a seller-client's willingness to accept less than the list price is confidential information and should not be disclosed to prospective buyers.

Personal Information about Buyer-Clients. It is less common for the issue of disclosure of personal information about a client to arise in connection with a *buyer* of property, but the same rule applies. Examples of personal information that if disclosed might adversely affect the buyer-client's bargaining position include the buyer's willingness to pay more than the price stated in the buyer's offer, the buyer's motivation for purchasing the property, or the buyer's plans for future use of the property.

Reminder: This *"duty of confidentiality" only applies to personal information about a client-principal* that should not be disclosed to a third person so long as the information is not a material fact as previously defined. *Personal information known to an agent about a third party that might influence the agent's principal in a transaction must be disclosed to the principal.*

Accounting

Generally, any agent is obligated under the law of agency to maintain accurate records of any transactions or dealings involving the principal and to account to the principal for all funds handled by the agent in which the principal has an interest. In addition to this general agency duty to account, brokers must also comply with accounting and safeguarding obligations under License Law and Commission rules when receiving goods or monies belonging to others while acting as an agent. For example, License Law requires a broker to account to any party, not just the principal, for whom the broker handles monies. These statutory and rule provisions define the responsibilities of brokers with regard to recordkeeping and accounting for the funds of others.[7]

Duties of a Broker-in-Charge

While all licensees have a duty to safeguard and protect the money or property of others coming into their possession under License Law, Commission rules make the designated broker-in-charge of each real estate office primarily responsible for the handling of trust monies and the maintenance of trust accounts and all records pertaining thereto. The broker-in-charge has the following specific duties with regard to recordkeeping and accounting for that office:

- Retaining records of all transactions, including copies of all documents.
- Maintaining a properly designated trust or escrow account for all "trust monies" (*e.g.,* earnest money deposits, down payments, tenant security deposits, rents, money received from final settlements, etc.) that come into the company's possession. The broker is the temporary custodian of these trust monies and holds them as a fiduciary for the parties to the transaction.

Trust monies must be maintained in a separate demand deposit account in a federally insured depository institution lawfully doing business in North Carolina that agrees to make the account records available to the Commission if requested. The account must be properly designated as a "trust account" or "escrow account" and those words must appear on all bank statements, checks, and deposit tickets for the trust or escrow account. Trust funds may not be "commingled" with the broker's own personal or business funds. The broker-in-charge also has final responsibility for ensuring that detailed financial records are maintained for the trust account in conformity with Commission Rule 58A.0117.

Duties of Provisional Brokers Only

Commission Rule 58A.0116(b)(1) states: "... *All monies received by a provisional broker shall be delivered upon receipt to the broker by whom he or she is employed ....*" Thus, trust monies received by a provisional broker acting on behalf of the company should be delivered immediately to the broker-in-charge for safekeeping and deposit, if applicable.

Duties of All Licensees (Brokers)

All licensees share certain accounting responsibilities under License Law and Commission rules regardless of their license status. For example, General Statute §93A-6(a)(14) requires a broker to furnish a detailed, accurate closing statement to the client accounting for the receipt and disbursement of all monies relating to the transaction about which the broker knows or reasonably should know. Commission Rule 21 NCAC 58A.0116(g) states:

> Every broker shall safeguard any money or property of others that comes into the broker's possession in a manner consistent with the Real Estate License Law and Commission rules. A broker shall not convert the money or property of others to his or her own use, apply such money or property to a purpose other than that it was intended for, or permit or assist any other person in the conversion or misapplication of such money or property.

A broker's recordkeeping obligations are found in Commission Rule 21 NCAC 58A.0108 which provides in part:

> Brokers shall retain records of all sales, rental, and other transactions conducted in such capacity, whether the transaction is pending, completed, or terminated prior to its successful conclusion. The broker shall retain records for three years after all funds held by the broker in connection with

the transaction have been disbursed to the proper party or parties or the successful or unsuccessful conclusion of the transaction, whichever occurs later....

The rule then lists 15 categories of records that must be retained, including contracts of sale, written leases, agency contracts, options, all offers to purchase, trust or escrow account records, earnest money receipts, disclosure documents, closing statements, and the final catch-all category "… any other records pertaining to real estate transactions."

Agent's Duty to Principal after Termination of Agency Relationship

Generally, a real estate broker has no continuing duty to the principal after the termination of their agency contract, absent some agreement to the contrary or other "unusual circumstances."[8] After the termination date specified in the listing or buyer agency contract has passed, or a transaction contemplated in those contracts has been successfully concluded, the broker usually has no further obligation to the principal.

Under certain circumstances, however, a broker will have obligations to the principal that continue even after the formal termination of their relationship. If in the agency contract with the principal an agent expressly promises to perform some act or service after the termination date, then the broker will be expected to keep this express promise. A continuing obligation also may be implied. For example, an agent who still holds a client's money after the termination of the agency relationship still owes the client the duty to safeguard and account for the money.

Another common example where a broker's obligations to the principal would survive the formal termination date in the agency contract is in a sales transaction when the listing or buyer agency contract expires *after* the buyer and seller have entered into a contract, but *before* the transaction has closed. Under such circumstances, the broker will continue to owe agency duties to the buyer or seller-client until the transaction either closes or terminates in some other way.

Courts across the country have held that a real estate agent's fiduciary obligations also survive the termination of the agency relationship in certain transactions where the agent seeks to deal on their own behalf with former principals. In such circumstances the courts have held that real estate brokers have a continuing duty of loyalty and good faith to the former principals to the extent that the brokers may not use their former position of confidence to profit or gain an unfair advantage over former clients.

Example: Owner lists property with Broker for $200,000. The property attracts little interest during the course of the listing and Owner becomes desperate to sell for financial reasons. Immediately prior to the termination date of the listing contract, Broker finds a buyer willing to pay Owner's full asking price. Broker does not inform Owner about the prospective purchaser, but instead allows the listing to expire. Then Broker offers Owner $150,000 for the property without mentioning the prospective purchaser's interest. Owner accepts Broker's offer and Broker then enters into a contract to sell the property to the interested purchaser for $200,000. Under these circumstances, Broker breached the duty of loyalty to Owner by failing to inform the Owner about the buyer willing to pay $200,000. Courts dealing with such cases almost uniformly have prevented agents from manipulating their position of superior knowledge to obtain a secret profit for themselves, even though the listing contract had expired.

In the absence of special circumstances similar to the three categories described above—that is, (1) express promise or implied obligation, (2) pending transaction at termination date of agency agreement, or (3) self-dealing—termination of the agency contract ends a real estate agent's duty to the principal. The broker later may represent a new client whose interests compete with those of the broker's former client.

> *Example*: Oscar and Olga Owner list their house for sale with Barry Broker for $250,000. During the listing period, Broker learns that the Owners are separating and really need to sell their house as soon as possible. The listing period expires without a sale and the Owners list their house with another broker. A few weeks later, Barry Broker is working with Bobby Buyer as a buyer's agent and Buyer shows an interest in the house owned by Oscar and Olga. Barry tells Bobby that the Owners are separating and that they very well may accept an offer that is well below the listing price. Barry now has an agency relationship with Bobby Buyer and is obligated to disclose to Buyer all information that might benefit Buyer or influence Buyer's decision concerning the purchase of the Owner's property.

It not only is appropriate for the broker to share information about the owners' situation with the buyer, but the broker is obligated under agency law to do so. This is the logical result because to hold otherwise would prohibit Barry Broker and other brokers in similar situations from fulfilling their agency obligations to a *current* client because they had a previous agency relationship with the party with whom their current client is dealing. The former client is aware of what the broker knows and can decide whether to negotiate with the broker's current client.

AGENT'S DUTIES TO THIRD PERSONS–COMMON LAW

Although a real estate agent's primary legal obligation is to the principal, the agent also owes certain duties to other parties (that is, "third persons") with whom the agent deals in any real estate transaction. Brokers' duties to third persons with whom they do not have an agency relationship under the common law ("case law") may be best described as a **general duty of "honesty and fairness."** As a practical matter, this common law duty has essentially been supplanted by the much more far-reaching duties to both principals and third persons imposed on a real estate broker by the North Carolina Real Estate License Law.

AGENT'S DUTIES UNDER REAL ESTATE LICENSE LAW

Virtually *any violation of the law of agency will constitute a violation of one or more License Law or Rule provisions.* The License Law and rules not only complement the common law of agency, but impose additional responsibilities on brokers beyond those duties mandated by the common law. In describing prohibited conduct by a real estate broker in a real estate transaction, License Law does not distinguish between a broker's "principal" under an agency contract and a "third party" with whom the broker does not have an agency contract. *Rather a broker's duties under License Law when dealing with parties to a transaction apply regardless of the broker's agency relationship to such parties.*

Broker's Duties to Parties under License Law [G.S. §93A-6(a)]

- Duty to avoid any willful or negligent misrepresentation or omission of a material fact to any party to a transaction. This includes a duty to disclose all material facts about which the broker has knowledge or should reasonably have acquired knowledge.
- Duty to avoid making false promises that are of a character likely to influence, induce, or persuade a party to a transaction.
- Duty to avoid any undisclosed conflict of interest.
- Duty to properly account for funds held in trust for others.
- Duty to act competently in the performance of services.
- Duty to avoid improper conduct and to be honest in all dealings with the parties.
- Duty to promptly deliver all offers and contracts to a party to the transaction.
- Duty to disclose to parties any commissions, referral fees, kickbacks, and similar payments from third parties.[9]

Misrepresentation and Omission

It is essential that real estate brokers thoroughly understand G.S. §93A-6(a)(1) that authorizes the Real Estate Commission to discipline a broker for "*. . . making any willful or negligent misrepresentation or any willful or negligent omission of a material fact.*"

When discussing misrepresentation and omission of material facts, it is perfectly natural to focus on seller agency situations because, as a practical matter, problems of this nature are more likely to arise in connection with the actions (or inaction) of a seller's agent when dealing with a buyer who is a "third party." Therefore, most of the discussion and examples in this section address situations involving improper actions by a seller's agent dealing with a third-party buyer. *It is important to remember, however, the following points when reading this material:*

1. Real estate brokers are prohibited from making any misrepresentations or failing to disclose a material fact to *any* party involved in a real estate transaction (seller, buyer, lender, attorney, etc.). This fundamental standard applies regardless of whether the licensee has an agency relationship with the party.

2. A buyer's *agent owes the exact same duties to a third-party seller as a seller's agent owes to a third-party buyer.* The law applies equally to all brokers regardless of who they represent.

Categories of Misrepresentation and Omission

Under General Statute §93A-6(a)(1) quoted above, there are four separate but closely related categories of conduct that a real estate broker must avoid when dealing with third persons (as well as when dealing with the broker's principal). These are: (1) willful misrepresentation, (2) negligent misrepresentation, (3) willful omission, and (4) negligent omission.

Understanding Some Basic Terms

- A "willful" act is one that is done intentionally and deliberately.
- A "negligent" act is one done unintentionally, but with a failure to exercise reasonable care as required under the circumstances at the time.
- A "misrepresentation" is the communication of false or incorrect information.
- An "omission" is the failure to disclose material information.

- "Material fact," as defined earlier, includes facts: 1) about the property itself, or 2) directly affecting the property, or 3) concerning a principal's ability to complete the transaction, or 4) of special importance to a party.

"Indirect" Misrepresentation through the Agent of a Third Person

Most of a real estate agent's communications in transactions are made to another broker working with consumers in a transaction. Recall that an agent stands in the place of the principal. Therefore, *an "indirect" misrepresentation— one made to a party's agent that is then passed on to the party—is the same as a misrepresentation made directly to that party.* Similarly, a misrepresentation made by an agent of one party (for example, the seller) to another broker working as a seller's "subagent" with the buyer that subsequently is passed on to the buyer by the subagent is the same as a misrepresentation made directly by the seller's agent to the buyer.

> *Example:* Sarah Seller is represented by Roberta Rocca, the listing broker. Steven Smith, an affiliated with another real estate firm, is working with Betty Buyer as a seller's subagent and is showing Sarah Seller's house to Betty Buyer. Although Roberta knows that the house has serious hidden structural problems, she tells Steven that the house is in great shape with no significant problems. When Steven relays this incorrect information to Betty Buyer, Roberta will be responsible for the misrepresentation communicated to Betty Buyer by Roberta's subagent, Steven.

"Puffing"

It is a common practice in the real estate business for brokers to promote the sale or rental of property by making complimentary statements about the property to prospective purchasers or tenants. This practice of boasting about a property's features, often to the point of exaggeration, is commonly referred to as "puffing." *Puffing,* which is essentially an expression of a broker's *opinion* about the property, *does not constitute misrepresentation.* However, a broker should beware of making any statement of *fact* without first being certain of its accuracy, as making an incorrect statement of fact may constitute either willful or negligent misrepresentation.

> *Example:* A real estate broker tells a prospective purchaser that, in his opinion, they are looking at "the prettiest farm in Harnett County." Even if the property would win an "ugly farm contest," the nature of the broker's statement was one of sales prowess or puffing. Buyers are not justified in relying on these types of representations.

Willful Misrepresentation

Willful misrepresentation of a material fact has long been treated as a fraudulent and illegal practice. Willful misrepresentation may involve either of the two types of situations discussed below.

Intentional Misrepresentation with Actual Knowledge

Where a real estate broker has "actual knowledge" of a material fact in a transaction and intentionally misinforms a party to the transaction (either the broker's principal or a third party) concerning such fact, the broker is guilty of willful misrepresentation.

> *Example:* A seller's agent is aware that the present owners of the listed property have had serious problems with electrical wiring. Nevertheless, the broker tells a prospective purchaser that all

mechanical systems, including the wiring, are in excellent condition. The broker, having actual knowledge of a material fact, has intentionally misinformed a prospective purchaser, and is guilty of willful misrepresentation.

This principle applies equally to a buyer agent's conduct.

Example: Beth Broker represents the Happy Land Amusement Corporation, a company interested in building an electronic theme and amusement park in New Hanover County. The corporation is interested in buying a farm located adjacent to Interstate 40 owned by Zeke Zappa. The farm's value as farmland is approximately $3,000/acre. The farm's value as an amusement park site is approximately $40,000/acre. Beth approaches Zeke and tells him that she has a party interested in buying Zeke's farm and that she is that buyer's agent. When Zeke asks Beth what the prospective purchaser's plans are for the property, Beth replies that the purchaser plans to operate a timber farm on the land and hold it for long-term investment purposes. Zeke sells the farm to the corporation for $3,000/acre. Beth has intentionally misinformed the seller of a material fact relating to the real estate transaction and is guilty of willful misrepresentation. A buyer's agent, like a seller's agent, has a duty to refrain from willful misrepresentation.

Note: A buyer agent has no duty to disclose to a seller the buyer's plans for a property—and, in fact, should not do so without the buyer's permission as it may place the buyer in a disadvantageous bargaining position. However, in this example, Beth Broker, the buyer's agent, lied to the seller about a matter that obviously was material to the seller, thus creating the intentional misrepresentation. The broker should have declined to disclose the buyer's plans on the grounds that this was confidential information she was not permitted to disclose.

Representation Made Without Regard for the Actual Truth

When a real estate broker who does not have actual knowledge of a material fact provides incorrect information to a party involved in the real estate transaction (either the broker's principal or a third party) without regard for the actual truth of the matter, the broker may nevertheless be guilty of **willful misrepresentation**. In other words, *when a broker recklessly makes an incorrect statement of fact without knowing whether it is true and without making any reasonable effort to verify its truth*, the broker may be treated the same as if the statement had been one of intentional misrepresentation. In the following example, the broker is considered to have acted in a highly irresponsible manner by failing to verify in advance the truth of the matter being represented and by intentionally making the statement without regard to its truth or falsity. The broker's failure to make any reasonable effort to verify the truth of this statement goes beyond ordinary negligence.

Example: While looking at an old house, a prospective buyer asks the seller's agent if the exterior walls and floors are insulated. The broker, who does not know the answer, states that the walls and floors are fully insulated without first checking with the owner or taking any other action to ascertain the truth. In fact, the walls and floors are not insulated. Because the broker intentionally made the statement, which was false, and because the broker showed a complete disregard for the truth, the broker is considered to have made a willful misrepresentation.

A buyer's agent also can be guilty of willful misrepresentation to the seller when the buyer's agent intentionally provides information to the seller without regard for the actual truth.

Example: Betty Broker, a buyer's agent representing Pat and Paula Prospect, shows them a home in Greensboro, North Carolina. During negotiations, the seller asks Betty about the financial background of the Prospects. Although Betty has made no inquiries regarding this matter, Betty promptly replies: "These are solid people from Kernersville with plenty of 'old money.'" In reality, the Prospects do not have any assets other than a minimal down payment. Because of Betty's representation, the seller agrees to sell the property to the Prospects and to finance part of the sales price directly. Betty Broker, the buyer's agent, has acted recklessly in responding to the seller's inquiry and likely will be considered to have made a willful misrepresentation to the seller.

Negligent Misrepresentation

Negligent misrepresentation of a material fact is an entirely different concept than willful misrepresentation. Willful misrepresentation is an intentional act; negligent misrepresentation is an unintentional act. The legal concept of "negligence"—the failure to exercise reasonable care under the circumstances—forms the basis for the improper conduct.

A real estate broker is legally obligated to act as other reasonably prudent real estate brokers would act in the same or similar situation. Therefore, *if a broker unintentionally misinforms a third party in a real estate transaction (or the broker's principal) concerning a material fact, and if the broker "should reasonably have known" the truth of the matter being represented, the broker will be guilty of negligent misrepresentation, even if the broker was acting in good faith.* Since an essential component of negligent misrepresentation is the *unintentional* conduct of the broker, it is not a defense that the broker was acting in "good faith."

The "Reasonableness" Standard

*The **key issue** in determining negligent misrepresentation is whether a reasonably prudent broker should have known that the information being provided to another party was incorrect.* In other words, would a reasonably prudent broker in the same or similar circumstances have known that the information being provided was incorrect? If a broker is relying on information from another source (such as the property owner or a multiple listing information sheet), the question is whether the broker acted reasonably in relying on the source without independently investigating the matter to verify the accuracy of the information.

Example: Bobbi Buyer is working with Ben Broker, who is acting as a buyer's agent, to find and purchase a house. While looking at a house with a large wooded lot in a relatively new subdivision, Buyer indicates she would want to build a large detached garage/storage building in the backyard and asks if that would be permissible. Ben Broker calls Nita Sale, the listing agent, to ask. Nita responds that most houses in the subdivision have garages and she also has seen some storage buildings, so she is sure that Buyer could build the garage/storage building. Ben Broker relays this information to Buyer, who subsequently purchases the house. Neither broker checks to see if there are any subdivision restrictive covenants nor suggest that Buyer investigate. Buyer is not given a copy of any restrictive covenants.

Buyer discovers a few months after purchasing the house that the subdivision restrictive covenants prohibit detached garages and strictly limits the size, architectural style, and location of storage buildings. The question is whether Nita Sale and Ben Broker acted reasonably.

Real estate brokers are expected to know that most subdivisions, especially relatively new subdivisions, not only have restrictive covenants, but that such covenants typically include restrictions on the construction of structures such as garages and storage buildings. Further, because Bobbi Buyer specifically asked whether she could build a detached garage/storage building, the issue became a "material fact" that a reasonably prudent broker would have been expected to check before responding. Thus, BOTH real estate brokers were negligent in not checking the restrictive covenants before answering Buyer's question. *At the very least*, the brokers should have advised Buyer that it was very possible, if not likely, that subdivision restrictive covenants existed governing construction of garages and storage buildings and should have strongly recommended that Buyer check with the homeowners' association and, if still uncertain, consult an attorney about this matter *before making an offer to purchase.*

Disclaimers May Not Be a Defense

The issue of negligent misrepresentation is further complicated by the placement of "disclaimer" statements on property information sheets such as MLS information sheets. These disclaimers warn the reader that the information provided is believed to be correct, but that the reader should make an independent investigation of the disclosed facts. *A broker cannot avoid responsibility for communicating incorrect information by arguing that the source of information was the seller-principal, another broker, a MLS information sheet, computerized data, or some other source.* In each situation, the broker will be held accountable according to the "reasonableness" test previously described. *Even if a "disclaimer" is provided when giving information to a party, the agent still has a "duty to investigate" facts whenever a reasonably prudent broker should have questioned the accuracy of the information at hand.* If the agent does not investigate the facts in such a situation, the broker may be guilty of negligent misrepresentation.

Standard for Listing Agents

The North Carolina Real Estate Commission will hold the listing agent accountable for the accuracy of information about the property that is included in advertising or provided directly or indirectly to buyers and brokers working with buyers. This includes property information: 1) communicated directly to buyers and other brokers, 2) placed in a listing information sheet or entered into a computer data bank such as those used by multiple listing services, and 3) included in promotional flyers or advertising. Because the seller's listing agent compiles the information that will be conveyed to prospective purchasers, the Commission expects *the seller's listing agent to take reasonable steps to verify all property data when taking the listing and to accurately report such information to prospective buyers and other brokers.* The listing broker is in a much better position to verify most property data than other brokers involved in a transaction.

A listing agent must not only take great care to acquire accurate data on listed property but also must assure that such information is accurately communicated to interested parties. *A seller's agent may be guilty of negligent misrepresentation when s/he makes a mistake in compiling or communicating information about a property.* The test in this situation is whether a reasonably prudent broker would have made the mistake. If not, then the listing agent will be answerable for the mistake and may be guilty of negligent misrepresentation when a purchaser relies on the misinformation.

Example: When listing a house, the listing broker states that the house is 20 years old and the lot is 0.57 acres. However, when entering the listing data into the MLS property information file, the office manager writes that the house is ten years old and the lot has 0.75 acres. The listing broker fails to check the information before it is sent to the MLS. A buyer, working with another broker in the same firm, purchases the house believing the MLS data to be correct. If the house had been very well-maintained and the lot's shape made it difficult to detect the error in reported size, the broker working with the buyer might not reasonably be expected to detect these errors. However, the listing agent and company are guilty of negligent misrepresentation because of the failure to verify the accuracy of the data entered into the MLS system.

Standard for Selling Agents

For a selling agent (broker working with a buyer as either a buyer's agent or a seller's subagent), the Real Estate Commission will apply a different standard than that applied to a listing agent. *Generally a selling agent may rely on the accuracy of property information provided by a listing agent, whether on a listing information sheet or in an MLS computer data bank,* **unless** *the selling agent should reasonably suspect that the information may be inaccurate.* Thus, a selling agent is not expected to personally verify the accuracy of information provided by the listing agent in most instances. It should be emphasized, however, that *a selling agent will still be judged according to the general "reasonableness" standard and is not automatically relieved of responsibility by relying on data provided by the listing agent.*

When selling agent is aware of a matter of special importance to a buyer. Whenever an agent working with a buyer is aware of the buyer's special needs or desires with regard to a property, the agent has a duty to take reasonable steps to verify the relevant information reported by the listing agent and to assure that the property under consideration will in fact satisfy the buyer's special concerns.

> *Example:* A broker is working with buyers who tell the broker that their previous house had a septic tank that gave them a great deal of trouble and that they do not want to buy another house with a septic tank. The buyers become interested in a house listed by another broker and the MLS information shows that the house is served by a community sewer system. Because of the buyer's stated special desires, the selling agent may NOT rely on the listing information provided by the listing agent. Rather, the selling agent has a duty to personally investigate to assure that the house in fact is served by a community sewer system and not a septic tank. One reasonable approach might be for the selling agent to ask the listing agent for the name of the utility company that serves the community and to personally call the utility company to check on the sewer system.

Note: The situation described in this example is not uncommon. It is not unusual for a subdivision to have water service provided by a utility company, but to have septic tanks rather than a community sewer system.

When there is a "red flag." Any time a situation exists that should make a reasonably prudent broker working with a buyer suspect that the information provided by the seller or another party may be incorrect—that is, whenever there is a "red flag" regarding reported information—the broker has a duty to investigate the accuracy of the reported information. The following example involves a seller's listing agent and a selling agent acting as the seller's subagent.

> *Example:* Burley Barnes, a broker, lists a rectangular-shaped, two-story house with no unusual or irregular design features for sale. Burley represents the living area to be 2,500 square feet based on what the owner has told him but does not verify the information. Sally Smith, another broker with Burley's firm, is working as a seller's agent with a buyer who is interested in the listed house. The buyer makes an offer that the seller accepts. Sally and the buyer rely on the square footage reported in the listing information. When the house is appraised, the buyer

learns the house only has 2,000 square feet, nearly 20 percent less than the advertised 2,500 square feet. The appraised value is less than the sale price. Needless to say, the buyer is unhappy and may terminate the contract unless the seller will reduce the sale price.

The listing agent failed to properly verify the reported square footage and is guilty of negligent misrepresentation. Sally, the selling broker, may also be guilty of negligent misrepresentation because given the size of the error and uncomplicated design of the house, she should have suspected that the reported square footage was erroneous and, *at a minimum*, asked the listing agent the source of the square footage figure. Of course, Sally should also advise the buyer and, if necessary, personally verify the reported square footage. In other words, the reported square footage should have been a "red flag" to a reasonably knowledgeable and prudent broker.

Misrepresentation by a Buyer's Agent to a Seller

Although it does not occur very frequently, *negligent misrepresentation by a buyer's agent to a seller (or seller's agent) is possible and is prohibited by the North Carolina Real Estate License Law.*

Example: Sue Seller lists her house for sale with Billy Broker. Sue wants to have a contract for the sale of her present house before purchasing a new house. Bobby Buyer submits an offer to purchase Seller's house through Clara Carver, a broker acting as a buyer agent. Sue Seller counters Buyer's offer, and Buyer wants to think it over. The next day, Clara calls Buyer and asks if he is going to accept the counteroffer and he replies "I've decided to accept the counteroffer." Clara immediately calls Billy Broker, the listing agent, and tells him "The buyer has accepted the seller's counteroffer." Billy conveys this information to Sue Seller, and, the next day, assists Sue in submitting an offer on another house. The offer is immediately accepted. Three days later, Clara Carver visits Bobby Buyer to pick up the signed contract, only to learn that Bobby changed his mind and *never signed the counteroffer from Sue Seller.* Bobby has no further interest in buying Sue's house unless Sue agrees to the terms of his original offer.

In this situation, Sue Seller acted to her detriment based on the representation by Clara Carver, the selling agent, that the buyer had accepted Sue's counteroffer. Clara's failure to assure that the counteroffer had been signed prior to advising the seller (or seller's agent) that it had been accepted constitutes negligent conduct on her part. Clara, therefore, is guilty of negligent misrepresentation to the seller while acting as a buyer's agent.

Willful Omission

When any broker involved in a real estate transaction has "actual knowledge" of material facts and intentionally fails to disclose those facts to all parties, the broker is guilty of "willful omission" (that is, intentional failure to disclose).

The "duty to disclose material facts to third persons" may seem to conflict at times with the agent's duties to the principal and thus may be a confusing concept to real estate licensees. Seller's agents frequently are confronted with situations where they know of some material property defect or other fact about the property that, if disclosed to a prospective purchaser, may discourage the prospect from buying the property. If a seller's agent acts solely for the benefit of the property owner who is the agent's principal, then the broker may not want to disclose information that might be adverse to the property owner. ***Despite the strong agency law duty requiring an agent to act in the best interest of the principal, the broker cannot withhold material facts about the property from a third party.*** *The* *agent's duty to represent the principal is not absolute, and, in the case of real estate brokers, is tempered by the statutory duty for brokers to disclose material facts about the property to third persons.* The duty to disclose material facts about a property is an *"affirmative"* duty. Thus, a broker representing a property owner is obligated to disclose material facts to a prospective purchaser even if the prospective purchaser does not inquire about them and even if the property owner instructs the broker not to disclose them. The following examples illustrate the concept of willful omission.

> *Example:* A seller's agent knows that a highway-widening project has been approved that will cut through part of the front yard of a residence and adversely affect the value of the property. The broker does not disclose this information to a prospective purchaser. The broker has violated License Law by failing to disclose a material fact to the prospective purchaser and is guilty of a willful omission. (It is irrelevant whether the prospective purchaser asked the broker a direct question about the matter.)

> *Example:* A seller's agent is aware that the listed property has suffered extensive termite damage that is not easily detectable. Regardless of whether a prospective purchaser actually inquires about possible termite infestation or damage, the broker has a duty to disclose this material fact. Even if the seller has instructed the broker "to keep quiet about the damage," the broker must disclose the problem.

The above discussion and examples focus on the willful omission of/intentional failure to disclose a material fact by a seller's agent when dealing with prospective purchasers because prospective buyers most frequently are affected by a seller's agent's failure to disclose material facts. Nevertheless, it should be clearly understood that *a* **buyer's agent** *is subject to the same material facts disclosure requirements as an owner's agent.* If a buyer agent has knowledge of material facts relating to a property, s/he must disclose those facts to a seller.

> *Example:* Sue Broker is aware of a recent decision by the State Board of Transportation to build a new bypass around a town. Sue obtains maps showing the planned route for the bypass. She then contacts Ivan Investor, a local real estate speculator, and asks Ivan if he is interested in trying to acquire land near planned interchanges for the proposed bypass to hold for resale at what would likely be a large profit. Ivan hires Sue to act as his buyer agent in acquiring such parcels. Sue then negotiates the purchase of a large tract of land adjacent to the path of the planned bypass directly with the owner, but never mentions the planned bypass to the property owner, who lives in another state. Sue may be guilty of willful omission by not disclosing the plans for the bypass, a material fact, to the property owner.

Negligent Omission

In addition to having a duty to disclose to all parties in a transaction all known material facts pertaining to the transaction, *a broker also has a duty to "discover and disclose" to all parties material facts relating to the transaction about which the broker "reasonably should have known."* The duty to disclose is not limited to situations where a broker has actual knowledge of a material fact. If a broker "reasonably should have known" of a material fact about a transaction, then a nondisclosure of such fact will constitute a "negligent omission" under the License Law. It is the statutory prohibition against negligent omission that creates the *duty to discover and disclose material facts.*

Negligent omission involves a broker's unintentional failure to discover and disclose a material fact (such as a property defect) about which the broker had no actual knowledge, in circumstances where the broker "should reasonably have known" about such fact. The same negligence standards as were discussed in the section on negligent misrepresentation apply to the concept of negligent omission. If a reasonably prudent broker would have been aware of or discovered the fact in question in the same or similar circumstances, the broker who was not aware of the fact and, therefore, did not disclose it, will be guilty of negligent omission.

As was the case with negligent misrepresentation, a negligent omission by a broker involves an *unintentional* act. Therefore, it is not a defense to a charge of negligent omission that the broker was acting in "good faith." Good faith may be an issue with regard to a willful misrepresentation or omission, but is not an issue where the broker's conduct was unintentional.

> *Example:* A broker is inspecting a house in January to list. The house is unusually cold, but the broker does not turn on the heat pump to see if it is working or even ask about its condition. In fact, the heat pump is inoperative; the broker fails to discover this fact and thus does not mention it in the information provided to other brokers. The property goes under contract; the buyer is never informed prior to closing that the heat pump does not work. An inoperative heat pump is clearly a material fact to most homebuyers. Under these facts, the listing agent is guilty of negligent omission as the broker clearly should have discovered the inoperative heat pump.

Negligent Failure to Disclose a Known Fact

Negligent omission may also involve a broker's *unintentional* failure to disclose a material fact when the broker has actual knowledge of the fact but *negligently fails to disclose the known fact.*

> *Example:* Assume the listing broker in the previous example discovers the inoperative heat pump, but then forgets to note the defect in the information provided to other brokers and the buyer is not advised of the defect. The broker in this situation had actual knowledge of the defect. Because the broker forgot to disclose it, the broker is guilty of negligent omission due to negligence in not providing the information to other brokers and the buyer.

> *Example:* Suppose the listing agent noted the defective heat pump in the MLS data, but the broker working with the buyer failed to notice the information about the defective heat pump and therefore failed to advise the buyer of the defect. In this scenario, the listing agent has done all that is reasonably expected of a listing agent by discovering the defect and noting it in the MLS data. It is the broker working with the buyer who is negligent in not noting the information about the heat pump in the MLS data and advising the buyer of the problem.

Facts of Particular Importance to a Party

Even if a particular fact would not normally be one that is sufficiently significant to rise to the level of being a "material fact," it becomes a material fact when a broker is aware that the matter in question is especially important to a party.

> *Example:* The fact that the previous occupants of a house had indoor pets normally would not be a material fact requiring disclosure. However, if a buyer tells her agent that she is allergic to pet hair and does not want a house previously occupied by pets, then whether pets previously

occupied a house becomes a material fact to that buyer. The broker has a duty to discover whether the house was previously occupied by pets and, if so, to disclose that fact.

Example: A seller has a 30,000-square-foot commercial property for sale that cannot be expanded under local zoning laws. The buyer is looking for property in the 25,000 to 30,000 square-foot range, but has informed her buyer agent that she needs a property where she can expand to 50,000 square feet or more in the future. The seller does not think to tell the buyer agent that the property cannot be expanded, and the buyer agent does not ask even though he is aware of the buyer's special needs. The buyer agent is guilty of negligent omission for failing to discover and disclose a special circumstance that he knew was important to his client.

It is fairly obvious that a buyer agent would have the duty to investigate matters of special concern to the client under agency law. Note, however, that *under Real Estate License Law, the broker's status as a buyer agent or seller agent does not matter when it comes to disclosing material facts.* Any broker working with a buyer is required to discover and disclose any material facts, including any matter that is of special importance to a party.

The "Reasonableness" Standard

Whether a broker has a duty to discover any particular material fact depends on whether a "reasonably knowledgeable and prudent broker" would have discovered the fact in the course of the transaction and acquiring information about the property. If a broker *has no knowledge* of a fact *and has no duty to discover* the fact, then the broker has no duty to disclose it, even though it is "material."

Example: A building listed for sale has serious structural damage, but the damage is such that it can only be detected by an experienced inspector, builder, or engineer from underneath the building. The structural damage is clearly a "material fact" that any prospective purchaser would want to know. If the listing agent has actual knowledge of the defect, it must be disclosed to all prospective purchasers and failure to do so would be a willful omission. However, if the listing agent does not know of the defect, the question is whether the listing agent reasonably should have known about it. In this scenario, a reasonably prudent broker clearly could not have discovered the defect. Thus, the listing agent had *no duty to discover and disclose the defect.*

UNFAIR AND DECEPTIVE PRACTICES ACT

While a real estate agent's duties stem primarily from the "common law" (court decisions) and the North Carolina Real Estate License Law, it is extremely important to note in the context of this discussion that brokers are also subject to the consumer protection provisions of North Carolina General Statute §75-1.1, sometimes referred to as the North Carolina Unfair or Deceptive Practices Act. (See discussion in Chapter 10 on Basic Contract Law.) This law prohibits unfair or deceptive acts or practices in commerce and applies primarily to the sale or rental of real estate and to real estate brokerage. The types of unfair conduct in business prohibited by the Act also are prohibited by the North Carolina Real Estate License Law and case law. "Unfair or deceptive acts" *include giving a misleading opinion or false inducement, failing to disclose a material fact, using misleading advertising, and misrepresentation.* The most important point to note about this law is that it creates a separate legal cause of action (in addition to common law causes of action such as fraud or breach of contract), and **a person**

found to be injured by an unfair or deceptive trade practice may be entitled to *three times the amount of actual damages*.

RESPONSIBILITIES OF SELLERS AND PURCHASERS

Doctrine of *Caveat Emptor*

The responsibilities of sellers and purchasers of real estate with regard to disclosure of information about the property being sold are governed primarily by the old common law legal doctrine of *caveat emptor*, which literally means "let the buyer beware." *The doctrine of* caveat emptor *basically holds that— except in cases involving fraud by the seller or the seller's agent—the seller has no affirmative obligation to disclose information about the property being sold to the purchaser and places the burden on the buyer to investigate the property before contracting to purchase the property.* Under the doctrine of *caveat emptor,* real estate *buyers are expected to make their own inspection of the property (or employ someone to do this for them) and to discover for themselves those facts that typically would be found by a reasonable inspection of the property.*

Seller Has Very Limited Obligation to Buyer

The seller's only obligation to the buyer concerning disclosure of information about a property's condition or about a matter that might affect the property's value or desirability is to avoid any fraudulent acts. A limited exception to the doctrine of *caveat emptor* is that the seller must avoid engaging in any sort of artifice or fraud intended to induce the buyer to forego an investigation that might reveal facts the seller does not want to be disclosed. In a suit by a purchaser against a seller for fraud, the courts will consider whether the information in question was reasonably discoverable through a diligent inspection by the buyer, as well as whether the seller engaged in conduct intended to induce the buyer to avoid an inspection that might reveal the information.

Effect of Residential Property Disclosure Act. As will be discussed shortly, sellers in most residential transactions have an obligation under North Carolina law to provide buyers with a "Residential Property and Owners' Association Disclosure Statement;" however, *a seller is not compelled to actually disclose any problems on the disclosure statement*. A seller may simply choose to make "No Representation" about all items listed on the disclosure form, rather than answer "yes" or "no."

Effect of *Caveat Emptor* Doctrine on Real Estate Broker's Duties

The above discussion addresses only the responsibilities of sellers with regard to disclosure of information about a property being sold and the responsibility of buyers who are attempting to sue the seller for fraud or misrepresentation by the seller. The situation is very different when a broker is involved in a transaction. *A broker is accountable under the North Carolina Real Estate License Law for both willful and negligent misrepresentations and omissions to both buyers and sellers.* Because a broker has an affirmative duty to disclose material facts to buyers, a buyer will have a much easier time maintaining a civil action for misrepresentation against a broker than against a seller.

Even though a broker must disclose material facts to buyers, in civil lawsuits for misrepresentation against brokers, the courts do not fully relieve buyers of responsibility to inspect the property they are buying through a broker. *The buyer is expected to verify information that is easily verifiable and to make at least a cursory inspection of the property prior to signing a purchase contract.* For example, if a defect that is not disclosed by an agent is so obvious that a buyer of reasonable intelligence, acting in a reasonable manner, should have discovered the defect, then the courts may find that the agent's failure to disclose the defect is not actionable in a civil lawsuit under the common law. Similarly, if an agent's representation regarding some fact about the property is so obviously wrong that a reasonably prudent buyer should have known or discovered its inaccuracy, then the courts may find that the buyer was not justified in relying on the agent's statement and that the broker, therefore, was not guilty of misrepresentation under the common law. A buyer is not entitled to rely on advice or opinions of an agent concerning matters in which the agent possesses no expertise.

Caution: Brokers should understand that while a buyer's failure to verify information or inspect a property in some cases may relieve an agent of civil liability for misrepresenting or failing to disclose a material fact, it will not necessarily excuse the broker from responsibility for his or her actions under North Carolina Real Estate License Law in a disciplinary inquiry.

> *Example:* When listing a house, Brenda Broker does not check the heating/cooling system and the seller does not tell her that the heat pump is not functioning. When viewing the house with Brenda Broker in late May, Bobby Buyer notices that it is unusually warm and that the thermostat is registering 82 degrees. He adjusts the thermostat to 72, but nothing happens. Despite this, Bobby makes no further inquiry and proceeds to buy the house. After moving in, he discovers that the heat pump is inoperable and files a lawsuit for damages against the seller and Brenda Broker based on their failure to disclose the condition of the heat pump.
>
> The standard form offer to purchase and contract signed by the parties states that the heating and cooling system is in good working order, *but* adds that the buyer has the option to inspect the system (all systems) prior to closing and that failure to inspect constitutes an acceptance of the system in its then existing condition. Buyer's failure to inspect the condition of the heat pump, especially after being alerted that there may be some problem, probably will preclude any award of damages to Bobby because of the contract's language and the application of the doctrine of *caveat emptor.* Note, however, that this doctrine operates only in the application of the common law by the courts. It does not relieve a real estate broker of the responsibility to discover and disclose material facts under North Carolina Real Estate License Law. Brenda Broker still could face disciplinary action by the Real Estate Commission for negligent omission of a material fact.

Where a purchaser is represented by a buyer agent and pursues a civil action against the agent for misrepresentation or breach of agency contract duties, it is unclear at this point whether North Carolina's courts would today place a greater duty on a buyer's agent to verify information and discover material facts than they would a seller's agent working with a buyer. Although such a conclusion would certainly seem logical, there are no cases directly on point at the present time. At any rate, all brokers, whether acting as a buyer's agent or seller's agent when working with a buyer, need to remember that the Real Estate License Law imposes an affirmative duty on all brokers to discover and disclose material facts, rather than hope the Real Estate Commission will hold the buyer accountable for failing to independently inspect a property or investigate some matter of importance to the buyer. (See earlier discussion of "Negligent Misrepresentation" and "Negligent Omission.")

SALE OF PROPERTY "AS IS"

Selling a property "as is" simply means that the seller does not intend to make repairs. A seller's desire to list property for sale in "as is" condition or to place an "as is" provision in the sales contract does not affect a broker's duty under the Real Estate License Law to disclose material facts to prospective purchasers. *An "as is" provision in a listing or sales contract does not relieve the broker of the responsibility to discover and disclose property defects and other material facts about a property.* This is why it is extremely important that listing agents explain this legal obligation to prospective sellers prior to executing a listing contract. Sellers need to understand that the broker's duty to not disclose personal, confidential information about the seller does not include material facts about the property.

> *Example:* A seller contacts a broker about listing the seller's home for sale. The seller informs the broker that there is a substantial crack in one of the foundation walls and that the seller has placed paneling over that wall. The seller informs the broker that the home must be sold "as is" and that the broker should "keep quiet" about the cracked foundation. The broker's duty under the Real Estate License Law to reveal all material facts to prospective purchasers is not superseded by an "as is" provision. The broker cannot take the listing under the circumstances demanded by the seller. [If the broker participates in the marketing of this property and fails to reveal this material defect, the broker violates the License Law (General Statute §93A-6(a)(1)), the Unfair and Deceptive Practices Act (General Statute §75-1.1), and also might be guilty of fraud.]

OTHER STATE DISCLOSURE LAWS

THE RESIDENTIAL PROPERTY DISCLOSURE ACT

In an effort to encourage more open disclosure by property owners of defects and problems with residential properties they are selling, the North Carolina General Assembly enacted Chapter 47E of the General Statutes, known as the Residential Property Disclosure Act, effective January 1, 1996. The Act was amended to require the disclosure form to also address information about any owners' association and mandatory covenants affecting the property as of January 1, 2012. The Act was amended again effective January 1, 2015 to address mineral, oil, and gas rights.[10]

Basic Requirement of Act

The central requirement is that sellers of residential one-to-four-unit properties provide prospective purchasers with a "Residential Property and Owners' Association Disclosure Statement" and a "Mineral and Oil and Gas Rights Disclosure." In spite of its title, the Residential Property Disclosure Act is not a true mandatory property condition disclosure law, because it only requires the seller to provide a prospective buyer with the disclosure statements on forms prescribed by the North Carolina Real Estate Commission. *The law does not require the seller to actually disclose any known information about the property's condition or whether the mineral, oil, and gas rights were severed from the property by a previous owner.* With regard to whether the seller has knowledge of the conditions listed on the disclosure forms, the seller has the option of checking "Yes," "No" or "No Representation."

Because the seller has the option to sell the property without making any representations as to the property's condition or as to the severance of mineral, oil, and gas rights by a previous owner, the North Carolina law is actually a voluntary disclosure law. However, it is mandatory that the seller provide the buyer with the disclosure statements, copies of which appear as Figures 8-1 and 8-2 at the end of this chapter.

The Disclosure Forms

The disclosure forms, officially called the ***"Residential Property and Owners' Association Disclosure Statement" (RPOADS)*** and ***"Mineral and Oil and Gas Rights Disclosure," (MOG)*** are issued by the North Carolina Real Estate Commission pursuant to Commission rules that supplement the Act.[11] *The prescribed forms may not be altered or amended in any way, and no other disclosure forms may be used as a substitute for the prescribed forms.* The forms contain instructions to property owners, including a summary of the owner's duties under the law and directions for completing the form. A space is provided for the seller(s) to sign each form. Also included is a note to purchasers regarding their cancellation rights, a space for the buyer to sign the form acknowledging its receipt, and a recommendation that purchasers obtain a property inspection from a licensed home inspector or other professional.

Applicability of the Act

The law applies to the following transfers of residential real property consisting of one to four dwelling units, whether the transaction is accomplished with or without the assistance of a broker:

- Transfers by sale or exchange, including transfers by installment land contract.
- Transfers by an option contract.
- Transfers by lease with an option to purchase, except where the lessee occupies or intends to occupy the dwelling.

The law applies to "For Sale By Owner" (FSBO) sales even without a broker, as well as to sales involving a real estate broker, unless the transaction is listed as exempt in General Statute §47E-2, partially reprinted on the RPOADS form. The following transfers are exempt from the law and thus the owner from the obligation to provide the Residential Property and Owners' Association Disclosure Statement.

- Transfers involving the first sale of a dwelling never inhabited, i.e., new construction.
- Transfers by lease with option to purchase where the lessee occupies or intends to occupy the dwelling.
- Transfers to or from the State or any political subdivision of the State (county or city).
- Transfers from one or more co-owners solely to one or more other co-owners.
- Transfers made solely to a spouse or a person in the lineal line of consanguinity.
- Transfers between spouses in conjunction with a decree of divorce or equitable distribution.
- Transfers made pursuant to a court order.
- Transfers made in connection with a default on a mortgage or with foreclosure.
- Transfers by a fiduciary (estate executor, guardian, trustee, etc.)
- Transfers in connection with the owner's failure to pay federal, state, or local taxes.
- Transfers where the parties agree that the owner not provide a disclosure statement.
- Lot sales. [**Note:** This is *not* a specific statutory exemption; however, since the statute applies only to property containing a dwelling unit(s), it would not apply to lot sales.]

Transactions Exempt from the Mineral and Oil and Gas Rights (MOG) Disclosure. Transactions that are exempt from providing the new MOG disclosure are the same as above <u>EXCLUDING</u> the following:

- Transfers involving the first sale of a dwelling never inhabited.
- Lease with option to purchase contracts where the lessee occupies or intends to occupy the dwelling.
- Transfers between parties when both parties agree not to complete a Residential Property and Owners' Association Disclosure Statement.

While sellers of residential property in the above three categories are not required to provide the Residential Property and Owners' Association Disclosure Statement, they must still provide the Mineral and Oil and Gas Rights Disclosure to a prospective buyer.

Who Is an "Owner?" The law applies to each owner having a recorded present or future interest in a property subject to the law, except that it specifically exempts from the definition of "owner" trustees under a deed of trust, mortgage holders (mortgagees), lien holders, and owners of any easement or license. Note that a relocation company that holds title to a property is an "owner" and is subject to the requirement to provide the disclosure statement, even though the company only intends to hold title temporarily for the purpose of resale.

Time for and Method of Delivery of Disclosure Statements

The seller must deliver the disclosure statements to the prospective buyer *no later than the time the buyer makes an offer to purchase,* exchange or option the property, or exercises an option pursuant to a lease with an option to purchase. While delivery of the disclosure statements to a *buyer's agent* in a timely manner would satisfy the delivery requirement, the form must be signed by the buyer, not the buyer's agent. The statute makes no mention of the method of delivery of the disclosure statements. Transmission by facsimile (FAX) or email are simple and effective methods of delivery that could be done immediately after the broker working with the buyer contacts the listing firm to make an appointment to show a listed property. In modern practice, the listing agent often will post all required seller-disclosure documents as attachments to the MLS listing information so they are readily available to brokers working with buyers. The broker working with the buyer should return to the listing agent a copy (in electronic or hard copy) of the statements that have been signed by the buyer. This can be done at the time an offer to purchase is submitted.

Buyer's Right to Cancel Contract

The Act gives the buyer a right to cancel a sales contract when either of the disclosure statements is not delivered in a timely manner, but in most transactions, the buyer's right to cancel for the seller's failure to timely provide the statements expires three days after contract formation. General Statute §47E-5(b) says if the statements are not delivered in a timely manner, the buyer may cancel upon the *first to occur* of four events:

1. The end of the third calendar day following the purchaser's receipt of the disclosure statement;
2. The end of the third calendar day following the date the contract was made;
3. Settlement or occupancy by the purchaser in the case of a sale or exchange; or
4. Settlement in the case of a purchase pursuant to a lease with option to purchase.

The buyer's only remedy - i.e., the right to cancel the contract solely due to the seller's failure to timely provide the required disclosures - is waived (lost) if not exercised prior to the occurrence of any of the foregoing events. A buyer who does not receive the required disclosure prior to extending an offer and chooses to cancel any resulting contract because of that failure must so notify the seller or the seller's agent in writing, *either by hand delivery or by depositing the written notice into the United States mail, postage prepaid and properly addressed to the seller or the seller's agent.* The law says that a buyer who timely cancels the contract is entitled to a refund of any deposit she or he may have paid.

Note that the buyer's right to cancel only arises if the seller fails to comply with the statute. *If the disclosure statements are delivered to the buyer prior to or at the time the buyer makes an offer, the buyer has no right under this law to cancel any resulting sales contract.* Also understand that the buyer's right to cancel within the brief timeframe allowed by state law for the seller's failure to timely provide the mandatory disclosures is independent of any right the buyer may have to unilaterally terminate a contract to purchase under the terms of the contract.

Real Estate Broker's General Duty

A real estate broker has certain statutory duties under the law. General Statute §47E-8, titled "Agent's Duty," states:

> A real estate broker acting as an agent in a residential real estate transaction has the duty to inform each of the clients of the real estate broker of the client's rights and obligations under this Chapter. Provided the owner's real estate broker has performed this duty, the broker shall not be responsible for the owner's willful refusal to provide a prospective purchaser with a residential property disclosure statement, the mineral and oil and gas rights mandatory disclosure statement, or an owners' association and mandatory covenants statement. Nothing in this Chapter shall be construed to conflict with, or alter, the broker's duties under Chapter 93A of the General Statutes.

Listing Agent's Basic Statutory Duty

The Residential Property Disclosure Act specifically charges a listing broker with the duty to *inform the owner of the owner's rights and obligations under this law.* To fulfill this duty, the listing broker should do the following:

1. Advise the seller whether the seller has an obligation to provide prospective buyers with the disclosure statements in the particular transaction and, if so, perform the acts listed below.
2. Advise the seller of the seller's statutory duties.
3. Advise the seller that the buyer has a three-day right to terminate (rescind) a sales contract when the seller (or seller's agent) fails to deliver the disclosure statements to the buyer (or buyer's agent) prior to or at the time the buyer makes an offer. Also explain that the buyer has no recourse if the disclosure statements are delivered in a timely manner or if the buyer agrees that the Residential Property and Owners' Association Disclosure Statement is not necessary. While the parties may agree to waive the Residential Property and Owners' Disclosure Statement requirement, they cannot waive the seller's duty to provide the Mineral and Oil and Gas Rights Disclosure.

The listing agent should find the "Instructions to Property Owners" and the "Note to Purchasers" on the front of the Residential Property and Owners' Association Disclosure Statement form very useful in explaining to the seller his or her duties and the buyer's right to cancel. An agent who fails to fulfill the statutory duty imposed by the law quoted above not only violates that statute but may also violate Real Estate License Law by engaging in unworthy or incompetent behavior that endangers the interest of the public and/or conduct that constitutes improper, fraudulent, or dishonest dealing.

In view of the broker's specific duty under General Statute §47E-8, a listing agent who advises the seller-client of the applicability of the disclosure law, the seller's duties under the law, the consequences of the seller's failure to perform such duties, and the seller's options for completing the disclosure statements shall not be considered by the Real Estate Commission to be improperly engaged in the practice of law within the meaning of other applicable statutes.[12]

Buyer Agent's Basic Statutory Duty

A buyer agent must explain to the buyer-client her or his right under this law to cancel any contract within three days of contract formation if the seller fails to provide the disclosure statements prior to or at the time the buyer makes an offer. As a practical matter, if the seller provides the disclosure statements in a timely manner, the buyer has no special rights or recourse under the law; therefore, where the disclosure statements are timely provided, no explanation is needed. A buyer agent should explain the disclosure law to the buyer *before* the broker begins showing the buyer properties so the buyer knows to expect and request the disclosure forms for each property.

Additional Duties of Brokers Related to the Disclosure Act

The Real Estate Commission expects each licensee to support the Residential Property Disclosure Act and the public policy of this State that encourages residential property sellers to provide disclosure statements to prospective buyers. Such support includes performing "additional duties" that the Commission views as flowing naturally from both a basic broker duty under the Act and under the common law of agency. A licensee who fails to perform these additional duties may violate Real Estate License Law in some circumstances.

Additional Duties of Listing Agent in Connection with the Disclosure Act. A listing agent's additional duties under the Residential Property Disclosure Act include the following:

1. Provide the seller with copies of the "Residential Property and Owners' Association Disclosure Statement" and "Mineral and Oil and Gas Rights Disclosure" forms as required by law.

2. Explain to the seller that a broker is required by License Law to disclose to each prospective buyer any material fact about a property of which the broker is aware or should reasonably be aware, even if the seller chooses not to disclose such material fact or makes no representation concerning the matter.

3. Assist the seller in assessing the property and completing the form. This could include (but not necessarily be limited to) the following:

   A) Gather property data. (This is mandatory for brokers under the License Law "duty to discover and disclose material facts.") A thorough "walkthrough" inspection of the property with the owner is a prudent method of obtaining this information.

   B) Identify items of possible concern and review with the seller her or his options for addressing such items. The listing agent should clearly explain to the seller which defects or conditions are "material facts" that the broker must disclose to prospective buyers.

   C) Advise the seller, if necessary, on the proper completion of the form. A listing agent is not expected to tell a seller how to answer any item or category but may provide such advice if he or she wishes.

4. Assist in delivering the completed disclosure forms to prospective buyers and their brokers. This may be accomplished by uploading the disclosure statements to the property information displayed on a cooperative listing website or by leaving copies at the property.

5. Monitor the property to ensure the continuing accuracy of the disclosure statements and to assist the seller in preparing corrected statements, if necessary.

6. If working directly with a prospective buyer, explain the statements to the buyer and review the "Note to Purchasers" section with the buyer.

7. Obtain from the buyer or selling agent, at the time the buyer submits an offer, copies of the

disclosure statements that have been signed by the buyer and retain these documents in the broker's transaction records.

Additional Duties of a Seller's Subagent Working with a Buyer. A seller's subagent working with a buyer should perform the following duties related to implementing the Residential Property Disclosure Act. The seller's subagent should:

1. Obtain completed disclosure statements from the listing broker/firm and deliver the statements to the prospective buyer. Make a note on the form or elsewhere of the date and time the disclosure statements were delivered to the buyer.
2. Explain the disclosure statements to the buyer and review the "Note to Purchasers" section with the buyer.
3. Procure the buyer's signature on the disclosure statements. The seller's subagent should retain a copy and provide a copy of each signed by the buyer to the seller or listing agent at the time an offer is submitted.

Additional Duties of a Buyer Agent. In addition to advising the buyer of the buyer's rights under the law, a buyer agent additionally should:

1. Obtain completed disclosure statements from the listing broker/firm and deliver the statements to the buyer-client, noting on the forms the date and time the statement was delivered. (If buyers have not previously been advised of their rights under the disclosure law, do this now using the "Note to Purchasers" section of the form.)
2. Have the buyer sign the disclosure statements, keep copies in the broker's transaction records, and return copies with the buyer's signature to the listing broker at the time an offer is submitted.
3. Assist the buyer in assessing the disclosure statements and the property, identify items of concern, and recommend that the buyer obtain appropriate inspections.

Broker's Duty to Disclose Material Facts Unaffected by Disclosure Act

It is extremely important to emphasize that *the Residential Property Disclosure Act does not in any way affect a broker's duty to discover and disclose material facts under Real Estate License Law or the common law* discussed earlier in this chapter. This is true regardless of the broker's role in the transaction—that is, as listing agent, seller's subagent working with a buyer, buyer's agent, or dual agent. **If a seller answers "No Representation" to a question, but the seller's agent is aware of a material defect, the seller's agent must disclose the defect to prospective buyers.**

RESIDENTIAL LEAD-BASED PAINT DISCLOSURES

Based on extensive research, the scientific and medical communities long ago concluded that lead poisoning is a major environmental health hazard. The use of lead in gasoline and food cans was restricted many years ago, and the use of lead in paint used for residential property was banned in 1978. However, it is estimated that 83 percent of the privately owned housing units built in the United States before 1980 contain some lead-based paint. Continuing research indicates the hazard from this old lead-based paint continues to be a serious problem. Although anyone can be harmed by excessive exposure to lead, it is especially harmful to children under the age of six, fetuses, and women of childbearing age.

To address this continuing problem, Congress passed the Housing and Community Development Act of 1992, Title X of which is titled the "Residential Lead-Based Paint Hazard Reduction Act of 1992." This law authorized the Department of Housing and Urban Development (HUD) and the Environmental Protection Agency (EPA) to develop and issue rules addressing the lead-based paint hazard problem. The resulting rules *became effective in 1996.* The two sets of rules are absolutely identical. The HUD rules may be found at 24 CFR Part 35 and the EPA rules may be found at 40 CFR Part 745.

Basic Disclosure Requirement

Before a buyer or renter is obligated under any contract to purchase or lease "target housing" (which is most residential housing built prior to 1978), a seller or lessor must:

1. provide the purchaser or lessee with a copy of the EPA pamphlet entitled *Protect Your Family from Lead in Your Home* (EPA747-K-99-001; www.epa.gov/lead) or an equivalent state publication approved by EPA.
2. disclose to the buyer or lessee the presence of any known lead-based paint or lead-based paint hazard, and provide the any records or reports available to the seller or lessor pertaining to lead-based paint or lead-based paint hazards. [Note: An owner must also provide the disclosures and any available information to any agent of the owner.]

In addition to potential liability of sellers, real estate brokers are also subject to liability. If a broker represents an owner of pre-1978 housing, the broker has a legal duty to ensure compliance with the lead paint disclosure requirements.[13]

Effect of Compliance after Offer is Made. An owner who fails to perform either of the above disclosure activities before the buyer or lessee makes an offer to purchase or lease, must complete the required disclosures and allow the buyer or lessee to review the information and amend the offer.

Buyers Have 10-Day Evaluation Period. A seller must permit the buyer a ten-day period to conduct a risk assessment or inspection for lead-based paint or related hazards before the buyer becomes obligated to purchase under any purchase contract; however, the buyer may waive the opportunity to conduct the risk assessment or inspection for the presence of lead-based paint or lead-based paint hazards, or the buyer may agree to a different inspection period (more or less than ten days).[14]

Applies to Tenants Renewing Leases. The disclosures need not be made to existing tenants, but when they renew their leases, the disclosures must be made.

"Target Housing" Affected by the Law/Rules

"Target housing" means *any housing constructed prior to 1978* and includes the "common areas" in multi-family housing structures. The only exceptions are:

1) *Housing for the elderly or persons with disabilities* (unless a child under six (6) years of age resides or is expected to reside in such housing).
2) *0-bedroom dwellings,* defined as any residential dwelling in which the living room is not separated from the sleeping area. This includes efficiencies, studio apartments, dormitory housing, military barracks, and rentals of individual rooms in residential dwellings.

The rules apply to *all transactions to sell or lease "target housing,"* including subleases, with the following exceptions:

- Sales of target housing at foreclosure.
- Leases of target housing where the housing has been found to be *lead-based paint free* by an inspector certified under the federal certification program or an accredited state or tribal certification program.
- Short-term leases of 100 days or less with no option to renew or extend the lease.
- Renewals of existing leases if the disclosure requirements were previously satisfied.

Disclosure and Certification by Parties as Part of Contract or Lease

Each sales contract or lease for target housing must have an addendum that includes a specified "Lead Warning Statement" and signed statements from all parties and agents of the seller or lessor certifying that all requirements were completed. As an alternative, the disclosures and certifications may be included in the body of the contract or lease. A copy of the completed addendum must be retained by the seller, lessor, and any broker for three years.

Sample Disclosure Formats. HUD and EPA have published separate sample disclosure formats for use with target housing sales (Figure 8-3) and rentals/leases (Figure 8-4) reprinted at the end of this chapter.

Note: The NC REALTORS® and the North Carolina Bar Association have published an addendum ("Lead-Based Paint or Lead-Based Paint Hazard Addendum," Standard Form No. 2A9-T) to accompany the standard "Offer to Purchase and Contract" Form (Standard Form No. 2-T). NC REALTORS® also has a similar addendum for use in lease transactions.

Agent Responsibilities

Federal rules define an "agent" as:

> … any party who enters into a contract with a seller or lessor, including any party who enters into a contract with a representative of the seller or lessor, for the purpose of selling or leasing target housing. This term does not apply to purchasers or any purchaser's representative who receives all compensation from the purchaser.

According to the official comments to the federal rules, the term "agent" includes all of the following in sales transactions:
1) Listing agents Presumably both the individual listing broker and the firm in whose name the listing is taken.
2) Selling agents (As used in the comments, this term appears to refer to sellers' subagents who are working with a buyer but being compensated from the brokerage fee paid by the seller to the listing broker/firm. If the selling broker is affiliated with a firm other than the listing firm, the selling agent's firm would also be included in the definition.)
3) *Buyer agents, if paid by the seller or through a cooperative brokerage agreement with the listing agent.* A buyer agent is specifically excluded if compensated solely by the buyer.

As for rental transactions, the comments do not provide any additional information. It is clear from the rule itself, however, that any individual agent employed by the broker-property manager to assist in the renting of the affected housing would be considered an "agent" under the rule. (Presumably, the property management firm would be included as well as the individual broker contracting with the owner in the firm's behalf.)

Each agent must ensure compliance with all requirements of the rules. The agent must:
1) Inform the seller or lessor of the seller's/lessor's obligations under these rules;   and
2) Either ensure that the seller or lessor has performed all activities required the rules *or personally ensure compliance with the requirements of the rules.*

Under the law, an agent shares legal responsibility for compliance with the seller or lessor. It is critically important that brokers understand their obligation to ensure compliance with these rules to avoid the consequences discussed in "Enforcement and Penalties." If the broker ensures compliance with the rules, the broker will not be liable for the owner's failure to disclose to a buyer or lessee the presence of lead-based paint and/or lead-based paint hazards known by a seller or lessor but not disclosed to the broker.

Enforcement and Penalties

Sellers, lessors, and their agents who fail to comply with the federal law/rules may be subject to one or more of the following enforcement sanctions:

- Warnings (for first-time, unintentional offenders).
- Injunctive relief to force compliance.
- Civil monetary penalties in an amount up to $10,000 per violation (for one who knowingly violates the rules).
- Civil suits for actual damages. Any person knowingly violating the rules can be held jointly and severally liable for treble (triple) damages. Plaintiffs may be awarded court costs, attorney fees, and expert witness fees if the plaintiff prevails.
- Criminal prosecution. Maximum penalty is one-year imprisonment and $10,000 fine.

FOR MORE INFORMATION

For a copy of *Protect Your Family from Lead in Your Home* (also available in Spanish), a copy of the rule, or to get answers to specific questions, call the National Lead Information Center (NLIC) at (800)424-LEAD, or TDD (800)526-5456 for the hearing impaired, or the EPA Lead Information Line at (202)566-0500. A copy of the pamphlet and other information may also be accessed and downloaded at www.epa.gov/lead.

Bulk copies of the pamphlet are available from the Government Printing Office (GPO) at (202)512-1800. Refer to the complete title or GPO stock number 055-000-00632-6. The pamphlet may also be ordered online from the U.S. Government Online Bookstore at www.gpo.gov/about/bookstore.htm.

LIABILITIES AND CONSEQUENCES OF AGENT'S BREACH OF DUTIES

A real estate broker who breaches or fails to fulfill duties to the principal or to third persons risks one or more of the following consequences.

1. The broker may be disciplined by the North Carolina Real Estate Commission. Virtually any breach of duty owed by an agent to a principal or third person will violate North Carolina Real Estate License Law, regardless of whether the breach gives rise to a civil lawsuit. If, after inquiry, the Commission finds that an agent has violated Real Estate License Law, the Commission may publicly reprimand the broker or, for more serious transgressions, may suspend or revoke the broker's license.

2. The broker may be liable for b*reach of duty in a civil action in court.* Either the principal or third parties may sue the broker in court for damages proximately caused by the broker's breach of duty to that person. Recall, however, that the elements of a cause of action under civil law frequently are higher or more rigorous than those necessary to prove a violation of License Law. A breach of duty by a broker affiliated with a firm or broker-sole proprietor may result in a lawsuit against both the individual broker and the employing firm or brokerage company. The fact that the affiliated broker may be an "independent contractor" for income tax purposes will have no bearing on the complaining party's ability to include the employing real estate company as a party to the lawsuit. Damages in these lawsuits vary depending on the type of breach that is involved. (Under the Unfair or Deceptive Practices Act, an injured party may be entitled to treble (triple) damages against a real estate broker.[15])

3. *Loss of commission.* In almost every case where a broker violates an agency duty to the principal, the broker will lose the commission. If the commission has already been paid, the broker will be required to refund it.

    - If the broker is guilty of undisclosed self-dealing, perhaps by buying property from the principal through a "strawman," any profits from the transaction, such as profits obtained by reselling the property, will be deemed the property of the principal.

    - If an agent is guilty of representing two parties to a transaction who have adverse interests without disclosure to and the informed consent of both parties, the broker will be denied compensation from either. Further, the consummated transaction may be voidable at the option of any principal who did not consent to dual agency. If a principal disaffirms a transaction because the broker has represented an adverse interest to the detriment of the principal, the principal is entitled to rescind the contract and to recover the property and any other damages the principal has sustained because of the broker's wrongful acts.

    - If a broker fails to exercise that reasonable skill, care, and diligence customarily used by reasonable, prudent brokers and that failure results in damages to the principal, the broker may be sued and held liable for those damages.

    - If the broker has misrepresented or withheld information regarding a material fact, an injured seller or buyer may have a legal claim against the broker for any resulting damages.

4. *The broker may be subject to criminal prosecution for the breach.* Criminal actions are instituted by district attorneys in the name of the state. North Carolina Real Estate License Law states that any person violating the provisions of Chapter 93A "... shall upon conviction thereof be deemed guilty of a Class 1 misdemeanor," which is punishable by a fine or imprisonment, or both, at the discretion of the court. Although it occurs infrequently, brokers can be criminally prosecuted for violating Real Estate License Law. Other offenses, such as embezzlement, misappropriation of funds, or fraudulent conduct are punishable under other criminal statutes and may result in stricter fines and longer periods of imprisonment upon conviction.

5. *The **principal** may be legally liable for the broker's breach of duty to a third person.* A breach of an agent's duty to a third person *by either an agent or subagent* may cause the principal

to be liable for the agent's or subagent's actions. This is true even if the principal did not know about the agent's activities, so long as the agent's wrongful act was within the apparent authority of the agent acting within the scope of agency employment. In practical terms, almost any representation or omission by a seller's agent concerning a material fact about the listed property will be a representation or omission made within the apparent authority of the broker.

DUTIES AND LIABILITIES OF PRINCIPALS

The principal in a brokerage agency relationship also has certain legal duties and liabilities to both the principal's own agent and third persons involved in the real estate transaction. These duties and liabilities are discussed below.

Principal's Duties to Agent

Agency law is not one-sided. While agents owe duties to their principals as previously discussed, principals also have duties to their agents. *A principal owes an agent the duties of good faith and compensation, whether the principal is the seller or the buyer.*

Under a listing contract, the property owner, as principal, must exercise good faith in all dealings with the broker-agent and, like the agent, must faithfully perform the principal's obligations under the contract. The owner must cooperate with the agent and not do anything to hinder the agent's performance.

> *Example:* Property owner Jones lists her home for sale with Broker Brown under a six-month listing contract. Thirty days later, after Broker Brown has shown the house to several prospects without success, Jones tells Brown that she does not want to be bothered anymore by people coming to look at the house and that Brown may only show prospects the outside of the house. The owner has breached the duty of "good faith" owed by Jones to Brown. Brown may be able to recover damages from the owner for Brown's expenses incurred in advertising and attempting to sell Jones's house.

A principal also has the duty to compensate the agent as provided in their agency contract, for the broker's performance under the contract. Under most listing contracts, the broker is entitled to receive and the owner is obligated to pay the commission when the broker has produced a ready, willing, and able buyer for the owner's property. Compensation can come from the principal or from third parties involved in the real estate transaction.

Where the broker is acting as a buyer agent, the method of compensation can vary. The source of compensation may be the buyer or may be the seller through a commission-sharing arrangement between the listing agent and buyer's agent. Under most buyer-agency agreements, a buyer agent earns a commission when that broker has located a property that meets the buyer's requirements and the buyer makes an offer to purchase the property that is accepted by the seller. A buyer's agent may have other arrangements for compensation with the buyer. A flat fee for the buyer's agent's efforts in locating a property may be paid regardless of the ultimate success of the broker in locating a suitable property for the buyer. A combination of both a flat fee and a commission in the event of success is also possible.

Principal's Duties to Third Persons

A property owner has a duty not to misrepresent the property being sold or rented, and may have a duty to disclose known defects or other material facts regarding the property to prospective purchasers or tenants in certain situations. For a discussion of the effect of fraud and misrepresentation on real estate contracts, see Chapter 10, "Basic Contract Law."

Principal May Be Liable for Conduct of Agent

Understand that *a principal-property owner may be liable to a third person not only for the principal's own acts, but also for the wrongful acts of a broker acting as the principal's agent*, as long as the wrongful act was committed by the agent while acting within the scope of the agency employment agreement. For example, if an agent, while attempting to sell the principal's property, misrepresents a material fact to a prospective purchaser, and the latter relies on the misrepresentation to her or his detriment, then the principal (as well as the agent) may be liable under civil law to the purchaser for the agent's wrongful act.

DISCLOSURE OF AGENCY RELATIONSHIPS IN REAL ESTATE SALES

AGENCY DISCLOSURE—THE COMMISSION RULE

North Carolina Real Estate Commission Rule 58A.0104 addresses agency agreements and disclosure. The rule provisions related to agency agreements are covered in Chapter 9. Those related to disclosure of agency status by brokers are summarized below and then discussed.

Summary of Major Agency Rule Provisions

- All brokers must give to and review with all sellers and buyers at "first substantial contact" the Commission's *Working with Real Estate Agents* brochure.

- All seller agents or subagents must disclose *in writing* their agency status to a prospective buyer at "first substantial contact" with the prospective buyer.

- All buyer agents must at least orally disclose their agency status to the seller or seller's agent at "initial contact" with the seller or seller's agent.

- Real Estate License Law and the common law of agency require that the consent and authorization for dual agency generally must be obtained *in writing* prior to a broker acting as a dual agent. However, where a broker is working with a buyer or tenant under a nonexclusive oral agency agreement with oral dual agency authorization (in those limited situations where this is allowed by the rule—see Chapter 9), the dual agency authorization must be reduced to writing when the buyer agency agreement is reduced to writing, *i.e.*, no later than when one of the parties wants to extend an offer to any other party.

- Note that the rule *applies to all **sales** transactions, residential and commercial.*

Required Use of *Working with Real Estate Agents* Brochure

Real Estate Commission Rule 58A.0104(c) reads

> (c) In every real estate sales transaction, a broker shall, at first substantial contact with a prospective buyer or seller, provide the prospective buyer or seller with a copy of the publication "*Working with Real Estate Agents*," set forth the broker's name and license number thereon, review the publication with the buyer or seller, and determine whether the agent will act as the agent of the buyer or seller in the transaction. If the first substantial contact with a prospective buyer or seller occurs by telephone or other electronic means of communication where it is not practical to provide the *Working with Real Estate Agents* publication, the broker shall at the earliest opportunity thereafter, but in no event later than three days from the date of first substantial contact, mail or otherwise transmit a copy of the publication to the prospective buyer or seller and review it with him or her at the earliest practicable opportunity thereafter . . .

Under this rule, *at the first substantial contact with a buyer or seller, a broker must: (1) discuss agency relationship options, and (2) determine in what capacity, if any, they will work with the consumer. The Commission-mandated brochure* **Working with Real Estate Agents** *must be given to and reviewed with each prospective buyer or seller by the broker.*

The text of the mandatory *Working with Real Estate Agents* brochure may be found on the Commission's website. The brochure is designed to be consumer friendly while still explaining and educating consumers about the various agency relationships, the duties arising out of each, and the options available to consumers in deciding how they wish to work with any given broker/firm. The final page of the brochure is a perforated panel on which the name of the consumer, the date, the real estate company's name, and the individual broker's name are printed or typed and the panel signed by the consumer acknowledging both receipt and review of the brochure by the broker. The consumer retains the brochure itself, and the broker retains the signature panel in the transaction file to evidence compliance with Rule A.0104(c).

The panel also contains a "Disclosure of Seller Subagency" box at the bottom, which should be checked if the broker and buyer decide that the broker will work with the buyer as a seller's subagent. It should be noted that the consumer is not required to sign acknowledging receipt of the disclosure form, although they should be encouraged to do so. However, if a consumer refuses to sign the form acknowledging its receipt, then the broker should note the person's refusal on the form and retain the form in the transaction file.

The brochure is simply a disclosure form and is not a contract. Signing the brochure only signifies that the broker has complied with the agency disclosure rule and that the buyer/seller has received the form, but it does not obligate the consumer to work with the broker.

The Meaning of "First Substantial Contact"

The key to complying with this rule is recognizing when the broker must make the disclosure. At what point does a contact with a prospective buyer or seller become "substantial"? The Commission adopted this somewhat flexible standard recognizing that it is not necessary or even appropriate for a broker to make this disclosure at every "first" contact with a consumer. In fact, many initial contacts may be informational only and not rise to the level of first substantial contact.

"*First substantial contact*" can be defined as the point in time when a consumer, whether a prospective seller or buyer, *begins to act as though an agency relationship exists or to disclose their particular needs, desires, or wants about property to be sold or purchased or any confidential personal information about them, such as financial circumstances, family matters, employment situations, etc.* First substantial contact also occurs when the broker begins to speak or act in such a way that a reasonable person would believe that an agency relationship exists. One of the primary goals of agency disclosure is to prevent a consumer from revealing personal or confidential information to a broker *before* the consumer is aware who the broker represents and the duties the broker owes to the principal.

Electronic or Telephonic First Substantial Contact. Under Rule A.0104(c), if the first substantial contact with a prospective seller or buyer occurs by telephone or other electronic means that make it impractical to give the person the written brochure, the broker is required "*at the earliest opportunity thereafter, but in no event later than three days* from the date of first substantial contact, mail, or otherwise transmit a copy of the publication [brochure] to the prospective buyer or seller *and review it with him or her at the earliest practicable opportunity thereafter*."

If the first contact is by telephone, the broker should inform the consumer that there is a brochure explaining various agency relationships that the broker will send to the consumer, which the broker and consumer must review and discuss before the broker can proceed very far in assisting the consumer. *The broker should warn the consumer not to reveal any confidential or personal information to any broker until the consumer decides who to hire as their agent, as there is no confidentiality until a principal-agent relationship is created.* Once the broker has sent the *Working with Real Estate Agents* brochure to the consumer, the broker should:

- contact the consumer and review the brochure with him or her,
- determine whether and how they will work together, and
- enter into the appropriate agency agreement or give the required notice to buyer from seller's agent/subagent *before* they begin to discuss the customer's/client's specific needs.

If the initial contact by the consumer is by email, fax, or other written communication, the broker should include the brochure in the written reply or indicate it will be forthcoming. Once that is done, the broker should contact the consumer to review the brochure, determine their agency relationship, and enter into the appropriate agency agreement or give the required notice to buyer from seller's agent/subagent. This should happen *before* the broker and customer/client begin to discuss the customer's/client's specific needs.

Listing Agent Working with a Prospective Seller

Generally first substantial contact with a prospective seller will occur at the initial listing presentation; the broker must give the seller the *Working with Real Estate Agents* brochure and *must review and discuss the brochure* with the prospective seller, preferably earlier rather than later in the listing presentation. While it need not be the very first words out of a broker's mouth, the broker must inform the consumer from the outset that *nothing the consumer tells the broker is confidential* unless the consumer decides to hire the broker's company. The broker is there to discuss the services the broker could offer the seller if the seller ultimately chooses to retain the broker/firm.

The brochure must be given to and reviewed with the prospective seller *before the seller reveals any personal or confidential information about the seller or the property*; if at any time during the listing presentation the seller begins disclosing confidential information, then the broker must *immediately* stop the presentation and review the *Working with Real Estate Agents* brochure and determine whether the seller wishes to retain the broker's services. If the seller wants to employ the broker/firm, then the broker must obtain a written listing agreement with the seller before the broker may provide any services to the owner. Typically a seller's only choices are 1) which company to hire, and 2) whether to authorize some form of dual agency.

Working with a Prospective Buyer

Buyers have more agency options to consider, since a broker may work with a buyer as *either* a buyer's agent, *or* a seller's agent/subagent (if permitted by the listing company), *or* a dual agent. Because of these choices, each with attendant duties owed to different principals, a broker who is contacted by a prospective buyer must give to and review with the consumer the *Working with Real Estate Agents* brochure at the outset of the first substantial contact with that customer *before eliciting any information about the customer's needs or wants or any personal information about the customer.* Once the broker has reviewed the brochure with the customer, the two then must decide whether and in what capacity they will work together *before they do anything else.* Will the broker work with the buyer as a buyer's agent under either an oral or written buyer-agency agreement (and if so, does the buyer authorize dual agency if the situation arises), or will the broker work with the buyer as a seller's agent/subagent?

This discussion and decision must be made **before** *a broker begins to work with a prospective buyer.* If the buyer and the broker decide that the licensee will work as a buyer's agent, then the buyer and broker must enter into either an oral or written buyer-agency agreement that also addresses whether any form of dual agency is authorized. If the buyer rejects buyer agency and chooses seller subagency, then *written* notice disclosing the broker's seller subagent status must be given to the buyer before showing the buyer any properties.

Disclosure by Seller's Agent/Subagent to Prospective Buyer

In addition to the Rule 58A.0104(c) mandate, Real Estate Commission Rule 58A.0104(e) requires disclosure of agency status when a seller's agent or subagent is dealing with a prospective buyer. The rule reads:

> (e) In every real estate sales transaction, a broker working directly with a prospective buyer as a seller's agent or subagent shall disclose *in writing* to the prospective buyer at the *first substantial contact* with the prospective buyer that the broker represents the interests of the seller. The written disclosure shall include the broker's license number. If the first substantial contact occurs by telephone or by means of other electronic communication where it is not practical to provide written disclosure, the broker shall immediately disclose by similar means whom he or she represents and shall immediately mail or otherwise transmit a copy of the written disclosure to the buyer. In no event shall the broker mail or transmit a copy of the written disclosure to the buyer later than three days from the date of first substantial contact with the buyer. [Emphasis added.]

The rule requires a broker acting as a seller's agent or subagent to disclose *in writing* at the **first substantial contact** with the prospective buyer that the broker represents the interests of the seller. *The primary purpose of the disclosure is to immediately notify prospective buyers that the broker with whom they are dealing is NOT "their agent"* **before** *the prospective buyer discloses personal information to the broker that the buyer would not want the seller to know.* Therefore, the disclosure must **always** occur before the buyer, either voluntarily or in response to questions from the broker, discloses any confidential information.

A broker working with a prospective buyer as a seller's agent must avoid soliciting "confidential" information from the buyer prior to making the required disclosure, and the broker should immediately stop any buyer who voluntarily offers such information prior to the disclosure being made. This is important because while a buyer agent has a duty to keep all personal information about his/her buyer-client confidential, a seller's agent (or subagent) has a duty to disclose to the seller any personal information about the buyer if it might influence the seller's decisions or improve the seller's bargaining position.

More often than not, "first substantial contact" will occur when the broker and prospective buyer first discuss the prospect's interest in buying a property, which may be before or after the first "in-person" meeting.

Complying with the "First Substantial Contact" Requirement

Disclosure must always occur prior to showing a property to the buyer. A broker working with a prospective buyer as a seller's agent/subagent should never show a property to the prospective buyer—or even search for possible properties to show—until after the written notice of seller agency has been given. To identify possible properties to show, the broker must elicit information from the prospective buyer, such as the buyer's price range. In the process, the buyer could inadvertently disclose information that s/he might not if the buyer understood that the broker was representing the seller and not him/her.

A broker affiliated with a firm that offers both seller agency and buyer agency must explain the firm's agency policies to the buyer ***at the earliest possible time*** and determine if the broker (and firm) will be working with the buyer as a seller's agent/subagent or as a buyer's agent. If after reviewing the Commission's *Working with Real Estate Agents* brochure, the buyer decides to work with the broker as a seller's agent or subagent, the broker must immediately give the buyer the required *written* disclosure. This can be accomplished by checking the box at the bottom of the perforated panel and obtaining the buyer's initials. If the buyer wants time to decide, the broker should delay identifying possible properties to show the buyer until the buyer decides on the agency relationship.

> *Example*: Brenda Buyer wants to buy a lot on which to build a house. Brenda goes to ABC Realty and asks Bill Broker to show her available properties that will meet her needs. Before identifying possible properties or otherwise discussing Brenda's needs, Bill reviews the *Working with Real Estate Agents* brochure with Brenda and informs her that the company can act as her broker—that is, as a buyer's agent—or can show her properties as a seller's subagent. Brenda declines to enter into a buyer-agency agreement of any kind, oral or written, with ABC Realty. Given Brenda's choice, Bill can only function as a seller's subagent and must deliver written notice of seller subagency to Brenda. This may be accomplished by checking the box next to the "Disclosure of Seller Subagency" clause at the bottom of the panel and asking Brenda to sign the panel before proceeding to work with Brenda.

Important Note: *Brokers must understand that before they can assist a prospective buyer with locating a property, the broker must either have: (1) an express oral or written buyer-agency agreement with the prospective buyer, or (2) disclosed in writing to the prospective buyer that the broker will be working with the buyer as a seller's agent or subagent.* ***There are no other options under the Commission's rule!***
Even if a prospective buyer contacts a listing agent directly about one of the broker's listings, the listing agent must promptly disclose that she or he represents the seller prior to showing the prop-

erty. The listing broker should not assume that the prospective buyer knows the listing broker is the seller's agent.

Open Houses. The open house scenario creates a more difficult situation for the listing agent. Obviously, not every person who comes to see the property is a serious prospect, but some will be. The disclosure rule does not require the listing agent to disclose his or her status as a seller's agent to everyone who walks into an open house. However, once a person shows any genuine interest in possibly purchasing the property (or any other property), the listing broker must provide and review the *Working with Real Estate Agents* brochure, explain the prospect's options for agency representation, and either create a buyer-agency/dual agency relationship or provide the prospect with a written seller agency/subagency disclosure notice. This must be done before the broker obtains any confidential information from the person, particularly information about the individual's financial situation or their ability to purchase a property.

Telephone or Other Electronic Contacts. Frequently, the initial contact with a prospective buyer will be by telephone. As a rule, brokers should keep initial telephone contacts general and *arrange to meet the consumer in person to review the company's agency policies and make any necessary disclosures.* Recognizing, however, that brokers sometimes must communicate with prospects by telephone or other electronic means because the prospect lives in another city or state and cannot meet with the broker prior to the appointment to show properties, the Commission revised its original rule to permit an initial explanation of agency options and disclosure of agency status to be made using the same electronic means (telephone, email, fax, etc.) utilized by the consumer in contacting the broker. The broker must send the *Working with Real Estate Agents* brochure to the prospect immediately, but in no event more than three days after first substantial contact.

In these situations, it is imperative that the broker fully explain the agency options described in the *Working with Real Estate Agents* brochure, determine the agency relationship with the prospect, and either create a buyer-agency relationship or properly disclose the agent's status as a seller's agent/subagent before soliciting any confidential information from the prospect concerning the prospect's housing needs or financial resources.

Disclosure by Buyer Agent to Seller/Seller's Agent

A broker acting as a buyer agent must notify the seller or seller's agent at least orally of his/her buyer-agent status upon initial contact with the seller or seller's agent. Commission Rule 58A.0104(f) reads:

> (f) In every real estate sales transaction, a broker representing a buyer shall, *at the initial contact with the seller or seller's agent,* disclose to the seller or seller's agent that the broker represents the buyer's interests. In addition, in every real estate sales transaction other than auctions, the broker shall, no later than the time of delivery of an offer to the seller or seller's agent, provide the seller or seller's agent with a written confirmation disclosing that he represents the interests of the buyer. The written confirmation may be made in the buyer's offer to purchase and shall include the broker's license number. [Emphasis added.]

"*Initial contact*" typically will occur when the buyer agent first telephones or emails the listing firm (or seller, if FSBO) to schedule an appointment. If appointments are made through a centralized showing service, rather than by contacting the seller or listing company, the broker buyer-agent's contact with the centralized showing service is *not* considered initial contact with the seller or listing company.

Because the Commission recognizes the impracticality of requiring a written disclosure of buyer agency when appointments are made to show property, the initial disclosure may be oral. This oral disclosure should be given prior to any discussion with any agent of the listing firm about the property or the parties. If a buyer agent for some reason has contact directly with an owner, s/he must immediately disclose her or his status as a buyer's agent to the owner. The buyer agent must confirm the oral disclosure *in writing no later than the time of delivery of an offer*. Standard Form 2-T, "Offer to Purchase and Contract," has a place below the signature lines for each broker to confirm agency status both to the principals (seller and buyer) and to each other.

Disclosure of and Consent to Dual Agency

If offered by their company, brokers must also discuss dual agency while reviewing the *Working with Real Estate Agents* brochure at first substantial contact with a consumer and determine whether the prospective seller or buyer will authorize the broker/firm to function as a dual agent if the situation arises.

Listing Agents. As will be discussed in Chapter 9, Commission rules require listing agreements to be in writing from the inception of the owner-broker relationship; thus, the listing broker should review dual agency with the seller and either obtain the seller's written consent in the listing agreement for the firm to practice dual agency or note in the agreement that the seller does not authorize the listing firm to act as a dual agent when selling the owner's property.

Buyer's Agents. Buyer agents must review dual agency with a prospective buyer when reviewing agency options. If a buyer agent initially works with a buyer under an express oral buyer-agency agreement, the parties nonetheless should clearly understand whether the buyer will permit dual agency if the situation arises. Absent express oral consent by the buyer to dual agency, the buyer agent could only show that buyer-client properties listed with other companies but could not show properties listed with the buyer-agent's company. All oral agreements, whether authorizing buyer-agency and/or dual agency, must be reduced to writing no later than the time an offer is presented, as will be discussed in Chapter 9.

Endnotes

1. *Brown v. Roth*, 133 N.C. App. 52, 514 S.E.2d 294 (1999), quoting Corpus Juris Secundum *Brokers* §53, at 160 (1980).

2. *Prall v. Corum*, 403 So.2d 991 (1991). While this is not a North Carolina decision, the enunciated principles apply equally to this State.

3. *Starling v. Sproles*, 66 N.C. App. 653, 311 S.E.2d 688 (1984).

4. N.C. Gen. Stat. §§39-50 and 42-14.2.

5. *Gelfand v. Horizon Corp.*, 675 F.2d 1108 (Tenth Cir. 1982).

6. *Brown v. Roth, supra.*

7. The Real Estate License Law sections and Commission rules that govern this subject are: N.C. Gen. Stat. §93A-6(a)(7), (12), and (14); N.C. Gen. Stat. §93A-6(d) and (g); Rules 21 NCAC 58A.0108, A.0116, A.0117 and B.0501 (timeshare trust funds). In addition, the North Carolina Tenant Security Deposit Act, N.C. Gen. Stat. §42-50 *et. seq.*, applies to all lessors of residential rental property located in North Carolina.

8. *Hardy v. Davis*, 223 Md. 229, 164 A.2d 281 (1960); *Olson v. Brickles*, 203 Va. 447, 124 S.E.2d 895.

9. 21 NCAC 58A.0109.

10. SL2014-120 (9/18/2014); N.C. Gen. Stat. §47E-4.1; 21 NCAC 58A.0119.

11. 21 NCAC 58A.0114 and 58A.0119.

12. N.C. Gen. Stat. §93A-6(a)(11) and §84-2.1.

13. Pancak, Miceli and Sirmans, *Legal Duties of Property Owners Under Lead-Based Paint Laws*, 24 Real Estate Law Journal 7 (Summer 1995).

14. See 42 U.S.C. §485d(A)(2) of the Act, which reads as follows:
    (2) Contract for purchase and sale
    Regulations promulgated under this section shall provide every contract for the purchase and sale of any interest in target housing shall contain a Lead Warning Statement and a statement signed by the purchaser that the purchaser has - A. read the Lead Warning Statement and understands its contents; B. received a lead hazard information pamphlet; and C. had a 10-day opportunity (unless the parties mutually agreed upon a different period of time) before becoming obligated under the contract to purchase the housing to conduct a risk assessment or inspection for the presence of lead-based paint hazards.

15. N.C. Gen. Stat. §75-1.1 and §75-16.

STATE OF NORTH CAROLINA
RESIDENTIAL PROPERTY AND OWNERS' ASSOCIATION DISCLOSURE STATEMENT

Instructions to Property Owners

1. The Residential Property Disclosure Act (G.S. 47E) ("Disclosure Act") requires owners of residential real estate (single-family homes, individual condominiums, townhouses, and the like, and buildings with up to four dwelling units) to furnish purchasers a Residential Property and Owners' Association Disclosure Statement ("Disclosure Statement"). This form is the only one approved for this purpose. A disclosure statement must be furnished in connection with the sale, exchange, option, and sale under a lease with option to purchase where the tenant does not occupy or intend to occupy the dwelling. A disclosure statement is not required for some transactions, including the first sale of a dwelling which has never been inhabited and transactions of residential property made pursuant to a lease with option to purchase where the lessee occupies or intends to occupy the dwelling. For a complete list of exemptions, see G.S. 47E-2.

2. You must respond to each of the questions on the following pages of this form by filling in the requested information or by placing a check (√) in the appropriate box. In responding to the questions, you are only obligated to disclose information about which you have actual knowledge.

    a. If you check "Yes" for any question, you must explain your answer and either describe any problem or attach a report from an attorney, engineer, contractor, pest control operator or other expert or public agency describing it. If you attach a report, you will not be liable for any inaccurate or incomplete information contained in it so long as you were not grossly negligent in obtaining or transmitting the information.

    b. If you check "No," you are stating that you have no actual knowledge of any problem. If you check "No" and you know there is a problem, you may be liable for making an intentional misstatement.

    c. If you check "No Representation," you are choosing not to disclose the conditions or characteristics of the property, even if you have actual knowledge of them or should have known of them.

    d. If you check "Yes" or "No" and something happens to the property to make your Disclosure Statement incorrect or inaccurate (for example, the roof begins to leak), you must promptly give the purchaser a corrected Disclosure Statement or correct the problem.

3. If you are assisted in the sale of your property by a licensed real estate broker, you are still responsible for completing and delivering the Disclosure Statement to the purchasers; and the broker must disclose any material facts about your property which he or she knows or reasonably should know, regardless of your responses on the Disclosure Statement.

4. You must give the completed Disclosure Statement to the purchaser no later than the time the purchaser makes an offer to purchase your property. If you do not, the purchaser can, under certain conditions, cancel any resulting contract (See **"Note to Purchasers"** below). You should give the purchaser a copy of the Disclosure Statement containing your signature and keep a copy signed by the purchaser for your records.

Note to Purchasers: If the owner does not give you a Residential Property and Owners' Association Disclosure Statement by the time you make your offer to purchase the property, you may under certain conditions cancel any resulting contract without penalty to you as the purchaser. To cancel the contract, you must personally deliver or mail written notice of your decision to cancel to the owner or the owner's agent within three calendar days following your receipt of the Disclosure Statement, or three calendar days following the date of the contract, whichever occurs first. However, in no event does the Disclosure Act permit you to cancel a contract after settlement of the transaction or (in the case of a sale or exchange) after you have occupied the property, whichever occurs first.

---

5. In the space below, type or print in ink the address of the property (sufficient to identify it) and your name. Then sign and date.

    Property Address: _____

    Owner'sName(s):_____

    Owner(s) acknowledge(s) having examined this Disclosure Statement before signing and that all information is true and correct as of the date signed.

    Owner Signature:_____ Date _____, _____

    Owner Signature:_____ Date _____, _____

    Purchasers acknowledge receipt of a copy of this Disclosure Statement; that they have examined it before signing; that they understand that this is not a warranty by owners or owners' agents; that it is not a substitute for any inspections they may wish to obtain; and that the representations are made by the owners and not the owners' agents or subagents. Purchasers are strongly encouraged to obtain their own inspections from a licensed home inspector or other professional. As used herein, words in the plural include the singular, as appropriate.

    Purchaser Signature:_____ Date _____, _____

    Purchaser Signature:_____ Date _____, _____

REC 4.22
REV 7/14

Figure 8-1

PropertyAddress/Description:_____

The following questions address the characteristics and condition of the property identified above about which the owner has _actual knowledge_. Where the question refers to "dwelling," it is intended to refer to the dwelling unit, or units if more than one, to be conveyed with the property. The term "dwelling unit" refers to any structure intended for human habitation.

<u>Yes</u> <u>No</u> <u>No Representation</u>

1. In what year was the dwelling constructed? _____.
   Explain if necessary: _____ ☐

2. Is there any problem, malfunction or defect with the dwelling's foundation, slab, fireplaces/chimneys, floors, windows (including storm windows and screens), doors, ceilings, interior and exterior walls, attached garage, patio, deck or other structural components including any modifications to them?... ☐☐ ☐

3. The dwelling's exterior walls are made of what type of material? ☐ Brick Veneer ☐ Wood ☐ Stone ☐ Vinyl ☐ Synthetic Stucco ☐ Composition/Hardboard ☐ Concrete ☐ Fiber Cement ☐ Aluminum ☐ Asbestos ☐ Other _____ (Check all that apply) ☐

4. In what year was the dwelling's roof covering installed?_____ (Approximate if no records are available) Explain if necessary: _____ ☐

5. Is there any leakage or other problem with the dwelling's roof?.. ☐☐ ☐

6. Is there any water seepage, leakage, dampness or standing water in the dwelling's basement, crawl space, or slab? ☐☐ ☐

7. Is there any problem, malfunction or defect with the dwelling's electrical system (outlets, wiring, panel, switches, fixtures, generator, etc.)?... ☐☐ ☐

8. Is there any problem, malfunction or defect with the dwelling's plumbing system (pipes, fixtures, water heater, etc.)? ☐☐ ☐

9. Is there any problem, malfunction or defect with the dwelling's heating and/or air conditioning?................... ☐☐ ☐

10. What is the dwelling's heat source? ☐ Furnace ☐ Heat Pump ☐ Baseboard ☐ Other _____ _____ (Check all that apply)................. ☐
    Age of system: _____

11. What is the dwelling's cooling source? ☐ Central Forced Air ☐ Wall/Window Unit(s) ☐ Other _____ _____ (Check all that apply) .... ☐
    Age of system: _____

12. What are the dwelling's fuel sources? ☐ Electricity ☐ Natural Gas ☐ Propane ☐ Oil ☐ Other _____ _____ (Check all that apply) If the fuel source is stored in a tank, identify whether the tank is ☐ above ground or ☐ below ground, and whether the tank is ☐ leased by seller or ☐ owned by seller. (Check all that apply)... ☐

13. What is the dwelling's water supply source? ☐ City/County ☐ Community System ☐ Private Well ☐ Shared Well ☐ Other _____ (Check all that apply)... ☐

14. The dwelling's water pipes are made of what type of material? ☐ Copper ☐ Galvanized ☐ Plastic ☐ Polybutylene ☐ Other _____ (Check all that apply)... ☐

15. Is there any problem, malfunction or defect with the dwelling's water supply (including water quality, quantity, or water pressure)?... ☐☐ ☐

16. What is the dwelling's sewage disposal system? ☐ Septic Tank ☐ Septic Tank with Pump ☐ Community System ☐ Connected to City/County System ☐ City/County System available ☐ Straight pipe (wastewater does not go into a septic or other sewer system [note: use of this type of system violates state law]) ☐ Other _____ (Check all that apply)... ☐

17. If the dwelling is serviced by a septic system, do you know how many bedrooms are allowed by the septic system permit?
    If your answer is "yes," how many bedrooms are allowed? _____ ☐☐ ☐
    ☐ No records available

18. Is there any problem, malfunction or defect with the dwelling's sewer and/or septic system?.......................... ☐☐ ☐

19. Is there any problem, malfunction or defect with the dwelling's central vacuum, pool, hot tub, spa, attic fan, exhaust fan, ceiling fans, sump pump, irrigation system, TV cable wiring or satellite dish, garage door openers, gas logs, or other systems?... ☐☐ ☐

20. Is there any problem, malfunction or defect with any appliances that may be included in the conveyance (range/oven, attached microwave, hood/fan, dishwasher, disposal, etc.)?.. ☐☐ ☐

Owner Initials and Date_____ Owner Initials and Date_____

Purchaser Initials and Date_____ Purchaser Initials and Date_____

Figure 8-1

	Yes	No	No Representation

21. Is there any problem with present infestation of the dwelling, or damage from past infestation of wood destroying insects or organisms which has not been repaired?.. ☐ ☐   ☐

22. Is there any problem, malfunction or defect with the drainage, grading or soil stability of the property?.......... ☐ ☐   ☐

23. Are there any structural additions or other structural or mechanical changes to the dwelling(s) to be conveyed with the property?.. ☐ ☐   ☐

24. Is the property to be conveyed in violation of any local zoning ordinances, restrictive covenants, or other land-use restrictions, or building codes (including the failure to obtain proper permits for room additions or other changes/improvements)?.. ☐ ☐   ☐

25. Are there any hazardous or toxic substances, materials, or products (such as asbestos, formaldehyde, radon gas, methane gas, lead-based paint) which exceed government safety standards, any debris (whether buried or covered) or underground storage tanks, or any environmentally hazardous conditions (such as contaminated soil or water, or other environmental contamination) which affect the property?.. ☐ ☐   ☐

26. Is there any noise, odor, smoke, etc. from commercial, industrial, or military sources which affects the property? ☐ ☐   ☐

27. Is the property subject to any utility or other easements, shared driveways, party walls or encroachments from or on adjacent property?.. ☐ ☐   ☐

28. Is the property the subject of any lawsuits, foreclosures, bankruptcy, leases or rental agreements, judgments, tax liens, proposed assessments, mechanics' liens, materialmens' liens, or notices from any governmental agency that could affect title to the property?... ☐ ☐   ☐

29. Is the property subject to a flood hazard or is the property located in a federally-designated flood hazard area? ☐ ☐   ☐

30. Does the property abut or adjoin any private road(s) or street(s)?.. ☐ ☐   ☐

31. If there is a private road or street adjoining the property, is there in existence any owners' association or maintenance agreements dealing with the maintenance of the road or street?.. ☐ ☐   ☐

If you answered "yes" to any of the questions listed above (1-31) please explain (attach additional sheets if necessary):

_____

_____

_____

In lieu of providing a written explanation, you may attach a written report to this Disclosure Statement by a public agency, or by an attorney, engineer, land surveyor, geologist, pest control operator, contractor, home inspector, or other expert, dealing with matters within the scope of that public agency's functions or the expert's license or expertise.

The following questions pertain to the property identified above, including the lot to be conveyed and any dwelling unit(s), sheds, detached garages, or other buildings located thereon.

	Yes	No	No Representation

32. To your knowledge, is the property subject to regulation by one or more owners' association(s) or governing documents which impose various mandatory covenants, conditions, and restrictions upon the lot, including, but not limited to obligations to pay regular assessments or dues and special assessments? If your answer is "yes," please provide the information requested below as to each owners' association to which the property is subject [insert N/A into any blank that does not apply]: ☐ ☐   ☐

•(specify name)_____ whose regular assessments ("dues") are $_____ per _____. The name, address, and telephone number of the president of the owners' association or the association manager are_____

_____

_____

_____.

•(specify name)_____ whose regular assessments ("dues") are $_____ per _____. The name, address, and telephone number of the president of the owners' association or the association manager are_____

_____

_____

_____.

* If you answered "Yes" to question 32 above, you must complete the remainder of this Disclosure Statement. If you answered "No" or "No Representation" to question 32 above, you do not need to answer the remaining questions on this Disclosure Statement. Skip to the bottom of the last page and initial and date the page.

Owner Initials and Date_____   Owner Initials and Date_____

Purchaser Initials and Date_____   Purchaser Initials and Date_____

Figure 8-1

		Yes	No	No Representation

33. Are any fees charged by the association or by the association's management company in connection with the conveyance or transfer of the lot or property to a new owner? If your answer is "yes," please state the amount of the fees:_____   ☐ ☐   ☐

34. As of the date this Disclosure Statement is signed, are there any dues, fees, or special assessments which have been duly approved as required by the applicable declaration or bylaws, and that are payable to an association to which the lot is subject? If your answer is "yes," please state the nature and amount of the dues, fees, or special assessments to which the property is subject: _____   ☐ ☐   ☐

35. As of the date this Disclosure Statement is signed, are there any unsatisfied judgments against, or pending lawsuits *involving the property or lot to be conveyed*? If your answer is "yes," please state the nature of each pending lawsuit, and the amount of each unsatisfied judgment:_____   ☐ ☐   ☐

36. As of the date this Disclosure Statement is signed, are there any unsatisfied judgments against, or pending lawsuits *involving the planned community or the association to which the property and lot are subject*, with the exception of any action filed by the association for the collection of delinquent assessments on lots other than the property and lot to be conveyed? If your answer is "yes," please state the nature of each pending lawsuit, and the amount of each unsatisfied judgment:_____   ☐ ☐   ☐

37. Which of the following services and amenities are paid for by the owners' association(s) identified above out of the association's regular assessments ("dues")? (Check all that apply).

	Yes	No	No Representation
Management Fees..	☐	☐	☐
Exterior Building Maintenance of Property to be Conveyed.................	☐	☐	☐
Exterior Yard/Landscaping Maintenance of Lot to be Conveyed..........	☐	☐	☐
Common Areas Maintenance...	☐	☐	☐
Trash Removal...	☐	☐	☐
Recreational Amenity Maintenance (specify amenities covered)_____ _____	☐	☐	☐
Pest Treatment/Extermination..	☐	☐	☐
Street Lights..	☐	☐	☐
Water...	☐	☐	☐
Sewer...	☐	☐	☐
Storm water Management/Drainage/Ponds...	☐	☐	☐
Internet Service...	☐	☐	☐
Cable..	☐	☐	☐
Private Road Maintenance...	☐	☐	☐
Parking Area Maintenance...	☐	☐	☐
Gate and/or Security...	☐	☐	☐

Other: (specify) _____

Owner Initials and Date_____   Owner Initials and Date_____
Purchaser Initials and Date_____   Purchaser Initials and Date_____

Figure 8-1

STATE OF NORTH CAROLINA
MINERAL AND OIL AND GAS RIGHTS MANDATORY DISCLOSURE STATEMENT

Instructions to Property Owners

1. The Residential Property Disclosure Act (G.S. 47E) ("Disclosure Act") requires owners of certain residential real estate such as single-family homes, individual condominiums, townhouses, and the like, and buildings with up to four dwelling units, to furnish purchasers a Mineral and Oil and Gas Rights Disclosure Statement ("Disclosure Statement"). This form is the only one approved for this purpose.

2. A disclosure statement is not required for some transactions. For a complete list of exemptions, see G.S. 47E-2(a). **A DISCLOSURE STATEMENT IS REQUIRED FOR THE TRANSFERS IDENTIFIED IN G.S. 47E-2(b),** including transfers involving the first sale of a dwelling never inhabited, lease with option to purchase contracts where the lessee occupies or intends to occupy the dwelling, and transfers between parties when both parties agree not to provide the Residential Property and Owner's Association Disclosure Statement.

3. You must respond to each of the following by placing a check √ in the appropriate box.

MINERAL AND OIL AND GAS RIGHTS DISCLOSURE

Mineral rights and/or oil and gas rights can be severed from the title to real property by conveyance (deed) of the mineral rights and/or oil and gas rights from the owner or by reservation of the mineral rights and/or oil and gas rights by the owner. If mineral rights and/or oil and gas rights are or will be severed from the property, the owner of those rights may have the perpetual right to drill, mine, explore, and remove any of the subsurface mineral and/or oil or gas resources on or from the property either directly from the surface of the property or from a nearby location. With regard to the severance of mineral rights and/or oil and gas rights, Seller makes the following disclosures:

		Yes	No	No Representation
_____ Buyer Initials	1. Mineral rights were severed from the property by a previous owner.	☐	☐	☐
_____ Buyer Initials	2. Seller has severed the mineral rights from the property.	☐	☐	
_____ Buyer Initials	3. Seller intends to sever the mineral rights from the property prior to transfer of title to the Buyer.	☐	☐	
_____ Buyer Initials	4. Oil and gas rights were severed from the property by a previous owner.	☐	☐	☐
_____ Buyer Initials	5. Seller has severed the oil and gas rights from the property.	☐	☐	
_____ Buyer Initials	6. Seller intends to sever the oil and gas rights from the property prior to transfer of title to Buyer.	☐	☐	

Note to Purchasers

If the owner does not give you a Mineral and Oil and Gas Rights Disclosure Statement by the time you make your offer to purchase the property, or exercise an option to purchase the property pursuant to a lease with an option to purchase, you may under certain conditions cancel any resulting contract without penalty to you as the purchaser. To cancel the contract, you must personally deliver or mail written notice of your decision to cancel to the owner or the owner's agent within three calendar days following your receipt of this Disclosure Statement, or three calendar days following the date of the contract, whichever occurs first. However, in no event does the Disclosure Act permit you to cancel a contract after settlement of the transaction or (in the case of a sale or exchange) after you have occupied the property, whichever occurs first.

Property Address: _____

Owner's Name(s):_____

Owner(s) acknowledge having examined this Disclosure Statement before signing and that all information is true and correct as of the date signed.

Owner Signature:_____ Date _____, ____

Owner Signature:_____ Date _____, ____

Purchaser(s) acknowledge receipt of a copy of this Disclosure Statement; that they have examined it before signing; that they understand that this is not a warranty by owner or owner's agent; and that the representations are made by the owner and not the owner's agent(s) or subagent(s).

Purchaser Signature:_____ Date _____, ____

Purchaser Signature:_____ Date _____, ____

REC 4.25
1/1/15

Figure 8-2

Disclosure of Information on Lead-Based Paint and/or Lead-Based Paint Hazards

Lead Warning Statement

Every purchaser of any interest in residential real property on which a residential dwelling was built prior to 1978 is notified that such property may present exposure to lead from lead-based paint that may place young children at risk of developing lead poisoning. Lead poisoning in young children may produce permanent neurological damage, including learning disabilities, reduced intelligence quotient, behavioral problems, and impaired memory. Lead poisoning also poses a particular risk to pregnant women. The seller of any interest in residential real property is required to provide the buyer with any information on lead-based paint hazards from risk assessments or inspections in the seller's possession and notify the buyer of any known lead-based paint hazards. A risk assessment or inspection for possible lead-based paint hazards is recommended prior to purchase.

Seller's Disclosure

(a) Presence of lead-based paint and/or lead-based paint hazards (check (i) or (ii) below):

    (i) _____ Known lead-based paint and/or lead-based paint hazards are present in the housing (explain).

    _____

    (ii) _____ Seller has no knowledge of lead-based paint and/or lead-based paint hazards in the housing.

(b) Records and reports available to the seller (check (i) or (ii) below):

    (i) _____ Seller has provided the purchaser with all available records and reports pertaining to lead-based paint and/or lead-based paint hazards in the housing (list documents below).

    _____

    (ii) _____ Seller has no reports or records pertaining to lead-based paint and/or lead-based paint hazards in the housing.

Purchaser's Acknowledgment (initial)

(c) _____ Purchaser has received copies of all information listed above.

(d) _____ Purchaser has received the pamphlet *Protect Your Family from Lead in Your Home.*

(e) Purchaser has (check (i) or (ii) below):

    (i) _____ received a 10-day opportunity (or mutually agreed upon period) to conduct a risk assessment or inspection for the presence of lead-based paint and/or lead-based paint hazards; or

    (ii) _____ waived the opportunity to conduct a risk assessment or inspection for the presence of lead-based paint and/or lead-based paint hazards.

Agent's Acknowledgment (initial)

(f) _____ Agent has informed the seller of the seller's obligations under 42 U.S.C. 4852d and is aware of his/her responsibility to ensure compliance.

Certification of Accuracy

The following parties have reviewed the information above and certify, to the best of their knowledge, that the information they have provided is true and accurate.

Seller	Date	Seller	Date
Purchaser	Date	Purchaser	Date
Agent	Date	Agent	Date

Figure 8-3

Disclosure of Information on Lead-Based Paint and/or Lead-Based Paint Hazards

Lead Warning Statement

Housing built before 1978 may contain lead-based paint. Lead from paint, paint chips, and dust can pose health hazards if not managed properly. Lead exposure is especially harmful to young children and pregnant women. Before renting pre-1978 housing, lessors must disclose the presence of known lead-based paint and/or lead-based paint hazards in the dwelling. Lessees must also receive a federally approved pamphlet on lead poisoning prevention.

Lessor's Disclosure

(a) Presence of lead-based paint and/or lead-based paint hazards (check (i) or (ii) below):

 (i) _____ Known lead-based paint and/or lead-based paint hazards are present in the housing (explain).

 _____

 _____

 (ii) _____ Lessor has no knowledge of lead-based paint and/or lead-based paint hazards in the housing.

(b) Records and reports available to the lessor (check (i) or (ii) below):

 (i) _____ Lessor has provided the lessee with all available records and reports pertaining to lead-based paint and/or lead-based paint hazards in the housing (list documents below).

 _____

 _____

 (ii) _____ Lessor has no reports or records pertaining to lead-based paint and/or lead-based paint hazards in the housing.

Lessee's Acknowledgment (initial)

(c) _____ Lessee has received copies of all information listed above.

(d) _____ Lessee has received the pamphlet *Protect Your Family from Lead in Your Home.*

Agent's Acknowledgment (initial)

(e) _____ Agent has informed the lessor of the lessor's obligations under 42 U.S.C. 4852d and is aware of his/her responsibility to ensure compliance.

Certification of Accuracy

The following parties have reviewed the information above and certify, to the best of their knowledge, that the information they have provided is true and accurate.

Lessor	Date	Lessor	Date
Lessee	Date	Lessee	Date
Agent	Date	Agent	Date

Figure 8-4

9 | AGENCY CONTRACTS AND BROKERAGE PRACTICES

INTRODUCTION

Whenever a consumer wants to hire a real estate broker either to sell or lease property, or assist in buying or leasing a property, this brokerage relationship must be established by a real estate **agency contract**. *An agency contract creates an agency relationship between the parties and describes the terms of the agent's (broker's) employment by the principal (property owner or prospective buyer or tenant).* There are five basic types of agency contracts used in contemporary real estate transactions.

Types of Real Estate Agency Contracts

Listing Contract. When a property owner employs a real estate broker or firm to obtain a buyer for his or her property, the property owner does so by entering into a listing contract with the broker or firm.

Buyer Agency Contract. When a prospective buyer employs a real estate broker or firm to represent the buyer in finding an acceptable property to purchase, a buyer agency contract is used.

Contract to Procure Tenant. When a property owner wants to enlist the assistance of a real estate broker or firm only to locate an acceptable tenant, but not to perform any ongoing service after procuring a tenant, a contract to procure tenant may be utilized.

Property Management Contract. When a property owner wants to enlist the assistance of a real estate broker or firm to locate an acceptable tenant AND also to perform ongoing services connected with the operation of the rental property, he or she does so by entering into a property management contract.

Tenant Representation Contract. When a prospective tenant wants to employ a real estate broker to assist in locating a suitable property to lease or rent, a tenant representation contract is used. This type of agreement is used primarily in commercial real estate brokerage and is rarely encountered in residential leasing.

As discussed in Chapter 8, it also is possible for a broker or firm to concurrently represent two parties with adverse interests in the same real estate transaction – i.e., act as a **dual agent.** The authority for such "dual agency" must be granted by both parties *in writing*. This is most frequently accomplished by including dual agency authority language in the basic agency contracts described above, but it may also be accomplished by utilizing a separate **dual agency contract**.

This chapter will address the agency contracts commonly used in **residential sales.** **Agency contracts in general** are addressed first, then **listing contracts.** **Buyer agency contracts** are addressed in the section on "Working with Buyers." Property management contracts are covered in Chapter 17.

This chapter also addresses many common brokerage practices, including the various services expected of a conscientious agent when working with sellers and buyers up to the point when a sales contract is formed. These practices are presented and discussed in "transaction sequence" – that is, the order in which they are performed in a typical transaction. Details relating to some of these practices may be addressed in other parts of this *Manual* and where that is the case, the reader is referred to the appropriate discussion of the matter in question.

AGENCY CONTRACTS AND BROKER COMPENSATION

This section focuses on the general requirements for all types of real estate agency contracts and the legal requirements for a real estate broker to be entitled to compensation in a sales transaction. *Before entering into an agency agreement with a prospective client, a broker should ask the prospective client whether he or she already has an agency agreement with another broker.* **If the prospective client says "Yes," then the broker should delay entering into an agency agreement with the prospective client until the existing agency agreement expires or the prospective client provides written evidence indicating that the existing agency agreement has been terminated.**

GENERAL REQUIREMENTS FOR AGENCY CONTRACTS

An agency contract must satisfy the minimum requirements for formation of any enforceable contract as described in Chapter 10 on Basic Contract Law. Additionally, several other requirements for agency contracts in any brokerage transaction are prescribed by Real Estate Commission rules. **Commission Rule 21 NCAC 58A.0104(a) and (b)** read as follows:

(a) Every agreement for brokerage services in a real estate transaction and every agreement for services connected with the management of a property owners association shall be in writing and signed by the parties thereto. Every agreement for brokerage services between a broker and an owner of the property to be the subject of a transaction shall be in writing and signed by the parties at the time of its formation. Every agreement for brokerage services between a broker and a buyer or tenant shall be express and shall be in writing and signed by the parties thereto not later than the time one of the parties makes an offer to purchase, sell, rent, lease, or exchange real estate to another. However, every agreement between a broker and a buyer or tenant that seeks to bind the buyer or tenant for a period of time or to restrict the buyer's or tenant's right to work with other agents or without an agent shall be in writing and signed by the parties thereto from its formation. A broker shall not continue to represent a buyer or tenant without a written, signed agreement when such agreement is required by this Rule. Every written agreement for brokerage services of any kind in a real estate transaction shall be for a definite period of time, shall include the broker's license number, and shall provide for its termination without prior notice at the expiration of that period, except that an agency agreement between a landlord and broker to procure tenants or receive rents for the landlord's property may allow for automatic renewal so long as the landlord may terminate with notice at the end of any contract period and any subsequent renewals. Every written agreement for brokerage services that includes a penalty for early termination shall set forth such a provision in clear and conspicuous manner that shall distinguish it from other provisions of the agreement. For the purposes of this Rule, an agreement between brokers to cooperate or share compensation shall not be considered an agreement for brokerage services and, except as required by Rule .1807 of this Subchapter, need not be memorialized in writing.

(b) Every listing agreement, written buyer agency agreement, or other written agreement for brokerage services in a real estate sales transaction shall contain the following provision: "The broker shall conduct all brokerage activities in regard to this agreement without respect to the race, color, religion, sex, national origin, handicap or familial status of any party or prospective party." The provision shall be set forth in a clear and conspicuous manner that shall distinguish it from other provisions of the agreement. For the purposes of this Rule, the term "familial status" shall be defined as it is in G.S. 41A-3(1b).

Requirement for Written Agency Agreement

In 1995, the use of written agency contracts became mandatory, rather than voluntary, with the amendment of Commission Rule 58A.0104 that required written agency agreements in all **sales** transactions. Since September 1, 2002, ***written agency agreements have been required by Commission rule in ALL real estate transactions***. This regulatory mandate gained statutory support with the enactment of General Statute 93A-13, captioned "Contracts for broker services," *effective October 1, 2011*. It states:

> No action between a broker and the broker's client for recovery under an agreement for broker services is valid unless the contract is reduced to writing and signed by the party to be charged or by some other person lawfully authorized by the party to sign.

Thus, it is now a settled point of law that *a broker may only collect a brokerage fee from a consumer if there is a written agreement for brokerage services between the broker and the consumer providing for such fee.*

Point in Time an Agency Agreement Must Be in Writing

Under the Commission's agency rule, there are different points in time by which various agency agreements must be reduced to writing, as noted below.

Agency Agreements with Property Owners. Rule A.0104(a) requires the agency agreement to be *in writing from the inception of the relationship whenever a broker represents a **property owner** in any capacity*, whether in a sales or lease situation. Thus, *all **listing contracts** and **property management contracts** must be in writing from the outset of the agency relationship.*

Agency Agreements with Buyers or Tenants. Commission Rule A.0104(a) allows a **limited exception** to the general written agency agreement requirement by permitting a *temporary* ORAL **buyer or tenant agency agreement** provided that:

1. the oral agreement must be "express" (meaning there must be a clear understanding of the oral agreement's terms);
2. the oral agreement must be "nonexclusive" (meaning it may not restrict the buyer's or tenant's right to work with other agents or without an agent);
3. the oral agreement must be "open-ended" and must not obligate the buyer or tenant to the broker for any period of time (i.e. buyer or tenant may terminate the oral agreement at any time); and
4. *any oral buyer agency agreement must be* **reduced to writing not later than the time any party** *in the transaction* **seeks to extend any offer** *to any other party.*

If the oral buyer or tenant agency agreement attempts to be "exclusive" (i.e., restrict the buyer's/tenant's right to work with other agents or independently) or attempts to bind the buyer/tenant to the broker for any period of time, then the agreement must be in writing from the inception of the restricted relationship. Additional comments relating to this exception and how it may be utilized properly are included later in this chapter under "Working With Buyers."

Other Requirements for Agency Agreements

Understand that the parties, namely, the consumer and the broker, may agree on whatever terms and services they wish in the agency agreement. The Commission's rule does not dictate the content of any agency agreement, other than to require the following components.

1. **Signed by parties**. Agency contracts must be signed by the parties and must include the broker's license number.
2. **Fixed termination date.** Agency contracts must be for a definite period of time and must terminate without prior notice at the expiration of that period. LIMITED EXCEPTION: Agreements to procure tenants or property management agreements may contain automatic renewal provisions *so long as* the owner may terminate with notice at the end of any contract period and any subsequent renewals.
3. **Nondiscrimination clause.** Agency contracts must contain the specific nondiscrimination language required by the rule and that language must appear in a clear and conspicuous manner.

EARNING A REAL ESTATE SALES COMMISSION

A real estate broker earns a brokerage fee (sales commission or flat fee) in a sales transaction when he or she accomplishes what the agency contract (listing contract or buyer agency contract) between the broker and the principal (seller or buyer) calls for as performance by the broker. The traditional rules regarding a broker's right to a brokerage fee developed over the many years that "seller agency" was used almost exclusively in the real estate industry as the preferred method of agency practice. Under the traditional seller agency system, a broker's right to a brokerage fee was based on the terms of the **listing contract**. Consequently, the primary body of law governing a broker's right to a brokerage fee is based on the application of contract law to listing contracts, and most of this section deals with the right of a **listing broker** to a brokerage fee pursuant to the listing contract. *A later section will discuss a broker's entitlement to a brokerage fee when acting as a* **buyer's agent**.

Earning a Brokerage Fee as a Listing Broker

An agent is entitled to receive a fee when the agent has performed the services required under the terms of the agency agreement with the principal. In the context of a listing agreement, to earn the fee a listing broker must:

- have a current North Carolina real estate license on active status; and
- have a valid *written* listing contract with the seller-principal; and
- procure a purchaser who is "ready, willing and able" to buy the listed property on the terms stipulated in the listing contract (unless the listing contract provides for a different standard).

If the individual listing broker is an affiliated broker with a real estate **firm**, then the agency agreement is between the firm and the consumer; accordingly, both the real estate *firm's license as well as the individual broker's license must be on active status at all times during the period that services are being provided.* If the firm continues to provide services after its license expires or becomes inactive, then neither the firm nor any of its affiliated agents may be paid. Similarly, if the firm allows an affiliated broker whose license is expired or inactive to perform the contracted brokerage services, then both the individual broker and the firm may forfeit any fee because the broker was not eligible to engage in brokerage services without an active license.

Under a typical listing agreement, the broker (or firm) becomes entitled to a brokerage fee when the broker procures a prospective purchaser who is **"ready, willing and able"** to purchase on the terms stipulated in the listing contract or upon such other terms as the owner may accept.[1] Under established contract law governing real estate listing contracts, it usually is **not** essential that the seller accept the buyer's offer or actually enter into a contract of sale, or that the sale close. The broker's entitlement to compensation also is not affected because the seller voluntarily fails to comply with an agreement to sell or is unable to convey a good title.

Any broker negotiating for a listing with an owner should ensure that the owner understands the meaning of this ready, willing and able provision. If the owner desires to pay a brokerage fee only if there is an actual consummation of the sale, and the broker agrees, the particular listing agreement should be modified to state in clear and unambiguous language the exact conditions on which the fee is earned and due. Where the listing contract does not clearly define when a brokerage fee shall be payable, then the broker has done all that the law has required under the contract when he or she produces to the owner-principal a buyer ready, willing and able to purchase on the exact terms specified by the owner in the listing contract.

The Meaning of "Ready, Willing and Able"

The term *"ready, willing and able," means that the prospective buyer desires to buy, is willing to enter into an enforceable contract to purchase the property involved, and has the financial and legal capacity to buy on the terms specified by the owner-principal within the time required.*

"Ready and Willing." The purchaser generally indicates that he or she is **"ready and willing"** by submitting a valid offer to purchase. If a buyer legally withdraws from a transaction in accordance with the contract's provisions, the buyer was not "ready and willing" to proceed with the purchase and the listing broker did not satisfy the "ready, willing and able" standard.

Other conditions in sales contracts commonly impact the issue of whether a buyer is *"ready and willing"* to complete a transaction. Take, for example, an **"option to terminate" provision in a sales contract** that permits the buyer to terminate the contract by some stated date prior to closing at the option of the buyer. The current version of the standard "Offer to Purchase and Contract" form provided by the North Carolina Bar Association and the North Carolina Association of REALTORS® allows the buyer a "due diligence period" to investigate the property and gives the buyer the right to terminate the contract for any reason or no reason during that period. This is an "option to terminate" provision and a buyer under such contract is not "ready and willing" until the due diligence period has passed without the option to terminate being exercised by the buyer.

Another common sales contract contingency provision is one conditioning the buyer's purchase on the buyer being able to close the sale of property currently owned by the buyer by a specified date, commonly referred to as a **"contingent sale provision."** If the buyer is not able to satisfy this condition in a timely manner, and does not waive the condition, the buyer is not "ready and willing" to consummate the purchase and the listing broker would not be entitled to a commission. The buyer only becomes "ready and willing" upon either completing the sale of the buyer's property by the specified date or waiving the condition.

"Able." A buyer procured by a real estate listing broker (or by a cooperating broker) also must be **"able"** to complete the transaction. From a financial perspective, this means that *the buyer must be able to marshal the funds necessary to close the transaction*. It is not necessary that the buyer have the cash in hand to complete the purchase. It is sufficient that the buyer can definitely produce the necessary funds at the scheduled closing. A buyer who has sufficient funds to make the prescribed down payment and pay the closing expenses, and who has obtained **loan approval** from a lender for a mortgage loan in an amount sufficient to pay the balance of the purchase price is financially "able" to complete the transaction.

The current version of the NCBA/NCAR standard Offer to Purchase and Contract form advises the buyer to pursue and obtain loan approval during the "due diligence period" as obtaining any requisite financing no longer is a condition of the purchase contract that will excuse the buyer's performance. However, even if a buyer does not terminate the contract prior to the expiration of the "due diligence period," that buyer still most likely will not be considered "able" to complete the transaction until he or she has obtained final loan approval. This means the listing broker/firm will not have earned its brokerage fee until the buyer obtains final loan approval. [Note: Under the current sales contract form, a buyer who allows the due diligence period to expire and who is not able to obtain loan approval, even after a diligent effort to do so, is not relieved of his or her obligation to honor the contract and will be in breach if he or she fails to complete the purchase.]

Understand as well that the *"able"* standard also applies to a **buyer's legal capacity**. Although such problems are relatively rare, if a buyer under a sales contract is found to lack the legal capacity to enter into an enforceable contract (for example, a buyer who is legally insane or is a minor), then the buyer is not considered "able" to complete the transaction and no fee is earned by the listing broker/firm.

When the Transaction Does Not Close

When the broker produces a buyer ready, willing and able to buy under the terms specified in the listing contract, the broker remains entitled to a brokerage fee even if the transaction fails because:

(a) the seller's spouse will not sign the contract or deed.

(b) the seller has a defect in title.

(c) the seller will be unable to deliver possession within a reasonable time.

(d) the seller insists on sale terms and conditions not stated in the listing contract.

(e) the buyer and seller get together after the contract has been signed and agree to cancel the contract.

In other words, the broker does not, in the absence of a special provision to the contrary in the listing contract, insure that a particular transaction will actually close as a condition precedent to his or her entitlement to a brokerage fee. So long as the "ready, willing and able" standard is specified in the listing contract, the broker is entitled to receive the brokerage fee simply upon producing a buyer ready, willing and able to purchase the property from the seller under the terms of the listing.

The "Procuring Cause" Doctrine

In addition to finding a *"ready, willing and able"* buyer, a real estate broker who has been employed by an owner to procure a purchaser for the owner's property as a general rule must be able to show that his or her efforts have been the **"procuring cause"** of the sale of the property.

The term *"procuring cause,"* as used in describing a broker's activity entitling him or her to a brokerage fee, refers to: *a cause originating a series of events that, without break in their continuity, result in the accomplishment of the prime objective for which the broker was employed, usually to procure a purchaser ready, willing and able to buy the property on the owner's terms.*[2] In order for a broker's efforts to be considered the procuring or effective or proximate cause of a sale, it must be established that the broker's activity was the originating cause that not only started negotiations for the transaction, but also ultimately resulted in its consummation; *the broker's activity must be the primary foundation upon which the negotiations were begun and the predominant factor in bringing about the transaction.* The procuring cause agent may not necessarily be the first broker who shows a property to a buyer, but rather the broker who assists the buyer in assessing the property and writing an offer for the buyer that becomes a contract leading to the sale of a property who can claim to be the procuring cause of the sale.

The Real Estate Commission does not have the authority to decide procuring cause disputes between brokers and their clients or between competing brokers. Such disputes must be resolved in a court of competent jurisdiction. Some boards of Realtors have arbitration committees for settling procuring cause disputes between competing brokers.

Type of Listing Contract. *The type of listing agreement is paramount when considering the issue of procuring cause* and its terms will govern the compensation issue because it is the contract between the seller and listing broker.

- **Open Listing:** In an *open listing agreement* the property owner basically is offering to compensate the broker who produces a purchaser. Because the property is placed for sale in the hands of a number of brokers, it becomes material to determine which broker is the procuring cause of a sale of the property.

- **Exclusive Agency:** An *exclusive agency* listing agreement grants a named broker (individual or firm) the exclusive or sole right to advertise and attempt to sell the property, but still permits the owner to sell the property through his or her own efforts without paying a brokerage fee to the broker. In such case it is essential to determine whether the broker or the owner is the procuring cause to determine whether a brokerage fee must be paid to the broker. Under an *exclusive agency* listing contract, the broker *will be* entitled to compensation from his principal if the principal, during the term of the listing contract, hires another broker who succeeds in selling the property. This is true even though the first broker was not the procuring cause because the seller-principal breached the agency contract that imposed a duty upon the owner to refrain from hiring other brokers.

- **Exclusive Right to Sell:** If the listing contract gives the broker the *exclusive right to sell,* the broker will be entitled to compensation no matter who sells the property.

Effect of a "Protection Period" Clause. Another frequent occurrence with respect to procuring cause is where a listing contract is for a definite time and the broker starts negotiating with a prospective purchaser but is unable to persuade the prospect to buy before the listing expires. Then, after the listing terminates, the owner sells the property directly to the prospect initially produced by the broker, reducing the purchase price because the seller thinks that a broker's commission will not be due. Since the listing has expired, the broker ordinarily would not be entitled to a brokerage fee, despite the fact that the broker was the procuring cause of the sale as result of the broker's efforts to negotiate a sale. To avoid this result, *most brokers now include in their listing contracts a "protection period" provision stating that a brokerage fee will be earned and due on any sales made within a certain period of time after the date of expiration of the listing when such sales are made directly by the seller to prospects with whom the broker has negotiated or who have been introduced to the seller by the broker before the listing expiration date.* Such provisions are discussed further in the "Major Listing Contract Provisions" section later in this chapter.

Splitting the Brokerage Fee of the Listing Broker/Firm

An independent broker who works alone and who both lists and sells a property for a seller-principal gets to retain the entire brokerage fee payable under the listing contract. In reality, however, most real estate brokers are associated with real estate firms having a number of affiliated licensees. Moreover, most sales transactions are "co-brokered" transactions involving brokers affiliated with different firms. Except for the unusual situation where the selling agent is a buyer's agent who will be compensated in full by the buyer, all firms and individual brokers involved in a transaction normally are compensated by splitting the brokerage fee paid to the listing broker/firm.

Only the Listing Firm May Sue the Seller for a Brokerage Fee

Since the listing firm has the listing contract with the property owner, **only the listing firm has the contractual right to a brokerage fee** upon performance pursuant to the terms of the listing contract. The right to compensation of any individual agent or any firm cooperating with the listing firm is dependent upon their agreement with the listing firm, and does not arise from the listing contract to which only the seller and the listing firm are parties.

Thus, *an individual agent associated with the listing firm has no right independently to sue the property owner for a brokerage fee under the listing contract, even if the agent is the listing agent.* Since the listing firm is the party to the contract, it is the firm's right to sue the seller for any brokerage fee which may be due the firm under the listing agreement. This is true even if the individual agents with the listing firm are legally considered to be subagents of the seller. The subagency status of agents affiliated with a listing firm results from their *employment agreement* with the firm, rather than any agreement with the seller.

Similarly, a cooperating firm (or any of its agents) who finds a buyer has no right to receive a brokerage fee under the listing firm's listing contract, because the cooperating firm and its agents are not a party to the listing contract. Any right to a brokerage fee of a cooperating firm (and its agents) results from an agreement with the listing firm to cooperate and share the listing firm's brokerage fee, not from the listing contract itself. *Only the listing firm has "privity of contract" with the property owner under a listing contract, and only the listing firm can enforce the provisions of the listing contract.*

The "In-House" Sale

The right of an agent affiliated with a firm to receive compensation when one of the firm's listings is sold is determined by the employment agreement between the firm and the agent. A firm may have a standard fee-split policy applicable to all affiliated agents or it may have a separate compensation agreement with each agent. *Typically, when an agent "sells" (finds a buyer for) one of the firm's listings, both the selling agent and the listing agent receive a designated percentage of the total earned brokerage fee, with another designated portion going to the firm.*

The Co-brokered Sale

The right of a cooperating firm to receive compensation from the listing firm when the cooperating firm finds a buyer for one of the listing firm's listings is determined by the **cooperation and fee-sharing agreement between the two firms**. Real estate firms frequently have standing agreements with other firms in their area to cooperate and share brokerage fees. For example, brokers who participate in a local multiple or cooperative listing service agree by virtue of their membership in the listing service to cooperate and share brokerage fees. If there is no such standing agreement, then a fee-sharing agreement must be negotiated on a case-by-case basis. The listing firm can refuse to cooperate with another firm and share the brokerage fee; however, such refusal should come *before* the cooperating firm's agents are allowed to show a property. As a practical matter, a firm wanting to show a property listed with another firm would be foolish to proceed without a clear agreement to cooperate and share the listing broker's fee in the event of a sale.

*As for the right to a share of the brokerage fee of an individual "selling agent" with a cooperating firm who obtains a buyer, one must look to the **employment agreement between the firm and the agent**.* The listing firm will pay a portion of the total earned brokerage commission to the cooperating firm, and the cooperating firm typically will retain a portion for its share and pay the remainder to the individual selling agent.

Co-brokerage with a Broker Licensed in Another State

While a broker must be licensed in North Carolina to earn a brokerage fee as a listing broker on the sale of property located in North Carolina, a North Carolina listing broker may cooperate and share a brokerage fee with a selling broker from another state who is licensed in his resident state, but not in North Carolina, *so long as the nonresident broker does not physically enter North Carolina and engage in conduct which would require a North Carolina real estate license.* For example, a Virginia broker may find a prospective buyer for a North Carolina property listed by a North Carolina broker, and the North Carolina broker can split his or her brokerage fee with the Virginia broker if a sale results; however, the Virginia broker may not come into North Carolina to show the listed property, to conduct negotiations, or to perform any other service requiring a North Carolina real estate license; rather the broker must remain in and negotiate the transaction from the state where the broker is licensed, namely, Virginia. All showings and negotiations performed *in North Carolina* must be performed by a broker who has an active North Carolina license.

Earning a Brokerage Fee as a Buyer's Agent

Buyer Agent's Right to Compensation

The use of buyer agency contracts between a consumer and a broker or firm is now a common practice. Despite this, there is no developed body of North Carolina case law specifically dealing with the right of a buyer's broker to compensation in a sales transaction. Nevertheless, it is clear that the **basic requirement** for a buyer's broker to earn a fee is very similar to that for a listing broker. *A buyer's broker must have a current active real estate license, must have a valid buyer agency contract and must* *perform the service required by the contract, namely, locate a property that the buyer agrees by enforceable contract to purchase, to be entitled legally to a fee.*

In the absence of case law, the authors express the opinion that, when Standard Form 2T is used, a buyer's agent most likely will not have earned a brokerage fee until expiration of the "buyer's due diligence period" without the buyer exercising the right to terminate the sales contract. On the other hand, if the buyer breaches the contract to purchase or agrees with the seller to cancel the contract after expiration of the due diligence period, the buyer's agent may be entitled to the compensation called for in the buyer agency contract. Similarly, if the seller improperly backs out of (breaches) the sales contract through no fault or participation of the buyer or buyer's agent, it is likely the buyer's agent would legally be entitled to compensation, but the buyer agent cannot sue the seller.

Methods of Compensating Buyers' Brokers

The issue of compensating a buyer's broker is a particularly confusing aspect of buyer brokerage. There is a major difference in the **source of the brokerage fee for a buyer's broker under a buyer agency contract** as compared to the situation where the agent working with a buyer is a seller's agent or subagent. When there is no buyer's agent agreement (all agents are seller's agents), the fee for the selling agent/firm always comes, directly or indirectly, from the seller. On the other hand, with a buyer agency agreement, the fee for the buyer's agent may either come directly from the buyer-principal or be paid by the seller (through the listing firm for a listed property) or be paid by both the seller and buyer. *One must look to the specific terms of the buyer agency contract and cooperation agreement between the firms involved in the sale to ascertain how a buyer's broker will be compensated.*

The Real Estate Commission's *Working with Real Estate Agents* brochure addresses the issue of a buyer agent's compensation as follows:

> . . . A buyer's agent can be compensated in different ways. For example, you can pay the agent out of your own pocket. Or the agent may seek compensation from the seller or listing agent first, but require you to pay if the listing agent refuses. Whatever the case, be sure your compensation arrangement with your buyer's agent is spelled out in a buyer agency agreement before you make an offer to purchase property and that you carefully read and understand the compensation provision.

"Retainer Fee" Plus "Success Fee" Approach. The prevailing approach to compensating buyer's brokers is the one employed by the North Carolina Association of REALTORS® Form #201 **"Exclusive Buyer Agency Agreement" reprinted as Figure 9-2**. This is a two-pronged approach that might be referred to as a "Retainer Fee" Plus "Success Fee" Approach. Under this approach, the agency contract allows the buyer and broker to agree to a **nonrefundable "retainer fee"** of a specified amount that is paid by the buyer upon entering into the oral or written buyer agency contract and to agree whether the retainer fee will or will not be credited toward any additional compensation that the broker will receive upon satisfying the terms of the agreement (i.e., finding a suitable property for the buyer). Some brokers/firms routinely require such a retainer fee, especially with an *oral* buyer agency contract that is for an indefinite period and may be terminated by the buyer at any time.

The second prong of this approach is the **"success fee."** Form #201 provides that the buyer's broker/firm will seek compensation first from the cooperating listing firm or from the seller if there is no listing firm. The dollar amount, percentage of purchase price or other method of determining the buyer's broker/firm's compensation must be stated in the buyeer agency agreement. This form states that if the buyer purchases property where the compensation offered to the selling broker/firm by the listing firm and/or seller is less than the amount stated in the buyer agency contract, or where no compensation is offered by either the listing firm or the seller, then the buyer must pay the difference between the fee amount stated in the agency contract and the compensation offered.

There is potential conflict of interest when the buyer's agent's compensation is a percentage of the purchase price; namely, the higher the purchase price, the greater the buyer's agent's fee. Despite the possible conflict of interest, there is no evidence of any significant problem with buyer agents failing to diligently seek the lowest possible price for their buyer-principals, as required by their fiduciary responsibilities, although Form #201 has a "Note" to the buyer concerning the potential conflict.

LISTING CONTRACTS, MLS OPERATIONS AND ANTITRUST LAWS

INTRODUCTION

The most common method of entering into an real estate agency relationship is by use of a **listing contract**, which is a contract between a property owner and a real estate broker/firm whereby the broker/firm agrees to market the owner's property and produce a buyer for the property on terms agreeable to the owner in return for payment to the broker/firm for services provided in acquiring such a buyer. A listing contract expressly creates an agency relationship between the property owner and the broker/firm. When a property owner enters into a listing contract with a broker/firm to market the property, both the property and the listing contract are commonly referred to in the real estate industry as a "**listing**." This section discusses the types of listing contracts, common listing contract provisions, and multiple listing service (MLS) operations.

TYPES OF LISTING CONTRACTS

There are several types of listing contracts. Contracts between brokers/firms and their principals, like all contracts, are interpreted according to the exact provisions of their agreements. It is important to categorize the particular type of listing contract involved in a specific case to determine the respective rights of the broker and the principal. The basic types of listing contracts are summarized below and then discussed in this section.

Basic Types of Listing Contracts
- "Full Service" Listing Contracts
  - Open Listing Contract
  - Exclusive Agency Listing Contract
  - Exclusive Right to Sell Listing Contract
- "Limited Service" Listing Contracts
- Protection Agreement

"Full Service" Listing Contracts

"Full service" listing contracts are those under which a broker/firm will "list" an owner's property for sale and perform a variety of traditional services associated with selling the owner's property, including listing the property for sale in a "multiple listing service" operated by a regional group of cooperating real estate brokers, advertising the property for sale in newspapers, real estate publications, etc. and on the Internet, placing a sign on the property, providing a lock/key box to facilitate showings by various brokers, showing the property to prospective buyers, conducting open houses, presenting and reviewing offers to purchase with the owner, and advising the seller on any matter relating to the sale. The various full-service listing contracts discussed below differ less in the scope of services provided than in the terms related to the relationship between the owner-principal and listing broker/firm, especially the terms describing the broker's entitlement to compensation for finding a buyer.

Open Listing Contract

An **open listing contract** *grants a broker/firm the* **nonexclusive** *right to obtain a purchaser for the listed real property.* Open listing contracts permit the owner to personally sell the property or hire other brokers. Thus, the owner may enter into open listing contracts with as many brokers as desired **and** the owner may sell the property personally without being obligated to pay anything to any broker. Where two or more brokers are employed to obtain a buyer for a property using open listing contracts, the seller is obligated to pay a commission only to the first broker who produces a buyer ready, willing and able to purchase the property on terms acceptable to the seller. The sale of the property by any one of the brokers, or by the owner, terminates the authority of all of the other brokers immediately, regardless of whether they have actual notice of the sale. If the owner personally sells the property to a purchaser who has not been produced by any of the employed brokers, the owner is under no obligation to pay a commission to anyone.

Although open listing contracts were common many years ago, they are rarely used today, as they frequently caused controversy and litigation because problems are inherent in this type of listing. In a number of court decisions, several competing brokers operating under separate open listings from the same property owner sue for a brokerage fee with each broker claiming to have been the procuring cause of the sale. Other cases involve disputes between the owner-principal and broker concerning who actually procured the purchaser. Once upon a time, there was a benefit to owners to list with multiple brokers because there was limited cooperation and fee splitting among brokers. The modern approach to marketing properties featuring widespread cooperation among brokers has largely eliminated the need for open listings. *Note that multiple listing services do not permit open listings to be advertised in the MLS.* Before entering into this type of agreement, both property owners and brokers should keep in mind its disadvantages.

Exclusive Agency Listing Contract

An **exclusive agency listing contract** *gives to only one broker/firm the right to market and sell the owner's property, but allows the owner to personally sell the property without being obligated to the broker/firm for a brokerage fee.* The broker employed under this form of listing is the *only agent* employed by the seller and will not have to compete with other brokers for the period of time designated in the exclusive agency listing contract. Obviously, an exclusive agency is infinitely more desirable for the broker than the open listing. The broker need not fear that the investment of time and money in locating a buyer will be frustrated by another broker's prior sale, thereby avoiding the main practical shortcoming of open listing contracts. A broker with an exclusive agency listing may list the property in a multiple listing service (MLS) and cooperate with other brokers in selling the property.

It should be noted, however, that under an exclusive agency contract, the owner-principal can personally negotiate a sale of the listed real estate without incurring liability to the broker for a commission. If the principal consummates a real estate transaction through his or her own efforts, the exclusive agency of the broker automatically comes to an end and the principal has no liability to pay any brokerage fee to the broker regardless of the employment period specified in the listing contract.

Exclusive Right to Sell Listing Contract

An **exclusive right to sell listing contract** not only makes the employed broker the only agent of the principal-seller, but also gives the broker the exclusive right to sell the property during the term of the contract.[3] An exclusive right to sell contract precludes the principal-seller (the owner) from competing with the agent. *If the owner sells the property through the owner's own efforts during the term of the contract, the owner still pay a commission to the broker who has been given the exclusive right to sell.* A broker who desires the protection of an exclusive right to sell contract, as distinguished from an exclusive agency contract, should be very careful about the language used in the listing contract. Where any ambiguity exists as to whether the owner has retained the right to personally sell the property, the courts favor an interpretation protecting the owner, especially where the contract was prepared by the broker. The reader is referred to the North Carolina Association of REALTORS® Standard Form 101 "Exclusive Right to Sell Listing Agreement" shown in Figure 9-1 for an example of clear and appropriate language.

Broker Typically May Not Obligate the Seller. The title "exclusive right *to sell*" is, in part, a misnomer. Despite the name, the broker does not have the right to obligate the owner by signing a sales contract for the owner. A broker's authority to effect a sale on the owner's behalf would require a power of attorney from the owner. A North Carolina Supreme Court decision addressed a misunderstanding over the meaning of this language and concluded as follows:

> ....While the listing agreement states that the agent shall have an exclusive "right to sell" the property, such a provision does not imply authority to enter into a contract binding on the owners for the sale of the property. When used in contracts between real estate agents and owners of land, the term "to sell" is generally given the restricted meaning of power to find a purchaser, and alone is not sufficient to empower a real estate agent to enter into a contract of sale.[4]

Limited Service Listing Contract

Some brokers specialize in providing "**limited listing services**" to sellers who primarily want the benefit of MLS advertising and who are willing to show their own properties, negotiate their own sales contracts, and handle their own preparations for closing. Limited service brokers typically *offer to provide, for a fixed or "flat" fee that is less than brokerage fees under full service listing arrangements, only only certain services to a seller, such as to place a "for sale" sign on the seller's property and list the property in the MLS and perhaps on Internet sites. The seller is usually responsible for fielding inquiries, scheduling and conducting showings, negotiating a contract, and other tasks associated with selling the property.* Such brokers advertise that their approach will save the seller substantial amounts of money in brokerage fees as compared to listing with a traditional "full service" broker.

The primary target market for limited services brokers consists of homeowners who are inclined to sell their homes using the "For Sale By Owner" (FSBO) approach, possibly because they want (or need) to reduce the amount of any brokerage fee or because they do not feel they need the full range of services offered under a full service agreement. The increasing popularity of Internet house shopping by prospective buyers and Internet advertising of listed real estate and real estate brokerage services seems to have given rise to new interest in the practice of limited or "unbundled" listing services.

While limited service brokerage arrangements may not be popular with traditional full service brokers, *limited service listing contracts are perfectly legal.* A broker should carefully specify in the written agency agreement those services that will be provided and clearly indicate that the broker's services are limited to those described in the contract.

Limitations Apply Primarily to Services, Not Duties

It is very important to note that limiting a listing broker's *services* by contract generally does not limit the broker's legal *duties.* Consider the points listed below:

1.   A broker MAY lawfully limit by contract the **services** he will provide to a client.
2.   A broker may NOT contractually limit or waive the **duties** imposed by statute and Real Estate Commission rules.
3.   *A contract that limits agency* **services** *may be found by a court to limit the agent's* **duties** *under the common law of agency* **only** *to the extent that such duties may not apply because of the limitation in services.* For example, if a limited service listing contract calls for the broker to only place a sign on the seller's property and place the listing in the MLS, then the seller is made responsible for all advertising other than the "for sale" sign and placing the listing in the local MLS.

Limited Service Listing Broker's Duties under Real Estate License Law and Commission Rules

No listing broker, whether providing full services or limited services, may waive or limit by contract the duties imposed by North Carolina Real Estate License Law and Commission rules. Thus, even though the parties' limited listing agreement only requires the broker to list the owner's property in a cooperative listing service, the broker still must use skill, care and diligence in servicing that listing and owes the owner-principal all the other traditional agency fiduciary duties (loyalty and obedience, disclosure of information and accounting) to the extent necessary to properly provide the contracted service. The *major* duties that a listing broker may NOT waive or limit by contract include:

- Duty to discover and disclose any material fact to any party about which the agent has knowledge or reasonably should have acquired knowledge (i.e., duty to avoid any willful or negligent misrepresentation or omission of a material fact). [G.S. § 93A-6(a)(1)] This duty is not limited to material facts related to the limited service being performed. It applies to any fact related to the property or a party's ability to fulfill his/her contractual obligation. Thus, the limited service listing agent is responsible for taking reasonable steps to assure the accuracy of all advertised information about the property (such as MLS information) and to discover and disclose any material facts that would be discovered by any reasonably prudent listing agent. For example, if a reasonable examination of the property at the time of listing would have revealed a leaking basement, the limited service listing agent would be responsible if this defect is not disclosed to prospective buyers.
- Duty to avoid making false promises of a character likely to influence, induce, or persuade the seller or a buyer. [G.S. § 93A-6(a)(2)&(3)] This would include false promises made to acquire the listing.
- Duty to avoid any undisclosed conflict of interest. [G.S. § 93A-6(a)(4) and Rule 58A.0104] As with any listing broker, the limited service listing broker must comply with agency disclosure requirements and obtain the seller's express written consent to represent a buyer interested in the seller's property.
- Duty to properly account for any funds held in trust for the principal. [G.S. § 93A-6(a) (7), (12) & (14) and Rule 58A.0116 and A.0117.] No matter what the contract says about handling trust monies, if a limited service listing broker receives any such monies, he/she must handle and account for the funds as required by the License Law and Commission rules. Of course, the brokers and parties in any transaction may agree that a particular

broker will or will not handle trust monies, and this is also true when a limited service list-ing broker is involved.

- Duty to act competently in the performance of services. [G.S. § 93A-6(a)(8)] Any ser-vices that are performed by the broker under the limited service listing contract must be performed competently. This includes providing accurate information (including square footage) in the MLS listing and servicing the listing in accordance with MLS rules.
- Duty to promptly deliver all copies of offers and contracts to parties to a transaction. [G.S. § 93A-6(a)(13) and Rule 58A.0106] As is the case with any licensee, a limited service list-ing agent must promptly deliver a copy of any offer, counteroffer or contract received by the agent to the appropriate party (seller or buyer). A limited service listing broker may contractually structure his/her relationship with a seller in a way that allows offers to be presented directly to the seller by buyers or other agents, and the limited service listing agent may direct other agents to present offers directly to the seller. However, if an offer is sent directly to the limited service listing broker in spite of his/her arrangements to the contrary, he/she must pass it on to the appropriate party in a timely fashion.

Duty to Comply With The Residential Property Disclosure Act

A limited service listing broker must remember that all listing brokers have certain non-waiv-able duties under both the Residential Property Disclosure Act and the Real Estate License Law. The reader is referred to the in-depth discussion of a listing agent's duties in this respect in Chapter 8.

No Standard Limited Service Listing Contract Form

No standard limited service listing contract form is provided by the North Carolina Associa-tion of REALTORS®. It is highly recommended that any broker who proposes to offer limited listing services consult a real estate attorney for assistance in drafting an appropriate contract.

"Protection Agreement"

At times, a broker who represents a buyer may contact an owner of a property *not* listed with a broker to inform him or her that the broker knows a prospective purchaser who might be interested in purchasing the owner's property. This is a fairly common occurrence with properties that are adver-tised by the owners as "For Sale by Owner (FSBO)." The owner may not want to enter into any of the previously mentioned listing arrangements with the broker, but may agree to let the broker show the property to the broker's buyer-client and to pay the broker a commission if the property is sold to that client. While no special term of art has been created for this type of agreement, it is frequently referred to as *"protection agreement"* since the broker will be protected insofar as earning a commission if the property is sold to the broker's named prospective buyer. A clear agreement to pay a commission must exist between the owner and the agent, as with all forms of listing contracts.

> *Example:* Adams is advertising her home for $140,000 without listing it with any real estate broker. Bob Broker contacts Adams and informs her that he has a client who may be inter-ested in buying Adams' home and would like to show the home to the prospect provided that Adams agree to pay a 4% commission if the prospect buys Adams' home. Adams signs an agreement to that effect. That afternoon, Broker brings the prospect through the house and the prospect offers to purchase it for $130,000. Adams accepts. Assuming all contract conditions are met, Bob Broker is legally entitled to a $5,200 commission.

The North Carolina Association of REALTORS® has a standard form for use by its members when dealing with an owner selling his or her own property who is willing to compensate the broker but does not want to sign a standard listing agreement.

MAJOR LISTING CONTRACT PROVISIONS

To avoid arguments, unnecessary controversy, and resulting ill feelings or legal disputes, every contractual agreement should be as clear and unambiguous as possible. Brokers usually prepare listing contracts by completing preprinted forms which they provide. Since any uncertainty or ambiguity in a written contract is interpreted against the party who prepares it, the broker who prepares a listing or employment contract must be very careful to ensure that the contract accurately and adequately sets out the significant terms of the parties' agreement and eliminates any doubt or ambiguity about its meaning. *It is strongly suggested that brokers have listing contract forms drafted by experienced real estate attorneys and that associated brokers be thoroughly trained in how to properly complete the contract forms and how to explain the contract's provisions to clients.* This section discusses the basic essential provisions of a **"full service" listing contract** and will refer to the sample **North Carolina Association of REALTORS®** Standard Form 101 **"Exclusive Right to Sell Listing Agreement"** reprinted as **Figure 9-1** at the end of this chapter. Not every provision of Standard Form 101 is addressed in this discussion. For convenience, this section will refer simply to "Standard Form 101."

Names and Signatures of the Parties

It is essential that the names of all property owners be included on the listing contract and that all owners sign the contract. A common broker error is to fail to name all of the owners of the property in the listing contract and to obtain all of their signatures on the listing contract.

Property Owned by Tenants by the Entirety

When a property is owned by a husband and wife as *tenants by the entirety,* each has an equal, undivided interest in the property and are treated legally as if they are one for the purpose of property ownership. Both owners' names should be included and both should sign the listing contract.

Property Owned by Tenants in Common or Joint Tenants

If two or more parties own property as *tenants in common* or as *joint tenants,* and one of the cotenants signs a listing contract, the contract may be enforceable by the listing broker for brokerage fee purposes against the cotenant who signed the listing contract, but no sale will result without the remaining co-owners' cooperation and consent. The broker may earn his commission if he produces a ready, willing and able buyer, even though the one signing cotenant will breach one of the seller's duties under the Standard Form 101 listing contract because he or she will not be able to convey fee simple marketable title to the entire property. A cotenant may be able to convey his or her individual proportionate interest in the property to a third party who then would own the property jointly with the other original cotenant-owners, but no sale of the entire tract can occur without **all** of the co-owners' signatures.

A cotenant-owner whose signature has not been obtained on the listing contract has not agreed to sell the property and cannot be compelled to cooperate in the sale if an offer is received. Thus, while the property technically might be listed, no sale of the parcel will occur without the consent and participation of all co-owners, whether spouses or unrelated persons, and the agent cannot argue breach of the listing contract to compel the non-signing co-owners to accept the offer or proceed with a sale because those owners never signed the listing agreement and are not bound by its terms. It is just plain bad practice not to obtain the names and signatures of **all** the property owners (and their spouses, if applicable) on the listing agreement.

Property Owned in Severalty by a Married Person

It is also recommended that an agent follow the same practice and *obtain the signature of a **non-titled** spouse on any listing agreement for a property owned in severalty by only one spouse.* While the non-titled spouse may not have any legal ownership interest in the property, he or she nonetheless has an interest in or potential claim against the property by mere virtue of being married to the titled owner, and this marital claim will not be extinguished unless he or she joins in the conveyance to the purchaser by signing the warranty deed. The refusal of a non-titled spouse to sign the warranty deed would impair, if not preclude, the seller from conveying marketable title, as the non-titled spouse's potential claim would remain a cloud on the title. A non-titled spouse who has not signed the listing agreement can not be compelled to cooperate in the sale of the property.

Property Description

A description of the real estate that is the subject of the listing should be set out in the contract. While this property description should be clear and specific, it does **not** have to be a formal "legal description" of the property in order for the listing contract to be valid. Courts customarily have recognized that descriptions in listing contracts are often more informal than those in contracts to convey, deeds, and deeds of trust. This does not mean that any informal description of the property will do. *The description must be sufficient to describe a particular tract of land as distinguished from other lands.* To avoid any possibility of confusion about the specific property to be sold, *brokers should obtain and include the legal description of the property in the listing contract.*

Urban/Subdivision Real Estate

*If the property which is the subject of the listing contract is located in an urban area or a residential subdivision, the street address will **usually** be legally sufficient, but is not recommended.* An example of a situation where a street address may not be sufficient is where the seller of a property owns more than one lot with the same street address and possibly has a house or other building on only one of the lots. In such a situation, it is critically important that the contract be clear about which of the lots is being sold. A lack of precision is an invitation to trouble. Thus, using an informal description is a sloppy practice considering the legal description should be readily available at the time of listing. *A listing broker should routinely include the legal description of the property in the listing contract.*

Rural Real Estate

If rural property is the subject of the listing, the description must be adequate to locate the property either from the description alone or from the description plus other documents clearly identified in the description. At times, it may be sufficient to use an informal description. For example, use of the description "the William P. Jackson farm, located between highway 421 and state road 1006 near Buies Creek, North Carolina" will be an adequate description for the listing contract if the parcel of land is referred to in the community by that name or if William P. Jackson owns only one farm in that vicinity. However, complete informality invites a legal disaster. Again, *a listing broker should routinely include the legal description of the property in the listing contract.* [See Chapter 4 as to methods of describing real estate.]

Fixtures and Personal Property

Fixtures automatically transfer with the real property. In practice, however, there is frequently a great deal of confusion among sellers, buyers and agents as to exactly which items are fixtures and which are not. Misunderstandings about this matter have historically been very commonplace. Thus, *it is very important for the listing contract (and any subsequent sales contract) to be clear about which items are fixtures and will transfer with the real property and which items are personal property that will be retained by the seller unless specifically purchased by the buyer.* The Standard Form 101 listing contract (Figure 9-1) provides a comprehensive list of items that are presumed to be fixtures unless the contract specifies otherwise. This is a very effective way to deal with this potential problem. Note, however, that *it is important to list any fixture the seller does **not** want to convey in the space provided on the form for this purpose.*

In addition to describing the fixtures that will convey with the real property, *the listing contract should also include a list of the items of personal property which the seller is willing to sell along with the real property.* In resort areas, houses and condominiums are frequently sold fully furnished. In such cases, all the personal property items should be listed on a separate sheet and attached to the listing contract. [See Chapter 2 for a fuller discussion of "fixtures" versus "personal property."]

Listing Price and Terms of Sale

A listing contract should specify the price at which the seller is willing to sell the property and any other conditions or terms of sale required by the seller. It is critically important to state the price and terms of sale in the listing contract so if the broker subsequently tenders to the seller an offer from a bona fide buyer who agrees to pay the exact price and to buy upon the exact terms as specified in the contract, the broker will have earned a commission even if the seller refuses to accept the offer. The listing price and complete terms of sale must be definitely stated in the contract listing agreement to determine when a broker has produced a buyer "ready, willing and able" to buy on the terms fixed by the principal. Where the listing agreement fails to fix the terms for the sale or exchange of property, or specifies only parts of the terms with the understanding that further details are subject to negotiation between the principal and the customer, courts have held that the principal is free to terminate the negotiations without any liability to the broker.

If a listing contract specifies a definite purchase price but does not include additional terms relating to payment of the purchase price, the law implies a "cash" sale. Brokers should be careful to insist that their principals state explicitly in the written listing contract the definite price and any other terms on which they will sell. Brokers should never enter into listing contracts that leave some of the terms to further negotiation between the buyer and the seller with respect to what the seller will accept. To leave room for negotiation eliminates any standard by which the broker's performance can be measured to determine if the broker has earned a commission, even if there is no sale. Note that Standard Form 101 in Figure 9-1 has check boxes for the purpose of indicating acceptable and unacceptable methods of payment and financing by the buyer.

Contract Term (Duration of Listing)

As mentioned at the outset, Real Estate Commission Rule 21 NCAC 58A.0104(a) requires: *"...Every written agreement for brokerage services of any kind in a real estate transaction shall be for a definite period of time...and shall provide for its termination without prior notice at the expiration of that period...."* (Italics added.)

To avoid unnecessary problems, the listing contract should always specify *a definite date* on which the initial listing period will terminate. There are times when merely stating that a listing is to run for "six months" or "90 days" creates a misunderstanding where the broker locates a purchaser at the end of the period. Precisely when does the six-month or 90-day period end? The problem can and should be avoided by simply stating the last day of the listing period. For example, a listing contract might simply state: "Broker is hereby given the exclusive right to sell the property commencing on January 1, 2018, and ending at midnight on June 30, 2018."

Length of Listing Period

An employment contract (listing agreement) between a broker and a principal can be for whatever period of time the parties mutually agree. As a practical matter, the broker should not try to tie up property for an unreasonably long period, especially when an exclusive listing is involved. However, the employment contract should allow the broker ample time to procure a buyer before it terminates. A six-month listing period is widely used in the industry for most residential properties and would seem appropriate for most markets. It is common to list land and commercial, industrial and farm properties for longer periods. Of course, the optimum reasonable period of time for a listing depends on varying circumstances such as the location and type of property. Exclusive right to sell listing contracts for excessive periods of time are discouraged by the Real Estate Commission and may be frowned upon by a court, unless supported by adequate consideration, because these contracts restrict the owner's right to sell his or her own property.

Owner Has No Right to Terminate Listing Contract Early

Where the listing contract stipulates a definite period of employment, the owner-principal has no "right" to terminate the broker's agency prior to the expiration of the term and, upon a wrongful termination, may incur liability to the broker. In other words, where a valid employment contract is for a definite time, the principal can withdraw from the agency relationship (i.e., "cancel" the listing), but by so doing breaches the contract and renders himself legally liable for all damages to the broker that result from the early termination of the broker's employment.

> *Example:* On July 1, 2018, a property owner lists her home with a broker under a listing contract which runs until October 1, 2018. The broker advertises and makes numerous efforts to sell the property. In August of 2018, the owner contacts the broker and cancels the listing contract, explaining that she has decided to remodel rather than sell the property. The broker's authority as the seller's agent is effectively revoked and the broker has no right to continue in his efforts to sell the property. The seller, however, has breached the listing contract with the broker and is liable for all damages caused by the breach of contract, such as the broker's expenditure of time and money in attempting to sell the property.

If a listing agent induces a seller to enter into a listing agreement by promising to allow the seller to terminate the listing agreement at any time, whether with or without penalty, then this promise and any related terms or conditions should be clearly specified in the written listing agreement.

Owner May Not Wrongfully Avoid Compensating Broker

The law will not permit an owner to avoid payment of a brokerage fee to a broker by terminating the broker's listing contract after the broker has fully performed by producing a buyer ready, willing and able to buy the principal's property, then selling the property directly to the buyer produced by the broker. *In such case, the broker will be entitled to the total brokerage fee specified in the contract.* The broker is entitled to his or her fee upon accomplishing the purpose of the contract within the time limit specified in the listing contract.

The broker's right to compensation may even extend to certain transactions occurring after the expiration of the listing period specified in the agreement. For instance, if the principal deliberately postpones agreeing with the prospective purchaser produced by the broker until after the listing contract expires for the purpose of defeating the broker's claim for compensation, the broker may be entitled to his compensation even though no contract was formed during the listing period. If the listing agreement provides for a protection period, then the broker should take whatever action is necessary to preserve his or the company's rights under that clause.

If *during the listing term* a seller enters into a contract with a ready, willing and able buyer, then the listing broker will be entitled to a sales commission *even if the transaction closes after the expiration of the listing agreement* as the fee was earned upon procuring a ready, willing and able buyer during the listing period. This is true particularly if the delay in consummating the transaction is due to the fault of the owner-principal or is occasioned by a defect in title.[5] An offer received from a buyer who cannot close within a reasonable time of contract formation may be rejected and will not give rise to a claim for compensation, as the buyer arguably is not "ready."

If a listing agreement expires *prior to the formation of any sales contract* between the owner and a buyer, then the listing broker must cease all efforts to represent the owner until the broker renews or extends the listing agreement, as the broker no longer is the authorized agent of the owner. Oral consent to extend the listing agreement is insufficient because Commission Rule A.0104 requires all agency agreements with owners to be in writing from the outset, *i.e.*, before the broker may provide any brokerage services. A listing broker must be aware of the date the listing agreement expires and renew or extend it if an offer is being negotiated near the expiration date of the listing agreement. Any broker who continues to actively represent a seller after a listing agreement expires and before the seller has accepted any offer will be ineligible to receive compensation in accordance with General Statute 93A-13.

Other Bases for Early Termination of Listing Contract

A broker's employment also may be terminated (i.e., the listing contract becomes void) upon the **death or insanity of the owner principal**, or upon the **dissolution of the brokerage firm** with which the property is listed. The same would be true upon the death or insanity of the broker if the listing was with an *individual broker* (a sole practitioner); however, if the listing was with a brokerage firm, then the listing most likely is *not* terminated by the individual broker's death because the listing contract is with the firm and there are other agents in the firm who can perform under the listing contract. If the **listed property is totally destroyed** (e.g., a condominium unit completely destroyed by fire), then the listing is terminated (void). On the other hand, partial destruction of the listed property (e.g., **destruction of an improvement** on land listed for sale – remember that land is "indestructible") may only make the listing contract voidable at the option of either party. Of course, any **material breach of agency duties** by either the broker or owner-principal may render the listing contract voidable at the option of the injured party. An **open listing** is immediately terminated by the sale of the listed property by the owner or another broker.

See the section on "Discharge of Contracts" in Chapter 10 for a more complete discussion of the general rules regarding termination of contracts.

Renewal of Listing

If the listing period expires without the broker producing a ready, willing and able buyer, the listing agent must enter into a new listing agreement in order to resume marketing a property. Prior to the expiration of a listing agreement, the agreement may be renewed or extended in writing for another fixed period of time. This can be accomplished either by executing a new listing contract for the additional desired time period or by executing a document that references the existing agreement, states the new listing period (including specific expiration date) and changes any terms that the parties would like to change (e.g., the listing price). *Any extension or renewal must be in writing and carefully drawn to show the exact terms of the new contract* to avoid any possibility of controversy insofar as practicable. There is no *"automatic" extension or renewal of listing contracts* under Commission Rule A.0104(a).

Compensation of Listing Broker/Firm

The listing contract should specify the brokerage fee to be paid to the listing broker/firm for services rendered in procuring a buyer for the listed property. Brokerage fees may take various forms as discussed below. Regardless of form, however, *brokerage fees must always be negotiable.* It is a violation of antitrust law for brokers to conspire to fix brokerage fees. Consequently, *a broker must never justify his fee by explaining that it is "the going rate" or "customary rate" in the community or region.*

Percentage of Sale Price (Commission)

A vast majority of listing contracts provide for the seller-principal to pay the listing broker/firm a fee based upon a *percentage of the sale price* as stated in the *sales* contract. This type of fee is commonly referred to as a sales commission or brokerage commission.

> *Example:* A listing contract states that the brokerage commission will be 5 percent of the gross sales price. If the listed property sells for $200,000, the commission is calculated as follows: .05 x 200,000 = 10,000. The broker's commission is $10,000.

Fixed or Flat Fee

Listing contracts may also provide for the seller-principal to pay the listing broker/firm a *fixed* or *flat fee* for brokerage services. One possibility is to pay a stated specific sum of money to the listing broker/firm *upon sale of the property.* This type of arrangement is rare.

Another flat fee arrangement that is used in connection with **limited services listing contracts** calls for the property owner to pay the listing broker/firm a *flat listing fee* in advance in exchange for the broker providing certain specific limited services for the seller, such as listing the owner's property in a Multiple Listing Service (MLS) and/or on an Internet site, perhaps providing a yard "for sale" sign, flyers, forms, etc. and possibly a few other services. (See previous discussion of these types of listing contracts in this chapter.)

Net Listing

A rarely used method of broker compensation is the *net listing* arrangement. A listing contract featuring this type of fee arrangement will provide for the seller-principal to receive a fixed price for the property, with the broker to receive any amount realized (i.e. the "net") in excess of that fixed price.

> *Example:* Smith lists her property with Jones Realty under a listing contract calling for Smith to receive the fixed amount of $85,000 for her property, with Jones Realty to receive as its fee any amount realized over and above $85,000. If Jones Realty sells Smith's property for $90,000, then Jones Realty has earned a fee of $5,000 ($90,000-$85,000).

The use of net listing arrangements is strongly discouraged because of the great potential for abuse and fraud. It is too easy for a broker to take advantage of a seller by intentionally undervaluing the seller's property to obtain a favorable net listing agreement and then selling the property at a much higher price, thereby providing a large fee for the broker. Brokers who use the net listing arrangement are inviting trouble. They should not be surprised that anytime a broker realizes a net listing fee which is substantially higher than the fee the broker would have earned under a common commission arrangement, the seller may complain to the Real Estate Commission and may pursue legal action against the broker.

Broker Compensation "Protection Period"

Any well-drafted listing contract should include *a "**protection period**" clause (sometimes also called an "**override**" or "**extender**" clause) that protects the broker from the possibility that a seller and a prospective purchaser procured by the broker may postpone the ultimate purchase to avoid the seller having to pay a brokerage fee and possibly also to reduce the purchase price.* The most common way of protecting the broker is to include language in the listing agreement requiring the seller-principal to pay a commission if the broker has produced a purchaser who viewed the property during the listing period, who subsequently purchases the property within a specified period (the "protection period") after the listing expires. The following language is an example of a "protection period" clause:

> If all or any part of the Property is sold or exchanged within _____ days after the expiration date of this listing contract to any person, or to anyone acting on behalf of said person, with whom the Broker or any of his agents negotiated during the term of this listing contract and whose name the Broker has submitted to the Seller in writing not later than _____ days after the expiration of this agreement, the Seller agrees to pay the Broker a commission as set forth above.

Under this or similar language, it becomes very important for a broker whose listing contract is expiring to disclose to the seller-principal a list of parties with whom the broker has communicated concerning the sale of the property.

Note that Standard Form 101 (see Figure 9-1), includes a provision very similar to the one cited above, but also creates an **exception** where the owner enters into a listing contract with another broker and sells the property to a prospect on the previous broker's prospect list during the protection period. After providing for the protection period, the form states: *"...HOWEVER, Seller shall NOT be obligated to pay the fee if a valid listing agreement is entered into between Seller and another real estate broker and the Property is subsequently sold, optioned, exchanged, conveyed or transferred during the Protection Period."* This language apparently is an attempt to clarify the respective rights of the brokers when the owner of property lists with another broker after the first broker's listing period expires without a sale. Even if the first broker has an interested prospect and has left the prospect's name with the owner, the subsequent broker is given the entire commission based upon the quoted clause.

Cooperation with and Compensation of Other Brokers/Firms

It is a very good practice to include in the listing contract a provision such as the one in Standard Form 101 that asks the seller to indicate whether he or she authorizes the listing broker/firm to cooperate and share the brokerage fee with other real estate firms/brokers acting as the seller's subagents and other firms/brokers acting as a buyer's agent. Having such a provision is very helpful in that it provides the broker an opportunity to educate the seller on this matter.

Firm's Duties/Services

A listing contract should describe the listing firm's duties and services to be provided under the contract. The Standard Form 101 describes the firm's **duties** only in a very general manner by saying that the firm will provide the seller the benefit of the firm's knowledge, experience and advice in the marketing and sale of the property and that the *firm agrees to use its best efforts to find a buyer that is ready, willing and able to purchase the seller's property.* Although a more specific statement of the firm's duties would be much more informative to the seller, the general statements in the standard form are likely legally sufficient given that execution of the listing contract automatically triggers an agency relationship and means that the firm has certain general duties under the law of agency.

Similarly, a description of the firm's services to be provided under the contract would be desirable, but the Standard Form 101 does not really address specific services other than to include a list of marketing activities (placing "for sale" sign on property, using listing service (MLS), etc.) that the seller is asked to "authorize" by checking boxes. Arguably, these listed marketing activities could be construed as services to be provided by the listing firm.

The lack of specificity regarding the listing firm's duties/services in the Standard Form 101 listing contract is offset to some extent by the fact that the seller will have been given the Real Estate Commission's *Working with Real Estate Agents* brochure which provides an explanation of a listing agent's duties and a short list of common services that are provided.

Seller's Duties

A listing contract needs to address the duties of the seller under the contract. Standard Form 101 state the seller's general duty to cooperate with the listing broker in the marketing and sale of the property and also lists a number of specific examples of what this general requirement includes, such as making the property available for showings, providing any disclosure forms required by law, providing the listing broker with copies of restrictive covenants and homeowner association documents, providing a copy of title documents (deed, deeds of trust, title insurance policy, etc.), and executing a general warranty deed conveying marketable title at closing.

Seller Representations

Although not essential for a valid and complete listing contract, Standard Form 101 includes a lengthy new "Seller Representations" provision asking the seller to answer a long list of questions about various matters relating to the property and the seller's ownership. Included among the matters addressed are: 1) location of property in a flood zone, 2) existence of synthetic stucco, 3) owner's association information, 4) seller's ownership period and residence status, 5) current liens, 6) whether the seller is involved in or contemplating bankruptcy proceedings, 7) legal access, 8) existence of leases, 9) recent appraisals, and 10) existence of special assessments.

There are several reasons for this provision. One purpose is to gather up front information that any buyer agent would need to properly complete the offer. Another reason is to assist the listing firm in determining whether it wants the listing – for example, the fact that any sale of the property is likely to be a "short sale" or that there may a question as to whether the seller will be able to convey a fee simple marketable title free of encumbrances. Still another reason is to assist the listing broker in identifying any material facts that must be disclosed to prospective buyers.

Dual Agency Authorization

The listing agreement itself establishes the agency relationship between the seller and the listing firm. However, if the firm practices both seller and buyer agency, the listing broker also must address the potential dual agency situation, which should have been explained during the review of the mandatory Working with Real Estate Agents brochure. So, when the firm practices dual agency for in-house transactions, the listing contract must include a provision that allows the seller to indicate whether he or she will authorize dual agency, if the situation arises.

The NCAR Standard Form 101 includes a comprehensive provision that explains the possibility of dual agency situations and how dual agency would work, including how the listing firm's duties would be modified to accommodate the dual agency. The seller is asked to indicate whether dual agency is authorized should that potential situation arise and, if authorized and if the firm also practices "**designated agency**," then whether designated agency is also authorized

MULTIPLE LISTING SERVICES

Most real estate listed for sale today is marketed through a **multiple listing service (MLS)**, **cooperative listing service (CLS)**, or similar listing service. An MLS or CLS is a common feature of a voluntary association of real estate brokers in a local area who have agreed to share information about their listed properties, to cooperate in the sale of such properties, and to share real estate commissions earned on sales. An overwhelming majority of such listing services have been formed by brokers who are members of the National Association of REALTORS® (NAR), the country's largest real estate trade organization. Local boards of REALTORS® form an MLS and adopt operating rules and procedures that must comply with MLS guidelines established by NAR. In addition to licensed real estate brokers, licensed or certified appraisers are also typically allowed to be members of a local NAR affiliated association and to be a member of the MLS.

Basic MLS Operations

Local MLS operations must comply with the general guidelines promulgated by NAR, but each MLS has the authority to adopt a specific set of operating rules or guidelines which can vary from one MLS operation to another. Member brokers/firms must pay a regular membership fee and are usually required to submit all their *exclusive listings* (no open listings are permitted) to the MLS within a specified time after taking the listing (most frequently 72 hours). The MLS has a detailed standardized property data sheet (may be only in electronic form for computerized MLS operations) which must be completed and submitted by listing brokers/firms for each listed property. Either the listing broker/firm or the MLS will also provide a photograph of the property for inclusion with the data sheet.

With today's computerized MLS systems, the listing agent enters all the data about a newly listed property into the system's computer data base. All member brokers can then access all MLS data directly by computer and can print a hard copy of a data sheet on each property as needed. Computer programs also allow brokers to search for properties to show to prospective buyers by entering the basic requirements of the prospect (price range, area, size, age, basic features, etc.) into the computer. Similarly, the MLS system can be used to select possible comparable sales for use by brokers in preparing a comparative market analysis or by an appraiser in performing an appraisal.

Computerized MLS operations today commonly use videodisc technology to store MLS data which allows the viewing of property photos by computer. Another popular marketing practice makes use of so-called "virtual reality" technology to show all aspects of a property on a computer screen and to enable prospective buyers to perform a "walk-through" viewing of the property by computer. Some of these programs even allow the viewer to place simulated furnishings to see, for example, what the inside of a house would look like furnished.

Broker Relationships and Cooperation in the MLS

Rules of the National Association of REALTORS® governing local MLS operations require that MLS member firms cooperate with other member firms who are acting as seller subagents and buyer agents unless the seller specifically instructs the listing firm to not cooperate with other firms. (Rejection of cooperation with other firms by sellers is actually quite rare because the seller does not want to limit his or her opportunities to sell the listed property.) Listing brokers/firms must now indicate at the time of placing a listing in the MLS whether they are cooperating with other member firms and must indicate the portion of their brokerage fee they will share with cooperating brokers/firms who produce a buyer.

Advantages of an MLS

There are many advantages of MLS operations for sellers, buyers and real estate brokers. The seller gains the advantage of broad market coverage by having his or her property accessible to a large number of real estate offices by means of a single listing contract. Buyers also have the advantage of being able to see much of the available property in the market in a particular locality by dealing with only one broker/firm of the buyer's choice without the necessity of explaining needs and desires over and over again to brokers with different firms. The MLS also provides a larger stock of listings to each broker/firm and makes it easier for brokers/firms to secure exclusive listings, since sellers know they are getting the large combined sales forces of numerous member brokers/firms at the same time. At the same time, brokers working with buyers have access to all the listings in the MLS rather than just those listed with their firm and, because MLS members with posted listings must cooperate with all other firms wishing to sell one of these listings, the brokers working with buyers do not have to negotiate a cooperation agreement with other firms in order to sell the listings of those firms. Moreover, sellers benefit because MLS-listed properties generally sell much faster than properties not listed in the MLS. Additionally, some MLS systems have agreements with national websites making properties accessible to any person with Internet access.

ANTITRUST LAWS

As with any other business, real estate brokerage is subject to federal antitrust laws, particularly the Sherman Antitrust Act. Antitrust laws are intended to prohibit anti-competitive practices that impair the operation of open markets. There are two primary types of practices that must be avoided in real estate brokerage practice because they violate antitrust laws: **"Price fixing"** and **"boycotting."**

"Price fixing" in the real estate industry involves *collaboration in setting brokerage fees by any group of two or more brokers/firms (i.e., two or more real estate brokerage firms or two or more brokers affiliated with two or more firms)*. Price fixing is considered to be an especially egregious anti-competitive conduct that, when shown to exist, constitutes an automatic violation of antitrust laws and subjects the perpetrators to both civil and criminal penalties. **For this reason, real estate firms/brokers absolutely must avoid any collaboration with other firms/brokers when setting brokerage fees.** Each firm should establish its own policy as to the amount of fees or rate of commissions charged to consumers and the sharing of any fees with cooperating selling agents. Most REALTOR® groups, as well as individual agents, are extremely sensitive to and scrupulously guard against any appearance of price fixing, both in establishing their fee structure as well as commission splits with cooperating brokers/

firms. Many MLS groups state in their rules that the MLS shall not fix, control, recommend or suggest commission rates or fees for agents' services or for the division of commissions or fees between cooperating brokers. Individual brokers repeatedly are reminded that discussions resulting in a conspiracy or restraint of trade regarding commissions, costs, marketing strategies or sales policies are illegal and are cautioned to disassociate themselves immediately from any persons engaging in such discussions.

"Boycotting" in the real estate industry is most likely to occur when any group of brokers collaborate in treating certain categories of brokers in a manner that restricts the ability of those brokers to be competitive. An example of such conduct would be an MLS group following a policy of excluding from membership part-time brokers or limited service ("discount") brokers, or charging such categories of brokers higher membership fees. Another example might be a group of brokers agreeing to refuse to refer clients to a particular service provider, such as an appraiser or attorney. Boycotting is also a violation of antitrust laws and must be completely avoided.

WORKING WITH SELLERS

*This section focuses on the **practices and services**, based on a listing agent's duties, that a conscientious **listing agent** should follow/provide when **working with a seller** of a **residential property**.* Most of the coverage is in summary form because many of the practices and services listed are covered in depth elsewhere in this text. Consequently, the reader will frequently be referred to other parts of the text for more detailed coverage of certain matters. Also covered are those less frequent situations where a buyer's agent is working directly with a seller who is not represented by an agent or who is represented by a limited service listing agent.

When working with sellers of **commercial** real estate, there are many additional steps that a prudent agent should take. The reader is referred to Chapter 19 on "Introduction to Commercial Real Estate Brokerage" to gain a basic understanding of the practices and services for a commercial real estate agent.

LISTING AGENT PRACTICES AND SERVICES

*The following discussion of practices and services of listing agents is presented in "**transaction sequence**" – i.e., the sequence in which the described practice or service would occur in a typical residential sales transaction – and focuses on how to work with sellers in a manner that complies with the law and good ethical practices and that best serves the interests of sellers.* Topics that relate primarily to sales skills and how to be successful in the real estate business are beyond the scope of this text, as well as real estate prelicensing and postlicensing courses. Thus, topics such as how to effectively solicit listings, market personal services, utilize computer programs or the Internet, manage one's time, design effective marketing and eliminate client/customer objections when negotiating are not addressed in this text.

Solicitation of Listings

The first step in working with a prospective seller is to identify a prospective seller-client. As mentioned above, the various methods for soliciting seller-clients (commonly referred to as "soliciting listings") are not addressed in this text. However, there are certain important legal and ethical issues that an agent needs to keep in mind when soliciting listings.

Soliciting the Active Listings of Other Firms/Brokers

Licensees who are members of the National Association of REALTORS® should be aware of the restriction in the REALTOR® Code of Ethics (Article 16) against soliciting the business of a property owner who has an active (unexpired) exclusive listing with another REALTOR®. Regardless of whether the broker/firm wanting to solicit a particular property owner or the broker/firm that has a current listing agreement with that property owner is a REALTOR®, solicitation of such a property owner is prohibited. A broker/firm engaging in such conduct will not only create ill will within the local community of real estate brokers, but also may risk being the subject of a lawsuit since soliciting the listing of another broker/firm may be found to constitute the **tortious interference with contractual relations** if the property owner breaches his or her existing listing contract, thereby damaging the broker who holds that listing. This civil wrong may be defined as a third party's intentional inducement of a contracting party to breach the contract, thereby causing damage to the other contracting party. It is sometimes also referred to as an "unlawful interference with a contractual relationship" or by similar terms.

Compliance with "Do Not Call" Laws and Rules

Real estate brokers must comply with the "Do Not Call" rules prescribed by state law and federal rules when soliciting real estate listings by "cold calling" prospects.[6] A real estate broker calling a homeowner in an attempt to obtain a listing (i.e., promote the services of the broker/firm to the homeowner) falls within the definition of a regulated telephone solicitation. Therefore, **a real estate broker generally is prohibited from "cold calling" a homeowner to solicit the homeowner's business when the homeowner's telephone number appears on the national Do Not Call Registry.**

The Federal Communications Commission (FCC) has specifically ruled that calls by real estate brokers to homeowners advertising their home as *"for sale by owner"* and calls to homeowners with **e**xpired *listings with another broker/firm* (i.e., whose listings with another real estate broker/firm have *expired*) for the purpose of soliciting a listing are **not** excluded from the Act's provisions. In other words, brokers may **not** call persons attempting to sell their own property nor listings previously belonging to other companies if the individuals have registered their telephone number and if the purpose of the call is to solicit their business.

On the other hand, a **buyer's agent** *may* call "for sale by owner" homeowners whose phone numbers are on the Do Not Call Registry if the agent's buyer-principal is interested in seeing the homeowner's property and the broker is calling in his/her role as a buyer's agent and does not attempt to solicit the homeowner's business for himself or his or her firm.

Brokers must be extremely careful to comply with the law/rules, as the penalties can be quite severe (discussed below). The old practice of soliciting listings by cold calling must now be undertaken very carefully in order to avoid a violation. Many brokers have shifted their emphasis when soliciting listings to Internet advertising and, yes, even solicitation by old-fashioned regular mail. (NOTE: Unsolicited faxes are also prohibited as discussed below.)

"Safe Harbor" Practices

- Understand the law and rules!
- Establish written procedures for compliance with the do not call rules and implement training for all employees and independent contractors who may be making calls to solicit business.
- Monitor and assure compliance with law/rules and company procedures.
- Properly maintain a company do not call list for those who request not to be called.
- Check the national Do Not Call Registry at least once every 31 days.
- Maintain complete records, especially for any unpermitted calls inadvertently made.

Penalties

The fines under federal rules for calling a person whose name appears on the Do Not Call Registry is **up to $11,000 per call** (for interstate calls if a lawsuit is filed by the federal government) and up to $500 per call if a lawsuit is filed by a state attorney general or a private lawsuit is filed by a consumer (with the possibility of treble fines in the case of willful violations.) Fines under North Carolina law can be up to $500 for the first violation, $1,000 for the second, and $5,000 for the third violation and any other violation that occurs within two years of the first violation.

Compliance with " Junk Fax" Laws and Rules

Since 1991, the Telephone Consumer Protection Act and the rules of the Federal Communications Commission (FCC) have restricted **unsolicited facsimile ("fax") transmissions** sent to fax machines. An **"unsolicited advertisement"** is *"any material advertising the commercial availability or quality of any property, goods, or services which is transmitted to any person without that person's prior express invitation or permission."* Private citizens were given the right to sue for injunctive relief and damages of $500 per fax, trebled if the violation was willful, and the FCC and the FCC and state attorneys general could also enforce the act.

    Considerations for Real Estate Brokers. Basically, a real estate broker/firm may not advertise its services through the use of unsolicited fax transmissions unless the broker/firm has a clearly established business relationship or the express permission (preferably written, faxed or perhaps emailed) with the party to whom the fax is sent.

Preparing for Prelisting Meeting with Prospective Seller

Before a real estate agent ever meets with a prospective seller to discuss the possibility of listing the seller's property, there are certain things that both the agent and seller need to do in order for the prelisting meeting to be as productive as possible.

Documents to Be Acquired by Listing Agent

- A Well-Drafted Listing Contract Form. It is important that real estate firms have a well-prepared listing contract form not only to protect their own interests but also to promote a good working relationship with their seller-clients. The form must conform with the requirements of Real Estate Commission rules. REALTORS® should seriously consider using the North Carolina Association of REALTORS® Standard Form 101.
- Copy of Commission's Working with Real Estate Agents Brochure. This will be needed at the agent's first meeting with the seller.
- Copies of the "Residential Property and Owners' Association Disclosure Statement" and "Mineral and Oil and Gas Rights Disclosure" forms. Remember that the Commission considers it to be a duty of the listing agent to provide the seller copies of these forms.
- Property Data Sheet. If the property will be listed in the MLS, then the listing agent should use the MLS property data sheet. If not to be listed in an MLS, then a property data sheet appropriate for gathering all the information the listing agent will need to properly market the property, including information buyers typically will want to know.

Documents/Information to Be Gathered by Seller

The current version of the NCAR Form #101 calls for the seller to make a number of representations regarding the status of the seller's title. Additionally, the Standard Form #2-T (reprinted and discussed in Chapter 11) requires the seller to provide title insurance policies, attorney's opinions on title, surveys, covenants, deeds, notes and deeds of trust and easements relating to the Property.

Having the seller provide the title-related documents indicated below at the outset of the agency relationship will not only assure that these documents are available to provide later to a buyer, but also will greatly assist the listing agent in completing a listing contract and determining whether the listing firm will want to take the listing and whether the seller will likely be able to deliver fee simple marketable title. If all the documents cannot be made available by the seller at the agent's initial meeting with the seller, then the agent should advise the seller to make every effort to gather such information by the time the listing agent subsequently has a follow-up meeting with the seller to actually list the property. Several of the most important documents or pieces of information to be acquired from the seller are discussed below.

1. **Seller's Deed.** It is important that the listing agent obtain a copy of the seller's deed and verify the seller's legal interest. (Normally this will be a fee simple interest, but it is important to verify this early to avoid wasting time marketing a property without a marketable title.) The deed also will indicate all the owners (as "Grantees" in the deed), thus the deed identifies who must sign the listing contract (and subsequently the sales contract). In addition, the deed usually will provide either a metes and bounds legal description or a description by reference to a recorded plat. If, however, the deed merely describes the property by reference to a description in another recorded deed, the listing agent should ask the seller to provide a copy of the referenced deed containing the more complete description. A complete legal description will be needed not only to assist the agent in verifying the lot acreage (metes and bounds descriptions almost always indicate the acreage) claimed by the seller but also to have the description available when it comes time for the listing agent or another selling agent to prepare an offer to purchase.

2. **Survey.** It is always helpful to have a copy of a recent survey available early in the transaction to assist the listing agent in identifying property boundaries at the prelisting meeting and often to provide additional verification of lot acreage. (Surveys frequently, but not always, show the amount of acreage determined by the surveyor.)

3. **Restrictive Covenants**. Most residential subdivisions have restrictive covenants containing important restrictions on the use of property in the subdivision. Having these available for buyers, who will almost certainly inquire about such covenants, will expedite the transaction later, possibly at a critical point where the buyer has a sufficient interest in the seller's property to request to see the covenants. Having a copy of restrictive covenants that the listing agent can reference and provide to the buyer if asked a question about permitted property uses may save the listing agent from the temptation to respond without checking the covenants or based only on the seller's understanding of restrictions. If the agent's response is incorrect, it will constitute at least a negligent misrepresentation and may even be considered a willful misrepresentation if made without regard for the actual truth.

4. **Homeowners Association Bylaws, Rules and Regulations, Dues and Assessment Information.** Many residential subdivisions, including virtually all newer subdivisions also have homeowners associations that are established by the developer's declaration of restrictive covenants, and these associations typically have bylaws and rules as well as regular monthly homeowners' dues and sometimes pending assessments. It is a good practice to have all

this information available for reference by the listing agent and to provide to prospective buyers, at least those who are considering making an offer. MLS data sheets typically ask about homeowners' dues and assessments, but homeowners' dues and unpaid assessments are clearly material facts that should be disclosed to prospective buyers in any event.

5. **Balance Due on Seller's Existing Mortgage(s) and Status of Mortgage(s).** The listing agent needs to know this information at the time he or she discusses with the seller a possible listing price and estimated net proceeds to the seller prior to signing a listing contract. Homeowners with little or no equity in their homes, may not be able to pay off their existing mortgage(s). Some may not be current on mortgage payments and may be facing foreclosure. There can be very serious consequences in such situations, as discussed in the next paragraph and also later in this section under the heading "Advise Seller on Listing Price," as well as in Chapter 13 under the heading "Short Sales."

Note: It is very important to know the balance due on the seller's existing mortgage(s) prior to listing a property so that the listing agent can recognize, upon performing a comparative market analysis, if the sale of the property is unlikely to produce sufficient money to pay off the mortgage and pay the brokerage fee and all other seller closing expenses. When a proposed purchase price is less than the net amount the seller needs, it is not uncommon for the listing broker to find himself or herself pressured to reduce the brokerage commission to "make the sale work." Even worse is a situation where there are insufficient proceeds to even pay off the balance on the seller's existing mortgage, not to mention other closing costs (including the brokerage fee).

In such a situation, the seller will be unable to convey marketable title unless he or she is able to make up the shortage from other personal funds or possibly to convince his or her lender (or mortgage note holder) to forgive some portion of the outstanding mortgage debt. Moreover, there will still be the issue of whether the listing broker will be able to collect the brokerage fee. Worst of all is the situation where the prospective seller is in danger of foreclosure. When the potential exists for sale proceeds to be insufficient to pay off outstanding mortgage debt and closing expenses (including the brokerage fee), and/or when the possibility of foreclosure exists, it is imperative that the listing agent have an honest discussion with the seller and his or her broker-in-charge about these matters before a listing contract is signed. It is very possible that a firm may not want to list a property in such a situation, or that the property can only be sold using the *"short sale"* process.

Prelisting Meeting with Prospective Seller

It is at this meeting that the listing agent and seller not only get to know each other (assuming they are not already acquainted), but commence their working relationship. There are many things the listing agent must do at this meeting, which typically is and should normally be held at the seller's property.

Remember to take appropriate safety precautions before and during any meeting with prospective sellers! Review the Commission's Safety Guide for helpful tips.

Explain Agency Relationship and Company Policies/Services

This is most frequently the listing agent's **"first substantial contact"** with the seller and, therefore, the point in time when the listing agent must comply with the Real Estate Commission's Rule 58A.0104(c)). [See "Disclosure of Agency Relationships in Real Estate Sales" in Chapter 8, and particularly note the discussions of what constitutes "first substantial contact."]

1. **Review with sellers the Real Estate Commission's *Working with Real Estate Agents* brochure and explain to sellers the firm's agency policies.** It is extremely important to "educate" most sellers at the time a listing presentation is made. The listing agent should explain thoroughly the various duties and relationships of real estate agents and his company's policies regarding agency, particularly dual agency and, if appropriate, designated agency. The broker should obtain the seller's signature acknowledging receipt and review of the *Working with Real Estate Agents* disclosure form and keep this acknowledgment for the three years required by Commission Rule 58A.0108. If the company allows the seller to make choices regarding cooperation with other real estate firms, explain each option so the seller can make an appropriate choice. *Be sure to explain the listing agent's legal duties to prospective buyers to disclose all material facts about the seller's property as well as his duties to the seller.*

   Many sellers, especially those who are not that experienced in real estate transactions, will appreciate a patient, thorough explanation of agency relationships. At worst, an experienced seller might simply say he or she understands and that you can move on. Even then, the seller will appreciate your attempt to educate them on this matter.

2. **Discuss how the property will be marketed.** Explain the various ways (MLS, publications, Internet, etc.) the property will be marketed. The less knowledgeable the seller is about real estate transactions, the greater the listing agent's responsibility to educate the seller regarding these and other related matters.

3. **Discuss the brokerage fee.** Advise the seller of the listing firm's proposed brokerage fee. Fee negotiation, if permitted by firm policies, should be accomplished in accordance with guidelines established by the firm's management. The extent to which the firm's brokerage fee is negotiable is up to the firm's management. *Never imply in any way that any cited fee is the "standard" or "customary" fee within the brokerage industry or the local area.* Only discuss the listing company's fee and, if questioned about brokerage fees charged by others, respond that each firm sets its own fees.

4. **Caution seller about providing confidential information.** Until the seller signs a listing agreement, an agency relationship has not been established between the listing firm and the seller, so the seller should be cautioned against providing personal, confidential information to the prospective listing broker or any other prospective listing broker with whom the seller might meet before a listing contract is signed.

5. Obtain and review the documents and information the seller was requested to gather in advance of the prelisting meeting.

Inspect Property and Verify Information

1. **Inspect the Property.** Perform a careful "walk-through" inspection of the seller's property in the presence of the seller, noting all major features of the property. The physical features of the property are needed in order to complete the property data sheet, to prepare advertising for the property, and to assist the seller in completing the property disclosure form. Moreover, the listing agent has a duty to be fully informed about the features of the property.

2. **Identify personal property to be sold and fixtures to be removed**. It is extremely important to make a list and include in the listing contract and property data sheet all items of personal property that the seller wants to sell with the real estate and to note in the listing contract and property data sheet any fixtures that the seller intends to keep. (These matters also will need to be addressed subsequently in any sales contract.) Identifying these issues initially will avoid confusion and problems later. Make certain the seller understands which items will transfer with the property and which will not.

3. **Note all significant property defects**. The listing agent must especially note all material property defects or encroachments that would be observed by a reasonably prudent listing agent conducting a thorough "walk-through" inspection of the property. Inquire about any signs that indicate major problems (examples: excessive moisture or water damage, sagging ceilings, cracks in walls or foundation, chimney pulling away from house, etc.).

4. **Suggest needed repairs and improvements**. A broker learns fairly quickly in the real estate business what features are attractive to buyers and what features tend to be found objectionable by most buyers. The listing agent should suggest repairs and improvements (cleaning, painting, "staging," landscaping, etc.) that are needed to either correct defects or to make the property more marketable.

5. **Inquire as to Construction/Alteration/Repair Permits.** Property owners are required under the North Carolina State Building Code to obtain a permit from the appropriate county or city code enforcement official for many additions, renovations or major repairs to a property. The law broadly requires a permit for:
   a. The construction, alteration, repair, removal or demolition of a building (e.g., room addition, renovations, deck addition, outbuilding construction, etc.).
   b. The installation, extension, alteration or general repair of a plumbing system, HVAC system or electrical wiring, devices, appliances or equipment.

Work costing less than $5,000 in a single family residence is exempt from the permit requirement *unless* it involves: addition, repair or replacement of load-bearing structures; change in plumbing design or additional plumbing; addition, replacement or change in the design of heating, air conditioning, or electrical wiring, devices, appliances, or equipment; or the addition of roofing.

The fact that construction, alterations, repairs, etc. requiring a permit have been performed on a property listed for sale without the property owner having obtained the required permit is a **material fact** *that a real estate broker must disclose to prospective buyers.* A **listing agent** is expected to ask the seller whether there have been any additions, renovations or repairs such as those described above and whether the seller obtained the required permit(s). *If it appears based on the seller's statements and/or the broker's observation during his or her property inspection that unpermitted work may have been performed, the listing broker should contact the local building code inspector's office to verify whether a permit was required, whether it was obtained, and what remedial action, if any, needs to be taken.* Any unresolved permit issues should either be resolved prior to listing the property or be disclosed to any prospective buyer.

A seller's failure to have obtained a required permit may result in a transaction failing if the buyer discovers this before closing. If the buyer discovers a permit problem after closing, it may be very difficult and expensive for the buyer to rectify the problem, and the buyer may have a cause of action against the seller and the listing broker/firm.

6. **Inquire as to Septic System Capacity.** Information about a dwelling listed for sale (or rent) that is advertised by a broker (in MLS data or other advertising) will virtually always indicate the number of bedrooms in the dwelling. Therefore, when a dwelling to be listed is served by a septic system, then the listing agent, prior to listing and advertising the property, should check with the county health department to verify the capacity allowed by the septic system permit for the property. The permit should indicate the number of bedrooms for which the septic system is approved and there is an assumption of two persons per bedroom to determine the maximum number of regular occupants that can be served by the septic system. If there is a problem, then it should either be resolved prior to listing the property or be disclosed to any prospective buyer. The listing agent needs to make certain that any advertisement does not improperly promote the use of a property in violation of health department regulations.

Assist Seller with Residential Property and Owners' Association Disclosure and Mineral and Oil and Gas Right Disclosure Statements

All requirements of the Residential Property Disclosure Act and the listing agent's duties in connection with that law are covered in depth in Chapter 8. While a listing agent could wait until after a listing contract is signed to assist the seller with completing the required disclosure statements, it is highly recommended that this be done prior to completing the listing contract because in the process of the seller completing the documents, the broker may become aware of issues that might affect not only the listing price but also the listing agent's decision as to whether to take the listing. For example, if the seller indicates to the broker that there is a major hidden defect but he/she does not want that information disclosed to prospective buyers or that gas rights have been sold, then the broker must remind the seller of the broker's duty to disclose all material facts. If the seller will not accept this, then the broker may have to refuse the listing, at least until the defect is repaired.

Comply with the Residential Lead-Based Paint Hazard Reduction Act

The requirements of the Residential Lead-Based Paint Hazard Reduction Act, including the listing agent's duties in connection with that law are discussed in depth in Chapter 8. Assure full compliance with this law if applicable (if the property was constructed prior to 1978 and is not an exempt property.) As with completion of the Residential Property Disclosure form, it is wise to address this disclosure, when required, prior to listing so that any adverse condition related to the presence of lead-based paint can be taken into account by the listing agent when recommending a listing price or making suggestions as to needed repairs or other corrective action.

Verify the Acreage of the Lot or Tract of Land

A listing agent is *not* generally expected to *measure* lots or tracts of land and calculate the acreage or square footage. However, the broker should attempt to *verify* the acreage of a lot or tract of land by checking the seller's deed and/or a recent survey. (Tax records/maps may not be a reliable source for acreage.) If the deed or survey does not state the acreage, as is sometimes the case, the listing agent is advised to avoid advertising such unconfirmed acreage and be extremely careful to emphasize in any statement to prospective buyers about acreage that the acreage has not been confirmed. Tour the lot with the seller and physically locate corners and property lines if possible in order to avoid subsequently making a misrepresentation to a prospective buyer or agent working with a buyer about such matters.

Verify and Properly Report Building Square Footage

Real estate brokers are *not* required by the Real Estate License Law or Real Estate Commission rules to affirmatively report (make unsolicited representations about) the square footage of buildings on properties being sold or leased; however, *when a real estate broker makes a representation about the square footage of a property to a prospective buyer or renter, it is important that the information provided be accurate.* This is true regardless of whether the representation is made directly to the prospective buyer/renter or indirectly through advertising, MLS data, flyers, another agent, or some other means. Consequently, a listing agent is expected to take reasonable steps to assure that any reported square footage is accurate.

To assist real estate brokers with understanding their responsibilities in determining and reporting the square footage of **residential 1-4 unit properties**, the North Carolina Real Estate Commission publishes a booklet entitled *Residential Square Footage Guidelines*, and the reader is referred to that booklet for a more detailed discussion of this matter. The *Guidelines* contain instructions for measuring and calculating square footage, with numerous illustrations, and address the responsibilities of agents working with buyers regarding the reporting of square footage.

The *Guidelines* point out that *a real estate broker is expected to possess the knowledge and skills necessary to accurately measure and calculate the square footage of most dwellings.* The Real Estate Commission understands that minor differences in square footage derived by different persons that may result from an agent's thoughtful judgment reasonably founded on these *Guidelines* will not be considered by the Commission to constitute error on the agent's part.

The *Guidelines* strongly recommend that a **listing agent** personally measure any listed dwelling and calculate the square footage when the dwelling is not particularly unusual or complex in its design and the square footage is being reported in any manner by the broker. It is also appropriate for a broker to rely upon measurements and calculations performed by *other professionals with greater expertise in determining square footage,* such as a licensed real estate appraiser or another broker who has greater experience in determining square footage. Such reliance might be especially appropriate in situations involving a house with an unusual measurement problem or with a complex design. The other professional whose calculations are relied upon must have used the *Guidelines* (or comparable standards) and the square footage must have been specifically determined in connection with the current transaction. Also, a broker who relies on another's measurements and calculations would still be expected to recognize an obvious error and to alert any interested parties.

As a general rule, an agent working with a buyer may rely on the listing agent's square footage representations except in those unusual instances when there is an error in the reported square footage that should be obvious to a reasonably prudent broker. For example, an agent showing a house described as having 3200 square feet when the house actually contains only 2300 square feet usually should be able to recognize such a discrepancy and should point out the suspected error to the buyer and the listing agent. On the other hand, a broker would not be expected to recognize that a house reported as having 2200 square feet actually contains only 2000 square feet.

The broker should *not* rely on sources of square footage information that are by their very nature unreliable. For example, a broker should *not* rely on square footage information provided by the property owner, blueprints used to build the property, or property tax records. An agent also should *not* rely on square footage information included in a listing, appraisal report or survey prepared in connection with an *earlier* transaction.

The Real Estate Commission's *Guidelines* permit the square footage of a dwelling to be reported as a single figure for the total *"living area,"* which is sometimes referred to as "heated living area" or as "heated square footage." **"Living area"** refers to the portion of a dwelling that is intended for human occupancy and which is:

(1) *heated* by a permanently installed heating system(s) sufficient to make the space suitable for year-round occupancy;

(2) *finished*, with walls, floors and ceilings of materials generally accepted for interior construction and with a ceiling height of at least seven feet (except under beams, ducts, etc. where the height must be at least six feet four inches); and

(3) *directly accessible from other "living area"* (through a door or by a heated hallway or stairway).

Under the *Guidelines*, "living area" generally includes all the heated and finished rooms and parts of the dwelling used for general living, such as living room, den, kitchen, dining room, study, bedrooms, bathrooms, pantry, foyer, utility ("mud") room, and hallways. Features that are not part of the heated living area (e.g. sun rooms directly accessible from living areas but having no heat source, bonus rooms over garages which are heated and finished but not directly accessible from other living areas, etc.) should *not* be included in the total square footage reported for the dwelling, but instead should be reported separately. *As a general rule, the amount of living area and other area in dwellings should be based on* ***exterior measurements***.

Note: The Commission's ***Residential Square Footage Guidelines*** do *not* apply to determining and reporting the square footage of **commercial properties**. Nevertheless, a broker involved with the sale or leasing of a commercial property who makes a representation as to square footage is also expected to take reasonable steps to assure that the information reported is accurate, and any such agent is expected to possess the necessary expertise to accurately determine the square footage of the commercial building being sold or leased. When confronted with a report of square footage for a commercial property determined by someone else, it is especially important for a broker to understand how the square footage was determined, since it is common for different methods to be utilized when determining and reporting the square footage of such properties.

Prepare a Comparative Market Analysis (CMA) for the Seller

A listing agent has an affirmative duty to provide his or her seller-client with competent advice as to an appropriate listing price for the seller's property, based on the broker's knowledge of the seller's property, the local real estate market for such properties and other relevant factors. To fulfill this duty, **a listing agent must formulate a reliable estimate of the approximate or probable selling price of the seller's property**. A real estate broker will need to perform a **comparative market analysis (CMA)** to formulate a reliable estimate of a property's probable selling price. The subject of "Comparative Market Analysis (CMA)" and "Broker Price Opinion (BPO)," is addressed in depth in Chapter 15, and the reader is referred to that chapter.

It is not a specific legal requirement under the Real Estate License Law or Commission rules or under the common law agency for every listing agent to perform a comparative market analysis (CMA) on every property he or she is listing. However, *it is a listing agent's obligation to derive in some manner a reasonably accurate estimate of the probable selling price of the seller-principal's property*. It is possible that a highly experienced broker who is extremely knowledgeable about the local real estate market and the current market values of other properties ("comparable" properties) similar to the property in question (i.e., the "subject" property), may be able to derive a reasonably accurate estimate of a subject property's probable selling price without going through all the steps normally associated with properly performing a CMA. However, **any broker, even one who is highly experienced, who "shortcuts" the normal process of estimating the value of a principal's property and significantly misses the mark, thereby harming the client's interest, may be found to have failed to act in a competent manner thereby subjecting the broker to discipline by the Real Estate Commission and possible liability for monetary damages in a civil lawsuit.** For the foregoing reasons, *it is highly recommended that every listing agent, regardless of his or her level of experience, perform a full comparative market analysis (CMA) for the seller prior to advising the seller on an appropriate listing price.*

Advise Seller on Listing Price

A variety of factors should be considered when determining an appropriate listing price, including the following:

Estimated probable selling price of property. The estimated probable selling price (either a single amount or a price range) indicated by a CMA is one important factor. Great care should be taken in advising the owner regarding probable selling price and listing price. If the broker is not completely confident of the estimated probable selling price, then perhaps the owner should be advised to have the property appraised by an appraiser before setting a listing price.

Current market conditions. The market for properties of the type being listed varies according to the property's location (with regard to both general area and specific location) and also varies over time depending on many other factors (the general and local economy, interest rates, etc.). In a "hot" market, a listing price may need to be near the high end of an estimated price range, whereas the opposite approach may be more appropriate in a "slow" market.

Seller's Needs and Desires. The seller's personal circumstances may be a significant factor in determining an appropriate listing price. The seller may have a number of reasons for needing a "quick sale" (job transfer or loss, marital separation, family member illness, etc.). In such a situation, it might be appropriate to list the property at a price near the lower end of the estimated price range. On the other hand, a seller may not be in a hurry to sell and may be resolved not to accept less than the best possible price. In that case, a price near the higher end of the estimated price range may be more appropriate. Remember, it is the seller's property and the seller's decision as to what the listing price should be. The listing broker's duty is to provide informed advice, not determine the listing price.

Likelihood of Sale Proceeds Being Insufficient. If the listing agent's comparative market analysis indicates that the likely sale price will not be sufficient to pay off the sellers' existing mortgage(s), the brokerage fee and other seller closing expenses, then the listing broker should fully discuss the potential consequences of a short sale with the seller. The seller will be unable to convey marketable title to a buyer unless the seller has funds from another source to pay the deficiency or the lienholder consents to the sale. The listing broker also should consult the broker-in-charge prior to accepting the listing since a sale price that is too low may also mean insufficient proceeds for the seller to pay the brokerage fee (not to mention other expenses). The broker-in-charge will decide whether it is feasible for the firm to list the property.

Agent's Needs. If the listing agent believes the seller is demanding a listing price that is unreasonably high and that this will result in the property either not selling or just sitting on the market for an extended period of time, the listing broker always has the option to refuse the listing if he or she determines it will not be worth the time and expense the broker will be required to devote to promoting the listing.

Estimating Net to Seller

During the process of setting a listing price, owners may inquire as to the minimum sale price necessary to "net" the owner a certain amount of money after paying the brokerage commission and closing costs. *The broker should be able to calculate the necessary sale price for the owner to "net" a certain amount of money.* These calculations are performed as shown in the example below.

> *Example:* Owner wants to "net" approximately $70,000 after paying the brokerage commission and closing expenses. The commission is to be six percent of the sale price and the broker estimates that the seller's closing expenses will be approximately $400. The broker should set up a simple algebraic formula to solve the problem. Use "P" to represent the unknown sales price. P is 100 percent of the sale price. Thus, the formula:
>
> $$(100\% \times P) - (6\% \times P) - \$400 = \$70,000$$
>
> Convert the percentages to decimals and we have: $(1.00 \times P) - (.06 \times P) - \$400 = \$70,000$
>
> Move the $400 to the right side of the equation by adding $400 to each side:
>
> $$(1.00 \times P) - (.06 \times P) - \$400 + \$400 = \$70,000 + \$400$$
>
> Simplify both sides of the equation: $.94 \times P = \$70,400$
>
> Divide each side by .94 to obtain the answer: P= $74,894

The sale price must be at least $74,894 in order for the owner to net $70,000 (assuming there is no mortgage or other encumbrance against the property).

Calculating Net Profit to Seller

Prior to setting a listing price or accepting an offer, sellers may want to know what their "profit" or "gain" will be upon the sale of the property. *The broker should be able to calculate the "profit" the seller may realize on a given sale.* To calculate *gross profit,* simply deduct the seller's "cost" (price seller paid for the property) from the proposed sale price. For example, if the Seller's cost was $120,000 and the proposed sale price is $180,000, the seller's gross profit would be $60,000 ($180,000 - $120,000 = $60,000). To determine the amount of gross profit expressed as a percentage, simply divide the amount of gross profit by the cost ($60,000 ÷ $120,000 = .50 = 50%).

Net profit is calculated similarly, except that the seller's closing expenses on both the previous purchase and the proposed sale are taken into consideration. Net profit is calculated as follows:

1. Deduct the seller's estimated closing expenses (including the brokerage fee) from the proposed sale price to determine the *adjusted sale price.*
2. Add to the seller's cost (purchase price) of the property the closing expenses paid by the seller when he purchased the property to determine the *adjusted cost.*
3. Deduct the adjusted cost (2) from the adjusted sale price (1) to determine the *net profit.*

> *Example:* A seller purchased his house for $120,000 and paid an additional $2,700 in closing expenses. The seller proposes to sell his house for $180,000 and the listing broker estimates that total closing expenses (including a 6% brokerage fee) on such sale would be $11,250. The seller's projected net profit on this sale is calculated as follows:
>
> (1) $180,000 (proposed sale price)   (2) $120,000 (cost of house)
>
>   - 11,350 (brokerage fee & closing expenses)   + $ 2,600 (Closing expenses at purchase)
>
> $168,650 (adjusted sale price) $122,600 (Adjusted cost)
>
> (3) $168,650 (adjusted sale price)
>
>   -$122,600 (adjusted cost)
>
> $46,050 (Net profit)

It is better to consider the seller's projected **net profit** rather than projected gross profit because in every case net profit will be considerably lower than gross profit due to the inclusion of expenses. It is important that the seller have reasonable expectations as to the anticipated profit or gain on the sale of the property. Note, however, that the actual **"net cash-in-hand" proceeds** to the seller generally should exceed the estimated net profit figure due to principal mortgage reduction during the ownership period, unless the owner has encumbered the property with additional deeds of trust or liens having a cumulative total in excess of the original purchase price.

> *Example*: Using the facts from the preceding example, assume that of the original $120,000 purchase price, the owner had paid $20,000 down, financing $100,000. He has lived in this house for eight years and the outstanding principal balance on his original mortgage now is only $81,590 and there are no other liens. He is selling the property for $180,000 and his total closing costs and brokerage fees are $11,350. His expected net cash-in-hand proceeds should be approximately: $180,000 - $11,350 - $81,590 (mortgage payoff) = $87,060 cash-in-hand (even though his capital gain should not exceed $46,050, as calculated in the preceding example).

Review and Complete the Listing Contract

*Completing the listing contract should be done only **after** all the other steps previously discussed have been completed.* As a general rule, all this cannot be done adequately at the initial meeting with the seller and it will be necessary to have a second meeting with the seller to review the agent's comparative market analysis (CMA,) determine an appropriate listing price and complete the listing contract. Some trainers and firms teach agents that they should get the seller's signature on the listing contract at their initial meeting with the seller. In most situations, however, this is not a wise practice. Having a seller sign a listing contract prior to performance of all the other duties previously discussed, especially performing a CMA, may not be in the seller's best interest and may very well constitute incompetence and improper dealing on the part of the agent. As the prospective agent of the seller, the listing agent should not have the seller obligate himself prematurely to a listing contract.

With today's technology, it is possible to perform a CMA using a laptop computer or other portable electronic device and portable printer while at the seller's house after completing the property inspection. If a CMA is properly done in this manner, and all other required steps are followed and all needed information is gathered, it *may* be feasible to complete a listing contract at the initial meeting with the seller. Note that *an abbreviated "quickie" CMA with limited comparable selection factors and no adjustments to comparables is **not** an acceptable CMA under standards expected by the Commission.* See the coverage of Comparative Market Analysis (CMA) in Chapter 15.

Complete all provisions. *All provisions of the listing contract should be appropriately filled in before it is signed by the seller. A listing agent should NEVER ask the seller to sign an incomplete contract –* for example, one with the listing price left blank, to be filled in later after the broker performs a CMA and advises the seller on an appropriate listing price. If a broker engages in this undesirable practice, the broker should not compound the problem by leading the seller to believe that the seller is obligated under the signed incomplete contract. For one thing, leaving a critical contract term out of a contract may mean that the contract has no legal effect because there is not a complete meeting of the minds of the parties on all material terms. All material terms of a listing contract must be agreed upon *in writing* for a valid contract to exist. The listing price is unquestionably a material term and the fact that the incomplete contract signed by the seller may be legally unenforceable is clearly a "material fact" requiring disclosure to the seller by the seller's broker under the Real Estate License Law and agency law. Give the seller a copy of the signed listing contract.

Provide copy of sales contract form. It is probably also a good idea to provide the seller at this point with a copy of the sales contract form (offer to purchase and contract form) that a buyer will likely use so the seller has an opportunity to review the form in advance and know what to expect when an offer is submitted.

Prepare Property Data Sheet and Place Listing in Multiple Listing Service

A listing agent must carefully prepare the property data sheet and enter all property data into the MLS data bank (assuming advertising via the MLS was authorized). Information included on the property data sheet and entered into the MLS data bank will subsequently be provided to prospective buyers. Therefore, all information must be accurate. The data reported to the MLS should be verified personally by the listing broker. Remember, *a listing broker will be held accountable for the accuracy of property information reported to prospective buyers from the property data sheet or MLS data bank, even if another person (including a licensee) actually enters the data into the MLS data bank.* Keep in mind that disclaimers published in MLS system will not protect a listing agent who willfully or negligently misrepresents a material fact.

In the case of *Crawford v. Mintz, et.al.*[7] in which the listing agent incorrectly stated in the MLS that the listed residential property was connected to the city sewer system when in fact it was connected to a septic system. The purchasers, despite pre-closing home inspections, did not discover this fact until two years after the closing when they had raw sewage in the back yard. They ultimately obtained a jury verdict against the brokerage company and listing agent for their costs to repair the septic system and connect to the city sewer system and were allowed to assert a claim for their attorney fees incurred in the protracted litigation of the case which was appealed to the North Carolina Supreme Court.

Marketing Listed Property – Legal Compliance

Effective marketing of a seller's listed property is beyond the scope of this text; however, the following discussion addresses the important issues of compliance with laws and Commission rules when marketing a property. Key points to remember are noted below.

- **Owner's consent required to display "for sale" or "for rent" signs.** This requirement is self-explanatory. Consent provisions are typically included in standard listing contract forms. Signs should be removed promptly after closing or upon the expiration of a listing agreement. [See Commission Rule 58A.0105(a)(2).]
- **Comply with laws/rules on sign placement.** State law prohibits placing any private signs on rights-of-way, medians or other state-owned property. Subdivision restrictive covenants may address the placement of for sale signs (including directional signs). Additionally, city and county ordinances commonly address the display of signs on streets and city or county owned property.
- **"Blind" advertisements are prohibited.** Commission Rule 58A.0105(b) requires that all advertisements for the sale, purchase, exchange, rent or lease of real estate by a licensee conspicuously indicate that it is the advertisement of a broker or brokerage firm and include the name of the broker or firm with which the individual broker is associated.
- **Truth-in-Lending Advertising Requirements.** The federal Truth-in-Lending laws and Regulation Z require certain disclosures in any advertisement for consumer credit placed by anyone, including real estate agents, if the ad contains certain "trigger terms." [See the coverage of "Truth in Lending Act" in Chapter 13.]

- **Fair Housing Advertising Restrictions**. Federal and state fair housing laws prohibit any advertisement that contains language or information that has a discriminatory effect on any of the fair housing protected classes. Licensees should be especially careful to avoid using words or phrases which have been determined to be discriminatory. [See Chapter 18.]
- **Internet Advertising.** *All legal requirements and restrictions on advertising apply equally to Internet advertising.* Internet advertising of a broker's or firm's listings should be regularly updated to remove expired listings (just as should be done with other advertising, such as MLS listings). Additional points to remember: Internet advertising by a broker or firm that shows or provides access to listings that are NOT the broker's or firm's listings should assure that the advertising does not convey the impression that such listings are the broker's or firm's listings. If the advertising does improperly convey the impression that the listings of others are the listings of the broker or firm responsible for the advertisement, this constitutes misrepresentation.

Marketing Listed Property – Duties of Listing Agent/Firm

This section focuses on the duty of a listing agent to his/her seller-principal under agency law to exercise "skill, care and diligence" in the performance of his/her contractual obligations under a typical "full-service" listing contract such as the North Carolina Association of REALTORS® Standard Form 101 – Exclusive Right to Sell Listing Agreement, which requires the listing agent to exercise his/her best efforts to find a buyer for the seller's property. This discussion assumes that the seller has not restricted the listing agent/firm in any significant manner with regard to marketing the property – in other words, that the seller has not prohibited the listing agent/firm from taking such actions as placing a "for sale" sign on the property, placing the listing in the MLS, cooperating with agents of other firms, etc.

The Basic Standard

A real estate agent must exercise the care, skill and diligence that is generally exercised by other real estate agents.[8] Therefore, *a listing agent/firm should take those steps to market a listed property that are customary within the real estate brokerage community for the type of property involved and the prevailing market conditions.*

Customary Marketing Practices for Most Residential Properties

- Place a "for sale" sign on the property.
- Place the listing in the local MLS.
- Provide a reasonable means for the property to be shown by other agents of the same or a different firm (for example, by using a lockbox, if permitted by the seller).
- Utilize available local print media (for example, local newspaper or real estate for sale publication) commonly used to advertise properties for sale.
- Prepare and make available to prospective buyers a promotional flyer about the property (for example, by having copies of flyers available for prospective buyers at the property).
- Advertise the property on the Internet either through a personal or firm website or Internet listing service. [Note: A majority of listed properties are now advertised on the Internet and a majority of home purchasers use the Internet to identify prospective properties, thus now making this method of advertising a "customary" practice in most locales.]
- Conduct an open house if appropriate and needed for the particular property.

- Be available to show the property to prospective buyers in a reasonable and timely manner.
- Fully cooperate with other agents wanting to show the property (to the extent authorized by the seller and if a commission sharing agreement satisfactory to the listing agent can be reached with the other agents).

Other Points to Consider

- A listing agent may want to obtain permission from his or her seller-client prior to using photographs or videos of the inside of the seller's home in advertising (e.g., in flyers or on websites). Some potential thieves could utilize such information to identify potential targets.
- While the common practice of providing to prospective buyers a copy of a survey of the seller's property with promotional flyers is fine, care should be taken not to mislead buyers into thinking they should not obtain a survey.

Educating Sellers on Their Role in Selling Their Property

- As part of their services to their seller-principals, listing agents should advise their sellers about a number of matters that affect a seller's interests and educate them on how to handle various situations, including the following:
- How to make the property more attractive to prospects. A few examples: Keeping grass mowed, adding mulch, adding some annual flowering plants, removing "junk," etc. to enhance "curb appeal"; repairing broken items; repainting with neutral colors; keeping house clean and neat at all times; getting rid of "clutter," etc.
- The importance of safeguarding personal valuable items while the property is on the market. Point out that, although prospects will always be accompanied by an agent, it may be difficult for the agent to watch every member of the viewing party at all times.
- The need to have the property available for showings every day, including early evenings and weekends. Determine any times that the seller does not want the property to be shown.
- If the listing agent prefers that the seller not be present for showings, discuss this with the seller.
- Handling prospects who arrive without an appointment (with and without an agent).
- How to handle contacts from other agents.
- How to respond to inquiries from prospects and buyer's agents in a manner that protects their bargaining position.

WORKING WITH A SELLER AS A BUYER'S AGENT

Occasionally, a **buyer's agent** encounters a situation where his or her buyer-client is interested in a property that is **not** listed for sale and the buyer's agent needs to work directly with a property owner (seller) in behalf of the buyer. *The most common situation is where a buyer represented by a buyer's agent is interested in a property advertised as "* **For Sale By Owner"** *("FSBO")* and the buyer's agent contacts the owner to ask if the owner will consider dealing with the agent and his or her buyer principal. At first substantial contact with the property owner, the broker should provide the owner a copy of the Commission's *Working with Real Estate Agents* brochure, review the brochure with the owner, and fully disclose the broker's status as a buyer's agent. Following agency disclosure, the buyer's agent should do the following:

- obtain a written agreement signed by the seller.
- avoid engaging in acts on behalf of the seller or when dealing with the seller that might result in the broker being found to be acting as the agent of the seller as well as the buyer (i.e., acting as an undisclosed dual agent). Primarily, this means not saying anything to the seller that would reasonably lead the seller to believe that the broker is working for the seller.

Working as Disclosed Dual Agent

Following agency disclosure, if permitted by the broker's buyer agency agreement and company policy, and if desired by the seller, a buyer agent could enter into a limited listing agreement with the seller (limited to the transaction with the buyer represented by the agent) that includes a dual agency addendum. The listing agreement should be completed in a manner that limits the agreement to the transaction with the named buyer, unless the seller is willing to give the agent a regular unrestricted listing.

Working as Buyer's Agent with a Seller Who Listed with a Limited Service Broker

Some buyer agents are reluctant to work directly with a seller whose property is listed with a limited service broker who has contracted only to advertise the seller's property, even to the point of avoiding selecting such a seller's property for showing to the buyer. This reluctance seems to stem from a fear of having to deal directly with the seller rather than through the listing broker. A particular concern of some buyer agents is how to handle situations where the seller asks the buyer's agent for advice.

The first thing that should be noted is that *there is nothing improper about a buyer's agent working directly with a seller who has employed a limited service listing broker so long as the buyer's agent discloses to the seller his/her status as a buyer's agent and is fair and honest in his/her dealings with the seller.* The buyer's agent needs to keep in mind that it may not be in the best interest of his or her buyer-client to avoid showing a property listed with a limited service broker.

As for compensation of the buyer's agent in this situation, limited service listing contracts typically call for the seller to pay the selling agent a specified commission at closing. If this isn't the case, most buyer agency contracts provide for the buyer to pay the buyer's agent a commission whenever the buyer's agent will not be compensated by the seller or listing agent. In any event, it is a good idea for a buyer's agent to obtain authorization from the limited sevice listing agent to communicate directly with the seller and to discuss the terms of the compensation arrangement before committing to a transaction.

WORKING WITH BUYERS

A broker may agree to work with a buyer in one of the following three ways: 1) as a **buyer's agent**; 2) as a **seller's subagent** (broker may be affiliated either with the listing firm or selling firm)**; or** 3) as a disclosed **dual agent** (agent of both seller and buyer in an "in-house" sale).

Summary of Agency Disclosure Requirements When Working with Buyers

At "first substantial contact" with a prospective buyer, a real estate broker must:
- Provide prospective buyer a copy of the Commission's Working with Real Estate Agents brochure AND
- Explain the substantive information in the brochure about agency relationship options and duties of real estate agents to the prospective buyer AND

- Explain to the prospective buyer the agency policies of the broker's firm AND
- Determine the type of agency relationship the broker (and firm) will have with the buyer before proceeding to provide any service to the prospective buyer.

[See Commission Rule 58A.0104(c) and (e) and the section on "Disclosure of Agency Relationships in Real Estate Sales" in Chapter 8 for a detailed discussion of these requirements.]

WORKING WITH BUYERS AS A SELLER'S AGENT OR SUBAGENT

If, after a real estate broker provides and explains to a prospective buyer the Commission's *Working with Real Estate Agents* brochure, the prospective buyer *does not want to enter into a buyer agency agreement, either oral or written, with the broker's firm,* then **the broker's only option is to work with the buyer as a seller's agent or subagent (if the broker's firm's policies permit this and the buyer is also agreeable).** If a prospective buyer will not agree to a buyer agency agreement and also does not consent to the broker working with the buyer as a seller's agent, the broker may not continue to work with the buyer.

Disclose and Document Agency Relationship

When the buyer and broker agree that the broker will work with the buyer as a seller's agent (or subagent), the broker must *disclose **in writing** his or her status as a seller's agent or subagent* as required by Commission Rule 58A.0104(e). To accomplish this, the broker should check the box on the signature panel of the brochure indicating that he or she will be working as a seller's subagent, write his or her broker license number on the signature panel, obtain the buyer's signature, and then make a copy of the signature panel for the buyer to retain as the written disclosure to him or her. The broker may then proceed to identify and show the buyer properties. If the buyer refuses to sign the brochure acknowledging this disclosure, the broker should carefully document the buyer's agreement and refusal to sign before proceeding. Having another broker (preferably even the office's broker-in-charge) witness the arrangement is recommended in the event the buyer should subsequently decide to claim the broker is supposed to be the buyer's agent.

"In-house" Situations

If a buyer chooses to work directly with the listing broker/firm, then the listing broker/firm may only work with the buyer as *either* a **seller's agent** (which requires disclosure of their seller agency status in writing) *or* a **dual agent**, if authorized by *both* the firm's existing seller-client *and* the new buyer-client.

Switching from a Seller's Subagent to a Buyer's Agent

If a broker works with a buyer as a seller's agent or subagent for a period of time and then the buyer asks the broker to represent him or her as a buyer's agent, the broker may switch from a seller's subagent to a buyer's agent only if the seller of any property already shown the buyer as a seller's agent or subagent knowingly consents to the broker becoming a buyer's agent, after first being informed of the resulting change in the agent's allegiance and duties. This consent of the seller is absolutely necessary and should be documented in writing because it is possible that while acting as the seller's agent or subagent, the broker may have acquired personal information about the seller that would be damaging to the seller's interests if disclosed to the buyer. (Remember, if the broker knows information about the seller that would benefit the buyer's interest, the broker must disclose such information to the buyer if he or she becomes a buyer's agent.) If the broker has *actually acquired confidential information about the seller,* the broker should make the seller aware of the information acquired when asking for the seller's permission to switch to being a buyer's agent.

The greater concern is where it is a *broker with the listing firm* who is asked to switch to acting as a buyer's agent. It is more likely that such a broker would have acquired confidential information about the seller than would a broker with a cooperating firm working with the buyer as a seller's subagent. In either event, such switching of agency relationships is **not recommended,** and should be done only with the seller's fully informed consent.

WORKING WITH BUYERS AS A BUYER'S AGENT

If, after a broker has reviewed and explained to a prospective buyer the Commission's *Working with Real Estate Agents* brochure, the buyer wants the broker to work with him or her as a buyer's agent, then the broker and buyer need to agree on the scope and terms of that representation.

Requirement for a Buyer Agency Contract

Real Estate Commission Rule 58A.0104(a) requires that *a real estate broker (or firm) proposing to work with a prospective buyer as a buyer's agent must have an express agreement regarding all terms of the working relationship prior to the agent providing brokerage services to the buyer as a buyer's agent. The agreement must be in writing, but there is a provision in the rule for an* **oral** *buyer agency agreement for a limited period of time under certain circumstances.* [See text of Rule and discussion of the oral buyer agency contract limited exception under "General Requirements for Agency Contracts" earlier in this chapter.]

Temporary Oral Buyer Agency Agreement Option

If a buyer wants a broker/firm to be his or her agent, but is unwilling to enter into a written buyer agency agreement at the beginning of the relationship, then *Commission rules permit the broker/ firm to temporarily work with the buyer under an* **oral buyer agency agreement**, as was discussed earlier in this chapter. *If an agent wishes to 1) bind a buyer to work only with the agent's firm for a period of time or 2) otherwise restrict the buyer's right to work with other agents or independently,* **then the buyer agency agreement must be in writing from the inception** of the relationship.

It should be remembered that *all the terms of the temporary oral agreement must be clearly understood by both the broker and the buyer.* To avoid confusion, *the Commission strongly recommends that the broker send the buyer a* **letter confirming the terms of their oral buyer agency agreement**. The letter not only should confirm that the broker will be working with the buyer under an oral buyer agency agreement, but additionally should set forth the terms of the parties' oral agreement, such as the names of all buyers and the broker, the type, price range and general location of the property sought, the services to be provided, the amount and method of compensation, whether the buyer authorizes dual agency, as well as any other agreed upon terms, and might further mention that a written buyer agency agreement will be required before any offer to purchase may be tendered on the buyer's behalf. *Note especially that the oral buyer agency agreement must include an authorization of* **dual agency** *if the broker is going to show the buyer any property listed with the broker's firm!*

Understand that the rule provision which allows oral buyer agency agreements was designed to address the initial reluctance of some buyers to enter into a written buyer agency agreement before they have had an opportunity to become acquainted with the broker. Nonetheless, *written agency agreements remain highly desirable and are preferred.* Brokers are urged to *obtain written buyer agency agreements at the earliest possible opportunity.*

Firms may require all buyer agency agreements to be in writing. Further, just because the rule allows temporary, oral buyer agency agreements does not mean that brokerage companies **must** allow oral agreements; rather, companies may decide as a matter of their internal office policy that they will not allow their agents to work under oral buyer agency agreements, but instead will require written agency agreements in all sales transactions from the first substantial contact. Alternatively, a company may decide that it will allow its agents to work with a buyer under an oral buyer agency agreement only for a maximum period of time, for example, up to two weeks, after which the buyer either must sign a written buyer agency agreement (whether exclusive or non-exclusive, or limited to certain specified properties or for a very limited duration, such as one month, etc.) or the company will terminate the agency relationship.

Terminating an Oral Buyer Agency Agreement. An oral buyer agency agreement may be terminated by oral notice from either party to the other at any time, although prudence would dictate a follow-up letter from the buyer to the broker or the broker to the buyer confirming the oral notice terminating the relationship.

Consequences If Buyer Refuses to Reduce Oral Agreement to Writing. If the buyer refuses to sign a written buyer agency agreement *prior* to writing an offer, then the broker may not continue to represent the buyer as a buyer's agent and may not write or present the offer to the seller on the buyer's behalf.

If a seller presents an offer to a buyer's agent working under an oral agreement with the buyer, the buyer's agent should not accept the offer for presentation to the buyer until the buyer signs a written buyer agency agreement. The buyer's agent must cease working with the buyer at this point until such a written agreement is obtained.

Switching from a Buyer's Agent to a Seller's Subagent. If the buyer under an oral buyer agency agreement absolutely refuses to reduce the agreement to writing, even if the agreement is limited to the particular property in which the buyer is interested, then *the broker may not continue to represent the buyer as a buyer's agent*, and may be compelled to walk away from the transaction.

While it is ***highly undesirable and is neither recommended nor encouraged***, an alternative to this dilemma would be for the broker to switch from working with the buyer as a buyer's agent to working with the buyer as a seller's subagent. It is not a violation of either Commission rules or statutes for a buyer's agent to terminate that buyer agency and convert to a seller's subagent ***if very specific conditions are first observed, namely:***

1. The broker must **clearly explain** to his or her buyer client that if the broker changes roles and switches to a seller's subagent, then the broker will be representing *the seller's interests and not the buyer's interests* and will owe a duty to the seller to ***reveal any and all confidential information the broker may have learned about the buyer during the course of their relationship***.

2. The broker must officially terminate the oral buyer agency relationship and obtain the now former buyer-client's written consent to work with him or her as a seller's subagent

3. The broker must have the *consent of the seller/listing firm to act as a seller's subagent in the transaction*.

If all of the foregoing three criteria are satisfied, then the broker may proceed to draft and present an offer to the seller as a seller's subagent.

Written Buyer Agency Contracts

The elements required to create a valid written buyer agency contract are very similar to those required for a valid written listing contract and are summarized below.

Summary of Essential Elements of a Written Buyer Agency Contract

---

- All parties should be named in the contract (including the names of all persons who will be purchasing the property) and all parties should sign the contract.
- The type and general location of the desired property should be described, and it is helpful to also address any special conditions of purchase required by the buyer (such as price range, intended special property use, etc.).
- The duties of both the firm and the buyer should be clearly described, as well as a description of the services to be provided by the firm.
- The amount and method of compensation of the buyer's broker should be clearly defined, as well as when the firm's brokerage fee will be earned.
- The duration of the agency contract must be stated and the contract must terminate automatically at the expiration of the time period. [See Commission Rule 58A.0104(a).]
- The contract must include the non-discrimination provision required by Commission Rule 58A.0104(b), and the provision must be set forth in a clear and conspicuous manner which shall distinguish it from other provisions of the contract.

Dual Agency Provision. If the brokerage firm practices dual agency in "in-house" transactions, it will be necessary to include a provision that enables the buyer to authorize or reject the firm acting as a dual agent in such transactions. This provision should clearly describe the firm's revised role as a dual agent and how the firm's duties will be modified in that situation.

Types of Buyer Agency Contracts

There are two primary types of buyer agency contracts used in residential sales: an **exclusive** agreement and a **non-exclusive** agreement. The North Carolina Association of REALTORS® has devised standard forms for these two types of buyer agency agreements for use by its members practicing buyer agency in residential sales, namely: **Standard Form #201, "Exclusive Buyer Agency Agreement," reprinted as Figure 9-2, and Standard Form #203, "Non-Exclusive Buyer Agency Agreement," reprinted as Figure 9-3** at the end of this chapter.

Exclusive Buyer Agency Contract

In an **exclusive** buyer agency contract, the prospective buyer retains a broker to act as the *exclusive* agent of the prospective buyer in locating and effecting the purchase of a property. Under this type of agreement, the employed buyer's broker is the **only real estate agent** with whom the prospective buyer can work in connection with the purchase of a property described in the agreement. The prospective buyer may not employ another buyer's broker to assist in purchasing a property described in the agreement, nor may the prospective buyer bypass his buyer broker and purchase property directly through a broker acting as a seller's agent or subagent. If the buyer purchases property of the type described in the buyer agency agreement during the term of the agreement through any real estate agent other than his or her broker, then the buyer may be liable to his or her broker for the agreed commission.

Whether the buyer is liable to his buyer's broker for a commission if the buyer purchases property without the assistance of any real estate agent, i.e. directly from a seller, depends on the provisions of the buyer agency agreement. The North Carolina Association of REALTORS® Standard Form #201 **"Exclusive Buyer Agency Agreement" (Figure 9-2)** provides in Paragraph 2 that the buyer "... agrees to conduct all negotiations for such property through Firm, and to refer to Firm all inquiries received in any form from other real estate firms, *prospective sellers or any other source*, during the time this Agreement is in effect." The Agreement further states that the firm's fee is deemed earned (1) if the Buyer, during the term of the Agreement, "...directly or indirectly enters into an agreement to purchase, option, and/or exchange any property of the type described above *regardless of the manner in which Buyer was introduced to the property...*" or (2) if the buyer within a certain prescribed time following the expiration of the agreement "...enters into a contract to acquire property *introduced to Buyer during the term of this Agreement by Firm or any third party...*" (Italics added.)

It seems clear that the contract is intended to entitle the buyer's broker/firm to compensation if the buyer purchases a property described in the agency agreement no matter how the buyer finds the property. NCAR's "Exclusive Buyer Agency Agreement" restricts a buyer from being able to independently purchase a property of the type described in the agency agreement prior to its expiration without incurring an obligation to pay a fee to the broker.

Nonexclusive Buyer Agency Contract

A **nonexclusive** buyer agency contract is one where the prospective buyer retains a broker to locate and effect the purchase of a property for the prospective buyer, but the contract permits *the prospective buyer to enter into similar nonexclusive buyer agency agreements with other buyer's brokers, to purchase a property through another broker acting as a seller's agent or subagent, or to purchase a property directly from a property owner.* Under this type of agreement, the buyer would be obligated to pay the buyer's broker a fee **only** if the buyer's broker is the procuring cause of the purchase.

The compensation should be clearly explained in the contract. The North Carolina Association of REALTORS® **Standard Form #203 Non-Exclusive Buyer Agency Agreement** specifically states that the buyer does **not** obligate himself or herself to pay the broker *any* of the fee stated in the contract, anticipating instead that the buyer's broker will be paid under an offer of compensation by a cooperating seller/listing firm. In the event the buyer is interested in purchasing property through the broker from a cooperating seller/listing firm and the offered compensation is less than the broker expected, then the broker has the right to terminate the agreement if unable to negotiate a modification of compensation terms with the buyer.

Note that Standard Form #203 has an option under the "Property" provision to specify a specific property if the buyer is only willing to sign a written agreement to consider one or more named specific properties.

Alternate Options For Working with Buyers

Brokers may find that some buyers are reluctant to enter into an exclusive buyer agency agreement at the outset of the relationship, particularly where it eliminates the buyer's right to function independently for as long as three to six months. However, the broker may want more assurance of a client's loyalty, as it were, than an oral agreement or a written non-exclusive agency agreement may provide. Thus, brokers may wish to consider options other than an oral agency agreement or nonexclusive buyer agency agreement, namely using an exclusive buyer agency agreement with special limitations as described below.

Limit Duration of Agreement. A broker could employ a standard exclusive buyer agency agreement form, but *limit its duration* to whatever period the parties agree, whether one day, a few days, a week, two weeks, one month, or whatever. During that period, the buyer is contractually obligated to refrain from using any other real estate broker and the broker likely also will be entitled to a commission if the buyer enters into a contract to purchase, option or exchange a property directly from a seller without any broker's assistance during the stated period.

A variant of this arrangement is to utilize an exclusive buyer agency agreement for a longer term, for example, three to six months, but include an early termination provision allowing the buyer to withdraw from and terminate the agency relationship prior to the expiration of the stated term. The agreement should specify any conditions affecting the buyer's right to terminate the agency agreement and how the buyer is to exercise that right.

Limit Agreement to Specific Properties. Another alternative is to identify specific properties to which the exclusive buyer agency agreement shall apply. In other words, the broker operates as the buyer's exclusive agent only for the named properties. The broker may be entitled to a commission if the buyer enters into a contract to purchase any of the named properties, but the buyer remains free to use other agents or view other properties independently without breaching his contractual obligations to the broker-agent.

DUTIES TO BUYER OF BUYER'S AGENT VERSUS SELLER'S AGENT

A buyer's agent will be held to a higher standard under the common law with regard to protecting and serving the buyer's interest than will a seller's agent dealing with a buyer as a third party. Because a buyer's agent has a fiduciary agency relationship with his or her buyer-principal and a seller's agent does not have such a relationship with a buyer (absent a dual agency situation), the buyer's agent's obligations to the buyer are considerably greater than the obligations of a seller's agent to a buyer.

It is true that when a seller's agent is working with a buyer, the seller's agent may, in fact, perform many of the same services to the buyer (for example, show a buyer properties for sale, assist a buyer in completing and offer to purchase, assist the buyer in locating financing or property inspections, etc.) that are routinely provided by a buyer's agent. However, the seller's agent is not performing such services due to any legal obligation to the buyer. Rather, the seller's agent is attempting to effect a sale of the seller's property in accordance with the agent's legal obligations to the **seller**, not to mention for the purpose of earning a brokerage commission! *To the extent that providing assistance to a buyer as a seller's agent contributes to the successful sale of the seller's property without compromising the seller's interest in any way, the seller's agent has a duty* **to the seller** *provide such assistance. The important distinction is that the seller's agent is providing the service because of his or her duty to the seller, not because of any duty owed to the buyer.*

PRACTICES OF AGENTS WORKING WITH BUYERS

This section focuses on the **practices and services** that a conscientious **buyer's agent** would follow or provide when working with a buyer *up to the point in time when an offer to purchase is prepared for the buyer.*

Educate the Prospective Buyer

Educate the prospective buyer as necessary about the process of buying a home and the current real estate market. This is especially important with first-time homebuyers. The less experienced the homebuyer, the greater the buyer's agent's responsibility to inform them about what is involved in buying a home. All buyers need to be informed about current market conditions.

Determine the Buyer's Specific Housing Needs and Desires

It is important to learn as much as possible about the buyer's needs and desires. Many questions must be asked to ascertain this information. What size house is needed? Size and type of lot? Design? Geographic area? Aesthetic desires? Amenities? Price range? And so on. Not only does obtaining such information enable the agent to better serve the buyer by identifying appropriate possible choices, it also will save the agent many wasted hours showing inappropriate properties.

"Qualify the Buyer"

It is especially critical to "qualify the buyer" — i.e., determine the maximum price the buyer is able and willing to pay for a residence. Procedures for financially qualifying a buyer are discussed in depth under "Loan Underwriting Practices" in Chapter 13. Even if the agent refers the prospective buyer to a loan officer for formal advance loan qualifying (i.e., "loan prequalifying"), which is an excellent practice, the agent still needs to understand the qualification requirements and procedures for major types of loans. Properly qualifying a buyer will help the agent avoid wasting the time of the buyer, the agent working with the buyer, the listing agent and owners of listed properties.

Select Properties for Showing

Select from listed property information (such as the MLS) appropriate possible choices of homes for the buyer to view based on the information gathered about the buyer's needs, desires and financial qualifications. Do not limit the properties selected to those listed by the buyer's agent's firm. Remember, a buyer's agent is primarily obligated to serve the best interest of the buyer, and arbitrarily limiting selected properties to "in-house" listings may not necessarily be in the buyer's best interest. Similarly, do not routinely exclude any listed property because it is listed with a limited service listing broker. This is an inappropriate approach which also may very well not be in a buyer's best interest.

Obtain Cooperation Agreement If Needed

Once potential properties are selected, if they include properties listed with other firms, and those other firms and the firm of the buyer's agent are not both members of an MLS or similar listing service, the buyer's agent should contact the listing agent and obtain an agreement on cooperation and fee-sharing. It is important that this be done *prior to scheduling a showing appointment and showing a property.*

Schedule Showing Appointments and Show Selected Properties

Contact the listing firm or MLS appointment service to schedule showing appointments, honoring any restrictions requested by the seller. Show the selected homes to the buyer. Always strive to adhere as closely as possible to the showing schedule and keep the listing firm advised if there is any problem. Remember common courtesies you would like for selling agents to demonstrate when showing your listings.

Remember to take appropriate safety precautions before and during any showings and securely lock all doors when you leave!

Discover and Disclose Material Facts

At the point that the buyer indicates an interest in possibly making an offer on a property (or narrows his/her choices to two or three properties), perform a **thorough "walk-through" inspection** of each property looking for any obvious property defects or inconsistencies in the property information provided by the listing agent. Remember that *agents basically have the same duty to discover and disclose material facts to a buyer under the Real Estate License Law regardless of whether they are acting as a buyer's agent or seller's agent; however, a buyer's agent is much more likely to be aware of a buyer's special interests or concerns and, therefore, is more likely to encounter situations where he or she needs to make a special effort to check into the matters of special interest or concern to the buyer.*

Perform a Comparative Market Analysis

Perform a comparative market analysis for the property. This will assist the buyer in determining an appropriate offer amount by identifying the approximate value of the property. This is one of the single most important services a buyer's agent can provide to a buyer-client. *[See Chapter 15 for detailed coverage of Comparative Market Analysis.]* **Note:** A **seller's agent** may, upon request of the buyer, provide the buyer with information on the sales prices of comparable sales; *however, the seller's agent should be careful not to provide the buyer with advice as to an appropriate offering price, as this might well be found to be acting against the best interest of his or her seller-client.*

Check Land Use Restrictions

An agent must make certain that any representations he or she makes regarding the property's use are accurate. A conscientious buyer's agent will routinely make certain his or her buyer-client knows to check into land use restrictions and will assist the buyer in doing so when circumstances exist that should lead a reasonably prudent agent to think there may be an issue about which the buyer should be aware.

Protective Covenants. Determine if the property is subject to protective covenants, homeowners association bylaws and/or homeowners association dues. Any house located in a subdivision is highly likely to be subject to protective covenants and may also have homeowners association and homeowner dues. If any of these are applicable, *advise the buyer that he/she should obtain copies of and review the relevant information as this may very well affect the buyer's decision about a property.* If requested by the buyer, obtain such information for the buyer. The best source for accurate information of this nature is the subdivision's homeowners association, if such an association exists. *[See the discussion of an agent's responsibilities in this regard under "Private Land Use Controls" in Chapter 7.]*

Zoning. *The agent should verify the zoning of the property under consideration anytime the buyer is planning to use the property for a purpose different than its current use, anytime the prospective buyer raises a question about a permitted use that might be affected by zoning, or anytime there is any reason ("red flag") to suspect there might be a zoning problem.* An example of a "red flag" situation might be a house located in an older neighborhood where there are mixed uses (for example, single-family residential, multi-family residential, office and retail uses all in the immediate vicinity). Another example might be a property located close to a city limit. Such property might be within the city's "extraterritorial jurisdiction" for land use regulation purposes. Zoning may be verified through the office of the city or county planning department (or building inspector).

Flood Hazard Area. Anytime a property under consideration is located in an area the agent knows to be flood-prone, the agent should advise the buyer of this fact and assist the buyer in verifying whether the property is located in a designated flood hazard area (check with local planning office) and in determining the cost of flood insurance. The same is true when the property is located near any body of water or river or creek. Agents who work in areas likely to have special environmental regulations (such as coastal areas) should be aware of where such regulations apply and advise buyers accordingly. When a particular type of property is generally known to possibly have an environmental issue (such as a property used for a service station which likely has underground fuel storage tanks), then the agent should advise the buyer to inquire about such matter.

Important Note: *For coverage of agent practices that should be followed with regard to sales contracts and related matters, see Chapter 11 on "Sales Contracts and Practice" and for agent practices related to preparation for closing (i.e., "buyer's due diligence") and closing, see Chapter 14 on "Closing the Transaction."*

WORKING AS A DUAL AGENT

Dual agency involves acting as an agent for two or more parties with adverse interests in the same transaction. In real estate brokerage, this occurs when a broker or firm agrees to act as the agent of both the seller and prospective buyer in a sales transaction or as the agent of both the property owner or landlord and prospective tenant in a rental/lease transaction. In real estate sales, dual agency situations arise primarily in the context of "in-house sales where a firm's buyer client is interested in a property that is listed for sale with the firm.

Requirements for Brokers in Dual Agency Situations

Because of the inherent conflict of interest between the principals in a dual agency situation, the North Carolina Real Estate License Law in General Statute §93A-6(a)(4) prohibits a broker (or firm) from *"acting for more than one party in a transaction without the knowledge of all parties for whom he or she acts."* Thus, **disclosure** *of the dual agency to all parties is required.* Although not explicitly stated in this provision, the necessity for the parties to **consent** to dual agency is clearly implied since otherwise there would be no purpose in requiring an agent to *disclose* the dual agency situation. Thus, **dual agency agreements** *between the agent and each of the affected parties are required by law before a broker may act as a dual agent for multiple parties.* This statutory requirement *applies to all real estate transactions*, not just real estate sales transactions.

Requirement for Written Agreement Authorizing Dual Agency
Real Estate Commission Rule 58A.0104(d) takes the statutory requirement a step further by requiring that *all dual agency agreements must be **in writing**. The rule provides in part: "A real estate broker representing one party in a transaction shall not undertake to represent another party in the transaction without the written authority of each party." The written authority (i.e., "dual agency agreement") must be in writing as of the time of formation of the dual agency relationship, with one exception noted below*

Exception Allowing Temporary ORAL Dual Agency Agreement. *Where a broker is already working with a buyer under an **oral** buyer agency agreement as authorized by Commission rules, a broker may work with the buyer and seller under **oral** dual agency agreements until such time as the oral buyer agreement is reduced to writing, i.e., no later than presentment of an offer by either party. At that point, the broker/firm must have written consent for dual agency from each party.*

Authorizing Dual Agency in Listing and Buyer Agency Contracts
Three possible situations may occur:
1. **Advance Written Consent by Both Seller and Buyer.** If the seller and buyer consented to dual agency in their listing and buyer agency contracts, then it is sufficient for the firm's

agent(s) to simply advise the seller and buyer orally when a dual agency situation arises. No further expression of consent is needed.

2. **Advance Consent by One Party Only.** If only one of the parties consented to dual agency in their agency contract, then the firm/agent must obtain the non-consenting party's consent for dual agency in writing prior to proceeding with the transaction. This may be accomplished by amending the agency contract where dual agency was initially rejected (and having the change dated and signed) or by executing a separate dual agency agreement.

3, **No Advance Consent by Either Party.** In this case, both the buyer and the seller will have to agree to dual agency **in writing** (at least for this particular transaction) before the buyer is shown the in-house listing. Again, this may be done by amending the initial agency contract (and dating and signing the change) or by executing a separate dual agency agreement.

The Major Practical Problem with Dual Agency

Both the North Carolina Association of REALTORS® and the North Carolina Real Estate Commission have developed approaches to help real estate licensees address the dual agency problem. These are listed below and then discussed separately.

(1)   *Limiting a dual agent's duties by contract.* The real estate brokerage industry has adopted a method of practicing dual agency which appears likely to be found legally acceptable and to reduce some of the risk of being a dual agent.

(2)   *Practicing "designated dual agency" under Real Estate Commission rules.* The Commission adopted rules which permit real estate agents in a firm to practice a form of dual agency known as "designated agency," which may provide an acceptable way to practice dual agency without limiting the agent's obligations and services to the clients..

(3)   *Limiting individual dual agent's duties by Real Estate Commission rule.* The Commission adopted a rule that permits an individual agent who is a dual agent to deal with disclosure of information in the same manner as an individual "designated agent."

Limiting the Dual Agent's Duties by Contract

The North Carolina Association of REALTORS® has included comprehensive "Dual Agency" provisions in its standard listing and buyer agency contract forms. The reader is referred to the Exclusive Right to Sell Listing Agreement form #101 (Figure 9-1) and the Exclusive Buyer Agency Agreement form #201 (Figure 9-2) that appear in this chapter for the specific language of the dual agency provisions.

One purpose of the dual agency provision in these agency contract forms is to permit the seller and buyer to authorize (or reject) in writing dual agency at the outset of the agency relationship. *The most important point about this dual agency provision in the REALTOR® agency contract forms is that it modifies and limits by contract the duties of the agent (real estate firm and affiliated individual licensees) to the principal (seller or buyer) when the agent (firm) is acting as a dual agent in an in-house sale situation.*

Limiting Disclosure of Certain Information to Principals

The following language appears in Standard Form #201 (with similar language in Standard Form #101) concerning the disclosure of certain information by the dual agent:

> Disclosure of Information. In the event Firm serves as a dual agent, Buyer agrees that without permission from the party about whom the information pertains, Firm shall not disclose to the other party the following information:
> (a) that a party may agree to a price, terms, or any conditions of sale other than those offered;
> (b) the motivation of a party for engaging in the transaction, unless disclosure is otherwise required by statute or rule; and
> (c) any information about a party which that party has identified as confidential unless disclosure is otherwise required by statute or rule.

Note that the above provision deals primarily with **"personal" information** about a party that does not relate directly to the property or affect a party's ability to complete the transaction. Paragraph (a) addresses the common question that sellers and buyers have in virtually every transaction. Paragraph (b) addresses the parties' *motivation*. This would probably come into play more often with regard to a *seller's* motivation and might include a motivation to sell due to a *pending foreclosure;* however, this would be required to be disclosed in any case under the Real Estate License Law because it deals with the seller's ability to complete the transaction.

Assuming the above limitations on the duty to disclose information are legally permissible, the form resolves, from the agent's perspective, the major problem encountered by agents in dual agency situations, namely the dilemma of how to handle personal information about one of the clients that might hurt that client if disclosed, but help the other client.

Limiting the Duties of Loyalty and Skill, Care and Diligence

The NCAR agency contract forms, in the "dual agency" provision, takes an additional step in attempting to limit the dual agent's duties to the two principals. The Exclusive Buyer Agency Agreement form states as follows under the heading "Firm's Role as Dual Agent:

> If Firm serves as agent for both Buyer and a seller in a transaction, Firm shall make every reasonable effort to represent Buyer and seller in a **balanced and fair manner**. Firm shall also make every reasonable effort to encourage and effect communication and negotiation between Buyer and Seller. [Emphasis added.]

Also included in the same provision under "Buyer's Role" is the following statement:

> Buyer is fully aware of and understands the implications and consequences of Firm's dual agency role as expressed herein to provide balanced and fair representation of Buyer and seller and to encourage and effect communication between them **rather than as an advocate or exclusive agent or representative**. [Emphasis added.]

The clear purpose of the foregoing language is to modify the standard agency duties of loyalty and skill, care and diligence that require an agent to fully serve the best interest of the principal to the exclusion of other adverse interests, and to seek the most advantageous bargain possible for the principal. *The language calls for the agent to be a conduit of information rather than to advise the client on how to obtain the best bargain or to advocate for the client's interest.*

Effect of This Approach

Assuming the limitations on a dual agent's duties set forth in the dual agency provisions of the NCAR standard agency contract forms prove to be legally effective, then the use of such a contract form will reduce somewhat the risks associated with acting as a dual agent. Many real estate firms obviously have decided that the potential risks associated with the practice of dual agency are necessary business risks. In essence, these companies have decided they cannot afford to lose business to other firms which specialize in buyer agency or which are willing to practice dual agency with the written consent of the seller and buyer.

Designated Dual Agency

Another approach some real estate companies are taking to alleviate some of the inherent problems involved with practicing dual agency is to utilize a form of dual agency called **"designated agency."** Designated agency was authorized by North Carolina Real Estate Commission rules effective in 1997 and offers an innovative approach to dealing with the dual agency problem. This concept has yet to be tested in the courts.

Under this *optional* approach, a *firm* that is a *dual agent* of both the seller and buyer may appoint or "designate" one or more *individual* agents (usually the listing agent) to continue to *fully* represent the interests of only the *seller* and one or more other *individual* agents (usually the agent working with the buyer) to continue to *fully* represent the interests of only the buyer in the transaction. [Typically, only one agent will be designated to represent each party.] In their dealings with the seller and buyer, the individual designated agents function as though they are agents of different firms representing different principals, even though they are both affiliated with the same firm which represents both principals.

The Major Rule Provisions

The basic rule provision, 21 NCAC 58A.0104(j), authorizing designated dual agency states:

> (j) When a firm represents both the buyer and seller in the same real estate transaction, the firm may, *with the prior express approval of its buyer and seller clients*, designate one or more individual brokers associated with the firm to represent only the interests of the seller and one or more other individual brokers associated with the firm to represent only the interests of the buyer in the transaction. The authority for designated agency must be reduced to writing not later than the time that the parties are required to reduce their dual agency agreement to writing in accordance with paragraph (d) of this rule. An individual broker shall not be so designated and shall not undertake to represent only the interests of one party if the broker has actually received confidential information concerning the other party in connection with the transaction. A broker-in-charge shall not act as a designated broker for a party in a real estate sales transaction when a provisional broker under his or her supervision will act as a designated broker for another party with a competing interest. [Italics added.]

Designated Agent's Duty. The Real Estate Commission rules prescribe that *a designated agent's duty is to represent only the interest of his or her designated client.* Consistent with this concept, the rule also *prohibits a designated agent from making certain disclosures of confidential information about his or her designated principal to the other principal in the transaction, just as a single agent may not disclose* *confidential information about his or her client to a third party.* Commission Rule 21NCAC58A.0104(k) provides that a broker (including a provisional broker) designated to represent only the **seller:**

> . . . shall represent only the interest of the seller and shall not, without the seller's permission, disclose to the buyer or a broker designated to represent the buyer:
>
> (1) that the seller may agree to a price, terms, or any conditions of sale other than those established by the seller;
>
> (2) the seller's motivation for engaging in the transaction unless disclosure is otherwise required by statute or rule; and
>
> (3) any information about the seller that the seller has identified as confidential unless disclosure of the information is otherwise required by statute or rule.

Virtually identical language appears in 21 NCAC 58A.0104(l) as to brokers (or provisional brokers) designated to represent only the **buyer.** The effect of designated dual agency is to provide, in an in-house sales transaction, a firm's seller and buyer clients, which the firm represents as a "dual" agent, the benefit of having a designated agent of the firm to represent them in essentially the same manner as seller and buyer clients are represented in "single" agency situations. Thus, designated dual agency has the effect of restoring the ability of the agents working with the seller and buyer to fully advise their clients and advocate for their clients' interests, something that is lost in normal dual agency where all agents working with the seller and buyer must only be a conduit of information and represent both clients in a fair and balanced manner without favoring or advocating for the interests of one client over the interests of the other client.

Disclosure of Identity of Designated Agents. One important theme found throughout the rules of the Real Estate Commission is the public policy concept of timely and meaningful disclosure of agency relationships to parties dealing with real estate agents. Real Estate Commission Rule 58A.0104(m) reads in part: "A broker designated to represent a buyer or seller ... shall disclose the identity of all of the brokers so designated to both the buyer and the seller. The disclosure shall take place no later than the presentation of the first offer to purchase or sell."

Advance Authority for Designated Agency

Note that the NCAR standard agency contract forms (see Figures 9-1 and 9-2) include a "Designated Agency Option" paragraph as part of the "Dual Agency" provision. This allows the seller or buyer to authorize (or reject) designated agency at the same time a choice is made about dual agency when the agency contract is being formed.

Special Features of Designated Dual Agency

Discussed briefly below are several features of designated dual agency practice that firms and individual agents need to keep in mind.

- Designated dual agency does not eliminate dual agency. It is merely a form of dual agency. The designation of individual agents to act as the "designated agents" for the seller and buyer does not change the status of the firm as a dual agent. As a dual agent, the firm is obligated to serve both seller and buyer equally.

- The designated agency option may be used only for in-house dual agency sales situations. Remember, there is no dual agency when an agent is showing one of his or her firm's listings as a seller's subagent.

- Prior approval of both seller and buyer is mandatory. Rule 58A.0104(j) continues to require prior written approval of both parties before designated agency may be employed. The authorization of the seller and buyer must be reduced to writing not later than the time the parties are required to reduce their dual agency agreement to writing. (Normally, the written designated agency authorization is included as part of the written dual agency agreement.)

- Individual designated agents will be considered by the Commission as having an obligation to act as the agent ONLY for the principal who the agent has been appointed or designated to represent in the particular transaction. Even though an individual designated agent is a type of dual agent, in order for the designated agency approach to be functional, it is necessary to view the agent as being obligated only to the party he or she is designated to represent. This assumes, of course, that the firm's designated agency policy is implemented in accordance with Commission rules. As the designated agency alternative is still relatively new, there are no North Carolina appellate decisions dealing with the duties and obligations of these agents. It is likely, however, that existing case law dealing with the duties of a seller's agent in most cases will be applicable to the duties of a designated seller's agent. Similarly, a designated buyer's agent should have the duties and obligations of a regular buyer's agent.

- An individual agent may not be appointed or undertake to serve as the designated agent of one party if the agent actually has received confidential information about the other party in the transaction. The reason for this restriction is that a designated agent is treated under this rule as the agent of only the party he or she is designated to represent and, as such, the agent owes the full scope of agency duties to the principal he or she is designated to represent. This includes full disclosure to the principal of all information known to the agent that might influence the principal's decision in the transaction. Thus, a designated agent should not possess confidential information about the other party, who is also the firm's client. Further, an individual agent, after having been designated to represent a party, neither should nor may actively seek confidential information about the other party to the transaction. To do so would undermine the firm's effort under the designated agency policy to provide the best representation possible for both clients while fulfilling the firm's obligations to both principals as dual agent. Where, for example, a buyer's agent who normally would be appointed as the designated agent for the buyer possesses confidential information about the seller, it will be necessary to appoint another agent in the firm to work with the buyer as the buyer's designated agent, OR the firm may continue to function more neutrally under the firm's standard dual agency policy rather than practice designated agency in that transaction.

- A comprehensive firm policy on designated agency practice in accordance with Commission rules is necessary. The policy should establish internal office procedures which minimize the possibility of confidential information about one client from accidentally falling into the hands of the designated agent for the other client in the same transaction. Additional matters to be addressed include record keeping systems and access to office files, access to agents' desks/offices, and communications among agents about client confidences.

- Multiple agents can be designated to represent a principal. Although this might be unusual in residential transactions, the rules allow more than one agent to be appointed to represent a party. If a proposed designated agent has a licensed personal assistant, then both should be designated.

- The firm must specify in its policy who is authorized to appoint designated agents. The rule says the "firm" may appoint designated agents, but it obviously is necessary for the firm to name an individual broker to do this. In firms with only one office, the broker making the designations will most likely (and probably should) be the broker-in-charge. Where a firm has multiple offices, especially in the same geographical area, the firm must address this issue in the firm's policy.

- A broker-in-charge cannot serve as a designated agent in the same transaction where a provisional broker under the supervision of the broker-in-charge is a designated agent for the other party. Rule 58A.0104(j) specifically prohibits this. As previously mentioned, a designated agent for one party may not have confidential information about the other party to the transaction nor should they have access to the other party's file. Yet a broker-in-charge is required to actively and personally supervise all provisional brokers in their office and thus must have access to the provisional brokers' files and oversee the provisional brokers' representation of clients. Thus, the broker-in-charge's mandatory supervisory obligations of provisional brokers in his or her office defeat the necessary separation required between designated agents. Because a broker-in-charge does not have the same supervisory obligations over his or her associated brokers whose licenses are not on provisional status (i.e., who are not provisional brokers), the conflict does not exist and the broker-in-charge may be the designated agent for one party so long as the designated agent for the other party is not a provisional broker.

- Designated agency must be commenced not later than presentation of the first offer to buy or sell. Remember that advance permission of the parties is necessary to practice designated agency. While the most logical time to commence designated agency is right after a buyer-client has expressed serious interest in a firm listing, designations must be established prior to the time the first offer is extended, which also is the deadline by which any oral buyer agency agreements with dual agency authorization must be in writing as well. Without prior authorization of both parties for designated agency, a firm may function only under its standard dual agency policy.

Individual Broker Dual Agent

When adopting the rules on "designated agency," the Real Estate Commission determined that in fairness to the individual broker who has a buyer client interested in one of the broker's personal listings, such individual broker should have the same benefit as a "designated agent" with regard to not having to disclose to a party certain personal and confidential information about the other party. Consequently, the Commission adopted Rule 21 NCAC 58A.0104(n) which reads:

(n) When an *individual broker* represents both the buyer and seller in the same real estate sales transaction pursuant to a *written agreement* authorizing dual agency, the parties may provide in the written agreement that the broker shall not disclose the following information about one party to the other without permission from the party about whom the information pertains:

(1) that a party may agree to a price, terms or any conditions of sale other than those offered;

(2) the motivation of a party for engaging in the transaction, unless disclosure is otherwise required by statute or rule; and

(3) any information about a party which that party has identified as confidential, unless disclosure is otherwise required by statute or rule.

By adopting this rule, the Commission recognized the very difficult situation an agent encounters when a buyer-client becomes interested in one of the agent's listings. The rule attempts to provide some limited relief by making it a little easier for a broker to lawfully practice dual agency when selling his or her own listings. However, *the nondisclosure of confidential client information in this particular dual agency situation must be specifically authorized in the agency agreements with both parties.*

Alternatives to Dual Agency in Other States

In an effort to avoid some of the dual agency problems described above, some jurisdictions have adopted statutes permitting real estate licensees to act as a "middle man," "limited agent," "transaction agent" or "facilitator" in real estate transactions. These statutory creations operate somewhat like a "limited" dual agency, where the real estate agent performs limited functions and owes limited obligations to each party to the real estate transaction. *North Carolina does **not** have any legislation or case law authorizing this middleman or facilitator concept.* As a practical matter, the method by which dual agency actually is being practiced in North Carolina at the present time — by use of agency agreements which purport to limit the agent's duties where dual agency is practiced for in-house sales — is extremely similar to these other approaches and probably render them unnecessary. Consequently, dual agency practice in North Carolina continues to be governed by the traditional law of agency as it applies to dual agency, combined with the requirements of the North Carolina Real Estate License Law and the rules of the North Carolina Real Estate Commission.

Dual Agency Agreement Without Pre-existing Agency Relationship

It is also possible to enter into a dual agency agreement with a property owner and prospective buyer or tenant where there may not be a pre-existing written agency agreement with either party. Where there is no existing agency contract with either party, or where the dual agency agreement is intended to *supercede*, rather than *supplement*, a pre-existing written agency agreement, the dual agency agreement must contain all the provisions essential to formation of a listing contract or buyer agency contract, in addition to clearly explaining the consequences of the broker or firm acting as a dual agent. A written dual agency *agreement* should address the following matters:

- The agreement should identify both the property owner and the buyer as well as the broker.
- The purpose of the agreement should be clearly explained. If it modifies and supercedes an existing listing contract with the owner and buyer agency agreement with the buyer with regard to the agency relationship between the firm (and its affiliated agents) and the parties to the transaction then it should explicitly state that.

- The agreement should clearly explain the consequences of the firm acting as a dual agent. If the firm is proposing to modify the duties it owes to the seller and buyer under existing agency contracts, it is especially important that any such proposed modification be clearly spelled out. Note: The failure to adequately explain the consequences of dual agency to clients could lead a court to conclude that there was no "informed consent."
- The proposed amount or method of compensation of the firm by either or both the owner and buyer/lessee should be stated, particularly if it alters the compensation arrangements described in any pre-existing agency contracts.
- The duration of the dual agency must be specified. The agreement should provide that the dual agency will terminate either upon the successful completion of the transaction between the parties or as of a specific date, whichever occurs first. Any provisions allowing earlier termination by providing notice should be specified.

The agreement must include the non-discrimination provision required by Commission Rule 58A.0104(b). All other essential terms must be included. The agreement should be signed by all principals and by an agent(s) on behalf of the real estate firm.

Endnotes

1. *Thompson-McLean, Inc. v. Campbell*, 261 N.C. 310, 134 S.E.2d 671 (1964).

2. *Resort Realty of the Outer Banks v. Brandt*, 163 N.C.App. 114, 593 S.E.2d 404; *Hecht Realty Inc. v. Whisnant*, 41 N.C. App. 702, 255 S.E.2d 647 (1979); *Realty Agency Inc. v. Duckworth & Shelton, Inc.*, 274 N.C. 243, 162 S.E.2d 486 (1968). See *Sessler v. Marsh*, 144 N.C.App. 623, 551 S.E.2d 160 (2001), where the Court of Appeals finds that the broker is the procuring cause of the sale when the broker's prospect does not purchase the property individually but later joins with other parties in the purchase. While there is conflicting authority nationally on this issue, the Court of Appeals found that the dispositive issue in these cases is one of proximate cause, and that the ultimate sale in this case was the proximate result of the broker's efforts. Thus the broker was the procuring cause of sale and was entitled to the commission.

3. *RWSP Realty, LLC v. Augusta*, 42 A.D. 3d 490 (Sup.Ct.App.Div. 2nd Dep. N.Y. 2007).

4. *Weber, Hodges & Goodwin Commercial Real Estate Services, LLC v. Cook*, 186 N.C. App. 288, 650 S.E.2d 834 (2007) *disc. review denied* 362 N.C. 374, 662 S.E. 2d 551 (2008) WL 2827584.

5. See, for example, the North Carolina Court of Appeals decision in *Adaron Group v. Industrial Innovators*, 90 N.C. App. 758, 370 S.E.2d 66 (1988), allowing the broker a commission when the purchase of the property was contracted for during the listing period but the actual sale did not take place until after its expiration.

6. 16 C.F.R., Part 310; 47 C.F.R. §64.1200; N.C. Gen. Stat. §75-100 through 75-105; www.donotcall. gov.

7.   *Crawford v. Mintz,* 187 N.C. App. 378, 653 S.E.2d 222 (2007), *reversed for reasons stated in the dissent and remanded,* 362 N.C. 666, 669 S.E.2d 738 (2008); 195 N.C. App. 713, 673 S.E.2d 746 (2009).

8.   *Brown v. Roth,* 514 S.E.2d 294, 233 N.C.App. 52 (1999).

EXCLUSIVE RIGHT TO SELL LISTING AGREEMENT
[Consult "Guidelines" (Form 101G) for guidance in completing this form]

This EXCLUSIVE RIGHT TO SELL LISTING AGREEMENT ("Agreement") is entered into between _____ as Seller(s) ("Seller") of the property described below (the "Property"), and _____ as Listing Firm ("Firm"). The individual agent who signs this Agreement shall, on behalf of the Firm, be primarily responsible for ensuring that the Firm's duties hereunder are fulfilled; however, it is understood and agreed that other agents of the Firm may be assigned to fulfill such duties if deemed appropriate by the Firm. For purposes of this Agreement, the term "Firm," as the context may require, shall be deemed to include the individual agent who signs this Agreement and any other agents of the Firm.

In consideration for Firm's services and efforts to find a buyer for the Property, Firm is hereby granted the exclusive right to sell the Property on the terms and conditions set forth in this Agreement.

Seller represents that as of the Effective Date the Seller is not (or will not be, if the Property is currently listed) a party to a listing agreement with any other real estate firm regarding the Property. Seller also represents that Seller has received a copy of the "WORKING WITH REAL ESTATE AGENTS" brochure and has reviewed it with Firm.

1. **TERM OF AGREEMENT.**
    (a) **Term**. The term of this Agreement ("Term") shall begin on its Effective Date and shall end at midnight on its Expiration Date.
    (b) **Effective Date**. This Agreement shall become effective and the Seller and Firm's respective rights and obligations under this Agreement shall commence ("Effective Date") as follows (*check appropriate box*):
    ❏ The Effective Date shall be the date that this Agreement has been signed by both Seller and Firm
    ❏ The Property is currently listed for sale exclusively with another real estate firm. Seller represents that the current listing agreement expires on _____. The Effective Date of this Agreement shall commence immediately upon the expiration of the current listing agreement. (**NOTE**: According to Article 16 of the REALTORS® Code of Ethics: *"REALTORS® shall not engage in any practice or take any action inconsistent with exclusive representation or exclusive brokerage relationship agreements that other REALTORS® have with clients."*)
    (c) **Expiration Date**. This Agreement shall terminate at midnight on _____ ("Expiration Date").

2. **PROPERTY**. The Property that is the subject of this Agreement shall include all that real estate described below together with all appurtenances thereto including the improvements located thereon and the fixtures and personal property listed in Paragraphs 3 and 4 below.
    Street Address: _____ Zip _____
    City: _____
    County: _____, North Carolina

    > **NOTE**: Governmental authority over taxes, zoning, school districts, utilities and mail delivery may differ from address shown. Legal Description: (Complete *ALL* applicable)

    - Plat Reference: Lot/Unit _____, Block/Section _____, Subdivision/Condominium _____, as shown on Plat Book/Slide _____ at Page(s) _____
    - The PIN/PID or other identification number of the Property is: _____
    - Other description: _____
    Some or all of the Property may be described in Deed Book _____ at Page _____

3. **FIXTURES AND EXCLUSIONS.**
    (a) **Specified Items:** Unless identified in subparagraph (d) below, the following items, including all related equipment and remote control devices, if any, are deemed fixtures and shall convey, included in the Purchase Price free of liens:

    - Alarm and security systems (attached) for security, fire, smoke, carbon monoxide or other toxins with all related access codes, sensors, cameras, dedicated monitors, hard drives, video recorders, power supplies and cables; doorbells/chimes
    - All stoves/ranges/ovens; built-in appliances; attached microwave oven; vent hood
    - Antennas; satellite dishes and receivers
    - Basketball goals and play equipment (permanently attached or in-ground)

    - Ceiling and wall-attached fans; light fixtures (including existing bulbs)
    - Fireplace insert; gas logs or starters; attached fireplace screens; wood or coal stoves
    - Floor coverings (attached)
    - Fuel tank(s) whether attached or buried and including any contents that have not been used, removed or resold to the fuel provider as of Settlement. **NOTE:** Seller's use, removal or resale of fuel in any fuel tank is subject to Seller's obligation under Paragraph 8(c) to provide working, existing

Page 1 of 10

STANDARD FORM 101
Revised 7/2017
© 7/2017

REALTOR®   Individual agent initials _____   Seller initials _____ _____

Figure 9-1

utilities through the earlier of Closing or possession by Buyer.
- Garage door openers with all controls
- Generators that are permanently wired
- Invisible fencing with power supply, controls and receivers
- Landscape and outdoor trees and plants (except in moveable containers); raised garden; landscape and foundation lighting; outdoor sound systems; permanent irrigation systems and controls; rain barrels; landscape water features; address markers
- Mailboxes; mounted package and newspaper receptacles
- Mirrors attached to walls, ceilings, cabinets or doors; all bathroom wall mirrors

- Storage shed; utility building
- Swimming pool (excluding inflatable); spa; hot tub
- Solar electric and solar water heating systems
- Sump-pumps, radon fans and crawlspace ventilators; de-humidifiers that are permanently wired
- Surface-mounting brackets for television and speakers; recess-mounted speakers; mounted intercom system
- Water supply equipment, including filters, conditioning and softener systems; re-circulating pumps; well pumps and tanks
- Window/Door blinds and shades, curtain and drapery rods and brackets, door and window screens and combination doors, awnings and storm windows

(b) **Items Leased or Not Owned:** Any item which is leased or not owned by Seller, such as fuel tanks, antennas, satellite dishes and receivers, appliances, and alarm and security systems must be identified here and shall not convey:
_____
_____
_____
_____

(c) **Other Fixtures/Unspecified items:** Unless identified in subparagraph (d) below, any other item legally considered a fixture is included in the Purchase Price free of liens.

(d) **Other Items That Do Not Convey:** The following items shall not convey (*identify those items to be excluded under subparagraphs (a) and (c)*): _____
_____ .
Seller shall repair any damage caused by removal of any items excluded above.

4. **PERSONAL PROPERTY.** The following personal property shall be transferred to Buyer at no value at Closing:
_____
_____

5. **HOME WARRANTY.** Seller ❑ agrees ❑ does not agree to obtain and pay for at settlement a one year home warranty for the Property at a cost not to exceed $_____. If Seller agrees to obtain and pay for a home warranty at any time, Firm hereby discloses that a fee of _____ will be offered to Firm by the person or entity through or from which any home warranty is obtained as compensation to Firm for its assistance in obtaining the home warranty, and Seller hereby consents to Firm's receipt of such fee.

6. **LISTING PRICE.** Seller lists the Property at a price of $_____ on the following terms: ❑ Cash ❑ FHA ❑ VA ❑ USDA ❑ Conventional ❑ Loan Assumption ❑ Seller Financing ❑ Other_____ .
Seller agrees to sell the Property for the Listing Price or for any other price or on any other terms acceptable to Seller.

7. **FIRM'S COMPENSATION.**
   (a) **Fee.** Seller agrees to pay Firm a total fee of _____ % of the gross sales price of the Property, OR_____ ("Fee"), which shall include the amount of any compensation paid by Firm as set forth in paragraph 8 below to any other real estate firm, including individual agents and sole proprietors ("Cooperating Real Estate Firm").
   (b) **Fee Earned.** The Fee shall be deemed earned under any of the following circumstances:
       (i) If a ready, willing and able buyer is procured by Firm, a Cooperating Real Estate Firm, the Seller, or anyone else during the Term of this Agreement at the price and on the terms set forth herein, or at any price and upon any terms acceptable to the Seller;
       (ii) If the Property is sold, optioned, exchanged, conveyed or transferred, or the Seller agrees, during the Term of this Agreement or any renewal hereof, to sell, option, exchange, convey or transfer the Property at any price and upon any terms whatsoever; or
       (iii) If the circumstances set out in (i) or (ii) above have not occurred, and if, within _____ days after the Expiration Date ("Protection Period"), Seller either directly or indirectly sells, options, exchanges, conveys or transfers, or agrees to sell, option, exchange, convey or transfer the Property upon any terms whatsoever, to any person with whom Seller, Firm, or any Cooperating Real Estate Firm communicated regarding the Property during the Term of this Agreement or any renewal hereof, provided the names of such persons are delivered or postmarked to the Seller within 15 days after the Expiration Date. HOWEVER, Seller shall NOT be obligated to pay the Fee if a valid listing agreement is entered into between Seller and another real estate broker and the Property is subsequently sold, optioned, exchanged, conveyed or transferred during the Protection Period.

STANDARD FORM 101
Revised 7/2017
© 7/2017

Individual agent initials _____ Seller initials _____ _____

Figure 9-1

(c) **Fee Due and Payable**. Once earned as set forth above, the Fee will be due and payable at the earlier of:

(i) Closing on the Property;

(ii) The Seller's failure to sell the Property (including but not limited to the Seller's refusal to sign an offer to purchase the Property at the price and terms stated herein or on other terms acceptable to the Seller, the Seller's default on an executed sales contract for the Property, or the Seller's agreement with a buyer to unreasonably modify or cancel an executed sales contract for the Property); or

(iii) Seller's breach of this Agreement.

(d) **Transfer of Interest in Business Entity**. If Seller is a partnership, corporation or other business entity, and an interest in the partnership, corporation or other business entity is transferred, whether by merger, outright purchase or otherwise, in lieu of a sale of the Property, and applicable law does not prohibit the payment of a fee or commission in connection with such sale or transfer, the Fee shall be calculated on the fair market value of the Property, rather than the gross sales price, multiplied by the percentage of interest so transferred, and shall be paid by Seller at the time of the transfer.

(e) **Additional Compensation**. If additional compensation, incentive, bonus, rebate and/or other valuable consideration ("Additional Compensation") is offered to the Firm from any other party or person in connection with a sale of the Property, Seller will permit Firm to receive it in addition to the Fee. Firm shall timely disclose the promise or expectation of receiving any such Additional Compensation and confirm the disclosure in writing before Seller makes or accepts an offer to sell. (**NOTE**: NCAR Form #770 may be used to confirm the disclosure of any such Additional Compensation)

(f) **Attorney Fees and Costs**. If Firm is the prevailing party in any legal proceeding brought by Firm against Seller to recover any or all of the Fee, Firm shall be entitled to recover from Seller reasonable attorney fees and court costs incurred by Firm in connection with the proceeding.

8. COOPERATION WITH/COMPENSATION TO OTHER FIRMS. Firm has advised Seller of Firm's company policies regarding cooperation and the amount(s) of any compensation that will be offered to other brokers, including but not limited to, seller subagents, buyer agents or both, brokers who do or do not participate in a listing service and brokers who are or are not REALTORS®. Seller authorizes Firm to (*Check ALL applicable authorizations*):

❏ Cooperate with subagents representing the Seller and offer them the following compensation:_____% of the gross sales price or $_____; and/or,

❏ Cooperate with buyer agents representing the buyer and offer them the following compensation:_____ % of the gross sales price or $_____; and/or,

❏ Cooperate with and compensate other Cooperating Real Estate Firms according to the Firm's attached policy.

Firm will promptly notify Seller if compensation offered to a Cooperating Real Estate Firm is different from that set forth above. Agents with Cooperating Real Estate Firms must orally disclose the nature of their relationship with a buyer (subagent or buyer agent) to Firm at the time of initial contact with Firm, and confirm that relationship in writing no later than the time an offer to purchase is submitted for the Seller's consideration. Seller should be careful about disclosing confidential information because agents representing buyers must disclose all relevant information to their clients.

9. FIRM'S DUTIES. Firm agrees to provide Seller the benefit of Firm's knowledge, experience and advice in the marketing and sale of the Property. Seller understands that Firm makes no representation or guarantee as to the sale of the Property, but Firm agrees to use its best efforts in good faith to find a buyer who is ready, willing and able to purchase the property. In accordance with the REALTORS® Code of Ethics, Firm shall, with Seller's approval, in response to inquiries from buyers or Cooperating Real Estate Firms, disclose the existence of offers on the Property. Where Seller authorizes disclosure, Firm shall also disclose whether offers were obtained by the individual agent who signs this Agreement, another agent of the Firm, or by a Cooperating Real Estate Firm. Seller acknowledges that real estate brokers are prohibited by N.C. Real Estate Commission rule from disclosing the price or other material terms contained in a party's offer to purchase, sell, lease, rent or option real property to a competing party without the express authority of the party making the offer.

Seller acknowledges that Firm is required by law to disclose to potential purchasers of the Property all material facts pertaining to the Property about which the Firm knows or reasonably should know, and that REALTORS® have an ethical responsibility to treat all parties to the transaction honestly. Seller further acknowledges that Firm is being retained solely as a real estate professional, and understands that other professional service providers are available to render advice or services to Seller, including but not limited to an attorney, insurance agent, tax advisor, surveyor, structural engineer, home inspector, environmental consultant, architect, or contractor. Although Firm may provide Seller the names of providers who claim to perform such services, Seller understands that Firm cannot guarantee the quality of service or level of expertise of any such provider. Seller agrees to pay the full amount due for all services directly to the service provider whether or not the transaction closes. Seller also agrees to indemnify and hold Firm harmless from and against any and all liability, claim, loss, damage, suit, or expense that Firm may incur either as a result of Seller's selection and use of any such provider or Seller's election not to have one or more of such services performed.

Page 3 of 10

Individual agent initials _____ Seller initials _____ _____

STANDARD FORM 101
Revised 7/2017
© 7/2017

Figure 9-1

THE AGENT (FIRM) SHALL CONDUCT ALL BROKERAGE ACTIVITIES IN REGARD TO THIS AGREEMENT WITHOUT RESPECT TO THE RACE, COLOR, RELIGION, SEX, NATIONAL ORIGIN, HANDICAP OR FAMILIAL STATUS OF ANY PARTY OR PROSPECTIVE PARTY TO THE AGREEMENT. FURTHER, REALTORS® HAVE AN ETHICAL DUTY TO CONDUCT SUCH ACTIVITIES WITHOUT RESPECT TO THE SEXUAL ORIENTATION OR GENDER IDENTITY OF ANY PARTY OR PROSPECTIVE PARTY TO THIS AGREEMENT.

10. **MARKETING.**

(a) **Commencement of Marketing**. The Firm is authorized to commence marketing the Property as described in subparagraph (b) below on the Effective Date OR, if selected ❑ on (insert date only if applicable) _____ ("Delayed Marketing Date").

NOTE: If a Delayed Marketing Date is selected, Seller understands and acknowledges the following:
- THE PROPERTY MAY NOT BE SHOWN BY ANY REAL ESTATE AGENT, INCLUDING FIRM'S AGENTS, PRIOR TO THE DELAYED MARKETING DATE.
- FIRM IS OBLIGATED TO PRESENT TO SELLER ANY OFFERS ON THE PROPERTY THAT MAY BE SUBMITTED TO FIRM PRIOR TO THE DELAYED MARKETING DATE.
- IT IS IN THE BEST INTEREST OF MOST SELLERS TO GET THE HIGHEST POSSIBLE PRICE ON THE BEST TERMS FOR THEIR PROPERTY, AND MAXIMIZING EXPOSURE OF THEIR PROPERTY ADVANCES THAT INTEREST. ACCEPTING AN OFFER ON THE PROPERTY BEFORE IT IS FULLY EXPOSED TO THE WIDEST GROUP OF POTENTIAL BUYERS MAY DENY SELLER THE BEST OPPORTUNITY TO ATTRACT OFFERS AT THE HIGHEST PRICE AND BEST TERMS.

(b) **Marketing Authorization.** Seller authorizes Firm (*Check ALL applicable sections*):

❑ **Signs**. To place "For Sale," "Under Contract," "Sale Pending," or other similar signs on the Property (where permitted by law and relevant covenants) and to remove other such signs.

❑ **Open Houses**. To conduct open houses of the Property at such times as Seller and Firm may subsequently agree.

❑ **Listing Service**. To submit pertinent information concerning the Property to any listing service of which Firm is a member or in which any of Firm's agents participate and to furnish to such listing service notice of all changes of information concerning the Property authorized in writing by Seller. Seller authorizes Firm, upon execution of a sales contract for the Property, to notify the listing service of the pending sale and the expiration date of any due diligence period, and upon closing of the sale, to disseminate sales information, including sales price, to the listing service, appraisers and real estate brokers.

❑ **Lock/Key Boxes**. The Seller ❑ does ❑ does not authorize Firm to place lock/key boxes on the Property.

❑ **Advertising Other Than On The Internet**. To advertise the Property in non-Internet media, and to permit other firms to advertise the Property in non-Internet media to the extent and in such manner as Firm may decide.

❑ **Internet Advertising**. To display information about the Property on the Internet either directly or through a program of any listing service of which the Firm is a member or in which any of Firm's agents participate. Seller further authorizes other firms who belong to any listing service of which the Firm is a member or in which any of Firm's agents participate to display information about the Property on the Internet in accordance with the listing service rules and regulations, and also authorizes any listing service of which the Firm is a member or in which any of Firm's agents participate to use, license or sell to others information about the Property entered into the listing service. Seller specifically authorizes the display of the address of the Property, automated estimates of the market value of the Property and third-party comments about the Property. If seller desires to limit or prohibit Internet advertising as set forth above, seller must complete an opt-out form in accordance with listing service rules.

NOTE: NCAR Form #105 may be used to limit or prohibit Internet advertising and explains how such limitations may or may not be effective.

(c) **"Coming Soon" Advertising**. ❑ (Check only if applicable). If applicable, Firm is authorized to market the Property as "Coming Soon," commencing on the Effective Date, in any media Firm may in its discretion select, provided that any "Coming Soon" advertising shall be conducted in accordance with any restrictions and requirements of any listing service in which the Property will be included, a copy of which ❑ are ❑ are not attached to this Agreement.

(d) **Seller Acknowledgement**. Seller acknowledges and understands that while the marketing services selected above will facilitate the showing and sale of the Property, there are risks associated with allowing access to and disseminating information about the Property that are not within the reasonable control of the Firm, including but not limited to:

(i) unauthorized use of a lock/key box,

(ii) control of visitors during or after a showing or an open house, including the taking and use of photographs and videos of the Property

(iii) inappropriate use of information about the Property placed on the Internet or furnished to any listing service in which the Firm participates, and

Individual agent initials _____ Seller initials _____ _____

Figure 9-1

(iv) information about the Property placed on the Internet by or through any listing service in which the Firm participates which is inaccurate or dated.

Seller therefore agrees to release and discharge Firm and Firm's agents from any and all claims, demands, rights and causes of action of whatsoever kind and nature not caused by Firm's negligence arising directly or indirectly out of any such marketing services.

WARNING: IT MAY BE A CRIME UNDER FEDERAL AND STATE LAWS TO LISTEN TO OR RECORD AN ORAL COMMUNICATION THROUGH THE USE OF ANY ELECTRONIC, MECHANICAL, OR OTHER DEVICE WITHOUT THE CONSENT OF A PARTY TO THAT COMMUNICATION. If there is a video/audio/surveillance device(s) on the Property, Seller is advised: (i) that no audio surveillance device may be turned on during any showings, open houses, investigations, examinations or inspections of the Property; and (ii) that the placement of any video surveillance device should not violate a visitor's reasonable expectation of privacy.

---

11. **EARNEST MONEY**. Unless otherwise provided in the sales contract, any initial and additional earnest money deposits and any other earnest monies paid in connection with any transaction shall be held by the Firm, in escrow, until the consummation or termination of the transaction. Any earnest money forfeited by reason of the buyer's default under a sales contract shall be divided equally between the Firm and Seller. In no event shall the sum paid to the Firm because of a buyer's default be in excess of the fee that would have been due if the sale had closed as contemplated in the sales contract. In accordance with NC General Statutes Section 93A-12, if a dispute regarding the return or forfeiture of any earnest money deposit arises between Seller and the buyer, the escrow agent holding the deposit may deposit the disputed monies with the appropriate Clerk of Court following written notice to the parties. In the event of any such dispute, Seller directs Firm to disclose Seller's last known mailing address to the escrow agent upon request to enable the escrow agent to comply with the notice requirement of such law.

12. **SELLER REPRESENTATIONS**.

(a) **Flood Hazard Disclosure/Insurance.** To the best of Seller's knowledge, the Property ❏ is ❏ is not located partly or entirely within a designated Special Flood Hazard Area. The Seller ❏ does ❏ does not currently maintain flood hazard insurance on the Property.

(b) **Synthetic Stucco.** To the best of Seller's knowledge, the Property has not been clad previously (either in whole or in part) with an "exterior insulating and finishing system," commonly known as "EIFS" or "synthetic stucco", unless disclosed as follows: _____.

(c) **Owners' Association**.

(i) Complete ONLY if the Residential Property and Owner's Association Disclosure Statement is required: The name, address and telephone number of the president of the owners' association or the association manager is: _____

_____

Owners' association website address, if any: _____

The name, address and telephone number of the president of the owners' association or the association manager is: _____

_____

Owners' association website address, if any: _____

(ii) Complete ONLY if New Construction or where the Residential Property and Owner's Association Disclosure Statement is NOT required: To the best of Seller's knowledge there ❏ is ❏ is not an owners' association which imposes various mandatory covenants, conditions and restrictions upon the Property. If there is an owners' association, Seller agrees to promptly complete an Owners' Association Disclosure and Addendum For Properties Exempt from Residential Property Disclosure Statement (Standard Form 2A12-T) at Seller's expense and to attach it as an addendum to any contract for the sale of the Property.

(d) **Termite Bond**. To the best of Seller's knowledge there ❏ is ❏ is not a termite bond on the Property. If there is a termite bond, it ❏ is ❏ is not transferable. If transferable, the transfer cost is $ _____, and the bonding company is: _____.

(e) **Ownership**. Seller represents that Seller:
  ❏ has owned the Property for at least one year;
  ❏ has owned the Property for less than one year
  ❏ does not yet own the Property

If Seller does not yet own the Property, Seller agrees to promptly provide Firm information pertaining to Seller's acquisition of the Property, such as a copy of a sales contract or option for the Property, and to keep Firm timely informed of all developments pertaining to Seller's acquisition of the Property.

(f) **Receipt of Sample Forms**.
  ❏ Seller acknowledges receipt of a sample copy of an Offer to Purchase And Contract (form 2-T) or Offer to Purchase and Contract—New Construction (form 800-T), as may be appropriate for review purposes.
  ❏ Seller acknowledges receipt of a sample copy of a Professional Services Disclosure and Election form (form #760) for review purposes.

Individual agent initials _____ Seller initials _____ _____

Figure 9-1

(g) **Current Liens**. Seller represents to the best of Seller's knowledge:

(1) The Property ❑ is ❑ is not encumbered by a deed of trust or mortgage. *Complete any of the following where applicable:*

(i) There is a first deed of trust or mortgage on the Property securing a loan held by:
Lender Name: _____
Approximate balance: $_____ Lender Phone#: _____
Lender Address: _____

(ii) There is a second deed of trust or mortgage on the Property securing a loan held by:
Lender Name: _____
Approximate balance: $_____ Lender Phone#: _____
Lender Address: _____

(iii) There is a deed of trust or mortgage on the Property securing an equity line of credit held by:
Lender Name: _____
Approximate balance: $_____ Lender Phone#: _____
Lender Address: _____

(2) Seller is current on all payments for the loans identified in numbered items (i), (ii) and (iii) above except as specified in (7) below.

(3) Seller is not in default on any loan identified in numbered items (i), (ii) and (iii) above and has not received any notice(s) from the holder of any loan identified in numbered items (i), (ii) and (iii) above or from any other lien holder of any kind, regarding a default under the loan, threatened foreclosure, notice of foreclosure, or the filing of foreclosure except as specified in (7) below.

(4) There are not any liens secured against the Property for Federal, State or local income taxes, unpaid real property taxes, unpaid condominium or homeowners' association fees, mechanics', laborers' or materialmen's liens, or other liens affecting the Property, and Seller has no knowledge of any matter that might result in a lien affecting the Property except as specified in (7) below.

(5) There are not any judgments against Seller affecting the Property, and Seller has no knowledge of any matter that might result in a judgment that may potentially affect the Property except as specified in (7) below.

(6) There are not any Uniform Commercial Code (UCC) fixture filings affecting the Property, and Seller has no knowledge of any matter that might result in a UCC fixture filing affecting the Property except as specified in (7) below.

(7) Specify any information, including approximate balances, required by Seller representations (2) through (6) above

NOTE: Outstanding liens may affect Seller's net proceeds: _____
_____
_____

(h) **Bankruptcy**. Seller currently:

(1) ❑ is ❑ is not under bankruptcy protection under United States law.

(2) ❑ is ❑ is not contemplating seeking bankruptcy protection during the term of this Agreement.

(i) **Access**. Seller represents that the Property has legal access to a public right of way. If access is by private road/easement/other, Seller further represents that there ❑ is ❑ is not an agreement regarding the maintenance of such private road/easement/other means of access. If applicable, Seller agrees to promptly provide Firm information pertaining to any such agreement.

(j) **Lease(s)**. To the best of Seller's knowledge, the Property ❑ is ❑ is not subject to any lease(s). If applicable:

(i) Seller agrees to promptly provide Firm a copy of any such lease(s) or a written statement of the terms of any oral lease(s);

(ii) If the Property is managed by someone other than Seller, the manager's name and contact information is as follows:_____.
Seller authorizes any such manager to release and disclose to Firm any relevant information about any leases(s) and to cooperate with Firm in the sale of the Property.

(k) **FHA Appraisal**. To the best of Seller's knowledge, an FHA appraisal ❑ has ❑ has not been performed on the Property within four months prior to the Effective Date. If applicable, Seller agrees to promptly provide Firm a copy of any such appraisal if available.

NOTE: Any such appraisal may or may not be binding on a buyer who intends to obtain FHA financing.

(l) **Special Assessments**. To the best of Seller's knowledge, there are no Proposed or Confirmed Special Assessments (as defined in the sample contract form provided to Seller) regarding the Property except as follows (Insert "none" or the identification of such assessments, if any):
_____
_____

(m) **Manufactured (Mobile) Home**. Complete ONLY if there is a manufactured (mobile) home(s) on the Property that Seller intends to include as a part of the sale of the Property: VIN(s): _____ or ❑ VIN(s) unknown. Other description (*year, model, etc.*): _____

(n) **Fuel Tank/Fuel**. To the best of Seller's knowledge, there ❑ is ❑ is not a fuel tank(s) located on the Property. *If "yes" complete the following to the best of Seller's knowledge:*

Ownership of tank 1: ❑ owned ❑ leased. If leased, the name and contact information of tank lessor is:
_____

Location of tank 1:   ❑ above ground ❑ below ground
Type of fuel: ❑ oil ❑ propane ❑ gasoline and/or diesel ❑ other: _____

STANDARD FORM 101
Revised 7/2017
© 7/2017

Individual agent initials _____ Seller initials _____

Figure 9-1

Refilling schedule: ☐auto-refill *(insert frequency)*: _____ ☐ other *(describe)*: _____
Name and contact information of fuel vendor: _____
Ownership of tank 2: ☐ owned ☐ leased If leased, the name and contact information of tank lessor is:

_____

Location of tank 2: ☐ above ground ☐ below ground
Type of fuel: ☐ oil ☐ propane ☐ gasoline and/or diesel ☐ other: _____
Refilling schedule: ☐auto-refill *(insert frequency)*: _____ ☐ other *(describe)* : _____
Name and contact information of fuel vendor: _____

If, during the term of this Agreement, Seller becomes aware that any of the representations set forth in this paragraph 12 are incorrect or no longer accurate, Seller shall promptly notify Firm and cooperate with Firm in taking appropriate corrective action.

13. **SELLER'S DUTIES.** Seller agrees to cooperate with Firm in the marketing and sale of the Property, including but not limited to:
   (a) providing to Firm, in a timely manner, accurate information including but not limited to the following:
      (i) Residential Property and Owner's Association Disclosure Statement (unless exempt);
      (ii) Mineral and Oil and Gas Rights Mandatory Disclosure Statement (unless exempt); and
      (iii) Lead-Based Paint or Lead-Based Paint Hazard Addendum with respect to any residential dwelling built prior to 1978.
   (b) making the Property available for showing (including working, existing utilities) at reasonable times and upon reasonable notice;
   (c) providing Firm as soon as reasonably possible after the execution of this Agreement copies of the following documents (where relevant) in the possession of Seller:
      (1) restrictive covenants affecting the Property;
      (2) bylaws, articles of incorporation, rules and regulations, and other governing documents of the owners' association and/or the subdivision;
      (3) title insurance policies, attorney's opinions on title, surveys, covenants, deeds, notes and deeds of trust and easements relating to the Property.

Seller authorizes (1) any attorney presently or previously representing Seller to release and disclose any title insurance policy in such attorney's file to Firm, (2) the Property's title insurer or its agent to release and disclose all materials in the Property's title insurer's (or title insurer's agent's) file to Firm, and (3) the owners' association manager (or other authorized representative) to release and disclose copies of all documents referenced in subparagraphs (c)(1) and (c)(2) above. Seller acknowledges and understands that Firm is under no obligation to acquire any of the information referenced in this subparagraph (c) or to verify the accuracy of any such information that may be provided to Firm.
   (d) immediately referring to Firm all inquiries or offers it may receive regarding the Property; showing the Property only by appointment made by or through Firm; and conducting all negotiations through Firm;
   (e) executing and delivering at settlement a GENERAL WARRANTY DEED conveying fee simple marketable title to the Property, including legal access to a public right of way, free of all encumbrances except ad valorem taxes for the current year, utility easements, rights-of-way, and unviolated restrictive covenants, if any, and those encumbrances that the buyer agrees to assume in the sales contract.

Seller represents that the Seller has the right to convey the Property, and that there are currently no circumstances that would prohibit the Seller from conveying fee simple marketable title as set forth in the preceding sentence, except as follows *(insert N/A if not applicable)*: _____
_____

NOTE: If any sale of the Property may be a "short sale," consideration should be given to attaching NCAR form 104 as an addendum to this Agreement.

   (f) providing Firm, in a timely manner, any information necessary (including any information omitted under Paragraph 12) to enable Firm to prepare an estimate of Seller's net proceeds at settlement. Seller acknowledges and understands that any such estimate is an approximation only and that Seller should verify the accuracy of the calculations.
   (g) if required by N.C.G.S. §44A-11.1, timely designating a Lien Agent, and providing Firm as soon as reasonably possible a copy of the appointment of Lien Agent.

14. **HOME INSPECTION.** Seller is advised to obtain a home inspection for the purpose of evaluating the condition of the Property in order to enhance its marketability and to help reduce concerns of prospective buyers. Seller ☐ agrees ☐ does not agree to obtain and pay for a home inspection by a licensed NC Home Inspector within _____ days after the execution of this agreement.

☐ Seller acknowledges receipt of a copy of *Questions and Answers on: Home Inspections* by the NC Real Estate Commission.

15. **PHOTOGRAPHS AND OTHER MATERIALS:** Firm is specifically authorized to use, for any purposes whatsoever, any and all photographs, drawings, video, advertising copy or other information obtained by or provided to Firm pursuant to this Agreement (including but not limited to any information concerning the price and terms of the sale of the Property, the description of the Property

STANDARD FORM 101
Revised 7/2017
© 7/2017

Individual agent initials _____   Seller initials _____ _____

Figure 9-1

and the length of time the Property is on the market) ("Materials"), both before and after the sale or, in the event there is not a sale, after this Agreement has expired. Seller shall not have or acquire any rights to use any of the Materials created by, on behalf of, or at the direction of Firm or an agent of Firm either during or after the Term of this Agreement without Firm's written consent. If Seller provides any Materials to Firm ("Seller Materials"), Seller represents that Seller owns the Seller Materials or otherwise has the legal right to provide the Seller Materials to Firm, and Seller grants to Firm and any listing service in which Firm or its agents participate a non-exclusive, perpetual license to use the Seller Materials, including the rights to display, reproduce, distribute or make derivative works from the Seller Materials. Seller agrees to indemnify and hold Firm and its agents harmless for any and all claims resulting from use of the Seller Materials under the terms of this license.

16. **ADDITIONAL TERMS AND CONDITIONS.** The following additional terms and conditions shall also be a part of this Agreement: _____

_____

_____

17. **DUAL AGENCY.** Seller understands that the potential for dual agency will arise if a buyer who has an agency relationship with Firm becomes interested in viewing the Property. Firm may represent more than one party in the same transaction only with the knowledge and informed consent of all parties for whom Firm acts.

(a) Disclosure of Information. In the event Firm serves as a dual agent, Seller agrees that without permission from the party about whom the information pertains, Firm shall not disclose to the other party the following information:

(1) that a party may agree to a price, terms, or any conditions of sale other than those offered;

(2) the motivation of a party for engaging in the transaction, unless disclosure is otherwise required by statute or rule; and

(3) any information about a party which that party has identified as confidential unless disclosure is otherwise required by statute or rule.

b) Firm's Role as Dual Agent. If Firm serves as agent for both Seller and a buyer in a transaction involving the Property, Firm shall make every reasonable effort to represent Seller and buyer in a balanced and fair manner. Firm shall also make every reasonable effort to encourage and effect communication and negotiation between Seller and buyer. Seller understands and acknowledges that:

(1) Prior to the time dual agency occurs, Firm will act as Seller's exclusive agent;

(2) In its separate representation of Seller and buyer, Firm may obtain information which, if disclosed, could harm the bargaining position of the party providing such information to Firm;

(3) Firm is required by law to disclose to Seller and buyer any known or reasonably ascertainable material facts.

Seller agrees Firm shall not be liable to Seller for (i) disclosing material facts required by law to be disclosed, and (ii) refusing or failing to disclose other information the law does not require to be disclosed which could harm or compromise one party's bargaining position but could benefit the other party.

(c) Seller's Role. Should Firm become a dual agent, Seller understands and acknowledges that:

(1) Seller has the responsibility of making Seller's own decisions as to what terms are to be included in any purchase and sale agreement with a buyer client of Firm;

(2) Seller is fully aware of and understands the implications and consequences of Firm's dual agency role as expressed herein to provide balanced and fair representation of Seller and buyer and to encourage and effect communication between them rather than as an advocate or exclusive agent or representative;

(3) Seller has determined that the benefits of dual agency outweigh any disadvantages or adverse consequences;

(4) Seller may seek independent legal counsel to assist Seller with the negotiation and preparation of a purchase and sale agreement or with any matter relating to the transaction which is the subject matter of a purchase and sale agreement.

Should Firm become a dual agent, Seller waives all claims, damages, losses, expenses or liabilities, other than for violations of the North Carolina Real Estate License Law and intentional wrongful acts, arising from Firm's role as a dual agent. Seller shall have a duty to protect Seller's own interests and should read any purchase and sale agreement carefully to ensure that it accurately sets forth the terms which Seller wants included in said agreement.

(d) Authorization *(initial only ONE)*.

_____   _____   Seller authorizes the Firm to act as a dual agent, representing both the Seller and the buyer, subject to the terms and conditions set forth in Paragraph 17.

_____   _____   Seller desires exclusive representation at all times during this agreement and does NOT authorize Firm to act in the capacity of dual agent. *If Seller does not authorize Firm to act as a dual agent, the remainder of this paragraph shall not apply.*

(e) Designated Agent Option *(Initial only if applicable)*.

_____   _____   Seller hereby authorizes the Firm to designate an individual agent(s) to represent the Seller. The individual designated agent(s) shall represent only the interests of the Seller to the extent permitted by law.

Individual agent initials _____   Seller initials _____   _____

STANDARD FORM 101
Revised 7/2017
© 7/2017

Figure 9-1

NOTE: When dual agency arises, an individual agent shall not practice designated agency and shall remain a dual agent if the individual agent has actually received confidential information concerning a buyer client of the Firm in connection with the transaction or if designated agency is otherwise prohibited by law.

18. **MEDIATION.** If a dispute arises out of or related to this Agreement or the breach thereof, and if the dispute cannot be settled through negotiation, the parties agree first to try in good faith to settle the dispute by mediation before resorting to arbitration, litigation, or some other dispute resolution procedure. If the need for mediation arises, the parties will choose a mutually acceptable mediator and will share the cost of mediation equally.

[THIS SPACE INTENTIONALLY LEFT BLANK]

STANDARD FORM 101
Revised 7/2017
© 7/2017

Individual agent initials _____ Seller initials _____ _____

Figure 9-1

19. **ENTIRE AGREEMENT/CHANGES/TERMINATION.** This Agreement constitutes the entire agreement between Seller and Firm and there are no representations, inducements, or other provisions other than those expressed herein. This Agreement may be signed in multiple originals or counterparts, all of which together constitute one and the same instrument. All changes, additions, or deletions to this Agreement must be in writing and signed by both Seller and Firm. Seller acknowledges and understands that this Agreement constitutes a binding contract between Seller and Firm. Although Seller may at any time withdraw from the fiduciary relationship existing between Seller and Firm, the contract created by this Agreement may not be terminated by Seller or Firm prior to its Expiration Date without legally sufficient cause. Any such termination shall be by mutually-acceptable written agreement signed by both Seller and Firm. **Seller and Firm each acknowledge receipt of a signed copy of this Agreement.**

THE NORTH CAROLINA ASSOCIATION OF REALTORS®, INC. MAKES NO REPRESENTATION AS TO THE LEGAL VALIDITY OR ADEQUACY OF ANY PROVISION OF THIS FORM IN ANY SPECIFIC TRANSACTION.

Seller: _____ _____ _____
                          Print Name   Signature   Date

Contact Information: _____ _____ _____ _____
                                        Home   Work   Cell   Email

Mailing Address: _____

Seller: _____ _____ _____
                          Print Name   Signature   Date

Contact Information: _____ _____ _____ _____
                                        Home   Work   Cell   Email

Mailing Address: _____

Entity Seller: _____
                    (Name of LLC/Corporation/Partnership/Trust/etc.)

By:_____ Date: _____

Name: _____ Title: _____

Contact Information: _____ _____ _____ _____
                                        Home   Work   Cell   Email

Mailing Address: _____

Firm:_____ Phone:_____
              Print Real Estate Firm Name

By: _____ _____ _____
        Individual Agent Signature   Individual License Number   Date

Office: _____

Address: _____

Office Phone: _____ Fax: _____ Email: _____

Figure 9-1

EXCLUSIVE BUYER AGENCY AGREEMENT
[Consult "Guidelines" (Form 201G) for guidance in completing this form]

This EXCLUSIVE BUYER AGENCY AGREEMENT ("Agreement") is entered into (Date)_____,
between_____ as Buyer(s) ("Buyer"),
and_____ ("Firm")
as the Buyer's exclusive agent to assist the Buyer in the acquisition of real property which may include any purchase, option and/or exchange on terms and conditions acceptable to Buyer. The individual agent who signs this Agreement on behalf of the Firm shall, on behalf of the Firm, be primarily responsible for ensuring that the Firm's duties hereunder are fulfilled; however, it is understood and agreed that other agents of the Firm may be assigned to fulfill such duties if deemed appropriate by the Firm. For purposes of this Agreement, the term "Firm," as the context may require, shall be deemed to include the individual agent who signs this Agreement and any other agents of the Firm.

Buyer represents that, as of the commencement date of this Agreement, the Buyer is not a party to a buyer representation agreement with any other real estate firm. Buyer has received a copy of the "WORKING WITH REAL ESTATE AGENTS" brochure and has reviewed it with Firm. Buyer further represents that Buyer has disclosed to Firm information about any properties of the type described in paragraph 1 below that Buyer has visited at any open houses or that Buyer has been shown by any other real estate firm.

1. **TYPE OF PROPERTY.** ❑ Residential (improved and unimproved) ❑ Commercial (improved and unimproved)
   ❑ Other _____
   (a) General Location: _____
   (b) Other: _____

2. **EFFECT OF AGREEMENT.** Buyer intends to acquire real property of the type described in paragraph 1. *By employing Firm as Buyer's exclusive agent, Buyer agrees to conduct all negotiations for such property through Firm, and to refer to Firm all inquiries received in any form from other real estate firms, prospective sellers or any other source, during the time this Agreement is in effect.*

3. **DURATION OF AGENCY.** Firm's authority as Buyer's exclusive agent shall begin _____, and subject to paragraph 4, shall expire at midnight, _____, or when Buyer acquires real property of the type described in paragraph 1, whichever occurs sooner.

4. **COMPENSATION OF FIRM.**
   (a) Firm acknowledges receipt of a non-refundable retainer fee in the amount of $_____ which
   ❑shall ❑ shall not be credited toward any compensation due Firm under this Agreement.
   (b) Buyer agrees that Firm's fee for services hereunder shall be in the amount of _____
   _____ ("Fee")
   (Insert dollar amount, percentage of purchase price, or other method of determining Firm's compensation for each type of property the Buyer may purchase, such as resale, new construction, land/lot and/or unrepresented seller. Do not insert N/A or a zero ($0)).
   (i) Firm shall seek the Fee from a cooperating listing firm (through the listing firm's offer of compensation in MLS or otherwise) or from the seller if there is no listing firm, and Buyer agrees that Firm shall be entitled to receive same in consideration for Firm's services hereunder.
   (ii) If Buyer purchases property where the compensation offered by the listing firm and/or seller is less than the Fee, or where no compensation is offered by either the listing firm or the seller, Buyer and Firm agree that Buyer will pay the difference between the Fee and the compensation offered unless prohibited by law. Firm will timely inform Buyer if the compensation offered is less than expected.
   (iii) If additional compensation, incentive, bonus, rebate and/or other valuable consideration *("Additional Compensation")* is offered through the MLS or otherwise, Buyer will permit the Firm to receive it in addition to the Fee. Firm shall timely disclose the promise or expectation of receiving any such Additional Compensation and confirm the disclosure in writing before Buyer makes or accepts an offer to buy. (Note: NCAR Form #770 may be used to confirm the disclosure of any such Additional Compensation)
   (c) The compensation shall be deemed earned under any of the following circumstances:
   (i) If, during the term of this Agreement, Buyer, any assignee of Buyer or any person/legal entity acting on behalf of Buyer directly or indirectly enters into an agreement to purchase, option, and/or exchange any property of the type described above regardless of the manner in which Buyer was introduced to the property; or
   (ii) If, within _____ days after expiration of this Agreement, Buyer enters into a contract to acquire property introduced to Buyer during the term of this Agreement by Firm or any third party, unless Buyer has entered into a valid buyer agency agreement with another real estate firm; or

Page 1 of 6

North Carolina Association of REALTORS®, Inc.

STANDARD FORM 201
Revised 7/2017
© 7/2017

REALTOR®

Buyer initials _____ _____ Individual agent initials _____

Figure 9-2

(iii) If, having entered into an enforceable contract to acquire property during the term of this Agreement, Buyer defaults under the terms of that contract.

(d) The compensation will be due and payable at closing or upon Buyer's default of any purchase agreement. If Buyer defaults, the total compensation that would have been due the Firm will be due and payable immediately in cash from the Buyer. No assignment of rights in real property obtained for Buyer or any assignee of Buyer or any person/legal entity acting on behalf of Buyer pursuant to this Agreement shall operate to defeat any of Firm rights under this Agreement.

> **NOTE:** Buyer understands and acknowledges that there is the potential for a conflict of interest generated by a percentage of price based fee for representing Buyer. The amount, format or rate of real estate commission is not fixed by law, but is set by each broker individually, and may be negotiable between Buyer and Firm.

(e) Attorney Fees and Costs. If Firm is the prevailing party in any legal proceeding brought by Firm against Buyer to recover the Fee, Firm shall be entitled to recover from Buyer reasonable attorney fees and court costs incurred by Firm in connection with the proceeding.

5. **OTHER POTENTIAL BUYERS.** Buyer understands that other prospective purchasers represented by Firm may seek property, submit offers, and contract to purchase property through Firm, including the same or similar property as Buyer seeks to purchase. Buyer acknowledges, understands and consents to such representation of other prospective purchasers by Firm through its agents.

6. **FIRM'S DUTIES.** During the term of this Agreement, Firm shall promote the interests of Buyer by: (a) performing the terms of this Agreement; (b) seeking property at a price and terms acceptable to Buyer; (c) presenting in a timely manner all written offers or counteroffers to and from Buyer; (d) disclosing to Buyer all material facts related to the property or concerning the transaction of which Firm has actual knowledge; and (e) accounting for in a timely manner all money and property received in which Buyer has or may have an interest. Unless otherwise provided by law or Buyer consents in writing to the release of the information, Firm shall maintain the confidentiality of all personal and financial information and other matters identified as confidential by Buyer, if that information is received from Buyer during the brokerage relationship. In satisfying these duties, Firm shall exercise ordinary care, comply with all applicable laws and regulations, and treat all prospective sellers honestly and not knowingly give them false information. In addition, Firm may show the same property to other buyers, represent other buyers, represent sellers relative to other properties, or provide assistance to a seller or prospective seller by performing ministerial acts that are not inconsistent with Firm's duties under this Agreement.

Upon closing of any sale of property not entered in a listing service of which Firm is a member, Buyer authorizes Firm to submit pertinent information concerning the property, including sales price, to such listing service.

7. **DISCLOSURE OF BUYER'S NAME/MAILING ADDRESS.**
(a) Unless otherwise stated in Paragraph 13 below, Firm has Buyer's permission to disclose Buyer's name.
(b) In accordance with NC General Statutes Section 93A-12, if a dispute regarding the return or forfeiture of any earnest money deposit arises between Buyer and the seller of any real property Buyer may agree to purchase, the escrow agent holding the deposit may deposit the disputed monies with the appropriate Clerk of Court following written notice to the parties. In the event of any such dispute, Buyer directs Firm to disclose Buyer's last known mailing address to the escrow agent upon request to enable the escrow agent to comply with the notice requirement of such law.

8. **NON-DISCRIMINATION. THE AGENT (FIRM) SHALL CONDUCT ALL BROKERAGE ACTIVITIES IN REGARD TO THIS AGREEMENT WITHOUT RESPECT TO THE RACE, COLOR, RELIGION, SEX, NATIONAL ORIGIN, HANDICAP OR FAMILIAL STATUS OF ANY PARTY OR PROSPECTIVE PARTY TO THE AGREEMENT. FURTHER, REALTORS® HAVE AN ETHICAL DUTY TO CONDUCT SUCH ACTIVITIES WITHOUT RESPECT TO THE SEXUAL ORIENTATION OR GENDER IDENTITY OF ANY PARTY OR PROSPECTIVE PARTY TO THIS AGREEMENT.**

9. **BUYER'S DUTIES.** Buyer agrees to cooperate with Firm in the acquisition of real property of the type described in paragraph 1, including but not limited to:
(a) working exclusively with Firm during the term of this Agreement;
(b) immediately referring to Firm information about any properties Buyer may have an interest in examining;
(c) complying with the reasonable requests of Firm to supply any pertinent financial or personal data needed to fulfill the terms of this Agreement;
(d) being available for reasonable periods of time to examine properties;
(e) examining properties only by appointments made by or through Firm and accompanied by an agent of Firm;
(f) conducting all negotiations and communications through Firm;
(g) conducting all due diligence on property in consultation with Firm; and

Page 2 of 6

STANDARD FORM 201
Revised 7/2017
© 7/2017

Buyer initials _____ _____ Individual agent initials _____

Figure 9-2

(h) paying for all products and/or services required in the examination and evaluation of properties (examples: surveys, water/soil tests, title reports, property inspections, etc.).

10. **OTHER PROFESSIONAL ADVICE.** In addition to the services rendered to Buyer by the Firm under the terms of this Agreement, Buyer is advised to seek other professional advice in matters of law, taxation, financing, insurance, surveying, wood-destroying insect infestation, structural soundness, engineering, and other matters pertaining to any proposed transaction. Although Firm may provide Buyer the names of providers who claim to perform such services, Buyer understands that Firm cannot guarantee the quality of service or level of expertise of any such provider. Buyer agrees to pay the full amount due for all services directly to the service provider whether or not the transaction closes. Buyer also agrees to indemnify and hold Firm harmless from and against any and all liability, claim, loss, damage, suit, or expense that Firm may incur either as a result of Buyer's selection and use of any such provider or Buyer's election not to have one or more of such services performed.

❑ Buyer acknowledges receipt of a sample copy of an Offer to Purchase And Contract for review purposes.
❑ Buyer acknowledges receipt of a copy of the brochure *Questions and Answers on: Home Inspections.*
❑ Buyer acknowledges receipt of a sample copy of a Professional Services Disclosure and Election form (form #760) for review purposes.

11. **HOME WARRANTY.** The seller of any property Buyer may be interested in buying may or may not provide a home warranty as a part of any sale. If the seller does not provide a home warranty, Buyer may elect to purchase one. Buyer understands that although Firm will assist Buyer in identifying available home warranty products, Buyer must refer specific questions regarding coverage afforded by any such product to the provider thereof. If Firm assists Buyer in obtaining a home warranty, a fee of _____ will be offered to Firm by the person or entity through or from which any home warranty is obtained as compensation to Firm for its assistance in obtaining the home warranty, and Buyer hereby consents to Firm's receipt of such fee.

12. **CONFIDENTIALITY OF OFFERS.** Real estate brokers are prohibited by N.C. Real Estate Commission rule from disclosing the price or other material terms contained in a party's offer to purchase, sell, lease, rent or option real property to a competing party without the express authority of the party making the offer. However, sellers may elect not to treat the existence, terms, or conditions of any offers Buyer may make as confidential. Additionally, sellers may elect not to disclose or authorize seller's agent to disclose the existence of any other offer(s).

13. **ADDITIONAL PROVISIONS.** _____
_____
_____

14. **DUAL AGENCY.** Buyer understands that the potential for dual agency will arise if Buyer becomes interested in viewing property listed with Firm. Firm may represent more than one party in the same transaction only with the knowledge and informed consent of all parties for whom Firm acts.

(a) **Disclosure of Information.** In the event Firm serves as a dual agent, Buyer agrees that without permission from the party about whom the information pertains, Firm shall not disclose to the other party the following information:
(1) that a party may agree to a price, terms, or any conditions of sale other than those offered;
(2) the motivation of a party for engaging in the transaction, unless disclosure is otherwise required by statute or rule; and
(3) any information about a party which that party has identified as confidential unless disclosure is otherwise required by statute or rule.

(b) **Firm's Role as Dual Agent.** If Firm serves as agent for both Buyer and a seller in a transaction, Firm shall make every reasonable effort to represent Buyer and seller in a balanced and fair manner. Firm shall also make every reasonable effort to encourage and effect communication and negotiation between Buyer and seller. Buyer understands and acknowledges that:
(1) Prior to the time dual agency occurs, Firm will act as Buyer's exclusive agent;
(2) In its separate representation of Buyer and seller, Firm may obtain information which, if disclosed, could harm the bargaining position of the party providing such information to Firm;
(3) Firm is required by law to disclose to Buyer and seller any known or reasonably ascertainable material facts.

Buyer agrees Firm shall not be liable to Buyer for (i) disclosing material facts required by law to be disclosed, and (ii) refusing or failing to disclose other information the law does not require to be disclosed which could harm or compromise one party's bargaining position but could benefit the other party.

Page 3 of 6

STANDARD FORM 201
Revised 7/2017
© 7/2017

Buyer initials _____ _____ Individual agent initials _____

Figure 9-2

(c) **Buyer's Role**. Should Firm become a dual agent, Buyer understands and acknowledges that:

(1) Buyer has the responsibility of making Buyer's own decisions as to what terms are to be included in any purchase and sale agreement with a seller client of Firm;

(2) Buyer is fully aware of and understands the implications and consequences of Firm's dual agency role as expressed herein to provide balanced and fair representation of Buyer and seller and to encourage and effect communication between them rather than as an advocate or exclusive agent or representative;

(3) Buyer has determined that the benefits of dual agency outweigh any disadvantages or adverse consequences;

(4) Buyer may seek independent legal counsel to assist Buyer with the negotiation and preparation of a purchase and sale agreement or with any matter relating to the transaction which is the subject matter of a purchase and sale agreement.

Should Firm become a dual agent, Buyer waives all claims, damages, losses, expenses or liabilities, other than for violations of the North Carolina Real Estate License Law and intentional wrongful acts, arising from Firm's role as a dual agent. Buyer shall have a duty to protect Buyer's own interests and should read any purchase and sale agreement carefully to ensure that it accurately sets forth the terms which Buyer wants included in said agreement.

(d) **Authorization** *(initial only ONE)*.

_____ _____   Buyer authorizes the Firm to act as a dual agent, representing both the Buyer and the seller, subject to the terms and conditions set forth in this Paragraph 14.

_____ _____   Buyer desires exclusive representation at all times during this agreement and does NOT authorize Firm to act in the capacity of dual agent. *If Buyer does not authorize Firm to act as a dual agent, the remainder of this paragraph shall not apply.*

(e) **Designated Agent Option** *(Initial only if applicable)*.

_____ _____   Buyer hereby authorizes the Firm to designate an individual agent(s) to represent the Buyer, to the exclusion of any other individual agents associated with the Firm. The individual designated agent(s) shall represent only the interests of the Buyer to the extent permitted by law.

> **NOTE:** When dual agency arises, an individual agent shall not practice designated agency and shall remain a dual agent if the individual agent has actually received confidential information concerning a seller client of the Firm in connection with the transaction or if designated agency is otherwise prohibited by law.

(f) **Dual Agency Compensation**. If the Firm acts as a dual agent (including designated agency), the total fee the Firm expects to receive for its services in representing Buyer and the seller shall be _____ .

_____
(Insert dollar amount, percentage of purchase price, or other method of determining Firm's compensation for each type of property such as resale, new construction and/or land/lot the Buyer may purchase.). THIS WILL IN NO WAY AFFECT OR MODIFY THE AMOUNT OF THE FEE SET FORTH IN PARAGRAPH 4 ABOVE THAT FIRM EXPECTS TO RECEIVE FOR ITS SERVICES IN REPRESENTING BUYER UNDER THIS AGREEMENT. In the event Buyer is interested in purchasing a property where the Firm's total fee is different from that described in this subparagraph (f), the Firm shall timely disclose the fee to Buyer and confirm it in writing before Buyer makes or accepts an offer to buy or sell any such property.

15. **MEDIATION.** If a dispute arises out of or related to this Agreement or the breach thereof, and if the dispute cannot be settled through negotiation, the parties agree first to try in good faith to settle the dispute by mediation before resorting to arbitration, litigation, or some other dispute resolution procedure. If the need for mediation arises, the parties will choose a mutually acceptable mediator and will share the cost of mediation equally.

16. **ENTIRE AGREEMENT/CHANGES/TERMINATION.** This Agreement constitutes the entire agreement between Buyer and Firm relating to the subject thereof, and any prior agreements pertaining thereto, whether oral or written, have been merged and integrated into this Agreement. This Agreement may be signed in multiple originals or counterparts, all of which together constitute one and the same instrument. No modification of any of the terms of this Agreement shall be valid, binding upon the parties, or entitled to enforcement unless such modification has first been reduced to writing and signed by both Buyer and Firm. Buyer acknowledges and understands that this Agreement constitutes a binding contract between Buyer and Firm. Although Buyer may at any time withdraw from the fiduciary relationship existing between Buyer and Firm, the contract created by this Agreement may not

STANDARD FORM 201
Revised 7/2017
© 7/2017

Buyer initials _____ _____   Individual agent initials _____

Figure 9-2

be terminated by Buyer or Firm prior to its Expiration Date without legally sufficient cause. Any such termination shall be by mutually-acceptable written agreement signed by both Buyer and Firm.

NOTE: Buyer should consult with Firm before visiting any resale or new homes or contacting any other real estate firm representing sellers, to avoid the possibility of confusion over the brokerage relationship and misunderstandings about liability for compensation.

17. **SURVEILLANCE:** Buyer is advised to be mindful of the fact that there could be video/audio/surveillance device(s) located on any property examined by Buyer and that Buyer or Buyer's representatives may be under surveillance during any such examination. Federal and State laws prohibit the interception of an oral communication through the use of any electronic, mechanical, or other device, whether or not recorded, without the consent of a party to that communication. However, video surveillance without consent is not illegal.

18. **USE OF PHOTOGRAPHS AND VIDEO**: Unless a property owner has notified the public that photography and video recording is prohibited, it is permissible to photograph or video the interior of private property since the owner's permission to enter the property implies permission to do so. However, under no circumstances may Buyer take photographs or videos that intrude on a property owner's reasonable expectations of privacy.

Buyer should only photograph or video things that are in "plain view". For example, taking a photo or video of the contents of a medicine cabinet or of financial records in a desk drawer would be impermissible. In addition, any permitted photography or video should be used only in a manner related directly to Buyer's examination and purchase of a property. TAKING IMPERMISSIBLE PHOTOGRAPHS OR VIDEOS OR USING THEM FOR AN IMPERMISSIBLE PURPOSE COULD SUBJECT BUYER TO CIVIL LIABILITY.

[THIS SPACE INTENTIONALLY LEFT BLANK]

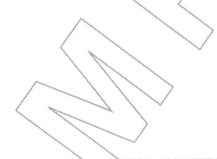
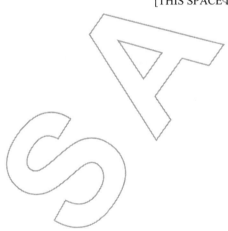

Page 5 of 6

Buyer initials _____ _____ Individual agent initials _____

Figure 9-2

Buyer and Firm each hereby acknowledge receipt of a signed copy of this Agreement.

THE NORTH CAROLINA ASSOCIATION OF REALTORS®, INC. MAKES NO REPRESENTATION AS TO THE LEGAL VALIDITY OR ADEQUACY OF ANY PROVISION OF THIS FORM IN ANY SPECIFIC TRANSACTION.

Buyer: _____   _____   _____
                Print Name   Signature   Date

Contact Information: _____   _____   _____   _____
                      Home   Work   Cell   Email

Mailing Address: _____

Buyer: _____   _____   _____
                Print Name   Signature   Date

Contact Information: _____   _____   _____   _____
                      Home   Work   Cell   Email

Mailing Address: _____

Entity Buyer: _____
          (Name of LLC/Corporation/Partnership/Trust/etc.)

By:_____   Date: _____

Name: _____   Title: _____

Contact Information: _____   _____   _____   _____
                      Home   Work   Cell   Email

Mailing Address: _____

Firm: _____   Phone: _____
              Print Real Estate Firm Name

By: _____   _____   _____
          Individual Agent Signature   Individual License Number   Date

Office: _____

Address: _____

Office Phone: _____   Fax: _____   Email_____

Page 6 of 6

STANDARD FORM 201
Revised 7/2017
© 7/2017

Figure 9-2

NON-EXCLUSIVE BUYER AGENCY AGREEMENT

This NON-EXCLUSIVE BUYER AGENCY AGREEMENT ("Agreement") is entered into (Date) _____,
between_____ as Buyer(s) ("Buyer"),
and_____ ("Firm").
The individual agent who signs this Agreement shall, on behalf of the Firm, be primarily responsible for ensuring that the Firm's duties hereunder are fulfilled; however, it is understood and agreed that other agents of the Firm may be assigned to fulfill such duties if deemed appropriate by the Firm. For purposes of this Agreement, the term "Firm," as the context may require, shall be deemed to include the individual agent who signs this Agreement and any other agents of the Firm.

> The purpose of this form is to properly establish a written buyer agency relationship. The various forms of agency relationships are discussed in the "Working with Real Estate Agents" brochure, a copy of which Buyer has received and reviewed with the agent. Buyer's execution of this form confirms that Buyer has read and understands the contents of that brochure, and is making a decision to request buyer agency for the period of time set forth below. Buyer represents that, as of the commencement date of this Agreement, Buyer is not a party to an exclusive buyer representation agreement with any other real estate firm.

1. **PROPERTY.** Firm agrees to act as a non-exclusive buyer's agent representing Buyer in the acquisition of real property by **[Check all that apply]**: ❑ locating suitable real estate ❑ showing the following specific property_____
_____

2. **DURATION OF AGENCY.** Firm's authority as Buyer's non-exclusive agent shall begin _____, and shall expire at midnight, _____.

3. **COMPENSATION OF FIRM.**
   (a) **Fee.** This agreement does not obligate Buyer to pay a brokerage fee or assure the payment of a brokerage fee to Firm. Buyer acknowledges and understands that Firm expects to receive and will seek a fee for Firm's services under an offer of compensation from a cooperating seller/listing firm in the amount of _____
   _____ ("Fee")
   (Insert dollar amount, percentage of purchase price, or other method of determining Firm's compensation for each type of property the Buyer may purchase, *such as resale, new construction, land/lot and/or unrepresented seller. Do not insert N/A or a zero ($0)).*
   (b) **Modification of Fee.** Provided, however, Firm may inform Buyer that the compensation offered is less than expected and, if Buyer is so informed prior to making an offer to purchase, Firm may seek a reasonable modification of the compensation terms herein and, if unable to reach such a modification, Firm may unilaterally terminate this Agreement.
   (c) **Additional Compensation.** If additional compensation, incentive, bonus, rebate and/or other valuable consideration ("Additional Compensation") is offered through the MLS or otherwise, Buyer will permit the Firm to receive it in addition to the Fee. Firm shall timely disclose the promise or expectation of receiving any such Additional Compensation and confirm the disclosure in writing before Buyer makes or accepts an offer to buy. (Note: NCAR Form #770 may be used to confirm the disclosure of any such Additional Compensation)
   (d) **When Compensation Earned.** The compensation shall be deemed earned if, during the term of this Agreement, Buyer, any assignee of Buyer or any person/legal entity acting on behalf of Buyer directly or indirectly enters into an agreement to purchase, option, and/or exchange property introduced to Buyer by Firm.

> **NOTE:** Buyer understands and acknowledges that there is the potential for a conflict of interest generated by a percentage of price based fee for representing Buyer. The amount, format or rate of real estate commission is not fixed by law, but is set by each broker individually, and may be negotiable between Buyer and Firm.

4. **ACKNOWLEDGMENTS OF RECEIPT.**
   ❑ Buyer acknowledges receipt of a sample copy of an Offer to Purchase and Contract for review purposes.
   ❑ Buyer acknowledges receipt of a copy of the brochure *Questions and Answers on: Home Inspections*.
   ❑ Buyer acknowledges receipt of a sample copy of a Professional Services Disclosure and Election form (form #760) for review purposes.

Page 1 of 4

North Carolina Association of REALTORS®, Inc.

Buyer initials _____ _____ Individual agent initials _____

STANDARD FORM 203
Revised 7/2017
© 7/2017

Figure 9-3

5. **CONFIDENTIALITY OF OFFERS.** Real estate brokers are prohibited by N.C. Real Estate Commission rule from disclosing the price or other material terms contained in a party's offer to purchase, sell, lease, rent or option real property to a competing party without the express authority of the party making the offer. However, sellers may elect not to treat the existence, terms, or conditions of any offers Buyer may make as confidential. Additionally, sellers may elect not to disclose or authorize seller's agent to disclose the existence of any other offer(s).

6. **DISCLOSURE OF BUYER'S NAME/MAILING ADDRESS.**
    (a) **Name**. Unless otherwise stated herein, Firm has Buyer's permission to disclose Buyer's name.
    (b) **Mailing Address**. In accordance with NC General Statutes Section 93A-12, if a dispute regarding the return or forfeiture of any earnest money deposit arises between Buyer and the seller of any real property Buyer may agree to purchase, the escrow agent holding the deposit may deposit the disputed monies with the appropriate Clerk of Court following written notice to the parties. In the event of any such dispute, Buyer directs Firm to disclose Buyer's last known mailing address to the escrow agent upon request to enable the escrow agent to comply with the notice requirement of such law.

7. **DUAL AGENCY.** Buyer understands that the potential for dual agency will arise if Buyer becomes interested in viewing property listed with Firm. Firm may represent more than one party in the same transaction only with the knowledge and informed consent of all parties for whom Firm acts.
    (a) **Disclosure of Information**. In the event Firm serves as a dual agent, Buyer agrees that without permission from the party about whom the information pertains, Firm shall not disclose to the other party the following information:
        (1) that a party may agree to a price, terms, or any conditions of sale other than those offered;
        (2) the motivation of a party for engaging in the transaction, unless disclosure is otherwise required by statute or rule; and
        (3) any information about a party which that party has identified as confidential unless disclosure is otherwise required by statute or rule.
    (b) **Firm's Role as Dual Agent**. If Firm serves as agent for both Buyer and a seller in a transaction, Firm shall make every reasonable effort to represent Buyer and seller in a balanced and fair manner. Firm shall also make every reasonable effort to encourage and effect communication and negotiation between Buyer and seller. Buyer understands and acknowledges that:
        (1) Prior to the time dual agency occurs, Firm will act as Buyer's exclusive agent;
        (2) In its separate representation of Buyer and seller, Firm may obtain information which, if disclosed, could harm the bargaining position of the party providing such information to Firm;
        (3) Firm is required by law to disclose to Buyer and seller any known or reasonably ascertainable material facts.

Buyer agrees Firm shall not be liable to Buyer for (i) disclosing material facts required by law to be disclosed, and (ii) refusing or failing to disclose other information the law does not require to be disclosed which could harm or compromise one party's bargaining position but could benefit the other party.

    (c) **Buyer's Role**. Should Firm become a dual agent, Buyer understands and acknowledges that:
        (1) Buyer has the responsibility of making Buyer's own decisions as to what terms are to be included in any purchase and sale agreement with a seller client of Firm;
        (2) Buyer is fully aware of and understands the implications and consequences of Firm's dual agency role as expressed herein to provide balanced and fair representation of Buyer and seller and to encourage and effect communication between them rather than as an advocate or exclusive agent or representative;
        (3) Buyer has determined that the benefits of dual agency outweigh any disadvantages or adverse consequences;
        (4) Buyer may seek independent legal counsel to assist Buyer with the negotiation and preparation of a purchase and sale agreement or with any matter relating to the transaction which is the subject matter of a purchase and sale agreement.

Should Firm become a dual agent, Buyer waives all claims, damages, losses, expenses or liabilities, other than for violations of the North Carolina Real Estate License Law and intentional wrongful acts, arising from Firm's role as a dual agent. Buyer shall have a duty to protect Buyer's own interests and should read any purchase and sale agreement carefully to ensure that it accurately sets forth the terms which Buyer wants included in said agreement.

    (d) **Authorization** *(initial only ONE).*

_____ _____   Buyer authorizes the Firm to act as a dual agent, representing both the Buyer and the seller, subject to the terms and conditions set forth in this paragraph.

_____ _____   Buyer desires exclusive representation at all times during this agreement and does NOT authorize Firm to act in the capacity of dual agent. *If Buyer does not authorize Firm to act as a dual agent, the remainder of this paragraph shall not apply.*

Buyer initials _____ _____ Individual agent initials _____

STANDARD FORM 203
Revised 7/2017
© 7/2017

Figure 9-3

(e) **Designated Agent Option** (*Initial only if applicable*).

_____ _____ Buyer hereby authorizes the Firm to designate an individual agent(s) to represent the Buyer. The individual designated agent(s) shall represent only the interests of the Buyer to the extent permitted by law.

> **NOTE:** When dual agency arises, an individual agent shall not practice designated agency and shall remain a dual agent if the individual agent has actually received confidential information concerning a buyer client of the Firm in connection with the transaction or if designated agency is otherwise prohibited by law.

(f) **Dual Agency Compensation**. If the Firm acts as a dual agent (including designated agency), the total fee the Firm expects to receive for its services in representing Buyer and the seller shall be _____.

(Insert dollar amount, percentage of purchase price, or other method of determining Firm's compensation for each type of property such as resale, new construction and/or land/lot the Buyer may purchase.). THIS WILL IN NO WAY AFFECT OR MODIFY THE AMOUNT OF THE FEE SET FORTH IN PARAGRAPH 3 ABOVE THAT FIRM EXPECTS TO RECEIVE FOR ITS SERVICES IN REPRESENTING BUYER UNDER THIS AGREEMENT. In the event Buyer is interested in purchasing a property where the Firm's total fee is different from that described in this subparagraph (f), the Firm shall timely disclose the fee to Buyer and confirm it in writing before Buyer makes or accepts an offer to buy or sell any such property.

8. **NON-DISCRIMINATION. THE AGENT (FIRM) SHALL CONDUCT ALL BROKERAGE ACTIVITIES IN REGARD TO THIS AGREEMENT WITHOUT RESPECT TO THE RACE, COLOR, RELIGION, SEX, NATIONAL ORIGIN, HANDICAP OR FAMILIAL STATUS OF ANY PARTY OR PROSPECTIVE PARTY TO THE AGREEMENT. FURTHER, REALTORS® HAVE AN ETHICAL DUTY TO CONDUCT SUCH ACTIVITIES WITHOUT RESPECT TO THE SEXUAL ORIENTATION OR GENDER IDENTITY OF ANY PARTY OR PROSPECTIVE PARTY TO THIS AGREEMENT.**

9. **EXECUTION.** This Agreement may be signed in multiple originals or counterparts, all of which together constitute one and the same instrument.

10. **SURVEILLANCE; USE OF PHOTOGRAHS AND VIDEO**: Federal and State laws prohibit the interception of an oral communication through the use of any electronic, mechanical, or other device, whether or not recorded, without the consent of a party to that communication. However, video surveillance without consent is not illegal. Buyer is advised to be mindful of the fact that there could be surveillance/audio device(s) located on any property examined by Buyer and that Buyer or Buyer's representatives may be under surveillance during any such examination.

Unless a property owner has notified the public that photography and video recording is prohibited, it is permissible to photograph or video the interior of private property since the owner's permission to enter the property implies permission to do so. However, under no circumstances may Buyer take photographs or videos that intrude on a property owner's reasonable expectations of privacy. Buyer should only photograph or video things that are in "plain view". For example, taking a photo or video of the contents of a medicine cabinet or of financial records in a desk drawer would be impermissible In addition, any permitted photography or video should be used only in a manner related directly to Buyer's examination and purchase of a property. TAKING IMPERMISSIBLE PHOTOGRAPHS OR VIDEOS OR USING THEM FOR AN IMPERMISSIBLE PURPOSE COULD SUBJECT BUYER TO CIVIL LIABILITY.

THE NORTH CAROLINA ASSOCIATION OF REALTORS®, INC. MAKES NO REPRESENTATION AS TO THE LEGAL VALIDITY OR ADEQUACY OF ANY PROVISION OF THIS FORM IN ANY SPECIFIC TRANSACTION.

Buyer: _____   _____   _____

                 Print Name   Signature   Date

Contact Information: _____   _____   _____   _____   _____

                      Home   Work   Cell   Email

Mailing Address: _____

Buyer: _____   _____   _____

                 Print Name   Signature   Date

Contact Information: _____   _____   _____   _____   _____

                      Home   Work   Cell   Email

STANDARD FORM 203
Revised 7/2017
© 7/2017

Buyer initials _____ _____ Individual agent initials _____

Figure 9-3

Mailing Address: _____

Entity Buyer:_____
              (Name of LLC/Corporation/Partnership/Trust/etc.)

By:_____ Date:_____

Name: _____ Title:_____

Contact Information: _____ _____ _____ _____
                     Home   Work   Cell   Email

Mailing Address: _____

Firm: _____ Phone: _____
             Print Real Estate Firm Name

By: _____ _____ _____
         Individual Agent Signature   Individual License Number   Date

Office: _____

Address:_____

Office Phone: _____ Fax: _____ Email_____

[THIS SPACE LEFT INTENTIONALLY BLANK]

Page 4 of 4

STANDARD FORM 203
Revised 7/2017
© 7/2017

Figure 9-3

10 | CONTRACT LAW

Virtually every real estate transaction is based on a contract, whether to lease, sell, purchase, or exchange an interest in real property. Real estate brokers must also have an agency contract with the consumer, as discussed in the preceding chapter. Thus, they must understand basic contract law and important contract principles, which this chapter will explore. Other chapters discuss more specifically the real estate contracts brokers encounter when conducting their brokerage business, namely, agency contracts, sales contracts, and leases.

BASIC CONTRACT TERMS AND CLASSIFICATIONS

Definition of a Contract

A **contract** *is a deliberate agreement between two or more competent parties supported by legal consideration to perform or abstain from performing some act.* If the agreement meets legal requirements, it is legally enforceable. In other words, a contract is simply a legally enforceable agreement between at least two persons. In general, contracts may be either written or oral. However, a law known as the **Statute of Frauds** requires that most real estate contracts be in writing and properly signed to be legally enforceable.

Express and Implied Contracts

An **express** *contract is one that is stated in words, either orally or in writing. An* **implied** *contract is one that is suggested from the conduct of the parties indicating the parties' intent to be bound.* Almost all real estate contracts are express contracts.

Requirement of a Writing

Most real estate contracts must be in writing as required by the Statute of Frauds. The Statute of Frauds, codified at General Statute 22-2, is discussed in detail later in this chapter. In a nutshell, it requires all contracts to convey real property to be in writing and signed by the "party to be charged" or an authorized agent of that party. The purpose of the Statute of Frauds is to prevent perjury, forgery, dishonest conduct and false testimony regarding the subject matter of contracts.

Unilateral and Bilateral Contracts

Contracts are also classified as *unilateral* or *bilateral.* In a *uni*lateral contract, only one party has promised to do or not do something; in a *bi*lateral contract, both parties have promised to do or not do something. *Most real estate contracts are bilateral, e.g.,* the seller promises to sell and the buyer promises to purchase the property for a stated sum, or the owner promises to lease the property and the tenant promises to pay periodic rent.

An option to purchase is an example of a *unilateral contract*, as only the owner-optionor is bound; the owner has promised not to sell to any other person during the prospective buyer-optionee's option period, but the optionee has *not* agreed or promised to purchase the property; the optionee has agreed to consider purchasing it for an agreed price. If the optionee decides to purchase the property, then s/he must affirmatively notify the optionor of that election prior to the expiration of the option period and must sign a contract to purchase, creating at that point a *bilateral* contract to purchase.

Executed and Executory Contracts

*An **executed** contract is one that has been fully performed.* All obligations under the contract have been fulfilled by all parties. However, the term "executed" has a second meaning used to refer to the fact that a contract or other legal document has been "signed" by the parties; thus, when the word "executed" is encountered in connection with contracts, a broker should ascertain whether the word is used to refer to the mere signing of the contract or the full performance of its terms.

> *Example:* A purchaser signed ("executed") a written offer to purchase a seller's home for $295,000. The seller signed ("executed") a written acceptance of the offer and a binding contract formed. The real estate closing took place one month later. Prior to the closing, the contract was "executory," meaning that its terms remained to be performed or fulfilled. With the completed real estate closing, the contract became "executed," the contract terms having been fulfilled. This example illustrates the two different uses of the verb "executed."

*All contracts that have not been fully performed are considered to be **executory** contracts.* A real estate sales contract that has been signed by both parties is an executory contract until the transaction closes, at which time it becomes an executed contract. In the preceding example, the contract between Henrietta and Zippy was "executory" from March 1 until the March 28 closing was completed.

Valid, Voidable and Void Contracts

*A **valid** contract satisfies all legal requirements for a contract and is fully enforceable in a court of law. A **voidable** contract is one where performance can be avoided by one of the parties based on some legal principle.* A voidable contract is valid until the party with the right to avoid performance actually disaffirms the contract. In other words, one party has the option to either avoid or ratify (honor) the contract. A number of circumstances that may result in voidable contracts are discussed later in this chapter but include, for example, a contract entered into with a minor.

*A **void** contract is unenforceable in a court of law.* Even so, some legally unenforceable contracts may be honored by agreement of or full performance by both parties. In other words, a contract that is "legally" void is *not* "automatically" void in the sense of having no effect. One or both of the parties must disaffirm the contract.

> *Example:* A and B orally agree that A will sell B his house for $175,000. Neither A can enforce the oral contract against B, nor B against A. Nevertheless, A and B together may voluntarily carry out their agreement and complete the sale, but if either refuses, the other has no legal remedy.

Certain illegal contracts, discussed later in this chapter, are void and cannot be enforced.

Example: A person forges the name of a property owner on a contract to convey it to a friend who has no knowledge of the forgery. The contract is totally void and cannot be enforced.

ESSENTIAL ELEMENTS OF A CONTRACT

Under contract law, any agreement between two or more parties must meet certain minimum requirements to be legally valid. The basic essentials for a contract are summarized and discussed below.

Essential Elements of a Contract
- Mutual assent (offer and acceptance)
- Consideration (the bargained for exchange)
- Legal contractual capacity of the parties
- Lawful objective (purpose) and means of accomplishing objective
- In writing (for most real estate contracts)

MUTUAL ASSENT: THE OFFER AND ACCEPTANCE

Every contract requires **mutual** assent, i.e., a "meeting of the minds." *There must be an agreement on definite material terms.* Mutual assent is gathered from a reasonable meaning of the words and acts of the parties and not from their unexpressed intentions or understandings. The parties' state of mind is not the controlling factor.

Example: A seller agrees to sell a home on a large lot to a purchaser. The contract complies with the Statute of Frauds and contains a precise legal description of the lot's boundaries. The rear boundary of the lot, as described in the legal description, is located 20 feet short of a line of trees. The purchaser, however, is under the mistaken impression that the rear boundary coincides with the line of trees. The seller never made any representation concerning that boundary, and the purchaser never made any inquiry. By signing the contract, the purchaser has agreed to the express terms as written. The purchaser's mistake of fact and uncommunicated thoughts do not make the contract unenforceable by the seller.

A person who accepts or signs an instrument that on its face is a contract is deemed to agree to all of its terms and cannot escape liability on the ground that he or she has not read it. The terms of the written agreement will control unless there is a legally recognized mistake of fact or a person has been induced to sign an instrument because of undue influence, duress, overreaching, or an unfair or deceptive trade practice. Manifestation of mutual assent is usually accomplished through an *offer* communicated to a person and that person's *acceptance* communicated back to the person who made the offer.

The Offer
Under basic contract law, an offer:
1) is a promise by an offeror
2) calling for a promise, an act, or forbearance by an offeree
3) that is definite and certain in its terms.

A Promise by an Offeror to an Offeree

An **offer** is a promise by one party, coupled with a request for something from a second party that is to be the agreed exchange for the promise or its performance. The "something" referred to is called the **consideration.** Consideration may be an act, a forbearance, a promise to act, or a promise to forbear acting in a particular way. The person making an offer is known as the ***offeror*** and the person to whom an offer is made is known as the ***offeree***. *A simple exchange of promises between an offeror and offeree provides sufficient consideration to support the formation of a binding contract.*

Definite and Certain in its Terms

An offer must be definite and certain in its terms or it may be ruled void for lack of certainty. *It must not be "illusory" in character, i.e.,* appear to have consideration where in fact there is none. *A valid offer must be an unequivocal promise, certain in its terms, that manifests a present, serious contractual intent.* The offeror must intend to be legally bound if the offer is accepted. If the offer pertains to real property, it must also comply with the Statute of Frauds.

> *Example:* A property owner writes to a broker, "I am very interested in selling my house and would like to get $265,000." The broker phones the owner immediately with the news that the broker has a purchaser who has accepted the owner's offer to sell for $265,000. The owner, however, declines to sell. No contract has come into being. The owner did not make a firm offer to sell; rather, s/he was inviting the broker to come with some offers, or was merely engaging in "preliminary negotiations" concerning the possible sale of his property. Parties often confuse preliminary communications with a legally binding offer.

Because a contract requires an offer, and an offer must contain a promise before it is binding at law, **conditional offers** (often called **contingent offers**) must carefully specify the details of any conditions to the offer. For instance, if a purchaser's offer to buy real property is intended to be binding, but only upon the condition that the buyer is able to sell other property, the condition clause in the offer to purchase should specifically set out the terms of the condition that must occur before the offer becomes binding.[1]

The typical real estate **listing** contract is NOT an offer to sell. *The listing contract specifies the terms under which a seller will be bound to pay the broker a commission, but does NOT bind the seller to sell even if the broker produces a purchaser who makes an offer that meets all the terms specified in the listing agreement.* Other actions that do not constitute offers to sell include *preliminary negotiations.*

> *Example:* A prospective purchaser emails a lot owner and asks her, "Would you be willing to sell your vacant lot for $5000?" The owner responds by email, "Sold!" The prospective purchaser did not make a valid offer to purchase under contract law and the lot owner's response was not a legal acceptance. The prospective purchaser's question was merely an inquiry or preliminary negotiation.

Advertisements of property for sale are **not** offers to sell as a matter of contract law; rather, they are merely invitations to those who read the advertisement to make an offer that the seller can then accept or reject.

> *Example:* A seller advertises a house for sale for $232,000. A buyer sends a text message informing the seller that the buyer "accepts" the seller's offer to sell. The advertisement is a mere invita-

tion to the public to submit offers to purchase to the seller. It does not bind the seller to sell to the buyer at the price advertised, even though the buyer's text message can qualify as a writing.

Typically in the sale of real property the seller usually is *not* the initial offeror; rather, **the *buyer* is the initial *offeror* and the *seller* is the *offeree*.**

Acceptances and Counteroffers

An **acceptance** is a promise by an offeree to be bound by the terms of an offer. Just as an offer cannot be accepted unless it is communicated to the offeree, *the acceptance of an offer must be communicated to the offeror in a manner indicated or implied in the offer.* If the offer indicates that the offeree is to promise something, then notice of the acceptance is required; but where the offer requests that the offeree perform some act, as distinguished from making a promise, simply performing the act may be sufficient. *An acceptance must be absolutely identical with the terms of the offer;* in other words, the acceptance must mirror the offer.

> *Example:* A property owner offers to sell to a prospective buyer. There are no conditions in the offer. The buyer accepts the offer subject to the inspection and approval of the property by an inspector of the buyer's choice. The buyer has not legally accepted the offer to sell because the acceptance includes an additional provision not in the original offer. The purported acceptance in reality is a counteroffer.

As the example illustrates, *if an intended acceptance places a condition on the acceptance or in any other way changes the terms presented in the offer, it is a **counteroffer**, not an acceptance.* The slightest change in the terms of an offer will prevent a proposed acceptance from becoming an acceptance that will form a legally binding contract. There is no mutual assent at that point to the additional or changed term, and thus no binding contract, until both parties have indicated their agreement to **all** the terms of the contract.

A **counteroffer** *constitutes a rejection of an offer* and starts anew the process of negotiation. If an offeree changes a term of an offer, such as the proposed purchase price, then signs the changed offer and returns it to the offeror, the offeree has rejected the original offer and has made a counteroffer, which in essence is a new offer. The original offeree now has become the offeror and the original offeror has become the offeree. *Once an offeree makes a counteroffer, he cannot subsequently change his mind and "accept" the original offer.* The original offer has been rejected and is gone forever unless a party revives it by making a subsequent offer containing identical terms as the original offer. Counteroffers in real estate sales transactions are very common and are discussed more thoroughly in Chapter 11.

Communication of Offer and Acceptance

Under contract law, offers and acceptances may be communicated in a variety of ways — orally, by personal delivery in writing, by mail, by email or text message, or by other electronic means. However, an offer can specify the exact manner in which acceptance is to be communicated, in which case the offeree must communicate acceptance in the manner directed to create a contract.

> *Example:* An owner offers to sell to a prospective buyer. The offer states that acceptance must be made by email message only. Instead, the prospective buyer leaves a phone message informing the seller that he has accepted and signed the offer. The offer has not been legally accepted.

Offers commonly specify that an *acceptance* must be made "in writing" or by signing the written offer. Even so, t*he offeree must not only sign the written offer (or write down his acceptance in the manner specified) but also must "communicate" the acceptance to the offeror to create a binding contract.* Generally, contract law allows this communication of acceptance to be made in any of the following ways.

Methods of Communicating Acceptance

1. *Oral communication.* The offeree may personally or by telephone notify the offeror that the offer has been signed by all offerees and thus accepted.

2. *Personal delivery.* The offeree may personally deliver the written acceptance to the offeror or may have the acceptance delivered to the offeror by another person.

3. *Mail (traditional or special mail).* The offeree may place the written acceptance in the mail *properly addressed* to the offeror. Once the acceptance has been mailed (placed in the control of the mail service and out of the control of the offeree), the *offer is considered to be accepted as of the date and time of mailing.* Even though the offeror does not receive the acceptance until several days later, the offeror cannot withdraw or revoke the offer after an acceptance has been mailed. Similarly, the offeree cannot withdraw or revoke the acceptance after it has been mailed. This rule of law is known as the "**mailbox rule.**" It is less important in today's world of instant electronic communication than it once was, but the legal principle remains the same.

4. *Electronic methods of communication.* The use of electronic communication methods, whether email, text message, or fax, is commonplace and perfectly legal <u>unless</u> the terms of the offer expressly provide otherwise. *An acceptance of an offer communicated by email, text message, or fax is effective* **upon receipt** *by the offeror's communication equipment or computer.*[2]

Mailbox Rule

The "mailbox rule" has some qualifications, including the requirement that the envelope must be properly addressed; if the envelope is addressed incorrectly, the mailbox rule does not apply. The mailbox rule also will not apply if the offer expressly so states or if the offer specifies certain methods of communicating acceptance and does not include acceptance by mail as an option. *The mailbox rule basically operates* **only as a method of communicating acceptance of an offer**. It does **not** apply to any other situation. Thus, the rejection of an offer or the making of a counteroffer will be effective only upon *receipt* by the addressee, not at the time of mailing.

The current standard residential contract form allows the buyer to unilaterally terminate the contract for any or no reason by delivering written notice of termination to the seller prior to the expiration of the buyer's due diligence period. *The mailbox rule does not apply to the delivery of the buyer's termination notice.* Pursuant to the contract terms, the notice of termination must be **delivered** to the seller or his agent prior to the expiration of the due diligence period. Similarly, notice that a buyer is exercising a right to purchase under a traditional option to purchase contract will be effective only upon receipt by the owner-optionor, not upon the mailing of the notice. (The latter two issues will be discussed in greater detail in Chapter 11.)

Communication to an Agent

In real estate practice *communicating an offer or acceptance to a principal's agent is the same as communicating directly to the principal.*[3] Remember that an agent stands in the place of the principal, at least for communication of notice purposes (although agents rarely, if ever, will have the authority to sign and accept an offer on behalf of their principal, thereby creating a contract). Suppose a seller receives an offer from a prospective buyer and makes a counteroffer to sell his property to that prospective buyer. If the prospective buyer signs the counteroffer and informs the seller's listing agent by telephone of his acceptance, that constitutes communication of the acceptance to the seller and a contract is formed at the time the offeree telephones the seller's agent.

Termination of Offers

Once an offer is made, how is it terminated? Any of the following acts may terminate an offer.

1. An offer is terminated by a counter offer or by a conditional or partial acceptance.
2. An offer is terminated if the offeree rejects the offer or fails to accept it within the period of time stipulated in the offer, or, if none is stipulated, within a reasonable period of time.
3. Unless the contract provides otherwise, an offeror may revoke the offer, thereby terminating it, at any time prior to communication of acceptance by the offeree.
4. The death or insanity of an offeror immediately terminates an offer without notice to the offeree.
5. An offer made to the general public, such as a newspaper or webpage advertisement, can be revoked by a subsequent notice given equal publicity as the original offer.

Exceptions to Ability to Revoke

There are certain exceptions to the rule that an offer may be revoked or withdrawn by the offeror at any time before notice of acceptance by the offeree. One exception is a traditional **option contract.** *An option to purchase is a contract to keep an offer to sell open for a certain period of time.* An option contract cannot be revoked by the seller because the prospective purchaser provides consideration in exchange for the seller's promise to keep the offer open for a stated period of time (the option period). Ordinarily an option gives a prospective purchaser the right to purchase property under stated terms if the purchaser chooses to exercise the right within a specified period of time.[4] Under the traditional option contract, the purchaser must affirmatively notify the seller (optionor) by the stated date that s/he (the optionee) is exercising the option to purchase and the parties must enter into a purchase contract. If an option is not timely exercised, it expires.

Another exception is the case of a **unilateral offer** where an offeror invites acceptance by performance of some act. While only complete performance is an acceptance, once an offeree begins to perform the requested act, the offer becomes irrevocable, thus allowing the offeree time to complete performance without risking a forfeiture.

CONSIDERATION

In addition to the offer and acceptance, *a valid contract must be supported by* **consideration.** A mere promise to another is not enforceable without consideration. *Anything that is bargained for and given in exchange for a promise is consideration.* Consideration might be payment of a sum of money, the performance of an act, such as procuring a purchaser for the seller's property, or the making of reciprocal promises.[5] Typically, the consideration for most sales contracts is the owner's promise to sell and the buyer's promise to purchase the property that is the subject of the transaction. The fact that a promise is conditional rather than absolute will not necessarily render it insufficient consideration for a return promise nor will the fact that the relative worth of two promised performances is unequal defeat otherwise good consideration.   Generally speaking, the parties are left with the bargain they negotiated, whether good or bad. Courts usually do not evaluate the sufficiency of the consideration, only whether it exists. However, a grossly inadequate consideration may be a circumstance that, together with other facts, may tend to show fraud or undue influence.

CAPACITY OF THE PARTIES

For a contract to be enforceable, the parties must have the "**legal capacity**" to create a contract. *If there is any indication that a contracting party may not have legal capacity, legal advice should be sought prior to allowing the party to execute an offer, acceptance, or contract.* The following persons do not have legal capacity to contract, and the contracts they sign are either void or voidable.
- Minors (persons under age 18)
- Contracts by persons legally declared to be mentally incompetent by a court of law
- Contracts by persons mentally incompetent in fact but not legally declared to be incompetent by a court of law
- Persons intoxicated or under the influence of drugs who do not understand what they are doing when signing a contract

Minors

Except for a category of contracts for "necessaries" and a limited exception for emancipated minors, a minor lacks legal capacity to enter into contracts. *A minor is a person under age 18. A minor* who executes a contract to purchase, lease, or sell real property *may disaffirm the contract* once they are 18 years old, i.e., the age of majority. Because a minor has the option to affirm, thereby accepting, or disaffirm, thereby rejecting, contracts entered into during minority, these contracts are said to be "*voidable.*"

Mentally Incompetent Persons

The test of mental capacity to contract is whether the individual's mental faculties are so impaired that the individual is incapable of understanding the nature or consequences of his or her acts in the transaction. There are three contract law categories of mentally incompetent persons.

1. Contracts executed by a person who has been *legally declared mentally incompetent by a court of law.* These contracts are **void**. A legal declaration of mental incompetency is often accompanied by the appointment of a guardian for the incompetent ward.[6] A guardian can petition the clerk of court to sell, mortgage, exchange, or lease the ward's real estate.[7]

2. *Contracts executed by a person who is mentally incompetent in fact but who has not been legally declared incompetent by a court of law.* These contracts are **voidable** if it is proved the mental incompetency prevented the person from understanding the nature and consequences of the transaction.

3. *Contracts executed by an intoxicated person or a person under the influence of drugs.* If a person is so intoxicated or under the influence of drugs that the person does not know what he or she is doing, the contract is "**voidable**" for want of capacity. If someone takes advantage of a person with either of these incapacities, the contract may also be set aside for fraud.

LAWFUL OBJECTIVE

As a matter of public policy, the law requires that all contracts must have a **lawful objective or purpose**. A party to an *illegal* contract cannot sue and ask a court to enforce the illegal purpose of the contract. "Illegality" takes many forms. A contract that violates any criminal or civil law will make all or part of the contract unenforceable. Examples of illegal contracts include those calling for immoral performance or discrimination against members of a protected class. Where the illegal provision is central to the contract, courts will void the entire agreement. If an illegal provision is merely collateral to the main purpose of the contract, courts may void only the offending provision while enforcing the remainder of the contract.

WRITTEN CONTRACTS

All contracts may be oral except those specifically required by law to be in writing. *If the law requires a written agreement, then no legally enforceable contract is created unless it is in writing.* As mentioned earlier in this chapter, the law of primary interest to real estate brokers is General Statute §22-2, the Statute of Frauds, that requires all contracts for the sale or conveyance of real property to be in writing and signed by the party against whom the contract is sought to be enforced.

NECESSITY OF MUTUAL CONSENT

A contract may comply with all of the foregoing elements and still be either void or voidable due to certain circumstances summarized below. When one of these circumstances exists, there is said to be no real "mutuality of consent" between the parties. In other words, the parties do not have an agreement because there has not been a true "meeting of the minds" regarding the contract.

Circumstances That May Render a Contract Void or Voidable
- Mistake
- Fraud
- Misrepresentation
- Unfair or Deceptive Practices
- Duress
- Undue Influence

MISTAKE OF FACT

A **mistake** is an erroneous impression on the part of one or both parties regarding some material aspect of a contract. *A contract may be **voidable** if the mistake of fact:*
1. involves some "material" term or aspect,
2. is **mutual**, and
3. is not the result of fraud or negligence.

The mistake may relate to the instrument signed, the identity of a contracting party, the existence or characteristics of the subject matter, or some similar matter. Understand that the mistake of fact must be **mutual**. Where there is a genuine mutual mistake concerning a material term of a contract, such mistake may make the contract voidable by one of the parties.

Example: B negotiates with A to purchase a tract of mountain land A owns. A honestly believes and tells B that the tract contains 260 acres. B relies on A's representations and the parties sign a contract. Prior to settlement, it is discovered that the tract contains only 160 acres. The contract most likely will be held voidable at B's election due to the magnitude of the mistake relating to a material term that both parties mistakenly believed.

In contrast, most *unilateral* mistakes of fact will *not* relieve a party from contractual obligations. Recall the earlier example of the buyer who mistakenly thought that the rear boundary of the property he was under contract to purchase extended to a line of trees, when in fact it was 20 feet in front of the line of trees. That buyer's unilateral mistake of fact would not enable him to have the contract declared voidable.

North Carolina courts are extremely hesitant to apply the mistake doctrine to *completed transfers*. It is one thing to rescind a contract to convey prior to the real estate closing; it is quite another to rescind a deed after the closing. To allow parties to legally attack completed transfers on a mistake theory could create uncertainty in titles.

MISTAKE OF LAW

Unlike mutual mistakes of material fact, *a **mistake of law** does **not** excuse a party's obligation under a contract, since everyone is presumed to know the law.* Thus, where there is no mistake of *fact* with respect to the making of a contract, a mistaken understanding of its legal effect does not excuse performance. A prime example is the case of *Willis v. Willis*[8] in which a widow, after signing her Last Will and Testament, later signed a warranty deed conveying real property she owned to one of her two sons, reserving a life estate for her. Unfortunately, the grantee son died before his mother, at which point the mother wanted to give the real property to her surviving son. Had she devised the property to her son in her Will, she could have changed the terms of the Will, but once she conveyed the property to her son by *Deed*, she could not later change her mind and rescind the deed. The North Carolina Supreme Court held that a unilateral mistake by the grantor as to the law will not support reformation of a deed. Thus, the grantee son's surviving spouse owned the property subject to the mother's life estate.

FRAUD AND MISREPRESENTATION

If a party or a party's agent engages in **fraud**, then any resulting contract may be *voidable* at the option of the party deceived. **Fraud** consists of the following elements:
1. either a false representation or nondisclosure of a material fact,
2. made with knowledge of its falsity or in reckless disregard of its truth,
3. with the intent that it be acted upon by the other party, and
4. that is acted upon by that party to his or her injury.

All four elements must be proved for the deceived party to avoid a contract on the ground of fraud.[9] A representation is *fraudulent* if it is made with knowledge of its falsity or without belief in its truth. *A representation made by a person believing it to be true, when it is untrue, may be the basis for rescission on the ground of **innocent misrepresentation**, but it is not fraud.* However, if a person represents a fact pretending to know it when in fact s/he does not know whether it is true, that representation is fraudulent if all of the other elements of fraud are proved. *Real estate brokers and property owners must not make statements concerning matters about which they are ignorant.*

Example: A listing broker tells an interested buyer that the developer is working with the county to pave the gravel road leading into the subdivision. In fact, the developer never intended to pave the road, never contacted the county, and refuses to pave it. The listing broker did not make this representation to other lot purchasers who did not ask about the road. If the broker's misrepresentation induced this buyer to purchase the lot, the buyer may bring an action for damages because the lot is worth less with a gravel road than a paved road. The buyer also may be able to rescind the contract. The purchasers of other lots do not have a right to sue for fraudulent misrepresentation because no assertions about the road were made to them.

Historically, the law did not impose any obligation on a property owner to tell a prospective buyer any material fact about the property. This doctrine was known as "**caveat emptor**" or "let the buyer beware." Similarly, a buyer who knows facts that enhance a property's value need not disclose those facts to a seller before entering into a contract to purchase the property at less than its potential value. Where a seller and buyer are dealing "at arm's length," the traditional understanding of the marketplace is that each must look after his or her own interests if the means of obtaining information are equally open to both parties. However, sellers rather than buyers are usually in a better position to know facts affecting the property being sold.

While most sellers of residential property are required to provide prospective buyers with the Residential Property and Owners' Association Disclosure Statement, the statement itself does not compel unlicensed sellers to disclose any problems or defects related to the property, as they have the option of checking "no representation." If they choose to answer yes or no, their answer must be honest or they may be guilty of fraud. Even though the seller may not be obligated to disclose material facts concerning the property, *the seller's broker must affirmatively disclose any and all material facts that he or she is or should be aware of to prospective purchasers.* Further, *the duty to disclose material facts pertaining to the property applies to **all** licensees*, regardless of whether they are acting as a seller agent or buyer agent. A licensee's failure to disclose a material fact to a seller or buyer (or lessor or lessee) may violate the Real Estate License Law and the deceptive practices statute.

Mere expressions of opinion usually are neither innocent misrepresentation nor fraud. To invalidate a contract, *the misrepresentation must be of a past or existing fact.* Of course, the dividing line between "representation of a fact" and "opinion" may be difficult to draw.

To disaffirm a contract and have it declared unenforceable due to fraud, *the injured party must show they believed the representation to be true, reasonably relied on it, and that it played a substantial part in inducing them to make the contract.* Where a purchaser ordered a home inspection prior to closing, but ignored the existing and potential problems disclosed by the report and did not pursue additional recommended inspections, that purchaser could not later prevail in a lawsuit against the seller for unfair and deceptive practices, fraud, or negligent misrepresentation. The Court of Appeals held that the purchaser could not prove reasonable reliance where she ignored information from her own home inspector that the roof might leak and chose not to have additional recommended inspections prior to closing, regardless of any representations the seller may have made.[10]

Fraud does not *automatically* make a contract absolutely void. *The defrauded party has the option to avoid the contract or to enforce it.* If a buyer finds that it is unprofitable to purchase because of the fraud, the buyer may rescind the contract. If the transaction remains beneficial despite the fraud, the buyer may affirm and enforce the contract.

A principal is responsible for his agent's misrepresentations. An agent who knowingly misrepresents a material fact may be personally liable for fraud and may be sued for damages if the individual relied on the misrepresentation and suffered injury.

UNFAIR OR DECEPTIVE PRACTICES IN COMMERCE

North Carolina law declares unfair methods of competition and unfair or deceptive acts or practices in or affecting commerce to be unlawful (General Statute §75-1.1, sometimes referred to as the **Unfair or Deceptive Practices Act**). An act by a seller or seller's agent that does not amount to fraud may still be found to be an unfair or deceptive act in commerce. Acts that violate the statute include providing a misleading opinion or false inducement, failing to disclose a material fact, misleading advertising, or misrepresenting the nature or extent of a guarantee or warranty that occur in the conduct of a trade or business. A person injured by the unfair or deceptive practices of another is entitled to treble damages (i.e., three times the amount of damages) under General Statute §75-16. It is also possible that a contract to convey real property could be invalidated if the seller or seller's agent has violated this statute. The purpose of this law is to encourage ethical conduct between persons engaged in commerce and consumers of those goods or services.[11]

The Unfair or Deceptive Practices Act does not apply to all sales of real estate. For example, the Act does not apply to a person who is selling their own property who does not generally engage in the trade or commerce of selling real estate. However, *owners who regularly sell real estate and real estate brokers are covered by the Act.*

The Unfair or Deceptive Practices Act provides an injured party to a real estate contract with a legal action separate and distinct from other legal actions such as fraud, breach of contract or breach of warranty. While a party need not prove fraud to prevail under this Act, proof of fraud automatically will constitute proof of an unfair or deceptive practice. Misrepresentations, whether fraudulent or innocent, made by a listing broker to a prospective purchaser may not only constitute grounds for the buyer to rescind the sales contract (since the principal/seller may be liable for the improper actions of his agent), but may also violate both the deceptive practices statute and License Law.

DURESS

Duress is overcoming the will of a person and forcing the person into a contract by violence or a threat of violence, imprisonment or a threat of imprisonment, threat of physical injury to a family member or others, threat of wrongful destruction, injury, seizure, or withholding of one's property, or any other wrongful act that compels a person against his or her will to enter into a contract. When a person enters into a contract out of fear or because another's actions prevent that person from exercising free will and judgment, the contract is *voidable* by the injured person who must initiate legal action within a reasonable time after the duress is removed.

UNDUE INFLUENCE

Undue influence may also invalidate a contract. Undue influence occurs when one person takes unfair advantage of another in a contractual relationship because of the parties' particular and peculiar relationship, or one party's weakness of mind, or due to a party's particular necessities or distress. Persons acting in a fiduciary capacity, such as attorney-client, guardian-ward, physician-patient, clergyman-parishioner, trustee-beneficiary, may have an unfair advantage because the other party relies upon and gives undue weight to the fiduciary's counsel. A contract may be *voidable* if it was induced by reason of the fiduciary's undue influence over the other party.

Similarly, if one takes advantage of another's weakness of mind and induces him or her to enter into a contract, the contract may be voidable if undue influence was used. If one takes advantage of another's distress or particular necessities that force that person to enter into a particular contract that is oppressive or unfair, it may be set aside because of undue influence.

OTHER CONTRACT LAW ISSUES

STATUTE OF FRAUDS

The Statute of Frauds, which comes from the English common law, is considered the most important statute dealing with real estate law in history. While many contracts are valid and enforceable even though oral, most contracts to transfer an interest in real property must be in writing to be enforceable because of the Statute of Frauds. Its purpose was to prevent perjury, forgery, dishonest conduct, and manufactured and false testimony with respect to certain types of contracts. The language of the present-day Statute of Frauds pertaining to real property transactions is similar to the original English statute. In North Carolina it is found in General Statute §22-2 which states in part:

> All contracts to sell or convey any lands ...and all other leases and contracts for leasing land exceeding in duration three years from the making thereof, shall be void unless said contract, or some memorandum or note thereof, be put in writing and signed by the party to be charged therewith. . . .

While the statute states that a contract not in compliance is "void" if not in writing, courts treat an oral or incomplete agreement as voidable and unenforceable, rather than void from the outset.

> *Example:* An owner offers in writing to sell her lot to a buyer, and the buyer accepts in writing. They agree to a closing date one month away. Although both agree orally on the lot that is being sold, neither the seller's nor the buyer's writing contains an adequate legal description. One month later, the transaction closes and a deed containing a precise legal property description is delivered to the buyer. Even though the contract was voidable by either the seller or buyer, they completed the transaction and the failure of the contract to comply with the Statute of Frauds became irrelevant.

As the example illustrates, if the parties choose to voluntarily perform an oral or incomplete written agreement, there is nothing that prevents the property interest from being transferred; it is only when either party refuses to do what he or she orally agreed to do that the non-breaching party will not be able to enforce the oral agreement in a lawsuit.

The Statute of Frauds also requires a written agreement for leases that will not be concluded within three years from the making of the lease agreement. For example, in one case two brokers purchased property anticipating that a friend of theirs would lease it from them for a bank the friend intended to open. The parties exchanged several letters negotiating the terms of a proposed five year commercial lease and later met and orally agreed on the final terms, but no lease agreement was actually signed prior to the Bank's Board of Directors rejecting the location. The broker-owners sued alleging breach of a commercial lease and negligent misrepresentation. The Court of Appeals held that the various writings did not "...evidence the mutuality of assent and intention to be bound necessary to comply with the statute of frauds. To the contrary, it shows on its face that defendants had not yet agreed to enter into the lease...." that had to be in writing to be enforceable because its duration exceeded three years from its making.[12]

The Statute of Frauds does not require that a formal written contract cover every detail of a transaction, although a well drafted and complete contract is much more desirable and will avoid future misunderstandings. A contract or memorandum will be sufficient if there is signed, written evidence of the agreement stating with reasonable certainty the items listed below.

Necessary Elements to Comply with Statute of Frauds

- The names of the parties to the contract
- The subject matter of the contract
- Material terms and conditions
- The signature of the party to be charged with the contract, or an authorized agent.[13]

One North Carolina decision provides a startling example of how informal a document might be and still comply with the Statute of Frauds. In that case, the seller gave the buyer an option to purchase land for $45,000. The buyer paid for the option by a check in the amount of $500 and the check was endorsed and cashed by the seller. On the front of the check the buyer wrote "For option on rest of Tuttle Tract at $45,000." Some weeks later, the seller refused to convey the property claiming that the option contract did not comply with the Statute of Frauds and was therefore unenforceable. The Court of Appeals found that the check met the minimum requirements under the Statute of Frauds and that the option contract was enforceable. The check contained the names of the parties, the subject matter of the contract ("rest of Tuttle Tract"), all material terms (courts are willing to imply some of these), and was signed by the party to be charged (since the seller endorsed the check when he cashed it).[14]

This example is provided not to encourage the use of checks or sketchy memoranda as contracts, but to illustrate that the courts at times will honor very informal written arrangements between parties if what is written contains minimum essentials. Sometimes a contract is evidenced by several interrelated written instruments, rather than in one document. Invoices, order blanks, receipts, entries in books of account, letters, electronically transmitted messages, and various other writings may be used to satisfy the Statute of Frauds if they are connected or refer to each other or the contract to be proved in some way.

> *Example:* X was the high bidder on a parcel of land at an auction sale and signed a written certification that X had purchased the lot subject to confirmation by the sellers. The sellers then signed a record sheet prepared by the auctioneer confirming the sale. The auctioneer then stapled together the document signed by X, the confirmation sheet signed by the sellers, and a plat fully describing the lot sold. The sellers now refuse to transfer the property to X, claiming failure to comply with the Statute of Frauds. The sellers are wrong. No formal contract is necessary as the separate but related writings constitute a sufficient written memorandum. No essential feature of a contract to convey has been left uncertain; the material terms are present, the parties are named, the land is adequately described, and the "party to be charged" (here, the seller) has signed.

A confusing aspect of the Statute of Frauds for sellers, buyers, and brokers is the legal distinction between *contract **modification*** and the *waiver* of contract provisions. A contract *modification* must be in writing to comply with the Statute of Frauds, because the parties are agreeing to change a term of their original contract. In contrast, a waiver of a contract provision may be oral, because a waiver is the voluntary release of a contractual benefit, but does not change the terms of the contract.[15] Because the distinction between modification and waiver can be a close call, brokers are advised to *put* *all changes to the contract in writing and have all sellers and buyers affirm the changes with their signatures or initials and date.*

ELECTRONIC TRANSACTIONS

A series of federal and state laws facilitate electronic real estate transactions. They include:
- Uniform Electronic Transactions Act (UETA)
- Electronic Signatures in Global and National Commerce Act (ESIGN)
- Uniform Property Electronic Recording Act (UPERA)
- Uniform Electronic Notarization Act

(The last two acts listed are discussed in Chapter 6.)

North Carolina adopted a version of the *Uniform Electronic Transactions Act (NCUETA) in* 2000.[16] UETA is a "uniform law" designed to deal with important unresolved issues involving electronic commerce, computer programs, electronic signatures, electronic agents, and electronic records. Because of the increasing use of electronic means when conducting commerce, UETA is important to real property lawyers and brokers. Its scope clearly includes real estate transactions if electronic means are used to facilitate the transaction.

A corresponding federal law, the *Electronic Signatures in Global and National Commerce Act (ESIGN),*[17] became effective June 30, 2000. Many of the provisions and definitions in both UETA and ESIGN are similar, but ESIGN regulates interstate or foreign commerce, *i.e.,* commerce across state lines, rather than *intra*state commerce, *i.e.,* commerce within a state. The North Carolina e-commerce laws generally apply to intrastate transactions, rather than the federal law.

NCUETA expressly states that an electronic signature satisfies a law requiring a signature, that a signature may not be unenforceable solely because it is in electronic form, and that a contract may not be denied legal effect or enforceability solely because an electronic record was used in its formation.[18] The Act defines an "***electronic signature***" as "*an electronic sound, symbol, or process attached to, or logically associated with, a record and executed or adopted by a person with the intent to sign the record.*" An "***electronic record***" is similarly broadly defined as "*…a record that is created, generated, sent, communicated, received or stored by electronic means.*"[19] Under General Statute 66-314, the Act "*…* applies to any electronic record or electronic signature created, generated, sent, communicated, received or stored on or after …" October 1, 2000 relating to a transaction.

NCUETA adopts the standard definition of "transaction" as "*…an action or set of actions occurring between two or more persons relating to the conduct of consumer, business, commercial, or governmental affairs.*" However, the NCUETA, like ESIGN, separately defines a "***consumer transaction***" as "*…a transaction involving a natural person with respect to or affecting primarily personal, household or family purposes.*"[20]

The primary consequence of this distinction relates to how parties' consent to conduct the transaction using electronic means is evidenced. General Statute 66-315(b) states that in a "transaction," "*…*Whether the parties agree to conduct a transaction by electronic means is determined from the context and surrounding circumstances, including the parties' conduct." However, in a "*consumer* transaction," NCUETA requires that a clear and conspicuous statement be given to the consumer regarding the consumer's rights before the consumer consents to utilize electronic means in the transaction, and that a consumer's consent to utilize electronic means may be evidenced by conduct under the regular transaction standard "*…*only when accomplished in compliance with …." the consumer disclosures required under General Statute 66-327(c)(1)-(4). The Act does not specify the consequences of failing to give the required special consumer disclosures in a consumer transaction.

In the non-consumer transaction arena the parties' consent will be evidenced by and inferred from their conduct. However, few cases or legal articles have discussed the applicability of NCUETA to real estate brokerage transactions, particularly in the consumer transaction realm. The North Carolina Real Estate Commission addressed this topic in its 2014-2015 *General Update Course* materials and noted that a "consumer transaction" requires NCUETA consumer disclosures **if** electronic means are used in a transaction involving at least one natural person who was:

1. purchasing or selling an owner-occupied dwelling, or
2. leasing a vacation rental property for personal use, or
3. leasing a pre-1978 dwelling to use as his or her residence[21]

While North Carolina law now validates electronic contracts and signatures where all parties consent to use electronic means, brokers should caution their principals/clients to be wary of electronic exchanges directly with the other party as a series of communications *between the parties* may be deemed sufficient to form a contract. *Communications sent electronically that are intended for discussion and negotiation purposes only should be clearly identified as such, whether sent by a party or a broker on behalf of his or her principal.*

A contract may also be created automatically by electronic means based on a pre-programmed computer response.

> *Example:* Golf Mountain Development (GMD) advertises lots for sale on the Internet. GMD's web page includes maps and pictures of the development, price lists for various lots, and a procedure for making an electronic offer on any unsold lot. Brenda Buyer fills out an electronic "offer to purchase" form on the web page for Lot #423. Brenda's e-offer is for $40,000, the full asking price for the lot. Without any review by any person at GMD, GMD's computer program automatically sends a confirming e-mail message to Brenda that simply reads: "Your offer to purchase Lot #423 in Golf Mountain Development is hereby accepted. GMD Corporation" The message from GMD also includes a series of real estate disclosures required by state and federal law. (Brenda had expressly agreed to accept disclosures by email by filling out an electronic consent form before she submitted her e-offer to purchase.)

Can a person enter into a binding contract with a computer? Brenda never dealt with any human at GMD. Can GMD's computer "accept" Brenda's offer to purchase without any review by an employee or agent of GMD? The answer is "yes" when you supplement traditional contract law with the provisions of UETA. GMD's computer can function as an "electronic agent" of GMD.[22] UETA authorizes "automated transactions,"[23] including those between a person and an electronic agent even if no individual was aware of or reviewed the electronic agent's actions.

DISHARGE OF CONTRACTS

The *discharge* of a contract is the termination of the agreement. Contracts may be terminated in several ways, the most common of which are by (1) agreement of the parties; (2) full and complete performance; (3) material breach; (4) impossibility of performance; and (5) operation of law.

Agreement of the Parties

A contract may be discharged in the same way it was formed, namely, by *agreement of the parties*. At any time the parties may enter into an agreement releasing each other from their contract and agreeing that neither is bound any longer by its terms. An agreement to terminate contractual obligations may take many forms and, depending on the form, may be given any of a number of labels under contract law, *i.e.*, a release, novation, modifying agreement, accord and satisfaction, or cancellation, each of which is summarized below.

Forms of Discharge of Contract by Agreement

Release — Each party to the contract "releases" the other from contractual duties. A release must comply with all requirements of a valid contract. It is, in effect, a contract to destroy the earlier contract.

Novation — A novation is the substitution of a new contract for the former one. All obligations under the old contract are discharged and replaced by the terms of the new contract. In the new contract, the parties may remain the same but the terms may change or, conversely, the terms may remain the same, but the parties may change.

Subsequent Modifying Agreement — As the title implies, the parties to the original contract enter into a new contract modifying the terms of their original understanding. This can be accomplished even though the original contract states that it cannot be thereafter altered or modified.

Accord and Satisfaction — An accord and satisfaction involves a settlement or compromise of a dispute between parties to a contract with one party providing some other or different performance that is accepted by the other party.

Cancellation — Some documents may be canceled by various physical acts such as marking "canceled" across the document, destroying it, or surrendering possession with the intent that the underlying obligation be discharged.

A study of these methods of discharge by agreement will reveal overlap between the various terms and definitions. While contract law carefully distinguishes between each category, the primary point is that a later agreement between the parties discharges the original contract. The later agreement may have to be in writing if the original agreement was required to be written.

Full Performance

The most frequent way that a contract will be discharged is by *complete performance* of all of its terms by each party. Each party does what each is obligated to do and the contract is fulfilled or fully performed.

Breach of Contract

A contract also may be discharged when one party breaches or refuses to perform his or her part of the contract. A material breach of contract by one party will discharge the other party from any obligation that he or she may have under the contract. *In the context of a real estate transaction, the failure of a purchaser to pay the seller for the property (within a reasonable time) discharges the seller's duty to convey the property to the purchaser.* In this instance, the purchaser's failure to perform is a material breach of the contract. This example may be especially applicable in contracts where the parties have agreed that "time is of the essence" as to the performance of the contract. In such a situation, the failure by one party to meet the "time is of the essence" condition discharges the other party's duty to perform his end of the agreement.[24] In most real estate contracts, time is not of the essence as to the closing date, and the parties have a reasonable time to close unless the contract specifies otherwise.

In some instances, a party's breach may not be material. For example, a home builder's failure to install a certain kind of appliance specified in the contract may constitute a breach, but not necessarily a material breach. The fact that the buyer contracted for a gas oven instead of an electric oven does not relieve the buyer of his obligation to purchase the home, although the builder may be liable for damages as a result of the breach or required to install a gas stove as promised.

Impossibility of Performance

Impossibility of performance **may** discharge a contract. *Generally, impossibility of performance does **not** avoid liability under a contract or discharge it.* The parties' rights are governed by the terms of their contract. They may legally bind themselves to perform what is in fact impossible. If one finds it impossible to do the thing he has promised, he still may be called upon to answer to the other party in damages for breach of contract. Performance is not excused by unforeseen difficulties, by unusual and unexpected expenses, by strikes, by the difficulty of obtaining raw materials, by fire, or by accidents. Such contingent events should have been considered before the contract was made, and if *they were to excuse a party from liability, an express language to that effect should have been included in the contract.*

However, there are some rare situations where impossibility of performance will discharge a party from liability under a contract. For instance, *if the contract is made on the basis of the existence or continued existence of a specific thing, the destruction or nonexistence of that specific thing will excuse the performance of the contract insofar as the destroyed or nonexistent thing is concerned.* If the destroyed or nonexistent thing represents the *sole* object of the contract, then performance under the contract is impossible and the contract is void.

> *Example:* The owner of an old warehouse contracts to convey it to a buyer. Between the signing of the contract and the closing date, the warehouse burns to the ground through no fault of either party. The destruction of the warehouse makes performance by the seller impossible; i.e., there no longer is a warehouse to convey. Although performance of the contract in its original form by the seller is excused, the buyer may be primarily interested in the land and thus may still insist upon transfer of the property as is. (A "risk of loss" statute governs this fact situation in North Carolina if the contract to convey does not specify what happens in the event of destruction of all or part of the property.)

The defense of impossibility of performance must be in the nature of the thing to be done and not the inability of the promisor to do it. For instance, if the promisor dies before the completion of performance, the liability of his estate is determined by the nature of the contract.

> *Example:* A property owner agrees to sell property to another but dies before the scheduled closing date. The seller's estate remains liable to sell the property; the contract to convey is not discharged on an impossibility theory because the land still exists and is now in the seller's estate which can convey it to the buyer.

Operation of Law

A contract may be discharged by operation of law in the following ways:
- Bankruptcy of a contracting party
- Statutes of limitation
- Government action prior to the contract's performance

A contract can be discharged by *operation of law.* For example, if a party to a contract files for *bankruptcy* prior to performing contractual obligations, the effect of the bankruptcy filing may extinguish any right of action on the contract. Technically, the bankruptcy does not discharge the contract, but it makes recovery from the bankrupt party difficult or impossible because the bankruptcy may release the debtor from all contractual obligations and debts owing as of the date the bankruptcy petition was filed.

Statutes of limitation may also result in a practical discharge of contracts. Statutes of limitation establish time periods within which a party must sue or the right to sue will expire. While statutes of limitation do not themselves extinguish contractual obligations, they bar legal remedies to enforce them. Thus, they effectively discharge contracts for most practical purposes.

Sometimes a purpose that is legal becomes illegal by *governmental action* prior to the contract's performance. In this case, to complete the contract would be to violate the law. In cases where there is a change in the law or an exercise of governmental authority that prohibits performance, the obligations under the contract cease and the contract is discharged.

ASSIGNMENT OF CONTRACTS

The topic of **assignment of contracts** involves an important distinction between an assignment of a contractual *right* and an assignment of a contractual *duty.* While an assignment often involves the transfer of both rights and duties, the distinction between these elements can become important. Whether a contract *right* is assignable depends on the nature and terms of the contract.

Ordinarily, a contract right is assignable by the person entitled to that right (the "contract obligee"), **unless** *performance by the person with the duty to perform (the "contract obligor") would materially change the obligor's burden of performance if the right was assigned to a person other than the obligee.*

Example: X, the owner of an apartment building, contracts with the Kleen Janitorial Service to have Kleen perform specified cleaning duties each week at X's apartments pursuant to a contract that is to run for three years. X agrees to pay Kleen $400/month for its services. Six months after the effective date of this agreement, X sells the apartments to Y and also assigns his rights under the cleaning contract to Y. The assignment is valid. Kleen's duties under the contract have not increased or materially changed in any way.

A contract might expressly provide that it *cannot* be assigned, or it may prevent assignment by one party without the consent of the other party, or contain other qualifying language.

The person assigning a contract is an *"assignor."* The person to whom the assignment is made is the *"assignee." The effect of an assignment is to transfer to the assignee all the rights and interests of the assignor.* The assignee stands in the shoes of the assignor, taking his or her rights and remedies, subject to any defenses that the obligor (the person with the duty to perform) may have against the assignor.

Where the assignor attempts to transfer *duties and obligations* as well as rights, the assignor will *not* be able to escape his or her obligations to the original party merely by delegating his duty to perform to the assignee. The assignee will be primarily liable for fulfilling the assignor's duties and obligations under the contract, but if the assignee fails to perform, then the assignor remains secondarily liable to the original party for the promised performance, unless the original party has consented to the assignment and has released the assignor from further liability.

Example: X leases property to Y for a three year term at a rental of $600/month. The lease contains no restrictions on assignments. Y assigns the lease to Z, and, after several months pass, Z defaults on the rent payments. Although Y can assign the obligation to pay rent to Z, Y cannot assign away his liability to X for the rent payments. As between Y and Z, Y remains secondarily liable for the rent and Z is primarily liable. In order to have relieved himself from future liability, Y would have needed a release or novation from X. Thus, X can compel payment from Y for any months in which Z fails to pay rent, and Y is left to seek reimbursement from Z.

Example: A seller and buyer enter into a contract for the purchase of the seller's warehouse. Prior to closing, the buyer executes a valid assignment "of all right, title, and interest in the contract" to an investor with the seller's consent. The investor then defaults on the contract and the seller suffers $40,000 in damages because the transaction fell through. While a valid assignment has taken place, it does not release the buyer from responsibilities and liabilities under the original contract.

In the example immediately above, *unless the seller who agreed to the assignment also agreed to release the buyer of all future obligations under the contract, the buyer remains legally liable to the seller for the investor's default.* As between the buyer and the investor, the buyer is secondarily liable. If the buyer is required to pay $40,000 in damages to the seller, the buyer will have a legal claim against and be entitled to judgment for the $40,000 from the investor under their assignment.

RULES FOR INTERPRETATION OF CONTRACTS

Over time, courts have developed rules concerning the interpretation and construction of written contracts to aid in determining by relatively uniform standards the parties' intentions from the words used in their contracts.

A rule known as the *"parol evidence rule"* applies where parties have entered into a final and complete contract. This rule states that *earlier informal and tentative agreements and negotiations are no longer valid where they have been replaced by a final and complete contract between the parties.* Thus, earlier agreements and negotiations will not be admitted as evidence in a legal action to contradict or change the terms of a final contract. Accordingly, it is very important that parties place their entire agreement, including *all* desired terms, in writing.

It is not uncommon for a written contract to contain language stating that the contract "... contains the entire agreement of the parties and there are no representations, inducements, or other provisions other than those expressed herein." Such language is known as a *"merger clause." Preliminary negotiations inconsistent with the terms in the final contract are not admissible in evidence to alter the terms of the contract.* Under the parol evidence rule, all prior negotiations are deemed to be superseded by and merged in the final written contract.

Example: During the course of negotiations between a seller and buyer involving the sale of a large tract of land, the buyer asked the seller how many acres of timber land were on the property. The seller, who honestly believed that the tract included 250 acres of timber land, told the buyer that she was pretty sure her tract contained that amount. However, the final written sales contract included the following clause:

> "Seller believes that the tract contains 250 acres of timber land but makes no guarantee that this figure is correct. Buyer is advised to obtain a survey of the tract to determine the precise acreage."

The final written sales contract also contained a merger clause. Under these facts, the seller's original oral representation of 250 acres of timber land is superseded by the express contract provision to the contrary. The parol evidence rule prohibits admission into evidence at trial of the seller's oral representation.

The most important rules for the interpretation of contracts are summarized below.[25]

Rules for Interpreting Contracts

1. Preliminary negotiations inconsistent with the terms of a final written contract are not admissible to alter the terms of the contract.
2. A contract is interpreted as a whole, and all writings forming a part of the same transaction are interpreted together.
3. Ordinary words will be interpreted in their ordinary, popular sense unless circumstances show that the parties intended to use them in a different or special sense.
4. Where there is a conflict between preprinted versus written provisions of a contract, the preferred interpretation is to give effect to the written provisions over the preprinted language.
5. Ambiguities will be construed against the party who prepared the provision or chose the words that now raise doubts.

CONTRACT REMEDIES

An important legal consequence of a valid contract is the availability of remedies in the event that a party to the contract breaches it. Where a party, without legal justification, breaches a contract, that breach may discharge the other party from performing some or all of his duties under the contract. Additionally, the nonbreaching party may have other legal remedies, such as those listed below.

Contract Remedies
- Money Damages
- Specific Performance
- Rescission

Money Damages

A nonbreaching party may seek money damages from the breaching party. The main category of money damages allowed by the courts is **compensatory damages**, the purpose of which is to place the injured party in the same position that he or she would have been had the contract been performed. The goal is to make the injured party whole, rather than penalize the breaching party.

For example, when a contract to convey real estate has been breached, the formula for compensatory damages is the difference between the contract price and the fair market value of the real estate at the time of breach, plus other incidental damages flowing from the breach.[26]

COMPENSATORY DAMAGES - PUTS INJURED PARTY BACK TO SAME POSITION AS IF BREACH HAD NOT OCCURRED.

Example: Seller and Buyer enter into a valid contract to purchase Seller's home for $395,000. Seller breaches the contract on December 12. If the property was worth $410,000 on that date, Buyer's damages amount to the $15,000 difference between the contract price of $395,000 and the fair market value at the time of breach of $410,000. (Buyer may also recover incidental damages, *e.g.*, costs of procuring a loan for the property, inspection costs, *etc.*) If, on the other hand, the home was worth $390,000 at the time of breach, Buyer's damages under the traditional formula are *zero,* although Buyer may be allowed to recover incidental damages.

Besides compensatory damages, special damages known as **consequential damages** also might be obtained where additional damages were or should have been reasonably foreseeable by the breaching party at the time of the contract.

A third category of damages, known as **liquidated damages**, occurs when parties to a contract specify in advance *a specific amount of damages recoverable by **either** party in the event of breach.* Where it is difficult to precisely determine actual damages and where the liquidated damages figure is reasonable, courts tend to enforce the liquidated damages provision and prohibit either party from suing for actual money damages. For example, a seller and a buyer stipulate in their purchase contract that in the event of a material breach by either party, damages will be liquidated at $10,000. If the $10,000 sum is reasonable, it will be the automatic measure of damages in the event of breach, even if the innocent party suffered no monetary damages or suffered more than $10,000 in damages resulting from the other party's breach.

Specific Performance

When real estate is the subject of a contract, a remedy known as **specific performance** is regularly granted to *purchasers* by the courts. Specific performance is an *equitable remedy* (rather than a legal remedy) in which the aggrieved party seeks to enforce the contract by requesting that a court order the other party to do what he or she is obligated to do, i.e., to specifically perform the contract. *When a seller refuses to conclude the sale, the purchaser may sue for specific performance to force the seller to honor the contract and convey the property.*[27] However, specific performance *rarely* is granted in favor of a seller trying to compel the buyer to purchase the property, because there are too many issues as to whether the buyer has the ability to perform what he or she promised. (The residential purchase contract most commonly used in North Carolina prohibits a seller from suing a buyer for specific performance, as will be discussed in Chapter 11.)

A variation of the remedy of specific performance is a remedy called **specific performance plus abatement** of the purchase price. This legal action might be used to remedy a deficiency in quality of title or quantity of land.

Example: A seller agrees to sell a parcel of land to a buyer for $500,000 and warrants that the parcel contains 800 acres. A subsequent survey reveals that the parcel only contains 760 acres, but the seller refuses to adjust the purchase price. Under these circumstances, the buyer may be entitled to specific performance of the original contract coupled with a $25,000.00 abatement in the purchase price to reflect the five percent deficiency in acreage.

Rescission

There are times when one of the parties to a binding contract will seek the remedy of **rescission**. *This remedy declares the contract invalid and returns the parties to the position they were in prior to entering into the contract.* Rescission may be granted where there has been a *mutual* mistake of fact, or in fraud and misrepresentation cases, and is a particularly appropriate remedy where one of the parties entered into the contract because of undue influence or duress.

> *Example:* Seller and Buyer enter into a contract to convey a vacant lot, both understanding that the land is suitable for an onsite sewage disposal system. If post-contract tests reveal that the land is not suitable for onsite sewage disposal, Buyer should be able to rescind the contract.

> *Example:* A seller believes and the listing broker states that a parcel of land is zoned multifamily. After signing the contract, the buyer discovers that the land is zoned single-family residential only. The buyer should be able to rescind the contract.

A rescission returns the parties to their original positions prior to entering into the contract. This means that the contract is voided and any monies paid by the buyer are refunded.

RELATIONSHIP OF CONTRACT LAW TO AUCTION SALES

Real estate auctions are common in North Carolina. Thus, a broker should have a basic understanding of the relationship of contract law to auction sales. An "auction" is defined as

"The sale of goods or real estate by means of exchanges between an auctioneer and members of an audience, the exchanges consisting of a series of invitations for offers made by the auctioneer, offers by members of the audience, and the acceptance by the auctioneer of the highest and most favorable offer."[28]

Thus, when a person participates in an auction, whether in person or electronically, and makes a bid, he or she is making an offer to purchase the property. When someone else participating in the auction makes a higher bid, this constitutes another offer to purchase that has the legal effect of superseding the prior lower bid. When the auctioneer yells "Sold!," slaps down the gavel, or engages in any words or conduct or electronic communication signifying acceptance of a bid, a legal acceptance under contract law has occurred and a binding contract of purchase and sale has been formed.

Must the auctioneer accept the high bid? This depends upon whether the auction is *with reserve* or *without reserve*. If an auction is held **with reserve**, then the owner of the property being sold at auction has reserved the right to reject bids for any reason or subject to specific guidelines (such as a minimum bid requirement). If, on the other hand, the auction is advertised as **without reserve**,[29] then the highest bidder will be entitled to purchase the property no matter how unfavorable the price is from the seller's standpoint because the seller did not set any minimum value.

An auctioneer is an *agent of the seller*. Unlike the typical real estate broker, an auctioneer usually has full authority to bind the owner of the property to sell. Since real estate is involved, the contract must comply with the Statute of Frauds. The successful high bidder must sign an adequate *written* sales contract to protect the bidder's rights, but a failure to do so will not relieve the bidder from liability on the bid. The North Carolina Association of REALTORS® has adopted a set of recommended forms for its members' use in voluntary auction transactions, including a standard auction listing agreement, an auction sale contract, and a buyer premium agreement.

Use of a buyer premium as a marketing tool has increased in North Carolina. A bidder, as a condition of being allowed to bid, agrees that the final purchase price will be the amount of the high bid *in addition to* paying a buyer premium, typically a percentage of the high bid paid to the auctioneer. The seller usually also owes a commission to the auctioneer.

> *Example:* A real estate auction is advertised as including a 5% buyer's premium. Assume that the seller also contracts to pay the auctioneer a 6% commission for the sale. The high bid for the property was $100,000; to conclude the purchase, the buyer must pay the $100,000 purchase price, plus a $5,000 buyer's premium to the auctioneer. The seller owes a $6,000 commission to the auctioneer.

The rights and obligations of a bidder can be substantially different, depending on whether the auction is a voluntary auction or a judicial auction held under court authority. When the auction is held under court order, the high bidder's rights and obligations are controlled by statutes and court orders that can require judicial confirmation or approval of the sale. Whether participating in a voluntary or judicial auction, it is the responsibility of each bidder to determine the conditions of the sale before making a bid.

Regulation of Auctions and Auctioneers

Subject to statutory exceptions,[30] all persons who sell or offer to sell goods or real estate by auction in North Carolina must hold a valid auctioneer license.[31] Individual and firm auctioneer licenses are issued and their conduct regulated by the North Carolina Auctioneers Commission.[32] A person who actually calls the bids or "cries the sale" must have at least an individual auctioneer license. *While a person acting **solely** as a cryer of sales is not required to have a real estate license, any other activity, such as advertising the sale of real property, making representations about the property, or soliciting persons to attend the auction, requires a real estate broker's license.* Therefore, most voluntary real property auctions are conducted by persons and firms holding both a real estate license and auctioneer license. Persons conducting judicial auctions may be exempt from licensing altogether, although ordinary practice is to use licensed persons and firms due to their expertise.

Endnotes

1.   *Poor v. Hill*, 138 N.C.App. 19, 530 S.E.2d 838 (2000).

2.   The Uniform Electronic Transactions Act (UETA) deals extensively with the time and place of sending and receipt of electronic messages. See N.C. Gen. Stat. §66-325.

3.   *Dysart v. Cummings*, 181 N.C.App. 641, 640 S.E.2d 832 (2007).

4.   *Lewis v. Jones*, 132 N.C. App. 368, 515 S.E.2d 87 (1999); *Lawing v. Jaynes*, 285 N.C. 418, 206 S.E.2d 162 (1974).

5.   See, for example, the case of *Sessler v. Marsh*, 144 N.C. App. 623, 551 S.E.2d 160 (2001), where the Court of Appeals reiterates the basic rule that a contract must be supported by consideration to be enforceable. After defining consideration as "any benefit, right, or interest bestowed upon the promisor, or any forbearance, detriment, or loss undertaken by the promisee," the Court refers to the listing contract involved and notes, in part: "The listing contract provides that defendant will pay plaintiff a commis-

sion if plaintiff procures a buyer who is ready, willing and able to purchase the property upon the seller's terms, specified in the contract. On its face, the document provides valuable and legal consideration." 551 S.E.2d 160, 167. [Citations omitted.]

6.   *See,* N.C.Gen.Stat. Chapter 35A, "Incompetency and Guardianship," North Carolina Department of Health and Human Services, "Guardianship Services," www.ncdhhs.gov/.../afs_g

7.   N.C.Gen.Stat. § 35A-1301(b).

8.   *Willis v. Willis,* 365 N.C. 454, 722 S.E.2d 505 (2012).

9.   *John v. Robbins,* 764 F. Supp. 379 (M.D.N.C. 1991).

10.   *MacFadden v. Louf,* 182 N.C.App. 745, 643 S.E.2d 432 (2007).

11.   *Poor v. Hill, supra.*

12.   See *Howlett v. CSB, LLC,* 164 N.C. App. 715, 596 S.E.2d 899, *disc. review denied* 359 N.C. 68, 604 S.E.2d 313 (2004).

13.   Examples of two Court of Appeals decisions involving disputes over whether the contract was properly executed by all of the owners: *Burgin v. Owen*, 181 N.C.App. 511, 640 S.E.2d 427 (2007) [contract signed by only one tenant by the entirety]; and *Parker v. Glosson*, 182 N.C.App. 229, 641 S.E.2d 735 (2007) [only one of two named sellers signed the contract].

14.   *Hurdle v. White,* 34 N.C. App. 644, 239 S.E.2d 589 (1977).

15.   *Ball v. Maynard,* 184 N.C.App. 99, 645 S.E.2d 890 (2007). The Court of Appeals held that the seller's conduct was in the nature of a waiver of a contract condition rather than a modification that would have required compliance with the Statute of Frauds.

16.   UETA is located at Article 40, Chapter 66 of the North Carolina General Statutes. It became effective on October 1, 2000. The United States Congress had previously passed legislation dealing with similar issues in 2000. The *Electronic Signatures in Global and National Commerce Act* (known popularly as ESIGN) became effective June 16, 2000. Among other things, ESIGN recognizes the legal validity of electronic contracts and signatures in interstate commerce. In 2005, North Carolina enacted the Uniform Property Electronic Recording Act (URPERA). This cutting-edge legislation authorizes the Secretary of State to adopt e-recording standards with an adequate information security system to ensure that electronic documents are accurate, authentic, adequately preserved, and resistant to tampering. As a necessary supplement to various e-commerce acts, including URPERA, discussed immediately above, the General Assembly enacted the 2005 Electronic Notarization Act setting forth procedures for electronic notary acts. These Acts are discussed in Chapter 6.

17.   See 15 U.S.C. §7001, *et.seq.*.

18.   N.C. Gen. Stat. §66-317, "Legal recognition of electronic records, electronic signatures, and electronic contracts."

19. N.C. Gen. Stat. §66-312(8)&(9): definition of electronic record and electronic signature, respectively.

20. N.C. Gen. Stat. §66-312(4)&(17): definition of consumer transaction and transaction respectively.

21. For a more in-depth discussion of NCUETA and brokerage, readers are referred to the article "Electronic Signatures and Documents" from the NC Real Estate Commission's *2014-2015 General Update* course which may be found at the Commission's website, www.ncrec.gov under "Publications" and then "Update/BICAR."

22. N.C. Gen. Stat. §66-312(7) defines "electronic agent" as meaning "a computer program or an electronic or other automated means used independently to initiate an action or respond to electronic records or performances in whole or in part, without review or action by an individual."

23. N.C. Gen. Stat. §66-324. ESIGN also authorizes these transactions. 15 U.S.C. § 7001(h).

24. *Midulla v. Howard A. Cain Co.*, 133 N.C. App. 306, 515 S.E.2d 244 (1999). In addition, obligations of a buyer and seller under a real estate contract are concurrent conditions, and neither party is in breach until the other party tenders performance, even though the designated closing date has passed. *Ball v. Maynard*, 184 N.C.App. 99, 645 S.E.2d 890 (2007).

25. For a recent summary of many of the key rules for interpreting contracts, see *42 East, LLC v. D. R. Horton, Inc.*, 218 N.C. App. 503, 722 S.E.2d 1 (2012).

26. *Pleasant Valley Promenade v. Lechmere, Inc.*, 120 N.C. App. 650, 464 S.E.2d 47 (1995).

27. *Lamberth v. McDaniel*, 131 N.C. App. 319, 506 S.E.2d 295 (1998). In *Curran v. Barefoot*, 183 N.C.App. 331, 645 S.E.2d 187 (2007), the North Carolina Court of Appeals held that, when a vacation home package is involved, the buyer can obtain specific performance of both real and personal property where the seller refuses to transfer some of the personal property after the closing.

28. N.C. Gen. Stat. §85B-1(1).

29.   N.C.Gen.Stat. § 85B-1(4) uses the term "absolute auction" and defines it as meaning "the sale of real or personal property at auction in which the item offered for auction is sold to the highest bidder without reserve, without the requirement of any minimum bid, and without competing bids of any type by the owner, or agent of the owner, of the property."

30. N.C. Gen. Stat. §85B-2.

31. N.C. Gen. Stat. §85B-4.

32. N.C. Gen. Stat. §§85B-3, 85-3.1, 85-3.2.

11 | SALES CONTRACTS AND PRACTICES

A written contract for the sale of real estate is a legally binding agreement between a seller and buyer whereby the seller agrees to sell and the buyer agrees to buy a parcel of real estate. This contract is perhaps the most important document in a real estate transaction. The contract of sale reflects in writing the agreement of the seller and purchaser and establishes their rights and obligations with respect to the sales transaction. It is extremely important that real estate brokers have a thorough working knowledge of contracts for the sale of real estate, especially since they routinely assist sellers and purchasers in contract preparation.

In a majority of *residential sales transactions* in North Carolina, the "standard form" Offer to Purchase and Contract will be the contract used. Because of the importance and common usage of the standard form, this chapter will focus on it in depth. The Joint Forms Task Force, comprised of members of the North Carolina Association of REALTORS® and members of the Real Property Section of the North Carolina Bar Association, promulgate **Standard Form 2-T**, the **Offer to Purchase and Contract**, (hereafter **Standard Form 2-T**) which is jointly copyrighted by both organizations.

In addition to the standard **offer to purchase and contract**, two other types of contracts for the sale of real estate will be encountered less frequently: the **installment land contract** and the traditional **option to purchase** contract. There are no "standard" forms for either of the latter two types of real estate sales contracts, which most commonly are referred to by their specific names. This chapter discusses in depth each of these three basic types of contracts for the sale of *residential* real estate.[1]

This chapter covers the following topics: sales contract preparation, the legal concept of offer and acceptance as it relates to real estate sales contracts, procedures related to handling earnest money, presenting offers to sellers, and handling contract modifications and counteroffers. The reader should keep in mind that the general principles of contract law discussed in Chapter 10 apply to contracts for the sale of real estate.

Introductory Concepts

A broker working with a prospective purchaser usually assists the prospective purchaser in completing a preprinted "offer to purchase and contract" form expressing the terms the purchaser wants to propose to the seller. When the prospective buyer signs the completed form and it is delivered to the seller, the document becomes an **offer**. If the seller subsequently **accepts** the offer by signing the form (or by any other legally acceptable method) and **communicates** the acceptance to the buyer, the buyer's offer coupled with communication of the seller's written acceptance create a completed contract binding both the seller and the buyer to the mutually agreed terms set forth in the written document.

The *"standard" contract most commonly used in North Carolina for the sale of residential real estate is called an* **offer to purchase and contract**. This offer to purchase and contract may also be referred to by a number of different descriptions or shorthand terms, such as real estate **sales contract**, **purchase contract**, **earnest money contract**, or **binder**. Most frequently, the term "sales contract" will be used to refer to the "offer to purchase and contract."

SALES CONTRACT PREPARATION

One of the most crucial moments in the entire real estate transaction is when a prospective purchaser wants to make an offer to purchase a seller's property. Real estate brokers must be knowledgeable about the legal rights and obligations that flow from the proper completion and execution of a sales contract. Brokers should realize that a poorly prepared contract not only may lead to dissatisfaction, controversy, and bad public relations with the parties involved, but worse, may result in expensive litigation, and possible proceedings before the North Carolina Real Estate Commission. *The North Carolina Real Estate Commission expects all real estate brokers to possess the competence necessary to properly prepare a sales contract.* "Proper preparation" means to competently and accurately complete an approved preprinted sales contract form; to do so requires an understanding of all provisions in the preprinted form.

In some respects, the sales contract is more important than a deed. This is because the contract determines the rights and obligations of the parties and, to a certain extent, the nature and content of the deed. *All ambiguities should be eliminated when completing a sales contract form.* If there is any ambiguity with respect to the meaning, interpretation, or construction of the language in an offer to purchase and contract completed by a broker who is the seller's agent, those ambiguities will be construed against the seller. If the broker who prepared the offer to purchase and contract is the buyer's agent, then any ambiguities will be construed against the buyer.

A real estate broker who completes a sales contract form improperly and thereby fails to adequately protect the interests of the client fails to exercise the skill, care and diligence owed a principal under agency law and also violates the Real Estate License Law by acting incompetently as a real estate broker.[2] *The required competence includes the ability to properly complete approved standard forms.*

"Drafting" of Sales Contracts by Agents Prohibited

The drafting of contracts or contract forms for others is the exclusive domain of attorneys under the law. *Thus, real estate brokers are prohibited by law from "drafting" real estate sales contract forms for others, as to do so constitutes the unauthorized practice of law.*[3] However, the legal profession has long acknowledged that requiring an attorney to prepare every offer to purchase and contract in every real estate sales transaction would unnecessarily impede the conduct of real estate brokerage. Consequently, the legal profession and the real estate profession reached a compromise on this issue *permitting real estate brokers to "fill in" or "complete" preprinted real estate sales contract forms that have been drafted by an attorney.*

A sales contract form may be one drafted by an attorney specifically for use by a particular real estate firm, or it may be a "standardized" form drafted by attorneys and approved for use by an organization such as a bar association (a professional trade organization for attorneys) or a real estate trade organization, or it may be a "standardized" form drafted by attorneys and marketed for general use. These preprinted forms consist mostly of standardized language with blanks to be filled in by the parties (or a real estate broker acting on behalf of one or both parties) regarding specifics about the particular transaction, such as the names of the parties, property description, purchase price, amount of earnest money, closing date, etc.

Sources of Contract Forms

The North Carolina Association of REALTORS® has worked with the North Carolina Bar Association to develop a series of standard contract forms and addenda that will be appropriate for use in virtually all sales of residential single-family properties, as well as other forms designed for use in certain other sales transactions. North Carolina Association of REALTORS® members may contact their local REALTOR® organization to learn where they may obtain these forms. Non-REALTOR® licensees may use the forms that have only the North Carolina Bar Association's logo.

OFFER TO PURCHASE AND CONTRACT

It is of vital importance that real estate brokers use the appropriate contract form in each transaction. *Real estate brokers must thoroughly understand every provision of any offer to purchase and contract form or addendum they recommend for use by a consumer and must be able to properly complete such forms on behalf of sellers and buyers. Above all, brokers must remember the importance of assuring that every detail is addressed in the completed contract. Every condition or point of agreement regarding the transaction should be included in the offer to purchase and contract or, when appropriate, addenda, to ensure that it accurately reflects the parties' agreement.*

Requirements for Offer to Purchase and Contract Forms

Buyers and sellers of residential property typically expect real estate brokers to provide an appropriate offer to purchase and contract form for use in the transaction. *When a broker provides such a preprinted contract form, the form suggested by the broker must comply with North Carolina Real Estate* **Commission Rule 21 NCAC 58A.0112** *titled "Offers and Sales Contracts."* This rule requires the form to address nineteen (19) separate matters, all of which are important issues on which the seller and buyer need to agree. A broker who proposes using a form that does not comply with this rule may be subject to disciplinary action. The standard forms jointly authored by the North Carolina Association of REALTORS® and the North Carolina Bar Association are intended to comply with the requirements of Real Estate Commission Rule A.0112, and the Commission strongly encourages real estate brokers to use these forms when appropriate.

Prohibition Against Certain Contract Provisions

In addition to requiring certain matters to be addressed in preprinted contract forms utilized by brokers, Commission Rule A.0112(b) also prohibits real estate brokers from including in an offer to purchase and contract *any provision relating to brokerage commissions or any provision disclaiming the liability of a broker for his representations in a transaction.* This rule states:

> (b) A broker acting as an agent in a real estate transaction shall not use a preprinted offer or sales contract form containing:
> (1) any provision concerning the payment of a commission or compensation, including the forfeiture of earnest money, to any broker or firm; or
> (2) any provision that attempts to disclaim the liability of a broker for his or her representations in connection with the transaction.
> A broker or anyone acting for or at the direction of the broker shall not insert

or cause such provisions or terms to be inserted into any such preprinted form, even at the direction of the parties or their attorneys.

The reason for prohibiting provisions relating to brokerage commissions is that the real estate broker is not a party to the sales contract and such contracts should not be used by real estate brokers to define their agreement regarding the sharing of real estate brokerage commissions ("commission splits").

We saw in Chapter 9 that it is common practice for real estate listing firms to share their earned brokerage commission with brokers of other real estate firms who produce a ready, willing and able buyer. The decision as to commission splits, however, is solely that of the listing firm. The listing firm can dictate when it will share a commission and what the split will be. In the past, some brokers working with buyers would attempt to improperly force the listing firm to give them a more favorable commission split by including a commission split provision in the offer to purchase presented to the listing firm for presentation to the seller. Real Estate Commission Rule A.0112(b) prohibits this practice, as it is not in the best interest of sellers and buyers. *Commission-split agreements must be negotiated separately between real estate firms and such agreements may not be included by real estate brokers in an offer to purchase and contract.*

The reason for prohibiting any provision that disclaims the liability of a broker for his representations in a transaction is obvious. A real estate broker's duties regarding representations to sellers and buyers are established by the North Carolina Real Estate License Law (see Chapter 8). The inclusion of a provision in a sales contract attempting to avoid a statutorily imposed duty has no legal effect and is entirely inappropriate.

Using Standard Contract Forms and Addenda Forms

The most frequently used form in residential sales is Standard Form 2-T, Offer to Purchase and Contract, which will be discussed in depth in these materials. However, brokers should be aware that there are different standard transactional forms available for their use in residential transactions, all of which are promulgated by the Joint Forms Task Force and copyrighted by the North Carolina Association of REALTORS® and the North Carolina Bar Association. (There also is an "Agreement for Purchase and Sale of Real Property," Standard Form 580-T, for use in commercial transactions which will be discussed in Chapter 19.) Brokers should have a thorough working knowledge of the various forms available and any attendant guidelines, which include:

- *Offer to Purchase and Contract*, **Standard Form 2-T** and the *Guidelines For Completing Offer to Purchase and Contract*, **Standard Form 2-G**.
- *Offer to Purchase and Contract - Vacant Lot/Land*, **Standard Form 12-T** and the *Guidelines for Completing the Vacant Lot Offer to Purchase and Contract*, **Standard Form 12-G**.
- *Offer to Purchase and Contract – New Construction*, **Standard Form 800-T**, and the *Guidelines for Completing the New Construction Offer to Purchase and Contract*, **Standard Form 800-G**.

Various **addenda forms** also have been developed to assist brokers to competently deal with common fact situations or contingencies where the standard contract forms require additional language. Each addendum has a standard form number. These addenda are revised or eliminated as necessary to conform to revisions in the standard form contracts. An **addendum** literally can be translated from the original Latin to mean simply "something added." In the context of the "Offer to Purchase and Contract" form, an addendum is an addition to the contract that must be carefully selected for appropriateness, competently completed by the broker, and appended to the contract.

    In the past, real estate brokers who needed specialized provisions sometimes drafted their own. These home-made clauses often failed to adequately address the specialized fact situation at hand and also exposed the broker to accusations of the unauthorized practice of law. Standard form addenda were developed to provide brokers with adequate language for many of the most common special fact situations in real estate transfers. Examples of addenda jointly approved by the North Carolina Bar Association and the North Carolina Association of REALTORS® include:

        Back-Up Contract Addendum (Standard Form 2A1-T)
        Contingent Sale Addendum (Standard Form 2A2-T)
        New Construction Addendum (Standard Form 2A3-T)
        FHA/VA Financing Addendum (Standard Form 2A4-T)
        Seller Financing Addendum (Standard Form 2A5-T)
        Loan Assumption Addendum (Standard Form 2A6-T)
        Lead-Based Paint Or Lead-Based Paint Hazard Addendum (Standard Form 2A9-T)
        Additional Provisions Addendum (Standard Form 2A11-T)
        Owners' Association Addendum (Standard Form 2A12-T)
        Vacation Rental Addendum (Standard Form 2A13-T)
        Short Sale Addendum (Standard Form 2A14-T)

    Two other standard forms exist, which technically are agreements, rather than addenda; these are: the Buyer Possession Before Closing Agreement (Standard Form 2A7-T) and the Seller Possession After Closing Agreement (Standard Form 2A8-T). New addenda are developed in response to specialized situations commonly encountered in real estate transfers or as laws add new requirements, such as disclosure requirements. Various addendum forms are periodically updated and revised.

Using the Appropriate Form

    As previously noted, the standard form most commonly employed by brokers in residential sales transactions is **Standard Form 2-T, Offer to Purchase and Contract**. The purpose of this form is described by its drafters in the Guidelines thereto as follows:

> This form may be used in a variety of real estate sales transactions, but it was developed primarily for use in the sale of existing single-family residential properties. Do not use this form as a substitute for a lease-option agreement, lease-purchase agreement or installment land contract. Also, if the sale involves the construction (or completion of construction) of a new single-family dwelling, use the current standard New Construction Addendum (NCAR/NCBA Form 2A3-T) or consult a NC real estate attorney for an appropriate form.[4]

    There no longer is an approved standard form Option to Purchase for real estate brokers to use. Parties engaging in options to purchase, including lease-option agreements, should be referred to an experienced real estate attorney who will draft an option contract suitable for the specific transaction. Similarly, there is no standard form contract for an installment land sale and parties desiring to use that method of purchase should be advised to consult a real estate attorney. As the *Guidelines* above expressly state, Standard Form 2-T was not intended to be used in either of those situations. It may also be necessary or advisable to have a contract drafted by an attorney for transactions involving sales of commercial properties, multifamily residential properties, or vacant land. While brokers might be tempted to use Standard Form 12-T when negotiating the purchase of a large tract of land, the opening paragraph of that form states:

> **NOTE:** This contract is intended for unimproved real property that Buyer will purchase only for personal use and does not have immediate plans to subdivide. It should not be used to sell property that is being subdivided unless the property has been platted, properly approved and recorded with the register of deeds as of the date of the contract. If Seller is Buyer's builder and the sale involves the construction of a new single family dwelling prior to closing, use the standard Offer to Purchase and Contract—New Construction (Form 800-T) or, if the construction is completed, use the Offer to Purchase and Contract (Form 2-T) with the New Construction Addendum (Form 2A3-T).

Real estate brokers are expected to know when it is appropriate to use a particular contract form and to recognize situations where sellers and buyers should be referred to an attorney to have a suitable contract drafted. If the transaction requires that extensive changes be made to a preprinted form or involves the insertion of atypical special provisions, then the standard form may not be appropriate for the situation. *Remember, real estate brokers can "fill in" blanks on preprinted contract forms, but if it is necessary to draft special provisions or change the form itself, a broker who proceeds to draft such special provisions or modify standardized contract terms is engaging in the unauthorized practice of law.*

In many specialized fact situations, Standard Form 2-T should be used in conjunction with an appropriate addendum or addenda. For example, if a sale involves the completion of construction of a single-family residence, Standard Form 2A3-T, "New Construction Addendum," should be appended to Standard Form 2-T, or perhaps the new Standard Form 800-T might be more appropriate if the seller also is buyer's builder and the sale involves the construction of a new single family dwelling prior to closing. If a seller is financing all or part of the purchase price, then the "Seller Financing Addendum" (Standard Form 2A5-T) should be properly completed and attached. If the buyer is taking physical possession of the property a few days prior to the closing date, then the "Buyer Possession Before Closing Agreement" (Standard Form 2A7-T) should be utilized.

Brokers will commonly encounter situations where it will be necessary to attach one or more sappropriate addenda. Accordingly, real estate brokers must be familiar with the proper combination of addenda to use with the standard form "Offer to Purchase and Contract."

General Instructions for Completing the Form

The Standard Form 2-T is not a static document; rather, it periodically is revised by the Joint Forms Task Force in an attempt to address perceived needs within the real estate brokerage industry. ***It is imperative that brokers have a thorough understanding and working knowledge of the most current version of Standard Form 2-T and that they promptly educate themselves as to any revisions in the form.*** The July 1, 2017 version of Standard Form 2-T is reprinted herein as Figure 11-1 and will be the basis of discussion for the remainder of this Chapter.

As the old saying goes, "When all else fails, read the directions." The instructions for completing the "Offer to Purchase and Contract" standard form are clearly set forth in Standard Form 2G, "Guidelines For Completing The Offer To Purchase And Contract." The "**General Instructions**" from the "Guidelines" bear repeating here. They read:

1. Type this form if possible; otherwise print or write legibly in ink.

2. Fill in all blank spaces. If any space is not used, enter "N/A" or "None" as appropriate.
3. Be precise. Avoid the use of abbreviations, acronyms, jargon, and other terminology that may not be clearly understood.
4. Every change, addition or deletion to an offer or contract must be initialed and should be dated by both Buyer and Seller.
5. If numerous changes are made or if the same item (such as the purchase price) is changed more than once, complete a new contract form to avoid possible confusion or disputes between the parties. If, *after the parties have entered into a valid contract*, you prepare a new form for the parties to sign because the existing contract contains so many changes that it is difficult to read, then do not discard the existing contract. Keep it with the new form.
6. Review with the parties all contract provisions. Advise the parties to consult their respective attorneys if they have any questions about the legal consequences of the contract or any particular provision.

These instructions may seem to be nothing more than common sense, but they were developed in response to mistakes commonly made by brokers completing the form. Perhaps the reader has encountered a form that has been revised so many times with so many initials, crossed out language and handwritten amendments scribbled in spaces and margins that it is difficult to ascertain what the parties agreed to on key points. Some of these transactions are completed more in spite of the contract than because of it. Others fail because a clear meeting of the minds was never evidenced in a written contract.

Note the sage advice to type the terms or to print *legibly* in ink, as pencil can be erased, and to make an entry in *all blanks* to clearly indicate that the blank was not omitted by oversight, but rather was considered and deemed inapplicable. Writing "N/A" or "none" or "0" in a blank also prevents later alteration or insertion of a term that was not intended by the parties. In the event that terms are altered, all such changes must be initialed by all parties to evidence their consent and the preferred practice is to write the date of the initialing as well to show the sequence of consent.

Persistent Problems

In the course of reviewing consumer complaints, the Real Estate Commission's legal staff has noted a variety of ongoing mistakes brokers commonly make in preparing and submitting Standard Form 2-T. A few of the most persistent and serious problems include:

- using the phrase "owner of record;"
- failing to clearly list fixtures the seller does not want to convey;
- failing to clearly specify personal property the buyer wants the seller to convey as part of the sale, even if identified in the MLS information as personal property that will convey;
- failing to clearly define all critical dates, preferably by stating a date certain, rather than vague descriptions of time periods;
- failing to timely present offers or provide all parties with copies of the fully executed contract;
- confusion as to the timing of requesting and negotiating repair issues versus the completion of agreed repairs as it relates to the due diligence period.

Although the proper completion of Standard Form 2-T, appropriate addenda, and other standards forms may require a little extra effort at the outset, it can save significant time, effort, and perhaps expense later. When a contract clearly sets forth the obligations of the parties and avoids confusing and improper language, smooth transactions are generally the rule, rather than the exception.

REVIEW OF MAJOR PROVISIONS IN STANDARD FORM 2-T

As can be seen by a review of Standard Form 2-T, shown as Figure 11-1, a well-drafted contract form must address a multitude of matters related to a typical residential real estate sales transaction. These forms change frequently, often annually, reinforceing the need for brokers to ensure that any form they suggest a consumer use is in fact the most current approved form.

Terms and Definitions

Paragraph One of Standard Form 2-T contains numerous subparagraphs defining most, if not all, of the major terms used in the contract. Note that *whenever a **term** appears in the body of the contract and **begins with capital letters** that normally would not be capitalized, it indicates that **the word or phrase is a "defined term"** that usually will be found somewhere in Paragraph 1*. Occasionally, the term may be defined elsewhere in the form.

Names

An essential element in any contract is the proper identification of the parties to the contract, in this instance, the buyers and sellers. Subparagraph (a) identifies the sellers and subparagraph (b) identifies the buyers. All parties should be identified by their current *individual legal names*, including full first and last names and at least the initial of their middle name, as well as any suffix, e.g., Jr, Sr, III, etc. Spouses may be identified as such, although it is not mandatory, i.e., Sally R. Doe and husband, Robert M. Doe. Do *not* identify spouses as Mr. and Mrs. Robert M. Doe because even though married, they remain two separate individuals with separate legal identities. It is important to use the correct legal name of each individual because:

a. Proper identification of all parties is an essential element of any contract. The broker preparing the offer should ascertain the correct legal names of **all** parties and include those names.

b. The closing attorney will need the correct legal names of all parties to prepare the deed and other closing documents. While a party's signature will appear at the bottom of the contract form, it may not be clearly legible.

There is no excuse for a broker preparing an offer to use the term "owner of record" to identify the seller. The owner's name should be easily ascertainable from the listing agent or listing data or from public records. Thus, avoid using the term "owner of record." Entities selling or purchasing property should be identified by the complete *legal* name of the entity and not the trade name, e.g., Built4U, LLC, Smith Brothers, LLP, Sunshine Enterprises, Inc. etc.

Brokers should also exercise caution when a property is being sold to liquidate a decedent's estate. The "owners" of the property are the heirs, not the executor, and the written consent of all of the heirs will be required to have a valid contract, unless all of them have conveyed the authority to sell the property to one individual through a power of attorney or the will grants the executor the authority to sell the property. If any of the heirs are married, their spouses' signatures will be required on the Warranty Deed and the consent of any minor heirs must be conveyed through their guardian.

Undisclosed Buyer-Principal

There are situations where a real estate broker is making an offer for an undisclosed buyer-principal. For example, a buyer agent may have a client (e.g., a corporate client) who does not want to be identified prior to entering into a contract because disclosure of the buyer's identity may result in an increase in the asking price for the property. In these fact situations, it is permissible for the buyer's agent to insert his or her own name as agent for an undisclosed principal in the space for the buyer's name. For example, "John A. Doe, agent for an undisclosed principal."

However, brokers should be cautious about undisclosed buyer-principal fact situations. If a broker signs a sales contract as a buyer agent for an undisclosed buyer-principal, the broker may be vulnerable to a lawsuit and liability for damages in the event the buyer-principal decides not to complete the purchase. A broker should seek legal advice in this situation. A seller's agent, on the other hand, should advise his seller to exercise caution when an offer by an undisclosed buyer-principal is made. Why does the buyer not want its identity revealed? The seller may want to investigate and ascertain whether facts exist that render the property more valuable. *A broker acting as a dual agent for both buyer and seller may not act as the agent for an undisclosed buyer-principal.* This is the case because a dual agent's duties to the seller-principal are the same as those owed to the buyer-principal. Failure to disclose the buyer's identity, information that clearly could impact the seller's decision, would violate agency law.

Property

The real estate broker must include in the offer to purchase and contract a description of the **real property** that is sufficiently definite and certain to identify the property from the written legal description alone. It is first identified in paragraph 1(c) by street address, city, county and zip code and then all available legal descriptions should be completed. The instructions in the "*Guidelines,*" Standard Form 2-G, on this topic are:

> **(c) PROPERTY/LEGAL DESCRIPTION:** Fill in street address of the Property, if there is one (**NOT** the mailing address, which may be different from the street address). In addition to a street address, include a legal description sufficient to identify and distinguish the Property from all other property. Fill in all applicable blanks as completely as possible.
>
> **(1) Plat reference:** If the Property is a lot in a subdivision or a condominium unit, include the lot number or condominium unit number, the block or section number of the subdivision or condominium, the name of subdivision or condominium, and recording reference for the plat as recorded in the Register of Deeds office.
>
> **(2) PIN/PID or other identification number: CAUTION**: Although helpful, reference to a **PIN/PID** alone is generally not an adequate legal description.
>
> **(3) Other description:** A survey attached as an Exhibit or an abbreviated description such as 10+/- acres at the northeasterly quadrant of the intersection of Route 41 and Jackson Boulevard may be helpful. A copy of Seller's deed may be attached as an Exhibit. Do not attempt to complete a metes and bound description as an Exhibit. A North Carolina real estate attorney should be consulted if a metes and bounds description is necessary or if the information available is inadequate to clearly describe the Property.
>
> **(4) Reference to a recorded deed:** If known, insert the book number and page number of Seller's deed as recorded in the office of the Register of Deeds office.

After the property description, the form contains the cautionary note that "Governmental authority over taxes, zoning, school districts, utilities and mail delivery may differ from address shown."

Brokers should remember that a vague or incomplete property description may result in the contract being unenforceable, as in the example below.

> *Example:* Seller entered into a purchase contract with Buyer in which the property was described as: "Located in the City of Raleigh, State of North Carolina, and more particularly described as follows: Street Address: Industrial Boulevard. Legal Description: See Book 340, page 187 for a complete metes and bounds." Actually, Seller owned only a portion of the land described in the plat book referred to in the description. Upon discovering this, Buyer refused to go through with the transaction. The North Carolina Court of Appeals held that Buyer did not have to perform, as the contract was unenforceable because the property description was in a state of absolute uncertainty.[5]

Although not mandatory, *a formal, legal description as required in deeds or mortgages (deeds of trust) is highly desirable and should be included if available.* The legal description need not be a full metes and bounds description. Reference to a recorded plat or map is sufficient where the referenced description is identical to the real property being conveyed.

> *Example:* A parcel is described in a sales contract as "Lot 42, Block 12, Hilly Hole Hollow Subdivision, Book 2744, page 190, Wake County Register of Deeds." This is an adequate legal description.

Reference to the book and page number of the seller's recorded deed to the property or using the parcel identifier number (PIN) is also legally sufficient where the seller is selling all of the property described in that deed. Because tax maps are historically less accurate as a source of property descriptions, *reference to a tax map alone may not provide an accurate legal description.* The listing agent should have obtained an adequate legal description at the time of listing and would be the logical first source to consult for a proper description. If the listing agent does not have the legal description, it can be obtained from the seller's deed to the property, which is a public record.

If for some reason it is not possible for the broker preparing the offer to purchase to obtain the actual legal description of the property (although such reason is hard to fathom), the broker should at least provide as much detail as possible. In this event, it might be advisable to state following the description that the seller will provide the purchaser with a complete legal description within a short, specified time after contract formation. The broker should assure that such description is delivered promptly to the buyer.

Purchase Price

It should be apparent that the offer to purchase and contract must clearly state the amount to be paid for the real property, as it is a material term of the contract. It is also important, however, to state how and when the sale price will be paid by the buyer. The total amount of the purchase price is stated on the first line in Paragraph 1(d), followed by lines on which to detail how much of that purchase price will be paid by each of the following: a due diligence fee, an initial earnest money deposit, an (additional) earnest money deposit, an assumption of seller's existing loan, seller financing, a building deposit (for new construction), and the balance to be paid in cash at Settlement. If the buyer is obtaining third-party financing for a portion of the sale price, this nonetheless is considered to be "cash" to the seller. If no terms are indicated as to method of payment, it will be presumed to be "cash." As for the time of payment, this normally will be "at closing" unless it is specifically stated otherwise.

The subparagraph expressly references the applicable addenda that should be completed and attached to the offer in the event loan assumption, seller financing, or new construction is involved. It also states that in the event the buyer fails to deliver either the due diligence fee or *initial* earnest money deposit by their due dates or if any other checks or funds paid by buyer are dishonored, then seller must first provide buyer with written notice of the default and buyer will then have *one **banking** day* after written notice to deliver good funds to the seller or seller will have the right to unilaterally terminate the contract upon written notice to buyer. "Good funds" may include cash, money orders, bank checks, certified checks or wire transfers.

The "balance due" entered on the last line of Paragraph 1(d) should be the difference between the amount stated on the first line, minus the amounts stated on the lines between the first and last line. Alternatively stated, the numbers entered below the first line of Paragraph 1(d) should *always* equal the amount stated on the first line. The *Guidelines* further caution brokers that if a counteroffer alters any of the numbers in 1(d), then *the parties must initial and should date all altered figures* and again check to confirm that the total of the amounts in the second through last lines equals the amount stated on the first line.

Earnest Money Deposit

Earnest money *is an amount of money deposited by the buyer with the broker or other escrow agent to evidence the buyer's good faith.* While earnest money is **not** essential to a valid offer and a valid enforceable contract may be formed without any earnest money being paid, sellers' agents generally should seek to obtain earnest money for their principal's benefit when negotiating the sale of property. A substantial, rather than token, amount of money usually is sought for several reasons. For one thing, if the prospective purchaser really is serious in making an offer for the seller's property, the purchaser should be willing to make a substantial payment toward the property's eventual purchase as the earnest money deposit will be credited towards the purchase price at closing. The depositing of earnest money not only is an indication of the prospective purchaser's worthiness and sincerity of purpose, but it also may serve as an indicator of the purchaser's ability to raise the cash or otherwise obtain the monies that will be needed to consummate the transaction.

Another very practical reason for requiring the prospective purchaser to make a substantial earnest money deposit is to have it available should the purchaser later default and either refuse or be unable to complete the transaction. This is particularly true under the terms of the Standard Form 2-T contract form, in that, as will be discussed shortly, the seller's sole remedy in the event of the buyer's default is the retention of any due diligence fee and earnest money deposits paid. A substantial, rather than nominal, earnest money deposit may also discourage the purchaser from backing out of the agreement after the expiration of the due diligence period. If the purchaser does later renege or default, the earnest money will be available to compensate the seller, and possibly the agent, for their losses due to the buyer's default.

Standard Form 2-T Paragraph 1(e) provides that the term "Earnest Money Deposit" includes any amounts listed in Paragraph 1(d) under either initial or additional deposits. Note that in the fourth line of Paragraph 1(d) "(additional)" is in parentheses to provide some flexibility. The intent is to address both the situation where there is an initial earnest money deposit *and* a subsequent deposit, as well as the situation where no earnest money is paid initially, but a later deposit is expected. Thus, the later deposit actually is the only earnest money deposit received, but it is not paid at the time of contract formation. The initial earnest money deposit still may be paid in cash, by personal check, official bank check, wire transfer or electronic transfer and is tendered either 1) with the offer or 2) paid within five days of the Effective Date. The current standard form not only continues the "time is of the essence" requirement as to payment of any additional earnest money deposit, it also specifies acceptable *modes of payment*, namely "... by cash, official bank check, wire transfer, or electronic transfer"

Do not be confused about the interplay between the contract language allowing the earnest money deposit to be paid within five days of the Effective Date and a broker's general obligation under Rule 58A.0116(b) to deposit trust monies into a trust/escrow account within three banking days of receipt. There really is no conflict, as a broker cannot deposit funds that have not been received. Note too that Rule A.0116(a) allows (but does not require) a broker to hold and safeguard an earnest money deposit paid by check or other negotiable instrument *without depositing it into an escrow account **pending contract formation***. Once the seller and buyer are actually under contract, the three banking day clock starts to tick if the check is in the possession of a broker/escrow agent. If Paragraph 1(d) states that the initial earnest money is being tendered "with this offer," *then the check or payment to the escrow agent should accompany the offer.* If the escrow agent is the listing company, then its three-banking-day clock would begin to tick upon contract formation as it already has the check in its possession.

If the buyer does not wish to give the earnest money deposit to the escrow agent until after a contract has been formed, then 1(d) should indicate that the earnest money deposit will be delivered within five days of the Effective Date. In this case, the buyer may not even write the earnest money check payable to the named escrow agent until two days after the Effective Date (contract formation) and give it to his/her buyer agent on Day 3 who in turn delivers it to the escrow agent on Day 4. If the escrow agent is a broker, then the clock begins to tick from the receipt of the check on Day 4 and the broker would have three *banking days* from that date to deposit the earnest money check into its trust account. Understand as well that *the three banking day rule only applies to escrow agents who are brokers.*

Disposition of Earnest Money Deposit

Paragraph 1(e) continues prior practice to the extent that *all earnest monies are to be held by the named escrow agent and credited to buyer at closing against the purchase price **unless** the contract is otherwise terminated.* Additionally, as will be discussed when reviewing Standard Form 2-T Paragraph 4, "Buyer's Due Diligence Process," if the buyer timely exercises the right to terminate the contract prior to the expiration of the due diligence period, then all earnest money deposits are refunded to the buyer. If the offer is not accepted or some condition of the resulting contract is not satisfied, then the earnest money deposit is to be *refunded* to the buyer. Buyers and their agents must understand that the current standard form contains considerably fewer *conditions* than earlier versions did and several conditions, such as the financing appraisal, and flood hazard conditions, have been eliminated and are replaced by and subsumed within the buyer's due diligence period.

If the **seller** *breaches* the contract, then all earnest money deposits are to be refunded to the buyer upon buyer's request, but "... shall not affect any other remedies available to Buyer for such breach." Pursuant to Paragraph 8(l) of the contract, if buyer elects to terminate the contract due to seller's breach (rather than sue for specific performance), buyer is also entitled to a refund of any due diligence fee paid, as well as reimbursement from the seller of the buyer's reasonable costs expended during the due diligence period and may pursue any other remedies s/he may have against the seller.

If the transaction closes, then the earnest money deposit is credited to the buyer against the purchase price. If the buyer does not elect to terminate the contract prior to the expiration of the due diligence period, but then later is unable or unwilling to consummate the transaction, then the buyer will be in breach of the contract. If the **buyer** *breaches* the contract, then *the **earnest money deposit** is to be "... paid to Seller ... as **liquidated damages and as Seller's sole and exclusive remedy for such breach** ..." except for seller's right to retain any due diligence fee and to seek compensation for any actual damage to the property caused by buyer or his/her agents.* Legally, "liquidated damages" means an amount of money the parties agree at the outset will adequately compensate a non-breaching party if the other party fails to perform his/her obligations under the contract. The non-breaching party receives the stipulated amount in settlement of any and all claims arising out of the transaction.

Understand that if the seller cannot or will not convey marketable and insurable title or fails to fulfill other material obligations imposed upon them, then the buyer may sue the seller, if necessary, for his actual out-of-pocket expenses for surveys or appraisals or home or pest inspections or other fees incurred in preparing to purchase the property or may sue the seller for specific performance of the contract, if appropriate. ***However, the seller may not sue the buyer for specific performance or other damages if the buyer breaches.*** This is unequivocally stated in the concluding sentences of Paragraph 1(e), namely:

> It is acknowledged by the parties that payment of the Earnest Money Deposit to Seller in the event of a breach of this Contract by Buyer is compensatory and not punitive, such amount being a reasonable estimation of the actual loss that Seller would incur as a result of such breach. The payment of the Earnest Money Deposit to Seller shall not constitute a penalty or forfeiture but actual compensation for Seller's anticipated loss, both parties acknowledging the difficulty determining Seller's actual damages for such breach.

Why this apparent disparity? The reasons are at least twofold.

1) Buyers typically must expend funds for inspections, fees, loan applications, appraisals, etc., in anticipation of purchasing the property and should be entitled to recover sums expended in good faith to move forward with the transaction, whereas sellers are not as likely to incur such preliminary expenses. In most cases, a seller's damages are non-existent or inconsequential. Even if a seller makes repairs requested by a buyer who then fails to purchase, the seller still has the benefit of the improvements to the property s/he still owns.

2) Courts *rarely* grant sellers specific performance against buyers, but are more likely to grant buyers specific performance against sellers. Why? In part, because the buyer has lost something unique (the property) that may not be readily replaceable, but the seller has simply lost money. Moreover, to prevail in an action for specific performance the plaintiff must show that the defendant has the *present ability to do (perform) that which s/he agreed to do in the contract.* When attempting to compel a buyer to perform, there are too many variables that influence a buyer's ability that may not be within the buyer's control, e.g., ability to obtain a loan on the terms represented, or inability to qualify because the property is in a flood zone, or the appraisal comes back too low, etc.. As to the sellers' performance however, typically all that is required is the owners' signature(s) on the General Warranty Deed, which normally is within their ability and relatively easy.

Thus, because sellers typically 1) have limited prospects for sustaining damages during the pendency of a contract if the buyer breaches and 2) are unlikely to prevail in a specific performance action, the current standard contract attempts to give sellers a more realistic understanding of the consequences of a breach by the buyer. Brokers representing sellers should be mindful that if the transaction fails to close after the expiration of the due diligence period because the buyer fails to perform, the ***only monies the seller will receive are any sums paid as the due diligence fee and as earnest money deposits.*** Not only should *seller agents* be aware of this fact, but they *should attempt to ensure that the* *seller fully understands that whatever the seller agrees to accept as the due diligence fee and earnest money deposit will be the only compensation the seller receives if the buyer fails to consummate the transaction **after** the due diligence period has expired.* Thus, brokers should encourage their seller clients to carefully consider the amount of the due diligence fee and earnest money deposit(s) before accepting an offer and evaluate whether it will be enough to adequately compensate the seller in the event the buyer breaches the contract. Sellers should also keep in mind that if the buyer timely exercises his/her right to terminate the contract, the only compensation the seller will retain is the due diligence fee.

Attorney Fees

Lastly, a sentence in the earnest money deposit section of the standard form expressly recognizes that if either party is compelled to sue the other for a determination of who is entitled to the earnest money deposit under the contract, then the prevailing party (i.e., the one who wins the lawsuit) "... ***shall*** *be entitled to recover from the non-prevailing party reasonable attorney fees and court costs incurred in connection with the proceeding.*" In most civil actions, each side must pay their own attorney fees absent special circumstances or statutory allowance and breach of contract typically is not one of those circumstances. In this instance, however, the right to recover attorney fees and costs is now expressly conferred by the parties' contract. The threat of additional costs may help dissuade persons who are not entitled to the earnest money deposit from refusing to consent to its release to the other party. Whether this provision will be held to be enforceable by North Carolina courts remains to be seen.

Escrow Agent

Earnest money is held "in trust" by an escrow agent while the transaction is pending. The "escrow agent" acts for both the seller and buyer and has fiduciary obligations to both parties with regard to the earnest money, which is considered to be "trust monies," particularly when held by a real estate broker. The escrow agent is to be identified by name in Paragraph 1(f). Typically this will be the name of a real estate company or a title company or an attorney.

If the earnest money is paid by check, the check should be made payable to the person or entity acting as escrow agent, using language such as "ABC Realty, escrow agent." It should also be noted on the check's memo line that it is earnest money for a particular transaction, such as "earnest money for 333 Elm Street" or "EMD - 333 Elm St." Persons or entities serving as *escrow agents should not sign acknowledging receipt of the earnest money deposit if in fact they have not yet received it!* While this may seem obvious, it occasionally happens. When asked to produce the earnest money deposit, the agent cannot and claims it was never received, yet has signed a document stating it *was* received.

Prudent real estate brokers will attempt to ensure that both the seller and buyer thoroughly understand the purpose of the earnest money deposit, how it will be handled while the transaction is pending, and who will be entitled to receive it under the various situations that may arise. It is important that the parties understand these procedures up front in order to avoid possible problems later. *The handling of earnest money, as well as other trust funds, by a real estate broker is strictly regulated by the North Carolina Real Estate License Law and Real Estate Commission Rules 58A.0116 and 58A.0117.* For a detailed discussion of the requirements and procedures associated with handling and accounting for trust funds (including earnest money), see the Real Estate Commission's *Trust Account Guidelines*.

Depositing Earnest Money into Trust Account

Whenever a real estate broker is acting as the escrow agent, the broker must deposit the buyer's earnest money (as well as all funds belonging to others) into a properly identified trust or escrow account. As of January 2012, General Statute 93A-6(g) was added and requires the escrow account to be a demand deposit account, but allows it to be opened in any federally insured depository institution lawfully doing business in North Carolina that agrees to make the broker's account records available for inspection to the Commission's representatives. Earnest money received by a provisional broker from a prospective buyer must be delivered immediately to the provisional broker's broker-in-charge. If a broker associated with a real estate company receives earnest money, he or she also should immediately deliver such funds to the broker-in-charge. The broker (or firm) named as escrow agent in the offer to purchase may hold an earnest money deposit *other than cash*, i.e., paid by check or other negotiable instrument, until a contract actually is formed, that is, until the seller accepts an offer or the buyer accepts a counteroffer. *Once a contract is formed, the broker or firm named as escrow agent must deposit the earnest money check or instrument into a trust or escrow account within three banking days of contract formation, if the deposit already is in the broker's possession, or within three banking days from receipt, if the earnest money is to be paid within five days of the Effective Date.*

If a broker receives an earnest money deposit in *cash*, then the *standard three banking days from* **receipt** *rule applies* and the broker must deposit those funds into a trust account within three banking days of receipt, regardless of contract formation. Note also that while the rule *permits* a broker to wait until contract formation to deposit non-cash earnest money deposits tendered, it does not *require* a broker to wait until contract formation to deposit non-cash earnest money deposits. Thus, a broker who receives a check for an earnest money deposit may immediately deposit that check into his/her trust account while the parties negotiate an agreement. However, if the parties never reach an agreement or the buyer withdraws the offer prior to seller's acceptance, the broker may not be able to immediately refund the buyer's deposit if the buyer's check has not yet cleared the trust account. It is for this reason that the Rule permits brokers to hold and safeguard an earnest money deposit check until a contract is formed before they are required to deposit it into their trust account. Such delay is unnecessary with deposits of cash, as cash is immediately refundable.

Interest-Bearing Trust Accounts

The general rule is that a *broker's* **trust account** *must be a separate, custodial demand deposit account that contains only monies belonging to others received by the broker when acting as an agent in a transaction.* The account must not contain the broker's business or personal funds. *The mixing of monies belonging to others (i.e., trust funds) with a broker's personal or business funds in the same account constitutes unlawful* **commingling** *of funds.* However, brokers may have interest-bearing trust accounts where the interest belongs to the broker, so long as they comply with the conditions set forth in Commission Rule 21 NCAC 58A.0116(c). Brokers who are entitled to receive interest on interest-bearing trust accounts must transfer the accumulated interest from their trust account to their operating account each month upon receipt of the bank statement indicating the amount of interest credited to avoid commingling monies that belong to them with monies belonging to others. Standard Form 2-T contains language expressly authorizing the escrow agent to place any earnest monies received into an interest-bearing trust account which interest will belong to the escrow agent and disbursed monthly.

Disputed Earnest Money Deposits

Standard Form 2-T unambiguously states who is entitled to receive any earnest money deposits under various situations. To summarize the previous discussion, if no contract is achieved, any earnest money deposit tendered by the buyer is returned to the buyer. If the parties reach an agreement and enter into a written contract, but the buyer timely exercises his right to terminate the contract prior to the expiration of the due diligence period (which will be discussed shortly) *or* if the transaction fails to close because the *seller* ultimately cannot or will not convey the property to the buyer, then the buyer is entitled to a refund of all earnest money deposits paid. If, however, after the expiration of the due diligence period, the transaction fails to close because the *buyer* cannot or will not perform, then the seller is entitled to receive all earnest monies deposited. Lastly, if a contract is formed and the transaction is successfully consummated, then any earnest money deposits are paid to the seller and credited to the buyer against the purchase price.

In theory then, there should *rarely* be a dispute over which party is entitled to receive the earnest money. The contract unambiguously expresses the general proposition that *the Buyer receives a refund of the earnest money deposit if Buyer timely delivers written notice of termination to the Seller/listing agent prior to the expiration of the due diligence period; otherwise, the Seller is entitled to the earnest money deposit in all other cases* **unless** *the seller breaches or fails to materially perform.* Thus, the primary question will be: *did the buyer* **timely deliver written notice** *of termination to the seller/listing company?* If yes, then the buyer receives the earnest money deposit; if no, then the seller receives the earnest money deposit, *unless* the transaction fails to close due to the seller's material breach. A party who stubbornly refuses to consent to the release of the earnest money deposit without any legitimate foundation should be reminded that s/he may be liable for a portion of the other party's attorney fees if the party entitled to the earnest money deposit must sue to recover it. Gone, however, are the squabbles over whether requested repairs were "legitimate" or whether the buyer's estimated cost of repairs was reasonable, which frequently arose under previous versions of the standard contract form.

Nonetheless, while brokers should use their best efforts to assure that the contract's provisions regarding the disposition of earnest money are followed, they also are obligated to abide by Real Estate License Law and Real Estate Commission Rules governing trust funds. One such rule concerning *disputed trust funds* bears special mention here. Commission Rule 21 NCAC **58A.0116(d)** states in part:

> *In the event of a dispute* between buyer and seller or landlord and tenant over the return or forfeiture of any deposit *other than a residential tenant security deposit* held by the broker, the broker shall retain the deposit in a trust or escrow account until the broker has obtained a written release from the parties consenting to its disposition or until disbursement is ordered by a court of competent jurisdiction. Alternatively, the broker may deposit the disputed monies with the appropriate Clerk of Superior Court in accordance with the provision of G.S. 93A-12 .... [Italics added.]

To determine whether a dispute exists, the broker holding the earnest money deposit should first notify the party of the broker's intent to release the money to the buyer or seller, as applicable, and gain the other party's oral or written assent prior to disbursing the earnest money deposit to the party entitled to it under the contract. *Where the seller and buyer disagree as to who should receive the earnest money, the broker is prohibited from making an independent decision in the matter,* even if it is apparent to the broker who should receive the earnest money under the clear and unambiguous language of the contract. Instead, the broker must hold the earnest money deposit in his or her trust account until the parties either reach a written agreement concerning disbursement or someone obtains a court order stating who is to receive the earnest money deposit. Usually these situations can be avoided by fully explaining to both parties at the outset of the transaction the procedures for handling and disbursing earnest money and by properly conducting the transaction as a whole.

The requirement quoted above concerning disputed funds is imposed by Commission rule; however, *Commission rules, like License Law, only apply to and govern the conduct of real estate brokers.* Non-broker escrow agents, such as attorneys or title insurance companies, are not necessarily bound by this requirement. However, Standard Form 2-T attempts to obtain the same result for disputed funds from non-broker escrow agents by stating in Paragraph 1(f) that any "(... Escrow Agent, if not a Broker, hereby agrees) to retain the Earnest Money Deposit in the Escrow Agent's trust or escrow account ..." pending written agreement of the parties or issuance of a court order.

Alternate Procedures for Broker and Attorney Escrow Agents Only

Commission Rule A.0116(d) quoted above also refers to G. S. §93A-12, a License Law statute enacted effective October 1, 2005 to provide an alternate procedure for brokers when the parties fail to reach an agreement or sue the other regarding disputed funds. Briefly, the law requires that, prior to depositing any disputed monies with the Clerk of Court, the broker must first notify all parties claiming ownership of or entitlement to the monies *in writing* that the broker intends to pay the monies to the Clerk of Court of the county in which the property is located ninety days following the notice and that the parties may initiate a special proceeding with the Clerk to recover the disputed funds within one year following the deposit. The statute requires that the notice either be delivered to the person or sent "... by first class mail, postpaid, properly addressed to the person at the person's last known address." If there still is no resolution after the ninety day period, the broker may then write a check from his or her trust account to the Clerk of Superior Court of the county where the property is situated and submit it with the appropriate form (AOC-SP-260) that may be obtained from the Clerk, thereby removing the funds from the broker's trust account which allows the broker's three year record retention period to begin.

If any party files a special proceeding with the Clerk within one year of the funds being deposited, then the Clerk will proceed to hear the case, determine "rightful ownership" and disburse the funds. If no party initiates a special proceeding with the Clerk within one year of the monies being deposited, then the Clerk is to escheat the funds to the State Treasurer.

While this procedure originally was only available to real estate brokers, General Statute 93A-12 was revised by the General Assembly in 2011 to include attorneys serving as escrow agents who, as of January 1, 2012, may use the same process as broker escrow agents to pay disputed funds to the Clerk of Court.

One other alternative allowed by Commission **Rule 58A.0116(d)** recognizes that with the passage of time, a party may abandon any claim to the disputed funds, in which event the broker "... may disburse the money to the other claim and according to the written agreement..." [i.e., the contract] aftern the broker first makes ("...a reasonable effort to notify the absent party and provide that party with an opportunity to renew his or her claim to the funds." Prudent brokers should be able to document how they provided the required notice to the party of the broker's intent to disburse the monies to the other party and that the abandoning party failed to renew his/her objection within the time provided in the broker's notice.

Effective Date

Standard Form 2-T defines "Effective Date" in Paragraph 1(g); the definition itself remains unchanged and is consistent with basic contract law concepts in North Carolina. The "Effective Date" is the date the contract comes into being and is defined as: "The date that: (1) the last one of Buyer and Seller has signed or initialed this offer or the final counteroffer, if any, and (2) such signing or initialing is communicated to the party making the offer or counteroffer, as the case may be." This concept will be more fully explained later in this chapter, but brokers must understand that *until the last offeree's signing or initialing of any changes has been* **communicated** *to the last offeror, there still is no contract.* To form a binding contract, not only must all parties' signatures appear on the document, as well as their initials and preferably dates as to any changes, but *the assent of the party to whom the last offer/counteroffer was made, whether the seller or the buyer, must be communicated to the party who made the last offer/counteroffer before the offer becomes a contract.*

Oral assurances that everyone is in agreement are meaningless when it comes to the conveyance of real property because the Statute of Frauds requires contracts to convey real property to be *in writing* to be enforceable. *Any notions that oral negotiations of real estate sales contracts are binding or that a seller must complete negotiations with a buyer who has made a written offer before entertaining another offer are simply wrong.*

Due Diligence, Due Diligence Fee and Due Diligence Period

The "**Due Diligence Period**" is defined in Paragraph 1(j) as a period of time commencing on the Effective Date of the contract and ending at 5:00pm on whatever date is inserted in the blank in that subparagraph. The definition expressly states "... **TIME BEING OF THE ESSENCE** with regard to said date" namely, the termination date (emphasis in the original). During the due diligence period, the buyer has the unbridled right to engage in any investigations, inspections or inquiries concerning the property itself or limitations on its permissible uses imposed by zoning requirements, restrictive covenants, or owners' association bylaws, rules, or regulations. "**Due diligence fee**" is defined in Paragraph 1(i) as:

> A negotiated amount, if any, paid by Buyer to Seller with this Contract for Buyer's right to terminat the contract for any reason or no reason during the Due Diligence Period. It shall be the property of Seller upon the Effective Date and shall be a credit to Buyer at Closing. The Due Diligence Fee shall be non-refundable except in the event of a material breach of this Contract by Seller, or if this Contract is terminated under Paragraph 8(n) or Paragraph 12, or as otherwise provided in any addendum hereto. Buyer and Seller each expressly waive any right that they may have to deny the right to conduct Due Diligence or to assert any defense as to the enforceability of this Contract based on the absence or alleged insufficiency of any Due Diligence Fee, it being the intent of the parties to create a legally binding contract for the purchase and sale of the Property without regard to the existence or amount of any Due Diligence Fee.

The due diligence fee is paid directly to the seller upon contract formation and generally is retained by the seller regardless of whether the transaction closes. If the transaction does close, then the amount of the due diligence fee is applied against the purchase price. The only two exceptions under current Standard Form 2-T to the seller's right to retain the due diligence fee regardless of the outcome of the transaction are: 1) if the seller either is unable or refuses to convey the property [Paragraph 8(n)] or 2) if the improvements on the property are materially damaged or destroyed prior to closing due to fire or other casualty [Paragraph 12]. In these situations, the buyer is entitled to a refund of the due diligence fee, if the buyer elects to terminate the contract.

The amount of the due diligence fee and the length of the due diligence period are subject to negotiation by the parties prior to contract formation. How much time or money is adequate is up to the parties to decide, who obviously may have different perspectives. Presumably a buyer will want to pay as little as possible for as long a period as possible, whereas a seller would prefer a larger fee for a shorter period. As indicated, it is up to the parties to negotiate.

Must a due diligence fee be paid? The express language in the first sentence of 1(i) defines a **due diligence fee** as "[a] negotiated amount, *if any...*" and the last sentence states that it is "... the intent of the parties to create *a legally binding contract* for the purchase and sale of the Property *without regard to the existence or amount of any Due Diligence Fee.*" [Italics added.] Thus, the contract form acknowledges the possibility that no fee will be paid. The latter provision was added to combat the concern of some legal minds that the contract might be held by a court to be illusory where the buyer has the unilateral ability to terminate and walk away for any or no reason ("in the *buyer's sole discretion*"), yet has not given the seller any consideration for that right. Since there is a split in jurisdictions on this issue, the safest course, and that which is recommended in order to protect against an illusory contract argument, is to include a reasonable due diligence fee until such time as the issue is decided by a North Carolina appellate court.

The consequences of a buyer's failure to timely deliver written notice to the seller by 5:00 p.m. on the date stated in 1(j) that s/he is electing to terminate the contract is addressed in the discussion of Paragraph 4 herein.

Settlement, Settlement Date and Closing

Paragraphs 1(k), (l), and (m) define more precisely the distinction between "settlement," "settlement date," and "closing." "**Settlement**" is defined as:

> (k) The proper *execution and delivery to the settlement agent of all documents* necessary to complete the transaction contemplated by this Contract, including the deed, settlement statement, deed of trust and other loan or conveyance documents, *and* the closing attorney's *receipt of all funds* necessary to complete such transaction.

[Emphasis added.]

Under this standard, the parties may not physically come together for a settlement meeting as long as each has provided the settlement agent with everything s/he needs to consummate the transaction. The "**settlement date**" is the date stated in Paragraph 1(l) on which settlement, as defined above, shall occur, unless otherwise agreed in writing. Closing is now defined in Paragraph 1(m) as "The completion of the legal process which results in the transfer of title to the Property from Seller to Buyer...." While it enumerates various steps that may precede the actual transfer of title, the transfer of title, i.e., the recording of the deed, remains the linchpin and it is only *after the recording of the deed and deed of trust* that the settlement agent is authorized to disburse the funds s/he is holding.

Special Assessments

Paragraph 1(n) defines a special assessment as a charge against the property by a governmental authority other than for taxes or by an owners' association other than for dues that may become a lien upon the property. A *"proposed"* special assessment is one that is under formal consideration but has not been approved prior to Settlement, whereas a *"confirmed"* special assessment is one that *has been approved* prior to Settlement, even if payable in installments that extend beyond the settlement date. Who pays what is addressed in later paragraphs that basically provide that the buyer takes the property subject to all disclosed proposed assessments [Paragraph 6(a)] and the seller pays all confirmed assessments, as long as the amount can be reasonably determined or estimated [Paragraph 8(k)].

Fixtures

Paragraph 2 of Standard Form 2-T sets forth numerous items that, if present on the property and owned by seller, will automatically convey as fixtures unless excepted. The current form expressly holds that the enumerated items "including all related equipment and remote contgrol devices, if any, are deemed fixtures and shall conveny included in the Purchase Price free of liens." See the lengthy bulleted list on page 3 of Figure 11-1 of the items that will convey as a fixture under the current standard form.

The parties may identify which items 1) are leased or not owned by seller or 2) that seller does not intend to convey or 3) may be considered fixtures, but are not expressly mentioned in the list of enumerated items. The *Guidelines* (Standard Form 2-G) state that while it is not necessary to cross out items that are listed in the fixtures clause but are not on the property, if in doubt as to whether an item that Seller wishes to exclude from any sale is a fixture, the more prudent course is to list it as an exception to eliminate any doubt and thereby avoid a later dispute. Lastly, language specifically requires the seller to repair any damage caused by the removal of any excepted items.

Personal Property

Any personal property, other than fixtures as defined in Paragraph 2, that is to convey with the real property should be identified in Paragraph 3 of Standard Form 2-T. There is no presumption that any personal property will convey with the real property, even if the advertisement for the real property stated that certain personal property would convey. The advertisement is not part of the parties' contract. The *Guidelines* offer the following advice:

> **3. PERSONAL PROPERTY:** List all items of personal property that are to be included in the sale. (EXAMPLES: Curtains, draperies, etc.; free standing appliances such as a refrigerator or a microwave oven; fireplace tools; window air conditioner; etc.) It is advisable to list any item included in the sale about which some dispute may arise. **NOTE: Care should be taken to ascertain that any personal property included in the sale is owned by Seller and is not merely rented or leased.**

Mistakes are commonly made in this section where the broker should describe any personal property that is to convey with the property. Although the omission of items of personal property to be included in the sale will not affect the validity of the real estate sales contract as between seller and buyer, it can result in unnecessary misunderstanding and dissatisfaction on the part of both parties. As mentioned in the quoted instructions, refrigerators still are not fixtures, since most are not built-in, so if the buyer wants the refrigerator, it needs to be specified in Paragraph 3. What about microwave ovens? If it is a "built-in appliance" then it would convey under Paragraph 2; if it sits on top of the counter, then it would not convey unless it was stated in Paragraph 3. Good business practices dictate that the description of personal property in sales contracts should be as clear and accurate as possible to avoid controversy, bad public relations, and litigation. For example, writing in a refrigerator description such as "18 cubic foot deluxe Amana refrigerator/freezer" may prevent an unscrupulous seller from leaving a 6 cubic foot "student" model in its place.

Value of Personal Property

The language in Paragraph 3 specifically states that any personal property identified shall transfer to the buyer at Closing "*at no value*." However, inclusion of personal property that is not usually conveyed with a house in a sales contract, even if stated to be at "no value," may create significant issues for mortgage lenders and should be avoided unless approved by the lender. Small items may not pose any problem for lenders, but larger items that do not typically convey with houses can be very problematic. The language in the contract expressly cautions the buyer to consult with his/her lender to assure that the enumerated personal property can be included in the contract. Some lenders may be inclined to reduce the purchase price stated in the contract by the value the lender ascribes to the personal property being transferred and to then calculate the amount of the loan for which the borrower is eligible based on the reduced purchase price.

As long as the contract specifies the personal property to be conveyed with the real property, whether itemized in the body of the contract or in an addendum expressly referenced in and attached to the contract, there would not appear to be any loan fraud, as the contract discloses the personal property items and the lender is free to alter the loan terms based on its assessment of the personal property being conveyed. However, a more difficult situation is presented if the lender requires that the personal property be removed from the real property sales contract and the parties then attempt to enter into a separate bill of sale transferring those items to buyer "at no value," which separate bill of sale is not mentioned in the real property contract. If the seller is willing to and does transfer the personal property to the buyer for no value even if the buyer fails to close on the real property, then there may not be any loan fraud involved. However, if the transfer of the personal property to the buyer is contingent upon the buyer purchasing the real property, then it would appear that the separate undisclosed bill of sale is ancillary to the real property sales contract and failure to openly disclose it in the real estate sales contract could result in charges of loan fraud.

Because it is common practice for owners to sell ocean, lake or mountain vacation homes fully furnished, an adequate description of the personal property included in the sale of the real property can avoid misunderstandings and possible litigation after the sale. The North Carolina Court of Appeals in a 2007 case held that the buyer can obtain specific performance of a contract to convey both real and personal property where the seller refuses to transfer some of the personal property after the closing. In that case, the Court held that the plain language of the contract, as well as other competent evidence in the record, proved that the owner of a lake house intended and contracted to convey personal property and watercraft identified in an addendum referenced in and appended to the contract that identified the personal property to be conveyed.[6]

Buyer's Due Diligence Process

Paragraph 4 of Standard Form 2-T outlines many *activities a buyer should perform prior to the expiration of the due diligence period,* as once that period expires, the buyer loses the right to terminate for any or no reason and is bound by the contract terms. The list does not purport to be exhaustive, as a buyer is free to engage in any inquiries or investigations s/he wishes during the due diligence period. Buyers and their agents must also understand, however, that buyer's opportunity to conduct any inspections, investigations, inquiries or examinations during the due diligence period and to terminate the contract if not satisfied with any of the results of buyer's due diligence is in lieu of and has replaced a number of specific conditions or contingencies previously found in predecessor forms that could excuse buyer's performance virtually up until the closing. ***There no longer are any loan conditions, appraisal conditions, or flood hazard conditions in Standard Form 2-T that will excuse the buyer's performance after the expiration of the due diligence period***. If the buyer has any reservations about the property or his or her ability to perform his or her obligations under the contract, then buyer must exercise the right to terminate the contract prior to the expiration of the due diligence period or risk forfeiting any earnest monies paid if buyer later fails to close.

Standard Form 2-T clearly states in Paragraph 4 that the buyer may terminate the contract for "any reason or no reason" simply by delivering written notice of termination to the seller during the due diligence period or any extension thereof. The contract specifies, however, that "time is of the essence" regarding the delivery of this written notice. If the buyer successfully delivers the termination notice to the seller or the seller's listing agent prior to 5pm on the date the due diligence period expires, then buyer is entitled to receive the earnest money deposit. The standard form attempts to emphasize how important the timeliness feature is through a "**WARNING**" further advising the buyer that the seller is not obligated to grant any extension of the due diligence period and failure to terminate prior to its expiration constitutes a "waiver" by the buyer to terminate for any matter related to the buyer's due diligence.

Scope of Due Diligence

Paragraph 4 recommends that, prior to the expiration of the due diligence period, the buyer "... conduct all desired tests, surveys, appraisals, investigations, examinations and inspections of the Property as Buyer deems appropriate ..." and further advises the buyer "... to consult with Buyer's lender *prior to signing this offer* to assure that the Due Diligence Period allows sufficient time for the appraisal to be completed and for Buyer's lender to provide Buyer sufficient information to decide whether to proceed with or terminate the transaction," i.e., whether Buyer will qualify for any needed financing on terms acceptable to the buyer. It is suggested that buyer review any zoning regulations, restrictive covenants, owners' association bylaws, rules and regulations, availability and cost of insurance, potential flood hazards and whether flood insurance may be required by buyer's lender. Buyer has virtually an unqualified right to explore any issue or matter that interests him during the due diligence period. The breadth and scope of buyer's due diligence is explored in detail in Chapter 14, since most of these activities occur post-contract formation, but prior to closing. Thus the reader is referred to the discussion in Chapter 14, "Buyer's Due Diligence Process," which will not be repeated here.

Repair Negotiations and Buyer's Liability for Damages

During the due diligence period, the parties may, but are not compelled to, negotiate any repair or remediation issues they wish. The buyer is free to request without limitation any repairs or remediation desired and the seller may agree or decline. If the parties agree on certain repairs to be performed by the seller, such agreement should be reduced to writing, signed by both parties and dated, and will be considered an addition to the contract. Negotiated repairs are to be performed in a good and workmanlike manner and buyer has the right to verify the adequacy of the repairs or remediation prior to settlement, as well as to conduct a walk-through inspection prior to closing.

Pursuant to Paragraph 4(d), the buyer is obligated to "promptly" repair any damage caused to the property by buyer's agents and inspectors or contractors, other than damage resulting from accepted practices approved by the Home Inspector Board or other licensed professionals. The buyer shall indemnify, defend and hold the seller harmless from any claims, suits, loss, damage, or injury to person or property resulting from the activities of buyer or his agents or contractors *except* for any loss, damage, claim or suit arising from pre-existing property conditions or from the seller's negligence or willful acts or omissions. The buyer's duty both to repair and to indemnify the seller expressly survive the termination of the contract.

Delivery of Termination Notice

Paragraph 4(f) gives Buyer right to unilaterally terminate the contract by ***timely* delivering** *written notice of termination to the seller prior to the expiration of the due diligence period.* Brokers must understand that, absent an agreed extension, buyer must **deliver** *written notice* to the seller of his election to terminate the contract no later than 5:00pm on the date stated in Paragraph 1(j). Otherwise, the buyer will have lost the ability to unilaterally terminate the contract. If the buyer subsequently is unable or unwilling to consummate the transaction for whatever reasons, then the buyer generally will forfeit to the seller any earnest monies paid. Buyer's performance usually will only be excused thereafter if the seller materially breaches the contract or if the property is destroyed or materially damaged prior to closing, or if there is some factor that might render the contract voidable under general North Carolina contract law principles discussed in Chapter 10 herein.

Pursuant to Paragraph 21 of Standard Form 2-T, any notice or communication required to be given to either party in connection with the contract may be given to the party or the party's agent by sending or transmitting it to a mailing or email address or fax number provided in the "Notice Information" section on page 12 of the contract. If no contact information is provided for a party, then it would appear that all notices must be given through the party's agent. If the agent provides his or her telephone number and office address, but no fax number or email address is stated, then based on the language of the contract, it would appear that the only authorized methods of delivering notice or communications would be to either personally deliver written notice to the office or mail the notice several days prior to the expiration of the due diligence period so it is timely received, even if the brokers have exchanged emails or faxes during the pendency of the transaction. Note that the *mailbox rule does **not** apply to delivery of the termination notice*; thus, depositing the notice into the United States Mail at 4:00pm on the final date is insufficient; the buyer would remain bound under the contract as the written notice must be **delivered** prior to the expiration of the due diligence period. (Recall that the *"mailbox rule" generally applies **only** to contract acceptance*.)

More likely, brokers will provide not only a physical address and telephone number, but also a fax number or email address or both in the Notice Information section, thereby authorizing communication by any of those means. Thus, faxing a notice of termination at 2:00pm on the last day of the due diligence period to the listing agent would constitute timely delivery as long as the sender retains a transmission report to show that the fax was successfully transmitted. If an email address is provided, then sending the termination notice via email prior to 5:00pm on the final day should constitute delivery, as long as the sender can show that the email was received by the recipient's server. Typically, *email notices are deemed "delivered" upon receipt by the addressee's server*, regardless of when read by the recipient. Prudent brokers not only will *retain some proof of delivery* in their transaction file, regardless of the method used, but also will not wait until the last minute to deliver the termination notice.

As with prior standard forms, ***closing constitutes acceptance of the property in its then existing condition, absent other written agreement***.

Buyer Representations

Paragraph 5 contains various disclosures or representations the buyer makes to the seller that may influence the seller's decision and upon which the seller is entitled to rely. In Paragraph 5(a) the buyer discloses whether finaning must be obtained financing to purchase the property and, if so, the type and terms of that loan, e.g., fixed or adjustable rate, conventional or FHA/VA, interest rate, duration, etc. However, ***this is not a loan*** condition as in earlier standard forms and does not excuse buyer's performance if buyer is unable to obtain a loan on the stated terms. It is primarily for informational purposes as it bears directly on buyer's ability to perform his/her obligations under the proposed contract and thus is a material fact that seller is entitled to know. If it appears that buyer may not be able to obtain financing on terms acceptable to the buyer, then the buyer must exercise the right to terminate the contract prior to the expiration of the due diligence period to avoid losing the earnest money deposit. The form cautions the seller, *prior to accepting the offer*, to request some verification or documentation of buyer's ability to purchase in the event the buyer represents that no financing will be required.

Buyer discloses in Paragraph 5(b) whether s/he must sell other property in order to qualify for a loan. If so, then the Contingent Sale Addendum (Form 2A2-T) should be referenced in Paragraph 15 and attached to the contract to make it a condition of the contract. *Buyer's mere assertion in 5(b) that s/he must sell other property first does not make the sale of the other property a condition of the contract that will excuse buyer's performance in the event the property does not sell.* Buyer further represents in 5(c) whether there are any other circumstances or conditions that would prevent buyer from fulfilling his/her financial obligations under the contract. If such circumstances or conditions exist, they should be specified. Such facts and circumstances may include bankruptcy proceedings involving the buyer, outstanding judgments against the buyer, or the necessary receipt of a gift, inheritance or other source of purchase funds, all of which pertain to buyer's ability to purchase the subject property and thus are material facts that a buyer agent is obligated to disclose to a seller. This provision helps brokers fulfill that obligation. The buyer discloses in 5(d) whether s/he received a Residential Property & Owners' Association Disclosure Statement from the seller prior to making the offer or whether the property is exempt from this requirement and if so, for what reason, with almost identical language appearing in (5e) giving the same three options regarding the buyer's receipt of the Minteral and Oil and Gas Rights Mandatory Disclosure form prior to signing an offer.

The *foregoing information is merely a representation or disclosure by the buyer to the seller of the buyer's plans or needs. The seller is entitled to rely upon these representations as true and the buyer may be liable to the seller if the representations are inaccurate. Nonetheless, in and of themselves, **they are not conditions of the contract**, unless other addenda are attached.* Thus, if the buyer cannot obtain a loan on the stated terms, s/he may not be able to consummate the transaction, but his/her performance is not excused and s/he is not entitled to a refund of any earnest money deposits *unless* s/he terminates the contract prior to the expiration of the due diligence period. As noted in Paragraph 1(d), if the buyer is assuming the seller's mortgage or if the seller is financing any portion of the purchase price, the applicable addenda (Standard Forms 2A6-T and 2A5-T respectively) should be attached to the contract and referenced in Paragraph 15.

Buyer Obligations

Buyer is responsible for paying the following fees or expenses pursuant to Paragraph 6:

- All *Proposed* Special Assessments which the seller is to list in Paragraph 7(c); however, seller does not *warrant* that there are no proposed assessments, but merely represents that "to the best of seller's knowledge" there are no proposed assessments other than those indicated.
- Any charges by an owners' association for Buyer's use of the common elements or services, move-in fees, membership fees, working capital contributions, or charges for providing information required by buyer's lender.
- All costs associated with any loan buyer must obtain, as well as the costs for an appraisal, title search, title insurance, recording the deed, and preparation and recording of all instruments required to secure the balance of the purchase price unpaid at Settlement.

Seller Representations

Paragraph 7 addresses various **disclosures** the seller is required to make under either federal or state law or representations that are critical to the financing or adequate evaluation of the property. In Paragraph 7, Seller indicates:

- whether s/he has owned the property at least one year, less than one year, or does not yet own the property;

- whether the residential property was built prior to 1978, in which case the lead-based paint disclosure form should be attached (Standard Form 2A9-T).

- that *to the best of seller's knowledge* there are no proposed special assessments and, except those listed, seller *warrants* that there are no confirmed special assessments except those specifically listed. If seller is not aware of any proposed or confirmed assessments, then "N/A" or "none" should be inserted on each line; and

- the amount of dues, the name, address and telephone number of the president of any owners' association and the manager of any association, the association's website address and authorizing the association to release various information to the buyer.

Note that the seller "warrants" that there are no *confirmed* assessments, but as to *proposed* assessments, seller merely states that there are none to the "best of seller's knowledge." The seller generally will be liable for all confirmed assessments, even if not disclosed, but usually the buyer takes the property subject to all *proposed* assessments. The buyer minimally would have to show that the seller knew or should have known that proposed assessments were being discussed at the time the parties were negotiating their contract to have a claim against the seller for fraud or misrepresentation. If the property is subject to regulation by an owners' association, then the seller must provide certain contact information for the association president and manager.

As with the buyer's representations, if any of the seller's representations are inaccurate, the seller may be liable to the buyer, as the expectation is that the representations are accurate and others may rely on that information. If the information later turns out to be erroneous or false, then the person making the inaccurate statement may be held accountable.

Seller Obligations

The seller's various duties and obligations under the contract are detailed in the 14 subsections of Paragraph 8(a) through (n). Virtually all of these obligations have been in earlier versions of Standard Form 2-T, but instead of being sprinkled throughout the form, they are all gathered in one paragraph. The seller must:

(a)   deliver to the closing attorney copies of all title information available to seller including title insurance policies, attorney's title opinions, surveys, easements, covenants, deeds, notes and deeds of trust, and designate the closing attorney as the sellers agent for obtaining payoff statements from seller's lenders.

(b)   authorize the seller's attorney to release any title insurance policy and the title insurer to disclose any materials in its file to the buyer and each party's agent.

(c)   to provide buyer reasonable access to the property, *including working, existing utilities*, through the earlier of closing or buyer's possession and allow a final walk-through inspection.

(d)   to remove all garbage and debris from the premises and all personal property not transferring to buyer .

(e) provide an affidavit *and indemnification agreement* signed by the seller *and* any person or entity who has performed or furnished labor, services, materials or rental equipment to the property within 120 days prior to the Settlement Date verifying that the person or entity has been paid in full and agreeing to indemnify buyer, buyer's lender and buyer's title in-surer from any loss arising from any claim related to the services or goods provided. This provision has been slightly expanded to account for the fact that title insurance companies sometimes require contractors, sub-contractors and vendors to waive lien rights as part of this affidavit and indemnification.

(f) designate a lien agent if required by G.S. 44A-11.1, provide lien agent information to buyer, pay any and all deeds of trust or other liens against the property not assumed by buyer at closing, and to promptly obtain cancellation of such liens or deeds of trust.

(g) to convey marketable and insurable title to the buyer by General Warranty Deed free from all encumbrances except ad valorem taxes (prorated), utility easements, and unviolated restrictive covenants that do not materially affect the value of the property. The property must have access to a public right of way.

(h) pay for preparation of the General Warranty Deed, any state or county excise taxes, and any local conveyance fees.

(i) pay a stated sum towards any of the buyer's expenses to purchase the property, if applicable. Such expenses may include discount points, fees for loan origination, appraisal, inspec-tions, attorneys, and "pre-paids" (taxes, insurance, owners' association dues, etc.), but are *not* limited to "qualified closing costs" as some have mistakenly assumed about similar language in past forms. However, mortgage lenders sometimes do impose restrictions on such payments, in which event the amount paid by seller may need to be reduced at settle-ment for the buyer to obtain the loan.

(j) pay an owners' association any fees charged for account payment information or related to the transfer to buyer except fees buyer is obligated to pay under Paragraph 6.

(k) pay all *confirmed* special assessments, so long as the amount can be reasonably determined or estimated.

(l) pay all property tax late listing penalties.

(m) make any agreed repairs in a good and workmanlike manner and allow the buyer to verify same prior to Settlement.

(n) refund to buyer all earnest money deposits *and the due diligence fee and reimburse the buyer for reasonable costs actually incurred in connection with his/her due diligence* in the event seller fails to materially comply with any of the aforementioned obligations or materially breaches the agreement **and** the buyer elects to terminate as a result of seller's failure or breach.

The problem sought to be addressed by the seller's obligation to remove all garbage, debris and personal property not transferring to the buyer should be apparent, although the remedy for seller's breach is not specified and might be somewhat elusive. The best scenario would be to address the issue at the settlement conference and attempt to resolve it in writing – either the seller will remove it by a specified date or buyer may discard it or seller pays to have the debris removed or the like. *Buyers would be well-advised to notify sellers in writing of what the buyer intends to do with the seller's property **before** the buyer discards it or gives it to charity or otherwise disposes of it to avoid legal claims by the seller against the buyer.*

Waiver of Lien Affidavit

Settlement agents (attorneys) routinely require an affidavit from the seller to the effect that there are no unpaid bills for labor or goods furnished to the property within the preceding four to six months to avoid the possibility of a mechanic or materialmen's lien being filed post-closing that would have priority over the buyer's deed of trust to his/her lender. Such liens may not be discovered in a pre-closing title search because they may be filed up to 120 days after the final date on which services or goods were provided, yet the lien relates back to the date on which services or goods first were provided and thus takes ahead of the buyer's mortgage lender's lien. Seller continues to have an obligation to provide a lien affidavit.

Seller's Breach

The current Standard Form 2-T clearly states that *in the event of **seller's breach** or failure to materially perform any of his/her obligations, **both the due diligence fee and all earnest money deposits are to be refunded to the buyer** if buyer chooses to terminate the contract because of seller's breach.* Additionally, the seller is obligated to *reimburse the buyer for reasonable costs* the buyer incurred in preparing to move forward with the purchase. What costs are "reasonable" remains to be seen, but most likely would at least include expenses reasonably incurred for any of the buyer's due diligence or loan application. While these expenses have always been an element of compensation to which a buyer was entitled as damages in the event of seller's breach, the standard form now contractually confirms this entitlement and requires payment by the seller. While the seller is obligated under the contract to pay these expenses, should s/he fail to do so voluntarily, the buyer still must sue the seller to enforce this provision. If the buyer wins the lawsuit, she/he may request reimburswement for his/her court costs and attorney's fees.

Short Sales

The Standard Form 2-T also includes a cautionary note under 8(g) suggesting that if the seller is in a short sale situation, s/he should seriously consider attaching to the contract the ***Short Sale Addendum*** form (**Standard Form 2A14-T**) created by the Joint Forms Task Force. A "short sale" situation is where the seller owes more on the property than the property presently is worth — a very common occurrence around 2010 as property values declined and many owners faced foreclosure. Without the addendum, the seller is destined for failure, as s/he will not be able to convey marketable and insurable title free from all encumbrances *without the lender's consent*, and thus will be in breach of contract, requiring not only the return of the due diligence fee and earnest money deposits to the buyer, but paying the buyer's reasonable costs incurred as well. Brokers must understand that ***the parties are under contract as soon as all parties, i.e., sellers and buyers, have signed the offer;*** *the lender is not technically a party to the contract,* but its consent becomes a *condition* of the contract that may excuse performance *only if the short sale addendum or similar language is included in or attached to the contract.*

Type of Conveyance and Quality of Title

Any contract to convey real property should specify the type of deed the seller must furnish the buyer. The Standard Form 2-T requires the seller to provide the buyer with a general warranty deed free and clear of all encumbrances such as deeds of trust, judgment liens, mechanics' liens, and delinquent taxes. If the property is being sold subject to one or more encumbrances, then those encumbrances should be specified; otherwise, the offer should state that the conveyance shall be free and clear of all encumbrances (particularly those encumbrances which secure financial obligations which if unpaid could result in foreclosure upon the property), except those encumbrance(s) expressly specified. Frequently there are public utility easements or rights-of-way across residential property which, while still encumbrances, may not as onerous to the parties as encumbrances that secure financial obligations.

Standard Form 2-Tcontains a number of important clauses relating to the type of conveyance and quality of title, most of which are found in Paragraph 8, "Seller Obligations," discussed above.

> *Example:* Sam Seller agrees to sell Bob Buyer his oceanfront cottage for $426,000 and they both execute a contract using Standard Form 2-T. Before the closing date, Buyer discovers after a title search that Herman Tuo, the owner of an inland cottage across the road from the subject property, has a right-of-way easement for access to the ocean that runs through the north ten feet of Seller's property. Because this private easement is not excepted from the title promised by Seller in Paragraph 8(g) (it clearly does not qualify as a "utility" easement), Buyer, at his option, may refuse to go through with the transaction and obtain his earnest money back, as well as the due diligence fee and his reasonable costs incurred during the due diligence period. His offer to purchase was *conditioned* upon Seller delivering the title promised in Standard Provision 8(g). Seller should have added a special provision in the contract informing Buyer that the title, in addition to the standard exceptions, also was subject to the private easement of Herman Tuo.

Building setback lines and other restrictive covenants on real property may serve to make the property more desirable than would be the case in their absence. Since they are encumbrances, however, it should be emphasized that, unless they are excepted from the title to be delivered, the buyer will be able to reject the seller's title and obtain the damages allowed under the contract. This is why Paragraph 8(f) in Standard Form 2-T wisely contains an automatic exception for "unviolated restrictive covenants that do not materially affect the value of the Property."

Finally, if an existing mortgage (deed of trust) on the real property is not going to be paid in full with the funds received by the seller at the real estate closing, its existence must be noted along with a statement that the purchaser is taking the property subject to the mortgage and Standard Form 2A6-T, Loan Assumption Addendum, should be completed and attached to the contract. Similarly, if there are any other liens against the property that will not be paid in full by Seller at closing, but rather assumed by the buyer, they should be expressly noted in the contract or buyer will have the right to refuse to perform the contract due to the seller's failure to deliver marketable and insurable title free from all encumbrances other than ad valorem taxes for the current year, utility easements, and unviolated restrictive covenants that do not materially affect the value of the property.

Prorations and Adjustments

Any well drafted real estate sales contract should specify the method of allocating all closing expenses and items traditionally prorated at the settlement. Specifically, how will real estate taxes, special assessments, personal property taxes, homeowners' association dues (if any), rents (if any), interest on an assumed mortgage (if applicable) and other items be prorated or otherwise handled at closing? Paragraph 9 of Standard Form 2-T addresses some of these issues as follows:

> **9. PRORATIONS AND ADJUSTMENTS.** Unless otherwise provided, the following items shall be prorated through the date of Settlement and either adjusted between the parties or paid at Settlement: (a) **Taxes on Real Property:** Ad valorem taxes and recurring governmental service fees levied with such taxses on real property shall be prorated on a calendar year basis; (b) **Taxes on Personal Property:** Ad valorem taxes on personal property for the entire year shall be paid by the Seller unless the personal property is conveyed to the Buyer, in which case, the personal property taxes shall be prorated on a calendar year basis; (c) **Rents:** Rents, if any, for the Property; (d) **Dues:** Owners' association regular assessments (dues) and other like charges.

Although the foregoing language reflects the customary practice in North Carolina for allocating prorations of taxes, rents and association fees in sales of existing homes, note that the language of the form begins with the words "Unless otherwise provided ..." Therefore, such matters are *fully negotiable* between seller and buyer. In the event the parties negotiate a proration or allocation of cost different from the standard form, it is important that the parties clearly express the negotiated change and modify the applicable language in Paragraph 9 of Standard Form 2-T.

Condition of Property at Closing

An offer to purchase should contain a provision similar to Paragraph 11 of Standard Form 2-T, which conditions the buyer's obligation to complete the purchase on *the property being in substantially the same or better condition at Closing as on the date of this offer, reasonable wear and tear excepted."* This provision is intended to protect the purchaser in the event the property is damaged, by the seller or otherwise, after the contract is signed but before closing. Suppose a storm severely damaged the property or the seller crashed his car through the garage door. In such case the buyer, relying on Paragraph 11, could be relieved of his obligation to purchase the property unless the seller restores the property to its previous condition prior to closing. This provision is closely related to and complements the "risk of loss" provision discussed below. Closing continues to constitute acceptance of the property in its then existing condition, absent written provisions to the contrary. Note, however, that this clause does not excuse a buyer from liability for damage to the property caused by the buyer or any of his or her agents, which is governed by Paragraph 4(d) and (e) of Standard Form 2-T.

Risk of Loss

The **Uniform Vendor and Purchaser Risk Act**[7] is in effect in North Carolina. The substantive provision of that Act relating to risk of loss reads as follows:

> **§39-39. Risk of loss** — Any contract hereafter made in this State for the purchase and sale of realty shall be interpreted as including an agreement that the parties shall have the following rights and duties, unless the contract expressly provides otherwise:
>
> (1) If, when neither the legal title nor the possession of the subject matter of

the contract has been transferred, all or a material part thereof is destroyed without fault of the purchaser, the vendor cannot enforce the contract, and the purchaser is entitled to recover any portion of the price that he has paid; (2) If, when either the legal title or the possession of the subject matter of the contract has been transferred, all or any part thereof is destroyed without fault of the vendor, the purchaser is not thereby relieved from a duty to pay the price, nor is he entitled to recover any portion thereof that he has paid.

In the Absence of a Contractual Provision

The foregoing statute supplies the rule, *in the absence of other contractual provision*, and holds that when neither legal title nor possession has passed to a buyer and all or a material part of the subject matter of a real estate contract is destroyed without the fault of the purchaser, the seller cannot enforce the purchase contract and the buyer may recover any portion of the price already paid. On the other hand, if legal title or possession of the real estate has been transferred pursuant to a contract and all or any part of the property is destroyed without the fault of the seller, the purchaser is not relieved of the duty to pay the price and is not entitled to recover any portion of the price already paid.

In other words, if a buyer tenders an offer to purchase and the seller subsequently accepts it, and the seller retains legal title and possession pending the closing, the risk of loss will remain on the owner-seller in the absence of a contrary stipulation in the contract. But if, as sometimes happens, the buyer goes into possession prior to closing, the buyer will bear the risk of loss of the property by fire or other reason, in the absence of a contrary provision in the sales contract. Thus, *if the parties desire to shift the risk of loss in any way, so that it will be on a person other than as provided by statute, the offer to purchase and contract must so state.* The buyer certainly should be apprised that if the buyer takes possession of the premises prior to the closing, the buyer assumes the risk of loss of the premises, even prior to taking legal title, and would have to go through with the contract even though the property is completely destroyed, unless the contract provides otherwise. It will be very important for the property to be insured in the buyer's name if the risk of loss has been shifted to the buyer.

Example: On December 1, A agrees to buy B's real property and both parties sign a valid contract to convey setting the closing date as January 15. According to the contract, transfer of both legal title and physical possession is to take place on the closing date. The contract is silent on risk of loss. On January 3, the residence on the property is destroyed by fire. The risk of loss under Section 39-39 falls upon the seller who cannot enforce the contract against the purchaser. (This does not mean that the purchaser cannot waive the defect and enforce the contract. The purchaser may be entitled to the fire insurance proceeds or may have been primarily interested in the land itself and not the structures on the land.)

Example: Same facts as immediately preceding with this change: The contract transfers physical possession to the purchaser two weeks before the legal closing date. After the purchaser takes physical possession of the property on January 1, fire destroys the residence on January 3. Under subsection (2) of Section 39-39, the risk of loss falls on the purchaser. Hopefully, the purchaser was prudent enough to have insurance in force as of the day he or she took occupancy.

Example: On January 5, X agrees to purchase Y's 150-acre farm and both parties sign a valid contract to convey setting the closing date as January 25. Both legal possession and physical occupancy are to transfer to the buyer on the closing date. The contract contains an additional provision noting that the farm buildings are now vacant, that the purchaser assumes the risk of loss from fire or the elements, and that the purchaser assumes responsibility for obtaining insurance. On January 10, all of the farm buildings are destroyed by a fierce windstorm. The risk of this loss falls on the buyer even though neither legal title nor possession has been transferred. Why? Because the contract expressly allocates the risk of loss, thus rendering the Uniform Vendor and Purchaser Risk Act's provisions inapplicable.

A careful analysis of General Statute 39-39 will reveal that certain possibilities are not covered because they do not legally constitute destruction of the property. If all or part of the property is rezoned or taken by eminent domain, for example, the statute is inapplicable. If the contract is silent on these possibilities, it will be up to a court to allocate the risk of loss in the event the parties cannot agree. The subjects of rezoning and eminent domain should be mentioned in contracts to convey where the purchaser is only interested in the property for a specific reason and cannot afford a change in the status of the property because of governmental action. While court decisions go both ways on the allocation of risk of loss due to governmental action, clear draftsmanship in the contract to convey will avoid the expense and time delay of litigation.

Risk of Loss Under Standard Form 2-T

Paragraph 12 clearly addresses the risk of loss. It reads:

> **12. RISK OF LOSS:** The risk of loss or damage by fire or other casualty prior to Closing shall be upon Seller. If the improvements on the Property are destroyed or materially damaged prior to Closing, Buyer may terminate this Contract by written notice delivered to Seller or Seller's agent and the Earnest Money Deposit and any Due Diligence Fee shall be refunded to Buyer. In the event Buyer does NOT elect to terminate this Contract, Buyer shall be entitled to receive, in addition to the Property, any of the Seller's insurance proceeds payable on account of the damage or destruction applicable to the Property being purchased. Seller is advised not to cancel existing insurance on the Property until after confirming recordation of the deed.

Thus, the "risk of loss" provision in the standard form clearly places the risk of loss or damage "by fire or other casualty prior to Closing" on the seller. *It therefore supersedes General Statute 39-39 on these matters.* Paragraph 12 does not address the subject of allocation of risk due to government action, probably because the form is designed for a residential transaction and it is extremely rare that eminent domain or rezoning will intervene to cause a problem. Note that under Paragraph 12, the buyer can only terminate the contract where **material** damage has occurred. The term "material" is subject to varying interpretations and could pose a problem in some fact situations. Since this is a legal issue, it should be referred to an experienced real estate attorney.

NOTE: both Paragraphs 11 and 12 regarding Condition of Property at Closing and Risk of Loss survive the expiration of the buyer's due diligence period and remain binding through the date of Closing.

Settlement Date

The standard contract form has never contained a "time is of the essence" provision as to the closing date. If time is not "of the essence," then there is no "drop dead date;" rather, courts generally will allow parties a reasonable time to perform after the stated deadline has passed, so long as the parties are working in good faith towards full performance of the contract. Standard Form 2-T has attempted to establish some parameters as to what constitutes a "reasonable time."

Under the current Offer to Purchase and Contract form, if a party is not prepared to proceed on the settlement date, but intends to proceed with the transaction and is acting in good faith and with reasonable diligence to that end (the Delaying Party), and the other party is ready, willing and able to complete the transaction on the stated Settlement Date (the Non-Delaying Party), then the Delaying Party is to give as much advance notice as possible of his/her inability to proceed to both the Non-Delaying Party and to the settlement agent and may have up to fourteen (14) days from the stated Settlement Date within which to complete the transaction.

If the parties do not agree *in writing* to an additional extension of the Settlement Date and have not completed settlement within fourteen days of the last stated Settlement Date, then the Delaying Party shall be in breach and the Non-Delaying Party may terminate the contract at his/her election and will be entitled to whatever remedy is provided under the contract. If the Non-Delaying Party is the seller, s/he is entitled to both the due diligence fee and any earnest money deposit paid. If the Non-Delaying Party is the buyer, s/he is entitled to a refund of both the due diligence fee and any earnest money deposits paid, as well as reimbursement of his/her reasonable costs incurred during the due diligence period as discussed previously under "Seller Obligations." No other fee, charge or interest is payable on account of the period of delay.

Caution about Using a "Time is of the Essence" Provision with Settlement Date

If it is absolutely essential to one of the parties that closing take place no later than the date specified in the contract, then the words *"time is of the essence"* may be included following the Settlement Date inserted in Paragraph 1(l) when preparing the contract. *However, brokers are **strongly cautioned against** suggesting the inclusion of a "time is of the essence" provision regarding the settlement date unless it is absolutely imperative to one of the parties that the transaction close by a specific date.* Where time is of the essence and the sale does not close by the specified date, the transaction could easily fall through unless the parties agree in writing to extend the time for settlement. The inclusion of a "time is of the essence" provision could prove to be adverse to the best interest of a broker's client. Since it is very common for settlement dates to be delayed for a multitude of reasons, it generally is better not to include a "time is of the essence" provision unless it is absolutely necessary.

Possession

Paragraph 14 still states that possession will be delivered to buyer at Closing (i.e., recording of the Deed) and that if buyer takes possession prior to closing or seller remains in possession after the closing, then the parties should attach the applicable addendum. Thus, if seller is to remain in possession for some period after closing, then the contract should specify that the seller pay appropriate rent to the buyer for such period. Similarly, if the buyer is to assume possession prior to closing, then a clause should be included requiring the buyer to pay rent to the seller for the period between transfer of possession and closing. The North Carolina Association of REALTORS® and the North Carolina Bar Association have drafted forms which address each scenario, namely, **Standard Form 2A7-T**, "Buyer Possession Before Closing Agreement," and **Standard Form 2A8-T**, "Seller Possession After Closing Agreement."

Contingency Provisions

As noted earlier in this chapter, real estate brokers are assisted in preparing contingency provisions by the existence of a number of approved **addenda** forms, e.g., "New Construction Addendum,"

"FHA/VA Financing Addendum," "Seller Financing Addendum," and "Additional Provisions Addendum." Problems commonly result when a broker attempts to draft a home-made condition and insert it on Standard Form 2-T, usually at Paragraph 15, which now is limited primarily to an itemization of the attached addenda, but it also is where brokers sometimes add or make reference to attached conditions that are not on any approved standard forms.

The need to insert qualifications or conditions pertaining to financing, or a spouse's approval, or satisfactory inspections or whatever the perceived need is, should be greatly diminished given the new "due diligence" standard under which the buyer has the unilateral right to terminate the contract for any or no reason prior to the expiration of the due diligence period and receive a refund of the earnest money deposit. However, when necessary, Paragraph 15 is the proper place on Standard Form 2-T to add a provision or condition or, more frequently, to make clear and unequivocal reference to a provision or condition or standard form addendum attached to the contract. All such properly identified provisions, conditions, and standard form addenda must be signed by the parties and then attached to Standard Form 2-T. For example, if the sale is contingent upon the sale of real property owned by the buyer, and if Standard Contingent Sale Addendum Form 2A2-T is used, then check the appropriate box in Paragraph 15. If any added provisions conflict with another provision already in Standard Form 2-T, clarify which provision is to govern. It should be carefully noted that all addenda to the Offer to Purchase *or any ancillary agreements* the parties may enter into, such as a repair agreement, *are a part of the contract and must be provided to the buyer's lender and to the settlement agent or attorney*.

Caution: Brokers must be extremely careful when adding contract provisions other than standard form addenda. The drafting of specialized provisions can constitute the unauthorized practice of law and could result in disciplinary action against the broker by the North Carolina Real Estate Commission, as could the inclusion of an inadequate or inappropriate provision. Brokers are especially cautioned against suggesting the deletion of standard provisions and the substitution of other provisions. Any time a broker personally drafts and inserts additional provisions on Standard Form 2-T (or any other approved form), the broker assumes some risk of being found to have acted incompetently and to have improperly engaged in the practice of law.

With these warnings in mind, the following guidelines for adding contract provisions or modifying or deleting standard contract language are provided. An understanding of all standard form provisions is part of the basic competence every licensee is expected to possess. A broker should not insert additional provisions or change standard language in an attempt to modify the contract form to a use for which it is not intended (e.g. option, lease-purchase, etc.). A broker should never attempt to draft lengthy, complicated provisions. This is a task that lawfully must be performed by an attorney. When a standard addendum form is appropriate to use, the broker *always* should use the form instead of attempting to draft the desired provisions. If a broker is unsure of the appropriateness of a change or possible additional provision, the party should be told to consult an attorney. If a party wants to delete or modify the wording of standard contract language or wants to insert additional provisions desired to satisfy some need or protect an interest, then let *the party/principal* delete the preprinted language or add the provision.

Concluding Standard Form Provisions

The content of the remaining paragraphs 16 through 23 in the Standard Form 2-T Offer to Purchase and Contract has not changed, other than the paragraph numbers. A summary of these provisions follows.

Assignments. The contract can not be assigned without the written consent of all parties, unless the assignment is in connection with a tax-deferred exchange. If the contract is assigned, its terms bind the assignee and his/her heirs.

Tax-Deferred Exchange. The parties agree to cooperate with each other and to execute whatever other documents may be required in the event either party is attempting to accomplish a tax-deferred exchange, but the non-exchanging party assumes no additional liability and any additional costs associated with the exchange are to be paid by the exchanging party.

Parties. The contract binds and inures to the benefit of the seller and buyer and their respective heirs, successors and assigns.

Survival. Any provision which by its nature is to be observed, kept or performed after Closing, shall survive the Closing and shall continue to bind the parties until fully performed. An example of this would be the seller's obligation to ensure that all liens against the property are properly satisfied and canceled of record.

Entire Agreement. Paragraph 20 provides that the parties' agreement is as stated in the contract, along with any referenced addenda, and that there are no conditions, representations or terms other than those expressed in the document itself. Any changes, additions or deletions must be in writing and signed by all parties.

Notice. As mentioned earlier, Paragraph 21 states that any notice or communication required to be given to either party may be given to the party or the party's agent by sending or transmitting it to a mailing or email address or fax number provided in the "Notice Information" section of the contract. If a fax number or email address is not provided, then it would appear that it is not an authorized or approved method for delivering notices, even if the parties or brokers have communicated via that method during the pendency of the transaction. Paragraph 21 states: "Seller and Buyer agree that the "Notice Information" and "Acknowledgment of Receipt of Monies" sections below shall not constitute a material part of this Contract, and that the addition or modification of any information therein shall not constitute a rejection of any offer or the creation of a counteroffer."

The *Guidelines* (Standard Form 2-G) recommend that "N/A" or "none" be inserted in the appropriate blank if a party or agent does not wish to authorize a particular method of communicating notices. It should also be noted that the Individual Selling Agent and Individual Listing Agent Notice Information now allow the agent to specify not only the agency capacity, but whether the agent is acting as a designated dual agent. If utilized and included as part of the first offer, this should satisfy the obligation to identify the designated agents for each party no later than presentation of the first offer to purchase or sell pursuant to Commission Rule A.0104(m). Note that there are no signature lines for the brokers to sign. Lastly, the *Guidelines* remind REALTORS® that if a party is represented by a broker, the REALTOR® Code of Ethics require them to conduct all dealings through the broker-agent and not the party directly, even if contact information is provided for the party.

Execution. While the contract *may* be signed in multiple originals or counterparts, taken together it still constitutes one contract. Thus, both parties may sign the same piece of paper once and multiple copies may then be made, or both may physically sign four duplicate originals, or other combinations may occur. Technically, now that "counterparts" are recognized, all parties no longer need to sign the same piece of paper. So long as the content of all the documents is identical, the sellers could sign one piece of paper and the buyers another, or with multiple sellers, each may sign separate physical documents with the buyers signing yet another, but so long as the content in all the documents is identical, they will all be construed together as forming one contract.

Computation of Days. Paragraph 23 continues the practice of the last several years by providing that the term *"days" refers to **calendar days*** with no exceptions for weekends or holidays, and that day 1 begins on the day following the day on which any act or notice was required to be performed or made.

Signatures and Dates

The offer to purchase and contract must be signed by all buyers and sellers. If the property being sold is owned by a husband and wife as tenants by the entirety, or by two or more persons as tenants in common, then *all co-owners must sign the contract.* Similarly, if the property is being purchased by a husband and wife who will take title as tenants by the entirety, or by two or more persons who will take title as tenants in common, then *all purchasers must sign the contract.*

Where One Spouse Is Selling His or Her Property

Although one might think it unnecessary to have the signature of the seller's spouse on the contract if the seller owns the property in severalty, this is not the case, as previously discussed. Even where one spouse holds title in his or her individual name only, the other spouse has the right to claim a "marital life estate" under certain circumstances.[8] (See the discussion of "marital life estates" in Chapter 1.) Where contracts to convey real property are concerned, a practical interpretation of North Carolina law dictates that *both husband and wife should always sign the offer to purchase contract as sellers, even though only one spouse owns the property.* This will obligate the non-titled spouse who does not have an ownership interest in the property to join in signing the deed at closing and will enable the buyer to force that spouse to sign the deed in a suit for specific performance should such action be necessary.

Where only the spouse owning the property has signed the contract, and the other spouse subsequently refuses to join in signing a deed conveying the property, the buyer would be entitled to either (1) rescind the contract due to the seller's inability to convey clear title free of encumbrances or (2) specifically enforce the contract with an abatement (reduction) in price because of the title defect. Of course, the buyer could honor the contract and accept a deed signed only by the spouse owning the property, but this could be risky from a property law point of view, since the buyer would be receiving title encumbered by the possibility that the nonsigning spouse might exercise his or her right to a marital life estate in the property in the future. The buyer also may have difficulty obtaining financing under these circumstances. Note that the non-owning spouse's marital life estate will be extinguished automatically and the cloud on title thereby dispelled, if he or she divorces the owner spouse or if he or she predeceases the owner-spouse, but relying on either is a gamble. The seller-spouse who owns the property can not specifically enforce the contract against the buyer because the seller is not able to provide clear title.

> *Example:* Bob Buyer offered to purchase a parcel of land owned solely by Sue Seller. Sue accepted Bob's offer by signing the sales contract, but Sue's husband, Bo, did not sign the contract. When the closing date approached, Bo made it clear that he would not sign the deed to Buyer. Even though Sue Seller solely owns the property, she cannot convey clear title without her husband's signature. His potential "marital life estate" constitutes an *encumbrance* on title. Bob Buyer does not have to proceed with the closing (since the contract to convey promised him clear title free of encumbrances); alternatively, Bob Buyer might seek to specifically enforce the contract with an abatement in price because of the title defect. Sue Seller cannot specifically enforce the contract against Bob Buyer. (Note: The result in this example would be identical if Bo Seller solely owned the property and his wife did not sign the contract and refused to sign the deed.)

Any time a married person is selling property that he or she owns in his or her individual name, whether purchased or inherited before or after marriage, and the sales contract is not signed by both husband and wife as sellers, the real estate broker has a duty to inform both the seller and buyer of the potential problem created by this situation and to advise both parties *to seek legal advice on the matter.* It should be pointed out that it is extremely rare that a surviving spouse ever elects a statutory marital life estate. Nevertheless, the mere possibility that it could happen constitutes a legal encumbrance on title.

Where One Spouse Is Buying Property

Unlike the seller's situation, it is *not* necessary to have the signature of the buyer's spouse on the sales contract if the buyer is to solely own the property. However, any lender will require the buyer's spouse to sign the deed of trust acknowledging the lender's security interest in the property, even though the spouse's signature may not be required on the underlying promissory note.

Escrow Agent's Signature

Whoever is acting as the escrow agent should sign the offer acknowledging receipt of the buyer's earnest money deposit, if any. Where the listing company is acting as the escrow agent, the acknowledgment may be signed by the individual broker working with the sellers or by any other affiliated broker or person with the listing company, as may be permitted by company policy. If the closing attorney or a title insurance company is acting as the escrow agent, then either the attorney or someone affiliated with the company should sign acknowledging receipt of the earnest money deposit. The escrow agent's signature is not required for any purpose other than to acknowledge receipt of the deposit; a prudent escrow agent will refrain from signing until s/he has actually *received* the check or negotiable instrument or cash or wire transfer, since one can not deposit an electronic copy of an earnest money check.

Dates

The date of the offer and the date of the acceptance should be shown on the contract, although their absence does not affect the legal validity of the contract. However, brokers are required to indicate the date of acceptance in the contract by Real Estate Commission Rule 21 NCAC 58A.0116 to determine when the three banking days within which to deposit the earnest money after acceptance begins to run.

CONTINGENT SALE ADDENDUM

A common scenario in contemporary residential real estate transactions is the buyer who must sell his or her present home in order to have sufficient funds to purchase another. To make it a condition of the contract, "contingent sale" language must be in the buyer's offer to purchase.[9] An article in the North Carolina Real Estate Commission Real Estate Bulletin[10] summarizes potential problems and good practice in this area, in part, as follows:

> . . . In the past, many licensees were disciplined for drafting their own "contingent sale" clauses in sales contracts. Often, these clauses were inadequate to address all the events which can occur when the buyers must sell their home before they can purchase another one. Even after the North Carolina Bar Association and the North Carolina Association of REALTORS® introduced a standardized Contingent Sale Addendum, some licensees continued to draft their own contingency forms. Serious problems can result from the improper use of such forms or the failure to use an appropriate form.

When dealing with a contingent sale, real estate brokers should use **Standard Form 2A2-T**, the ***Contingent Sale Addendum***, in conjunction with the standard Offer to Purchase and Contract form. Standard Form 2A2-T is set forth at **Figure 11-2** at the end of this chapter. As noted in the discussion under Buyer Representations, there no longer is any loan condition that will excuse buyer's performance, and even though buyer may indicate in Paragraph 5(b) that buyer must sell property currently owned, that representation does not make the sale of buyer's currently owned property a condition of the contract to purchase seller's property. *The sale of buyer's property only becomes a condition of the contract with seller if Standard Form 2A2-T* (or some similar addendum prepared by an attorney) *is incorporated by reference in Paragraph 15 and attached to the standard Offer to Purchase.*

If the buyer is not not already under contract to sell his/her property at the time s/he enters into a contract to purchase, then s/he basically has the due diligence period within which to find a buyer for the buyer's property. The buyer must deliver a copy of the sales contract for the buyer's property to the seller prior to the expiration of the buyer's due diligence period. Buyer may mark through any confidential information in the contract for the buyer's property, such as the purchase price and the name of the buyer. If buyer fails to deliver to seller a copy of a contract to purchase buyer's property prior to the expiration of the due diligence period, then the parties' contract automatically becomes "null and void" and the earnest money deposit is refunded to the buyer.

If buyer finds a buyer for his property and goes under contract, then the sale of buyer's property should close prior to the Settlement Date stated in buyer's contract with seller. If the sale of buyer's property fails to close prior to the Settlement Date stated in buyer's contract with seller, and the parties do not negotiate an extension of that Settlement Date, then buyer still has the right under Paragraph 1(b) to terminate the contract with the seller by providing written notice of termination to the seller within three days of their stated Settlement Date, *time being of the essence*, and still receive a refund of the earnest money deposit, even though the due diligence period has expired. If the buyer fails to exercise this option and ultimately can not close on the purchase of seller's property within the fourteen days allowed under Paragraph 13 of the standard contract form, then buyer will lose the earnest money deposit.

Lastly, if a contract to purchase buyer's property is terminated at any time, then buyer "... shall within 3 days promptly provide Seller written notice and reasonable documentation of such termination ...." Either buyer or seller may terminate their contract by written notice to the other, and buyer will be entitled to a refund of the earnest money deposit. If the seller elects to terminate the contract prior to the expiration of buyer's due diligence period, then seller must also refund buyer's due diligence fee.

Example: Betty Buyer makes an offer to purchase Stan Seller's property, contingent on Betty selling her house which has been on the market for 3 weeks and has had several showings. Betty attaches the standard Contingent Sale Addendum to her offer. Stan and Betty enter into a contract on August 10. Betty's due diligence period expires on September 10 and the parties' Settlement Date is September 29. Betty accepts an offer to purchase her property on August 20; the purchaser's due diligence period expires September 15 and the Settlement Date in that contract is September 28. Betty provides a copy of the contract to purchase her property to Stan on August 23, whiting out the name of the buyer and the amounts in Paragraph 1(d).

Betty's buyer informs her on September 27 that she will not be able to close until October 5. Betty has a dilemma. If Stan is willing to extend in writing the Settlement Date in their contract to October 6, then Betty's problem may be solved, but if Stan is unwilling to agree to an extension, then Betty needs to decide whether to notify Stan in writing no later than October 2 that she is terminating their contract in order to receive a refund of her earnest money deposit. If Betty fails to notify Stan in writing by October 2 that she is terminating the contract, and later fails to close that transaction on or before October 13, then Stan may terminate the contract any time thereafter and he will be entitled to receive the earnest money deposit paid by Betty. However, if Betty elects not to terminate the contract with Stan by October 2, and Betty's buyer closes on Betty's property on October 5 or 6, Betty will then be able to close on her purchase of Stan's property prior to October 13, the expiration of her 14 day grace period under contract Paragraph 13.

Had Betty's buyer notified Betty on September 12 that she was terminating the contract to purchase Betty's property, then Betty would have been obligated to "promptly" notify Stan and to provide him with reasonable documentation of this development. Presumably, reasonable documentation could be a copy of the written termination notice Betty's buyer gave her. Pursuant to Paragraph 2 of the Contingent Sale Addendum, either Stan *or Betty* would then have the option of terminating their contract by providing written notice to the other and Betty still would be entitled to a refund of her earnest money deposit *even though her due diligence period had expired*. Had the Contingent Sale Addendum *not* been attached to Stan and Betty's contract and Betty received a termination notice from her buyer on September 12, then Stan and Betty may have voluntarily agreed to terminate their contract if Betty could not otherwise proceed with the purchase due to inability to obtain financing, but Stan would be entitled to receive Betty's earnest money deposit, as Betty had lost her right to unilaterally terminate the contract because her due diligence period expired on September 10.

BACK-UP CONTRACT ADDENDUM

While some property owners may stop actively marketing or showing their property once they are under contract, they have never been required to "take the property off the market". However, if the listing company is a member of a Multiple Listing Service, the rules of that organization may require the listing broker to indicate that the property being advertised is now "under contract" or "contract pending," which may diminish interest by other prospective buyers who may believe that the proposed sale is a "done deal." Of course no pending transaction is ever final until it closes and many transactions are never consummated, whether due to the buyer's inability to obtain the requisite financing, or the failure of the property to appraise for the purchase price, or disputes between the parties as to necessary repairs, or for various other reasons. (If the buyer's performance was excused and the buyer thus was entitled to a refund of the earnest money deposit, then the seller received nothing as a result of the unsuccessful former contract.)

While the *fact that the seller has accepted an offer and is thus under contract is a material fact that must be disclosed by the listing broker*, the playing field changed with the introduction of the due diligence standards in residential sales. Both brokers and buyers should recognize that virtually all pending contracts are subject to unilateral termination by the buyer for any or no reason for a stated period of time. While sellers may receive some consideration in the form of the due diligence fee for the period of time allowed the buyer, they may not be as inclined to stop marketing their property until after the buyer's due diligence period has expired.

In the past, if a listing broker received an offer on a property that was already under contract, the broker first was obliged to inform the prospective buyer of that fact, but if the prospective buyer insisted on having his offer considered by the seller, then the broker was obligated to present the offer to the seller. *The broker had and has a duty to inform the seller of the serious legal problems that might result from accepting another offer when already under contract and to advise the seller to seek legal advice from an attorney if the seller wants to consider the offer.*

However, it is possible, perhaps more so now than previously, that a seller may want to accept a properly drafted "back-up" offer, especially when the current buyer's due diligence period has not yet expired or there is some question about whether the buyer under the existing contract will proceed to close. The North Carolina Association of REALTORS® and the North Carolina Bar Association have devised a "***Back-Up Contract Addendum***" form, **Standard Form 2A1-T**, to address this situation, but a seller still may wish to confer with an attorney if he or she has any questions concerning its legal effect or to prepare an appropriate addendum.

The addendum allows a seller and a second buyer to actually complete and sign a standard Offer to Purchase and Contract form to which the addendum is then attached, with the express understanding that the contract will remain in a secondary position until the pending contract, referred to as the "Primary Contract," is either terminated or performed. The addendum clarifies that any initial earnest money deposit to be paid under the secondary contract will be deposited by the named escrow agent within three banking days of back-up contract formation. If the primary contract is performed, rather than terminated, then the secondary contract automatically becomes "null and void" and the earnest money deposit is refunded to the back-up buyer. The seller is to "promptly" notify the back-up buyer in writing if the primary contract is terminated and to provide written evidence of that termination, at which point the secondary contract becomes primary.

Buyer may specify a date in the addendum by which seller must notify buyer that the primary contract has been terminated, time being of the essence as to that date, *or the back-up contract becomes null and void*. The addendum also gives the back-up buyer the right to terminate the back-up contract at any time prior to the atuomatic termination date by providing written notice to seller of buyer's election, *as long as* buyer has not received written notice from seller that the back-up contract has become primary. In both instances, buyer is entitled to a refund of the earnest money deposit. The back-up contract addendum also states that any due diligence fee due under the secondary contract will be payable within five days after delivery of notice to the buyer that the primary contract has been terminated and that the back-up contract is now primary. The addendum also instructs that when submitting a back-up offer, the parties should not insert dates for the expiration of the due diligence period or the Settlement Date in Standard Form 2-T, but write instead "See attached Back-Up Contract Addendum." The addendum then establishes each date as x number of days following Seller's delivery of notice to buyer that the back-up contract is now primary.

SALES CONTRACT PROCEDURES

Now that the reader is familiar with the standard Offer to Purchase and Contract form, this section will briefly review the necessary elements and the process to create a valid, legally binding contract for the sale of real estate.

OFFER AND ACCEPTANCE

To create a valid real estate sales contract, there must be an **offer**, an **acceptance** of the offer, and **communication of acceptance** to the last offeror. The formation of most real estate contracts begins with the making of an offer to purchase. The question of whether the offer to purchase (or counteroffer to sell) has been accepted is important since acceptance is a prerequisite to formation of a contract. The essential elements of a contract have been discussed in Chapter 10, "Basic Contract Law." This discussion provides a brief review of offer and acceptance requirements as they apply to the standard real estate contract and focuses on several points that are frequently misunderstood, as well as the subject of electronically transmitted offers and acceptances.

The Offer

A person making an offer to enter into a contract is known as the **offeror.** Thus both a prospective purchaser making an offer to purchase and a seller of property making a counteroffer to sell are offerors. The person to whom the offer is made is known as the **offeree.** Some of the more important points about offers to purchase real estate are summarized below.

The Offer - Key Points

- An offer must be definite and certain in its terms.
- To have legal effect, an offer must be communicated to the offeree (or the offeree's agent).
- An offeror can withdraw (revoke) his or her offer at any time prior to acceptance by the offeree. An offer is not considered legally revoked until notice of revocation is given to the offeree (or the offeree's agent).
- The offeror can specify in the offer a deadline for acceptance and the method of acceptance. Where the offer is silent on this point, an offer terminates after the passage of a reasonable period of time.
- Death (or insanity) of the offeror prior to acceptance of the offer terminates the offer as a matter of law.
- A counteroffer terminates the original offer.

Offers Are Revocable

One of the most misunderstood points concerning offers to purchase real estate is the fact that *an offer, until accepted, is revocable and the prospective buyer can withdraw sthe offer to purchase at any time before acceptance by the seller in the designated manner or within the designated time period.* The buyer is not bound to keep the offer open *even for the designated time.* The buyer can withdraw the offer *at any time.* The inclusion of a date by which the seller must accept simply indicates that the offer will expire automatically at the termination of the named period if the seller does not accept before then. The same rule applies to an offer to sell made by a seller, and to any counteroffer made by a seller or buyer.

It becomes readily apparent that a broker who procures or receives an offer to purchase should promptly deliver it to the owner-seller of any offer. Similarly, the owner-seller's signed acceptance should be communicated and delivered to the buyer as soon as possible in the manner prescribed, if any, in the offer of purchase. *Until the owner-seller's acceptance has been communicated to the buyer, the buyer may still withdraw his offer.*

> *Example:* X makes an offer to purchase Y's home on March 1, giving Y until midnight of March 3 to accept X's offer. At noon on March 2, X notifies Y that the offer to purchase is revoked. Y protests that he has until midnight of the next day to accept the offer. Y is incorrect. As long as Y has not notified X that he accepts X's offer, X has the power to revoke it under contract law. X need not express any reason for the revocation.

A more complicated example, based in part on a North Carolina Supreme Court decision,[11] is set forth below.

> *Example:* Sue Seller listed her house for sale with Bob Broker. Art Able submitted a written offer to purchase Sue's house on August 4. The offer called for $1,000 earnest money, an additional $9,000 at closing, and a 30-year purchase money mortgage financed with the seller. The offer stated it was valid only until August 9 at 5:00 P.M. When Seller received the offer, she made a series of material changes, placed her initials next to each one of the changes made, and had Bob Broker return the offer as changed to Art Able. Art Able believed he then had an option to purchase Sue's property on the changed terms, but decided to wait a few days before exercising what he thought was his "option" to purchase Sue's property.
>
> Meanwhile, Bob Broker found another purchaser, Carol Cook, who signed an offer to purchase the property on terms completely satisfactory to Sue Seller. Bob Broker informed Art Able that Seller's counteroffer was revoked and that Seller was selling the property to Carol Cook. On August 7, Seller accepted Cook's offer. Able then signed Seller's original counteroffer to Able and delivered it to Bob Broker before the August 9 deadline.
>
> Sue Seller's counteroffer to Able constituted a *rejection* of Able's offer to purchase. Able did not have any type of "option" to purchase Sue's property for a set period of time. Able did have the power to accept Seller's counter-offer, but a counteroffer can be revoked prior to acceptance just like an offer, and Sue clearly revoked her counteroffer when she had Bob Broker notify Able of her revocation.

This example illustrates how easily misunderstandings can arise between potential parties to a contract for the sale of real estate. Note the tricky legal situation a seller can face where the possibility of multiple acceptances are concerned. In the above example, the mere fact that Sue Seller accepted another offer to purchase did not constitute a revocation of her prior counteroffer. Art Able must have *direct or indirect notice that the counteroffer to him has been revoked.* Sue's direct notice to Able through Bob Broker clearly constituted a revocation of her counteroffer.

If Sue simply had accepted Carol Cook's offer and Able somehow had accidentally acquired knowledge that she had done so, that "indirect" notice probably would constitute an indirect revocation of Sue's counteroffer in North Carolina. It is, however, a poor operating procedure for a seller to accept an offer to purchase while the seller has a counteroffer outstanding. One unhappy legal result could be that the seller may obligate herself to sell the property to two different buyers where the seller accepts an offer to purchase and the offeree accepts the counteroffer before the seller notifies him that the counteroffer has been revoked. Thus, the better practice is to revoke the counteroffer first, and then accept the desired offer to purchase.

The Acceptance

As previously stated, an offer must be accepted *and* the acceptance must be appropriately communicated to the offeror before a contract for the sale of real estate is created. Once the offer is accepted and acceptance communicated, a contract is formed and the acceptance cannot be undone or recalled except by the consent of both parties to the contract. Some of the more important legal points about the law of acceptance are summarized below.

The Acceptance - Key Points

- The offeree must agree to *all* of the precise terms of the offer, (i.e., acceptance must mirror offer).
- An attempted acceptance that adds to or changes the terms of an offer revokes the offer and constitutes a counteroffer.
- There customarily is no acceptance of an offer to purchase real estate until the last offeree has accepted in writing. However, the acceptance is still not effective until communicated to the last offeror. (Communication by a seller to the seller's agent is not communication to the purchaser.)
- If the offeror has specified that acceptance must be made prior to a certain deadline or in a particular manner, then the offeree's acceptance must comply with these specifications. If the offer does not specify how the acceptance must be communicated to the offeror, the acceptance may be communicated in any legal manner (orally, in person or by phone; by delivery of written acceptance; by mail; by electronically transmitted message; etc.).

Remember, *a seller who modifies or adds terms to an offer to purchase is making a **counteroffer** and is rejecting the original offer.* Once rejected, the offer is gone forever unless the purchaser offers it again. Some sellers (and, unfortunately, their agents) have the erroneous impression that they can "fall back" on the original offer if the counteroffer is rejected. They are clearly wrong as the following example illustrates.

Example: Y has property listed with a broker at an asking price of $178,000. X offers to purchase the property for a price of $171,000. Y responds with a counteroffer to sell for $174,000. X rejects the counteroffer. Y then notifies X that the original offer of $171,000 is accepted. Y cannot accept X's original offer because that offer was rejected by Y's counteroffer. Unless X reaffirms the original offer, no contract exists between the parties.

Communication of Acceptance

Since an offer can be revoked at any time prior to acceptance and communication of that acceptance to the offeror, real estate brokers should promptly communicate acceptances.

Example: X makes an offer to purchase Y's property. Y accepts X's offer on October 23 by signing the standard form contract. Y then hands the contract to Y's listing agent and tells the broker to inform the purchaser. The broker is very busy for the rest of that day and intends to personally deliver the contract to the purchaser the next morning. Meanwhile, on the evening of October 23, X informs Y that he has changed his mind and that the offer is revoked. No contract for the sale of real estate was ever created because the offeror (X) revoked the offer prior to communication to X of Y's acceptance. Remember, *communication of acceptance by the seller to a real estate broker legally representing the **seller** is not communication to the purchaser.* This is why broker should promptly notify the purchaser or a broker legally representing the purchaser when the seller has accepted the offer to purchase.

Recall that communications or notices to a party's agent are deemed communications to the party. Thus, if a seller makes a **counteroffer**, *communication by the prospective purchaser to the seller's listing agent that the purchaser has signed the counteroffer is the same as communication of acceptance to the* *seller, upon the occurrence of which a contract is formed.* While counteroffers are discussed later in this chapter, an additional example at this juncture will be helpful.

> *Example:* X makes a written offer to purchase Y's property for $196,000. Y crosses out the $196,000 figure, inserts $210,000, and signs the contract. Y's action constitutes a rejection of X's offer and a counteroffer to sell the property to X for the higher figure. Upon receipt of the counteroffer, X initials and dates the change, thereby accepting seller's counteroffer, and delivers the accepted contract to Y's listing broker. Communication of the acceptance to the listing broker constitutes communication to Y, the principal, at which point a binding contract is created and Y has lost the power to revoke the counteroffer.

Remember that under the "**mailbox rule**," *an acceptance becomes binding when it is mailed* to the offeror, not when it is received by the offeror. The next example illustrates the mailbox rule. (See also the discussion in Chapter 10.)

> *Example:* X makes an offer to purchase Y's property on March 15. Y accepts X's offer by signing the offer and mails the signed offer to X on March 17. On March 18, before X receives the signed offer, X contacts Y and informs her that X is revoking the offer. The attempted revocation is of no effect. Under contract law, a binding contract was formed on March 17 when Y mailed the signed offer to X. By custom, an acceptance is considered "communicated" when an offeree deposits a properly addressed envelope into a mailbox or other receptacle under the control of the United States Postal Service. This is true even though it may be several days before the acceptance is actually received by the offeror.

However, when the offeror specifies the form and manner of acceptance, the offeree must carefully comply with the specifications or run the risk that a contract will not be formed.

> *Example:* X submits an offer to purchase Y's property. The offer specifies that Y is to accept by delivering a signed acceptance to X's place of business not later than 5:00 p.m. the next day. Y signs the contract, thereby accepting X's offer, but Y's agent mails the acceptance to X's residence instead of delivering it to X's place of business. Unless X wants to waive the requirements set forth in the offer, a contract has not been formed. An offeror is free under contract law to specify the time and manner of acceptance.

Understand that *the mere signing of an offer by the offeree is not sufficient to create a binding contract, even if the offer states that a binding contract is formed when the offer is signed by both parties. Nevertheless, the offeree must* **communicate** *acceptance to the offeror* **after** *signing the offer in order for a valid contract to be created.* The offeree may communicate acceptance to the offeror in any reasonable manner unless the offer specifies a particular method by which acceptance is to be communicated to the offeror. It is highly recommended that any oral communications be followed by prompt delivery of a copy of the signed contract to the offeror.

Electronically Submitted Offers and Acceptances

The availability today of nearly instant electronic communication has revolutionized the real estate business as well as commerce in general. In this regard, two distinct options exist: (1) communication by facsimile (fax) machine; and (2) communication via e-mail. Since the law in this area continues to develop, especially with regard to e-mail and digital signatures, this discussion will distinguish between communications by fax and e-mail.

Recall that federal and state laws address the use of electronic means in transactions and supplement in important respects the traditional Statute of Frauds. The federal law is the Electronic Signatures in Global and National Commerce Act (often referred to as "ESIGN").[12] The North Carolina legislation is the Uniform Electronic Transactions Act (often referred to as "UETA").[13] The thrust of both Acts is that **if** parties consent to use electronic means in effectuating their transaction, they cannot later deny the validity of those transactions by arguing that other laws required certain documents to be in writing. The Notice Information Section of Standard Form 2-T allows the parties and agents to insert contact information as to any address, electronic delivery address, or telephone or facsimile numbers approved for the receipt of any notice contemplated by the contract.[14]

Facsimile (FAX) Communications

As a general rule, an offer to purchase real estate can be communicated by fax, assuming that the offeree has a fax machine that will allow the intended recipient to receive such faxed offers. Logically, a faxed offer can also be made to a seller's agent who, in turn, is bound to promptly deliver it to the seller. Standard Form 2-T, Offer to Purchase and Contract, when signed by the prospective purchaser/offeror and properly transmitted by fax transmission, will comply with all requirements of General Statute §22-2, the Statute of Frauds. When communicating via fax, it is prudent for brokers to seek prompt confirmation from the recipient that the complete faxed document was in fact received. A follow-up phone call can easily confirm this fact.

Counteroffers and revocations of offers and other communications related to the formation or termination of a contract also can be faxed and will be as valid as if the document was hand delivered or mailed. Acceptances of offers can be communicated by fax.

Example: Barry and Brenda Buyer attend an open house. Several days later, they decide to make an offer to purchase the property. Their agent, Mary, fills out an "Offer to Purchase and Contract" (Standard Form 2-T) that Barry and Brenda sign and Mary immediately faxes the offer to the home of Steve and Stella Sellers (or to the real estate office of the Sellers' agent). A successful transmission of the offer via facsimile machine is valid under both contract law and the Statute of Frauds. Barry and Brenda are bound by the faxed offer to purchase if Steve and Stella duly accept it and communicate that acceptance to them. (Steve and Stella can send their acceptance by fax to Barry and Brenda or their agent, assuming all parties involved have fax machines and have authorized that method of communications in the contract.)

Electronic Mail (E-Mail)

An offer to purchase real estate can be communicated as an attachment (attached document) to an e-mail transmission.[15] This could be accomplished by scanning the completed signed offer into a computer file that can be transmitted via e-mail. Of course, the offeree must have a computer and be able to receive the transmission and attachment in complete and proper format. The recipient should be advised to print both the e-mail cover message and the attached document and promptly respond in the event that formatting or related problems have rendered the transmission ineffective. The Statute of Frauds requirement that the contract be "signed by the party to be charged therewith" (General Statute §22-2) would appear to be fully satisfied by a successful electronic transmission. A signed copy of the actual Offer to Purchase and Contract form could then promptly be delivered to the seller.

Likewise, counteroffers and revocations of offers and other communications related to the formation or termination of a contract can also be sent as e-mail messages or attachments to e-mail messages. *It is always prudent to follow-up any electronic communications with oral confirmations and to promptly deliver original signed documents,* if such exist.

Electronically Submitted Acceptances

As a general rule, an acceptance of an offer to purchase real estate can be communicated by fax or as an attachment to an e-mail transmission, assuming that the offeror has a fax machine, computer or other electronic device that will allow the intended recipient to receive such faxed or e-mailed acceptances. Logically, a faxed acceptance can also be sent to a buyer's agent who, in turn, is bound to promptly deliver it to the buyer. Standard Form 2-T, Offer, when accepted with the signatures of the sellers and properly transmitted by fax or as an attachment to e-mail, will comply with all requirements of General Statute §22-2, the Statute of Frauds. An acceptance transmitted by fax or e-mail will be deemed legally communicated when the transmission has been received by the offeror's fax machine or computer, as appropriate.

> *Example:* Sam Seller received an offer to purchase his residence from Betty Buyer on Standard Form 2-T. Sam unequivocally accepted the offer by properly completing and signing the acceptance portion of the form. His broker then immediately sent Standard Form 2-T as an attachment to an e-mail message to Carole Cook, the broker for the buyers. Carole Cook received the e-mail transmission and the complete copy of Standard Form 2-T as an attachment. A valid contract between the parties was formed when the electronic transmission was successfully received by Carole's server.

Again, *it is always prudent to follow-up electronic communications with oral confirmations and to promptly deliver original signed documents.* Parties should also be warned that **exchanges of e-mail messages directly between prospective seller and buyer could result in a binding contract to convey real estate. Under proper circumstances, e-mail messages themselves can constitute all or part of a binding sales contract between seller and buyer.**[16] Brokers negotiating or offering terms on behalf of their principal in e-mail exchanges would be wise to include a disclaimer that the contents of the email are for negotiation purposes only and are not binding on the principal, although under the standard agency contract in North Carolina, brokers do not have the authority to bind their principal to a contract.[17]

Electronic vs. Digital Signatures

In the less than two decades since North Carolina's Uniform Electronic Transactions Act was enacted, technological advancements in communication have exploded. Some real estate brokerage companies are now "going paperless;" all documents, files and related materials are generated and stored electronically, whether on external or internal hard drives or in "the cloud."

Such policies, however, do not reduce a broker's obligation to have paper copies of all required disclosures and other documents available for those consumers who choose not to use electronic means in a transaction.

Understand as well that "electronic" and "digital" signatures are not synonymous terms. *All digital signatures are "electronic signatures" under the Act, but* **not all electronic signatures are digital**. Non-digital electronic signatures are easy to use, involving the click of a mouse or using a finger to "write" one's name, but they are uncoded images affixed to a document and do not seal the document, as a digital signature does. For this reason, some non-digital electronic signature providers may apply a digital signature technology to the document after signing to tamper seal the document. Digital signatures are coded images permanently linked to a document at the time of "signing" that tamper seal the document, ensuring the security of the signature.

SUBMITTING OFFERS TO SELLER

*Under the law of agency, a seller's agent (**listing** agent or **seller's subagent**) has a duty to communicate (present) all offers on a listed property to the seller (principal) as soon as possible and to disclose to the seller all information in the agent's possession that might affect the seller's decision to accept an offer.* In addition, Real Estate Commission Rule 21 NCAC 58A.0106 requires all brokers to " ...immediately, but in no event later than five days from the date of execution, deliver to the parties thereto copies of any... contract, offer, lease, or option affecting real property." It is important to note that this Commission rule *applies to all brokers involved in a transaction regardless of whom they represent or from whom they will receive compensation.*

These requirements mean very simply that a *seller's* agent (or subagent) must *immediately* **present** all offers to the seller and must inform the seller of any matter that might affect the seller's decision. The broker should not withhold or delay the delivery of offers or information. Orally communicating the terms of offers to an offeree does not excuse the broker from delivering the offer within the five days required by the rules.

> *Example:* Sally Seller lists her property with Bob Broker for $319,500 and authorizes him to list the property with a multiple listing service. Bob finds a prospect who is fairly interested in the property and who probably will make an offer of $315,900 after checking with his father about help with a down payment. In the meantime, Zippy Smith, a competing broker who is also a member of the multiple listing service, contacts Bob Broker and delivers to him an offer to purchase the property from a third party who is willing to pay $315,500 for the property. Because Bob does not want to split the commission with Zippy, he places the offer in his desk drawer and does not tell Seller about it. Bob hopes that his prospect will come through with an offer soon and that he won't have to present the offer from Zippy's prospect. Bob's action constitutes both a violation of agency laws and of Real Estate Commission Rule A.0106.

In addition to presenting signed offers, a seller's agent (or subagent) must promptly inform the seller of any *possible* offers that may be forthcoming. Such information may be extremely important to the seller.

> *Example:* X has interested Smith in purchasing a residence listed with X's firm although Smith has not signed an offer to purchase the property yet. Y, a broker with another firm, phones X and informs him that he has a prospect who is very interested in purchasing, and that he will be preparing an offer with the prospect that evening. After this phone call, X hurries over to Smith's house, convinces Smith to make a formal offer to purchase the property, and promptly delivers Smith's offer to the seller without informing the seller that another offer probably will be submitted very shortly. X has breached his agency duty to disclose all relevant information to his principal. Even oral offers or expressions of strong interest by third persons should be disclosed.

The duty of a broker to deliver offers to a seller is quite clear where the broker is the *listing* agent, but what if the broker is a *buyer's* agent, or even a broker proposing to act as a seller's subagent, but without an advance agreement with the listing firm to cooperate and share in the listing firm's commission? How does the Real Estate Commission's rule on delivery of instruments apply in these circumstances?

The Commission's delivery of instruments rule imposes an absolute requirement applicable to all brokers regardless of whom they represent or who will compensate them. If a buyer's agent or broker proposing to act as a seller's subagent has a signed offer to purchase, the broker must deliver such offer to the seller (or seller's listing agent), *even if there is no agreement to cooperate with the listing firm and share the listing firm's brokerage commission.* As a practical matter, this means that any broker working with a buyer who wants to cooperate with a listing firm and share the listing firm's brokerage commission should have an *advance agreement* with the listing firm regarding cooperation and commission-splitting *prior to assisting a prospective buyer with preparing an offer on a property listed with the listing firm.* Otherwise, the Commission's rule could have the effect of forcing a broker working with the buyer to work without compensation because once the buyer has prepared an offer, the broker is compelled to deliver it promptly to the seller. [Recall, however, that a buyer's agent is prohibited from conveying any offer to the seller unless the buyer has signed a *written* buyer agency agreement. Thus, buyer agents are advised not to even draft an offer unless they first have a written buyer agency agreement to avoid any conflict between Rules A.0104(a) and A.0106.]

It is not permissible for a buyer's agent or broker acting as a seller's subagent to use the threat of withholding an offer to purchase as a means of forcing a listing firm into an agreement to cooperate and share a commission. Such compensation agreements should be worked out in advance between the brokers (or firms) involved *prior to preparing any offers on the buyer's behalf* to avoid the situation where the seller accepts the buyer's offer, but the listing firm declines the selling agent's request for compensation.

A seller's agent has no authority to reject an offer on behalf of the seller, even if the offer is clearly disadvantageous to the seller. Rather, **all offers** *must be presented to the principal and the broker should point out the disadvantages of any given offer.* If, for example, the broker is aware that the prospective buyer (offeror) may be financially unqualified, this fact should be disclosed to the seller when the offer is presented.

In a transaction involving more than one broker, the broker who is not presenting an offer may have to relay information to the seller through another broker. For example, *if the selling agent who prepares an offer has information that should be disclosed to the seller, but the offer is to be presented to the seller by the listing agent, then the selling agent should provide such information to the listing agent.*

Concurrent Multiple Offers

Where a broker receives multiple offers on a listed property about the same time, all offers should be presented to the seller at the same time. The broker should not present one offer to the seller and withhold a second offer until the seller makes a decision on the first offer. In this situation, it makes no difference which offer was received first, or which offers the highest price, or which company procured the offer. It also makes no difference whether the offer has been submitted through a seller's agent or subagent or a buyer's agent.

When a seller is considering several offers, may the listing broker disclose the terms of some offers to some of the competing buyers, but not to other competing buyers? No. The Commission has maintained for years that listing brokers who are in a multiple offer situation have a duty to treat all buyers fairly, honestly and equally. This duty arises out of the common law of agency and since July 1, 2008 has been reinforced by Commission Rule 58A.0115 which states:

> A broker shall not disclose the price or other material terms contained in a party's offer to purchase, sell, lease, rent, or to option real property to a competing party without the express authority of the offering party.

To disclose terms of an offer to one or two buyers, but not to other competing buyers, gives the first two buyers an advantage over the others. If the seller is not inclined to accept any of the offers as presented, s/he may instruct the listing broker to notify all buyers that the seller has received multiple offers and invite each buyer to submit his/her highest and best offer, if they have not done so already, by a certain time and date at which point the seller will reevaluate the offers received and make a decision. *The listing agent, with the seller's permission, may also outline any terms* **the seller** *might favorably consider, so long as the information is given to all.* Note that **the rule is not limited to sales transactions, but applies to ANY offers received by a broker, including offers to lease or rent or an option to purchase property.**

Understand as well that the mere fact that the owner has received more than one offer is *not a material fact* that the listing broker must disclose to any of the prospective buyers. *A listing broker must first obtain the owners consent before mentioning to anyone that the owner has received or is considering more than one offer.* In a seller's market, the owner may want this information disclosed so buyers are aware that there are several people who are interested in the property. However, in a buyer's market, where there are numerous available properties that satisfy a buyer's needs, a buyer may decide not to make an offer on a property if s/he knows another offer is pending or is coming in, as s/he does not want any competition when negotiating a purchase or lease. Rather than assume s/he may disclose that there are multiple offers, the listing broker must obtain the owner's consent to share that information and should share the same information with everyone to treat all fairly, equally, and honestly.

CONTRACT MODIFICATIONS AND COUNTEROFFERS

It is extremely common for a seller of real estate to insist on changes to and substitutions for some of the terms proposed by a prospective buyer in an offer to purchase. If a counteroffer is made to the prospective buyer, he or she in turn may insist upon further changes and modifications. Most commonly, written alterations to a proffered contract are made by hand-writing in the modifications and additions on the contract itself. Since it is inevitable that brokers frequently will find themselves in situations where offers and counteroffers will be modified, a number of legal principles and practical pointers should be mentioned.

When a seller receives an offer to purchase property, *makes changes to the offer*, initials the changes, signs the offer, and returns it to the prospective buyer, the seller has made a **counteroffer** under the law of contracts. **A counteroffer is a rejection of the offer to purchase which** *terminates the original offer*. Unless the seller's changes are truly trivial, the seller has substituted his or her own terms for the deal proposed by the prospective buyer. *Brokers would be well advised to assume that any change made to an offer by a seller is a material one that will result in a counteroffer.* Unless the prospective buyer accepts the seller's counteroffer (by initialing and preferably dating each modification to the original offer), a contract does not come into existence. If the prospective buyer agrees to and initials some of the changes, but does not agree to all changes or makes further material changes in terms and then returns the form to the seller, the process of counteroffer has repeated itself; i.e., the prospective buyer's response to the seller's counteroffer has resulted in a new counteroffer, this time from the prospective purchaser to the seller.

A seller may want to inquire as to a prospective buyer's willingness to accept changes to a submitted offer without making a formal counteroffer. For example, a seller might reply to a prospective purchaser that the offer to purchase is being studied by the seller. At the same time, the seller might inquire orally or in writing whether the prospective purchaser would consider certain changes to the offer. The seller essentially is attempting to keep the buyer's offer on the table, while simultaneously seeking to determine whether the buyer will do better. While this is possible in theory, in order to avoid misunderstanding, *it is important for any written memorandum or oral communication to the prospective buyer to carefully indicate that it is **not** an acceptance, rejection or counteroffer of the buyer's offer*, but rather is merely an inquiry from the seller as to whether the prospective purchaser is willing to negotiate on matters relating to the transaction. Otherwise, the seller's inquiries may well be viewed as a rejection of the buyer's offer. Indeed, the North Carolina Association of REALTORS® Standard Form *#340-T, "Response to Buyer's Offer"* expressly states that it **is** a rejection of the offer. Thus, using this form to inquire whether the buyer will consider other terms will terminate the buyer's original offer.

> *Example:* Betsy Buyer offers to purchase Sam Seller's home for $275,000. Seller's home was listed for sale at $285,000. The offer calls for the closing to take place on April 10. Seller's broker informs Betsy that Sam is considering her offer and has not accepted or rejected it, but would like to know whether Betsy is willing to negotiate two matters: the closing date and sales price. Seller's three children are in local schools, and it would be more convenient for seller to remain in the house until the end of the school year. Seller's broker also inquires whether Betsy might be willing to increase her offer by $5,000. *Under these facts*, Betsy's offer has not been accepted or rejected, nor has a counteroffer been made to her. Seller has simply made an inquiry through his broker as to whether Buyer is willing to negotiate terms of the proposed sale.

A number of practical pointers regarding how brokers should deal with contract modifications and counteroffers are suggested below.

Practical Pointers

(1) When preparing a counteroffer, the party making the counteroffer should initial each change made to the original offer. If the seller is making the counteroffer to an original written offer, the seller should sign and date the offer to purchase and contract form or the signature page at the end of the form. If the counteroffer is a second counteroffer, each change should be dated as well as initialed.

(2) When a counteroffer is made, it is extremely important that it be communicated promptly to the other party. If the other party agrees with the counteroffer, his or her clear assent to the new terms should be indicated by either initialing and dating each change, or by clear language of agreement to the changes followed by a signature and date, or by both methods. Acceptance of the new modified terms must be communicated to the party who made the counteroffer.

(3) If a series of negotiations between the parties results in numerous changes to the original offer to purchase, it is far better for the broker to take a blank standard form and complete it anew based upon the latest understanding of the parties. The temptation to save time by squeezing proposals and counter-proposals (with initials and dates) into margins or between lines, and by including confusing references to additional sheets of paper can result in a contract that will be impossible to interpret in a later dispute between seller and buyer. A broker does the parties a disservice if the broker allows the only evidence of the purchase and sale agreement to be a cluttered, incomprehensible document that may be legally unenforceable because of its ambiguities.

(4) Closely related to item three is the inadvisability at times of engaging in negotiations through successive written modifications of the original offer to purchase. Frequently, a phone call or oral request for clarification by one party to another will quickly and conveniently determine the acceptability of proposed modifications and changes to a contract. If there is a meeting of the minds during these oral communications, the original written proposal can be amended accordingly and both parties to the contract then can assent to the amendments by signature or initial, as appropriate. A carefully worded written inquiry, as described earlier, also may be used for this purpose.

(5) Where a seller or seller's agent is responding to an offer to purchase with a written or oral inquiry as to whether the buyer might consider different terms of sale, *the seller or broker should make it clear that the inquiry does not constitute a counteroffer or an acceptance or rejection of the buyer's initial offer.* The North Carolina Association of REALTORS® standard form #340-T, "Response to Buyer's Offer," should *not* be used for this purpose as it will constitute a rejection of the buyer's offer.

(6) If negotiations lead to complex or unusual contract or financing proposals, the broker should cease attempting to integrate the proposals into the standard form and should advise the parties to seek legal assistance from an attorney.

FURNISHING COPIES OF OFFERS AND CONTRACTS

Real estate brokers are reminded again of Real Estate Commission Rule 21 NCAC 58A.0106 titled "Delivery of Instruments" that imposes on brokers certain obligations regarding the furnishing of copies of executed documents. When a buyer signs an offer to purchase, the broker must provide that buyer with an exact and complete copy of what he or she has signed and delivers copy to the seller. When the seller accepts the buyer's offer to purchase, that seller also must be provided with an exact copy of what he or she has signed, and the broker must promptly deliver a copy to the buyer showing that the contract is complete and binding. This prompt furnishing of copies of these significant instruments to all persons involved is a sound business practice and should keep misunderstandings and criticism to a minimum. The furnishing of copies of these documents to all parties involved as well as retaining a copy for the broker's file, should be routine for every broker.

However, while the rule requires that all parties be provided a copy of various instruments (i.e., agency agreements, contracts, offers, leases or options), recognize that only one contract signed by all parties is required to form a legally valid enforceable contract. See the earlier discussion of Standard Form 2-T Paragraph 22, "Execution", regarding multiple originals or counterparts. Whether duplicate originals or copies of the "originals," the contract should be retained by each party and broker. The lender and closing attorney will also want copies.

INSTALLMENT LAND CONTRACT

An **installment land contract** (also known as a **land contract, land sales contract,** or **contract for deed**) *is an agreement whereby real property is sold on the installment payment method with the seller retaining legal title to the property until all of the purchase price is paid or until some other agreed upon point in the timetable of payments.* An installment land contract has a dual legal personality. It is a contract by which the seller agrees to sell and the buyer agrees to buy, and it is also a financing device that can be used in place of a purchase money deed of trust or mortgage. Use of the installment land contract is common in some states but is relatively rare in North Carolina.

The relationship between seller (sometimes called "vendor") and buyer (sometimes called "vendee") under an installment land contract is substantially the same as that existing between a mortgagee and mortgagor under a mortgage or deed of trust. The seller is doing the financing and therefore is in a position analogous to a mortgagee. The buyer is under an obligation to pay the installment payments as they come due and is therefore in a position analogous to a mortgagor, although *the buyer does not have the same legal rights and protections afforded a mortgagor under deed of trust foreclosure statutes.*

Basic Characteristics

The installment land contract should be contrasted with Standard Form 2-T. Standard Form 2-T is an interim device, a binder contract that defines the rights and obligations of seller and buyer up until the closing date for the real estate transaction, at which time the deed to the property is delivered to the buyer. The buyer then normally executes a deed of trust to secure repayment of the funds he has borrowed to pay the purchase price. The installment land contract, on the other hand, defines the rights and obligations of the parties over a long period of time. No deed passes at a closing, and the buyer has not paid the seller the purchase price before moving onto the property. *The buyer occupies the property under the terms of the land contract and makes installment payments until the buyer has eventually paid the entire purchase price or a predetermined percentage of the purchase price, at which time he or she obtains a deed to the property from the seller.* The installment land contract gives the buyer *"equitable"* title to the property and serves as a long-term financing device. The seller retains *"legal"* title until it is time to convey such title to the buyer under the terms of the contract.

At present, there is no approved standard form in North Carolina for installment land contracts, *and it is **never** appropriate to use Standard Form 2-T as an installment land contract form.* Standard Form 2-T and other standard contract forms are not designed to cover long-term financing arrangements and are inadequate and incomplete for that purpose. *Because the installment land contract is also a financing device, the parties should always be advised to consult with an attorney for legal advice and drafting expertise.* As is discussed below, there remain significant disadvantages to installment land contract financing from the vendee's perspective. In addition, there may be situations where a vendor's attorney would also advise against utilizing the land contract approach to financing.

The following examples are taken from the terms of payment paragraphs of typical installment land contracts and may help the reader to envision the nature of this type of contract. Note that the following constitute only part of a complete installment land contract.

Example of Land Contract Involving 20-Year Repayment Period

The purchaser, in consideration of all the covenants and agreements contained in this land contract, agrees to purchase the real property described below, and to pay therefor to the seller the sum of $105,000 in the following manner: $5,000 at the execution of this land contract, and the balance of $100,000, together with interest on such portions thereof as shall remain from time to time unpaid, at the rate of 12 percent per annum, until paid in full. Said principal and interest shall be payable in 240 installments of not less than $1101.09 per month, beginning on the 5th day of March, 2015.

Example of Land Contract with Payments Amortized Based on a 20-Year Period, But with a Balloon Payment Due After 5 Years

The purchaser, in consideration of all of the covenants and agreements contained in this land contract, agrees to purchase the real property described below, and to pay therefor to the seller the sum of $105,000 in the following manner: $5,000 at the execution of this land contract, and the balance of $100,000, together with interest on such portions thereof as shall remain from time to time unpaid at the rate of 12 percent per annum, until paid in full. Said principal and interest shall be payable in equal monthly installments of $1101.09 per month beginning March 5, 2015; provided, however, that the entire unpaid principal balance is due and payable on the fifth anniversary of this land contract.

In the first example, the buyer will not actually receive a deed from the seller until the year 2035, after making installment payments for 20 years. In the second example, a balloon payment of the entire unpaid balance is required after 5 years even though the payments up until that time are amortized based upon a 20-year period. At the end of the 5-year period the buyer will have to refinance the purchase price, probably by a conventional deed of trust, in order to make the balloon payment. When the buyer pays the seller in full, the seller will convey title by deed to the buyer.

Chapter 47H: Contracts for Deed

As of October 1, 2010, state laws found in General Statutes Chapter 47H apply to "contracts for deed" **if** the property either contains a 1-4 family dwelling structure on it or one will be erected that will be *used as the purchaser's principal dwelling*. The Act also applies to the sale of property on which a manufactured home used as the purchaser's principal dwelling will be situated. General Statute 47H-1(1) defines a "*contract for deed*" as:

> An agreement ...in which the seller agrees to sell an interest in property to the purchaser and the purchaser agrees to pay the purchase price in five or more payments, exclusive of the down payment, if any, and the seller retains title to the property as security for the purchaser's obligation under the agreement.

G.S. 47H-2 lists 17 points that represent the *minimum contents of a contract for deed for a principal dwelling*. In addition to the obvious material terms, e.g., parties, property description, purchase price, interest rate, duration, etc., the statute also requires the contract for deed to state the purchaser's right to cure a default, and provisions indicating who is responsible for repairs to the property and payment of taxes, hazard insurance premiums, flood insurance premiums, and owners' association dues. If the property is encumbered by a lien, the amount of the lien and the amount and due date of any periodic payments must be included in the contract for deed. The purchaser has the statutory right to cancel the contract within three business days following execution or receipt of a copy of the contract, whichever is later. If the purchaser elects to cancel, then the seller must return to the purchaser within ten days any property exchanged or payments made, less any offset for the fair rental value of the property for the period of the purchaser's possession and any sums required to repair damages to the property caused by the purchaser beyond normal wear and tear.

The law requires the *seller* to record the contract for deed or a Memorandum thereof within five business days of execution. Additionally, the seller must provide the buyer with an *annual accounting* stating the amount paid under the contract, the amount still due, the number of payments remaining, amounts paid for taxes and hazard insurance, any insurance proceeds received for property damage and how the funds were spent, and the outstanding balance of any lien secured by the property. Late fees may not exceed 4% of the payment due and the payment must be at least 15 days past due.

General Statute 47H-6 imposes certain limitations on the seller's title and requires a prominent warning (14 point, boldface, caps) to the purchaser prior to executing the contract that there is more than one lien on the property and that if the seller defaults in his/her payments, the lienholders may foreclose on the property even if the purchaser has made all required payments. If a seller breaches his/her obligations under the statute to timely pay existing encumbrances, then the buyer has the right to sue for damages or rescind the installment land contract and recover all sums previously paid, minus an offset for the fair rental value of the property during the period of buyer's possession. The statute also allows the purchaser to sue for declaratory or equitable relief, and acknowledges that each has "... any other rights and remedies provided by law or equity." It also excepts a seller from liability under the unfair and deceptive trade practices act when selling his/her primary residence directly to a buyer.

If the purchaser defaults on any of his/her obligations specified in the contract, then the seller must provide written notice specifying with particularity all breaches/defaults claimed, and allow the purchaser not less than 30 days to cure the default(s). If the purchaser fails to cure the default and will not voluntarily surrender possession, the seller will need to consult an attorney regarding his/her legal options.

Advantages and Disadvantages

Discussed below are the advantages and disadvantages to sellers and buyers of using a contract for deed or an installment land contract rather than the traditional approach involving transfer of title at closing coupled with a purchase money mortgage given by the buyer to the seller.

Advantages to Buyer

The installment land contract offers a number of advantages to the buyer. One is the availability of an alternative means of financing during times of tight conventional money supply. The down payment is often lower in installment land contracts than with conventional methods of financing. The closing costs can be lower, although the fact that this type of contract is not that common in North Carolina may produce added legal expenses. The buyer also can claim the usual tax advantages that ownership of real property brings.

Disadvantages to Buyer

On the other hand, a number of disadvantages exist when a buyer goes the installment land contract route. Remedies can be harsh if the buyer defaults on installment payments. *Most land contracts give the seller the option of calling the entire amount of unpaid principal due and payable if the buyer defaults on even one payment. A buyer in default does have the right to exercise an "equity of redemption" and pay the unpaid balance (including any accrued interest and pre-payment penalties) to keep the property.*[18] If the buyer cannot come up with the balance, then the buyer often loses all rights to the real estate and to payments previously made. *The protections of the deed of trust foreclosure statutes generally are not available to the defaulting buyer.* If the property is the purchaser's residence, then the new laws require written notice from the seller to the buyer specifying the default and allowing thirty days to cure.

There is another major disadvantage to the buyer. Since the seller keeps legal title until some future date (often the date when the final payment is made), the title ultimately delivered to the buyer may be encumbered or defective in some way. Special legal precautions need to be taken to protect a land contract vendee with regard to title. Specifically, ***the installment land contract should be recorded in the Register of Deeds office immediately after execution in order to protect the buyer's (vendee's) interest from the claims of others related to the land.***

Additionally, the buyer under an installment land contract who later decides to sell or borrow money on his or her interest in the property may encounter some legal and practical difficulties. In some instances, installment land contracts may not be freely assignable.[19] Even where land contract forms authorize assignment, potential purchasers may shy away from this method of land transfer. Should the vendee under a land contract wish to pledge the property as security to borrow money, he or she may find that traditional lenders are reluctant to accept a vendee's interest in a land contract as collateral to secure the loan.

Advantages to Seller

The seller under an installment land contract may see a number of advantages in selling property by this method. Income tax advantages flowing from the installment sale of property may appeal to sellers who need tax relief. The seller still has bare legal title and holds the deed to the property as security. *If the buyer defaults, the seller may be able to both obtain clear title to the land once again and also retain all payments previously made by the buyer.* Finally, the installment land contract device may be the only viable way that the seller has of selling the real estate; i.e., the seller may have a buyer who can purchase only if this method of financing is used.

Disadvantages to Seller

One disadvantage to the seller is that a land contract is frequently characterized by a low down payment. Also, the purchase price is paid in installments instead of one lump sum. To a seller who needs money rather than a tax advantage, this installment method will be disadvantageous. While legal remedies most certainly favor the seller in the event of default by the buyer, the seller may encounter extensive legal fees and a time delay before he actually forecloses the buyer's rights under the land contract and clears the title of the defect of an outstanding land contract.

OPTION TO PURCHASE REAL ESTATE

In the typical contract to convey, the seller of real estate is legally obligated to sell and the purchaser is legally obligated to buy. In contrast, an **option to purchase contract** (or **option**) *binds the owner of real estate* (called the "**optionor**") *to hold an offer to sell open for a set period of time and gives the other party to the option contract* (called the "**optionee**") *a legal right to either accept or not accept the optionor's offer to sell during the time period of the option.* Why would an owner of property bind oneself to sell in a contract where the other party, the optionee, is not legally bound to purchase? The answer is that *the optionee pays a fee or other valuable consideration for the option.* Indeed, if no consideration is paid, the option is not a binding contract.[20]

Do not confuse the separate and distinct "option to purchase" with the due diligence determination feature contained in the current Offer to Purchase and Contract forms discussed extensively earlier in this chapter. This discussion focuses on the traditional "option to purchase".

Options have a very practical utility in the realm of real estate practice. Real estate brokers frequently run into the situation where a prospective purchaser is not immediately prepared to make a decision to buy the property. At the same time, the prospective purchaser desires to obtain a legally enforceable right to purchase the property at his or her option at some future date. The owner, however, usually is not willing to forego opportunities to sell the property to other persons unless the owner is compensated for withdrawing the property from the market. Hence, the prospective purchaser may find it advantageous to procure an option from the seller.

The prospective purchaser pays the property owner a negotiated and specified amount of money for the exclusive privilege of buying the property upon specified terms and conditions within a designated time period. If no consideration has been paid, the option is invalid. When a valid option to purchase exists, the optionee is given the exclusive privilege of buying the property within the allotted time, for the price and upon the terms and conditions specified in the option contract. Remember that *while an option binds the optionor-owner to keep the offer to sell open to the optionee-prospective purchaser, it imposes no obligation on the optionee to purchase the property.* The optionee is given the exclusive right to buy if the optionee elects to exercise the option within the term specified.

The option to purchase has a number of other practical uses. One of the most common fact situations is where a lessee has negotiated an option to purchase as part of the lease agreement.[21]

Elimination of Standard Form Option to Purchase

While simple in concept, option contracts are often complex legal documents that can tie up title to real property and affect the rights of parties in significant ways. Because of this complexity and because "one size does *not* fit all". there has not been a standard form "Option To Purchase" for years. Thus, real estate brokers should advise sellers and buyers to obtain the services of an experienced real estate attorney when an option to purchase agreement is contemplated.

Rights of Parties

An option does not give the optionee any title or legal interest in the property. The optionee merely receives an opportunity to accept or decline the temporarily irrevocable offer of the optionor to sell the property.

The optionor, by granting an option to the optionee, gives up only the right to sell the property to anyone other than the optionee during the specified period of time. The optionor also gives up the right to withdraw his offer to sell to the optionee prior to the expiration of the option period. *The optionee has the exclusive right to exercise the option and purchase the property during the stated option period, but only upon the terms and conditions prescribed by the option contract.* The optionee can not change the terms in any way upon exercise of the option (unless, of course, the optionor agrees to any proposed change in terms).

The validity of an option is not, however, endangered by further negotiations. In fact, one advantage of obtaining a valid option contract is that *negotiations during the option period do not affect the optionor's continuing offer to sell at the originally stated option price. The optionee may make an offer to buy on different terms than those stated in the option without giving up the right to exercise the option.*

Example: A, an owner of property, agrees to grant to X a 60-day option to purchase A's property for a total price of $180,000 cash. All essential terms are contained in a well-drafted option agreement. During the option period, X notifies A that credit is extremely tight and that X would like to offer A $150,000 for the property with A taking back a second mortgage for $25,000 of the price. A flatly rejects this proposal and claims that the option has ended because of X's "counteroffer." A is incorrect. Subsequent negotiations during the option period will not alter the validity of the original option (unless, of course, the parties mutually agree to an amendment).

Options Must Be in Writing and Recorded

An option to purchase must be in writing to satisfy the Statute of Frauds. In addition, *the option must be recorded to protect the optionee from third persons who may deal with the owner-optionor and who are unaware of the outstanding option.* To secure the protection of the recording statutes, the option must be legally acknowledged before an appropriate officer.

The legal formalities of drafting an option are the same as those for all contracts and documents involving real property. As with other real estate contracts, when the subject matter of an option is property owned by the entireties, the signatures of both tenants by the entirety are necessary to make the option effective.

Consideration

There are two types of consideration involved in an option. One is the consideration paid by the optionee to the optionor for the option itself. The other type of consideration involved in an option is the price the optionee must pay in order to purchase the property. *Both monetary amounts, the amount paid by the optionee for the option and the price to be paid if the optionee elects to consummate the purchase, should be definitely and separately stated in the option.*

For instance, the option may provide that the optionee is to pay $2000 to the optionor for the option itself and that the optionee will pay $120,000 if the optionee elects to purchase the property within the specified period. It is also desirable from the standpoint of clarity to state whether the consideration paid for the option is to be applied toward the purchase price in the event that the option is exercised.

Other Option Provisions

The **total purchase price** the optionee agrees to pay if the option is exercised, together with **terms regarding the method of payment**, should be clearly spelled out. If a part of the purchase price concerns a mortgage, its interest rate, maturity date, and terms of payment should be clearly stated, as well as any forfeiture provisions in the event of any default. As with contracts to convey, the option should describe the quality of **title** to be conveyed, including any reservations or exceptions desired by the optionor.

The **duration of the option** (i.e., the "option period"), is the time during which the optionee may elect to exercise the option and purchase the property and must be stated with precision in the option agreement. ***Time is of the essence with respect to the option period and exercise of the option.*** Because time is of the essence, an experienced real estate attorney will specify both the date and the time at which the option is to expire. That attorney will avoid language such as "sixty days from the date hereof" or "for three months from today" as these descriptions can lead to disputes over the last date that the option can be exercised. Specifying both the date and time elimiinates misunderstandings concerning the expiration of the option period.

The **manner of notification** to the optionor that the optionee elects to exercise the option and purchase the property is an important provision. An option must be exercised in accordance with the terms of the option contract. The various methods of notification, including the possibility of e-mail, should be described in a properly drafted option contract. Note that it will *not* be sufficient to send notice on the final day of an option period by regular first class or next day delivery express mail, since *the option must be exercised **prior** to expiration of the time period* and a notice mailed on the last day but not received until after expiration of the option period is legally inadequate. ***Contrary to the general mailbox rule for acceptances, a mailed notice of option exercise is <u>not</u> effective as of the date of mailing or postmark.***

In addition to the language related to exercise of the option, some option contracts require an additional payment of money to accompany the exercise of the option or even a tender of the full purchase price. The leading North Carolina Supreme Court decision on this issue states the rule of law, in part, as follows:

> . . . Whether tender of the purchase price is necessary to exercise an option depends upon the agreement of the parties as expressed in the particular instrument. The acceptance must be in accordance with the terms of the [option] contract. Where the option requires the payment of the purchase money or a part thereof to accompany the optionee's election to exercise the option, tender of the payment specified is a condition precedent to the formation of a contract to sell unless it is waived by the optionor. On the other hand, the option may merely require that notice be given of the exercise thereof during the term of the option.[22]

The all important lesson is a basic one: *Notification of exercise of the option must be made in the manner specified in the option contract unless the optionor waives the provision.*

The option contract should provide for the **form of conveyance** by which the optionor is to convey title and the **type of title** that is to be conveyed by the optionor. It is in the optionee's best interest that the option require conveyance by warranty deed of a fee simple title free and clear of all encumbrances. The option should allow the optionee-purchaser a certain period of time after the election to purchase (exercise of the option) to have title to the property examined before closing the transaction. It also is good practice to include a **prorations** provision in the option contract stating how taxes, assessments, insurance, and similar matters are to be prorated between the parties at closing following the exercise of the option.

Unless there is an express provision in the option contract to the contrary, *options may be assigned by the optionee to a third person*, thereby giving the third person the right to exercise the option and purchase the property. *The right to exercise the option is also inheritable.*

Thus, if the optionor desires to prevent the optionee from assigning the option contract, the optionor should specifically restrict assignment in the option agreement. As discussed in Chapter 10, nonassignability is sometimes implied under contract law. If the terms of the option clearly indicate that it was entered into in reliance on the personal integrity, skill, or credit of the optionee, it may be held nonassignable even in the absence of a provision restricting assignment. An example might be where the optionor will be providing seller financing for the optionee-purchaser. However, to avoid disputes and litigation and to eliminate all doubt, a nonassignability clause should be included in the agreement, if it is important to the seller.

Options should not be too informal or sketchy. If the option is to be of any value to either the prospective seller or buyer, it should reflect the complete agreement between the parties. A full and adequate **legal description of the property** that is the subject of the option should be included. Options are often declared invalid as a result of legally deficient descriptions.

Example: A grants to B an option to purchase property described in the option contract as: "200 acres of timberland near Smith's property in Harnett County." The option agreement is void under the Statute of Frauds, since the legal description is hopelessly ambiguous. There may be hundreds of Smiths who own property in Harnett County. Even if the correct Smith can be located, the precise shape and location of the optioned property still cannot be determined from this patently ambiguous description.

An expertly drafted option contract will cover essential matters that must be included to make a valid and binding contract. Once again, the importance and complexity of option contracts dictates that an experienced real estate lawyer be retained to prepare them. One mistake occasionally made when laypersons attempt to draft option contracts is failing to set a definite price to be paid for the property in the event the option is exercised. In these poorly drafted agreements, the parties agree that the optionee shall have the option to purchase the property "at a price to be mutually agreed upon by the parties." This kind of price provision is meaningless because either party may decide not to agree for any or no reason at all. Thus, *the price that ultimately will be paid must be determined and specified at the time the option is prepared.*[23] Similarly, an agreement that the purchase will be made at "current fair market value" is an invitation to legal controversy and disagreement and should be avoided.

Residential Lease with Option to Purchase

The foregoing discussion applied to option contracts in general. However, as noted, options frequently may be coupled with a preceding lease term. There are no North Carolina laws at present dictating minimum terms or conditions that must be addressed in a commercial lease with option to purchase transaction; the lessor-optionor and tenant-optionee are free to negotiate whatever terms are mutually acceptable and the rights and obligations of each will be governed by the terms of their written agreements.

However, *when an option contract is entered into simultaneously with a lease agreement for a* **residential property that will be the principal dwelling of the lessee-optionee,** *consumer protection laws found in* **Chapter 47G** *of the General Statutes will apply.* Chapter 47G does *not* apply to leases or options on commercial property; rather it applies to "**covered lease agreements**" defined as a "residential lease agreement that is combined with, or is executed concurrently with, an option contract..." for the *purchase of property on which a 1-4 family structure is located that will be* **used as the purchaser's primary dwelling**. The law requires that the lease-option contract be in writing and contain certain minimum terms or disclosures including: full names and addresses of all parties and the date each signs the contract; a legal description of the property to be conveyed; the sales price of the property and the amount of any option fee or other amounts to be paid by either party; all obligations imposed on the purchaser that, if breached, will trigger a forfeiture of the option; the time period within which the purchaser must exercise the option; a statement of the purchaser's right to cure a default, including the right to cure a default once in any 12-month period during the covered lease agreement; and notice in 14-point boldface type above the purchaser's signature that the *purchaser* has the *right to cancel* the option contract anytime *until midnight of the third business day following execution or delivery of the option contract, whichever is later.* As with Contracts for Deeds under Chapter 47H, the statute requires the **seller to record the option contract**, or a Memorandum of Option Contract, with the appropriate Register of Deeds *within five business days after contract execution.*

General Statute 47G-3 expressly states that the *landlord-tenant laws found in Chapter 42 of the General Statutes apply to covered lease agreements.* Thus, the lessor will be responsible for fulfilling all of a residential landlord's obligations under state law and the lessee will have the statutory duties of a residential tenant during the lease period until the lessee either exercises the option to purchase the property or the option expires.

The purchaser's option rights can only be forfeited if the purchaser has breached one or more of his/her express obligations set forth in the lease-option contract *and* the contract allows the seller to declare a forfeiture in the event of purchaser's breach. However, the seller must first provide the purchaser with a written notice specifying the purchaser's default, including the amount of any monies due if payments are in default, and the date by which any cure must be made to avoid forfeiture of the purchaser's interest, which date may not be less than 30 days from service of the notice. The law specifically allows the lessee-optionee the right to cure a default once every 12 months during the term of the lease. A lessor faced with a lessee who fails to cure a default under the lease terms and refuses to surrender possession of the premises must resort to the summary ejectment process found in Article 3 of Chapter 42 of the General Statutes and discussed in Chapter 16 herein.

PREEMPTIVE RIGHTS

In the real estate law context, a preemptive right is one that gives a person the first right to purchase real property. It is a generic term that can take a number of forms. The two primary examples of preemptive rights are the **right of first refusal** and the **first opportunity to purchase**.

Right of First Refusal

Under a right of first refusal, *an owner of property legally promises to the other contracting party that, in the event the owner decides to sell the property at some time in the future, the owner will give the other contracting party the opportunity to match a bona fide offer to purchase received by the owner from a third party.*

There are both similarities and differences between preemptive rights and the option to purchase. The main difference is that with a preemptive right, the property owner does not make a present binding offer to sell the property. The chief similarity is that the right of first refusal operates similarly to an option to purchase, in that the property owner first must offer the property to the person holding the first right of refusal if the owner decides to sell at some future date, before he or she may sell to the public at large.

Preemptive rights have a number of practical uses. For example, a purchaser of part of a larger parcel of land may want the first right to buy the remainder of the parcel in the event the owner decides to sell. A lessee may desire to have a preemptive right in a lease enabling the lessee to purchase the property if the lessee does not like a prospective purchaser. The following is an example of part of a right of first refusal provision contained in a lease:

> If the Lessor shall receive, during the term of this lease, a bona fide offer to purchase the leased property from a third party, the Lessee shall have the right to purchase the property upon terms as favorable to the Lessor as appear in the third party offer to purchase. The Lessee shall have 30 days after personal delivery of the offer to purchase to exercise this right of first refusal or it shall be deemed waived by Lessee and be of no further force and effect.

Additional terms essential to the right of first refusal would be set forth in the lease.[24] As with other real estate contracts, the *right of first refusal* must be a right that has been clearly granted and *must be supported by adequate consideration*. Not every right of first refusal is valid and enforceable in North Carolina. Property can only be tied up with this type of agreement for a *reasonable period of time*.[25]

In addition, the price or formula for determining the purchase price must be clear and reasonable. If these requirements are not satisfied, the right of first refusal is void. For these reasons, an experienced real estate attorney always should be consulted when drafting this type of contractual right.

The right of first refusal form of agreement has been criticized as having the potential to trigger a number of practical and legal problems. As a practical matter, rights of first refusal can have an adverse effect on sales to third parties. A potential purchaser may be reluctant to negotiate a purchase contract and spend money on matters such as due diligence if that purchaser knows that these efforts, time and expense may be wasted because its offer may be matched by the person holding the right of first refusal. In addition, there are many cases litigating issues involving rights of first refusal. Because of the shortcomings of the right of first refusal, the current trend is to prefer the first opportunity to purchase form of preemptive right.

Right of First Opportunity to Purchase

Because of practical and legal problems that can occur when a right of first refusal is used, a relatively new form of contract provision that may lead to a purchase of property has evolved. It is known as the right of first opportunity to purchase. Under a first opportunity to purchase, *an owner of property legally promises to the other contracting party that, in the event the owner decides to sell the property at some time in the future, the owner will give the other contracting party the first opportunity to purchase at a price to be determined at that time.* As with the right of first refusal, the most common fact situation in which this type of agreement is utilized involves a commercial lease. Under a right of first opportunity to purchase, a lessee who may be interested in purchasing the property if the owner ever decides to sell negotiates a provision in the lease to the effect that, if the lessor decides to sell the property during the lease term, the lessor will first notify the lessee and offer to sell the property to the lessee for a designated price. If the lessee opts not to exercise the right to purchase at the designated price, the lessor is free to sell the property to a third party at the designated price. (The agreement may allow the lessor to then sell for a percentage of the designated price; e.g., 90% or more of the designated price.) If, however, the lessor does not then sell to a third party at the designated price during a specified period of time, the lessor cannot sell the property without once again making a new offer to the lessee pursuant to the right of first opportunity to purchase agreement.

Endnotes

1.   Other specialized types of contracts known as preemptive rights are discussed at the end of this Chapter.

2.   N.C. Gen. Stat. §93A-6(a)(8). This License Law provision authorizes the Real Estate Commission to discipline a licensee who is found to be "... unworthy or incompetent to act as a real estate broker in a manner as to endanger the interest of the public."

3.   N.C. Gen. Stat. §93A-6(a)(11) and Real Estate Commission Rule 21 NCAC 58A.0111; also N.C. Gen. Stat. §84-2.1.

4.   *Guidelines for Completing the Offer to Purchase and Contract*, Standard Form 2-G, Copyright 7/2017.

5.   This example is based on *Bennett v. Fuller*, 67 N.C. App. 466, 313 S.E.2d 597 (1984). The serious problem with the description in this case was that the vendors did not own all of the property recorded in the book and page of the register of deeds land records specified in the contract to convey. The Court held that this resulted in a patently ambiguous legal description that could not be corrected because of the Statute of Frauds.

6.   *Curran v. Barefoot,* 183 N.C. App. 331, 645 S.E.2d 187 (2007).

7.   N.C. Gen. Stat. §§39-37 through 39-39.

8.   See N.C. Gen. Stat. §29-30 which gives a surviving spouse an option to take a life estate in one third of all property which the deceased spouse owned during their marriage. This potential life estate is *not* extinguished by the owner-spouse's conveyance of the property unless the non-owner-spouse also signed the deed.

9.   For a case in which a dispute arose over a contingent sale addendum see *Carson v. Grassman,* 182 N.C. App. 521, 642 S.E.2d 537 (2007).

10.   See *"When Sale of Present Home' is a condition for buying ... How do you handle the Offer to Purchase?"* Vol. 31, No. 1 Real Estate Bulletin, Spring, 2000, p. 7, by Blackwell M. Brogden, Jr., Chief Depute Legal Counsel, North Carolina Real Estate Commission.

11.   *Normille v. Miller,* 313 N.C. 98, 326 S.E.2d 11 (1985).

12.   15 U.S.C. §7001 *et seq.* (2000).

13.   N.C. Gen. Stat. §66-323 *et seq.* For a more in-depth discussion of UETA and its applicability to real estate transactions, see the article *Electronic Signatures and Documents* from the 2014-2015 *General Update* course materials available on the Commission's website under Publications at www.ncrec.gov.

14.   The legal and practical issues revolving around e-mail transmissions and electronic signatures are addressed in Chapter 10, Basic Contract Law. Standard Form 2-T states in paragraph 21 that any action related to the transaction, including signatures, may be done electronically.

15.   There is no North Carolina appellate decision directly on point, but precedent in analogous fact situations clearly reinforce this conclusion. See, for example, the landmark case of *Yaggy v. BVD Company,* 7 N.C. App. 590, 173 S.E.2d 496 (1970). See also the North Carolina Uniform Electronic Transactions Act ("UETA"), N.C. Gen. Stat. §66-323 *et. seq.*

16.   See, for example, a 2001 Massachusetts court decision, *Shattuck v. Klotzback,* 14 Mass.L.Rptr. 360, 2001 WL 1839720 (Mass.Super., 2001), a case where a prospective purchaser of a 1.8 million dollar home sued to enforce a contract to convey based upon an exchange of e-mail. The seller moved to dismiss, arguing that the electronic communications did not satisfy the Statute of Frauds because they were not signed. Other legal defenses were also raised by the seller. The court correctly denied the seller's motion to dismiss and held that an e-mail signature deliberately typed at the end of an e-mail message can be sufficient to satisfy the Statute of Frauds. Likewise, other essential terms of a sales contract could be contained in an e-mail message. The court's decision is consistent with legal precedent dealing with other forms of electronic communication, including the telegraph. It predates federal and state legislation dealing with electronic documents and signatures that would now deal favorably with the same fact situation.

17.   *Manecke v. Kurtz,* _____ NC App. _____, 731 S.E.2d 217 (2012). In this case, the buyers (residents of New Jersey) signed an offer to purchase the seller's property in North Carolina and their North

Carolina buyer's agent emailed it to the listing agent. The seller increased the price and added a repair allowance, signed the counteroffer and the listing agent emailed it to the buyer agent who forwarded it to the buyers. The buyers' agent replied via email to the listing agent that the buyers "…were excited about their new home and agree to the counteroffer…." The next day the buyer agent emailed a copy of the earnest money check to the listing agent and commented that he "should have the initialed changes to the contract tomorrow." The buyers ultimately never signed the counteroffer and the sellers sued for specific performance (pre-2011 Standard Form 2-T) based on the buyer agent's statement that the buyers agreed to the counteroffer. The Court of Appeals affirmed the trial court's ruling in buyers' favor, stating that the general rule is: "A real estate agent in North Carolina, absent special authority, does not have the power to bind his principal in a contract to convey real property." In this case, the buyer agent had neither the actual nor apparent authority to bind his principals and since the buyers never accepted the counteroffer in writing per the Statute of Frauds, there was no contract.

18. *Lamberth v. McDaniel*, 131 N.C. App. 319, 506 S.E.2d 295 (1998).

19. *Parkersmith Properties v. Johnson*, 136 N.C. App. 626, 525 S.E.2d 491 (2000). In this case, the North Carolina Court of Appeals held that non-assignment clauses in installment land contracts are not void as against public policy.

20. *McLamb v. T.P. Inc.*, 173 N.C. App. 586, 619 S.E.2d 577 (2005).

21. While most options are for relatively brief periods of time, they can be created to be effective for much longer periods of time. Free standing options to purchase, called "options in gross," become invalid if they are not exercised within 30 years after creation. N.C.Gen.Stat. § 41-29. Options that are part of lease agreements and options relating to oil, gas or mineral rights are not subject to this 30-year rule.

22. *Kidd v. Early*, 289 N.C. 343, 222 S.E.2d 392 (1976). See also, Christopher, *"Options to Purchase Real Property in North Carolina,"* 44 N.C. L. Rev. 63 (1966).

23. It is possible for the parties to agree to establish a price based on a report by one or more appraisers or some other objective basis. Complicated price terms should be avoided. If they are deemed necessary by the parties, an experienced real estate attorney should draft them.

24. See *Chapel Hill Cinemas, Inc. v. Robbins*, 143 N.C.App. 571, 547 S.E.2d 462 (2001), *reversed on other grounds in* 354 N.C. 349, 554 S.E.2d 644 (2001), where the lessor/owner of property conveyed it to a third person without honoring the terms of a valid right of first refusal held by a lessee. The holder of the right of first refusal was awarded substantial damages for the lessor/owner's breach of the agreement.

25. Free standing rights of first refusal or preemptive rights (referred to as being "in gross") become invalid if they are not exercised within 30 years after creation. N.C.Gen.Stat. § 41-29. Rights of first refusal (preemptive rights) that are part of lease agreements or those relating to oil, gas or mineral rights are not subject to this 30-year rule.

OFFER TO PURCHASE AND CONTRACT
[Consult "Guidelines" (Form 2G) for guidance in completing this form]

For valuable consideration, the receipt and legal sufficiency of which are hereby acknowledged, Buyer offers to purchase and Seller upon acceptance agrees to sell and convey the Property on the terms and conditions of this Offer To Purchase and Contract and any addendum or modification made in accordance with its terms (together the "Contract").

1. **TERMS AND DEFINITIONS**: The terms listed below shall have the respective meaning given them as set forth adjacent to each term.

　　(a) "**Seller**": _____

　　(b) "**Buyer**": _____

　　(c) "**Property**": The Property shall include all that real estate described below together with all appurtenances thereto including the improvements located thereon and the fixtures and personal property listed in Paragraphs 2 and 3 below.

> **NOTE**: If the Property will include a manufactured (mobile) home(s), Buyer and Seller should consider including the Manufactured (Mobile) Home provision in the Additional Provisions Addendum (Standard Form 2A11-T) with this offer.

Street Address: _____
City:_____　　Zip:_____
County: _____, North Carolina

> **NOTE**: Governmental authority over taxes, zoning, school districts, utilities and mail delivery may differ from address shown.

Legal Description: (Complete *ALL* applicable)
Plat Reference: Lot/Unit_____, Block/Section _____, Subdivision/Condominium _____
_____, as shown on Plat Book/Slide _____ at Page(s) _____
The PIN/PID or other identification number of the Property is: _____
Other description: _____
Some or all of the Property may be described in Deed Book _____ at Page _____

(d) "**Purchase Price**":

$ _____　paid in U.S. Dollars upon the following terms:
$ _____　BY DUE DILIGENCE FEE made payable and delivered to Seller by the Effective Date
$ _____　BY INITIAL EARNEST MONEY DEPOSIT made payable and delivered to Escrow Agent named in Paragraph 1(f) by ❑ cash ❑ personal check ❑ official bank check ❑ wire transfer, ❑ electronic transfer, EITHER ❑ with this offer OR ❑ within five (5) days of the Effective Date of this Contract.
$ _____　BY (ADDITIONAL) EARNEST MONEY DEPOSIT made payable and delivered to Escrow Agent named in Paragraph 1(f) by cash, official bank check, wire transfer or electronic　　　　transfer　　　　no　　　　later　　　　than _____, *TIME*
　　　　　　　　　　　　　　　　BEING OF THE ESSENCE with regard to said date.
$ _____　BY ASSUMPTION of the unpaid principal balance and all obligations of Seller on the existing loan(s) secured by a deed of trust on the Property in accordance with the attached Loan Assumption Addendum (Standard Form 2A6-T).
$ _____　BY SELLER FINANCING in accordance with the attached Seller Financing Addendum (Standard Form 2A5-T).
$ _____　BY BUILDING DEPOSIT in accordance with the attached New Construction Addendum (Standard Form 2A3-T).
$ _____　BALANCE of the Purchase Price in cash at Settlement (some or all of which may be paid with the proceeds of a new loan)

Should Buyer fail to deliver either the Due Diligence Fee or any Initial Earnest Money Deposit by their due dates, or should any check or other funds paid by Buyer be dishonored, for any reason, by the institution upon which the payment is drawn, Buyer shall

Page 1 of 13

This form jointly approved by:
North Carolina Bar Association
North Carolina Association of REALTORS®, Inc.

REALTOR®

EQUAL HOUSING OPPORTUNITY

STANDARD FORM 2-T
Revised 7/2017
© 7/2017

Buyer initials _____ _____　　Seller initials _____ _____

Figure 11-1

have one (1) banking day after written notice to deliver cash, official bank check, wire transfer or electronic transfer to the payee. In the event Buyer does not timely deliver the required funds, Seller shall have the right to terminate this Contract upon written notice to Buyer.

(e) "**Earnest Money Deposit**": The Initial Earnest Money Deposit, the Additional Earnest Money Deposit and any other earnest monies paid or required to be paid in connection with this transaction, collectively the"Earnest Money Deposit", shall be deposited and held in escrow by Escrow Agent until Closing, at which time it will be credited to Buyer, or until this Contract is otherwise terminated. In the event: (1) this offer is not accepted; or (2) a condition of any resulting contract is not satisfied, then the Earnest Money Deposit shall be refunded to Buyer. In the event of breach of this Contract by Seller, the Earnest Money Deposit shall be refunded to Buyer upon Buyer's request, but such return shall not affect any other remedies available to Buyer for such breach. In the event of breach of this Contract by Buyer, the Earnest Money Deposit shall be paid to Seller as liquidated damages and as Seller's sole and exclusive remedy for such breach, but without limiting Seller's rights under Paragraphs 4(d) and 4(e) for damage to the Property or Seller's right to retain the Due Diligence Fee. It is acknowledged by the parties that payment of the Earnest Money Deposit to Seller in the event of a breach of this Contract by Buyer is compensatory and not punitive, such amount being a reasonable estimation of the actual loss that Seller would incur as a result of such breach. The payment of the Earnest Money Deposit to Seller shall not constitute a penalty or forfeiture but actual compensation for Seller's anticipated loss, both parties acknowledging the difficulty determining Seller's actual damages for such breach. If legal proceedings are brought by Buyer or Seller against the other to recover the Earnest Money Deposit, the prevailing party in the proceeding shall be entitled to recover from the non-prevailing party reasonable attorney fees and court costs incurred in connection with the proceeding.

(f) "**Escrow Agent**" (insert name): _____

> **NOTE**: In the event of a dispute between Seller and Buyer over the disposition of the Earnest Money Deposit held in escrow, a licensed real estate broker ("Broker") is required by state law (and Escrow Agent, if not a Broker, hereby agrees) to retain the Earnest Money Deposit in the Escrow Agent's trust or escrow account until Escrow Agent has obtained a written release from the parties consenting to its disposition or until disbursement is ordered by a court of competent jurisdiction. Alternatively, if a Broker or an attorney licensed to practice law in North Carolina ("Attorney") is holding the Earnest Money Deposit, the Broker or Attorney may deposit the disputed monies with the appropriate clerk of court in accordance with the provisions of N.C.G.S. §93A-12.

THE PARTIES AGREE THAT A REAL ESTATE BROKERAGE FIRM ACTING AS ESCROW AGENT MAY PLACE THE EARNEST MONEY DEPOSIT IN AN INTEREST BEARING TRUST ACCOUNT AND THAT ANY INTEREST EARNED THEREON SHALL BE DISBURSED TO THE ESCROW AGENT MONTHLY IN CONSIDERATION OF THE EXPENSES INCURRED BY MAINTAINING SUCH ACCOUNT AND RECORDS ASSOCIATED THEREWITH.

(g) "**Effective Date**": The date that: (1) the last one of Buyer and Seller has signed or initialed this offer or the final counteroffer, if any, and (2) such signing or initialing is communicated to the party making the offer or counteroffer, as the case may be. The parties acknowledge and agree that the initials lines at the bottom of each page of this Contract are merely evidence of their having reviewed the terms of each page, and that the complete execution of such initials lines shall not be a condition of the effectiveness of this Agreement.

(h) "**Due Diligence**": Buyer's opportunity to investigate the Property and the transaction contemplated by this Contract, including but not necessarily limited to the matters described in Paragraph 4 below, to decide whether Buyer, in Buyer's sole discretion, will proceed with or terminate the transaction.

(i) "**Due Diligence Fee**": A negotiated amount, if any, paid by Buyer to Seller with this Contract for Buyer's right to terminate the Contract for any reason or no reason during the Due Diligence Period. It shall be the property of Seller upon the Effective Date and shall be a credit to Buyer at Closing. The Due Diligence Fee shall be non-refundable except in the event of a material breach of this Contract by Seller, or if this Contract is terminated under Paragraph 8(n) or Paragraph 12, or as otherwise provided in any addendum hereto. Buyer and Seller each expressly waive any right that they may have to deny the right to conduct Due Diligence or to assert any defense as to the enforceability of this Contract based on the absence or alleged insufficiency of any Due Diligence Fee, it being the intent of the parties to create a legally binding contract for the purchase and sale of the Property without regard to the existence or amount of any Due Diligence Fee.

(j) "**Due Diligence Period**": The period beginning on the Effective Date and extending through 5:00 p.m. on _____
_____ *TIME BEING OF THE ESSENCE* with regard to said date.

(k) "**Settlement**": The proper execution and delivery to the closing attorney of all documents necessary to complete the transaction contemplated by this Contract, including the deed, settlement statement, deed of trust and other loan or conveyance documents, and the closing attorney's receipt of all funds necessary to complete such transaction.

Page 2 of 13

Buyer's Initials _____ _____ Seller's Initials _____ _____

Figure 11-1

(l) **"Settlement Date":** The parties agree that Settlement will take place on _____
_____(the "Settlement Date"), unless otherwise agreed in writing, at a time and place designated by Buyer.

(m) **"Closing":** The completion of the legal process which results in the transfer of title to the Property from Seller to Buyer, which includes the following steps: (1) the Settlement (defined above); (2) the completion of a satisfactory title update to the Property following the Settlement; (3) the closing attorney's receipt of authorization to disburse all necessary funds; and (4) recordation in the appropriate county registry of the deed(s) and deed(s) of trust, if any, which shall take place as soon as reasonably possible for the closing attorney after Settlement. Upon Closing, the proceeds of sale shall be disbursed by the closing attorney in accordance with the settlement statement and the provisions of Chapter 45A of the North Carolina General Statutes. If the title update should reveal unexpected liens, encumbrances or other title defects, or if the closing attorney is not authorized to disburse all necessary funds, then the Closing shall be suspended and the Settlement deemed delayed under Paragraph 13 (Delay in Settlement/Closing).

> **WARNING:** The North Carolina State Bar has determined that the performance of most acts and services required for a closing constitutes the practice of law and must be performed only by an attorney licensed to practice law in North Carolina. State law prohibits unlicensed individuals or firms from rendering legal services or advice. Although non-attorney settlement agents may perform limited services in connection with a closing, they may not perform all the acts and services required to complete a closing. A closing involves significant legal issues that should be handled by an attorney. Accordingly it is the position of the North Carolina Bar Association and the North Carolina Association of REALTORS® that all buyers should hire an attorney licensed in North Carolina to perform a closing.

(n) **"Special Assessments":** A charge against the Property by a governmental authority in addition to ad valorem taxes and recurring governmental service fees levied with such taxes, or by an owners' association in addition to any regular assessment (dues), either of which may be a lien against the Property. A Special Assessment may be either proposed or confirmed.

"Proposed Special Assessment": A Special Assessment that is under formal consideration but which has not been approved prior to Settlement.

"Confirmed Special Assessment": A Special Assessment that has been approved prior to Settlement whether or not it is fully payable at time of Settlement.

2. FIXTURES AND EXCLUSIONS:

(a) **Specified Items:** Unless identified in subparagraph (d) below, the following items, including all related equipment and remote control devices, if any, are deemed fixtures and shall convey, included in the Purchase Price free of liens:

- Alarm and security systems (attached) for security, fire, smoke, carbon monoxide or other toxins with all related access codes, sensors, cameras, dedicated monitors, hard drives, video recorders, power supplies and cables; doorbells/chimes
- All stoves/ranges/ovens; built-in appliances; attached microwave oven; vent hood
- Antennas; satellite dishes and receivers
- Basketball goals and play equipment (permanently attached or in-ground)
- Ceiling and wall-attached fans; light fixtures (including existing bulbs)
- Fireplace insert; gas logs or starters; attached fireplace screens; wood or coal stoves
- Floor coverings (attached)
- Fuel tank(s) whether attached or buried and including any contents that have not been used, removed or resold to the fuel provider as of Settlement. **NOTE:** Seller's use, removal or resale of fuel in any fuel tank is subject to Seller's obligation under Paragraph 8(c) to provide working, existing utilities through the earlier of Closing or possession by Buyer.
- Garage door openers with all controls

- Generators that are permanently wired
- Invisible fencing with power supply, controls and receivers
- Landscape and outdoor trees and plants (except in moveable containers); raised garden; landscape and foundation lighting; outdoor sound systems; permanent irrigation systems and controls; rain barrels; landscape water features; address markers
- Mailboxes; mounted package and newspaper receptacles
- Mirrors attached to walls, ceilings, cabinets or doors; all bathroom wall mirrors
- Storage shed; utility building
- Swimming pool (excluding inflatable); spa; hot tub
- Solar electric and solar water heating systems
- Sump-pumps, radon fans and crawlspace ventilators; de-humidifiers that are permanently wired
- Surface-mounting brackets for television and speakers; recess-mounted speakers; mounted intercom system
- Water supply equipment, including filters, conditioning and softener systems; re-circulating pumps; well pumps and tanks
- Window/Door blinds and shades, curtain and drapery rods and brackets, door and window screens and combination doors, awnings and storm windows

Page 3 of 13

STANDARD FORM 2-T
Revised 7/2017
© 7/2017

Buyer's Initials _____ _____   Seller's Initials _____ _____

Figure 11-1

(b) **Items Leased or Not Owned:** Any item which is leased or not owned by Seller, such as fuel tanks, antennas, satellite dishes and receivers, appliances, and alarm and security systems must be identified here and shall not convey:

_____
_____
_____

(c) **Other Fixtures/Unspecified items:** Unless identified in subparagraph (d) below, any other item legally considered a fixture is included in the Purchase Price free of liens.

(d) **Other Items That Do Not Convey:** The following items shall not convey (*identify those items to be excluded under subparagraphs (a) and (c)*): _____
_____.

Seller shall repair any damage caused by removal of any items excluded above.

3. **PERSONAL PROPERTY:** The following personal property shall be transferred to Buyer at no value at closing:_____
_____.

> **NOTE:** Buyer is advised to consult with Buyer's lender to assure that the Personal Property items listed above can be included in this Contract.

4. **BUYER'S DUE DILIGENCE PROCESS:** WARNING: **BUYER IS STRONGLY ENCOURAGED TO CONDUCT DUE DILIGENCE DURING THE DUE DILIGENCE PERIOD.** If Buyer is not satisfied with the results or progress of Buyer's Due Diligence, Buyer should terminate this Contract, PRIOR TO THE EXPIRATION OF THE DUE DILIGENCE PERIOD, unless Buyer can obtain a written extension from Seller. SELLER IS NOT OBLIGATED TO GRANT AN EXTENSION. Although Buyer may continue to investigate the Property following the expiration of the Due Diligence Period, Buyer's failure to deliver a Termination Notice to Seller prior to the expiration of the Due Diligence Period will constitute a waiver by Buyer of any right to terminate this Contract based on any matter relating to Buyer's Due Diligence. Provided however, following the Due Diligence Period, Buyer may still exercise a right to terminate if Seller fails to materially comply with any of Seller's obligations under Paragraph 8 of this Contract or for any other reason permitted under the terms of this Contract or North Carolina law.
    (a) **Loan:** Buyer, at Buyer's expense, shall be entitled to pursue qualification for and approval of the Loan if any.

> **NOTE:** Buyer's obligation to purchase the Property is not contingent on obtaining a Loan. Therefore, Buyer is advised to consult with Buyer's lender prior to signing this offer to assure that the Due Diligence Period allows sufficient time for the appraisal to be completed and for Buyer's lender to provide Buyer sufficient information to decide whether to proceed with or terminate the transaction.

    (b) **Property Investigation**: Buyer or Buyer's agents or representatives, at Buyer's expense, shall be entitled to conduct all desired tests, surveys, appraisals, investigations, examinations and inspections of the Property as Buyer deems appropriate, including but NOT limited to the following:
        (i) **Inspections**: Inspections to determine the condition of any improvements on the Property, the presence of unusual drainage conditions or evidence of excessive moisture adversely affecting any improvements on the Property, the presence of asbestos or existing environmental contamination, evidence of wood-destroying insects or damage therefrom, and the presence and level of radon gas on the Property.
        (ii) **Review of Documents**: Review of the Declaration of Restrictive Covenants, Bylaws, Articles of Incorporation, Rules and Regulations, and other governing documents of any applicable owners' association and/or subdivision. If the Property is subject to regulation by an owners' association, it is recommended that Buyer review the completed Residential Property and Owners' Association Disclosure Statement provided by Seller prior to signing this offer. It is also recommended that the Buyer determine if the owners' association or its management company charges fees for providing information required by Buyer's lender or confirming restrictive covenant compliance.
        (iii) **Insurance**: Investigation of the availability and cost of insurance for the Property.
        (iv) **Appraisals**: An appraisal of the Property.
        (v) **Survey**: A survey to determine whether the property is suitable for Buyer's intended use and the location of easements, setbacks, property boundaries and other issues which may or may not constitute title defects.
        (vi) **Zoning and Governmental Regulation**: Investigation of current or proposed zoning or other governmental regulation that may affect Buyer's intended use of the Property, adjacent land uses, planned or proposed road construction, and school attendance zones.
        (vii) **Flood Hazard**: Investigation of potential flood hazards on the Property, and/or any requirement to purchase flood insurance in order to obtain the Loan.

Page 4 of 13

Buyer's Initials _____ _____ Seller's Initials _____ _____

Figure 11-1

(viii) **Utilities and Access**: Availability, quality, and obligations for maintenance of utilities including water, sewer, electric, gas, communication services, stormwater management, and means of access to the Property and amenities.

(ix) **Streets/Roads**: Investigation of the status of the street/road upon which the Property fronts as well as any other street/road used to access the Property, including: (1) whether any street(s)/road(s) are public or private, (2) whether any street(s)/road(s) designated as public are accepted for maintenance by the State of NC or any municipality, or (3) if private or not accepted for public maintenance, the consequences and responsibility for maintenance and the existence, terms and funding of any maintenance agreements.

(x) **Fuel Tank**: Inspections to determine the existence, type and ownership of any fuel tank located on the Property.

> **NOTE:** Buyer is advised to consult with the owner of any leased fuel tank regarding the terms under which Buyer may lease the tank and obtain fuel.

(c) **Repair/Improvement Negotiations/Agreement**: Buyer acknowledges and understands that unless the parties agree otherwise, THE PROPERTY IS BEING SOLD IN ITS CURRENT CONDITION. Buyer and Seller acknowledge and understand that they may, but are not required to, engage in negotiations for repairs/improvements to the Property. Buyer is advised to make any repair/improvement requests in sufficient time to allow repair/improvement negotiations to be concluded prior to the expiration of the Due Diligence Period. Any agreement that the parties may reach with respect to repairs/improvements shall be considered an obligation of the parties and is an addition to this Contract and as such, must be in writing and signed by the parties in accordance with Paragraph 20.

> **NOTE:** See Paragraph 8(c), Access to Property and Paragraph 8(m), Negotiated Repairs/Improvements.

(d) **Buyer's Obligation to Repair Damage**: Buyer shall, at Buyer's expense, promptly repair any damage to the Property resulting from any activities of Buyer and Buyer's agents and contractors, but Buyer shall not be responsible for any damage caused by accepted practices either approved by the N.C. Home Inspector Licensure Board or applicable to any other N.C. licensed professional performing reasonable appraisals, tests, surveys, examinations and inspections of the Property. This repair obligation shall survive any termination of this Contract.

(e) **Indemnity**: Buyer will indemnify and hold Seller harmless from all loss, damage, claims, suits or costs, which shall arise out of any contract, agreement, or injury to any person or property as a result of any activities of Buyer and Buyer's agents and contractors relating to the Property except for any loss, damage, claim, suit or cost arising out of pre-existing conditions of the Property and/or out of Seller's negligence or willful acts or omissions. This indemnity shall survive this Contract and any termination hereof.

(f) **Buyer's Right to Terminate**: Buyer shall have the right to terminate this Contract for any reason or no reason, by delivering to Seller written notice of termination (the "Termination Notice") during the Due Diligence Period (or any agreed-upon written extension of the Due Diligence Period), ***TIME BEING OF THE ESSENCE***. If Buyer timely delivers the Termination Notice, this Contract shall be terminated and the Earnest Money Deposit shall be refunded to Buyer.

(g) **CLOSING SHALL CONSTITUTE ACCEPTANCE OF THE PROPERTY IN ITS THEN EXISTING CONDITION UNLESS PROVISION IS OTHERWISE MADE IN WRITING.**

5. **BUYER REPRESENTATIONS**:

(a) **Loan**: Buyer ❑ does ❑ does not intend to obtain a new loan in order to purchase the Property. If Buyer is obtaining a new loan, Buyer intends to obtain a loan as follows: ❑ FHA ❑ VA (attach FHA/VA Financing Addendum) ❑ Conventional ❑ Other: _____ loan at a ❑ Fixed Rate ❑ Adjustable Rate in the principal amount of _____ plus any financed VA Funding Fee or FHA MIP for a term of _____ year(s), at an initial interest rate not to exceed _____ % per annum (the "Loan").

> **NOTE:** Buyer's obligations under this Contract are not conditioned upon obtaining or closing any loan.

> **NOTE:** If Buyer does not intend to obtain a new loan, Seller is advised, prior to signing this offer, to obtain documentation from Buyer which demonstrates that Buyer will be able to close on the Property without the necessity of obtaining a new loan.

(b) **Other Property**: Buyer ❑ does ❑ does not have to sell or lease other real property in order to qualify for a new loan or to complete the purchase.

> **NOTE:** This Contract is not conditioned upon the sale of Buyer's property unless a contingent sale addendum such as Standard Form 2A2-T is made a part of this Contract.

(c) **Performance of Buyer's Financial Obligations**: To the best of Buyer's knowledge, there are no other circumstances or conditions existing as of the date of this offer that would prohibit Buyer from performing Buyer's financial obligations in accordance with this Contract, except as may be specifically set forth herein.

STANDARD FORM 2-T
Revised 7/2017
© 7/2017

Buyer's Initials _____ _____   Seller's Initials _____ _____

Figure 11-1

(d) **Residential Property and Owners' Association Disclosure Statement** (*check only one*):
❑ Buyer has received a signed copy of the N.C. Residential Property and Owners' Association Disclosure Statement prior to the signing of this offer.
❑ Buyer has NOT received a signed copy of the N.C. Residential Property and Owners' Association Disclosure Statement prior to the signing of this offer and shall have the right to terminate or withdraw this Contract without penalty (including a refund of any Due Diligence Fee) prior to WHICHEVER OF THE FOLLOWING EVENTS OCCURS FIRST: (1) the end of the third calendar day following receipt of the Disclosure Statement; (2) the end of the third calendar day following the Effective Date; or (3) Settlement or occupancy by Buyer in the case of a sale or exchange.
❑ Exempt from N.C. Residential Property and Owners' Association Disclosure Statement because (SEE GUIDELINES):_____
_____.

(e) **Mineral and Oil and Gas Rights Mandatory Disclosure Statement** (*check only one*):
❑ Buyer has received a signed copy of the N.C. Mineral and Oil and Gas Rights Mandatory Disclosure Statement prior to the signing of this offer.
❑ Buyer has NOT received a signed copy of the N.C. Mineral and Oil and Gas Rights Mandatory Disclosure Statement prior to the signing of this offer and shall have the right to terminate or withdraw this Contract without penalty (including a refund of any Due Diligence Fee) prior to WHICHEVER OF THE FOLLOWING EVENTS OCCURS FIRST: (1) the end of the third calendar day following receipt of the Disclosure Statement; (2) the end of the third calendar day following the Effective Date; or (3) Settlement or occupancy by Buyer in the case of a sale or exchange.
❑ Exempt from N.C. Mineral and Oil and Gas Rights Mandatory Disclosure Statement because (SEE GUIDELINES): _____
_____.

Buyer's receipt of a Mineral and Oil and Gas Rights Mandatory Disclosure Statement does not modify or limit the obligations of Seller under Paragraph 8(g) of this Contract and shall not constitute the assumption or approval by Buyer of any severance of mineral and/or oil and gas rights, except as may be assumed or specifically approved by Buyer in writing.

> **NOTE**: The parties are advised to consult with a NC attorney prior to signing this Contract if severance of mineral and/or oil and gas rights has occurred or is intended.

6. **BUYER OBLIGATIONS**:
   (a) **Responsibility for Proposed Special Assessments**: Buyer shall take title subject to all Proposed Special Assessments.
   (b) **Responsibility for Certain Costs**: Buyer shall be responsible for all costs with respect to:
   (i) any loan obtained by Buyer, including charges by an owners association and/or management company as agent of an owners' association for providing information required by Buyer's lender;
   (ii) charges required by an owners' association declaration to be paid by Buyer for Buyer's future use and enjoyment of the Property, including, without limitation, working capital contributions, membership fees, or charges for Buyer's use of the common elements and/or services provided to Buyer, such as "move-in fees";
   (iii) determining restrictive covenant compliance;
   (iv) appraisal;
   (v) title search;
   (vi) title insurance;
   (vii) any fees charged by the closing attorney for the preparation of the Closing Disclosure, Seller Disclosure and any other settlement statement;
   (viii) recording the deed; and
   (ix) preparation and recording of all instruments required to secure the balance of the Purchase Price unpaid at Settlement.
   (c) **Authorization to Disclose Information**: Buyer authorizes the Buyer's lender(s), the parties' real estate agent(s) and closing attorney: (1) to provide this Contract to any appraiser employed by Buyer or by Buyer's lender(s); and (2) to release and disclose any buyer's closing disclosure, settlement statement and/or disbursement summary, or any information therein, to the parties to this transaction, their real estate agent(s) and Buyer's lender(s).

7. **SELLER REPRESENTATIONS**:
   (a) **Ownership**: Seller represents that Seller:
   ❑ has owned the Property for at least one year.
   ❑ has owned the Property for less than one year.
   ❑ does not yet own the Property.

   (b) **Lead-Based Paint** (*check if applicable*):
   ❑ The Property is residential and was built prior to 1978 (Attach Lead-Based Paint or Lead-Based Paint Hazards Disclosure Addendum {Standard Form 2A9-T}).

STANDARD FORM 2-T
Revised 7/2017
© 7/2017

Buyer's Initials _____ _____   Seller's Initials _____ _____

Figure 11-1

(c) **Assessments**: To the best of Seller's knowledge there are no Proposed Special Assessments except as follows (Insert "None" or the identification of such assessments, if any): _____ .

Seller warrants that there are no Confirmed Special Assessments except as follows (Insert "None" or the identification of such assessments, if any): _____ .

(d) **Owners' Association(s) and Dues**: Seller authorizes and directs any owners' association, any management company of the owners' association, any insurance company and any attorney who has previously represented the Seller to release to Buyer, Buyer's agents, representative, closing attorney or lender true and accurate copies of the following items affecting the Property, including any amendments:

- Seller's statement of account
- master insurance policy showing the coverage provided and the deductible amount
- Declaration and Restrictive Covenants
- Rules and Regulations
- Articles of Incorporation
- Bylaws of the owners' association
- current financial statement and budget of the owners' association
- parking restrictions and information
- architectural guidelines

❑ (specify name of association): _____ whose regular assessments ("dues") are $_____ per_____. The name, address and telephone number of the president of the owners' association or the association manager is: _____
_____ .
Owners' association website address, if any: _____

❑ (specify name of association): _____ whose regular assessments ("dues") are $_____ per_____. The name, address and telephone number of the president of the owners' association or the association manager is: _____
_____ .
Owners' association website address, if any _____

8. **SELLER OBLIGATIONS**:
   (a) **Evidence of Title, Payoff Statement(s) and Non Foreign Status**:
   (i) Seller agrees to use best efforts to provide to the closing attorney as soon as reasonably possible after the Effective Date, copies of all title information in possession of or available to Seller, including but not limited to: title insurance policies, attorney's opinions on title, surveys, covenants, deeds, notes and deeds of trust, leases, and easements relating to the Property.
   (ii) Seller shall provide to the closing attorney all information needed to obtain a written payoff statement from any lender(s) regarding any security interest in the Property as soon as reasonably possible after the Effective Date, and Seller designates the closing attorney as Seller's agent with express authority to request and obtain on Seller's behalf payoff statements and/or short-pay statements from any such lender(s).
   (iii) If Seller is not a foreign person as defined by the Foreign Investment in Real Property Tax Act, Seller shall also provide to the closing attorney a non-foreign status affidavit (pursuant to the Foreign Investment in Real Property Tax Act). In the event Seller shall not provide a non-foreign status affidavit, Seller acknowledges that there may be withholding as provided by the Internal Revenue Code.

   (b) **Authorization to Disclose Information**: Seller authorizes: (1) any attorney presently or previously representing Seller to release and disclose any title insurance policy in such attorney's file to Buyer and both Buyer's and Seller's agents and attorneys; (2) the Property's title insurer or its agent to release and disclose all materials in the Property's title insurer's (or title insurer's agent's) file to Buyer and both Buyer's and Seller's agents and attorneys and (3) the closing attorney to release and disclose any seller's closing disclosure, settlement statement and/or disbursement summary, or any information therein, to the parties to this transaction, their real estate agent(s) and Buyer's lender(s).

   (c) **Access to Property**: Seller shall provide reasonable access to the Property (including working, existing utilities) through the earlier of Closing or possession by Buyer, including, but not limited to, allowing Buyer and/or Buyer's agents or representatives, an opportunity to (i) conduct Due Diligence, (ii) verify the satisfactory completion of negotiated repairs/improvements, and (iii) conduct a final walk-through inspection of the Property.

Buyer's Initials _____ _____ Seller's Initials _____ _____

STANDARD FORM 2-T
Revised 7/2017
© 7/2017

Figure 11-1

NOTE: See WARNING in paragraph 4 above for limitation on Buyer's right to terminate this Contract as a result of Buyer's continued investigation of the Property following the expiration of the Due Diligence Period.

(d) **Removal of Seller's Property**: Seller shall remove, by the date possession is made available to Buyer, all personal property which is not a part of the purchase and all garbage and debris from the Property.

(e) **Affidavit and Indemnification Agreement**: Seller shall furnish at Settlement an affidavit(s) and indemnification agreement(s) in form satisfactory to Buyer and Buyer's title insurer, if any, executed by Seller and any person or entity who has performed or furnished labor, services, materials or rental equipment to the Property within 120 days prior to the date of Settlement and who may be entitled to claim a lien against the Property as described in N.C.G.S. §44A-8 verifying that each such person or entity has been paid in full and agreeing to indemnify Buyer, Buyer's lender(s) and Buyer's title insurer against all loss from any cause or claim arising therefrom.

(f) **Designation of Lien Agent, Payment and Satisfaction of Liens**: If required by N.C.G.S. §44A-11.1, Seller shall have designated a Lien Agent, and Seller shall deliver to Buyer as soon as reasonably possible a copy of the appointment of Lien Agent. All deeds of trust, deferred ad valorem taxes, liens and other charges against the Property, not assumed by Buyer, must be paid and satisfied by Seller prior to or at Settlement such that cancellation may be promptly obtained following Closing. Seller shall remain obligated to obtain any such cancellations following Closing.

(g) **Good Title, Legal Access**: Seller shall execute and deliver a GENERAL WARRANTY DEED for the Property in recordable form no later than Settlement, which shall convey fee simple marketable and insurable title, without exception for mechanics' liens, and free of any other liens, encumbrances or defects, including those which would be revealed by a current and accurate survey of the Property, except: ad valorem taxes for the current year (prorated through the date of Settlement); utility easements and unviolated covenants, conditions or restrictions that do not materially affect the value of the Property; and such other liens, encumbrances or defects as may be assumed or specifically approved by Buyer in writing. The Property must have legal access to a public right of way.

NOTE: Buyer's failure to conduct a survey or examine title of the Property, prior to the expiration of the Due Diligence Period does not relieve the Seller of their obligation to deliver good title under this paragraph.

NOTE: If any sale of the Property may be a "short sale," consideration should be given to attaching a Short Sale Addendum (Standard Form 2A14-T) as an addendum to this Contract.

(h) **Deed, Taxes and Fees**: Seller shall pay for preparation of a deed and all other documents necessary to perform Seller's obligations under this Contract, and for state and county excise taxes, and any deferred, discounted or rollback taxes, and local conveyance fees required by law. The deed is to be made to: _____
_____.

(i) **Agreement to Pay Buyer Expenses**: Seller shall pay at Settlement $_____ toward any of Buyer's expenses associated with the purchase of the Property, at the discretion of Buyer and/or lender, if any, including any FHA/VA lender and inspection costs that Buyer is not permitted to pay.

NOTE: Parties should review the FHA/VA Addendum prior to entering an amount in Paragraph 8(i). Certain FHA/VA lender and inspection costs CANNOT be paid by Buyer at Settlement and the amount of these should be included in the blank above.

(j) **Owners' Association Fees/Charges**: Seller shall pay: (i) any fees required for confirming Seller's account payment information on owners' association dues or assessments for payment or proration; (ii) any fees imposed by an owners' association and/or a management company as agent of the owners' association in connection with the transaction contemplated by this Contract other than those fees required to be paid by Buyer under paragraph 6(b) above; and (iii) fees incurred by Seller in completing the Residential Property and Owners' Association Disclosure Statement, and resale or other certificates related to a proposed sale of the Property.

(k) **Payment of Confirmed Special Assessments**: Seller shall pay all Confirmed Special Assessments, if any, provided that the amount thereof can be reasonably determined or estimated. The payment of such estimated amount shall be the final payment between the Parties.

(l) **Late Listing Penalties**: All property tax late listing penalties, if any, shall be paid by Seller.

(m) **Negotiated Repairs/Improvements**: Negotiated repairs/improvements shall be made in a good and workmanlike manner and Buyer shall have the right to verify same prior to Settlement.

Page 8 of 13

Figure 11-1

(n) **Seller's Failure to Comply or Breach**: If Seller fails to materially comply with any of Seller's obligations under this Paragraph 8 or Seller materially breaches this Contract, and Buyer elects to terminate this Contract as a result of such failure or breach, then the Earnest Money Deposit and the Due Diligence Fee shall be refunded to Buyer and Seller shall reimburse to Buyer the reasonable costs actually incurred by Buyer in connection with Buyer's Due Diligence without affecting any other remedies. If legal proceedings are brought by Buyer against Seller to recover the Earnest Money Deposit, the Due Diligence Fee and/or the reasonable costs actually incurred by Buyer in connection with Buyer's Due Diligence, the prevailing party in the proceeding shall be entitled to recover from the non-prevailing party reasonable attorney fees and court costs incurred in connection with the proceeding.

9. **PRORATIONS AND ADJUSTMENTS**: Unless otherwise provided, the following items shall be prorated through the date of Settlement and either adjusted between the parties or paid at Settlement:
(a) **Taxes on Real Property:** Ad valorem taxes and recurring governmental service fees levied with such taxes on real property shall be prorated on a calendar year basis;
(b) **Taxes on Personal Property:** Ad valorem taxes on personal property for the entire year shall be paid by Seller unless the personal property is conveyed to Buyer, in which case, the personal property taxes shall be prorated on a calendar year basis;
(c) **Rents**: Rents, if any, for the Property;
(d) **Dues**: Owners' association regular assessments (dues) and other like charges.

10. **HOME WARRANTY**: Select one of the following:
❑ No home warranty is to be provided by Seller.
❑ Buyer may obtain a one-year home warranty at a cost not to exceed $_____ which includes sales tax and Seller agrees to pay for it at Settlement.
❑ Seller has obtained and will provide a one-year home warranty from _____
at a cost of $ _____ which includes sales tax and will pay for it at Settlement.

> **NOTE:** Home warranties typically have limitations on and conditions to coverage. Refer specific questions to the home warranty company.

11. **CONDITION OF PROPERTY AT CLOSING**: Buyer's obligation to complete the transaction contemplated by this Contract shall be contingent upon the Property being in substantially the same or better condition at Closing as on the date of this offer, reasonable wear and tear excepted.

12. **RISK OF LOSS**: The risk of loss or damage by fire or other casualty prior to Closing shall be upon Seller. If the improvements on the Property are destroyed or materially damaged prior to Closing, Buyer may terminate this Contract by written notice delivered to Seller or Seller's agent and the Earnest Money Deposit and any Due Diligence Fee shall be refunded to Buyer. In the event Buyer does NOT elect to terminate this Contract, Buyer shall be entitled to receive, in addition to the Property, any of Seller's insurance proceeds payable on account of the damage or destruction applicable to the Property being purchased. Seller is advised not to cancel existing insurance on the Property until after confirming recordation of the deed.

13. **DELAY IN SETTLEMENT/CLOSING**: Absent agreement to the contrary in this Contract or any subsequent modification thereto, if a party is unable to complete Settlement by the Settlement Date but intends to complete the transaction and is acting in good faith and with reasonable diligence to proceed to Settlement ("Delaying Party"), and if the other party is ready, willing and able to complete Settlement on the Settlement Date ("Non-Delaying Party") then the Delaying Party shall give as much notice as possible to the Non-Delaying Party and closing attorney and shall be entitled to a delay in Settlement. If the parties fail to complete Settlement and Closing within fourteen (14) days of the Settlement Date (including any amended Settlement Date agreed to in writing by the parties) or to otherwise extend the Settlement Date by written agreement, then the Delaying Party shall be in breach and the Non-Delaying Party may terminate this Contract and shall be entitled to enforce any remedies available to such party under this Contract for the breach.

14. **POSSESSION**: Possession, including all means of access to the Property (keys, codes including security codes, garage door openers, electronic devices, etc.), shall be delivered upon Closing as defined in Paragraph 1(m) unless otherwise provided below:
❑ A Buyer Possession Before Closing Agreement is attached (Standard Form 2A7-T)
❑ A Seller Possession After Closing Agreement is attached (Standard Form 2A8-T)
❑ Possession is subject to rights of tenant(s)

> **NOTE:** Consider attaching Additional Provisions Addendum (Form 2A11-T) or Vacation Rental Addendum (Form 2A13-T)

15. **ADDENDA:** CHECK ALL STANDARD ADDENDA THAT MAY BE A PART OF THIS CONTRACT, IF ANY, AND ATTACH HERETO. ITEMIZE ALL OTHER ADDENDA TO THIS CONTRACT, IF ANY, AND ATTACH HERETO.

❑ Additional Provisions Addendum (Form 2A11-T)   ❑ Loan Assumption Addendum (Form 2A6-T)
❑ Additional Signatures Addendum (Form 3-T)   ❑ New Construction Addendum (Form 2A3-T)

Buyer's Initials _____ _____   Seller's Initials _____ _____

STANDARD FORM 2-T
Revised 7/2017
© 7/2017

Figure 11-1

❑ Back-Up Contract Addendum (Form 2A1-T)
❑ Contingent Sale Addendum (Form 2A2-T)
❑ FHA/VA Financing Addendum (Form 2A4-T)
❑ Lead-Based Paint Or Lead-Based Paint Hazard Addendum (Form 2A9-T)

❑ Owners' Association Disclosure And Condominium Resale Statement Addendum (Form 2A12-T)
❑ Seller Financing Addendum (Form 2A5-T)
❑ Short Sale Addendum (Form 2A14-T)
❑ Vacation Rental Addendum (Form 2A13-T)

❑ Identify other attorney or party drafted addenda: _____

NOTE: UNDER NORTH CAROLINA LAW, REAL ESTATE BROKERS ARE NOT PERMITTED TO DRAFT ADDENDA TO THIS CONTRACT.

16. **ASSIGNMENTS**: This Contract may not be assigned without the written consent of all parties except in connection with a tax-deferred exchange, but if assigned by agreement, then this Contract shall be binding on the assignee and assignee's heirs and successors.

17. **TAX-DEFERRED EXCHANGE**: In the event Buyer or Seller desires to effect a tax-deferred exchange in connection with the conveyance of the Property, Buyer and Seller agree to cooperate in effecting such exchange; provided, however, that the exchanging party shall be responsible for all additional costs associated with such exchange, and provided further, that a non-exchanging party shall not assume any additional liability with respect to such tax-deferred exchange. Buyer and Seller shall execute such additional documents, including assignment of this Contract in connection therewith, at no cost to the non-exchanging party, as shall be required to give effect to this provision.

18. **PARTIES**: This Contract shall be binding upon and shall inure to the benefit of Buyer and Seller and their respective heirs, successors and assigns. As used herein, words in the singular include the plural and the masculine includes the feminine and neuter genders, as appropriate.

19. **SURVIVAL:** If any provision herein contained which by its nature and effect is required to be observed, kept or performed after the Closing, it shall survive the Closing and remain binding upon and for the benefit of the parties hereto until fully observed, kept or performed.

20. **ENTIRE AGREEMENT**: This Contract contains the entire agreement of the parties and there are no representations, inducements or other provisions other than those expressed herein. All changes, additions or deletions hereto must be in writing and signed by all parties. Nothing contained herein shall alter any agreement between a REALTOR® or broker and Seller or Buyer as contained in any listing agreement, buyer agency agreement, or any other agency agreement between them.

21. **CONDUCT OF TRANSACTION**: The parties agree that any action between them relating to the transaction contemplated by this Contract may be conducted by electronic means, including the signing of this Contract by one or more of them and any notice or communication given in connection with this Contract. Any written notice or communication may be transmitted to any mailing address, e-mail address or fax number set forth in the "Notice Information" section below. Any notice or communication to be given to a party herein, and any fee, deposit or other payment to be delivered to a party herein, may be given to the party or to such party's agent. Seller and Buyer agree that the "Notice Information" and "Acknowledgment of Receipt of Monies" sections below shall not constitute a material part of this Contract, and that the addition or modification of any information therein shall not constitute a rejection of an offer or the creation of a counteroffer.

22. **EXECUTION:** This Contract may be signed in multiple originals or counterparts, all of which together constitute one and the same instrument.

23. **COMPUTATION OF DAYS/TIME OF DAY**: Unless otherwise provided, for purposes of this Contract, the term "days" shall mean consecutive calendar days, including Saturdays, Sundays, and holidays, whether federal, state, local or religious. For the purposes of calculating days, the count of "days" shall begin on the day following the day upon which any act or notice as provided in this Contract was required to be performed or made. Any reference to a date or time of day shall refer to the date and/or time of day in the State of North Carolina.

Page 10 of 13

Buyer's Initials _____ _____   Seller's Initials _____ _____

STANDARD FORM 2-T
Revised 7/2017
© 7/2017

Figure 11-1

THE NORTH CAROLINA ASSOCIATION OF REALTORS®, INC. AND THE NORTH CAROLINA BAR ASSOCIATION MAKE NO REPRESENTATION AS TO THE LEGAL VALIDITY OR ADEQUACY OF ANY PROVISION OF THIS FORM IN ANY SPECIFIC TRANSACTION. IF YOU DO NOT UNDERSTAND THIS FORM OR FEEL THAT IT DOES NOT PROVIDE FOR YOUR LEGAL NEEDS, YOU SHOULD CONSULT A NORTH CAROLINA REAL ESTATE ATTORNEY BEFORE YOU SIGN IT.

This offer shall become a binding contract on the Effective Date. Unless specifically provided otherwise, Buyer's failure to timely deliver any fee, deposit or other payment provided for herein shall not prevent this offer from becoming a binding contract, provided that any such failure shall give Seller certain rights to terminate the contract as described herein or as otherwise permitted by law.

Date: _____   Date: _____

Buyer: _____   Seller: _____

Date : _____   Date: _____

Buyer: _____   Seller: _____

Entity Buyer: _____   Entity Seller: _____

_____   _____
(Name of LLC/Corporation/Partnership/Trust/etc.)   (Name of LLC/Corporation/Partnership/Trust/etc.)

By: _____   By: _____

Name: _____   Name: _____

Title: _____   Title: _____

Date: _____   Date: _____

[THIS SPACE INTENTIONALLY LEFT BLANK]

STANDARD FORM 2-T
Revised 7/2017
© 7/2017

Figure 11-1

NOTICE INFORMATION

NOTE: INSERT AT LEAST ONE ADDRESS AND/OR ELECTRONIC DELIVERY ADDRESS EACH PARTY AND AGENT APPROVES FOR THE RECEIPT OF ANY NOTICE CONTEMPLATED BY THIS CONTRACT. INSERT "N/A" FOR ANY WHICH ARE NOT APPROVED.

BUYER NOTICE ADDRESS:

Mailing Address: _____

_____

Buyer Fax#: _____

Buyer E-mail: _____

SELLING AGENT NOTICE ADDRESS:

Firm Name:_____
Acting as ❑ Buyer's Agent ❑ Seller's (sub)Agent ❑ Dual Agent
Firm License #:_____
Mailing Address: _____

_____

Individual Selling Agent: _____
❑ Acting as a Designated Dual Agent (check only if applicable)

Selling Agent License #:_____

Selling Agent Phone#: _____

Selling Agent Fax#:_____

Selling Agent E-mail:_____

SELLER NOTICE ADDRESS:

Mailing Address: _____

_____

Seller Fax#:_____

Seller E-mail:_____

LISTING AGENT NOTICE ADDRESS:

Firm Name:_____
Acting as ❑ Seller's Agent ❑ Dual Agent
Firm License #:_____
Mailing Address: _____

_____

Individual Listing Agent: _____
❑ Acting as a Designated Dual Agent (check only if applicable)

Listing Agent License #:_____

Listing Agent Phone#:_____

Listing Agent Fax#:_____

Listing Agent E-mail:_____

[THIS SPACE INTENTIONALLY LEFT BLANK]

Page 12 of 13

Buyer's Initials _____ _____ Seller's Initials _____ _____

STANDARD FORM 2-T
Revised 7/2017
© 7/2017

Figure 11-1

ACKNOWLEDGMENT OF RECEIPT OF MONIES

Seller:_____("Seller")

Buyer:_____("Buyer")

Property Address: _____("Property")

❑ **LISTING AGENT ACKNOWLEDGMENT OF RECEIPT OF DUE DILIGENCE FEE**

Paragraph 1(d) of the Offer to Purchase and Contract between Buyer and Seller for the sale of the Property provides for the payment to Seller of a Due Diligence Fee in the amount of $_____, receipt of which Listing Agent hereby acknowledges.

Date_____   Firm:_____

                                                  By:_____
                                                                      (Signature)

                                                  _____
                                                                      (Print name)

❑ **SELLER ACKNOWLEDGMENT OF RECEIPT OF DUE DILIGENCE FEE**

Paragraph 1(d) of the Offer to Purchase and Contract between Buyer and Seller for the sale of the Property provides for the payment to Seller of a Due Diligence Fee in the amount of $_____, receipt of which Seller hereby acknowledges.

Date_____   Seller: _____
                                                                      (Signature)

Date_____   Seller: _____
                                                                      (Signature)

❑ **ESCROW AGENT ACKNOWLEDGMENT OF RECEIPT OF INITIAL EARNEST MONEY DEPOSIT**

Paragraph 1(d) of the Offer to Purchase and Contract between Buyer and Seller for the sale of the Property provides for the payment to Escrow Agent of an Initial Earnest Money Deposit in the amount of $_____. Escrow Agent as identified in Paragraph 1(f) of the Offer to Purchase and Contract hereby acknowledges receipt of the Initial Earnest Money Deposit and agrees to hold and disburse the same in accordance with the terms of the Offer to Purchase and Contract.

Date_____   Firm:_____

                                                  By:_____
                                                                      (Signature)

                                                  _____
                                                                      (Print name)

❑ **ESCROW AGENT ACKNOWLEDGMENT OF RECEIPT OF (ADDITIONAL) EARNEST MONEY DEPOSIT**

Paragraph 1(d) of the Offer to Purchase and Contract between Buyer and Seller for the sale of the Property provides for the payment to Escrow Agent of an (Additional) Earnest Money Deposit in the amount of $_____. Escrow Agent as identified in Paragraph 1(f) of the Offer to Purchase and Contract hereby acknowledges receipt of the (Additional) Earnest Money Deposit and agrees to hold and disburse the same in accordance with the terms of the Offer to Purchase and Contract.

Date: _____   Firm:_____

Time: _____ ❑ AM ❑ PM   By:_____
                                                                      (Signature)

                                                  _____
                                                                      (Print name)

Page 13 of 13

STANDARD FORM 2-T
Revised 7/2017
© 7/2017

Buyer's Initials _____ _____   Seller's Initials _____ _____

Figure 11-1

CONTINGENT SALE ADDENDUM

Seller's Property: _____

Seller: _____

Buyer: _____

This Addendum is attached to and made a part of the Offer to Purchase and Contract ("Contract") between Seller and Buyer for the Seller's Property.

1. **Closing Contingency for Buyer's Real Property located at:** _____
_____ ("Buyer's Property"):

   (a) **Contract For Buyer's Property**: If Buyer's Property is under contract as of the Effective Date of this Contract with Seller OR goes under contract after the Effective Date of this Contract, then Buyer shall deliver a copy of the contract for Buyer's property ("Contract for Buyer's Property") to Seller and it shall be a condition of this Contract that closing on the sale of Buyer's Property occurs on or before the Settlement Date of this Contract, subject to the terms of this Addendum. If Buyer fails to deliver to Seller a copy of a Contract for Buyer's Property by the expiration of the Due Diligence Period this Contract shall be null and void and the Earnest Money Deposit shall be refunded to Buyer. In any instance when Buyer is providing to Seller a copy of a Contract for Buyer's Property, Buyer may mark out any confidential information, such as the purchase price and the buyer's identity, prior to providing the copy to Seller.

   (b) **Closing on Contract For Buyer's Property**: If there is a Contract For Buyer's Property, but the closing on the sale of Buyer's Property has not occurred by the Settlement Date of this Contract, then Buyer may terminate this Contract within three days following the Settlement Date of this Contract by written notice to Seller, *TIME BEING OF THE ESSENCE*, and the Earnest Money Deposit shall be refunded to Buyer.

   (WARNING: If Buyer does not terminate this Contract as set out in (b) above, and Buyer fails to timely complete Settlement and Closing as provided in this Contract, Buyer risks the loss of the Earnest Money Deposit).

2. **Termination of Contract for Buyer's Property**. If any Contract for Buyer's Property previously delivered to Seller terminates for any reason, Buyer shall within 3 days provide Seller written notice and reasonable documentation of such termination. In the event of any such termination, then Buyer may terminate this Contract by written notice to Seller any time prior to Buyer's delivery of another Contract for Buyer's Property or the expiration of Buyer's 3-day right of termination set forth in subparagraph 1(b) above, and Seller may terminate this Contract by written notice to Buyer any time prior to Buyer's delivery of another Contract for Buyer's Property. In either event, the Earnest Money Deposit shall be refunded to Buyer. If Seller elects to terminate the Contract under this paragraph during the Due Diligence Period, Seller also must refund any Due Diligence Fee as a condition of such termination.

3. **Listing of Buyer's Property for Sale.**   If Buyer has not entered into a Contract For Buyer's Property as of the Effective Date of this Contract, Buyer's Property (*check only ONE of the following options*):
   ❑ is listed with and actively marketed by _____
   ❑ will be listed with and actively marketed by _____ on or before _____
   ❑ Buyer is attempting to sell the Buyer's Property without the assistance of a real estate broker.

IN THE EVENT OF A CONFLICT BETWEEN THIS ADDENDUM AND THE CONTRACT, THIS ADDENDUM SHALL CONTROL, EXCEPT THAT IN THE CASE OF SUCH A CONFLICT AS TO THE DESCRIPTION OF THE SELLER'S PROPERTY OR THE IDENTITY OF THE BUYER OR SELLER, THE CONTRACT SHALL CONTROL.

Page 1 of 2

This form jointly approved by:
North Carolina Bar Association
North Carolina Association of REALTORS®, Inc.

STANDARD FORM 2A2–T
Revised 7/2016
© 7/2017

REALTOR®

EQUAL HOUSING
OPPORTUNITY

Buyer initials _____   _____   Seller initials _____   _____

Figure 11-2

THE NORTH CAROLINA ASSOCIATION OF REALTORS®, INC. AND THE NORTH CAROLINA BAR ASSOCIATION MAKE NO REPRESENTATION AS TO THE LEGAL VALIDITY OR ADEQUACY OF ANY PROVISION OF THIS FORM IN ANY SPECIFIC TRANSACTION. IF YOU DO NOT UNDERSTAND THIS FORM OR FEEL THAT IT DOES NOT PROVIDE FOR YOUR LEGAL NEEDS, YOU SHOULD CONSULT A NORTH CAROLINA REAL ESTATE ATTORNEY BEFORE YOU SIGN IT.

Date:_____

Buyer:_____

Date: _____

Buyer:_____

Date: _____

Buyer: _____

Entity Buyer:
_____
(Name of LLC/Corporation/Partnership/Trust/etc.)

By: _____

Name: _____

Title: _____

Date: _____

Date: _____

Seller: _____

Date: _____

Seller: _____

Date: _____

Seller : _____

Entity Seller:
_____
(Name of LLC/Corporation/Partnership/Trust/etc.)

By: _____

Name: _____

Title: _____

Date: _____

[THIS SPACE INTENTIONALLY LEFT BLANK]

Figure 11-2

STANDARD FORM 2A2–T
Revised 7/2016
© 7/2017

12 | MORTGAGES AND DEEDS OF TRUST

Real estate brokers must have a basic understanding of mortgage law. Purchasers of real estate rarely pay cash, typically because they lack the financial ability, but also because financing a purchase may have tax advantages. When a buyer borrows money to finance a real estate purchase, the loan typically is secured by a mortgage on the real property. This chapter covers basic mortgage concepts, mortgage financing instruments, rights of mortgage lenders and borrowers, sales of mortgaged properties, and mortgage priorities.

BASIC MORTGAGE THEORIES

SUMMARY OF THE MORTGAGE PROCESS

In a typical mortgage transaction, the borrower — or **mortgagor** — signs a **promissory note** promising to repay the loan, as well as a **mortgage** or **deed of trust** pledging real property as collateral to secure the loan. Generally, the collateral securing a loan to purchase real property is the property purchased with the loan proceeds. If the borrower fails to repay the loan, the lender — or **mortgagee** — may initiate a **foreclosure** proceeding unless some other settlement with the borrower is made. A foreclosure is a forced sale of the real property by public auction with the sale proceeds applied to the balance owed on the loan.

MORTGAGE TERMS AND THEORIES

Lien Theory of Mortgage Law

Most states follow the **lien theory of mortgage law. Under** this theory, the borrower-property owner (the "**mortgagor**") holds both *"legal title"* and *"equitable title"* to the real property during the term of the loan, but the lender (the "**mortgagee**") holds a *"lien"* on the real property until the borrower repays the loan. The borrower-property owner has the right to possess and use the mortgaged real property during the term of the loan. The legal document used is a **mortgage**. The mortgage lien is canceled once the loan is paid in full.

Title Theory of Mortgage Law

Some states, including North Carolina, follow the **title theory of mortgages**.[1] Technically, the borrower-property owner (called the **"grantor"**) conveys *"legal title"* to the real property to a third party (called the "trustee") to hold for the benefit of the lender (called the **"beneficiary"**) until the loan is repaid. The legal instrument used to accomplish this is a **deed of trust**. Under this concept, the borrower holds *"equitable title"* to the property and has the right to possess and use the pledged real property during the term of the loan. Upon loan repayment, the trustee cancels the deed of trust. Despite the deed of trust terminology, the borrower-property owner is often generically referred to as a "mortgagor," the mortgage lender as a "mortgagee," and the document as a "mortgage."

Common Usage of the Term "Mortgage"

Although there are technical differences between the lien and title theories of mortgage law, each theory has the same practical effect. Both deeds of trust and mortgages encumber real property. It is common practice in North Carolina to refer to a "deed of trust" as a "mortgage" and to refer to property pledged by a deed of trust as security for a loan as "mortgaged property." The authors follow this common practice by using the terms *mortgagor, mortgagee, mortgage,* and *mortgaged property* when generally discussing mortgage law and financing. However, ***real estate brokers should be aware of the technical distinction between a mortgage and a deed of trust.***

MORTGAGE DOCUMENTS AND RIGHTS OF PARTIES

A borrower-buyer signs a multitude of forms when obtaining a mortgage loan and closing a real estate purchase transaction. Chapter 13 discusses real estate lending practices and procedures. As noted above, the primary legal documents involved with a mortgage loan are the **mortgage note** (promissory note) and the **mortgage** or **deed of trust**.

THE MORTGAGE NOTE (PROMISSORY NOTE)

The **mortgage note** *evidences the indebtedness* **secured by a mortgage** or **deed of trust**. The promissory note, true to its name, is an IOU by which one party acknowledges a debt owed to another party and promises to repay the debt in accordance with the terms expressed in the note. When a mortgage or deed of trust secures payment of the debt, the promissory note may also be called the "mortgage note."

Essential Elements of a Mortgage Note

To be legally sufficient, a mortgage note must contain:

- a promise by the borrower to pay the lender a fixed sum,
- payment terms, and
- the borrower's signature.

A mortgage note typically states the principal amount of the loan, the interest rate, the amount of each payment, the due date of payments, late payment fees, default procedures, and all other loan terms. To be enforceable, all material terms must be clearly stated.

Personal Liability of Borrower

Any person signing a mortgage note is personally liable for payment of the note, even though the debt is secured by a mortgage or deed of trust. *This personal liability continues until the note is paid in full.* A promissory note under which the debtor has personal liability for payment of the debt is known as a **note with recourse.** Even if the mortgage or deed of trust is foreclosed, the lender can sue the borrower and obtain a personal judgment for any deficiency between the foreclosure sale price and the amount of indebtedness remaining unpaid. This general rule regarding a borrower's personal liability for the full amount of a mortgage loan applies to virtually all *home buyers.*

A different situation is encountered in some *commercial real estate loans.* It is not unusual for a lender to accept a **nonrecourse note** (i.e., a **note without recourse**), which means that the borrower is *not* personally liable on the note. When a borrower defaults on a nonrecourse mortgage note, the lender can only foreclose upon the mortgaged property. If the proceeds from the sale of the pledged property do not satisfy the debt, the lender has *no recourse against the borrower* and cannot obtain a deficiency judgment against the borrower for the remaining balance of the debt.

Negotiability of Note

Promissory notes are either *"negotiable"* or *"nonnegotiable."* A **negotiable promissory note** is an unconditional promise made by one person to another, signed by the borrower, promising to pay on demand or at a future time a sum of money "to order" or "to bearer." The note is *negotiable* because of the words "to bearer" or "to order," rather than to a named person or entity. This makes the note payable to any party lawfully holding the note. A negotiable note is transferable by simple indorsement — in other words, it is "salable" by the lender to others. This is an important legal distinction as most first mortgage notes are sold by the initial lenders to investors in the secondary mortgage market. Therefore, most mortgage notes are negotiable.

A **nonnegotiable note** is *not* payable "to order" or "to bearer" but only to a specific named party. Nonnegotiable notes may not be sold to a third party.

Other Common Provisions in Mortgage Notes

Most mortgage notes also contain two other provisions — an acceleration clause and a prepayment penalty clause — of significant importance to the parties involved but not technically essential to the validity of the note itself.

Acceleration Clause

Virtually every promissory note, especially those prepared using a standard form, contains an "acceleration clause." An acceleration clause provides that, *in the event of any default in payment of any installment of principal or interest or upon breach of any other condition specified, the holder of the note has the option of declaring the entire principal sum of the note immediately due and payable.* The holder of the note also has the option of instituting legal proceedings to recover the entire principal sum plus accrued interest and costs.

Example: In 2015, a bank loaned a home purchaser $350,000 at 4 percent interest, repayable in monthly installments for 30 years. The loan was secured by a mortgage to the bank. In 2017, when the purchaser still owed $338,000 on the mortgage loan, he materially defaulted by missing four monthly payments. After communicating a notice of default and providing the purchaser an opportunity to cure by catching up on missed payments, the bank declared the entire unpaid balance of the loan due and payable. By materially defaulting on payments, the purchaser now owes the bank the entire unpaid balance of the mortgage loan.

In the above example, the purchaser who missed four payments probably will not be able to pay the entire unpaid balance. Absent a "short sale" approved by the bank or some other settlement of the matter, the bank will proceed with a foreclosure sale. While acceleration clauses can appear to be harsh in operation, they are legally valid.

Prepayment Penalty Clause

Some promissory notes contain a *prepayment penalty clause requiring the borrower to pay additional money to the creditor if the borrower repays the debt prematurely.* Prepayment penalties can adversely affect a property owner-borrower who wants to sell the mortgaged property or one who borrows money when interest rates are high and later wants to refinance when rates drop. *North Carolina General Statute §24-1.1A prohibits lenders from charging a prepayment penalty on a "home loan" with a principal amount of $150,000 or less, if the loan is secured by a first mortgage or a deed of trust on real estate that contains or will contain a 1-4 family dwelling(s) that will be occupied by the borrower as the borrower's principal dwelling.* Federal law prohibits prepayment penalties on loans insured by the Federal Housing Administration (FHA) or guaranteed by the Veterans Administration (VA). Additionally, many loans that lenders sell in the secondary mortgage market are not permitted to have prepayment penalty provisions in the note. Nevertheless, borrowers should be alert to the possibility of prepayment penalties being included in a mortgage note, especially if the loan is not a "home loan" (as defined in the statute) or exceeds $150,000.

Although rarely called "penalties" in commercial mortgage documents and usually referred to as "prepayment charges" or "fees," prepayment penalties are generally enforceable in *nonresidential* mortgage loans. As a general proposition, prepayment charges or fees must be reasonable.

THE MORTGAGE (OR DEED OR TRUST) DOCUMENT

A **mortgage** or **deed of trust** on real property *is a document conveying an interest in real estate that is pledged as security for the payment of a debt.*[2] It provides collateral for a promissory note, elevating its status to that of a "secured note." A default on the note triggers foreclosure.

Essential Elements of a Mortgage or Deed of Trust

A valid mortgage or deed of trust must:[3]
- Secure the payment of an identified and valid debt;[4]
- Be in writing under the Statute of Frauds;[5]
- Identify the mortgagor and mortgagee;
- Be executed by a mortgagor with legal capacity who owns property that may be mortgaged;
- Contain a legal description of the mortgaged property;
- Expressly grant a security interest in the property
- Be properly executed (signed just as in the case of a deed); and
- Be legally delivered and accepted (in the same manner as for deeds).

The mortgage or deed of trust is enforceable between the parties[6] even if it is not recorded in the register of deeds office. However a prudent mortgagee will insist on immediately recording the mortgage lien or deed of trust to secure priority of that debt and protect the lender-mortgagee's interest against any party who subsequently acquires an interest in the property, whether a future purchaser or lienholder.[7]

The above list of essential elements assumes a typical real estate transaction where the purchaser obtains a mortgage loan and executes a promissory note and deed of trust or mortgage note against the property, but there are other possibilities. For example, a person may execute a mortgage to secure the debt of another.

> *Example:* A husband inherited land and holds title in his name alone. His wife borrows $400,000 from a bank to finance the purchase of a commercial building. She signs a promissory note, and her husband executes a mortgage of his land to the bank to secure repayment of the loan but does not sign the promissory note. Under these facts, the bank has a valid mortgage on the husband's land, but the husband is not personally liable on the loan.

As the above example illustrates, a person signing only a mortgage or deed of trust is not personally liable for the mortgage debt unless he or she also signs the promissory note. The husband's liability is limited to the value of his land. If his wife defaults on the mortgage loan, he could lose his land in a foreclosure sale, but he would not be personally liable for any deficiency. Thus, a property owner may execute a mortgage against their land to secure or provide additional security for the loan obligation of another without incurring any liability to the creditor on the underlying debt. The most common situation involves one family member or spouse helping out another.

Other Common Provisions in Mortgages and Deeds of Trust

In addition to the essential provisions mentioned above, mortgages and deeds of trust include other provisions, including the following:

- Power of sale provision
- Due-upon-sale clause
- Insurance requirement
- Taxes, assessments, and charges requirement
- Requirement of property maintenance

Power of Sale Provision

For the lender to be able to foreclose by power of sale, a deed of trust must contain a provision authorizing the trustee to sell the mortgaged property at auction in the event of default by the borrower. Virtually all standard form deeds of trust in North Carolina have a power of sale provision.

Due-on-Sale Clause

A due-on-sale clause provides that, *if the borrower transfers the mortgaged property without the mortgagee's prior consent, the entire mortgage loan becomes immediately due and payable.* Generally, in a voluntary sale the owner's existing mortgage is paid in full at closing from the sale proceeds to enable the seller to convey marketable and insurable title; however, if the purchaser wants to assume the balance of the seller's existing mortgage, the owner's mortgagee must consent to the buyer's assumption of the existing loan, rather than having it paid in full at closing as required under the due-on-sale clause.

Mortgages and deeds of trust routinely include due-on-sale clauses. Their use is authorized by federal law and their validity has been upheld.[8]

Parties sometimes attempt to avoid a due-on-sale clause in the seller's mortgage by hiding or camouflaging a sale from the seller's mortgagee, which violates the terms of the mortgage loan, and may constitute mortgage fraud. A real estate broker should never advise a purchaser to evade the due-on-sale clause and should never knowingly participate in a transaction where the sale is hidden or camouflaged from the seller's mortgagee.

Insurance

A mortgagor must maintain adequate property insurance on any improvements on the property in an amount sufficient to cover the amount of the mortgage loan. If the mortgagor fails to insure the property, the mortgagee may obtain insurance and add it to the principal loan amount. In most residential mortgage transactions, the mortgagor makes monthly payments into an escrow fund maintained by the mortgagee to pay the property insurance premiums annually.

Taxes, Assessments, and Charges

A mortgagor usually must pay property taxes, special assessments, and homeowners' association dues or assessments related to the mortgaged property, although the mortgagor's monthly payments usually include an amount for estimated taxes that will be held in escrow by the mortgagee until the real property taxes are due. If the owner fails to pay any of these expenses, the lender may pay the amounts due and add those amounts to the principal loan amount.

Property Maintenance

A mortgagor must maintain the mortgaged premises in good repair. Failure to do so authorizes the mortgagee to make necessary repairs and add the repair cost to the loan principal and may also subject the mortgagor to liability for damages under the law of "waste."

Mortgage Cancellation

The closing attorney must assure that the mortgagee properly cancels the seller's mortgage debt and mortgage or deed of trust. *A broker should never give an opinion to a client regarding the legal requirements for cancellation.* When a mortgage note is paid in full, the lender can acknowledge payment and cancellation of the note by a number of methods (for example, by stamping "Paid" on the original note and returning it to the borrower). However, cancellation of the mortgage or deed of trust instrument must be recorded.

North Carolina law provides detailed procedures for cancellation of a mortgage or deed of trust. The closing attorney must confirm proper cancellation of the seller's mortgage or deed of trust after the attorney pays the loan balance in full at closing. As a practical matter, the attorney must wait for the seller's lender to process the seller's loan payoff and provide the necessary documents to cancel the seller's mortgage or deed of trust. Thus, the seller's mortgage or deed of trust may not be cancelled in the county land records until several weeks after closing.[9]

FORECLOSURE OF A MORTGAGE OR DEED OF TRUST

Lender's Right to Foreclose

A mortgagee's primary remedy for a mortgagor's default is **foreclosure,** *a procedure that allows a mortgagee to force a sale of the mortgaged property and apply the sale proceeds to pay the mortgage indebtedness.*

The following important foreclosure topics are discussed below:
- Foreclosure by judicial action
- Foreclosure by power of sale
- General foreclosure procedures
- Seller financing and the anti-deficiency judgment statute

Foreclosure by Judicial Action

If the mortgagor defaults on the loan, this method requires the lender to file a lawsuit pursuant to the foreclosure statutes. If the court finds that the borrower has substantially defaulted on the loan, it will order that the property be sold at public auction and the sale proceeds be applied to the debt. This method is used occasionally in North Carolina and involves closer judicial scrutiny than does the more popular North Carolina foreclosure by power of sale method.[10]

Foreclosure by Power of Sale

Almost all mortgage loan transactions in North Carolina use this method of foreclosure. *All standard form deeds of trust used in North Carolina grant a trustee the "power" to sell the property in the event of default by the borrower.* Compared to the *foreclosure by judicial action* procedure, *foreclosure by power of sale* expedites the foreclosure process because the lender does not file a typical civil lawsuit, but the process still is conducted under the auspices of the clerk of court. Procedurally, it requires a hearing before the clerk with a right to appeal to district or superior court. Under the foreclosure by power of sale procedure, the trustee under the deed of trust sells the property at a public auction with the proceeds applied to satisfy the debt, interest, and other costs.[11]

General Foreclosure Procedures

Statutory procedural requirements apply to **all** foreclosures. Failure to strictly comply with state law can result in invalidation of the foreclosure sale.[12] In any type of foreclosure proceeding, there is a hearing before either a judge or the clerk of court, and proper notice of the foreclosure sale must be given to the debtor-borrower and to the general public. After the sale at public auction, a 10-day *statutory redemption period* must pass without "upset bids" before the sale is final. Once the foreclosure sale is final, the sale proceeds are applied to the debt and the costs of the foreclosure, and the purchaser (high bidder) at the sale receives a trustee's deed to the property.

Foreclosure Sale Proceeds

Foreclosure sale proceeds are applied *first to satisfy the underlying debt plus accrued interest and expenses, and next to any liens that have attached to the property.* Junior mortgagees and judgment lien creditors, if any, receive any remaining sale proceeds and then, finally, the mortgagor. If, however, the proceeds from the foreclosure sale are insufficient to pay the mortgage debt, the lender then has the right to sue the borrower-property owner for a judgment for the unpaid balance of the debt. This judgment is called a **deficiency judgment.** It gives the lender the right to levy against any other property (real or personal) of the debtor-borrower to recover the "deficiency."

Example: A mortgagor defaults in making payments under a mortgage note and a properly conducted foreclosure sale is held. The unpaid balance on the loan, legal fees, and other costs related to the foreclosure total $240,000, but the sale brings only $180,000. The mortgagee may sue the debtor for a deficiency judgment for the $60,000 difference. Once judgment is entered, the mortgagee may proceed against the mortgagor's other real or personal property, if any, to satisfy the deficiency judgment.

The Anti-Deficiency Judgment Statute

North Carolina law prohibits a seller from obtaining a deficiency judgment against a purchaser who financed the purchase of real property entirely or in part with **seller financing**. In other words, a seller who agrees to finance a portion of the buyer's purchase of the seller's property, rather than requiring the buyer to obtain third party financing for the entire purchase price, will not be entitled to a deficiency judgment against the buyer. If the buyer defaults on the loan and the seller forecloses under the mortgage or deed of trust, and the foreclosure sale proceeds are insufficient to satisfy the outstanding loan balance due the seller, the seller cannot sue the buyer for the difference. [13]

Example: A married couple sells their farm to a buyer for $700,000. The buyer paid $35,000 down, and the sellers agreed to finance the remaining purchase price balance of $665,000. At the real estate closing, the sellers deeded the farm to the buyer, and the buyer executed a promissory note and deed of trust back to the sellers. A few years later, the buyer still owes $650,000, but defaults on the loan payments, and the sellers initiate a foreclosure by power of sale proceeding. At the foreclosure sale, the property sells to the highest bidder for $600,000, leaving $50,000 still owed on the loan. The anti-deficiency judgment statute prohibits the sellers from suing the buyer for a $50,000 deficiency judgment.

The only realistic way for sellers to protect themselves in the above example is to obtain a larger down payment and, in the event of foreclosure, bid on the property up to the amount they are owed and take their farm back. The sellers cannot require that the buyers waive the statute as a condition for providing the financing.

The statute applies regardless of whether the seller's mortgage is a first or junior mortgage on the property conveyed. The anti-deficiency judgment statute poses a particular problem for sellers who are partially financing the purchase of real property, but are subordinating their mortgage to third-party financing and thus hold a junior mortgage.

The statute does *not* apply to third party lenders who loan the buyer the money to purchase the property and take back a mortgage or deed of trust as security.

A real estate broker should never advise a seller about the legal implications of seller financing and should never recommend that a seller finance the buyer's purchase of the sellers' real property. Rather, a seller contemplating seller financing should seek legal advice from an experienced real estate attorney. (Indeed, an experienced real estate attorney will not advise a seller to engage in seller financing without thoroughly explaining the serious potential disadvantage to the seller given the anti-deficiency judgment statute.)[14]

Mortgagee's Right to Assign (Sell) Mortgage

A lender holding a negotiable note secured by a mortgage or deed of trust may assign (i.e., sell or transfer) the note and the mortgage or deed of trust securing it to a third person. The lender who transfers the debt and its security is an "assignor" and the person who receives the instruments is an "assignee." The note typically is transferred by the holder endorsing it on the back. Since a mortgage or deed of trust conveys an interest in real estate, it is assigned by a formal writing signed by the assignor and recorded at the register of deeds office. The assignee of the indebtedness will notify the debtor-borrower of the assignment. The original lender (assignor) may continue to service the loan and receive payments to transmit to the assignee.

Original lenders often sell residential mortgages on the secondary mortgage market, a process facilitated by the securitization of residential mortgages by government-sponsored enterprises (GSE) such as the Government National Mortgage Association and the Federal National Mortgage Association. To issue residential mortgage-backed securities for sale on the capital markets, the government-sponsored enterprises acquire pools of mortgages by a transfer of the mortgage loan and by an assignment of each mortgage, which is recorded at the register of deeds office of the county in which the real estate is located. In addition to local recordation, MERS® (Mortgage Electronic Registration System), a national electronic registry system created by the mortgage banking industry, tracks the transfer and ownership of mortgages. MERS® does not replace local recording requirements; it simply is a registry that tracks changes in servicing rights and beneficial ownership interests in mortgage loans.[15]

Borrower's Right to Possession and Use

Under a mortgage or deed of trust, a mortgagor retains the right to possess and enjoy the property prior to any default and foreclosure. Subject to rare exceptions (such as abandonment of the property or a court-ordered receivership), the mortgagee is not entitled to possession.

Borrower's Right of Redemption

All states recognize a mortgagor's **right of redemption, also called an "equity of redemption,"** under which a defaulting mortgagor has the right to pay off the full mortgage debt plus accrued interest and keep the land free of the mortgage or deed of trust. Even after default, *at any time before a valid foreclosure process is complete, the borrower may "redeem" his or her title in the mortgaged property* by paying to the mortgagee the total amount owed plus accrued interest.

Lenders cannot require a borrower to waive this right of redemption and if such language is included in a deed of trust or promissory note it will not be enforced. The equity of redemption continues in the debtor-mortgagor, who has a legal right to pay in full and recover his land back at any time before a valid, completed foreclosure cuts off that right. The only way a lender can terminate the borrower's equity of redemption is to fully complete a foreclosure in accordance with state law.

Statutory Redemption Period

In addition to the protection afforded a debtor by the common-law equity of redemption doctrine, borrower-mortgagors in many states also enjoy the benefit of a **statutory redemption period.** Other states have enacted laws that grant the mortgagor (borrower) the right to redeem the mortgaged property within a specified period of time *after the foreclosure sale.* The time period can be as long as six months or even one year. North Carolina has no similar statutory right of redemption.

North Carolina Upset Bid Period

In North Carolina, a statutory process allows a mortgagor (borrower) or others, including members of the public, to submit an *"upset bid"* within 10 days following a foreclosure sale. The *"upset bid"* must exceed the highest bid at the foreclosure sale by at least five percent but no less than $750. A successful upset bidder becomes the new high bidder, triggering another 10 day upset bid period.[16] This process continues until no upset bid is submitted during the 10 day period. Anyone may submit upset bids increasing the foreclosure sale proceeds.

When there are no more upset bids, the foreclosure sale becomes final and the mortgagor's right to redeem the property ends. While insignificant as a mortgagor's right when compared to the statutory redemption laws of other states, the upset bid window briefly extends the mortgagor's right of redemption beyond the actual foreclosure sale as the borrower could submit an upset bid, if s/he can marshal the financial resources.

Homeowner and Homebuyer Protection Act

In July of 2010, the General Assembly enacted the **Homeowner and Homebuyer Protection Act**, sweeping legislation dealing with egregious abuses caused by what the legislation terms "home foreclosure rescue scams." The Act prohibits home foreclosure rescue scams in which a property owner, hoping to avoid a foreclosure that has commenced, is induced to sell the mortgaged property for less than 50 percent of its fair market value. The Act regulates, in great detail, lease-option contracts (Chapter 47G of the General Statutes) and contracts for deed (Chapter 47H of the General Statutes), as well as prohibits — under specifically defined circumstances and subject to enumerated exceptions — foreclosure rescue transactions (Article 6, Chapter 75 of General Statutes).

IMPORTANT NOTE: This law is detailed and lengthy. Brokers dealing in any way with a transaction that seeks to save a property from foreclosure via a lease with an option to purchase, a contract for deed, or any other purported rescue transaction should tell the parties to seek legal advice from an attorney.

SALES OF MORTGAGED PROPERTY

Most sellers own property encumbered by a mortgage or deed of trust. The sale of mortgaged property may be accomplished in a number of ways, including the following three:
- Cash sale (with existing mortgage paid off)
- Assumption of existing mortgage by buyer
- Sale subject to the existing mortgage

Cash Sale

In the vast majority of residential property sales where the seller's property is encumbered by a mortgage, the buyer arranges new financing and the seller's existing mortgage or deed of trust is paid in full at closing and then cancelled. This is the safest procedure for the seller because it terminates the seller's liability as to that indebtedness. Additionally, the buyer's mortgagee wants to have a first mortgage on the property and will require payment in full of the seller's mortgages and liens.

Assumption of Existing Mortgage

If interest rates are high, financially able buyers may prefer to assume the seller's existing mortgage if that mortgage is assumable and has an interest rate substantially lower than current rates. It also may work to the seller's advantage to accept this arrangement rather than insist on a cash sale, because the property may not sell as quickly due to potential purchasers' reluctance to arrange new financing when interest rates are unfavorably high.

If a mortgage or deed of trust does not address whether a purchaser of the property can assume the seller's mortgage, then a buyer has the right and may agree to assume and pay the mortgage indebtedness — *without the consent of the lender.* When this occurs, the *purchaser who assumes an existing mortgage becomes personally obligated to pay the mortgage debt.* The purchaser may be sued and judgment entered against him or her, and the mortgage or deed of trust may be foreclosed.

Even if a buyer assumes an existing mortgage, the original borrower (seller) remains liable to the lender unless the lender releases him from liability.[17] The seller can sidestep this problem by asking the mortgagee to sign a written "release" that relieves the seller of future liability.

Sale Subject to Existing Mortgage

While rare in residential sales transactions, a buyer may offer to purchase a property "subject to" an existing mortgage. When a sale of real property is made "subject to" an existing mortgage debt, the buyer is *not* personally liable for the debt or any deficiency if the land is sold by foreclosure. *When a purchaser of land takes expressly "subject to" a mortgage debt (or impliedly without the mortgage debt being mentioned), the debt can be satisfied only out of the land itself or by suit against the seller (the original borrower/mortgagor), and the purchaser of the mortgaged land does **not** become personally liable either to the mortgagee or the seller.*[18] The buyer does not assume the mortgage debt, so the seller of the mortgaged premises remains the only one personally liable on the indebtedness. Since the seller cannot sue the buyer if the buyer does not pay the debt, a "subject to" transfer is not desirable from the seller's perspective.

While rare, transfers of property "subject to" an existing mortgage or deed of trust occur when there is a valid preexisting mortgage on the property of which the purchaser is unaware. While a purchaser in this situation may have legal recourse against the seller (or may be able to recover under a title insurance policy if the defect is not excepted from coverage), the land nonetheless is subject to the mortgage and can be sold by foreclosure if the indebtedness is not paid when due. This underscores why an adequate title search should be made before real property is purchased.

Effect of Due-on-Sale Clauses on Mortgage Assumptions

Most contemporary forms used by institutional lenders now contain a *due-on-sale clause that effectively prohibits the assumption of the mortgage or deed of trust by a purchaser of the mortgaged property without the lender's prior consent.*

It is unlikely that a lender will consent to the purchaser's assumption of an earlier mortgage or deed of trust with a substantially lower interest rate unless the purchaser agrees to pay the lender a higher interest rate. If the lender does obtain a higher interest rate from the assuming purchaser, then it probably will release the seller from further liability under the original indebtedness as part of the transaction. This assumes, of course, that the lender is satisfied with the credit worthiness of the assuming purchaser. It is important to emphasize, however, that *a lender is not legally required to release the original debtor after consenting to the assumption by a new purchaser.* Thus, a seller is well-advised to make any proposed sale involving assumption of the seller's mortgage conditional upon release of the seller by the lender from further liability under the assumed mortgage.

MORTGAGE PRIORITIES

The Broker's Role

A broker is prohibited from giving legal advice and should tell sellers and buyers to confer with an attorney when a question of mortgage law or priorities arises.

The Basic Rule

The priority of real estate title documents is determined by the recording act. "Title Recordation" is discussed in detail in Chapter 6. By way of review, any grantee of an interest in real property must record the document to properly protect that interest.

A properly executed mortgage or deed of trust is valid and enforceable between the parties even if not recorded, but *unless a mortgage or deed of trust is recorded, it is **not** valid against the following:*

- subsequent lien creditors of the grantor who record first
- subsequent mortgages given by the grantor of the same land that are recorded first
- subsequent purchasers of all or part of the same land from grantor who record first.

To obtain priority for a mortgage or deed of trust, the mortgage lender and title insurance company will require immediate recordation of the mortgage or deed of trust. This provides "constructive notice" to all persons who subsequently deal with the property and gives the recorded mortgage priority.

> *Example:* On September 14, 2017, a bank loaned a farm owner $200,000, taking back a first mortgage on the farm to secure repayment of the debt. The bank, however, failed to record the mortgage until September 19, 2017. On September 18, a judgment creditor filed a lien against the farm owner. The judgment lien is a first lien on the farm. The bank's delay in recording results in the judgment lien creditor having a first lien because it was filed prior to recording the mortgage. The bank continues to have a valid mortgage, but it is a "second" mortgage junior in priority to the judgment lien.

Special Priority of Purchase-Money Mortgages

*A purchase-money mortgage given to a seller or third-party lender to secure the purchase of property has a special priority over all previous mortgages and other liens against the **purchaser** of that property.* (The term "purchase-money mortgage" includes purchase-money deeds of trust.) Even though recorded *after* previous liens filed against the purchaser before he or she took title to the property, a purchase-money mortgage receives first priority because it secures repayment of the funds that enabled the purchase of the property.

A purchase-money mortgage secures a loan to a buyer for the purchase of real property. The purchase may be for vacant or improved land, and it may involve the purchase of a lot on which the buyer also finances construction of a home or other building. It must be executed at the same time as the deed from the seller or as part of one continuous sales transaction.

> *Example:* A valid judgment lien exists against a married couple. Several years after the lien was properly filed, the couple buys a home for $300,000 and signs a deed of trust to a bank for a $240,000 mortgage loan. The deed to the couple and the mortgage are promptly recorded. Even though the judgment lien against the couple is prior *in time* to the bank's mortgage, the bank's deed of trust is given a special priority. The judgment lien is valid and attaches to the title to the home, but it is junior to the bank mortgage.

Do not confuse the special priority of purchase-money mortgages with fact situations involving prior liens against the **seller**. The seller obviously cannot convey more title than he or she has. If, for example, there is a prior judgment lien against the seller, it takes priority over the buyer's purchase-money mortgage. The same will be true if a preexisting mortgage is not paid off at closing.

> *Example:* A seller of property subject to a recorded mortgage agrees to sell to a buyer, who obtains a purchase-money mortgage from a bank to enable her to purchase the property. The bank will insist that the seller's mortgage be paid off at closing and then cancelled. Otherwise,

the bank's mortgage, even though a purchase-money mortgage, will be a second mortgage, junior to the seller's mortgage.

Types of Mortgages by Priority of the Mortgage

The order in which mortgages are recorded determines their priority. A mortgage on property recorded prior to recordation of any other mortgage on that property is called a "**first mortgage**," meaning it is first in priority. Even if there is only one mortgage recorded on a property, it still is referred to as a first mortgage.

Any mortgage on property that is not a first mortgage is a "**junior mortgage**." If a junior mortgage is second in priority, it is commonly called a "**second mortgage**." While it is possible to have additional lower-priority mortgages on a property numbered according to their priority (third, fourth, etc.), this is uncommon in residential transactions. Any mortgage *higher* in priority than another may be referred to as a "**senior mortgage**." For example, if a property has three outstanding recorded mortgages, the first and second mortgages are senior to the third. A junior mortgage moves up in priority when the borrower pays off and cancels a senior mortgage. Thus, if a first mortgage is paid off, the second mortgage (if one exists) becomes the first mortgage.

Importance of Mortgage Priority at Foreclosure

When more than one outstanding mortgage (or other lien) exists, their priority determines the order in which mortgage and lien holders will be paid at foreclosure.

Foreclosure by Holder of First Mortgage

If the senior mortgagee forecloses, *the foreclosure sale proceeds will be applied first to pay off the first mortgage and expenses of sale and then to pay off any other junior outstanding mortgages (and other liens) in the order of their priority.* The holder of a *junior* mortgage (or other lien not ranking first in priority) might be paid in full or might receive nothing, depending on the amount of the sale proceeds.

Regardless of the foreclosure sale price, **foreclosure by the first mortgage holder will have the effect of "clearing the title" to the property from all other outstanding liens** so that the trustee conducting the foreclosure sale can convey clear title to the successful high bidder. This means that *all outstanding mortgages (and other liens) on the property are extinguished by a foreclosure even if they are not paid.*

Since a junior mortgage can be satisfied from the proceeds of a sale to foreclose only after the senior mortgage has been fully satisfied, a lender taking a junior mortgage as security incurs a greater risk than one who holds a first mortgage. For this and other legal reasons, mortgage lenders require a first mortgage.

Foreclosure by Holder of a Junior Mortgage

The holder of a *second* (or other junior) mortgage can foreclose and force a foreclosure sale, even if the first mortgage is not in default. If the holder of the first mortgage joins in the foreclosure proceeding, which is usually the case, then the result is the same as if the foreclosure proceeding had been initiated by the first mortgage holder. If, however, the first mortgage holder does *not* join the foreclosure proceeding, then the foreclosure will only extinguish the second mortgage and any liens subordinate to it. In this case, the purchaser at the foreclosure sale would take the property *subject to the first mortgage,* which would remain outstanding. As a practical matter, it is very unusual for a first mortgage holder not to join a foreclosure proceeding initiated by a junior mortgage holder.

Special Mortgage Arrangements Affecting Priority

Future Advances Mortgage.

A *"future advances mortgage"* secures both present funds given to the borrower at the time of the mortgage, as well as future funds that will or may be given to the borrower (future advances). Future advances mortgages most commonly is used in construction financing.

> *Example:* A married couple seeks a loan to help finance the purchase of a vacant lot and the construction of a home. A bank agrees to loan them $200,000 — $50,000 to be advanced to them upon execution of the mortgage and note and $150,000 to be advanced to them in future installments as construction on their home progresses. The couple has obtained a future advances mortgage.

A common legal issue involved with future advances mortgages involves priority problems. What if, after the married couple received the initial advance of $50,000 and take title to the lot, but before they receive any future advances, a creditor obtains a judgment lien against them (and thus their property) or the couple borrows money from another lender and gives that lender a second mortgage on their property? Will the judgment lien or second mortgage take priority over the bank's first mortgage to the extent of the $150,000 in future advances? If the bank provides future advances to the couple as construction proceeds, will those future advances be protected against the lien and second mortgage? The answer is "yes."[19]

Home Equity Loan (Equity Line of Credit)

In a *"home equity loan"* (*"equity line of credit"*), the borrower uses the equity that has accrued in his or her home to secure a line of credit.[20] The borrower then has the right to withdraw funds up to the agreed home equity loan limit. As the borrower repays the funds, they become available to the borrower again. Thus, the home equity loan acts as a revolving fund from which the borrower borrows and repays monies over a period of time. A home equity loan is secured by a mortgage, often a second mortgage, on the borrower's property. Thus, a default in paying the home equity loan may cause the lender to initiate a foreclosure on the borrower's home.

Due to the revolving nature of a home equity loan, the bank's mortgage on the borrower's property does not end when the balance of the loan returns to zero.[21]

> *Example:* A homeowner obtains a home equity loan from a bank in the total amount of $50,000 and executes a home equity loan agreement and mortgage to the bank to secure repayment of any loan funds. The homeowner then borrows $30,000 from the home equity line of credit to construct a swimming pool. Several years later, the homeowner repays the entire $30,000 to the bank. The bank continues to have a mortgage on (security interest in) the home, and the homeowner is free to borrow up to $50,000. The reduction of the home equity loan to zero does not automatically cancel the bank's mortgage. As long as the term of the mortgage/home equity loan agreement has not expired, the mortgage will not be canceled of record unless the homeowner requests cancellation.

Home equity loans that comply with statutory requirements receive a priority similar to future advances loans. All advances secured by the home equity mortgage take priority as if they were made at the time that the home equity mortgage was executed.[22]

Reverse Mortgage

The North Carolina Reverse Mortgage Act is designed to enable persons 62 years of age or older who have substantial equity in their home to access that equity to supplement their income.[23] For example, an elderly couple has paid off the mortgage on their principal residence, where they wish to stay, but now requires more money for expenses than their retirement funds can provide. Rather than sell their home, the couple may obtain a reverse mortgage under which the bank makes a payment or periodic payments to them secured by the equity in their home.

> *Example:* A married couple long ago paid the mortgage on their personal residence in full. They are retired and now need to supplement their modest retirement income. They enter into a reverse mortgage transaction with a bank in which the bank agrees to send them a monthly payment of $500 for the next ten years. They are obligated to repay the loan with interest when they sell their home or at the end of the 10-year period, whichever comes first. The couple will still be responsible for paying the property taxes, insurance premiums, and maintaining the property.

The Act defines a "reverse mortgage loan" as:

> … a loan for a definite or indefinite term (i) secured by a first mortgage or deed of trust on the principal residence of the mortgagor located in North Carolina, (ii) the proceeds of which are disbursed to the mortgagor in one or more lump sums, or in equal or unequal installments, either directly by the lender or the lender's agent, and (iii) that requires no repayment until a future time, upon the earliest occurrence of one or more events specified in the reverse mortgage loan contract.[24]

Because of the potential for abuse in loans involving the elderly, the Act regulates reverse mortgage loans very strictly. Requirements include various disclosures and reverse mortgage counseling for the borrower(s) prior to the loan closing.[25]

Subordination

Priorities between different mortgages, liens, and encumbrances on land can be changed or rearranged via a "*subordination agreement.*" In this context, "subordination" means to move a superior lien below a junior lien in priority. The holder of a first mortgage may agree for various reasons to subordinate it to an existing or proposed mortgage on the same property, or where a homeowner wants to refinance his first mortgage but also has a home equity line of credit (HELOC).[26] Upon refinancing, the existing first mortgage will be paid in full, moving the HELOC from second place into first place in priority and the refinanced loan would be in second place unless that lender insisted that the entity holding the HELOC must agree to subordinate the HELOC to the new first mortgage.

> *Example:* An investor proposes to purchase vacant land from a seller for $400,000 and construct a commercial building. The terms of the sale include:
> 1) The investor will make a 10 percent down payment.
> 2) The seller will finance the remaining 90 percent and receive a purchase-money mortgage.
> 3) The bank will loan the investor-buyer $1.5 million to construct the building.
> 4) The seller agrees to subordinate his recorded purchase-money mortgage (which is first in time) to the bank's later construction loan deed of trust.

Once the seller and the bank enter into the written subordination agreement that is then filed in the register of deeds office, the seller's senior mortgage will become junior and second in priority to the bank's construction loan which will become senior and first in priority.

*A broker should **never** offer advice on whether to subordinate*, because the question raises significant legal issues. Instead, a broker should strongly recommend that the consumer consult an experienced real estate attorney. This is particularly true where seller financing is involved and the seller is being asked to subordinate a purchase money mortgage. (Recall that a seller who finances all or a portion of the buyer's purchase is precluded by law from obtaining a deficiency judgment against the buyer if the collateral securing the debt is insufficient to satisfy the debt.)

Endnotes

1. Some experts argue that North Carolina actually follows an **"intermediate theory" of mortgages,** a hybrid theory striking a middle position between the pure title and lien theories of mortgage law, but the specifics of this theory are beyond an introductory discussion of North Carolina mortgage law.

2. In addition to securing a debt, a mortgage or deed of trust can secure an obligation, but since this chapter only discusses mortgage debts, the secured obligations topic is omitted.

3. For a comprehensive discussion of this area, see Hetrick and McLaughlin, *Webster's Real Estate Law in North Carolina, 6th ed. (LexisNexis),* Chapter 13, *"Mortgages and Deeds of Trust."*

4. *In re Head Grading Co., Inc.,* 353 B.R. 122 (Bankruptcy Ct. E.D.N.C. Wilson Div. 2006), citing three North Carolina appellate decisions.

5. N.C. Gen. Stat. §22-2. *In re Hudson,* 182 N.C. App. 499, 642 S.E.2d 485 (2007)

6. *Leggett v. Bullock,* 44 N.C. 283 (1853); *Ellington v. Raleigh Bldg. Supply Co.,* 196 N.C. 784, 147 S.E.2d 307 (1929).

7. The recording act dealing with deeds of trust and mortgages is found at N.C. Gen. Stat. §47-20.

8. For the leading North Carolina case on "due-on-sale" clauses, see *Crockett v. Savings and Loan Association,* 289 N.C. 620, 224 S.E.2d 580 (1976). See also *In re Foreclosure of Bonder,* 306 N.C. 451, 293 S.E.2d 798 (1982) and *Davis v. Vecaro Dev. Corp.,* 101 N.C. App. 554, 400 S.E.2d 83 (1991).

9. The North Carolina statutes related to the satisfaction of mortgages and deeds of trust were revised in 2005 with minor revisions in 2011. See Article 4, Chapter 45 of the North Carolina General Statutes.

10. Hetrick and McLaughlin, *Webster's Real Estate Law in North Carolina, 6th ed. (LexisNexis),* §§13.29-13.31, pp. 13-55 to 13-63.

11. *Id.,* pp. 581-626.

12. N.C. Gen. Stat. Chapter 1, Article 29A and Chapter 45. For an example, see *In re Foreclosure by David A. Simpson, P.C.*, 211 N.C. App. 483, 711 S.E.2d 165 (2011), where the entity in possession of the original mortgage note could not prove the note had been properly endorsed to the entity, and thus, the entity had no standing to pursue foreclosure on the property securing the debt evidenced by the note.

13. N.C. Gen. Stat. §45-21.38. Leading cases interpreting the anti-deficiency judgment statute include *Ross Realty Co. v. First Citizens Bank & Trust Co.*, 296 N.C. 366, 250 S.E.2d 271 (1979); *In re Gulledge*, 17 B.R. 311 (Bankr. M.D.N.C. 1982); *Blanton v. Sisk*, 70 N.C. App. 70, 318 S.E.2d 560 (1984); *Chemical Bank v. Belk*, 41 N.C. App. 356, 255 S.E.2d 421 (1979).

14. A North Carolina statute provides limited protection to a mortgagor against a deficiency judgment sought by a third-party lender, but that statute is of little practical value and is beyond the scope of this Manual. See, **N.C. Gen. Stat. §45-21.36.** For one of the few instances where the mortgage debtor has been successful in asserting this defense, see *First Citizens Bank & Trust Co. v. Cannon*, 138 N.C. App. 153, 530 S.E.2d 581 (2000) where the mortgage debtor successfully raised the defense. Mere unsubstantiated and unproven assertions, however, will not help the debtor. *Lexington State Bank v. Miller*, 137 N.C. App. 748, 529 S.E.2d 454 (2000).

15. For more information on MERS®, see "Information for Homeowners" on www.mersinc.org. A MERS® Commercial system is also in place for commercial mortgage loans and the securitization process.

16. N.C. Gen. Stat. §45-21.27 through §45-21.30.

17. See, for example, *Investors Title Ins. Co. v. Montague*, 142 N.C. App. 696, 543 S.E.2d 527 (2001), where the Court of Appeals reviews the rules concerning the liability of a person assuming a mortgage and the liability of the original mortgagor.

18. See, for example, *Arnold v. Howard*, 29 N.C. App. 570, 225 S.E.2d 149 (1976).

19. Article 7, Chapter 45 of the North Carolina General Statutes, titled "Instruments to Secure Future Advances and Future Obligations," sets forth requirements and guidelines for future advances mortgages. N.C. Gen. Stat. §45-70(a) provides:
    > Any security instrument which conforms to the requirements of this Article shall, from the time and date of registration thereof, have the same priority to the extent of all future advances secured by it, as if all the advances had been made at the time of the execution of the instrument.

20. See Article 9, Chapter 45 of the North Carolina General Statutes, titled "Instruments to Secure Equity Lines of Credit." N.C. Gen. Stat. §45-81(a) defines "equity line of credit" as follows:
    > (a) The term "equity line of credit" means an agreement in writing between a lender and a borrower for an extension of credit, pursuant to which:
    > (1) At any time within a specified period not to exceed 30 years, the borrower may request and the lender is obligated to provide, by honoring negotiable instruments drawn by the borrower or otherwise, advances up to an agreed aggregate limit;
    > (2) Any repayments of principal by the borrower within the specified

period will reduce the amount of advances counted against the aggregate limit; and

(3) The borrower's obligation to the lender is secured by a mortgage or deed of trust, relating to real property, that shows on its face the maximum principal amount which may be secured at any time and that it secures an equity line of credit governed by the provisions of this Article.

21. N.C. Gen. Stat. §45-81(c); §45-82.

22. N.C. Gen. Stat. §45-82. The first sentence of this statute reads: "A mortgage or deed of trust which shows on its face that it secures an equity line of credit governed by the provisions of this Article, shall, from the time of its registration, have the same priority to the extent of all advances secured by it, as if the advances had been made at the time of the execution of the mortgage or deed of trust, notwithstanding the fact that from time to time during the term of the loan, no balance is outstanding."

23. Article 21 of Chapter 53 of the North Carolina General Statutes. The purpose of the Reverse Mortgage Act is set forth at N.C. Gen. Stat. §53-256 as follows:

It is the intent of the General Assembly that reverse mortgage loans be available so that elderly homeowners may use the equity in their homes to meet financial needs. The General Assembly recognizes that there may be restrictions and requirements governing traditional mortgage transactions that should not apply to reverse mortgages. The purpose of this Article is to authorize reverse mortgage transactions and to clarify other provisions of North Carolina law that might otherwise apply to reverse mortgage loans, and to provide protection for elderly homeowners who enter into reverse mortgage loans.

24. N.C. Gen. Stat. §53-257(6).

25. See N.C. Gen. Stat. §53-264: "Disclosure of loan terms;" §53-269: "Counseling provisions;" and §53-270: "Prohibited Acts."

26. "Subordination" of mortgages is governed by N.C. Gen. Stat. §39-6.6.

13 | FINANCING LEGISLATION AND PRACTICES

This chapter addresses various federal and North Carolina laws that apply to real estate financing and then provides an overview of basic real estate lending practices and procedures, including a discussion of fraudulent practices by borrowers, licensees, and others in connection with real estate lending. The focus is on residential real estate financing – more specifically, laws and practices related to first mortgage loans on owner-occupied homes.

FEDERAL LEGISLATION

To protect members of the public seeking consumer credit, Congress has enacted a series of laws prohibiting certain discriminatory activities by lenders and requiring disclosure of specific information to assist a prospective home buyer in making better informed decisions. Major federal legislation applicable to residential financing includes the Truth in Lending Act, the Fair Credit Reporting Act, the Equal Credit Opportunity Act, legislation requiring certain loan servicing disclosures, and the Dodd-Frank Wall Street Reform and Consumer Protection Act, all of which are addressed in this section. The Real Estate Settlement Procedures Act (RESPA), a very important federal consumer disclosure act pertaining to financing and loan closing, is covered in Chapter 14, "Closing Real Estate Transactions."

DODD-FRANK WALL STREET REFORM AND CONSUMER PROTECTION ACT

Background

In 2007, the United States and global economies suffered a long-smoldering financial crisis and ensuing recession caused by excessive risk-taking and abuses by many major players in the financial community, including banks and other mortgage lenders, the secondary mortgage market, institutional investors, investment firms and others. This crisis resulted in bank failures, business failures, high unemployment, sharply declining real estate values, historic levels of loan foreclosures, and other conditions that, in turn, led to massive bailouts of banks and businesses by U. S. taxpayers, a massive federal debt and a long-running recession. Many experts believe the financial crisis was due largely to inadequate regulation and oversight of the financial sector, notably the mortgage lending and investment (securities) sectors.

Passage of Dodd-Frank Wall Street Reform and Consumer Protection Act

To address the perceived regulatory failures in the financial and investment sectors, Congress passed the Dodd-Frank Wall Street Reform and Consumer Protection Act (hereafter the **"Dodd-Frank Act"**) effective July 12, 2010.[1] This massive piece of legislation called for the most comprehensive financial regulatory system reforms since the 1930s, when similar major legislation was needed to address abuses in the banking and investment sectors. This law established a new consumer protection and financial regulatory agency, the *Bureau of Consumer Financial Protection*, to take over the consumer protection and financial regulatory activities previously handled by several different federal agencies. The scope of this law is extremely broad and goes far beyond regulating matters directly related to real estate financing. The coverage here will summarize a few of the major subjects addressed by Dodd-Frank, but will then focus on regulation in the real estate finance area. Legislation and regulations affecting various aspects of mortgage lending and real estate settlement practices were enacted that substantially altered settlement closing practices, discussed in Chapter 14.

Major Matters Addressed by Dodd-Frank Act

Some of the most significant subjects addressed by the Dodd-Frank Act include:
- Capital requirements for banks.
- Minimum standards for originating mortgages and disclosures to borrowers.
- Compensation of mortgage brokers.
- The sale of mortgage loans.
- Creation of the Bureau of Consumer Financial Protection(CFPB) having broad authority over most consumer financial products.
- Creation of the Financial Stability Oversight Council charged with identifying and responding to emerging risks throughout the financial system.
- Federal Deposit Insurance Corporation standards and requirements.
- Federal Reserve's Board's emergency lending powers and various Federal Reserve Board operations.
- Banking entities' ability to engage in certain investment transactions.
- Regulation of the market for securities known as "derivatives" and of "hedge funds" and private equity funds.
- Liquidation of failing banks and entities primarily engaged in financial activities and prohibition of a "bailout" by taxpayers (i.e., ends "too big to fail bailouts").
- Governance of publicly-traded financial services companies, including mandatory disclosure of executive compensation and shareholder approval of "golden parachutes" for executive officers.
- Regulation of credit rating firms.

CONSUMER FINANCIAL PROTECTION BUREAU

Although the Dodd-Frank Act established a new major financial oversight agency named the *Bureau of Consumer Financial Protection*, the agency (and virtually everyone else) uses the name ***Consumer Financial Protection Bureau (CFPB)***. Thus, the coverage in this text will use the name and acronym used by the agency itself.

While the CFPB technically is an agency of the Federal Reserve Board and is housed with and funded by the Federal Reserve Board, it has the authority to operate independently of any control or influence of the Federal Reserve Board. The director of the CFPB is appointed by the President and confirmed by the Senate.

Purposes and Functions of the CFPB

The primary purposes of the CFPB include: 1) the prevention of lender abuses such as predatory lending or the use of inappropriate fees, and 2) the integration of federal regulations protecting individual borrowers and other consumers into one agency. It has broad authority to develop and implement rules regarding most *consumer* financial products. The CFPB can independently write and enforce rules for consumer protection governing all financial institutions – banks and non-banks – that offer consumer financial services or products. The *consumer protection responsibilities* of several other federal agencies (listed below) were transferred to the CFPB, thereby consolidating these responsibilities under one powerful agency with the authority to act quickly to address bad business practices without having to wait for Congress to pass a law.

Agencies Whose Consumer Protection Responsibilities Were Transferred to the CFPB

- Office of the Comptroller of the Currency (OCC)
- Office of Thrift Supervision (OTS) – agency abolished
- Federal Reserve Board ("Fed")
- Federal Deposit Insurance Corporation (FDIC)
- National Credit Union Administration (NCUA)
- Department of Housing and Urban Development (HUD)
- Federal Trade Commission (FTC)

The CFPB has the authority to examine and enforce regulations for banks and credit unions with assets over $10 billion and all mortgage-related businesses (lenders, servicers, mortgage brokers, and even foreclosure scam operators), payday lenders, and student lenders, as well as other non-bank financial companies such as debt collectors and consumer reporting agencies. The CFPB must, however, coordinate with other bank regulators (i.e., the Federal Reserve Board or the National Credit Union Administration) when examining banks to prevent undue regulatory burdens. (Banks and credit unions with assets of less than $10 billion will be examined for consumer complaints by the Federal Reserve Board or NCUA, as appropriate.)

Laws/Regulations Now Administered by the CFPB

The consumer financial protection laws and implementing regulations currently administered by the CFPB are shown in the table below, along with the former responsible regulatory agency. These regulations have long been referred to by a designated letter, such as "Regulation Z" for Truth in Lending regulations, and these letter designations have been retained in the regulations that have been republished by the CFPB. In addition to those laws listed below, the Dodd-Frank Act assigned regulatory responsibility for the *Home Mortgage Disclosure Act* and the *Home Ownership and Equity Protection Act* to the CFPB.

Law	Rule	Former Agency
Equal Credit Opportunity Act (ECOA)	Regulation B	Federal Reserve Board
Fair Credit Reporting Act (FCRA)	Regulation V	Federal Reserve Board
Truth in Lending Act (TILA)	Regulation Z	Federal Reserve Board
Real Estate Settlement Procedures Act (RESPA)	Regulation X	HUD
Secure and Fair Enforcement for Mortgage Licensing Act (SAFE Act)	Regulations G & H	Interagency for Mortgage Licensing Act (SAFE Act)
Interstate Land Sales Full Disclosure Act Land Registration Purchaser's Revocation Rights Sales Practices and Standards Special Rules of Practices	 Regulation J Regulation K Regulation K Regulation L	 HUD HUD HUD HUD

TRUTH IN LENDING ACT

The **Truth in Lending Act (TILA)** was enacted by Congress as Title I of the Consumer Credit Protection Act of 1968.[2] The general thrust of all federal consumer protection laws in the consumer credit area generally can be characterized as combining two regulatory approaches:

(1) **Disclosure** — Creditors are required to disclose certain information to consumers in a prescribed manner and timeframe.

(2) **Market Protections** — Creditors are required to perform certain acts, or prohibited from engaging in certain acts, in their relations with consumers in the marketplace.[3]

The Truth in Lending Act emphasizes the first of the above approaches rather than the second. Its basic purpose is to provide a full disclosure of credit charges to the consumer to enable consumer-borrowers to shop and compare various credit sources, understand the cost of credit, and decide for themselves whether the charge for credit is reasonable.

The Truth in Lending Act was amended effective 1982 by the **Truth in Lending Simplification and Reform Act (TILSRA)**[4] and was further amended in 2009 by the **Mortgage Disclosure Improvement Act**, which expanded the TIL early disclosure requirements. This discussion will refer both to the initial law and its amendments collectively as the "Truth in Lending Act" (or "Act" or "TILA)." Until 2010, the Federal Reserve Board was responsible for enforcing TILA and did so through rules commonly known as **Regulation Z**. *As of 2010, responsibility for rulemaking and enforcing TILA was transferred to the* **Consumer Financial Protection Bureau (CFPB)** *by the* **Dodd-Frank Act.** The moniker of "Regulation Z" was retained with the CFPB rules.

Brokers must be familiar with the required credit disclosures and rules relating to advertising credit terms.

Applicability

The *truth in lending laws and regulations apply both to those who **advertise** or extend* the following types of loans *if the loan 1) involves a finance charge **OR** 2) is payable in more than four installments*:

A) All "closed end" real estate mortgage loans to natural persons where the loans are not made for business, commercial or agricultural purposes, regardless of the amount of the loan. This includes loans on second homes and vacation homes as well as loans on a personal residence.

B) Personal consumer loans of $54,600 or less through 2017. Under the Dodd-Frank Act, this threshold must be adjusted annually by any annual percentage increase in the consumer price index.

Loans *exempt* from truth in lending disclosure requirements are those made primarily for commercial, agricultural, or business purposes (including most loans on residential *rental* property) and loans for more than $54,600 secured by personal property.

Any person, company or institution that regularly extends consumer credit in exchange for a finance charge (interest and/or other charges) must comply with truth in lending laws and regulations. In addition to traditional lending institutions (such as banks and savings associations), this legislation also applies to finance companies, mortgage companies, and anyone who extends such credit more than five times a year. Mortgage brokers and real estate brokers are not directly affected by this law when "arranging" financing, provided they are not lending the money themselves, thereby becoming a creditor in the transaction. However, real estate brokers are impacted by and must comply with Regulation Z if they include any financing terms when advertising property.

Disclosure of Credit Information

The primary purpose of the truth in lending laws and regulations is to inform the borrower of the true cost of credit. Lenders are required to *disclose certain information no later than three business days after receiving the borrower's loan application.*

Chief Disclosures to Borrower

The four most important disclosures are the: **annual percentage rate, finance charge, amount financed, and total of payments**. These major disclosures must appear prominently and separately from other information on the disclosure form provided to borrowers, previously called a Truth-in-Lending Disclosure.

Annual Percentage Rate (APR). The APR is arguably the single most important component of the truth in lending disclosures because it provides the borrower with a figure that the borrower can use to easily compare the cost of credit from various sources. The APR is *the cost of credit expressed as a yearly rate*. The APR is a function of the amount financed by the consumer, the finance charge, and the payment schedule set forth by the lender.[5] Although the interest rate for most loans will be very close to the APR, the APR is *not the interest rate. The APR is the simple interest rate **plus** certain specified "finance charges" over the life of the loan expressed as a yearly rate*. Thus, the APR will always be slightly higher than the interest rate (unless there are no lender fees). Another definition of the APR is the relation between the total finance charge and the net amount borrowed expressed as an annualized percentage rate.

The formulas for calculating the APR are very complex. Real estate brokers do not need to be able to calculate the APR, but they must understand what is included in the calculation. *Not all charges relating to the property purchase may be included in the APR.* If an APR seems unusually low compared to other quotes, a prudent borrower will ask for an itemization of *all* projected closing charges, as costs may be higher for charges that are not subject to inclusion as a "finance charge" and thus not included in the APR calculation.

Finance Charge. The finance charge is the *total dollar amount the credit will cost the borrower over the life of the loan,* assuming the loan is not paid off early and that each scheduled payment is made on the actual due date. Basically, the finance charge is the cost for obtaining a loan, rather than paying cash and includes *any charges or fees payable by the consumer imposed by the lender as a condition of extending credit.* For example, interest, origination fees, discount point(s), processing or administrative fees, and mortgage insurance premiums, to name a few, are considered finance charges. Fees for services that may be required, but are not a condition of extending the credit, such as fees for a credit report, appraisal, inspections, title binder and insurance, and fees to prepare loan related documents, e.g., deeds, deeds of trust, reconveyances, notary fees, recording fees, etc., are not included as part of the finance charge.[6] However, where the lender not only requires the service, but chooses the third party service provider, then the fees charged by that provider may be included in calculating the finance charge.[7]

Prospective buyers may be shocked by the finance charge amount as the total finance charge over the life of the loan may be two or three times the amount financed (depending on prevailing interest rates). For example, on a 30-year loan for $175,000 at a fixed 5 percent interest rate, the total cost for *interest alone* over the full loan term would be $163,198. Even at a 4 percent interest rate, the total interest would still be $126,772.

Amount Financed. The amount financed is simply *the net amount of credit actually provided to the borrower.* It is the loan amount, plus any amounts financed by the lender that are not included as part of the finance charge, minus any prepaid finance charge, which are monies paid prior to or at closing or withheld from the credit proceeds. The *amount financed typically* results in a disclosed figure that actually *is less than the loan amount* specified on the loan application and promissory note.

Total of Payments. This disclosure is *the total dollar amount the borrower will pay to the lender over the life of the loan* and is the sum of the **amount financed** plus all **finance charges**. In other words, the total of payments is the amount of each periodic payment multiplied by the number of periodic payments. For example, a $175,000 loan at a 5 percent fixed rate for 30 years will have 359 monthly payments of $939.75 and one final payment of $827.37. Thus, assuming the borrower makes all scheduled payments when due, the total of payments will be $338,197.62.

Other Disclosures

Various additional disclosures are required under TILA and Regulation Z including the ***identity of the creditor*** and whether the loan involves an ***adjustable rate.*** If the interest rate may increase in the future, then the borrower must be told what circumstances will cause an increase, any limitations on the increase, the effect of an increase, and an example of payment terms that would result from an increase.

A creditor must also disclose the ***payment schedule*** (the number, amounts, and timing of payments to repay the loan obligation). If the loan has a ***demand feature*** (if it is payable "on demand") that must be disclosed. Prepayment penalties, late charges, credit insurance matters, loan assumption policies, and required deposits for items such as taxes, insurance or repairs also must be disclosed when applicable.

Timing of Disclosures, Collection of Fees and Consummation

Since enactment of the **Mortgage Disclosure Improvement Act (MDIA) effective July 30, 2009**, consumers who apply for a closed end real estate mortgage loan subject to TILA must be given an *"early" TIL disclosure*, *i.e.*, at the time of loan application or within three business days following application. The lender cannot collect any fees, other than a reasonable fee for obtaining the consumer's credit history, until the consumer receives the early TIL disclosure. Once the consumer receives the disclosure, the lender may collect other fees such as a lock-in fee, application fee, appraisal fee, etc. The lender may not close the loan until seven business days after the early disclosures are given, thereby effectively eliminating rushed closings. The MDIA "also requires disclosure of payment examples if the loan's interest rate or payments can change, as well as disclosure of a statement that there is no guarantee the consumer will be able to refinance in the future."[8]

If the APR on the early TIL disclosure becomes inaccurate, the lender must provide corrected disclosures to the consumer with a revised APR. To remain accurate, the final APR cannot be more than 1/8 of one percent above or below the APR initially disclosed. To allow ample time for the consumer to digest the final disclosures, the consumer must receive the corrected disclosures **no later than three *business* days before loan consummation.** This allows consumers to review the material loan terms *before* the settlement meeting.

Any significant change in the **finance charge** most likely will require a new TIL disclosure and an additional waiting period. To add to the delay, *if corrected disclosures are mailed to the consumer, another three business days must be added* to allow the disclosures to reach the consumer. The TIL regulations go on to describe several specific circumstances that can trigger corrected TIL disclosures and thus delay the consummation of the loan transaction:

- The consumer fails to "lock in" the initial interest rate offered by the lender and interest rates later increase.
- Any estimated component of the finance charge increases after the initial disclosure, e.g., interim interest, origination fee, discount points, mortgage insurance, etc.
- The closing meeting is delayed and the consumer's interest rate lock period expires.
- Subsequent to the initial application, the consumer switches to a different loan product.
- Fees charged by third-parties increase, such as the settlement agent's fees.

Both the timing and content of lender disclosures under TILA (the early TIL and final TIL) and under RESPA (the Good Faith Estimate and HUD-1 settlement statement) were very similar, but lenders were required to provide both if the transaction was subject to TILA and RESPA. The Dodd-Frank Act, in consolidating both rule-making authority and enforcement of TILA and RESPA into one agency, directed the CFPB to integrate the separate disclosure forms required under TILA and RESPA into one form that would satisfy both laws. Thus, for loan applications made on or since October 3, 2015, applicant-borrowers have received a "Loan Estimate" in lieu of the early TIL and a "Closing Disclosure" form instead of the final TIL, both of which will be discussed in greater detail in Chapter 14.

Additional Protections for Consumers With "Higher Priced Mortgage Loans"

Regulation Z was amended effective October 1, 2009 to address undesirable lending practices in connection with "higher priced mortgage loans" (not to be confused with predatory "high cost mortgages").

Spurred by low interest rates during the 2000s, both the prime and subprime[9] mortgage markets underwent dramatic change. With property values appreciating in the housing market up until 2007, refinancing accelerated as homeowners were anxious to extract equity. Less qualified borrowers were attracted to "non-traditional"[10] mortgage loans. Many borrowers thought that the appreciation in property values would enable them to refinance their loans well before the lower initial fixed rate period ended and the new (much higher) adjustable rate period began. Underwriting standards were loosened in many sectors of the mortgage market as lenders, particularly non-depository institutions, many of which no longer exist, competed aggressively for market share.

Regulation Z's 2009 requirements for higher priced mortgage loans were crafted to apply to all subprime loans, although the scope of the rule is broad enough to reach some segments of the prime lending market as well. A ***higher priced mortgage loan*** is defined as a *consumer-purpose closed-end loan secured by a consumer's principal dwelling and having an annual percentage rate (APR) that exceeds the average prime offer rates for a comparable transaction by at least 1.5 percentage points for first-lien loans, or 3.5 percentage points for subordinate lien loans.* Among the protections afforded consumers who obtain higher-priced mortgage loans, the rules:

- prohibit mortgage lenders from extending credit without regard to a consumer's ability to repay from sources other than the collateral itself;
- require creditors to verify income and assets they rely upon to determine repayment ability;
- prohibit prepayment penalties except under certain conditions; and
- require creditors to establish escrow accounts for taxes and insurance, but permit creditors to allow borrowers to cancel escrows 12 months after loan consummation.

The revised regulation prohibits mortgage lenders from structuring closed-end mortgage loans as open-end lines of credit to evade the rules because the rules do not apply to open-end lines of credit. Regulation Z "higher priced mortgage loans" are called "rate spread home loans" under a 2007 North Carolina law discussed shortly under Predatory Lending, "Consumer's Ability to Repay."

Disclosures in Credit Advertising

To prevent misleading advertising of credit terms, *Regulation Z governs **any** advertisement for consumer credit, **regardless of who places the advertisement**.* Thus, real estate brokers who include certain terms related to possible financing of real estate in their advertising are subject to the requirements of Regulation Z.

Trigger Terms

Regulation Z requires that any advertisement for consumer credit include certain information (basically, *all* major financing terms) if any of four "trigger terms" are included in an advertisement. These *"trigger terms"* are:

1. The down payment, whether expressed as a dollar amount or as a percentage. Examples: "10% down;" "$1,000 down;" or "90% financing."
2. The amount of any payment, whether expressed as a dollar amount or percentage. Examples: "Payments only $700 per month" or "Payments of $8.66 per $1,000 borrowed."
3. The number of payments or the period of repayment. Examples: "Only 120 low monthly payments" or "30-year mortgages available."
4. The dollar amount of any finance charge. Examples: "Interest averages less than $300 per month" or "$10 per month carrying charge." (This is rarely a problem with real estate advertisements.)

As can be seen above, when the advertisement contains *specific* financing terms the advertiser must fully disclose **all** credit terms, whereas general statements related to financing do *not* trigger additional disclosures. A few examples of general statements that *are acceptable* include:

"No down payment" or "Low down payment"

"Easy monthly payments" or "Low monthly payments"

"Financing available" or "Long-term financing available"

"Low financing charges"

"No closing costs"

Required Disclosures

If any of the four "trigger terms" listed above appear in an advertisement, then *the following specific disclosures concerning the financing must appear in the same advertisement:*

1. The amount or percentage of the down payment (or a statement that none is required).
2. The terms of loan repayment (i.e., repayment obligations over the full loan term).
3. The annual percentage rate, using that specific term or the abbreviation "APR." If the APR may be increased after consummation of the credit transaction, that fact must be stated.

Advertising Finance Rates

The only number that may appear in advertising (other than the purchase or lease price that has nothing to do with financing terms), is the *finance charge expressed as an "annual percentage rate," using that term or the abbreviation "APR."* This is true *even if the APR is the same as the simple interest rate.* Of course, the reported APR must be correct! Thus, unless they have a background in finance, real estate brokers almost certainly will need a lender's assistance to properly calculate the APR. If the advertisement includes the APR, then the interest rate also may be reported, but not in a manner that makes it more conspicuous than the APR. If the credit involves a variable or adjustable rate, the fact that the rate is subject to change must be stated in the advertisement. Calculation of the APR when the interest rate is subject to change is very complicated and should only be undertaken by a qualified finance person.

Guideline for Real Estate Brokers

Real estate brokers who include credit terms in their real estate advertisements should follow the general rule that *if **any** specific credit terms are included in the advertisement, then **all** required credit disclosures must be included.* Brokers should seek assistance from qualified finance experts to calculate any annual percentage rate (APR) to be used in an advertisement or they may *avoid Regulation Z issues by not including any numbers in their advertising, other than the list or lease price.*

FAIR CREDIT REPORTING ACT

A federal court decision[11] has summarized the purpose of the **Fair Credit Reporting Act**[12] (FCRA) as follows:

> ... A central purpose of the FCRA is to ensure the confidentiality and accuracy of consumer credit information and to require that reasonable procedures are in place to meet these goals. Under the FCRA, Congress imposed obligations on three entities: (1) consumer reporting agencies; (2) users of consumer reports; and (3) furnishers of information to reporting agencies. The FCRA defines a "consumer reporting agency" as "any person which, for monetary fees ... regularly engages in ... assembling or evaluating consumer credit information ... for the purpose of furnishing consumer reports to third parties ..." [Citations omitted.]

Detailed records of individuals' consumer credit are maintained by companies called "credit bureaus" that clearly are a "consumer reporting agency" under FCRA. There are three major national credit bureaus: Equifax, TransUnion, and Experian. Creditors may contact these agencies to check the credit standing of an individual applying for credit.

The **Fair Credit Reporting Act** was passed in 1970 to set standards on how credit bureaus handle their consumer credit information and to require certain disclosures to individuals. Consumer accounts are referred to as "trade lines." Unfavorable or adverse credit information may only be reported for seven years from the date of last account activity, or for ten years from the filing of a civil judgment or discharge in bankruptcy. Individuals have the right to examine their own credit reports and to demand the correction of erroneous data. Obviously, a credit bureau has the right to require reasonable proof that information is incorrect before it can be altered or deleted.

If an individual has been denied credit because of an unacceptable credit report, that person has the right to examine the credit record at no charge. Otherwise, the reporting bureau may collect a fee for its services in providing the consumer's credit report if the consumer already has received his/her free annual credit report. Only persons and companies who are in the business of extending credit and are members of the credit bureau itself are authorized to examine the credit records of others, and then only for the specific purpose of approving or disapproving a credit applicant.

It is **highly recommended** *that real estate brokers advise prospective buyers to contact at least one of the credit bureaus and examine their credit reports* **before** *applying for a loan.* Eliminating erroneous information before it is disclosed to a lender can avoid subsequent problems and can positively affect a consumer's credit score. Should a problem arise, the agency now responsible for administering and enforcing the Fair Credit Reporting Act is the CFPB.

In 2003, the ***Fair and Accurate Credit Transaction Act*** [13] **(FACTA)** added new sections to the Fair Credit Reporting Act intended primarily to help consumers fight the growing crime of identity theft. It attempts to enhance the accuracy of consumer credit information, enables identity theft victims to place "fraud alerts" in their credit files, and limits customer information sharing among corporation's affiliates for marketing purposes. FACTA also is the source of the right to a *free credit report every year from each of the three consumer reporting agencies.* [14]

EQUAL CREDIT OPPORTUNITY ACT (ECOA)

The **Equal Credit Opportunity Act (ECOA)**, [15] implemented by Regulation B and passed in 1974, initially *prohibited discrimination in the granting of credit on the basis of sex or marital status.* A 1976 amendment expanded the prohibition to include *race, color, religion, national origin, sex, marital status, age, receipt of public assistance, and the exercise of rights under the Consumer Credit Protection Act,* of which ECOA is a part.

While ECOA is directed at other forms of consumer credit, it had a profound effect on mortgage lending. A borrower's potential for future income factors more heavily when considering a borrower for a mortgage loan, given the duration, than when considering borrowers for short-term loans. Dodd-Frank amendments to Regulation B implemented by the CFPB in January 2014 also require creditors to provide mortgage loan applicants with free copies of appraisals and other written valuations and to notify applicants that they will receive copies of all appraisals.

ECOA recognizes two different theories of discriminatory conduct that violate the Act. The first is *disparate treatment*; it occurs when a creditor treats an applicant differently because the applicant is a member of one of the ECOA protected classes that include age, marital status, and receipt of public assistance (which are not protected classes under the Fair Housing Act). The second is *disparate impact*; this occurs when a creditor's policies or practices appear to be facially neutral, but in fact have an adverse effect or impact on a member of a protected class.[16]

Implementing the ECOA has not been easy, but one of the early steps was to limit the questions a lender could ask a loan applicant. No questions could be asked about certain income such as alimony, child support, or separate maintenance payments *unless that income would be used to help repay the loan.* No discounting of income by sex or marital status is permitted — each applicant must be considered as an individual whose income is measured separately. Credit histories of married or divorced persons should be separated so that adverse credit of one party does not unfairly impact the other. Various attempts have been made to expand the protected ECOA classes to prohibit discrimination on the basis of sexual orientation or gender identity when extending credit, but these attempts have been unsuccessful thus far.

FAIR HOUSING ACT

The Fair Housing Act[17] prohibits discrimination in residential real estate related transactions based upon a person's race, color, religion, sex, handicap, familial status, or national origin and clearly includes residential loan transactions. The Fair Housing Act specifically prohibits a lender from discriminating based on a protected class either when making loan transactions available or in the proffered terms and conditions of loan transactions. Prohibited lender practices include failing to provide information as to the availability of loans or providing information that is inaccurate or different from that provided others because of a person's race, color, religion, sex, handicap, familial status or national origin.[18]

LOAN SERVICING DISCLOSURE REQUIREMENTS

The Cranston-Gonzalez **National Affordable Housing Act** passed in 1990 amended the **Real Estate Settlement Procedures Act (RESPA)** and brought a number of changes to the lending industry, including a *servicing disclosure requirement* that became effective in 1991. *The purpose of the law is to provide consumers with both information and protection against the widespread practice of a servicing company transferring the responsibility for servicing the loan to another company.* "Servicing" includes receiving monthly mortgage payments, accounting for and remitting the principal and interest portion to the holder of the note, maintaining the escrow accounts for property insurance and real estate taxes, paying such real estate taxes and insurance premiums as they come due, and handling any collection actions as may be needed.

Required Disclosures

The following disclosures are required regarding the transfer of loan servicing and a borrower's rights.

- *Servicing Disclosure Statement.* The servicing disclosure statement must be given to persons applying for a federally related first lien mortgage loan. The disclosure must be given at the time of application, but in no event later than three business days following application. As modified in 1997, the abbreviated servicing disclosure statement merely states whether the servicing of the loan may be assigned, sold, or transferred at any time while the loan is outstanding. There no longer is a requirement that the applicants acknowledge receipt of the statement.
- *Transfer Requirements.* If servicing is transferred, the lender must provide a notice containing the name, address, and a toll-free or collect-call telephone number for the

new servicing company not less than 15 days prior to the date of transfer. Once servicing is transferred, the new servicer must send the borrower a written notice acknowledging the transfer within 15 days after the date of transfer.

- *Complaint Resolution.* If a borrower sends a qualified written request to the servicer, a written acknowledgment must be provided within five (5) business days of receipt. Any appropriate corrections to the account must be made within thirty (30) business days.
- *Damages and Costs.* The law provides for damages and costs to be assessed against servicers who violate the disclosure requirements.

NORTH CAROLINA LEGISLATION

In 1999, North Carolina became the first state in the United States to enact comprehensive predatory lending laws designed to protect North Carolina consumers from unscrupulous real estate financing practices that separate consumers from their money or the equity in their homes. Additionally, North Carolina has enacted legislation requiring the licensure of lending professionals, mandating additional disclosures, and in 2007, a series of laws regarding mortgage lending practices. The goal has been to eliminate abuses in home loan lending and loan collection practices, reduce home loan foreclosures, and require mortgage companies to ensure that they do not offer loans the consumer does not have the ability to repay.

Predatory Lending

It is difficult to define the term "predatory lending" because it can take so many forms. In general, the term refers to loans made on highly unfavorable terms to the consumer accompanied by lending practices that usually involve varying amounts of deception and outright fraud by the lender, resulting in loans with exorbitant costs and highly disadvantageous terms for consumers. In most instances, the victims of predatory lending are borrowers who are having financial difficulties and are ignorant of their legal rights. Most predatory lending practices are an unfair or deceptive trade practice under North Carolina General Statute § 75-1.1. An article on common predatory lending practices states:

> Commonly mentioned predatory terms include prepayment penalties
> for paying off the loan before the term ends; balloon payments that are greater
> than the borrower is able to raise except with even higher interest loans; high
> interest rates; negative amortization; high appraisal costs; requirement of up
> front credit insurance; mandatory pre-dispute arbitration clauses that result
> in borrowers waiving rights to trial and appeal if a dispute arises; yield spread
> premiums that are really prohibited "kickbacks" to [loan] brokers.[19]

The same article notes that predatory lending can also involve the following practices.
- Materially inflated appraisals.
- Equity-stripping loans that totally disregard the ability of the borrower to repay.
- Encouraging loan applicants to exaggerate or submit false information about their ability to repay the loan.
- A closing settlement statement that discloses a mortgage loan on more onerous terms and at a higher cost than the borrower reasonably expected.
- A practice known as "loan flipping" where the loan is refinanced repeatedly to the detriment of the borrower in the form of additional up-front fees.

"**Loan flipping**" and other abusive home loan practices are prohibited by North Carolina General Statute §24-10.2. These prohibitions include no prepayment penalties for home loans of $150,000 or less and no financing of upfront single premium credit, life, unemployment, disability, or health insurance coverages. A broker who knowingly participates in a predatory lending practice, including but not limited to the above listed practices, may violate the Unfair and Deceptive Practices Act (General Statute §75-1.1), federal legislation and regulations, the North Carolina Real Estate License Law, and North Carolina Real Estate Commission Rules.

High-Cost Home Loans

In 1999, North Carolina was a pioneer in enacting laws intended to curtail predatory home lending practices. With the enactment of General Statute §24-1.1E, the General Assembly targeted "high-cost home loans," known as "high cost mortgages" or "HOEPA loans" when Regulation Z addressed the topic several years later. By restricting these predatory loans, the legislature made it extremely difficult for lenders to extend high-cost home loans, effectively making them economically unattractive to mortgage lenders. State law continues to define a "*high-cost home loan*" as one involving:

1) a natural person for
2) an open or closed end loan that is not a reverse mortgage
3) incurred primarily for personal, family or household purposes
4) that does not exceed $300,000 and
5) is secured by a lien against either
   a) a manufactured home occupied by the borrower as his principal dwelling or
   b) real property on which there is or will be a 1-4 family residential structure occupied
   by   the borrower as his/her principal dwelling.

Additionally, the loan must exceed one or more of the following thresholds listed in the statute.
High fees – loans of $20,000 or more where the borrower is charged more than 5% of the loan amount in upfront points, fees, or other charges, although certain bona fide loan discount points or prepayment penalties may be excluded from this 5% calculation under specified circumstances; or
High interest rate – loans where the borrower is charged 8% more than the comparable Treasury securities rate; or
Prepayment penalty (if permitted), longer than 30 months or more than 2% of the amount pre-paid.

Other limitations and prohibited practices imposed by state law on lenders extending high-cost home loans include: no financing of upfront fees and insurance premiums; no balloon payments or negative amortization allowed; no early call or acceleration provision absent default or sale and no increased interest rate after default; required counseling for high-cost home loan borrowers prior to closing; and no lending without considering the consumer's ability to repay.

Consumer's Ability to Repay

By 2007, it became apparent that North Carolina's "high-cost home loan" statute directed at predatory lending did not afford adequate protection for borrowers from subprime lenders. Thus, the General Assembly added important new protections to Chapter 24 of the General Statutes including General Statute §24-1.1F that was crafted to regulate (but not prohibit) a category of subprime loans defined as "rate spread home loans."[20] A ***rate spread home loan*** has an interest rate that is clearly above the current market rate, but it is not so high as to trigger the anti-predatory lending provisions of the high cost home loan discussed above.

Under state law, rate spread home loans 1) cannot have a prepayment penalty, thus enabling a borrower to escape the onerous terms of a subprime loan by refinancing; and 2) the lender must consider the borrower's ability to repay the loan, including the borrower's credit history, current and future reasonably expected income, employment, assets (other than the home), debt-to-income ratio, and mortgage-related obligations, including property taxes, hazard insurance, and private mortgage insurance. *The lender must document the borrower's ability to repay.*

In September 2009, the statute was amended to conform to federal Regulation Z's newly created "higher priced mortgage loan" rule, the rationale being that to require a mortgage lender to apply one standard for federal purposes and a different standard for state purposes would be unreasonably burdensome on mortgage lenders without any corresponding benefits to consumers. Additional revisions to General Statute §24-1.1F effective October 1, 2013 adopted the TILA standards for defining a "higher priced mortgage loan" to define a rate spread home loan under state law, including treatment of prepayment penalties, determining APR, and other aspects of making a rate spread home loan. Since October 1, 2013, if it violates TILA/Regulation Z's requirements for a high-cost home loan (15 U.S.C. §1639c), then it violates North Carolina law for rate spread home loans.

North Carolina Amortization Notice and Disclosure

To better educate North Carolina mortgage loan applicants about different factors affecting loan amortization, state law requires lenders to provide certain information to consumers applying for a closed-end loan for less than $300,000 made for consumer, family or household purposes that will be secured by a first lien on the consumer's principal dwelling.

For these loan applications, mortgage lenders must provide at least one, and sometimes two, disclosures. First, mortgage lenders must provide information and examples of amortization of loans having different terms to these applicants. The North Carolina Commissioner of Banks has created a "Notice of Information and Examples of Amortization of Home Loans" to satisfy this first disclosure requirement. The lender must deliver the notice to applicants at the time of loan application or within three business days thereafter. Second, if the loan is a **fixed rate** loan requiring periodic payments, the mortgage lender must give the borrower an amortization schedule of his/her specific loan at closing or within three business days thereafter.

Residential Mortgage Fraud Act

The General Assembly enacted a new criminal Article 20A, titled the "Residential Mortgage Fraud Act," of Chapter 14 of the North Carolina General Statutes effective December 1, 2007. A key section, General Statute §14-118.12(a), provides:

> (a) A person is guilty of residential mortgage fraud when, for financial gain and with the intent to defraud, that person does any of the following:
>
> (1) Knowingly makes or attempts to make any material misstatement, misrepresentation, or omission within the mortgage lending process with the intention that a mortgage lender, mortgage broker, borrower, or any other person or entity that is involved in the mortgage lending process relies on it.
>
> (2) Knowingly uses or facilitates or attempts to use or facilitate the use of any misstatement, misrepresentation, or omission within the mortgage lending process with the intention that a mortgage lender, borrower, or any other person or entity that is involved in the mortgage lending process relies on it.

(3) Receives or attempts to receive proceeds or any other funds in connection with a residential mortgage closing that the person knew, or should have known, resulted from a violation of subdivision (1) or (2) of this subsection.

(4) Conspires or solicits another to violate any of the provisions of subdivision (1), (2), or (3) of this subsection.

Committing even one mortgage loan violation is a felony punishable by incarceration, forfeiture of property, and/or restitution. District attorneys may criminally prosecute violations on their own initiative or based on evidence of possible wrongdoing received from the North Carolina Commissioner of Banks, the North Carolina Real Estate Commission, the North Carolina Appraisal Board, the Attorney General, or other sources. Real or personal property gained through the fraudulent transaction may be subject to forfeiture under the provisions of General Statutes §14-2.3 and §14-7.20, subject to certain claims of good faith lienholders and innocent bona fide purchasers who had no knowledge of the violation. Real estate brokers should be alert to mortgage fraud, never participate in it, passively or actively, and should report suspected mortgage fraud to the proper governing or regulatory authority.

Identification of Loan Originator

General Statute §45A-4, titled "Duty of Settlement Agent," requires settlement agents to identify the loan originator on the deed of trust and lenders must identify the loan originator in the loan closing instructions.[21] If the settlement agent has received information from the lender or has actual knowledge that a mortgage broker or other person acted as a mortgage broker in the origination of the loan, then information identifying that mortgage broker or other person shall be placed on the first page of the deed of trust and shall not be considered confidential information.

Conduct of Loan Collectors and Ability to Contest Foreclosures

Session Law 2007-351 revised various real property and foreclosure statutes and added a major new article to Chapter 45 of the General Statutes titled "Mortgage Debt Collection and Servicing." This consumer-oriented legislation regulates the conduct of loan collectors, limits fees they can charge, and increases borrowers' ability to contest foreclosures.

N.C. Secure and Fair Enforcement (S.A.F.E.) Mortgage Licensing Act

In July 2008, Congress passed the Housing and Economic Recovery Act (HERA) to help the residential housing market recover. The primary goal of the federal *Secure and Fair Enforcement for Mortgage Licensing Act of 2008" (the SAFE Act)*[22] was to enhance consumer protection and reduce mortgage loan fraud by requiring the licensing of mortgage brokers and the registration of state-licensed mortgage originators and financial institution mortgage loan employees. The licensing requirement sets qualification standards for mortgage loan originators that include training and testing. The federal SAFE Act requires states to adopt minimum standards consistent with the Act's requirements.

In July, 2009, the North Carolina General Assembly enacted the **"North Carolina Secure and Fair Enforcement Mortgage Licensing Act."**[23] Although North Carolina has regulated and licensed mortgage loan originators and the companies that employ them since 2002, the North Carolina SAFE Act was intended to bring the state's mortgage lending laws into compliance with the federal SAFE Act. The state Act grants the North Carolina Commissioner of Banks broad authority to administer, interpret, and enforce the requirements of the Act and to adopt rules governing the licensure and practices of mortgage loan originators.

Both the federal and state SAFE Acts establish a means of monitoring the performance of mortgage loan originators. Any unfair practices will be recorded in the national registry and follow the individual originator from job to job. The registry system provides consumers with easily accessible information at no charge regarding the employment history of, and publicly adjudicated disciplinary and enforcement actions against, mortgage loan originators. The Act includes education, testing, and continuing education requirements for mortgage loan originators. It also specifies mortgage broker duties, mortgagor servicer duties, and prohibited acts.[24]

RESIDENTIAL REAL ESTATE LENDING PRACTICES AND PROCEDURES

To function competently, real estate brokers involved with residential real estate sales should have a thorough understanding of current real estate lending practices and procedures. This section addresses buyer loan prequalification, the loan application, general loan underwriting practices, borrower qualification requirements, and loan fraud. Because the majority of licensees assist others in residential sales, the focus of this coverage is on *residential lending practices – more specifically,* **practices associated with first mortgage loans for owner-occupied single family homes**. The lending practices and procedures for loans on income-producing or commercial real estate or land are very different and are beyond the scope of this text.

IMPORTANT NOTE: Real estate brokers are expected to understand basic real estate finance concepts (principal and interest, discounting, yield, calculation of mortgage interest and payments, etc.), sources of real estate financing (the primary mortgage market), the secondary mortgage market, the many types of mortgage loans available, and the government's role in real estate financing. That said, these topics either are not addressed in this Manual or are addressed only briefly. Readers should consult a real estate principles and practices text or a real estate finance text for coverage of these topics. The following discussion assumes some understanding of the topics listed in this note.

BUYER LOAN PREQUALIFICATION

Although some homebuyers may have experience with real estate lending practices and requirements, most prospective buyers need advice at the outset of their property search regarding the *maximum loan amount* for which the buyer can qualify and the *maximum purchase price* the buyer can afford to pay, not to mention the *type of loan* best suited for their situation. The process of helping a prospective buyer answer these questions commonly is referred to as "qualifying a buyer," although it is more accurate to refer to this procedure as *"prequalifying a prospective buyer."*

Importance of Buyer Prequalification

Prequalify a prospective buyer as soon as possible after the prospect has contacted a broker before beginning to select properties to show the buyer. Failure to prequalify a prospective buyer may result in the buyer entering into a contract to purchase a property, but failing to qualify for a loan amount sufficient to buy the property at the contracted price. In such a case, the broker has not acted in the best interest of either the buyer or the seller and also has wasted the broker's time and efforts. If it turns out that $150,000 is the maximum loan amount for which the buyer can qualify and the buyer only has $7,500 for a down payment, this means that the maximum purchase price the buyer could afford is actually *less than* $157,500 because of the closing costs the buyer also must pay. (Five percent of the maximum loan amount will yield a *rough estimate* of the buyer's closing costs.) Thus, a broker who has shown this buyer properties listed for sale for more than $160,000-$165,000 has wasted everybody's time due to not prequalifying the buyer.

Prequalification Options

When prequalifying a buyer, a broker may: (1) personally obtain the necessary personal financial information from the buyer and perform the appropriate income/expense analysis; or (2) refer the buyer to a mortgage lending officer to prequalify the buyer.

Brokers who thoroughly understand the types and characteristics of various mortgage loans may be comfortable with personally prequalifying a buyer by analyzing the buyer's income and recurring expenses; this analysis is better than no prequalification at all. There are, however, disadvantages to prequalification by the broker; many buyers may understandably be reluctant to provide detailed personal financial information to the broker unless acting as a buyer's agent. Brokers who are working with a buyer as a seller's agent should be very cautious about asking the buyer for such information and must ensure that the prospective buyer understands that the broker is the *seller's* agent, not the buyer's agent, and the broker must disclose any information to his or her seller client that might benefit the seller in the transaction.

Other disadvantages of broker prequalification are that the broker may not be as informed about available loan products as a mortgage lending officer and the fact that a lender can access a buyer's credit record, but a broker cannot access such information. Thus, a broker will not be able to analyze a buyer's creditworthiness, one of the most important factors considered by lenders.

For these reasons, most brokers prefer to refer the buyer to a lender or mortgage broker for prequalification. This can be done either by dealing directly with a local lender (or multiple local lenders), dealing with a mortgage broker who can place loans with various lenders, or by loan shopping via the Internet. This approach to prequalification has the additional advantage of speeding up the loan application process. If the buyer already is pre-approved for a particular maximum loan amount the loan approval process may be expedited if the buyer's requested loan does not exceed that amount. *A broker's best approach to prequalifying a buyer is to refer the buyer to one or more lenders or mortgage brokers.*

Referring Buyers to Lenders

Any referral to lenders or mortgage brokers must be made in good faith with the buyer's best interest in mind. Usually, a broker will want to refer a buyer to lenders offering the lowest interest rates and/or other loan costs, although the quality of service and financing options available through a particular lender or mortgage broker are also factors that might influence the referral.

Referral Fees Prohibited. *It is **illegal** for a real estate broker to receive a "referral fee" or "kickback" or anything of value in exchange for the referral to a mortgage lender.* The Real Estate Settlement Procedures Act (RESPA) and regulations of the Consumer Financial Protection Bureau (CFPB) specifically prohibit both 1) the payment by lenders of fees (or other valuable consideration) for loan referrals, as well as 2) the receipt of any such loan referral fee by a real estate broker. Violators are subject to criminal penalties. This topic is discussed further in Chapter 14.

THE LOAN APPLICATION

A prospective buyer should contact a lender or mortgage broker before negotiating a purchase contract. If the buyer has been prequalified by a lender, s/he may already have completed a loan application. If not, the first formal step in obtaining a mortgage loan is to complete a loan application.

If the loan is to finance the purchase of residential 1-4 unit property (1-4 family), there is a standard application form that is used for conventional/conforming, FHA, and VA loans (Fannie Mae #1003/Freddie Mac #65). Brokers should be familiar with these loan application forms so they can advise buyers, at least in general terms, of the information they must provide a lender, thus speeding up the loan approval process.

Note: There is no standardized application form generally used by lenders if the loan is to finance the purchase of commercial property. Each lender requires its own information including complete identification of the borrower (company structure, its owners, etc.), the purpose of the loan, an evaluation of the collateral offered, and financial statements for the past several years.

Prequalification, Good Faith Estimate, and Rate Lock

The common practice in residential lending is for a potential borrower to submit an initial application to a lender to obtain what amounts to a conditional "pre-approval" subject to a full review of the borrower's qualifications and final decision on the borrower's application. Depending on the lender, this initial application is done either on the regular, full application form (usually the standard Fannie Mae/Freddie Mac approved form) or on a less detailed form. The borrower does not pay an application fee at this point and the only permissible fee a lender may charge at this juncture is for the cost of a credit report.

Based on the information provided by the borrower, the credit report, and the type of loan the borrower is seeking, the lender will provide to the borrower a **"Loan Estimate (LE),"** formerly known as a "Good Faith Estimate" under RESPA and the "early TIL" under the MDIA/TILA. In addition to disclosing up front all expected closing costs, the LE describes the basic terms of the proposed loan and advises the borrower of when s/he must "lock" the loan interest rate quoted in the LE to get that rate for the loan. The Real Estate Settlement Procedures Act (RESPA) and the Loan Estimate are discussed in Chapter 14.

LOAN UNDERWRITING PRACTICES

Once the loan application is submitted and the Loan Estimate is issued, the lending institution will evaluate the application and determine whether it will approve the loan. This process is known as "underwriting" the loan. The loan underwriting guidelines followed by lenders are generally very similar for most major types of residential first mortgage loans. An overwhelming majority of residential first mortgage loans are made by institutions that are in the business of making such loans, and a majority of these loans are then "sold" by the lending institutions in the "secondary mortgage market" (discussed later in this chapter). As a consequence, reasonably consistent standards have evolved for making mortgage loans that are "salable" in the secondary mortgage market and these standards are followed by most mortgage lenders.

During the real estate boom of the early 2000s, loan underwriting standards became relatively lax, resulting in many loans being made to persons who were not truly qualified (financially able to maintain and repay the loan). This led directly to widespread loan defaults and foreclosures that in turn was a major cause of the collapse of the real estate market and general economy in 2007. Since that crisis, loan underwriting standards have been raised back to a level that will reasonably assure that borrowers are properly qualified and will be able to make their loan payments.

Loan underwriting involves an analysis of borrower credit and collateral risk. A common practice in the mortgage industry today is automated underwriting (or at least automated analysis of submitted data) where information is entered into a program that performs certain calculations and analysis and determines whether the application should be approved, though manual review by lending officials still occurs to supplement, approve or override a proposed decision made by an automated underwriting program. Any loan approval will be subject to the borrower producing documents acceptable to the lender verifying the borrower's claimed assets and income. The major differences in underwriting practices usually involve borrower expense-to-income ratios and/or loan-to-value ratios. This discussion will address the *general underwriting guidelines applied when qualifying a borrower for any type of first mortgage loan on a dwelling that will serve as the borrower's principal residence.*

Evaluation of Borrower's Qualifications for a Loan

The ability of the borrower to repay the loan while continuing to pay all other debts and living expenses is of paramount concern to the lender, especially if the loan has a high loan-to-value ratio. When evaluating a borrower's financial condition and ability to repay the loan, lenders will consider factors such as the type, stability and adequacy of the borrower's income. If the loan is part of a pool of loans that the lender intends to sell in the secondary market, then the lender will follow the investors' standards for borrower qualifications. The secondary market will be discussed later under "Major Types of Residential Mortgage Loans."

Loan to Value Ratio

No matter what type of loan a party seeks, the lender will analyze the loan to value (LTV) ratio to determine whether the borrowers are qualified for the loan. The loan to value ratio is simply a comparison of the loan amount to the *lesser of:*

    1) the appraised value of the property that secures the loan *or*

    2) the purchase price of the property.

Usually, this ratio is expressed as a percentage. Thus, a loan with a 90:100 loan to value ratio is expressed as a 90% loan. This means that the maximum loan amount will be 90% of the appraised value of the property *or* the purchase price, *whichever is lower.* The simplest example of a 90% loan to value is a loan of $90,000 for a house appraised at $100,000. Even if the purchase price was $105,000, $90,000 still would be the maximum the purchaser could borrow, as 90% of the appraised value ($100,000) is less than 90% of the purchase price of $105,000 ($90,000 versus $94,500). Generally, loans with higher loan to value ratios (i.e. smaller down payments) carry stricter qualification requirements than loans with low loan to value ratios because the lender's risk increases as the loan to value ratio rises, decreasing the borrower's interest/equity in the property.

Type of Income

As a general rule, *"acceptable"* income to a lender is *income that, based on the borrower's income history, is regular and stable.* Salary or regular hourly wages from full-time employment consistently earned for the past two to three years clearly is acceptable. Overtime pay from a full-time job or wages from a part-time second job likely will be acceptable only if the borrower can show that such income has been regularly received over a number of years. For regular commission income, the lender will consider the amount of such income over the past several years to determine what amount to include as "regular" and thus "acceptable." Similarly, the income of a self-employed person will be considered based on the amount of income reported for income tax purposes over the past several years, as will investment income (such as interest or dividends).

Child support and alimony may be acceptable as income if they are: 1) paid pursuant to a court order or legally enforceable agreement, 2) the past payments have been regular, and 3) the payments will continue for at least an additional 36 months. A lender will *not* consider income that is not reported for tax purposes, or the possibility of future increases in income. All eligible income of a co-borrower (e.g., a spouse) is also acceptable as described above. Note too that because lenders consider gross income in making their calculations, income that is not taxable to the recipient, e.g., child support, social security benefits, or disability benefits, may be increased by the lender by 25-30% to approximate what the equivalent gross income would be in determining the amount of the borrower's loan eligibility.

Stability of Income

Because most first mortgage loans involve a long repayment period (15 to 30 years), the lender is very concerned about the stability of a borrower's income. *In assessing income stability, lenders consider the borrower's type of work, type of income, and length of time in current job or occupation.* Lenders obviously prefer borrowers who have both a relatively stable employment history and level of income, as well as good future employment prospects. For example, assuming income levels are comparable, a teacher or nurse with a regular salary will be preferred over a person working on commission or an hourly non-union manufacturing worker who is subject to periodic layoffs. Likewise, one who has a stable work history in a particular job or field of work will be preferred over one who has made frequent career changes without advancing himself or herself. Lenders will verify employment and income with employers and/or require income tax returns as evidence of income. For self-employed borrowers, lenders will require and must rely upon copies of income tax returns for the previous few years.

Expense-to-Income Ratios

One important factor considered by lenders is whether the borrower's regular income is sufficient to enable the borrower to comfortably pay the loan payment and other housing expenses as well as all other recurring debts and living expenses. In determining adequacy of income, the lender first will ascertain the amount of the borrower's *acceptable income, expected "housing expenses," and expected expenses for "other recurring obligations."* The lender will then apply certain prescribed *expense-to-income ratios* that vary depending on the type of loan to determine if the borrower is eligible under the adequacy of income standard. All loan applications, regardless of loan type, involve analysis of the proposed monthly housing expense and a borrower's existing or recurring debt after loan closing.

Housing Expense-to-Income Ratio. When determining the **housing expense-to-income ratio**, sometimes called simply the "housing expense ratio" or "front-end ratio," the *projected monthly housing expense includes not only the minimum required loan payment for principal and interest, but also projected costs for property taxes, hazard insurance, flood insurance, private mortgage insurance, special assessments, and homeowners association dues, if applicable.* Not all loans will have each of these payment elements, but if applicable to the subject property, these amounts will be included as a projected housing expense. *Historically, qualifying guidelines stipulate a* **housing expense-to-income ratio in the 28-32% range**, *depending on the type of loan.* The borrower's housing expense ratio is calculated by dividing the total proposed monthly housing expense by the verified gross income (e.g. $1,000 monthly housing expense with $5,000 monthly gross income results in a 20% housing expense ratio).

Debt-to-Income Ratio. When determining the **debt-to-income ratio**, the *projected debt (total monthly recurring obligations) includes the borrower's proposed monthly housing expense plus any recurring payments for outstanding debt or obligations that will remain after the loan has closed.* Historically, qualifying guidelines stipulate a **debt-to-income ratio in the 36-43% range**, *depending on the type of loan.* The borrower's debt ratio is calculated by dividing the total projected monthly debt expense by the verified gross income (e.g. $2,000 in housing and other debt payments with $5,000 monthly gross income results in a 40% debt-to-income ratio).

Ratios Depend on Type of Loan. Slightly differing expense-to-income ratios may apply depending on the type of loan sought. For example, the ratios for most **conventional-conforming loans are 28%/36%**, while the ratios for **FHA loans are 31%/43%**. However, lenders are also allowed to exceed these ratios, especially the debt-to-income ratio, in certain situations. These ratios will be discussed further under "Major Types of Residential Mortgage Loans" and see the application of the expense-to-income ratios under "Conforming Conventional Loans."

Adequacy of Assets to Close the Transaction

The borrower must have sufficient liquid assets (cash or assets immediately convertible to cash) to complete the purchase (i.e., pay at settlement the down payment and all closing costs for which the borrower is responsible). *Lenders usually will not permit the borrower to borrow money from other sources to pay the minimum down payment or closing costs* (including the loan origination fee and any discount points required by the lender). Lenders will consider the source, "seasoning" and ownership of "cash" assets. The source of funds may be earnings, gifts, savings, etc. "Seasoning" refers to how long an applicant has possessed the specific asset and ownership refers to the applicant's percentage of asset ownership. Most lenders will require copies of bank or other financial statements or direct lender verification with the bank or other asset institution.

In most cases, loan program guidelines do not permit an applicant to borrow unsecured monies to pay the down payment or other closing costs. If the borrower is obtaining funds from a parent, for example, for a portion of the down payment or closing costs, the lender may require the parent to sign a statement declaring that the money provided to the borrower is a gift rather than a loan (commonly called a "gift letter"). If a borrower has significant verified assets other than "cash" assets, (e.g., real estate), this can be helpful in loan qualifying and may influence a lender to be more flexible with regard to other loan qualification standards, such as the expense-to-income ratios previously discussed.

Credit History

Of primary importance to a lender and loan underwriter is *the borrower's ability to efficiently manage his or her financial affairs and a demonstrated willingness to pay his or her debts promptly*. Consequently, the lender will perform a credit check on the borrower to determine the past history of handling credit arrangements. Evaluating credit characteristics can be very difficult in some cases, yet credit checks may reveal a background of credit problems that serve as a legitimate basis for denying a loan application. A poor credit record is very difficult to overcome when attempting to obtain a mortgage loan at a reasonable interest rate. On the other hand, an exemplary credit record frequently will persuade a lender to make a loan to a borrower who may not qualify fully under other guidelines, such as the expense-to-income ratios.

The mortgage lender will obtain a three bureau **credit report**, commonly referred to as a "3-merged" or "triple merged" credit report. This report will contain historical credit data for the applicant as provided by the major credit bureaus. Lenders require not only "trade line" information such as payments, balances, and limits on credit card accounts, automobile loans, etc., but also credit scores and matters reflected in public records. Information maintained by credit bureaus covers the past seven years (10 years in the case of bankruptcies). Most loan programs have written minimum credit score requirements and those that do not often will have an "unwritten" minimum required **credit score**. Fannie Mae currently requires a FICO score of at least 620 out of 850 for conventional-conforming loans. The borrower usually is charged a fee for the credit report at initial loan application.

Under the Fair Credit Reporting Act, an individual has the right to review his credit information on file with a credit bureau or repository and has the right to have incorrect information removed from the record upon satisfactory proof of the error. Any consumer is entitled to request and receive one free copy of his or her credit report from each of the credit bureaus annually. Consumers may be charged for additional copies. Lenders may, but are not required to, provide loan applicants with a copy of the applicant's credit report, but *lenders are required to notify applicants of the **credit score** reported by the credit bureaus.*

*A broker working with a buyer should advise the buyer to obtain a copy of his or her credit report from at least one of the national repositories **prior to** applying for a loan.* Considering the devastating effect a bad credit report may have on a loan application, a buyer should determine as early in the process as possible if there is a problem with his or her credit record that needs attention.

Occupancy

There are three primary occupancy categories for lending purposes: 1) primary residence, 2) vacation or second home, and 3) non-owner occupied. Typically, *the highest loan-to-value ratios and more permissive underwriting practices have been permitted with owner-occupied primary residences*, as they historically had the lowest default statistics. Defaults on mortgages secured by vacation or second homes exceed those on primary residences, but still number fewer than loan defaults on non-owner occupied or "investment" property. The high rate of foreclosures nationally between 2005 and 2015 influenced the loan-to-value ratio lenders offer; presently the loan-to-value for a conventional loan on a vacation or second home generally will not exceed 90%, if that high, and will be no more than 80% or less for an investment property, while a conventional loan on a primary residence might be as high as 95%.

Property Analysis (Appraisal)

A mortgage lender must have satisfactory assurance that the property offered as collateral for the loan will be sufficient to compensate the lender in the event of borrower default. Therefore, *lenders routinely require an **appraisal** of the property **by an appraiser the lender selects** and the borrower is charged for the appraisal.* All appraisals of property in North Carolina made for loan qualification purposes must be performed by a state-certified or state-licensed real estate appraiser. (See Chapter 15, "Real Estate Valuation.")

The appraiser conducts a thorough analysis of the property, examining all of the property characteristics (age, size, location, condition, special features, etc.), and compares the property to other similar properties that have sold in the recent past. Every factor that might affect the value of the property is considered by the appraiser. The appraiser then submits to the lender an appraisal report detailing all facts about the property and stating his opinion (estimate) as to the current market value of the property. The appraisal report is one factor the lender considers when determining whether to approve the requested loan. If the appraisal is performed for a VA loan, then a VA Certificate of Reasonable Value (CRV) will be issued stating the reasonable value of the property based on the appraisal report.

The lender usually will require that the appraised property value be equal to, or greater than, the sale price. If the property value is less than the sale price, the lender will be reluctant to approve a loan with a high loan-to-value ratio and probably will insist that the borrower make a larger down payment. In any event, *the appraised value must be high enough to justify the loan in accordance with established policies on loan-to-value ratios.* For example, if the requested loan amount is $190,000 and the maximum permissible loan-to-value ratio is 95 percent, then the appraised value must be at least $200,000 (190,000 ÷ .95 = 200,000) regardless of the purchase price.

Although borrowers usually pay for an appraisal, *the lender selects the appraiser and is the appraiser's client* since the purpose of the appraisal is help protect the lender's interest (and that of subsequent secondary mortgage market investors) by providing reasonable assurance that, in the event of default by the borrower and foreclosure on the property, a sale of the property would likely produce sufficient funds to pay off the outstanding mortgage balance.

The appraiser's rules of professional conduct prohibit the appraiser from discussing the property appraisal directly with the borrower or providing the appraisal report directly to the borrower. However, due to changes in ECOA effective January 18, 2014, *if the property is a 1-4 family dwelling, federally regulated lenders are required to make a copy of the appraisal report available to the applicant promptly upon completion, or at least three business days before closing, whichever is earlier.* The lender must notify applicants in writing within three business days of application that the applicant has the right to receive a copy of any appraisal developed in connection with the application. Previously, lenders were only required to provide a copy of the appraisal upon the applicant's request.

Other Requirements

*In addition to being satisfied as to the borrower's qualifications and the property's value, the lender will require that the borrower receive a **clear title** to the property and that the lender receive a **first mortgage** on the property.* Consequently, the lender will require a satisfactory **title opinion** from an attorney (usually the closing attorney) as well as a policy of **title insurance** (lender's policy) to protect the lender against title defects. The lender also may require the closing attorney to provide, after the deed and mortgage (deed of trust) have been recorded, a second opinion to the effect that the lender has a first lien on the property.

Loan Commitment and Closing

If the lending institution is satisfied that the loan meets all its underwriting requirements, it will issue to the borrower a "letter of commitment" agreeing to make the loan under certain specified conditions. This **loan commitment** (sometimes referred to as a "firm commitment") will specify the loan amount, interest rate (and discount points, if any), the loan term, the amount of the regular loan payments, escrow requirements for real estate taxes and property insurance, origination and other fees, and any other key loan terms and conditions. The commitment will indicate a specific period of time (usually 45-90 days) within which the loan must be closed. If closing does not take place during the period specified, the lender is not obligated to make the loan. For *FHA loans* (loans insured by the Federal Housing Administration), the FHA must review and approve the loan package (unless the lender has been pre-approved by the FHA for "direct endorsement") and issue a commitment to insure the loan. Similarly, for *VA loans* (loans guaranteed by the Veterans Administration), the VA must review and approve the loan package (unless the lender has been pre-approved by the VA) and issue a commitment to guarantee the loan.

The loan principal is not disbursed by the lender until the settlement of the transaction (often called the "loan closing"). Lenders now usually require that the closing be conducted by an attorney; the lender provides detailed loan closing instructions to the attorney who collects all monies due from the lender and the parties and disburses all funds to the proper payees, thereby "closing" or "settling" the transaction.

THE "MORTGAGE MARKETS"

Most licensees are introduced to how real estate mortgage markets operate in their prelicensing or postlicensing courses. The primary and secondary mortgage markets are briefly described below; those desiring more information are referred to a general real estate prelicensing text or the wealth of information that is available online.

The Primary Mortgage Market

The *"primary mortgage market"* is the term used to describe the marketplace in which mortgage loans are made or "originated." The primary entities involved in mortgage lending are: (1) **"banking" institutions** who are actively involved in making mortgage loans directly to borrowers using funds on deposit with the institutions, such as banks, savings institutions, and credit unions; (2) **mortgage bankers**, which are companies that make mortgage loans with funds belonging to other entities such as insurance companies, pension funds or endowment funds, and sometimes their own funds; and (3) **mortgage brokers**, who do not use their own funds but rather place loans for borrowers with other entities such as mortgage banking companies, various lenders, and even insurance companies, pension funds, endowment funds, etc.

A prospective buyer applies for a mortgage loan to one of these entities and it approves or denies the loan application based on the loan underwriting standards prescribed by the entity providing the funds.

The Secondary Mortgage Market

Prior to the 1930s, residential mortgage loans made by banks, savings and loan associations, and other primary lenders were simply held as long-term investments by the originating lender until paid by the borrower. This meant that monies loaned to borrowers only became available again to the lender to make more loans as the earlier loans were slowly repaid. But mortgage promissory notes are "negotiable," meaning the note and the right to receive the loan payments under the note can be "sold" by the note holder (i.e., the lender) to another person or entity. The entity buying the note pays the lender an amount somewhat less than the total amount the lender would receive if the note was held for the full loan term. This allows the buyer of the mortgage note to receive the loan payments and make a profit. The tradeoff to the original lender is that it gets back the amount of money loaned and can make another loan with those funds.

Applying this concept on a broad scale, Congress created a system to enable the orderly sale of mortgage notes by primary lenders in what became known as the *secondary mortgage market*. The initial secondary mortgage market was established in 1938 by the creation of a federally-chartered quasi-governmental organization known as the Federal National Mortgage Association (FNMA – widely known as **"Fannie Mae"**) tasked with "buying" government-insured Federal Housing Administration (FHA) loans and government guaranteed Veterans Administration (VA) loans from lenders originating such loans. A similar organization known as the Government National Mortgage Association (GNMA or **"Ginnie Mae"**) was spun off from Fannie Mae in 1968 as an agency of HUD primarily to liquidate old FHA and VA loans held by Fannie Mae to enable Fannie Mae to expand its operations. Subsequently, in 1970, the Federal Home Loan Mortgage Corporation (FHLMC, which became known as **"Freddie Mac"**) was established as a quasi-governmental organization authorized to purchase loans not insured by the government that were made by savings and loan associations (thrift institutions).

These government initiatives were tremendously successful in creating a very active and prosperous secondary mortgage market that continuously replenished funds available to primary lenders to make mortgage loans. This made loans more readily available and fueled the long-term growth of the real estate market in the country. *"Fannie Mae" and "Freddie Mac" together constitute the heart of the country's* **secondary mortgage market** *by serving as the principal source of funds for originating mortgage loans.* They purchase huge "pools" of mortgage loans from primary mortgage lenders (mortgage companies, thrift institutions, banks, etc.) and issue "mortgage-backed securities" that are then sold to investors, thereby creating more funds to purchase additional pools of loans from primary lenders and, in turn, providing more funds for primary lenders to make additional mortgage loans.

Although they compete in the secondary market, *"Fannie Mae" and "Freddie Mac" cooperate in establishing uniform underwriting guidelines for non-government insured residential mortgage loans (known as "conventional" loans) and these guidelines must be followed by primary lenders who want to sell their loans in the secondary market.* Thus, any conventional loan made by a primary lender that meets these loan underwriting guidelines is said to be a *"conforming"* loan. Most residential mortgage loans fall into this category.

The legal status and functions of these three major secondary mortgage market players have evolved dramatically over the years. Ginnie Mae remains a government agency. Fannie Mae and Freddie Mac became giant private stock-issuing companies that purchase loans of all types from various lenders who originate the loans, but they remain subject to federal government oversight. Due to the real estate and financial crisis beginning in 2007-08, Fannie Mae and Freddie Mac lost billions of dollars and were in danger of failing until their oversight agency, the Federal Housing Finance Agency (FHFA), a totally independent agency created in 2009, placed both companies under a governmental conservatorship to stabilize their operations and the entire secondary mortgage market.

MAJOR TYPES OF RESIDENTIAL MORTGAGE LOANS

An understanding of the major types of residential mortgage loans will enhance the reader's understanding of borrower qualifications for such loans as discussed in the previous section on "Loan Underwriting Practices." There is no uniformly accepted system for classifying residential mortgage loans; however, the prevailing view seems to be that all such loans fall into two general categories. One category may be referred to as "**government loans**," meaning loans that are insured or guaranteed by a federal government agency. The other is a much broader category called "**conventional loans**," generally defined as loans that are *not* insured or guaranteed by a federal government agency. These general loan categories, the types of loans that fall within each, their basic characteristics, and borrower qualification requirements are briefly reviewed in this section.

Conventional Loans

This broad category includes a wide variety of loans that are similar only by virtue of the fact that loan repayment by the borrower is not insured or guaranteed by the federal government. The "**conventional**" loan category may be divided into two subcategories of loans called "**conforming**" and "**nonconforming.**"

Conforming Loans

"Conforming" or "conventional conforming" loans are loans that are made by lenders according to the underwriting guidelines of the Federal National Mortgage Association (FNMA or "Fannie Mae") and the Federal Home Loan Mortgage Corporation (FHLMC or "Freddie Mac"). "**Conforming**" **conventional loans** have the following major characteristics:

- Loan amount generally may not exceed $424,100 for a single family home in 2017.*

- Loan must be secured by 1-4 unit residential property (attached or detached).
- Borrower must have private mortgage insurance if the loan to value ratio exceeds 80%.
- Maximum loan to value ratio is 95%.
- Borrower's qualifications must be verified and the borrower must be found to have a good credit history.
- Borrower's expense to income ratios typically must not exceed 28% for the housing expense to gross income ratio and 36% for the recurring debt to gross income ratio; however, the latter ratio may be as much as 45% for some particularly well-qualified borrowers.

*The loan limits for conventional loans are revised periodically and the maximum limit increases as the size of the property increases from single family, to two-unit, three-unit, and four-unit. Additionally, Fannie Mae and Freddie Mac have designated certain high-cost areas in the country where the limits are higher. For example, a single family home located in Seattle Washington could have a maximum loan up to $592,250 (rather than $424,100) and the same home in Los Angeles could have a maximum loan up to $636,150 and still be a conforming conventional loan.

While many conventional lenders today place greater emphasis on credit scores and income stability, they still must consider the expense-to-income ratios to sell these loans in the secondary market. The historical rule for calculating the adequacy of income requirements for conventional/conforming loans continues to be the 28%/36% rule, namely:

> the borrower's projected **monthly housing expenses** must not exceed **28 percent** of his regular **gross** monthly income, and the borrower's projected **total monthly recurring obligations** (housing expenses plus other recurring obligations) must not exceed **36 percent** of his regular gross monthly income.

"**Monthly housing expenses**" include the monthly loan principal and interest payment, one-twelfth (1/12) of the annual real estate taxes, one-twelfth (1/12) of the annual property (homeowner's) insurance premium, the monthly private mortgage insurance premium (if applicable), and homeowners association fees (if applicable).

"**Total monthly recurring obligations**" include the housing expenses *plus* installment obligations that extend for more than six months (such as automobile loan and personal loan payments), any other mortgage loan payments, credit card and revolving charge account payments, alimony or child support payments, and other similar recurring debts.

To determine whether an applicant's income is adequate, two separate calculations are required. This is best illustrated by an example using the 28/36 qualifying ratio typically used with conventional/conforming loans.

Example: A husband and wife apply for an 80% conventional first mortgage loan and a 10% second mortgage loan, for total loans of $180,000, on a house valued at the purchase price of $200,000. There is *no private mortgage insurance*, but there are homeowner association dues of $100 per month. The housing expenses will be $1,560 per month (PITI +HOA) and the couple's other recurring obligations amount to $675 per month. Thus, their total monthly recurring obligations are $2,235. The couple's combined regular gross monthly income is $5,600. To apply the 28/36 ratio:

Step 1: Divide the monthly housing expenses by the monthly gross income: 1560 ÷ 5600 = .2786 or 27.86%. This is less than 28%, so the couple qualifies under this ratio.

Step 2: Divide the total monthly recurring obligations by the monthly gross income: 2235 ÷ 5600 = .3991or 39.9%. This is more than 36 percent, so the couple does *not* qualify under this ratio.

Conclusion: Since the couple did not qualify under *both* ratios, their loan application may be denied as submitted. The couple may need to reduce the loan amount (increase their down payment) or pay off some of their debts in order to obtain the desired loan.

Note, however, that both Fannie Mae and Freddie Mac guidelines currently allow lenders to exceed the 36% benchmark as to the total debt-to-income ratio up to a maximum of 45% if there are other "strong compensating factors." Compensating factors may include an excellent credit score and history, stable employment for numerous years with a reliable salary and little prospect of termination within the foreseeable future, the amount of equity in the collateral, and the presence of other assets, e.g., investments, savings, retirement accounts, etc..

Nonconforming Loans

*"Nonconforming" loans simply are loans that do **not** conform to (meet) the Fannie Mae and Freddie Mac guidelines.* This broad subcategory of conventional loans includes "jumbo" loans (loans exceeding the guideline cap), loans with loan-to-value ratios exceeding 95%, "subprime" or "nonprime" loans, and "home equity" loans. During the real estate "boom" period of the late 1990s and early 2000s, there was a tremendous increase in not only the number of nonconforming loans, but also the proportion of total residential mortgage loans that fell into the nonconforming category. This period saw rapid growth in the number of housing units and residential property values, fueled in large part by historically low interest rates and a substantial easing of loan qualification standards for nonconforming loans. The expansive real estate market led lenders and secondary mortgage market investors, including "Fannie Mae" and "Freddie Mac," to lower their borrower qualification requirements for residential loans and substantially increase the number of "nonconforming" loans made to borrowers. This practice has been dramatically curtailed and lending requirements have tightened given the large number of defaulting borrowers and resulting foreclosures these practices spawned. The major types of "nonconforming" loans are briefly discussed below.

Jumbo Loans

"Jumbo" loans are simply loans for amounts that exceed the $424,100 single family home maximum permitted for "conforming" loans. Specific borrower qualification requirements vary according to the lender or the investor to whom the lender plans to sell the loan; generally, borrower qualification requirements are similar to those for conforming loans.

Subprime Loans

"Subprime" or "nonprime" loans include a wide variety of loans made primarily to borrowers who cannot qualify for "conforming" or "government" loans, often due to poor credit histories and/or limited assets. These loans may take many forms, but frequently involve a high loan to value ratio, higher loan fees (often financed in with the base loan), higher interest rates and/or an adjustable interest rate. They sometimes feature interest-only payments, and may have a balloon payment. Not all subprime loans are made to borrowers with poor credit. For example, a borrower with good credit may just not have enough assets to make a traditional down payment and may want a loan. Typically though, subprime loans involve borrowers with relatively low credit scores who are considered a greater credit risk.

It is not surprising then that *subprime loans have higher foreclosure rates than conforming loans and substantially higher rates of payment delinquency by borrowers.* One issue has been adjustable rate mortgages (ARMs), loans with low initial interest rates (below the prevailing rates for fixed-rate loans) that may be adjusted after an initial period of one, two or three years and again at regular intervals thereafter. A substantial number of borrowers who could barely afford to make the loan payment based on the low initial interest rate found that when the interest rate (and payment) were adjusted upward to (or closer to) the prevailing interest rate for fixed-rate loans, they no longer could afford the higher loan payment, forcing them into payment delinquency and default. The problem is heightened if prevailing interest rates rise during the period that the ARM's interest rate is subject to adjustment.

Excessive subprime lending and the high payment delinquency and foreclosure rates for subprime loans fueled a major financial crisis in this country involving not only subprime lenders but the entire financial community that led to a substantial tightening of credit standards and reduction in funds available for residential mortgage loans as investors became wary of investing in subprime mortgages. The crisis also spawned some of the federal legislation mentioned earlier defining "high cost mortgage" and "higher priced mortgage loan."

Home Equity Loans

A *"home equity" loan is a loan whereby a homeowner accesses the "equity" in his or her home (the value of the home in excess of the balance due on the first mortgage loan) by obtaining a second mortgage loan on the home.* Home equity loans became increasingly popular beginning in the late 1980s after the Tax Reform Act of 1986 removed the federal tax deduction for interest paid on debts other than home mortgages. *A home equity loan is simply a **"second"** or **"junior"** mortgage that is subordinate (inferior) to a first mortgage.* Traditional second mortgages resemble first mortgages in that they are made for a fixed amount (a "closed end" mortgage) for a specified period of time at a stated interest rate (may be fixed or variable).

Unlike a traditional closed-end second mortgage, the widely used **"home equity line of credit" (HELOC)** is secured by an "open end" second mortgage, meaning that the borrower may draw funds in varying amounts as s/he chooses up to a maximum loan limit or "line of credit." These loans operate much like a revolving credit account, except that they are secured by a second mortgage/deed of trust against the real property. (See also the discussion of "Home Equity Loan" in Chapter 12.)

Whether a HELOC or traditional second mortgage, loan terms and qualification requirements are determined by individual lenders and may vary substantially. For example, most home equity loans require that the combined loan-to-value ratio of the first mortgage and home equity loan may not exceed 90% of the home's market value; however, it may be possible to obtain a home equity loan with a higher LTV ratio. Home equity loans typically have an interest rate that is lower than common rates for credit cards but higher than common rates for first mortgage loans. *Interest rates* may be fixed or adjustable, but *usually are adjustable for home equity lines of credit.* Loan terms are 10-20 years, which is shorter than the terms of most first mortgage loans. As with nonconforming first mortgage loans, a home equity loan may also be a "subprime" loan, meaning it has an unusually high loan-to-value ratio and/or is being made to a borrower with less than stellar credit and may feature an interest rate or loan fees that are higher than is customary.

Home equity loans trigger special legal rules. For example, *an applicant for a home equity loan has three days to reconsider his or her decision under the Truth in Lending Act.*[25] This right to cancel or rescind can be exercised without penalty if exercised within the three-day period. The three-day period begins after the applicant has received the credit contract, the Truth in Lending disclosure form, and two copies of a Truth in Lending notice explaining the right to rescind. During this time period, activity related to the contract cannot take place. In order to rescind, the applicant must notify the creditor in writing. This right to rescind does *not* apply to a loan to purchase or build a principal residence, nor does it apply when a loan is being refinanced with the same lender and no additional funds are being borrowed. It also does not apply when a state agency is the creditor for a loan.

Government Loans

The three primary types of "government" loans are **"FHA loans," "VA loans"** and **"Rural Development loans,"** and each of these is discussed below.

Federal Housing Administration (FHA) Loans

The Federal Housing Administration (FHA) is a federal agency established by the **National Housing Act** of 1934.[26] *The FHA provides mortgage insurance on loans made by FHA-approved lenders on single-family and multi-family homes including manufactured homes.* It is the largest insurer of mortgages in the world, insuring over 40 million home mortgages since its inception in 1934.[27] The purpose of the FHA is to make residential mortgage loans more accessible to homebuyers who have good credit but have difficulty accumulating sufficient cash to make the down payment and pay the closing costs associated with a conventional conforming loan, and to assure that these loans will be attractive to investors in the secondary mortgage market.

Major Features of FHA Loans

A major advantage of FHA loans over conventional conforming loans is that FHA loans permit a lower down payment, allowing the *borrower to finance up to 96.5% of the purchase price (or appraised value, whichever is less)*. To counter the increased risk to lenders and investors purchasing FHA mortgages in the secondary mortgage market that results from a higher loan-to-value ratio, *the FHA provides mortgage insurance at a cost that is lower than that charged to borrowers for private mortgage insurance on a conventional conforming loan.* The mortgage insurance premium includes an upfront premium that may be financed as part of the loan and a continuing monthly premium paid over a five-year period or until the loan balance reaches 78%, at which time mortgage insurance no longer is required and mortgage insurance premium payments terminate.

Eligibility Requirements

Eligibility requirements are set forth at the HUD website, *www.hud.gov*, and *www.fha.gov*. The borrower qualification requirements are very similar to those for conventional conforming loans, except the housing expense and recurring debt to income ratios and standards for borrower assets are more lenient. *Generally, the housing expense to gross income ratio should not exceed* ***31%*** *and the recurring debt to gross income ratio should not exceed* ***43%***. Gifts from third parties and contributions from the seller are permitted to assist the borrower in paying closing costs, something that is not allowed with conventional conforming loans. Eligible properties are one-to-four unit residential structures. The mortgage amount limit for FHA loans depends on the geographic location of the property.[28]

Major FHA Loan Programs

FHA mortgage loan programs include but are not limited to those listed below.

Fixed-Rate Mortgage Loan [Section 203(b)]. The best known FHA-insured loan is the fixed-rate Section 203(b) loan that allows buyers to finance up to 96.5% of their home purchase. This is the only loan in which 100% of the closing costs can be a gift from a relative, non-profit, or government agency.

Adjustable Rate Mortgage (ARM) [Section 251]. The FHA adjustable rate mortgage (ARM) program provides insured mortgage loans with adjustable interest rates for purchases or loan refinances. The initial interest rate usually is significantly lower than the prevailing rate for fixed rate loans. As with any ARM, it may not be a wise choice in times when interest rates are expected to rise in the near future.

Graduated Payment Mortgage (GRM) [Section 245]. The graduated payment loan program is designed for first-time and other buyers with low and moderate income who cannot meet standard payments but who expect an increase in income over the next five to ten years. Under the graduated payment loan, payments will increase each year in amounts that depend upon the plan for which the borrower qualifies.

FHA Condominium Unit Loans [Section 243(C)]. This program insures loans specifically geared toward purchasers of condominium housing units. One purpose of this program is to assist moderate and low income renters who wish to avoid being displaced when their apartments are converted into condominiums.

FHA Energy Efficient Mortgages. The FHA Energy Efficient Mortgage Loan program helps current or potential homeowners lower their monthly utility bills by enabling them to incorporate the cost of adding energy efficient improvements into their new or existing home loan.

Reverse Mortgages for Seniors [Section 255] - Home Equity Conversion Mortgages (HECM). Under the HECM-FHA reverse mortgage program, senior homeowners (age 62 and older who meet additional eligibility requirements) can convert the equity in their primary residence into monthly streams of income or a line of credit to be repaid when they no longer occupy the home. The loans are funded by private FHA-approved lenders. A homeowner applying for a HECM loan must participate in consumer education and counseling by a HECM counselor.

Veteran Administration (VA) Loans

The U.S. Department of Veterans Affairs (VA) guarantees home loans to veterans of the United States Armed Services under the **Servicemen's Readjustment Act** of 1944.[29] The VA guarantee, known as an "entitlement," makes restitution to the lender in the event of default. The amount of guarantee available is regularly adjusted and is available on the VA website, *www.va.gov*. The home loan must be for the borrower's principal residence.

VA guidelines require the use of both an expense-to-income ratio and an analysis of "residual income." Under the **residual income** method, housing expenses, other recurring obligations, plus federal and state income taxes are all deducted from the borrower's gross income to determine the amount of "residual income" the borrower will have. The minimum acceptable amounts of residual income vary depending on the loan amount, the region of the country where the borrower resides, and the borrower's family size.

In addition to looking at residual income, the lender also must apply an income ratio, but the VA only looks at the ratio of total monthly recurring obligations to monthly gross income and applies a maximum acceptable ratio of **41%**. If the borrower's ratio exceeds 41%, the borrower may still qualify if the borrower's residual income exceeds the minimum acceptable amount by 20% or more.

VA guidelines also permit consideration of other factors in making the loan decision about a borrower's financial qualifications and are generally more lenient than the guidelines for either conventional/conforming or FHA loans. A qualified borrower may obtain a VA loan with no down payment which, until recently, was unique.

Rural Development (RD) loans

The Rural Housing Services Agency of the U. S. Department of Agriculture operates both direct and guaranteed home loan programs for low- to moderate-income individuals or families purchasing, repairing, or rehabilitating a home in a rural area (defined as a community of up to 20,000 persons). The primary loan program provides both subsidized and unsubsidized direct loans, commonly referred to as **rural development (RD) loans**, to qualified borrowers. Like VA loans, these loans permit a 100% loan-to-value ratio (i.e., no down payment), and like FHA loans, the expense to income ratios are more lenient than with conventional loans. Currently, monthly housing expenses may not exceed 29% of gross monthly income and monthly recurring debts (including housing expenses) should not exceed 41% of gross monthly income. Borrowers' income must not exceed stated limits and the home must be in a permitted geographic area.

LOAN SERVICING PRACTICES

The mortgage industry is very complicated and ever changing. *There are two components to mortgage lending: lending funds and servicing the loan.* The "lender" is the source of the original loan and may be a bank, a savings institution, a credit union, a mortgage banker, or some other entity. A lender charges the borrower fees that usually are collected from the borrower at closing, and this accounts for a portion of the lender's revenue (in addition to interest that will be earned on the loan). The lender may also "service" the loan, but frequently may sell the loan (technically the mortgage note) which transfers the right to the loan payments to the note purchaser (investor). By doing this, the lender can earn some additional income while getting back the money that was loaned without having to hold the loan for its full term.

The borrower sends the periodic mortgage payments to the "loan servicer," the entity responsible for administering the loan. The loan servicer forwards the principal and interest payment to the mortgage note holder, collects the escrow monies, pays the taxes and hazard insurance, and monitors timely payment of all sums due. The investor pays the servicer a fee for administering the loan that the servicer deducts from the funds it sends to the investor. The lender may choose to service the loans it makes or sell the servicing responsibilities to another entity, but must notify the borrower of the probability that servicing will be transferred. See the discussion of the required disclosures under "Loan Servicing Disclosure Requirements." Servicing a loan can be a fairly smooth and lucrative business as long as the borrower pays regularly. Individuals and entities who purchase closed loans are referred to as "investors."

LOAN FRAUD

Occasionally a buyer-borrower will attempt to bend the loan qualifying rules in his favor by providing false personal, financial, or transaction information in connection with a loan application. Sometimes this is done at the suggestion or with the assistance of the real estate broker and/or the loan officer (or others). Such conduct constitutes "loan fraud," is illegal, and can have severe consequences for the parties involved.

The Extent of Loan Fraud. Loan fraud continues to be a widespread problem hurting homeowners, businesses, and the national economy. The Federal Bureau of Investigation relies in part on "Suspicious Activity Reports" (SARS) filed by financial institutions and information from the Department of Housing and Urban Development's Inspector General to estimate the prevalence of loan fraud. The number of Suspicious Activity Reports filed by financial institutions pertaining to mortgage fraud rose 31% from 2006 to 2007, 36% from 2007 to 2008, and 5% from 2008 to 2009.[30] The full extent of loan fraud and its repercussions continues to unfold.

Why Loan Fraud Is a Problem. Some people may think loan fraud is no big deal and that nobody is really hurt if a big lending institution makes a loan for a few thousand dollars more than is legal under lending guidelines. The truth is that everyone is hurt. Remember the great savings and loan crisis of the 1980s when thousands of thrift institutions and banks failed *due to bad loans* (mostly real estate loans) and it cost hundreds of billions of dollars in taxpayer money to bail out our thrift and banking system? Our entire economy is adversely affected by loan fraud. Any time a loan is made based wholly or in part on false information, the risk of loan default is increased. This increases the costs for all borrowers and if there are too many borrowers who are barely able to make their mortgage payments, there could be major problems in the future if general economic circumstances change.

Loan Fraud: A Serious Felony and License Law Violation. Loan fraud in virtually *any loan transaction* involving a lending institution in the United States is a felony under federal criminal law. 18 U.S.C. §1001 states that any person under the jurisdiction of the federal government who knowingly and willfully falsifies, conceals, covers up by trick, scheme or device a material fact, or who makes a *materially false statement or uses a writing or document knowing that it is false* is guilty of a felony punishable by fine or up to five years imprisonment or both. The statute is intentionally broad to prevent easy circumvention. Anyone who participates in a fraudulent transaction, even if they are not the one making the misrepresentation, may be guilty of conspiracy. 18 U.S.C. §1014 is even more severe. It punishes one who:

> "...knowingly makes any *false statement or report*, or *willfully overvalues any land, property or security*, for the purpose of influencing in any way the action of ... [any governmental agency, lender, bank, credit union, corporation, etc.] ... upon any application, advance, discount, purchase, purchase agreement, repurchase agreement, commitment, or loan, or any change or extension of any of the same, by renewal, deferment of action or otherwise, or the acceptance, release, or substitution of security therefor, *shall be fined not more than $1,000,000 or imprisoned not more than 30 years, or both*.

NOTE: Pursuant to the Fraud Enforcement and Recovery Act of 2009, these loan fraud statutes apply to transactions made by any mortgage lending business or any person or entity that makes in whole or in part a federally related mortgage loan and *all submissions involving virtually any governmental entity*. Thus, the reach of the loan fraud statutes applies not only to residential transactions, but also to sales of subsidized housing, business, commercial, agricultural, and other transactions that may be exempt under RESPA.

A **borrower** who obtains a loan by fraudulent means not only may have his loan canceled (called due early), but in some cases may be criminally prosecuted under federal law. Loan fraud by a **loan officer** not only exposes the loan officer to possible criminal prosecution, but also may endanger the approval of the lending institution by federal government agencies (such as the FHA or VA) to make certain types of loans, and may make it difficult for the lender to sell future loans in the secondary mortgage market. If a **seller** or a **closing attorney** is actively involved in loan fraud, they too are subject to criminal prosecution, and the attorney could be disciplined by the North Carolina State Bar.

A **real estate broker** who participates in loan fraud may be criminally prosecuted and subject to disciplinary action by the North Carolina Real Estate Commission for violating License Law. General Statute §93A-6(a)(1) prohibits any "willful or negligent misrepresentation or omission" to anyone involved in a real estate transaction, including a lender. General Statute §93A-6(a)(10) prohibits any "improper, fraudulent or dishonest dealing" by a real estate broker in connection with any transaction. **Licensees have an affirmative duty to disclose material facts not only to their buyer and seller clients and customers, but also to the lenders and other persons participating in the transaction.** A licensee also has a duty to advise clients to avoid fraudulent transactions, as it is not in a client's best interests to be exposed to potential criminal and civil liability for loan fraud. *Licensees should remove themselves from any transaction if the licensee believes the transaction is being handled in a fraudulent manner and the parties are unwilling to make full disclosures to the lender.*

Elements of Loan Fraud

Loan fraud involves making false representations to obtain a larger loan amount than the borrower is entitled to under the lender's guidelines. The primary elements of loan fraud are:

1) an intentional misrepresentation of fact
2) to a lender, mortgage broker, other loan originator, underwriter, governmental agency, or any person or agency serving a lender, underwriter, or government guarantor
3) for the purpose of obtaining more money than the borrower could otherwise obtain
4) with the expectation that the mortgage broker, originator, lender, government agency, or underwriter will rely on the false information.

In almost every loan fraud, false documents are created and supplied to lenders, closing attorneys, real estate brokers, and others involved in the transaction. *The loan-to-value ratio is a factor in virtually every loan fraud case,* because the borrower attempts to manipulate the ratio to obtain more money than the amount for which s/he otherwise qualifies.

It is extremely important that licensees understand the difference between mortgage brokers and lenders. Mortgage brokers are often independent parties who are paid by the lender only if the transaction closes. If a mortgage broker suggests making a disbursement outside closing that is not reflected on the settlement statement, a licensee should not assume that the lender knows of or approves the payment. The settlement statement documenting the closing must reflect all monies received and disbursed related to the transaction. If a lender refuses to allow a receipt or disbursement to be shown on the settlement statement, then that payment cannot be made; handling the payment outside of the settlement statement is simply illegal.

Finally, brokers should never assume that the settlement statement is accurate and that funds are being handled appropriately just because an attorney is conducting the settlement. Attorneys may not be aware of all of the discussions between the parties. If a broker is aware of an agreement between the parties to handle funds in a different manner than that shown on the settlement statement, the broker should disclose the agreement to the closing attorney and the lender.

Unfortunately, closing attorneys are sometimes involved in mortgage fraud transactions. If a broker believes anything less than full disclosure is being made to the lender, the broker should insist that the settlement statement be changed to represent the true nature of the deal, disclose in writing to the lender the true nature of the transaction, and advise the client to seek separate legal counsel to discuss the potential liability they may face if the transaction is completed without full disclosure to the lender.

Some Examples of Loan Fraud

Below are a few examples of "loan fraud" brokers should avoid. **Note:** *this is not an all-inclusive list* by any means and there are many variations of the schemes mentioned below.

False Gift Letter

It is not uncommon for buyers to lack sufficient funds either for the minimum down payment needed to qualify for a particular loan or to pay closing costs and to receive financial assistance from a relative or other person in order to meet these cash demands. As long as the lender is aware of the nature and source of the funds, this is not loan fraud. However, occasionally the buyer-borrower obtains a *loan* that is described to the lender as a "gift" to deceive the lender into thinking the buyer is qualified. This is loan fraud.

Example: A buyer is applying for a first mortgage loan that requires the buyer to have at least $7,500 in cash for the down payment. The buyer actually has only $4,000 available for the down payment, but the buyer's aunt is willing to temporarily lend him the other $3,500. Knowing that the lender will not approve the mortgage loan if the $3,500 is a loan, the broker working with the buyer suggests that the aunt provide a letter to the lender stating that the $3,500 is a "gift" to the buyer and that the buyer does not have to repay the money. The buyer gets the letter from his aunt and the lender approves the requested loan because of the false gift letter. In this situation, the buyer, the aunt and the real estate broker have all engaged in loan fraud.

Falsification of Debt Reduction

Frequently, a buyer-borrower has total recurring obligations that are too high for the buyer to qualify under the expense-to-income ratios. Misleading the lender into thinking that certain of these obligations have been paid and should not be considered in calculating the expense-to-income ratios is loan fraud.

False Claim of Owner Occupancy

In order to obtain a Farmers Home Administration, a Veterans Administration loan, or a Federal Home Administration loan, a borrower must certify that he or she will own and occupy the property him or herself for a specific period of time. A common loan fraud scheme involves the borrower making a false statement that s/he intends to occupy the subject property when in fact s/he does not. *Many conventional loans require a borrower to sign an affidavit affirming personal occupancy for a prescribed period.* The ***false statement of personal occupancy*** when in fact the borrower does not intend to live there, but rather use the property for rental or other investment purposes ***constitutes loan fraud*** in that it may induce a lender to issue a loan at owner-occupied interest rates that usually are lower than interest rates offered on investment property.

False Employment and/or Income History

This category of loan fraud includes lies about borrower income, debt, employment, and/or assets. In a typical case, the agent and/or other persons involved falsify or alter documents to show that the buyer is qualified when s/he is not.

In one case before the Commission, a woman who had never worked outside the home was approved for a $125,000 loan after the loan originator and real estate broker fabricated an entire employment history for her. This included business cards and letterhead showing her as a self-employed "housekeeper" and submitting false income tax returns, made by substituting her name on copies of her ex-husband's tax returns.

In another case, a father was selling property to his son, who was required to pay 15% down unless the son could show that he had paid rent on the property, in which event his down payment would be only 5%. The mortgage broker and real estate licensee fabricated a tax Schedule E to reflect the father's alleged receipt of rents the son never actually paid.

Secret Second Mortgage

A long-used scheme that is similar to the false gift letter in purpose, but considerably more complex, is the use of a secret second mortgage (deed of trust). As is usually the case in most loan fraud situations, this occurs when the buyer-borrower does not have sufficient funds to make the necessary down payment and pay all closing costs. The seller, the broker, or some third party agrees to advance the buyer-borrower the additional funds needed to qualify for the loan in exchange for a second mortgage on the property being purchased. The *lender*, or at least the underwriter, *is not made aware of the second mortgage and no reference to it appears in any of the closing documents*. Some other subterfuge (such as a false gift letter) may be necessary to explain to the lender the borrower's sudden acquisition of substantial funds.

After the closing, the second mortgage may or may not be recorded, but the buyer's obligation to make payments on the secret second mortgage may interfere with his/her ability to timely pay the first mortgage, increasing the risk unknowingly assumed by the lender (and secondary mortgage market investors). The agreement between the buyer and the provider of the funds may or may not be in writing. Sometimes, the closing attorney may be involved in, or at least aware of, the scheme. Anybody who participates in such a scheme is guilty of loan fraud.

> *Example:* A buyer contracts to purchase a house for $100,000 and will incur an additional $4,000 in closing costs, for a total due at closing of $104,000. The buyer only has $5000 cash and thus needs a loan of $99,000, which would represent a 99% loan to value ratio. The lender will only give a 90% loan, namely, $90,000 maximum. Some individual, whether the seller, a broker, a loan originator, whoever, agrees to fund $9,000 of the buyer's settlement costs in exchange for a second deed of trust against the property, which arrangement is not disclosed to the lender.

Typically, the deed of trust evidencing the second "secret" mortgage is recorded a day or two after the first deed of trust held by the lender. Nonetheless, the paper trail exists and the evidence can be found by a simple search of the grantor index, part of the public records in the Register of Deeds office (now accessible online for many counties).

A slight wrinkle on the foregoing scheme, but equally illegal, is where someone advances monies to an inadequately funded buyer, but rather than take a second mortgage against the property that is the subject of the transaction, the advanced funds purportedly will be secured by a deed of trust/mortgage against some other real property owned by the buyer. The buyer may or may not disclose the source of these funds to the lender, who may or may not have a copy of the prepared deed of trust against the other property in its file. Often the parties' intent is to substitute the subject property to the second lien after closing. Thus, two deeds of trust are prepared, one against the non-subject property and a second against the subject property. The deed of trust against the non-subject property is never recorded; the deed of trust against the subject property is recorded after closing, thus becoming a secret (i.e. undisclosed) second mortgage as in the first scenario.

Again, the key distinction between this practice and current conventional loan practices involving a first and second mortgage previously described is that in the latter instance, the lender is fully aware of the legitimate existence of the second mortgage which also appears on the settlement statement and is in fact recorded. *Loan fraud arises where the lender is not aware of the second mortgage against the subject property.*

Advance Brokerage Commission Rebate

It is not unusual for buyers to run a little short of cash needed to close a deal. Closing expenses may prove to be more than anticipated and the buyers just cannot come up with the additional money. Occasionally, a broker may be willing to effectively reduce his brokerage commission by secretly advancing the buyer the additional funds needed. If the lender is not told, and the brokerage commission reduction and borrower credit are not shown on the settlement statement, this is loan fraud. Understand that as long as the lender knows that the broker is sharing part of his/her commission with the buyer *and* the payment is reflected on the settlement statement as a credit to buyer, it is entirely permissible.

False Earnest Money Deposit

The loan-to-value ratio is designed to ensure that the buyer-borrower is financially committed to the transaction. In a false deposit case, the intent is to convince the lender that the buyer has made a sizeable earnest money deposit or down payment, when in fact he has not. In a simple false deposit case, the sales contract recites earnest money being paid, but no one can produce any records to substantiate payment or receipt. The broker may falsely inform the closing attorney that the earnest money was applied to the broker's commission and the settlement statement will show the earnest money as "paid outside of closing." More complex schemes attempt to create a false paper trail to support the deception, such as *false checks*, (proffering a check supposedly written for the earnest money knowing that it was never negotiated).

Concealed Concessions

In secret or concealed concession cases, the seller or broker pays or gives certain monies to the borrower that are not disclosed on the settlement statement. A typical case is where the property does not appraise at the desired value so the borrower cannot obtain the loan amount originally contemplated. The seller or broker agrees to pay certain concessions to the buyer, e.g. $2000 towards closing costs, which concessions are not reflected on the settlement statement. This failure to tell the lender, an intentional omission, constitutes a "false statement" and is loan fraud.

Contract Kiting

Contract kiting is another complex loan fraud scheme. It involves the use of two sales contracts, one real and one fake, to deceive the lender into thinking the terms of a transaction are different than is actually the case. The real contract may or may not be in writing. The point of all such schemes is to have the lender make the loan based on a sale price that is higher than the actual agreed price. In this situation, the seller, the buyer, the real estate brokers, and/or the closing attorney may be involved in the scheme.

Example: The contract given to the lender states the contract price as $200,000, but the parties have actually agreed (may be written or oral) to a purchase price of $195,000. The buyer is applying for a 90% loan-to-value loan amount. The buyer needs the sale price to be higher because he needs a $180,000 loan rather than a $175,500 loan. If the appraised value is at least $200,000, the buyer will get $4,500 more than he should get based on the actual sales price.

Note: There are many variations of the contract kiting scheme, some quite complex. Often, these schemes combine different approaches discussed above, but all have the same basic purpose — to defraud the lender.

Organized Mortgage Fraud

Organized mortgage fraud has increased substantially in the market. These schemes are perpetrated by unlicensed "promoters," real estate brokers, mortgage brokers, attorneys, builders, and appraisers working together to accomplish the fraud on a wide-scale basis.

Example: An unlicensed "promoter" partners with a builder having difficulty selling a new home inventory. The promoter has investor-buyers lined up to purchase properties. The promoter negotiates with the builder to get the properties at the lowest possible price — the "real" price. The promoter then finds an investor-buyer who enters into a contract with the builder to purchase the property at an inflated price. The builder already has agreed that the difference will be kicked back to the promoter either outside closing (and therefore not disclosed on the settlement statement) or misrepresented on the settlement statement as a repair or renovation expense when no repairs or renovations have been undertaken.

In some situations, the first two or three lots in subdivisions are transferred among members of the developer company, falsely increasing the price of the lots with each transaction. This builds a base of comparable properties for appraisers to use for future lot sales, creating false "comps" for the entire subdivision. A licensee should never suggest or pressure an appraiser to inflate the value of a property nor should they place misleading, fraudulent, inaccurate, or incomplete information in the MLS that might mislead appraisers.

Promoters usually get investors to purchase by misrepresenting the true value of the property, making it appear the investors are getting the property for a good price with instant equity. In some cases, promoters even pay the buyers kickbacks for purchasing properties. Promoters may promise investors to find tenants for the properties under lease-to-own contracts, but often tenants are never placed in the properties. If they are, they usually cannot qualify to purchase the properties and cannot afford the rent. These transactions usually result rapidly in foreclosure.

In most of these schemes, appraisals are inflated and false documents are submitted to the lender to qualify the investor/buyers, including false paystubs, tax returns, W-2's, and verifications of deposit, employment, or rent. Sometimes the investor/buyer falsely claims the property will be their principal residence, in which case a false lease often is created to demonstrate to the lender that the investor/buyer is renting their existing principal residence to a tenant and intends to move into the new property.

Sometimes the difference between the "real" price and the contract price is paid to the real estate broker as an additional commission or marketing fee. After closing, the licensee kicks back the additional commission or marketing fee to the investor/buyer as payment for purchasing the property. The fee is usually enough to reimburse the investor/buyer for all closing costs and down payment. Thus, while the lender believes it has made a 90% loan, the buyer really has no investment in the property at all, and sometimes even profits from the purchase.

Loan fraud has cost the lending industry billions of dollars, but lenders are not the only victims. Schemes that falsely inflate the value of properties result in increased housing costs, property tax assessments, and foreclosures. This leads to higher costs for mortgages and decreased availability of mortgage credit. Licensees should be aware of mortgage fraud in the marketplace and avoid any involvement in such transactions.

SHORT SALES

When the value of a property is less than the outstanding indebtedness secured by the property, the property and the owner are commonly said to be "underwater" in that the total debt exceeds the property's value. Since the national real estate and financial crisis began in 2007, many homeowners with low equity in their homes became "underwater" with their mortgages as home values declined, resulting in huge numbers of properties either threatened with or subjected to foreclosure since 2007. To avoid having a foreclosure on their credit record, many homeowners attempted to obtain their lender's consent to sell the home for an amount less than the outstanding mortgage balance, but still have the lender release the lien. Such an arrangement is known as a "short sale."

What is a "Short Sale"?

A "short sale" is a sale of real property where the proceeds from the sale are insufficient to pay in full the seller's outstanding mortgage and any other liens against the property **and** *the seller lacks sufficient other assets to pay the remaining amounts due on the secured debts after the sale proceeds are applied to the loan.* Because the seller lacks the financial resources to remove these encumbrances in order to convey marketable and insurable title as required by most purchase contracts, the seller's lender, as well as all other lienholders, must consent to the sale and agree to voluntarily release the liens. Unless all lienholders formally agree to accept an amount less than the full indebtedness due and to release their lien, the seller will not be able to sell the property.

It is not uncommon for a property to have a second mortgage loan, such as a home equity line of credit (HELOC), in addition to the first mortgage. If the value of the property is less than the combined balances of both mortgages, then the holder of the second mortgage must also agree to release its lien in order for a short sale to occur. There may be other liens against the property, such as owner association liens for unpaid fees and assessments or judgment liens, that also must be paid or a release obtained. The more lienholders there are, the less likely it is that the property will be a viable candidate for a short sale, as *all lienholders* must voluntarily agree to release their respective liens or the owner cannot convey marketable and insurable title and thus cannot sell the property.

Consequences of Short Sale for Seller. There are financial consequences for a short sale seller other than simply avoiding foreclosure by selling the property. One possibility is that a lienholder will approve the short sale, but NOT forgive the portion of the secured debt that is not satisfied by the sale proceeds, otherwise known as the "deficiency." The lienholder may sue to obtain a deficiency judgment against the seller for the unpaid portion of the debt. Thus, the seller has avoided foreclosure, but still owes and is liable to the lienholder for the unpaid amount remaining on the debt.

Another possibility is that all lienholders consent to the short sale and one or more lienholders also *agree to forgive the remaining debt not satisfied by the short sale proceeds.* This appears to be good news until one realizes that in most cases the forgiven debt will be treated by the Internal Revenue Service as "income" and subject to taxation.

Congress created an exception to the foregoing rule by enacting the **Mortgage Forgiveness Debt Relief Act of 2007.** It provided that debt forgiven through mortgage restructuring, short sale, or foreclosure *may* be excluded from income *if* the debt was used to buy, build, or substantially improve the borrower's principal residence, was secured by the residence, and the loan balance was less than two million dollars. Debt used to refinance qualifying debt was also eligible for the exclusion, but only up to the amount of the old mortgage principal just before refinancing. Originally, this tax relief applied to eligible debt forgiven in 2007 through 2012, but the Act was extended twice through December 31, 2016. A bill was introduced in Congress in January 2017 to again extend the Act to apply to eligible mortgage debt forgiven after December 31, 2016 through December 31, 2018, but as of June 2017, the bill had not been enacted.

Even under the former exception, not all of the forgiven debt was excludable from income. For example, if $10,000 of the home equity line of credit was used to purchase an automobile, rather than for improvements to the real property, that was not excludable, or if in the refinance three years ago the owner borrowed $20,000 more than the outstanding principal balance of the previous mortgage to pay off credit card and other debts, that was not excludable from income. Further, *debt forgiven on second homes, rental property, business property, credit cards, or car loans did **not** qualify for this tax relief— only debt secured by a borrower's* **principal residence** *which debt was used to purchase, build, or substantially improve the principal residence.* Because of the intricacies of these calculations and ever-changing tax laws, **real estate brokers should not attempt to advise seller-clients on any of these matters, but instead should recommend that the seller seek advice from a competent tax lawyer or accountant.**

Why Lienholders Might Consent to a Short Sale. Lenders and mortgage investors generally like to avoid foreclosure proceedings because the expenses associated with a foreclosure may be substantial and frequently the highest bid at a foreclosure sale is less than the amount of the outstanding loan balance, meaning that the lienholder is going to take a loss, possibly substantial. It is not uncommon that a lienholder may be forced to buy the mortgaged property at the foreclosure sale and then attempt to sell the property in the open market in an effort to recover more of the amount due on the debt than would be realized in the foreclosure sale. When facing such a situation, a lienholder may be willing to accept an amount less than the full outstanding balance in full or partial satisfaction of the debt to avoid the trouble and expense of a foreclosure proceeding and the possibility of losing even more money.

Responsibilities of Brokers

The existence of a possible short sale situation is a "material fact" that any broker must disclose to the parties to a transaction in a timely manner. Any broker participating in a short sale transaction is expected to be familiar both with short sale procedures and possible consequences to properly advise and assist real estate consumers in these situations.

Listing Broker. As was discussed in Chapter 9, a listing broker has a responsibility to the seller-client to identify any potential "short sale" situation prior to completing a listing contract and setting a listing price and to alert the seller to the possible consequences of a "short sale." If a short sale appears likely, the listing broker should explain how a short sale works and suggest that the seller discuss the situation with his or her lender or loan servicing company to determine if some sort of "workout" arrangement is possible. A broker should explain the brokerage aspects of a short sale (i.e., the seller's inability to convey marketable and insurable title without lienholders' consent), but must avoid counseling the seller on the legal consequences of a short sale (e.g., deficiency judgment and taxation of forgiven debt). Instead, the broker should only mention these possible consequences and recommend that the seller consult an attorney or an accountant for advice concerning such consequences. If a listed property is going to involve a short sale, the listing agent must disclose this fact to any prospective buyers and brokers working with buyers.

Broker Working with a Buyer. Unlike a listing broker, a broker working with a buyer has less ability to discover many facts about a property, particularly whether a short sale situation exists. A broker working with a prospective buyer (other than the listing broker) is not expected to independently discover if a listed property will involve a short sale. While short sales have diminished in frequency, *a broker working with a buyer may still want to ask the listing broker whether a property involves a short sale.* If a buyer wants to purchase a short sale property, the broker should explain to the buyer how a short sale works and should provide the buyer with appropriate short sale sales contract addenda, if available, to use in formulating an offer.

The Short Sale Process

Seller Contact with Lender

Once the likelihood of a short sale situation becomes apparent, the seller-property owner should contact his or her lender or loan servicer, explain his or her financial situation, and inquire whether the lender would consider approving a short sale and under what parameters. The lender may not be receptive to the idea of a short sale initially, but at least the seller will have given the lender notice of the seller's distressed situation. Even if a lender is not favorably inclined towards a short sale, this does not mean the lender will not consider a short sale if a specific proposal is presented.

The Sales Contract

The first step is to have a buyer who is willing to purchase the property through a short sale process that can become quite protracted (4 to 8 weeks or even longer to obtain lender approval is not unusual). The sales contract should include a contingency requiring approval by *all* lienholders. Brokers using Standard Form 2-T should also append the Short Sale Addendum, Standard Form 2A14-T. If a standard form short sale addendum is not available, the broker working with the buyer should suggest that the buyer consult an attorney to draft an appropriate addendum. The broker should **not** draft a short sale addendum, as this would be the unauthorized practice of law. Once the parties have successfully negotiated the terms of and have signed a contract, it should be submitted to the loan servicer (who may or may not be the lender) with a request that all lienholders accept and approve the parties' contract and release their respective liens.

The Approval Process

Any workout arrangement will require the approval of the lienholder and possibly any mortgage insurer. The initial contact for the seller probably should be the primary lender (if the lender services the loan) or the loan servicer (if the loan is being serviced by a third party servicing company). The approval process will involve "qualifying the seller" considering whatever factors the loan servicer, lienholder, and mortgage insurer may require. This is somewhat similar to the process of underwriting a mortgage loan for a borrower, although there are no uniform guidelines for approving a seller's request for a short sale arrangement. Some of the typical factors considered in assessing a "short sale" request include:

Loan status. Typically, the loan must be in default or default must be imminent.

Hardship. The seller may be required to demonstrate that he or she is facing a financial hardship resulting from circumstances beyond his or her control that adversely impacts his or her ability to make the mortgage payments. Examples might include separation/divorce, loss of employment, illness or disability. Each situation is evaluated on a case-by-case basis.

Seller's financial status. The seller's financial status will be evaluated to determine whether the seller has other resources or assets from which to pay all or some portion of any shortage (deficiency) resulting from the "short sale." The seller will be required to provide documentation of income (e.g., copies of tax returns, pay stubs, bank statements, etc.) and likely a statement of assets and liabilities (such as is provided by a borrower on a loan application).

Brokerage fee. Workout arrangements typically consider the amount of any brokerage fee that the seller must pay to market and sell the property.

Possibility of loan fraud. The loan servicer and lienholder may scrutinize a short sale request for possible loan fraud where the owner defaults on the loan within the first 12 months of the loan term.

Property value. The loan servicer typically will obtain an appraisal to assist in evaluating the short sale request.

Lender's/Investor's Loss. The lienholder will consider how the loss involved with the short sale compares to the projected loss and additional work and expenses involved to pursue a foreclosure.

If the lender/investor and mortgage insurer, if applicable, agree to a "short sale" arrangement, the lender or loan servicer will issue a "Short Sale Approval Letter" outlining the conditions for the sale and specifying the period of time within which the sale must be closed.

Brokers' Roles

The listing broker may communicate with the seller's lender or loan servicer about the status of the short sale approval process; however, *the **listing broker** should **not** negotiate with the lender, servicer, or any other lienholder on the seller's behalf* to avoid engaging in the unauthorized practice of law and possibly violating federal regulations governing mortgage assistance relief service providers. Once the parties' contract is submitted to the lienholder, the role of a **broker working with a buyer** in a short sale is quite passive – basically, just waiting to hear from the lienholder(s) about the requested short sale. If the short sale is approved, the brokers will perform the same tasks as with any other sale transaction.

HOME FORECLOSURE RESCUE SCAMS

In July of 2010, the North Carolina General Assembly enacted the **Homeowner and Homebuyer Protection Act**, sweeping legislation dealing with egregious abuses caused by what the legislation terms "home foreclosure rescue scams." The Act prohibits home foreclosure rescue scams in which a property owner, in hopes of avoiding a foreclosure that has commenced, is induced to sell the mortgaged property for less than fifty percent of its fair market value. The Act seeks to protect homeowners facing foreclosure by regulating in great detail lease option contracts (Chapter 47G of the General Statutes) and contracts for deed (Chapter 47H of the General Statutes), as well as by prohibiting foreclosure rescue transactions under specifically defined circumstances and subject to enumerated exceptions (Article 6, Chapter 75 of General Statutes).

IMPORTANT NOTE: This law is a detailed and lengthy addition to the North Carolina General Statutes. Brokers dealing in any fashion with a transaction seeking to save a property from foreclosure through a lease with an option to purchase, a contract for deed, or any other purported rescue transaction should advise the parties to seek legal counsel from an experienced real estate attorney.

SELECTED RESOURCES

North Carolina Commissioner of Banks: www.nccob.gov. This agency regulates mortgage lending in North Carolina; it sets the standards that individuals within the industry must meet, addresses consumer complaints, and has a voice in proposing or revising legislation to protect the consumer. Its website contains a wealth of information that readers may find helpful. Other useful agencies and websites include:

Federal Reserve Board: www.federalreserve.gov;

Federal Deposit Insurance Corporation: www.FDIC.gov;

Housing and Urban Development: www.HUD.gov; (NC regional office in Greensboro, telephone (336) 547-4000);

US Department of Justice, Civil Division: www.USDOJ.gov;

North Carolina Department of Justice: www.ncdoj.gov;

Federal Housing Administration: www.fha.gov;

US Department of Veteran Affairs: www.homeloans.va.gov;

US Department of Agriculture: www.usda.gov;

Fannie Mae: www.fanniemae.com;

Freddie Mac: www.freddiemac.com.

Endnotes

1.   Public Law 111-203, 124 Stat. 1376 (2010); to be codified in scattered sections of the United States Code.

2.   Public Law 90-321, 15 U.S.C. 1601, *et.seq.* (1968).

3.   See "Regulatory Analysis of Revised Regulation Z," 46 Federal Register 20941 (April 8, 1981).

4.   TILSRA is Title VI of the Depository Institutions Deregulation and Monetary Control Act of 1980 (Public Law 96-221).

5.   Consumer Financial Protection Bureau. Consumer Laws and Regulations: Truth in Lending, ON-LINE.   See   http://files.consumerfinance.gov/f/201306_cfpb_laws-and-regulations_tila-combined-june-2013.pdf.

6.   See 12 C.F.R. 1026.18 for more examples and further discussion.

7.   Consumer Financial Protection Bureau. Consumer Laws and Regulations: Truth in Lending, ON-LINE.   See   http://files.consumerfinance.gov/f/201306_cfpb_laws-and-regulations_tila-combined-june-2013.pdf.

8.   *Id.*

9.   "Subprime" or "nonprime" refers to the credit characteristics of individual borrowers. Subprime borrowers typically have weakened credit histories that include payment delinquencies and possibly more severe problems such as charge-offs, judgments, and bankruptcies. They may also display reduced repayment capacity as measured by credit scores, debt-to-income ratios, or other criteria that may encompass borrowers with incomplete credit histories. Subprime loans are loans to borrowers displaying one or more of these characteristics at the time of origination.

10. "Non-traditional" mortgage loans, sometimes referred to as "alternative" or "exotic" mortgage loans are loans with special features such as: (1) low initial payments based on a fixed introductory rate that expires after a short period and then adjusts to a variable index rate plus a margin for the remaining term of the loan; (2) very high or no limits on how much the payment amount or the interest rate may increase ("payment or rate caps") on reset dates; (3) Limited or no documentation of borrowers' income; (4) Product features likely to result in frequent refinancing to maintain an affordable monthly payment; and/or (5) Substantial prepayment penalties and/or prepayment penalties that extend beyond the initial fixed interest rate period.

   Many non-traditional mortgage loans also were characterized as "reduced documentation," a loan feature that is alternatively referred to as "low doc/no doc", "no income/no asset", "stated income" or "stated assets." For mortgage loans with this feature, a mortgage lender set reduced or minimal documentation standards to substantiate the borrower's income and assets.

   Non-traditional loans were first designed to meet special needs of higher-end customers, but were widely marketed to all borrowers, including sub-prime borrowers.

11. *Banks v. Stoneybrook Apartment*, 2000 WL 1682979 (M.D.N.C. 2000).

12. 15 U.S.C. §1681-1681u.

13. Public Law 108-159.

14. www.annualcreditreport.com.

15. 15 U.S.C. §1691. For a case in which a group of African-American farmers brought a class action under the ECOA against the United States Department of Agriculture see *Pigford v. Glickman*, 185 F.R.D. 82 (D.D.C. 1999) affirmed by *Pigford v. Glickman*, 206 F.3d 1212 (2000). The plaintiffs alleged that the USDA systematically discriminated against them on the basis of their race in the administration of credit benefit programs. A consent decree in favor of the plaintiffs was approved by the court.

16. CFR Part 1002 Supp. I Sec. 1002.4(a)-1 and Sec. 1002.6(a)-1.

17. 42 U.S.C. §3605. The Fair Housing Act is discussed in Chapter 18*infra*.

18. See HUD Regulations at 24 C.F.R. §100.120(b) (2002).

19. Celeste M. Hammond, *Predatory Lending - A Legal Definition And Update*, 34 REAL ESTATE LAW JOURNAL 176, 179 (Fall, 2005).

20. Session Law 2007-352 (House Bill 1817), amending and adding significant sections to Chapter 24 of the General Statutes.

21. Session Law 2007-176 (House Bill 313). N.C. Gen. Stat. § 45A-4(b). Under N.C. Gen. Stat. §45A-5(b), the lender is required to include in the loan closing instructions to the settlement agent the name of the mortgage broker or other person, if any, who acted as a mortgage broker in the origination of the loan.

22.   Public Law 110-289, July 30, 2008. Title V of 12 United States Code, 12 U.S.C. §§5101-5116.

23.   See Article 19B of Chapter 53 of the North Carolina General Statutes.

24.   See N.C. Gen. Stat. §§53-244.109, 53-244.110, and 53-244.111 respectively.

25.   For more information as to the three-day cancellation rule, see
       www.ftc.gov/bcp/edu/pubs/consumer/alerts/alt037.htm.

26.   12 U.S.C.A. §§1701 *et. seq.*.

27.   See generally the official HUD and FHA website: *www.hud.gov,* and *www.fha.gov.*

28.   *Id.* The official HUD website contains a detailed description of mortgage limits by geographic loca-
       tons.

29.   38 U.S.C.A. §1081 *et.seq.*.

30.   Mortgage Asset Research Institute Twelfth Periodic *Mortgage Fraud Case Report*, April 2010.

14 | CLOSING REAL ESTATE TRANSACTIONS

The real estate "closing" is the consummation of a real estate sales transaction. Many people think the closing occurs when the parties meet with the settlement agent to sign all the required legal documents (warranty deed, promissory note, deed of trust, settlement statement, disclosure acknowledgements, etc.) and pay all the funds necessary to complete the sale, but this meeting more properly is referred to as the "settlement meeting" and is defined as such in Standard Form 2-T. *"Closing" is actually a legal process that culminates in the transfer of title from seller to buyer.* It includes not only the "settlement," but also other activities and typically is not fully accomplished in one day. Closing involves the completion of a satisfactory title update by the closing attorney following the settlement meeting, the closing attorney's receipt of permission from the buyer's lender to disburse the loan funds, recordation of the deed and deed(s) of trust in the county registry, and finally disbursement of the sale proceeds to the seller and others in accordance with state law, the sales contract, and the settlement statement. *It is only at this point that the closing and transfer of title is considered complete.*

Competent handling of a real estate closing requires extensive knowledge of general real estate practices, real property law, title examination/transfer/recordation, real estate mortgage law, real estate contract law, and closing procedures and practices. Because so many of the functions to close a transaction require the services of an attorney, **virtually all real estate closings in North Carolina are conducted by attorneys.** However, *real estate brokers are obligated to assist buyers and sellers with the entire sale transaction, including performing "pre-closing" tasks to prepare for settlement.* Brokers working with buyers should guide the buyers through the "buyer's due diligence" process and brokers working with both parties should explain to those parties all the pre-closing and settlement procedures and what each party must do to facilitate the closing. The less experienced the buyer and seller, the greater the need for careful explanation of these procedures. *Thus, real estate brokers should possess a thorough understanding of closing practices and procedures, as well as the competence to properly assist buyers, sellers, and closing attorneys with the closing process.*

This chapter focuses on the closing process for sales of **residential 1-4 family properties**, but many of the principles and practices discussed also apply to closings for other types of properties.

PRE-CLOSING PROCEDURES

Numerous issues must be addressed by the parties after signing the sales contract and prior to settlement, the most important of which are discussed in this section.

GENERAL ISSUES

Respective Responsibilities of the Parties

The respective responsibilities of the buyer and seller for obtaining and/or paying for various settlement services are governed by the terms of the sales contract, or in the absence of a contract provision, by custom. Statements in this text regarding which party typically is responsible for a given matter are based on the provisions of the **Offer to Purchase and Contract, Standard Form 2-T, jointly approved by the North Carolina Bar Association (NCBA) and the North Carolina Association of REALTORS® (NCAR)** and used in the vast majority of residential single-family property transactions in North Carolina. (hereafter, Standard Form 2-T) Comments about each party's responsibilities for matters not addressed in this standard form are based on customary practice.

Selecting the Closing Attorney

The buyer has the right to select the closing attorney of his/her choice. *Usually, the closing attorney will represent both the buyer and the buyer's lender and will provide very limited services to the seller, such as preparing the deed.* The seller may, however, elect to have his/her own attorney. This is rarely done in residential transactions, but is more common in commercial transactions. Buyers frequently ask real estate brokers to recommend a closing attorney, and *a broker may recommend one or more attorneys as long as the broker does not receive any referral fee and has no undisclosed special relationship with the attorney.* The closing attorney should be selected as soon as possible after a sales contract is signed. Closing attorneys are frequently very busy, especially near the end or beginning of a month, so making early arrangements with the attorney is important.

Providing Information to Closing Attorney

The buyer or the broker working with the buyer should immediately provide the selected closing attorney a copy of the sales contract and schedule the settlement on or before the date specified in the contract. Both parties and the listing and selling brokers should provide whatever information is needed to the attorney as that information becomes available (or to the paralegal who will be preparing the closing documents for the attorney). Information the attorney will need includes: copy of sales contract, the parties' contact information and social security numbers, copy of seller's deed, payoff information on the sellers' loans secured by the property, copies of any required inspection reports, contact information for the buyer's lender who the attorney also represents and from whom the attorney must obtain the loan closing documents and instructions, etc. Working closely with the closing attorney's office will help ensure smooth closings and avoid delays.

Settlement Date and Delays

The settlement date usually is specified in the sales contract. The parties and the closing attorney will attempt to close on or before the specified date if at all possible. However, closings are commonly delayed for one reason or another, often because of the buyer's failure to seek or obtain loan approval in a timely manner and/or the buyer's lender's failure to provide the loan closing "package" (all necessary loan related documents and closing instructions) to the closing attorney in a timely manner. The contract settlement date can be delayed by agreement of the parties or, in the absence of an agreement, for a reasonable period of time unless the contract states that "time is of the essence" as to the settlement date or specifies that settlement delays will be handled differently. The NCBA/NCAR Standard Form 2-T allows the delaying party 14 days beyond the stated settlement date, if that party has been acting diligently and in good faith and notifies the non-delaying party. Any other delay must be agreed to by both seller and buyer to avoid the delay becoming a breach of the contract by the de-laying party.

While rare, if the sales contract does not specify a settlement date, then the parties must agree on a settlement date, or lacking agreement, the transaction simply must close within a "reasonable time." The closing cannot take place until all required preliminary matters have been accomplished.

BUYER'S DUE DILIGENCE PROCESS

Most post-contract pre-settlement matters are the responsibility of the buyer, with assistance from the broker working with the buyer. The buyer has always been expected to exercise "due dili-gence" in attending to those matters he or she must resolve to proceed to settlement. This responsibility is even more important since the standard sales contract form allows the buyer a "due diligence period" to obtain satisfactory financing and to conduct all tests, surveys, appraisals, investigations, and inspec-tions required by the lender or desired by the buyer. The buyer has a right to terminate the contract within the stated due diligence period for any reason or no reason, all as discussed in Chapter 11.

This section discusses the major issues that the buyer should explore *at the buyer's expense* dur-ing the "due diligence period." Investigating these issues has always been a buyer's responsibility be-cause it is the buyer who must decide whether to proceed with the purchase or terminate the contract.

General Responsibility of Broker Working with Buyer

A broker working with a buyer, whether as a buyer's agent or a seller's agent, should assist the buyer in completing the "due diligence" process. Under Real Estate License Law, **all brokers** have the duty to discover and disclose all material facts to the buyer (and seller); act in a competent manner; avoid any undisclosed conflict of interest; avoid any improper, fraudulent or dishonest dealing; and otherwise comply with all applicable provisions of License Law and Commission rules, as well as the common law duty to treat third parties honestly and fairly. A broker acting as a **seller's agent** also has a duty to his or her seller-principal under agency law to assist the buyer in performing those tasks necessary to achieve the consummation of the transaction to further the seller's interest in closing the sale. Further-more, a **buyer's agent** also owes his or her buyer-principal the standard agency law duties, meaning that a buyer's agent has an even higher level of responsibility for advising and assisting the buyer in the due diligence process. [See Chapters 8 and 9.]

Buyer's Loan

Perhaps the most critical issue many buyers face is obtaining a loan to finance the real estate purchase. The buyer who needs financing should begin this process before they even start to look at properties for sale. As discussed in Chapter 9 under "Working with Buyers" and also in Chapter 13 under "Real Estate Lending Practices and Procedures," *the real estate broker working with a buyer should encourage the buyer to meet with a mortgage loan officer to "prequalify" the buyer for a loan before look-ing for property.* This will enable the buyer and broker to focus on properties the buyer can afford and will have the additional benefit of speeding up the loan approval process when a formal application is submitted.

Broker's Responsibility

Real estate brokers should be prepared to advise buyers about possible loan sources and the informa-tion they will need when seeking loan prequalification and making a loan application, such as proof of in-come (copies of recent tax returns), list of debts and recurring payments, bank account information, etc. This is true even if the broker working with the buyer is the seller's agent since it is also in the best interests of the seller for the buyer to obtain satisfactory financing in a timely manner. Brokers should, however, be cautious about suggesting any specific type of loan or one particular lender, and should remember that they cannot receive any "kickback" of any type from a recommended lender. It would be prudent to recommend that the buyer contact at least two or three different lenders to obtain information on loan terms, especially interest rates. This can be easily accomplished today by "loan shopping" online. *A prudent broker, especially a buyer's agent, should also caution a buyer if the broker becomes aware that the buyer is considering a loan that may be disadvantageous to the buyer,* such as a loan with an "above market" interest rate, a loan with an adjustable interest rate during a period when interest rates are rising or expected to rise in the near future, an "interest-only" loan (with no amortization of principal), or a loan featuring "negative amortization."

Appraisal

In virtually every transaction involving financing of a real estate purchase, the lender will require an appraisal of the property by a certified real estate appraiser to provide reasonable assurance that the property is worth the purchase price and that the lender's interest will be protected in the event the buyer defaults on the loan. Moreover, a buyer will want some assurance of the value of the property being purchased. Thus, a formal appraisal by a licensed or certified appraiser is almost always necessary. *With residential loans involving a lender, the lender selects the appraiser, the buyer pays for the appraisal (typically by paying the appraisal fee to the lender at the time of loan application), and the appraisal report is sent directly to the lender by the appraiser.* Since January 18, 2014, the lender is required by federal law to provide the buyer of a 1-4 family dwelling a copy of any appraisals obtained in that transaction. The lender will order the appraisal shortly after the loan application is received because the lender must have an appraisal with a satisfactory estimate of the property's value before the buyer's loan can be evaluated and approved.

Property Survey

Mortgage lenders used to require a current survey by a licensed surveyor before they would extend a loan, but this practice has decreased. Even if the buyer is not required by his/her lender to obtain a current survey, or if the buyer pays cash or obtains seller financing, there are numerous reasons why a prudent buyer may want one anyway. A survey will provide accurate measurements of the property boundaries and the precise total area of the property. The typical survey of an improved property will also locate buildings and other improvements on the property. A survey will reveal the existence of encroachments (such as fences, driveways, landscaping or outbuildings) and easements (such as utility easements) as well as any building setback violations and whether any portion of the property lies in a designated special flood hazard area. Be aware that many properties located in a normally dry area may actually be wholly or partially located in a special flood hazard area. This is one reason why lenders might require a survey as a condition of loan approval. *Even if not required, a survey is advisable if there are any questions about boundaries, area, encroachments, easements or any other matter discoverable by a survey.*

Since the buyer (as the prospective new owner of the property) is the party most interested in learning of such problems *before* the closing, *the buyer usually bears the cost of a survey unless the sales contract provides otherwise.* The Standard Form 2-T calls for the buyer to be responsible for obtaining and paying the cost of a survey. If the survey discloses any problem, it usually will be the seller's responsibility to correct the problem. Otherwise, the buyer may be able to opt out of the transaction. A copy of any survey should be provided to the closing attorney as soon as it is obtained.

Property Insurance

In sales of improved property involving a loan, the lender will require that the buyer obtain a property insurance policy (homeowner's policy for residential property) to protect both the buyer and the lender. While an assignment of the seller's policy is possible, insurance companies today generally will not allow this. *The contemporary practice is for the buyer to arrange for a new property insurance policy effective on the settlement date.* The buyer will be required to prove to the lender that the property is adequately insured as of the settlement date. A copy of the property insurance binder must be provided to the closing attorney, who will send it to the lender with the closing package.

In those rare instances where the buyer is paying cash for the property or is obtaining private financing, it is equally important that the buyer (and private financier) be protected by a property insurance policy. *Brokers should always strongly recommend that buyers have adequate insurance coverage effective on the date of the closing.*

Flood Insurance

Flood insurance is required when improved real estate is located in an area designated by the Federal Emergency Management Agency (FEMA) as a "special flood hazard area" and a government-insured mortgage loan is being made on the property. Flood insurance subsidized by the National Flood Insurance Program may be available through insurance agents. FEMA maps (available online) may be consulted to help determine if a property is located in a flood zone; however, it may be necessary to have a survey by a licensed surveyor to conclusively determine if a property is in a special flood hazard area, especially since it is not uncommon for only a portion of a property to be in a flood zone. This is one of several reasons why lenders require a survey as a condition of loan approval and frequently require a flood certification certificate indicating whether the property is in a designated flood zone and, if so, what zone category.

Inspections/Inquiries

As discussed in Chapter 8, a seller of a residential 1-4 unit property must provide the buyer with a Residential Property and Owners Association Disclosure Statement, *but the seller has no affirmative duty to disclose defects or other information about the property* since s/he may choose "No Representation" for any item on the disclosure form. Basically, the seller's only obligation is to avoid misrepresenting facts about the property, whereas *a real estate broker has an affirmative obligation to disclose to prospective buyers any material facts relating to the property that the broker actually knows or should reasonably discover through a "walk-through" inspection of the property.* Brokers may have no actual knowledge of problems with a property and do **not** have a duty to discover and disclose problems that are not readily apparent from a walk-through inspection of the property. A prudent buyer will not only personally inspect the property, but will also have appropriate inspections made by qualified professionals.

The various major inspections and inquiries that a buyer should consider conducting during his or her due diligence period in a residential transaction are discussed below.

Wood-Destroying Insect Inspection

Typically, a residential mortgage lender will require an inspection by a licensed pest control operator who reports the inspection results on a standard form pursuant to regulations of the North Carolina Structural Pest Control Committee. A favorable report is not a guarantee that there is no infestation; rather, it is a report that there is no *visible* evidence of wood-destroying insects and no visible damage from wood-destroying insects. The buyer usually is allowed to choose the inspector.

Standard Form 2-T makes the *buyer* responsible for obtaining and paying for this inspection and report. The cost for any extermination services that may be required or any structural repair of damage caused by wood-destroying insects is negotiable between the buyer and seller. If the property is newly constructed, the seller must provide a new construction termite guarantee at his or her expense. A copy of the inspector's report should be provided to the closing attorney.

General Property Inspection by a Qualified Professional

A broker working with a buyer should strongly recommend that the buyer have the property inspected by a qualified professional. Under Standard Form 2-T, the buyer has the option of inspecting, or obtaining at the buyer's expense, inspections to determine the condition of the property. *For a residential property, the inspection would best be accomplished by a licensed home inspector.* Home inspectors perform a thorough check of the dwelling's condition and provide a report to the buyer. If a commercial property is involved, the buyer may want to employ a general contractor, engineer, or other qualified person to inspect the property. Such an inspection should be performed as soon as possible after contract formation to allow time for addressing any problems that may be discovered.

Physical Inspection by Buyer

A buyer should always make a careful physical inspection of the property prior to expiration of the due diligence period. Any broker working with a buyer should strongly recommend this to the buyer and accompany the buyer when making the inspection. Ideally, an initial physical inspection should be performed as soon as possible after contract to identify potential problems that need to be examined by a qualified professional. A follow-up inspection by the buyer is advisable after the buyer has received copies of any survey and all inspection reports and should be completed prior to expiration of the buyer's due diligence period. In addition to looking for physical defects, the buyer may also want to investigate the following matters.

Tenants. Recall that leases of real property for less than three years from the date the lease was made need not be in writing or recorded. Hence, if the seller previously has leased all or part of the real property being sold, that lease will be valid, even though oral, if it is for three years or less from the time it was made. Physical inspection of the property may disclose a tenant under a valid oral lease, and the buyer can inquire as to the lease terms and what rights, if any, the tenant claims to any personal property or fixtures on the property.

Easements and Encroachments. Physical inspection by the buyer may reveal the existence of possible encroachments or visible easements that have not been recorded and would not be revealed by a title search. For example, an inspection might raise a question about whether a neighbor's fence, driveway or structure actually encroaches on the property to be purchased, indicating the need for a survey. *This is especially important if the buyer has not had a survey performed.*

Recent Construction or Renovations and Violations of Zoning or Restrictive Covenants. A physical inspection might reveal evidence of recent construction or renovations, triggering the question of whether there are outstanding mechanics' liens against the property in favor of contractors who did the construction work. Although closing attorneys routinely have sellers sign an affidavit that there are no mechanics' liens, a buyer should tell the closing attorney if there has been recent construction or renovation so the attorney can contact the designated lien agent.

The inspection might reveal possible violations of building codes, zoning ordinances, or restrictive covenants. Most structural additions and renovations require a county/city building permit. [There is a $5,000 exemption for single-family residences unless the work involves repair/replacement of load-bearing structures or changes in the design of plumbing, HVAC systems, or electrical wiring.]

When it appears that work requiring a permit has been done, the seller should be asked to produce the permit to prove that the improvements were done lawfully. Similarly, most residential subdivisions have restrictive covenants with setback requirements and construction standards for structures. Purchasers might want to read the restrictive covenants before conducting a detailed property inspection.

Note: *A broker working with a buyer is expected to recognize "red flag" situations relating to possible violations of zoning, restrictive covenants, or building permit requirements that warrant further inquiry and to assist the buyer in checking into such situations.*

Sewage Disposal Systems

A buyer should have the waste disposal system inspected if the property currently is or will be served by an on-site septic system.

Unimproved Land. If the property is unimproved and does not have access to a municipal, county, or community sewage disposal system, the buyer should have the appropriate local health department determine whether the land is "suitable," "provisionally suitable" or "unsuitable" for an on-site septic system. The health department having jurisdiction over the property must determine that the property has suitable soils to accommodate a septic system and, if so, issue a permit before the property may be legally improved and a septic system installed. When granted, these permits usually allow a "conventional" septic system, but sometimes a permit is issued with conditions that will only allow a special septic system that is more elaborate and expensive. This frequently occurs when a property borders a body of water or creek, or has an unusually steep slope, but other property conditions can be problematic. Buyers will not have the answers to these issues without an inspection by the local health department.

If a septic system permit has been issued, the buyer should obtain a copy of the permit to verify exactly what type of septic system is allowed. Health department regulations require that septic systems be located a certain distance from each other, from wells, and from dwellings, and comply with regulations pertaining to drain fields and "repair areas" (*i.e.,* an area that can be used as an alternate drain field if the primary drain field fails). *If the buyer is buying vacant land and plans to build on it, the buyer should promptly have an inspection by the county health department to confirm that the land is suitable for an on-site septic system,* preferably a "conventional" septic system, during the due diligence period. If the sales contract does not include a due diligence period, the buyer should make the sales contract contingent on the land satisfying health department standards for a septic system. Alternately, the sales contract could require the property owner to provide proof of proper septic permitting.

Even if the vacant land being purchased is a lot in a subdivision, a buyer should always check with the county health department to assure that the lot has been approved for a septic system because the subdivision's developer may not have obtained approval of that lot for a septic system. Moreover, *the buyer needs to determine the system's capacity (number of bedrooms the system can support) and any restrictions on the type of system that can be used.* Subdivision approval is handled at the county and city levels in North Carolina and there is no state law requiring that developers have septic system approval of all lots prior to obtaining approval of the subdivision. Thus, **subdivision approval may have been granted to the developer without advance approval of all lots (or any of the lots) for a septic system**.

Improved Property. Even for an improved property with an existing on-site septic system, it is important that a buyer ascertain the type of septic system (conventional or other) and verify the "improvement permit" issued by the health department to confirm the system's approval *and determine the system's capacity. The capacity of a septic system is stated in terms of the number of bedrooms (assuming two persons per bedroom) that the system can support,* and this should be noted on the permit. Use of the property by more than two persons per bedroom can overload the system and lead to failure. Should that happen, the health department can prevent further use of the system and, even if the system is repaired, impose lower limits on it use.

Buyers should verify that the septic system will accommodate the number of people who will be living in the house. A real estate **broker** should not make any statement to a buyer regarding the adequacy of the septic system without first checking the septic permit. A broker working with a buyer may rely on the listing broker's representations regarding septic system capacity; however, should any question arise as to whether the represented number of bedrooms and/or occupancy is correct, the broker must verify the accuracy of the information provided by the listing broker.

Well or Water Quality

If an unimproved property is not serviced by a municipal, county, or community water system and will need an onsite well to provide water to a planned building, a well permit must be obtained from the local health department. Water samples from the well must meet water quality standards. A buyer must investigate this issue (as well as all other issues of interest or concern) prior to the expiration of his/her due diligence period, unless the contract specifically requires the seller to provide proof of compliance and water quality.

If a buyer has a question about the quality of the water on any property, s/he should have the water tested by the local health department or a qualified private company.

Lead-Based Paint Inspection

If a residential structure was built prior to 1978, the seller should have provided the buyer with the lead-based paint disclosure form required by federal law. [See Chapter 8.] Regardless of what the seller discloses on the form, the buyer may want to have the property inspected by a certified lead-based paint inspector. This is especially true if the buyer has small children or anticipates having children; expects future renovations or repainting that would disturb existing lead-based paint; or is aware that existing lead-based paint is deteriorating or likely to deteriorate.

Radon Inspection

If there is some reason to suspect that a property may have high radon levels, or if the buyer simply wants to have radon levels checked, the buyer may have a radon test performed by the home inspector or a certified radon tester to determine if there is a problem and the cost of remediation. Testing devices include short-term test kits (3-7 days), long-term test kits (90-365 days), and continuous radon monitors (2-3 days), and may be either passive or active. Passive detectors include charcoal canisters and alpha-track detectors that do not need power to operate, whereas active detectors require both electricity and regular calibration. As a practical matter, the typical timetable in a residential sales transaction generally will only permit a short-term radon test.[1]

Asbestos Inspection

If the buyer has reason to suspect some potential problem with asbestos or is planning to renovate a building (especially an older structure), the buyer may want to have an asbestos inspection performed by a qualified professional to determine if there is a problem and the cost of remediation.

Resolution of Inspection/Repair Issues Related to Property Condition

The seller and buyer should resolve any issues related to the property's condition discovered during the buyer's due diligence inspections/inquiries *prior to expiration of the due diligence period.* Buyers must understand that while Standard Form 2-T allows the buyer to terminate the contract within the due diligence period for any reason or no reason, it does not obligate the seller to make any repairs. Thus, the parties must negotiate as to any repairs requested by the buyer. If the due diligence period expires without any agreement, the buyer will lose the right to terminate the contract without penalty. If the buyer later refuses to close, s/he may be in breach of the contract and most likely will forfeit the earnest money deposit (and may be liable for attorney fees, if the seller must sue for the earnest money and wins).

Property condition is fertile ground for disputes in real estate sales, especially sales of residential single-family properties. Buyers and sellers frequently disagree about conditions that the buyer or home inspector may perceive to be a problem, but the seller does not. Early resolution of any disputes is encouraged. The seller must provide proof of any repairs the seller agreed to make to the buyer and possibly the closing attorney.

Review of Restrictive Covenants and Governing Documents of any Homeowners Association

Preferably prior to making an offer, the buyer should obtain and review any subdivision restrictive covenants and homeowners association articles of incorporation, bylaws, or regulations to learn the permitted property uses/improvements, construction and setback restrictions, rules for common area use, association dues and assessments, etc. This is especially important if the buyer intends to add structures (outbuilding, fence, pool, etc.), expand an existing structure, or use a residential property for a business purpose. Recognizing that sellers may not be a reliable source for information on covenants and homeowners association documents, buyers and brokers working with buyers should go directly to the homeowners association for such information. While brokers may assist buyers in obtaining these documents, they should not interpret covenants and homeowners association documents for buyers, as that would constitute the unauthorized practice of law. Instead, buyers should consult their attorney on such matters.

Review of Zoning and Other Matters Affecting the Property That Are Subject to Government Regulation

Planned Property Use. The buyer should check that county/city zoning regulations and subdivision covenants allow the buyer's planned uses of the property. Know that a particular use may be allowed by the covenants, but prohibited by zoning regulations (and vice-versa). If an **adjacent property** is undeveloped or has a use different from the property being purchased, the buyer should inquire as to the zoning of that property to know what use may be made of the adjacent property in the future. For example, there may be a wide, undeveloped wooded area behind a house that appears to be a "buffer" zone, but has zoning that will allow it to be developed for a commercial or industrial use that would adversely affect the enjoyment of the house.

Roads and Schools. If a house being purchased is in a subdivision, the buyer should always determine whether the subdivision's streets are "public" or "private." In other words, has the state assumed responsibility for permanent maintenance of the streets or is street maintenance the responsibility of subdivision homeowners? If the streets are "private," then the expense of future maintenance could become quite costly for homeowners. If the buyer is concerned that an adjacent or nearby road may be widened in the future, or that a new road may be located nearby, the buyer should investigate to learn if there are any plans by the city, county, or state. Finally, if school assignment is important to the buyer, the buyer should check into the county's or city's policies and plans for school assignment.

OTHER PRE-CLOSING MATTERS

Title Search

Well before the settlement meeting, the closing attorney will search the seller's title to assure that the seller owns marketable title to the property, subject only to encumbrances permitted by the contract of sale. Technically, the *buyer* is responsible for determining whether the seller has a satisfactory marketable title, but the buyer's lender is equally concerned about the quality of title, so the closing attorney performs the title search for both the buyer and the lender since the attorney represents both these parties in handling the closing. The attorney's search will reveal if the seller has good record title through the chain of conveyances, whether there are any outstanding encumbrances, deeds, contracts, deeds of trust, mortgages, judgments, tax or assessment liens, easements, or other title defects that will prevent the buyer from getting that for which he bargained, namely, marketable and insurable title. The title search should be performed well in advance of the settlement date to allow the seller time to clear any title defects.

Clearing of Title Defects by Seller

If the closing attorney discovers "defects" (any matter affecting the quality of the title, such as existing liens) in the seller's title that are not listed as exceptions in the sales contract, the defects must be cured by the seller by the settlement date. The **seller's existing first mortgage (deed of trust)** will be paid in full by the closing attorney out of the sale proceeds at closing, as will any existing **home equity loan (second deed of trust)** the seller may have. Those deeds of trust will be canceled to remove them as liens against the property. A fairly common problem is an old home equity loan or line of credit secured by the property that was in fact paid, often years earlier, but the creditor failed to cancel or mark the deed of trust satisfied at the register of deeds office within 60 days as required by state law. Because sellers at times had difficulty in obtaining the timely cancellation and release of security instruments, the General Assembly enacted laws creating a procedure for consumers to compel a creditor's release of a lien and allowing an attorney to act as a satisfaction agent and cancel outstanding liens and deeds of trust in certain circumstances.[2]

Another common example of a title defect is a **mechanic's lien** filed by a provider of services for an unpaid balance due on recent construction, remodeling or repairs made to the seller's property. The seller will be required to provide receipts or lien waivers to show that no outstanding or potential encumbrance or lien exists. Even if there is no recorded mechanic's lien as of the settlement date, a mechanic's lien may be filed against the property after the closing, since a provider of materials or services may file the lien within 120 days after the last date services or materials were provided and the lien relates back to the first date services or materials were provided. Therefore, closing attorneys routinely require sellers to execute an **affidavit as to mechanic's liens** assuring the buyer, lender, and title insurance company that **either** (1) no labor, services or materials have been provided to the seller in connection with the property within the past 120 days (statutory lien filing period) or (2) certain specified labor, services or materials have been provided within the lien filing period, but each potential lien claimant has been fully paid and has signed a paid receipt for the work or materials or has otherwise waived in writing his lien rights. (See Chapter 2 for a detailed discussion of mechanic's liens.)

Preparation for Assignment of Outstanding Leases

If the property being sold is currently rented to a third party, the *outstanding lease must be assigned by the seller to the buyer*. The seller should provide copies of all outstanding leases to his attorney (or the closing attorney) and the attorney should prepare the appropriate document assigning such leases to the buyer, along with the right to any unpaid rents. The seller should give the buyer a list of all tenants and the status of rent payments as of the settlement date. If a *residential* property is involved, the seller will want to eliminate future liability to the tenants by complying with the "Tenant Security Deposit Act." General Statute §42-54 states that the seller will be relieved of liability if he either: (1) transfers the security deposits to the buyer and notifies the tenants by mail of the transfer and the buyer's name and address; or (2) returns the security deposits to the tenants. The seller and buyer should agree on how this will be handled at the time they enter into the sales contract.

Final Pre-Closing Procedures

The following actions are performed shortly prior to the settlement date. This discussion, as well as the following section titled "Closing Procedures," reflects custom and practice for the past few decades, although the timetable, the required documents, and other aspects of closing a residential transaction changed slightly as of October 3, 2015 when the Loan Estimate and Closing Disclosure forms were implemented in residential transactions subject to the CFPB's "TRID" rules discussed shortly.

Transfer of Earnest Money from Broker/Firm to Closing Attorney

If a broker/firm is holding the purchaser's earnest money deposit in its brokerage trust account, it may *disburse the earnest money from the broker's/firm's trust account to the closing attorney no earlier than 10 days prior to the scheduled settlement date,* pursuant to Commission Rule 58A.0116(e). No other disbursement is permitted under Commission rules without the written consent of both parties. In some areas, a practice has developed between brokers and attorneys where, rather than transferring the earnest money deposit to the settlement agent, the company holding the earnest money retains it as partial commission and *after closing* writes a check to the company from its trust account for the amount of the earnest money. On the settlement statement, the closing attorney credits the amount of the earnest money against the brokerage fee due the broker/firm and pays the balance of the brokerage fee to the broker/firm at closing.

Arrange for Title Insurance

In North Carolina, title insurance is arranged by the closing attorney and will be required if there is a lender involved. The closing attorney searches the title and submits a preliminary opinion on title (report on the status of title) to a title insurance company as an application for a policy of title insurance. After examining the application, the title company will issue a preliminary binder of insurance prior to the closing. After the closing and final title search update by the attorney, a final *mortgagee's (lender's) policy* will be issued to the lender. The common practice in North Carolina is for an *owner's policy* to be issued to the buyer at the same time the lender's policy is issued. The *buyer* pays the one-time premium for both the lender's policy and the owner's title insurance policy; the additional cost for an owner's policy versus simply a lender's policy is negligible. *Even if a lender's title insurance policy is not required because no lender is involved in the transaction, it is highly advisable for the buyer to obtain an owner's policy.*

Notify Buyer of Money Needed to Close

The final preliminary matter is to notify the buyer how much money the buyer must pay from his/her own funds at closing to complete the sale. The closing attorney will have prepared a draft of the settlement statement and will inform the buyer (usually through the broker working with the buyer) of the amount the buyer needs to bring as "certified funds" (certified or official bank check) to the settlement meeting.

Loan Closing "Package" and Document Review

The settlement statement is completed, if not prepared, by the closing attorney once the attorney receives the loan closing package from the buyer's lender. The loan closing "package" includes a multitude of forms and instructions for closing the loan. The lender will transmit the loan funds needed by the buyer to the attorney either as part of the loan package or separately. The principal loan documents are the promissory note and the deed of trust, but there are numerous other loan-related documents. The attorney reviews and finalizes all settlement documents as part of the settlement services included in the attorney's fee the buyer will pay at closing.

Prior to the **TILA-RESPA Integrated Disclosure ("TRID") rule** effective October 3, 2015, closing attorneys frequently did not receive the loan closing package from the lender until either the day before or the morning of the settlement meeting, effectively eliminating review by the parties or their agents prior to the settlement meeting. As discussed shortly, the TRID rule *requires the creditor/ lender to give the "Borrower's Closing Disclosure" to the borrower* **at least three (3) business days before the borrower consummates the loan,** thereby providing the borrower with adequate time to review the loan terms and closing costs.

CLOSING PROCEDURES

After all preliminary preparations are complete, it is time to finalize or "close" the transaction. This section provides a brief overview of the events on the settlement date and immediately thereafter.

CLOSING METHODS

There are two basic methods of closing real estate sales transactions: the **settlement meeting method** and the **escrow closing method.** *The settlement meeting method is used in the vast majority of real estate closings in North Carolina* as well as a number of other states and will be the focus of this discussion. However, an overview of the escrow closing method is included to acquaint North Carolina brokers with this method since it is used in some specialized fact situations in North Carolina and is the prevalent closing method in many parts of the country, especially the western and Midwestern states.

Escrow Closing Method

The parties to the sales contract (seller and buyer) do not attend an escrow closing. Instead, all funds and legal documents necessary for settlement and closing are deposited with an impartial third party, known as the *escrow agent* or *escrowee,* who pursuant to written instructions from the parties, is authorized to handle all closing matters, including the delivery of all legal documents and payment of funds to the appropriate parties. Of necessity, the escrow agent must be a disinterested party. In states where escrow closing is the common practice, a title insurance company or escrow division of a lending institution typically will serve as the escrow agent. In North Carolina, attorneys occasionally serve as an escrow agent in this capacity when closing a transaction.

Escrow Agreement and Procedures

After the seller and buyer have entered into a sales contract, they also enter into an escrow agreement containing instructions to the escrow agent from both seller and buyer. This agreement may bear any of a number of titles including but not limited to "Escrow Agreement," "Escrow Instructions," or "Deed and Money Escrow." The escrow agent then performs the specified closing functions in accordance with the escrow agreement independently of any further control by either the seller or the buyer.

The seller and buyer each must attend to pre-closing matters as required in the escrow agreement. All information is furnished to the escrow agent. When both parties have complied with the escrow agreement and have furnished all necessary documents, the escrow agent will complete the transaction after first verifying by an updated title search that the seller's title conforms to the contract terms and obtaining certified funds for the balance due from the buyer. Depending on the terms of the escrow agreement, the escrow agent may also handle a number of the closing details, including obtaining title insurance, preparing a settlement statement, paying the brokers' commissions, and recording and delivering documents to each party. Since neither seller nor purchaser must be present, the escrow closing method is well suited for closings involving out-of-state parties.

> *Example*: A New Jersey resident who owns a North Carolina beach cottage may enter into a contract to sell that property to a North Carolina resident. The seller might appoint a North Carolina attorney as escrow agent and deliver the signed deed and other necessary documents to that escrow agent with instructions to perform certain closing functions and to deliver the deed to the buyer when the buyer has delivered the purchase price to the escrow agent.

Relation Back Doctrine

One of the benefits of the escrow closing is the "relation back" doctrine. While the deed technically is not effective as a conveyance until the escrow agent has delivered it to the purchaser, *the deed will be treated as having been delivered for certain purposes when the seller gives it to the escrow agent.* This is the "relation back" doctrine. Perhaps the most common fact situation triggering the relation back doctrine is if the grantor dies.

> *Example:* On April 15, a seller delivers a warranty deed into escrow to be conveyed to the buyer when certain conditions are met, including the buyer's delivery of a certified check for $100,000 to the escrow agent. On April 20, the buyer delivers the check and by April 25, all documents and conditions are satisfied and the escrow agent can proceed. However, the seller dies on April 22. In this situation, the transfer of the deed to the buyer legally is treated as "relating back" to April 15, the date the deed was delivered into escrow. Thus the escrow agent does not lose his authority to deliver the deed to the buyer and the buyer will obtain good title even though the seller died prior to consummation of the escrow closing or the recording of the deed.

Settlement Meeting Method

Most real estate closings in North Carolina use the settlement meeting method with an attorney conducting or supervising the closing. The attorney coordinates the closing process, assures that all requirements of the contract and lender are met, prepares all legal documents and the settlement statement(s), records the deed and any deed of trust, and disburses funds. *It is common in residential transactions for only one attorney to supervise and handle the entire closing process.* The closing attorney usually represents the buyer and lender while also performing limited functions for the seller (such as preparing the deed). By comparison, in complex real estate transactions, including most commercial and industrial property closings, the buyer and the seller will each have an attorney.

The Role of Nonlawyers in Closings

Historically, settlement meetings for residential properties were always conducted personally by an attorney with a paralegal or assistant often coordinating the closing and physically preparing the documents under the attorney's direction. In 2003, the North Carolina State Bar ruled in an ethics opinion that *attorneys need not be physically present at settlement meetings in residential real estate closings. A* **nonlawyer assistant** *acting under the direct supervision of an attorney may conduct the settlement meeting without the attorney being present.* At the settlement meeting, the nonlawyer assistant may identify the documents to be signed, show the client where to sign, and write checks disbursing the proceeds.[3] While the majority of real estate settlement meetings continue to be conducted by an attorney, the use of nonlawyer assistants has become commonplace.

The State Bar ethics opinion should not be interpreted to mean that attorneys will not be involved in real estate closings. In another ethics opinion dealing with unauthorized practice of law issues, the North Carolina State Bar made it clear that numerous aspects of residential real estate transactions involve the practice of law and nonlawyers may not perform these services.[4] The ethics opinion lists as examples eight functions related to a real estate closing that would constitute the unauthorized practice of law if performed by a nonlawyer. The list is nonexclusive. According to the opinion, a nonlawyer is engaged in the unauthorized practice of law if he or she performs any of the following functions related to a transaction.

1. Abstracting or providing an opinion on title to real property.
2. Explaining the legal status of title to real estate, the legal effect of anything found in the chain of title, or the legal effect of an item reported as an exception in a title insurance commitment, except as necessary to underwrite a policy of insurance and except that a licensed title insurer, agency, or agent may explain an underwriting decision to an insured or prospective insured, including providing the reason for the decision.
3. Explaining or giving advice about the rights or responsibilities of parties concerning matters disclosed by a land survey under circumstances that require the exercise of legal judgment or that have implications with respect to a party's legal rights or obligations.
4. Providing a legal opinion or advice in response to inquiries by any of the parties regarding legal rights or obligations of any person, firm, or corporation, including but not limited to the rights and obligations created by a promissory note, the effect of a pre-payment penalty, the rights of parties under a right of rescission, and the rights of a lender under a deed of trust.
5. Advising or instructing a party to the transaction regarding alternative ways to take title to the property or the legal consequences of taking title in a particular manner.
6. Drafting a legal document for a party to the transaction or assisting a party in completing a legal document, or choosing or assisting a party in selecting a form legal document from among several forms having different legal implications.
7. Explaining or recommending a course of action to a party that requires the exercise of legal judgment or that impacts the party's legal rights or obligations.
8. Attempting to settle or resolve a dispute between the parties to the transaction that affects their respective legal rights or obligations.

Closing Coordinated by Real Estate Broker

Real estate brokers should note that the North Carolina State Bar's ethics opinion allowing settlement meetings to be conducted by nonlawyer assistants acting under an attorney's supervision should not be interpreted to mean that real estate brokers can now conduct real estate closings. While a broker may infrequently be called upon to coordinate certain aspects of closing a transaction they have brokered, **brokers are strongly discouraged from attempting to act as a settlement agent. A broker acting as a settlement agent will be held strictly accountable by the North Carolina Real Estate Commission for assuring that all aspects of the closing are handled properly and that the broker uses an attorney to perform all closing functions that require a law license.** Such functions include, but are not limited to, preparing deeds and other documents, explaining the parties' rights and obligations, and offering an opinion about the nature or quality of the title to be transferred. A real estate broker should be extremely careful not to engage in the unauthorized practice of law.

If a broker personally coordinates a real estate closing (using an attorney to perform those functions requiring a law license), the broker **must** *deposit all funds paid by or in behalf of the buyer into his or her brokerage trust account and make all required disbursements directly from the trust account.* It is not proper for a broker/firm to use a business or personal account for this purpose, as this would constitute illegal "commingling" of the parties' funds with the broker's funds. A broker/firm coordinating a closing may disburse the entire brokerage fee earned to his/its business account and then compensate the broker's/firm's agents or a cooperating broker/firm, as appropriate, or it may pay all earned brokerage fees to the broker's agents and to a cooperating broker (i.e., another firm) directly from the brokerage trust account. Historically, the settlement agent generally paid the brokerage fees due each real estate company from the escrowed funds and each company paid its affiliated brokers the agreed percentage from the company's operating account. At a minimum, the brokerage commission split between the listing broker and any cooperating selling broker or firm should be shown on the settlement statement.

Settlement Meeting Procedures

Parties Attending the Settlement Meeting

The parties attending the settlement meeting may include: (1) the seller(s), (2) the buyer(s), (3) the closing attorney and/or a nonlawyer assistant supervised by the closing attorney, (4) the listing real estate broker, and (5) the selling real estate broker. Sometimes a representative of the mortgage lender may be present, especially if the lender is a local institution. It is possible for the closing to be conducted without one or both of the principal parties (seller and buyer) present; for example, a seller could sign the deed in advance and deliver it to the closing attorney to hold until the closing or a buyer might give another person a power of attorney to sign all settlement documents on behalf of the buyer, but the latter is not typical. *Buyers in a residential transaction usually attend the settlement meeting, while the sellers' presence may be optional as long as they have provided the closing attorney with all necessary documents.* The closing attorney may meet with all the parties and their respective agents when conducting the settlement meeting or may meet separately with each party and their agent, rather than having them all in one room at the same time.[5]

The listing broker and selling broker should attend the settlement meeting. A broker who neglects to attend the settlement meeting for a sale he or she brokered may be found derelict in the performance of his or her duties. [**Note:** A broker whose license becomes inactive or expires or is suspended or revoked between contract formation and settlement should *not* attend the settlement meeting because a broker may not engage in any brokerage activities when his or her license is not on active status. The broker may receive any earned commission as long as the broker's license was on active status while providing brokerage services and the broker stopped providing any services the moment s/he no longer had an active license.]

Location of Settlement Meeting

Where a settlement meeting is conducted may be based on the nature of the transaction, local custom, and/or convenience to the parties. There is no legal dictate as to location. *The most common practice in North Carolina is to have the settlement meeting at the office of the buyer's attorney.* The lending institution financing the purchase also may be used for the meeting or the meeting may be held in the office of a real estate broker involved in the transaction.

Final Review of Settlement Statement

Usually the first item of business at a settlement meeting is to review the settlement statement. It is important that the parties and the real estate brokers agree on the accuracy of the settlement statement before proceeding with the closing. Brokers involved in the transaction should obtain a copy of the settlement statement as soon as possible and review it with each party with whom they are working. The closing attorney must collect all amounts due from the buyer, whether paid with a certified check or wire transfer or comparable method that guarantees payment. A broker's responsibility regarding preparation and review of settlement statements will be discussed shortly.

Review and Signing of All Closing Documents; Furnishing Copies to Parties

The closing attorney or nonlawyer assistant will conduct the settlement meeting pursuant to the detailed instructions from the buyer's lender and in accord with the terms of the sales contract. All documents, including various disclosure forms, will be reviewed with the buyer and/or seller and signed as appropriate. The modern real estate closing involves a multitude of forms and documents, but the most important are the warranty deed transferring title from the seller to the buyer and the promissory note and deed of trust executed by the buyer in connection with the buyer's loan to finance the purchase. While specific practices among attorneys differ, attorneys generally provide buyers with unsigned copies of most, if not all, documents at the settlement meeting.

No Disbursement of Funds at Settlement Meeting

*Funds will **not** be disbursed to anyone at the settlement meeting.* The **North Carolina Good Funds Settlement Act** (Chapter 45A of the General Statutes) requires the settlement agent (closing attorney) to: 1) *verify funds paid to the settlement agent by the buyer, lender, or other party for the transaction and* 2) *record the deed and deed of trust **prior to** disbursing any funds.* The funds paid to the settlement agent are acceptable if they have been irrevocably credited to the settlement agent's escrow account or if they were paid by certified check, cashier's check, teller's check, official bank check, wire transfer, check drawn on an attorney's trust account, check drawn on a real estate broker's trust account, or certain other specified types of checks. After verifying available funds, the closing attorney must update the title search, record the deed and deed of trust, and only then may disburse funds to the seller, brokers, and any other payees as noted on the settlement statement.

Procedures after the Settlement Meeting

Title Update, Document Recording, and Funds Disbursement

As soon as possible after the settlement meeting (typically the same day or the next business day), the closing attorney will "update" the earlier title search to assure that no encumbrances (such as a mortgage or other lien) have been recorded against the property or the seller since the previous title search. *If no problem is found during the title update search, the closing attorney will record the deed and the deed of trust, if any, and disburse all funds as indicated on the settlement statement.* Thus, the seller and real estate brokers usually do not receive funds due until a day or two after the settlement meeting.

As mentioned at the outset, *"closing" technically is not complete until the deed and deed of trust are recorded*, as recognized by the definition of "closing" in Standard Form 2-T discussed in Chapter 11.

Transmitting Documents to Lender and Buyer

After recording the deed and deed of trust and disbursing all funds, the closing attorney promptly submits all relevant financing documents (including the original note and certified copy of the recorded deed of trust) to the lender. *The original general warranty deed commonly is mailed to the buyer by the register of deeds office after it has been imaged into the document recording system*, although some attorneys have it sent to them and they transmit it to the buyer.

Income Tax Reporting Requirements

The seller's proceeds from the sale or exchange of real estate must be reported to the Internal Revenue Service on an informational return, Form 1099-S. This informational return must be filed in all voluntary sales or exchange transactions involving individual or partnership sellers of improved or unimproved real property. Excluded from the reporting requirements are refinancings not involving sales, sales by corporate grantors or governmental units, gift transfers, bequests, leases, options, foreclosures or deeds in lieu of foreclosure, and certain other transfers specified within the voluminous Internal Revenue Code and related regulations.

The closing attorney, as the settlement agent, has the primary obligation to file the 1099-S form reporting the seller's proceeds. IRS regulations assign responsibility for filing Form 1099-S as follows: (1) the person responsible for the closing, (2) the lender, (3) the seller's broker, (4) the buyer's broker or, lastly, (5) the buyer.

Informational returns must be filed with the IRS between January 1 and February 28 of the year following the year of sale. Usually these returns are filed electronically, unless fewer than 250 returns are expected to be filed in a calendar year, in which case reporting can be by the paper Form 1099-S.

North Carolina requires that a state informational form be filed for any purchase of real property located within North Carolina from a *non-resident seller*. **Form NC-1099NRS** *must be filed by the buyer within 15 days of the closing.* The closing attorney is primarily responsible for assuring compliance with North Carolina revenue laws and regulations.

REAL ESTATE SETTLEMENT PROCEDURES ACT (RESPA)

INTRODUCTION

The Real Estate Settlement Procedures Act (RESPA)[6] was enacted by Congress to protect buyers when they obtain a "federally related mortgage loan" to purchase real property on which a 1-4 family dwelling is or will be situated within two years of purchase. Originally passed in 1974, RESPA has been amended several times and is now administered by the Consumer Financial Protection Bureau (CFPB) that assumed administrative and rulemaking responsibilities from the Department of Housing and Urban Development (HUD) in 2010 pursuant to the Dodd-Frank Wall Street and Consumer

Protection Act ("Dodd-Frank Act"). The RESPA rules are commonly referred to as *"Regulation X"*[7] (versus Regulation Z for TILA rules). Most of the current regulations under both TILA and RESPA were strengthened, rather than significantly altered, by the Dodd-Frank reforms.

Applicability of Law

RESPA applies to **residential** transactions involving a federally related mortgage loan. Simplified, Regulation X basically defines a *"federally related mortgage loan" as:*

- any loan made by a lender insured, regulated, or guaranteed by the federal government **or** that will be sold in the secondary mortgage market

    and

- is secured by a lien on residential real property on which a 1-4 family dwelling is or will be constructed or placed (including a manufactured home) within two years of settlement.

Although there are a few exemptions, *the law applies to virtually all mortgage loans secured by real property having a 1-4 family dwelling made by institutional lenders,* including home purchase loans, home improvement loans, home equity loans, reverse mortgages, and refinancing loans. RESPA does not apply to loans for a commercial, business, or agricultural purposes. Note that loans secured by residential rental or investment properties may be excluded from RESPA coverage under the "business purpose" exception.

RESPA REQUIREMENTS/CONSUMER PROTECTIONS

The major RESPA consumer protections are summarized below and then discussed in more detail, as is the impact that the TILA-RESPA Integrated Disclosure (TRID) rules had upon duplicate disclosures required under TILA and RESPA. Consumer protections under RESPA include the following requirements.

1) If a loan is originated by a mortgage broker who receives a fee from the lender for making a loan with an above-market interest rate (i.e., a *"yield-spread premium"*), then the fee must be disclosed and the borrower must receive a full credit toward their loan origination charges in the amount of any yield spread premium paid to the mortgage broker.

2) Loan servicers must provide *loan servicing disclosures* informing the borrower (1) if the loan servicing may be transferred to another entity during the life of the loan and (2) when the loan servicing is actually transferred and to whom.

3) RESPA rules establish *limits on* the amount that lenders/servicers may collect from a borrower and maintain in the borrower's *escrow account* for payment by the lender of real estate taxes and property insurance premiums, and provide detailed regulations governing the operation of such escrow accounts.

4) RESPA prohibits the payment or receipt of any *fees or kickbacks* to or from any person for the referral of business related to any real estate settlement service for which the buyer-borrower or seller is required to pay.

5) Loan originators (lenders and mortgage brokers) must provide borrowers a *special information booklet* about shopping for a house and a loan and information about the closing process within three business days of loan application.

6) Loan originators must provide borrowers with an estimate of settlement charges they

will incur and related loan information within three business days of loan application. RESPA still refers to this document as a ***Good Faith Estimate (GFE),*** although the GFE has been replaced by the Loan Estimate (LE) under the TRID rules.

7) RESPA still defines the ***HUD-1 or HUD-1A settlement statement*** as the statement prescribed for setting forth settlement charges in the purchase or refinance of a federally related mortgage loan secured by real property on which a 1-4 family dwelling is situated, but this too was impacted by the TRID rules.

While all of the above protections continue under RESPA, the last three were impacted by the TILA-RESPA Integrated Disclosure rule created by the CFPB that became effective October 3, 2015 and will be discussed shortly.

Borrower Credit for "Yield Spread Premiums"

In the 1990s and early 2000s, a lending practice developed whereby loans allegedly having very low or even no upfront closing costs or origination fees were offered to borrowers when in fact the proposed loan was at an interest rate higher than the normal rate for which the borrower qualified. The inflated interest rate made the loan more attractive to loan investors and enabled the lender to sell the loan at a higher price. Lenders began to pay mortgage brokers a substantial fee (e.g., 1% of the loan amount) for placing the loan with an above-market interest rate. *This fee is known as a "yield spread premium" because it is a premium paid to the mortgage broker by the lender for making a loan with an "above-market" interest rate that will produce an increased yield to the lender and investor.*

This practice of using yield spread premiums to make low/no closing cost loans that were more susceptible to foreclosure contributed greatly to the financial industry crisis, and subsequent crises in the entire housing industry and the economy at large of the mid-2000s. Borrowers frequently did not understand that they were agreeing to a loan with a higher interest rate than they were qualified to obtain. Excessive yield spread premiums sometimes would be charged without increasing the interest rate by disguising the yield spread premium as some kind of necessary fee associated with making the loan. The result was the same — borrowers were paying more than necessary to obtain the loan.

Abuses in the use of yield spread premiums by some players in the lending community led HUD to adopt a rule effective January 1, 2010 requiring the loan originator to give the borrower a credit against loan origination charges for the full amount of any yield spread premium. This credit must be shown in the loan origination section of the former Good Faith Estimate (GFE) form (now the Loan Estimate [LE] form) as reducing the borrower's loan origination charge in exchange for the cited interest rate. It is easiest to think of this credit as the opposite of "discount points" that are paid by a borrower to obtain a lower interest rate. Of course, mortgage brokers could simply increase the amount of the base origination fee so that the adjusted origination fee still provides the desired amount of excess profit. *The real advantage of this rule is that with the standardized cost estimate form, the borrower can much more easily compare the adjusted origination charges of loans from different lenders* and avoid choosing the loan offered by a mortgage broker who seeks an excessive profit.

Loan Servicing Disclosure Requirements

RESPA requires servicers of all federally related mortgage loans to disclose to borrowers at the time of loan application whether the servicing of the loan may be sold, transferred, or assigned to another entity during the term of the loan. If at any time during the loan term, the loan servicing is transferred, both the transferor servicer and the transferee or subsequent loan servicer must notify the borrower in writing prior to transferring the loan servicing responsibilities of the effective date of transfer, the new payment address, and telephone numbers for both the old and new loan servicer so the borrower may call if s/he has any questions. These written disclosures must occur each time loan servicing is transferred.

Escrow Account Restrictions

It is common practice for lenders (and others who service mortgage loans) to maintain an escrow account from which to pay real estate taxes and property insurance premiums on the property securing the loan as taxes and insurance premiums come due. In addition to the monthly principal and interest payment, the borrower must pay a specified amount monthly to the escrow account so there will be sufficient funds available to pay the taxes and insurance at the appropriate time. Hence the term "***PITI payment***" that represents "*principal, interest, taxes and insurance.*" This protects the interests of the lender and any investor who may have purchased the loan in the secondary mortgage market. If taxes are not paid, a tax lien will attach to the property and would take precedence (have priority) over the mortgage loan in the event of foreclosure. If the property is damaged or destroyed by fire, wind, or other causes, current hazard insurance is needed to cover repairs or compensate for the loss. Note that lenders frequently are the named loss payees on the insurance policy, in conjunction with the borrower, in the event the property is completely destroyed.

RESPA establishes limits on the amounts that mortgage lenders (or other servicers) may require a borrower to deposit into any escrow account for taxes and insurance. The maximum amount that may be collected monthly is an amount equal to one-twelfth (1/12) of the total disbursements for taxes and insurance premiums that are anticipated in a year (as well as any other escrowed expenses, such as private mortgage insurance). When establishing the escrow account (usually done at closing) the lender may collect an amount equal to one-sixth (1/6) of the expected annual disbursements (i.e., two months advance escrow payments) to serve as a "cushion," and may also collect amounts that will assure there are sufficient funds, when considered along with the monthly payments, to pay the taxes and insurance premiums when they next come due. Usually, the hazard insurance premium for the first year is paid at closing, so only the cushion amount is escrowed. However, the next tax bill might be due just a few months after closing, thus requiring an additional up-front contribution, as the monthly payments escrowed by that time would not be sufficient to pay the tax bill. The permitted cushion of one-sixth of the annual disbursement may be maintained throughout the life of the loan.

Prohibited Kickbacks or Referral Fees

RESPA prohibits the payment or receipt of any fee, kickback, or other "thing of value" to or from any person pursuant to any agreement or understanding, oral or otherwise, that business incident to a real estate settlement service shall be referred to any person. Note that ***both the payment and the receipt of such referral fees or any unearned fees are prohibited.*** The underlying reason for these restrictions is to prevent higher loan acquisition costs to borrowers due to inflated loan settlement charges that might result from the payment of referral fees or kickbacks between settlement service providers. *Thus,* ***no fee can be paid for mere referrals of business — any fee paid must be for services, goods or facilities actually provided and the amount of the fee must be reasonably related to the value of the service, goods or facility.***[8]

"Settlement Service." The term "settlement service" applies to *any service related to a real estate settlement (closing) for which the buyer-borrower or seller is required to pay* and includes real estate brokerage, loan application processing, loan origination, mortgage brokering, credit report, appraisal, home inspection, pest inspection, survey, insurance (homeowner's, mortgage or mortgage life), legal services (document preparation, title search, closing, etc), title insurance and others.

Applies to ALL Service Providers, including Real Estate Brokers. These provisions apply to all settlement service providers, not just to lenders, and prohibit payments to any person for referring business to a settlement service provider. Lenders may not be paid referral fees by appraisers, credit reporting companies, attorneys, inspectors, or anyone else providing a settlement service nor may they give any person any "thing of value" for referring business to them. Real estate brokers are settlement service providers and may not be paid or accept *any referral fee from a lender, appraiser, inspector, insurance agent, attorney, home warranty company, or other settlement service provider nor may they pay any person for referring business to them.* The lone exception under RESPA is that ***referral fees between real estate brokers for brokerage activity are expressly permitted.*** Other than real estate brokerage referral fees, it is completely inappropriate for real estate brokers to request, pay, or receive any referral fee from a settlement service provider in a RESPA governed transaction.

Any "Thing of Value" Prohibited. While the terms "kickbacks" and "referral fees" are used throughout this discussion for convenience, understand that the RESPA prohibition is not limited to the payment of fees, but prohibits *any "thing of value" that is given in exchange for a referral.* This includes, for example, not only money, but also any personal property item of value, discounts, coupons, reduced fee or free services, the chance to win a prize through a lottery or drawing, etc.

Payment Pursuant to an "Agreement or Understanding." To be prohibited, the payment must have been made pursuant to some agreement or understanding that there would be consideration for referrals; however, no formal agreement is necessary to be considered a prohibited arrangement. An informal oral agreement or even a tacit understanding will be sufficient. If there is a pattern of payments for referrals, the understanding component will be inferred from the parties' conduct.

Payment in Exchange for a Referral Is the Problem. The prohibition is for compensation made in exchange for a referral. If a lender or other service provider has a marketing program that gives away something of value to all real estate brokers in a particular area (or all agents belonging to a particular trade organization or attending an educational program) rather than just to those who refer business to the lender, that may not violate RESPA. That said, be aware that the CFPB is closely scrutinizing "marketing service agreement" arrangements between various settlement service providers and has determined several to be illegal.

Under RESPA, only brokerage fees between real estate brokers, whether commission splits or referral fees, are permitted, including referral fees paid to a licensed relocation company. Two examples of illegal payments to real estate brokers for referring business to a settlement service provider are below.

- A home inspector pays a real estate broker a $25 referral fee for each buyer the broker refers to the home inspector. (Note: the payment does not have to be in money. A gift certificate, lunches/dinners, a leather note pad holder, a cellular phone, a financial calculator, or anything else of value is equally illegal.)
- For each borrower referred by a real estate broker, a mortgage loan officer places a numbered drawing ticket into a box and gives the broker the stub. At a predesignated point in time, a ticket is drawn and the broker with the winning ticket receives an all-expense paid cruise. Awarding a prize or gift of any sort after a designated number of referrals is also a problem. ***Any arrangement that results in some form of consideration for referrals is prohibited.***

Affiliated Business Arrangements. The rules also address the referral of consumers to other settlement service providers where the referring individual has an ownership interest in both the company making the referral and the company to which the referral is made, but these can be complex.

One example of an affiliated business arrangement is where an individual has an ownership interest in both a real estate company and in a mortgage company or an appraisal company or a home inspection company. RESPA allows certain affiliated business arrangements as long as: 1) the existence of the relationship is *disclosed* and a *written estimate* of the provider's charges or range of charges is given to the person being referred, 2) the person is *not required to use* any particular provider, and 3) the only "thing of value" received by the person making the referral is a return on his/her ownership interest in the affiliated business entity or franchise relationship.

There are various arrangements that may be considered affiliated business arrangements under RESPA. Situations where different service providers, such as a real estate broker and an attorney or a mortgage broker, share office space are particularly suspect, especially if the rent paid is related in any way to the volume of business referred. Real estate brokers/firms with any kind of special arrangement with another settlement service provider should seek the advice of an attorney regarding RESPA compliance.

Special Information Booklet for Homebuyer/Borrowers

When a consumer submits an application for a loan subject to RESPA, the lender or mortgage broker must either personally deliver or mail a copy of a "special information booklet" to the consumer *within three business days following receipt of the loan application,* unless the loan is denied within that three day period. From January 1, 2010 through October 3, 2015, the HUD-prescribed booklet was titled *Shopping for Your Home Loan.* As of October 3, 2015, the TRID-prescribed booklet is titled *Your Home Loan Toolkit.* The information booklet addresses shopping for a house, a loan, settlement service providers, the settlement process, sample forms, and other matters related to the residential lending and closing processes. The booklet is very informative, and real estate brokers are urged to advise potential buyers to study the booklet so they can better understand the process and especially the relevant forms.

Written Estimate of Closing Costs

In addition to the information booklet, RESPA requires *the lender or mortgage broker to personally deliver or mail a written estimate of settlement charges the borrower will incur to a loan applicant either at or within three business days of application.* RESPA still refers to this written expense estimate as a "**Good Faith Estimate (GFE),**" but since October 3, 2015, it is now called a "Loan Estimate" (LE).

Definition of "Loan Application"

The potential borrower's "application" for the purpose of triggering the written cost estimate requirement does not have to be a formal detailed application on a prescribed form. RESPA defines an "application" as the lender's receipt of the following financial information submitted in anticipation of a credit decision.

1) Applicant's legal name
2) Applicant's gross income
3) Applicant's Social Security number (to obtain a credit report)
4) Address of property that will be pledged as security for the loan
5) Estimated value of the property
6) Requested loan amount

Upon the lender's receipt of the above information, the written estimate must be provided within three business days, unless the lender denies the application within that three business day period or the borrower withdraws the application. Although the lender may initially require some additional basic information, such as the applicant's birthdate, the type of property involved, or whether the property will be owner-occupied, the lender may not at the application stage insist on verifying the applicant's income/employment and may not charge an application fee other than the cost for obtaining a credit report. Limiting the permissible fee to the cost of a credit report at initial loan application is intended to encourage potential borrowers to use the written cost estimate to shop for a loan from various lenders.

HUD-1 Settlement Statement

For decades RESPA also required the use of a standardized uniform settlement statement known as the HUD-1 form (or HUD-1A for a refinancing). While RESPA continues to define what a HUD-1 settlement statement is, it no longer is used in most residential transactions where the purchase is subject to either RESPA or TILA, having been replaced by required "Closing Disclosures" under the TILA-RESPA Integrated Disclosure Act.

Penalties for Violating RESPA

The law prescribes criminal and civil penalties that may be sought by individuals or a federal or state government enforcement agency. These include:

- Criminal fines of up to $10,000 per violation.
- Imprisonment for up to one year.
- Injunctions against illegal activity and orders to compensate victims for any illegal profits.

The law also permits civil lawsuits, including class action lawsuits, and may award monetary damages up to three times the amount of the overcharge, plus court costs and attorneys' fees.

License Law Violation

A violation of RESPA by a real estate licensee is considered to be a violation of General Statute §93A-6(a)(10) prohibiting "improper, fraudulent or dishonest dealing."

TILA-RESPA INTEGRATED DISCLOSURE ("TRID") RULE

As mentioned in Chapter 13, the Dodd-Frank Wall Street Reform and Consumer Protection Act (hereafter "Dodd-Frank Act") effective July 10, 2010 created the CFPB and transferred the administration and regulation of various consumer protection laws from other agencies to the CFPB. One of the express mandates of the Dodd-Frank Act directed the CFPB to consolidate or integrate the duplicate disclosures required by TILA and RESPA into one disclosure form that would satisfy both laws.

Recall that under TILA, lenders must provide the borrower with an early Truth-in-Lending disclosure of all loan related costs within three business days of application while RESPA required the Good Faith Estimate to be provided within the same time frame. Similarly, at settlement, lenders must provide a final Truth-in-Lending disclosure to the borrower while RESPA required the HUD-1 settlement statement. These duplicate disclosures with very similar information that lenders were required to provide at roughly the same time in the transaction were thought to be unduly burdensome to lenders and confusing to consumers.

After two years of consumer and industry research, public feedback, usability testing and other public outreach, the CFPB published its final rule in November 2013. *The TRID rule* became effective October 3, 2015, amidst much concern in the lending and brokerage industry, and *applied to loan applications received on or after October 3, 2015*. As a practical matter, any residential sale transaction that is governed by TILA or RESPA now uses the disclosure documents required by TRID, namely, the Loan Estimate and the Borrower's and Seller's respective Closing Disclosure documents.

Real estate brokers should have a general awareness of what residential sales transactions are covered by the new rules, but it is the lenders or persons/entities extending the consumer credit that must ensure compliance with the integrated disclosure requirements and suffer the consequences of noncompliance. The TRID rules are directed at the persons/entities extending consumer credit and/or dealing with federally insured mortgage loans. Lenders who permit mortgage brokers to issue the Loan Estimate or who permit settlement agents to prepare or modify the Closing Disclosures are liable for the actions of these agents, including clerical errors. Violations can be costly — minimally $5,000 per day per occurrence and $25,000 per day if reckless, if not more.

THE LOAN ESTIMATE

The Loan Estimate (LE) replaces the former Good Faith Estimate and must be personally delivered or sent to the borrower within three business days following the lender's receipt of a "loan application" as previously defined under RESPA, i.e., the borrower's legal name, gross income, Social Security number to order a credit report, the property address and estimate of value, and the requested loan amount. The Loan Estimate clearly identifies the: 1) loan amount, 2) interest rate, 3) existence of a prepayment penalty or a balloon payment, 4) projected monthly principal and interest payment, 5) projected real property taxes and homeowner's insurance, 6) estimated borrower settlement charges, and 7) estimated cash needed to close. A completed Loan Estimate available on the CFPB's website is reprinted as **Figure 14-1** at the end of this chapter, as is the related Borrower's Closing Disclosure for the same transaction (**Figure 14-2**). As with the former GFE, the only fee the lender may charge initially is the cost to obtain a credit report. A lender need not provide a Loan Estimate if it denies the application within three business days or the borrower withdraws the application within that period.

Permissible Variations/Tolerance Limits

Lenders remain bound by the "tolerance limits" first imposed in 2009/2010, although the former tolerance limits are now called **permissible "*variations*"** for loans subject to the new TRID rules. Understand that *costs estimated on the LE may be **less** at settlement/consummation without causing any problem, but they may not increase beyond the permissible variations* that continue to fall into one of three categories.

No Variation Allowed
1) any fee paid to the lender, mortgage broker, or affiliates of either;
2) lender required services for which the borrower may not shop; and
3) transfer taxes (in North Carolina, buyers don't typically pay a "transfer tax" as in some other States. The primary "transfer tax" in NC is excise tax paid by the seller, although a few counties may impose a transfer tax that also is paid by the seller.)

Ten Percent (10%) Variation Allowed

1) recording fees;
2) charges for third party services *if:*
   A) no part of the charge is paid to/retained by the lender or the lender's affiliates (as it otherwise would be in the zero variation category);
      and
   B) the consumer is permitted to shop for the service *but chooses a provider on the lender's written list of providers.*

NOTE: Costs in the no variation category may not be more at settlement than the amount stated on the LE. Costs for any particular service in the ten percent variation category may be more at settlement than reflected on the LE *as long as the total costs at settlement for services in the 10 percent category do not exceed the total costs for those services as stated on the LE by more than 10 percent.* If there is a violation in either category, the lender must reimburse the borrower the excess costs, generally within sixty (60) days of settlement. As a practical matter, the "cure" for the violation most often will occur at the settlement meeting.

Services for Which the Borrower May Shop

Lenders may allow borrowers to shop for certain required settlement services but must provide the borrower with a list of those services and identify at least one provider for each settlement service. If the borrower chooses a service provider listed by the lender, then that cost is included in the 10% variation category. If the borrower uses a provider not on the lender's list, then the lender has no responsibility for the amount of the fee the service provider charges the borrower. Lenders have no liability for fees charged by providers of services that are not required by the lender/creditor, *e.g.*, home inspection, owner's title insurance.

Accuracy of Loan Estimate

The Loan Estimate must be accurate, as within the variation limits, lenders will be bound by the estimated costs stated, unless changes occur that permit issuance of a revised LE. Revisions may be permitted due to changed circumstances (i.e., unexpected events or events beyond a person's control), or if the borrower's eligibility changes, or if the borrower requests a change, such as a different loan product or loan term (e.g., a 20-year mortgage rather than a 30-year mortgage). Loan Estimates typically may not be revised by a lender unless changed circumstances permit or require a revised LE, in which case it must be delivered to the borrower within three business days after the lender's receipt of the information that caused the revision and the revised loan estimate must be *received* by the borrower *at least four business days prior to consummation.*

Brokers' Responsibility for Loan Estimate

Brokers should have a general understanding of what transactions are subject to TRID and the timing and purpose of the Loan Estimate. Brokers working with buyers in covered transactions should be aware that the buyer-borrower is entitled to receive the Loan Estimate within three business days of loan application (i.e., the lender's receipt of six items of information) and that the purpose is to allow buyers to compare the cost of the desired credit. *Note:* most of the information on the Loan Estimate relates to the loan itself and there is no information regarding the borrowers' amount or source of income, monthly expenses, or credit score. See Figure 14-1.

THE CLOSING DISCLOSURES

The TRID rule also replaced the HUD-1 settlement statement (RESPA) and final Truth-in-Lending statement (TILA) with two ***Closing Disclosure (CD)*** documents, one for the borrower and a separate one for the seller. The Borrowers' Closing Disclosure (BCD) is five pages and contains information about the loan itself on pages one, four, and five. Pages two and three resemble the HUD-1 settlement statement and disclose *all transaction-related expenses paid by either the buyer or the seller*, whether at or before settlement, *and expenses paid by third parties.* [See Figure 14-2.] The Sellers' Closing Disclosure (SCD)reflects monies due to and from the seller and the names, license numbers, and contact information for the settlement agent and the real estate brokers representing each party on the first page and only seller-paid expenses, whether at or before closing, are shown on page two.

Because the Borrowers' Closing Disclosure now contains non-public TIL information about the buyers' loan, such as the interest rate, term, down payment, amount financed, etc, there were concerns that allowing the seller to see the Borrowers' Closing Disclosure might violate privacy issues under the Gramm-Leach-Bliley Act. Thus, the CFPB opted to provide separate Closing Disclosures for each party, but the rule allows the lender/settlement agent to decide whether to issue two separate closing disclosures or allow the seller to see the Borrowers' Closing Disclosure, as long as it contains all of the seller's transaction information. If two separate CDs are used, then the settlement agent must provide a copy of the sellers' CD to the borrower's lender, but not to the borrower. Even if the borrower does not receive a copy of the sellers' CD, s/he should be able to confirm the expenses paid by the seller as they should be entered in the sellers' columns on page three of the BCD.

Delivery of Borrowers' Closing Disclosure

One of the more significant impacts of TRID was the requirement that the ***lender deliver the completed BCD to the borrower not less than three business days prior to consummating the loan***. Technically, the loan is "consummated" when the borrower becomes obligated on the loan, which in North Carolina occurs at "closing," i.e., recording of the deed and deed of trust and disbursement of the loan proceeds. For practical purposes, the *borrower must receive the completed CD three business days prior to settlement to permit settlement to occur on the third business day*. This was a substantial departure from prior practice that allowed the borrower to see the HUD-1 one business day prior to settlement "if it was available," which often it was not.

How Delivered and Timeline

If the lender personally delivers the completed CD to the borrower, then receipt is immediate, and settlement may occur three business days later. If the CD is mailed or delivered electronically or by any method other than personal delivery, then the lender must add three business days to the period to ensure *receipt* by the borrower at least three business days prior to settlement. Thus, the completed CD must be mailed or delivered *six business days* prior to settlement. However, if the lender has proof that the borrower received the CD earlier than three business days after the lender mailed or sent it electronically, then it will be deemed received on that date. **Note:** *creditors are only required to ensure the* ***borrower receives their Closing Disclosure three business days prior to settlement***; *there is no similar requirement for delivery of or receipt by the seller of either Closing Disclosure prior to settlement.*

*For closing disclosure purposes, **"business day"** excludes only Sundays and the 10 federal public holidays*, namely, (New Year's Day, Martin Luther King Day, Washington's birthday, Memorial Day, July 4th, Labor Day, Columbus Day, Veterans' Day, Thanksgiving, and Christmas). Understand as well that the triggering event is the borrowers actual receipt of the CD and the first business day will be the next day, not the day of receipt.

> *Example 1:* The lender hand-delivers the completed BCD to the borrower on Monday. Assuming no federal holidays, when may settlement occur? Settlement may occur three business days later. Thus, if the BCD is *received* by the borrower Monday, Tuesday is day 1, Wednesday is day 2, so settlement may occur on Thursday, business day 3.

> *Example 2:* The lender delivers (i.e., sends) the completed BCD to the borrower by overnight delivery on Friday. The borrower receives and signs for the package on Saturday, thereby providing proof of earlier delivery. When may settlement occur, assuming no intervening federal public holidays? Settlement may occur the following Wednesday, the third business day following the borrower's actual receipt, rather than Friday, the sixth day after delivery.

Understand that "delivery" and "receipt" are separate events; delivery occurs when the lender mails or transmits or otherwise sends the document to the borrower, but it is not *received* until the borrower has actual possession. Depending on the delivery method chosen, receipt may occur the same day as delivery or a day or two later.

While it is the lender's responsibility to comply with these requirements (not the broker's), brokers should educate their clients and customers about these disclosure timelines, and caution that settlement cannot occur unless the borrowers timely receive their Closing Disclosure (which is not within a real estate broker's control). The three/six business days prior to settlement delivery requirement applies **only to the Borrower's Closing Disclosure**, not the sellers' Closing Disclosure. *There is no rule requiring delivery of the seller's closing disclosure to the seller prior to the settlement meeting.*

The lender, not the settlement agent, will decide whether to issue separate Closing Disclosures and any other settlement statements authorizing disbursement of the proceeds. If the lender decides to issue two separate Closing Disclosures, a broker acting as a dual agent should only give each party that party's CD, and not the other party's CD, as the lender chose to issue separate CDs for a reason. **Delivery must be to the borrowers personally**, not just to a broker acting as a buyer agent.

Corrected/Revised Closing Disclosure

The CFPB recognizes three categories of changes that require a corrected Closing Disclosure. They are:
>1. changes that occur pre-consummation that require a new three business day period;
>2. changes that occur pre-consummation that do not require a new three business day period;
>3. changes that occur post-consummation.

According to the CFPB, the **only three changes** that will **require** a new Closing Disclosure and **a new three business day waiting period** are:
>1. An increase in the apr;
>2. A change in the loan product;   or
>3. The addition of a prepayment penalty.

As to other changes, the CFPB counsels in its *Small Entity Compliance Guide* available on its website:

12.3: For any other changes before consummation that do not fall under the three categories above (i.e., related to the APR, loan product, or the addition of a prepayment penalty), the creditor still must provide a corrected Closing Disclosure with any terms or costs that have changed and ensure that the consumer receives it. For these changes, there is no additional three-business-day waiting period required. The creditor must ensure only that the consumer receives the revised Closing Disclosure at or before consummation.

Broker Access to Closing Disclosures

In the first few months following TRID's implementation, there were questions as to whether real estate brokers, particularly those acting as buyer agents, could be provided with a copy of their client's Closing Disclosure without violating the Gramm-Leach-Bliley Act. After various groups expressed concerns, the CFPB issued a press release on July 29, 2016, announcing proposed clarifying amendments to the TRID rule, including the release of Closing Disclosures to real estate brokers. The CFPB stated:

> The Bureau understands that it is usual, accepted, and appropriate for creditors and settlement agents to provide a closing disclosure to consumers, sellers, and their real estate brokers or other agents. The Bureau is proposing additional commentary to clarify how a creditor may provide separate disclosure forms to the consumer and the seller.

Public comment on the proposed rules closed in late fall of 2016 and the CFPB announced in early July 2017 that the above proposal was adopted. The final rules will be published in the Federal Register and may be found at www.consumerfinance.gov/policy-compliance/rulemaking/final-rules. It appears that lenders, settlement agents/closing attorneys, consumers, and real estate brokers agree that a real estate broker representing a buyer or seller should be permitted to see his/her client's closing disclosure. *Even if a broker is denied the opportunity to see/review the closing disclosure,* **there still should be some comprehensive settlement statement that details all monies received and disbursed related to that transaction that the broker must review.**

Closing *Disclosure* versus Settlement Statement

Real estate brokers must understand that closing disclosures are exactly that — *they are disclosures only* and are not equivalent to a settlement statement. Note that only the borrower's CD must be signed by the borrower, whereas there is no signature line on the seller's CD, and *neither closing disclosure authorizes the settlement agent to disburse funds according to the allocations shown on the closing disclosures.* Accordingly, the settlement agent must use some other document that must be signed by all sellers and buyers authorizing the disbursement of funds as indicated either in the settlement statement or referencing the applicable closing disclosure. While the HUD-1 no longer is used as the settlement statement in TRID-governed transactions, it appears that settlement/closing statements created and published by the American Land Title Association (ALTA) are gaining in popularity. Real estate brokers may well continue to see the HUD-1 used as the settlement statement in non-TRID-governed transactions, such as cash transactions, construction loans, or purchases of investment property.

It is the lender's responsibility to issue and ensure the borrower's timely receipt of the borrower's Closing Disclosure over which the real estate broker has no direct control. However, a buyer agent should assist the buyer in gathering and submitting to the lender as soon as possible information concerning expenses the buyer has paid or will pay related to the closing, e.g., home inspection, pest inspection, survey, owner's title insurance, hazard insurance and provider, etc., to facilitate the lender's early preparation of the BCD. The buyer also should be advised to notify his/her closing attorney and buyer agent if s/he has not received the Closing Disclosure at least three business days prior to the settlement meeting, e.g., the buyer must receive the BCD by Monday to allow a Thursday settlement meeting to proceed.

BROKER'S RESPONSIBILITY

Brokers' duties concerning the provision and accuracy of closing statements when they are not acting as the settlement agent are not substantially altered by the new forms. As mentioned, the Closing Disclosures will be prepared by the lender/creditor in-house or perhaps through an attorney-settlement agent, depending on the lender's practices. The real estate broker has little control over preparation and delivery of the BCD. Although a buyer agent is expected to review the Borrower's Closing Disclosure if provided to the broker and notify the closing attorney/settlement agent if the broker believes there are errors, License Law speaks only to a broker's obligation concerning delivery of the settlement statement. A broker may be subject to disciplinary action for:

> (14) Failing, at the time a sales transaction is consummated, to deliver to the broker's client a detailed and accurate closing statement showing the receipt and disbursement of all monies relating to the transaction about which the broker knows or reasonably should know. <u>If a closing statement is prepared by an attorney or lawful settlement agent, a broker may rely on the delivery of that statement,</u> *but the broker must review the statement for accuracy and notify all parties to the closing of any errors.* [Emphasis added.]

Thus, a broker's duty to provide a party with a copy of the settlement statement is satisfied if the broker ensures that the closing attorney/settlement agent has provided a copy of the closing/settlement statement to the party.

Broker's Settlement Statement Obligations

- A broker must confirm the accuracy of all ***entries about which s/he has direct knowledge***. Such items include, but may not be limited to:
  - the sale price;
  - amount of the due diligence fee and earnest money deposit;
  - amount of the brokerage commission and split;
  - any amounts due either party under the offer to purchase and contract, e.g., closing costs paid by seller, as well as any sums paid by or due to third parties related to the transaction, if the broker knows or should know about the expense.
- As to amounts paid by or due to third parties, brokers generally may assume that the amounts for charges and fees as stated on the settlement statement are correct unless there is something that would lead a reasonable broker to suspect that an amount is incorrect. As to all debits and credits related to the transaction, whether paid before or at closing, the broker must:
  1) review and confirm that all charges and credits have been properly debited or credited to the seller or buyer and are entered in the correct column; and
  2) review and confirm the accuracy of the calculations for all prorated items, escrow reserves, interim interest, excise tax and the "bottom line figures," i.e., total settlement charges to each party, cash from borrower-buyer, and cash to seller.

- If a broker is aware of *any expense* related to the transaction paid to or by either party or any third party that is not included on the settlement statement, the broker must notify both the settlement agent and the lender of the omission, as **the settlement statement should reflect all expenses and payments related to the transaction**, not just monies the settlement agent disburses. Failure to notify the lender of any such expense or payment would be considered willful failure to disclose a material fact, e.g., not telling the lender that the buyer's friend loaned them money for closing costs, or that the builder-seller is giving the buyer a $200 gift card, or that the $450 paid to the home inspector prior to closing was paid by the borrower's parents. Understand, none of the foregoing acts is illegal **as long as it is disclosed to and approved by the lender and** it appears in the proper column on the settlement statement/Closing Disclosure. If the lender doesn't approve the payment, then the borrower/buyer can't accept it.

A broker should notify the settlement agent if the broker believes there are any errors or omissions on the disclosure statement.

THE SETTLEMENT STATEMENT

The **settlement statement** *is a detailed report of all monies received and disbursed by the settlement agent in connection with a real estate sales transaction.* It is essential that the settlement statement be accurate and that a copy be provided to each party. The settlement statement is prepared by the settlement agent – the individual conducting the closing, which in North Carolina is almost always the **closing attorney** or a nonlawyer assistant working under the supervision of the closing attorney. Due to a real estate broker's obligation to review the settlement statement for accuracy as discussed in the preceding section, including prorated expenses, a brief review is warranted.

Basic Terminology

Since the settlement statement is an accounting document, each entry is referred to as either a "debit" or a "credit."

- *A* **debit** is a *"charge"* against a party. It indicates an amount that a party is responsible for paying at closing.
- A **credit** is a sum entered in favor of a party. It indicates an amount that a party is to receive or be reimbursed for at closing.

While these terms do not appear on the settlement statement, brokers must understand when an entry is a "debit"("charge") or "credit." Settlement charges are "debits" because they are a "charge" to a party. Items listed as paid by or on behalf of a party (typically the buyer-borrower) are a "credit" to the borrower against the purchase price. For its prelicensing and postlicensing education courses, the Commission has instructed schools to use pages two and three of the Borrower's Closing Disclosure as a worksheet to prepare for their review of whatever settlement statement the closing attorney or lender chooses to use, as all credits and debits on those two pages of the BCD should also appear as credits or debits on the settlement statement, assuming the BCD includes seller-paid expenses.

Prorations at Closing

One purpose of the settlement statement is to resolve all financial matters between the seller and buyer relating to the property transfer. There are a few property-related items for which property owners either make payments or receive payments on an annual or monthly basis. These items must be allocated or "prorated" for the amount of the obligation or entitlement due the seller and the buyer according to the time each owns the property during the payment period (monthly or annually). *Prorations are made based on the settlement date and* **in North Carolina the actual settlement date is allocated to the seller**. Thus, the seller is treated as if he or she owns the property through the day of settlement. (The reverse practice is true in some states, where the settlement date is allocated to the buyer.)

In **residential** transactions, the items commonly needing proration are **real estate taxes** (which are assessed and paid on an annual basis), **homeowners association dues**, if any, (which are assessed on an annual basis but may be paid on either an annual or monthly basis), and rent from a tenant (which is typically paid on a monthly basis). These are the items to be prorated under the standard provisions of the NCBA/NCAR Standard Form 2-T discussed in Chapter 11.

Prorations always involve a "double entry" on the settlement statement. The amount entered will be the same for entries in both the seller's statement and the borrower-buyer's statement, but whether the entry is a debit or credit will depend on whether the item is an obligation or entitlement and whether the obligation is paid or unpaid or the entitlement has been received or not received.

Proration Methods

The **365-Day Year Method** of prorating is the most accurate method and is the method commonly used in real estate closings in North Carolina. Under this method, **yearly amounts** are prorated by dividing the annual amount by 365 days (366 in leap years) to arrive at a daily rate. The number of days allocated to the seller is then determined by counting from January 1 through and including the day of closing, which is allocated to the seller under North Carolina practice. The remaining days in the year are allocated to the buyer. The daily rate is then multiplied by the number of days of the seller's ownership and the buyer's ownership to arrive at their respective prorata shares of the annual expense. Alternatively, once either the seller's or the buyer's prorata share is determined, that amount can be subtracted from the annual amount and the remaining amount represents the other party's share of the yearly amount. For **monthly amounts** (such as rent and sometimes homeowners dues), the exact same method is followed using the actual days in the month of closing.

A simpler proration method is the **360-Day Year Method** that assumes 30 days in each month. The method is slightly less accurate and is not typically used in real estate settlements, although it is commonly used in real estate prelicensing instruction and license examinations (including North Carolina's examination) because of its simplicity.

Nonetheless, the following proration examples are based on the 365-day year method routinely used by settlement agents in real estate closings.

Proration of Real Estate Taxes for Current Year

The item most commonly prorated in any real estate sales transaction is real estate taxes for the current year. Although such taxes are levied to fund governmental operation for a fiscal year (July 1-June 30), *the overwhelming custom and practice in closing residential real estate sales transactions in North Carolina is to prorate ad valorem real property taxes on a* **calendar year basis.** Regardless of whether real estate taxes for the calendar year of sale have been paid by the seller prior to closing, will be paid at closing, or will be paid by the buyer after closing, *the amount of the taxes for which each party is responsible will be based on the period of ownership by each.* Thus, if the seller is the owner for 200 days during the year, the buyer is the owner for 165 days, the total tax bill is $1,095, and the daily amount of taxes is $3 ($1,095 ÷ 365), then the seller's share is $600 (200 days x $3) and the buyer's share is $495 (165 days x $3).

In North Carolina, counties handle the real property tax billing for municipalities within their counties. Thus, for property located in a municipality, the real property tax bill from the county will include both the county taxes and the city/town taxes. Closing attorneys typically will enter the prorated amounts for the combined county and city/town taxes in the appropriate county taxes line of the settlement statement, rather than breaking down and separately reporting the prorated amount for county and city/town taxes.

When Taxes Have Been Paid by Seller Prior to Closing

If the seller already has paid the taxes for the year, then the seller will receive a credit for the amount of taxes for which the buyer is responsible, and the buyer should have a corresponding debit (charge). This occasionally happens with a closing that occurs after September 1, especially when the property does not have an existing mortgage with an escrow account for taxes and insurance.

> *Example:* Closing is on October 15. Real property taxes for the current year are $1,350 and have been paid by the seller. The calculation of taxes is as follows:
>
> $1,350 ÷ 365 days = $3.70 per day (rounded to nearest cent)
>
> October 16 – December 31 = 77 days (buyer's ownership)
>
> 77 days x $3.70 = $284.90 (buyer's share of taxes)

Since the seller has paid the taxes, the buyer must reimburse the seller for the $284.90. Thus, the settlement statement will reflect a *debit (charge) to the buyer* for this amount and *a credit to the seller* for the same amount.

When Taxes Have NOT Been Paid Prior to Closing

In most situations, the real estate taxes will not have been paid by the seller prior to closing. This certainly is the case when closing is prior to September 1, but it will also frequently be true for closings occurring after September 1 as well. For one thing, the tax bill is not due until September 1 and does not become delinquent until the following January; thus many property owners do not pay their tax bill until sometime in the fall or early winter. For the many property owners who have a mortgage on the property and pay a monthly amount that is escrowed by the lender to pay real estate taxes, the lender usually will not pay the tax bill until December.

Tax Bill Not Issued: When the tax bill has not been issued, i.e., closings prior to July 1, the taxes obviously will not be paid at closing, but will be paid by the buyer later in the year to protect his or her property interest. In this situation, most closing attorneys will charge (debit) the seller for the portion of the taxes attributable to the seller's period of ownership and credit the buyer in that same amount. The buyer will then be responsible for paying the taxes for the entire year by the due date.

Tax Bill Issued: When taxes are unpaid, *but the tax bill has been issued*, most closing attorneys will pay the taxes for the current year at closing; however, some attorneys may not pay the taxes at closing and instead handle the tax proration at closing exactly the same as noted above for situations where the tax bill has not been issued, i.e., charge the seller for his/her share of the taxes and credit the buyer for the same amount, with the buyer paying the full year's taxes later.

Estimating Taxes When Tax Rate Is Not Known. County and city governments typically do not complete their annual budgets and set the real property tax rate until shortly before July in each year. This means there is no way to accurately prorate the taxes on any real estate sold *prior to July 1* of each year, because the tax rate is unknown until just before the new fiscal year begins. *For closings prior to establishment of the tax rate (generally closings prior to July 1), closing attorneys typically use the known taxes on the property for the previous year to prorate the taxes for the current year,* as this is the best estimate available for such taxes. The parties may, of course, agree between themselves to a different basis for prorating the taxes, but typically they accept using the previous year's taxes for this purpose.

Taxes Unpaid — To Be Paid by Buyer Later in Year. If the taxes have not been paid, the seller is responsible for the taxes owed for the period up to and including the settlement date and the buyer is responsible for the taxes for the remainder of the year. *If the buyer is to pay the full tax bill after closing, the buyer should have a credit which is deductible from the purchase price at closing for the seller's share of the taxes and the seller should have a corresponding debit (charge) in the same amount.*

> *Example*: The settlement date is February 20 and the previous year's county real estate taxes of $2780 are used to prorate the taxes for the current year. The calculation of the taxes for the period the property is owned by the seller is as follows:
> Yearly tax of $2780 ÷ 365 = $7.616 per day
> January 1 through February 20 = 51 days. 51 x $7.616 = $388.42

The seller's prorated share of the taxes is $388.42. Since the taxes will have to be paid by the buyer later in the year after the tax bill is issued and the taxes become due, the seller owes the buyer $388.42. Thus, the settlement statement will reflect *a debit (charge) to the selle*r for that amount and a *credit to the buyer* for the same amount.

Taxes Unpaid — To Be Paid at Closing. Closing attorneys take different approaches to recording the tax proration on the settlement statement when closing occurs after the tax bill for the current year is issued and the taxes are to be paid at closing. However, the bottom line result is the same under either approach.

> *Example*: Closing is on October 15. Real property taxes for the current year are $1,350. The calculation of taxes is as follows:
> $1,350 ÷ 365 days = $3.6986 per day
> January 1 – October 15 = 288 days (seller's ownership)
> October 16 – December 31 = 77 days (buyer's ownership)
> 288 days x $3.6986 = $1,065.1968 rounded to $1065.20 (seller's share of taxes)
> 77 days x $3.6986 = $284.7922 rounded to $284.80 (buyer's share of taxes)

Approach #1: When paying the real property taxes at closing, many closing attorneys will simply charge each party for their share of the taxes by making "double debit" entries on the settlement statement charging each party their prorata share.

Approach #2: Some closing attorneys will accomplish the same result by charging the buyer the full amount of the taxes ($1,350 in the example) and then debit the seller for his/her share ($1,065.20) and credit the buyer for the same amount ($1,065.20).

Delinquent Taxes Not Prorated. In the case of taxes for *previous* years which have *not* been paid by the seller and are therefore "delinquent," the *seller* is solely responsible for all such taxes. There is *no proration of delinquent taxes.* The seller will be debited (charged) on the settlement statement for the full amount of the taxes and any interest or penalties due. Any delinquent taxes must be paid at closing to clear the tax lien that is a cloud on the title.

Proration of Rents

Rents are prorated where the property sold is being rented at the time of the sale. *Most commonly, rent is payable in advance for each month.* Thus, if a seller who is closing on September 5 has already received the rent in the amount of $600 for the entire month of September from the lessee, the seller is entitled to five (5) days rent and the purchaser is entitled to 25 days rent. $600 ÷ 30 = $20 per day. Since the seller has received rent for 25 days that the property will belong to the purchaser, the seller is debited on the settlement statement in the amount of $500 (25 days x $20 per day) and the purchaser is credited with the same amount.

There may be instances where rent is paid to the owner at the end of a rental period (i.e. *in arrears)*. In this event, the charges would be reversed. If the September rent in the above example was to be paid after closing to the purchaser, then the seller will be credited and the purchaser will be debited $100 (the amount of rent that the seller is entitled to due to his ownership of the property from September 1 through 5).

Proration of Homeowner's Dues

Property owners associations for subdivisions, condominium complexes, townhouse communities, etc. typically can assess regular dues that must be paid by property owners. These dues are most commonly assessed annually but may be payable either annually or monthly. Whether paid or unpaid at the time of closing, these dues should be prorated between the seller and buyer in the same manner as property taxes and rents are prorated. If paid in advance by the seller, the buyer's share will be charged to the buyer and the same amount will be credited to the seller. If not paid prior to closing, the buyer will have to pay the unpaid assessment after closing, so the seller's share will be charged to the seller and the same amount will be credited to the buyer.

Other Items and Proration Methods

The sales contract may provide for proration of other items not discussed here and may provide for adjustment or proration of various items in a manner different from those previously discussed. Where the purchaser and seller agree by contract on how to allocate certain obligations, their agreement will govern.

Facts and Comments about the CFPB's Sample Forms

The fact situation below is based on information gleaned from the CFPB's sample Loan Estimate (LE) and pages 2 and 3 of the Borrowers' Closing Disclosure (BCD) reprinted as Figures 14-1 and 14-2. This exercise is included to assist brokers in reviewing the accuracy of whatever settlement statement may be used by the closing attorney. Whatever information appears on pages 2 and 3 of the Borrower's Closing Disclosure should also appear somewhere on the settlement statement. Recall that these forms were prepared by the CFPB in 2013, which may account for the low interest rate.

For those accustomed to the HUD-1 settlement statement, know that the information on page 1 of the HUD-1 is found on page 3 of the BCD, and the itemized expenses found on page 2 of the HUD-1 are on page 2 of the BCD.

These forms are designed for a national audience and may contain charges that are not customary in North Carolina. Note too that the settlement agent is a title insurance company, whereas in North Carolina, a residential closing generally is handled by an attorney in private practice. Compare the $1300 the title insurance company is receiving in fees to conduct the title search and act as settlement agent to fees charged by a closing attorney (not to mention the $650 it charged for the insurance binder and the $500 for the lender's policy). Additionally, while there is no transfer tax in North Carolina, the seller does pay an excise tax on the sale price which is omitted on the CFPB's sample forms, and it is unusual for a buyer to pay $1,000 for an owner's title insurance policy. Lastly, most lenders would require the borrowers to maintain private mortgage insurance until they have at least 20% equity in the property, but that too is omitted from the CFPB sample forms.

Facts underlying Sample Forms

Settlement date: April 15, 2013
Sellers: Steve Cole and Amy Doe
Buyers: Michael Jones and Mary Stone
Purchase price = $180,000
Buyers obtained a conventional 30-year fixed loan, 90% financing, at 3.875% interest.
Buyer's deposit (earnest money in NC) = $10,000
Loan discount points = .25% of loan amount
Loan application fee = $300
Loan underwriting fee = $1097
Monthly HOA dues = $160 (prepaid by seller for April)
Annual real estate taxes = $1263.60   (plus six months prepaid by buyer at settlement)
Annual hazard insurance = $1209.96 (prepaid by buyer at settlement)
Credit report = $29.80   paid at loan application
Flood monitoring fees = $51.75 total
Tax search and monitoring fees = $155.00 total
HOA transfer fees = $650 total
Rebate to buyer from title insurance company = $750
Recording fees = $85 total   ($40.00 Deed and $45 = Mortgage/Deed of trust)
Pest inspection fee = $120.50
Survey = $85
Fees to the Title Insurance Company: title search = $800; settlement agent fee = $500;
     Insurance binder = $650; lender title insurance policy = $500
Owner's title insurance policy = $1,000
Home inspection fee = $1500 (divided equally between the parties by agreement)
Calculate interim interest and prorated taxes.
Borrowers' Escrow Account: 2 months hazard insurance premium and 2 months of real property taxes.
Brokerage commission = $11,400 (divided equally between listing and selling brokers)
Home warranty fee = $450 to be paid by seller
Seller credit to buyer's closing costs = $2500 (presumably pursuant to the sales contract)
Seller's loan payoff = $100,000
Transfer tax = $950 (paid by seller)

Endnotes

1. For more information concerning radon and a broker's duties pertaining thereto, readers are referred to the article on radon in the Commission's 2017-2018 General Update materials that may be found on the Commission's website at: https://www.ncrec.gov/Publications/BicarTopics.

2. Procedures for the discharge and release of deeds of trust are found in North Carolina General Statutes Chapter 45, Article 4. A "satisfaction agent" must be an attorney under Gen. Stat. §45-36.13.

3. North Carolina State Bar Formal Ethics Opinion 2002-9 (January 24, 2003).

4. North Carolina State Bar Formal Ethics Opinion 2002-1 (January 24, 2003). Opinion 1 answers the question: "May a nonlawyer handle a residential real estate closing for one or more of the parties to the transaction?" The first paragraph of the response is as follows:

    > No. Residential real estate transactions typically involve several phases, including the following: abstraction of titles; application for title insurance policies, including title insurance policies that may incorporate tailored coverage; preparation of legal documents, such as deeds (in the case of a purchase transaction) and deeds of trust; explanation of documents implicating parties' legal rights, obligations, and options; resolution of possible clouds on title and issues concerning the legal rights of parties to the transaction; execution and acknowledgment of documents in compliance with legal mandates; recordation and cancellation of documents in accordance with North Carolina law; and disbursement of proceeds after legally-recognized funds are available. These and other functions are sometimes called, collectively, the "closing" of the residential real estate transaction. As detailed below, the North Carolina General Assembly has determined specifically that only persons who are licensed to practice law in the state may handle many of these functions. [The opinion cites *State v. Pledger*, 257 N.C. 634, 127 S.E.2d 337 (1962) for the exception that allows a party having a "primary interest" in a transaction to prepare deeds of trust and other documents to effectuate it.

5. According to North Carolina State Bar Formal Ethics Opinion 2002-9, dealing in part with the execution of closing documents and disbursement of proceeds:

    > "... the execution of the documents and the disbursement of the proceeds may be accomplished by mail, by e-mail, by other electronic means, or by some other procedure that would not require the lawyer and the parties to be physically present at one place and time."

6. 12 U.S.C. §2601 et. seq.

7. The Dodd-Frank Act is Public Law 111-203. Regulation X as republished by the Consumer Financial Protection Bureau may be found at 12 C.F.R. §1024.

8. The information on RESPA referral fees in this section is based in part on the following two publications of the Real Estate Services Providers Council, Inc. (RESPRO), 1090 Vermont Ave., N.W., Suite 800, Washington, D.C. 20036: *RESPA Guide to Referral Fees: Do's and Don'ts for Salespersons* (2000); and *How to Prevent (and Defend) a RESPA Enforcement Action* (1998).

FICUS BANK

4321 Random Boulevard · Somecity, ST 12340

Save this Loan Estimate to compare with your Closing Disclosure.

Loan Estimate

DATE ISSUED	2/15/2013	**LOAN TERM**	30 years
APPLICANTS	Michael Jones and Mary Stone	**PURPOSE**	Purchase
	123 Anywhere Street	**PRODUCT**	Fixed Rate
	Anytown, ST 12345	**LOAN TYPE**	☒ Conventional ☐ FHA ☐ VA ☐ _____
PROPERTY	456 Somewhere Avenue	**LOAN ID #**	123456789
	Anytown, ST 12345	**RATE LOCK**	☐ NO ☒ YES, until 4/16/2013 at 5:00 p.m. EDT
SALE PRICE	$180,000		

*Before closing, your interest rate, points, and lender credits can change unless you lock the interest rate. All other estimated closing costs expire on **3/4/2013** at 5:00 p.m. EDT*

Loan Terms

		Can this amount increase after closing?
Loan Amount	$162,000	**NO**
Interest Rate	3.875%	**NO**
Monthly Principal & Interest *See Projected Payments below for your Estimated Total Monthly Payment*	$761.78	**NO**

		Does the loan have these features?
Prepayment Penalty		**YES** • **As high as $3,240** if you pay off the loan during the first 2 years
Balloon Payment		**NO**

Projected Payments

Payment Calculation	Years 1-7	Years 8-30
Principal & Interest	$761.78	$761.78
Mortgage Insurance	+　82	+　—
Estimated Escrow *Amount can increase over time*	+　206	+　206
Estimated Total Monthly Payment	**$1,050**	**$968**

		This estimate includes	In escrow?
Estimated Taxes, Insurance & Assessments *Amount can increase over time*	**$206** a month	☒ Property Taxes ☒ Homeowner's Insurance ☐ Other:	**YES** **YES**

See Section G on page 2 for escrowed property costs. You must pay for other property costs separately.

Costs at Closing

Estimated Closing Costs	$8,054	Includes $5,672 in Loan Costs + $2,382 in Other Costs – $0 in Lender Credits. *See page 2 for details.*
Estimated Cash to Close	$16,054	Includes Closing Costs. *See Calculating Cash to Close on page 2 for details.*

Visit **www.consumerfinance.gov/mortgage-estimate** for general information and tools.

Closing Cost Details

Loan Costs

A. Origination Charges	$1,802
.25 % of Loan Amount (Points)	$405
Application Fee	$300
Underwriting Fee	$1,097

B. Services You Cannot Shop For	$672
Appraisal Fee	$405
Credit Report Fee	$30
Flood Determination Fee	$20
Flood Monitoring Fee	$32
Tax Monitoring Fee	$75
Tax Status Research Fee	$110

C. Services You Can Shop For	$3,198
Pest Inspection Fee	$135
Survey Fee	$65
Title – Insurance Binder	$700
Title – Lender's Title Policy	$535
Title – Settlement Agent Fee	$502
Title – Title Search	$1,261

D. TOTAL LOAN COSTS (A + B + C)	$5,672

Other Costs

E. Taxes and Other Government Fees	$85
Recording Fees and Other Taxes	$85
Transfer Taxes	

F. Prepaids	$867
Homeowner's Insurance Premium (6 months)	$605
Mortgage Insurance Premium (months)	
Prepaid Interest ($17.44 per day for 15 days @ 3.875%)	$262
Property Taxes (months)	

G. Initial Escrow Payment at Closing		$413
Homeowner's Insurance $100.83 per month for 2 mo.		$202
Mortgage Insurance per month for mo.		
Property Taxes $105.30 per month for 2 mo.		$211

H. Other	$1,017
Title – Owner's Title Policy (optional)	$1,017

I. TOTAL OTHER COSTS (E + F + G + H)	$2,382

J. TOTAL CLOSING COSTS	$8,054
D + I	$8,054
Lender Credits	

Calculating Cash to Close

Total Closing Costs (J)	$8,054
Closing Costs Financed (Paid from your Loan Amount)	$0
Down Payment/Funds from Borrower	$18,000
Deposit	– $10,000
Funds for Borrower	$0
Seller Credits	$0
Adjustments and Other Credits	$0
Estimated Cash to Close	$16,054

Figure 14-1

Additional Information About This Loan

LENDER	Ficus Bank	
NMLS/__ LICENSE ID		
LOAN OFFICER	Joe Smith	
NMLS/__ LICENSE ID	12345	
EMAIL	joesmith@ficusbank.com	
PHONE	123-456-7890	

MORTGAGE BROKER	
NMLS/__ LICENSE ID	
LOAN OFFICER	
NMLS/__ LICENSE ID	
EMAIL	
PHONE	

Comparisons

Use these measures to compare this loan with other loans.

In 5 Years	$56,582	Total you will have paid in principal, interest, mortgage insurance, and loan costs.
	$15,773	Principal you will have paid off.
Annual Percentage Rate (APR)	4.274%	Your costs over the loan term expressed as a rate. This is not your interest rate.
Total Interest Percentage (TIP)	69.45%	The total amount of interest that you will pay over the loan term as a percentage of your loan amount.

Other Considerations

Appraisal	We may order an appraisal to determine the property's value and charge you for this appraisal. We will promptly give you a copy of any appraisal, even if your loan does not close. You can pay for an additional appraisal for your own use at your own cost.
Assumption	If you sell or transfer this property to another person, we ☐ will allow, under certain conditions, this person to assume this loan on the original terms. ☒ will not allow assumption of this loan on the original terms.
Homeowner's Insurance	This loan requires homeowner's insurance on the property, which you may obtain from a company of your choice that we find acceptable.
Late Payment	If your payment is more than *15* days late, we will charge a late fee of *5% of the monthly principal and interest payment.*
Refinance	Refinancing this loan will depend on your future financial situation, the property value, and market conditions. You may not be able to refinance this loan.
Servicing	We intend ☐ to service your loan. If so, you will make your payments to us. ☒ to transfer servicing of your loan.

Confirm Receipt

By signing, you are only confirming that you have received this form. You do not have to accept this loan because you have signed or received this form.

_____   _____   _____   _____
Applicant Signature   Date   Co-Applicant Signature   Date

LOAN ESTIMATE

Figure 14-1

Closing Disclosure

This form is a statement of final loan terms and closing costs. Compare this document with your Loan Estimate.

Closing Information

Date Issued	4/15/2013
Closing Date	4/15/2013
Disbursement Date	4/15/2013
Settlement Agent	Epsilon Title Co.
File #	12-3456
Property	456 Somewhere Ave Anytown, ST 12345
Sale Price	$180,000

Transaction Information

Borrower	Michael Jones and Mary Stone 123 Anywhere Street Anytown, ST 12345
Seller	Steve Cole and Amy Doe 321 Somewhere Drive Anytown, ST 12345
Lender	Ficus Bank

Loan Information

Loan Term	30 years
Purpose	Purchase
Product	Fixed Rate
Loan Type	☒ Conventional ☐ FHA ☐ VA ☐ _____
Loan ID #	123456789
MIC #	000654321

Loan Terms

Loan Terms		Can this amount increase after closing?
Loan Amount	$162,000	**NO**
Interest Rate	3.875%	**NO**
Monthly Principal & Interest *See Projected Payments below for your Estimated Total Monthly Payment*	$761.78	**NO**
		Does the loan have these features?
Prepayment Penalty		**YES** • As high as **$3,240** if you pay off the loan during the first 2 years
Balloon Payment		**NO**

Projected Payments

Payment Calculation	Years 1-7	Years 8-30
Principal & Interest	$761.78	$761.78
Mortgage Insurance	+ 82.35	+ —
Estimated Escrow *Amount can increase over time*	+ 206.13	+ 206.13
Estimated Total Monthly Payment	**$1,050.26**	**$967.91**

Estimated Taxes, Insurance & Assessments *Amount can increase over time* *See page 4 for details*	$356.13 a month	**This estimate includes**	**In escrow?**
		☒ Property Taxes	**YES**
		☒ Homeowner's Insurance	**YES**
		☒ Other: Homeowner's Association Dues	**NO**
		See Escrow Account on page 4 for details. You must pay for other property costs separately.	

Costs at Closing

Closing Costs	$9,712.10	Includes $4,694.05 in Loan Costs + $5,018.05 in Other Costs – $0 in Lender Credits. *See page 2 for details.*
Cash to Close	$14,147.26	Includes Closing Costs. *See Calculating Cash to Close on page 3 for details.*

Figure 14-2

Closing Cost Details

Loan Costs		Borrower-Paid		Seller-Paid		Paid by Others
		At Closing	Before Closing	At Closing	Before Closing	
A. Origination Charges		**$1,802.00**				
01 0.25 % of Loan Amount (Points)		$405.00				
02 Application Fee		$300.00				
03 Underwriting Fee		$1,097.00				
04						
05						
06						
07						
08						
B. Services Borrower Did Not Shop For		**$236.55**				
01 Appraisal Fee	to John Smith Appraisers Inc.					$405.00
02 Credit Report Fee	to Information Inc.		$29.80			
03 Flood Determination Fee	to Info Co.	$20.00				
04 Flood Monitoring Fee	to Info Co.	$31.75				
05 Tax Monitoring Fee	to Info Co.	$75.00				
06 Tax Status Research Fee	to Info Co.	$80.00				
07						
08						
09						
10						
C. Services Borrower Did Shop For		**$2,655.50**				
01 Pest Inspection Fee	to Pests Co.	$120.50				
02 Survey Fee	to Surveys Co.	$85.00				
03 Title – Insurance Binder	to Epsilon Title Co.	$650.00				
04 Title – Lender's Title Insurance	to Epsilon Title Co.	$500.00				
05 Title – Settlement Agent Fee	to Epsilon Title Co.	$500.00				
06 Title – Title Search	to Epsilon Title Co.	$800.00				
07						
08						
D. TOTAL LOAN COSTS (Borrower-Paid)		**$4,694.05**				
Loan Costs Subtotals (A + B + C)		$4,664.25	$29.80			

Other Costs						
E. Taxes and Other Government Fees		**$85.00**				
01 Recording Fees	Deed: $40.00 Mortgage: $45.00	$85.00				
02 Transfer Tax	to Any State			$950.00		
F. Prepaids		**$2,120.80**				
01 Homeowner's Insurance Premium (12 mo.) to Insurance Co.		$1,209.96				
02 Mortgage Insurance Premium (mo.)						
03 Prepaid Interest ($17.44 per day from 4/15/13 to 5/1/13)		$279.04				
04 Property Taxes (6 mo.) to Any County USA		$631.80				
05						
G. Initial Escrow Payment at Closing		**$412.25**				
01 Homeowner's Insurance $100.83 per month for 2 mo.		$201.66				
02 Mortgage Insurance per month for mo.						
03 Property Taxes $105.30 per month for 2 mo.		$210.60				
04						
05						
06						
07						
08 Aggregate Adjustment		– 0.01				
H. Other		**$2,400.00**				
01 HOA Capital Contribution	to HOA Acre Inc.	$500.00				
02 HOA Processing Fee	to HOA Acre Inc.	$150.00				
03 Home Inspection Fee	to Engineers Inc.	$750.00			$750.00	
04 Home Warranty Fee	to XYZ Warranty Inc.			$450.00		
05 Real Estate Commission	to Alpha Real Estate Broker			$5,700.00		
06 Real Estate Commission	to Omega Real Estate Broker			$5,700.00		
07 Title – Owner's Title Insurance (optional) to Epsilon Title Co.		$1,000.00				
08						
I. TOTAL OTHER COSTS (Borrower-Paid)		**$5,018.05**				
Other Costs Subtotals (E + F + G + H)		$5,018.05				

J. TOTAL CLOSING COSTS (Borrower-Paid)		**$9,712.10**				
Closing Costs Subtotals (D + I)		$9,682.30	$29.80	$12,800.00	$750.00	$405.00
Lender Credits						

Calculating Cash to Close

Use this table to see what has changed from your Loan Estimate.

	Loan Estimate	Final	Did this change?	
Total Closing Costs (J)	$8,054.00	$9,712.10	YES	• See **Total Loan Costs (D)** and **Total Other Costs (I)**
Closing Costs Paid Before Closing	$0	− $29.80	YES	• You paid these Closing Costs **before closing**
Closing Costs Financed (Paid from your Loan Amount)	$0	$0	NO	
Down Payment/Funds from Borrower	$18,000.00	$18,000.00	NO	
Deposit	− $10,000.00	− $10,000.00	NO	
Funds for Borrower	$0	$0	NO	
Seller Credits	$0	− $2,500.00	YES	• See Seller Credits in **Section L**
Adjustments and Other Credits	$0	− $1,035.04	YES	• See details in **Sections K and L**
Cash to Close	$16,054.00	$14,147.26		

Summaries of Transactions

Use this table to see a summary of your transaction.

BORROWER'S TRANSACTION

K. Due from Borrower at Closing	$189,762.30
01 Sale Price of Property	$180,000.00
02 Sale Price of Any Personal Property Included in Sale	
03 Closing Costs Paid at Closing (J)	$9,682.30
04	
Adjustments	
05	
06	
07	
Adjustments for Items Paid by Seller in Advance	
08 City/Town Taxes to	
09 County Taxes to	
10 Assessments to	
11 HOA Dues 4/15/13 to 4/30/13	$80.00
12	
13	
14	
15	

L. Paid Already by or on Behalf of Borrower at Closing	$175,615.04
01 Deposit	$10,000.00
02 Loan Amount	$162,000.00
03 Existing Loan(s) Assumed or Taken Subject to	
04	
05 Seller Credit	$2,500.00
Other Credits	
06 Rebate from Epsilon Title Co.	$750.00
07	
Adjustments	
08	
09	
10	
11	
Adjustments for Items Unpaid by Seller	
12 City/Town Taxes 1/1/13 to 4/14/13	$365.04
13 County Taxes to	
14 Assessments to	
15	
16	
17	

CALCULATION	
Total Due from Borrower at Closing (K)	$189,762.30
Total Paid Already by or on Behalf of Borrower at Closing (L)	− $175,615.04
Cash to Close ☒ From ☐ To Borrower	**$14,147.26**

SELLER'S TRANSACTION

M. Due to Seller at Closing	$180,080.00
01 Sale Price of Property	$180,000.00
02 Sale Price of Any Personal Property Included in Sale	
03	
04	
05	
06	
07	
08	
Adjustments for Items Paid by Seller in Advance	
09 City/Town Taxes to	
10 County Taxes to	
11 Assessments to	
12 HOA Dues 4/15/13 to 4/30/13	$80.00
13	
14	
15	
16	

N. Due from Seller at Closing	$115,665.04
01 Excess Deposit	
02 Closing Costs Paid at Closing (J)	$12,800.00
03 Existing Loan(s) Assumed or Taken Subject to	
04 Payoff of First Mortgage Loan	$100,000.00
05 Payoff of Second Mortgage Loan	
06	
07	
08 Seller Credit	$2,500.00
09	
10	
11	
12	
13	
Adjustments for Items Unpaid by Seller	
14 City/Town Taxes 1/1/13 to 4/14/13	$365.04
15 County Taxes to	
16 Assessments to	
17	
18	
19	

CALCULATION	
Total Due to Seller at Closing (M)	$180,080.00
Total Due from Seller at Closing (N)	− $115,665.04
Cash ☐ From ☒ To Seller	**$64,414.96**

Additional Information About This Loan

Loan Disclosures

Assumption

If you sell or transfer this property to another person, your lender

☐ will allow, under certain conditions, this person to assume this loan on the original terms.

☒ will not allow assumption of this loan on the original terms.

Demand Feature

Your loan

☐ has a demand feature, which permits your lender to require early repayment of the loan. You should review your note for details.

☒ does not have a demand feature.

Late Payment

If your payment is more than *15* days late, your lender will charge a late fee of *5% of the monthly principal and interest payment.*

Negative Amortization (Increase in Loan Amount)

Under your loan terms, you

☐ are scheduled to make monthly payments that do not pay all of the interest due that month. As a result, your loan amount will increase (negatively amortize), and your loan amount will likely become larger than your original loan amount. Increases in your loan amount lower the equity you have in this property.

☐ may have monthly payments that do not pay all of the interest due that month. If you do, your loan amount will increase (negatively amortize), and, as a result, your loan amount may become larger than your original loan amount. Increases in your loan amount lower the equity you have in this property.

☒ do not have a negative amortization feature.

Partial Payments

Your lender

☒ may accept payments that are less than the full amount due (partial payments) and apply them to your loan.

☐ may hold them in a separate account until you pay the rest of the payment, and then apply the full payment to your loan.

☐ does not accept any partial payments.

If this loan is sold, your new lender may have a different policy.

Security Interest

You are granting a security interest in
456 Somewhere Ave., Anytown, ST 12345

You may lose this property if you do not make your payments or satisfy other obligations for this loan.

Escrow Account

For now, your loan

☒ will have an escrow account (also called an "impound" or "trust" account) to pay the property costs listed below. Without an escrow account, you would pay them directly, possibly in one or two large payments a year. Your lender may be liable for penalties and interest for failing to make a payment.

Escrow		
Escrowed Property Costs over Year 1	$2,473.56	Estimated total amount over year 1 for your escrowed property costs: *Homeowner's Insurance Property Taxes*
Non-Escrowed Property Costs over Year 1	$1,800.00	Estimated total amount over year 1 for your non-escrowed property costs: *Homeowner's Association Dues* You may have other property costs.
Initial Escrow Payment	$412.25	A cushion for the escrow account you pay at closing. See Section G on page 2.
Monthly Escrow Payment	$206.13	The amount included in your total monthly payment.

☐ will not have an escrow account because ☐ you declined it ☐ your lender does not offer one. You must directly pay your property costs, such as taxes and homeowner's insurance. Contact your lender to ask if your loan can have an escrow account.

No Escrow		
Estimated Property Costs over Year 1		Estimated total amount over year 1. You must pay these costs directly, possibly in one or two large payments a year.
Escrow Waiver Fee		

In the future,

Your property costs may change and, as a result, your escrow payment may change. You may be able to cancel your escrow account, but if you do, you must pay your property costs directly. If you fail to pay your property taxes, your state or local government may (1) impose fines and penalties or (2) place a tax lien on this property. If you fail to pay any of your property costs, your lender may (1) add the amounts to your loan balance, (2) add an escrow account to your loan, or (3) require you to pay for property insurance that the lender buys on your behalf, which likely would cost more and provide fewer benefits than what you could buy on your own.

Figure 14-2

Loan Calculations

Total of Payments. Total you will have paid after you make all payments of principal, interest, mortgage insurance, and loan costs, as scheduled.	$285,803.36
Finance Charge. The dollar amount the loan will cost you.	$118,830.27
Amount Financed. The loan amount available after paying your upfront finance charge.	$162,000.00
Annual Percentage Rate (APR). Your costs over the loan term expressed as a rate. This is not your interest rate.	4.174%
Total Interest Percentage (TIP). The total amount of interest that you will pay over the loan term as a percentage of your loan amount.	69.46%

 Questions? If you have questions about the loan terms or costs on this form, use the contact information below. To get more information or make a complaint, contact the Consumer Financial Protection Bureau at **www.consumerfinance.gov/mortgage-closing**

Other Disclosures

Appraisal
If the property was appraised for your loan, your lender is required to give you a copy at no additional cost at least 3 days before closing. If you have not yet received it, please contact your lender at the information listed below.

Contract Details
See your note and security instrument for information about
• what happens if you fail to make your payments,
• what is a default on the loan,
• situations in which your lender can require early repayment of the loan, and
• the rules for making payments before they are due.

Liability after Foreclosure
If your lender forecloses on this property and the foreclosure does not cover the amount of unpaid balance on this loan,

☒ state law may protect you from liability for the unpaid balance. If you refinance or take on any additional debt on this property, you may lose this protection and have to pay any debt remaining even after foreclosure. You may want to consult a lawyer for more information.

☐ state law does not protect you from liability for the unpaid balance.

Refinance
Refinancing this loan will depend on your future financial situation, the property value, and market conditions. You may not be able to refinance this loan.

Tax Deductions
If you borrow more than this property is worth, the interest on the loan amount above this property's fair market value is not deductible from your federal income taxes. You should consult a tax advisor for more information.

Contact Information

	Lender	Mortgage Broker	Real Estate Broker (B)	Real Estate Broker (S)	Settlement Agent
Name	Ficus Bank		Omega Real Estate Broker Inc.	Alpha Real Estate Broker Co.	Epsilon Title Co.
Address	4321 Random Blvd. Somecity, ST 12340		789 Local Lane Sometown, ST 12345	987 Suburb Ct. Someplace, ST 12340	123 Commerce Pl. Somecity, ST 12344
NMLS ID					
ST License ID			Z765416	Z61456	Z61616
Contact	Joe Smith		Samuel Green	Joseph Cain	Sarah Arnold
Contact NMLS ID	12345				
Contact ST License ID			P16415	P51461	PT1234
Email	joesmith@ ficusbank.com		sam@omegare.biz	joe@alphare.biz	sarah@ epsilontitle.com
Phone	123-456-7890		123-555-1717	321-555-7171	987-555-4321

Confirm Receipt

By signing, you are only confirming that you have received this form. You do not have to accept this loan because you have signed or received this form.

_____   _____   _____   _____
Applicant Signature   Date   Co-Applicant Signature   Date

Figure 14-2

15 | REAL ESTATE VALUATION

Estimates of the value of real property are used for a wide variety of purposes, a few of which include real estate financing, investment analysis, selling or buying real estate, taxation of real estate, property insurance and others. In the area of real estate sales, a formal estimate of value, known as an "appraisal," most often is developed to assist lenders in determining maximum real estate mortgage loan amounts for loans made to purchasers of real estate. An appraisal may only be performed by a licensed or certified real estate appraiser. (NOTE: Appraisals can be developed for buyers, sellers, attorneys, accountants, government agencies, and others and used for multiple reasons other than lending.)

Real estate brokers routinely perform a "comparative market analysis" as part of their brokerage services to an owner-client or buyer/tenant-client to estimate the "probable selling or leasing price" of a property to assist the client in pricing a property for sale or lease or in deciding how much to offer as a prospective buyer or lessee. Since 2012, only brokers with a "non-provisional" license may legally perform a "broker price opinion" or "comparative market analysis" for various persons and entities for a fee. Thus, real estate brokers must understand basic valuation concepts and procedures to competently perform these common brokerage services. This chapter introduces the reader to the basic concepts and methods of real property valuation used by real estate appraisers when performing an appraisal and those used by real estate brokers when performing a broker price opinion or comparative market analysis.

INTRODUCTION

The reader must have a clear understanding of certain basic terms. According to the dictionary, the term **"appraisal"** simply means an "evaluation" or "estimate" of something. When it refers to something's "value," an appraisal may be defined as an "estimate of value." While the term "appraisal" sometimes is used to refer to "the act or process of estimating value," it is less confusing to refer to the process as "appraising" rather than appraisal.

For an "estimate of value" related to **real estate** in North Carolina, specific definitions are provided by statute to differentiate between an in-depth **"appraisal"** performed by a licensed or certified real estate appraiser and a **"broker price opinion"**(BPO) or **"comparative market analysis"**(CMA) performed by a licensed real estate broker.

Key Definitions
Real Estate Appraisal

The North Carolina Appraisers Act is found in Chapter 93E of the North Carolina General Statutes. General Statute §93E-1-4(1) defines a "real estate appraisal" as:

> "Appraisal" or "real estate appraisal" means an analysis, opinion, or conclusion as to the value of identified real estate or specified interests therein performed for compensation or other valuable consideration.

Under the Appraisers Act, only a State certified or licensed real estate appraiser or registered appraiser trainee may perform real estate appraisals in accordance with strict guidelines imposed by federal and state law. An appraiser must develop an independent, impartial, and objective opinion of value that represents the appraiser's best judgment based on all relevant factual data reasonably available, derived utilizing appropriate analytical methods.

Broker Price Opinion or Comparative Market Analysis

General Statute §93A-82 of the North Carolina Real Estate License Law and General Statute §93E-1-4(7c) of the North Carolina Appraisers Act have identical definitions of a "broker price opinion," commonly referred to as a "BPO," and a "comparative market analysis," commonly referred to as a "CMA:"

> ... the terms "broker price opinion" and "comparative market analysis" mean an estimate prepared by a licensed real estate broker that details the probable selling price or leasing price of a particular parcel of or interest in property and provides a varying level of detail about the property's condition, market, and neighborhood, and information on comparable properties, but does not include an automated valuation model.

NOTE: Broker price opinions (BPOs) and comparative market analyses (CMAs) will be discussed in depth later in this chapter. At this point, the reader only needs to know a few basic points about a broker price opinion (BPO) and comparative market analysis (CMA) resulting from the major revisions to the Real Estate License Law and Appraisers Act effective October 1, 2012.

- "Broker price opinion (BPO)" and "comparative market analysis (CMA)" are synonymous, having the same legal definition.

- Only a licensed "non-provisional" real estate broker on active status may perform a BPO or CMA *for a fee*.

- A BPO or CMA may only estimate the *"probable selling price"* or *"probable leasing price"* of a property, not the "value" of a property. ***The difference in terminology is key***. If a BPO or CMA purports to estimate the "value" or "worth" of a property, then legally it is a "real estate appraisal" that may only be prepared by a State licensed or certified real estate appraiser and the broker could be subject to disciplinary action for violating both License Law and the Appraisers Act. Brokers must not use the words "appraisal," or "value," or "worth" in a BPO or CMA.

- A BPO or CMA provided for a fee must be performed in compliance with License Law and standards set forth in rules adopted by the North Carolina Real Estate Commission.

While a broker employs similar valuation concepts and methodology when performing a BPO/CMA as an appraiser does when performing an appraisal, the analysis associated with a BPO/CMA is less comprehensive and detailed than with an appraisal and the regulatory standards for BPOs/CMAs are less stringent.

Regulation of Appraisers and Appraisals

In the 1980s many savings and loan associations failed due to bad loans, mostly real estate loans, many of which were based on poor, and in some cases fraudulent, real estate appraisals. In the aftermath of this debacle, Congress enacted the **Financial Institutions Reform, Recovery and Enforcement Act of 1989 (FIRREA)**. Among other things, the law established a complex system for regulating real estate appraisers when performing appraisals of real property in connection with "federally related transactions," which include most real estate loans made in the United States. While a detailed explanation of the federal regulatory system is unnecessary here, real estate brokers should know a few basics about the regulatory process.

Key Regulatory Agencies

The key agencies involved in the appraiser regulatory process are listed below.

Federal Financial Institutions Examination Council (FFIEC). The agencies comprising the FFIEC are: 1) the Board of Governors of the Federal Reserve System (FRB or the "Fed"), 2) the Federal Deposit Insurance Corporation (FDIC), 3) the Office of the Comptroller of the Currency (OCC), and 4) the National Credit Union Administration (NCUA). These four banking regulatory agencies are joined by the Federal Housing Finance Agency (FHFA), the Bureau of Consumer and Financial Protection (CFPB), and the Department of Housing and Urban Development (HUD). These seven agencies appoint the members of the **Appraisal Subcommittee** and oversee the operations of that organization.

The *Appraisal Subcommittee* is the primary federal oversight agency for appraiser regulation. As mentioned, its members are appointed by the heads of the four FFIEC agencies and the FHFA, CFPB and HUD. The Appraisal Subcommittee is responsible for: 1) monitoring the activities of The Appraisal Foundation, 2) approving and monitoring the licensing and certification programs established by the various states, and 3) coordinating the appraisal rules of the various federal agencies.

The Appraisal Foundation is a private, nonprofit corporation formed by several of the leading appraiser trade organizations. It also has a number of affiliate members from the financial community. The Appraisal Foundation is the congressionally approved source of appraisal standards and appraiser qualifications. It functions primarily through two independent boards.

1. **The Appraiser Qualifications Board (AQB)** issues minimum qualification requirements for appraisers to be licensed or certified by state appraiser regulatory agencies and creates or endorses examinations for licensure/certification.

2. *The Appraisal Standards Board (ASB)* sets minimum standards of practice for **appraisals** performed in connection with federally related transactions. The ASB authors and distributes the *"Uniform Standards of Professional Appraisal Practice (USPAP)."*

State Appraiser Regulatory Agencies. Each state has an agency and system for licensing and certifying real estate appraisers in accordance with federal law and regulations. *The North Carolina*

Appraisal Board (NCAB) is the independent state governmental board responsible for real estate appraiser licensing and regulation in North Carolina.

Mandatory Real Estate Appraiser Licensing/Certification

The North Carolina Appraisers Act states that to act as a real estate appraiser or to engage in any way in the business of real estate appraising in North Carolina, one must hold a real estate appraiser license or certification issued by (or be registered as an appraiser trainee with) the North Carolina Appraisal Board.[1] Thus, with certain limited exceptions, *all real estate appraisals performed for compensation in North Carolina must be performed by a North Carolina licensed or certified real estate appraiser (or appraiser trainee working under the supervision of a certified real estate appraiser).* Currently, there are three categories of real estate appraiser registration, licensing, and certification in North Carolina listed below from the lowest level to the highest level.

1. Registered Appraiser Trainee
2. Certified Residential Appraiser
3. Certified General Appraiser

A fourth license category called "Licensed Residential Appraiser" formerly existed. That license category was terminated in 2008, but persons already holding that license were allowed to retain the license by continuing to renew it.

Appraisal Management Companies. Until recently, North Carolina only regulated the activities of **individual** appraisers. Following widespread problems in North Carolina and other states with unregulated *appraisal management companies* that were coordinating appraisal services to lenders and providing inaccurate or otherwise substandard appraisals, a law was passed requiring such companies to register with and be regulated by the North Carolina Appraisal Board effective January 1, 2011.[2] An appraisal management company is a business entity that provides appraisal services to lenders and others by utilizing an "appraisal panel" or "fee panel" consisting of licensed or certified appraisers who are independent contractors to the company.

Property Tax "Appraisals"

As discussed in Chapter 3, an "*assessment*" of property is the process of determining property value for the purpose of *ad valorem* taxation. Assessment is a specialized form of appraising. County assessors, county appraisers, and private appraisal firms providing appraisals for real estate taxation purposes must be certified by the North Carolina Department of Revenue. While property assessments share certain basic appraisal principles and concepts, they employ different techniques and specialized methods that are used only when appraising large numbers of similar properties for tax purposes, a process known as "*mass appraisal.*" Since real estate brokers are not directly involved with property tax assessments, the subject of mass appraisal is not explained in this text. Those desiring more information are referred to the International Association of Assessing Officials (www.IAAO.org), a nonprofit educational and research association founded in 1934 by government officials and others interested in property tax administration. It offers professional development and research in property appraisal, assessment administration, and property tax policy.

BASIC VALUATION CONCEPTS

"Value" is a key concept that links the real estate brokerage and appraisal businesses and is extremely important in virtually all real estate transactions. Real estate brokers need to understand the valuation concepts that underlie both the processes followed by appraisers to produce an appraisal and the processes followed by brokers to produce a broker price opinion (BPO) or comparative market analysis (CMA).

"**Value**" may be defined generally as *the quantity of one commodity that can be obtained in exchange for another.* This represents the "**value-in-exchange**" concept utilized in the sale of real estate (the value of goods or services depends on what or how much can be obtained for them in exchange for other goods or services). This is only one of the "value" concepts. "**Value-in-place**" is the amount a purchaser would pay for an item (e.g., equipment, fixture) in place, determined by the use the item contributes to the whole. "**Value-in-use**" relates to the productivity of an economic good to its owner-user, i.e., the value a specific property has to a specific person or entity as opposed to the value to persons or the market in general. Special-purpose properties such as churches, schools, and public buildings that are seldom sold in the open market can be valued in use to a specific person and may include sentimental value.

Consider the value-in-exchange and the value-in-use concepts as they relate to a specialized manufacturing plant. The value in use to a specific entity may be the value the manufacturing plant contributes as part of an integrated manufacturing facility. If there is no competitive demand for the building, its value-in exchange might be nominal. However, if the building is fulfilling an economic demand and is likely to continue to do so, its value-in-use might be substantial. In such a situation, the value-in-use represents the amount the owner of the operation would be willing to pay for assurance against being deprived of its use.

Elements of Value

The emphasis in appraising is on the relationship between a desired commodity and a potential purchaser of that commodity. An object has no inherent value until others need or want it. Typically, the item must also have **utility** to arouse the needs and desires of the consumer. Need alone does not create value. If it did, bread and water would be intrinsically valuable because they are needed to satisfy hunger and thirst, but if the availability of bread and water exceeds the need, their value decreases. *Value, therefore, is not intrinsic, but depends on the relationship between supply and demand.* Stated differently, an object must be relatively **scarce** to have value. While no commodity, including real estate, can have value unless it has both **utility** and **scarcity**, these two factors alone do not create value. The consumer must have the **desire** and the **capacity** (**purchasing power**) to purchase before value is created. This may be referred to as "*effective demand.*" A commodity may have utility and scarcity, but it will have little value if no one has the ability to buy it.

Estimating the value of real estate is complicated by the **permanence of real estate**. Unlike other consumer goods that are rapidly consumed, the benefits of real property often are realized over a long period of time. Thus, *the value of real property* may be thought of as the "*present value of the future benefits to be derived from the property.*" Thus, any estimate of a property's value must consider social and economic trends that may influence people's needs or desire for that property, the long-term utility of the property, the relative scarcity of competing properties, and the capacity of the marketplace to purchase the property. In considering these factors, the appraiser should never lose sight of the fact that he or she is interpreting reactions of typical users and investors. The appraiser does not create value, but rather interprets it, chiefly from market evidence.

Value Versus Cost And Price

"Value" is not always the same as "cost" or "price." **Cost** represents a measure of past expenditures in labor, materials, or sacrifices of some nature. While it is a factor on which value is often based, at least in part, it need not be. For example, the cost of an oil well might be the same whether it turns out to be a dry hole or a big producer of oil. While they may cost the same to develop and drill, only one will have any appreciable value.

Price is the amount one pays for a commodity (i.e., the "sale price" or "purchase price"). The sale price may represent the value of the item, or the actual value of the item may be higher or lower than the sale price. For example, a person might pay $10,000 for a purportedly flawless one-carat diamond; however, the diamond actually has serious flaws and an informed buyer would only pay $5,000 for it. The diamond's value in this instance was substantially lower than its price. This distinction between price and value is discussed further in the next section on market value.

Market Value

A thorough understanding of "market value" is critical for anyone who will be appraising real property. *The ultimate purpose of most appraisals is to derive an accurate estimate of market value.* The *Uniform Standards of Professional Appraisal Practice* ("USPAP") promulgated by the Appraisal Standards Board of The Appraisal Foundation, describes ***market value*** as *"…a type of value, stated as an opinion, that presumes the transfer of a property (i.e., a right of ownership or a bundle of such rights), as of a certain date, under specific conditions set forth in the definition of the term identified by the appraiser as applicable in the appraisal."* USPAP cautions appraisers to identify an exact definition and cite its source for all assignments stating:

> … conditions for defining value may vary from definition to definition
> but will generally fall into three categories:
>
> 1. the relationship, knowledge, and motivation of the parties (i.e., seller and buyer);
>
> 2. the terms of sale (e.g., cash, cash equivalent, or other terms); and
>
> 3. the conditions of sale (e.g., exposure in a competitive market for a reasonable time prior to sale).

Market price may not represent value for a variety of reasons. A seller may have been under some pressure to sell quickly, whether due to a job transfer/loss, a divorce, a potential foreclosure, etc., or may have been mistakenly advised by an inexperienced broker to list a property at a price that was too low, or a property may have been sold privately without being exposed to the open market. A market price may not represent market value if the property was not advertised in the customary manner, was not allowed a reasonable time on the market, or if the financing involved was sufficiently favorable so as to cause the price to be higher than would be expected under "typical" financing arrangements. Since most transactions can be considered typical, proper market research should lead to a proper market value estimate. That research, however, must include some investigation into the circumstances surrounding individual sale prices.

An older but perhaps more easily understood definition of "market value" than the USPAP definition quoted above (which is for professional appraisers) is the one still cited in the Uniform Residential Appraisal Report form promulgated by Fannie Mae and Freddie Mac (2005 edition):

> The most probable price which a property should bring in a competitive
> and open market under all conditions requisite to a fair sale, the buyer and
> seller, each acting prudently, knowledgeably and assuming the price is not

affected by undue stimulus. Implicit in this definition is the consummation of a sale as of a specified date and the passing of title from seller to buyer under conditions whereby: (1) buyer and seller are typically motivated; (2) both parties are well informed or well advised, and each acting in what he or she considers his or her own best interest; (3) a reasonable time is allowed for exposure in the open market; (4) payment is made in terms of cash in U. S. dollars or in terms of financial arrangements comparable thereto; and (5) the price represents the normal consideration for the property sold unaffected by special or creative financing or sales concessions granted by anyone associated with the sale.

Although the above definition of "market value" is intended for appraisers estimating "value," the underlying principles apply to broker price opinions and comparative market analyses performed by real estate brokers to determine a "probable selling price."

Forces and Factors That Influence Value

The value of real property is created, maintained, modified, or destroyed by the interplay of four basic forces that affect human behavior with respect to real estate. These forces may be categorized generally as follows:

1. Social Trends
2. Economic Circumstances
3. Government Controls and Regulations
4. Environmental Conditions

These forces set the pattern for the variables affecting real estate market values. They influence the value, in a general sense, of every parcel of real estate, because they affect the demand and supply sides of the market. Each general force is composed of many complex factors that are in a constant state of change.

Social trends include population trends, geographical distribution of social groups, family sizes and attitudes toward educational and social activities, as well as many other factors. **Economic circumstances** include employment trends, wage levels, interest rates, and tax burdens, to name but a few. **Government controls and regulations** include zoning laws, building codes, environmental regulations, rent controls, and police and fire regulations, and many others. **Environmental conditions** may be created either by nature or by society, and include natural resources, climate, topography, soil characteristics, flood conditions and others. Because all of these individual factors affect cost, price and value, they are the basic underlying considerations when performing an appraisal. Individual factors often appear in two or more categories and all continually interact with one another in the marketplace.

Basic Economic and Appraisal Principles Relating to Value

To properly understand the concept of value and to competently estimate real property value or probable selling or leasing price, an appraiser or real estate broker must understand various economic and appraisal principles relating to value and estimating value. Several of the more important basic economic and appraisal principles are discussed below.

Supply and Demand

The principle of **supply and demand** involves the interrelationship of the desire for a commodity and its scarcity. *The principle asserts that decreasing supply or increasing demand tends to enhance the price obtainable in the market, whereas increasing supply or decreasing demand tends to lower prices.* The value of housing is affected by factors such as population changes, income levels, price levels, housing starts, interest rates, zoning and other government regulations, etc., all of which bear directly on either or both sides of the supply-demand relationship. Certain factors must be present in the housing market to stimulate additions to the housing supply. There must be a shortage in the supply of units, a relatively strong demand for housing, and effective purchasing power generated by adequate availability of financing. When the effective demand is sufficiently high relative to income levels and to existing supply, builders are encouraged to construct new units. If demand is very strong and purchasing power is increasing faster than the ability of the supply to satisfy the increased need, the price of available units will tend to rise until more builders are attracted to the market, accelerating the pace of additions to the housing supply. If this results in an excess of housing units, prices will tend to decline or stabilize until the oversupply subsides or until demand increases sufficiently to absorb the supply.

Anticipation

The principle of *anticipation* maintains that *value is created by the expectation of benefits to be obtained sometime in the future.* Homebuyers are largely influenced by the anticipation of future benefits of home ownership such as appreciation, increasing equity through periodic mortgage payments reducing the loan balance, tax savings through deductible mortgage interest, as well as basic housing considerations. On the other hand, the value of an income-producing property is based primarily on the purchaser's anticipation or expectation of future rental income to be derived from operation of the property.

Most value estimates must focus on future use and benefits; what occurred in the past is relevant only insofar as it assists in projecting future trends. The analysis of comparable sales is a primary use of past experience to forecast value trends, but present value is a function of market expectations for the future.

Substitution

Substitution asserts that *when several commodities with substantially the same utility or benefit are available in the marketplace, the commodity with the lowest price will attract the greatest demand.* With respect to residential real estate, when two or more homes offer approximately the same advantages, the prospective buyer will tend to select the one with the lowest price. Stated differently, substitution posits that a prudent and rational purchaser would not pay more to acquire a given property than he would be required to pay to obtain an equally desirable substitute property, assuming no costly delay is encountered in making the substitution. Hence, the market value of a property tends to match the value indicated by the actions of informed buyers in the market for comparable real estate having similar physical and locational characteristics. The principle of substitution is a cornerstone of the sales comparison approach in estimating market value, but also applies to aspects of the cost approach and income approach.

Conformity

Conformity holds that *maximum value of an improved property is realized when the other properties in the immediate area have compatible uses and characteristics.* In other words, houses in a single family residential neighborhood should be of reasonably similar design, construction, size, and age, and residents should be of similar social and economic status. Value often is adversely affected when land uses in a particular area are mixed. For instance, dwellings adjacent to commercial areas typically sell for less than their otherwise similar counterparts not exposed to commercial influences. Dwellings that are unusually large or more costly than surrounding homes often sell for less than similar homes located in neighborhoods with other large costly homes. The reverse is true for dwellings that are smaller and less costly than surrounding homes. While the principle of conformity implies some degree of harmonious similarity in architectural styles and designs, it does not mean monotonous architectural uniformity. Some differences in the size and design of structures not only are tolerable, but frequently are desirable. However, a property's maximum value usually is realized when it conforms generally to the standards governing the area in which it is located.

Contribution

Contribution **maintains** that *the value of any part of a property is dependent on the degree to which it contributes to the value of the entire property or the degree to which its absence detracts from the value of the entire property.* For example, the principle of contribution may apply in estimating the value of lots of varying depths since it may be necessary to estimate the value, if any, additional depth contributes over and above the value of a lot of standard depth. This principle may also be fundamental to any consideration of the feasibility of remodeling or modernizing a structure. For example, if the cost of installing an air conditioning system exceeds the increase in value resulting from the installation, then installing the system may be an "over-improvement" to the property that might not be justified.

Swimming pools may be an excellent example of contribution. In an expensive neighborhood where many homes have in-ground swimming pools, a pool might contribute value approximating its cost, but in neighborhoods with less expensive homes where pools are not standard, they may represent an over-improvement and increase the property's value by only a fraction of the cost to install.

Competition

The **principle of** *competition* asserts that *profits tend to attract competition and excess profits tend to encourage ruinous competition.* Competition is a product of supply and demand. When demand is strong relative to existing supply, prices increase and competition is encouraged. The greater the demand relative to supply, the greater are the resulting profits until they reach a point where competition increases supply beyond the demand, thereby lowering prices and profits.

Change

Change holds that *changes in the many forces and factors that influence value are inevitable.* Changes in the social, economic, governmental, or environmental forces that affect property value may be sudden and obvious, or they may be so slow and subtle that they are barely noticeable. Relatively sudden changes that can affect property value include the addition of a large new manufacturing facility, business layoffs of employees, changes in tax laws, zoning changes, or environmental accidents. *It is the inevitability of change and especially the prospect of relatively sudden changes that force* **appraisers to limit the applicability of their value estimates to the date an appraisal is performed**. Because there are so many changeable factors that can affect the value of a property, no appraiser can provide assurance that his value estimate will be accurate for any period of time after the appraisal date.

Because of the principle of anticipation, an appraiser must be particularly sensitive to changes that are slow and subtle. For example, a residential appraiser must understand the well-known pattern of change in residential neighborhoods referred to as the "**neighborhood transition cycle**" or "**neighborhood life cycle**." Neighborhoods undergo constant change and normally follow a pattern of

growth, stability, decline, and **renewal.** The **growth** stage is the initial development period in which the neighborhood gains acceptance in the market. The **stability** phase is then a period of equilibrium that may last for any number of years before the neighborhood begins declining in public acceptance. In the **decline** phase, demand diminishes and price levels tend to decline (or not increase as rapidly as inflation). While not necessarily true of all neighborhoods, many neighborhoods will eventually reach a point of deterioration that either public or private groups begin programs of revitalization. The widespread purchase and rehabilitation of these old homes constitutes the **renewal** phase that effectively initiates the cycle all over again.

Highest and Best Use

The principle of "highest and best use" is fundamental to the estimate of value of any real property in that the price a buyer will pay for a given property is a function of the buyer's anticipated use of the property. The most likely use will tend to be the most profitable legal use possible for the property and considering that "highest and best use" is critical to valuing the property. **Highest and best use** is defined as *"the reasonably probable and legal use of property, which is physically possible, appropriately supported, financially feasible, and that results in the highest value."*[3]

The highest and best use of **land** is almost always considered *as if the site were vacant* and available to be put to its highest and best use. Even if a large structure is located on the land, it can be demolished and the land utilized for another purpose. Hence, it is the highest and best use of the site, considered as if vacant, that determines the value of the land.

The highest and best use of an **entire improved property** (i.e., both land and buildings) may well be different than the highest and best use of the land, considered as if vacant. Existing buildings should be retained as long as they continue to productively contribute to the total market value of the property. When it becomes more profitable to demolish the existing improvements and build new ones, the existing improvements no longer productively contribute value in which case the highest and best use of the entire property as improved becomes synonymous with the highest and best use of the land. The existing use of the property should continue, however, unless and until the land value in its highest and best use exceeds the total value of the property in its existing use.

Land cannot be valued on the basis of one use while the buildings are valued on the basis of another use. For instance, if a dwelling located on a lot where a commercial use is permissible and the potential for commercial development of that lot are such that the lot proved more valuable vacant than the combined worth of the lot and dwelling for residential purposes, then no value could be attributed to the structure in the appraisal. The lot would be valued in the context of a commercial highest and best use less the cost of removing the dwelling. On the other hand, if the lot and dwelling are worth more for residential purposes than the lot, considered as if vacant, is worth for commercial uses, then the property would be valued for its residential use.

In any appraisal of an *improved* property, the appraiser must consider **both** the highest and best use of the *land as though vacant* **and** the highest and best use of the *land as improved.* Only in this way can the appraiser determine the appropriate highest and best use.

For a particular property use to be the highest and best use for that property, the use must be: (1) legally permissible, (2) physically possible, (3) financially feasible, and (4) maximally productive. The "maximally productive" use is the use projected to be the "most profitable" for the property owner. It most likely will be a long-term use that produces a reasonable rate of income and preserves the value of the land. Sometimes a short term "interim" use is the highest and best use at a particular point in time. Just as the principle of change serves to produce different property values over time, so can the highest and best use of a property change over time.

The Valuation Process

A proper appraisal must be based on a careful analysis of all data and factors that can influence the value of a particular property. According to the Uniform Standards of Professional Appraisal Practice (USPAP), an appraiser must be aware of, understand, and correctly employ those recognized methods and techniques that are necessary to produce a credible appraisal and must be able to document the steps taken to do so. Over the years, professional appraisers have developed a step-by-step process considered to be the appropriate procedure to follow when performing any appraisal assignment. This process is called "the valuation process" and includes the following steps.

Defining the Problem (Task)

The first step in performing any appraisal assignment is to clearly define the problem or task. A critical first step is for the appraiser to gather and analyze information related to six assignment elements that must be identified.

1. *Who is the client and are there any other intended users?* In the typical residential appraisal for mortgage loan purposes, the client is the lender.
2. *What is the intended use of the appraiser's opinions and conclusions?* Is it for a lender to use in establishing a maximum loan amount, or a prospective buyer to use in determining the amount of an offer? Is it for use in litigation?
3. *What type and definition of value is to be determined?* Most often this will be "market value."
4. *What is the effective date of the appraiser's opinions and conclusions?* Usually, the value estimate will be for the date the appraisal is actually performed because appraisers usually are estimating *current* value, and *unless otherwise specified, the appraisal is considered valid only for the date it was performed.* However, an appraiser occasionally is asked to estimate value for some specified past or future date.
5. *What is the subject of the assignment and its relevant characteristics?* The appraiser will define what is being appraised and will look at those characteristic (size, location, utility, etc.) that create value in the marketplace.
6. *Are there any conditions that may exist with the assignment?* These conditions may include extraordinary assumptions or hypothetical conditions.

Scope of Work

After defining the problem, an appraiser must then determine an acceptable scope of work that is sufficient to produce a credible appraisal. It is the appraiser's responsibility to determine and perform a proper scope of work for each assignment.

Data Collection and Analysis

An appraiser must have current and accurate data to use as the basis for his analysis. Some of this data is general and will apply to a wide variety of appraisal assignments, while other data will be specific data on the property being appraised (i.e., the "subject" property) and on similar properties (i.e., "comparable" properties) being compared to the subject property. This step includes the following:

1. *Collecting "general" data.* This includes data on social, economic, governmental, and environmental forces affecting the nation, the region, and the neighborhood. Especially important is demographic data and data on the local real estate market.
2. *Applying general data to appraisal of subject property and performing a neighborhood or area analysis.* A careful analysis of the local real estate market is especially important.

3. *Collecting specific data.* This includes obtaining a detailed description of the subject property and identifying comparable properties to be used in the appraisal. In this connection, the appraiser will inspect the subject property, verify square footage, and gather information on the characteristics and condition of improvements to use in estimating depreciation. Information on comparable properties will be obtained primarily from the closed sales files of the local multiple listing service, if available. This specific data is analyzed when applying the three approaches to value.

Highest and Best Use Analysis

This critical step in the valuation process was covered previously in the discussion of highest and best use.

Application of Approaches to Value

There are three general approaches to value that will be discussed shortly. These approaches are: **1) sales comparison approach, 2) cost approach,** and **3) income approach.** It is in this step that the appraiser utilizes established methodology to derive specific indications of value for the subject property.

Reconciliation and Final Value Estimates

After deriving separate estimates of value using the three approaches, the appraiser must determine a single, final estimate of value based on these separate estimates. Discussion of this important step is deferred to the end of the section on "Approaches to Value" to enable the reader to better understand what is involved.

Appraisal Report

The appraiser's conclusion as to the final estimate of value may, in some instances, be reported in letter form or even orally, but most frequently a written report is provided. For single-family residential properties, the report is usually presented using the **Uniform Residential Appraisal Report (URAR)** form issued jointly by the Federal National Mortgage Corporation ("Fannie Mae") and the Federal Home Loan Mortgage Corporation ("Freddie Mac"). For appraisals of income-producing properties and most other appraisals, the report usually will be a comprehensive written narrative report.

APPROACHES TO VALUE

A real estate appraisal is an estimate of value derived through the application of one, two, or all three of the generally accepted approaches to value—the **sales comparison approach, cost approach**, and **income approach.** The three approaches to value, or methods of deriving value, utilize different information and analysis techniques to derive an estimate of value.

Sales Comparison Approach. The basic theory underlying this approach is that value is related to the selling prices of recently sold comparable properties when differences are properly considered for various factors such as property location, physical characteristics, age, design, date of sale, and conditions of sale. This approach rests on the substitution principle that a prudent and reasonable purchaser would not pay more to buy a given property than he would be required to pay to buy an equally desirable substitute property.

Cost Approach. The theory underlying this approach is that value is related to the current costs of reproducing or replacing a building, less the loss in value from the various forms of depreciation, plus the underlying land value. The cost approach develops an indication of value by examining these factors.

Income Approach. This approach is based on the theory that value is related to the rental income that the property is capable of generating for the owner. The income approach explores this relationship in the marketplace and applies the findings to the subject property for an indication of value.

An appraiser generally considers all three approaches in any assignment. For a particular property type, the value indications obtained through one of the approaches may be more accurate than the values indicated by the other two approaches. *Whenever possible, all three approaches should be used, but greater consideration should be given to the approach that uses the most relevant and reliable data for the type of property being appraised.*

SALES COMPARISON APPROACH

The ***sales comparison approach*** *to estimating value involves the comparison of the property being appraised with recently sold similar properties.* The theory is simply that the best indicators of the market value of a property are the prices buyers have paid in the recent past for similar properties sold in the open market. Thus, the sales comparison approach best reflects the value of property based on the actions of buyers and sellers in the marketplace. The sales comparison approach is an extremely reliable approach to estimating the value of any type of property that is sold frequently. *It is the most reliable and commonly used approach when appraising single-family residential properties because such properties are sold frequently.* The sales comparison approach may also be a reliable method for appraising other types of properties (multifamily residential, commercial, industrial, farm land, etc.) if there has been sufficient market activity in the area to provide the appraiser with data on recently sold similar properties. The sales comparison approach should always be considered for any type of property when recent sales of comparable properties are available. The sales comparison approach is used not only by appraisers but also by real estate brokers when performing a comparative market analysis (CMA) or broker price opinion (BPO) to estimate a probably selling price of a property.

It would be especially helpful at this point to understand certain commonly used appraisal terms. Appraisers refer to the property being appraised as the "**subject property**" or simply the "**subject.**" The recently sold similar properties the appraiser will compare to the subject property are referred to as "**comparable properties**" or, more frequently, as "**comparables**" or "**comps.**" This terminology is also applicable to broker price opinions (BPOs) and comparative market analyses (CMAs) performed by real estate brokers.

Selecting Comparables

For the sales comparison approach to be reliable, *the comparable properties selected for analysis should be similar to the subject property in most respects such as property type, usage, age, location, physical characteristics, condition, amenities, utility, and conditions of sale.* The selected properties should 1) have been sold in the recent past, 2) reflect current market conditions, and 3) have involved typical financing. If all of these conditions are met, then the comparable sale will be a good indicator of the market value of the subject property. If not, then the proposed comparable may not be truly "comparable" and may not provide a reliable indication of the subject property's value.

An "ideal" comparable property to compare to a residential single-family subject property is one that is very similar to the subject property in age, size, condition, amenities and general physical characteristics, is located in the same neighborhood, and was recently sold on the open market under typical conditions involving typical financing. While "ideal" comparable properties may not always be available, the goal still is to select comparables that are as close as possible to the ideal. A recently sold comparable that is very similar to the subject property and was inspected by the appraiser usually will be a particularly good comparable because the appraiser's familiarity with the comparable will enable him or her to make more accurate adjustments.

After inspecting and compiling detailed data on the subject property, the next step is to look for recently sold properties that are as similar as possible to the subject property in the same or a similar area. For residential properties, the best comparables often are located in the subject property's neighborhood or subdivision, or in a similar neighborhood in the general area of the subject property. Properties that are substantially different from the subject property should not be used. Below is a summary of factors to consider when selecting comparables for properties with improvements (buildings or structures) followed by a brief discussion of the various factors.

Factors to Consider When Selecting Comparables

1) Property Type and Use (residential house, townhouse or condominium; multi-family residential property, commercial office building, etc.)
2) Age of Building
3) Condition of Building (state of repair and functional utility)
4) Location (including effect of external influences)
5) Size (of lot and building)
6) Physical Characteristics (lot and building) and Amenities
7) Date of Sale/Changes in Market Conditions
8) Conditions of Sale (typical open market, foreclosed property, short sale, special financing, etc.)

Property Type and Use. Comparables must be the same type of property and used for the same purposes as the subject property, *e.g.,* a single-family house should be compared to sold similar single-family houses, a retail commercial property should be compared to sold similar retail commercial properties, etc.

Age and Condition. Ideally, selected comparables should have structures similar in **age** as structures on the subject property; it generally is more important that the age of the structures on comparable and subject properties be very similar where the subject property is relatively new. Where the subject property is an older property, age differences are usually less important than the condition of the properties. For example, a 30-year old house that has been particularly well maintained or remodeled may have the same "effective age" as a 20-year-old house; thus, the **condition** of a property is just as important to consider as the property's age. The condition of the building includes not only its *state of repair*, but also its *functional utility*. For example, if a possible comparable is a three-bedroom house with only one bathroom while the subject property is a three-bedroom house with 2 bathrooms, this property might not be an appropriate comparable (depending on other factors).

Location. Where property is located is an *extremely* important factor when selecting comparable properties. Ideally, the comparable property should be located in the same neighborhood (or business district for commercial property) as the subject property. If there are no recently sold similar properties in the same neighborhood, then a property located in a similar neighborhood in the same general area should be selected. A property's location can have a tremendous effect on its market value. Two properties that are virtually identical in every respect except for location can have very different values. For example, *external factors* may have had a positive or negative effect on a possible comparable property's sale price, yet the subject property may not be affected by such factors. Thus, a property's location must be carefully considered before selecting that property for use as a comparable.

Size. One of the most significant physical characteristics to consider is the **size** of the subject and comparable properties. For single-family dwellings, it is important that the dwelling units on the comparable properties and the subject property be approximately the same size. Lot size should also be comparable. For purposes of selecting comparables, however, differences in size of structures may be less important than other factors if the subject property is, for example, a tract of undeveloped land, a warehouse, an industrial plant, or a multi-story office building.

Major Physical Characteristics. Some major physical characteristics that should be considered when selecting comparables are: **1) type and quality of construction, 2) exterior and interior design, 3) number of rooms, 4) heating/cooling systems, 5) garage/carport, 6) porch/deck, 7) lot characteristics, and 8) outbuildings or other structures**. The subject property and comparable properties should be similar with regard to these features. For example, do not use a two-story house as a comparable for a one-story house, or an ultra-modern house with unusual design features or materials as a comparable for a traditional-style house, or a townhouse as a comparable for a free-standing house. *Relatively minor differences in physical characteristics are acceptable* and represent the usual situation.

When selecting comparables for a subject house, for example, a small difference in the number of rooms due to interior design is usually acceptable. Likewise, the presence or absence of a garage or carport in an otherwise similar property would not be objectionable. The fact that an otherwise similar property has a lot with more or fewer improvements (e.g., landscaping, paved driveway, etc.) probably is not a sufficient difference to eliminate the property as a comparable. Differences in siding may be acceptable if there are not sufficient comparables with the same type of siding. *As a general rule, the best comparables will be those with the fewest differences when compared to the subject property.*

Date of Sale/Changes in Market Conditions. Comparable properties not only should be "similar" but also should be "recently sold." The more recently a comparable sold, the more likely it is to reflect current market conditions. Thus, the **date of sale** is a very important consideration. Some markets are relatively stable and changes in property values occur slowly, but market conditions can sometimes change very quickly due to changes in economic circumstances. For example, when a relatively small community loses a major industry, the adverse effect on local housing values can be dramatic. In that case, the appraiser may need to adjust the sale prices of all comparables due to the major **changes in market conditions**. In areas where there is a great deal of economic growth and real estate activity, values can increase significantly in a very short period of time. In such active markets, a person should only use comparable properties that sold within the previous few months. In markets with less real estate activity, or when dealing with an unusual or relatively scarce type of real property, you may need to use somewhat older sales, but rarely, if ever, should you use properties that sold more than one year ago as comparables.

Conditions of Sale. A comparable property should have been sold under **typical open market conditions** where the buyer and seller were well informed and acting without undue pressure. Comparable properties should have been advertised in the customary manner, listed and sold through a broker, and exposed to the market for a reasonable period of time. A property that is sold privately without exposure to the open market may not be a good indicator of market value for various reasons. Similarly, a property sold quickly by a seller who is under pressure to sell (e.g., due to a job transfer or financial problems) may not be a good comparable.

The United States experienced an historic real estate market decline between 2007-2011 resulting in record numbers of foreclosed residential and other properties being placed on the market, as well as **"distressed sales"** or **"short sales"** by owners acting under the threat of foreclosure. In some markets, the number of foreclosed and distressed sale properties outnumbered regular open market sales, forcing sale prices of non-distressed properties downward due to the glut of foreclosed and distressed sale houses in the market. The question arises, should sales of foreclosed or distressed sale properties ever be used as comparables? There may be some situations when it would be appropriate to include one or more distressed sales as a comparable. While it is preferable that all comparables be open market sales with no adverse factors affecting the sales, that may not be possible in some markets.

During periods when sale prices of properties not sold under duress are adversely affected by distressed sales in the local market where a subject property is located, then it might be appropriate for one or more of the comparables used to be a distressed sale. The number of distressed sales used should be no more than necessary to accurately reflect local market conditions. Certainly, *anytime a distressed sale is used as a comparable, the appraiser must clearly note this information in the appraisal report.*

Comparable sales also should have involved **financing** typically available in the community rather than some unusual financing method or term that is not commonly available. For example, suppose a buyer is unable to qualify for a typical mortgage loan from a lender due to poor credit. A seller may finance the purchase price at a competitive interest rate but only if the buyer is willing to pay a higher purchase price. In such case, the sale price may exceed what the property's actual market value would have been if typical financing had been involved. Unusual financing terms will be very difficult to discover in most situations, however, because appraisers most frequently acquire their information from MLS files that usually do not include financing information.

Number of Comparables

How many comparable sales should be selected? **Three or four comparables may be sufficient**, provided that these comparables have been carefully selected. As a general rule, the more comparables that are used, the more accurate the appraisal. It is always better to use too many comparables than not enough.

Sources of Comparables

The best single source for finding and gathering information about potential comparables is the local multiple listing services. Most MLS organizations retain information on recently sold properties specifically for the purpose of assisting member agents in performing broker price opinions and comparable market analyses and appraisers in performing appraisals. If there is no MLS in the area, then the task of finding comparables and gathering data is more difficult. The appraiser's own office files of appraised properties will often be an excellent source of comparables and the appraiser's familiarity with the properties should enable the appraiser to make more accurate adjustments. Real estate firms are required to retain transaction records for three years and may be willing to provide an appraiser access to these records to search for possible comparable sales. Valuable information can also be obtained from local tax offices and register of deeds offices, as well as directly from property owners if necessary. Pending sales contracts may also be used as a source of comparables, although such contracts are not completely reliable as a data source until the sales are closed. Listing data should be avoided as a source for comparables since a listing price, obviously, can be very different from a property's actual sale price or market value.

Data to Be Collected

Whatever sources are used, the data that is compiled on comparable properties should be very detailed and include both *sales data* and *property data.* The **sales data** includes the sales price, conditions of sale, and the date of sale. The **property data** includes information such as the property's location, age and condition, size of the heated useable area and other areas such as garages, porches, decks, basements, etc., quality of construction, lot size and description, number of rooms, and special features. In other words, the appraiser attempts to be equally familiar with the comparable property and the subject property, since this approach involves comparing one property with the other.

Adjustments to Sale Prices of Comparables

As noted above, virtually every comparable property that is selected will be different in some respect from the subject property. Reasonable differences are tolerable for the purpose of selecting comparables, but you still must account for these differences when deriving an estimate of value for the subject property. Once data has been collected on several recently sold comparable properties, the data on each property sale is individually compared to the subject property. **Adjustments** *are made to the sale price of each comparable property to reflect differences between the comparable property and the subject property. Adjustments are always deducted from or added to the sale price of the* **comparable property** so that the resulting adjusted price can be thought of as the presumed price for which the comparable property would have sold had it been identical to the subject property.

Where the subject property is superior to the comparable sale property, the sale price of the comparable property is adjusted upward. (If the subject property is superior, it would be expected to sell for more.) Conversely, *where the subject property is inferior to the comparable sale property, the sale price of the comparable property is adjusted downward.*

Factors for Which Adjustments May Be Necessary

Individual adjustments are made to the sales price of the comparable property for each *significant* difference (i.e., each difference likely to affect market value) between the subject property and the comparable property. *Factors for which adjustments may be needed are essentially the same as the factors to consider when selecting comparables.*

Age and Condition of Building. These factors must be considered together to determine the appropriate adjustment if a comparable is significantly different from the subject in age or condition. For example, if the subject property is 20 years old but has been very well maintained and has upgraded finishes (such as hardwood floors replacing carpet) and appliances, then the sale price of a 20 year old comparable that has had only average maintenance and no upgrades will need to be adjusted higher to serve as a viable comparable in estimating the subject property's value.

Location. A property's value is definitely influenced by where it is located, yet location is a difficult factor for which to make an adjustment. It is far better to be careful when selecting comparables to avoid comparables with locational features that are significantly different from the subject. Nevertheless, if a comparable with substantially different locational features must be used, an adjustment may be needed. This might be indicated if two highly similar comparables, one in the same neighborhood as the subject property and the other in a different neighborhood, sold for significantly different prices at about the same time. Also, when there are *external factors* affecting a comparable property, such as the property's location on a major thoroughfare (negative) or location convenient to shopping (positive), then such factors should alert the appraiser to the possible need for an adjustment, depending on the subject property's location and whether the market indicates the external factor(s) is significant.

Size of Building or Lot. Unless the buildings on the subject and comparable properties are extremely close in size, an adjustment is appropriate. Substantial differences in lot size may also require an adjustment. An evaluation of the market should be made to determine if an adjustment is warranted. In other words, is the market treating highly similar houses on lots of different size differently in the sale price of the houses? If so, then an adjustment may be needed.

Major Physical Characteristics. Adjustments usually will be necessary for *significant* differences in physical characteristics or features such as the type and quality of construction (e.g., brick veneer vs. fiber cement vs. vinyl siding), number and type of rooms, presence or absence of major features (such as a basement, garage, carport, deck, porch, pool, fireplace, or storage building), major mechanical systems (such as exceptional or substandard heating/cooling systems), presence of central vacuum or audio system, architectural design features, interior design features (floor coverings, countertops, trim, etc.), and lot features (including landscaping, slope/drainage, unusual shape, etc.).

Date of Sale. An adjustment may also be necessary for the date of sale, depending on how much time has passed since the comparable was sold and whether market conditions have changed (e.g., whether property values in the area have been increasing, decreasing or stable during the period since the comparable was sold).

Conditions of Sale. In addition, adjustments may be necessary where there were other factors affecting the sale price of the comparable, such as unusual financing, a private sale (not on the open market), or undue pressure on the seller. Except where the property listing and sale record indicated the property was a "short sale" or "foreclosure," the biggest challenge for the appraiser may be discovering when these factors exist, since they often will not be obvious from the sales data typically available. *To the extent possible, it is far better to address the issue of conditions affecting a sale in the process of selecting comparable properties, rather than in the process of adjusting sale prices of comparables.*

No Adjustment Is Usually Needed for Minor Differences. Adjustments are not made for all differences between the subject property and a comparable property. Minor differences that when considered individually do not have a significant impact on value, do not require adjustments. A few examples include *minor differences* in: 1) room, garage or deck size; 2) quality of trim, fixtures or floor coverings; and 3) heating/cooling systems or kitchen appliances/surfaces. If there are a number of such minor differences that when considered together may as a whole affect property value, then a more general adjustment may be made for these differences, if not already taken into account when making other adjustments.

Amount of Adjustment

The *amount* of the adjustment to be applied for any given dissimilarity requires considerable judgment and experience, which is why *there is no substitute for experience when it comes to appraising real estate.* Recognizing the importance of experience, the North Carolina Appraisal Board requires significant appraisal experience as a trainee or apprentice before a person qualifies for appraiser certification. *There is no set formula for making adjustments and certainly no standard chart or list of adjustments — the appraiser must utilize his or her training and experience to research sales/property data and estimate the appropriate amount for any adjustment.* Selecting comparable properties as similar as possible to the property being appraised lessens both the number and amounts of needed adjustments, thereby reducing the margin for error. That said, seldom will there be such similarity that no adjustments are needed.

Paired Sales Analysis. Where possible, one can be reasonably assured that an adjustment reflects market behavior if the amount of the adjustment is based on a comparison of comparable sales with one another. This method of determining the amount of an adjustment is referred to as "**paired sales analysis**" and is most effective when using pairings of properties located within the same subdivision or immediate neighborhood. The properties used in the comparison must be extremely similar and must have only a very few differences (preferably only one or two) to which the variance in their sale prices can be attributed. *Examples of how to determine the amount of an adjustment due to **differences in various characteristics or factors** follow.*

Presence/absence of garage. Two recently sold houses are virtually identical in all respects except that one has a two-car garage and the other has no garage. It is reasonable to assume that any difference in their sale prices is due to the garage. All differences with respect to garages on any of the comparable sales could then be adjusted on the basis of that one comparison. If the house with the two-car garage sold for $250,000 and the house with no garage sold for $235,000, then it is reasonable to assume that a $15,000 adjustment is appropriate for the presence or absence of a two-car garage, although it is preferable to have multiple examples to support a conclusion as to the appropriate amount of an adjustment.

Date of sale. Two houses have no appreciable differences, but one sold a year ago for $200,000 and the other just sold for $204,000. If a similar increase in sales prices for other comparable houses can be confirmed through analysis of other sales within the past year, then the $4,000 difference may be attributed to appreciation in house prices. The sale prices of comparable sales from less than a year ago that are used in the appraisal of the subject property might be reasonably adjusted upward at the rate of 2 percent per year ($4,000 ÷ $200,000 = 2 percent).

Size of building. Two extremely similar houses in the same subdivision sold within the same month. One has 2,400 heated square feet of living area and sold for $280,000. The other has 2,600 square feet and sold for $290,000. The $10,000 difference in sale price may be reasonably attributed to the 200 square foot difference in size. $10,000 ÷ 200 = $50 per square foot. If an analysis of other sales confirms that the $50 per square foot figure is reasonable, then an adjustment for square footage difference between a subject property and comparables may be based on that figure.

Note: It is not appropriate when making adjustments for square footage differences under the sales comparison approach to use an estimated replacement cost per square foot. The replacement cost per square foot almost always will be higher than the amount derived through a paired sales analysis.

Age of Building. A comparable house highly similar to and located in the same subdivision as the subject house recently sold for $250,000. The two houses are both well-maintained, but the comparable house is five years older than the subject house. Using the paired sales analysis method on recent home sales data in the area, the appraiser finds that the subject house's market value is likely about $10,000 more than the comparable due to the age difference. Thus, the appraiser adjusts the comparable's sale price upward by $10,000.

Condition of Building. A comparable house located in the same subdivision as and highly similar to the subject house recently sold for $230,000. It is only one year older than the subject house, but the comparable house recently had been painted, had numerous small repairs, had the roof replaced, and generally had been better maintained than the subject house. Based on his or her knowledge of market information, the appraiser estimates that the condition of the comparable house makes it worth $20,000 more than the subject house. Thus, the appraiser adjusts the comparable's sale price downward by $20,000.

Location. A comparable house recently sold for $170,000. It is highly similar to the subject house in most respects, but is located about two miles from the subject house on a main thoroughfare across from a convenience store, while the subject house is located on a side street with other similar houses. The appraiser does not have sufficient comparables near the subject house, so he examines recent sales of houses in nearby vicinities, including the comparable in question. The appraiser concludes that the comparable's less desirable location resulted in a sale price that is $20,000 lower than it would have been had the comparable been in the same neighborhood as the subject house; accordingly, the appraiser adjusts the comparable's sale price upward by $20,000.

Major Physical Characteristics. The example involving the presence or absence of a garage illustrates the need for adjustments due to differing physical characteristics of the subject and comparable properties. There are so many possible differences in physical characteristics that it is not feasible to address them all. Basically, the appraiser determines based on his/her experience and knowledge of the market the appropriate amount of adjustment to make for each significant difference in physical characteristics.

Conditions of Sale. Property sold under circumstances that may have affected the sale price generally should be avoided as a comparable. However, if the appraiser must use as a comparable a sale that was, for example, a private sale, or the seller was forced to sell quickly for some reason resulting in a lower than typical sale price, then the appraiser must make an appropriate adjustment to the sale price for the adverse conditions of sale, with the amount of adjustment being based on the appraiser's comparison of the comparable's characteristics and sale price with other highly similar comparables.

*Note on "**Distressed Sales**."* When local market conditions dictate that a "distressed sale" must be used as a comparable, the appraiser will first make adjustments to the comparable's sale price for factors other than conditions of sale just as with normal comparables. Since distressed sale properties frequently have been poorly maintained and are not in good condition, the adjustment made for the property's condition may be sufficient to account for the lower sale price of the distressed sale, but this may not be the case.

The appraiser may have to take one of two approaches. One is to determine by market analysis of other comparable sales an appropriate adjustment to make for "conditions of sale" as a result of the distressed sale circumstance (foreclosure, short sale, etc.). The other approach is to include the unadjusted sale price of the distressed sale comparable, but clearly indicate in the appraisal report that this comparable sale represents the low end of the possible value range and to afford that comparable considerably less weight in reconciling the indications of value derived for all the comparables.

Reconciling Indications of Value

By making adjustments to the sale price of each comparable, the appraiser will produce an *"adjusted sale price" for each comparable.* Each of these adjusted sale prices is an indication of value, but each will be a different amount. The various adjusted sale prices of the comparables should form a fairly tight range of value within which the value of the subject property will fall. The greater the difference between the lowest and highest of the adjusted sale prices, the more difficult it will be for the appraiser to derive an accurate estimate of value.

At this point in the appraisal process, the appraiser must use his or her best judgment to derive a single value estimate based on the sales comparison approach. This estimate should fall within the range formed by the adjusted sale prices of the comparables. It is important to note, however, that *the estimate of value based on the sales comparison approach should **not**, as a general rule, be derived by "averaging" the adjusted sale prices of the comparables.* Some of the adjustments made to the sale prices of the comparables will be more subjective than others, and some will be larger than others. The greater the number and size of adjustments, the greater is the chance of error. Therefore, *"weighted" (i.e., greater) consideration generally should be given to the adjusted sale prices of those comparables requiring the least amount of adjustment (in both number and size) and the least subjective adjustments.* In other words, if one comparable is more comparable than the others, then that comparable should be given greater weight in deriving the value estimate. Thus, the value estimate may fall at the low end of the range in adjusted sale prices, at the high end of the range, or somewhere in the middle. The appraiser is expected to include comments in the report to explain the reconciliation, how the comparables were weighted, and why the final opinion of value is justified.

COST APPROACH

The **cost approach** may be used by appraisers to estimate the value of properties that are improved by one or more buildings. Unlike the sales comparison approach, this method involves *separate estimates of value for the building and the land.* These separately derived estimates are added together to obtain the value estimate for the entire improved property. This approach involves three basic steps.

Steps in the Cost Approach

1. Estimate the current replacement cost or reproduction cost of the subject building.
2. Estimate the amount of depreciation (loss in value) to the subject building and deduct this amount from the building cost estimate to determine the estimate of building value.
3. Estimate the value of the land (including land improvements) using the sales comparison approach and add this amount to the estimate of building value to determine the estimate of property value based on the cost approach.

Like the sales comparison approach, the basic theory underlying the cost approach reflects the principle of "substitution" discussed earlier in the chapter. This theory assumes that a reasonable and prudent buyer would not pay more for an existing improved property than the amount it would cost to buy a comparable parcel of land and construct a new building that is comparable to the existing building in desirability and usefulness.

The cost approach is, as a general rule, a less desirable appraisal method than the sales comparison approach because of the great difficulty and subjectivity involved in estimating depreciation and because the estimate of building value is not based directly on the actions of sellers and buyers in the marketplace. *When the subject property is a type of property not frequently sold and it does not produce income, the cost approach can be an especially useful method.* A few examples of such properties are schools, churches, hospitals and government buildings.

The cost approach can be a reliable method when estimating the value of *new or relatively new buildings,* including residential structures. This is because the cost to construct a building is most likely to be close to the market value of the building when the building is new. The cost approach is much less reliable when estimating the value of older buildings, primarily because of the difficulty in estimating depreciation. Other situations where the cost approach is useful include estimating the market value of a *proposed* new building and estimating building value for insurance purposes.

The cost approach is *not* used by real estate brokers when performing a comparative market analysis (CMA) or broker price opinion (BPO) to estimate a probable selling price for a property.

Estimating Building Cost

When estimating building cost, the appraiser calculates either "**reproduction cost**" or "**replacement cost**." These are very different concepts, however, and it is important to understand each and when their use is appropriate. **Reproduction cost** *is the cost of creating an exact replica of the improvement based on current prices for labor and materials.* **Replacement cost** *is the cost of creating an improvement having the same or equal utility using current standards of material and design and based on current prices for labor and materials.*

Reproduction cost may be difficult to estimate for older buildings because materials and standards of design and construction tend to change. Some components of the structure may no longer be sufficiently available in the market making it difficult to accurately estimate cost without consulting with builders. By the same token, the cost of a component may be very high by current standards and may not contribute value commensurate with such cost. Using reproduction cost may only further complicate estimating the functional obsolescence category of depreciation.

For example, suppose the subject of the appraisal was a 75-year-old house with solid brick walls. Since this type of construction is rarely, if ever, used today, the cost of reproducing it would not generally be available to the appraiser. The cost of frame construction and brick veneer would be lower and just as acceptable to the market. After all the extra effort to estimate the cost of the solid brick wall, the excess cost over the brick veneer frame wall would be deducted in the depreciation estimate, since it would not contribute value commensurate with its cost. The use of replacement cost would include only the cost of the brick veneer frame wall (easily determined since it is the standard of masonry residential construction) and would eliminate the need to deduct the depreciation inherent in the solid brick wall. For these reasons, **replacement cost** *is the more practical of the two concepts and is the concept most commonly used by appraisers.*

Cost estimating can be accomplished in several ways. It can range from a comprehensive *quantity survey method* usually used by contractors to bid specific jobs to the simpler *square foot method* most often used for appraisals. Somewhere in between is the *unit-in-place method,* which is a blend of the other two methods.

Quantity Survey Method

The **quantity-survey method** involves a complete breakdown of all the materials, equipment, labor, indirect costs (permits, licenses, fees, interest, taxes, overhead, etc.) and builders' profit. Used by building contractors when estimating the cost of proposed construction, such an estimate will rarely be utilized by appraisers. If such a detailed estimate is needed, the services of a trained estimator should be employed.

Unit-in-Place Method

The **unit-in-place method** breaks down the construction cost into the various building components, the cost for each being estimated on the basis of workable units such as the square foot or lineal foot. For instance, the cost of the masonry foundation wall might be established on the basis of dollars per square foot of wall area by consulting a masonry contractor. The cost of the roof covering might be estimated in dollars per 100 square feet, and the cost of interior partitions on the basis of dollars per lineal foot. Contractors' overhead and profit may be included in the unit cost figures or computed separately.

Square Foot Method

One of the more widely used methods of cost estimating for appraisal purposes is *based on square footage*. Licensed and certified appraisers typically refer to square footage as "gross living area" (GLA) or "gross building area" (GBA) and can be utilized as a comparative unit of measurement method. This method involves estimating the cost per square foot of an entire structure based on known costs per square foot for similar structures adjusted for time and physical differences.

Sources of Cost Information

The primary sources for such information are building contractors, market sales of new homes, and cost services.

Building Contractors. Building contractors do not customarily price or bid homes without carefully estimating the job using a quantity survey method. However, they do generally take note, after the fact, of the actual cost to construct their dwellings. Since costs are somewhat proportional to size, the actual costs are expressed in terms of square feet for comparison purposes. Most builders know the cost per square foot that their construction involves and will share the information with appraisers. However, such consultations can be misleading unless everyone involved has an understanding of what is included and excluded in the figures being discussed. For instance, a builder might state that it cost $110 per square foot to build a given house. Before the appraiser can use that figure to estimate the cost of another dwelling, he must first know whether that figure includes builder's profit and overhead, land, site improvements, porches, garages, etc.

New Home Sales Data. Since the *cost per square foot used for appraisal purposes must include builder's profit and overhead*, actual sales of new homes provide excellent data on cost. Once the cost of the site, site improvements, and appurtenant structures are estimated and deducted from the sales price and the remainder is divided by the size of the heated livable area, the resulting cost per square foot can be used as a gauge of cost for similar construction. Since the cost per square foot of heated living area constitutes most of any sales price or value estimate, some error may be acceptable in the estimate of site value, site improvements, or appurtenant structures since such minor errors will not significantly distort the resulting extracted cost per square foot of heated living area.

Cost Services. There are also a number of cost services that publish data on building costs. Most of the services provide basic costs for various types of construction and also provide adjustments to modify the published data for considerations of time, location, size, shape, quality, and other factors that influence construction costs. When using such services, comparisons must periodically be made with actual costs to ensure the accuracy of the manuals. However, the informed practitioner generally utilizes all sources of data to remain current on building costs.

Depreciation Concepts

Once replacement or reproduction cost is estimated, it is converted to an indication of improvement value by deducting *"accrued depreciation."* Depreciation is often misunderstood, and accurately estimating it is usually the most difficult part of the cost approach. **Depreciation** *is a loss of utility and, hence, value from any cause.* It is the difference between cost new on the date of appraisal and present market value. It may be caused by "deterioration" or by "obsolescence." **Deterioration** is a physical impairment caused by wear and tear, decay, dry rot, cracks, encrustations, or structural defects. **Obsolescence** is an impairment of desirability or usefulness brought about by changes in design standards *(functional obsolescence)* or factors external to the property *(economic or external obsolescence)*. All of these terms will be discussed shortly.

The concept of depreciation applies **only** *to improvements (structures) and* **not** *to the land on which the improvements are situated.* Even if the value of a parcel of land decreases over time, this is not considered "depreciation" for appraisal purposes. Because there is no depreciation applied to land value, the cost approach involves separate calculation of land value using the sales comparison method.

Depreciation is sometimes estimated as a percentage of cost new, the percentage reflecting the ratio between "effective age" and "economic life." The **economic life** of an improvement is the period over which the improvement declines in value from 100 percent of cost new to zero percent. In other words, it is the total period of time during which the improvements contribute value to the property.

The **effective age** of the structure is the age that the structure appears to be, considering its age, condition, design, and economic forces that affect value.

For example, if a building looks like a 12-year-old building and market conditions affect it as if it were a 12-year-old building, then it is a 12-year-old building for appraisal purposes. The chronological or actual age should be noted but is not as significant to the value of the building. Generally speaking, *if a building is in average condition for buildings of similar age and design, its effective age and chronological age will be the same.* A building that has had a better-than-average level of maintenance, rehabilitation, or modernization will have an effective age less than its chronological age. Conversely, a building that has not received at least an average level of maintenance, rehabilitation, or modernization will have an effective age greater than its chronological age.

Depreciation Methods

The appraiser must distinguish between depreciation for appraisal purposes versus accounting and/or tax purposes. Depreciation for appraisal purposes as stated earlier reflects an *"actual loss in value"* from cost new of the improvements. Depreciation estimates for accounting and tax purposes are more academic in nature and may not actually simulate the market. They may reflect more or less depreciation than is reflected in the market for a particular structure.

There are three basic methods commonly used by appraisers in estimating depreciation. These are listed below and then discussed.

Depreciation Methods

- Age/Life Method
- Market Abstraction Method
- Breakdown Method

Age/Life Method

The **age/life method** of estimating depreciation is based primarily on observation and judgment. *The method assumes that the percentage of depreciation is the same percentage as the effective age is to the total economic life.* If a building has an effective age of 25 years and an economic life of 50 years, then depreciation is estimated at 50 percent. Another building in the same area may have the same design and chronological age but may have been better maintained such that its effective age is only 20 years, and its accrued depreciation would therefore be estimated at 40 percent. Still a third building in the same neighborhood might have similar effective age but be of superior design and construction such that its economic life would be estimated at 60 years and accrued depreciation would be estimated at 20 divided by 60, or 33 percent.

The age/life method is widely utilized because it is easy to understand and simple to use, but is subjective and highly dependent upon the appraiser's judgment and experience. While it can be an effective way to estimate depreciation accrued to date, it should not be considered a reliable indication of the rate of depreciation the property will suffer in the future.

Market Extraction Method

Much of the subjectivity can be removed from the depreciation estimate by extracting the depreciation from the market. The **market extraction method** involves analysis of current sales to see to what extent the market has penalized them. By analyzing sales of properties similar to and in the same area as the subject, the average annual rate of depreciation can be calculated for each. *This method* *assumes that similar properties will depreciate at similar rates such that a rate extracted from recently sold comparable properties provides the best reflection of depreciation for the subject building.*

Breakdown Method

The **breakdown method** is the most analytical and most difficult to perform in an appraisal analysis. It is *rarely used in residential appraising* and thus will receive scant treatment here, but even the novice should have a basic understanding of the types or categories of depreciation addressed by the breakdown method of estimating depreciation. These basic types of depreciation are listed and discussed below.

Types of Depreciation

- Physical Deterioration (Curable and Incurable)
- Functional Obsolescence (Curable and Incurable)
- Economic or External Obsolescence (Incurable Only)

Physical deterioration occurs from *wear and tear on improvements* and consists of two types: "*curable*" and "*incurable.*" "**Physical-curable**" items refer to those details that need repair and should be cured immediately, such as a broken light fixture, peeling paint on siding, broken gutter, etc. Another type of physical-curable depreciation is referred to as "**physical-curable postponed.**" This refers to items that do not need immediate replacement, but which must be replaced prior to the end of the economic life of the total structure. For example, the roof may not need replacing as of the date of the appraisal, but it might be half way through its economic life, or 50 percent depreciated. Thus, the amount chargeable to physical-curable postponed depreciation would be 50 percent of the cost to replace the roof covering.

"**Physical-incurable**" deterioration refers to deterioration of the basic "bone structure" of the improvements. It is termed "incurable" because typically it is not economically feasible to replace the basic building structure prior to the end of its economic life. The measure of physical-incurable deterioration is based on the age/life method as previously discussed. However, prior to computing the actual amount of depreciation, the amount of physical-curable postponed items must be deducted from the overall reproduction or replacement cost of the structure to avoid double depreciation.

Functional obsolescence *is a loss in value due to physical design features that no longer are, or perhaps never were, desirable to most purchasers in the market.* Outmoded plumbing fixtures or a bedroom adjacent to a kitchen might be classified as functional obsolescence for a house. Features that are functionally obsolescent usually are considered "*curable*" since they can be corrected for a relatively modest cost. However, some features may be too costly to remedy and thus be deemed "*incurable.*" A house with only one bathroom or that has a tiny kitchen with very little cabinet space may be examples of incurable functional obsolescence. The test between curable and incurable is still somewhat subjective but often is determined by the economic prudence of correcting the functional deficiency as of the date of appraisal.

Economic or external obsolescence *is caused by factors external to the property* and is sometimes referred to as "*locational obsolescence.*" *It is of an "incurable" nature only.* One example might be where most of the traffic utilizing a thoroughfare with many retail establishments is diverted to a new bypass, thereby adversely affecting the desirability and value of the retail properties. Another example might be the establishment of a hog farm or waste dump near dwellings in a rural area. Still another might be the rezoning of a former residential neighborhood adjacent to a second residential neighborhood to permit commercial uses. The measure of this type of loss in value is difficult to determine because of the subjective judgment required, and extreme caution is urged if attempting an estimate of this type.

Estimating Land Value

Land value is estimated using the sales comparison approach. If recent sales of comparable *unimproved* parcels of land are available, the process is very simple. The appraiser will use the comparable land sales to derive the land value for the parcel of land being appraised. If, however, there are inadequate recent sales of comparable unimproved parcels of land, the appraiser will have to "extract" the land value from recent sales of *improved* properties. This is accomplished by estimating the building cost and deducting accrued depreciation for *each* comparable. The depreciated replacement cost is then deducted from the actual sale price to estimate the value of each comparable's land. The results are then reconciled into an estimate of land value for the subject property.

Illustration of Cost Approach

An appraiser is estimating the value of a 10-year old house with 2,000 square feet of heated living area. The house is in above average physical condition and the appraiser notes no functional or external obsolescence. The appraiser estimates the "effective age" of the house to be eight (8) years. There have been several sales of comparable houses in the neighborhood during the past year. Therefore, the appraiser decides to use the age/life depreciation method and to extract the depreciation rate from comparable sales in the neighborhood. First, the appraiser determines that the current replacement cost for the house should be based on $110 per square foot, which figure was obtained from consultations with local building contractors and reference to an appropriate cost reporting publication. The appraiser then uses the market abstraction method described earlier in this chapter to determine that the appropriate depreciation rate is two (2) percent per year. Using the same comparables, the appraiser then extracts the land value from the market by deducting the depreciated replacement cost (estimated) of each comparable from the sale price of that comparable. The result is an indicated land value of $35,000. The calculations would then proceed as follows:

Estimate of Replacement Cost	$220,000
(2,000 SF x $110 per SF)	
Estimate of Depreciation	- 35,200
(8 years @ 2% per year = 16%;	
16% x $220,000 = $35,200)	
Depreciated Replacement Cost	$184,800
Land Value (by sales comparison approach)	+ 35,000
Estimate of Value by Cost Approach	**$219,800**

INCOME APPROACH

The **income approach** is used to estimate the value of *income-producing properties*, i.e., properties typically purchased for investment purposes. It is used most frequently with five-or-more-unit residential properties (e.g., apartment complexes) and commercial/industrial/ agricultural and other income-producing properties. The projected net operating income is the principal factor affecting the value of such properties. An investor purchasing such a property is actually purchasing the rights to that future income, and there is a relationship between the income stream to be acquired and the value of the property which generates it. Although an appraiser will utilize all three approaches to value when estimating the value of an income-producing property, the greatest weight typically will be given to the result derived by using the income approach.

There are actually multiple income approaches or income analysis methods employed by appraisers depending on the nature of the property and the specific appraisal assignment.

Income "Approaches" or "Analysis Methods"

Gross Rent Multiplier (GRM) Method. This is a simple income analysis method that involves examining the relationship between gross rental income and value. It is commonly used when estimating the value of **residential 1-4 unit properties**. The method is used by both appraisers estimating property value and real estate brokers performing a comparative market analysis (CMA) or broker price opinion (BPO) to estimate a property's probable selling price.

Direct Capitalization Method. This method involves converting the estimate of projected future income into an estimate of current market value. It is commonly used when estimating the value of **income-producing properties other than residential 1-4 unit properties.** The method is used by both appraisers estimating property value and real estate brokers performing a comparative market analysis (CMA) or broker price opinion (BPO) to estimate a property's probable selling price.

Discounted Cash Flow Analysis (or Yield Capitalization). This very complicated advanced method of income analysis is used to analyze income when the direct capitalization method may not produce a reliable result, particularly when the subject property's future income and expenses are either not very predictable or it is known that future income and/or expenses will vary substantially over time. This method (and variations of it) is used only by professional appraisers with highly specialized training and experience in appraising commercial properties who can apply the method in compliance with the competency rule of the Uniform Standards of Professional Appraisal Practice. The advanced techniques used with this method and its variations are far beyond the scope of this manual and will not be mentioned further. Real estate brokers performing a comparative market analysis (CMA) or broker price opinion (BPO) should *not* attempt to use this method of analysis.

Gross Rent Multiplier Method

The **gross rent multiplier (GRM) method** is an income analysis method commonly used to estimate the value of residential 1-4 unit properties. This method may also be used for other income-producing properties; however, an income capitalization approach is usually preferred for such properties because it considers more specific information and tends to yield a more reliable result.

When adequate comparable sales are available in which gross rental income and sale prices are known, the sale price of each comparable can be divided by its gross rental income to derive a **gross rent multiplier (GRM). A gross rent multiplier is determined using the following formula:**

$$\text{Sales Price} \div \text{Gross Rental Income} = \text{Gross Rent Multiplier}$$

Either annual or monthly rental income may be used, but typically annual income is used. Where consistency is noted in the multiplier obtained from several sales of comparable properties, it can be assumed that a similar relationship would exist between the subject property's gross income and value. *By multiplying the subject property's gross income by the gross rent multiplier derived from the comparables, an indication of the subject property's value is obtained.*

The GRM method is used in addition to the sales comparison approach for residential 1-4 unit properties, and it is likely that the same comparable properties used in the sales comparison approach can be used with the GRM method if the gross rental income for the comparables is known. If different comparables are used, then it is necessary to make adjustments to their sale prices for differences between the comparables and the subject property, just as is done with the sales comparison approach.

Example of Gross Rent Multiplier (GRM) Method

Assume the subject property is a single-family rental house with annual gross rental income of $14,700. The appraiser has found three recent sales of very similar rental houses in the subject property's neighborhood. Minor adjustments are made to the sale prices to reflect differences in characteristics between the comparables and the subject property. The adjusted sale prices, gross annual rent and GRM for the comparables are shown below:

Sale #	Sales Price	Gross Annual Rent	Gross Rent Multiplier
1	$232,500	$15,600	14.90
2	$230,000	$15,000	15.33
3	$211,900	$14,340	14.78

The sale price of each comparable was divided by the annual gross income (rent) to determine the gross rent multipliers shown in the right column above. The GRMs average about 15, and this seems to be an appropriate figure to use in this case. By multiplying the subject property's annual gross income by the derived GRM of 15, an indication of the subject property's value is obtained:

$$\$14,700 \times 15 = \$220,500$$

Direct Capitalization

"**Capitalization**" *is a process that converts an estimate of a property's future income into an estimate of current property value.* "**Direct Capitalization**" is a relatively simple and straightforward capitalization method that assumes the future income and expenses of the subject property will be stable. The method is widely used to estimate the value of *all types of income-producing properties other than residential 1-4 unit properties.*

The **direct capitalization** method involves selecting recently sold comparable properties for which the *sale price* and annual *net operating income (NOI)* are known, then dividing the NOI by the value (sale price) to derive a *capitalization rate* for each comparable. A "capitalization rate" is a rate of return on investment. After analyzing the capitalization rates for each comparable and selecting an appropriate expected capitalization rate for the subject property, the projected average annual net operating income of the subject property is divided by the derived capitalization rate to determine an estimate of the subject property's value.

Direct Capitalization Formula. The relationship between these variables is expressed algebraically as:

$$\text{Value} = \frac{\text{Net Operating Income}}{\text{Capitalization Rate}} \quad \text{or} \quad V = \frac{I}{R}$$

The above formula can also be used in reverse. When looking at the known NOI and sale price of a comparable property, one can determine the overall capitalization rate (as mentioned above and discussed further below) by dividing the NOI by the sale price. For example, if a property sold for $922,000 and has NOI of $83,000, the capitalization rate is $83,000 divided by $922,000, which is 0.09, or 9 percent.

Capitalization Rate

A variety of "rates of return" can serve as a capitalization rate when appraising income property. However, when using the **direct capitalization** method, the rate typically used is the "**overall capitalization rate**," which is the relationship, expressed as a percentage, that the net operating income bears to value (indicated by the sale price of recently sold comparable properties.)

It is extremely important that the appraiser use an appropriate capitalization rate. The best way to assure this is to extract the rate from recent sales of comparable income-producing properties, known as "extracting a capitalization rate from the market." When adequate comparable sales are available for which net operating income and sale price are known net operating income may be divided by the sale price to derive a rate from each sale. Where general consistency is found in the rates extracted from several sales of properties of a class similar to the subject property, it can be assumed that a similar relationship would exist between the subject property's net income and value. Thus, the subject property's net income can be capitalized at the given rate to produce an indication of market value. Note that the capitalization rate for the various comparables may or may not be accorded equal weight, depending on the characteristics of the comparables as compared to the subject property. It may be more appropriate to give differing weight to the rates derived from the various comparables.

Note that, just as with the sales comparison approach, the *selection of comparable properties* is important to producing an accurate result. Comparables must be just as carefully selected based on their similarity to the subject property as is the case with the sales comparison approach. In fact, for many income properties, the appraiser will be using both the sales comparison and income capitalization approaches, in which case the same comparables selected for the sales comparison approach may be used in the income capitalization approach if income and expense information is available. As is done with the sales comparison approach, *the sale prices of comparables used to extract a capitalization rate must also be adjusted for differences between the comparables and the subject property.*

The more similar the comparables are to the subject, the fewer adjustments that are needed to the sales prices, net income or capitalization rates for the comparables.

Income and Expense Estimates

It should be obvious that the income projections are also critical to the reliability of the approach. Income and expenses must be projected for the subject property based on actual data from both the subject property and comparable properties. The typical basis for *gross income* estimates is "market rent." *Market rent* can be defined as the amount of rent that tenants most probably would be willing to pay in an open market. Such estimates are best made through a comparison process with actual rents of similar properties. **Gross rental income** is actually the "potential" income assuming 100% occupancy and no losses due to failure to collect rent that is due. If, for example, an apartment complex has 40 units that all rent for $800 per month, the gross potential rental income is 40 x $800 = $32,000 per month x 12 months = $384,000 per year.

Estimates of **net operating income (NOI)** are made by deducting from the gross income estimate the estimated *vacancy and collection losses* and *operating expenses*, again based on the known experience of both the subject and comparable properties. "**Operating expenses**" are those expenses necessary to maintain and operate the property, such as taxes, insurance premiums, maintenance and repair costs, reserves for replacement, management fees, and other expenses. They do *not* include book depreciation, debt service, or capital improvements. Thus, ***net operating income*** *equals gross rental income less (minus) vacancy and collection losses and operating expenses.*

Direct Capitalization Example

Assume the subject property is a 4,000 square foot office building. Research has found recent sales of three very similar office buildings in the area and the sales prices have been adjusted for differences between the comparables and the subject property, yielding the data below on the three comparables:

Sale #	Adj. Sales Price	Size (SF)	Rent/SF	Vacancy	Annual Expenses	Net Income	Capitalization Rate
1	$375,000	3,750	$14.50	0%	$6,500	$47,875	12.8%
2	$355,000	3,900	$14.00	5%	$7,500	$44,370	12.5%
3	$370,000	4,300	$13.50	10%	$7,000	$45,245	12.2%

Given the similarity of the comparables to the subject property, the adjustments made to the comparables' sale prices and similar market conditions for the properties, it seems appropriate in this case to give equal weight to the gross income (market rent) for each of the three comparables, which would yield approximately $14.00 per square foot. Using this figure, the gross rental income for the subject property may be estimated to be about $56,000 per year (4,000 SF @ $14/SF). Vacancy and collection losses for the comparables, expressed as a percentage of gross income, ranged from 0-10 percent, and averaged 5 percent, which also seems to be an appropriate rate to use for the subject property. Applying this rate to the gross income estimate for the subject property produces an effective gross income of $53,200 ($56,000 less 5%). Annual expenses per square foot for the three comparables (divide annual expenses by size) are $1.73, $1.92 and $1.63, respectively. The average for the three comparables is $1.76 per square foot and this seems to be the appropriate rate to use in projecting annual operating expenses for the subject property. The calculation of net operating income for the subject property may be summarized as follows:

Gross Income (4,000 SF at $14/SF)	$56,000
Less Vacancy and Collection Losses (5 percent)	-2,800
Effective Gross Income	$53,200
Less Operating Expenses (4,000 SF at $1.76/SF)	-7,040
Net Operating Income (NOI)	$ 46,160

The relationship between net income and sales price is expressed as a capitalization rate. By dividing the net income for each comparable sale by the sales price, the resulting rates ranged from 12.2 percent to 12.8 percent, or ±12.5 percent. By capitalizing the subject property's net income estimate at 12.5 percent, an indication of the subject property's value is derived:

$46,160 Net Operating Income ÷ .125 Capitalization Rate = $369,280 Value

RECONCILIATION OF THE THREE APPROACHES TO VALUE

In actual appraisal practice, the conscientious development of all three approaches to value often will present three separate indications of subject property value, ideally within a reasonably narrow range. **Reconciliation** *is the process by which the appraiser evaluates each approach to value to derive a single conclusion of value.*

The various indications are seldom averaged, as that implies equally weighted consideration to each approach, which is seldom realistic. Usually there will be one approach that is considered to be more reliable than the others and on which greater reliance should be placed. This determination involves consideration of the quantity, quality, and reliability of the data processed in each approach as well as the applicability of the approach to the property type being appraised. The value of income-producing properties usually will be based largely on the income capitalization approach. Thus, the value indication derived by the income approach will likely be given more weight for income properties.

Valuation of residential single-family properties and vacant land is usually based primarily on the sales comparison approach and the value indicated by that approach will almost always be given the greatest weight. Valuation of special-purpose properties such as school buildings often must be based on the cost approach, due to the lack of sufficient data for other approaches. These are only general rules of thumb, however, and they may be modified if an otherwise relevant approach is rendered less reliable by the absence of suitable data. For instance, both the sales comparison and cost approaches might apply to the valuation of a new dwelling. However, if the quantity or quality of the comparable sales was insufficient for a reliable conclusion, perhaps weighted consideration would be given to the cost approach.

Appraisal Report

The appraiser's conclusion of value for the subject property will be presented in an appraisal report provided to the appraiser's client. This report should explain clearly each approach to value utilized by the appraiser as well as the reasons for relying more heavily on any given approach to value. Appraisals of residential properties performed for loan purposes will be prepared utilizing the *Uniform Residential Appraisal Report* form prescribed by the Federal National Mortgage Association (Fannie Mae) and the Federal Home Loan Mortgage Corporation (Freddie Mac). Reports for appraisals of other properties may use a variety of formats.

BROKER PRICE OPINION OR COMPARATIVE MARKET ANALYSIS

LAW AND PRACTICE PRIOR TO OCTOBER 2012

Since the advent of appraisal and appraiser regulation in North Carolina (and nationally) in 1990, most appraisals of real property have been (and still are) required to be performed by a licensed or certified real estate appraiser. Prior to October 1, 2012, the North Carolina Appraisers Act, like the laws of many other states, had a limited exception that allowed real estate licenses to perform a "comparative market analysis (CMA)" so long as the real estate licensee did not represent himself or herself as a licensed or certified appraiser or registered appraiser trainee. This limited exception read: "A real estate broker may perform a "comparative market analysis" for compensation or other valuable consideration *only for actual or prospective brokerage clients or for real property involved in an employee relocation program."* The Act defined a **"comparative market analysis"** as "...the analysis of sales of similar recently sold properties in order to derive an indication of the probable sales price of a particular property by a licensed real estate broker." In practice, the term **"broker price opinion (BPO)"** was considered to be synonymous with the term "comparative market analysis."

The key limitation on a broker's ability to perform a comparative market analysis (CMA) for compensation under prior law was that it must be performed *for actual or **prospective** brokerage clients.* The primary issue became whether the party for whom the CMA was being performed was a legitimate "prospective" client. The Commission's position was *for a broker to be able to perform a CMA for a fee under the "prospective client" concept, there must be a genuinely reasonable possibility that the broker will enter into a brokerage agreement as a seller's or buyer's agent for the property that is the subject of the CMA.* [Understand that CMAs could always be performed by real estate licensees *without charging a separate fee for the CMA* if it was being performed for an actual brokerage client (i.e., for sellers by listing agents or for buyers by buyer agents).]

Despite the efforts of the Commission and the North Carolina Appraisal Board to enforce the restriction against brokers performing CMAs or BPOs for parties who are not "actual or prospective clients," some brokers violated the law, performing a BPO for a fee for parties with whom they not only had no brokerage (agency) agreement, but with whom there was no reasonable expectation of having such an agreement. These situations most commonly occurred when a lender wanted an estimate of a property's current probable selling price for some reason other than making a mortgage loan (e.g., to make a decision regarding foreclosure or a short sale), but did not want to pay hundreds of dollars for an appraisal that by law must be performed by a licensed or certified appraiser. Thus, some lenders sought brokers who were willing to provide a BPO for a much lower fee than an appraisal might cost.

The incidence of "illegal" BPOs increased substantially in the aftermath of the real estate market collapse in 2007 as the number of "distressed" properties ballooned. With the large number of properties in foreclosure or in danger of foreclosure and the huge increase in "short sale" situations, the demand from lenders for low-priced BPOs substantially increased. As a consequence, the real estate brokerage industry across the country began to seek legislative changes in those states, such as North Carolina, that restricted the performance of CMAs or BPOs for a fee by real estate licensees to those performed for actual or prospective clients.

BPO/CMA LAWS EFFECTIVE OCTOBER 1, 2012

The North Carolina General Assembly amended both the Real Estate License Law and the Appraisers Act (Senate Bill 521, 2012 Session Law 163) substantially changing the law regarding when broker price opinions (BPOs) or comparative market analyses (CMAs) may be performed *for a fee* by licensed brokers. These amendments were **effective October 1, 2012. Remember that the terms** "broker price opinion" **(BPO)** and "comparative market analysis" **(CMA) are synonymous, as the definition of each under state law is identical.**

Summary of Major Law Changes
- **Primary Change.** *A "non-provisional" broker* (i.e., a broker who has completed all postlicensing courses, thereby removing "provisional" status) whose license is on active status may prepare a broker price opinion (BPO) or comparative market analysis (CMA) and charge and collect a fee for the opinion. The BPO may be performed for a fee *for persons and entities for a variety of reasons, not just for actual or prospective brokerage clients.*

  Note: Unlike under former law, a ***provisional broker*** may not perform a BPO or CMA for a fee for anyone, even for an actual or prospective client. Provisional brokers may not perform a BPO/CMA for a fee due to concern that many will not have either adequate instruction or sufficient experience in brokerage to exercise the judgment necessary to properly perform a BPO/CMA. [G.S. §93A-83(a) and (b)]

- **Important Restriction.** Just as was the case under former law, a broker may NOT prepare a BPO (or CMA) for an existing or potential lienholder or other third party where the BPO is to serve as the basis to determine the **value** of a property for the purpose of originating a mortgage loan, including first and second mortgages, refinances or equity lines of credit. [G.S. §93A-83(b)(6)]

- **Other Restrictions.** Note that a BPO or CMA that estimates the "**value**" or "**worth**" of a parcel of, or interest in, real estate rather than the "probable sales or leasing price" *is deemed to be an **appraisal** and may NOT be prepared by a broker.* A BPO or CMA may NOT be called a "valuation" or "appraisal" and a broker may NOT knowingly prepare a BPO or CMA for any purpose in lieu of an appraisal when an appraisal is required by federal or state law. [G.S. §93A-83(f)]

- **Use of Income Analysis Methodology Now Permitted Where Appropriate.** The revised statutes eliminated the Appraisers Act restriction that a broker's CMA for actual or prospective clients and for compensation was permitted only if the analysis involved sales of similar recently sold properties in order to derive an indication of the probable sales price. A broker performing a BPO or CMA to determine an estimated *"probable selling price or leasing price"* is now permitted to utilize methods involving the analysis of income where appropriate (i.e., for income-producing properties) as well as the sales comparison method. [G.S. §93A-83(c)(3)] **Note:** As will be addressed in the coverage of Commission rules, the use of income analysis methodology (e.g., income capitalization or gross rent multiplier) is actually **required** by Commission rule where appropriate. [Rule 58A .2202(e)]

- A BPO or CMA must be *in writing* and must address those matters specifically required by the statute or Commission rule. [G.S. §93A-83(c)]

- The amended Real Estate License Law authorizes the Commission to adopt and implement rules not inconsistent with provisions of the statute. [G.S. §93A-83(d)]

Real Estate Commission's BPO/CMA Rules

Brokers must understand that *License Law and Commission rules must be read in conjunction with each other.* The rules expand on and supplement License Law, but cannot replace or contradict state law. Brokers who attempt to perform BPOs for a fee should seek special instruction in how to competently perform a BPO/CMA, as coverage of this topic in required prelicensing and postlicensing education courses is limited. A broker who attempts to perform this service should also have read and be familiar with License Law and Commission rule requirements, with which s/he must comply. The two additions to License Law and the changes in the Appraisal Act are reprinted at the end of this chapter. However, because the standards to which brokers will be held when performing BPOs for a fee are found in Rule 58A.2202, it is dissected in some depth.

The Commission's BPO/CMA rules are found in Section 58A.2200. The rules apply "... *to broker price opinions and comparative market analyses provided for a fee by a real estate broker whose license is not on provisional status* pursuant to Article 6, Chapter 93A of the General Statutes." Thus, whenever the term "broker" appears in this section, it should be read as meaning "**non-provisional broker**" (i.e., a broker whose license is not on provisional status).

21 NCAC 58A .2202 STANDARDS

This rule sets compliance standards for brokers when performing BPOs. Each subparagraph of the rule will be reprinted, followed by comments about the rule where warranted.

> (a) A broker performing a broker price opinion or comparative market analysis for a fee shall comply with all the requirements in G.S. 93A-83 and in this Rule.

Comment

As previously stated, when performing BPOs brokers must comply with **both** License Law **and** the rule currently under review, both of which describe the minimum standards for BPOs.

> (b) A broker shall only accept an assignment to provide a broker price opinion or comparative market analysis for a property if the broker has knowledge of the real estate market, direct access to real estate market sales or leasing data, and brokerage or appraisal experience in the subject property's geographic location.

Comment

A broker performing a BPO/CMA for a fee must have all of the following *in the area of the subject property's geographic location:* (1) knowledge of the real estate market (i.e., current market conditions); (2) direct access to current market sales or leasing data; and (3) actual brokerage or appraisal experience. The "subject property's geographic location" means *the **local** area where the subject property is located* – NOT anywhere in North Carolina or the general region where the property is located. This means, for example, that a broker whose only brokerage experience is in the Charlotte area may not accept an assignment to perform a BPO/CMA for a property in the Triangle area.

> (c) A broker shall not provide a broker price opinion or comparative market analysis for a property unless the broker can exercise objective, independent judgment free of any influence from any interested party in the performance of his or her analysis of the facts relevant to determination of a probable selling or leasing price.

Comment

The requirement for a broker to exercise objective, independent judgment free of any influence from any interested party applies to all BPO/CMA assignments performed for a fee, including those performed for an actual or prospective brokerage client. Under no circumstances should a broker's analysis be influenced in any manner by the client or by any other party. While the broker may for good reason (e.g., marketing or negotiating strategy) recommend to his or her client a listing or offer price or leasing price different from his or her estimate of probable selling or leasing price, the broker must not allow the estimate itself to be influenced by that client.

> (d) A broker shall not provide a broker price opinion or comparative market analysis for a property unless the broker has personally inspected the

exterior and interior of that property, provided, however, that an inspection
of the exterior or interior is not required if this is waived in writing by the
party for whom the opinion or analysis is being performed.

Comment

If the party for whom a BPO/CMA is being performed indicates in writing that the party does
not desire an exterior and/or interior inspection of the subject property, then the broker is not required
to perform such inspection; however, an inspection waiver should not be suggested by the broker.
*The Real Estate Commission strongly encourages brokers to perform both exterior and interior inspections
whenever feasible in order to produce a more accurate estimate of probable selling or leasing price, even if a
property inspection is waived by the client.*

(e) When developing a broker price opinion or comparative market analysis
for a property or interest therein, a broker shall utilize methodology such
as analysis of sales or income of sold or leased properties comparable to the
subject property or capitalization as is appropriate for the assignment and
type of subject property.

Comment

A broker is expected to utilize methodology when developing a BPO/CMA that is appropriate
for the particular assignment and type of subject property.

Residential 1-4 Unit Properties. An analysis of sold comparable properties utilizing the **"sales
comparison"** approach is clearly needed for all residential single-family subject properties for which
the assignment is to estimate a probable selling price. If the subject single-family residence being sold
is also a rental property, or if the assignment is only to estimate a probable leasing price for a residential
1-4 unit property, the broker must analyze rents of comparable properties (i.e., use the **"gross rent
multiplier"** method).

Income Properties. For most income-producing properties (other than residential 1-4 unit
properties), the broker who is asked to estimate a probable selling price must utilize both the **"sales
comparison"** approach and the **"income capitalization"** approach. Generally, for income properties,
the income capitalization approach is considered to be the more reliable method for estimating a probable selling price. If the broker is only requested to estimate a probable leasing price, then it may be
sufficient to only analyze income and expense data of comparable properties. The methodology used
will be dictated by the particular assignment and type of property.

NOTE ON COMPETENCE: While Article 6 and Section 2200 of the Commission's rules do not
specifically state that a BPO or CMA must be competently performed, underlying the provision of
all brokerage services are the License Law prohibitions against willful or negligent misrepresentation,
undisclosed conflict of interest, and being unworthy or incompetent to act as a broker. Thus, a broker
is expected to perform all BPOs and CMAs in a competent manner that produces a reasonably reliable
result without any undisclosed conflict of interest. If a broker is not properly qualified by way of education and/or experience to use certain methodology (e.g., income capitalization methodology) that may
be required to properly perform an assignment, then the broker is expected to decline the assignment.

(f) When analyzing sales of properties comparable to the property that is the
subject of a broker price opinion or comparative market analysis assignment,
a broker shall comply with the following standards:

(1) The broker shall select from reliable information sources a minimum
of three sold or lease comparable properties for use in his or her analysis

that are similar to the subject property with regard to characteristics such as property type, use, location, age, size, design, physical features, amenities, utility, property condition and conditions of sale. The comparable properties selected shall reflect the prevailing factors or market conditions influencing the sale or lease prices of similar properties in the subject property's local market.

(2) The broker shall make adjustments to the selling or leasing price of selected comparable properties for differences between the characteristics of the comparable properties and the subject property as necessary to produce a credible estimate of the probable selling or leasing price. Adjustments shall be considered for differences in property characteristics such as location, age, size, design, physical features, amenities, utility, condition, economic or functional obsolescence and conditions of sale. The amounts of adjustments shall reflect the values that the local real estate market places on the differences in the characteristics in question.

Comments

This rule sets forth the methodology a brokers is expected to employ when analyzing sales (or leases) of properties comparable to the subject property in connection with a BPO/CMA assignment. These basic procedures for analyzing sales of comparable properties when performing a BPO/CMA are far from new! On the contrary, they are the same as the procedures long required of real estate appraisers performing appraisal assignments which the Commission long ago applied to any CMA/BPO performed by a licensee, even if not performed for a fee.

Standard for Analyzing Comparables with BPOs/CMAs versus Appraisals. Although the procedures prescribed in these rules for selecting and analyzing sale or lease prices of comparables are the same as those used by professional appraisers, this does not mean the Real Estate Commission expects a broker performing a BPO/CMA to be as detailed and precise in his or her analysis as a real estate appraiser must be when performing an appraisal assignment. Not only does a licensed or certified real estate appraiser have far more education and experience in real property valuation than most real estate brokers, but a real estate appraiser also must adhere to very strict standards of practice which demand that the appraiser perform an appraisal assignment in an extremely detailed manner.

For these reasons, the Commission does not expect a real estate broker to be as detailed in following procedures for analyzing comparable properties when performing a BPO/CMA as the appraiser regulatory authorities expect of an appraiser when performing an appraisal, even though the basic procedures followed in both processes are the same. **Rather, a broker performing a BPO/CMA subject to License Law is expected to select comparables and make adjustments to the sale or lease prices of comparables in a manner that would be expected of a reasonably knowledgeable, experienced, and competent real estate non-provisional broker.**

(g) A broker price opinion or comparative market analysis provided to the party for whom the opinion or analysis is being performed shall address, in addition to matters required to be addressed by G.S. 93A-83 and other provisions of this Rule, the following items:
(1) a description of the comparable properties used in the analysis (including any unsold properties listed for sale or rent that were used as comparable properties);
(2) the adjustments made to the selling or leasing prices of comparable properties;

(3) local real estate market conditions;

(4) if the date on which the sale or lease of a comparable property became final is more than six months prior to the effective date of the broker price opinion or comparative market analysis, an explanation of why the comparable property was used in the analysis and a description of the market conditions affecting the comparable property at the time the sale or lease became final; and

(5) each method used in deriving the estimate of probable selling or leasing price.

(h) In connection with a broker price opinion or comparative market analysis, an estimated probable leasing price may be reported by a broker as a lease rate and an estimated probable selling or leasing price may be reported by a broker either as a single figure or as a price range. When the estimated probable selling or leasing price is stated as a price range and the higher figure exceeds the lower figure by more than 10 percent, the broker shall include an explanation of why the higher figure exceeds the lower figure by more than 10 percent.

Comment

The typical appraisal prepared by a licensed or certified appraiser cites a specific figure as the appraiser's conclusion as to the subject property's value. Such specificity is considered appropriate because of the thorough analysis done by an appraiser to support that specific conclusion. Since the estimate of "probable selling or leasing price" derived by a broker performing a BPO/CMA is not based on an analysis as thorough as an appraiser's analysis, the Commission allows brokers to report their estimate of probable selling or leasing price as a **price range** rather than a single figure, provided that the higher figure in the range does not exceed the lower figure by more than 10 percent. If the client wants a specific probable selling or leasing price rather than a range, the broker should comply with the client's request.

Record Retention

Commission Rule 58A.0108 requires licensees to retain records of all sales, rental, and other transactions conducted in a brokerage capacity, regardless of whether the transaction was completed or terminated prior to its successful conclusion, for three years after all funds held by the licensee in connection with the transaction have been disbursed to the proper party or parties or until the successful or unsuccessful conclusion of the transaction, *whichever occurs later.* To eliminate any doubts, the rule expressly requires retention of "… **broker price opinions and comparative market analyses prepared pursuant to G.S. 93A, Article 6, including any notes and supporting documentation** …." Recall as well that all such records shall be made available for inspection and reproduction by the Commission or its authorized representatives without prior notice.

BPOs/CMAs Performed for NO FEE

Any broker *(non-provisional or provisional)* has always been permitted to perform a BPO/CMA for any party when NO FEE is charged, and this continues to be true under the revised law and rules. Note that *the Commission does not consider compensation of a broker for general brokerage services under a brokerage agreement to constitute a "fee" under Article 6 of N.C.G.S. §93A.* "General brokerage services" means services provided under a brokerage agreement to property owners in connection with listing/

selling/leasing property and to prospective buyers or tenants in connection with purchasing or leasing a property. Such services may include the provision by a licensee of a CMA or BPO. Similarly, the possibility of entering into a brokerage agreement (and earning a brokerage fee) does not constitute a "fee" when a licensee performs a CMA/BPO for a *prospective* client without charging a fee for the CMA/BPO.

Brokers must remember, however, that the Commission expects every CMA/BPO performed by a licensee to be performed in a competent manner and without any undisclosed conflict of interest, even if no fee is received for the CMA/BPO. Thus, as a practical matter, a broker performing a CMA/BPO for no fee should still look to the standards described in Commission Rule 58A .2202 for guidance regarding the proper performance of a CMA/BPO.

REAL ESTATE BROKER'S DUTY REGARDING A CMA/BPO

A real estate broker's duty with regard to providing a CMA/BPO to a client (1) for a fee as a non-provisional broker or (2) for no fee for an actual or prospective client as either a non-provisional or provisional broker arises from two sources: the Real Estate License Law and the law of agency. More importantly, ***a broker's basic duty is the same regardless of whether the CMA/BPO is being provided for a fee or no fee or by a non-provisional broker or provisional broker.***

Duty under the Law of Agency

Owners of real estate usually need the expert advice and assistance of a real estate broker to determine an appropriate listing or leasing price for their property and to help them decide what selling or leasing price they are willing to accept. Similarly, prospective buyers or renters routinely need for a broker to advise them of the probable selling price or leasing price of a property they are considering in order to determine how much they are willing to pay. In addition, other parties may employ a non-provisional broker specifically to estimate the probable selling or leasing price for a variety of reasons.

*Under the law of agency, a real estate agent owes his or her client a duty to serve the client with **skill, care and diligen**ce and to disclose to the client any inf**ormation likely to influence the client's decision**.* This means that a real estate agent has a duty to provide competent expert advice and assistance, and this includes the duty to provide the client with reliable information relating to the probable selling or leasing price of a property being sold, leased, purchased or rented by the client or a property for which the client has contracted with the agent for a CMA/BPO. It necessarily follows that a real estate broker must possess the **competence** needed to properly perform a CMA/BPO for the type of property involved in a transaction involving the client.

Duty under the License Law

The License Law authorizes the Commission to take disciplinary action against a broker for "…making any willful or negligent misrepresentation or any willful or negligent omission of material fact…" [N.C.G.S. §93A-6(a)(1)] and for "…being unworthy or incompetent to act as a real estate broker in a manner as to endanger the interest of the public…" [N.C.G.S. §93A-6(a)(8)]. Thus, a real estate broker performing any brokerage service, including a CMA/BPO, must perform such service in a **competent** manner that avoids making a misrepresentation or omission of a material fact such as the probable selling or leasing price of a property in a transaction.

CMA/BPO of Residential 1-4 Unit Properties

Any licensed broker, even a newly licensed provisional broker, is expected to possess the minimum level of expertise needed to perform a CMA/BPO of a residential 1-4 unit property. For residential 1-4 unit properties, any real estate broker generally has ready access to market data on such sold properties and is expected to possess the expertise to analyze such sales data and perform an appropriate CMA/BPO for such properties.

CMA/BPO of Residential 5+ Unit Properties and Other Income-Producing Properties

For residential 5+ unit properties and commercial/industrial/agricultural and other income-producing properties (hereafter, simply "income producing properties), deriving any kind of reliable value estimate is a much more complex process than that used for a residential 1-4 unit property. The analysis in the case of income-producing properties relies heavily on the income approach (discussed previously in the "Approaches to Value" section of this chapter), not just a simple analysis of comparable sales or use of the relatively simple gross rent multiplier method. A non-provisional broker is not, simply by virtue of his/her status as a non-provisional broker, expected by the Commission to possess the minimum competence necessary to perform a BPO/CMA related to an income-producing property. Brokers performing a CMA/BPO on an income-producing property must possess substantial education and experience dealing with the particular type of property in question to perform a CMA/BPO in a competent manner.

A broker should not accept a listing, agree to serve as a buyer's agent, or agree to perform a BPO/CMA for a property other than a residential 1-4 unit property unless the broker possesses the competence necessary to properly perform a CMA/BPO for the client, or, when acting as a listing agent or buyer's agent, the broker arranges for a qualified person to perform the CMA or BPO. A qualified person might be a commercial broker experienced in working with the type of property in question or a certified general appraiser. If hiring a qualified person to perform a CMA/BPO on an income-producing property is going to cost the client more than the client would have had to pay had the broker been fully qualified to undertake the representation, then the broker should disclose that cost to the client upfront and obtain his/her consent or should simply not accept the work assignment.

PERFORMING a BPO or CMA

As discussed earlier, a broker price opinion (BPO) or comparative market analysis (CMA) is clearly distinguished from an "appraisal" under the North Carolina Real Estate License Law and North Carolina Appraisers Act and there are significant differences between a BPO/CMA and an appraisal. Even so, there are more similarities than differences. Both are based on exactly the same valuation concepts and principles and both involve the use of virtually identical methodology in deriving their estimates of value (appraisal) or probable selling or leasing price (BPO/CMA). The differences between the two processes primarily involve the thoroughness and level of detail and precision employed in the process of deriving and reporting their respective estimates. A broker who intends to perform BPO/CMAs must thoroughly understand the valuation concepts and methodology addressed under the "Basic Valuation Concepts" and "Approaches to Value" sections of this chapter.

The similarities in the two processes also mean that it is unnecessary to repeat here the explanations regarding methodology covered in the section on "Approaches to Value." When reading the material in this section about the Sales Comparison Approach, Gross Rent Multiplier Approach and

Income Capitalization Approach, the reader should also refer to the detailed coverage of these topics under "Approaches to Value."

The BPO/CMA Process

This section summarizes the steps in the BPO/CMA process for BPOs/CMAs performed by non-provisional brokers for a fee under Article 6 of N.C.G.S., Chapter 93A.

Assuring the Broker is Qualified

When a broker is approached about performing a BPO/CMA *for a fee*, the broker must first make certain he/she is qualified to perform the assignment.

(1) The broker must have a "non-provisional" license (i.e., a license that is NOT on "provisional" status) that is in good standing (currently renewed) and on "active" status. [N.C.G.S. §93A-83(a)]

(2) The broker must determine if he/she possesses the knowledge and experience (i.e., **competence**) necessary to perform the assignment. Any non-provisional broker is expected to possess the minimum competence necessary to perform a BPO/CMA related to a **residential 1-4 unit property** using the sales comparison and/or gross rent multiplier approaches. This is NOT the case with a BPO/CMA on a **residential 5-or-more-unit property** or a **commercial/industrial/agricultural or other income-producing property;** if requested to perform a BPO/CMA on such a property, the broker must ensure, prior to accepting the assignment, that he/she possess the necessary education and experience in dealing with the specific type of property in question to competently perform the BPO/CMA, or to make arrangements satisfactory to the client for a qualified person to perform the BPO/CMA. A broker who performs a BPO/CMA incompetently may be subject to disciplinary action. [N.C.G.S. §93A-6(a)(8)]

(3) The broker must have all of the following *in the area of the subject property's geographic location (i.e., the subject property's* **local area***):* (A) knowledge of the real estate market (i.e., current market conditions); (B) direct access to current market sales or leasing data; and (C) actual brokerage or appraisal experience. [Commission Rule 21 NCAC 58A.2202(b)]

(4) The broker must assure that he or she discloses to the client any existing or contemplated conflict of interest. [N.C.G.S. §93A-83(c)(5)]

Identifying the Assignment

A broker must clearly identify the property (or property interest) to be priced and the purpose and scope of the assignment, including any assumptions or limiting conditions. The assignment must be one that is permissible under the law, which primarily means that the BPO/CMA must NOT be for an existing or potential lienholder who intends to use the BPO/CMA as a basis for determining the property's value for a mortgage loan origination, including first and second mortgages, refinances or equity lines of credit. [N.C.G.S. §93A-83]

Collecting Data on Subject and Local Market

A broker performing a BPO/CMA should already have general data on local market conditions and trends. He/she will collect data on the subject property. The data routinely compiled for listing purposes should be sufficient and readily available if the subject property is listed.

Inspecting the Subject Property. The Commission's rules require a broker to personally inspect the exterior and interior of the subject property unless such inspections are specifically waived in writing by the party for whom the BPO/CMA is being performed. [21 NCAC 58A.2202(d)] The Commission discourages brokers from suggesting to a client that inspection of the subject property be waived. It is extremely difficult to obtain a true understanding of a property's condition without actually inspecting the property. Personal inspection of the subject property by the broker greatly increases the likelihood of an accurate estimate of probable selling or leasing price.

Analysis Using the Sales Comparison Approach

For **any type of property** for which the broker is estimating a "probable selling price," the broker will likely utilize the Sales Comparison Approach as described in detail earlier in this chapter and summarized briefly below.

Selecting Comparables. Remember that *the most important part of the sales comparison approach is selecting good comparables.* The more similar the comparables are to the subject property and the fewer adjustments that have to be made for differences, the more accurate the indication of probable selling price will be. A minimum of three comparables is required by Commission Rule 21 NCAC 58A.2202(f), but more are encouraged, especially if most of the comparables have substantial differences in characteristics as compared to the subject property. A broker might be wise to consider this guideline: If the comparables are very good, then as few as three comparables may be sufficient, but if the comparables are not very good, more comparables should be used.

Making Adjustments to Sale Prices of Comparables. After carefully selecting appropriate comparables, the broker should compare each comparable to the subject property and make appropriate adjustments to the sale prices of the comparables for *significant* differences between the subject and comparable properties. The factors that are to be considered when making adjustments are exactly the same as those used by appraisers when applying the sales comparison approach discussed earlier. As noted earlier in the coverage of Commission rules on BPOs/CMAs, real estate brokers are not expected to be nearly as detailed and precise in making adjustments to the sale prices of comparables as an appraiser would be when performing a formal appraisal. Nevertheless, appropriate adjustments should be made for differences that might **significantly** impact the estimate of probable selling price.

The most difficult aspect of making adjustments is determining the appropriate amount of adjustment to make for the various significant differences between the subject and comparable properties. Experienced real estate brokers should have acquired considerable knowledge as to appropriate adjustments and should not have great difficulty in determining appropriate amounts. On the other hand, inexperienced brokers should consult with their broker-in-charge, other experienced brokers and/or appraisers for information on appropriate adjustments. Some firms will have guidelines they have developed for use by their affiliated brokers when performing CMAs/BPOs. The most important point is that there should be a reasonable basis for each adjustment.

Reconciling Indications of Value from Comparables. If the broker is providing a single figure as the estimate of probable selling price based on the sales comparison approach, it is important to remember all the indications of value usually do not warrant equal weight. *Generally, greater weight should be given to the adjusted sale price of the comparable that required the fewest adjustments and the smallest adjustments, and vice-versa.*

Analysis Using the Gross Rent Multiplier Approach

A BPO/CMA on a **residential 1-4 unit** *rental* **property** for the purpose of estimating probable selling price will typically also require the use of the gross rent multiplier approach described in the "Approaches to Value" section of this chapter in addition to the use of the sales comparison approach. As with the sales comparison approach, the broker must select recently sold properties that are very similar to the subject property to use as comparables. Selection will generally consider the same factors as those used in the sales comparison approach. The broker must also obtain the "gross annual rent" income for each comparable in order to determine a relationship between the gross rent and sale price for each comparable. This is accomplished by *dividing the sale price of each comparable by its amount of gross annual rent to determine a **gross rent multiplier.***

When there are significant differences in characteristics and market factors between a comparable and the subject property, the broker may need to make adjustments to the comparable's sale price, gross rent, or both, as may be appropriate in the particular situation. As with the sales comparison approach, selection of good comparables will minimize the need for making adjustments and improve the quality of the estimate of probable selling price.

Once the broker knows the gross rent multipliers for each comparable, he/she must select an appropriate gross rent multiplier to apply to the subject property. This process is referred to as "extracting a gross rent multiplier from the market." *The broker will then multiply the projected gross rent for the subject property by the gross rent multiplier extracted from the comparable sales to derive the estimate of probable selling price for the subject property.* The estimate derived via the gross rent multiplier approach will then be considered along with the estimate derived via the sales comparison approach to formulate the broker's estimate of probable selling price.

Analysis Using the Income Capitalization Approach

A BPO/CMA on **any income-producing property other than a residential 1-4 unit property** will typically require the use of the income capitalization approach (normally the "direct capitalization" method) to derive an estimate of probable selling price. Such a BPO/CMA may also require use of the sales comparison approach (unless not desired by the client). The reader is referred to the "Approaches to Value" section of this chapter for an explanation and example of deriving a value estimate using the direct capitalization method.

Once again, the broker's initial step will be to identify recently sold comparable properties to use in his/her analysis. *The same principles and considerations apply to the selection of comparables for income properties as residential 1-4 unit properties.* The more similar the comparables are to the subject property, the fewer the adjustments that will be necessary to the comparables' sale prices and the more accurate the estimate of probable selling price will be. Adjustments to the sale prices of the comparables will be made in the same manner as is done when using the sales comparison approach.

In addition to determining an **adjusted sale price**, the broker must also obtain actual income and expense data for each comparable that will enable the broker to determine the amount of annual **net operating income**. *The adjusted sale price of each comparable is then divided by the annual net operating income to derive the **capitalization rate** for each comparable.* Using the capitalization rates derived for the various comparables, the broker must use his/her best judgment to determine an appropriate capitalization rate to apply to the subject property to derive an estimate of probable selling price.

This process is referred to as *"extracting a capitalization rate from the market."* After deciding on an appropriate capitalization rate, *the projected net operating income of the subject property is divided by the extracted capitalization rate to derive an estimate of probable selling price for the subject property.* This estimate is then considered along with any estimate derived using the sales comparison approach to formulate an appropriate probable selling price. Most frequently, the estimate derived via the income capitalization approach for income-producing properties is given greater weight than the estimate derived by the sales comparison approach.

Analysis Relating to Estimating a Probable Leasing Price (Lease Rate)

Another common type of BPO/CMA assignment involves income analysis to estimate the probable leasing price (or lease rate or rental amount) for a subject income-producing property rather than to estimate probable selling price. This is a more limited analysis than estimating probable selling price, but utilizes much of the same methodology. In this situation, the subject property owner is not looking to sell the property, but only to establish an appropriate lease or rental rate.

The broker will identify the characteristics of the subject property and then identify comparable income-producing properties just as with the approaches previously described, except that in this case the comparables do NOT have to be recently sold. The broker must ascertain the lease or rental rates for each comparable and adjust those if necessary for differences in characteristics between the comparables and the subject property. If this process is being used to estimate a probable lease rate for a property that is only rented as a whole (e.g., a small free-standing retail store) and only has a single lease rate, then the process is relatively simple. On the other hand, when the subject and comparables are multi-unit buildings with different lease rates for various units (e.g., an apartment complex may have apartments of three or four different sizes/designs, each of which rents for a different amount), then the process can be very complicated.

Once the broker has considered all factors, he/she will formulate an estimate of an appropriate probable lease rate (or multiple rates) for the subject property.

Reporting Probable Selling/Leasing Price as a "Range"

Recognizing the former practice of brokers reporting their sale/lease price estimate as a range in value, the rules allow a broker some flexibility in reporting his or her estimate. First, as to reporting a probable leasing price, the rule allows use of the term *"lease rate."* Secondly, the broker's estimate of probable selling price or leasing price (lease rate) may be reported either as a single figure or as a **price range**. When the estimate states a price range and the higher figure exceeds the lower figure by more than ten percent (10%), the broker shall include an explanation as to why the variance is more than 10 percent. [See 21 NCAC 58A.2202(h)]

The BPO/CMA Report

N.C.G.S. §93A-83(c) specifically prescribes certain things that must be addressed in or attached to the written BPO/CMA report. Additionally, Commission Rule 21 NCAC 58A.2202(g) addresses the BPO/CMA report. *The BPO/CMA report must be **in writing** and include or attach the following:*

(1) A brief description of the subject property. [Note that BPO/CMA forms required by many clients may call for a substantial amount of information on the subject property rather than a "brief description." Generally the information in a typical listing will be sufficient except for any required description of the property's condition.]

(2) A description of the property interest to be priced. [Example: Fee simple.]

(3) A statement of the intended purpose of the BPO/CMA and any assumptions or limiting conditions related to the assignment.

(4) A copy of the assignment request (or engagement letter or agreement).

(5) A disclosure by the broker of any existing or contemplated interest of the broker issuing the BPO/CMA, including the possibility of representing the landlord, tenant, seller or buyer.

(6) A description of local market conditions and the basis of reasoning used to reach the price estimate, including a description of:
    a.   each method used in deriving the estimate;
    b.   the comparable properties used in the analysis (including any unsold properties listed for sale or rent that were used as comparables); and
    c.   the adjustments made to the selling or leasing prices of comparables.

(7) The effective date of the BPO/CMA.

(8) The name, license number and signature of the broker performing the BPO/CMA, the name of the brokerage firm for which the broker is acting, and the broker's signature date.

(9) The following disclaimer statement:

> "This opinion is not an appraisal of the market value of the property, and may not be used in lieu of an appraisal. If an appraisal is desired, the services of a licensed or certified appraiser shall be obtained. This opinion may not be used by any party as the primary basis to determine the value of a parcel of or interest in real property for a mortgage loan origination, including first and second mortgages, refinances, or equity lines of credit."

      Comments on "Assumptions and Limiting Conditions." The law requires that a broker's BPO/CMA report include, in addition to the other disclosures, disclaimers, and descriptions of purpose of assignment and methods utilized that are required by the law or Commission rules, "…any assumptions or limiting conditions."

      Note that the assumptions and limiting conditions addressed may be either matters intended to clarify what is required or not required from the **client's** perspective or to clarify issues related to the estimate of probable selling price or other matters from the **broker's** perspective. For example, if the client has indicated that the broker is not required to perform an interior inspection of the subject property, then this waiver of the broker's obligation to perform such an inspection should be clearly stated in the report. The broker should always indicate in the report whether exterior and interior inspections were performed. Another example might be if the broker wants to place any limitation on statements he or she has included in the report about adverse conditions affecting the subject property (such as presence of hazardous wastes, lead-based paint, etc. or whether the property is located in a designated flood hazard area), such limitation should be included. Still another example might be a statement that the broker's report assumes the validity of the subject property owner's legal interest described in the assignment. *It is in a broker's best interest to describe in the report any limiting condition regarding his or her performance of the assignment.*

      Form Reports. The Real Estate Commission does not require nor recommend a particular form for use in preparing BPO/CMA reports. Many clients will require the broker to provide the BPO/CMA report on a form prescribed by the client. When that is the case, the broker should use the client's form, but the broker must still assure that the report addresses all the matters noted above and required by the License Law and Commission rules. If there is no designated place on the form for a particular matter the broker is required to address, the broker should address the matter in the "Comments" section or in an attachment. If the client does not provide a form, then the broker should simply prepare a report of his/her own design that addresses all required matters in a logical manner.

Records. Brokers should remember the requirement of Commission Rule 21 NCAC 58A.0108 to retain for three years from the date of the report a copy of the report and any notes and supporting documentation.

Reminder about CMAs/BPOs Provided for No Fee

The above section on performing a BPO/CMA focuses on the requirements under the BPO/CMA law and rules for assignments performed **for a fee** by a **non-provisional broker**. The Commission expects every CMA/BPO to be performed in a competent manner, **even if no fee is received for the CMA/BPO**. Thus, as a practical matter, a licensee performing a CMA/BPO for no fee should abide by the standards described in Commission Rule 58A .2202 and discussed above, especially those relating to local market knowledge/experience, the necessity for objective independent judgment, personal inspection of the subject property, and the use of the sales comparison, gross rent multiplier, and income capitalization approaches in deriving an estimate of probable selling/leasing price.

Text of Real Estate License Law Added Effective October 1, 2012

Article 6
Broker Price Opinions and Comparative Market Analyses.

§ 93A-82. Definitions.

As used in this Article, the terms "broker price opinion" and "comparative market analysis" mean an estimate prepared by a licensed real estate broker that details the probable selling price or leasing price of a particular parcel of or interest in property and provides a varying level of detail about the property's condition, market, and neighborhood, and information on comparable properties, but does not include an automated valuation model.

§ 93A-83. Broker price opinions and comparative market analyses for a fee.

(a) Authorized. – A person licensed under this Chapter, other than a provisional broker, may prepare a broker price opinion or comparative market analysis and charge and collect a fee for the opinion if:

    (1) The license of that licensee is active and in good standing; and

    (2) The broker price opinion or comparative market analysis meets the requirements of subsection (c) of this section.

    (3) The requirements of this Article shall not apply to any broker price opinion or comparative market analysis performed by a licensee for no fee or consideration.

(b) For Whom Opinion May Be Prepared. – Notwithstanding any provision to the contrary, a person licensed under this Chapter may prepare a broker price opinion or comparative market analysis for any of the following:

    (1) An existing or potential seller of a parcel of real property.

    (2) An existing or potential buyer of a parcel of real property.

    (3) An existing or potential lessor of a parcel of or interest in real property.

    (4) An existing or potential lessee of a parcel of or interest in real property.

    (5) A third party making decisions or performing due diligence related to the potential listing, offering, sale, option, lease, or acquisition price of a parcel of or interest in real property.

    (6) An existing or potential lienholder or other third party for any purpose other than as the basis to determine the value of a parcel of or interest in property, for a mortgage loan origination, including first and second mortgages, refinances, or equity lines of credit.

    (7) The provisions of this subsection do not preclude the preparation of a broker price opinion or

comparative market analysis to be used in conjunction with or in addition to an appraisal.

(c) Required Contents of a Broker Price Opinion or Comparative Market Analysis. – A broker price opinion or comparative market analysis shall be in writing and conform to the standards provided in this Article that shall include, but are not limited to, the following:

(1) A statement of the intended purpose of the broker price opinion or comparative market analysis.

(2) A brief description of the subject property and property interest to be priced.

(3) The basis of reasoning used to reach the conclusion of the price, including the applicable market data or capitalization computation.

(4) Any assumptions or limiting conditions.

(5) A disclosure of any existing or contemplated interest of the broker issuing the broker price opinion, including the possibility of representing the landlord/tenant or seller/buyer.

(6) The effective date of the broker price opinion.

(7) The name and signature of the broker issuing the broker price opinion and broker license number.

(8) The name of the real estate brokerage firm for which the broker is acting.

(9) The signature date.

(10) A disclaimer stating that "This opinion is not an appraisal of the market value of the property, and may not be used in lieu of an appraisal. If an appraisal is desired, the services of a licensed or certified appraiser shall be obtained. This opinion may not be used by any party as the primary basis to determine the value of a parcel of or interest in real property for a mortgage loan origination, including first and second mortgages, refinances, or equity lines of credit."

(11) A copy of the assignment request for the broker price opinion or comparative market analysis.

(d) Rules. – The North Carolina Real Estate Commission shall have the power to adopt rules that are not inconsistent with the provisions in this Article.

(e) Additional Requirements for Electronic or Form Submission. – In addition to the requirement of subsection (c) of this section, if a broker price opinion is submitted electronically or on a form supplied by the requesting party, the following provisions apply:

(1) A signature required by subdivision (7) of subsection (c) of this section may be an electronic signature, as defined in G.S. 47-16.2.

(2) A signature required by subdivision (7) of subsection (c) of this section and the disclaimer required by subdivision (10) of subsection (c) of this section may be transmitted in a separate attachment if the electronic format or form supplied by the requesting party does not allow additional comments to be written by the licensee. The electronic format or form supplied by the requesting party shall do the following:

a. Reference the existence of a separate attachment.

b. Include a statement that the broker price opinion or comparative market analysis is not complete without the attachment.

(f) Restrictions. – Notwithstanding any provisions to the contrary, a person licensed pursuant to this Chapter may not knowingly prepare a broker price opinion or comparative market analysis for any purpose in lieu of an appraisal when an appraisal is required by federal or State law. A broker price opinion or comparative market analysis that estimates the value of or worth a parcel of or interest in real estate rather than sales or leasing price shall be deemed to be an appraisal and may not be prepared by a licensed broker under the authority of this Article, but may only be prepared by a duly licensed or certified appraiser, and shall meet the regulations adopted by the North Carolina Appraisal Board. A broker price opinion or comparative market analysis shall not under any circumstances be referred to as a valuation or appraisal.

(g) No Report of Predetermined Result. – A broker price opinion or comparative market analysis shall not include the reporting of a predetermined result.

Appraisers Act for BPOs/CMAs Effective October 1, 2012

§ 93E-1-3(c) was revised as follows:

Nothing in this Chapter shall preclude a real estate broker licensed under Chapter 93A of the General Statutes from performing a broker price opinion or comparative market analysis as defined in G.S. 93E-1-4, provided the person does not represent himself or herself as being a registered trainee or a licensed or certified real estate appraiser, and provided they follow the standards set forth in Article 6 of Chapter 93A.

§ 93E-1-3(f)(6) was revised by adding the following sentence:

The provisions of this Chapter shall not apply to certified real estate appraisers who perform a broker price opinion or comparative market analysis pursuant to G.S. 93E-1-3(c), so long as the appraiser is licensed as a real estate broker by the North Carolina Real Estate Commission and does not refer to himself or herself as an appraiser in the broker price opinion or comparative market analysis.

§ 93E-1-4(7c) – The definition of "comparative market analysis" in the statute was revised to be exactly the same as the definition in G.S. 93A-82 of the Real Estate License Law.

§ 93E-1-12 was revised by adding the following provision:

(e) No appraiser shall be disciplined for completing an appraisal that includes a reduced scope of work or reporting level as long as it is appropriate for the intended use and is performed in accordance with the Uniform Standards of Professional Practice.

BPO/CMA Sales Comparison Analysis Illustration

This illustration is provided to enhance understanding of a broker price opinion (BPO)/comparative market analysis (CMA) sales comparison approach analysis for a single-family house. The adjustment chart appears on the facing page. Presented below is basic information about the assignment, the subject property, local market conditions and the methodology used by the broker, as well as explanatory comments about the adjustments made by the broker to the sale prices of comparable properties.

Assignment: A property owner is considering whether to list her house for sale and engages the services of a non-provisional broker to perform a CMA *for a fee* on her single-family house located at 123 Apple Lane, Anywhere, NC. Since the CMA is being performed for a fee, it will be performed by the broker in accordance with Article 6 of the Real Estate License Law (Chapter 93A of the N.C. General Statutes) and Section 2200 of the Real Estate Commission's Rules (21 NCAC 58A.2200).

Subject Property Characteristics: The subject property is a 2200 square foot, traditional 2-story single-family house located in a medium-size suburban subdivision with a community pool and common area. The house is 15 years old, has 3 bedrooms, 2.5 baths, is of typical design, has average appeal and is in average condition for its age. The house has an attached 2-car garage and an average-size deck.

Local Market Conditions: Following a decline in house values due to the general market decline during the 2007-11 period, values have generally been stable during 2012. Sales of houses in or pending foreclosure have had some impact on keeping prices from rising.

Methodology: Using the sales comparison approach, the broker in this example identified a number of generally similar properties in the area that have sold within the past year and chose five comparable properties for further analysis. The broker's adjustments to the sale prices of the five chosen comparables and estimates of the subject's probable selling price are shown in the chart on the facing page and discussed below.

Comments on Selected Adjustments and Estimated Price Range

General: Figures used for adjustments were derived by market analysis. $48/SF used for adjustments due to differences in heated living area and $35/SF used for adjustments due to differences in deck size. No adjustments were made to any comps for date of sale due to stable market prices for the past year.

Comp #1: Highly similar to subject. Only two significant adjustments were made for house size (square footage) difference and the below average condition of the comp.

Comp #2: Adjustments were made for comp's larger size, bonus room, above average design/appeal, excellent condition and backyard fence. No adjustment was made for the comp's lack of community pool because the estimated adjustment amount of $1,000 was not considered that "significant."

Comp #3: Substantial adjustments were made for comp's pricier subdivision, superior design/appeal, excellent condition w/ kitchen and hardwood floor upgrades, 300 additional heated square footage and larger deck (by 60 SF).

Comp #4: Major adjustments were made for comp's location on a busy road and no garage, and significant adjustments were made for comp's fireplace and for comp having only 2 baths versus subject's 2.5 baths. Neither the $960 adjustment for the comp's slightly less square footage nor the $1,000 adjustment for no community pool were, *standing alone*, considered sufficient to necessitate an adjustment; however, because together they amount to a more significant adjustment of $1,960, adjustments for both were made.

Comp #5: Comp is highly similar to subject, but in view of other normal sales of comps in the area (i.e., without adverse conditions of sale), a major adjustment was warranted due to Comp #5's short sale. A square footage adjustment for difference in heated living area was also made.

Estimated Probable Selling Price Range for Subject: $232,400 - $244,000. High estimate exceeds low estimate by 5% ($11,600 ÷ $232,400), which is within the 10% allowed by Commission rule without the broker providing an explanation. Comp #1 is the most similar comp with the least amount of adjustment to its sale price and thus is likely the most reliable estimate of probable selling price indicated by the five comps.

BPO/CMA Sales Comparison Analysis Adjustments Example

Item	Subject	Comparable Sale #1 111 Peach		Comparable Sale #2 222 Plum		Comparable Sale #3 333 Cherry		Comparable Sale #4 444 Blueberry		Comparable Sale #5 555 Orange	
Address	123 Apple										
Proximity		2 blocks		0.2 miles		2 miles		0.5 miles		3 blocks	
Sales Price	$ N/A	$232,000		$257,000		$282,000		$202,000		$210,000	
Value Adjustment	Description	Description	+/- $ Adjust	Description	+/- $ Adjust	Description	+/- $ Adjust	Description	+/- $ Adjust	Description	+/- $ Adjust
Condition of sale	Normal	Normal	None	Normal	None	Normal	None	Normal	None	Short Sale	+ 20,000
Date of Sale	N/A	8/15/2012		5/6/2012		9/3/2012		2/20/2012		9/8/2012	
Location (Subdivision (SD))	Same SD	Same SD		Sim SD		Superior SD	- 10,000	No SD/Busy Rd	+ 15,000	Same SD	
Size & Features	0.5 acre	Similar		Similar		Similar		Similar		Similar	
Design & Appeal	2 Story/Average	Similar		Sim/Above avg	- 2,000	Sim/Above avg	- 2,000	Similar		Similar	
Actual Age	15 years	15 years		12 years		14 years		16 years		15 years	
Condition	Average	Below Avg	+ 4,000	Excellent	- 5,000	Excellent	- 7,500	Similar		Similar	
Room Count	8 - 3BR/2.5BA	8 - 3BR/2.5BA		9 - 3BR/2.5BA BONUS	- 2,000	9 - 3BR/2.5BA BONUS	- 2,000	8 - 3BR/2BA	+ 3,000	8 - 3BR/2.5BA	
Heated Living Area	2200 sq.ft.	2250 sq.ft.	- 2,400	2400 sq.ft.	- 9,600	2500 sq.ft.	- 14,400	2180 sq.ft.	+ 960	2150 sq.ft.	+ 2,400
Below Grade Area	None	Same		Same		Same		Same		Same	
Functional Utility	Good	Similar		Similar		Similar		Similar		Similar	
Garage/Carport	2-Car Garage	Same		Same		Same		None	+ 15,000	Same	
Porch/Patio/Deck Fence/Fireplace	Deck	Same		Deck/Fence	- 2,500	Larger Deck	- 2,100	Deck/Fireplace	- 2,500	Same	
Amenities	Community Pool	Same		None		Same		None	+ 1,000	Same	
Net Adj.		1 %		8 %		13 %		16 %		11 %	
Gross Adjustments		+$4,000 / - $2,400	+ $ 1,600	+ $ none / - $ 21,100	- $ 21,100	+ $ none / - $ 38,000	- $ 38,000	+ $ 34,960 / - $ 2,500	+ $ 32,460	+ $ 22,400 / - $ none	+ $ 22,400
Adjusted Sale Price of Comparables		$233,600		$235,900		$244,000		$234,460		$232,400	

Estimated Probable Selling Price Range: Low: $ 232,400   High: $ 244,000   High estimate exceeds low estimate by ___5___ %.

Endnotes

1. North Carolina Appraisers Act, N.C. Gen. Stat. §93E-1-2.1.

2. N.C. Gen. Stat. §93E-2-1.

3. Uniform Standards of Professional Appraisal Practice (USPAP) "Glossary," 2008, issued by the Appraisal Standards Board of The Appraisal Foundation.

16 | LANDLORD AND TENANT

This chapter focuses primarily on *residential* landlord-tenant law, with commercial leasing covered in Chapter 19. While residential and nonresidential tenancies share the same common-law roots, numerous state and federal laws enacted to protect the rights of residential tenants regulate residential leasing. Although the rental of residential property remains the product of contract and property law, statutes now supplement, if not supersede, these common-law principles.

A broker regularly engaged in leasing residential property should read and be familiar with the North Carolina Residential Rental Agreement Act and other key laws protecting North Carolina residential tenants.

Landlord- Tenant Terms and Theories

A **landlord** is an owner of real property, who agrees to rent all or part of the property to a **tenant**. The relationship of landlord and tenant is created by a rental agreement or lease. A lease is: 1) a contract between landlord ("**lessor**") and tenant ("**lessee**") that 2) conveys a nonfreehold estate in real property. The tenant receives a right to legal possession in exchange for paying rent to the lessor. In addition to the central matters of possession and rent, a lease may contain other legally binding promises made by the lessor and lessee to each other. Because a lease is both a conveyance and a contract, it gives rise to two sets of rights and duties between the parties:

1) those arising because of traditional property law rules, i.e., the "**privity of estate,**" and
2) those arising because of the express contractual promises of the lease, i.e., the "**privity of contract.**"

The rental of residential dwelling units also is subject to numerous state and federal laws enacted to protect the rights of residential tenants. *When a common-law property principle or a contract provision conflicts with state or federal law, the law governs and determines a residential tenant's rights and protections.*

LAWS PROTECTING RESIDENTIAL TENANTS

North Carolina legislation enacted for the protection of residential tenants includes the Acts listed on the following page.

- Residential Rental Agreements Act[1]
- Act Prohibiting Retaliatory Eviction[2]
- Tenant Security Deposit Act[3]
- Act Prohibiting Self-Help Eviction[4]
- Act Prohibiting Discrimination Against Tenants[5]
- Laws Allowing Early Termination of Lease.[6]
- Laws Protecting Victims of Domestic Violence, Sexual Assault or Stalking[7]
- Unfair and Deceptive Practices Act[8]

This chapter contains a summary of a landlord's duties under key statutes. A broker-property manager is strongly advised to go beyond the summary of these statutes and to read and understand all statutory requirements in their entirety. Chief among the federal laws protecting residential tenants is the **Fair Housing Act of 1968,** as amended.[9] (Fair housing and its prohibitions against discrimination are discussed in Chapter 18.) Military service members who are residential tenants receive certain protections under the federal Servicemembers Civil Relief Act (SCRA),[10] as well as under state law. Federal laws and regulations provide additional protections to tenants in government-subsidized housing.[11]

RESIDENTIAL RENTAL AGREEMENTS ACT

The **Residential Rental Agreements Act** (the "Act") is the primary state legislation enacted for the protection of residential tenants.[12] The Act's central purpose is to require the rental of only "habitable" residential rental units. It implements this purpose by imposing detailed requirements on landlords and creating, in essence, a statutory "warranty of habitability." These minimum landlord obligations promote public policy in seeking to ensure that all residential rental units are safe and habitable. All jurisdictions in the United States have adopted similar legislation.

The Act "determines the rights, obligations, and remedies under a rental agreement for a dwelling unit" located in North Carolina.[13] The term "dwelling unit" includes not only structures but also mobile homes and mobile home spaces and the "grounds, areas, and facilities normally held out for the use of residential tenants."[14]

The Act does not apply to commercial and industrial rentals, nor does it apply to transient occupancy in a motel, hotel, or similar lodging nor any dwelling furnished rent free. Simply labeling an apartment building a "hotel" will not, however, avoid application of the Act.

Example: A building called the "Downtowner Hotel" is the primary residence of many of its occupants. Some occupants live in the building for long periods of time. Each unit has a living area and kitchen. The occupants are residential tenants protected by the Act. The owner is in reality a residential landlord. The building is not a true "hotel" and is not exempt from the Act.[15]

Waiver of the Act is Prohibited

The statutory duty placed on the landlord cannot be waived or altered by lease provision or other arrangement between landlord and tenant.

Example: A landlord rents a deteriorating home to a tenant under a lease that provides: "Tenant hereby agrees to accept the leased home *as is*. Landlord is not responsible for the condition of the heating unit, electrical wiring, or plumbing. Tenant hereby agrees to be solely responsible for the habitability of the leased home and hereby waives any legal rights the tenant might have against the landlord relating to the habitability of the home." The tenant cannot waive his legal rights against the landlord under the Act. The "as is" provision is void and unenforceable.[16]

The Act does allow a very limited and rarely used "fix-up" exception. N.C. General Statute §42-42(b) states in part: "... the landlord and tenant are not prohibited from making a subsequent written contract wherein the tenant agrees to perform specified work on the premises, provided that said contract is supported by adequate consideration other than the letting of the premises and is not made with the purpose or effect of evading the landlord's obligations under this Article." Thus, *a tenant can contractually agree to make certain repairs to the premises.* The tenant must be paid for making the repairs, and the tenant is obligated to make the repairs as agreed.

Example: A landlord rents an apartment to a tenant for $600/month in an area with comparable rental rates. In a separate agreement, the landlord agrees to give the tenant a $300/month discount for the first five months of the lease if the tenant, a licensed plumber, repairs and remodels the two bathrooms in the apartment. Assuming that this agreement has not been made to evade the landlord's obligations under the Act, it is valid.

"Mutuality of Obligations"

The Act specifies that obligations of a landlord and tenant under the rental agreement and state laws are "mutually dependent." Thus, a breach of a primary obligation under the Act or rental agreement by the landlord excuses continued performance by the tenant.

Early landlord-tenant law significantly favored the landlord in many ways, including subjecting residential tenants to the doctrine of *caveat emptor.* The Act now supersedes the prior one-sided law in key areas, including placing a duty on the landlord to provide a residential tenant with a "habitable" place to live.[17]

Tenant's Statutory Duties

The Act is a two-way street that places specific obligations and duties on tenants as well as on landlords. In terms of a tenant's duties, however, the Act has had little impact because lease forms historically placed numerous legal obligations on a tenant. Under the Act a tenant must:
- keep the leased premises as clean and safe as conditions permit and cause no unsafe or unsanitary conditions in the common areas;
- properly dispose of ashes, rubbish, garbage, and other waste;
- keep plumbing fixtures as clean as their condition permits;
- not deliberately or negligently destroy, deface, damage, or remove any part of the premises;
- comply with obligations imposed by current building and housing codes;
- be responsible for all damage to the unit other than deterioration caused by ordinary

wear and tear, acts of the landlord or his agent, defective products supplied or repairs authorized by the landlord, acts of third parties not invitees of the tenant, or natural forces; and

- share duties with the landlord concerning the operation of smoke detectors and carbon monoxide alarms.[18]

Except in emergency situations, a landlord must notify a tenant in writing of any breaches of the above statutory obligations by the tenant.

Landlord's Statutory Duties

The Act fulfills its primary purpose of protecting residential tenants by detailing extensive standards for "habitability." Under General Statute 42-42(a), a landlord must:

- comply with current building and housing codes;
- make repairs and keep the tenancy in a fit and habitable condition;
- keep common areas in a safe condition;
- maintain in good and safe working order and promptly repair all electrical, plumbing, sanitary, heating, ventilating, and air conditioning systems;
- provide operable smoke detectors and carbon monoxide alarms and perform other duties with regard to those systems;
- notify a tenant if the landlord receives notification that a water system the landlord charges a tenant for exceeds a maximum contaminant level; and
- repair any "imminently dangerous condition" within a reasonable period of time based upon the severity of the condition.[19]

Imminently Dangerous Condition

The Act requires that a landlord repair or remedy an "imminently dangerous condition" on the leased premises within a reasonable period of time based on the condition's severity.[20] The reasonable period of time to repair commences when a landlord has actual knowledge of the condition or receives notice of it. A landlord can recover the reasonable cost of repairs caused by the tenant's damage. The Act's definition of *imminently dangerous condition* encompasses:

- unsafe wiring, flooring or steps, ceilings or roofs, or chimneys or flues;
- lack of potable water;
- lack of operable locks on exterior doors;
- broken windows or lack of operable locks on all ground-floor windows;
- lack of adequate heating facilities;
- lack of operable toilet, bathtub, or shower;
- rat infestation resulting from structural defects; and
- excessive standing water, sewage, or flooding problems caused by plumbing leaks, or inadequate drainage that contribute to mosquito infestation or mold.

Operable Smoke and Carbon Monoxide Alarms

Three subsections of the Act deal with the important safety feature of smoke and carbon monoxide alarms.[21] Under the Act, a landlord must:

- provide an operable smoke alarm in each residential rental unit;
- provide a minimum of one operable carbon monoxide alarm per rental unit per level;
- ensure that a carbon monoxide alarm is operable and in good repair at the beginning of

each tenancy;
- comply with statutory standards for providing and replacing alarm batteries; and
- comply with precise national minimum standards for replacement and installation of new alarms.

Victim Protection (Protected Tenant)

The Act defines a *protected tenant* as "a tenant or household member who is the victim of domestic violence under Chapter 50B of the General Statutes or sexual assault or stalking under Chapter 14 of the General Statutes."[22] A protected tenant has three specific rights listed below designed for victim protection.

1) ***Nondiscrimination substantially based on the tenant's victim status.*** Landlords may not terminate or fail to renew a tenancy, refuse to enter into a rental agreement, or otherwise retaliate in the rental of a dwelling unit based substantially on the status of the tenant as a victim of domestic violence, sexual assault, or stalking. In addition, a protected tenant may not be discriminated against for exercising a right to early termination of a rental agreement.

2) ***The right to have locks to the unit changed.***[23] The scope and nature of protections requiring the changing of locks to a dwelling unit of a victim depend upon whether the perpetrator is or is not a tenant in the same dwelling unit as the protected tenant.

   - *Perpetrator is not a tenant in the same dwelling unit.* Under this circumstance, a protected tenant can give oral or written notice to the landlord requesting that the locks to the unit be changed. Within 48 hours of receiving this request, the landlord is required to change the locks or give the tenant permission to do so. The tenant bears the cost of changing locks. A tenant who changes the locks is required to give a key to the new locks to the landlord within 48 hours of the locks being changed.

   - *Perpetrator a tenant in the same dwelling unit.* Under this circumstance, a protected tenant can give oral or written notice to the landlord requesting that the locks to the unit be changed. However, the protected tenant must also provide the landlord with a copy of the court order requiring the perpetrator to stay away from the dwelling unit. Unless a court order allows the perpetrator to return to the dwelling to retrieve personal belongings, the landlord has no duty to allow the perpetrator access and is not liable for civil damages to the excluded perpetrator.

3) ***The right to early termination of a rental agreement.***[24] A protected tenant has the right to terminate his or her rental agreement 30 days after providing the landlord with written notice of termination (which will be discussed in more detail later in this chapter).

Broker's Duties under the Residential Rental Agreements Act

A broker managing residential property must have a clear understanding of the Act, particularly the landlord's statutory duties. The Act's essence is expressed in the requirement that a landlord do "whatever is necessary to put and keep the premises in a fit and habitable condition."[25] Where a rental agent who has general authority to act for the landlord violates the Residential Rental Agreements Act, that rental agent may be liable to the tenant for damages. Know, too, that a real estate agent having actual or apparent authority to perform the landlord's duties is defined as a "landlord" under the Act.[26]

Allocation of Public Utility Costs

Public utility costs include the following:

- electric service
- natural gas service
- water and sewer services

Public utilities law[27] requires that service and meters for each individual apartment or dwelling unit be in the name of the tenant or other occupant, subject to the following exceptions:

1) Electrical or Natural Gas Service.

- The landlord and tenant can agree in the lease that the cost of electric or natural gas service or both be included in the tenant's rent payments with the service in the name of the landlord.

    or

- A landlord may apply to the Utilities Commission for a "certificate of public convenience and necessity," authorizing the landlord to provide *electric service* using individually metered units in the lessor's name to allocate the cost of electric service among tenants "when the lessor has a separate lease for each bedroom in the unit."

2) Water and Sewer Service. Similarly, the Public Utilities Act permits landlords to apply for a certificate of convenience and necessity that allows the landlord to charge tenants for *water and sewer services* provided through the landlord's account.

In each case, the law specifies in great detail how to determine each tenant's costs.[28] The Residential Rental Agreements Act expressly prohibits a landlord from disconnecting either the landlord-provided water/sewer service or the electric service due to a tenant's nonpayment.[29] In addition, any *arrearage in costs owed by a tenant for water or sewer services or electric service cannot be used as a reason to terminate the lease.* Any *payment* to the landlord *shall be applied first to the rent owed and then to charges* for electric service or water or sewer service, unless otherwise designated by the tenant.[30]

Further, General Statute 42-46 only allows a landlord to charge a late fee for **rent** and expressly prohibits assessment of any late charge for late utility payments. While a tenant's delinquency in paying either water/sewer service or electric service provided by the landlord may not be used to terminate the lease and may not be deducted first from future rent payments, the landlord may deduct the arrearage *from that tenant's tenant security deposit* **after the termination of that tenant's tenancy.**

Alternatively, the tenant and landlord may agree in the lease that the cost of electric or natural gas service in the landlord's name be included as part of the monthly rental payments.

Example: Rather than pay $1,000 per month rent plus the prorated amount of the actual electric service to the premises, a landlord and tenant agree that the tenant will pay a flat $1,200 per month rent that will include landlord-provided electric or natural gas service.

When utilities are included in the rental amount, the landlord is solely responsible for paying these utilities. If the tenant's consumption exceeds the landlord's estimate, the landlord is responsible for paying the excess charges and cannot later recoup any of it from the tenant.[31]

A broker managing residential property in which utilities are in the landlord's name and the costs allocated to the tenants should ensure that the landlord has obtained the required certificate of public conve-

nience and necessity and should be thoroughly familiar with all state law requirements, particularly concerning proper allocation of costs.

Tenant Remedies for Breach by Landlord

The material failure of a landlord to comply with the Residential Rental Agreements Act and provide a habitable rental unit to a tenant can result in serious consequences to the landlord, and, at times, the rental agent. *Tenants can bring an action against the landlord for damages, including the recovery of all or part of past rents paid while the unit was uninhabitable.*

Where the landlord has materially breached the Act, the tenant is entitled to **general damages** for any period of the tenant's occupancy during which the premises were uninhabitable.[32] General damages are measured by the following formula:

> **the fair rental value (FRV) of the unit as warranted**
> **minus**
> **the fair rental value (FRV) of the unit in its unfit condition**

A landlord suing a tenant for back rent might find the amount owed reduced by the foregoing formula for the landlord's violation of the Act. The landlord may also be ordered to correct the defects in the property.

While the law does not allow a tenant to unilaterally withhold rent prior to a court's determination that they have a right to do so, a tenant who does not pay rent because of the landlord's material breach is not precluded from recovering damages for the landlord's breach.

Common-Law Doctrine of Constructive Eviction

In addition to remedies under the Act, *the tenant may invoke the common-law doctrine of "constructive eviction" if the premises are uninhabitable and the landlord is unable or unwilling to correct the problem.* The constructive eviction doctrine allows a tenant to leave the leased premises and end the landlord and tenant relationship. A tenant arguing constructive eviction must establish the following elements:

1) A serious problem exists with the condition of the dwelling unit that makes the premises uninhabitable.
2) The tenant has given notice to the landlord of the problem and requested that the landlord correct it.
3) The landlord has failed to correct the problem within a reasonable period of time.
4) The tenant has moved out because the tenancy is uninhabitable.

If the above elements exist, the doctrine of constructive eviction allows the tenant to vacate the premises and cease paying rent. In addition, the tenant is relieved all future liability to the landlord for rent. The theory is that the landlord has "constructively evicted" the tenant through a failure to maintain fit and habitable premises.

> *Example:* A tenant leased a home for a two-year term. Several months later, the roof developed a major leak damaging the ceilings, walls, and floors of the house. In spite of numerous complaints to the landlord by the tenant during the next several weeks, the landlord made no effort to repair the roof and incorrectly claimed that roof maintenance was the tenant's responsibility. The tenant then vacated the house and rented elsewhere. Even though more than a year and a

half remains on the lease term, the tenant is relieved of all further liability under the lease because the landlord's inaction constitutes *constructive eviction.* The tenant may also be entitled to recover damages from the landlord.

An ancient common-law rule, the constructive eviction doctrine remains important because it applies to all types of tenancies—residential and nonresidential—where the landlord is responsible for the problem at issue. The doctrine will not operate to protect a tenant, however, unless the tenant vacates the leased premises within a reasonable period of time after the landlord's breach.[33]

Violation of Unfair or Deceptive Practices Act

If a violation of the Residential Rental Agreements Act by a landlord is also an **unfair and deceptive business or trade practice**, then the tenant who has suffered damages because of the landlord's violation can recover treble damages (three times the actual damages).[34] The North Carolina Real Estate Commission offer guidance for landlords, property managers, and tenants on these subjects in a consumer-information pamphlet.[35]

Landlord's Liability under the Law of Negligence

What if a tenant, a member of the tenant's family, or a tenant's guest suffers personal injury on the rented premises? Might the landlord be liable for damages under the law of negligence? Traditionally, negligence law distinguishes between two fact situations:

1) Common areas under the landlord's control
2) Rental unit occupied exclusively by a tenant

These two areas, as well as a landlord's potential liability for a tenant's injuries caused by the criminal acts of third persons, are discussed below.

Common Areas under the Landlord's Control

A landlord has a duty to maintain common areas under his or her control. Common areas include hallways, stairways, elevators, parking lots, sidewalks, and private parks or other amenities in the development. If a tenant or other person who has a right to be on the premises is injured because of the landlord's negligence in maintaining common areas, the injured party may be able to collect damages from the landlord (assuming that the injured party is not contributorily negligent.)[36]

> *Example:* A tenant leases an apartment. During a winter storm, snow and ice accumulate on the sidewalk leading from the tenant's apartment to the parking lot. The snow and ice remain on the sidewalk for several days after the storm, and more ice accumulates from the melting and refreezing of ice on the sidewalk. The tenant slips and falls on the icy sidewalk, fracturing her hip. Assuming the tenant did not contribute to her injury through her own negligence, the landlord may be liable under the law of negligence for the tenant's injuries.

In a landmark North Carolina Supreme Court decision,[37] a visitor to the common area of rental property was attacked and injured by a tenant's dogs. The Supreme Court held that the injured visitor was not required to show that the landlord was an owner or keeper of the dogs to prove that the landlord was negligent. The lease agreement gave the landlord some control over the tenant's dogs. The "landlord control" issue was reached because, under the terms of the lease, the tenant could keep one dog on the leased premises. Instead, the property manager permitted the tenant to keep two dogs.

The lease also required the tenant to "remove any pet ... within forty-eight hours of written notification from the landlord that the pet, in the landlord's sole judgment, creates a nuisance or disturbance or is, in the landlord's opinion, undesirable." The dogs frequently were not confined and had previously attacked a neighbor, a fact that the landlord knew.

Prudent landlords and property management companies carry insurance for protection against possible liability under the law of negligence. They also engage in risk management measures to prevent possible injuries to tenants in common areas.

Rental Unit Occupied Exclusively by a Tenant

The traditional rule is that *the landlord is not liable for the tenant's fail*ure to maintain the leased premises, that is, the actual area occupied exclusively by the tenant, his/her family members, and guests. Under this rule, a tenant's personal injury arising out of a defective or unsafe condition in the leased premises (as opposed to the common areas) does *not* ordinarily give rise to a negligence action for personal injury against the landlord.

What if a residential tenant is injured on the leased premises because of a landlord's failure to comply with the duties imposed on landlords under the Residential Rental Agreements Act? The Act itself states that a violation of it "shall not constitute negligence *per se*," which means that a violation of the Act is not automatically treated as negligence. North Carolina courts have held that, while not negligence per se, *a landlord's violation of the Residential Rental Agreements Act can be introduced in court as evidence of negligence.* [38]

> *Example:* A tenant who recently rented a house sends an email message informing the landlord that the only stairway to the upstairs bedrooms is sagging and has loose stairs. The landlord replies that the inside of the house is the tenant's sole responsibility. In spite of the tenant's repeated requests, the landlord refuses to repair the stairs. Several weeks later, a family member is injured when a step cracks and breaks. Under the Residential Rental Agreements Act, unsafe steps are an *imminently dangerous* condition. The landlord's failure to repair within a reasonable period of time is strong evidence of negligence. The landlord may be liable for the family member's personal injuries, if the landlord is found negligent.

Given a residential landlord's duties imposed by state law, the traditional distinction under the law of negligence between areas controlled by the landlord and areas controlled by the tenant is becoming blurred. A landlord renting residential units in North Carolina has certain legal obligations to provide for the safety of a tenant within the leased premises, and any failure to fulfill those obligations can result in liability under the law of negligence, in addition to liability under the Residential Rental Agreements Act itself.

Landlord's Liability for Criminal Acts of Third Persons

Is a landlord liable to a tenant injured by criminal acts of third persons occurring on the leased premises? In general, a landlord has no duty to protect a tenant against the criminal acts of third persons unless the landlord knows or has reason to know of a threat of harm to the tenants and fails to take reasonable precautions to protect the tenants.

> *Example:* A 40-unit apartment building is in an area with an ongoing crime problem. In recent months, several tenants have been the victims of armed robberies and beatings in the building's hallways. Police inform the owner-landlord that the locking systems at the building's entrances

can be easily opened with a plastic credit card and urge the owner to both replace the old locks with deadbolt locks and install a security system. Many tenants notify the landlord of the crime problem and demand that the landlord replace the locks and install a security system. The landlord refuses. Several weeks later, another tenant is robbed in a common-area hallway and seriously injured. Under these facts, the landlord may well be liable under the law of negligence for failing to take reasonable precautions to protect the tenants from the foreseeable criminal activity of third persons.

If the apartment building in the above example is located in North Carolina, the landlord has also breached a statutory duty under the Residential Rental Agreements Act to repair or remedy and *imminently dangerous condition* within a reasonable period of time. That failure also provides strong evidence of negligence.

ACT PROHIBITING RETALIATORY EVICTION

"**Retaliatory eviction**," the eviction of a tenant by a landlord in response to the assertion by the tenant of a legal right, is prohibited. Residential tenants (and other persons in residence) are protected by law when engaging in good faith in specified protected activities.[39]

Protected Activities of Tenants

- Complaining to a government agency
- Requesting repairs by the landlord
- Exercising legal rights under the lease
- Exercising rights under federal or state law
- Becoming involved in a tenants' rights organization

In addition, a tenant is protected from retaliatory action by a landlord where a government agency issues a formal complaint to a landlord concerning the rented premises.

If a landlord tries to evict a tenant within 12 months after the occurrence of a protected tenant activity, the tenant can raise the defense of retaliatory eviction. If the tenant prevails, the landlord will be prevented from evicting the tenant.

Example: In January 2017, a month-to-month residential tenant made a good faith complaint to the city concerning major housing code violations at the leased premises. In March 2017, the landlord gave notice to the tenant that the tenancy was terminated, citing the need to redecorate the premises. Other apartments in the building were also undergoing redecoration, but the landlord was not terminating those tenancies. It is highly likely that the landlord was evicting the tenant in retaliation for the earlier complaints to the city; if so, this constitutes impermissible retaliatory eviction.

TENANT SECURITY DEPOSIT ACT

The **Tenant Security Deposit Act** regulates and protects the security deposits of residential tenants.[40] It applies to *any* person, firm, or corporation renting or managing a **residential** dwelling unit or units (excluding single room) on a weekly, monthly, or annual basis. *All owners of residential rental* *property located in North Carolina must comply with the requirements of this Act, regardless of whether the owner is a licensed broker.* Brokers are subject to the Act whether leasing residential property they own or is owned by others. Requirements include the following:

- All residential tenant security deposits must be held in a properly designated trust or escrow account in a federally insured depository or trust institution authorized to do business in North Carolina, or the owner-landlord must furnish a bond in the amount of the deposit from a licensed insurance company authorized to do business in North Carolina.

- Within 30 days of the tenancy, the landlord must notify the tenant of the name and address of the depository institution where the landlord has deposited the tenant's security deposit or the name of the insurance company providing the bond.

- Where the owner has hired a licensed real estate broker to manage the property and collect the rents and other monies, the broker does not have the option of obtaining a bond but must deposit all monies received from the tenant into a trust or escrow account maintained in accordance with North Carolina License Law and Commission rules. The tenant must be notified in writing if the security deposit is transferred to an account at a different bank.

Permitted Uses of Security Deposits

North Carolina law allows residential landlords and their agents to deduct amounts from a tenant security deposit only for the following purposes:

(1) nonpayment of rent and costs for water, sewer, electric, or natural gas services provided by the landlord pursuant to state law;

(2) damage to the premises, including damage to or destruction of smoke alarms or carbon monoxide alarms, but excluding "ordinary wear and tear;"

(3) damages arising from nonfulfillment of the rental period (i.e., future rent due under the lease terms during landlord's diligent efforts to re-rent);

(4) any unpaid bills that become a lien against the property due to the tenant's occupancy;

(5) costs of re-renting the premises after breach by the tenant, including any reasonable fees or commissions paid by the landlord to a licensed real estate broker to re-rent the premises;

(6) costs of removal and storage of the tenant's property after a summary ejectment proceeding;

(7) court costs;

(8) late fees for any rental payments more than five days late;[41] and

(9) complaint filing fees or court appearance fees only as permitted by G.S. 42-46.42

Where Unit Is Re-rented

A common misconception among residential landlords and property managers is the belief that the landlord automatically may keep the entire security deposit when a tenant breaches the lease or abandons the rented unit prior to the lease termination date. This is not true; rather, the landlord (or agent) must use reasonable efforts to obtain another tenant and re-rent the unit as soon as possible. A landlord may only keep that portion of the security deposit equal to the rent that would have been received if the tenant had not breached the lease. Frequently, the amount of rent that would have been earned under the lease (i.e., the "lost rent") exceeds the amount of the security deposit. In that case, the landlord can keep the entire security deposit. If, however, the landlord finding a new tenant quickly, the landlord can only retain an amount from the security deposit equal to the "lost rent" plus the amount of the landlord's actual cost in re-renting the unit.

> *Example:* A tenant rented an apartment for one year at $800/month and gave the landlord a $1,200 security deposit (one and one-half the monthly rent). With six months remaining on the lease term, the tenant breached the lease and abandoned the apartment. The landlord finds a new tenant, who moves in one month later with five months remaining on the original tenant's lease term. The landlord's costs in obtaining the new tenant were $250. The landlord's total damages are $1,050: $800 (one month's rent) plus $250. The landlord is entitled to deduct $1,050 from the security deposit but must refund the remaining $150 to the tenant, unless other permissible deductions exist, such as unpaid utilities or damage to the unit.

Where Premises Are Damaged

The landlord may use the tenant security deposit to pay for repairing damage to the rented unit that occurred during the tenancy. *A landlord may **not**, however, keep any part of the security deposit for damages caused by "ordinary wear and tear" of the premises, nor can the landlord keep any amount from the deposit that exceeds the landlord's actual damages.*[43]

> *Example:* A tenant who has occupied an apartment for five years vacates with proper notice at the end of the lease term. The landlord retains the entire $600 security deposit because the apartment needs new carpeting. The carpeting in the apartment was 10 years old at the time the tenant took occupancy and is worn out from ordinary use. The tenant did not cause any unusual or special damage to the carpet. The landlord has violated the Tenant Security Deposit Act for retaining the $600 security deposit. The tenant is not responsible for the ordinary wear and tear of the carpet and has a claim for damages against the landlord for a refund of the security deposit.

> *Example:* A licensed real estate broker managing a large apartment complex routinely keeps 30 percent of each tenant security deposit as a "cleaning fee." This fee is charged regardless of how clean the tenant left the apartment. The broker is violating both the Tenant Security Deposit Act and his or her duties as a licensed real estate broker.

Disputes between landlords (or their rental agents) and tenants over what is *"damage due to ordinary wear and tear"* versus *"other damage"* in residential rental situations are common, in part because state law does not define "ordinary wear and tear" nor are there any North Carolina court decisions defining the term. Thus, such determinations must be made on a case-by-case basis. However, both the North Carolina Department of Justice and North Carolina Real Estate Commission have published consumer information pamphlets that offer guidance for landlords, property managers, and tenants on the Tenant Security Deposit Act.[44] Based primarily on the information in these publications, the following are common examples of "damage due to ordinary wear and tear" and "other damage":

Common Examples of "Damage Due to Ordinary Wear and Tear"

- Worn or dirty carpeting
- Faded or cracked paint

- Dirty windows
- Dirty walls
- Frayed or broken curtain or blind strings
- Leaking faucets or toilets
- Small nail holes in walls (from hanging pictures)
- Worn lavatory basin
- Burned-out range heating elements

*Landlords and property managers must **not** use a tenant security deposit to cover the expense of correcting problems resulting from "ordinary wear and tear."* These expenses are considered part of the landlord's cost of doing business.

Charges for routine house cleaning or routine carpet cleaning are not permissible deductions from a residential tenant security deposit. If a tenant promises in a lease to have the carpets professionally cleaned at the end of the tenancy and then fails to do so, the landlord may not deduct the cost of the professional carpet cleaning from the tenant's security deposit. The landlord must sue the tenant in court for damages related to the tenant's breach of the lease agreement.

Common Examples of "Other Damage"

- Crayon marks on walls
- Large holes in walls
- Broken windows
- Burned spots or stains on carpeting
- Bizarre or unauthorized paint colors
- Broken counter tops
- Filthy appliances (such as ovens or refrigerators) requiring extraordinary cleaning
- Exceptionally filthy premises (in general) requiring extraordinary cleaning

*Deductions may be made from a tenant security deposit to cover the expense of repairing "damage **not** due to ordinary wear and tear" that occurred during the tenancy.* Many of these disputes could be avoided if the property manager used property-condition checklists at the beginning and end of each tenancy. It would also help if rental agents explained to new tenants the expectations of them with regard to maintaining the property when the lease is signed.

Accounting to the Tenant

The tenant security deposit must remain in the escrow account until the end of the tenancy. At the conclusion of the tenancy, the landlord or landlord's agent *must mail or deliver a written accounting to the tenant* detailing how the tenant security deposit was disbursed. General Statute §42-52 requires that this written accounting must:

- be mailed or delivered to the tenant within ***30 days*** after termination of the tenancy. If the extent of a landlord's claim against the deposit cannot be determined within 30 days, the landlord must provide an interim accounting within 30 days and a final accounting within ***60 days***;

- itemize any deductions from the deposit for damage;
- detail any deductions for unpaid rent or other permissible deductions; and
- specify the balance of the deposit, if any, to be refunded to the tenant.

Often the tenant security deposit may be fully consumed by amounts owed for back rent, in which case the landlord may be able to provide an accounting within days of the tenant vacating the unit. Any amount due the tenant should be refunded within a reasonable period of time, defined as 30 days from the termination of the tenancy unless the landlord's claims are still being determined, in which case the refund must occur no later than 60 days after the termination of the tenancy. The only reason a landlord should ever have a tenant security deposit in a trust account more than 60 days after the tenancy terminated is if the landlord provided a written accounting and partial or full refund to the tenant at the last address provided by the tenant, but the notice was returned. In this case, the statute requires the landlord to hold the deposit in a trust account for at least six months. Note that the tenant's security deposit does not automatically become the landlord's property merely because the tenant has failed to claim it.

The willful failure of a landlord to comply with the Tenant Security Deposit Act, including a failure to maintain the deposit in a trust or escrow account or post a bond or account for and refund the balance of the tenant's security deposit, voids the landlord's right to retain any portion of the tenant security deposit. In other words, even if the tenant owes back rent or has damaged the property or owes money for utility services, if the landlord failed to comply with state law in maintaining and accounting for the deposit to the tenant, he or she cannot legally withhold any sums from the tenant security deposit and must refund the entire deposit to the tenant. Willful noncompliance is against public policy, and in addition to damages, a court may award the tenant attorney's fees incurred in suing the landlord.[45]

Security Deposit Limits

The Act also limits the maximum amount that a landlord can collect as a security deposit.

Security Deposit Limits

- Week-to-week tenancy: Two weeks' rent maximum
- Month-to-month tenancy: One & one-half months' rent maximum
- Terms greater than month-to-month: Two months' rent maximum

Example: An apartment rents for $600/month for a one-year term. The landlord can require a security deposit of up to $1200. (If the tenancy had been month-to-month at the same rental, the maximum security deposit allowed by law would have been $900.)

Pet Fee

The Act does permit the landlord to require a separate *reasonable and nonrefundable fee* for pets kept by the tenant on the premises.[46] The Act neither defines the term "reasonable" nor sets limits on the amount of the pet fee. This fee is for the privilege of having a pet and does not cover damages caused by the pet. Such damages may be deducted from the security deposit.

Limits on Late Payment Fee

When a tenant is five days or more late paying rent, the amount of a late payment fee is limited by General Statute §42-46 as follows:

- Rent due in monthly installments: Fee not to exceed $15.00 or 5% of the monthly rent, whichever is greater.
- Rent due in weekly installments: Fee not to exceed $4.00 or 5% of the weekly rent, whichever is greater.

A late fee may be imposed only once for each late rental payment and it may not be deducted from a tenant's next rental payment if it causes that payment to be in default.

SUMMARY EJECTMENT (EVICTION PROCEDURE)

A **small claim action** in district court for summary ejectment is the procedure by which most residential tenants are evicted.[47] The complaint must be in writing, signed either by the landlord as plaintiff, the plaintiff's attorney, or an agent for the plaintiff who has actual knowledge of the facts alleged in the complaint.[48] The law allows a property owner to file for summary ejectment whenever a tenant (or a tenant's assigns) refuses to vacate the property after a demand to vacate and surrender possession of the property has been made in either of the following cases:

- the tenant holds over after the lease term has expired.
- the tenant has done or omitted any act by which the estate has ceased according to the lease terms.

Can a broker initiate a summary ejectment action and sign a complaint on behalf of the owner whose property the broker is managing? The answer is "yes" if all of the following requirements are met:

1) The broker is an agent of the owner.
2) The property management agreement authorizes the broker to initiate legal proceedings on behalf of the owner.
3) The broker *has actual knowledge of the facts alleged in the complaint.*

Standard property management agreements authorize the broker, as the owner's agent, to initiate legal proceedings on behalf of the owner. A broker who does not want this responsibility should consider striking that provision from the agreement. A broker who accepts this responsibility must still have *personal knowledge of the facts underlying the legal action* to file the complaint. Generally, the broker will have personal knowledge if he or she is handling all aspects of managing the owner's property.

The complaint is filed in the small claims division of the office of the clerk of superior court in the county where the defendant/tenant resides.[49] Upon filing of the complaint, the clerk of court will issue a magistrate summons formally commencing the legal action and assigning a trial date of not more than seven days after the filing of the complaint, excluding holidays and weekends. A copy of the summons and filed complaint is then delivered to the sheriff's office for service on the defendant(s). A standard form magistrate summons and complaint in summary ejectment are set forth as Figures 16-1 and 16-2 at the end of this chapter. In most counties, a brief summary of eviction procedures, links to applicable forms, and information regarding fees may be found on the clerk of superior court's website.[50]

Self-help Eviction Prohibited

Historically, some residential landlords evicted tenants without going to court via methods such as padlocking a tenant's apartment, changing the locks on the apartment door, disconnecting utilities, or posting a false legal notice on the tenant's door ordering the tenant to leave immediately. *Now the **only** eviction remedy when residential tenancies are involved is the procedure established by state law; self-help evictions by residential landlords are expressly prohibited.*[51] A tenant wrongfully evicted by a landlord has a right to bring an action against the landlord.

> *Example:* A residential tenant is behind in rent. While the tenant is at work, the landlord changes the locks on the apartment door and leaves a notice on the door informing the tenant that, unless the back rent is paid, the tenant will not be allowed back into the apartment. The notice also says that the landlord's agent must be present and will assist the tenant in retrieving the tenant's personal belongings from the apartment. The landlord's actions constitute an illegal self-help eviction.

The prohibition against self-help eviction does **not** apply to a fact situation where a tenant has *voluntarily* vacated the apartment and abandoned his or her obligations under the lease, although there are other measures the landlord must take to confirm the tenant's abandonment and reclaim the rental unit.

> *Example:* A tenant is two months behind on rent payments. The tenant rents a truck, removes all personal belongings from the unit, and sends the landlord the apartment keys with a note informing the landlord that the tenant is recently unemployed, has abandoned the apartment, and is moving to another state. The tenant has voluntarily abandoned the property. Under these facts, the landlord can accept the tenant's abandonment and retake possession of the apartment without having to file a summary ejectment action.

Seizure of Tenant's Personal Property (Distress and Distraint)

"Distress" or "distraint" of the tenant's personal property by a landlord is prohibited. *The common-law doctrine of "distress" or "distraint" allowed a landlord to seize the tenant's personal property on the leased premises when the tenant had not paid the rent and to keep the property until the tenant cured the default. This common-law practice is expressly **prohibited by statute for landlords of residential property.*** General Statute **§42-25.7**, titled "Distress and distraint not permitted," reads:

> It is the public policy of the State of North Carolina that distress and distraint are prohibited and that landlords of residential rental property shall have rights concerning the personal property of their residential tenants only in accordance with G.S. 42-25.9(d), 42-25.9(g), 42-25.9(h), or 42-36.2.[52]

Lease provisions allowing a landlord to seize a tenant's personal property for nonpayment of rent are against public policy and void. While a residential landlord does *not* have an automatic lien on a residential tenant's personal property, the landlord is specifically authorized, after being placed in lawful possession by execution of a writ of possession, to throw away, dispose of, or sell items of personal property left behind by a tenant in accordance with state law. General Statute §42-25.9 distinguishes between: 1) abandoned personal property of $500 or less, 2) abandoned personal property of $750 or less, and 3) abandoned personal property valued at more than $750.

Abandoned Personal Property of Less than $500

Personal property of less than $500 is deemed abandoned five days after the time of execution of a writ of possession, and the landlord is authorized to throw away or dispose of it. *Note: If the tenant requests the property prior the expiration of the five-day period, the landlord is required to release the property during regular business hours at an agreed time.*

Abandoned Personal Property of $750 or Less

If a residential tenant has abandoned personal property having a value of $750 or less or fails to remove that personal property at the time of execution of a writ of possession in a summary ejectment action, the landlord has an option to deliver the tenant's property "into the custody of a nonprofit organization regularly providing free or at a nominal price clothing and household furnishings to people in need." The nonprofit must agree to identify and hold the property for 30 days and to return it to the tenant if requested during that 30-day period. A landlord using this procedure must post a notice with the name and address of the nonprofit at the leased premises and at the location where rent was paid.

Alternatively, the landlord can use the procedure of General Statute §42-25.9(g), which reads in part:

> Seven days after being placed in lawful possession by execution of a writ of possession, a landlord may dispose of personal property remaining on the premises ... During the seven-day period..., a landlord may move for storage purposes, but shall not throw away, dispose of, or sell any items of personal property remaining on the premises unless otherwise provided for in this Chapter. Upon the tenant's request prior to the expiration of the seven-day period, the landlord shall release possession of the property to the tenant during regular business hours or at a time agreed upon. If the landlord elects to sell the property at public or private sale, the landlord shall give written notice to the tenant by first-class mail to the tenant's last known address at least seven days prior to the day of the sale...

The seven-day notice period for the sale of the tenant's personal property can run concurrently with the seven-day period during which the tenant may request possession of the property. The statute specifies the contents of the notice of sale. Any surplus from the sale after the payment of unpaid rents, damages, storage fees, and costs shall be disbursed to the tenant upon request within seven days after the sale. If the tenant fails to request the surplus proceeds, then the law directs that the surplus funds be delivered to the government of the county where the property is located. However, if the tenant requests the return of the property within the initial seven-day period, the landlord must release the property to the tenant during regular business hours or at an agreed-upon time.

Personal Property Exceeding $750 in Value

When the value of a tenant's personal property exceeds $750, the personal property must be handled by the county sheriff. The sheriff must follow specific statutory procedures outlined in General Statute §42-36.2 before serving a writ for possession of real property and removing the tenant's personal property. The sheriff must give the tenant written notice of the approximate time that the order or writ for possession of the leased premises will be enforced by the sheriff and must inform the tenant that if the tenant fails to request possession of any personal property within seven days after execution of the writ, then the property may be thrown away, disposed of, or sold. The sheriff shall remove the tenant's property from the premises unless the landlord signs a statement saying that the personal property may remain on the premises, in which case the sheriff will merely lock the premises. If the sheriff removes the property and the tenant refuses to take possession, then the sheriff may deliver it to a storage warehouse, but may first require the landlord to advance both the cost of delivering the property and one month's storage fee. If the landlord refuses to pay these costs, then the sheriff may refuse to remove the property.

Note that *a residential tenant has an absolute right to recover any personal property left at the premises, regardless of value, so long as the tenant timely requests return of the property within the stated time periods, i.e., either five or seven days.*

Lien on Personal Property Permitted for Lessor of Space for Manufactured Home

A lessor of a space for a manufactured home has a statutory lien on the personal property of the tenant and the manufactured home itself titled in the name of the tenant.[53] There are very specific statutory notice requirements and guidelines that must be followed by the lessor.

Expedited Eviction for Criminal Activity

Article 7 of Chapter 42 of the General Statutes is an attempt to assure residential tenants of peaceable, safe, and quiet enjoyment of their homes by creating special rules applicable to the expedited eviction of tenants or other persons in specific situations.[54] Subject to statutory qualifications, a court is authorized to order the immediate eviction of a tenant and all other occupants of that tenant's unit where the court, as required by General Statute §42-63, finds any of the following:

- Criminal activity has occurred on or within the individual rental unit leased to the tenant.
- The rental unit leased to the tenant was used in any way in furtherance of or to promote criminal activity.
- The tenant, any member of the tenant's household, or any guest has engaged in criminal activity on or in the immediate vicinity of any portion of the entire premises.
- The tenant has given permission to or invited a person to return or reenter any portion of the entire premises, knowing that the person has been legally removed by statute and barred from the entire premises or barred by the reasonable rules and regulations of a publicly assisted landlord.
- The tenant has failed to notify law enforcement or the landlord immediately upon learning that a person who has been removed and barred from the tenant's individual rental unit pursuant to this Article has returned to or reentered the tenant's individual rental unit.

The term "criminal activity" is defined by statute.[55] There is also a "partial eviction" provision allowing the removal of someone other than the tenant, including a member of the tenant's household.[56] The nature of expedited eviction proceedings are described by statute,[57] as are defenses available to a tenant.[58]

Because the expedited eviction for criminal activity statutes contain detailed requirements and procedures, a landlord or landlord's agent seeking this type of eviction should seek legal advice before proceeding under these statutes.

ADDITIONAL LAWS PROTECTING RESIDENTIAL TENANTS

Additional laws that provide significant rights and protections to residential tenants are addressed below.

Fair Housing Laws

Landlords and the brokers who represent them must know and comply with the federal Fair Housing Act (FHAct) and the North Carolina Fair Housing Act,[59] both of which prohibit discrimination against a tenant or prospective tenant on the basis of race, color, religion, sex, national origin, handicap, or familial status in the rental of residential property.

With respect to handicapped or disabled tenants or prospective tenants, federal and state law require landlords to make *reasonable accommodations* in rules, policies, practices, and services when such accommodations may be necessary to afford a person with a disability the equal opportunity to use and enjoy a dwelling.[60]

Perhaps the request most frequently encountered by brokers or owners is from tenants who have assistance animals. An assistance animal may also be referred to as a "support animal," "therapy animal," or "service animal." Owners who have a "no pet" policy are prohibited by both state and federal law from refusing to rent to a person who has a legitimate assistance animal, whether in a vacation rental or short or long-term lease. Assistance animals are not "pets." Although the Americans with Disabilities Act (ADA) now defines a service animal as a canine, the Fair Housing Act imposes no such limitations on assistance animals; assistance animals may include cats, birds, ponies, monkeys, or guinea pigs, to name a few. Under certain circumstances, a landlord's prohibition against pets will not prohibit an assistance animal, and a landlord cannot charge a pet fee for an assistance animal. However, a tenant is responsible for any damage caused by an assistance animal.

(Fair housing laws and the statutory protections that exist to prevent housing discrimination are discussed in Chapter 18.)

Sexual Harassment Laws

It is a violation of law for any lessor of residential property, or the lessor's agent, to harass a lessee or prospective tenant on the basis of sex. The statute defines **sexual harassment** as "unsolicited overt requests or demands for sexual acts when (i) submission to such conduct is made a term of the execution or continuation of the lease agreement, or (ii) submission to or rejection of such conduct by an individual is used to determine whether rights under the lease are accorded."[61]

Laws Protecting Public Housing Tenants

Brokers dealing with rental property should be acutely aware of the distinction between private and government-subsidized housing. Tenants in government-subsidized housing (often called "Section 8 housing") are protected by the laws previously mentioned and have additional rights, procedures, and remedies under the federal and state federal and state constitutions, laws, and regulations.

Unlike a month-to-month tenant in a private apartment building, *a tenant in a government-subsidized apartment can be evicted only for "good cause."*[62] (Remember that a regular month-to-month tenant can be evicted for any reason, as long as it is not retaliatory or discriminatory.) Furthermore, tenants in Section 8 housing are entitled to "procedural due process" before they can be evicted.[63] Before a public housing tenant can be evicted, the tenant is entitled to notice, confrontation of any witnesses against him or her, legal counsel, and a decision by an impartial decision-maker based on evidence given at a hearing.

The 1988 Anti-Drug Abuse Act[64] requires local agencies responsible for the administration of federally funded public housing to include a lease provision providing that "any drug-related criminal activity on or off such premises, engaged in by a public housing tenant, or any member of the tenant's household, or any guest or other person under the tenant's control ... [is] cause for termination of tenancy." A ninth circuit federal court decision[65] has held that tenants in public housing may not be evicted for the criminal drug activities of guests of which the tenants were unaware or could not control. Federal law does allow public housing authorities discretion to make termination decisions in individual cases.[66]

A contractor who provides Section 8 housing but who does not keep the properties in a decent, safe, and sanitary condition and who fails to cooperate in efforts to improve the properties may be suspended and barred from future participation in covered transactions with the federal government.[67]

The additional protections available to residential tenants in the event of foreclosure under the Protecting Tenants at Foreclosure Act, discussed shortly, also apply to residential housing in which tenants receive Section 8 rental-voucher assistance.

Federal Servicemembers Civil Relief Act (SCRA)

There are a significant number of military servicemembers residing in North Carolina. Servicemembers who are tenants in residential leases have traditionally been entitled to rights and benefits of the Soldiers' and Sailors' Civil Relief Act. That Act has been amended and replaced by the federal Servicemembers Civil Relief Act (SCRA).[68]

It is important that landlords who rent residential property and their management agents understand the rights of servicemembers under the SCRA. These rights can be summarized as the right to terminate a residential lease under certain circumstances, the right of a dependent of a servicemember who has executed a joint lease to terminate, and protections in an eviction action. An expert on the SCRA provides the following helpful summary of the first two protections:

> Perhaps the most significant developments concern the SCRA's protections for servicemembers who need to terminate a residential lease. The SCRA allows servicemembers to terminate their leases upon "entry into military service." They can also terminate their leases when they "receive military orders for a change of permanent station or to deploy within a military unit, or as an individual in support of a military operation, for a period not less than 90 days." Under the SCRA as enacted in 2003, the deployment benefit was only for servicemembers mobilized with a unit. With its 2004 amendment, Congress acknowledged that individuals are often called to deploy as individuals and not as members of a unit.
>
> The second change provides a great benefit to servicemembers who have joint leases. The SCRA's protections now extend to joint leases entered into by a servicemember and a servicemember's dependent. This was added to assist those non-servicemember spouses (or other dependents) who were being held to a lease that they and their deployed spouse signed, but in a location where the non-servicemember spouse did not wish to reside without the servicemember.[69] *[citations omitted]*

In terms of eviction safeguards for residential tenants who are servicemembers, the SCRA provides that, except by court order, a landlord may not evict a servicemember (or his or her dependents) during a period of military service of the servicemember from a tenancy occupied primarily as a residence.[70] The SCRA also requires a stay of execution when a court-ordered eviction is involved.

Laws Protecting Tenants in Foreclosure Situations

State Law Allowing Early Termination of Lease in the Event of Foreclosure

North Carolina law allows tenants who rent residential real property containing less than 15 rental units to terminate a rental agreement by providing the landlord with a ten-day notice of termination after the tenant has received a notice of foreclosure.[71]

Example: A residential tenant renting an apartment in a ten-unit apartment building receives a notice that the building will be sold at a foreclosure sale. Although eight months remain on the tenant's lease term, the tenant has the option of terminating the tenancy by giving the landlord a ten-day notice. N.C. Gen. Stat. §42-25.2, the early-termination statute, requires that the rent be prorated to the effective date of the ten-day termination notice and adds: "The tenant is not liable for any other rent or damages due only to the early termination of the tenancy."

Special Notice to Tenants in Manufactured Home Communities Prior to Conversion of Use

Tenants living in manufactured homes in a manufactured home community, defined by statute as "a parcel of land, whether undivided or subdivided, that has been designed to accommodate at least five manufactured homes," are entitled, regardless of the term of their tenancy, to a 180-day notice to vacate in the event the owner of the manufactured home community intends to convert it or any part of it to another use that requires the movement of the manufactured homes. If a tenant is entitled to a longer notice or has more than 180 days remaining on a tenancy for a definite term, that tenant is not required to vacate within 180 days.[72]

LEAD-BASED PAINT HAZARD DISCLOSURE

The Residential Lead-Based Paint Hazard Reduction Act of 1992[73] imposes legal requirements on landlords of "target housing"[74] (pre-1978 housing). The primary focus of this federal legislation is disclosure, and landlords are required to make specified disclosures to potential lessees. For example, before a lessee is obligated under a contract to lease target housing, the lessor is required to provide the lessee with a lead-based paint hazard information pamphlet, disclose the presence of any known lead-based paint, and permit the lessee to conduct a risk assessment/inspection for the presence of lead-based paint hazards. If a real estate broker is acting as a leasing agent for the owner, that broker is required to ensure compliance with lead-based paint disclosure requirements on behalf of the lessor.[75]

There are substantial penalties for violating the Residential Lead-Based Paint Hazard Reduction Act of 1992, including significant civil liability for knowingly violating the Act. Any person who knowingly violates the disclosure provisions is jointly and severally liable to the lessee in an amount equal to three times the damages incurred.[76] Additional legal requirements exist for federally owned and assisted housing. The requirements under federal law are discussed in Chapter 8 and the disclosure form for lease transactions is Figure 8-3 at the end of that Chapter.

TYPES OF TENANCIES (aka NONFREEHOLD ESTATES)

A **tenancy** or **nonfreehold estate** is an estate in real property that is less than a freehold estate. A tenancy or nonfreehold estate is created by a lease or rental agreement, either oral or written; thus, it is also known as a **leasehold estate**. The holder of a nonfreehold estate (the "tenant" or "lessee") has the right to possess and use property in accordance with the terms of the lease agreement.

As indicated in Chapter 1, there are **four types of nonfreehold estates**:
- Tenancy for years (tenancy for a definite term)
- Tenancy from period to period (periodic tenancy)
- Tenancy at will
- Tenancy at sufferance

It is possible for different combinations of nonfreehold estates to apply to the same rental over a period of time. A tenant can start out with a two-year lease to expire on September 30, 2016. Thereafter the tenant may stay on the leased premises and keep paying rent and become a month-to-month tenant. A tenant for years, or a periodic tenant, or a tenant-at-will may all end up as a tenant at sufferance if the tenant defaults on rent but remains on the leased premises.

As you study the different types of tenancies, notice that *the primary difference between each category is how the tenancy is terminated.* A month-to-month tenancy on the same property may be valuable, but there is no guarantee that the landlord will continue the landlord-tenant relationship beyond the next month.

TENANCY FOR YEARS (TENANCY FOR A DEFINITE TERM)

By far the most common nonfreehold estate is the **tenancy for years** (also called **tenancy for a definite term**). This is an estate created by a lease whereby a tenant takes a "leasehold interest" in the real property for a specific term. *The chief characteristic of the estate for years is that the term or period must have a definite beginning and termination date.* Whether a leasehold interest is for 100 years or for only one year, or for a month, a week, or even a day, the estate of the lessee is termed in law an *estate for years* so long as the lease is for a *definite term.*[77]

Characteristics of a Tenancy for Years

The major characteristics or incidents of a tenancy or estate for years are discussed below.

Automatic Termination

A tenancy for years *terminates automatically* upon the expiration of the set period of time designated for the duration of the lease without the necessity of notice by either party to the lease.

Example: A landlord and tenant enter into a lease to commence on April 1, 2015, and to terminate on March 31, 2017. The lessee will have to vacate the premises on March 31, 2017, regardless of whether the lessor gives any kind of notice that the tenancy has ended.

Exclusive Right to Possession

A tenant (lessee) holding a tenancy for years has an exclusive right to possession, not only as against third persons but also as against the landlord (lessor). Leases frequently alter this rule to a limited extent by allowing the landlord the right to occasionally inspect the premises and to enter the premises, after prior notice, to make repairs. (See "Landlord's Right to Enter Premises during Lease Term" discussed under "Common Lease Provisions.") Without such a lease provision, a landlord or broker has no right to enter a leased property without the tenant's express permission.

Repairs

A *residential* tenant is protected by the Residential Rental Agreements Act, discussed earlier, and is not obligated to make repairs to the leased premises arising from normal wear and tear. The tenant is responsible and must pay for repairs caused by the tenant's misuse or negligence. *Nonresidential* tenants, on the other hand, generally have the obligation to make repairs to the leased premises unless the lease imposes this duty on the landlord.

Right to Transfer Leasehold Interest

The tenant under an estate for years may *assign* or *sublease* the leasehold interest to a third party unless the lease prohibits transfer. Most standard residential lease forms either prohibit or significantly restrict transfer by a tenant. Even if an assignment or a sublease is allowed, the original tenant is not relieved of liability under the original lease unless the lessor has agreed to release the tenant. (Assignments and subleases are discussed in Chapter 19.)

TENANCIES FROM PERIOD TO PERIOD (PERIODIC TENANCIES)

Tenancies from period to period (also called **periodic tenancies**) are estates that exist for an initial period and then automatically continue to exist *until the landlord or tenant gives proper notice of termination.* Thus, a periodic tenancy can be of very brief or very long duration. Month-to-month periodic tenancies are common but decreasing in popularity in favor of the tenancy for years (tenancy for a definite term). Historically, year-to-year periodic tenancies were common in agricultural tenancies.

Periodic tenancies may be created either by express contract or by implication of law. If the parties agree that the lease is to be "from month to month" (or other "period to period"), a periodic tenancy is created. Periodic tenancies also arise by implication when there is a rental of real property in which the lease does not specify a definite term but states an annual, monthly, or weekly rental amount. In these cases, a tenancy from year to year, month to month, week to week, or day to day is created, depending on the frequency of the required rent payments.

The law also creates a periodic tenancy where a tenant for a fixed period (a tenant for years) "holds over" after the expiration of the original lease term but continues to pay rent to the landlord, who accepts the rent.

> *Example*: A landlord leases a home to a tenant for a three-year term at a monthly rental of $1,500. The three-year term expired on April 30, 2017, but the tenant remained on the leased premises and sent the landlord a $1,500 check for May 2017, which the landlord accepted. The original tenancy for years (tenancy for a definite term) was converted into to a periodic month-to-month tenancy under these circumstances.

A periodic tenancy may also be implied by law when a lessee enters into possession under a lease void under the statute of frauds. If the tenant pays the agreed-upon monthly rent and it is accepted by the landlord, a month-to-month tenancy results.

Characteristics of a Periodic Tenancy

The characteristics of tenancies from month to month or other periodic tenancy are for the most part the same as those set out earlier with respect to tenancies for years. One significant difference between the two is how the tenancy terminates.

Tenancies for years terminate automatically at the end of a particular term, whereas *estates from year to year and other periodic tenancies are terminable only by giving an appropriate prior* **notice** *that the tenancy is being terminated.* Notice must be given by the tenant to the landlord or by the landlord to the tenant a certain period of time prior to the end of the current period, depending upon the type of periodic tenancy involved. General Statute §42-14 establishes the *minimum* notice required.

Period/Term	Minimum Notice
Year to Year	1 month
Month to Month	7 days
Week to Week	2 days

Leases may and often do provide for longer periods of advance termination notice than the statutory minimums shown above. *If proper notice is not given the required minimum time prior to the end of the current term, both parties will be bound to the periodic tenancy for at least one additional term.* The required notice need not be in any particular form; notice orally or by email or text message is sufficient unless the lease specifies how notice should be delivered.

As a practical matter, a month-to-month residential tenancy is not transferable. Most contemporary rental agreements prohibit tenant transfers or require the prior consent of the landlord. If a tenant transfers without prior permission, the landlord has the option of ending the tenancy by giving the proper minimum notice. Any transfer by a month-to-month tenant does not relieve the original tenant of liability under the rental agreement unless the landlord agrees to release the tenant.

TENANCIES AT WILL

A **tenancy at will** (also called an **estate at will**) is *one that is held at the pleasure of both the owner and the tenant,* pursuant to the "will" of both. *The tenancy at will may be terminated "at the will" of either party.* Tenancies at will are extremely rare.

> *Example:* An owner of a house that is in the projected path of a proposed highway widening rents it to a tenant who needs temporary housing and knows about the possible highway widening. The owner and tenant agree that the tenancy will continue "until the tenant wants to leave for any reason or until the landlord wants to terminate for any reason." The parties have created a tenancy at will.

A tenancy at will is not transferable by a tenant. It can be terminated at any time by either landlord or tenant. In theory, the tenancy terminates "instantly" when notice is given. In practice, a tenant will be entitled to a reasonable time to vacate the property. Because of their rarity and brief period of existence even when created, tenancies at will have little practical importance or impact today in real estate law and practice.

TENANCIES AT SUFFERANCE

A **tenancy at sufferance** (also called an **estate at sufferance**) is in reality not a true tenancy at all. It is never intentionally created and only occurs indirectly as the result of circumstance. *The term "tenancy at sufferance" simply describes the situation when one goes into possession of land lawfully but holds over without any right to do so and without the consent of the owner.* The only difference between a tenant at sufferance and a mere trespasser is that the tenant at sufferance went into possession lawfully but has now overstayed his or her welcome.

The simplest illustration of a tenancy at sufferance is where a tenant has a lease for a specified term and then holds over at the end of his lease without any consent or recognition on the part of the lessor. The tenant at sufferance is not a trespasser because his or her possession began with a lawful tenancy. The tenant is not a tenant at will, since the owner does not want the tenant to remain in possession and refuses to accept any rent payments. A tenant at sufferance can be evicted at any time by a summary ejectment action.

RESIDENTIAL LEASE FORMS

In most residential lease transactions, brokers may use standardized lease forms issued by trade organizations or drafted by an attorney for the broker's use. While brokers may not draft legal documents for others, they may fill in blank spaces on preprinted forms that cover essential details of the rental agreement, such as the names of the parties, a description of the leased premises, amount of security deposit, rent, duration of the lease, etc. Brokers managing property for others must know what forms are appropriate for different lease situations and should only use forms approved by a professional trade association or created specifically for the broker by an attorney. An attorney should be consulted when a rental transaction deviates from usual practices.

> *Example:* An owner hires a broker to find a renter for the owner's home. A prospective tenant wants to sign a three-year lease but also wants the lease to include an option to purchase the home with all rental payments applied toward the purchase price if the option is exercised. Most preprinted residential lease forms would be wholly inadequate to use in a lease-option transaction. The broker should advise the homeowner to retain an attorney for both legal advice and to draft a custom document that comports with state law.

An example of a well-drafted *standard residential* lease form is the NC REALTORS® Standard Form No. 410, "Residential Rental Contract," reproduced as Figure 16-3 at the end of this chapter. It is a very detailed *residential* lease form that is copyrighted and available only to individuals who are members of that trade association. Brokers who do not belong to a REALTOR® organization should not use Standard Form 410.

Essential Provisions

While many provisions that are both practical and desirable may be added to leases, *the following elements are essential to every valid lease:*

1) The parties must be identified.
2) The house or apartment must be identified. The lease must clearly state the exact residential dwelling unit or house being rented. Either a street address of a single family house or a street address and apartment number for an apartment is sufficient. Full legal descriptions are rarely used in residential leases.
3) The landlord and tenant must expressly agree on all material terms of the lease, such as the duration of the lease, the rent amount and payment terms, the amount of security deposit, and any other mutually agreed rights and obligations of either party. If a tenancy for years can be renewed, a provision describing the tenant's renewal right and procedure is a material term.

Landlord's Right to Enter Premises during Lease Term

Provisions giving the landlord the right to enter leased residential premises are common. The landlord typically retains a limited right during the lease term to enter the leased home or apartment to inspect it, to see if the tenant is complying with all lease obligations, to make necessary repairs, to place "for sale" or "for rent" signs on the premises, or to show the premises to prospective purchasers or tenants. In the absence of such a provision or understanding, the landlord has no right to enter the premises during the term of the lease.

REQUIREMENT THAT LEASES BE IN WRITING AND RECORDED

Under North Carolina law, short-term leases that will be fully performed within three years from the time of making need not be in writing or recorded. While most residential leases are for terms less than three years and thus could be oral, brokers managing rental property for others should require that *all rental agreements be in writing to lessen future disputes and misunderstandings between the parties.*

Recall that the statute of frauds, General Statute §22-2, requires that any lease that will not be fully performed within three years from the time of its making must be in writing and signed by the party to be charged therewith to be enforceable. *Leases that will not be completed within three years from the time of making (execution) not only* ***must be in writing, but they should be recorded*** *to protect the lessee's interest.* Even though a lease that lasts more than three years from its making is in writing, it still will be void against the lessor's purchasers for value and subject to subsequent lien creditors unless it is recorded pursuant to General Statute §47-18.[78]

NORTH CAROLINA VACATION RENTAL ACT

The **North Carolina Vacation Rental Act** (the "VRA") is found in Chapter 42A of the North Carolina General Statutes. The General Assembly enacted the VRA in 1999 to regulate the competing interests of landlords, brokers, and tenants in the vacation rental market. This market presents fact situations that differ from a normal residential dwelling unit rental. The VRA defines "***vacation rentals***" as: *The rental of residential property for vacation, leisure, or recreation purposes for fewer than 90 days by a person who has a place of permanent residence to which he or she intends to return.* Short term vacation rentals share characteristics with both residential landlord-tenant transactions and innkeeper-guest relationships.

"Residential property" includes condominiums, townhomes, single-family homes, cottages, apartments, or "… other property devoted to residential use or occupancy … for a definite or indefinite period." The VRA does *not* apply to hotels, motels, and other businesses regulated under innkeeper-guest laws. Other limited exceptions also exist.

The VRA applies to any *person, partnership, corporation, limited liability company, association, or other business entity acting as a landlord or real estate broker engaged in the rental or management of "vacation rental property."* It provides detailed and clear guidelines for any owner or agent leasing vacation property. Understand that owners must comply with the VRA regardless of whether they hire a broker. ***Brokers*** clearly are bound by the Act when managing vacation rentals for others and ***must have a written management agreement with the owner prior to providing any brokerage services*** pursuant to Commission rules. Written property management agreements will be discussed in Chapter 17.

Requirements for a Valid Vacation Rental Agreement

The VRA requires that all rental agreements for "vacation rentals" be in writing. A vacation rental agreement is not valid and enforceable unless the tenant has accepted the agreement by one of three statutory options: (1) signing the agreement; (2) paying any monies to the landlord or real estate property manager after the tenant's receipt of the agreement; or, (3) taking possession of the vacation rental property after the tenant's receipt of the agreement. State law dictates specific content requirements for vacation rental agreements, such as the special "notice" required by General Statute §42A-11(a), which reads:

> A vacation rental agreement executed under this Chapter shall contain the following notice on its face which shall be set forth in a clear and conspicuous manner that distinguishes it from other provisions of the agreement: 'THIS IS A VACATION RENTAL AGREEMENT UNDER THE NORTH CAROLINA VACATION RENTAL ACT. THE RIGHTS AND OBLIGATIONS OF THE PARTIES TO THIS AGREEMENT ARE DEFINED BY LAW AND INCLUDE UNIQUE PROVISIONS PERMITTING THE DISBURSEMENT OF RENT PRIOR TO TENANCY AND EXPEDITED EVICTION OF TENANTS. YOUR SIGNATURE ON THIS AGREEMENT, OR PAYMENT OF MONEY OR TAKING POSSESSION OF THE PROPERTY AFTER RECEIPT OF THIS AGREEMENT IS EVIDENCE OF YOUR ACCEPTANCE OF THIS AGREEMENT AND YOUR INTENT TO USE THIS PROPERTY FOR A VACATION RENTAL.'

The VRA also requires that the vacation rental agreement contain the following provisions:

- Manner in which funds will be received, deposited, and disbursed in advance of the tenant's occupancy of the property;
- Name and address of the depository or trust institution where the escrow account is maintained;
- Any processing or administrative fees permitted under the VRA;
- Any cleaning fee permitted under the VRA;
- Rights and obligations of the landlord and tenant;
- Applicability of expedited eviction procedures;
- Rights of the landlord or real estate broker and tenant if the property is transferred;
- Rights and obligations of the landlord or real estate broker tenant in the event of a mandatory evacuation; and
- Any other obligations of the landlord and tenant.

The NC Association of REALTOR® organization created a Vacation Rental Agreement (Form 411-T) that complies with state law. In a rare exception, it allows not only its Realtor members to use the form but also *owners who are personally managing their property for vacation rental purposes*. Brokers who are managing vacation rentals for others and who are not Realtors may *not* use Form 411-T. They must find another source for a vacation lease agreement that complies with state law or hire an attorney to create a compliant standard form for use in their brokerage activity.

Handling and Accounting of Funds

The VRA has detailed requirements regarding the receipt and accounting of funds received from a vacation rental tenant. The following is a concise outline of key points regarding funds.

1) Owners must deposit all advanced payments, whether for rent, security deposit, sales tax, fees, etc., into a ***trust or escrow account in a federally insured depository or trust institution*** authorized to do business in North Carolina ***within three banking days of receipt***.

2) Owner/landlords do not have the option of posting a bond for the security deposit; rather, it must be deposited into an escrow account.

3) No advanced funds received for sale or occupancy taxes or security deposit may be disbursed prior to the termination of the tenancy or material breach by the tenant except to refund the monies to the tenant.

The VRA details what advanced payments received may be disbursed and when. Briefly, the only sums that may be disbursed prior to the tenancy include: 1) any administrative fee charged for the cost of processing the tenant's reservation; 2) fees owed to third parties to pay for goods, services, or benefits for the tenant; and 3) up to 50% of any rents received. Understand that if the tenancy does not occur for reasons other than the tenant's breach, then the tenant may be entitled to a refund of all rents paid in advance. The Act also addresses an owner's accounting and transfer obligations for advanced payments received, if ownership of the property is transferred while there are future tenancies that have not yet occurred.

Transfer of Property Subject to a Vacation Rental Agreement

The VRA establishes a timetable for accounting by a former owner to a new owner if the vacation rental property is sold with outstanding vacation rentals pending. In essence, the VRA requires the new owner to honor all vacation rental agreements that end within 180 days of the new owner acquiring title. Whether the new owner chooses to honor vacation rental agreements that end more than 180 days after the title transfer is up to the owner; those vacation rental tenants have no right to enforce the rental agreement, but they are entitled to a full refund if the new owner declines to honor the agreement.

The landlord who is conveying the property has various disclosure obligations to the purchaser both prior to contract and after closing and must transfer all advance payments received for tenancies occurring post-transfer to the new owner within 30 days of closing.[79]

Expedited Eviction Proceedings

Unlike long-term rentals, an expedited eviction procedure is needed in vacation rentals to remove a tenant who is holding over, has failed to pay rent, is in material breach of the vacation rental agreement, or has obtained possession by fraud or misrepresentation. The details of the VRA's comprehensive expedited procedure are beyond the scope of this chapter. Brokers managing vacation rentals should be thoroughly familiar with the expedited procedure to competently represent their owners. The following summary is a brief introduction.

1. Four hours oral or written notice must be given to the vacation renter to leave the property. (Notice may be posted on the front door of the property if the first method of notice has failed.)

2. If the tenant fails to leave voluntarily, a summons and complaint may be filed to initiate legal proceedings. Within a relatively short time period (12-48 hours) after service

on the tenant, a hearing may be held before a magistrate in small claims court.

3. If the magistrate finds in favor of the landlord, an order to vacate is entered and the vacation renter has no less than two hours nor more than eight hours to vacate.

Landlord and Tenant Duties

Using language similar to the landlord's and tenant's duties under the Residential Rental Agreements Act, the VRA details a statutory warranty of habitability owed by a landlord to a vacation rental tenant. The vacation rental tenant has statutory duties to the landlord analogous to those owed by a regular residential tenant.

The Act describes the consequences of a landlord's failure to provide the property in a fit and habitable condition, in part, as follows:

> Except as otherwise provided in this subsection, if, at the time the tenant is to begin occupancy of the property, the landlord or real estate broker cannot provide the property in a fit and habitable condition or substitute a reasonably comparable property in such condition, the landlord and real estate broker shall refund to the tenant all payments made by the tenant.

The Vacation Rental Act further provides that "all funds collected from a tenant and not identified in the vacation rental agreement as occupancy or sales taxes, fees, or rental payments shall be consider a tenant security deposit and shall be subject to the provisions of the Residential Tenant Security Deposit Act" discussed earlier. In addition, the Act prohibits a vacation rental agreement from containing language compelling or permitting the automatic forfeiture of all or part of a security deposit in the event of breach of contract by the tenant. The Act requires that the vacation rental agreement "provide that a tenant security deposit may be applied to actual damages caused by the tenant" as permitted under the Residential Tenant Security Deposit Act.

Mandatory Evacuation

The Act addresses the very practical issue of the legal rights of the parties in the event of a mandatory evacuation. N.C. Gen. Stat. §42A-36 provides, in part:

> If State or local authorities ... order a mandatory evacuation of an area that includes the residential property subject to a vacation rental, the tenant under the vacation rental agreement, whether in possession of the property or not, shall comply with the evacuation order. Upon compliance, the tenant shall be entitled to a refund from the landlord of the rent, taxes, and any other payments made by the tenant pursuant to the vacation rental agreement as a condition of the tenant's right to occupy the property prorated for each night that the tenant is unable to occupy the property because of the mandatory evacuation order. The tenant shall not be entitled to a refund if: (i) prior to the tenant taking possession of the property, the tenant refused insurance offered by the landlord or real estate broker that would have compensated the tenant for losses or damages resulting from loss of use of the property due to a mandatory evacuation order; or (ii) the tenant purchased insurance offered by the landlord or real estate broker. The insurance offered shall be provided by an insurance company duly authorized by the North Carolina Department of Insurance, and the cost of the insurance shall not exceed eight percent (8%) of the total amount charged for the vacation rental to the tenant less the amount paid by the tenant for a security deposit.

Endnotes

1. N.C. Gen. Stat., Article 5, "Residential Rental Agreements," §42-38 *et seq.*

2. N.C. Gen. Stat. Article 4A, "Retaliatory Eviction," §42-37.1 *et. seq.*

3. N.C. Gen. Stat., Article 6, "Tenant Security Deposit Act," §42-50 *et. seq.*

4. N.C. Gen. Stat., Article 2A, "Ejectment of Residential Tenants," §42-25.6 *et. seq.*

5. Chapter 41A of the North Carolina General Statutes. See Chapter 18 for a complete discussion of state and federal fair housing legislation.

6. North Carolina statutes allow a residential tenant to unilaterally terminate the tenancy in three situations. *See* N.C. Gen. Stat. §42-45, "Early termination of rental agreement by military personnel," N.C. Gen. Stat. §42-45.1, "Early termination of rental agreement by victims of domestic violence, sexual assault, or stalking," and N.C. Gen. Stat. §42-45.2, "Early termination of rental agreement by military and tenants residing in certain foreclosed property."

7. N.C.Gen.Stat. §14-395.1; N.C.Gen.Stat. §§42-42.2, 42-42.3.

8. N.C.Gen.Stat. §75-1.1.

9. The Fair Housing Act of 1968, as amended, is found at 42 U.S.C. §§3601 *et. seq.* The North Carolina Fair Housing Act is located at Chapter 41A of the General Statutes.

10. 50 USC App. §§ 501-597b.

11. 12 U.S.C. §1715z-1b(b)(3)(2004); 24 C.F.R. § 247.4.

12. The Residential Rental Agreements Act is found at N.C. Gen. Stat. §42-38 *et. seq.* Additional references to it in this chapter will not be footnoted.

13. N.C.Gen.Stat. § 42-38.

14. N.C.Gen.Stat. § 42-40.

15. This example is based on *Baker v. Rushing*, 104 N.C. App. 240, 409 S.E.2d 108 (1991).

16. N.C. Gen. Stat. §42-42(b).

17. N.C. Gen. Stat. §42-42(a)(2) imposes a duty on the landlord to correct unfit conditions and not a duty to warn against them. *Brooks v. Francis*, 57 N.C. App. 556, 291 S.E.2d 889 (1982).

18. N.C. Gen. Stat. §42-43(a).

19. *Mudusar v. Murray & Co.*, 100 N.C. App. 395, 396 S.E.2d 325 (1990). For an excellent summary, see the nine-page publication, "Landlord Maintenance and Repair Duties: Your Rights as a Residential Tenant in North Carolina," revised October, 2007, published by the N.C. Department of Justice. http://www.ncdoj.gov/Files/Consumer/landlord-tenant-booklet.aspx

20. N.C. Gen. Stat. §42-42(a)(8), the "imminently dangerous condition" section was added by Session Law 2009-279.

21. N.C. Gen.Stat. §42-42(5)(5a)(7)

22. N.C.Gen.Stat. § 42-40(4).

23. N.C.Gen.Stat. §42-42.3.

24. N.C.Gen.Stat. §42-45.1.

25. N.C.Gen.Stat. §42-42(a)(2).

26. A real estate agent having actual or apparent authority to perform duties imposed on landlords by the Residential Rental Agreements Act is defined as a "landlord" under N.C. Gen. Stat. §42-40(3). That agent may be liable to the tenant for damages or other remedies where a material violation of the Act has occurred. *Surrat v. Newton*, 99 N.C. App. 396, 393 S.E.2d 554 (1990); *Baker v. Rushing, supra.* Liability of the agent for damages is not limited to the amount the agent was paid by the landlord for management services.

27. Chapter 62 of the North Carolina General Statutes. See also N.C. Gen. Stat. §143-151.42.

28. N.C. Gen. Stat. §62-110(g) and N.C. Gen. Stat. §42-42.1.

29. N.C. Gen. Stat. §42-42.1(b).

30. N.C. Gen. Stat. §42-26(b).

31. N.C. Gen. Stat. §62-110(h). N.C. Gen. Stat. §143-151.42. New subsection (b)(2) of this statute is effective on June 13, 2013, and is applicable "to leases entered into, amended, or renewed, including leases that are renewed by inaction, on or after the effective date." Session law 2013-168. For a more in-depth discussion of this issue, licensees are referred to an *Advice Letter for Residential Apartment Owners* updated by the Public Staff of the NC Utilities Commission in July 2013.

32. *Von Pettis Realty, Inc. v. McKoy*, 135 N.C. App. 206, 519 S.E.2d 546 (N.C. App. 1999) is the leading North Carolina case on the issue of calculating the proper measure of damages for a landlord's breach of implied warranty of habitability under the Act. For a North Carolina appellate decision in which a landlord was held liable for damages for breach of the implied warranty of habitability, see *Cardwell v. Henry*, 145 N.C. App. 194, 549 S.E.2d 587 (2001). In this case, the violations included unsafe electrical wiring resulting in an insufficient supply of electrical power often causing the leased premises' heat, hot water, and appliances to be useless. *Miller v. C.W. Myers Trading Post, Inc.*, 85 N.C. App. 362, 355 S.E.2d 189 (1987); *Cotton v. Stanley*, 86 N.C. App. 534, 358 S.E.2d 692 (1987); *Surrat v. Newton*, *supra*. The landlord who has materially breached the implied warranty is liable for both retroactive and prospective rent abatements during the period of the breach. Damages for rent abatement can only include offsets against rent actually paid by the tenant. *Allen v. Simmons*, 99 N.C. App. 636, 394 S.E.2d 478 (1990).

33. See, for example, *Gardner v. Ebenezer, LLC*, 190 N.C. App. 432, 660 S.E.2d 172 (2008), quoting as follows from *K & S Enter. v. Kennedy Office Supply Co., Inc.*, 135 N.C. App. 260, 520 S.E.2d 122 (1999): "[C]onstructive eviction takes place when a landlord's breach of duty under the lease renders the premises untenable. A tenant seeking to show constructive eviction has the burden of showing that he abandoned the premises within a reasonable time after the landlord's wrongful act."

34. Rental of residential property is "in or affecting commerce" for purposes of coverage under the deceptive practices statute. *Stolfo v. Kernodle*, 118 N.C. App. 580, 455 S.E.2d 869 (1995). N.C. Gen. Stat. §75-1.1. If the tenant prevails under this statute the tenant might also recover attorney's fees under N.C. Gen. Stat. §75-16.1.

35. See Question and Answer pamphlets entitled "*Renting Residential Real Estate*" and "*Tenant Security Deposits*" published by the N.C. Real Estate Commission.

36. Under the traditional law of North Carolina, a landlord is not liable for injuries on the premises unless the landlord has contracted to repair a condition, knowingly leaves the premises in a state of ruin or nuisance, authorizes a wrong on the premises, or maintains control over the premises. *Wilson v. Dowtin*, 215 N.C. 547, 2 S.E.2d 576(1939); *Rigsbee v. Special Flowers, Inc.*, 198 N.C. App. 703, 681SE2d 865 (2009). A contributorily negligent tenant may not recover damages if s/he is aware of a dangerous condition in a common area and fails to notify the landlord of the condition. *DiOrio v. Penny*, 103 N.C. App. 407, 405 S.E.2d 789 (1991). *Taylor v. Batts*, 201 N.C. App. 728, 689 SE2d 201 (2010) (holding that liability requires landlord's notice of the dangerous condition even if the alleged duty is enumerated in the Residential Rental Agreements Act and reiterating that violation of the Act is not negligence per se).

37. *Holcomb v. Colonial Associates, L.L.C.*, 358 N.C. 501, 597 S.E.2d 710 (2004): cf. *Walden v. Morgan*, 179 N.C. App. 673, 635 S.E.2d 616 (2006).

38. *Bradley v. Wachovia Bank & Trust Co., N.A.*, 90 N.C. App. 581, 369 S.E.2d 86 (1988). *Prince v. Wright*, 141 N.C. App. 262, 541 S.E.2d 191 (2000).

39. N.C. Gen. Stat., Article 4A, "Retaliatory Eviction." N.C.Gen.Stat. § 42-37.1(a).

40.   N.C. Gen. Stat. §42-50 *et. seq.*

41.   N.C. Gen. Stat. §42-46. If the rent is paid in monthly installments, late fees are limited to the greater of $15.00 or 5% of the monthly rent. If weekly rent installments are involved, late fees are limited to the greater of $4.00 or 5% of the weekly rent. N.C. Gen. Stat. §42-46(b) provides, in part:

> A late fee ... may be imposed only one time for each late rental payment.
> A late fee for a specific late rental payment may not be deducted from a subsequent rental payment so as to cause the subsequent rental payment to be in default.

42.   N.C. Gen. Stat. §42-46(e),(f)&(g). Subsection (h) of this statute lists limitations on the charging and collection of fees by a landlord. Included in this subsection is the following limitation: "Any provision of a residential rental agreement contrary to the provisions of this section is against the public policy of this State and therefore void and unenforceable."

43.   N.C. Gen. Stat. §42-52.

44.   *See*, the pamphlet titled "*Questions and Answers on Tenant Security Deposits*" published by the N.C. Real Estate Commission.

45.   N.C. Gen. Stat. §42-55.

46.   N.C. Gen. Stat. §42-53, appropriately titled "Pet Deposits."

47.   A "small claims action" is defined by N.C. Gen. Stat. §7A-210 as a civil action wherein:

> 1) The amount in controversy, computed in accordance with G.S. 7A-243, does not exceed five thousand dollars ($10,000); and
> 2) The only principal relief prayed is monetary, or the recovery of specific personal property, or summary ejectment, or any combination of the foregoing in properly joined claims; and
> 3) The plaintiff has requested assignment to a magistrate in the manner provided in this Article.
> 4) See Article 19 of Chapter 7A of the North Carolina General Statutes. That Article is titled "Small Claim Actions in District Court." See also Articles 2A of Chapter 42 of the General Statutes titled "Ejectment of Residential Tenants," and "*A Citizen's Guide to Small Claims Court*" published by the NC Department of Justice at this link: http://www.ncdoj.gov/getdoc/906abea4-5cb8-4d71-b014-522fa8a27806/Citizens-Guide-to-Small-Claims-Court-Josh-Stein-1.aspx

48.   N.C. Gen. Stat. §7A-216, titled "Form of Complaint."

49.   N.C. Gen. Stat. §7A-213.

50.   More detailed information regarding the residential eviction process and how to complete the summary ejectment complaint may be found in the Real Estate Commission's *2012-2013 Real Estate Update Course*, Section 3, "Summary Ejectment in Residential Tenancies," available on its website under "Publications" at https://www.ncrec.gov/Pdfs/bicar/SummaryEjectment.pdf

51.   *Stanley v. Moore*, 339 N.C. 717, 454 S.E.2d 225 (1995) recognizes the prohibition of "self-help" eviction measures by a landlord without resort to judicial process.

52.   N.C. Gen. Stat. §42-25.9(c) states: "The remedies created by this section are supplementary to all existing common-law and statutory rights and remedies." G.S. §44A-2 originally authorized liens on personal property for residential landlords, but that statute was revised to cover only nonresidential tenancies.

53.   N.C. Gen. Stat. §42-36.2.

54.   See the "Statement of Public Policy" at N.C. Gen. Stat. §42-59.1.

55.   N.C. Gen. Stat. §42-59(2). Other key terms also are described in this section.

56.   N.C. Gen. Stat. §42-63(b).

57.   N.C. Gen. Stat. §42-68, titled "Expedited Proceedings."

58.   N.C. Gen. Stat. §42-64, titled "Affirmative defense or exemption to a complete eviction."

59.   The federal Fair Housing Act is found at 42 U.S.C. §§3601 *et. seq.*, and the North Carolina Fair Housing Act is found in Chapter 41A of the North Carolina General Statutes.

60.   42 U.S.C. §3601-3619, Fair Housing Act. 42 U.S.C. §3604(f)(3)(B).

61.   See *Bragdon v. Abbott*, 524 U.S. 624, 632 (1998).

62.   *Charlotte Housing Authority v. Patterson*, 120 N.C. App. 552, 464 S.E.2d 68 (1995).

63.   *Roanoke Chowan Regional Housing Authority v. Vaughan*, 81 N.C. App. 354, 344 S.E.2d 578 (1986). See, also, *Lincoln Terrace Associates, Ltd. v. Kelly*, 179 N.C. App. 621, 635 S.E.2d 434 (2006), holding that the landlord failed to show that it complied with notice requirements for summary ejectment proceedings.

64.   42 U.S.C. §1437d(1)(5).

65.   *Rucker v. Davis*, 237 F.3d 1113 (Ninth Cir. 2001). The first paragraph of this decision reads:
            Many of our nation's poor live in public housing projects that, by many
            accounts, are little more than illegal drug markets and war zones. Innocent
            tenants live barricaded behind doors, in fear for their safety and the safety
            of their children. What these tenants may not realize is that, under existing
            policies of the Department of Housing and Urban Development ("HUD"),
            they should add another fear to their list: becoming homeless if a household

member or guest engages in criminal drug activity on or off the tenant's property, even if the tenant did not know of or have any reason to know of such activity or took all reasonable steps to prevent the activity from occurring ("innocent tenants"). Today we examine the statutory basis behind HUD's "One Strike and You're Out" policy, and hold that Congress did not intend to authorize the eviction of innocent tenants.

It is important to remember that North Carolina is located in the Fourth Federal Circuit, and the holding of the Ninth Circuit is not binding precedent for the Fourth Circuit.

66.   North Carolina has legislation applicable to all residential tenancies titled "Expedited Eviction of Drug Traffickers and other Criminals." See Article 7, Chapter 42 of the North Carolina General Statutes.

67.   *Marshall v. Cuomo*, 192 F.3d 473 (4th Cir. 1999).

68.   The federal Soldiers' and Sailors' Civil Relief Act is at 50 U.S.C. App. §501-594 (2000),and the Servicemembers Civil Relief Act is at 50 U.S.C. App. §501-596.

69.   Professor and Lieutenant Col. J. Thomas Parker, *Servicemembers Civil Relief Act (SCRA) and Uniformed Services Employment and Reemployment Rights Act (USERRA) Amendments and Updates*, 2005-March ARMY LAWYER, pp. 22-24.

70.   50 U.S.C. App. §531(a). A state statute also protects military tenants under certain circumstances. *See* N.C. Gen. Stat. §42-45, "Early termination of rental agreement by military personnel."

71.   See also, N.C. Gen. Stat. §45-21.17(4), requiring that a notice of a foreclosure sale be given to certain residential tenants. In addition, N.C. Gen. Stat. 45-21.16A requires the notice of foreclosure sale to state that any purchaser at the foreclosure sale takes subject to this tenant statutory right to terminate upon ten days' notice.

72.   N.C. Gen. Stat. §42-14.3.

73.   42 U.S.C. §4851 *et seq.*, 15 U.S.C. §2881. See, also, N.C. Gen. Stat. §130A-131.5 and rules adopted by the *N.C. Department of Environment Quality, Commision for Public Health* implementing the law in this area.

74.   "Target housing" is more precisely defined as "any housing constructed prior to 1978, except housing for the elderly or persons with disabilities (unless any child who is less than 6 years of age resides or is expected to reside in such housing for the elderly or persons with disabilities) or any 0-bedroom dwelling." 42 U.S.C. §4851b(27).

75.   42 U.S.C. §4852d(a)(4).

76.   42 U.S.C. §4852d(b)(3).

77. See, for example, *Nesbit v. Cribbs*, 203 N.C.App.149, 692 SE2d 194 (2010) (holding that an agreement to lease "indefinitely" failed to prescribe a lease term and resulted in a periodic tenancy).

78. See, for example, *National Advertising Co. v. NC Dept. Of Transportation*, 124 N.C. App. 620, 478 S.E.2d 248 (1996), where the plaintiff claimed, among other things, that it had a five-year sign lease. The Court of Appeals held that plaintiff's failure to record his lease under N.C. Gen. Stat. §47-18 made it invalid against a subsequent purchaser of the property for value who recorded first. See *Chapel Hill Cinemas, Inc. v. Robbins*, 143 N.C. App. 571, 547 S.E.2d 462, *reversed* 354 N.C. 349, 554 S.E.2d 644 (2001), where the lessee lost a valuable right of first refusal contained in a lease because of failure to record. (The lessee prevailed in a suit for damages against the lessor who sold the property without honoring the right of first refusal.)

79. For additional information regarding permissible disbursements from advanced payments and an owner's obligation to transfer advanced payments for future tenancies to a new owner, readers are referred to the Commission's "Sale of Vacation Rentals" from the *2015-2016 General Update* materials available on the Commission's website under "Publications," and then "Update/BICAR" at this link: https://www.ncrec.gov/Pdfs/genupdate/VacRentalSales.pdf

STATE OF NORTH CAROLINA

_____ County

File No.

In The General Court Of Justice
District Court Division - Small Claims

Plaintiff(s)

MAGISTRATE SUMMONS
☐ **ALIAS AND PLURIES SUMMONS (ASSESS FEE)**

VERSUS

G.S. 1A-1, Rule 4; 7A-217, -232

Defendant(s)

Date Original Summons Issued

Date(s) Subsequent Summons(es) Issued

TO

Name And Address Of Defendant 1

TO

Name And Address Of Defendant 2

A Small Claim Action Has Been Commenced Against You!

You are notified to appear before the magistrate at the specified date, time, and location of trial listed below. You will have the opportunity at the trial to defend yourself against the claim stated in the attached complaint.

You may file a written answer, making defense to the claim, in the office of the Clerk of Superior Court at any time before the time set for trial. Whether or not you file an answer, the plaintiff must prove the claim before the magistrate.

If you fail to appear and defend against the proof offered, the magistrate may enter a judgment against you.

Date Of Trial

Time Of Trial
☐ AM ☐ PM

Location Of Court

Name And Address Of Plaintiff Or Plaintiff's Attorney

Date Issued

Signature

☐ Deputy CSC   ☐ Assistant CSC   ☐ Clerk Of Superior Court

AOC-CVM-100, Rev. 10/14

(Over)

Figure 16-1

RETURN OF SERVICE

I certify that this summons and a copy of the complaint were received and served as follows:

DEFENDANT 1

Date Served	Time Served ☐ AM ☐ PM	Name Of Defendant

☐ By delivering to the defendant named above a copy of the summons and complaint.

☐ By leaving a copy of the summons and complaint at the dwelling house or usual place of abode of the defendant named above with a person of suitable age and discretion then residing therein.

☐ As the defendant is a corporation, service was effected by delivering a copy of the summons and complaint to the person named below.

Name And Address Of Person With Whom Copy Left (if corporation, give title of person copy left with)

☐ Other manner of service *(specify)*

☐ Defendant WAS NOT served for the following reason:

DEFENDANT 2

Date Served	Time Served ☐ AM ☐ PM	Name Of Defendant

☐ By delivering to the defendant named above a copy of the summons and complaint.

☐ By leaving a copy of the summons and complaint at the dwelling house or usual place of abode of the defendant named above with a person of suitable age and discretion then residing therein.

☐ As the defendant is a corporation, service was effected by delivering a copy of the summons and complaint to the person named below.

Name And Address Of Person With Whom Copy Left (if corporation, give title of person copy left with)

☐ Other manner of service *(specify)*

☐ Defendant WAS NOT served for the following reason:

FOR USE IN SUMMARY EJECTMENT CASES ONLY:	☐ Service was made by mailing by first class mail a copy of the summons and complaint to the defendant(s) and by posting a copy of the summons and complaint at the following premises:
	Date Served | *Name(s) Of The Defendant(s) Served By Posting*
	Address Of Premises Where Posted

Service Fee $	Signature Of Deputy Sheriff Making Return
Date Received	Name Of Deputy Sheriff Making Return (type or print)
Date Of Return	County Of Deputy Sheriff Making Return

AOC-CVM-100, Side Two, Rev. 10/14
© 2014 Administrative Office of the Courts

Figure 16-1

File No. |

COMPLAINT
IN SUMMARY EJECTMENT

G.S. 7A-216, 7A-232; Ch. 42, Art. 3 and 7

STATE OF NORTH CAROLINA

_____ County

In The General Court Of Justice
District Court Division-Small Claims

Name And Address Of Plaintiff

VERSUS

Name And Address Of Defendant 1

County | Telephone No.

☐ Individual ☐ Corporation

Name And Address Of Defendant 2

County | Telephone No.

☐ Individual ☐ Corporation

County | Telephone No.

Name And Address Of Plaintiff's Attorney Or Agent

1. The defendant is a resident of the county named above.
2. The defendant entered into possession of premises described below as a lessee of plaintiff.

Description Of Premises (Include Location)

Rate Of Rent	Date Rent Due	Date Lease Ended
$	per ☐ Month ☐ Week	

Type Of Lease
☐ Conventional
☐ Public Housing
☐ Section 8
☐ Oral ☐ Written

3. ☐ The defendant failed to pay the rent due on the above date and the plaintiff made demand for the rent and waited the 10-day grace period before filing the complaint.

☐ The lease period ended on the above date and the defendant is holding over after the end of the lease period.

☐ The defendant breached the condition of the lease described below for which re-entry is specified.

☐ Criminal activity or other activity has occurred in violation of G.S. 42-63 as specified below.

Description Of Breach/Criminal Activity (give names, dates, places and illegal activity)

4. The plaintiff has demanded possession of the premises from the defendant, who has refused to surrender it, and the plaintiff is entitled to immediate possession.

5. The defendant owes the plaintiff the following:

Description Of Any Property Damage

Amount Of Damage (If Known)	Amount Of Rent Past Due	► Total Amount Due
$	$	$

6. I demand to be put in possession of the premises and to recover the total amount listed above and daily rental until entry of judgment plus interest and reimbursement for court costs.

Date | Name Of Plaintiff/Attorney/Agent (Type Or Print) | Signature Of Plaintiff/Attorney/Agent

CERTIFICATION WHEN COMPLAINT SIGNED BY AGENT OF PLAINTIFF

I certify that I am an agent of the plaintiff and have actual knowledge of the facts alleged in this Complaint.

Date | Name Of Agent (Type Or Print) | Signature Of Agent

(Over)

AOC-CVM-201, Rev. 9/13
© 2013 Administrative Office of the Courts

Figure 16-2

INSTRUCTIONS TO PLAINTIFF OR DEFENDANT

1. The PLAINTIFF must file a small claim action in the county where at least one of the defendants resides.

2. The PLAINTIFF cannot sue in small claims court for more than $10,000.00 excluding interest and costs unless further restricted by court order.

3. The PLAINTIFF must show the complete name and address of the defendant to ensure service on the defendant. If there are two defendants and they reside at different addresses, the plaintiff must include both addresses. The plaintiff must determine if the defendant is a corporation and sue in the complete corporate name. If the business is not a corporation, the plaintiff must determine the owner's name and sue the owner.

4. The PLAINTIFF may serve the defendant(s) by mailing a copy of the summons and complaint by registered or certified mail, return receipt requested, addressed to the party to be served or by paying the costs to have the sheriff serve the summons and complaint. If certified or registered mail is used, the plaintiff must prepare and file a sworn statement with the Clerk of Superior Court proving service by certified mail and must attach to that statement the postal receipt showing that the letter was accepted.

5. In filling out number 3 in the complaint, if the landlord is seeking to remove the tenant for failure to pay rent when there is no written lease, the first block should be checked. (Defendant failed to pay the rent due on the above date and the plaintiff made demand for the rent and waited the ten (10) day grace period before filing the complaint.) If the landlord is seeking to remove the tenant for failure to pay rent when there is a written lease with an automatic forfeiture clause, the third block should be checked. (The defendant breached the condition of the lease described below for which re-entry is specified.) And "failure to pay rent" should be placed in the space for description of the breach. If the landlord is seeking to evict tenant for violating some other condition in the lease, the third block should also be checked. If the landlord is claiming that the term of the lease has ended and the tenant refuses to leave, the second block should be checked. If the landlord is claiming that criminal activity occurred, the fourth block should be checked and the conduct must be described in space provided.

6. The PLAINTIFF must pay advance court costs at the time of filing this Complaint. In the event that judgment is rendered in favor of the plaintiff, court costs may be charged against the defendant.

7. The PLAINTIFF must appear before the magistrate to prove his/her claim.

8. The DEFENDANT may file a written answer, making defense to the claim, in the office of the Clerk of Superior Court. This answer should be accompanied by a copy for the plaintiff and be filed no later than the time set for trial. The filing of the answer DOES NOT relieve the defendant of the need to appear before the magistrate to assert the defendant's defense.

9. Requests for continuances of cases before the magistrate may be granted for good cause shown and for no more than five (5) days per continuance unless the parties agree otherwise.

10. The magistrate will render judgment on the date of hearing unless the parties agree otherwise, or the case is complex as defined in G.S. 7A-222, in which case the decision is required within five (5) days.

11. The PLAINTIFF or the DEFENDANT may appeal the magistrate's decision in this case. To appeal, notice must be given in open court when the judgment is entered, or notice may be given in writing to the Clerk of Superior Court within ten (10) days after the judgment is entered. If notice is given in writing, the appealing party must also serve written notice of appeal on all other parties. The appealing party must PAY to the Clerk of Superior Court the costs of court for appeal within ten (10) days after the judgment is entered. If the appealing party applies to appeal as an indigent, and that request is denied, that party has an additional five (5) days to pay the court costs for the appeal.

12. If the defendant appeals and wishes to remain on the premises the defendant must also post a stay of execution bond within ten (10) days after the judgment is entered. In the event of an appeal by the tenant to district court, the landlord may file a motion to dismiss that appeal under G.S. 7A-228(d). The court may decide the motion without a hearing if the tenant fails to file a response within ten (10) days of receipt of the motion.

13. Upon request of the tenant within seven (7) days of the landlord being placed in lawful possession, the landlord shall release any personal property of the tenant. After seven (7) days, the landlord may sell, throw away or dispose of said property. If sold, the landlord must disburse any surplus proceeds to the tenant upon request within seven (7) days of the sale. If the total value of the property is less than $500.00, it is deemed abandoned five (5) days after execution.

14. This form is supplied in order to expedite the handling of small claims. It is designed to cover the most common claims.

15. **The Clerk or magistrate cannot advise you about your case or assist you in completing this form. If you have any questions, you should consult an attorney.**

AOC-CVM-201, Side Two, Rev. 9/13
© 2013 Administrative Office of the Courts

Figure 16-2

RESIDENTIAL RENTAL CONTRACT

RESIDENT: _____ ("Tenant")

OWNER: _____ ("Landlord")

REAL ESTATE MANAGEMENT FIRM: _____ ("Agent")

PREMISES: City:_____ County: _____ State of North Carolina
   ❑ Street Address:_____ Zip Code:_____
   ❑ Apartment Complex:_____ Apartment No. _____
   ❑ Other Description (Room, portion of above address, etc.):_____
_____

INITIAL TERM: Beginning Date of Lease: _____Ending Date of Lease: _____

RENT: $ _____ PAYMENT PERIOD: ❑ monthly ❑ weekly ❑ yearly ❑ other:_____

LATE PAYMENT FEE: $_____ OR _____% of rental payment, whichever is greater
(State law provides that the late fee may not exceed $15.00 or five percent (5%) of the rental payment, whichever is greater.)
RETURNED CHECK FEE: $ _____ *(The maximum processing fee allowed under State law is $25.00.)*
SECURITY DEPOSIT: $ _____ to be deposited with: (check one) ❑ Landlord ❑ Agent
LOCATION OF DEPOSIT: (insert name of bank): _____
BANK ADDRESS: _____

FEES FOR COMPLAINT FOR SUMMARY EJECTMENT AND/OR MONEY OWED (See paragraph 17) (NOTE: Landlord may charge and retain only one of the following fees in addition to any court costs):
- COMPLAINT-FILING FEE: $_____ OR _____% of rental payment, whichever is greater *(Fee may not exceed $15.00 or five percent (5%) of the rental payment, whichever is greater.)*
- COURT APPEARANCE FEE: _____% of rental payment *(Fee may not exceed ten percent (10%) of the rental payment.)*
- SECOND TRIAL FEE: _____% of rental payment *(Fee may not exceed twelve percent (12%) of the rental payment.)*

PERMITTED OCCUPANTS (in addition to Tenant):_____
_____

CONTACT PERSON IN EVENT OF DEATH OR EMERGENCY OF TENANT (name and contact information):_____
_____

    IN CONSIDERATION of the promises contained in this Agreement, Landlord, by and through Agent, hereby agrees to lease the Premises to Tenant on the following terms and conditions:

    1. **Termination and Renewal:** EITHER LANDLORD OR TENANT MAY TERMINATE THE TENANCY AT THE EXPIRATION OF THE INITIAL TERM BY GIVING WRITTEN NOTICE TO THE OTHER AT LEAST _____ DAYS PRIOR TO THE EXPIRATION DATE OF THE INITIAL TERM. IN THE EVENT SUCH WRITTEN NOTICE IS NOT GIVEN OR IF THE TENANT HOLDS OVER BEYOND THE INITIAL TERM, THE TENANCY SHALL AUTOMATICALLY BECOME A _____ (PERIOD) TO _____ (PERIOD) TENANCY UPON THE SAME TERMS AND CONDITIONS CONTAINED HEREIN. THEREAFTER, THE TENANCY MAY BE TERMINATED BY EITHER LANDLORD OR TENANT GIVING THE OTHER _____ DAYS WRITTEN NOTICE PRIOR TO THE LAST DAY OF THE FINAL PERIOD OF THE TENANCY. *(EXAMPLE: Assume tenancy is a calendar month-to-month tenancy and 30 days advance written notice of termination is required. Tenant desires to terminate lease at the end of the April period of the tenancy. Tenant would be required to give landlord written notice no later than March 31ˢᵗ. If the written notice of termination were to be given to the Landlord on the 10th of April, the notice would be effective to terminate the lease at the end of May rather than the end of April, since the monthly periods of the tenancy expire on the last day of the month and the notice was not given 30 days prior to the end of April.)*

Page 1 of 8

North Carolina Association of REALTORS®, Inc.

STANDARD FORM 410 – T
Revised 7/2015
© 7/2017

Tenant Initials _____ _____ Landlord Initials _____ _____

Figure 16-3

2. **Rent:** Tenant shall pay the Rent, without notice, demand or deduction, to Landlord or as Landlord directs. The first Rent payment, which shall be prorated if the Initial Term commences on a day other than the first day of the Payment Period, shall be due on _____ (date). Thereafter, all rentals shall be paid in advance on or before the **FIRST** day of each subsequent Payment Period for the duration of the tenancy, and shall be considered late if not paid on or before such date.

3. **Late Payment Fees and Returned Check Fees:** Tenant shall pay the Late Payment Fee if any rental payment is five (5) days or more late. *This late payment fee shall be due immediately without demand therefor and shall be added to and paid with the late rental payment. Tenant also agrees to pay the Returned Check Fee for each check of Tenant that is returned by the financial institution because of insufficient funds or because the Tenant did not have an account at the financial institution.*

4. **Tenant Security Deposit:** The Security Deposit shall be administered in accordance with the North Carolina Tenant Security Deposit Act (N.C.G.S. § 42-50 et. seq.). IT MAY, IN THE DISCRETION OF EITHER THE LANDLORD OR THE AGENT, BE DEPOSITED IN AN INTEREST-BEARING ACCOUNT WITH THE BANK OR SAVINGS INSTITUTION NAMED ABOVE. ANY INTEREST EARNED UPON THE TENANT SECURITY DEPOSIT SHALL ACCRUE FOR THE BENEFIT OF, AND SHALL BE PAID TO, THE LANDLORD, OR AS THE LANDLORD DIRECTS. SUCH INTEREST, IF ANY, MAY BE WITHDRAWN BY LANDLORD OR AGENT FROM SUCH ACCOUNT AS IT ACCRUES AS OFTEN AS IS PERMITTED BY THE TERMS OF THE ACCOUNT.

Upon any termination of the tenancy herein created, the Landlord may deduct from the Tenant Security Deposit amounts permitted under the Tenant Security Deposit Act. If there is more than one person listed above as Tenant, Agent may, in Agent's discretion, pay any balance of the Tenant Security Deposit to any such person, and the other person(s) agree to hold Agent harmless for such action. If the Tenant's address is unknown to the Landlord, the Landlord may deduct any permitted amounts and shall then hold the balance of the Tenant Security Deposit for the Tenant's collection for a six-month period beginning upon the termination of the tenancy and delivery of possession by the Tenant. If the Tenant fails to make demand for the balance of the Tenant Security Deposit within the six-month period, the Landlord shall not thereafter be liable to the Tenant for a refund of the Tenant Security Deposit or any part thereof.

If the Landlord removes Agent or Agent resigns, the Tenant agrees that Agent may transfer any Tenant Security Deposit held by Agent hereunder to the Landlord or the Landlord's designee and thereafter notify the Tenant by mail of such transfer and of the transferee's name and address. The Tenant agrees that such action by Agent shall relieve Agent of further liability with respect to the Tenant Security Deposit. If Landlord's interest in the Premises terminates (whether by sale, assignment, death, appointment of receiver or otherwise), Agent shall transfer the Tenant Security Deposit in accordance with the provisions of North Carolina General Statutes § 42-54.

5. **Tenant's Obligations:** Unless otherwise agreed upon, the Tenant shall:
(a) use the Premises for residential purposes only and in a manner so as not to disturb the other tenants;
(b) not use the Premises for any unlawful or immoral purposes or occupy them in such a way as to constitute a nuisance;
(c) keep the Premises, including but not limited to all plumbing fixtures, facilities and appliances, in a clean and safe condition;
(d) cause no unsafe or unsanitary condition in the common areas and remainder of the Premises used by him;
(e) comply with any and all obligations imposed upon tenants by applicable building and housing codes;
(f) dispose of all ashes, rubbish, garbage, and other waste in a clean and safe manner and comply with all applicable ordinances concerning garbage collection, waste and other refuse;
(g) use in a proper and reasonable manner all electrical, plumbing, sanitary, heating, ventilating, air conditioning, and other facilities and appliances, if any, furnished as a part of the Premises;
(h) not deliberately or negligently destroy, deface, damage or remove any part of the Premises (including all facilities, appliances or fixtures) or permit any person, known or unknown to the Tenant, to do so;
(i) pay the costs of all utility services to the Premises which are billed directly to the Tenant and not included as a part of the rentals, including, but not limited to, water, electric, telephone, and gas services;
(j) conduct himself and require all other persons on the Premises with his consent to conduct themselves in a reasonable manner and so as not to disturb other tenants' peaceful enjoyment of the Premises;
(k) not abandon or vacate the Premises during the Initial Term or any renewals or extensions thereof. Tenant shall be deemed to have abandoned or vacated the Premises if Tenant removes substantially all of his possessions from the Premises; and
(l) _____

_____
_____
_____
_____

STANDARD FORM 410 – T
Revised 7/2015
© 7/2017

Tenant Initials _____ _____ Landlord Initials _____ _____

Figure 16-3

6. **Landlord's Obligations:** Unless otherwise agreed upon, the Landlord shall:

(a) comply with the applicable building and housing codes to the extent required by such building and housing codes;

(b) make all repairs to the Premises as may be necessary to keep the Premises in a fit and habitable condition; provided, however, in accordance with paragraph 11, the Tenant shall be liable to the Landlord for any repairs necessitated by the Tenant's intentional or negligent misuse of the Premises;

(c) keep all common areas, if any, used in conjunction with the Premises in a clean and safe condition;

(d) promptly repair all facilities and appliances, if any, as may be furnished by the Landlord as part of the Premises, including electrical, plumbing, sanitary, heating, ventilating, and air conditioning systems, provided that the Landlord, except in emergency situations, actually receives notification from the Tenant in writing of the needed repairs; and

(e) within a reasonable period of time based upon the severity of the condition, repair or remedy any imminently dangerous condition on the Premises after acquiring actual knowledge or receiving notice of the condition. Notwithstanding Landlord's repair or remedy of any imminently dangerous condition, Landlord may recover from Tenant the actual and reasonable costs of repairs that are the fault of Tenant.

7. **Utility Bills/Service Contracts:** Landlord and Tenant agree that utility bills and service contracts ("Service Obligations") for the Premises shall be paid by the party indicated below as to each Service Obligation. The party agreeing to be responsible for payment of a Service Obligation agrees to timely pay the applicable Service Obligation, including any metering, hook-up fees or other miscellaneous charges associated with establishing, installing and maintaining such utility or contract in that party's name. Within thirty (30) days of the Beginning Date of this Lease, Tenant shall provide Landlord with a copy of any requested information about any Service Obligation for which Tenant has agreed to be responsible. Any Service Obligation not designated below shall be the responsibility of Tenant unless the parties agree otherwise in writing.

Service obligation	Landlord	Tenant	N/A
Sewer/Septic	❏	❏	❏
Water	❏	❏	❏
Electric	❏	❏	❏
Gas	❏	❏	❏
Telephone	❏	❏	❏
Security System	❏	❏	❏
Trash disposal/dumpster	❏	❏	❏
Landscaping	❏	❏	❏
Lawn Maintenance	❏	❏	❏
	❏	❏	❏
	❏	❏	❏
	❏	❏	❏

STANDARD FORM 410 – T
Revised 7/2015
© 7/2017

Tenant Initials _____ _____ Landlord Initials _____ _____

Figure 16-3

8. **Smoke and Carbon Monoxide Alarms:** Pursuant to North Carolina General Statutes § 42-42, the Landlord shall provide operable smoke alarms, either battery-operated or electrical. If the Premises has a fossil-fuel burning heater, appliance, or fireplace, or an attached garage, the Landlord shall provide and install a minimum of one operable carbon monoxide alarm per level in the Premises, either battery operated or electrical. The Tenant shall notify the Landlord, in writing, of the need for replacement of or repairs to a smoke or carbon monoxide alarm. The Landlord shall replace or repair the smoke or carbon monoxide alarm within 15 days of receipt of notification if the Landlord is notified of needed replacement or repairs in writing by the Tenant. The Landlord shall ensure that a smoke or carbon monoxide alarm is operable and in good repair at the beginning of the Initial Term of the Tenancy.

The Landlord shall place new batteries in any battery-operated smoke or carbon monoxide alarms at the beginning of the Initial Term of the tenancy **and the Tenant shall replace the batteries as needed during the tenancy**, except where the smoke alarm is a tamper-resistant, 10-year lithium battery smoke alarm.

9. **Rules and Regulations:**
(a) **Landlord Rules and Regulations:** The Tenant, his family, servants, guests and agents shall comply with and abide by all the Landlord's existing rules and regulations and such future reasonable rules and regulations as the Landlord may, at Landlord's discretion, from time to time, adopt governing the use and occupancy of the Premises and any common areas used in connection with them (the "Rules and Regulations"). Landlord reserves the right to make changes to the existing Rules and Regulations and to adopt additional reasonable rules and regulations from time to time; provided however, such changes and additions shall not alter the essential terms of this lease or any substantive rights granted hereunder and shall not become effective until thirty (30) days' written notice thereof shall have been furnished to Tenant. A copy of the existing Rules and Regulations are attached hereto and the Tenant acknowledges that he has read them. The Rules and Regulations shall be deemed to be a part of this lease giving to the Landlord all the rights and remedies herein provided.

(b) ❑ (*check if applicable*) **Owner Association Rules and Regulations:** The Premises are subject to regulation by the following owners/condo association:
- Name of association:_____ _____
- Name of association property manager:_____
- Property manager address and phone number:_____
- Association website address, if any: _____

Tenant agrees to abide by any applicable owners' association regulations as they now exist or may be amended.

10. **Right of Entry:** Landlord hereby reserves the right to enter the Premises during reasonable hours for the purpose of (1) inspecting the Premises and the Tenant's compliance with the terms of this lease; (2) making such repairs, alterations, improvements or additions thereto as the Landlord may deem appropriate; and (3) showing the Premises to prospective purchasers or tenants. Landlord shall also have the right to display "For Sale" or "For Rent" signs in a reasonable manner upon the Premises. Tenant acknowledges and understands that in the case of an emergency, the Landlord may need to enter the Premises at any hour to cause repairs to be made to preserve or prevent further damage from occurring to the Premises, and the Tenant agrees to cooperate reasonably with the Landlord in the event of any such emergency.

11. **Damages:** Tenant shall be responsible for all damage, defacement, or removal of any property inside a dwelling unit in the Tenant's exclusive control unless the damage, defacement or removal was due to ordinary wear and tear, acts of the Landlord or the Landlord's agent, defective products supplied or repairs authorized by the Landlord, acts of third parties not invitees of the Tenant, or natural forces. Tenant agrees to pay Landlord for the cost of repairing any damage for which Tenant is responsible upon receipt of Landlord's demand therefor, and to pay the Rent during the period the Premises may not be habitable as a result of any such damage. Such damage may include but is not limited to window panes or screens damaged by Tenant, filthy ovens, refrigerators, kitchen floors, cabinets or bathrooms, drink stains on carpet, and unauthorized paint colors.

. 12. **Pets:** Tenant agrees not to keep or allow anywhere on or about the Premises any animals or pets of any kind, whether on a temporary basis or otherwise and whether belonging to the Tenant or anybody else, including but not limited to, dogs, cats, birds, rodents, reptiles or marine animals, unless permitted under the terms of a Pet Addendum attached to this Agreement. Tenant shall be subject to a fine of $ _____ for any violation of this paragraph or of the terms of any Pet Addendum that may be a part of this Agreement, and Tenant agrees to pay any such fine upon receipt of Landlord's demand therefore.

STANDARD FORM 410 – T
Revised 7/2015
© 7/2017

Tenant Initials _____ _____ Landlord Initials _____ _____

Figure 16-3

13. **Alterations**: The Tenant shall not paint, mark, drive nails or screws into, or otherwise deface or alter walls, ceilings, floors, windows, cabinets, woodwork, stone, ironwork or any other part of the Premises, decorate the Premises, change or remove any existing locks or add any additional locks, or make any alterations, additions, or improvements in, to, on or about the Premises without the Landlord's prior written consent and then only in a workmanlike manner using materials and contractors approved by the Landlord. All such work shall be done at the Tenant's expense and at such times and in such manner as the Landlord may approve, and keys for any changed or additional locks shall immediately be provided to the Landlord. All alterations, additions, and improvements upon the Premises, made by either the Landlord or Tenant, shall become the property of the Landlord and shall remain upon and become a part of the Premises at the end of the tenancy hereby created.

14. **Occupants:** The Tenant shall not allow or permit the Premises to be occupied or used as a residence by any person other than Tenant and the Permitted Occupants. Tenant shall be subject to a fine of $ _____ for any violation of this paragraph, and Tenant agrees to pay any such fine upon receipt of Landlord's demand therefor.

15. **Rental Application:** In the event the Tenant has submitted a Rental Application in connection with this lease, Tenant acknowledges that the Landlord has relied upon the Application as an inducement for entering into this Lease and Tenant warrants to Landlord that the facts stated in the Application are true to the best of Tenant's knowledge. If any facts stated in the Rental Application prove to be untrue, the Landlord shall have the right to terminate the tenancy and to collect from Tenant any damages resulting therefrom.

16. **Tenant's Duties Upon Termination:** Upon any termination of the Tenancy created hereby, whether by the Landlord or the Tenant and whether for breach or otherwise, the Tenant shall: (1) pay all utility bills due for services to the Premises for which he is responsible and have all such utility services discontinued; (2) vacate the Premises removing there from all Tenant's personal property of whatever nature; (3) properly sweep and clean the Premises, including plumbing fixtures, refrigerators, stoves and sinks, removing there from all rubbish, trash, garbage and refuse; (4) make such repairs and perform such other acts as are necessary to return the Premises, and any appliances or fixtures furnished in connection therewith, in the same condition as when Tenant took possession of the Premises; provided, however, Tenant shall not be responsible for ordinary wear and tear or for repairs required by law or by paragraph 6 above to be performed by Landlord; (5) fasten and lock all doors and windows; (6) return to the Landlord all keys to the Premises; (7) restore the level of fuel in any fuel tank used by the Tenant to its level as of the Beginning Date of the Tenancy; and (8) notify the Landlord of the address to which the balance of the Security Deposit may be returned. If the Tenant fails to sweep out and clean the Premises, appliances and fixtures as herein provided, Tenant shall become liable, without notice or demand, to the Landlord for the actual costs of cleaning (over and above ordinary wear and tear), which may be deducted from the Security Deposit as provided in paragraph 4 above.

In the event Tenant desires to terminate the Tenancy prior to the end of its term then in effect, Tenant acknowledges and understands that the Landlord will use reasonable efforts to re-rent the Premises, but that the Tenant shall remain responsible for the performance of all the Tenant's obligations under this Agreement until such time as the Landlord may be able to re-rent the Premises, unless the Landlord and the Tenant agree otherwise in writing.

17. **Tenant's Breach:**
   (a) **Events Constituting Breach:** It shall constitute a breach of this Agreement if Tenant fails to:
      (i)   pay the full amount of rent herein reserved as and when it shall become due hereunder; or
      (ii)   perform any other promise, duty or obligation herein agreed to by him or imposed upon him by law and such failure shall continue for a period of five (5) days from the date the Landlord provides Tenant with written notice of such failure.
In either of such events and as often as either of them may occur, the Landlord, in addition to all other rights and remedies provided by law, may, at its option and with or without notice to Tenant, either terminate this lease or terminate the Tenant's right to possession of the Premises without terminating this lease.
   (b) **Landlord's Right to Possession:** Regardless of whether Landlord terminates this lease or only terminates the Tenant's right of possession without terminating this lease, Landlord shall be immediately entitled to possession of the Premises and the Tenant shall peacefully surrender possession of the Premises to Landlord immediately upon Landlord's demand. In the event Tenant shall fail or refuse to surrender possession of the Premises, Landlord shall, in compliance with Article 2A of Chapter 42 of the General Statutes of North Carolina, reenter and retake possession of the Premises only through a summary ejectment proceeding.
   (c) **Summary Ejectment Fees:** If a summary ejectment proceeding is instituted against Tenant, in addition to any court costs and past-due rent that may be awarded, Tenant shall be responsible for paying Landlord the relevant Complaint-Filing Fee, Court Appearance Fee or Second Trial Fee in accordance with NC General Statutes §42-46.
   (d) **Acceptance of Partial Rent:** Tenant acknowledges and understands that Landlord's acceptance of partial rent or partial housing subsidy will not waive Tenant's breach of this Agreement or limit Landlord's rights to evict Tenant through a summary ejectment proceeding, whether filed before or after Landlord's acceptance of any such partial rent or partial housing subsidy.

Tenant Initials   Landlord Initials

Figure 16-3

(e) **Termination of Lease:** In the event Landlord terminates this lease, all further rights and duties hereunder shall terminate and Landlord shall be entitled to collect from Tenant all accrued but unpaid rents and any damages resulting from the Tenant's breach, including but not limited to damages for Tenant's continued occupancy of the Premises following the Landlord's termination.

(f) **Termination of Tenant's Right of Possession:** In the event Landlord terminates the Tenant's right of possession without terminating this lease, Tenant shall remain liable for the full performance of all the covenants hereof, and Landlord shall use reasonable efforts to re-let the Premises on Tenant's behalf. Any such rentals reserved from such re-letting shall be applied first to the costs of re-letting the Premises and then to the rentals due hereunder. In the event the rentals from such re-letting are insufficient to pay the rentals due hereunder in full, Tenant shall be liable to the Landlord for any deficiency. In the event Landlord institutes a legal action against the Tenant to enforce the lease or to recover any sums due hereunder, Tenant agrees to pay Landlord reasonable attorney's fees in addition to all other damages.

18. **Landlord's Default; Limitation of Remedies and Damages:** Until the Tenant notifies the Landlord in writing of an alleged default and affords the Landlord a reasonable time within which to cure, no default by the Landlord in the performance of any of the promises or obligations herein agreed to by him or imposed upon him by law shall constitute a material breach of this lease and the Tenant shall have no right to terminate this lease for any such default or suspend his performance hereunder. In no event and regardless of their duration shall any defective condition of or failure to repair, maintain, or provide any area, fixture or facility used in connection with recreation or recreational activities, including but not limited to swimming pools, club houses, and tennis courts, constitute a material breach of this lease and the Tenant shall have no right to terminate this lease or to suspend his performance hereunder. In any legal action instituted by the Tenant against the Landlord, the Tenant's damages shall be limited to the difference, if any, between the rent reserved in this lease and the reasonable rental value of the Premises, taking into account the Landlord's breach or breaches, and in no event, except in the case of the Landlord's willful or wanton negligence, shall the Tenant collect any consequential or secondary damages resulting from the breach or breaches, including but not limited to the following items: damage or destruction of furniture or other personal property of any kind located in or about the Premises, moving expenses, storage expenses, alternative interim housing expenses, and expenses of locating and procuring alternative housing.

19. **Bankruptcy:** If any bankruptcy or insolvency proceedings are filed by or against the Tenant or if the Tenant makes any assignment for the benefit of creditors, the Landlord may, at his option, immediately terminate this Tenancy, and reenter and repossess the Premises, subject to the provisions of the Bankruptcy Code (11 USC Section 101, et. seq.) and the order of any court having jurisdiction thereunder.

20. **Tenant's Insurance; Release and Indemnity Provisions:**
(a) **Personal Property Insurance (*Tenant initial if applicable**):**
_____ _____ Tenant shall be required to obtain and maintain throughout the term of the tenancy a renter's insurance policy and to promptly provide Landlord evidence of such insurance upon Landlord's request. In addition to coverage for damage or loss to Tenant's personal property in such amount as Tenant may determine, the policy shall include coverage for bodily injury and property damage for which Tenant may be liable in the amount of _____
If not initialed, Tenant shall not be required to obtain a renter's insurance policy
(b) Whether or not Tenant is required to obtain a renter's insurance policy, Tenant shall be solely responsible for insuring any of his personal property located or stored upon the Premises upon the risks of damage, destruction, or loss resulting from theft, fire, storm and all other hazards and casualties. Regardless of whether the Tenant secures such insurance, the Landlord and his agents shall not be liable for any damage to, or destruction or loss of, any of the Tenant's personal property located or stored upon the Premises regardless of the cause or causes of such damage, destruction, or loss, unless such loss or destruction is attributable to the intentional acts or willful or wanton negligence of the Landlord.
(c) The Tenant agrees to release and indemnify the Landlord and his agents from and against liability for injury to the person of the Tenant or to any members of his household resulting from any cause whatsoever except only such personal injury caused by the negligent, or intentional acts of the Landlord or his agents.

21. **Agent:** The Landlord and the Tenant acknowledge that the Landlord may, from time to time in his discretion, engage a third party ("the Agent") to manage, supervise and operate the Premises or the complex, if any, of which they are a part. If such an Agent is managing, supervising and operating the Premises at the time this lease is executed, his name will be shown as "Agent" on the first page hereof. With respect to any Agent engaged pursuant to this paragraph, the Landlord and the Tenant hereby agree that: (1) Agent acts for and represents Landlord in this transaction; (2) Agent shall have only such authority as provided in the management contract existing between the Landlord and Agent; (3) Agent may perform without objection from the Tenant, any obligation or exercise any right of the Landlord imposed or given herein or by law and such performance shall be valid and binding, if authorized by the Landlord, as if performed by the Landlord; (4) the Tenant shall pay all rentals to the Agent if directed to do so by the Landlord; (5) except as otherwise provided by law, the Agent shall not be liable to the Tenant for the nonperformance of the obligations or

Figure 16-3

promises of the Landlord contained herein; (6) nothing contained herein shall modify the management contract existing between the Landlord and the Agent; however, the Landlord and the Agent may from time to time modify the management agreement in any manner which they deem appropriate; (7) the Landlord, may, in his discretion and in accordance with any management agreement, remove without replacing or remove and replace any agent engaged to manage, supervise and operate the Premises.

22. **Form**: The Landlord and Tenant hereby acknowledge that their agreement is evidenced by this form contract which may contain some minor inaccuracies when applied to the particular factual setting of the parties. The Landlord and Tenant agree that the courts shall liberally and broadly interpret this lease, ignoring minor inconsistencies and inaccuracies, and that the courts shall apply the lease to determine all disputes between the parties in the manner which most effectuates their intent as expressed herein. The following rules of construction shall apply: (1) handwritten and typed additions or alterations shall control over the preprinted language when there is an inconsistency between them; (2) the lease shall not be strictly construed against either the Landlord or the Tenant; (3) paragraph headings are used only for convenience of reference and shall not be considered as a substantive part of this lease; (4) words in the singular shall include the plural and the masculine shall include the feminine and neuter genders, as appropriate; and (5) the invalidity of one or more provisions of this lease shall not affect the validity of any other provisions hereof and this lease shall be construed and enforced as if such invalid provision(s) were not included.

23. **Amendment of Laws:** In the event that subsequent to the execution of this lease any state statute regulating or affecting any duty or obligation imposed upon the Landlord pursuant to this lease is enacted, amended, or repealed, the Landlord may, at his option, elect to perform in accordance with such statute, amendment, or act of repeal in lieu of complying with the analogous provision of this lease.

24. **Eminent Domain and Casualties:** The Landlord shall have the option to terminate this lease if the Premises, or any part thereof, are condemned or sold in lieu of condemnation or damaged by fire or other casualty.

25. **Assignment:** The Tenant shall not assign this lease or sublet the Premises in whole or part.

26. **Waiver:** No waiver of any breach of any obligation or promise contained herein shall be regarded as a waiver of any future breach of the same or any other obligation or promise.

27. **Joint and Several Liability:** If there are multiple persons listed as Tenant, their obligations under this Agreement shall be joint and several.

28. **Other Terms and Conditions:**
  (a) If there is an Agent involved in this transaction, Agent hereby discloses to Tenant that Agent is acting for and represents Landlord.
  (b) Itemize all addenda to this Contract and attach hereto:
    ❏ Disclosure of Information on Lead-Based Paint and Lead-Based Paint Hazards (form 430-T) (if Premises built prior to 1978)
    ❏ Maintenance Addendum (form 440-T)
    ❏ Pet Addendum (form 442-T)
    ❏ OTHER:_____
    _____

  (c) The following additional terms and conditions shall also be a part of this lease: _____
  _____
  _____
  _____
  _____
  _____

29. **Inspection of Premises:** Within _____ days of occupying the Premises, Tenant has the right to inspect the Premises and complete a Move-in Inspection Form.

30. **Tenant Information:** Tenant acknowledges and understands that during or after the term of this Agreement, the Landlord may, at the request of third parties, provide information about Tenant or relating to the Tenancy in accordance with applicable laws.

Figure 16-3

31. **Execution; Counterparts:** When Tenant signs this lease, he acknowledges he has read and agrees to the provisions of this lease. This lease is executed in_____ (number) counterparts with an executed counterpart being retained by each party.

32. **Entire Agreement:** This Agreement contains the entire agreement of the parties and there are no representations, inducements or other provisions other than those expressed in writing. All changes, additions or deletions hereto must be in writing and signed by all parties.

33. **Use of Electronic Means; Notice.** The parties agree that electronic means may be used to sign this Agreement or to make any modifications the parties may agree to, and that any written notice, communication or documents may be transmitted to any e-mail address or fax number set forth in the signature section below. Any notices required or authorized to be given hereunder or pursuant to applicable law may also be mailed or hand delivered to the Tenant at the address of the Premises and to the Landlord at the address of the Agent.

THE NORTH CAROLINA ASSOCIATION OF REALTORS®, INC. MAKES NO REPRESENTATION AS TO THE LEGAL VALIDITY OR ADEQUACY OF ANY PROVISION OF THIS FORM IN ANY SPECIFIC TRANSACTION.

LANDLORD: _____

LANDLORD: _____

BY: AGENT: _____
　　　　　　　[Name of real estate firm]

By:_____ Individual license #_____ Date: _____
　　[Signature of authorized representative]

Address:_____

Telephone: _____ Fax: _____ E-mail: _____

TENANT:_____ Date: _____
　　　　　[Tenant signature]
Contact information: _____
　　　　　　　　　　Home　　　　　　　Work　　　　　　　Cell　　　　　　　Email

TENANT:_____ Date: _____
　　　　　[Tenant signature]
Contact information: _____
　　　　　　　　　　Home　　　　　　　Work　　　　　　　Cell　　　　　　　Email

TENANT:_____ Date: _____
　　　　　[Tenant signature]
Contact information: _____
　　　　　　　　　　Home　　　　　　　Work　　　　　　　Cell　　　　　　　Email

TENANT:_____ Date: _____
　　　　　[Tenant signature]
Contact information: _____
　　　　　　　　　　Home　　　　　　　Work　　　　　　　Cell　　　　　　　Email

STANDARD FORM 410 – T
Revised 7/2015
© 7/2017

Figure 16-3

17 | PROPERTY MANAGEMENT

Real estate, like any other asset or investment, requires management. Many owners, whether working farmers, business operators, or homeowners, "manage" their own properties, performing normal maintenance and repairing damage or long term wear and tear. Other owners entrust management of their real property to professionals. Those entrusted with such tasks generally must either be licensed real estate brokers or employees of a licensed broker.

North Carolina has not adopted a separate license for "property managers," nor is the term "property manager" defined by statute or Commission Rule. Lacking definition, it may be used to describe various services, from mere maintenance and custodial services, to leasing and rent collection, to full-fledged management, planning and oversight of a property for an owner. Modern broker-property managers of large multi-tenant or mixed use properties are often so involved in the maintenance and operation of the physical aspects of a the property that those managers need licenses for overseeing construction or operation of complex infrastructure (water, sewer, telephone, and power systems), in addition to their real estate licenses.

Frequently included within the broad generic term "property management" is a related but even more complex business known as "association management." Persons and firms engaged in this area of property management are responsible for the daily operations of property owners' associations. Besides collecting, disbursing, and accounting for funds of an association, the association manager typically organizes and maintains the association's records, plans the annual budget, and may be responsible for overseeing the maintenance and repair of some portion(s) of the real properties subject to the recorded covenants.

While many brokers may not become full-fledged "property managers," most will have occasion to be involved in the rental or leasing of an owner's property. Thus, all brokers should have at least a basic understanding of property management, the functions and requirements of a property manager, and standard provisions of a property management agreement, which are the principal topics addressed in this chapter. *Any broker who is involved in any significant amount of real estate management should seriously consider acquiring additional specialized training in the field of property management.* The National Association of REALTORS® sponsors the Institute of Real Estate Management, which promotes the "Certified Property Manager" designation. Additionally, the Property Management Division of the North Carolina Association of REALTORS® has published the *Residential Property Management Legal Handbook*.

Any type of real estate with income-producing potential may be managed for property owners by real estate brokers. This chapter focuses on the management of residential properties, although the licensing requirements, applicability of agency, and principal functions of a property manager discussed herein generally apply to the management of any type of real property. Brokers working in specialized areas of property management should seek additional education in their particular areas.

Brokers who manage vacation rentals must be familiar with the specific requirements of North Carolina's Vacation Rental Act, Chapter 42A of the General Statutes. The Property Management Division of the North Carolina Association of REALTORS® and the Vacation Rental Managers Association offer educational courses and materials for their members that address the unique aspects of vacation rental management.

The Community Association Institute is a national non-profit organization that provides training and certification for persons in the business of association management, owners in an association, and those who are chosen to serve as association officers.

LICENSING REQUIREMENTS

When an owner of income-producing real estate desires professional assistance in leasing his or her property, he or she hires a "**property manager**." Since "managing" real property in the brokerage, rather than custodial, sense involves the leasing or renting of the property, i.e., the temporary transfer of an interest in real property for others, a property manager must be a **licensed real estate broker**. [See G.S. 93A-2(a).] Thus, *any individual or entity that undertakes to manage real property belonging to others for compensation or consideration must be a licensed real estate broker.*

Only the individual or entity that owns (holds title to) the property may show the property, procure tenants, enter into lease agreements, collect rents and security deposits, etc. without having a license because they are not doing it "for others." Understand that while unlicensed individual property owners may lease their properties themselves, they may not pay or give any consideration to unlicensed friends, siblings, children, relatives, etc. to assist them in leasing their properties, whether to show the property or collect rent or any other leasing-related activity. *Only the title owners of real property may buy, lease, sell, or exchange their property without having a broker license.* That said, corporations, limited liability companies, and partnerships that hold title to property may buy, lease, sell, or exchange that property through their officers, member-managers, managers, general partners, and any authorized W-2 employees, and neither the owner-entity nor the individuals employed by the owner-entity are required to have a license.[1]

Lastly, it is also recognized that managing homeowner or property owner associations (hereafter "**association management**") in North Carolina still does not require any license (as long as no sales, leasing or rent collection is conducted). However, the Commission has long required a *real estate broker who engages in association management for a fee must comply with all Real Estate License Laws and Commission rules when managing such associations, including having a written agency agreement and handling all monies received in compliance with the Commission's trust account rules.* Commission Rule 58A.0118(b) provides a very limited exception for a broker who is a property owner in and an officer of an association who has access to association funds in his or her official capacity and who receives no fee or other consideration for his or her services; in such instance, the broker may not be required to maintain the association account records in compliance with the Commission's trust account rules, but he or she may be subject to disciplinary action if association funds are converted or misapplied.

Although there are many real estate brokers and firms that are actively involved in both sales and property management, especially in small towns and rural areas, the modern trend is toward brokerage firms that specialize in property management (i.e. leasing). Even in those firms that engage in both sales and property management, there typically is a designated person or division which handles all property management activities. Property management firms often have a number of employees who perform various functions connected with managing any particular property, such as marketing, showing the property, leasing, maintaining grounds and facilities, maintaining records, and other sundry tasks.

A broker must clearly understand as to which of his or her employees working in property management must have a real estate license. *Generally, any employee who engages in or supervises other employees who engage in* **negotiating** *any terms of a lease or rental agreement on behalf of the owner must have a real estate license.*

Exemption of Certain Employees. G.S. 93A-2(c)(6) exempts from licensing certain salaried (W-2) employees *of a broker* and delineates the specific acts which the broker's unlicensed salaried employees may perform. The statute states:

> (c) The provisions of this Chapter shall not apply to and shall not include:
>
> (6) Any salaried person employed by a licensed real estate broker, for and on behalf of the owner of any real estate or the improvements thereon, which the licensed broker has contracted to manage for the owner, if the salaried employee's employment is limited to: exhibiting units on the real estate to prospective tenants; providing the prospective tenants with information about the lease of the units; accepting applications for lease of the units; completing and executing preprinted form leases; and accepting security deposits and rental payments for the units only when the deposits and rental payments are made payable to the owner or the broker employed by the owner. The salaried employee shall not negotiate the amount of security deposits or rental payments and shall not negotiate leases or any rental agreements on behalf of the owner or broker. However, in a vacation rental transaction as defined by G.S. 42A-4(3), the employee may offer a prospective tenant a rental price and term from a schedule setting forth prices and terms and the conditions and limitations under which they may be offered. The schedule shall be written and provided by the employee's employing broker with the written authority of the landlord.

This exception exempts the typical salaried employee of a broker who works solely as a **"leasing agent,"** perhaps on-site at an apartment complex, who has limited decision-making authority. Such a leasing agent may **not** be delegated the authority to solicit new property management business for the firm, negotiate property management agreements, or negotiate lease terms (including the amount of security deposits or rent) unless the employee has a real estate broker license on active status. The broker is responsible for the conduct of any unlicensed salaried employee the broker hires to assist in managing others' properties and may be subject to disciplinary action under G.S. 93A-6(b)(4) if "... the broker's unlicensed employee ... has committed, in the regular course of business, any act which, if committed by the broker, would constitute a violation of G.S. 93A-6(a) ...." Thus, brokers who hire unlicensed W-2 employees must supervise these employees and ensure that they are well trained and knowledgeable about the scope of their duties and what they may and may not do or say.

LAWS GOVERNING PROPERTY MANAGEMENT RELATIONSHIPS

The legal duties and responsibilities of a broker dealing with leasing "clients" and "customers" are established by both agency law and Real Estate License Law, discussed in depth in Chapters 8 and

9 of this text. The reader should review the coverage of these laws in the context of property management.

Relationships With Clients

When a property owner employs a broker or brokerage firm, he or she creates an **agency relationship** between the property owner (client) and the broker similar to that created when a property owner lists his or her property for sale with a broker or when a prospective real estate purchaser engages a broker as a buyer's agent. ***The duties owed by a broker to the owner-principal are exactly the same as the duties a seller's agent or buyer's agent owes to his or her principal under the law of agency and the North Carolina Real Estate License Law.*** Further, an employee of a broker is an agent of the property manager and a subagent of the owner, just as a real estate firm is the primary agent of its principals and all of the firm's affiliated agents are subagents of the company's principals. (See the discussions of agency relationships and duties and liabilities of agents in Chapter 8.)

Relationships With Customers

When a broker is acting as an owner's agent and has no contractual relationship with tenants or prospective tenants, the broker and his or her employees treat tenants as customers or "third parties," just as an agent listing property for sale deals with buyers who are "customers" rather than "clients." Like the listing agent dealing with a third person (e.g., prospective buyer), ***the broker-property manager and his or her employees and agents owe certain duties to tenants and prospective tenants that arise under North Carolina Real Estate License Law, landlord and tenant law, fair housing laws and court decisions.*** (See the discussions of agents' duties to third persons in Chapter 8, landlord and tenant law in Chapter 16, and fair housing laws in Chapter 18.)

Brokers routinely represent tenants (as clients) in commercial transactions and may even represent residential tenants (as clients) in some situations. While the *"Working with Real Estate Agents"* disclosure brochure is not required in lease transactions, brokers nonetheless are required to properly establish and/or disclose their agency relationships in property management/lease transactions. A broker must also clarify his/her agency relationship when/if an owner or tenant with whom he or she is working appears to misunderstand the broker's role.

Because cooperative or multiple listing services are not used as widely in property management as in sales, brokers who wish to share in compensation earned by other brokers or paid by a party other than the party the broker represents should understand the laws governing such agreements and establish written co-brokerage arrangements prior to negotiating leases or rental agreements.

A further caveat: Dual agency can arise in rental and leasing situations where a brokerage firm represents both the property owner and the tenant. Conflicts of interest can arise when a firm manages property of an owner and then seeks to represent their client-owner's current tenant in locating other property to rent or buy. A broker or firm in such situations must act in compliance with all laws and rules governing this conduct.

PROPERTY MANAGEMENT AGREEMENT

A property management agreement should clearly define the role and authority of the property manager as the agent of the owner, specify the term of the agreement, state the amount or method for calculating the property manager's fee, describe the procedures for handling tenant security deposits, and delineate the responsibilities of both the property manager and the owner.

Written Agreement Required

The Commission's agency rule, 58A.0104(a), requires that *an agency agreement between a broker and a property owner be in writing from the inception of the relationship.* Thus, the broker must obtain a *written* property management agreement signed by the broker and the property owner *before* rendering any services on the property owner's behalf. A broker who neglects to obtain a written agency agreement at the outset of the relationship will be precluded from asserting any claims for compensation against the owner-principal pursuant to General Statute 93A-13, discussed in Chapter 9. Commission Rule A.0106(a) requires a broker to give the owner-client a copy of the signed property management agreement.

Termination and Renewal

Like all agency agreements, the property management agreement must have a definite termination date. Unlike most agency agreements, however, a limited exception to this requirement exists for property management agreements. The relevant portion of Rule 58A.0104 states:

> ... Every written agreement for brokerage services of any kind ... shall be for a definite period of time, shall include the broker's license number, and shall provide for its termination without prior notice at the expiration of that period, except that an agency agreement between a landlord and broker to procure tenants or receive rents for the landlord's property may allow for automatic renewal so long as the landlord may terminate with notice at the end of any contract period and any subsequent renewals....

Thus, the duration of the initial term and the automatic termination date must be specified, but the agreement may allow automatic renewal of the agency relationship for a specified period as long as the property owner has the right to terminate the relationship by giving notice to the broker, preferably in writing, within a certain period prior to the automatic renewal date of the property owner's desire to terminate the agency relationship. See Paragraph 2 of Figure 17-3 reprinted at the end of this chapter. Recall as well that the non-discrimination language set forth in 58A.0104(b) also must be included in the property management agreement.

NCAR Standard Form 401

To illustrate a well-prepared agreement for management of a residential property, the North Carolina Association of REALTORS®, Inc. Standard Form No. 401 "Exclusive Property Management Agreement," is shown as Figure 17-3. This standard form agreement is designed for use when managing long-term residential properties and will be referenced during the discussion. The North Carolina Association of REALTORS®, Inc. (NCAR) has a similar form, #402, designed for use by its members when managing vacation rental property, NCAR Form #572 is intended for use in commercial leasing situations, and NCAR Form #591 is intended for commercial property management. It is not unusual for property managers of multi-tenant or mixed use properties to negotiate separate management agreements with owners to address unique specific needs of individual properties. Note too that Rule A.0104(a) requires a management agreement between a broker and a property owner association to be in writing from the inception of the relationship, although there does not yet appear to be a pre-drafted standard association management form.

Management Fee. The method for determining the property management fee can vary as indicated by the blank space for insertion of the fee arrangement in Figure 17-3. Although in some cases a fixed amount may be set as the monthly fee, the most common fee arrangement for residential properties is to express the broker's fee as a percentage of actual gross rents received. Often, as in Paragraph 3, the fee arrangement also will provide for a minimum monthly fee (fixed amount) that will apply if the fee calculated on a percentage-of-rents-received basis is lower than the prescribed minimum fee. Paragraph 4 addresses disposition of other fees the Agent may collect from the tenant on the owner's behalf

The fee needed to provide reasonable compensation for the broker's services will depend on a variety of factors, such as the property's past and projected vacancy rate, time required to manage the particular property, and expenses that the broker must pay out of the fee. For example, if the property manager must pay advertising expenses out of his or her fee, then the fee most likely will be higher than it would be if the owner pays the advertising expenses. Before setting a management fee, a broker should have a clear understanding with the owner of all services to be rendered and who will pay for advertising and other operating expenses.

PRINCIPAL FUNCTIONS OF PROPERTY MANAGERS

A summary of the principal functions of a broker is set forth below. Each of these leading functions is then discussed separately in the pages that follow.

PRINCIPAL FUNCTIONS OF PROPERTY MANAGERS

- Preparing a Management Plan
- Establishing a Rental Schedule
- Preparing an Operating Budget
- Marketing and Renting the Property
- Collecting Rents and Security Deposits
- Maintaining and Protecting the Property
- Preparing and Enforcing "Rules and Regulations"
- Performing Landlord's Duties
- Instituting Legal Actions
- Maintaining Property Insurance
- Maintaining Records and Accounting to Owner
- Preparing Income/Expense Reports

PREPARING A MANAGEMENT PLAN

The first thing a broker must do when preparing to manage a rental property for a property owner is develop a comprehensive **management plan.** Brokers anxious to obtain a property owners' business too often will sign property management agreements and then afterwards develop management plans. This is a bad business practice because the broker needs to thoroughly understand a property's condition, market potential and management needs, as well as the owner's plans and expectations, prior to committing to manage the property.

Development of a management plan involves a thorough property analysis and market analysis that together provide the basis for developing a proposed rental schedule and operating budget. A prudent property manager will develop a management plan while negotiating an agency agreement with the property owner. This is necessary for the broker to accurately project the owner's expenses and to set an appropriate management fee. Both the property owner and the broker should have a clear understanding as to the profit each can reasonably expect to earn from operation of the rental property.

The property manager's first step in developing a management plan is to perform a thorough **property analysis.** This involves an evaluation of such things as the number and size of the rental units, the physical condition of the property (including all equipment, appliances and fixtures), occupancy history, current leases, past and current financial data, staffing needs, and various features that make the property attractive or unattractive to current and prospective tenants. This will also enable the broker to acquire material facts which must be disclosed to prospective tenants.

The property manager must also perform a **market analysis.** This involves evaluating general economic trends, the local economy, the neighborhood where the property is located (neighborhood demographics, transportation, facilities, traffic patterns, etc,), and the local rental market (occupancy rates, trends, etc.). It also involves an analysis of other rental properties in the area that are "comparable" (similar) to the "subject property" (the property to be managed), and a careful comparison of the subject property with comparable properties as to property characteristics, condition, location and financial data.

If the subject property has been recently appraised by a qualified real estate appraiser (e.g., in connection with a recent purchase or refinancing), the property manager would be well advised to request a copy of the appraisal report. A recent appraisal would be extremely helpful to the property manager in the preparation of a management plan, as it will include an assessment of value from an income approach which also will reflect information on income and expenses for comparable properties.

The property analysis and market analysis will enable the property manager to formulate a management plan for the subject property that will include a proposed rental schedule, operating budget and capital budget. Establishing a rental schedule and preparing an operating budget are discussed below.

The broker should also inquire whether the property is subject to a loan and, if so, inquire about the status of the loan. The fact that a loan is in default should be a red flag to the broker. A pending foreclosure sale would be a material fact that the broker would have to disclose to prospective tenants and would impact the broker's ability to lease the property and receive compensation for doing so.

ESTABLISHING A RENTAL SCHEDULE

A broker is expected to establish, subject to the owner's approval, a rental schedule that will produce the greatest net profit for the owner. In order to properly establish the rental schedule, the property manager must know how to competently analyze the property and the market. This will require an accurate knowledge of such matters as the character of the neighborhood, the advantages and disadvantages of the location of the property, the character of competing rentals in the area, rents currently charged for similar properties and the potential demand. The property's physical condition and design (functionality), especially as compared to competing properties, are major factors to consider when determining appropriate rental amounts.

The most important factor for the broker to consider in establishing a rental schedule is the information gathered on rents charged for comparable properties in the area. Using all the information described above, the broker will determine the optimum rental schedule which will produce the highest net profit for the owner after considering projected vacancy, rent collection losses and operating expenses, including reserves for replacement. The establishment of an appropriate rental schedule in connection with a comprehensive management plan is not a job for the novice property manager, especially when large investment properties are involved. This critical task should only be undertaken by persons with the appropriate training or experience in the property management field.

PREPARING AN OPERATING BUDGET

Property managers are often expected to prepare a proposed annual operating budget for the owner at the beginning of each management period, typically yearly. The purpose of the budget is to estimate income and expenses for the coming year and to establish budget guidelines for that year, as well as to make any adjustments to the rental schedule that may be appropriate. Normally, the proposed budget prepared by the broker is subject to approval by the owner. Formal operating budgets usually will be required for multi-unit apartment complexes and commercial properties, but often are not required for single-family or other small properties.

Only an experienced property manager should attempt to prepare an operating budget for properties other than single-family or small multi-unit residential properties. Proper budget preparation requires considerable knowledge and research. Since the budget is for the coming year, all estimates are projections. Some income and expense items (such as salaries, debt service, property taxes, planned improvements, and property insurance premiums) may be estimated with a great deal of accuracy, but some items, such as repairs, are more variable and require careful consideration. For properties currently managed, heavy reliance may be placed on the actual income and expenses of the property during the past few years. For new properties, the property manager must rely primarily on information gathered on comparable properties.

Projecting Income

The first step in preparing an annual operating budget is to calculate the **gross potential rental income,** which is the maximum possible income based on 100 percent occupancy for the entire year. The broker will then deduct from this figure the projected **vacancy and rent collection losses** (i.e., unpaid rent) to determine the projected "actual" rental income. Any other income of the property (such as income from vending machines, coin operated laundry facilities, concessions, etc.) is then added to the projected actual income to provide the **effective gross income.** When projecting the vacancy rate, the broker should pay special attention to the historical vacancy rate for the property and to the current vacancy rates for comparable properties in the area. The prudent broker will avoid being overly optimistic when projecting vacancy and rent collection losses.

Projecting Operating Expenses

Next, the broker will estimate **operating expenses** (the cost of managing, operating and maintaining the property). Most of the operating expenses will be the responsibility of the property owner, although the broker normally will pay these expenses for the owner from the rents received. These include: ad valorem property taxes; property (hazard) insurance premiums; utilities (electricity for onsite office and common areas and water/sewer); legal expenses (associated with rent collection, tenant eviction, etc.); personnel cost (for full-time or part-time maintenance and/or security personnel); contract maintenance and repair expenses (for painting, redecorating, equipment/appliance repair or replacement, common area supplies, grounds maintenance, etc.) and advertising expenses.

Other operating expenses that relate to managing the property usually will be the responsibility of the broker and will be paid by the broker from his or her fee. These include personnel costs for resident manager/leasing agents and general administrative costs (for clerical/bookkeeping/accounting personnel and services, office equipment/supplies, telephone, etc.) These management expenses, as well as an amount representing the broker's "profit," are incorporated into the management fee.

The actual employer of unlicensed persons engaged in showing units, placing tenants, collecting rents and deposits, and completing preprinted form leases can be a pitfall for unwary brokers. The use of a "payroll" company to employ such personnel removes these persons from the exemption for the *broker's* salaried employees.

From the standpoint of the overall budget, it makes little difference whether a particular operating expense is the responsibility of the owner or the property manager, as all will be paid from the gross rent proceeds received. However, whether an expense is paid by the owner or the broker can make a significant difference in determining an appropriate management fee. Consequently, the broker must make certain that he/she and the owner have a clear agreement as to who is responsible for the various operating expenses.

Brokers should be cautious about estimating expenses for capital improvements and some types of repairs, particularly if they have little experience with such improvements or repairs. It may well be necessary to obtain estimates from contractors, repair persons, plumbers, etc. in order to properly project expenses for any planned construction or repair work. Additionally, anytime a broker undertakes to oversee, supervise, or coordinate major repairs, reconstruction, or renovations to properties the broker manages on behalf of an owner, the broker may be required to have a general contractor license, even though duly-licensed individuals are hired to perform the actual repairs, construction or renovations. *If the total cost of repairs or renovations equals or exceeds $30,000, State law requires the broker, as a non-owner, to have a general contractor license to supervise other licensed laborers on behalf of the owner. Most likely, buildings permits will be required for some repairs and improvements.*

The Bottom Line

Total *operating expenses* discussed above are deducted from *effective gross income* to determine projected **net operating income.** Deductions are then made for *debt service* (mortgage principal and interest payments) and for projected *capital expenditures* (building expansion, remodeling, roof replacement, parking lot paving, etc.). The result will be the **before tax cash flow** which represents cash flow to the owner *before* deducting depreciation for income tax purposes and before income taxes are paid by the owner. It is not unusual for a property owner to have a negative cash flow (loss) *for income tax purposes* after depreciation is deducted. Note that capital expenditures are shown in the budget as a separate item because an owner will not be able to deduct such expenditures as operating expenses for income tax purposes. Debt service also is listed separately because it is considered to be a cost of "owning" rather than "operating" the property, although the owner may be able to deduct *mortgage interest* as an operating expense for income tax purposes.

Sample Operating Budget

Figure 17-1 illustrates an annual operating budget for a 150-unit residential apartment complex. This budget assumes that the broker will compensate the resident manager and leasing agents and pay the general office administrative costs out of the broker's management fee, and that the property owner will pay for all other expenses associated with operating, maintaining and managing the property.

Sample Annual Operating Budget
Period: January 1 - December 31, 201X

Property:
Woodcrest Apartments (150 Units)
600 Woodcrest Rd.
Anywhere, NC

Income:

Gross Potential Rental Income	$1,458,000	
30 Units @ $900/mo = $324,000		
90 Units @ $800/mo = $864,000		
30 Units @ $750/mo = $270,000		
Less Vacancy and Collection Losses (5%)	- 72,900	
Plus Other Income (vending machines, laundry, etc.)	+ 10,800	
Effective Gross Income	$1,395,900	$1,395,900

Expenses:

Management Fee	$139,590	
[10% of effective gross income. Includes salaries and wages (for resident manager, leasing agents and clerical services), general administrative costs (office equipment, supplies, telephone, etc.), and broker's "profit."]		
Maintenance Personnel	$40,000	
Security Personnel	$29,200	
Ad valorem Property Taxes	$120,000	
Property Insurance Premiums	$25,600	
Utilities (electricity - office & common areas)	$12,000	
Utilities (water & sewer - entire complex)	$72,000	
Advertising	$12,000	
Maintenance and Repair	$45,000	
[includes contract maintenance/repair, replacement of appliances, equipment, supplies, etc.]		
Legal Services	$6,000	
Total Operating Expenses	$501,390	- $501,390
Net Operating Income		**$894,510**
Debt Service (mortgage principal and interest)		- 632,004
Capital Expenditures		- 60,000
Before Tax Cash Flow (to Property Owner)		**$202,506**

Figure 17-1

MARKETING AND RENTING THE PROPERTY

Property management agreements usually authorize the broker-agent to operate, manage, and lease the property to the best advantage of the owner, including advertising the property, displaying signs, and renting the property. For example, in paragraph 6 of the management agreement shown as Figure 17-3 the agent has the authority "... to negotiate, execute, extend and renew leases in Owner's name ..." for a certain leasehold term. Some brokers use lease agreements that do not identify the landlord; if they do so, they should have appropriate authority in the management agreement. In taking over an existing property, a broker may find a form lease in use that neither identifies the agent nor the landlord, but instead describes the lessor by a name associated with the property (for example: The Pines) which does not correspond to the legal name of any person or entity involved in the transaction.

Marketing

In order to lease vacant properties, brokers must usually market the properties. This means that the broker must, by advertising or other promotional methods, attract as many suitable tenants as possible. The broker must strive to keep vacancies as low as possible and must constantly endeavor to rent the property to reliable tenants.

Screening Prospective Tenants

Consumer Credit Checks

Although the specific criteria for determining the suitability of prospective tenants will vary according to property type, it is essential that a property manager "qualify" all prospective tenants to assure that they possess the ability to pay the rent and to review their history of paying debts. This is accomplished by verifying the prospective tenant's employment history and current income, checking with the tenant's current or former landlord, performing a credit check (usually by obtaining a credit report from a local credit bureau) and checking other references. The prospective tenant's "track record" with regard to paying rent and other obligations is extremely important.

More and more property managers are turning to consumer reporting agencies (CRAs) to obtain information about prospective tenants. Common types of CRAs include credit bureaus, tenant-screening services and reference-checking services. CRAs must comply with the Fair Credit Reporting Act (FCRA).[2] Established in 1970, the FCRA is designed to ensure the confidentiality and accuracy of consumer credit information.

The Federal Trade Commission's Business Center[3] has published various articles that contain useful information on this topic for property managers such as: "Using Consumer Reports: What Landlords Need to Know," "A basic 'tenant' of credit reporting," and "Disposing of Consumer Report Information? Rule Tells How."

If a property manager refuses to rent to a prospective tenant or changes the rental terms (e.g. increases the rent or the security deposit or requires a co-signor, etc.) based even partially upon information in a consumer credit report, then the property manager must give the prospective tenant an "adverse action notice." Although giving an oral notice is permitted, written notice is recommended, because it provides evidence of compliance with the FCRA. According to the FTC, an adverse action notice

> ... must include the name, address and telephone number of the CRA
> that supplied the consumer report, including a toll-free telephone number for
> CRAs that maintain files nationwide; a statement that the CRA that supplied

the report did not make the decision to take adverse action and cannot give the specific reasons for it; and a notice of the individual's right to dispute the accuracy or completeness of any information the CRA furnished, and the consumer's right to a free report from the CRA upon request within 60 days.

Property managers and landlords who fail to comply with the FCRA can be sued in federal court. If a broker or landlord loses such a case, then he or she may have to pay court costs, the plaintiff's reasonable legal fees and punitive damages. For more information on the FCRA or for a copy of the Act, you may call 1-877-382-4357 or go to www.ftc.gov/os/statutes/fcrajump.shtm.

Commission Rule A.0108 requires brokers to retain records of rental transactions for three years. If a tenant's rental application is rejected, then the broker should retain the tenant background information for three years from the rejection date. If a tenant's rental application is approved and the tenant enters into a lease, then the broker should retain the background information for three years following the termination of the tenant's lease or accounting for the tenant's security deposit, whichever occurs last.

When disposing of the information obtained from CRAs, landlords and property managers who acquired the information for business purposes must comply with the Disposal Rule that is enforced by the Federal Trade Commission. This rule requires proper disposal of information derived from consumer reports, and while the standard is flexible, property managers must take reasonable measures to ensure that all consumer information is disposed of in a manner that would prevent an unauthorized person from acquiring and using the information. For paper documents, shredding (so they cannot be read or reconstructed) and burning are two methods of disposal that would satisfy the requirements for proper disposal. For digital information, destroying or erasing electronic files so that the information cannot be read is also acceptable.

Use of Criminal Records

In April 2016 HUD's Office of General Counsel issued *Guidance on Application of Fair Housing Act Standards to the Use of Criminal Records by Providers of Housing and Real Estate-Related Transactions*.[4] For reasons stated in the treatise, HUD has concluded that a blanket policy that excludes anyone with a criminal conviction, regardless of what it was or how long ago, presents a housing barrier that has a disparate impact on minorities and therefore violates the Fair Housing Act when leasing residential property.

HUD specifically acknowledges that housing providers have a significant interest in protecting the safety and property of others and a prospective tenant's previous criminal convictions may be one factor in that evaluation, but they should not be the lone factor. According to HUD's *Guidance*:

> …where a policy or practice that restricts access to housing on the basis of criminal history has a disparate impact on individuals of a particular race, national origin, or other protected class, such policy or practice is unlawful under the Fair Housing Act if it is not necessary to serve a substantial, legitimate, nondiscriminatory interest of the housing provider, or if such interest could be served by another practice that has a less discriminatory effect.

HUD is not saying that landlords and property managers cannot consider criminal record histories; what will violate the Fair Housing Act is either 1) a blanket policy of not renting to anyone with a criminal record or 2) considering arrests, because arrests are not convictions. The one conviction recognized by the Fair Housing Act as justifying denial of housing is a conviction of illegally manufacturing or distributing a controlled substance as defined under federal law. [21 United State Code 802.] Note that it must be a ***conviction***, not merely an arrest, for the ***manufacture or distribution*** of a controlled substance, not just use or possession of a controlled or illegal substance.

Broker-property managers should create a written tailored criminal history use policy, be able to explain the rationale and how it supports a "substantial, legitimate, nondiscriminatory purpose," instruct all employees in its application, and then apply it uniformly to all. Factors to consider might include: 1) the nature of the crime (violent/nonviolent, intentional/negligent) and whether a misdemeanor or felony; 2) how long ago and the age of the individual; 3) the circumstances and whether there were mitigating factors; 4) whether the individual was incarcerated or received probation; and 5) the applicant's conduct since the incident or release. Three of the many statistics cited in HUD's General Counsel's *Guidance* included that:

- nearly one-third of the national adult population has a criminal conviction of some type,
- on average 650,000 inmates have been released annually from federal and state prisons since 2004, and
- studies indicate after six or seven years with no offenses, the risk that a former convict may commit a new offense begins to approximate the risk that a person with no prior record will commit a new offense.

Negotiating Rents

Frequently it is necessary for a broker to engage in rent negotiations with prospective tenants and existing tenants who are renewing their leases. The broker should have a clear understanding with the owner as to the broker's authority and latitude to deviate from the established rental schedule. Some owners may be willing to allow the broker some flexibility with regard to rent negotiations, while others may require the broker to strictly adhere to the rental schedule and to obtain the owner's approval for any deviation from that schedule.

COLLECTING RENTS AND SECURITY DEPOSITS

The broker is the owner's agent for the collection of all rents and any other charges or amounts due under the lease agreement. A fairly strict collection policy is basic tenet of successful management of real property. Uncollected rent is often worse than a vacancy, because a property suffers wear and tear from a tenant while that tenant enjoys shelter for which he or she is not paying. The broker should establish a rent collection policy to assure that all tenants pay regularly and promptly.

A procedure to collect past-due rents should be rigidly and uniformly followed. A statement for past due rents and late charges should be sent to delinquent tenants within five to ten days after the rental due date. The initial notice may be followed with a final notice a week or ten days later. If the tenant ignores the notice and does not pay, the property manager may need to initiate legal proceedings for possession of the premises and to collect or obtain a judgment against the tenant for the unpaid rent, if the broker has that authority under the property management agreement. [See Paragraph 6(i) in Figure 17-3.]

If **residential** property is involved, the broker should be thoroughly familiar with the provisions of the **Residential Rental Agreements Act** (Article 5, Chapter 42 of the North Carolina General Statutes). This Act, other relevant statutes, and summary ejectment proceedings are discussed in Chapter 16 of this text.

Paragraph 10 of the Exclusive Property Management Agreement shown in Figure 17-3 addresses the subject of tenant security deposits. Under that paragraph, the property manager has the discretion to require security deposits from tenants "... in an amount permitted by law." If **residential** tenancies are involved, both the owner and the broker are subject to and must comply with the **Tenant Security Deposit Act** found in Article 6, Chapter 42 of the North Carolina General Statutes. Recall that *all residential landlords must deposit their tenant security deposits into a trust or escrow account in a federally insured depository institution lawfully doing business in North Carolina.* If the property owner wants to hold the residential tenant security deposit, it must either be in a compliant trust or escrow account or the owner must post a bond in an amount equivalent to the tenant security deposit. (See G.S. §42-50.)

ALL monies belonging to others received by a broker acting in a fiduciary capacity must be deposited into a trust or escrow account maintained by the broker in a federally insured depository institution pursuant to General Statute 93A-6(g). Brokers and their employees may not accept rent checks payable to the owner and deposit them directly into their clients' accounts or deliver the rent payments directly to their clients. If a broker or his/her employee accepts possession of monies payable to or due others, those monies must first be deposited into the broker's escrow account.

A broker's trust account must be clearly designated as a trust or escrow account and must be maintained and managed in compliance with North Carolina Real Estate License Law and North Carolina Real Estate Commission rules with respect to the handling of trust funds (rents and security deposits) regardless of the type of property involved. The words "trust account" or "escrow account" must appear on all checks, deposit tickets, and monthly bank statements for the account. Brokers engaged in property management should be intimately familiar with the Commission's trust account rules, presently, 58A.0116, 58A.0117 and 58A.0118. Paragraph 13 in Figure 17-3 addresses interest bearing trust accounts which must comply with Rule A.0116(c).

MAINTAINING AND PROTECTING THE PROPERTY

The property manager is usually granted the authority to make any repairs necessary to preserve, maintain, and protect the property. The property management agreement should address the broker's duty to inspect the property and specify whether there is any limit on the funds that the broker may expend for necessary repairs or maintenance without first obtaining the owner's consent. The broker also must comply with any laws concerning the condition of the premises. In the case of **residential** tenancies, G.S. §42-42, "Landlord to Provide Fit Premises," defines a landlord's duties that the broker must ensure are fulfilled. See Chapter 16 for a complete discussion of these statutory requirements. Paragraphs 6(f) through (h) in Figure 17-3 address the agent's authority for repairs and expenses and Paragraph 9(a) and (b) discuss the owner's obligations.

The owner obviously has an interest in the broker devoting sufficient attention to the property to safeguard the owner's investment such that it may yield the highest possible net return over its economic life. Tenants also are more easily retained and better satisfied if a building or dwelling they are renting is kept in good repair. Thus, the property manager should develop a sound inspection and maintenance program for all properties being managed.

It should be noted, however, that the **tenant** also may have certain maintenance and repair duties, depending on the terms of the tenancy and the type of property involved. In **residential** tenancies, tenants have certain duties under G.S. §42-43. The reader is again referred to Chapter 16 for a discussion of these duties. The broker who manages a property must take all actions necessary to keep the premises in proper repair and must endeavor to maximize the owner's net return by prudently expending funds to accomplish these purposes. Operational practices should be reviewed often and economy must be practiced.

A wise practice is to routinely use a "**property condition checklist**" that is signed by the tenant prior to the tenant taking possession of the property. The manager and tenant should use the checklist to jointly inspect the premises and agree on its condition at the beginning of the tenancy. The property condition, and especially any defects, should be noted for each item on the checklist and the checklist should then be signed by the tenant. When the tenant moves out, the manager should inspect the property using the same checklist and compare the inspection results with the checklist signed by the tenant upon moving in. It would also be wise for brokers to photograph any damages or defects that will require repair or replacement. Such procedures enable, the property manager to better determine whether there is damage to the property that was not previously present and that is not the result of "ordinary wear and tear," and to more easily overcome refute a tenant's false claim that damages found upon surrender of the premises were present when the tenant took possession.

The property manager should regularly inspect the leased premises *during the course of the tenancy* to assure that the tenant is not abusing the property and is otherwise fulfilling any duties concerning the property's maintenance and condition that are imposed on the tenant under the lease terms and/or state law.

PREPARING AND ENFORCING RULES AND REGULATIONS

Even with a thorough, well-drafted lease, it usually is necessary to have supplemental "Rules and Regulations" for an apartment complex and multi-tenant commercial property. The lease should specifically refer to and incorporate by reference any such rules and regulations. Rules and regulations for an apartment complex may deal with a wide variety of matters, such as:

- Swimming pool hours and use by tenants and guests
- Use of clubhouse facilities
- Handling of personal items that are left in common areas
- Storage of personal belongings
- Conduct of tenants and guests (for example, noise restrictions/quiet hours)
- Parking
- Use of laundry facilities
- Assistance for tenants who lock themselves out of properties
- Prohibition against illegal or nuisance activities

Fair, strict, and uniform enforcement of established rules and regulations is very important in operating an apartment or multi-tenant complex in a manner that will retain desirable tenants.

PERFORMING LANDLORD'S DUTIES UNDER LEASES

The property manager typically is required to perform any duties and exercise any rights conferred upon the owner-landlord under the lease entered into in connection with the property, which may vary depending on property type. For example, a property manager of an office building may be required to provide window cleaning and janitorial services at specified intervals, while such services typically are not provided in residential leases. Similarly, providing heat, electricity, and other utilities may be common responsibilities of property managers of multi-tenant commercial properties, whereas residential tenants are typically responsible for acquiring and paying for their own utility services.

While the services an owner-landlord must provide may vary depending on property type, an owner's rights under virtually every lease include the enforcement of tenant obligations with respect to the property and the common legal remedies in the event of tenant breach.

Brokers must be responsive to tenants' concerns and repair requests. Brokers should develop and implement procedures for tenants to notify brokers regarding such issues and communicate the issues to owners when appropriate.

INSTITUTING LEGAL ACTIONS

The broker is routinely authorized to initiate and prosecute legal proceedings to recover possession of the property in the event of the tenant's breach of the lease agreement and/or rents and other sums owed to the owner by a tenant. Broad discretionary authority may be given to the agent to settle or compromise these legal proceedings. Brokers should understand that the Clerk of Court will require prepayment of court filing and service fees before the Clerk will accept and file a complaint. See paragraph 9(b) of the sample property management agreement set forth in Figure 17-3.

Residential property managers must be thoroughly familiar with the statutory residential eviction remedies and procedures that must be followed to legally eject a tenant who has breached the leaseand to know what a broker may and may not do regarding a tenant's personal property. These rules and procedures are discussed in greater detail in Chapter 16.

Present North Carolina laws governing the use of Small Claims Court allow an agent for a landlord to complete and sign a complaint for possession or past due rents and damages *when the action is prosecuted in the name of the owner* (not the name of the broker, management firm or property). The Commission recommends that *the broker sign such complaints as the agent of the owner, not the broker's exempt employee.* The role of a broker in the summary ejectment or collection action is limited to testifying to the facts known to the broker or having the broker's employee with personal knowledge testify. The broker and the employee cannot engage in the unauthorized practice of law. If the case is appealed to the District Court, or if the landlord is seeking some relief other than summary ejectment or a judgment for unpaid rents and damages, the landlord must retain an attorney to assist in the case. Similarly, if the monetary claim on behalf of the landlord exceeds the jurisdictional limit in Small Claims Court, the landlord must hire an attorney to pursue a remedy in the appropriate court.

MAINTAINING PROPERTY INSURANCE

Generally the property owner is responsible for obtaining hazard and liability insurance for his or her property even though the broker may assume responsibility for paying the periodic premiums for the insurance coverage from the rent proceeds. See paragraph 9(d) in Figure 17-3. If the broker assumes the responsibility for obtaining proper hazard, liability and other appropriate insurance for the property on behalf of the owner, then the broker must periodically review the insurance coverage to ensure that the owner's interests in the property are adequately protected. To do so competently, the broker should have some knowledge of the different types of insurance coverage available to property owners for investment (i.e., non-owner occupied) or commercial properties. Even when the owner is responsible for securing adequate insurance, the broker would be well advised to request a copy of the policy for the broker's transaction file and review any applicable policies annually to confirm that the coverage is sufficient.

Brokers should encourage tenants to obtain renter's insurance to cover damages which will not be covered by the owners' insurance policies.

MAINTAINING RECORDS AND ACCOUNTING TO OWNER

The property manager almost always is required to give *monthly statements of receipts, collections, expenses, charges, and disbursements to the owner* and to remit to the owner the balance of such receipts and collections. Thus the property manager must establish and maintain an adequate accounting system to facilitate an orderly and understandable presentation of all operations and activities concerning the property to the owner. Additionally, the broker must ensure that journals and ledger sheets for each property managed are properly maintained in accordance with the Commission's trust account rules and that all information required by the rules appear on the applicable documents. Know that *the broker will be held accountable for all monies received and for the proper maintenance and monthly reconciliation of all records, whether the broker personally maintains the records or delegates that function to a licensed or unlicensed employee.*

Regular monthly income/expense reports and detailed annual reports should be provided to the owner for accounting purposes. Cost accounting is quite important in property management for the manager and owner to assess fluctuations in income and expenses and to have a basis for future decisions with respect to rentals, maintenance, and productivity of the property as an investment.

On the following page is a sample monthly income and expense report for a 48-unit residential apartment complex. A similar report should be prepared at the end of each year to provide the owner with a proper accounting and a basis for projecting an operating budget for the following year.

All information and documentation generated, sent and/or received by a broker in the course of managing an owner's property should be made available to the owner upon request. A broker cannot refuse to give a current or former landlord-client tenant information or other information pertaining to the broker's management of a property.

Endnotes

1. N.C.Gen.Stat. 93A-2(c)(1) effective October 22, 2015.

2. 15 U.S.C. § 1681 et seq.

3. https://www.ftc.gov/tips-advice/business-center; https://www.ftc.gov/tips-advice/business-center/guidance/using-consumer-reports-what-landlords-need-know; https://www.ftc.gov/news-events/blogs/business-blog/2013/04/basic-tenant-credit-reporting; https://www.ftc.gov/tips-advice/business-center/guidance/disposing-consumer-report-information-rule-tells-how

4. The link below is to HUD's Office of General Counsel's *Guidance* document regarding use of criminal records in housing decisions referenced in the text. https://portal.hud.gov/hudportal/documents/huddoc?id=HUD_OGCGuidAppFHAStandCR.pdf .

   For a discussion of criminal background checks and a Model Policy for Screening Tenants created by the NC Housing Finance Agency in conjunction with the NC Justice Center and the NC Department of Health and Human Services for use by property managers participating in NCHFA programs, see pages 8-12 of the document at this link: http://www.nchfa.com/sites/default/files/page_attachments/TenantSelectionPlanPolicy.pdf

SAMPLE INCOME/EXPENSE REPORT
For September, 201X

Date: October 10, 201X

Property

    Pineview Apartments (48 units)

    300 Pineview Lane

    Anywhere, NC

Income

Gross Potential Rental Income @ $750/unit	$36,000	
Vacancy and Rent Collection Losses (3 units)	- 2,250	
Total Rent Collected (Effective Gross Income)	$33,750	$33,750

Expenses

Management Fee (10% of effective gross income)	$3,375	
Maintenance Personnel	$2,640	
Escrow for Property Taxes and Insurance	$2,875	
Utilities (electricity-office and common areas)	$1,000	
Utilities (water and sewer-entire complex)	$3,360	
Advertising	$500	
Maintenance and Repairs	$1,200	
Legal Services	$150	
Total Operation Expenses	$15,100	$15,100

Net Operating Income	$18,650
Debt Service (mortgage principal and interest payment)	- 14,600
Capital Expenditures	- 0
Contribution to Reserves	- 1,000
Net Paid to Owner (before tax cash flow)	**$3,050**

Figure 17-2

EXCLUSIVE PROPERTY MANAGEMENT AGREEMENT
Long-term Rental Property

This Exclusive Property Management Agreement is entered into by and between _____
_____ ("Owner")
and _____ ("Agent").

IN CONSIDERATION of the mutual covenants and promises set forth herein, Owner hereby contracts with Agent, and Agent hereby contracts with Owner, to lease and manage the property described below, as well as any other property Owner and Agent may from time to time agree in writing will be subject to this Agreement (the "Property"), in accordance with all applicable laws and regulations, upon the terms and conditions contained herein.

1. Property. City:_____County:_____, NC
Street Address:_____Zip Code:_____
Other Description:_____
_____

❑ **MULTIPLE PARCELS** (*check if applicable*). Additional parcels of real property are the subject of this Agreement, as described in the attached Multi-Parcel Addendum. The term "Property" as used herein shall be deemed to refer to all such parcels unless specifically indicated otherwise.

2. Duration of Agreement. This Agreement shall be binding when it has been signed and dated below by Owner and Agent. It shall become effective on _____ ("Effective Date") and shall be for an initial term of _____. NOT LESS THAN _____ DAYS PRIOR TO THE CONCLUSION OF THE INITIAL TERM, EITHER PARTY MAY NOTIFY THE OTHER PARTY IN WRITING OF ITS DESIRE TO TERMINATE THIS AGREEMENT, IN WHICH CASE IT SHALL TERMINATE AT THE CONCLUSION OF THE INITIAL TERM. IF NOT SO TERMINATED, THIS AGREEMENT SHALL AUTOMATICALLY RENEW FOR SUCCESSIVE TERMS OF _____ EACH UNLESS EITHER PARTY GIVES THE OTHER PARTY WRITTEN NOTICE OF ITS DESIRE TO TERMINATE THIS AGREEMENT AT LEAST _____ DAYS PRIOR TO THE CONCLUSION OF ANY SUCH RENEWAL TERM, IN WHICH CASE THIS AGREEMENT SHALL TERMINATE AT THE CONCLUSION OF SUCH TERM.

3. Agent's Fee. For services performed hereunder, Owner shall compensate Agent in the following manner:
   ❑ A fee ("Fee") equal to the greater of:
      (i) _____ percent (____%) of total gross rental income received on all rental agreements, or
      (ii) $_____ per month for each month of the Initial Term or any renewal term of this Agreement.
   ❑ Other *(describe method of compensation)*:_____
_____.

Note: No fees may be deducted from any tenant security deposit until the termination of the tenancy. Thereafter, any fees due Agent from Owner may be deducted from any portion of the security deposit due to Owner.

4. **Early Termination Fee:** IF, PRIOR TO THE END OF THE INITIAL TERM OR ANY RENEWAL TERM OF THIS AGREEMENT, (I) OWNER TERMINATES THIS AGREEMENT WITHOUT LEGALLY SUFFICIENT CAUSE OR (II) AGENT TERMINATES THIS AGREEMENT FOR LEGALLY SUFFICIENT CAUSE, OWNER SHALL PAY AGENT AN AMOUNT EQUAL TO THE FEE AGENT WOULD HAVE BEEN ENTITLED TO RECEIVE DURING THE BALANCE OF THE THEN-EXISTING TERM OF THIS AGREEMENT, TAKING INTO ACCOUNT ANY RENTAL AGREEMENTS IN EFFECT AT THE TIME OF SUCH TERMINATION.

5. **Other Fees:** Agent may charge tenants reasonable administrative fees permitted by law and retain any such fees, including but not limited to, fees to cover the costs of processing tenant rental applications. If, in Agent's discretion, tenant leases provide for late payment fees and/or returned check fees, such fees, when collected by Agent, shall belong to _____
_____(Owner or Agent). Fees for purposes covered under the Tenant Security Deposit Act will be collected, held and disbursed in accordance with the Act and paragraphs 10, 13 and 17 of this Agreement.

North Carolina Association of REALTORS®, Inc.

STANDARD FORM 401
Revised 7/2016
©7/2017

REALTOR®

Owner Initials _____ _____ Agent Initials _____ _____

EQUAL HOUSING OPPORTUNITY

Figure 17-3

6. **Authority and Responsibilities of Agent:** During the time this Agreement is in effect, Agent shall:

(a) Manage the Property to the best of Agent's ability, devoting thereto such time and attention as may be necessary;

(b) OFFER THE PROPERTY FOR RENT IN COMPLIANCE WITH ALL APPLICABLE FEDERAL AND STATE LAWS, REGULATIONS AND ETHICAL DUTIES, INCLUDING BUT NOT LIMITED TO, THOSE PROHIBITING DISCRIMINATION ON THE BASIS OF RACE, COLOR, RELIGION, SEX, NATIONAL ORIGIN, HANDICAP, FAMILIAL STATUS, SEXUAL ORIENTATION OR GENDER IDENTITY IN THE LEASING OF THE PROPERTY; USE AGENT'S BEST EFFORTS TO SOLICIT, SECURE AND MAINTAIN TENANTS, INCLUDING THE AUTHORITY TO NEGOTIATE, EXECUTE, EXTEND AND RENEW LEASES IN OWNER'S NAME FOR TERMS NOT IN EXCESS OF _____ ;

(c) Collect all rentals and other charges and amounts due under tenant leases and give receipts for amounts so collected;

(d) Deliver to Owner within 45 days following the date of execution of any rental agreement an accounting which sets forth the name of the tenant, the rental rate and rents collected, and promptly provide a copy of any rental agreement to Owner upon reasonable request;

(e) Provide Owner monthly statements of all monies received and disbursed in connection with Agent's management of the Property, and remit to Owner rental proceeds collected, less any deductions authorized hereunder; provided: (1) this shall not constitute a guarantee by Agent for rental payments that Agent is unable to collect in the exercise of reasonable diligence; (2) if, pursuant to this Agreement or required by law, Agent either has refunded or will refund in whole or in part any rental payments made by a tenant and previously remitted to Owner, Owner agrees to return same to Agent promptly upon Agent's demand; and (3) any rents pre-paid by a tenant shall be held in trust by Agent and disbursed to Owner as and when they become due under the terms of the tenant's lease;

(f) Make arrangements on Owner's behalf for any repairs which, in Agent's opinion, may be necessary to preserve, maintain and protect the Property; provided, Agent may not make arrangements for any repairs that exceed $_____ without prior approval of Owner, except that in the case of an emergency, Agent may, without prior approval, make arrangements for whatever expenditures on behalf of Owner that are reasonably necessary to preserve the Property or prevent further damage from occurring;

(g) Answer tenant requests and complaints and perform the duties imposed upon Owner by tenant leases or any local, state or federal law or regulations, including the authority to purchase such supplies and hire such labor as may be necessary in Agent's opinion to accomplish any necessary repairs;

(h) Retain such amounts from Owner's rental proceeds as may be necessary from time to time to pay expenses associated with the management and operation of the Property for which Owner is responsible hereunder. Agent will establish and maintain a fund on Owner's behalf in the amount of $_____ from which expenses may be paid, but Owner acknowledges and understands that Agent may from time to time retain additional amounts as Agent notifies Owner in advance in writing are reasonably necessary; Negotiate partial refunds with tenants if, in Agent's reasonable opinion, the tenant's use and enjoyment of the Property has been or will be materially and adversely affected as a result of a defect in the condition of the Property (such as a repair to the electrical, plumbing, sanitary, heating or ventilating facilities or a major appliance that cannot be made reasonably and promptly);

(i) Institute and prosecute such proceedings in small claims court as may be necessary and advisable, in Agent's opinion, to recover rents due the Owner from tenants or to evict tenants and regain possession, including the authority, in Agent's discretion, to settle, compromise and release any and all such small claims proceedings; provided, that with respect to any such small claims proceeding, Agent shall have actual knowledge of the facts alleged in the complaint; and

(j) _____

_____

_____

_____

7. **Cooperation With/Compensation To Other Agents:** Agent has advised Owner of Agent's company policies regarding cooperation and the amount(s) of any compensation, if any, that will be offered to subagents, tenant agents or both. Owner authorizes Agent to (*Check ALL applicable authorizations*):

❑ Cooperate with subagents representing only the Owner and offer them the following compensation: _____

_____

❑ Cooperate with tenant agents representing only the tenant and offer them the following compensation:_____

_____

❑ Cooperate with and compensate agents from other firms according to the attached company policy.

Agent will promptly notify Owner if Agent offers compensation to a cooperating agent(s) that is different from that set forth above.

8. **Marketing.** Owner authorizes Agent to advertise the Property in such manner as may be appropriate in Agent's opinion, including the authority to: (*Check ALL applicable sections*)

Page 2 of 7

STANDARD FORM 401
Revised 7/2016
©7/2017

Owner Initials _____ _____ Agent Initials _____ _____

Figure 17-3

❑ place "For Rent" signs on the Property (where permitted by law and relevant covenants) and to remove other such signs.

❑ submit pertinent information concerning the Property to any listing service of which Agent is a member or in which any of Agent's associates participates and to furnish to such listing service notice of all changes of information concerning the Property authorized in writing by Owner. Owner authorizes Agent, upon execution of a rental contract for the Property, to notify the listing service of the rental, and to disseminate rental information, including rental price, to the listing service, appraisers and real estate brokers.

❑ advertise the Property in non-Internet media, and to permit other firms to advertise the Property in non-Internet media to the extent and in such manner as Agent may decide.

❑ display information about the Property on the Internet either directly or through a program of any listing service of which the Agent is a member or in which any of Agent's associates participates, and to authorize other firms who belong to any listing service of which the Agent is a member or in which any of Agent's associates participates to display information about the Property on the Internet in accordance with the listing service rules and regulations. Owner also authorizes any listing service of which Agent is a member or in which any of Agent's associates participates to use, license or sell to others information about the Property entered into the listing service. Owner specifically authorizes the display of the address of the Property, automated estimates of the market value of the Property and third-party comments about the Property. If Owner desires to limit or prohibit Internet advertising as set forth above, Owner must complete an opt-out form in accordance with listing service rules.

(**NOTE**: NCAR Form #105 may be used to limit or prohibit Internet advertising and explains how such limitations may or may not be effective.)

9. **Responsibilities of Owner:** During the time this Agreement is in effect, Owner shall:

(a) Be responsible for all costs and expenses associated with the maintenance and operation of the Property in accordance with the requirements of tenant leases or any local, state or federal law or regulations, including but not limited to NC General Statutes Section 42-42, and advance to Agent such sums as may be necessary from time to time to pay such costs and expenses;

(b) Provide funds to Agent promptly upon Agent's request for any cost or expense for which Owner is responsible that Agent, in Agent's discretion, incurs on Owner's behalf, including but not limited to, the costs of advertising, emergency maintenance and repairs, utilities, property taxes, owners' association dues and assessments, court costs and attorney's fees; and further, pay interest at the rate of _____percent (%) per year on the amount of any outstanding balance thereof not paid to Agent within _____ days of Agent's written request therefore;

(c) NOT TAKE ANY ACTION OR ADOPT ANY POLICY THE EFFECT OF WHICH WOULD BE TO PREVENT AGENT FROM OFFERING THE PROPERTY FOR RENT IN COMPLIANCE WITH ALL APPLICABLE FEDERAL AND STATE LAWS, REGULATIONS AND ETHICAL DUTIES, INCLUDING BUT NOT LIMITED TO, THOSE PROHIBITING DISCRIMINATION ON THE BASIS OF RACE, COLOR, RELIGION, SEX, NATIONAL ORIGIN, HANDICAP, FAMILIAL STATUS, SEXUAL ORIENTATION OR GENDER IDENTITY IN THE LEASING OF THE PROPERTY;

(d) Carry, at Owner's expense, public liability insurance against any and all claims or demands whatever arising out of, or in any way connected with, the operation, leasing and maintenance of the Property, including property damage and personal injury, in the amount of not less than $_____, which policy shall, without cost to Agent, name Agent as an additional insured as its interest may appear, and provide at least annually a copy of such insurance policy or policies to Agent upon Agent's request;
(Name of insurance agent:_____; telephone no.:_____)

(e) Indemnify and hold Agent harmless to the extent allowable by law from any and all costs, expenses, attorneys' fees, suits, liabilities, damages or claims for damages, including but not limited to, those arising out of any injury or death to any person or loss or damage to any property of any kind whatsoever and to whomsoever belonging, including Owner, in any way relating to the management of the Property by Agent or the performance or exercise of any duty, obligation or authority set forth herein or hereafter granted to Agent, or arising out of a tenant's breach of any lease for the Property, except to the extent that such may be the result of gross negligence or willful or intentional misconduct by Agent;

(f) Be responsible for timely payment of all property taxes, mortgage payments, governmental or owners' association assessments associated with the Property, and any other expenses which could become a lien against the Property, and for promptly notifying Agent in the event that Owner receives any notice(s) from the holder of any loan or from any other lien holder of any kind, regarding a default in payment, threatened foreclosure or the filing of a foreclosure proceeding; and

Page 3 of 7

Owner Initials _____ _____Agent Initials _____ _____

Figure 17-3

(g) _____
_____
_____
_____
_____
_____
_____

10. **Tenant Security Deposits.** Agent may, in Agent's discretion, require tenants to make security deposits in an amount permitted by law to secure tenants' lease obligations (such security deposits shall hereinafter be referred to as "Tenant Security Deposits"). If the Agent requires Tenant Security Deposits, they shall be placed in a trust account in Agent's name in a North Carolina bank or savings and loan association. Upon the commencement of this Agreement, Owner shall deliver to Agent a list of any current tenants who previously made Tenant Security Deposits under existing leases and the amounts thereof. Simultaneously therewith, any such Tenant Security Deposits shall be placed in a trust account in Agent's name in a North Carolina bank or savings and loan association, and shall thereafter be administered in accordance with this Agreement.

11. **Pets.** Tenants *(check one of the following)* ❏ shall not be allowed to bring Pets onto the Property ❏ shall be allowed to bring pets onto the Property in accordance with Agent's company policy, a copy of which shall be provided to Owner and made a part of any rental agreement. Owner acknowledges and understands that whether or not pets are allowed, a person with a disability has the legal right to be accompanied by a service/assistance animal in the Property, that no pet fee may be charged to such person, and that such person would be liable for any damage done by the service/assistance animal to the Property.

12. **Owner/Condo Association** ❏ *(check if applicable)*.
   - Name of association: _____
   - Name of association property manager:_____
   - Property manager address and phone number: _____
   - Association website address, if any: _____

13. **Trust Account Interest. Agent may, in Agent's discretion, place gross receipts and collections, including Tenant Security Deposits, in an interest bearing trust account in the name of Agent in an insured bank or savings and loan association in North Carolina. Interest on any such amounts shall belong to _____(Owner or Agent), except that with respect to any Tenant Security Deposits, tenant leases shall specify, in Agent's discretion, whether such interest shall be payable to Owner or to the tenant. If the lease provides that such interest is payable to the tenant, Agent shall account for the interest in the manner set forth in such lease. If the lease provides that such interest is payable to Owner or as Owner directs, then such interest shall be paid to Owner or Agent as set forth above. Agent may remove any interest payable to Agent from the account at all times and with such frequency as is permitted under the terms of the account and as the law may require.**

14. **Entry by Owner.** Owner agrees that neither Owner nor any third party acting at Owner's direction, shall enter the Property for any purpose whatsoever during any time that it is occupied by a tenant in the absence of reasonable notice to Agent or tenant and scheduling by Agent or tenant of an appropriate time for any such entry.

15. **Lead-Based Paint/Hazard Disclosure**. If the Property was built prior to 1978, Landlord understands that Landlord is required under 42 U.S.C. 4852(d) to disclose information about lead-based paint and lead-based paint hazards, and that Agent is required to ensure Landlord's compliance with said law. Landlord agrees to complete and sign a "Disclosure Of Information On Lead-Based Paint And Lead-Based Paint Hazards" form (NCAR form #430-T), photocopies of which will be provided by Agent to prospective tenants. In the alternative, Landlord authorizes Agent, in Agent's discretion, to fulfill Landlord's disclosure obligations by completing and signing said form on Landlord's behalf based on information provided by Landlord to Agent.

16. **Tenant Information**. Owner acknowledges and understands: (i) that state and federal laws regulate the maintenance and disposal of certain personal information of consumers, such as social security numbers, drivers' license numbers, account numbers and other numbers that may be used to access a person's financial resources, and (ii) that contractual limitations with third-party providers of credit reports or other background information relating to prospective tenants may limit or prohibit Agent's dissemination of such reports/information. Owner agrees that Agent shall not be required to disclose any such information to Owner about a tenant or prospective tenant, and that if Agent does disclose any such information to Owner, Owner will indemnify and hold Agent harmless

STANDARD FORM 401
Revised 7/2016
©7/2017

Owner Initials _____ _____ Agent Initials _____ _____

Figure 17-3

from any and all costs, expenses, attorneys' fees, suits, liabilities, damages or claims for damages as set forth in paragraph 9(e) of this Agreement as a result of the disclosure of any such information to or by Owner.

17. **Duties on Termination.** Upon termination of this Agreement by either party, each shall take such steps as are necessary to settle all accounts between them, including, but not limited to, the following:
  (a) Agent shall promptly render to Owner all rents then on hand after having deducted therefrom any Agent's fees then due and amounts sufficient to cover all other outstanding expenditures of Agent incurred in connection with operating the Property;
  (b) Agent shall transfer any security deposits held by Agent to Owner or such other person or entity as Owner may designate in writing; provided, Owner understands and acknowledges that the Tenant Security Deposit Act requires Owner to either deposit any such deposits in a trust account with a licensed and insured bank or savings institution located in North Carolina, or furnish a bond from an insurance company licensed to do business in North Carolina; and provided further, Owner shall be responsible for any out-of-pocket transfer costs incurred by Agent;
  (c) Owner shall promptly pay to Agent any fees or amounts due the Agent under the Agreement or any current rental agreement and shall reimburse Agent for any expenditures made and outstanding at the time of termination;
  (d) Agent shall deliver to Owner copies of all tenant leases and other instruments entered into on behalf of Owner (Agent may retain copies of such leases and instruments for Agent's records); and
  (e) Owner shall notify all current tenants of the termination of this Agreement and transfer of any advance rents and security deposits to Owner.

18. **Sale of Property.** In the event Owner desires to sell the Property through Owner's own efforts or those of a firm other than Agent, Owner shall: (a) promptly notify Agent that the Property is for sale and, if applicable, disclose to Agent the name of the listing firm; and (b) promptly notify Agent if the Property goes under contract and disclose to Agent the agreed-upon closing date.

19. **Entire Agreement; Modification.** This Agreement contains the entire agreement of the parties and supersedes all prior written and oral proposals, understandings, agreements and representations, all of which are merged herein. No odification of this Agreement shall be effective unless it is in writing and executed by all parties hereto.

20. **Non-Waiver of Default.** The failure of either party to insist, in any one or more instances, on the performance of any term or condition of this Agreement shall not be construed as a waiver or relinquishment of any rights granted hereunder or of the future performance of any such term or condition, and the obligations of the non-performing party with respect thereto shall continue in full force and effect.

21. **Governing Law; Venue.** The parties agree that this Agreement shall be governed by and construed in accordance with the laws of the State of North Carolina, and that in the event of a dispute, any legal action may only be instituted in the county where the Property is located.

22. **Relationship of Parties.** Although Owner and Agent agree that they will actively and materially participate with each other on a regular basis in fulfilling their respective obligations hereunder, the parties intend for their relationship to be that of independent contractors, and nothing contained in this Agreement shall be construed to create a partnership or joint venture of any kind.

23. **Exclusivity.** Owner agrees that Agent shall be the exclusive rental agent for the Property, and that no other party, including Owner, shall offer the Property for rent during the time this Agreement is in effect. Any rent nevertheless received by Owner or any third party will be transferred to Agent and thereafter accounted for as if originally received by Agent, including the deduction therefrom of any fee due Agent hereunder.

24. **Default.** If either party defaults in the performance of any of its obligations hereunder, in addition to any other remedies provided herein or by applicable law, the non-defaulting party shall have the right to terminate this Agreement if, within thirty days after providing the defaulting party with written notice of the default and the intent to terminate, the default remains uncured. Notwithstanding the foregoing, Agent shall have the right to terminate this Agreement immediately on written notice in the event Owner seeks bankruptcy protection, or the Property becomes subject to a foreclosure proceeding, or Owner fails to promptly pay for any costs associated with Owner's obligations under NC General Statutes Section 42-42 or to advance to Agent such sums as may be necessary to pay such costs.

25. **Costs in Event of Default.** If legal proceedings are brought by a party to enforce the terms, conditions or provisions of this Agreement, the prevailing party shall be entitled to recover all expenses (including, but not limited to, reasonable attorney fees, legal expenses and reasonable costs of collection) paid or incurred by such prevailing party in endeavoring to enforce the terms, conditions, or provisions of this Agreement and/or collect any amount owing in accordance with this Agreement.

Page 5 of 7

STANDARD FORM 401
Revised 7/2016
©7/2017

Owner Initials _____ _____ Agent Initials _____ _____

Figure 17-3

26. **Authority to Enter into Agreement; Principal Contact.** Owner represents and warrants to Agent that Owner has full authority to enter into this Agreement, and that there is no other party with an interest in the Property whose joinder in this Agreement is necessary. Either _____ or _____ shall serve as Owner's principal contact for purposes of making all decisions and receiving all notices and rental payments contemplated by this Agreement, and all persons signing this Agreement as Owner hereby appoint either of said persons as Owner's agent and attorney-in-fact for the purposes set forth in this section.

27. **Use of Electronic Means; Notice.** The parties agree that electronic means may be used to sign this Agreement or to make any modifications the parties may agree to, and that any written notice, communication or documents may be transmitted to any mailing address, e-mail address or fax number set forth in the signature section below. Either party may change the address to which any notice or documents should be sent by written notification to the other party in a manner permitted by this paragraph.

28. **Binding Nature of Agreement.** This Agreement shall be binding upon and inure to the benefit of the heirs, legal and personal representatives, successors and permitted assigns of the parties.

29. **Assignments by Agent; Change of Ownership.** Owner agrees that at any time during the term of this Agreement, Agent may either assign Agent's rights and responsibilities hereunder to another real estate agency, or transfer to another person or entity all or part of the ownership of Agent's real estate agency, and that in the event of any such assignment or transfer, this Agreement shall continue in full force and effect; provided, that any assignee or transferee must be licensed to engage in the business of real estate brokerage in the State of North Carolina. In the event of any such assignment or transfer, Owner may, in addition to all other termination rights hereunder, terminate this Agreement without cause on sixty (60) days' prior written notice to the assignee or transferee of Owner's intent to terminate this Agreement.

30. **Other Professional Services.** Owner acknowledges that Agent is being retained solely as a real estate professional, and understands that other professional service providers are available to render advice or services to Owner at Owner's expense, including but not limited to an attorney, insurance agent, tax advisor, engineer, home inspector, environmental consultant, architect, or contractor. If Agent procures any such services at the request of Owner, Owner agrees that Agent shall incur no liability or responsibility in connection therewith.

31. **Addenda.** Any addenda to this Agreement are described in the following space and attached hereto: _____
_____
_____
_____.

The parties agree that any such addenda shall constitute an integral part of this Agreement. In the event of a conflict between this Agreement and any such addenda, the terms of such addenda shall control.

32. **Other.** _____
_____
_____
_____

[THIS SPACE INTENTIONALLY LEFT BLANK]

STANDARD FORM 401
Revised 7/2016
©7/2017

Owner Initials _____ _____Agent Initials _____ _____

Figure 17-3

THE AGENT SHALL CONDUCT ALL BROKERAGE ACTIVITIES IN REGARD TO THIS AGREEMENT WITHOUT RESPECT TO THE RACE, COLOR, RELIGION, SEX, NATIONAL ORIGIN, HANDICAP OR FAMILIAL STATUS OF ANY PARTY OR PROSPECTIVE PARTY TO THE AGREEMENT. FURTHER, REALTORS® HAVE AN ETHICAL DUTY TO CONDUCT SUCH ACTIVITIES WITHOUT RESPECT TO THE SEXUAL ORIENTATION OR GENDER IDENTITY OF ANY PARTY OR PROSPECTIVE PARTY TO THIS AGREEMENT.

THE NORTH CAROLINA ASSOCIATION OF REALTORS®, INC. MAKES NO REPRESENTATION AS TO THE LEGAL VALIDITY OR ADEQUACY OF ANY PROVISION OF THIS FORM IN ANY SPECIFIC TRANSACTION.

OWNER:

_____(SEAL)   DATE:_____

_____(SEAL)   DATE:_____

_____(SEAL)   DATE:_____

_____(SEAL)   DATE:_____

AGENT: _____
    [Name of real estate firm]

BY:_____ Individual license #_____ DATE:_____
    [Authorized Representative]

Address:_____

Telephone: _____ Fax:_____ E-mail:_____

Owner:_____

Address:_____

Contact information: _____
            Home   Work   Cell   Email

Owner:_____

Address:_____

Contact information: _____
            Home   Work   Cell   Email

Owner:_____

Address:_____

Contact information: _____
            Home   Work   Cell   Email

Owner:_____

Address:_____

Contact information: _____
            Home   Work   Cell   Email

STANDARD FORM 401
Revised 7/2016
©7/2017

Figure 17-3

18 | FAIR HOUSING

The **Federal Fair Housing Act**[1] and the **North Carolina Fair Housing Act**[2] prohibit discrimination against an individual based on race, color, religion, sex, national origin, handicap, or familial status in the sale, rental or advertising of residential property. Fair housing laws and regulations are explained in depth in this chapter. *Any violation of fair housing laws by a real estate broker is also a violation of the North Carolina Real Estate License Law.*[3]

The **Americans with Disabilities Act (ADA)** protects the civil rights of persons with mental and physical disabilities. It does not apply to the sale or rental of residential units. Included in the ADA's protections are extensive requirements designed to ensure adequate access for the disabled to commercial buildings and places of public accommodation. Another law prohibiting discrimination based on race is The **Federal Civil Rights Act of 1866 prohibits discrimination based on race**.

FAIR HOUSING LAWS

FEDERAL FAIR HOUSING ACT

The **Federal Fair Housing Act of 1968**, which is Title VIII of the Civil Rights Act, and the **Federal Fair Housing Amendments Act of 1988 (both referred to in this chapter as the "FHA")** prohibit discrimination against protected classes of persons. In 2015, the United States Supreme Court reviewed the history of past discrimination in the sale and rental of housing and reaffirmed its commitment to a broad interpretation of enforcement of the FHA.[4]

Protected Classes

Discrimination is prohibited both in the sale, rental, or advertising of a dwelling and in the provision of brokerage services to any member of a protected class. There are seven protected classes expressly listed under the Fair Housing Act:

- Race
- Color
- Religion
- Sex/gender
- Handicap/disability
- Familial status
- National Origin

Note on Status of LGBT Persons

Although lesbian, gay, bisexual, or transgender (LGBT) persons are not expressly listed as a protected class under the Fair Housing Act, the Department of Housing and Urban Development (HUD) has regulations and rules implementing policies "to ensure that its core programs are open to all eligible individuals and families regardless of sexual orientation, gender identity, or marital status."[5] Official HUD policy is summarized below, followed by examples provided by HUD at the same source.

> [A] lesbian, gay, bisexual, or transgender (LGBT) person's experience with sexual orientation or gender identity housing discrimination may still be covered by the Fair Housing Act. In addition, housing providers that receive HUD funding, have loans insured by the Federal Housing Administration (FHA), as well as lenders insured by FHA, may be subject to HUD program regulations intended to ensure equal access of LGBT persons.[6]

Example: A gay man is evicted because his landlord believes he will infect other tenants with HIV/AIDS. That situation may constitute illegal disability discrimination under the Fair Housing Act, because the man is perceived to have a disability, HIV/AIDS.

Example: A property manager refuses to rent an apartment to a prospective tenant who is transgender. If the housing denial is because of the prospective tenant's nonconformity with gender stereotypes, it may constitute illegal discrimination on the basis of sex under the Fair Housing Act.

Example: An underwriter for an FHA insured loan is reviewing an application where two male incomes are being used as the basis for the applicants' credit worthiness. The underwriter assumes the applicants are a gay couple and denies the application despite the applicants' credentials. This scenario may violate HUD regulations which prohibit FHA-insured lenders from taking actual or perceived sexual orientation into consideration in determining adequacy of an applicant's income.

The Code of Ethics of the National Association of REALTORS® states:

> Realtors® shall not deny equal professional services to any person for reasons of race, color, religion, sex, handicap, familial status, national origin, sexual orientation, or gender identity. Realtors® shall not be parties to any plan or agreement to discriminate against a person or persons on the basis of race, color, religion, sex, handicap, familial status, national origin, or gender identity.
>
> Realtors®, in their real estate employment practices, shall not discriminate against any person or persons on the basis of race, color, religion, sex, handicap, familial status, national origin, sexual orientation, or gender identity.[7]

Given HUD's expanding and clear public policy to ensure fair housing to all eligible individuals and families regardless of sexual orientation, gender identity, or marital status, real estate brokers should realize that any discrimination in housing based upon LGBT considerations may violate the federal Fair Housing Act. Brokers who are also Realtors® have an ethical duty to refrain from discriminating against LGBT persons.

Prohibited Practices

The prohibited practices below evidence an effort by Congress in the Fair Housing Act, as amended, to eradicate all forms of discrimination against protected classes of persons. Forms of illegal discrimination frequently encountered are then discussed, although the discussion is by no means exhaustive.

It is illegal to engage in any of the following practices because of a person's race, color, religion, sex, handicap, familial status, or national origin.

- Refuse to sell or rent a dwelling after a bona fide offer has been made, or refuse to negotiate for the sale or rental of a dwelling.[8]
- Discriminate in the terms, conditions, or privileges of the sale or rental of a dwelling, or in the provision of services or facilities in connection with such sale or rental.
- Engage in any conduct relating to the provision of housing which makes it unavailable.
- Discriminate in publications or advertising.
- Represent that a dwelling is not available for sale or rental when it is.
- Engage in blockbusting practices.
- Deny equal access to a multiple listing service or other brokerage organization or service.
- Discriminate in the making or purchasing of loans (1) for purchasing, constructing, improving, repairing, or maintaining a dwelling, or (2) where the security is residential real estate.
- Discriminate in the selling, brokering or appraisal of residential real property.

This section discusses specific acts that are prohibited in the sale or rental of housing. The language of the Fair Housing Act is constantly being refined, interpreted, and explained by court decisions and government regulations. The discussion below is a sampling of prohibited practices that violate the Fair Housing Act.

Responsibility for Compliance

Fair housing laws require compliance by sellers, landlords (lessors), real estate brokers, agents of sellers and landlords, multiple listing services, lenders, investors, appraisers, and anyone else involved with selling or leasing residential real estate. *A real estate broker cannot avoid liability for a prohibited discriminatory practice by claiming that he or she was acting upon the explicit instructions of his or her principal (usually a seller or landlord).*[9] Recall as well that an agent is only obligated to follow the *lawful* directives of his or her principal.

A property owner may be liable for his agent's violation of the fair housing laws and a broker-in-charge and/or a real estate company may be civilly liable for discriminatory actions by affiliated brokers committed within the apparent scope of the broker's employment.[10] Whether a broker-in-charge may be civilly liable for the acts of affiliated brokers under his/her supervision or subject to disciplinary action by the Commission may be influenced by such factors as the extent of the broker-in-charge's obligation to supervise the affiliated broker, how well he or she fulfilled that obligation, whether he or she knew or should have known about the affiliated broker's conduct and what, if any, remedial action the broker-in-charge took upon learning of any violation. Clearly, if the broker-in-charge participated in the discrimination, then he or she is liable for his or her conduct.

Blockbusting

"***Blockbusting***" is a term used to describe practices by real estate brokers and others directed at influencing and exploiting the racial turnover in a neighborhood. *The illegal object of this practice is to scare property owners in a neighborhood into selling their property below its fair market value by telling them that members of a minority group are moving into the area.* Another term for blockbusting is "*panic-peddling.*" The actions may be either direct or subtle and may include a variety of inducements for a homeowner to sell, such as representations regarding a decline in property values, a decline in the quality of education available in the neighborhood, or an increase in crime rate.[11]

Example: A broker, by means of phone calls and personal visits to residents of a white neighborhood, consistently made subtle references to changing neighborhoods, to the expansion of neighborhood ghettoes, to the real estate broker's personal fear of crime in the area, and to the increasing difficulty of finding purchasers for homes in the neighborhood. These actions constitute illegal blockbusting.[12]

Example: X Realty Company mailed notices to white residents of an integrated neighborhood stating that certain properties in that neighborhood had been sold and X Realty offered to sell the homes of the white residents who received the notices. At the same time, X Realty mailed different notices to the black residents of the neighborhood informing them that certain neighborhood homes were for sale and asking if a "friend" might be interested in purchasing these homes. These actions by X Realty constitute a subtle but equally illegal form of blockbusting.

Steering

Most cases involving "***steering***" have dealt with racial discrimination.[13] "Racial steering" has been defined as follows:

> "Racial steering" is a practice by which real estate brokers … preserve and encourage patterns of racial segregation by steering members of racial and ethnic groups to buildings occupied primarily by members of their own racial or ethnic group and away from buildings and neighborhoods inhabited by members of other races or groups.[14]

Example: Brokers at a real estate company show black prospective purchasers listings in predominantly black areas of the city and discourage them from looking for housing in white neighborhoods. White prospective purchasers are not shown listings in black or integrated neighborhoods. If interest is expressed in such a neighborhood, the prospective purchaser is cautioned about the racial makeup of the area and discouraged from purchasing there. These practices constitute illegal racial steering.

While steering most often involves racial factors, it is equally illegal when based on any other protected class such as color, religion, sex, handicap, familial status or national origin. Thus, a broker who steers a prospective purchaser or renter away from a neighborhood because it is predominantly occupied by members of a certain religion or nationality is practicing illegal steering under the Fair Housing Act. Know that steering, while illegal, is frequently practiced in both leasing and sales. Complaints continue to be filed against real estate companies for routinely steering white renters or buyers to white neighborhoods and making disparaging remarks about minority neighborhoods while steering minority renters or buyers to minority neighborhoods.

Discrimination in Advertising

Under the Fair Housing Act as amended, discriminatory advertising is prohibited. The Act and the federal regulations interpreting it *prohibit **anyone** from making, printing or publishing any notice, statement, or advertisement with respect to the sale or rental of a residential dwelling which indicates any preference, limitation, or discrimination because of a person's race, color, religion, sex, handicap, familial status or national origin.*[15] Real estate brokers involved in the sale or rental of residential property should carefully review all advertisements, notices, and commercials to assure compliance with the Act. Additionally, *brokers must be mindful of their statements, as "to publish" is not limited to printed media, but includes web page information, email and text message, and oral comments or statements.*

Advertising Guidelines

HUD advocates the following general rules to avoid violating fair housing laws, namely:

1. Describe the *property*, not the *person*. In other words, describe the physical attributes of the dwelling itself, not the persons who might live there; e.g., state the number of bedrooms, not the number of people who might live there; say "fixer-upper" rather than "handyman."
2. Mention the amenities, e.g., tennis courts, cycling/jogging paths, not the participants, e.g., tennis players, cyclists, joggers.
3. State the geographic location, rather than landmarks, e.g., 632 Main Street, rather than "across from Christ the King Episcopal Church."

Acceptable Words and Phrases[16]

- near bus/metro
- no drinking
- great for family
- near golf course
- luxury condo

- credit check required
- no drugs
- family room
- gated
- parks nearby

- den
- equal housing opportunity
- fixer-upper
- houses of worship nearby
- quiet residential area

Unacceptable Words and Phrases

- able-bodied
- adult only/living/community
- no blind
- couples only
- no impaired
- singles preferred

- agile
- no alcoholics/drinkers
- no crippled, deaf
- colored
- healthy only/no handicapped
- mature individual/persons

- bachelor (pad)
- near churches
- no children
- empty nesters
- restricted
- integrated

Obviously any reference to a particular race, religion, or national origin e.g., African, Latino, Hispanic, Asian, Catholic, Jewish, WASP, Irish, etc. or other protected class clearly violates fair housing laws, whether the words or phrases appear in print or whether they are uttered in person.

Not only must one be mindful of the words one uses, but also any photographs, pictures or models used in any advertising, including web Internet advertising, should reflect diversity, or at least avoid conveying a preference for a certain "type" of person. Similarly, choosing methods of advertising that clearly exclude large segments of protected classes may be deemed discriminatory. Some advertisers of residential property for rent or sale are required to display an affirmative statement, Equal Housing Opportunity logo, or other form of affirmative language informing the public of the nondiscrimination policy of the advertiser.

Recall that most advertising is done in the name of the real estate *company*. While the individual broker's name also may appear in the advertising, the broker is acting as an agent of the company with which he or she is affiliated and the company may be liable for any advertising that violates fair housing. While brokers are individually responsible for advertising they prepare, brokers-in-charge are responsible for "the proper conduct of all advertising by or in the name of the firm." Real estate companies should have a written fair housing policy and train their affiliated brokers in fair housing compliance practices.

Refusal to Sell, Rent, or Negotiate

It is illegal under the Fair Housing Act to refuse to sell[17] or rent[18] to a person who has made a bona fide offer, or to refuse to negotiate with any person based on race, color, religion, sex, handicap, familial status, or national origin. Both *direct* and *indirect* methods of discrimination are prohibited. Additionally, the Act prohibits a misrepresentation (to a protected person) that any dwelling is not available for inspection, as well as prohibiting discrimination in the terms, conditions, or privileges connected with the sale or rental of a dwelling.

Discrimination against minorities is often subtle, and fair housing agencies are authorized to enlist the assistance of "testers" to help prove illegal discrimination. The following is an example.

Example: A broker lists a condominium unit for sale at $179,500. The owner tells the broker that she would accept $175,000. An African-American woman expresses an interest in the unit and offers $176,000. The broker refuses to submit the offer to the seller and informs the prospective buyer that the $179,500 listing price is not negotiable. A fair housing organization then sends two testers, one African-American and one Caucasian, to inquire. The African-American tester is told by the broker that the $179,500 price is firm. Four days later the Caucasian tester meets with the broker and says, "It's about $180,000, isn't it?" The broker replies that the price is flexible and that the unit would sell for $175,000.

Example: A landlord refuses to rent to divorced women, but will rent to divorced men. This practice constitutes illegal sex discrimination under the Fair Housing Act.[19]

Example: A realty company that manages residential rental properties establishes a certain "minimum income" requirement as a prerequisite to renting an apartment. Numerous African-American families are turned away because their incomes fall short of the minimum standard. However, the "minimum income" standard is regularly waived for white prospective tenants, but never for African-American or Latino prospective tenants. This practice violates the Fair Housing Act.

Use of Criminal Records in Leasing

In April 2016, HUD released a 10-page guideline regarding the use of criminal records in housing decisions, primarily in residential leasing. HUD found that nationally, "across all age groups, the imprisonment rates for African American males is almost six times greater than for White males, and for Hispanic males, it is over twice that for non-Hispanic White males." HUD concluded:

Across the United States, African Americans and Hispanics are arrested, convicted, and incarcerated at rates disproportionate to their share of the general population. Consequently, criminal records-based barriers to housing are likely to have a disproportionate impact on minority homeseekers. While having a criminal record is not a protected characteristic under the Fair

Housing Act, criminal history-based restrictions on housing opportunities violate the Act if, without justification, their burden falls more often on renters or other housing market participants of one race or national origin over another (i.e., discriminatory effects liability). Additionally, intentional discrimination in violation of the Act occurs if a housing provider treats individuals with comparable criminal history differently because of their race, national origin, or other protected characteristic (i.e., disparate treatment liability).

HUD specifically acknowledged that housing providers have a significant interest in protecting the safety and property of others, and a prospective tenant's previous criminal convictions may be one factor in that evaluation, but it should not be the lone factor. What an owner may legitimately consider without violating the Fair Housing Act will be discussed in greater detail in Chapter 17, but for this discussion, understand HUD's position as expressed in the April 2016 *Guidance*:

> ... Thus, where a policy or practice that restricts access to housing on the basis of criminal history has a disparate impact on individuals of a particular race, national origin, or other protected class, such policy or practice is unlawful under the Fair Housing Act if it is not necessary to serve a substantial, legitimate, nondiscriminatory interest of the housing provider or if such interest could be served by another practice that has a less discriminatory effect.

Discrimination in the Financing of Housing

The Fair Housing Act contains sweeping prohibitions against discrimination in the financing of housing. *Banks and other mortgage lending institutions are prohibited from discriminating on the basis of race, color, religion, sex, handicap, familial status, or national origin in the granting of loans or in the terms and conditions of loans.*[20] Loans covered by the Act are those for the purpose of purchasing, constructing, improving, repairing, or maintaining a dwelling.

Redlining. One historic illegal practice that the Fair Housing Act sought to end was the "**redlining**" of certain areas by lenders based upon the area's racial composition.[21] Loan applications for housing within the "redlined" area were either denied or subjected to more onerous loan terms as a prerequisite for approval. The Fair Housing Act specifically prohibits discrimination in the fixing of the amount, interest rate, duration, or other terms and conditions of the loan. The Act has successfully eliminated most discrimination in the approval and terms of residential mortgage loans.

Discrimination in the Provision of Brokerage Services

The Act declares it unlawful "to deny any person access to membership or participation in any multiple-listing service, real estate brokers' organization, or other service, organization, or facility relating to the business of selling or renting dwellings, or to discriminate against him in the terms or conditions of such access, membership, or participation, on account of race, color, religion, sex, handicap, familial status, or national origin."[22]

Discrimination Based on Familial Status

The Fair Housing Act prohibits discrimination based on familial status. *"Familial status" means discrimination against* **families with children***, but the term encompasses more than the traditional family.*[23] Nondiscrimination protections based on familial status *apply to children* (individuals under the age of 18) domiciled with a parent or person having legal custody, or children domiciled with the designee of a parent or legal custodian with the written permission of the parent or legal custodian.[24] Familial status protections also apply to persons who are pregnant or about to obtain legal custody of a child.

Subject to limited exceptions for senior housing developments, it is illegal to discriminate against families with children by excluding them from housing developments or parts of developments.

Example: A complex contains three 40-unit apartment buildings. The complex manager has a policy that all families with children must live in Building 1 and Buildings 2 and 3 are designated as "adults only" buildings. This policy illegally discriminates based on familial status.

Example: The owner of a 25-story high-rise apartment building informs the property manager that families with children will be permitted on the bottom fifteen floors, but that the top ten floors are reserved for single persons and married couples without children. The owner cites safety reasons for the policy. Nonetheless, the policy illegally discriminates based on familial status.[25]

The main thrust of the addition of familial status to fair housing legislation is to prevent the exclusion of children from housing developments and likewise to prevent the segregation of children within such developments. HUD's official position is that segregated "dual housing" facilities that restrict families with children to designated areas within the building or community violate the federal Fair Housing Act.

A landlord's improper inquiry about marital status when a prospective tenant mentions that she has children can be evidence of unlawful discrimination under the Fair Housing Act.

Example: A landlord refused to show an apartment for rent to a woman after learning that she was the unmarried mother of two children. Later, the same apartment is again advertised for rent and this time the woman emailed the landlord. In her message, she pretended to be married with one child and the landlord agreed to show her the apartment. She then filed a complaint alleging familial status discrimination. The court held that while the Fair Housing Act does *not* prohibit discrimination based on marital status, the landlord's conversations and actions implied that the landlord would not rent to a single woman with children, which does violate the Fair Housing Act.[26]

Occupancy Restrictions. The Federal Fair Housing Act allows ***reasonable*** *maximum occupancy standards* restricting the number of people who will be allowed to live in a unit, *if* they are applied to all occupants of rental housing and *if* they do not directly or indirectly discriminate on the basis of familial status.[27]

Example: An apartment complex landlord has a policy of refusing to rent one-bedroom apartments to more than one person. While this policy does not directly prohibit children as tenants and appears to be facially neutral, the actual effect of the policy has what is legally known as a "disparate impact" on renters with children. The policy results in discrimination against a protected class, children, and therefore violates the Fair Housing Act.[28]

Not every occupancy restriction that affects *families with children violates th*e Fair Housing Act, but occupancy restrictions are considered suspect and can be combined with other factors to prove illegal discrimination. If the apartment complex has a history of encouraging "adults only" occupancy, that factor, combined with a one person per unit occupancy restriction, tends to prove illegal discrimination based on familial status.

The Fair Housing Act does not limit "the applicability of any reasonable local, State, or Federal restrictions regarding the maximum number of persons permitted to occupy a dwelling."[29] HUD acknowledges that, *as a general rule*, a reasonable occupancy policy is two persons per bedroom, but this should *not* be interpreted as an absolute rule of thumb. In reviewing complaints of familial status discrimination involving occupancy limits, HUD takes into account relevant factors, including bedroom sizes, ages of children, apartment configuration, and state and local law.[30]

Discrimination Based on Handicap/Disability

It is unlawful under the Fair Housing Act to refuse to sell or rent a dwelling to a handicapped person, to discriminate against the handicapped in the terms, conditions, or privileges in the sale or rental of a dwelling, or to otherwise impair reasonable access to housing by an individual with a handicapping condition. An individual has a handicapping condition, also referred to as a "disability" under HUD regulations, if the individual:

1) has a physical or mental disability (including hearing, mobility, or visual impairments; chronic alcoholism; chronic mental illness; AIDS, AIDS Related Complex; autism and mental retardation) *that substantially limits one or more major life activities*, or
2) has a record of such a disability, or
3) is regarded as having such a disability.

"*Major life activities*" include the ability to: care for yourself, perform manual tasks, walk, talk, see, hear, breathe, learn and work.[31] Because of the unique challenges faced by the handicapped and disabled in the area of housing, two major requirements of the Fair Housing Amendments Act of 1988 dealt with the physical design of multifamily dwellings, namely:

(1) reasonable accommodations and modifications must be made to existing buildings; and
(2) design and construction of new buildings must accommodate the handicapped.

The ramifications of these requirements as to the provision of housing are sweeping and impact real estate brokers as they engage in the sale, rental, and management of residential property.

"Reasonable Accommodations and Modifications"

Owners who lease residential property generally must grant reasonable tenant requests for accommodations or modifications necessary to enable a tenant with a disability to access and use the dwelling.[32] An *accommodation* is a *change or variance in rules, services, practices or policies that allows a person with a handicapping condition to enjoy the housing, but does not alter application of the rule, policy, service or practice as to other tenants.* Landlords *may not refuse to make reasonable **accommodations** in rules, policies, practices, or services if necessary for the disabled person to use the housing.* Examples of reasonable accommodations include:

- assigning a reserved parking space to a mobility-impaired tenant near his/her apartment when the complex offers tenants ample, unassigned parking;
- providing written material either orally or in large print or Braille to a visually-impaired tenant;

- reminding a developmentally challenged tenant that rent is due in three days;
- permitting a live-in aide to reside with a disabled tenant even if it violates "normal" policy;
- permitting "service animals" even if the apartment complex otherwise prohibits pets;
- altering chemicals used for pest control or maintenance or, if alternate chemicals are ineffective, at least providing an allergic tenant with several days' notice prior to using the chemicals;
- permitting a tenant who, after several surgeries, has difficulty walking up stairs to move from a fourth floor apartment to an available apartment on the first floor.[33]

A *modification alters the physical characteristics of the dwelling or common areas of a building.* These requests generally arise only in lease transactions, because in a purchase, the buyer acquires and controls the property and may make whatever changes s/he wishes. In *lease transactions,* prospective tenants with a handicapping condition may request a landlord to *allow reasonable modifications to the dwelling or common use areas to enable the tenant to use the housing.* Generally, landlords may not refuse such reasonable requests, but the landlord may require the tenant to pay for the modifications. Further, if internal modifications would interfere with a future occupant's use, then the landlord may require the tenant, if reasonable and necessary, to restore the dwelling to its original condition at the end of the tenancy. The same is not true of external modifications, such as a wheelchair ramp; typically tenants may not be required to remove the external modification at the end of the tenancy. Modifications fall within one of the following three classifications, namely:

1. ***Modifications that do not need to be restored to the original condition.*** These include modifications that do not interfere with future occupants' use of the unit and modifications to the public and common use areas (often external), such as widening interior doorways, grab bars in bathrooms, and ramps to afford ingress and egress.

2. ***Modifications that must be restored to original condition but don't require an escrow account.*** Typically these modifications are relatively minor, easy to restore, and inexpensive, such as replacing a cabinet underneath a bathroom sink that was removed to allow wheelchair access.

3. ***Modifications that must be restored but are moderately expensive and require an escrow account.*** An owner who permits more extensive modifications that will cost more to remediate, such as lowering kitchen and bathroom counters or replacing all the kitchen cabinets, may lawfully request the tenant to deposit a reasonable agreed sum into an escrow account that will be held until the end of the tenancy and used to pay for the restoration of the premises. Any unused funds from such deposits that are not needed to pay for the restoration should be returned to the tenant.

A landlord renting a residential unit must make or allow reasonable modifications to the unit, if the modifications are necessary to afford the handicapped person full enjoyment of the premises. A refusal to allow reasonable modifications or to make reasonable accommodations in rules, policies, or services that may be necessary to provide a handicapped tenant with an equal opportunity to use and enjoy a dwelling constitutes a violation of the Fair Housing Act.

The 2012 case of *Scott v. Croom*[34] illustrates how costly such a refusal can be. Mr. Scott and his wife and three children had been renting a single family home from the owner for three years when Mr. Scott unexpectedly was stricken with multiple sclerosis that within months relegated him to a wheelchair. He could no longer access many of the rooms in the house, including the bathrooms, with his wheelchair. Mr. Scott requested in writing that he be allowed to install a wheelchair ramp, to remove a shower door, to lower certain counters and sinks and install a higher commode, all using licensed contractors. He offered to pay all modification expenses as well as any costs to restore the property to its former condition at the end of the tenancy. The landlord refused all requests, other than the wheelchair ramp, and further refused to renew the lease for another year and ordered the Scotts to vacate, which they did. In a Consent Order entered in the lawsuit filed on the Scotts' behalf, the landlord (a retired attorney) agreed to pay $200,000 in damages to the Scotts and to implement certain training and policies and the report to counsel for the United States for three years.

Assistance and Service Animals

Brokers and housing providers are increasingly encountering requests from tenants who have or want an assistance or service animal. Due to this increasing frequency and the need to protect the rights of people with disabilities under the Fair Housing Act, a detailed discussion follows. *Brokers must clearly understand that "assistance" animals are not "pets."* In an April 2013 Notice[35] regarding assistance animals under the Fair Housing Act, HUD comments:

> An assistance animal is not a pet. It is an animal that works, provides
> assistance, or performs tasks for the benefit of a person with a disability, or
> provides emotional support that alleviates one or more identified symptoms
> or effects of a person's disability.

While the Americans with Disabilities Act (ADA) more narrowly defines the term "service animal," the Fair Housing Act imposes no such limitations. In addition to the most common examples of canines, assistance animals may include cats, birds, ponies, monkeys or guinea pigs, to name a few. Owners may not charge a pet deposit fee or apply apartment restrictions on pets to assistance or service animals, although they may deduct from the tenant security deposit any damage beyond ordinary wear and tear caused by the assistance animal.

Permissible Inquiries under the Fair Housing Act

As explained in the April 2013 HUD Notice referenced above, an "assistance animal" under the Fair Housing Act is not required to be individually trained or certified as an assistance animal. If the person's disability and the disability-related need the animal serves is either readily apparent or already known to the housing provider, then no further documentation may be requested. *If either the disability or the need for the animal is not readily apparent,* e.g., a person prone to seizures who has a seizure alert service animal, *then an owner/agent may ask the following two questions when faced with a request for an accommodation to allow an assistance animal under fair housing laws,* namely:

1) Does the person seeking to use the animal have a disability, i.e., a physical or mental impairment that substantially limits one or more major life activities?

and

2) Does the animal work, provide assistance, perform tasks or services for the benefit of the person with the disability or provide emotional support that alleviates one or more of the identified symptoms or effects of the person's disability?

If the answer to either question is "no," then the request for accommodation may be denied, but *if the answer to both questions is "yes," then the owner generally must grant an accommodation* to existing policy and allow the animal access to all areas of the premises where persons are permitted entry. If the disability is obvious, but the need for and tasks performed by the animal are not apparent, then the housing provider may only ask the tenant for documentation of the disability related need for the animal. As to an *emotional support animal,* the April 2013 HUD Notice says that the owner may request:

> ... documentation from a *physician, psychiatrist, social worker, or other mental health professional* that the animal provides emotional support that alleviates one or more of the identified symptoms or effects of an existing disability. *Such documentation is sufficient if it establishes that an individual has a disability and that the animal in question will provide some type of disability-related assistance or emotional support.*[36] *[Emphasis added].*

Owners **may not ask** an applicant or tenant to *provide access to his/her medical records or medical providers or to provide extensive information or documentation of the person's physical or mental impairments.* An otherwise substantiated request may be denied only if making the accommodation:

1) would impose an undue financial or administrative burden or would fundamentally alter the housing provider's services, or
2) if the specific animal poses a direct threat to the safety and health of others that can't be reduced by other reasonable accommodations, or
3) the specific animal would cause substantial physical damage to the property of others that can't be reduced or eliminated by other reasonable accommodations.

The determination of either #2 or #3 "... must be based on an *individualized assessment* that relies on *objective evidence about the specific animal's actual conduct* - <u>not</u> on mere speculation or fear about the types of harm or damage an animal may cause and <u>not</u> on evidence about harm or damage that other animals have caused." [Italics added.]

Typically, both *disability* and *need* must be present and verified before an owner is obligated to make an accommodation under fair housing. Persons owning residential rental property and their agents must comply with both federal and state fair housing laws and allow reasonable accommodations for persons with disabilities, including those who need an assistance animal. Owners or their agents must respond to all requests for modifications and accommodations as the failure to respond to a request violates the Fair Housing Act.

Design and Construction Requirements

The amended fair housing legislation imposes major requirements on the design and construction of "covered multi-family dwellings" certified for first occupancy after March 13, 1991.[37] "Covered multi-family dwellings" are: 1) buildings having one or more elevators and four or more units, and 2) ground floor units in buildings with four or more units, but no elevator. These buildings must be designed and constructed to have an accessible route into and through the building and must satisfy the following requirements, namely:

- Public and common areas must be accessible to persons with disabilities.
- Doors and hallways must be wide enough to accommodate wheelchairs.
- All affected units must have:
    1) accessible routes into and through the unit;
    2) reinforced bathroom walls to allow later installation of grab bars;
    3) kitchens and bathrooms usable by a person in a wheelchair; and
    4) accessible light switches, electrical outlets, thermostats, and other environmental controls. [38]

If a building first occupied after March 13, 1991 has four or more units *but no elevator* then *the foregoing standards only apply to the ground floor units.* If the building has four or more units and at least one elevator, then all units must meet the above standards. Buildings in compliance with design standards for handicapped access promulgated by the National Standards Institute in 1986 satisfy federal requirements on this issue. Further, *if building standards under state or local laws or ordinances are more stringent than the foregoing requirements, then the state or local standards prevail.*

Housing for Older Persons Exemptions

The Fair Housing Act exempts specified categories of "housing for older persons" from the Act's prohibitions against discrimination because of familial status. These exemptions are a result of a public policy that senior citizens have a right to reside in a child-free environment under certain circumstances. In spite of the prohibition of the Fair Housing Act against discrimination based upon familial status, senior adult buildings and communities are given an exemption. The "housing for older persons" exemptions are as follows:

- Housing built under state or federal programs to assist the elderly.[39]
- Housing intended for and solely occupied by persons 62 years of age or older.[40]
- Housing intended for occupancy by adults 55 years of age or older under specified circumstances.[41]

The most sweeping of the above exemptions is the "55 years of age or older" exemption. The Housing for Older Persons Act of 1995 (HOPA)[42] redefined and clarified the original exemption contained in the Fair Housing Act for housing designed and operated for occupancy by persons who are 55 years of age or older. Qualification of a housing development for the "55 years of age or older" category is a legal matter to be determined by an experienced real estate attorney.[43] Brokeers advertising property in such a communityu shall confirm the community qualifies before advertising it over 55 only.

Exemptions to Federal Law

In addition to the exemption for eligible senior housing, the Fair Housing Act has a few other very limited exemptions listed below.

1. Sale or lease of single-family dwelling by owner under limited circumstances
2. Rental of rooms or units in one-to-four unit dwellings if one unit is owner occupied.
3. Sale or lease of property owned or operated by a nonprofit organization for noncommercial purposes

The "***single-family dwelling exemption***" is limited to an owner who *personally* sells or rents his or her dwelling. *The sale or rental of a single-family dwelling is NOT exempted when the services of a real estate broker are involved.* A single-family dwelling owner who seeks the help of others to rent his or her property and compensates those others for their assistance also forfeits the exemption.[44] An owner wishing to claim this exemption cannot engage in discriminatory advertising and is subject to additional restrictions concerning the number of dwellings he or she can own and the number of exempt sales in which he or she can engage.

The ***one-to-four unit dwelling*** exemption applies to the rental of rooms or units in dwellings containing living quarters occupied by no more than four families, if the owner of the building actually maintains and occupies one of the living quarters as his or her residence.

The *religious organizations and private clubs* exemption applies to religious organizations when they wish to rent or sell noncommercial property to persons of the same religion. The exemption is inapplicable if membership in the religion is restricted on account of race, color, or national origin. A **private club** is exempted when, as an incident to its primary purpose, it provides lodging that it owns or operates for other than a commercial purpose. The club cannot qualify for the exemption if it is open to the public.

STATE FAIR HOUSING ACT

The North Carolina State Fair Housing Act, found at Chapter 41A of the North Carolina General Statutes, accomplishes on the state level what the federal Fair Housing Act does on the federal level. Because of substantial conformity between state and federal law on fair housing matters, *except for issues related to discrimination against LGBT persons, all violations of the Federal Fair Housing Act previously discussed also violate the State Fair Housing Act. Similarly, violations of North Carolina law are virtually always violations of federal law.*

Like its federal counterpart, the purpose of the State Fair Housing Act is to provide fair housing throughout North Carolina by making discriminatory practices based on race, color, religion, sex, national origin, handicapping condition, or familial status illegal. The Real Estate Commission publishes an informational pamphlet on Fair Housing answering common questions regarding discriminatory practices, handicapped persons, familial status, real estate agents, and fair housing and enforcement of the fair housing laws.[45]

ENFORCEMENT OF FAIR HOUSING LEGISLATION

Persons who believe they have been illegally discriminated against in violation of federal or state fair housing legislation effective and relatively prompt investigatory and enforcement options. A housing discrimination complaint can be filed with the *federal Department of Housing and Urban Development (HUD),* or it can be filed with the *North Carolina Human Relations Commission.* Housing complaints to HUD can be filed on the HUD webpage[46] and through HUD mobile applications.

If a complaint is filed with HUD, that agency is required to refer it to the North Carolina Human Relations Commission because North Carolina's Fair Housing Act is certified as being substantially equivalent to the Federal Fair Housing Act, as amended. HUD can also file a complaint alleging illegal housing discrimination on its own initiative. In other words, the agency itself can commence an action to enforce the Fair Housing Act.

Once a complaint is filed, an investigation takes place, after which a determination is made as to whether reasonable grounds exist to believe that an unlawful discriminatory housing practice has occurred. Efforts are made to resolve complaints by informal conferences and conciliation. If a finding is made that reasonable grounds do exist to believe that an unlawful discriminatory housing practice has occurred, both federal and state laws provide the victim of discrimination with a number of legal enforcement options. Legal actions against the party accused of housing discrimination can be brought either before a federal administrative law judge, in federal court, or, alternatively, in state court.

The intricate details, timetables, and procedures for enforcement of fair housing laws are beyond the scope of this chapter. What is important is that real estate brokers realize that two very powerful administrative agencies, one state and one federal, and the federal and state court system are at the disposal of victims of illegal housing discrimination.

Civil Penalties

Persons discriminated against can recover actual damages, punitive damages (where appropriate), and attorneys' fees against the person or persons who have engaged in illegal discrimination against them. Actual damages include items such as inconvenience, mental anguish, humiliation, embarrassment, and out-of-pocket expenses such as the higher cost of obtaining alternative housing. Punitive damages are a penalty assessed against persons whose conduct willfully violates the Act or blatantly disregards the fair housing laws.

Real Estate License Law Penalties

A real estate broker violating federal or state fair housing laws is also subject to disciplinary action by the North Carolina Real Estate Commission, which can include revocation of an agent's license. The Real Estate Commission has explicitly stated in its rules (21 NCAC 58A.1601) that any violation of the Federal Fair Housing Act or State (North Carolina) Fair Housing Act by a real estate broker also constitutes a violation of the North Carolina Real Estate License Law, General Statute §93A-6(a)(10).

FEDERAL CIVIL RIGHTS ACT OF 1866

The Federal Civil Rights Act of 1866[47] declares, *without exception*, that "all citizens of the United States shall have the same right, in every State and Territory, as is enjoyed by white citizens thereof, to inherit, purchase, lease, sell, hold, and convey real and personal property." In a landmark decision, *Jones v. Alfred H. Mayer Company*,[48] the United States Supreme Court held that the Civil Rights Act of 1866 provided a private right to sue to victims of racial discrimination in the sale and rental of housing.

The relationship between the Federal Civil Rights Act of 1866 and the Federal Fair Housing Act of 1968 may seem confusing to the layperson because both statutes appear, at times, to cover the same thing. In terms of protected classes of persons, *the older statute applies only to* **racial** *discrimination,* while the Fair Housing Act prohibits discrimination based on the protected classes listed in the Act. There is an overlap between the two statutes to the extent that both prohibit racial discrimination. The Fair Housing Act of 1968 is a detailed and comprehensive open housing law that in many respects provides a better method through which aggrieved citizens can obtain legal relief.

The Civil Rights Act of 1866 contains no exceptions, one advantage to persons discriminated against based upon race not available under the FHA. Thus, the exemptions in the Fair Housing *Act of 1968 are inapplicable to the Civil Rights Act of 1866*, and a victim of racial discrimination is not prohibited from bringing an action under the 1866 statute even though an exemption prohibits the victim from seeking relief under the FHA.[49]

FAIR HOUSING CASE STUDIES

Below are ten fair housing case studies to better understand how fair housing laws are applied in practice. Each case study describes a fact situation that the reader should consider and then answer the question: "Is there reasonable cause to believe that the Fair Housing Act has been violated?" The reader should be able to explain his or her answer. [**The answers for each case study and an analysis of each case study appear in Appendix C.**]

Case Study 1

A large condominium development has a strict, consistently enforced "no pets" policy. The condominium association board made an exception several years ago and allowed a seeing-eye dog in a unit as a reasonable accommodation to a blind tenant. Recently, a condominium unit owner with diagnosed post-traumatic stress disorder has submitted a request to the condominium association board for an "emotional support" service dog. The request is supported by written verification from the unit owner's psychiatrist and doctor that a dog will provide therapeutic nurture and support for the tenant's post-traumatic stress disorder. The proposed service dog has been professionally trained and will not pose a threat or disturbance to the other unit owners. The board members empathized with the unit owner's personal situation but denied the request.

Is there reasonable cause to believe that the Fair Housing Act has been violated?
- A. Yes, because allowing the service dog constitutes a reasonable accommodation under the Fair Housing Act.
- B. Yes, because the condominium association board has allowed a service dog in the past.
- C. No, because an exception to the "no pets" policy for unit owners with psychiatric disabilities would eventually render that policy meaningless.
- D. No, because the accommodation requirement for service dogs is limited to physical disabilities.

Case Study 2

A large apartment complex does not have assigned parking, although there are spaces reserved at various points in the parking areas for persons with state-issued handicap stickers. A tenant displays a handicap sticker from the tenant's car to the apartment complex manager and demands that an additional handicap parking space in the immediate area of the tenant's apartment be reserved exclusively for that tenant. Because the tenant appears to have no mobility issues, the apartment manager asks for additional written verification from the tenant's doctor concerning the nature of the tenant's handicap. The apartment manager also notes that there are several spaces reserved for the handicapped within 100 feet of the tenant's apartment. The tenant refuses to provide additional verification insisting that the state-issued handicap sticker is all that should be necessary. After consultation with the landlord, the apartment manager refuses to reserve an exclusive handicap parking spot for the tenant.

Is there reasonable cause to believe that the Fair Housing Act has been violated?
- A. Yes, because the actions of the landlord and apartment complex manager constitute a failure to reasonably accommodate a handicapped tenant.
- B. Yes, because the state-issued handicap sticker from the tenant's automobile is sufficient evidence that the tenant is legally handicapped.
- C. No, because it is reasonable under these circumstances to require that the tenant substantiate the purported handicap and the handicap sticker alone is not conclusive.
- D. No, because the landlord already provides handicapped parking space areas in the complex.

Case Study 3

A tenant has a child who now must use a wheelchair for approximately ten months as a result of major surgery. The bathroom and bedroom doors in the tenant's apartment are too narrow to permit a wheelchair to pass. The tenant emails the landlord asking for permission to widen the two doorways at the tenant's expense. The tenant assures the landlord that the work will be done by a licensed contractor in a workmanlike manner. The landlord grants permission for the modifications on the condition that the tenant pay to return the doorways to their original width at the end of the tenancy. The tenant disagrees with the landlord's condition and insists that the doorways can be left in their widened state at the end of the tenancy. The landlord then refuses to permit widening of the doors.

Is there reasonable cause to believe that the Fair Housing Act has been violated?

    A. Yes, because the tenant has requested a reasonable accommodation and wider doorways will not interfere with the landlord's or the next tenant's use and enjoyment of the premises.

    B. Yes, because the doorways must be widened at the landlord's, not the tenant's, expense.

    C. No, because the tenant is required to return the premises to their original condition at the tenant's expense.

    D. No, because the physical disability of the child is a temporary one.

Case Study 4

A woman who is five months pregnant applies to rent a third-floor efficiency apartment in a ten-unit building with no elevator. The apartment manager processing the application makes a notation that reads: "Pregnant applicant will have health problems using three sets of stairs and, once child is born, efficiency apartment may be too small." Several days later, the apartment is rented to a single man. Upon hearing of this, the woman files a complaint with a fair housing agency asserting illegal housing discrimination based on familial status.

Is there reasonable cause to believe that the Fair Housing Act has been violated?

    A. Yes, because the landlord failed to reasonably accommodate the pregnant woman.

    B. Yes, because the term "familial status" includes any person who is pregnant and the implied occupancy limitation is unreasonable.

    C. No, because pregnancy is not a handicap.

    D. No, because the "familial status" protections of the Act do not apply until a child is born.

Case Study 5

The owner of a two-unit duplex lives in the upper unit. Recently, the lower unit became vacant and the owner posted the following message on Craigslist:

> For rent: Two-bedroom-two-bath lower unit in luxury duplex. Perfect
> for a mature person. Upscale suburban location adjacent to exclusive private
> country club. Country club guest privileges for the right tenant. Reply with
> your picture and a picture of any children.

During the next several days, the owner ignored all responses that did not include a picture. One ignored response was from a Hispanic couple with two young children. Subsequently, the owner rented the unit to an elderly Caucasian man. The Hispanic couple contacted an attorney for legal advice.

Is the attorney likely to advise that there is reasonable cause to believe that the Fair Housing Act has been violated?

    A. Yes, because the owner rented to a single Caucasian man.

    B. Yes, because the posting on Craigslist constitutes a publication that indirectly indicates a limitation or discrimination based on race, national origin and familial status.

    C. No, because the owner-occupied dwelling is exempt from the Fair Housing Act.

    D. No, because there is no evidence of the owner's intent to illegally discriminate.

Case Study 6

The owner of a single family home lists the home for sale with a real estate broker. The owner lives in the home, does not own any other single family houses, and is not in the business of selling real property. After entering into the listing agreement, the owner informs the broker that the owner will not accept any offer from a member of any racial minority. The owner bases this assertion on research of the Fair Housing Act conducted on the Internet.

Is the homeowner's assertion correct?

A. Yes, because of the single-family home exemption in the Fair Housing Act.

B. Yes, because the owner is not in the business of selling real property.

C. No, because there are no exemptions to the Fair Housing Act.

D. No, because the owner's house is being sold with the services of a real estate broker.

Case Study 7

The owner of a single family home lists a home for sale with a real estate broker at a price of $455,000. An African American couple then tours the home and makes an offer to purchase the home at a price of $435,000. Because the broker feels that the owners may be adverse to selling to this couple, the broker holds the offer to purchase for several days. During that time, a Caucasian couple tours the home and makes an offer to purchase at a price of $450,000. The broker then presents both offers to the owner at the same time. The owner agrees to sell to the Caucasian couple because their offer is for an amount $20,000 above that of the African American couple.

Is there reasonable cause to believe that the broker has violated the Fair Housing Act?

A. Yes, because the broker did not process the offer of the African American couple in the usual manner.

B. Yes, because broker engaged in the practice of panic selling.

C. No, because the owner of the home did not unlawfully discriminate by accepting the higher offer.

D. No, because the Act applies only to sellers, not real estate brokers.

Case Study 8

The developers of a new residential development that will eventually include 800 homes, a golf course, tennis courts, swimming pool, health club, and other amenities, design and post an extensive web page extolling the many advantages of purchasing a new home in the development. The web page contains dozens of pictures of persons golfing, playing tennis, lounging around the pool, and working out in the health club. All web page pictures depict middle-aged Caucasian couples. There are no minorities, disabled persons, or children shown in any picture.

Is there reasonable cause to believe that the Fair Housing Act is being violated?

A. Yes, because the cumulative effect of the web page pictures sends a message of a preference that excludes persons because of race, color, national origin, or familial status.

B. Yes, because the web page proves a subjective intent on the part of the developers to illegally discriminate.

C. No, because there is no evidence that persons protected by the Fair Housing Act will refrain from purchasing homes in the development.

D. No, because the web page pictures standing alone constitute insufficient proof of discrimination.

Case Study 9

An owner of an 8-unit apartment building wishes to rent a vacant apartment but has had unfavorable experiences in the past with college students as tenants. The owner instructs the broker acting as rental agent and property manager that the owner will not rent to college students. Two Caucasian college students, one male and one female, 18 and 19 years of age, contact the broker and express an interest in renting the vacant unit. The broker frankly informs the students of the owner's instructions and refuses to show them the apartment. The students become very upset because of a shortage of rental housing in the area and contact a lawyer.

Will the lawyer conclude that there is reasonable cause to believe that the Fair Housing Act has been violated?

> A. Yes, because there is discrimination based on familial status.
> B. Yes, because there is discrimination based on the students' ages.
> C. No, because the owner has had bad experiences with college student renters in the past.
> D. No, because the Fair Housing Act does not include "college students" as a protected group.

Case Study 10

A home builder follows the practice of having a mortgage loan agent at the site during open houses. The agent represents a bank that works with the builder to provide mortgage loan financing for the builder's customers. The agent has a one-to-ten personal rating system based in part on credit worthiness and in part on the agent's face-to-face evaluation of the loan applicant's general reliability. Applicants with a score of 6 or higher receive loans; those earning a score of less than 6 do not receive loans. By this process, the agent rejects a majority of African American loan applicants while approving a majority of Caucasian applicants. One rejected African American couple discovers that their combined income and credit rating is superior to that of Caucasian friends who received a mortgage loan through the bank's agent. They complain, but the agent informs them that the process involves more than income and traditional credit ratings.

Is there reasonable cause to believe that the Fair Housing Act has been violated?

> A. Yes, because the agent's personal rating system appears to have a disparate impact on African Americans as a group.
> B. Yes, because the agent's personal rating system failed to make available a loan based on race.
> C. No, because some African American couples receive loans through the agent's personal rating system.
> D. No, because there is no evidence that the agent had an intent to discriminate based on race.

AMERICANS WITH DISABILITIES ACT (ADA)

The Americans with Disabilities Act and federal regulations implementing the ADA have the goal of protecting the civil rights of *"persons with mental or physical disabilities."* The ADA does *not* affect the sale or rental of *residential housing. Title III of the ADA, however, requires that most* **commercial facilities***"* and *"***places of public accommodation***"* comply with specifications designed to assure adequate **access** *for persons with disabilities.* In addition, Title I of the ADA prohibits employment discrimination against qualified individuals with disabilities in the private business sector.[50]

Importance to Real Estate Brokers

Although it may not be readily apparent, real estate brokers can be affected by the ADA. Consider the following:

1. Real estate brokers *selling, buying or leasing* "commercial facilities" or "places of public accommodation" *for others* have a legal obligation to *disclose to all parties* to the transaction *any failure of the property to comply with the ADA* when the broker has actual knowledge of such noncompliance or should reasonably be aware of such noncompliance.
2. Real estate offices are "places of public accommodation" and are subject to compliance with the ADA's accessibility requirements.
3. Real estate brokers (and firms) with 15 or more employees must comply with Title I of the ADA relating to employment discrimination.

ADA Definition of "Disability"

Laypersons tend to think of disabled persons as those with very obvious physical disabilities. However, the ADA definition of "persons with disabilities" is *much* broader than that.

A "person with a disability" is an individual who has a *physical or mental impairment* that *substantially limits* one or more of his/her *major life activities.* *"Physical or mental impairment"* is very broadly defined and can include virtually any physiological disorder and a broad range of mental or psychological disorders. *"Major life activities"* include functions such as caring for oneself, performing manual tasks, walking, seeing, hearing, speaking, learning and working.

Commercial Facilities and Places of Public Accommodation

The ADA applies to "public entities," i.e., federal, state, and local governmental programs, services, activities, and facilities (Title II), as well as to commercial facilities, educational facilities, and public accommodations (Title III), including leasing offices, shelters, assisted living facilities, guest lodging, most retail establishments, and many others.

Owners, tenants and operators of *"commercial facilities"* are responsible for assuring that such facilities comply with the ADA's *facility accessibility and use* requirements for new construction and existing facilities. *"Commercial facilities" include any privately owned, nonresidential facilities whose operations affect commerce.* Examples are office buildings, retail establishments, factories or warehouses.

A much broader category of facilities regulated by the ADA is that of **"places of public accommodation."** Owners, tenants and operators of "places of public accommodation" are responsible not only for assuring compliance with *facility accessibility and use* requirements for new construction and existing facilities, but also for assuring compliance with *numerous other provisions relating to access to and use of programs and services.*

The ADA defines *"places of public accommodation"* very broadly as any **privately owned** facility *whose operations affect commerce.* They include but are not limited to hotels and motels, restaurants and bars, theatres and stadiums, sales and retail establishments, service establishments, offices, schools, museums, zoos, parks, and sports facilities. The offices of a real estate company open to the public are "places of public accommodation" under the ADA.

"Service Animals" under the ADA

In 2010, the US Department of Justice revised the **ADA** regulations[51] to narrowly define a "**service animal**" as:

> ... any *dog* that is *individually trained to do work or perform tasks* for
> the benefit of an individual with a disability, including a physical, sensory,

psychiatric, intellectual, or other mental disability. *Other species of animals, whether wild or domestic, trained or untrained, are not service animals for the purposes of this definition.* The work or tasks performed by a service animal must be directly related to the individual's disability....

While only canines may be service animals under the ADA according to the foregoing definition, other ADA regulations provide a limited exception for **miniature horses** that also may be service animals that must be admitted to the public facility.

The regulations provide that *the work or tasks performed by the service animal must be **directly related** to the person's disability* and mention the following examples:

- assisting persons who are blind or have low vision to navigate and other tasks;
- alerting persons who are deaf or hard of hearing to the presence of people or sounds;
- providing non-violent protection or rescue work;
- assisting an individual having a seizure;
- pulling a wheelchair;
- alerting a person to the presence of allergens;
- retrieving items such as medicine, or the telephone;
- providing physical support and assistance with balance or stability to a mobility-impaired person;
- preventing or interrupting impulsive or destructive behaviors in persons with psychiatric or neurological disabilities.

NOTE: The ADA definition of service animal expressly states: "The crime deterrent effects of an animal's presence and *the provision of emotional support, well-being, comfort, or companionship **do not constitute** work or tasks for the purposes of this definition.*" Thus, "service animals" are now a defined term under the ADA and comprise a much smaller group than "assistance animals" under fair housing laws.

HUD's April 2013 Notice observes that if an animal meets the ADA definition of "service animal" then *public entities and public accommodations must allow the service animal into the covered facility.* **Where the individual's disability and the work or tasks performed by the animal are apparent, the ADA covered facility** (including broker-property managers and owners) **may not request any further documentation or verification.** However, *where either the disability or the work/tasks performed are **not** apparent,* then the only two questions the covered facility may ask are:

1) Does this person need this animal to accompany him/her due to a disability?
and
2) What work or tasks has the animal been trained to perform that relate to the disability?

There must be a nexus between the disability and the task performed by the trained service animal. The covered facility *may **not** ask about the nature or extent of the disability nor require medical records or proof that the animal is certified, trained or licensed as a service animal, nor may it charge any fee for the service animal's admittance.* If it either is apparent or the individual verifies the existence of a disability and the related work or tasks performed by the animal, then the service animal must be admitted to all areas of the facility to which the public has access *unless:*

1) the animal is out of control and the handler doesn't take effective action to control the animal; or

2) the animal is not housebroken;   or

3) the animal poses a direct threat to the health or safety of others that can't be eliminated or reduced to an acceptable level by a reasonable modification to other policies, practices, and procedures.

Housing Providers Subject to Both ADA and FHAct

Brokers managing commercial properties, whether shopping centers, office buildings or other commercial properties that do not provide any lodging, generally must only comply with the ADA laws and regulations regarding "service animals" and need not assess or address the assistance animal question under the FHA. The sale, purchase or lease of most residential property clearly will be subject to fair housing laws, but leasing certain residential property may also be subject to the service animal requirements under the ADA if the property is a "place of public accommodation." Thus, leasing rooms in a bed and breakfast, or vacation rental properties, or units in an apartment or condominium complex would qualify as a "place of public accommodation" (as would a broker's business office), requiring compliance with both laws.

When dealing with multiple laws, HUD's April 2013 Notice recommends that a provider first apply the ADA "service animal" test, because if the animal qualifies as a service animal then the animal **must** be permitted to accompany the individual in all areas of the facility that persons normally may go unless the animal is uncontrollable or not housebroken or presents a direct threat to others' health and safety.

If the animal does not qualify as a service animal, whether because it is not a canine or because it provides emotional support, then the housing provider must evaluate the request under fair housing's "assistance animal" standards. The preamble to the 2010 ADA regulations acknowledges this reality noting:

> … an individual with a disability may have a right to have an animal other than a dog in his or her home if the animal qualifies as a "reasonable accommodation" that is necessary to afford the individual equal opportunity to use and enjoy a dwelling, assuming that the use of the animal does not pose a direct threat…. [Further], *emotional support animals that do not qualify as service animals under the ADA may nevertheless qualify as permitted reasonable accommodations for persons with disabilities under the FHAct.*[Italics added.]

Broker's Duty to Disclose Noncompliance

As a general rule, a broker who *leases* or *manages* a commercial facility and/or place of public accommodation *as the agent of the property owner* is *not* directly responsible for assuring compliance with the ADA. As the case with Fair Housing Act building design and construction standards, real estate developers, builders, owners and architects are responsible for the design or construction of multi-family housing and may be liable for a Fair Housing Act violation if their buildings are not in compliance with design requirements. Accessibility design and construction standards are highly technical and should be left to experts.

However, any real estate broker acting as an agent in selling, buying, or leasing a "commercial facility" or "place of public accommodation" must disclose any failure of the property to comply with ADA requirements to all parties to the transaction when the agent has actual knowledge of such noncompliance or should reasonably be aware of such noncompliance.

The fact that the property does not comply with the ADA is a *"material fact"* that a broker has an affirmative duty to disclose to all parties involved. While a real estate broker would not be expected to know whether a regulated property complies with all details of the ADA, a broker would be expected to recognize *obvious* signs of noncompliance, such as a lack of access ramps, doors or elevators not accessible to persons in wheelchairs, or restrooms that are not equipped for the disabled.

Brokers' Responsibilities as Employers

Any business with 15 or more employees each working day in each of 20 or more calendar weeks in the current or preceding calendar year must comply with the comprehensive requirements of Title I of the ADA prohibiting *discrimination in employment* against a "qualified individual with a disability." A "qualified individual with a disability" is defined as a person with a disability who satisfies the requisite skill, experience, education, and other job-related requirements of the position held or desired, and who, with or without reasonable accommodation, can perform the *essential functions* of such position.

Title I not only prohibits discrimination in the hiring process and in the terms and conditions of employment, but also requires that employers provide "reasonable accommodation" allowing disabled persons equal opportunity in *all aspects of employment*. "Reasonable accommodation" might include modifying existing facilities for ready accessibility, job restructuring, acquiring special equipment, modifying training materials, or providing qualified readers or interpreters. Employers may be able to avoid making such provisions if they can demonstrate "undue hardship."

In determining the number of employees, *it is very important to note that affiliated real estate brokers who are treated as "independent contractors" (rather than "employees") under Internal Revenue Service guidelines very well may be considered "employees" for purposes of compliance with the ADA.* All real estate business owners who have a total of 15 or more employees and brokers combined would be well advised to consult their attorney.[52]

SEXUAL HARASSMENT BY LESSORS OR THEIR AGENTS

Any lessor (landlord) of residential real property *or the lessor's agent* who harasses a lessee or prospective tenant on the basis of sex violates North Carolina state law.[53] The statute defines **sexual harassment** as

> … unsolicited overt requests or demands for sexual acts when (i) submission to such conduct is made a term of the execution or continuation of the lease agreement, or (ii) submission to or rejection of such conduct by an individual is used to determine whether rights under the lease are accorded.[54]

Endnotes

1.   The Fair Housing Act of 1968, as amended, is found at 42 U.S.C. §§3601 et. seq. The Fair Housing Amendments Act was enacted as Public Law No. 100-430, 102 Stat. 1619 (1988). The Department of Housing and Urban Development has issued extensive regulations and commentary implementing the amendments at 54 Fed. Reg. 32232 (1989), amending 24 C.F.R. §§100.1 - 146.49. Most of the information in this chapter has been obtained from these statutes, regulations and commentary. The authors have chosen not to footnote this chapter extensively, since most of the notes would refer back to the above sources. Readers interested in more information about federal fair housing rules are encouraged to contact the Department of HUD and obtain the latest amended set of regulations and commentary. By its very nature, this area of law is evolving and subject to change.

2.   The North Carolina Fair Housing Act is found in Chapter 41A of the North Carolina General Statutes. Readers interested in all the specifics of this important legislation should read this relatively short and clearly written chapter of the statutes. Although language and procedural differences exist between state and federal law, the state law on fair housing is in conformity with federal law in all important respects. Thus, most of the discussion in this chapter on federal fair housing rules should accurately predict what the outcome under state law and the NC Fair Housing Act would be.

3.   See Rule 21 NCAC 58A.1601 and N.C. Gen. Stat. §93A-6(a)(10) and (15).

4.   *Texas Dept. of Housing And Community Affairs, et al, v. The Inclusive Communities Project, Inc., et al,* 576 U.S. __ (2015).

5.   Federal Register, Vol. 77, No. 23, Friday, February 3, 2012/Rules and Regulations.

6.   See: portal.hud.gov/hudportal/HUD?src=/program_offices/fair_housing_equal_opp/LGBT_Housing Discrimination

7.   Article 10, "Duties to the Public," (Amended 1/14).

8.   See *Michigan Protection and Advocacy Service, Inc. v. Babin,* 18 F.3d 337 (Sixth Cir. 1994), a case involving alleged discriminatory motivation in the sale of a home in violation of the Federal Fair Housing Act.

9.   Real estate companies have been held legally responsible for the discriminatory acts of the brokers they employ and the fact that agents were specifically instructed not to discriminate does not relieve the principal (namely, the firm or company) from liability. *City of Chicago v. Matchmaker Real Estate Sales Ctr.,* 982 F.2d 1086 (Seventh Cir. 1992).

10.   *Meyer v. Holley,* 123 S. Ct. 824, 154 L.Ed.2d 753 (2003). The legal term is "vicarious liability," defined as follows in Black's Law Dictionary, Fifth Ed., p. 1404: "Indirect legal responsibility; for example, the liability of an employer for the acts of an employee, or, a principal for torts and contracts of an agent." *Cleveland v. Caplaw Enterprises,* 448 F.3d 518 (Second Cir. 2006).

11. Definition adapted and paraphrased from "Blockbusting: Judicial and Legislative Response to Real Estate Dealers' Excesses," 22 DePaul Law Review 818 (1973).

12. Example adapted from Note, "Blockbusting," 59 Georgetown Law Review 170 at 171 (1970). The federal regulation defining "blockbusting" can be found at 24 C.F.R. §100.85.

13. For a case illustrating racial steering, see *Heights Community Congress v. Hilltop Realty, Inc.*, 774 F.2d 135 (Sixth Cir. 1985).

14. *Coles v. Havens Realty Corp.*, 633 F.2d 384 (4th Cir. 1980). For another example of a consent decree entered after a housing organization sued a real estate broker for racial steering, see *South Suburban Housing Center v. Berry*, 186 F.3d 851 (Seventh Cir. 1999).

15. See *Ragin v. Harry Macklowe Real Estate Co.*, 6 F.3d 898 (Second Cir. 1993). See also *Jancik v. HUD*, 44 F.3d 553 (Seventh Cir. 1995), where advertisement expressing preference with the phrase "mature person preferred" was discriminatory based on familial status. See "Discriminatory advertisements, statements and notices." 24 C.F.R. §100.75.

16. A more extensive list of acceptable, unacceptable and cautionary words and phrases may be found on the website of the Miami Valley Fair Housing Center Inc., in Dayton, Ohio, at http://www.mv-fairhousing.com/ad_word_list.php

17. *Green v. Century 21*, 740 F.2d 460 (Sixth Cir. 1984).

18. *Stewart v. Furton*, 774 F.2d 706 (Sixth Cir. 1985); *Hamilton v. Svatik*, 779 F.2d 383 (Seventh Cir. 1985); *Hayden v. Oak Terrace Apts.*, 808 F.2d 1269 (Seventh Cir. 1987); *Asbury v. Brougham*, 866 F.2d 1276 (Tenth Cir. 1989); *United States v. DiMucci*, 879 F.2d 1488 (Seventh Cir. 1989). For other cases dealing with racial discrimination in the rental of housing, see *Alexander v. Riga*, 208 F.3d 419 (3rd Cir. 2000); *Harris v. Itzhaki*, 183 F.3d 1043 (9th Cir. 1999); and *Cole v. Wodziak*, 169 F.3d 486 (Seventh Cir. 1999). For a case in which the government successfully brought an action against an apartment complex's owner and management company on behalf of prospective tenants whose rental applications had been denied based on race, see *United States v. Big D Enterprises, Inc.*, 184 F.3d 924 (Eighth Cir. 1999).

19. For an example of illegal discrimination based on sex, see *Walker v. Crigler*, 976 F.2d 900 (Fourth Cir. 1992).

20. See *Ring v. First Interstate Mortgage, Inc.*, 984 F.2d 924 (Eighth Cir. 1993). For another case involving racial discrimination in lending in which the lender and its president were found in violation of the Fair Housing Act and the Equal Credit Opportunity Act, see *Johnson v. Kakvand*, 192 F.3d 656 (Seventh Cir. 1999). See "Discrimination in the making of loans and in the provision of other financial assistance," 24 C.F.R. §100.120 & 100.130.

21. *Nationwide Mutual Insurance Co. v. Cisneros*, 52 F.3d 1351 (Sixth Cir. 1995).

22. *Singleton v. Gandason*, 545 F.2d 1224 (9th Cir. 1976).

23. See *Morgan v. Secretary, HUD*, 985 F.2d 1451 (10th Cir. 1993), where the Court of Appeals found discrimination against children in the leasing of mobile home spaces; see also *Hooker v. Weathers*, 990 F.2d 913 (Sixth Cir. 1993), *Massaro v. Mainlands Section 1&2 Civic Ass'n.*, 3 F.3d 1472 (11th Cir. 1993), cases involving alleged illegal discrimination based on familial status.

24. *Gorski v. Troy*, 929 F.2d 1183 (Seventh Cir. 1991), case holding that licensed foster parents in the State of Illinois have "familial status" under the Act.

25. See *Hamad v. Woodcrest Condominium Assoc.*, 328 F.3d 224 (Sixth Cir. 2003), involving alleged familial status discrimination in violation of the Fair Housing Act. Condominium bylaws restricted families with children to first-floor units. Although the condominium association reached a subsequent agreement with the federal government not to enforce discriminatory bylaws, the Sixth Circuit Court of Appeals held that a Fair Housing Act action was not rendered moot where plaintiffs sought damages under the Act.

26. Example based on *White v. U.S. Department of Housing and Urban Development*, 475 F.3d 898 (Seventh Cir. 2007)

27. See *City of Edmunds v. Oxford House, Inc.*, 514 U.S. 725, 115 S. Ct. 1776 (1995). *Fair Housing Advocates Assoc., Inc. v. City of Richmond Heights, Ohio*, 209 F.3d 626 (Sixth Cir. 2000).

28. *United States v. Badgett*, 976 F.2d 1176 (Eighth Cir. 1992); Civil Rights Act of 1968, §801 et. seq., as amended, 42 U.S.C.A. §3601 et. seq.

29. 42 U.S.C. §3607(b)(1). See also the regulations of the Department of Housing and Urban Development concerning this issue under the Fair Housing Act.

30. While the "two persons per bedroom" occupancy restriction may, *as a general rule,* be "reasonable," for a discussion of other factors HUD will consider in determining the reasonableness of occupancy restrictions as to familial status situations, see the "Keating Memo" issued in 1991 and formally adopted by HUD as its policy in late 1998. The Keating Memo is found at: www.hud.gov/offices/fheo/library/occupancystds.pdf . See also *Reeves v. Rose*, 108 F.Supp.2d 720 (E. D. Mich. 2000), where the court held that issues of fact existed as to whether familial status discrimination had taken place and as to the reasonableness of building occupancy restrictions.

31. 24 C.F.R. §100.201 defines in greater detail "physical or mental impairment" and "major life activities."

32. 42 U.S.C. §3604; 24 C.F.R. §100.203 (1989); N.C. Gen. Stat. §41A-4(f). See *Elliot v. Sherwood Manor Mobile Home Park,* 947 F. Supp. 1574 (M.D. Fla. 1996).

33. *Bentley v. Peach & Quiet Realty 2 LLC*, 367 F. Supp.2d 341 (E.D. N.Y. 2005). The court denied the landlord's motion to dismiss a tenant's action under the Fair Housing Act Amendments (FHAA). At 367 F. Supp.2d 341, 344, the Court notes, in part:

    > Whether a requested accommodation is required under the FHAA is "highly fact-specific, requiring case-by-case determination." *United States v. California Mobile Home Park Mgmt. Co.*, 29 F.3d 1413, 1418 (9th Cir.

1994) ... "Ordinarily, the duty to make reasonable accommodations is framed by the nature of the particular handicap." *Salute v. Stratford Greens Garden Apts.*, 136 F.3d 293, 301 (Second Cir. 1998) ... A defendant [landlord] must incur reasonable costs and take modest, affirmative steps to accommodate the handicapped, as long as the accommodations sought do not pose an undue hardship or a substantial burden. *Tsombanidis v. West Haven Fire Dept.*, 352 F.3d 565 (Second Cir. 2003) [some citations omitted.]

34.   *Scott v. Croom*, 12 CV-00680-MCA-ACT (2013) and companion case *United States v. Croom*, 12 CV-1132. A copy of the complaint and Consent Order entered in March 2013 may be found on the website of the law firm who represented Mr. Scott at http://www.relmanlaw.com/civil-rights-litigation/cases/Scott-v-croom-on-consent-order.php

.35.   The US Department of Housing and Urban Development issued a Notice on April 25, 2013, titled "*Service Animals and Assistance Animals for People with Disabilities in Housing and HUD-Funded Programs.*" [**FHEO-2013-01.**] The purpose of the Notice was to explain owners' obligations under both the Fair Housing Act and the ADA regarding assistance or service animals. In an April 30, 2013, press release (HUD No. 13-060A), John Trasvina, HUD Assistant Secretary for Fair Housing and Equal Opportunity, commented:

> The vital importance of assistance animals in reducing barriers, promoting independence, and improving the quality of life for people with disabilities should not be underestimated, particularly in the home. ... Disability-related complaints, including those that involve assistance animals, are the most common discrimination complaint we receive. This Notice will help housing providers better understand and meet their obligation to grant reasonable accommodations to people with disabilities that require assistance animals to fully use and enjoy their housing.

The Notice distinguishes between "assistance animals" under the Fair Housing Act (and Section 504 of the Rehabilitation Act of 1973), and "service animals" as defined under the Americans with Disabilities Act and "applies to all housing providers covered by the FHAct, Section 504 and/or the ADA." The Notice explains owners' obligations and the appropriate test to apply under each Act. For a copy of the Notice, go to www.hud.gov and enter **FHEO-2013-01** in the search field.

36.   FHEO-2013-01, pp. 3-4. Brokers and owners may find additional helpful information in a 2004 and 2008 HUD publication titled: *Reasonable Accommodations under the Fair Housing Act*, May 17, 2004, at www.hud.gov/offices/fheo/library/huddojstatement.pdf, and *Reasonable Modifications under the Fair Housing Act*, March 5, 2008, found at: www.hud.gov/offices/fheo/disabilities/reasonable_modifications_mar08.pdf

37.   For decisions involving the alleged failure of developers and architects to comply with the building and design requirements of the Fair Housing Act, see *U.S. v. Quality Built Construction*, 358 F.Supp.2d 487 (E.D.N.C. 2005); *Fair Housing Council, Inc. v. Village of Olde St. Andrews, Inc.*, 250 F.Supp.2d 706 (W.D. Ky. 2003); *U.S. v. Edward Rose and Sons*, 384 F.3d 258 (Sixth Cir. 2004). See also Consent Orders entered in administrative actions initiated by HUD, *e.g.*, *HUD v. H&H Development Group, et. al.*, FHEO 07-11-0533-8, and *HUD v. Fourth Street Realty Inc, et.al.*, FHEO -1-12-0064-8.

38. See, for example, "Accessibility Design and Construction Requirements For Covered Multifamily Dwellings Under the Fair Housing Act," Joint Statement Of The Department Of Housing And Urban Development And The Department Of Justice, April 30, 2013.

39. 42 U.S.C. §3607(b)(2)(A). N.C. Gen. Stat. §41A-6(e)(1).

40. 42 U.S.C. §3607(b)(2)(B). N.C. Gen. Stat. §41A-6(e)(2).

41. 42 U.S.C. §3607(b)(2)(C). N.C. Gen. Stat. §41A-6(e)(3). For a case dealing with the "over 55" exemption prior to amendments and clarifications enacted in the Housing for Older Persons Act, see *Simovits v. The Chanticleer Condominium Assoc.*, 933 F. Supp. 1394 (N.D. Ill. 1996), where a condominium association's "no children" covenant was found to be in violation of the Fair Housing Act and where the condominium complex failed to meet minimum requirements under the Fair Housing Act for an "over 55" exemption. For a comprehensive article discussing the rights of seniors under the Fair Housing Act, see Schwemm and Allen, "For The Rest of Their Lives: Seniors and the Fair Housing Act," 90 Iowa L. Rev. 121 (2004).

42. HOPA amended Section 807(b)(2)(C) of the Fair Housing Act (42 U.S.C. §3607(b)(2)(C)). In a federal case involving a mobile home owner who was refused rental space in a mobile home park because his age (41) did not qualify him for a space in a retirement community, see *Taylor v. Rancho Santa Barbara*, 206 F.3d 932 (9th Cir. 2000). Among other things, the Court upheld the validity of the new amended "over 55" exemption to the Fair Housing Act.

43. Important Department of Housing and Urban Development Regulations, including helpful examples, can be found at 24 CFR Part 100, Subpart E.

44. See 24 C.F.R. §100.90.

45. See pamphlet titled "Questions and Answers on Fair Housing" published by the North Carolina Real Estate Commission.

46. www.hud.gov/fairhousing.

47. 42 U.S.C. §1982.

48. *Jones v. Alfred H. Mayer Co.*, 392 U.S. 409, 88 S.Ct. 2186 (1968).

49. *Johnson v. Zeremba*, 381 F. Supp. 165 (N.D. Ill. 1973); *Morris v. Cizek*, 503 F.2d 1303 (Seventh Cir. 1974).

50. The Americans with Disabilities Act, 42 U.S.C. §12101-12213 (1991). Regulations implementing the ADA can be found at 56 Federal Register 35592 (1991).

51. 28 Code of Federal Regulations Part 35.104 and Part 36.104.

52.   For additional *information about the ADA, see:* Governor's Advocacy Council for Persons with Disabilities Raleigh 1-800-821-6922; U.S. Equal Employment Opportunity Commission (EEOC), Washington 1-800-669-EEOC; Raleigh 919-856-4064; Office on the ADA, Civil Rights Division, U.S. Department of Justice Washington, D.C. 202-514-0301; U.S. Architectural and Transportation Barriers Compliance Board Washington, D.C. 202-653-7834.

53.   See *Beliveau v. Caras*, 873 F. Supp. 1393 (C.D. Cal. 1995), *Honce v. Vigil*, 1 F.3d 1085 (10th Cir. 1993), *New York ex rel Abrams v. Merlino*, 694 F. Supp. 1101 (S.D. N.Y. 1988), cases where sexual harassment has been held to constitute impermissible housing discrimination under the Fair Housing Act.

54.   N.C. Gen. Stat. §14-395.1, titled "Sexual Harassment." Verbal and physical sexual harassment may also constitute a violation of the Fair Housing Act. See, for example, "Fair Housing Act: Physical and Sexual Harassment Is Violation," 34-May Real Estate Law Report 5 (2005).

19 | COMMERCIAL REAL ESTATE BROKERAGE

A majority of real estate brokers work exclusively in *residential* brokerage. Consequently, when addressing brokerage issues, this manual has focused primarily on residential brokerage. However, a significant number of brokers, especially in urban areas, practice exclusively in *commercial* real estate brokerage, and many brokers who work primarily in residential brokerage occasionally become involved with a transaction involving commercial property, especially in smaller towns and rural areas. The practice of commercial brokerage is a very important component of real estate brokerage.

With the sole exception of the *limited* **nonresident** *commercial real estate license* (discussed later in this chapter), a real estate broker license in North Carolina entitles the broker to engage in brokerage activities (selling, leasing or renting property for others for compensation) involving *any type of property*. Although brokers are legally authorized by their licensure to engage in both residential and commercial real estate brokerage, in reality there are very important differences between these two areas of practice, including practice methods, property types, client types, market factors, pricing and valuation issues and transaction cycles. As will be seen in the following pages, commercial real estate is a very broad and complex area.

This chapter provides only a *very basic* **introduction** to the subject of commercial real estate brokerage. It should be noted that the North Carolina Real Estate License Law requires *that any broker act competently when engaging in any aspect of real estate brokerage.*[1] The failure to act competently when dealing with real estate consumers is considered to be an act which endangers the public interest and constitutes grounds for disciplinary action against a broker. *To practice most aspects of commercial real estate brokerage competently, a broker will need substantial education and training beyond the introductory level instruction provided in this manual and in prelicensing and postlicensing courses.*

Brokers should also keep in mind that, in addition to the competency requirement of the Real Estate License Law, the common law of agency requires an agent to exercise appropriate skill, care and diligence under the circumstances. A residential agent who attempts to handle a commercial transaction will be held to the standard of practice of someone who routinely handles commercial transactions. A broker's incompetence or lack of care and skill may subject him or her not only to discipline under the License Law, but also to potential civil liability should he or she be sued by a client who is injured as a result of the agent's inadequate performance under the reasonably expected standard of care, skill and diligence by an agent. The below examples help illustrate this point.

Example: Ben Arounde is a very successful and long-time residential real estate broker, but has no experience in handling commercial transactions. His clientele includes many of the most affluent people in his town. While assisting Ima Bigdeel with the purchase of a new country estate, Ben learns that Ima's wife has recently purchased the franchise rights for a hobby shop. Ben asks about the hobby shop and Ima, being so pleased with how Ben has diligently handled his new house purchase, insists that Ben help his wife find a location in a mall or shopping center for the hobby shop. What should Ben do? Ben should decline the representation and refer Ima's spouse to a skilled retail leasing agent (from whom he may request a referral fee), Ben would be ill advised to attempt to attempt to handle this retail leasing assignment independently without assistance from an experienced commercial agent. Before any broker attempts to handle a commercial transaction, the broker should be completely confident he or she possesses the knowledge necessary to handle the transaction with the legally required care and skill.

Example: Several years later, the town near Ima's country estate has grown by leaps and bounds and Ima is suddenly surrounded by a new school, shopping centers, apartment complexes and new roads. Ima decides it is time to move. He has been told that his property is well located for future commercial development and might bring a tidy profit from developers who might be able to put this property to many different uses. Ima calls his old friend Ben, the residential broker, to ask for help in selling his home and buying a new home. Ben has not handled any commercial transactions since being involved with the acquisition of the hobby shop for Ima's wife several years earlier. Clearly Ben can help Ima with locating a new house, but what about the sale of his current house? See the previous example. The best option would be for Ben to refer Ima to a commercial broker experienced in land development (and take a referral fee), because that broker will be able to better assess the market for the property and maximize Ima's value. The highest and best use of Ima's property is probably no longer as a residential property. Consequently, it should be considerer as "land," and land is the most complicated commercial real estate product because it can be used for many different purposes. If Ben attempts to handle the sale of the house himself and his client is injured due to Ben's lack of knowledge and competence in handling land transactions, Ben will have a very difficult time defending himself before the Real Estate Commission or in a civil lawsuit.

INTRODUCTORY CONCEPTS AND ISSUES

There is no universal definition of the term "commercial real estate." As will be seen later in the section on the limited nonresident commercial license, North Carolina has adopted one regulatory definition of commercial real estate for the limited purpose of this licensing program. However, this definition is not necessarily portable into all other contexts. Therefore, to understand what is meant by this term, it is helpful to first understand what is meant by the term "residential real estate." **"Residential real estate"** is commonly understood to refer to *real property that either includes or is intended to include a residential one-to-four unit dwelling.* A widely accepted definition of **"commercial real estate"** is *any real property that is not "residential real estate."* As a general rule, this definition is satisfactory even though some types of properties classified generally as commercial real estate by this definition (e.g., industrial properties and special purpose properties such as hospitals, churches, parks, etc. are technically not "commercial" in nature). **"Commercial real estate brokerage"** *is considered* *as includes both the sale and rental of commercial properties.* Note, however, that *"commercial real estate brokerage" generally is **not** considered to include the leasing and management of **residential** income-producing properties,* even those with as few as five units. The leasing and management of residential properties, especially those with five or more dwelling units, is generally considered to fall within the specialty area of practice known as **"property management."** Nonetheless, in the commercial context, property management typically involves the management of a property (rent collection, supervision of maintenance and upkeep, lease administration) as distinct and apart from the ownership of or the leasing of space in a property. In fact, it is not uncommon for one company to be responsible for the management of a property and another company to be responsible for the leasing of a property.

BASIC DISTINCTIONS BETWEEN RESIDENTIAL AND COMMERCIAL PRACTICE

To begin our study of commercial real estate brokerage, it would be helpful to examine briefly some of the major differences between residential and commercial brokerage practice. Several significant differences are listed below and then separately discussed.

Major Differences Between Residential and Commercial Practice

- Multiple Product Types and Specialized Areas of Practice
- Transaction Cycle Time
- Multiple Listing Service (MLS)® versus Database
- Special Importance of Zoning and Other Land Use Restrictions
- Leasing
- Contracts and Contract Forms
- Financing
- Higher Stakes
- Business Relationships
- Working Hours
- Cooperating with Out-of-State Agents/Limited Nonresident Commercial Brokers
- Commercial Real Estate Broker Lien

Multiple Product Types And Specialized Areas of Practice

As will be seen later in this chapter, commercial real estate encompasses a number of very different types of real property, each with its own distinguishing terminology, characteristics and market factors that must be taken into consideration. The differences among types of commercial real estate reach all aspects of their use, marketing and pricing, all of which are essential to consider in determining the best use of a property, the proper market position of a property, and ultimately its value. Accordingly, knowledge of the relevant characteristics and factors for a particular type of property is required to effectively deal with that type of property. If a broker does not have a firm understanding of these matters, it is not possible to provide competent service to one's client or customer.

The breadth of knowledge needed for each type of commercial property is one reason *many commercial practitioners, especially those in larger metropolitan areas, choose to specialize in dealing with one particular type of commercial property.* It is very difficult to be adequately knowledgeable about all matters relevant to sale and leasing of several different types of commercial property. "Product" knowledge specialization (i.e., focusing on a particular type of commercial property such as hotels, retail clothing stores, fast food restaurants, small office buildings, etc.) often leads commercial practitioners to be more market mobile than residential agents, because there may be a limited amount of a given product (type of property) in a particular locale and because their clients and customers may be willing to examine a broader area to satisfy their needs. It is very common for a commercial broker to cover a large geographic region, even a state or states, with respect to a particular product (type of property) or a particular client.

It is said that knowledge is power and nowhere is that more true than in the commercial real estate market. If a broker does not understand the important features of a particular type of property and what uses are permissible and prohibited, he or she runs the risk of not properly marketing the property or not making a reliable determination as to whether a property is well suited for a client's or customer's use. If a broker does not understand and recognize the market factors that affect a property in its market place (such as its location, the linkages that affect it, and the demographics that surround it), he or she cannot realize the true benefit of the property for a client or customer or find the correct property for a client or customer. If a broker does not understand the factors involved in determining the value of a particular type of property, he or she run the risk of underselling a seller-client's property or permitting a buyer-client to overpay for a property. Accordingly, *the commercial real estate broker must be very well informed about the type of property he or she markets or seeks.*

At the same time, regulatory issues, product types, uses and market factors all change routinely in the commercial marketplace. Thus, the commercial broker must also keep abreast of changes which affect various properties. Given the length of a typical commercial listing and transaction cycle, the importance of this consideration cannot be understated.

Transaction Cycle Time

Apart from property type, perhaps the single largest distinction between residential and commercial real estate is the market and transaction cycle time. From the time of signing the listing to the time of closing, a typical residential transaction in North Carolina's larger real estate markets will have a three to six month time frame (assuming no unusual market or property factors). By comparison, *a typical commercial transaction will have a twelve to eighteen month time frame (sometimes even greater).* This cycle time difference has implications in a number of areas.

Listing agreements typically have a longer term in commercial transactions as a result of the longer transaction cycle - many listing agreements last a year or longer. In addition, marketing expenses may be dealt with as a reimbursable charge or as a separate charge, apart from the brokerage commission. This separation of marketing expenses occurs partially as a result of the longer time spent marketing the property, but also arises as a result of the fact that signage expenses (for signs advertising the property) are typically higher and the market is much broader, thus requiring a greater investment by the broker over a longer period of time.

The longer listing term also often has implications for what happens when the listing expires. The North Carolina Association of REALTORS® residential listing agreement form (Standard Form 101 – Exclusive Right to Sell Listing Agreement) provides that if the property is listed with another broker after expiration of the agreement, the broker with the expired listing has no entitlement to a commission, even if that broker had introduced the prospect who eventually purchased the property through the broker with the subsequent listing. On the other hand, the North Carolina Association of REALTORS® - REALTORS® Commercial Alliance[2] commercial listing agreement forms provide that an expiring listing agent may, if they register their prospects, still be entitled to all or a percentage of their commission even if the property is subsequently listed with another broker after expiration of the original listing agreement and a prospect registered by the first broker purchases the property. This provision is grounded in the fact that there is a longer and often financially significant investment in marketing the property.

Sales contract cycles are also often much longer in commercial real estate transactions. A typical residential transaction will have a six-week (45-day) time frame from signature to closing. As will be discussed later in more detail (see section on "The Transaction Cycle"), many commercial contracts have a four to five month (120-150 day) time frame from signature to closing, often with built-in rights to extend the time frames in the contract.

Multiple Listing Service® (MLS)® vs. Database

A majority of residential transactions are conducted through a Multiple Listing Service (MLS)® arrangement. See Chapter 9. *The vast majority of commercial listing systems are **databases** and not MLS® arrangements*, and there are no established or "built-in" rules or procedures regarding agent cooperation or commission splits. Further, a large number of commercial properties on the market are not listed even in available data bases. As a result, *commercial real estate agents must independently inquire about agency authority and cooperation when contacting a listing agent regarding a listed property, and must also negotiate and confirm their commission split arrangements prior to negotiating any offer on the property.* Even in areas where there is a commercial MLS®, a broker bringing a prospect for a property may often be from outside that market or not be a member of the commercial MLS®. Under those circumstances, the MLS® arrangement will not apply and the brokers must independently confirm their agency relationships and agree on commission splits.

Special Importance of Zoning and Other Land Use Restrictions

Zoning, deed restrictions and other land use regulations are important in residential real estate transactions, but take on a special importance in most commercial real estate transactions. A residential one-to-four unit property is nearly always suitable for use as only as a residence, and a residential one-to-four zoning classification does not often allow other uses. Also, changes in land use designations are increasingly scrutinized by planning officials, politicians and neighbors. Changes from residential uses to commercial uses are made infrequently and can be quite challenging to obtain. Similarly, protective covenants for residential subdivisions almost always prohibit non-residential uses of the houses in the subdivisions, and these covenants are rarely amended to allow commercial uses.

On the other hand, a non-residential property, especially undeveloped land, may be suitable for a wide variety of commercial (or residential) uses. For example, a tract of farm land near a city or town may be suitable for use as a site for a residential subdivision, a warehouse, a manufacturing plant, an office complex, a shopping center, a recreation facility, or many other uses. The feasibility of obtaining the appropriate zoning for such property to accommodate a buyer's desired use of the property is of critical importance to both the property owner and the buyer. Even a property that is already developed for a commercial use, such as a strip shopping center, may be suitable for a different use, such as offices, but the zoning would likely need to be changed in order to accommodate such use.

In addition to zoning and deed restrictions, there are many other land use and development regulations and restrictions that may affect a property's use and value. All these issues are so important in commercial transactions that they are discussed in greater depth in the section of this chapter titled "Special Considerations in Commercial Practice."

Leasing

While an overwhelming majority of residential real estate brokers are involved almost exclusively with sales transactions, *a substantial number of commercial real estate brokerage practitioners are very involved with lease transactions.* In fact, with some types of commercial property, such as office properties, the majority of transactions are lease transactions. Lease transactions have an entirely different set of guideposts than sales transactions. Considerations such as length of term, upfit requirements, the credit of the tenant, common area charges and apportionment between landlord and tenant of responsibility for the property and its costs of operation are unique to leasing transactions. Since there is no closing, the timing of payment of the brokerage commission may vary from one lease transaction to another. Some lease transactions have commissions payable at the signing of the lease, some pay at the tenant's occupancy of the space, some pay over the term of the lease and some use a mix of the above. It is important to make sure that these matters are resolved as early in the transaction as possible. As will be seen in more detail later (*see* "The Transaction Cycle- Lease"), the process of getting a tenant into a space once they have decided they are interested in it is significantly different than the process of closing on a sale.

Unlike residential tenancies, which are governed by the Residential Rental Agreements Act, there is no statute governing commercial leases. As a result, a commercial lease is purely a matter of contract and the parties can agree to anything that they desire so long as it does not offend public policy. A provision in a lease which would offend public policy would be any provision that tried to vary basic human rights and entitlements or other clear protections of citizens of the state of North Carolina. A provision which seeks to discriminate based upon any class of persons protected under the fair housing laws and civil rights laws, any restraint of trade provision, any usurious or any unconstitutional provision will all, among other provisions, not be enforceable. With commercial leases, virtually everything is negotiable and that flexibility should be taken into account. Not only does this mean that tenants are free to ask for virtually anything they desire, but it also means that landlords are free to deny virtually anything that is requested.

Contracts and Contract Forms

The contract forms for agency contracts, sales contracts and leases that are used in commercial transactions are very different from the contract forms commonly used in residential sales and leasing. For this reason, the North Carolina Association of REALTORS˙ - REALTORS˙ Commercial Alliance has a separate series of forms for use in commercial transactions.[3] Different forms are needed because commercial property transactions are so different from residential transactions. Typically, a commercial series form should not be used in a residential transaction, nor should a residential form be used in a commercial transaction. If there is a question about the character of the transaction or the usefulness of a form in a particular circumstance, the circumstances and form should be carefully examined to make sure it is appropriate under the circumstances; this review may often prudently involve the assistance of a real estate attorney.

A commercial brokerage practitioner is much more likely than a residential practitioner to have occasion to deal with institutional clients and customers with national or multi-state operations. Such institutional entities often have their own agency contract and transactional forms that they require to be used in transactions in which they are a party. When a North Carolina broker encounters such an agency contract form, they should be careful to assure that the form complies with North Carolina Real Estate Commission Rule 21 NCAC 58A.0104 regarding provisions that must be included in any such contract used by a North Carolina broker. If necessary, the agent should seek the assistance of a competent real estate attorney who is familiar with the North Carolina Real Estate Commission rules. REALTORS˙ may want to use the North Carolina Association of REALTORS˙ - REALTORS˙ Comercial Alliance Compliance Addendum (NCAR-RCA Form 560), which was designed to be attached to such institutional agency contract forms to bring them into compliance with the Commission's rule.

Although standard commercial sales contract and lease forms are available, the commercial practitioner is much more likely than a residential practitioner to encounter situations where a standard sales contract or lease form is completely inadequate for the transaction in question. In such cases, the agent must refer the parties to a real estate attorney to draft an appropriate sales contract or lease. Agents need to be able to recognize situations where a standard form is adequate.

It should also be mentioned that brokers in commercial transactions will more frequently encounter situations involving *option contracts*, particularly leases with an option to purchase.

Financing

Many aspects of financing the purchase of commercial properties are very different from residential financing. Underwriting standards, loan repayment periods, amortization periods, and loan-to-value ratios are just a few of the significant differences. It is also possible that the construction costs of improvements to existing property may be included as a part of the financing of a property purchase. These and other characteristics of commercial real estate financing are addressed further in the section on "Special Considerations in Commercial Practice."

Higher Stakes

It is critical that brokers keep in mind that commercial transactions are usually far more complex than residential transactions, require much more of a broker's time, involve higher marketing costs, and take much longer to consummate. A broker must be prepared mentally, emotionally and financially to cope with this aspect of the business.

Business Relationships

Commercial brokers rely more heavily on obtaining business as a direct result of personal relationships with property owners and potential buyers/tenants. Establishing oneself in the commercial brokerage business may, therefore, be more difficult than getting started in the residential business.

Working Hours

Residential real estate brokers must devote many evenings and weekends to working with prospective buyers and sellers because that is the time when they are typically available to tend to matters relating to their transaction. On the other hand, most commercial transactions involve business entities which generally have regular daytime business hours. Therefore, most matters relating to commercial transactions are handled during regular weekday business hours.

Cooperating with Out-Of-State Agents

It is not unusual for residential practitioners to have occasion to cooperate with agents who are resident brokers of another state and who have clients from out of state, especially in areas close to the state border. *However, in commercial practice, it is much more common to encounter client or customer representatives from out of state.* As our nation becomes increasingly retail franchise oriented and corporate operations are increasingly consolidated, the incidence of encountering national or regional representatives who travel the country handling real estate matters for companies and franchises is increasing. It is also increasingly the case that companies and franchisors are hiring a single broker or brokerage firm to oversee real estate operations nationally for the company and this broker or firm in turn hires other brokers as subagents to act as regional representatives and service a number of states in a region. Thus, the number of commercial practitioners from other states coming into this state seeking to purchase or lease property on behalf of their represented companies and the frequency of their visits is increasing. In addition, it is increasingly common for property outside the state of North Carolina to be managed or marketed from within North Carolina. It is, therefore, particularly important for commercial practitioners to be fully informed about North Carolina's real estate licensing requirements and the legal requirements and restrictions related to cooperation with and payment of compensation to persons from out of state.

The Licensing Requirement

North Carolina General Statutes §93A-3 requires that anyone who is physically present in the state of North Carolina conducting activity for which a real estate license is required must have a North Carolina Real Estate license. It is also a violation of the license law to pay any consideration or thing of value to an unlicensed person who performs any act for which a license is required.[4] Thus, when a broker in another state comes to North Carolina to assist in locating and acquiring a site for a client, if that broker seeks to be compensated, he or she must have a North Carolina real estate license. Otherwise, the out-of-state broker may not be paid a fee for his or her brokerage activities in North Carolina. It does not matter what the payment is called (e.g. a consulting fee, a finder's fee, etc.), it is the payment of consideration or giving of a thing of value that is prohibited. If, on the other hand, the out-of-state broker does not come to North Carolina, but stays in the state where he or she has a real estate license, a North Carolina broker is permitted to pay them. Again, it does not matter what it is called (a referral fee, commission split, etc.), it is permissible to pay an out-of-state broker as long as they did not come to North Carolina and engage in activities in North Carolina requiring a real estate license during the transaction. Note also that *a referral fee or other payment cannot be paid indirectly to an unlicensed person by "laundering" the payment through a broker of this or another state.* Finally, note that if an out-of-state broker engages in brokerage activity in North Carolina and is acting as the agent of a real estate firm, that firm must also have a North Carolina real estate *firm* license.

Similarly, if a person located in North Carolina is marketing and selling property located in another state, they must have a North Carolina real estate license in order to receive payments for that work. Even if they are licensed in the state where the property is located, they must also be licensed in North Carolina if they are conducting their real estate activities from North Carolina.

Licensing of a Person with a Real Estate License in Another State.   If a real estate broker in another state wishes to obtain a North Carolina individual broker license, he or she may do so by applying for a North Carolina license and passing the "State" section of North Carolina's license examination. The prelicensing education requirement and "National" section of the license examination are waived for such applicants. The North Carolina Real Estate Commission terminated all reciprocal licensing arrangements with other states effective March 1, 2012 and implemented the above-stated requirement for brokers of other states to obtain a North Carolina real estate license.

Verifying a Claim of North Carolina Licensure

When dealing with other persons who hold themselves out as being licensed in North Carolina, commercial agents (or, for that matter, residential agents) simply need to act in a reasonably responsible manner in determining whether such persons are, in fact, licensed in this state. *As a general rule, a broker may accept the word of another person who claims to have an active North Carolina license unless there exists some factor that would make a reasonably prudent agent question the validity of such claim.* At the commencement of dealings with another agent or representative, a broker should, however, at least inquire about the other person's licensure if such person does not affirmatively disclose such information. Thus, if the person is a North Carolina resident and claims to have an active license, one generally need not make further inquiry. If, for example, the other person does not appear to be affiliated with a real estate company and/or does not appear to be knowledgeable about how to handle the proposed transaction, the broker should verify the person's licensure. This can easily be accomplished by asking to see the person's pocket card (though this does not indicate active or inactive status) or even better, by calling the Real Estate Commission or accessing the Commission's interactive web site.

The same basic standard applies if the person claiming North Carolina licensure is from out of state, although a prudent North Carolina resident broker should probably be a little more diligent about verifying North Carolina licensure when the person is a nonresident. (This inquiry may also facilitate the introduction of the opportunity to obtain a Limited Nonresident Commercial License as discussed below.)

Example: Brenda Office, a broker, gets a phone call one day from Bob Dallas, a Texas real estate agent, who says he has the exclusive agent for Billy Bob's Office Supplies, which wants to open an administrative office in North Carolina. Dallas wants Brenda to locate potential office space for Billy Bob's, and he tells Brenda that he will come to North Carolina and personally inspect any office space identified as suitable so he can make sure his client's needs are met. Dallas also tells Brenda that she will have to pay him a consulting fee out of her part of the commission on any transaction. Brenda inquires if Dallas has a North Carolina real estate license. Dallas says no, he won't need one because he will be getting paid a consulting fee, not a commission. Brenda says she is sorry, it is the payment of consideration (a thing of value), not what the payment is called, that requires the North Carolina license. Brenda properly informs Dallas that she cannot pay him anything if he comes to North Carolina. Dallas slams down the phone.

Example: A few days later, Dallas calls Brenda back and says he has a solution for their "fee issue." Dallas' real estate company has an office in North Carolina and there are agents there who are licensed. Dallas will still come to North Carolina and inspect any potential properties, but Brenda will pay Dallas' company's local office the consulting fee and they will see that it is "allocated" appropriately. Brenda properly informs Dallas that he cannot engage in real estate activity in North Carolina without an individual North Carolina real estate license and also that she cannot pay a fee to another North Carolina broker with full knowledge that such broker is going to pay all or a portion of such fee to a person who is not licensed in North Carolina. To do so would make her part of an illegal scheme to circumvent the Real Estate License Law. She suggests that Dallas, who is licensed in Texas, simply stay in Texas and not come to North Carolina. She will be glad to provide him with whatever information he wants regarding any space or transaction and he can be as involved as he wants in the transaction and she will be glad to pay him a fee, as long as he does not come to North Carolina. Dallas reluctantly agrees and the transaction is thus structured to avoid any violation of the License Law.

Limited Nonresident Commercial License

Effective July 1, 2004, the Limited Nonresident Commercial License was created in North Carolina as an alternative to obtaining a regular license. The Law and Commission rules governing this special license provide that any *person* residing in a state or United States territory other than North Carolina who holds an *active license* in a "qualifying state" may obtain from the Commission a **"limited nonresident commercial real estate broker license"** without having to take any prelicense education or license examination in North Carolina. Under the statute and rules, a qualifying state is defined as "...the *state or territory* of the United States *where* an applicant for ... a limited nonresident commercial license issued under this Section is *licensed in good standing ... and maintains his or her primary place of business as a real estate broker or salesperson."*

The license will be for the limited purpose of entering North Carolina to engage in a commercial real estate transaction only, subject to restrictions discussed below. Practice in North Carolina is limited to transactions involving **"commercial real estate,"** which is defined by rule as *any interest in real property (freehold or non-freehold) which at the time of the transaction is used, or zoned (or under application to be zoned) to be used, or intended in good faith to be used "...primarily for sales, office, research, institutional, warehouse, manufacturing, industrial, or mining purposes or for multifamily residential purposes involving five or more dwelling units."* It should be noted that the definition of commercial real estate does NOT include bulk land purchases for the development of residential lots.

Only individuals, not business entities/firms, are allowed to apply for a limited nonresident commercial license. While business entities/firms are ineligible for the limited nonresident commercial license, a non-North Carolina entity/firm may apply for a standard firm broker license.

A couple of other significant features of this special licensing system are worthy of mention here. *Prior to entering North Carolina, the limited nonresident commercial broker must have a* **brokerage cooperation agreement** *and a* **declaration of affiliation** *with a resident North Carolina broker* (multiple simultaneous agreements are possible and the declaration of the affiliation and the brokerage cooperation agreement need not be with the same broker in each instance). Once that agreement is in place, *the North Carolina broker must actively and personally supervise the nonresident commercial broker* to reasonably assure that such broker conforms to the North Carolina Real Estate License Law and Commission rules. The North Carolina broker will also be required to retain all documents and hold and account for trust monies, to the extent that agents in the transaction hold the trust monies, relating to transactions conducted under the agreement.

Commercial Real Estate Broker Lien

Another distinction between residential and commercial brokerage practice is the right of a commercial broker to, under certain circumstances, place a **commercial real estate broker lien** on a property to protect the broker's right to a brokerage fee. The Commercial Real Estate Broker Lien Act (codified as Part 4 of Article 2 of NC General Statutes §44A or NCGS §44A-24.1-14) was enacted by the 2011 North Carolina General Assembly and became effective October 1, 2011.

Commercial sales and lease transactions commonly take months or years to negotiate and bring to fruition, requiring the broker(s) involved to devote massive amounts of time to a transaction. Such transactions also frequently involve large brokerage commissions. Not surprisingly, then, it has not been uncommon for commission disputes between brokers and clients to arise and not be resolved by the closing date. In that case, the disputes could lead to civil litigation because the broker had no right to place a lien on the property being transferred. Once title to the property was transferred, the broker had no "leverage" and could only resort to suing the former property owner who owed the brokerage fee.

The Commercial Real Estate Broker Lien Act attempts to mitigate this problem for commercial real estate brokers by granting a broker who is representing a property owner in a commercial real estate transaction a right to file a lien against the parcel of commercial real estate being sold or leased to protect the broker's right to recover a brokerage fee.

Major Features of the Commercial Real Estate Broker Lien

Important Note to Commercial Brokers. Note that coverage of the commercial real estate broker lien in this book is intended only to make brokers aware of the existence of the lien right and the major features of the lien. The statute establishing the lien contains many detailed provisions regarding requirements for filing and enforcement of the lien that are beyond the scope of coverage in this course. Brokers who deal in commercial real estate are strongly advised to seek further education on the lien and to promptly consult with their attorney regarding the filing of the lien when they perform the contracted service under a commercial brokerage services contract with a property owner. Brokers are also cautioned to make certain the brokerage services contract form they use contains language regarding their performance and compensation that will allow them to utilize the lien right.

Who Is Entitled to the Lien. The lien is available to real estate brokers licensed in North Carolina, including an out-state-broker who holds a North Carolina Limited Non-Resident Commercial License.

Property that May Be Subject to the Lien. The lien is permitted only in connection with services rendered by a broker in the sale or leasing of commercial real estate. "Commercial real estate" is defined in the statute as any real property or interest therein, whether freehold or leasehold, which is used "…primarily for sales, office, research, institutional, warehouse, manufacturing, industrial, or mining purposes or for multifamily residential purposes involving five or more dwelling units,…" or property which is zoned to permit such use, or which is subject to a petition for rezoning for such use, or which is in good faith intended to be immediately used for such purposes. [Note that the "good faith" provision is applicable only in areas of the state where there are no land use regulations governing the property's use.]

Lien Right Is Limited to Broker/Firm with Written Brokerage Services Agreement with the Owner. *The lien is available only to listing brokers/firms who have a written contract with the property owner to sell or lease the owner's property.* A cooperating broker who is acting as either a buyer's agent or a subagent of the owner pursuant to a cooperation agreement with the listing broker/firm has no right to the lien because the cooperating broker has no direct contractual relationship with the owner. Note that a cooperating broker acting under a cooperation agreement with a listing broker has never had any legal standing to sue the owner for a brokerage fee. Note also that it is the brokerage firm or the owner-broker of the sole proprietorship that has the listing who has the right to the lien, not an affiliated individual broker who may be the listing agent and who may have signed the listing agreement in behalf of his or her employing broker or firm.

Lien Applies Only to Property That Is Subject to the Transaction. The lien only applies to the parcel of commercial real estate that is being conveyed or leased and that is the subject of the brokerage services agreement, not to any other property of the owner.

Other Prerequisites for Filing a Lien. In order to be entitled to a lien, all of the following requirements must be met:

- The broker must have performed pursuant to the terms of the written brokerage services agreement;
- The written agreement must clearly set forth the broker's duties to the owner; and
- The written agreement for broker services must set forth the conditions upon which the compensation shall be earned and the amount of the compensation.

When Lien Must Be Filed. For a *sale* transaction, a lien must be filed *after* the claimant's performance under the written agreement and before the conveyance or transfer of the commercial real estate subject to the lien. Additionally, *a lien should not be filed more than 30 days prior to the closing date (for a sale) or possession date (for a lease)* because a lien filed more than 30 days prior to the closing or possession date shall be available only upon grounds of the owner's breach of the brokerage services agreement. **Caution:** These provisions have the effect of making the lien unavailable to a broker if the listing agreement provides that the broker's fee will be earned only upon closing because the lien must be filed after the fee is earned but prior to closing. If the fee is only earned at closing, the broker cannot meet the statutory requirement for timely filing of the lien.

For a **lease** transaction, the statute provides an exception to the requirement for filing the lien prior to transfer of possession by allowing, in the case of transfer of a nonfreehold (i.e., leasehold) interest, the lien may be filed no later than 90 days following the tenant's possession or 60 days after the due date of a payment pursuant to the brokerage services agreement.

There are also special provisions for lien filing after the transfer or conveyance for portions of a commission that are due after the transfer or conveyance, as well as provisions for a single filing to cover all installments due regarding the commission if the broker amends the lien after each paid installment to reduce the amount of the lien.

Time Limit for Lien Enforcement; Lien Priority. If a lien is not paid or otherwise satisfied, the lien claimant (broker/firm) has up to 18 months from the filing of the lien to file a suit to enforce the lien (basically to foreclose on the property subject to the lien).

The commercial broker's lien is effective only from the date of lien filing, meaning that other liens filed prior to the filing of the commercial broker's lien will have priority. Moreover, under the statute, *mechanic's and materialmen's liens are always superior to the commercial broker's lien even if filed after the filing of the broker's lien.* Thus, the broker's lien is lower in priority than any liens existing at the time the broker's lien is filed (e.g., a mortgage or tax lien) as well as any mechanic's lien filed after the broker's lien is filed.

Costs of Legal Proceeding to Enforce a Broker's Lien. Brokers should be aware that the statute provides that the costs *of any proceeding to enforce a lien, including reasonable attorneys' fees, shall be paid by the non-prevailing party.* This provision is obviously very beneficial to the broker who has a legitimate claim to a commission and has strictly adhered to all the statutory lien requirements. On the other hand, a broker who incorrectly or wrongfully files a lien and pursues enforcement not only will not be able to collect a fee, but also may be assessed court costs and attorneys' fees incurred by the owner in defending the broker's claim.

SPECIAL CONSIDERATIONS IN COMMERCIAL PRACTICE

Before delving into coverage of the various types of commercial properties and the factors that affect the value and desirability of such properties, it would perhaps be helpful to focus on a few subjects that warrant special consideration when dealing with commercial properties in general. These subjects are listed below and then discussed.

Subjects Warranting Special Consideration in Commercial Practice

- Zoning and Other Land Use Restrictions
- Financing
- Client and Customer Perspectives

Zoning and Other Land Use Restrictions

Zoning

Many commercial transactions involve clients or customers who conduct a particular type of business or engage in a particular use of property (e.g., manufacturing, retail sales, distribution). Often, the new user of the property will be putting the property to a different use than the previous user, and even a use that is only slightly different may raise an important zoning issue. **Zoning ordinances** regulate the use of property and detail what activities may or may not be conducted in a particular zone. They also address matters such as setbacks, building orientation, building size, screening, and parking, to name a few. Thus, *it is extremely important for the commercial practitioner to be aware of the existence of a zoning ordinance and, if there is an applicable ordinance, how it affects the property in question.* A broker must also be mindful of **extraterritorial jurisdiction**. It may be very possible that a property which is located outside the city limits may still be regulated by the nearby city's zoning ordinance. It should be noted, however, that there remain many areas (especially areas outside of cities and towns) in North Carolina where there are no zoning ordinances. It is a broker's responsibility to know if a land use ordinance is applicable to property they are marketing.

The zoning classification is included in the listing data and advertisements for most every commercial property, and is clearly a material fact in commercial transactions. It is thus important that an agent make accurate determinations and disclosures regarding zoning. The public official charged with enforcement of the zoning ordinance (most frequently, the county or city building inspector) is the best source of information regarding zoning. Such official can advise whether a particular property is affected by the ordinance, what zoning classification (if any) applies, and what use restrictions apply to that property.

If it is determined that a property's zoning classification does not meet a particular client's or customer's needs or intended use, it may be necessary to seek a rezoning of the property. Again, the public official charged with enforcement of the zoning ordinance is the best source for information on how the rezoning process works as well as what classification might best suit the client's or customer's intended needs or use. From a buyer's or tenant's perspective, determinations regarding zoning should be made as early as possible in a contemplated transaction. If it is determined that it is necessary to rezone a property, any offer made regarding the property will need to clearly provide that any proposed sale contract or lease will be contingent upon the successful rezoning of the property to the desired classification.

Increasingly, planning officials are requiring change of use or occupancy permits in connection with different ownership or usage of a property. Interpretations of land use regulations in this context may require significant changes to a property to permit its use (upgrades to current standards) or may actually prohibit a presumed "okay" use of a property. Brokers are cautioned when the tenant or use of a property will change in connection with a transaction to thoroughly investigate permitted use of the property. At a minimum, where such interpretive requirements may be present, a listing agent should disclose that fact and direct potential purchasers or tenants to investigate requirements that may be particular to their intended use.

Example: Nota Clu, a relatively new agent practicing commercial real estate, lists a vacant warehouse for lease or sale. Trying to "pump up" the potential market for the facility, Nota advertises that the building would be "great for use as an indoor recreational facility." Nota did not check the permitted uses for the industrial zoning classification of this property – indoor recreational use is not a permitted use under the current zoning classification and thus that use would require a zoning change. Nota is affirmatively misrepresenting the potential use of the facility. Uses that are not permitted under existing zoning classifications should not be represented in advertising as potential uses for a property.

Example: In the above example, let us presume that the facility is not vacant and is presently being used on a short term basis by a distributor who has filled the warehouse with materials. Nota logically targets similar distributors in marketing the building and finds one who signs a long term lease. As the tenant begins the permitting process for their improvements to the facility, they are informed by planning officials that their records show the building is vacant and in order to permit the occupancy of the building for the tenant's intended use, an occupancy permit will be required. (The existing tenant had not obtained an occupancy permit and was thus occupying the facility illegally.) Obtaining the occupancy permit will require substantial modifications to the building safety systems for fire code compliance which the tenant discovers will cost in excess of $100,000.00. Nota did not disclose that there were any regulatory requirements for occupancy of the property and use as desired by the tenant because he did not investigate this matter. Thus, he has failed to disclose a material fact (that there were conditions precedent to use of the facility for the represented purpose, namely an occupancy permit) to this tenant.

Private Use Restrictions

Private use restrictions on land may also have a significant impact on land use. Such restrictions may take the form of deed restrictions or conditions that limit the estate granted, but, more commonly, are created by **deed restrictive covenants** established when an owner of adjoining parcels conveys one of the parcels to a grantee with the understanding, stated in the deed (or a separate set of covenants referenced in the deed), that the grantee will only use the property in a specified manner. Restrictive covenants differ from zoning ordinances in three important respects.

      (1) They are not codified in an ordinance, but are instead found recorded in the Register of Deeds Office for the county where the property is located (in the chain of title for the property).

      (2) Their purpose is not limited to protecting and serving the public health, safety and welfare (as are zoning ordinances); they can regulate any matter, as long as such regulation is not against public policy.

      (3) They cannot be changed by public body action, but only by the property owners affected by the restrictive covenants, in the manner set forth in the restrictive covenants.

Brokers must understand the distinction between private use restrictions and zoning, particularly in commercial transactions where use plays such a big role in the suitability of a property.

Since private use restrictions are not codified like zoning ordinances, it can be much more difficult to determine what private use restrictions, if any, affect a property. Nonetheless, the determination must be made as private use restrictions are enforceable and can affect how a property can be used. A comprehensive title search conducted by an real estate attorney is the best way to determine for certain what private use restrictions affect a given piece of property. For this reason, determinations regarding private use restrictions are usually made during the term of a sales contract by an real estate attorney in the course of a title search. *Any offer to purchase or lease should contain a clear condition that the contract shall be contingent on the land use desired by the buyer (or tenant) being permissible under not only zoning ordinances but also any applicable private use restrictions.*

Restrictive covenants can regulate a wide variety of matters and are becoming increasingly detailed. In many instances, restrictive covenants provide for a property owners association which is given authority over many and diverse matters such as common area maintenance and architectural guidelines. Often the details of these regulated matters are not contained in the recorded restrictions (the restrictions merely create the authority), but instead are contained in unrecorded bylaws and guidelines implemented by the owners association. Under these circumstances, it is important for a prospective buyer or tenant to obtain copies of these bylaws and guidelines in their most current form. The importance and sophistication of private land use regimes controlled by property owners associations is on the increase, and association bylaws and guidelines may have a significant impact on an owner's or tenant's rights regarding a particular property. When marketing a property affected by restrictions which provide for a property owners association, a listing agent should undertake to obtain copies of those restrictions and any related bylaws and guidelines which may have been adopted pursuant thereto and deliver them to serious prospects. At the very least, any broker working with a buyer or tenant should advise the buyer or tenant to obtain and carefully review any applicable restrictive covenants or owners association bylaws and regulations.

A broker should be very careful in making any representations regarding private use restrictions. Interpreting restrictive covenants and advising a party as to the applicability and impact of such restrictive covenants constitutes the practice of law. If a broker should happen to have a copy of the owner's title insurance policy that details the matters affecting title, he or she should provide that policy to prospects *without comment other than to indicate the nature of the document.* The instruments referenced in the title insurance policy may also be copied and provided to prospects, but interpretation of those instruments as affecting the property should be left to a real estate attorney. Likewise, a broker may supply prospects with a copy of an opinion of title from an attorney (and copies of instruments referenced therein), but, once again, *without comment.* Brokers are also reminded that *under North Carolina law, only licensed attorneys are permitted to give opinions as to matters of title or the interpretation of recorded documents, such as restrictive covenants, easements and other agreements affecting rights in real property.*

Private use restrictions and related documents often regulate construction methods (through architectural guidelines), define the scope of common area maintenance obligations (which may include significant expenses such as roads and detention facilities) and regulate signage and permitted uses. Such restrictions and guidelines may have a significant financial impact on a property's owner and full awareness of such restrictions is thus critical with respect to commercial property.

Example: Big Gulp, Inc., a soft drink bottler, is looking for a new site for its headquarters, warehouse and manufacturing operations. John Doitall, the broker with Doitright Realty who is working with Big Gulp as a buyer's agent, has identified two sites that appear to meet Big Gulp's needs. In reviewing the information about the site, Doitall has verified with the seller's lawyer that Site A has no restrictive covenants affecting it. Doitall has also determined that Site B has restrictive covenants affecting it and has obtained a copy of them for Big Gulp. Doitall points out to Big Gulp that the restrictions on site B have very specific architectural guidelines that must be followed in connection with any construction on the site. Big Gulp turns these guidelines over to its general contractor who reports back that if Big Gulp selects Site B, the architectural guidelines will require changes in their proposed building plans. Big Gulp's contractor goes on to indicate that the changes in plans will increase the construction costs to Big Gulp by almost $25 per square foot. Big Gulp makes the decision to go with Site A, since the absence of restrictive covenants with architectural guidelines will allow them to save $25 per square foot.

Note that *zoning does not "overrule" restrictive covenants or other private use restrictions.* A property that is zoned for commercial use, but is subject to restrictive covenants which require "residential use only," can only be used for residential uses. The passage of time or a change in the uses around a property do not necessarily end the effect of a restrictive covenant. Often people mistakenly presume that a restriction is automatically terminated when a restricted area has been put to a use that violates the restrictive covenants governing the property. A restrictive covenant may be terminated by affirmative action of those owners affected by it in the manner set forth in the covenants (or by unanimous vote if no voting percentage is stated), may expire on a date certain as set forth in the covenants, or may be terminated by significant, long term change in use in violation of the covenants, but a court action is required to terminate any private use restriction on the grounds of changed circumstances. Under certain circumstances, title insurance companies may agree to insure an owner against enforcement of a restriction on the basis of changed use. The granting of this insurance is an assumption of risk by the title insurance company, not a termination of the restriction. This insurance protects the owner from the attempted enforcement of the restriction and will usually allow the transaction to go forward., but the increased incidence of lawsuits over restrictions has made obtaining insurance against enforcement of a questionable restriction more difficult. However, this insurance does not affect the restriction and someone may still sue to have it enforced, at which point the title insurance company will be required to defend the action against enforcement. If the enforcement action is successful, the owner will not be able to use the property in violation of the restriction.

Other Land Use and Development Regulations

In addition to zoning and private use restrictions, there are a number of other land use and development regulations that may impact the use and development of property and thus are of concern to commercial practitioners. Increasingly, municipalities are devising unique local land use regulations and, depending on the area in which a broker practices, there may be other types of regulations with which a broker must become familiar.

Subdivision Ordinances. Subdivision ordinances are adopted by counties and municipalities pursuant to authority given to them by the state. Subdivision ordinances regulate the division of land into more than one parcel.(See the discussion of this subject in Chapter 7 on "Land Use Controls") Typically, subdivision ordinances set forth requirements as to lot size (density), access and street width, sidewalk and other transportation and utility improvements and apply those requirements differently in each zoning classification. Knowledge and understanding of applicable subdivision ordinances is particularly important for commercial agents dealing with the development and marketing of land. Nonetheless, all commercial brokers should have a basic knowledge of the applicability of subdivision ordinances so that situations where the subdivision ordinance might apply can be readily recognized. As with zoning ordinances, the public official charged with enforcement of the subdivision ordinance is the most reliable resource for information regarding the ordinance.

Sign Ordinances. Sign ordinances have been adopted by many municipalities across the state to regulate the placement, type and size of signage. Since visibility and signage can often be deciding factors in many commercial transactions (particularly in retail transactions where signage can attract customers), it is important for a commercial broker to have an understanding of any sign ordinances applicable to a given property. It also may be important to understand how adjacent properties' use of the sign ordinance might affect a property's visibility. For example, can the owner of Property A erect a sign which obscures Property B's visibility? Sign ordinances typically also regulate the placement of and style of billboards (except along certain interstates and highways which are controlled and regulated by the North Carolina Department of Transportation). Again, the public official charged with enforcement of the sign ordinance (typically the zoning enforcement officer) is the most reliable source of information regarding the ordinance.

Watershed Regulations. Watershed regulations have been adopted by the state in an effort to protect the public drinking water supply.[5] In addition, some counties and municipalities have adopted their own, more restrictive watershed regulations. It is thus important to determine if the county or municipality has adopted a watershed regulation. Watershed regulations map out and classify the whole state into categories of watershed areas, which are classified depending upon the type of water source nearby.[6] Under certain watershed categories, the type of development as well as the permitted **"impervious surface"** (the amount of hard surface or surface not readily penetrable by water) is regulated.

Watershed regulations frequently affect new development. The regulations may prohibit the type of development contemplated or the development type contemplated may be affected by impervious surface limitations. For example, industrial facilities which have large building areas and large parking areas may require significantly more land in a watershed regulated area (since they have such a large area of impervious surface) than would be required in an area not subject to watershed regulations. Such regulations also may apply to the modification of an existing development since the permitted impervious surface of a property is fixed in accordance with how it is developed. If a property has the maximum permissible impervious surface, an expansion of the building or parking lot will not be permitted under the watershed regulations. Under certain circumstances, watershed regulations may allow an increased impervious surface or different types of development if certain **"best management practices" (BMPs)** are utilized. BMPs are structural or non-structural management-based measures (such as a detention pond) used singularly or in combination to reduce nonpoint source inputs to receiving waters in order to achieve water quality protection goals.

All commercial brokers should have a basic knowledge of the existence and applicability of watershed regulations and other water related regulations applicable in their area that affect a given property, such as Storm Water Improvement Management Buffers and flood way regulations. If a broker practices in an area where there are significant critical watershed areas, a good working knowledge of the applicability of the watershed regulations is necessary. Each county and municipality is required to designate a watershed enforcement officer,[7] who will be the most reliable source of information regarding watershed regulations.

Tree Ordinances. A number of municipalities have adopted ordinances to regulate the planting, removal and trimming of trees. At a minimum, a commercial broker should know whether the property he or she is dealing with is subject to a tree ordinance. One should also be prepared to direct clients and customers to information resources regarding the tree ordinance so that they may avoid fines and penalties that are levied for failure to comply with such ordinances.

Other Regulatory Issues. Any given transaction may also involve one or more of various regulations relating to environmental protection, development or other matters. A basic awareness of the existence and applicability of the regulations, to the extent that those regulations could apply to transactions in which the agent is involved, is necessary for the competent practice of commercial brokerage. Several of these regulatory issues are briefly mentioned below.

- The existence of **"wetlands"** may impact new development or expansion of existing development. Responsibility for determining what lands are subject to regulation as "wetlands" and how such lands may be utilized lies with the Army Corps of Engineers. It is important to note that land does not have to be consistently "wet" to be classified as "wetlands" and subject to stringent development restrictions. Brokers should not make assumptions about a property's "wetlands" status. Advise prospective developers or users considering redevelopment or expansion activities to have this checked.

- New construction or redevelopment of existing facilities may raise issues regarding the compliance of facilities with the **Americans with Disabilities Act (ADA)**. The ADA, among other things, regulates accessibility of structures for disabled persons and may require, as to new facilities or the redevelopment of a facility (look for definition of applicability), that certain features be installed to assist the disabled. (See also the discussion of the ADA in Chapter 18.)

- There are frequently a number of environmental considerations that must be taken into account in connection with the commercial use of a property. Typically, a buyer will have a **Phase I Environmental Assessment** performed during due diligence inspections while a contract is pending to determine if there are issues of an environmental nature with which to be concerned. The results of this assessment may lead to additional assessments and the potential implication of other regulations.

- The presence of any **hazardous substance** or **dangerous material** on a property is a material fact that must be disclosed to the parties to the transaction by a broker if a broker has knowledge, or should reasonably have knowledge, of its presence. A broker must also disclose the existence of any **underground storage tank** on the property. The State of North Carolina now requires an **asbestos report** prior to the issuance of a permit on any reconstruction, renovation or demolition of any structure, residential or commercial.

- Brokers should also be informed about any laws or regulations that are applicable to the particular area where they practice, such as the **Mountain Ridge Protection Law**[8] or the **North Carolina Coastal Area Management Act.**[9]

The foregoing discussion addresses only the most generally applicable and frequently encountered land use and development regulations. There may be other federal, state or local regulations which affect a particular type of property, a specific area or a specific property. *Commercial brokers should seek to stay aware of the regulations affecting property with which they deal and in instances where such regulation appears, a basic level of familiarity with the applicability and subject matter of the regulation should be acquired.*

Financing

Brokers must be familiar with the sources and types of financing for commercial real estate. The discussion in this manual of commercial real estate financing is very limited and is intended to merely provide an overview of the subject. Financing methods and terms are constantly changing and agents must strive to keep abreast of such changes. Brokers should also note the potential implications of securities laws and regulations briefly highlighted elsewhere in these materials.

Sources of Financing

Just as with residential loans, banks (both commercial and savings banks) and independent lenders are very actively involved in making loans on commercial real estate. In addition, insurance companies, pension funds, private investors and other capital sources also often make loans for commercial real estate, frequently through independent mortgage loan brokers. Just as is the case with residential lenders, different lenders have different levels of risk that they will undertake and, therefore, such lenders have different terms that they are willing to offer to borrowers. *Unlike residential lending, there is little standardization within the lending community with regard to qualifying guidelines for commercial loans.*

Characteristics of Commercial Loans

While most residential loans have a term of either 15 or 30 years, commercial loans have terms that vary greatly in length, often depending on the type of loan. *The terms of commercial loans typically range from 5 years (or less) to 20 years.* Loans with terms exceeding 20 years are available, but they are not nearly as common as they are in the residential marketplace. Most residential loans are amortized over the life of the loan in such a manner that the loan is fully repaid at the end of the loan term. On the other hand, *the amortization period for commercial loans often is much longer than the term of the loan.* For example, a lender may make a commercial loan that is for a term of 7 years with an amortization period of 30 years. What this means is that the borrower makes payments during the 7 years of the loan in an amount that is determined as if the loan were being paid off over 30 years (which creates lower payments that a 7 year amortization), and then one "balloon" payment of all the remaining balance on the loan at the end of 7 years. The length of the loan term and the amortization period will typically have an effect on the rate the lender charges. Often, depending on the credit strength of the borrower, these terms may be negotiable.

Adjustable (variable) interest rates are more common in commercial loans than in residential, although market factors present at any given time may affect the proportion of loans that have a fixed rate versus an adjustable (variable) rate. A broad number of indexes are used by lenders for determining the rate for any point in time on adjustable rate loans. An index is a published rate that is referenced in a promissory note as the basis for setting and/or adjusting the rate of interest charged on a loan. Quite often the determined rate will be defined as the index rate plus a stated number of "basis points." For example, a loan that determined its rate by using the average rate of one-month treasury bills as published in the Wall Street Journal (index), plus 250 basis points (margin), would be determined by taking the index rate and adding 2.5% to it to get the applicable percentage rate of interest. Some of the indexes often used in commercial real estate lending, to name but a few, are the prime rate, the London Interbank Offered Rate (LIBOR), and treasury bill rates (many maturities from 1-10 years are typically used).

Loan-to-value ratios on commercial loans are usually in the 60-80% range and while some loans are made at higher loan-to-value ratios, such loans are rare and usually limited to construction/development projects. There are no VA or FHA programs in commercial lending and no private mortgage insurance. Accordingly, lenders have no insurance to rely on in the event of borrower default, and they must rely more heavily on the real estate pledged or the income therefrom as security. Thus, loan to value ratios tend to stay in this range. There are certain programs that will allow a borrower to obtain loans with higher loan-to-value ratios, but a large majority of commercial real estate loans have loan-to-value ratios in the 60-80% range.

Commercial real estate loans are often made to entities rather than individuals. Quite often these entities are formed for the specific purpose of owning the real estate to be acquired. Accordingly, these entities may often not have a financial track record or any credit history. Under these (and other) circumstances, commercial real estate lenders will often require that principals or owners of the entity guarantee the loan. The purpose of this guaranty is to give the lender an individual or entity with a credit history and/or financial track record that they can rely upon and from whom they can recover in the event that the loan is not repaid. If a guaranty is not required and the lender is looking at the property as its only means of recovery in the event of loan default, the loan is called a **"non-recourse" loan**. The lender has no recourse against anyone or anything other than the property.

There are many other factors and issues which can impact commercial real estate financing and thus the success of a transaction. It is important for the broker working with the commercial client or customer to understand the basics of commercial real estate lending so that time is not wasted working on transactions that cannot be financed or working with clients or customers who have unrealistic expectations as to the cost and availability of funds for commercial real estate. The buyer hoping to get a 30-year term with a 30-year amortization period on a 95% loan is going to be sorely disappointed.

Client and Customer Perspectives

To properly serve real estate clients and customers, a broker must always understand the perspective of the party with whom he or she is working because the perspective that a client or customer brings to the transaction can dictate the factors that are important in the transaction.. In residential practice, this is a relatively simple matter — there is typically a seller and a user-buyer (a buyer who plans to personally use the property). In commercial practice, there can be additional perspectives, as discussed below.

Seller

When marketing a seller's commercial property, the listing agent has to take into account both types of purchasers — "users" and "investors." While the property may be very well suited for any number of users who may appear to be the logical buyers, and such potential users may be plentiful in the marketplace, there is also the possibility that an investor might find the property attractive. On the other hand, some properties may be attractive only to users or only to investors. The common law of agency requires the use of an agent's skill and knowledge in dealings with one's principal. This requirement makes it essential that an agent understand how to determine what the potential market for the seller's property may be. Another issue that should be discussed with the property owner is whether it is in the owner's best interest to sell the property or to lease the property.

Property Assessment by Listing Agent. In order to properly make a determination as to the market for a property, a thorough assessment of the property must be undertaken by the listing agent. In addition to simply gathering property information, the listing agent should carefully consider such factors as: the property's condition, land use restrictions, environmental issues, area demographics, market forces affecting the property, an assessment of the property's past and potential future financial performance, " linkages,"(to be discussed later in this chapter), and any other factor that might impact on marketing the property. Based largely on the foregoing factors, a marketing strategy to reach the potential users and investors will need to be developed (including discussion of a possible separate marketing budget/fee, if applicable). All of these undertakings should be made at the time of or before the listing is actually signed.

Landlord

When representing a landlord in a commercial transaction, a broker may encounter a number of different circumstances, depending on the property and the landlord's desires. The possibilities include: (1) leasing space in an existing building; (2) leasing space in a building to be built by the landlord; (3) leasing land for a tenant to build something on, or (4) leasing land but the landlord will build something for the tenant on the land ("build to suit"). There may well be other options or a mix of these options.

If the space to be leased is **existing space** or **space to be built by the landlord**, the broker (landlord's agent) must first gather all relevant property information and perform a property assessment similar to that described above in the discussion about a "Seller," then determine with the landlord the business terms of the lease offering. Terms which must be considered include: what amount of money will be available for "upfit" for the tenant (i.e., for making alterations necessary for the tenant to utilized the property), what occupancy arrangements will be made for the tenant, what will be the factor of "usable" and "rentable" square footage, what will be the rental rate, and who will be responsible for what charges as relates to the operation and maintenance of the structure (what type of lease will it be), among other matters.

As a practical matter, landlords will also want to take into account their approach to property management and lease administration when offering multi-tenant space in the market. A landlord will likely want to have a standard lease form so that their relationships with the various tenants in the property will generally be similar. Many landlords refuse to change the terms of a lease in the body of the lease and instead prefer to do so on a "rider" to the lease (an addendum) so that any changes of terms in their base lease with any particular tenant are readily identifiable by looking at the rider (without having to review the whole lease).

If the property to be leased is **land on which the tenant is to build something**, there are also a couple of other important matters be considered. One issue is who will be entitled to the improvements built by the tenant at the end of the lease term. Most likely, this will be the landlord. In any event, this issue has a significant impact on the amount of rent the tenant will be required to (or willing to) pay. In addition, zoning, private use restrictions and other regulations that impact on the property must be considered because those factors will define the market with regard to possible tenants for the property. For example, if the property is an outparcel in a shopping center with private use restrictions which prohibit financial institutions and zoning which prohibits drive-through windows, banks and many fast food restaurants will not be eligible tenants.

If the property is to be leased to a tenant and the **landlord will build to suit** for the tenant, the normal listing agent duties (see above discussion) must be performed and the zoning and private use restrictions must be taken into account in determining what will be built on the property. Typically, lease terms are defined by the use that is requested by the tenant, but the agent and the landlord should have done some homework and defined permitted uses and possible scenarios in order to have a valid negotiating position once a tenant brings a request for a permitted use. This process will typically involve an allowance for construction. If the allowance is exceeded based on a request from the tenant, the rate of rental will be increased by an amount sufficient to cover that amount over the term of the lease, including interest on the excess, since that amount is in essence being financed.

As should be apparent from the above discussion, in a commercial transaction it is very important for a landlord and the landlord's agent to work closely together to understand the property, the potentially available transaction structures and what the general business terms of those transaction structures will be.

User

Typically a user will define the type of commercial property they desire. *A user may be either a tenant or a purchaser.* In this instance, it is the job of the commercial broker to identify properties that meet the needs of the user, according to the specifications that they set forth. Whether they are seeking to lease space or buy, the client or customer's definition of what they are looking for is that which the agent seeks. In this circumstance, it is important that the broker understand the type of property that the client or customer seeks in order to be able to properly evaluate the choices in the marketplace. It may well be the case that a given property is perfectly suitable for the user, be they tenant or buyer, even if the property is not advertised as appropriate. This is where knowledge of the market, factors affecting property, linkages and demographics (among other matters) come into play with the commercial broker. As noted above, knowledge of the market, various types of properties and the factors affecting them is critical for the commercial real estate broker. This is especially true when representing the user.

Where the user is a tenant, a broker has a perhaps more complicated set of factors to consider in assisting their client or customer in evaluating property choices. As noted later, there are varying methods of calculating square footage. There are also varying costs associated with a tenancy apart from base rent (such as common area maintenance charges, utilities, parking, upfit, etc.) and these costs may or may not be associated with square footage. These costs may also be subject to adjustment and those adjustments may be limited (as where there is a cap on rent increases) or they may not be limited (as is often the case with increases in common area maintenance charges). All of these factors must be taken into account in assisting a tenant with a determination of their total cost of occupancy (what it will cost, in full, to occupy a space). The ultimate objective of a broker in these circumstances is to assist their client or customer in assessing the varying options on an "apples-to apples" basis considering these varying factors.

Investor

Many different types of individuals and entities make up the universe of investor buyers of commercial properties, but one thing all such investor buyers have in common is that the factor they consider most critical is the financial analysis of the property. Investor buyers make their decisions based upon the return or potential return on investment income that the property will likely provide. When working with an investor buyer, an agent should determine the client's risk parameters, their assumptions for financial analysis of the property and their desired results, among other considerations. Only with a firm understanding of the client's needs can an agent adequately assess and present properties that are suitable to the investor client.

Caution: Investment analysis is a very complex matter and should not be engaged in lightly. Financial analysis of real estate investments undertaken for a prospective buyer should only be attempted by agents who have substantial special training in the performance of such analyses. Such training is well beyond the scope of real estate prelicensing education and introductory level courses on commercial brokerage. Even with appropriate training and experience, investment analysis should be only be performed with thorough research, careful preparation and clear disclosure as to the assumptions made and methods of analysis used. As noted earlier, if a broker is presented with an investor client and does not have the knowledge and skills to represent them, the broker should seek the assistance of a more experienced broker or a person experienced in matters of investment valuation before proceeding.

COMMERCIAL PROPERTY CLASSIFICATIONS, UNIQUE FEATURES AND MARKET FACTORS

Commercial real estate is generally classified into four broad categories: **Office**, **Retail**, **Industrial** and **Land**. In addition to these broad categories, there are also "specialty properties" (such as churches or recreational facilities) and an increasing number of "hybrid" property types which mix features of different categories (such as "flex" warehouse space which has warehouse and office space combined). Increasingly, office, retail and residential uses are being combined in projects which are often referred to as "mixed use" projects. These mixed use projects also often include specialty and hybrid property types as well. While these materials seek to address some basic terminology and features related to each commercial property type, the information provided here should by no means be viewed as comprehensive. In addition, certain local markets develop their own "lingo" and factors for evaluation in connection with each type of property. Before dealing with a particular type of property, an agent should seek to gain understanding of all matters that are related to the property type in general and in their local market place.

Major Categories of Commercial Properties

- **Office**
- **Retail**
- **Industrial**
- **Land**
- **Specialty Properties**

OFFICE PROPERTIES OR SPACE

Office space is space that is used for clerical, management, professional or other similar functions. Office space may be found in properties where the whole building is used for office space, where only certain floors or areas are used for office space or where the property was once used for another purpose and has now been wholly or partially converted to an office use (e.g., an old warehouse which has been turned into office space). Office space can be found in buildings of many types. The most common building types in which office space is located are: (1) the tower or highrise; (2) the midrise; (3) the campus or garden building. **Highrise buildings** are characterized by a significant number of building floors, a shell of concrete or steel and a skin of pre-cast materials and remote or deck parking. **Midrise buildings** often are constructed in a similar fashion to highrise buildings but contain fewer floors (usually as a result of land use regulations or market conditions). **Garden** or **campus buildings** are the type most often found in business parks and are characterized by a limited number of floors, surface parking and construction and site placement that seeks to blend the building in with its surroundings.

In addition to these referenced types of construction, office space is often found in small freestanding buildings, houses which have been converted for use as office space, and "strip" office buildings (sometimes even old shopping centers). These types of office space are commonplace and are particularly prevalent in small-to-medium-size towns and areas of larger cities which may be undergoing a transition from one prevalent use in the area to another prevalent use.

While the condominium form of ownership (see discussion in Chapter 1) has traditionally been used mostly in the residential context, offerings of office condominiums have significantly increased in recent years. These offerings occur across many building types and include both newly constructed condominiums and conversions of existing properties from single ownership into the condominium form of ownership.

Office Space Classifications

In addition to references to the type of construction, *office space is often classified as Class "A," "B" or "C"*. Generally, these classifications refer to the age and functionality of the structure. **Class "A" office space** typically is no more than 20 years old, has modern features and amenities, is well maintained, and has excellent construction quality and finish materials. **Class "B" and "C" office**

space, on the other hand, typically is older than 20 years, may not have been well maintained and has features and amenities that are dated. The more pronounced the age, maintenance problems and lack of amenities or features, the more likely a building will be classified as "C" space as opposed to "B" space. The significance of the ABC classification is that most often, *Class "A" space rents are the highest in the market and Class "C" rents are at the bottom of the market.*

Factors Affecting the Value and Desirability of Office Space

Office properties exist primarily for the purpose of *leasing* space to tenants as a means of generating income to the property owner. Even if an office property is to be occupied and used by the purchaser of the property for the purchaser's own offices, its value in the sale transaction is largely determined by the income generated from existing leases and/or potential future leases. For this reason, this discussion of office properties focuses primarily on factors considered in *leasing* office space.

Nonetheless, as noted above, the condominium form of ownership has become increasingly popular in the office market. In assessing a potential condominium purchase, the factors noted below as affecting value and desirability will remain important considerations to an office user, with the rent consideration being replaced by an occupancy cost/cost of ownership consideration. The potential investment returns and tax advantages of ownership have increased consideration of ownership amongst particularly smaller office users and agents should be aware of this option when working with office clients or customers.

Size of the Space

Many of the critical definitions relating to office space concern floor or space configuration, since those factors most directly affect the price and true desirability of a space for a tenant's or purchaser's particular use.

The size of a **floor plate**, that is the area of each floor as determined by measuring along the exterior walls, can often be a significant factor for an office tenant. If a tenant is looking for a space larger than a given building's floor plate, they will have to occupy two floors in that property, which may mean the property is not desirable even though it has enough available space. Each floor typically has a **core area**, that is the area used up for building functions such as lobbies, elevators, stairs, restrooms, heating and cooling equipment and mechanical, plumbing and electrical functions. For each floor of a building, the floor plate minus the core area provides the floor's **usable area** (or usable square footage). Nonetheless, landlords do not typically charge rent only on usable area (or usable square footage). In order to account for the core area of the building and make sure that all tenants pay rent which covers those areas as well, landlords will apply a **core factor** to usable square footage. A core factor is a percentage that typically is calculated as the percentage of the overall building square footage that the core occupies. The usable area is multiplied times one plus the core factor to determine **rentable area** (or rentable square footage). *Rental rates for office space are usually quoted per* **rentable square foot**, *thereby taking the core factor into account.*

> *Example:* A landlord has his building measured and determines that the core factor of the building is 12%; that is, 12% of the space is taken up by building functions which qualify for treatment as core factor. The landlord also has each office suite measured for its actual square footage. A particular suite has 1,000 usable square feet. Since the core factor is 12%, the usable square feet (1,000) multiplied times 1.12 (1 + the core factor), determines rentable square footage of 1,120 that will be quoted for the suite in question.

Determination of Square Footage

An important factor for consideration in office leasing is determining how the square footage for the space was calculated. There is a standard for measurement of office space established by Building Owners and Managers Association (BOMA) and referred to as the *BOMA standard*. Nonetheless, this standard is not always used and accordingly, one may encounter a number of different methods of measuring and calculating the square footage of office space. *It is important that the square footage reported be accurate and that it be determined according to a clearly defined method, consistently applied (whether it is the BOMA standard or the broker's own system). A listing agent in particular will be held accountable for the accuracy of square footage he or she reports.*

If representing a prospective tenant, it is important that the broker assist his or her client in making an "apples-to-apples" determination. The tenant is going to be most interested in how much space the tenant can actually use and what it is going to cost. Thus, the broker should, in each instance, ask the listing agent how the space was measured and how the rentable and usable square footage figures were determined. Only by doing this for each prospective space under consideration does one provide the client with information that makes it possible to make a proper comparison of competing space.

Property Features and Amenities

There are many factors relating to the specific features and amenities of office space that are typically important to tenants. The **shape of the floor** may be of importance because an unusual shape may provide for an interesting design from the outside but leave irregular and unusable spaces on the interior. The **bay depth**, the distance from the tenant side of a corridor wall to the exterior face of the building (or the other corridor wall, if interior space, as applicable) is an important factor because it can significantly impact the ability to lay out offices and other uses. **Columns**, the interior structural supports between floors, may also have an impact on the usefulness of space. If the columns are large or not spaced far apart, this may adversely impact the tenant's ability to use certain layouts. **Floor load**, or the capacity of a floor to hold non-structural weight placed on it, can also be a significant factor. A tenant with a large number of heavy items such as books, file storage or equipment will need to examine the floor load to determine if there is enough capacity to support the weight that the tenant intends to place on the floor. **Ceiling height,** which can provide significant additional vertical space, is also of concern to many tenants who have storage or other unusual height needs.

The majority of office buildings have **elevators**, but the speed and capacity of the elevators may be a relevant factor for some tenants -- multiple tenant facilities tend to have higher elevator use than single tenant facilities. **Heating, ventilation, air conditioning (HVAC) systems** are also typical in today's market. However, the type of system and the layout of the building can affect the effectiveness of the system. While older buildings typically have a single HVAC unit for the whole building, many modern buildings have separate units for different areas of the building and often have a number of control zones within each area. Obviously, more specific HVAC control and regulation may be attractive to a tenant.

Today, access to the internet is an integral part of many businesses and thus the availability of internet access, the manner of access (wireless, broadband, etc.) and the capacity (bandwidth) available is an important consideration to many office users.

There are also external factors that are of importance to tenants. **Parking** is always an important consideration. On-site parking, deck parking or off-site parking are all common types of parking. Each arrangement has an impact on rent and may have an impact on a tenant if they have frequent client visits or other mobility issues. For example, off-site parking may not prove acceptable for the tenant who has regular visitors and the cost of parking for employees may be a job attractiveness factor. The **amenities** that are located in the building or very nearby may also be a factor for many tenants. Office buildings are increasingly offering retail, food service, health club, delivery service and security services as amenities that are readily available even if the use of these amenities is not included in the rent.

Rent

Of course, rent is one of the major factors for consideration by a tenant. *The majority of office space is leased by the square foot, with rent generally being quoted as an annual rate per square foot, typically an amount per rentable square foot.* There are, however, instances where office space is leased on a flat rate or on some other price factor. As noted previously, rental rates may actually reflect qualitative differences in the office space and/or building itself or in the features or amenities associated with the office space. A building with adjacent surface parking and 24- hour security may well rent for more than an identical building which has off-site parking and no security. Thus, property features and amenities are market factors that influence rent. The amount of rent may also be influenced by other factors discussed in this section, such as how square footage was calculated, location, upfit arrangements and level of landlord service, as well as other factors.

Location

As is the case with any type of real estate, location is also a major factor to tenants when considering office space. The appearance and impression of the building may be important to some tenants who engage in frequent public contact, while this factor may not be very important to a tenant who is telemarketing. Convenience is a factor for all tenants. It is important that the office be convenient for workers and it may be important, depending on the tenant's customer interaction, that it be convenient for the customer as well. Thus, it is important to assess both the facility and the client or customer's needs regarding convenience. Often, in addition to building amenities, nearby amenities such as a gym, hotels, recreational facilities, theaters or government offices may be important. In any event, a broker working with a prospective office tenant should inquire of the client or customer beyond the basic rent and space requirements to determine what market factors, in addition to those that affect rent directly, are important to the tenant. When representing the landlord, it is important to good marketing that one understand the factors that affect the building or space in order that appropriate rental rates may be established and appropriate tenants may be clearly identified.

Level of Landlord Service

When deciding to offer a tenancy or deciding between tenancies, the level of landlord service should also be considered. Services provided, or not provided, by the landlord can have a significant bearing on the total cost of space. Under a **full service lease** the landlord provides all cleaning services, utilities and other services attendant to the tenancy — basically, all expenses of occupancy are included in the rent. These leases obviously have higher rental rates than leases where the tenant is expected to separately arrange for these services. Thus, differences in the level of service provided by landlords are factors to be considered in positioning space for rent or deciding upon space.

Similarly, a landlord must consider if they will offer to make **tenant improvements** for a tenant or if they will require the tenant to make any desired improvements to a space. If a landlord offers to make tenant improvements, there is usually factored into the rent an **upfit allowance** for tenant improvements, expressed as a number of dollars per square foot.

Example: Landlord A tells a tenant that they will lease 1200 rentable square feet of space at $20.00 per square foot with an upfit allowance of $3.00 per usable square foot. If there is a core factor of 12%, there are 1071 usable square feet (1200   1.12= 1071). This means that the annual rent payable by the tenant will be $24,000 per year (1200 rentable square feet x $20.00 per rentable square feet) and the upfit allowance will be $3,213.00 (1071 x $3.00 per usable square foot).

From both the landlord's and the tenant's perspective, it is important to be clear if the allowance is granted per rentable square foot or per usable square foot. Obviously, an allowance per usable square foot is smaller than one on the same space calculated per rentable square foot. The positioning of rentable space in the marketplace or the comparison of options for lease provisions by a tenant is not complete without addressing tenant improvement issues, as well as the potential impact on total space cost of "financed" tenant improvements.

Common Special Office Lease Provisions

Even though the parties to commercial leases have great flexibility in negotiating lease terms, there are certain "business terms" in office leases that are regularly negotiated. A landlord should make decisions on how to handle these matters prior to putting space on the market and a tenant should take the different approaches to these matters into account when evaluating different proposals for office space. Two common special provisions frequently included in office leases are those relating to *rent increases* and a *tenant's sharing of property ownership and/or operation costs*. These are discussed briefly below.

Rent escalator provisions. *Office leases commonly include rent escalator provisions that call for the rent to increase (or decrease) a prescribed amount at set intervals.*

Example: A tenant's lease calls for rent in the amount of $20.00 per rentable square foot for an area of 2500 rentable square feet. The lease also provides that rent will increase at the end of the first year by 3% and at the end of each year thereafter the rent will be adjusted by an amount equal to the increase or decrease in the consumer price index (CPI) from the end of the first year of the term to the end of the second year of the term. The lease was signed on January 1, 2010. The original rent under this lease was $50,000.00 per year. On January 1, 2011 the rent increased to $51,500.00 ($50,000 x 1.03). On January 1, 2012, the rent will increase or decrease by a percentage that will be determined by taking the difference between the consumer price index for December 2011 and the consumer price index for December 2010. In this example, the lease provides for a **fixed rent escalator** (3%) for the increase at the end of the first year and an **indexed rent escalator** (based on increases or decreases in the CPI) for adjustments at the end of subsequent years.

Rent escalators have many variations but most often provide for either a fixed percentage or flat amount increase per period or provide for an increase that is tied to and determined by the increase (or decrease) in an index like the consumer price index. It should be noted that there are multiple consumer price indicators which change at different rates, such that the choice of a particular consumer price index is a business decision in and of itself.

Pass through provisions. Office leases also commonly contain provisions that allow a landlord to pass along to the tenant some or all of the cost of operating or owning the property. These **"pass through" provisions** can take many different forms. Matters that are typically passed through to the tenant are ad valorem property taxes, insurance, utility costs and operating and management costs. Such provisions may call for all of these expenses to be passed through to the tenants (usually in a ratio of their rentable square footage to the total square footage of the building), with the total amount of the expenses for the building being divided among the tenants based on the amount of space they occupy. The type and scope of expenses passed through continues to change and agents should be aware of what is included in "pass throughs". Today, some leases never call for capital expenditures (expansion or remodeling) to be included on pass throughs. In other circumstances, the landlord may agree to assume the liability for the current amount of each of these items and only will charge the tenant for their pro rata share of any increases in these amounts over a determined base year (usually the first year of the lease). This type of provision is known as a **"pass through with a base year stop."** It is also possible that a lease may "mix and match" the types of provisions, allowing, for example, for a total pass through of taxes and a pass through with a base year stop for operating expenses and insurance.

RETAIL PROPERTIES OR SPACE

Retail Space Classifications

Retail space is space that is used to offer and sell goods or services to the consuming public. Retail space is broadly classified into three categories of space, defined largely by the style and layout of the facility: (1) Shopping centers (which includes malls); (2) stand-alone retail facilities; and (3) strip or cluster retail facilities.

Shopping Centers. There are six general types of shopping centers:
1. the **super-regional shopping center,** which has three or more anchor tenants in excess of 100,000 square feet and a large variety of other products and services in smaller shops;
2. the **regional shopping center,** which usually has one or two anchor tenants in excess of 100,000 and a gross retail area of up to 1,000,000 square feet;
3. the **community shopping center,** which usually is built around a supermarket or junior department store, has a variety of shops and a gross retail area of up to 300,000 square feet;
4. the **neighborhood shopping center,** which is built around a grocery store or drug store, has goods and services targeted to the immediate neighborhood and gross retail area of up to 100,000 square feet;
5. the **strip center,** which has miscellaneous anchors and usually a gross retail area under 20,000 square feet;
6. the **specialty or theme center,** which usually has no anchor and is consistent in terms of either architecture or tenants, thus creating a desired theme or atmosphere.

Of course, there are other mixed formats of retail shopping centers in addition to these broad categories, and as well, there is an increasing incidence of the mixing of office, retail and residential uses in mixed use projects (as noted earlier).

Stand-alone retail facilities. As the classification name implies, these are single use buildings devoted to the sale of goods and services to the consuming public. A majority of retail space in this country falls into this category.

Strip or cluster retail facilities. These may be defined as a series of proximately located but independently developed retail facilities that have no common management or marketing.

Factors Affecting the Value and Desirability of Retail Space

Most retail space is leased from the property owner by the user of the space and most of the key factors relating to retail space concern factors important to retail tenants. In view of this, and the fact that the value of retail space being sold is determined primarily by the marketability of the space to tenants, this discussion of retail space focuses primarily on the leasing of such space.

Location

Location is by far the most important factor to retail tenants. While the factors considered by retailers in making their location determinations are somewhat similar, the mix of factors considered and the emphasis placed upon each is unique with each retailer. That is to say, each retailer has its own way of applying the "tools of the trade" to determine suitable locations. For example, most retailers use demographic information in some capacity to make location decisions. However, some retailers look at age statistics, some look at income statistics, some look at home ownership statistics; and some look at a mix of some or all of the above (or other matters such as level of education). Similarly, while traffic counts may be important to some retailers who rely upon a flow of traffic for their customers, other retailers are more interested in the number of people who are located within their defined trade area.

Even matters which may define a retailer's trade area may differ from retailer to retailer and many factors can determine a retailer's trade area, including traffic patterns, location of their competition, tenant mix in the area, employment patterns in the locale and income levels, to name but a few. While visibility and accessibility are important to most all retailers, some retailers who are "point of destination" retailers, are not as concerned with these matters because people coming to buy their goods and services seek them out specifically for their goods and services, not because of the relationship to another facility or their particular location. For example, a specialty cigar store may be a point of destination retailer, meaning their customers come for the product and for the specific store and thus seek the destination, not only convenience.

Many retail tenants rely heavily upon demographic information in making their decisions regarding location of a facility. **Demographic information** is information regarding the makeup of the population in a defined area surrounding the site. Demographic information may be derived using any number of criteria (income, age, social relationships, etc.) and may cover a number of areas such as an area with a certain number of miles radius, an area defined by a series of census tracts, or an area defined by the amount of time it takes to drive to the defined location. Demographic information often includes information such as age, racial composition, household makeup, religion, or other information which might be susceptible to being used improperly to discriminate. Agents using or working with demographic information which contains this type of information should be mindful of the manner in which they present and use the information (see also Chapter 18- Fair Housing & Laws Against Discrimination.). REALTORS' using demographic information should be aware of the guidance in Standard of Practice 10-3 under Article 10 of the *REALTOR' Code of Ethics* which indicates that **in a commercial transaction**, a REALTOR' is permitted to provide demographic information on the conditions that: (i) the information is needed to assist with the transaction; (ii) the information is not to be used for a discriminatory purpose in violation of Article 10; (iii) the information is obtained or derived from a recognized, reliable, independent, and impartial source; (iv) any additions, deletions, modifications, interpretations, or other changes shall be disclosed in reasonable detail.

Most retailers have developed (or should have developed) a profile of their typical customers and their willingness to travel to obtain the goods and services offered by the retailer. The travel profile of their typical customer defines a **trade area**, the area from which a retailer may draw customers. Trade areas differ greatly depending on the type of retailer. By studying demographic data regarding an area and by being familiar with retailers' general customer profiles and trade area definitions, an agent marketing a space or working with a retailer can adequately identify the potential of a market for a number of retail uses.

Of course, demographics are not the only location-related factors looked at by retailers. Many retailers rely upon automobile traffic for their customers (e.g., convenience stores and fast food restaurants) and, accordingly, **traffic counts** are important to them. Traffic counts are a determination of the average daily number of cars passing a site, usually made by the local or state department of transportation. Many retailers will require a certain traffic count before they will consider a site for their use.

Accessibility, that is the ease of access to the site or facility from major traffic arteries, is also important to retailers. Closely related to accessibility is the concept of **visibility**. Visibility means exactly what it sounds like — how readily apparent is the retailer to the public passing by or seeking to find it. A shop that is located in the far corner of a shopping center behind a number of trees and which cannot be seen from the road driving by has low visibility (and may prove to be an undesirable location).

"**Signage**," or the ability of a retailer to erect or install a readily visible sign is very important to most retailers. Often, the ability to obtain signage is regulated by local ordinance (a sign ordinance) and may also be regulated by private use restrictions. Sometimes, good signage rights may offset poor site visibility by making the retailer still easy to locate by the consuming public because the sign will be readily visible even though the retail location itself is not.

Size of the Space and Method of Square Footage Determination

The size of the property and how well that space suits a tenant's needs is obviously very important to any retail tenant, especially since *the majority of retail space is leased by the square foot, with rent being quoted as an annual dollar amount per square foot.*

A broker working with retail space also has to be concerned with how to measure the square footage of the space, or if working with a tenant or buyer, how the square footage of the space was determined. There is **not** a universally recognized standard for measuring retail space, as there is for office space (the BOMA Standard). Accordingly, the consistent application of a method of measurement by a listing agent and the inquiry by the buyer's or tenant's agent as to how the square footage number was determined becomes a very critical determination. As a listing agent, the requirement is that one be accurate and consistent if advertising or citing square footage. As a buyer's/tenant's agent, the requirement is that you assist your client in making an apples-to-apples determination regarding square footage.

Property Features and Amenities

In shopping center retail, **bay depth and width**, which is the depth and width of the available space, are very important factors because the retailer must be able to fit their offered goods and services into the space. **Frontage**, the width of the retail space that is exposed to customer traffic, and that may provide visibility, is also an important feature of retail space. Depending upon the type of retailer, the **storage area** and rear door or **loading area also** may be very important. Many retailers deal in goods that require large inventories and, therefore, storage is important. Many retailers also deal in goods that require frequent shipping by large trucks and thus the accessibility and availability of a loading area may be important as well.

Rent

The amount of proposed rent (for a prospective tenant) or possible rent (for a prospective buyer-investor) is obviously always a critical factor. As was noted in the discussion of office space rent, the amount of rent is affected by many other factors, including location, property features, and market conditions. *Rent in retail leases is most often quoted as an **annual dollar amount per square foot**. However, total space cost, including common area maintenance changes, upfit costs and proper due diligence on these costs must be taken into account.*

Retail or Tenant Mix

Another factor often considered by retailers is the **retail or tenant mix**, the number and type of retailers that are located in a shopping center, cluster or trade area. Some types of retailers are good draws for other retailers and other types are competition, so the tenant mix of a center or trade area can be a significant factor for a retailer looking to lease space and also should be considered by a landlord and their agent when marketing space.

Zoning and Other Land Use Regulations

Although zoning and land use restrictions are important factors for any type of property, these issues arise more frequently with regard to retail properties than office or industrial properties. For stand alone retailers, the suitability of the existing building for their use as well as any applicable zoning or land use regulations are very important. If the site is vacant and being considered for retail use, the applicable land use restrictions are paramount. Today, land use restrictions which prohibit or restrict certain uses are very common and must be investigated and taken into account in marketing or considering any particular space. Further these types of restrictions are becoming increasing complex. Most major retailers who build stand-alone facilities today have a prototype building and, accordingly, the suitability of the site for that building, taking into account land use restrictions, will be a determining factor, even if all other important factors favor the site.

Utilities

Typically, retail space is leased as vacant, unfinished space. An unfinished floor, demising walls (the walls between tenants) and basic utility sources are all that is provided. It is up to the tenant to "create" their space within that shell. Accordingly, the **utilities** that are provided (i.e., electric, plumbing and heating and air) are a significant issue. Often, access to these utilities will be provided and the tenant will be expected to install their own electrical systems and meter, their own plumbing systems (including any restrooms) and water meter, and their own HVAC system to serve their space. The cost of connecting to these facilities can often be a significant upfit cost which should not be overlooked.

Parking

Finally, **parking** is very important to retail tenants. Even if a retailer has good visibility, accessibility and signage, they may have problems if there is not adequate parking to accommodate the planned use. Many zoning ordinances regulate the number of parking spaces that must be provided. However, it must be kept in mind that the number of spaces that a retail establishment needs is often dictated by the use and may be greater than the number permitted by regulation. For example, a retail specialty store requires fewer parking spaces than a restaurant. While parking for the facility may have been adequate when the space was used as a specialty store, a change in use to a restaurant may cause parking problems.

Common Special Retail Lease Provisions

Just as with leases for other types of commercial property, commercial retail leases are not governed by any statute and are purely a matter of contract — the parties can agree to anything that they desire so long as it does not offend public policy. While this fact creates free negotiation as with office leases, there are certain "business terms" in retail leases that are regularly negotiated. A landlord should make decisions on how it intends to handle these matters prior to taking space to market and a tenant should take the different approaches to these matters into account when making a decision between tenancies. A few of these frequently included special retail lease provisions are discussed below. Most retail landlords will have their own form leases which deal with many considerations. Most significant retail tenants will have their own lease forms as well. Typically, such landlords and tenants are willing to negotiate on a limited number of items, but there are certain common subjects which all leases typically address.

Percentage Rent Provision. While percentage rent provisions can be structured in a number of fashions, the basic concept is that the landlord will receive, as additional rent, over and above the stated rent per square foot, a percentage of the tenant's sales over a certain predefined amount which is often referred to as the "breakpoint".

Common Area Maintenance (CAM) Charge Provision. Typically, retail leases in shopping centers or other multi-tenant facilities will have a common area maintenance (CAM) charge provision in the lease. The purpose of this provision is to require the tenants to pay, typically on a *pro rata* basis, some or all of the costs of operating and maintaining the shopping center. Items typically covered in a CAM charge are maintenance, landscaping, security, management fees, parking lot maintenance, trash removal and other common area expenses (sometimes including even capital improvements). While a budget for marketing the shopping center may be included among CAM charges, many modern shopping centers will provide separately in their leases for a **marketing fund charge**, which all tenants pay. The shopping center management then uses the monies collected through these charges to market the shopping center as a whole. CAM charges as a total of occupancy costs should be carefully considered by a tenant.

Tenant Exclusivity Provisions. Retail leases frequently contain tenant exclusivity provisions. Some landlords will promise to tenants, or may have already promised to other tenants, that certain stores or retail activities are prohibited in the property (and perhaps also on other property owned by the landlord nearby) for a period of time. For example, a landlord may agree with a restaurant that they will not allow any food preparation activities by any of the other tenants. When a drugstore with a lunch counter comes along as a prospective tenant, this previously granted exclusive food preparation rights provision in the restaurant's lease will not allow the drugstore lunch counter and may alter the drugstore's plans for the site or may cause them to go to another site. Such *"exclusives"* are often granted by reference to store names (to exclude specific competitors), store types (to exclude types of similar retailers), product lines (to exclude the sale of popular products by another store) or product types. Quite often these provisions can be very broad and at the same time very specific. Thus, it is always important when looking at any prospective retail tenancy to inquire as to any exclusives that may have been granted.

INDUSTRIAL PROPERTIES

Industrial facilities are typically defined as facilities used for the manufacturing, storage or distribution of goods.

Industrial Property Classifications

While industrial properties come in all shapes and sizes, there are some broad classifications that can be used a rule of thumb for typing industrial property.

Bulk Warehouse. Bulk warehouse space is probably the simplest type of industrial facility. Typically it involves no more than enclosed space that is used to store materials and/or finished goods.

Office Warehouse. Office warehouse space is warehouse space that contains some level of office space (perhaps for managing distribution) in the same facility as the warehouse. Both bulk warehouse and office warehouse space are typically very large and are of brick, block, tilt-up concrete or metal construction and are located near significant thoroughfares or rail lines for easy access and shipping.

Large Manufacturing. Large manufacturing facilities house operations that manufacture products, parts and finished goods. These facilities are typically extremely large, often as large as 2,000,000 square feet, and are on large tracts of land to accommodate the facility and the shipping and receiving that are necessary to the manufacturing operation. These facilities may often be located near rail lines in order to provide for receipt of bulk materials used in the manufacturing process.

Small Manufacturing. Small manufacturing facilities also house operations that manufacture products, parts and finished goods, but they are just smaller than large manufacturing facilities.

Multi-tenant Industrial. Multi-tenant industrial facilities are among the smallest facilities. They are often used for satellite distribution or small manufacturing operations and often have high ceilings to accommodate significant storage in a small space.

Research and Development. Research and development facilities are a hybrid of office and manufacturing and usually involve low pollution, clean manufacturing. The interior finishes of these buildings are usually of better quality than other industrial facilities since there is usually a high concentration of office personnel on site. These facilities are often found in business park settings and the buildings have a higher quality of construction than many other industrial facilities.

Industrial Park. A mix of the above-described types of industrial properties, or a cluster of facilities of any one type may be developed as an industrial park. An industrial park is akin to a planned residential community in that there is a master plan of development that is coordinated. Quite often there are architectural guidelines as to the type of construction that is permitted and there may be restrictions on the type of use that may be undertaken in the park. There may also be amenities associated with the park and even an owners association to administer and maintain the park and its amenities.

Factors Affecting the Value and Desirability of Industrial Space

As with office and retail space, industrial space is frequently leased to users and many of the key factors relating to industrial space are those that are especially important to tenants. Even the value of an industrial property occupied by an owner-user is greatly affected by the desirability of such space to prospective tenants. Thus, this discussion focuses primarily on the leasing of industrial space.

Size of the Space and Method of Square Footage Determination

As with other types of commercial properties, the size of the space is a very important factor to any user, whether a tenant or owner. Also, as is the case with retail space, special attention must be paid to the method of square footage determination because there is no universally recognized standard for measuring industrial space. Agents must always be sure they understand the method used for determining the square footage of industrial space for not only the particular property in question, but also for any similar properties being used for comparison purposes. Rents for industrial space are also generally quoted as an annual dollar amount per square foot, which makes size and method of square footage determination especially important.

Property Features and Amenities

Building features are a major consideration in industrial facilities since they are often used for activities such as manufacturing, warehousing and distribution where layout and functionality are primary considerations. Whether marketing a facility or attempting to locate a facility for a client or customer, it is very important to understand the features that are present or are important to a client or customer and how they might benefit or hinder the use of the facility by one's client or customer.

Most industrial facilities have simple structural features. Foundations are usually dirt, asphalt or concrete, with load-bearing concrete being the most common feature. Exterior walls are typically made of metal, brick, block or concrete. As the aesthetics of industrial facilities have become more important to users and regulatory authorities, types of exterior wall construction are often mixed to create a more attractive outside finish. Interior walls are often moveable walls or partitions, installed for flexibility in layout and use;, however, fixed, floor to ceiling walls are not uncommon.

A **free span** building, which has no supports across the building, provides the most clear and unobstructed space and thus is the most flexible with regard to potential uses. If a building is **spanned**, it has columns to support the structure and **column spacing** becomes important — the more columns and the closer together they are, the more limited the uses that may be made of the space. The number and type of **loading docks**, which have large doors and permit easy loading of trains and trucks for the delivery and transport of materials, may also be an important consideration. In some warehouse facilities, there may even be **drive-in doors** which allow for trucks to drive into the building to be loaded and unloaded. If a facility is to be used for warehousing, or if the facility is to have drive-in doors and truck traffic inside the facility, the **floor load capacity**, the ability of the floor to bear weight, becomes a significant factor. A facility built for the warehousing of foam rubber products may not have been constructed with sufficient floor load capacity to support the warehousing of textile machinery (without significant damage to the floor). It is important in dealing with industrial real estate seller/landlords and buyer/tenants to be aware of these considerations and the needs of the particular client or customer with respect to those considerations.

Ceiling height is of particular concern in industrial facilities. The **clear height** of a facility (the height at which no portion of the ceiling structure interferes with the use of the space) can be particularly important in warehouse and distribution facilities since that height will dictate how much storage is truly available.

HVAC systems are frequently zoned in industrial buildings, particularly office warehouse and manufacturing facilities. Different uses may require differing capacities for heating and cooling and thus zoning of the system is appropriate. For example, the office section of an office warehouse will often require more temperature regulation than the warehouse section that is used for storing a non-temperature sensitive material such as lumber. Capacity of the system to heat or cool may also be a special consideration for some intended uses. For example, a manufacturer whose intended use would produce heat will require more cooling capacity than one whose use does not produce heat.

The type of **power supply** can be important to industrial facilities. Significant manufacturing operations often require three-phase power which may or may not be available from the power company at any given location. In addition, different uses within an industrial facility may require either single-phase or three-phase power and accordingly the electrical design of the building may have been paneled so as to permit different power types in different areas of the facility. More often than not, the electrical layout of a facility is specifically designed to the user's needs and thus must be carefully examined if a change in use is contemplated. The **lighting array** and foot candle level (the unit of measurement for lighting) in an industrial facility may be of significance to many users as different uses require different levels of lighting. For example, warehouse uses may not require the level of lighting that electronics manufacturing requires.

Similarly, the availability of **water and sewer connections** can be an important factor. Many industrial facilities require large amounts of water for their operation and the existence of an adequate water supply may have an impact on the usability of the facility. As well, facilities that use large amounts of water generate large amounts of waste water and thus the capacity of the sanitary sewer or other disposal system can be a critical factor.

Fire protection systems are another common feature of industrial facilities that may pose special considerations. For example, manufacturing operations that use a significant amount of sensitive equipment may not find a water-based sprinkler system a satisfactory fire prevention/containment system since the water will damage the sensitive equipment. They may instead prefer a dry or gas-based fire prevention/containment system. Industrial facility features are often very specific to the user. Different uses may require different fire code compliance and thus the adequacy of the systems in place for potential uses may become a question which should be taken into account in the marketing of and disclosure about a given property.

Location

Manufacturers who generate a large amount of solid waste will be concerned about **proximity to waste disposal facilities** that can accept the type of waste that they generate. Warehouse, distribution and manufacturing uses are going to be particularly concerned about the **proximity and accessibility of rail, air, trucking and other transportation outlets** so that they can get their products readily to the markets that they are serving. While warehouse uses are often not very labor intensive, manufacturing uses are often very labor intensive and accordingly those type users are concerned with the facility's **proximity to a qualified and available labor force**. The type of labor force required may differ greatly from user to user. For example, research and development users typically are looking for an educated, white collar workforce while many manufacturing users are looking for skilled and unskilled blue collar workers. Thus, an understanding of the labor force available to a particular facility is important to its marketing or selection.

Environmental Considerations

*Existing industrial facilities are perhaps more prone to **environmental considerations** than any other type of commercial property.* This consideration becomes particularly acute where the facility is older and has been used for manufacturing for many years. Simply put, environmental regulations were not in existence or were not as stringent when many of these facilities were initially put into use as industrial facilities, and the likelihood that there may be environmental contamination on the site is more pronounced. Even with more recent facilities, the possibility for environmental contamination exists since industrial uses are more likely to involve hazardous materials. Thus, *when listing an industrial property, careful attention should be paid to making inquiry regarding environmental matters and disclosures regarding environmental matters should be handled very carefully. Agents representing tenants looking at industrial facilities should have an awareness of these issues and should make sure their clients are aware of the need to consider environmental factors with regard to industrial property.*

Rent

As with any type of commercial property, the amount of proposed rent (for a prospective tenant) or possible rent (for a prospective buyer-investor) is of paramount importance. An appropriate rental amount can only be determined by considering all property features and all relevant market factors, including the amount of rent being paid for comparable properties in the area. As previously mentioned, rent is most commonly quoted as an annual dollar amount per square foot.

Business Incentives

Finally, industrial facilities seem more likely than other types of property to bring users who may qualify for **business incentives**. The state of North Carolina and many municipalities will offer incentives for job creation and other economic activities (often related to industrial property) to businesses locating in their area. These incentives may involve *ad valorem* tax reductions, tax credits, job training and other matters. These incentive programs may also be targeted at specific areas of a municipality or the state.[10] Accordingly, when dealing with industrial facilities or industrial users, it is important, both as a landlord and as a tenant, to be aware of any available incentives.

Leases for Industrial Properties

Industrial leases are often the most "straight forward" of commercial leases. Often the lease is for the whole site and facility, which requires the parties to make a determination as to whom will be responsible for the various costs of ownership and maintenance of the facility.

An **industrial gross lease** is a type of industrial lease which commonly requires that the landlord be responsible for structural maintenance, taxes and insurance for the facility and that the tenant be responsible for landscaping and routine facility maintenance. An **industrial net lease** commonly makes the tenant responsible for most matters related to the ownership and use of the property including maintenance (often including paving of parking and driveway areas), taxes and insurance while the landlord retains responsibility for structural maintenance, including capital expenditures for replacement of major building systems such as HVAC systems. Of course, rents under an industrial net lease will be lower than under an industrial gross lease because the tenant has more financial responsibilities for the facility under the net lease as compared to the gross lease. There are many variations on these basic themes, and accordingly, an agent must be prepared to understand the impact on rental rate and expense obligations resulting from a change in allocation of responsibilities as to these items between a landlord and tenant.

LAND

Land is the most complex type of commercial property because it is possible to put land to any use that is permissible under applicable public land use regulations and private use restrictions. In addition, it is frequently possible to obtain a change in public land use restrictions, such as zoning, which may permit more or different uses. As can be seen from the previous discussions of other categories of commercial property, the factors that are important to users of each property type are varied. It is perhaps for this reason that many agents who deal with commercial land specialize in a particular category of use. Brokers dealing in land must have adequate knowledge to understand the various potential uses of a parcel of land, which potentially may include any commercial or residential use, and how the applicable regulations, restrictions and ordinances impact such potential uses and possible users. They must understand all the physical characteristics of and locational factors affecting the parcel of land in question because these are relevant with regard to every potential commercial or residential use. In this context, they must also understand the market factors which relate to the property and how those factors affect the ultimate usability of the property in the context of any potential user's needs.

Factors Affecting the Value and Desirability of Land

Highest and Best Use

In the context of a complete understanding of property characteristics, land use regulations/ restrictions, locational factors, economic/market and other factors, an analysis of the **highest and best use** of the property can be made. *A property's highest and best use is considered to be that reasonable and probable use of the land that results in the highest present value of the land in view of the various legally permissible, physically possible and economically feasible uses.* Highest and best use analysis is a complex, but critically important step that should be undertaken only by qualified persons. Such an analysis involves consideration of many factors, including financial analysis of different potential uses. A discussion of highest and best use analysis methodology is beyond the scope of this text. It should be noted, however, that a highest and best use analysis does not presume that the current permitted use of the property is its highest and best use. Rather, the analysis seeks to determine the use that will be most beneficial to the value of the property in its market context. If the perceived most beneficial use is currently not permitted, any analysis must also consider the feasibility of zoning or other land use regulation changes that would make such desired use permissible. A highest and best use analysis also does not seek to define a specific use (such as a drugstore), but seeks to define a category of use (such as retail) that would be the highest and best use. Even if an agent does not personally perform the highest and best use analysis of a parcel of land, it is imperative that the agent have a thorough knowledge of all the factors that affect the value and desirability of the land and that are considered in such analysis.

Land Use Restrictions

In determining what uses may be suitable for a piece of land, *it is essential to determine what private and public land use restrictions apply.* This determination should be one of the first steps taken by a listing agent when marketing a piece of land. A broker marketing a vacant tract of land must be familiar with the zoning of the property and the uses that are permitted under that classification. A broker must also have a general understanding of the zoning and regulatory structure applicable to the property in order to be able to assist a seller or buyer with a determination of potential additional uses of a property which might be obtained by taking advantage of any available procedures for obtaining a change in permitted land uses.

If a property is zoned to allow multifamily development but has a private use restriction that limits that property to single family residential uses, it cannot and should not be marketed as multi-family land. Admittedly, making the determination of what private use restrictions affect a property may be a significant undertaking and likely will require the assistance of a real estate attorney. However, it is only when armed with this information that a broker can properly market a tract of land. In addition to possibly causing a broker to advertise a property for a prohibited use, a lack of understanding of the property's restrictions may adversely affect the uses for which the property is marketed and the value of the property to the owner as either a seller or landlord.

A similar analysis must be undertaken with other land use regulations (for example, subdivision ordinances, wetlands regulations, watershed regulations, etc.) that may directly impact the use(s) available for the property.

Acreage and Encumbrances

One of the first determinations a broker needs to make in connection with evaluating land is the number of **net acres** that are available. The first step in this process is to examine the deed to the property or a survey of the property. Quite often, these instruments will state the property's acreage. A broker must also be careful to inquire as to whether the seller has acquired any additional property or disposed of any of the property since the deed or survey. In reviewing the deed or survey, an agent should look to determine if any of the property is within a public right of way or street. *Acreage within a public right of way is not included in net acres since it is not available for use by a purchaser of the property.* A visual inspection, a conversation with the seller and a review of any survey should also be undertaken to determine if there are other rights of way that may affect the property. (Note that a right of way may not be evident from a visual inspection.) For example, a 98-foot power company easement traversing the property may have a significant impact on what portion of the property may be used and what uses the remaining unaffected portion of the property may support for development. In the event that a per acre offering price is to be considered, the broker involved in the transaction should assure that an attorney is involved in the preparation of the definition of "net acres" for purposes of the sales agreement. Preparation of this type of definition constitutes the practice of law and there is no more significant provision in a per acre sales agreement than the definition of the basis for calculating the price.

Physical Features

In addition to the size of a tract of land, there are often other physical features of the property that are extremely important to a determination of its market position and value . A few of these include the **shape of the tract**, the **road frontage** of the tract, and its **topography**, **soil characteristics**, and **drainage**. A site's physical characteristics may greatly restrict or enhance possible uses or may substantially affect site preparation and infrastructure costs.

Location

Location is always a critically important characteristic of any parcel of land, and this is especially true if the property has any potential retail use, as noted previously in the discussion of retail properties. Factors such as traffic patterns and counts, visibility, and demographics are particularly important for potential retail properties. Regardless of the intended use, general compatibility of the proposed use with existing and likely future neighboring uses is an important consideration.

Site Access

While it may seem rather obvious, and in many cases the determination will be easy, a broker dealing with land should also verify a property's **legal access** to a public street and the nature of that legal access. More often than not, legal access to a public street or road exists because the property abuts the public street or road. However, access can at times be provided by an access easement or by easement over private streets that have access to a public street. Legal access is essential to property as it cannot be financed and may not be usable without it. The best way to determine if there is legal access if there is a question is to obtain a copy of the survey of the property (to see if access is shown). One may also obtain a copy of the owner's title insurance policy to determine if there is an exception for access (in which case there is not access).

Closely related to legal access is the concept of **practical access**. There are occasions where a property has practical access, for example, a driveway used to access the property, when in fact the property has no legal access because there is nothing in writing or on the public record to establish that access. There are also occasions where a property may have legal access but very little practical access.

A property with long frontage on a controlled access road and only a small frontage on a side street that may not be sufficient to meet driveway permit requirements may have very little practical access. Practical access to non-residential streets is controlled by the applicable department of transportation (state or municipal) through the **driveway permit** process. There are criteria which must be met, in the interest of traffic safety and welfare, in order to obtain a driveway permit to obtain practical access. Sometimes the value of a piece of land can be significantly impacted by the location(s) of permitted driveways and thus the nature of the practical access is a significant consideration. On a related note, the location of street intersections is also controlled by the applicable department of transportation and there are also established criteria for allowing these intersections. If the use and development of a piece of property could require a road and intersection, a determination regarding the ability to create the intersection is absolutely necessary.

Transportation Systems and Transportation Improvement Plans

The **transportation systems** supporting a tract of land have an immense effect on its use and value as a commercial property. The availability of an adequate road network and the proximity of major highways, rail transportation and air transportation all are important factors to consider in connection with any tract of land.

A broker also should become aware of any impact that transportation improvements may have on the property. The **transportation improvement plan (TIP)** for an area (there is usually a state and a local TIP) will provide information on pending transportation improvement plans for roads and other transportation facilities in the area. The TIP will also give some indication of the priority and proposed timing of these plans. Transportation improvements may directly affect a property, as is the case where the road the property is on is planned to be widened and part of the property taken, or may indirectly affect a property by providing better access or adversely affecting future access to the property (such as when all or a portion of the property frontage may be proposed to be controlled access).

It should be noted that some zoning ordinances have what are called **transitional setbacks**. Under a zoning ordinance, roadways are typically classified into types depending upon the amount of traffic that they carry or are expected to carry. *A transitional setback restriction provides for an area adjacent to the street within which no development is permitted because the area is expected in the future to be taken and used to widen the street.* Transitional setbacks are larger on streets with higher expected traffic flows. The current construction setbacks are determined from the boundary of the transitional setback, which may be several feet from the current public right of way. Accordingly, a property that is subject to a transitional setback may have significantly less usable area than would readily appear, because no development is permitted in the transitional setback area.

Marketing Considerations for Land

Since land can be put to so many uses, and since there is rarely only one specific use that is permissible or beneficial, a determination regarding the marketing of land involves consideration of all of the factors outlined above. It also involves, to a great extent, consideration of many of the relevant factors affecting the value and desirability of each of the major property types. Once a determination has been made as to the most desirable use of the land (office, retail, industrial, multifamily residential, single family residential, etc.), attention should be focused on the marketing considerations and factors for properties with that type of land use. *Brokers are again reminded and cautioned that land is the most complicated product type. The listing and marketing of land should never be taken lightly.*

SPECIALTY PROPERTIES

There are certain types of commercial real estate that constitute their own specialty niche. Often, the reason for the specialty niche is because there is a relatively narrow market for the type of property and, accordingly, there are not as many transactions or players in the marketplace as there are for other types of property. **Examples** of these property types include **golf courses**, **amusement parks**, **sports facilities** (and other recreational facilities), **churches and synagogues**, **entertainment facilities** and **hospitals**. As can be seen from the nature of the examples, there are not large numbers of these type facilities regularly marketed and there is not a large market for them. A broker attempting to deal with one of these types of property should make sure that they have available persons who have experience in dealing with these types of property to use as a resource.

There are also other areas of commercial real estate such as **hotel properties** and **multifamily (apartment) properties** that are becoming especially specialized. The hotel and multifamily markets have become increasingly nationalized. Institutional investors have increasingly become the primary players in these fields, which creates a different set of market factors and user and seller motivations than may be present in a typical commercial real estate transaction. Therefore, as is the case with the other specialty niche product types noted above, a broker presented with a hotel or multifamily property will be well served to seek the assistance of an agent with some significant level of experience in dealing with multifamily or hotel properties.

Hybrid Properties

Finally, there is an increasing tendency in the commercial real estate market to develop "**hybrid properties**;" that is, types of real estate development that contain some or all of a mix of the various types of commercial real estate. Increasingly in urban areas, retail, residential and office uses are being combined in variations on a "live-work" theme. In many of these properties, the same space is used for a retail or office venture and the residence of the business person is also in or above the same space. Office space and warehouse space are increasingly being combined in what is often referred to as **"flex" space** — space that is designed to provide quality office (and often showroom) space as well as warehouse space. This combination trend is not lost on retailers either as they seek to reduce warehouse space, using more and smaller distribution centers and increasing inventory capacity at their retail stores to reduce warehouse costs.

Thus, while the discussion in this section has focused on the four major types of commercial real estate, it is increasingly the case that properties are serving multiple uses. Dealing with properties that have multiple uses requires an agent bring to bear a depth of knowledge of each of the types of property involved, each type's significant market factors and the relevant points for negotiation in dealing with each type of property. The commercial real estate market changes on a daily basis and creative and hybrid property uses are only limited by imagination and land use regulation. A competent agent keeps abreast of these changes and understands what they mean for the property that the agent is marketing or seeking to find.

MARKET COMPREHENSION AND ANALYSIS

Understanding Market Factor Concepts

The value and usefulness of a parcel of commercial real estate is not determined solely by its own attributes and features. Rather, the value of a parcel of commercial real estate is determined as well by a number of factors external to the property — factors that define its place in the market. A basic understanding of certain key market factor concepts is the underpinning of a successful commercial real estate practice.

Linkages

"Linkages" are relationships between land uses and other components of the market or submarket. They concern how necessary inputs — employees, resources, raw materials, services, amenities, information — get to a location from other areas of the market, and how outputs- products and services *get from the location to other areas of the market.*"[11] The ability to define, understand and analyze relevant linkages for a particular property is the crux of having a solid understanding of the property. The linkages that are relevant to a particular property are defined by the nature of the property. For example, two important linkages for a manufacturing facility are the time and distance traveled by the labor pool who will work in the factory and the relevant wage scale of that labor pool in the area. Data can be obtained regarding the average travel time to the facility for the typical worker, and data can also be obtained regarding the salary level of workers who would be available for the facility. Obtaining data of this nature as to each of the relevant linkages for a particular property and for similar properties in the area provides the information necessary to understand and compare the linkages for the particular property to those of the other similar properties to determine the relative desirability of the properties.

Demographics

As noted earlier, demographic information plays an important part in the analysis of many sites by sellers and users. Demographic information is information about population, employment, income, wages, home values, retail sales, growth trends and other statistics that is collected and reported for any given area (often broken down by census tract). Demographic information is very helpful in analyzing linkages that are defined for a property. If a user already has a definition of the profile of its client or customer base, demographics may be used to determine the presence or absence of persons with that profile.

Absorption

Absorption is the number of units (square feet, acres, apartments, etc.) that are used up or occupied over a defined time period. In order to determine absorption, one must determine how many units were in use (what was the occupancy rate) at the beginning of the time period desired to be measured and how many units were in use at the end of the time period to be measured. By looking at absorption, an agent can determine how much of the unit that they are measuring was used during the defined time period. If one also looks at the number of units produced during that time period, a determination can be made as to whether production is running ahead of absorption. If production is running ahead of absorption (assuming there are no units being taken out of the marketplace), there is likely to be a reduction in prices because unused supply will be growing (there will be more vacancies — more of what is being measured on the market). This analysis can be very helpful in determining how the larger market may have an impact on the property being marketed. This analysis can also assist an agent in determining where there may be opportunities for a property. If there is a "shortage" of a particular unit type in the market, it may be possible to position one's property to fill that shortage.

Other Factors

Each of the types of commercial real estate will have its own market factors that will be important from an analysis standpoint. Retailers will want to know about their trade area, sales volumes per square foot, growth trends and a number of other demographic analyses based upon the customer profile. Office users will want to know about the service area, demographics of the area and employment ratios. Industrial users will be very concerned with the labor pool, the industrial service area and transportation facilities. In each instance, the commercial real estate broker will need to know where to obtain the desired information (a chamber of commerce is an excellent source for much of this information) and will then, once obtained, need to know how to recognize what the information is saying and/or how to analyze it. These are not simple undertakings and a discussion of how to analyze such information is outside the scope of these materials. Prior to attempting to conduct any of these analyses, a broker who is not experienced should seek the assistance of an agent who is skilled in making such determinations and analyses.

Understanding Your Market

Defining A Market

Given the complexity of the commercial real estate market and the level of knowledge required to deal with any given type of commercial real estate, it is particularly important that a commercial real estate broker define a "market" in which he or she are going to practice. This market may be defined by geography, such as a section of a metropolitan area or a state, or it may be defined by a product type such as industrial real estate. In many instances a broker's "market" will be defined by both criteria (e.g., industrial real estate in the Charlotte to Greensboro I-85 corridor). In any event, it is critically important that a broker obtain, in addition to an understanding of all of the specifics elsewhere mentioned, market knowledge and people knowledge regarding their chosen "market".

Market Knowledge

Having knowledge of one's market does not necessarily mean committing to memory all of the relevant statistics affecting one's chosen marketplace. In fact, that would prove a counterproductive exercise as the information relevant to a marketplace is constantly changing. Nonetheless, it is never too soon for a commercial real estate broker to become familiar with all of the sources of statistics and information available regarding his or her marketplace. Resources for information regarding employment, information regarding population, demographic information, information regarding traffic and transportation facilities and other information relevant to linkages that affect one's chosen marketplace are of critical importance. In many instances, a chamber of commerce is a good resource for this information. There also may be other resources such as regional or municipal economic development organizations, government agencies, the Federal Reserve Bank and private information providers who are equally as valuable. In any event, it is important that these resources be identified, cultivated and understood.

In addition to these statistical information sources, there are also public record information sources that all commercial brokers should be aware of and capable of using. A large number of counties in North Carolina now have all or some of their public tax and land records available on the Internet via a Geographic Information System (GIS) or other services. In many instances, these systems allow a person to obtain title, tax, zoning, utility and other information regarding a property at one online location, with the information being depicted in easy to view graphic format (in addition to text). In addition, most North Carolina state administrative agencies now have web pages that provide a huge amount of information regarding the professionals and professions they regulate or the subject matter that is their jurisdiction. Finally, general media and media specific to the real estate industry or a particular segment thereof are often excellent sources of information for trends in the market or significant events. All of these resources contain valuable information that may be relevant to an agent's chosen marketplace and accordingly they should be used as resources.

There are a staggering number of information resources available to brokers today. The important exercise for the commercial real estate broker is to identify those resources that are both useful and relevant to the broker's chosen marketplace. Then, armed with those information resources, brokers can gain an understanding of their chosen marketplace.

People Knowledge

It is not enough to simply define a marketplace, acquire resources regarding the chosen marketplace and "sit there and wait for the phone to ring." There is a huge amount of information affecting every aspect of the commercial real estate market that is possessed by people and is only accessible via people. Accordingly, it is very important that a commercial real estate broker know and understand the people in their chosen marketplace. Regulatory offices that are responsible for land use regulation implementation are staffed by people who interpret and apply the rules and regulations. A familiarity with these people and how they approach their jobs is of significant importance in being able to understand, interpret and apply land use regulations. As well, there are "major" players in every marketplace who have large amounts of experience and knowledge and who also impact many things that go on in a marketplace. The ability to learn from these major players is an opportunity to advance one's knowledge by a significant number of years. As well, these major players are often at the forefront of what is happening in a marketplace, and often their decisions can directly affect a marketplace. Thus, knowing and/or watching these "major" players can greatly assist an agent in acquiring knowledge about what is going on in their chosen marketplace, thereby making them more effective.

PRICING AND ANALYSIS ISSUES

Sale Pricing of Commercial Properties

Regardless of the type of property involved, a seller typically will need competent advice regarding a property's probable sale price to establish an appropriate listing price, and a buyer will need similar advice in order to determine an appropriate amount to offer to purchase the property. As is thoroughly discussed in Chapter 8 on Brokerage Relationships, Chapter 9, Agency Contracts and Brokerage Practices, and Chapter 15 on Real Estate Valuation, which includes detailed coverage of Broker Price Opinions (BPOs) and Comparative Market Analyses (CMAs), *a real estate broker is generally expected to perform a BPO/CMA and provide seller or buyer clients with a reasonably accurate estimate of the probable sale price of a property, regardless of property type, unless a broker's general inexperience, inexperience with a particular property type or inadequate training as to the methodology required for the particular property type renders him incompetent to independently perform a proper BPO/CMA in a particular situation.* If not capable of performing a particular BPO/CMA for any of these reasons, then a broker should decline the assignment or obtain appropriate assistance from qualified persons to perform the BPO/CMA. To do otherwise would violate the Real Estate License Law prohibition against acting in an incompetent manner, and may also violate the License Law duty to avoid negligent misrepresentation and the agency law duty to exercise reasonable skill, care and diligence to serve a client.

Non-provisional and provisional brokers are expected to be able to either independently perform a BPO/CMA for a **residential 1-4 unit property** in a minimally competent manner or to obtain any needed assistance from a more experienced broker in order to complete an appropriate BPO/

CMA. These BPOs/CMAs will involve use of the *sales comparison approach* and, if a rental property is involved, likely also the *gross rent multiplier approach.*

A different situation often arises when dealing with a **commercial income-producing property (including residential properties with 5 or more units).** First of all, a residential broker with little or no experience in commercial brokerage should never undertake to independently perform a BPO/CMA for a commercial property. Moreover, a commercial broker with experience with only one type of property (e.g., retail) should probably not attempt to independently perform a BPO/CMA on another type of property (e.g., office). The reasons for such restraint are many. Developing an estimate of probable sale price for a commercial property often involves many factors that aren't present with small residential properties. There are major differences in factors considered among the various types of commercial properties. Virtually every commercial income-producing property will require a BPO/CMA that not only uses the *sales comparison approach*, but also uses the *income capitalization approach.* And don't forget the previously mentioned License Law prohibition against acting incompetently.

A broker needs to be certain he or she possesses the necessary education and experience to perform a BPO/CMA on a particular commercial property. Even a non-provisional broker with some commercial experience needs to be careful to accept BPO/CMA assignments only for those types of properties with which he or she has experience and only if they possess the necessary expertise to utilize properly the necessary methodology, especially the income capitalization approach.

The reader is again referred to Chapter 15 for a detailed discussion of the law, rules and practices related to **broker price opinions (BPOs) and comparative market analyses (CMAs),** especially the law and rules related to performance of a BPO/CMA **for a fee by non-provisional brokers.**

Lease Pricing of Commercial Properties

Just as sellers and buyers of commercial real estate need advice regarding the probable sale price of property being sold or purchased, landlords and tenants of commercial real estate need advice regarding appropriate **rental rates (lease prices).** All of the preceding discussion under "Sale Pricing of Commercial Properties" about the expectations for a broker performing a BPO/CMA to determine an estimate of probable sale price applies equally to a broker determining a probable lease price (rental rate) for a property for the benefit of a client, and the reader is referred back to that discussion.

Many factors must be taken into account when setting rental rates and other charges to tenants. The permitted uses of the property, the condition of the property, the location of the property, the property's suitability for permitted uses, and the landlord's income requirements are all important factors that must be considered. Ultimately, however, *rental rates will primarily be determined by conditions in the local market affecting the particular type of property in question. The relative availability of comparable properties and current market rental rates for comparable properties will be the major determining factors in the establishment of rental rates.*

Lease pricing will differ depending on the type of property involved. For **office properties**, the rate, which is most often stated on a per-square-foot-per-year basis, is most often determined by analyzing the rental rates and characteristics of comparable properties, especially taking into account differences in the class of the property, the market factors affecting the property and whether the lease is a full service lease. The pricing of **retail properties** being leased is very similar to office pricing. Space is typically leased at rates that are determined by looking at market comparables. However, careful attention should be paid to market factors and leasing factors such as CAM charges and other "non-rent" expenses in comparing rents. For example, non-rent charges under a lease may make space significantly more expensive overall when the total cost is taken into account and if market factors do not support this additional cost, rental rates may have to be adjusted downward. If **land** is to be leased, the rental determination takes into account the market factors affecting the property and pricing is typically based upon a desired rate of return for the landlord, within the context of what a user might likely pay for land of the type and use in question.

Because a lease pricing determination requires consideration of so many factors, it is not to be taken lightly and a broker should seek the assistance of a more experienced broker if they do not have experience with pricing for lease purposes the type of property in question.

Lease versus Purchase Analysis

Clients and customers (sellers or buyers) are frequently uncertain as to whether it is more appropriate to lease or purchase/sell a property. Either way, the client or customer will incur substantial costs. In the context of a customer's or client's overall business plan, they will often want to seek the lowest cost alternative. *A lease versus purchase analysis attempts to compare the cost of ownership and the cost of leasing over a given period of time to determine which is least costly.* While leasing often involves using less of a client or customer's capital (because there is no need for a down payment and there is not significant investment in land or build-up), it necessarily carries with it a limited time frame and does not allow the tenant the benefits of ownership such as appreciation in value. Some potential users definitely want to own their property in order to benefit from appreciation, to control the property, or to take advantage of some other benefit of ownership. Others known they definitely want to lease. For these clients or customers, the analysis would not be useful. Nonetheless, for a client who is interested mainly in the cost of occupancy, the analysis often proves very useful.

Factors To Consider

When looking at a lease versus purchase comparison, it is most important to make sure that all of the costs regarding the two options are taken into account in order to get a valid comparison.

Leasing Option. The length of the lease must be considered as well as all of the costs that will be paid under the lease, including rent and non-rent items. Assumptions may need to be made regarding rent escalator provisions if the future adjustments under the lease are not presently calculable with certainty. (For example, if they are tied to an index, assumptions regarding the changes in that index must be made.)

Purchase Option. A holding period must be determined and assumptions will need to be made regarding costs of acquisition and costs of resale, as well as an "apples-to-apples" comparison of all factors affecting price. Assumptions will need to be made regarding the increase in value during the holding period (appreciation), the terms of any loan, and increases in the costs of ownership such as taxes, insurance, maintenance, etc. Depreciation will need to be taken into account since the building (but not the land) can be depreciated.

Methodology

Collecting information regarding all of the applicable costs that relate to a lease and a sale is a significant undertaking. Making reasonable assumptions regarding any changes in those costs over time involves even more complicated research and analysis. Making assumptions regarding changes in price indexes and changes in value involves researching historical data regarding these matters and discussing it with the party for whom the analysis is conducted to see if they are comfortable with the assumptions being made. Once all of these assumptions are made, they can be applied to costs to determine the assumed costs for each year of the lease or holding period. Arriving at these calculations will mean calculating the financing costs, calculating the depreciation, calculating the rent and non-rent costs (as affected by any assumptions), calculating other costs of ownership (as affected by any assumptions), and adding up all of these costs to determine the annual costs of leasing and the costs of ownership. At this point, the exercise is not over. The tax considerations and impacts of each of these costs must be determined to arrive at an *after tax cost of leasing* and an *after tax cost of ownership* for each year. (It should be noted that the overall tax considerations of the party for whom the analysis is being done will almost always differ from person to person and accordingly their tax advisors should be involved in the discussion.).

Once these calculations have all been made, a **present value determination** of the total costs for each year on each side of the analysis will need to be made. A present value determination involves calculating the value of future expenditures in terms of today's dollars. The calculation is made by applying a **discount factor** (a rate of return a person is comfortable they could achieve in any economic conditions) to determine how many of today's dollars will be needed to fund the future dollars needed. This present value calculation is normally done using a number of different discount rates so that the person for whom the analysis is done can see the impact of changes in rates. By comparing the present value of the two costs of occupancy (ownership or leasing) at a discount rate that a person is comfortable with, they can make a valid decision as to which is the least costly alternative. *Clearly, this is a complicated analysis and should not be undertaken without a great deal of experience in these matters or assistance from someone who has experience with lease versus purchase analyses.*

Investment Analysis

Investors play a significant part in the commercial real estate market, so it is highly likely that a commercial real estate broker will have occasion to deal with investors in their practice. Investors in real estate use a different set of tools for evaluating real estate than users. *Investors are most interested in the return that they can get from a property* and that return can come in a number of different forms. Investors use different tools to measure the return on a property depending upon what their objectives are in a given transaction. Many of these tools take market factors for the type of property into account directly or indirectly. Therefore, prior to using these tools, it is important for an agent to have a thorough understanding of the market factors that are important to a property type. In addition, many investment analysis tools involve the use of market statistical data. As previously noted, commercial brokers must know the sources of this information in order to obtain the necessary data for any given analysis. It thus becomes clear that investment analysis is not a simple or straightforward matter. *A broker, prior to undertaking investment analysis, must have a thorough understanding of all of the concepts and matters introduced to the reader in this chapter, how they relate to and influence one another, and how they affect determinations under an investment analysis.* **Brokers who do not have substantial experience with investment analysis should not attempt to provide investment analysis advice to clients or customers. They should refer the client or customer to more experienced agents or involve those agents in the analysis and advice.**

Time Factors

Perhaps the most complicated factor affecting investment analysis is the fact that it involves making determinations regarding the performance of a property over a period of time as opposed to a determination of price or value at a stated point in time. The passage of time affects every factor considered under an investment analysis, most importantly the value of money. A dollar today is not worth the same as a dollar yesterday or tomorrow. Accordingly, investment analysis has developed concepts such as "**present value**" to compare the relative value of dollars over a period of time. In addition to the value of money, the passage of time changes other factors that are important to investment analysis. As noted earlier, leases may have escalator clauses that cause rent to change based upon changes in an index.

Those projected changes have to be taken into account. Financing terms, tax rates, interest rates, market conditions, depreciation rates, laws affecting property uses and economic changes are all matters that may change with the passage of time and, accordingly, their potential for change must be factored into any sound investment analysis.

Variables and Assumptions

Matters that must be addressed in investment analysis are broad and far ranging and can change depending upon the objective of the client or the property being considered. In order for an investment analysis to be sound, each aspect of a property and each aspect of its relevant contractual relationships must be taken into account. Of course, any changes which are inherent in the terms of a transaction, such as a fixed increase in rents for a property, must be taken into account and are easily quantified and calculated. Any investment analysis exercise must necessarily involve determining all of the matters that are subject to such fixed adjustments. The more complex undertaking is to identify those matters that are subject to being changed by the passage of time or changes in market factors and the economy. Still more complex is making assumptions regarding how those factors will change over the period of time under consideration in any given analysis. For example, an office building with full service leases without any provision for passing through utility costs to tenants means that any increase in utility costs will be borne by the landlord. A sound investment analysis will have to make assumptions about changes in utility costs and factor those into the analysis. These utility costs may be a variable not only because there may be changes in the costs of utilities, there may also be changes in the amount of utilities consumed based upon the nature of the tenants in the building. For example, a software provider technical support center, open 24 hours a day and staffed with persons who are using computers around the clock will use significantly more power than the software sales office that the same tenant may have maintained in that space previously. As a result, the investment analysis of this property will need to take into account not only the increase in the cost of utilities, but also the likelihood of increased usage of utilities. Any unaccounted for expense can decrease value for a landlord or increase occupancy cost for a tenant.

Caution: *Investment analysis of commercial properties for a client or prospective client should only be undertaken by a broker who possesses appropriate training in this field.* Commercial real estate investors and analysts have developed many tools for assisting with the investment analysis of commercial properties. Prior to undertaking investment analysis, brokers should have a good understanding of these tools and their use. A good investment analysis can only be achieved with the proper understanding of all of the factors related to commercial real estate discussed in this chapter, a thorough understanding of the client's objectives, and sound application of the appropriate analysis tools using appropriate variables and assumptions for the given circumstances.

Like-Kind Exchanges

Another analysis that is frequently required in commercial sales transactions is one to determine the feasibility and desirability of structuring a sale in the form of an **exchange of properties** that may provide the seller with an income tax benefit by virtue of a deferral of tax liability. Such exchanges are common in commercial sales transactions. Therefore, it is important for a commercial real estate agent to have an understanding of the motivation for such transactions and a few of the basics about these exchanges.

What Is A Like-Kind Exchange

A *"like-kind exchange"* *is a method of transferring property that defers the tax impact of the* *transaction.* Such exchanges are commonly referred to as "tax-deferred exchanges" or "Section 1031 exchanges" after the section of the Internal Revenue Code that authorizes such exchanges. Sometimes these transactions are also called "tax-*free* exchanges," but this is a misnomer since these exchanges only involve a *deferral* of tax liability, not an avoidance of tax liability.

Basic Rules

There are certain requirements that must be met in order for a transaction to qualify as a like-kind exchange. Certain types of property are excluded from qualifying as a like-kind exchange.[12] This section of the chapter provides only a brief, basic overview of Section 1031 exchanges. There are more issues that must be considered in effecting a Section 1031 exchange and there may be other applicable regulations or considerations depending upon the nature of the particular taxpayer, property or transaction under consideration.

The relevant section of the Internal Revenue Code, Section 1031(a) has three major requirements for a transaction to qualify as a like-kind exchange: *(1) the property being sold (the "relinquished* *property") must have been held for productive use in a trade or business or for investment; (2) the property* *must be exchanged for property (the "replacement property") of like kind which is to be held for productive* *use in a trade or business or for investment; (3) there must be an exchange.*

Properties Exchanged Must Be of "Like Kind." The requirement that the relinquished property and replacement property be of "like kind" references the nature and character of the property and not the type or quality of the property. It is not required that the relinquished property and the replacement property be the exact same type of property, however, *both properties must be held for* *productive use in a trade or business or for investment.* For example, one may sell a drugstore that was held for investment and acquire raw land that will be held for investment. There is no set holding period to determine if a property is a qualified property. The question of whether a property meets the definition of eligible property is one not determined purely by time. The question is one of intent and circumstances involving a number of factors which have been examined in a number of cases and examples which are beyond the scope of these materials. There are a number of tests set forth in the regulations and related tax cases that give guidance in determining whether a taxpayer's use of property qualifies for treatment as property held for productive use in a trade or business or for investment.[13]

There Must Be an Exchange. The mere sale of one property and reinvestment of all of the proceeds in a replacement property will not qualify as an exchange. A straight swap of one property for another property of like kind involving only the properties themselves and no money (or other compensation) changing hands clearly can qualify as an exchange. Since direct swaps of property with no additional compensation ("boot") are rare, *a majority of Section 1031 exchanges are* **"delayed** **exchanges"** *(or* **"deferred exchanges"**) using an **"exchange agreement"** with a **"qualified intermediary,"** and the relinquished property and the replacement property are transferred pursuant to the terms of the exchange agreement.[14]

A **delayed or deferred exchange** *occurs where the taxpayer disposes of the relinquished property at* *one point in time and acquires the replacement property at some later point in time.* Section 1031(a)(3) of the Internal Revenue Code sets forth clear rules for deferred exchanges. In order to qualify as replacement property under this section, the replacement property must be (1) identified by the taxpayer, in writing, to the person obligated to transfer the replacement property to the taxpayer (or someone else involved in the exchange that is not the taxpayer) no later than midnight on the 45th day after the transfer date of the relinquished property (typically the date of recording of the deed transferring the relinquished property); and (2) the replacement property must be received by the taxpayer by the earlier of (a) 180 days after the transfer date of the relinquished property or (b) the due date of the taxpayer's tax return (including any extensions). *If the dates as determined under these time frames fall on a Saturday, Sunday or legal holiday, the taxpayer is NOT given until the next business day to meet the requirements of the rule.*

Since a delayed or deferred exchange is not a simultaneous exchange, it is important to make sure that the taxpayer does not actually or constructively receive the proceeds of the sale of the relinquished property in the interim. If actual or constructive receipt by the taxpayer occurs, the exchange is disqualified (even if the taxpayer does acquire a replacement property). For this reason, an **exchange agreement** typically is entered into by the taxpayer and a **qualified intermediary**. This exchange agreement will provide that the qualified intermediary hold the proceeds of the sale of the relinquished property and use them, under the terms of the exchange agreement, to acquire the replacement property for the taxpayer. The agreement will also address any other matters related to the structure of the exchange and the parties' obligations concerning the use of the proceeds of the relinquished property and the acquisition of the replacement property.

Guidance by the Internal Revenue Service[15] has increased the incidence of the use of **reverse exchanges** and **improvement exchanges**. A reverse exchange occurs where a taxpayer acquires the replacement property before the sale of the relinquished property. This circumstance may arise where there is a delay in the closing of the sale of the relinquished property or where the taxpayer finds a replacement property that market circumstances require immediate action to secure. Improvement exchanges involve exactly what the name implies- exchanges where the replacement property is either to be built or renovated or expanded. There are no black and white rules regarding these types of exchanges and discussion of them in detail is outside the scope of these materials.

In addition, tenancy in common interests in real property (see Chapter 1- Property Ownership) are increasingly being offered in the marketplace as investments or as replacement property for exchanging taxpayers. These offerings provide partial ownership of a property and often involve larger or more valuable properties than an individual investor could afford on their own. These offerings also typically involve a property which has nationally recognized or strong credit tenants. The benefit to investors is stated to be the ability to own a part of a quality property with a strong tenant or tenants. A detailed discussion of these investment vehicles is outside the scope of these materials. Agents advising clients or customers interested in these type interests should be experienced with these type transactions before advising clients or customers and should keep in mind the possible applicability of securities laws (see later discussion of Securities Laws and the Commercial Real Estate Professional in this chapter).

What Is The Benefit Of A 1031 Exchange

Sales of real property are subject to tax, most often at capital gains rates.[16] *The benefit of a Section 1031 exchange is that the tax is deferred because, under the IRS regulations, no gain or loss shall be recognized in an exchange completed in accordance with the section.* If a client or customer is facing a significant gain on the sale of a piece of real property, they may be able to benefit from a tax deferred exchange. If a taxpayer wants to *totally defer* tax liability using a Section 1031 exchange, the taxpayer must acquire replacement property with a value that equals or exceeds the value of relinquished property, and all of the proceeds from the sale of the relinquished property must be used to obtain the replacement property. If there was debt on the relinquished property, there must be at least as much debt on the new property (or the taxpayer must inject new money equal to the difference between the debt on the relinquished property and the debt on the replacement property). If the transaction does not meet these requirements, it may still be possible to qualify for partial non-recognition of gain under Section 1031 (b).

> *Example:* John Farmer has owned his family farm for fifteen years. He bought the land for the 150-acre farm fifteen years ago for $150,000.00 ($1,000.00 per acre). He and his family live on a small adjacent tract and have been making a living for the last fifteen years by working the family farm. Development has surrounded Farmer's land and he has developers knocking on his door offering him as much as $10,000.00 per acre for his land ($1,500,000.00). John Farmer has been reluctant to sell because he is afraid of the taxes he would have to pay. Since the land is not depreciable, he has a basis of $150,000.00 in the property and would have to pay tax of 18% on $1,350,000.00 for a total tax of $243,000.00. Jim Taxfree, a broker, tells John Farmer about a strip shopping center for sale for $1,500,000.00 which produces more income annually than John has been making as a farmer. John says he can't afford the property because he would have to borrow money to buy it (he hates debt) since he will only have $1,257,000.00 left over after taxes from the sale of his land. Jim Taxfree tells Farmer to go talk to his accountant about the possibility of a tax-deferred exchange. Farmer goes to talk to his accountant who tells him: 1) his farm qualifies for tax deferral because it is used in a trade or business; 2) the shopping center qualifies as a replacement property because it will be held for investment; 3) the value of the shopping center is at least that of his farm so he can totally defer his tax; 4) all he has to do is structure the transaction as an exchange and he can avoid paying any of the $243,000.00 in tax and still acquire the shopping center with no debt. Farmer excitedly calls Taxfree to thank him for the good recommendation and hires him to be his real estate agent for both transactions.

A detailed discussion of the tax consequences of a like-kind exchange is beyond the scope of these materials. A proper analysis of the tax consequences of an exchange involves determining the taxpayer's realized gain or loss, determining the taxpayer's recognized gain (boot) and any offsets that there may be to this recognized gain, as well as determining the basis of the replacement property (since an exchange requires the transfer of basis from the relinquished property to the replacement property so that tax liability may be ultimately captured).[17]

Brokers are especially cautioned not to give advice regarding the eligibility of property for a Section 1031 exchange or how to conduct such an exchange. While a broker may suggest that a client consider an exchange, the client should be directed to consult with their tax advisor or an attorney with experience in handling such exchanges.

THE COMMERCIAL TRANSACTION CYCLE

The transaction cycle for commercial transactions usually requires a substantial period of time and the nature of the transaction can be varied and complex. The coverage in this section will address briefly some of the more typical matters encountered in commercial sale and lease transactions and the procedures that are most commonly followed. Other sections of this chapter have discussed issues that must be addressed during the preliminary stages of any transaction, such as identifying client/customer needs, analysis of property characteristics, market analysis, pricing, advertising properties for sale or lease, locating suitable properties for prospective buyers/tenants, and investment analysis. Therefore, our coverage of the typical sales and lease transaction cycles begins with a discussion of negotiating contracts.

The Typical Cycle – Sale Transaction

Negotiation

Once a client or customer has identified a property that they are interested in purchasing, the negotiation part of the transaction cycle begins. Most often, this process begins with a discussion between agents regarding terms that will be agreeable to their principals. Sometimes, all preliminary discussions are accomplished orally, but frequently such negotiation will include use by one or both parties of a **letter of intent**. *A letter of intent is a statement of the terms and conditions under which a party will enter into a contract.* Agents assisting buyers or sellers with the preparation of a letter of intent should assure that any such letter clearly state that it is **non-binding.** Should the party who will sign the letter of intent desire to be bound by its terms, the party should be referred to a real estate attorney to have the letter drafted. Once negotiations, with or without use of a letter of intent, reach a stage where the parties are in agreement as to the material terms of the transaction, a contract is then negotiated. Because of the complexity of commercial transactions, contract negotiation is often handled by attorneys for the respective parties.

Contract Preparation Generally

Typically, the buyer and seller will turn over the letter of intent or a statement of their understanding of the proposed transaction to their attorneys who will negotiate and draft a purchase contract on behalf of their clients. *Brokers must remember that the drafting by real estate brokers of contract provisions which secure the rights of others is prohibited under the Real Estate License Law and Real Estate Commission rules.*[18] *Even under circumstances where a broker may have a number of provisions that have been drafted by an attorney, the use and arrangement of those provisions in connection with a contract (cutting and pasting) involves the practice of law and should not be undertaken by a broker.* The complexity of contract structure and issues dealt with in commercial sales contracts makes the use of "clause banks" problematic at best.

The North Carolina Association of REALTORS® - REALTORS® Commercial Alliance and the North Carolina Bar Association have developed a standard form "Agreement for the Purchase and Sale of Real Property" (NCAR-RCA/NCBA Form 580-T) for use in connection with commercial real property sales transactions. This form is useful in many transactions but is necessarily a lowest common denominator form and will not be appropriate in many commercial transactions which, by their nature, are much more complex than residential transactions. *When using the Form 580-T Commercial Sales Agreement, agents must be very careful to have a real estate attorney draft any additional provisions that the parties may need and review any other changes to the Form 580-T Commercial Sales Agreement.* The broker who negotiates a commercial transaction and has the parties sign a contract, even a standard form contract, without the involvement of real estate attorneys for each party is potentially inviting trouble. *A good broker will always advise sellers and buyers to consult a real estate attorney (and probably also a tax accountant) before signing a commercial sales contract.*

Selected Contract Provisions

Commercial sales contracts necessarily must address such basic matters as price, earnest money, property description, title to be conveyed, financing contingencies, closing, possession, etc. Aside from such basic terms, there are a number of matters that are routinely addressed in commercial sales contracts. A few of these are discussed briefly below.

Inspection/Evaluation Provisions. Most commercial sales contracts contain a provision that allows a buyer a period of time at the outset of the contract to conduct an inspection and evaluation of the property. *Such a provision typically will authorize the buyer to conduct, at the buyer's expense, a thorough evaluation of the property during the inspection period stated in the contract to determine if the property is suitable for the intended use (which may also be stated in the contract), and will further authorize the buyer to terminate the contract at any time before expiration of the inspection period if the buyer determines, in the buyer's sole discretion, that the property is unsuitable.* Such a provision will also typically provide for the buyer to have the earnest money returned if the buyer terminates under this provision. The inspection period under such a provision is commonly referred to as a **"free look" period** because the provision allows the buyer to terminate the contract without penalty if the buyer determines that the property is unsuitable.

It would seem that such a provision makes the buyer's promise to perform under the contact "illusory" in nature and thus a contract containing such a provision would be unenforceable due to the lack of mutual obligation to perform by both parties. However, the North Carolina Court of Appeals (as well as courts in a number of other states) has ruled that such provisions allowing one party the discretion to terminate do not necessarily render a contract unenforceable if it is clear from the nature of the contract that there is also an "implied promise" that the party having the discretionary right must *act reasonably and in good faith.* The court stated the rule as follows: "Where a contract confers on a party a discretionary power affecting the rights of the other, this discretion must be exercised in a reasonable manner based upon good faith and fair play."[19]

Based on the foregoing court ruling, *it seems that provisions allowing the buyer to terminate the contract, at the buyer's discretion, if the buyer finds the property to be unsuitable are valid provisions; however, a buyer terminating a contract under such provision should be prepared to demonstrate that he or she is acting reasonably and in good faith.*

From the seller's perspective, it is important that this inspection period not be unduly long and, from the buyer's perspective, it is critical that the provision afford enough time to adequately investigate the property. After the inspection period is over, the contract becomes "hard," meaning that the buyer usually is very limited as to circumstances that will allow the buyer to terminate the contract without penalty.

It should be noted that a seller may sometimes object to the buyer having such an unrestricted discretionary right to terminate the contract during the stated evaluation period *and* to have all the earnest money returned. If so, an alternative is for the buyer to be required by the contract to forfeit all or part of the earnest money if the buyer exercises the right to terminate the contract. Another alternative is to utilize an **option contract**, which would require the buyer to pay a non-refundable amount for the option to purchase at a stated price within a stated period of time. The buyer could then conduct the property evaluation during the option period and decide whether or not to exercise the option.

Conditions Regarding a Change in Use. Many commercial contracts also will have provisions making the contract conditional on the buyer being able to obtain a land use regulation change (often a zoning change). Since changes in land use regulations involve a public process that has a clearly defined timeline, it is important that any provisions respecting such contemplated changes be mindful of those time frames and contemplate sufficient time to achieve the desired decision. Similar type conditions may involve obtaining a building permit, obtaining a driveway permit, or obtaining approval of a proposed subdivision of the property, among other possibilities. Since land use regulations and private use restrictions can have such a significant impact on commercial property, a contractual provision regarding the intended use of the property often takes on added significance in a commercial transaction. *Brokers are reminded that it is never permissible for an agent to draft a land use change condition for use in a sales contract.*

Other Provisions. There are any number of other provisions that may be significant in any given commercial real estate transaction. While a broker is expected to be generally familiar with various types of provisions and their meaning and import, brokers should remember that *only attorneys can lawfully draft contract provisions or advise someone regarding interpretation or application of contract provisions.* It is for this reason that the statement "Note: Under North Carolina law, real estate agents are not permitted to draft conditions or contingencies to this Agreement" has been added to Section 1(i) of the standard Form 580-T Commercial Sales Agreement which references the attachment of an Exhibit B containing additional terms. Virtually every use of an Exhibit B with additional terms will require the involvement of a real estate attorney. It is important that brokers assist the parties' attorneys as much as possible by providing information regarding the property and the parties' concerns and positions. The brokers should also stay informed regarding the progress of the negotiations in order that they might offer suggestions where appropriate to move the process forward.

"Due Diligence" (Property Evaluation)

Once the parties have signed a contract, it is time to begin execution of the contract. Many contracts call for the seller to provide title, survey, loan, environmental and other information to the buyer within a short period of time after the signing of the contract. (See Section 4 of the Form 580-T Commercial Sales Agreement.) It is important that this information exchange take place because it assists the buyer with many aspects of the buyer's evaluation of the property, which is commonly referred to by practitioners as "due diligence." **"Due diligence"** *is a term of art referring to the process of the buyer duly investigating the property in a diligent manner so that all relevant information about the property might be adequately determined.* Typically, a buyer conducts the "due diligence" evaluation during the inspection period stated in the contract, but there may be a provision in the contract that provides a buyer additional time as to certain matters of due diligence, depending upon the circumstances. While matters evaluated during the course of performing a due diligence evaluation may vary from contract to contract, there are certain things that are typically done in every transaction.

A **title search** is almost always part of a buyer's evaluation of the property. This search will help determine if the seller has good title to the property and will also help determine any applicable easements or private use restrictions which might impact the proposed use of the property. Closely related to the title search is a **survey**. Depending on the type of survey performed, a survey may locate improvements on the property, may identify easements and also may graphically depict the impact of certain land use regulations such as setbacks and public rights of way. If the property is proposed to be developed, the survey may also include **topography** (the grade and elevation of the land). While a discussion of survey types in detail is outside the scope of these materials (see also the discussion in Chapter 4), brokers working in commercial real estate should be familiar with the different types of surveys and the information that will and will not necessarily be reflected on a survey based upon the type of survey in question.

Analysis of the property itself is also undertaken. This assessment frequently includes a Phase I Environmental Assessment which reviews the property and public records related to hazardous wastes to determine if there is reason to believe there may be environmental issues at the property. Buyers often also hire third party inspectors to evaluate the structure and systems of an existing facility. If new construction or the expansion of an existing facility is contemplated, **soil testing** may be done to determine the type of soils present on the property and if there are any conditions adverse to construction.

There also may be the need to have a **wetlands** evaluation done to determine if any of the proposed construction or expansion will affect wetlands.

There may be the need to verify certain other matters such as the existence of adequate **power facilities**, adequate **water and sewer**, availability of **driveway permits** and **verification of zoning and permitted uses** under applicable zoning classifications (see earlier discussion of change of use and oc-cupancy permits). If new construction is contemplated at the property, **demolition permits, grading permits, building permits and other regulatory compliance** may need to be obtained.

If any contractual relationships need to be established with reference to the acquisition of the property, such as a general contract for the construction of improvements or expansion of an existing facility, these matters should be undertaken during the inspection period as well, so they and their as-sociated costs are known and established prior to the buyer losing the right to terminate the contract. Assuming that the buyer does not turn up anything during this due diligence period that creates a problem for the property or the transaction or the buyer's intended use of the property, the buyer will not terminate the contract during the inspection period and the contract will go "hard" (i.e., become binding on the buyer).

Financing

Financing in commercial real estate transactions is generally much more complex than in resi-dential transactions, and financing terms are often much more negotiable. Typically, a borrower will apply for a loan and will receive a **commitment letter** from a financial organization willing to make the loan. This commitment letter sets forth the terms upon which the loan will be made and usually provides that it will expire unless accepted within a certain number of days. The letter also usually has an outside date by which the borrower must close or the commitment does not have to be honored.

The conditions set by a lender under a commitment letter usually involve a wide ranging checklist of items regarding the borrower and the property that must be provided to the lender before they will fund the loan. An appraisal, title insurance policy, survey, Phase I Environmental Assess-ment, financial statements, project budgets (if construction is involved), certificates of occupancy, utilities verification letters, zoning verification letters, corporate resolutions for the borrower, docu-mentation of the borrower's status as a legal entity (if not an individual), among other items, are all typical requirements.

The lender will also have loan documents which grant it the desired security under the transac-tion. These loan documents typically are not preprinted form documents as is the case in residential transactions and they are quite often negotiable. In many commercial real estate transactions, there are three lawyers involved: the buyer's lawyer, the seller's lawyer and the lender's lawyer. The buyer's lawyer and the lender's lawyer will negotiate the terms and provisions of the loan documents and any related documentation. It is typical for the lender to require the borrower to pay the legal fees of the lender's lawyer. Once all of the checklist items have been provided and there is agreement on the terms of the loan documents, the transaction is ready to close.

Closing

Commercial real estate closings take on many formats. There may be a traditional closing meeting where the buyer and seller and their lawyers and the lender's counsel meet, execute and ex-change all required documents, but this format is increasingly rare. After execution, the deed and other documents to be recorded are then taken to the courthouse for recording. Typically, only after the documents are recorded will the lender wire its money, and thus only after the lender's funds have been received may any disbursements (like the seller's proceeds) be made. Traditional closing meetings appear to be fading. In today's market, buyers and sellers often sign all required documents prior to the actual closing and the closing is actually handled by the lawyers, either at a meeting, or by a courier or mail delivery exchange of documents. Nonetheless, it is always required that all documents affecting title be recorded prior to any money changing hands. In some instances, a lender may even impose other conditions, such as receipt of the lender's title insurance policy, before allowing disbursement of the loan funds.

Post-Closing

In addition to the usual post-closing document distribution, it is often the case that there will be post-closing follow-up items to be dealt with in commercial real estate closings. Sometimes a lender's counsel will allow certain checklist items to be delivered after closing. In addition, it is not at all uncommon for there to be financial covenants in loan documents which require the borrower to make periodic reports to the lender regarding any number of matters. In the event that any such post-closing matters are present, it is important that they be dealt with in a timely fashion.

The Typical Cycle – Lease Transaction

Negotiation

The negotiation of a commercial lease transaction takes much the same path as that of a commercial sales transaction. While the subject matter of the negotiation is significantly different, once a prospective tenant becomes interested in a particular property, there is typically a discussion of terms, either orally or through a letter of intent. Once the parties have identified and tentatively agreed on the material terms of the lease, they turn to memorializing that agreement in a lease document.

Lease Preparation Generally

Commercial lease transactions can become very complex and involve complicated provisions. Again, as with commercial sales transactions, attorneys are very often involved in the negotiation of commercial leases. Many landlords in commercial transactions have a form lease that they use in connection with the leasing of their properties and, accordingly, the negotiations will focus on provisions in this form. As in the case of commercial sales contracts, **brokers are cautioned to avoid the practice of law in connection with lease preparation**. Many leasing agents have good form leases that were developed over the years or in connection with a particular transaction. Many leasing agents also have readily available attorney-approved clauses to deal with certain situations. Nonetheless, *a broker may not "cut and paste" a lease form, mixing and matching provisions from their clause bank — that is the practice of law. The assembling of provisions to create a lease should be left to competent real estate attorneys.* The North Carolina Association of REALTORS® - REALTORS® Commercial Alliance has developed a "Commercial Lease Agreement" (NCAR-RCA Form 590-T) for use in connection with commercial lease transactions. As is the case with the Form 580-T Commercial Sales Agreement ("Agreement for Purchase and Sale of Real Property") form, it is necessarily a lowest common denominator form and may not be suitable in a number of circumstances.

Selected Lease Provisions

As noted earlier, there are a number of business provisions that must be dealt with in a typical lease. In addition to rental and other basic terms, there may be CAM charges or other non-rent charge provisions in the lease. There may also be escalator provisions which increase the rent and other charges. Sometimes a landlord will want to put a provision in a lease that allows the landlord to relocate the tenant within the building to substantially similar space if the tenant's space is needed for another tenant. Particular attention should be paid to these provisions. Since the provisions in a commercial lease are limited only by the bounds of the common law of contract, the number and type of provisions that may appear in a commercial lease are innumerable. There are, however, three other matters of special significance which are addressed in virtually every lease: Provisions regarding **upfit** (or the lack thereof), provisions regarding **delivery of possession**, and provisions regarding the **lease term** or period.

Upfit/Construction. It is rare that a tenant will find a space that is completely satisfactory without the need for any changes. Typically, there will need to be modifications made to the premises. This is known as **"upfitting"** the premises. The first decision to be made is who is to make the changes, the tenant or the landlord. If the tenant makes the changes, typically the rent will be lower because the landlord cannot charge for the improvements. If the landlord makes the improvements, the rent will typically be higher since the landlord can charge for the improvements. There are two critical considerations when looking at upfit – ***detail* and *cost* – *and these are closely related.*** Upfit plans must be specified with sufficient detail to not only avoid controversy regarding what was to be done, but they must also be sufficiently detailed to allow correct pricing. Most landlords provide an allowance (a fixed amount of dollars) for upfit and most tenants (if they are doing it themselves) have a budget for upfit. Only with sufficient detail regarding upfit may the cost be determined so that an allowance or a budget is not overrun. Where the tenant bears any responsibility for upfit costs, tenants should be advised strongly to make these cost determinations thoroughly and carefully prior to signing a lease, since there is little a tenant can do, other than absorb the cost overrun, after lease execution. Another significant factor with upfit is timing. Adequate time must be provided for obtaining necessary permits and for the upfit changes to be completed prior to the tenant's need for the space. This timing consideration relates to another important consideration in most leases — when the tenant takes possession.

Taking Possession. A tenant typically starts paying rent when they take possession of the premises; but there are other determining factors for rent commencement, particularly when upfit is involved. The obligation to pay rent and the right to possession of the premises do not necessarily coincide. *Rent may be required to be paid from the date of the lease, from a date certain stated in the lease, from the issuance of a certificate of occupancy, from substantial completion of the upfit in accordance with the plans, or from actual possession by a tenant. The right to occupy the space may also be tied to any one of these factors (except occupancy, of course, because the right to occupy cannot be conditioned upon occupancy).* Accordingly, careful consideration should be given during negotiations to when rent will start and when occupancy will be allowed. For example, quite often, when space is to be upfit for a tenant, the rent will commence when a certificate of occupancy for the space is issued. Unfortunately, while a certificate of occupancy confirms that the improvements have been substantially completed in accordance with the building code, the state of completion may not be such that a tenant will want to occupy and conduct business from the space. Matters of this nature should be considered during negotiations. In addition, occupancy and rent are often determined by a date certain stated in a lease. Unfortunately, construction schedules and suppliers' schedules often do not comply with these timetables and the parties are left with a circumstance that is not contemplated by the lease. Again, consideration of these matters should take place during negotiations. The bottom line is that when considering occupancy and rent commencement issues, all of the circumstances surrounding the space and the parties should be taken into account to attempt to reach an agreement that works under the circumstances.

Lease Term.   A unique aspect of leases is that they stand in the present and look forward in time (often as much as 20 years) and try to contemplate all of the circumstances that might arise affecting the parties for the period of the lease. Accordingly, factors that may change over time must be taken into account. Is the tenant's business growing? Does that mean that they want a shorter term or does that mean they want a right of first refusal on adjacent space? When might that adjacent space become available? Is the tenant stable and not expecting any changes in its needs for space for an extended period of time? Does that mean that the tenant may want to have the right to extend the term of the lease? Does the tenant think rents are moving up or down? If they are moving up, does that mean a tenant wants to lock in a rate for a longer period of time (a longer term), or do escalators in the lease change that analysis? These are but a few of the considerations that must be contemplated when making a decision on the lease term. Circumstances will dictate how important each consideration may be, and a landlord's willingness to address these considerations will definitely be a factor. The important part of the exercise is to make sure that these questions are asked and answered. Asking these questions after the lease is signed is too late.

REAL PROPERTY LEASES

Statute of Frauds

Recall that a lease "that exceeds three years in duration from the time of making thereof" must be in writing to comply with *Statute of Frauds*.[20] Although the statute does not require short-term leases that will expire within three years from the time of making to be in writing, both common sense and preventive law considerations dictate the wisdom of putting all leases in writing. What does the language "from the time of making thereof" in the Statute of Frauds mean? *The time of making of the lease occurs when the parties have contractually bound themselves to the lease agreement.* It *does not* have to be the same date as the commencement date of the lease term.

> *Example:* On August 1, 2017, a lessor and lessee orally agree to all terms of a lease whereby the lessor agrees to lease a building to the lessee for a two-year period commencing on October 1, 2018 and ending on September 30, 2020. Although the lease term itself is only for two years, it will run for a period *exceeding three years* from the time the lease was entered into (*i.e.* August 1, 2017 until September 30, 2020). Because the lease must be in writing and signed by the party to be charged under the Statute of Frauds, either lessor or lessee can assert that the lease is not valid and enforceable.

It is incorrect, however, to assume that a lease that does not comply with the Statute of Frauds is automatically "void" and unenforceable. In the above example, both lessor and lessee may honor the lease with neither raising the statute as a defense to enforcement. If an incomplete or oral lease is honored and voluntarily performed by the parties, the statute has become irrelevant. What about a lease for exactly three years from the time of making?

> *Example:* On April 1, 2017, a lessor and lessee orally agree that the lessor will lease a building to the lessee for a term of exactly three years commencing on April 1, 2017, and ending on March 31, 2020. Since this lease runs for a period *not exceeding* three years from the time the lease is made, it is not subject to the Statute of Frauds and is not required be in writing to be valid.

As a precautionary practical matter, *all* leases should be in writing.[21] A lease must identify both lessor and lessee, contain an adequate legal description of the leased premises, state both a precise or computable starting date and termination date, include all material terms, and be signed by both parties to make it enforceable against the parties "to be charged therewith." If the lessor or lessee is an entity (corporation, limited liability company, limited partnership, etc.), the person signing the lease must have the authority to bind the entity to the lease.

Recording the Lease

A lease that lasts more than three years from its making will be void against the lessor's purchasers for value or his lien creditors unless it is recorded (also called "registered") pursuant to General Statute §47-18, known as the Conner Act.[22]

Example: An owner leases a warehouse to a lessee for a 10-year term to commence on January 1, 2017. The lease is in writing and fully complies with the Statute of Frauds, but is not recorded. On August 15, 2017 (with more than nine years yet to run on the lease), the lessor conveys the property to a purchaser for value who promptly records the deed. The purchaser takes title free and clear of the lease because it was not recorded.

If the lease is for less than three years *or* if a lease for three or more years has been properly recorded, the sale of the leased premises by the lessor to a purchaser for value will **not** extinguish the lessee's rights under his lease.

Example: Same facts as in the previous example, except that the lease is promptly recorded on January 2, 2017. Because the lease is recorded, the purchaser for value has notice and takes title to the property subject to the lease and may not disturb the lessee's possession for the remaining nine years of the lease term, as long as the lessee continues to comply with all lease obligations.

Recording a Memorandum of Lease

Commercial lease agreements can be dozens of pages in length. It is not necessary to record the entire agreement to protect the lessee's rights and put future purchasers and others dealing with the property on notice, and there may be practical reasons why a commercial lessor and lessee would not want every detail of their transaction in the public land records. North Carolina law authorizes the recordation of a ***memorandum of lease***, which is a summary of the lease agreement, instead of the entire lease. A recordation of a memorandum has the same effect as if the entire lease had been recorded.[23] The memorandum must include: 1) the names of the parties, 2) a description of the leased property, 3) the term of the lease (including extensions, renewals and options to purchase, if any), and 4) a reference sufficient to identify the complete agreement between the parties.

The statute includes a sample memorandum of lease and authorizes adaptation of the form to allow lessors and lessees to add other provisions.[24] If the duration of the lease is complicated because of various extension and renewal options, General Statute §47-118(b) states:

> If the provisions of the lease make it impossible or impractical to state the maximum period of the lease because of conditions, renewals and extensions, or otherwise, then the memorandum of lease shall state in detail all provisions concerning the term of the lease as fully as set forth in the written lease agreement between the parties.

Real Property Law versus Contract Law

While commercial leasing continues to be based on both real property law and contract law, many default rules of traditional property law are modified, qualified, or rendered inapplicable by express contract law provisions if inserted in a lease.

Example: Under traditional property law, a commercial lessee is entitled to remove trade fixtures at the end of the lease term. An express lease provision giving the lessor ownership of fixtures at the end of the lease term is enforceable and prevails over the property law default rule.

Example: A tenancy for years (tenancy for a definite term) terminates automatically and requires no prior notice by lessor or lessee under property law. However, for practical reasons, the lease requires that the lessee provide prior notice to the lessor of the lessee's intent to vacate at the end of the term.

Example: Under property law, a lessee receives title to and exclusive possession of a nonfreehold estate. A shopping mall or office lease may include a provision allowing a "substitution of space" within the mall or office building.

The moral of this story in the realm of commercial leasing is threefold: Read the lease! Read the lease! Read the lease! Modern commercial leasing is a complex area of practice and law. It is no accident that many leases are both lengthy and detailed.

MAJOR TYPES OF LEASES

Leases are often categorized or described according to the method by which rent is calculated. New forms of rent provisions are constantly evolving in response to changing economic conditions and the contemporary needs of both lessors and lessees. A summary of the more typical lease types follows. In some categories, infinite variations are possible. As the reader will quickly recognize, all of these lease types are used only in connection with *commercial* properties, except for fixed rental (flat) leases also used in residential leasing.

<u>**Major Types of Leases**</u>
- Fixed rental (flat) leases (residential and commercial)
- Percentage leases
- Net leases
- Graduated leases
- Index leases
- Full-service leases

Fixed Rental (Flat) Leases

A fixed rental (flat) lease involves the payment of a fixed amount of rent at regular intervals during the lease term, *e.g.*, the lease of a warehouse for five years at a rental of $3800 per month. A commercial lease with an annual fixed rent of $30 per square foot of rentable area is another example. The benefit of this form of rent calculation is its simplicity. A detriment is the inability of the rent amount to adjust to increased fair rental value and inflation in leases of lengthy terms.

Percentage Leases

Under a percentage lease, all or part of the rent is calculated with reference to a stated percentage of receipts from the business of the lessee. A common commercial lease involves a percentage of gross sales. Occasionally, a percentage of net profit is used as a system of rent calculation, although disputes often arise over defining that term.

A typical contemporary commercial lease involves a combination of fixed rental (sometimes called the "minimum rent") with a percentage of gross sales (sometimes called "additional rental"). A 1976 North Carolina Court of Appeals decision[25] involved a lease with a rent provision of this nature. The rental paragraph of the lease in that case called for a $9,000 per year fixed rent and further provided:

> ...In addition to the rental set out above, in the event the sales for the fiscal year of Lessee shall exceed NINE HUNDRED THOUSAND AND No/100 DOLLARS ($900,000.00), the Lessee will pay as additional rental one-half percent of all sales in excess of NINE HUNDRED THOUSAND AND No/100 DOLLARS ($900,000.00) for the original term of this lease and any extensions thereof, if any. By way of illustration only, if the sales for a fiscal year equal ONE MILLION SIX HUNDRED THOUSAND AND No/100 DOLLARS ($1,600,000.00), then the additional rental for the year will be THREE THOUSAND FIVE HUNDRED AND No/100 DOLLARS ($3,500.00).

Note the caution of the draftsman. To avoid any misunderstanding, the percentage rental provision sets forth an example of how the percentage formula operates. Despite comprehensive lease provisions, a legal problem developed between the lessor and lessee. The lessee moved to a different location during the term of the lease. Was the lessee liable under the above lease provision for both the fixed rental to his original lessor as well as a percentage of sales at its *new* location?

The Court of Appeals answered in the negative as to the percentage of sales based on the language used in the lease. The Court held that the lease agreement did not require the tenant to occupy or operate its business in the leased premises during the lease term. The lease agreement was also silent as to what would happen regarding the percentage rent if the tenant should move to a new location. Thus, the Court held that the lessee was required to pay only the fixed rental for the remainder of the lease term. This case illustrates the need for expert legal counsel whenever commercial leases are required. A provision that looks complete may be wholly inadequate in light of court decisions interpreting other leases.[26]

Good percentage leases define all key terms. A sample clause in a lease of space in a shopping center, for example, calls for a minimum rent combined with a percentage rent of 1.25 percent of gross sales. "Gross sales" is then defined in a full paragraph which reads as follows:

> The term 'gross sales' as used herein shall include all sales of merchandise from, through, or out of the leased premises, including performance of any service for any customer or patron for compensation by the Lessee, or by any salesman, saleswoman, or employee, and shall include all sales by every portion and department thereof, and sale by any sublessee, concessionaire, or broker in said premises for cash or on a charge basis, paid or unpaid, collected or uncollected, and including all business in which orders come by mail, telephone, or telegraph, and all business where goods are delivered directly by the supplier to the purchaser (whether or not actually handled by

the Lessee), less credit for returned merchandise, merchandise trade-ins, and credits of a similar nature; 'gross sales' shall not include sales tax. Transfers of merchandise between stores of sublessees are not Gross Sales.

Net Leases

In a net lease, the lessee, in addition to paying rent, is made responsible for some or all of the expenses and costs relating to the property. Long-term leases of commercial or industrial buildings are common examples of net leases. Numerous net lease variations exist depending upon the types of expenses and charges that the tenant is obligated to pay. In some net leases, the lease payment to the lessor is truly "net," i.e., the tenant is responsible for all costs and expenses associated with the leased premises. In other net lease arrangements, the lessor may pay for some of the expenses. The more property expenses that are paid by the *tenant*, the closer the lease is to being a true net lease. One excellent way to determine the extent to which a lease is a net lease is to review lease provisions relating to the following matters: repairs and maintenance, property taxes, property insurance, and other property operating expenses.

Graduated Leases

Graduated leases call for systematic increases in the rental rate at regular intervals over the lease term. There are various reasons why a lessor or a lessee might desire this arrangement. The lessor may be attempting to predict the return required in an inflationary economy by automatic periodic rent increases. The lessee may need the economic advantage of lower rent at the commencement of the lease term.

Index Leases

Index leases call for periodic increases or decreases in rent based upon some reliable government or private index or standard. Index leases must be drafted with great care. A 1977 court decision[27] involved a lease for 10 years with rent payable based on a number of factors. The lease had a minimum rent that automatically increased after four years. Added to the minimum rent was a percentage of gross sales provision. In addition, the minimum rent was to be annually adjusted upward based on the Consumer Price Index. The clause in the lease dealing with the index read as follows:

> 3.06. At the end of each one-year period subsequent to the execution of this lease, the fixed minimum rent shall be adjusted upward if the cost of living index as provided herein discloses an increase in the cost of living, according to the United States Consumer Price Index. Said rent shall be adjusted upward *by the percent which said price index has moved since the last adjustment in rent.* In any event, said fixed minimum rent shall not be less than provided in Section 3.03. The United States Consumer Price Index as of the effective day of this lease as represented by the United States Department of Labor, Bureau of Statistics for the United States area, is agreed by the parties to stand at 125.0 as of June, 1972, and *that this is to be used as the base hereinafter.* [Emphasis added.]

The lessor and lessee sued each other over the interpretation of the above clause. The lessor contended that the proper method of calculating the increases was to divide the current consumer price index by the base 125.0, multiply that by the fixed minimum rent, and add the resulting figure to the last adjusted rent. This argument emphasized the last phrase of paragraph 3.06 of the lease. The lessee, on the other hand, claimed that the proper method to interpret the index clause was to subtract the last applicable consumer price index from the current index figure, divide the difference by the last applicable index figure, apply the percentage to the fixed minimum rent, and add the resulting figure to the last adjusted rent. This interpretation emphasized the language "by the percent which said price index has moved since the last adjustment in rent."

The court ruled that the language of the index clause was ambiguous and therefore construed it against the lessor-draftsman. The court declared the proper computation to be as follows: the cost-of-living index published as of June of each year shall be annually compared with that as published for June of the preceding year, and if there has been an increase, the number of points of increase shall be divided by the index for June of the preceding year, and the resulting percentage shall be the percentage of increase for the year. During the first four years of the lease, the resulting percentage shall be multiplied times the base fixed rental of $3,250 with that product added to the last preceding monthly rental, and that sum shall be the monthly rental for the next ensuing year. After the fourth year, the percentage shall be multiplied times the base fixed minimum rental of $4,000 and added to the last previous monthly rental to produce the new monthly rental for the next ensuing year.

Once again, the lesson to be learned from court decisions is that *meticulous legal drafting is required when these specialized types of lease terms are employed.* Some index leases link rent increases to factors besides government indexes. Increases tied to tax increases or operating expenses (or both) are examples.

Full-Service Leases

In shopping centers, large office buildings and other multi-tenant buildings, full service leases are common. Under a full service lease, the lessor provides all utilities, cleaning services, ground maintenance service and other services related to the tenancy. In other words, all expenses related to occupancy are included. Such leases obviously have higher rent than leases where the lessee is responsible for these services. As a practical matter, the lessee indirectly is paying for these services by paying a higher rental. The rent paid to the lessor in a full-service lease is often determined by establishing a base rent for the particular space and adding to that figure the lessee's designated share of the building's operating expenses to determine the total rent paid by the lessee. The definition of "operating expenses" can vary from lease to lease, but it often includes the usual costs of building operation such as management fees, repair and maintenance costs, utility costs, ad valorem taxes, special assessments, and property insurance premiums. With many full-service leases, the lessor will estimate the operating expenses for the current year and establish the rental amount on that basis, then reimburse the lessee in the event actual expenses for the year are lower than the estimate.

LEASES FOR SPECIAL CIRCUMSTANCES

In addition to the previously discussed leases, some leases are classified based upon their use in special situations. Ground leases, mineral leases, and oil and gas leases are three examples.

Ground Leases

A ground lease is where a tenant leases a vacant parcel of land for an extended period of time. Some ground leases are for a 99-year period. The duration of a ground lease is calculated to enable the lessee to realize an adequate return on its investment. In a ground lease, the lessee agrees to construct a building on the property that the lessee will, in turn, lease or sell to a third party. A developer of real property may need to invest the cash otherwise required to purchase the land into developing the property and may find a ground lease advantageous as a form of equity financing. Additionally, rent paid under a ground lease provides a tax deduction to the lessee, whereas the value of the land would not be a depreciable asset for tax purposes if the developer purchased instead of leased the land.

Mineral Leases

A mineral lease entitles the lessee to explore for minerals and mine them if they are discovered. Under the North Carolina Statute of Frauds, General Statute §22-2, mineral leases *of any duration* must be in writing. While brokers rarely will encounter mineral leases in their daily real estate business, mineral rights can be a very important aspect of a real estate transaction.

A mineral lease should be distinguished from a mineral deed. When rights to minerals in land have been severed by deed from surface rights, two distinct estates in land are created. The question of what constitutes a "mineral" periodically arises and demonstrates a need for careful draftsmanship. A 1945 North Carolina Supreme Court decision, for example, held that kaolin, a fine, soft, white clay used in making china, was a mineral that could be mined by the open-pit method.[28] This result had dire consequences for the owner of the surface estate who had taken subject to a prior grant of mineral rights.

Oil and Gas Leases

As the title reveals, this type of lease transfers the right to extract oil or gas from the real property of the lessor. A separate and highly technical body of law exists with regard to oil and gas leases and expert advice should be sought if a broker encounters such a transaction.

COMMON LEASE PROVISIONS

As mentioned earlier, leases are contracts and must satisfy fundamental contract law principles as well as include all essential elements of a contract, as identified in Chapter 10. These essential elements include the identity of each party (each having the legal capacity to contract), an adequate description of the property to be leased and all material terms, such as rent amount, duration, and obligations of each party. Additional provisions commonly found in commercial leases may address the topics noted below. All sample clauses used herein are simplified examples for educational purposes only and should not be viewed nor relied upon as model language. Prudent parties will consult an attorney for assistance in preparing a lease agreement that meets the parties' needs.

1. The lessee's intended use of the premises.
2. Environmental provisions, including provisions prohibiting the use, storage or discharge of hazardous chemicals and substances.
3. Whether repairs or alterations of the premises are necessary to prepare for the lessee's intended use, and if so, who will make such repairs and alterations.
4. Whether the lessee has the right to remove fixtures or structures placed by him on the premises at the expiration of the term.
5. The rights and duties of the parties concerning maintaining the premises in good repair.
6. What utility charges, insurance, and taxes each party is to bear.
7. The effect upon the lease of the loss or destruction of the premises by fire or other hazards.
8. The services to be furnished by the lessor, if any, such as elevator service, hot water, heat, janitorial service, or others.
9. Any prohibition against the lessee assigning or subleasing the leased premises.

10. The right of the lessee to renew the lease or an option for the lessee to purchase the leased premises. A lessee has no implied right to renew his lease. A right of renewal must be expressly reserved in the lease.

11. The acts of the parties that will result in a termination of the lease, such as:
    a) lessee's failure to pay rent or insolvency or bankruptcy;
    b) lessee's failure to observe covenants in lease, such as a covenant to repair;
    c) lessee's commission of "waste";
    d) lessee's abandonment of premises;
    e) lessee's failure to obtain license or permit necessary for lessee's business;
    f) lessor's failure to supply stipulated services.

12. The lessor's right to enter the premises during the lease term. For instance, the lessor may reserve the right to enter the premises:
    a) to inspect the premises to determine if lessee is complying with lease terms;
    b) to make repairs, additions or alterations;
    c) to show the premises to prospective buyers or future lessees or to post "for sale" or "for rent" signs on the premises.

13. If a lessee is to share a building or property with the lessor or other lessees, whether:
    a) a covenant may exclude other occupants from engaging in a competing business or impose some other restriction on a party to the lease;
    b) a clause states the parties' duties with respect to parts of the building or property used in common.

14. Whether either party to the lease must post security to assure the other party of compliance with and full performance of the lease.

15. The condition in which the lessee is to leave the premises at the end of the term.

Although provisions relating to these matters may not be essential for a lease to be legally valid and binding, additional provisions usually are necessary to adequately reflect the agreement of the parties and to protect the parties' interests. A more detailed discussion of some of the more common types of additional or special lease provisions follows.

Lessee's Proposed Use

A lessor should consider a lessee's desired use of the leased premises, particularly in light of environmental laws and regulations discussed next. There are many practical situations where a lessor may want to restrict a lessee's use of the premises. A lessor who has expended extra funds to construct a restaurant building will want to restrict the use of that building to restaurant purposes. A lessor who operates a pharmacy in one part of a building may limit the use of another part of the building to ensure that the lessee does not also operate a pharmacy. *Absent a lease provision restricting the lessee's use, the lessee may make any use of the leased premises that is legal.*

Sometimes, it is the lessee who is interested in specifying conditions at the inception of the lease term. For example, if the lease is entered into conditioned on the lessee obtaining a license to sell alcoholic beverages, the lessee should specify the purpose of the lease and make the lease contingent on obtaining the necessary license or licenses. A lessee's proposed use may require approval by a zoning or planning board. The following is an example of a zoning contingency.

> *Zoning Contingency.* This lease is subject to Lessee's obtaining from the City of _____ authority and necessary permits to use the leased premises as a _____. This contingency will continue for a period of 90 days

after the date of this agreement. If Lessee is unable to obtain the requisite authority and permits within the 90-day period, Lessee either may waive this contingency or declare the Lease to be of no effect. Lessor agrees to cooperate fully with Lessee in an effort to obtain this approval.

Environmental Matters (Lessor's Perspective)

Lessors should be careful to prohibit the use, storage, or discharge by the lessee of any chemicals or substances harmful to the environment. *A lessor can be held legally responsible for environmental cleanup costs even though the problem was caused by the lessee. The storage, usage, and discharge of dangerous chemicals and hazardous materials should be expressly prohibited.* Sample language addressing these very important environmental matters follows.

> *Environmental Provisions.* Lessee shall not permit the storage or use of any dangerous or hazardous chemical, substance, or material on the leased premises, including but not limited to asbestos, toxic chemicals, radioactive materials, chemical waste, medical waste, or pollutants. Lessee shall not release or discharge any dangerous or hazardous chemical, substance, or material on the leased premises. In the event that lessee causes or allows any environmental discharge or damage to the leased premises, lessee shall be fully responsible for all environmental cleanup expenses, attorneys' fees and other costs of compliance with applicable environmental laws and regulations.

Where hazardous chemicals, substances, or materials must be used on the leased premises, special provisions requiring careful compliance with all environmental laws and regulations should be included in the lease.

Lessee's Environmental Due Diligence

An environmental due diligence investigation may be necessary prior to leasing industrial and warehouse facilities and may also be appropriate when leasing all or part of an older commercial building. Under the Comprehensive Environmental Response, Compensation and Liability Act of 1989 (known as CERCLA)[29] a lessee of property may be liable for environmental clean-up of a property even though the lessee did not cause the contamination. To avoid liability by qualifying as an innocent purchaser (in this case, an "innocent lessee"), a prospective lessee has a legal duty to engage in an *environmental site assessment (ESA).*

A prior lessee or the owner may have previously used hazardous substances on the property or improperly disposed of dangerous chemicals. Issues related to asbestos and lead paint are commonplace in older buildings. Former service station locations may have leaking underground storage tanks. In addition, the lessee's proposed use or development of land may be subject to wetlands regulations.

> *Example:* A prospective lessee negotiating to lease a small commercial building for use as a convenience store makes an inquiry concerning prior uses of the building. The lessor informs the lessee that the building was used for many years as a dry cleaning business. This fact raises a "red flag" concerning the need for an environmental site assessment of the property.

If the prospective lessee proceeds to lease without conducting a proper environmental site assessment and making what is known as an "all appropriate inquiry" of the environmental condition of the property, then the lessee may be jointly and severally liable with prior owners and lessees for the environmental clean-up costs if hazardous substances or pollution exists on the property, even though the lessee did not cause the contamination.

An environmental inspection of the property involves what is known as a "Phase I ESA." If environmental issues arise as a result of the Phase I ESA, a Phase II ESA may be necessary. Both Phase I and II ESAs should be conducted or supervised by a trained and experienced environmental professional who follows national and state standards.[30]

Environmental Phase I Assessment. This assessment is conducted for the purpose of making an initial determination of the environmental condition of the property[31] and includes the following:

- A site inspection of the property and an investigation of possible contamination from neighboring properties.
- A review of government records.
- Interviews with the property owner and current occupants of the property.
- Interviews with past owners and occupants.
- A review of the history of use of the property.
- Interviews with local government officials and determination of the environmental status of the property.

The results of this assessment may dictate that an Environmental Phase II Assessment is necessary, which would be more extensive and include testing and sample analysis.

Lessee's Trade Fixtures

A trade fixture is an item of personal property installed on the leased premises by a lessee for use in the lessee's trade or business. Examples include store display cases, special lighting, check-out counters, and shelving. The general law pertaining to fixtures is the opposite of the law of trade fixtures. Absent an agreement to the contrary in a contract to convey real estate, regular fixtures become part of the real estate and transfer to the new owner. Trade fixtures, on the other hand, are removable by a lessee at the end of the lease term if no material damage to the leased premises results and if the lease does not provide otherwise.

If the lessee desires to make changes in the premises or to add fixtures, the lease should cover the rights of the parties relating to ownership and removal of fixtures at the end of the lease term. Where improvements or equipment affixed to the premises by the lessee are to be removed by the lessee upon termination of the lease, specific provisions should deal with removal. Frequently, these trade fixture removal provisions in commercial leases require that the lessee return the leased premises to their condition at the inception of the lease. Below is a simple example of a clause dealing with alterations and improvements to the leased premises by a lessee.

> *Alterations & Improvements by Lessee.* Lessee shall not make any alterations or improvements to the leased premises, nor attach any fixtures, including trade fixtures, to the leased premises without obtaining the Lessor's prior written consent. All alterations, improvements, and fixtures, other than Lessee's trade fixtures, made or installed on the leased premises shall be the Lessor's property and shall remain on the leased premises at the end of the term. All trade fixtures attached to the leased premises may be removed at any time by the Lessee, provided the Lessee restores the leased premises to the condition of same prior to the attachment of the trade fixtures. All trade fixtures not removed by the Lessee prior to termination of this lease shall become the property of the Lessor. Lessor reserves the option to require Lessee, at Lessee's

expense, to remove all alterations, improvements, fixtures, and trade fixtures which were placed on the leased premises by Lessee and to repair any damage caused by such removals.

As this sample lease provision illustrates, the lessor may not want the lessee's alterations, fixtures, and trade fixtures left on the premises after termination of the lease.

Example: A lessor leases a 2,000-square-foot commercial building to a lessee, a bathroom remodeling business, for a 10-year term. The lessee converts the large showroom area into 20 "model bathrooms" by installing walls, fixtures, and trade fixtures. When the lessee vacates the leased premises at the end of the lease term, it is unlikely that the lessor will want the 20 display bathrooms and will insist that the lessee remove all alterations, fixtures, and trade fixtures and restore the leased premises to their original condition as one large showroom assuming the lease included a clause similar to the one above.

Repairs

In the absence of a specific lease provision regarding repairs to nonresidential property, *a lessor is not obligated to make ordinary repairs to the leased premises*. Matters related to upkeep and repair responsibilities should be carefully spelled out in any lease of commercial or industrial property.

Example: A lessee leased a 60,000-square foot warehouse for 20 years. The lease was silent concerning the condition of the leased premises and the lessor made no promises as to repairs. Several years later, vandals shattered 17 warehouse windows. The lessee is responsible for replacing the windows.

The longstanding property law rule in North Carolina has been that *a lessor has no duty to the lessee or others on the leased premises for injuries or property damage caused as the result of* **obvious (patent) defects** *in the leased premises that existed at the time the lessee took possession.* In the absence of a warranty, fraud, misrepresentation, or unfair or deceptive business practice, the nonresidential lessee takes the leased premises with all existing defects known or ascertainable by a reasonable inspection. *There is no implied promise that the premises are fit or suitable for occupation, or for the particular use intended, or that the premises are safe for use.* Because of this traditional view, lessees frequently obtain express promises in the lease from the lessor regarding condition of the leased premises, suitability for a particular use, and obligations for major and minor repairs.

Traditional property law places many obligations on a nonresidential lessee in the absence of a lease provision to the contrary, including a duty to make ordinary repairs. *If a lessee fails to make ordinary repairs, the lessee may be liable to the lessor for "waste," thereby breaching the lease.* A lessee is not liable to make extraordinary or major repairs to the leased premises unless the lease specifically places this burden on the lessee.

If the leased premises are part of a larger area owned by the lessor, such as a shopping center, office building, apartment building, or warehouse with multiple occupants, the *lessor* is deemed to have *retained control of the* **common areas** (hallways, lobbies, public restrooms, elevators, parking areas, etc.). *The lessor has an obligation to keep these common areas in proper repair and safe.*

In conclusion, the duties and responsibilities related to repair and upkeep of the leased premises are matters that should be clearly detailed in all nonresidential leases. In the event of accidental destruction of or damage to the leased premises, the lease should also describe the insurance obligations of both lessor and lessee.

Upfitting Improvements

An issue closely related to improvements by a lessee and repairs by a lessor or lessee is the issue of "upfitting improvements" by a lessor as a concession to obtain or retain a tenant. "**Upfitting**" *involves the providing of improvements to a **commercial** property by the lessor at the lessor's expense to prepare the property for the tenant's use.* The parties may have started with a large open area in a new building, with the lessor customizing a space for the lessee. As a condition for renewing an existing office building lease, a desirable commercial tenant with a strong credit rating may require that the lessor "upfit" the lease premises.

> *Example:* A stock brokerage agency leased a 5,000 square foot area in a medium-sized office building for 10 years, with the lease expiring on March 31, 2026. During negotiations for a new lease term, the lessee insisted that the lessor "upfit" at the lessor's expense the leased premises and the common area leading to it by recarpeting and wallpapering the lobby, recarpeting the leased premises, replacing the ceiling tiles throughout the leased premises, adding chair rails and wainscoting in designated rooms, and repainting and wallpapering parts of the leased premises. The lessor agreed to this upfitting because of new office buildings in the area and the possibility that this valuable lessee might consider relocating to a new building.

Assignments and Subleases

In the absence of a lease provision restricting or prohibiting the lessee's right to assign or sublease the premises, a lessee has the right to assign or sublease without the permission of the lessor. By assigning or subleasing, the lessee is simply transferring all or part of the lessee's remaining interest in the lease to a third party. *An "assignment"* is a transfer of the lessee's entire remaining interest in the lease. The lessee who assigns the lease (the **assignor**) to another person (the "**assignee**") does not retain any later interest (*"reversionary interest"*) *in the lease term. The new tenant (the **assignee**) replaces the former tenant for the remainder of the lease term.*

> *Example:* A lessor leases a restaurant building to a lessee for a 10-year term to end on September 30, 2026. The lease does not prohibit or restrict assignments or subleases. In June of 2017, the lessee assigns all of her remaining interest under the lease to a new owner. A valid assignment has taken place. The new owner is called the *assignee*, and the lessee is called the *assignor*.

Note *that a lessee who assigns his/her interest is **not** relieved from future liability under the lease to the lessor.* If the assignee does not pay the rent, the lessor can recover payment from the lessee (assignor). If possible, the lessee should seek a release (sometimes called a novation) from the lessor when an assignment is being made to relieve the lessee from any further liability under the lease. The lessor may or may not agree to that novation.

Where a lease is assigned, the assignee steps into the shoes of the original lessee and enters into a lessor and tenant relationship with the original lessor. *There are two types of assignments: a "bare assignment" and a "full assignment."* The law on this subject can be involved, but the essential difference between the two is that an assignee has more potential liability under a full assignment. Bare assignments are commonplace; full assignments are not found by the courts unless the parties expressly indicate in the assignment document that a full assignment is intended.

Bare Assignment. The assignee does not expressly assume all of the contractual promises in the original lease. Instead, the assignee agrees to abide by the important covenants in the lease (such as the payment of rent) only as long as the assignee remains in privity of estate with the lessor. If an assignee reassigns to another party, the assignee is no longer responsible for any lease covenants and is no longer liable to the lessor for compliance with them.

Example: A lessor leased a warehouse to lessee for a 10-year term. Two years later, the lessee assigned the lease to X for the remainder of the term. X simply agreed to an assignment of the lease and did not expressly assume the obligations under the lease contract. Five years later, with three years remaining on the original lease term, X assigned the lease to Y. Several months after taking possession of the warehouse, Y defaulted on the rent payments and abandoned the leased premises. The lessor's total damages, including unpaid rent for the rest of the lease term, total $40,000. The lessor can recover damages from Y or the lessee, but has no right to recover from X. While X had title to the nonfreehold estate (while X was in privity of estate), X complied with all lease covenants. Once X transferred the nonfreehold estate by a valid assignment to Y, X was no longer in privity of estate and was thereby relieved of all liability to the lessor for future breaches of lease covenants.

Why does the lessee remain liable to the lessor in the above example? *The original lessee remains liable to the lessor for the entire lease term under privity of contract absent an express agreement with the lessor to the contrary.* The lease is a contract, and the lessee is liable under that contract regardless of whether the lessee makes any kind of assignment or sublease during the lease term. In the above example, the lessee remains liable to the lessor as a surety. If Y fails to pay the rent and damages, the original lessee will be liable.

Full Assignment. Some assignees not only take an assignment but also expressly assume responsibility for all covenants and provisions in the original lease for the rest of the term. This means that an assuming assignee is responsible for compliance with the lease even after reassigning it to another person.

Example: Same facts as the example above, except, when the lessee assigned to X for the remainder of the term, X *expressly agreed to assume all obligations under the lease.* After the assignment to Y and Y's default and abandonment of the leased premises, the lessor can now hold the lessee, X and Y liable for the $40,000.

As with the previous example, the lessee remains liable under contract law and is not relieved of liability by any kind of assignment to a third party. Even though X, the assignee, paid rent while she was in privity of estate, she expressly agreed to assume all obligations under the lease with lessor, i.e., she took a full assignment of the leasehold estate and was therefore responsible under privity of contract for the rest of the lease term. Y, of course, is also liable. As a practical matter, if Y doesn't pay, X will; and if X doesn't pay, Y will.

"**Subleasing**" (sometimes called **subletting**) is, in effect, the making of a new lease in which the original lessee becomes a "**sublessor**" who has rented to a "**sublessee**" under a document separate from the original lease. In essence, a sublease carves a shorter-lease term out of the remainder of the main lease term. The sublessee is not substituted for the original tenant, but a new and lesser tenancy has been created. *In a sublease, the sublessor (the lessee under the original lease) reserves a period of time at the end of the lease term (called a "reversionary interest").*

When a lessee subleases and thereby becomes a sublessor, the lessee is **not** relieved from future liability under the lease. If the sublessee does not pay the rent under the sublease, the lessee (sublessor) is legally bound to pay the rent under the main lease (sometimes called the head lease). There can be disadvantages also to the sublessee. If a sublessee pays rent to the sublessor, but the sublessor fails to pay rent under the head lease, the head lease can be terminated and the sublease will cease to exist.[32]

Technically, there is no direct relationship between a sublessee and the lessor under the original lease. The sublessee pays rent to the sublessor who, in turn, pays rent to the original lessor. The rent paid by the sublessee may be and often is higher than the rent under the original lease. The sublessor pockets the profit and delivers the rent agreed upon in the original lease to the lessor.

> *Example:* A lessor leased a warehouse to a lessee for a 10-year term. Two years later, the lessee, as sublessor, subleased the warehouse to X, as sublessee, for a term ending one day prior to the remainder of the head lease term. As part of sublease agreement, X agreed to pay sublease rental payments to the lessee/sublessor who, in turn, agreed to pay the payments under the head lease to the lessor. Several years later, X defaulted on the rent payments and abandoned the warehouse. The lessee/sublessor has a right to enforce the sublease agreement against X and recover unpaid rent and damages. As long as the lessee continues to pay rent under the head lease, the lessor will be unconcerned with X's breach of the sublease agreement. If the lessee stops paying rent under the head lease, the lessor will be entitled to all appropriate remedies against the lessee but not against X.

The above example can appear complex until one realizes that there were two leasehold (non-freehold) estates created: 1) the original 10-year warehouse lease between lessor and lessee, and 2) a sublease for a shorter term between the lessee, as a sublessor, and X, as a sublessee.

Unless the lease specifically prohibits or regulates the assignment or subleasing of the leasehold interest, a lessee is free to do either. Restrictions on assigning and subleasing are construed strictly against the lessor. Indeed, a provision in a lease prohibiting assignments does prohibit subleases, and vice versa. In long-term leases, it is far more common for the lessor to restrict the transfer by assignment or sublease rather than prohibit it outright. Restrictions usually require the lessor's prior permission, and the lessor promises not to unreasonably withhold approval of a new sublessee or assignee. Restrictions may include the type of business or activity of the proposed sublessee or assignee. The credit rating or ability of the proposed sublessee or assignee to fulfill the financial obligations of the lease also is of concern to the lessor.

The title that a lessee places on an instrument transferring all or part of the lessee's interest under the lease usually will accurately reflect the nature of the transfer (i.e., a document titled "assignment" will normally be an assignment, and a document titled "sublease" normally will be a sublease). But regardless of what a transfer is titled, the above examples illustrate a very important point regarding North Carolina property law: *If a lessee transfers the entire leasehold term away, the lessee has created an "assignment" regardless of what the document is called.*[33] *If a lessee retains the right to possession for a period of time at the end of the lease term (reversion), the lessee has created a "sublease" regardless of what the document is called.*

As with all contractual provisions, great care must be taken in drafting a prohibition against or restrictions on assignment and subleasing; an example of such a clause, from the lessor's perspective, follows.

> *Assignment or Subleasing:* Lessee shall not sell, assign, sublease, mortgage, pledge, or in any manner transfer this lease, or any interest therein, or any part thereof, to anyone other than the lessee without the prior written consent of the lessor, which consent shall not be unreasonably withheld. Consent by the lessor to one assignment or subleasing of the leased premises shall not constitute a waiver of the lessor's rights as to any subsequent assignment or subleasing. No consent by the lessor to any transfer by the lessee shall relieve the lessee of lessee's obligations under this lease.

Lease Renewal

In the absence of an express provision in the lease, *a lessee does not have any implied right to renew the lease.* Covenants are often put into leases giving the lessee the option to renew by notifying his lessor a specified time prior to the termination of the initial term of the lease.[34] A renewal provision may be quite important to a tenant who makes an expensive improvement to leased property relying upon the expectation of continuing in possession for a longer period than provided by the original term. Leases are often very specific about the timing and methods of giving notice to exercise renewal options.

> *Example:* A lessor leases to a lessee for a five-year term. The lease gives the lessee a right to renew the lease at the same rental for another five-year term by giving written notice to the lessor at least 30 days prior to the expiration of the initial term. As the end of the initial term nears, the lessee has forgotten about the written notice requirement. The lessee remembers the lease renewal clause several days before the end of the lease term, and, with only two days remaining on the initial term, gives the lessor a late notice of intent to renew for the additional five year term. The notice is too late and does not comply with the lease! Unless the lessor decides to waive the lease provision and accept the late notice, the lessee has lost a valuable right to renew. This is true regardless of whether the lessor has been actually injured by the late notice.

There are several North Carolina court decisions where the lessor was held to have legally waived the notice of renewal requirements stated in the lease. In one case, the lessor had accepted oral notices of renewal twice in the past. The Court felt that this practice misled the lessee into believing that the lessee could continue to give oral notices of renewal in the future. The Court therefore allowed the lessee to renew for a third term after giving oral notice, even though the lease called for a written notice. Another instance of waiver of the lease requirements for renewal involves acceptance by the lessor of a higher rent after expiration of the initial lease term.

> *Example:* A lessor leases to a lessee for five years at a rental of $2,000/month. The lease gives lessee the right to renew for an additional five-year term at $2,300/month if the lessee gives the lessor written notice exercising the option to renew no later than 60 days prior to expiration of the initial lease term. The lessee forgets all about the notice requirement, but after the initial term expires, remains on the premises and sends the lessor the higher *$2,300 month* rent called for in the renewal provision. The lessor accepts the higher rent. Under these circumstances, the

lessor is deemed to have waived the lease notice requirements and to have accepted the lessee for the additional five-year term.

The lease may contain an "automatic renewal" clause whereby the original term is repeated for successive terms unless one of the parties indicates to the other his intention not to renew for another term within a specified time. Some leases contain clauses calling for "successive renewals" or language that could be construed to give the lessee a perpetual right to renew the lease for given periods of time. This type of provision is frowned upon by the courts because a lessor might unknowingly tie up property forever without intending to do so. In 1985, the North Carolina Supreme Court took a dim view of perpetual renewal clauses.[35] It adopted what is called a "***brightline rule***" for determining the validity of these clauses. This rule states that, unless the lease makes it absolutely clear that a lease renewal right is to be a perpetual one, the renewal clause will *not* be construed to run indefinitely. Words such as "perpetual," "for all time," or "forever" probably will be clear enough to create a valid perpetual renewal provision in North Carolina. Merely calling for "successive renewals" or "automatic renewals every five years," however, will not be interpreted as perpetual renewal provisions.

Options to Purchase and Preemptive Rights

When a lessee has constructed a building upon leased premises or made other improvements thereto, a lease provision often gives the lessee an option to purchase the real property. Sometimes the price to be paid by the lessee to the lessor is established in the lease provision. Occasionally, if the lessor and lessee cannot agree on a price, the lease states that each party shall appoint an appraiser, and the two appraisers will appoint another appraiser and the three appraisers will then value the property and set the price to be paid. *Every option to purchase must specify the purchase price or some reliable method to determine it.* Each option to purchase should also specify the type of conveyance to be made by the grantor-lessor, the time and manner in which the lessee must exercise his option and pay an option fee. The introductory paragraph in an option to purchase portion of a lease reads as follows:

> *Option to Purchase:* If the Lessee shall not then be in default in the performance or observance of any of the terms, covenants, or conditions to be performed or observed by the Lessee under this lease, the Lessee shall have an option to purchase the Leased Premises at any time during the term of this lease or any extended term thereof for One Million Fifty Thousand Dollars ($1,050,000). The Lessee shall pay an option fee of Five Thousand Dollars ($5,000) and shall exercise its option to purchase by giving written notice thereof to the Lessor.
>
> [The clause then describes in great detail the method of title protection, time limits, and the precise form that the final conveyance is to take.]

Leases may contain a provision granting the lessee a **preemptive right** to purchase the leased premises. This preemptive right may be in the form of a **right of first refusal**, an agreement giving the tenant the opportunity to match a bona fide offer to purchase from a third person in the event the lessor decides to sell, or, it may be in the form of a **first opportunity to purchase**. (See the discussion of these preemptive rights at the end of Chapter 11.)

Lessor's Right to Enter Premises During Lease Term

Leases often contain clauses giving the lessor the right to enter leased premises during the lease term to inspect the property to see if the tenant is complying with the tenant's obligations, to make necessary repairs, to place "for sale" or "for rent" signs on the premises, or to show the premises to prospective purchasers or tenants. In the absence of such language, the lessor has no right to enter the premises during the term of the lease.

Lessor's Implied Covenant of Quiet Enjoyment

There is an implied covenant of quiet enjoyment in every lease, even if the lease itself contains no express provision on point. This covenant is in reality a guaranty to the lessee that the lessor has good legal title to the property. Under this covenant, the lessor assures that the lessee shall have continuous, uninterrupted possession of the leased premises during the lease term. The covenant assures that the lessee's possession during the term of the lease will not be terminated or interfered with by the lessor, by a party whose claim stems from the lessor, or by a third party with title superior to that held by the lessor. *If the lessee is deprived of or removed from possession because of any of these circumstances, the lessor is liable to the lessee for breach of the covenant of quiet enjoyment.*

> *Example:* The owner of an office building, borrowed $2,000,000 and gave the bank a deed of trust on the office building to secure repayment of that amount. The owner then leased part of the building to a lessee for a 10-year term. Several years later, the owner defaulted on repayment of the mortgage loan, and the bank foreclosed. The bank was high bidder at the foreclosure sale and immediately proceeded to evict the lessee because the bank's original deed of trust was prior in time and superior to the leasehold interest. Because the lessee is being evicted by someone with superior title to the lessor, she can bring an action against the owner for breach of the covenant of quiet enjoyment.

The covenant of quiet enjoyment does **not** protect a lessee against the acts of third-party wrongdoers who interfere with the lessee's possession without having any legal right to do so. A lessee can, of course, sue the third party for trespass or pursue some other appropriate remedy. However, the *legal meaning* of the term "quiet enjoyment" is not what one would think based on the normal meanings of the words "quiet" and "enjoyment." A lessor does **not** assure by this implied covenant that the leased premises will be free from excessive noise caused by neighbors or that the lessee's possession will be enjoyable and serene. Rather, *it is a warranty of the lessee's leasehold title to possess and use the premises as called for in the lease.*

Breach of Lease by Lessor or Lessee

All well-drafted leases include remedies for the lessor against various acts of default by the lessee. The three most common examples of default are: nonpayment of rent, the lessee's abandonment of the leased premises, and the lessee's commission of waste. A lessor's remedies in the event of the lessee's default are governed by the terms of the lease, applicable statutes, and various North Carolina court decisions. *Default is a two-way street.* A lessor might be the party in default under a lease.

Lessee's Failure to Pay Rent

Even without a lease provision expressly on point, the lessor's common-law remedies for a lessee's material breach of the covenant to pay rent are the following:

- Terminate the lease and retake possession of the leased property;
- Reenter the leased premises and relet them for the lessee's account;
- Do not reenter the premises and sue for delinquent rent as it accrues.

Almost all well-drafted leases supplement and alter the common law by including detailed provisions giving the lessor additional remedies for a lessee's breach. Examples include clauses authorizing a lessor's actual damages, consequential damages, and/or liquidated damages. Under contract law, a lessor has the obligation to mitigate damages, rendering the lessor's third alternative at common law – leaving the premises vacant – an unwise one.

Lessee's Liability for Waste

A lessee may be liable for *"waste"* if the lessee destroys part of the premises or permits its value to be substantially diminished by negligence or failure to maintain and repair the premises as required by the lease.

Example: A lessor leases a warehouse to a lessee for 10 years. The lease placed the responsibility for all maintenance and repair of the structure on the lessee. During the lease term, the tenant noticed termite infestation but did nothing. By the time the term expired, the warehouse had suffered substantial structural damage because of the termites. The lessee is guilty of waste under these circumstances and will be liable to the lessor for damages.

Lien on Personal Property Permitted – Nonresidential Property

A lessor of *nonresidential* real property has a statutory lien on the personal property of a tenant. General Statute 44A-2(e) provides, in part:

> (e) Any lessor of nonresidential demised premises has a lien on all furniture, furnishings, trade fixtures, equipment and other personal property to which the tenant has legal title and which remains on the demised premises if (i) the tenant has vacated the premises for 21 or more days after the paid rental period has expired, and (ii) the lessor has a lawful claim for damages against the tenant. If the tenant has vacated the premises for 21 or more days after the expiration of the paid rental period, or if the lessor has received a judgment for possession of the premises that is executable and the tenant has vacated the premises, then all property remaining on the premises may be removed and placed in storage. If the total value of all property remaining on the premises is less than one hundred dollars ($100.00), then it shall be deemed abandoned five days after the tenant has vacated the premises, and the lessor may remove it and may donate it to any charitable institution or organization..

Subsection (e) of the statute continues with a proviso: The lessor is not entitled to a lien if there is an agreement with the tenant that the lessor shall not have a lien. The lien authorized by the above subsection is for unpaid rent and damages. The lien is enforceable by a public sale pursuant to the provisions of General Statute §44A-4(e).

Lien on Personal Property in Self-Service Storage Facilities

The widespread popularity of self-service storage facilities warrants a mention of liens on personal property stored in such facilities. Owners of these commercial facilities lease individual storage units of various sizes to renters who have exclusive possession of their units and secure them with a lock. Additional security is often supplied by the owner. The rental of a self-service storage unit can result in numerous issues, including default in rent payments by the unit lessee while the unit contains the lessee's personal property, criminal law issues, tenant bankruptcy, and self-storage liens. Article 4 of Chapter 44A of the General Statues, "Self-Service Storage Facilities," deals with the lien rights of a facility owner when the tenant has defaulted on unit rent payments. G.S. § 44A-41 provides:

> The owner of a self-service storage facility has a lien upon all personal property stored at the facility for rent, expenses necessary for the preservation of the personal property, and expenses reasonably incurred in the sale or other disposition of the personal property pursuant to this Article. This lien shall not have priority over any security interest which is perfected at the time the occupant stores the property at the self-service storage facility.

The self-service storage facility lien is enforced pursuant to the requirements of G.S. § 44A-43. Separate requirements exist if the property on which the lien is claimed is a motor vehicle. G.S. 44A-44.1 provides:

> Unless the rental agreement specifically provides otherwise, the exclusive care, custody, and control of all personal property stored in a storage space at a self-service storage facility shall remain vested in the occupant until the property is sold as provided in this Article or otherwise disposed of. The owner of a self-service storage facility is a commercial lessor who rents space. Unless the rental agreement specifically provides otherwise, while the personal property remains on the owner's premises, the owner is liable for damage caused by the intentional acts or negligence of the owner or the owner's employees.

Lessee's Remedies for Lessor's Breach

Damage: A well-drafted lease will detail the lessee's remedies in the event of breach by the lessor. The classic measure of damages for the lessor's breach is the difference between the fair rental value in the condition of the property specified in the lease and the diminished fair rental value because of the lessor's breach. A lessee is also entitled to consequential damages resulting from the lessor's default. In proper circumstances, the lessee may also recover lost profits.

Common Law Doctrine of Constructive Eviction. While more common in residential leasing, a commercial lessee may be able to invoke the common-law doctrine of *"constructive eviction"* if the premises are uninhabitable and the lessor is unable or unwilling to correct the problem. Under the constructive eviction doctrine, the tenant gives a lessor notice of a material breach by the lessor that renders the premises uninhabitable or unusable for the lessee's purposes. If the lessor fails to correct the problem within a reasonable time, the tenant may have the option of leaving the premises and ending all future liability to the lessor for rent. The theory is that the lessor has "constructively evicted" the tenant through his failure to maintain fit and habitable premises.

> *Example:* A doctor leased a medical office suite from a lessor for a five-year term. Under the terms of the lease, the lessor agreed to maintain the exterior and roof of the building. Several months later, the doctor discovered that the roof leaked after heavy rain storms. He notified the lessor of this fact and also noted that his medical equipment and waiting room furniture had been damaged during each storm. In spite of several additional complaints from the doctor over several more weeks, the lessor made no effort to repair the roof. After a final notice to the lessor, the doctor then vacated the leased premises, removed all of his equipment and furnishings, and rented elsewhere. Even though more than four and one-half years remained

on the lease term, the doctor is relieved of all further liability under the lease because the lessor's inaction constituted a *constructive eviction* of the tenant. The tenant may also be entitled to recover damages from the lessor.

The constructive eviction doctrine developed in every American jurisdiction through a series of early appellate court decisions. It is an important doctrine and remedy because it applies to all types of tenancies - residential and non-residential - where the lessor is responsible for the problem at issue. The doctrine will not operate to protect a tenant, however, unless the tenant vacates the leased premises within a reasonable period of time after the lessor's breach.[36]

SECURITIES LAWS AND THE COMMERCIAL REAL ESTATE PROFESSIONAL

There are aspects of commercial real estate practice that may implicate federal and state securities laws. Due to the severe penalties for violating the securities laws (including fines, imprisonment, and possible rescission of non-compliant transactions), attention to and compliance with these laws is advisable.

The Securities and Exchange Act of 1934 (the "34 Act") along with other statutes and agency rules regulate the nation's securities markets and the securities professionals who participate in those markets. The 34 Act creates the scheme of regulation for, among other things, the business of being a broker-dealer in securities. Any person or firm that qualifies as a "broker" or "dealer" in "securities", as those terms are defined by the 34 Act, must satisfy the threshold requirement of registration with the Securities and Exchange Commission or risk severe penalties. The 34 Act also regulates and may require registration with respect to certain securities and certain transactions. By way of clarification, consider the following definitions under the 34 Act.

Broker- A "broker" is defined in the 34 Act to mean any person engaged in the business of effecting transactions in securities for the account of others (excluding banks).

Dealer- A "dealer" is defined in the 34 Act to mean any person engaged in the business of buying and selling securities for his own account, through a broker or otherwise (excluding banks), or any person insofar as he buys or sells securities for his own account, either individually or in some fiduciary capacity, but not as a part of a regular business.

Security- A "security" is defined in the 34 Act to mean any note, stock, treasury stock, bond, debenture, certificate of interest or participation in any profit-sharing agreement or in any oil, gas, or other mineral royalty or lease, any collateral-trust certificate, preorganization certificate or subscription, transferable share, investment contract, voting trust certificate, certificate of deposit for a security, any put, call, straddle, option, or privilege on any security, certificate of deposit, or group or index of securities (including any interest therein or based on the value thereof), or any put, call, straddle, option, or privilege entered into on a national securities exchange relating to foreign currency, or in general, any instrument commonly known as a "security"; or any certificate of interest or participation in, temporary or interim certificate for, receipt for, or warrant or right to subscribe to or purchase, any of the foregoing...."

The purpose of reproducing the above definitions is to illustrate the wide swathe of transactions, instruments and economic arrangements covered by the securities laws. At first blush, some transactions that are conventionally viewed as real estate and not securities may not seem to fit squarely within the excerpted language above. Notwithstanding the belief held by many real estate professionals that real estate cannot be a security, the SEC has been aggressive in its application of the "securities" label to many real estate transactions.

Consider the National Association of Securities Dealer's (NASD) Notice to Members in March of 2005 regarding the popularity of using tenants-in-common (TIC) interests as replacement property in the IRC Section 1031 context. Many real estate professionals have been bundling TIC interests in rental or other commercial property with other arrangements (like, for example, a contract with a property manager who will manage the property on behalf of the investors) and selling the arrangement to investors as a 1031 vehicle. The NASD has made it clear that notwithstanding the fact that a TIC is an interest in real property, the arrangements are usually "investment contracts" (and therefore securities) under the federal securities laws.

Another common situation involves a client who retains a real estate professional to help them sell their business' real estate and building, but want the real estate professional to help them sell their inventory, equipment, customer accounts, etc. as well. When an intermediary plays an integral role in negotiating and effecting an acquisition or disposition of a business, securities are almost inevitably involved and therefore the securities laws are implicated and broker-dealer registration is required.

Finally, consider another type of transaction where a real estate broker plays an active role in finding investors to contribute money to an entity to acquire land for investment or development. The interests offered to the investors by the real estate professional would be securities and therefore bring the transaction under the securities laws.

Although these three scenarios raise different substantive legal issues under various securities law provisions, they all implicate the potential applicability of state and federal securities laws. Addressing these laws in detail is clearly outside the scope of this Manual. However, it is important for agents to be aware of the fact that these laws may apply to certain real estate transactions or aspects of certain real estate transactions. Brokers considering a commercial real estate practice should familiarize themselves with the basic applicability of the securities laws and should seek (and direct their clients and customers to seek) professional, legal assistance if questions arise regarding the possible application of securities laws to a particular circumstance.

Endnotes

1. N.C. Gen. Stat. §93A-6(a)(8).

2. The North Carolina Association of REALTORS˚ - REALTORS˚ Commercial Alliance is a division of the North Carolina Association of REALTORS˚ sometimes referred to as "NCAR-RCA" or "RCA" The purposes of the Alliance as stated in their bylaws are:

    (a) To unite those engaged in the commercial and investment real estate business for the purpose of exerting a beneficial influence upon matters affecting the commercial real estate business; to provide an organization for the collection and dissemination of information to promote professionalism which could prove helpful to members of this Alliance, to encourage and provide services and educational opportunities so that members may broaden their knowledge of the business; and to provide meetings and opportunities for members to exchange views and information on topics of common interest; (b) To protect and promote the welfare of commercial property and the ownership of same and promote private enterprise; (c) To advise, counsel and interact with committees and leadership of the North Carolina Association of REALTORS° to provide information, proposals, solutions and assistance with reference to commercial and investment real estate concerns.

The listing forms are designated as Form 570- Exclusive Right to Lease and or Sell Listing Agreement, Form 571- Exclusive Right to Sell Listing Agreement and Form 572- Exclusive Right to Lease Listing Agreement.

3.   The North Carolina Association of REALTORS° - REALTORS° Commercial Alliance series of forms are all numbered in the 500 series of the REALTORS° standard forms and contain agency disclosure and compliance forms, listing agreements, buyer-tenant agency agreements, inter-agent split agreements, unlisted property fee agreements and transactional forms.

4.   N.C. Gen. Stat. §93A-6(a)(9).

5.   N.C. Gen. Stat. §143-214.5, "Water Supply Watershed Protection."

6.   The complete system of classification of watershed areas and the related regulations are set forth in 15A NCAC Subchapter 2B.

7.   N.C. Gen. Stat. §143-214.5(d).

8.   N.C. Gen. Stat. §113A-205 et. seq.

9.   N.C. Gen. Stat. §113A-100 et seq.

10. N.C. Gen. Stat. §105-129.2, et. seq. Business Tax Incentives Article 3A- Tax Incentives for New and Expanding Businesses.

11. *Market Analysis for Commercial Real Estate- CI 201*, page 7-3,9.8 and 9.9 and other references Commercial Investment Real Estate CCIM Institute, 2005.

12. Internal Revenue Code Section 1031(a)(2) lists property types excluded from the use of Section 1031, namely:

> "(a) Stock in trade or other property held primarily for sale; (b) Stocks, bonds or notes; (c) Other securities or evidences of indebtedness or interest; (d) Interests in a partnership; (e) Certificates of trust or beneficial interest; or (f) Choses in action."

13. See Internal Revenue Code Regulations Section 1.1031(a)–1. Issues of a taxpayer's intent in holding the property, the amount of time the property was held and the type of property involved are factors which are reviewed to determine if the property qualifies as "like kind" (held for productive use in a trade or business or for investment) as to both the property sold and the property acquired.

14. The regulations for use of a qualified intermediary are set forth in Section 1.1031(b)-2. It is important that a Qualified Intermediary be truly independent. Use of a taxpayer's attorney, accountant or real estate agent to serve as the qualified intermediary is not advisable as they are typically disqualified persons, not able to serve as a qualified intermediary, (see Internal Revenue Code Regulations Section 1.1031(k)-1(k)) and thus their acting as the qualified intermediary will disqualify the exchange. It is also important to make sure that the exchange agreement is properly drafted to avoid constructive receipt of the money by the taxpayer (see Internal Revenue Code Regulations Section 1.1031(k)-1(f)) which will disqualify the exchange.

15. See Revenue Procedure 2000-37 and Revenue Procedure 2004-51.

16. Gain or loss realized on the sale or disposition of real property must be recognized for tax purposes under Section 1001 of the Internal Revenue Code.

17. For more detail on this and other matters related to Section 1031 exchanges, see *Tax Free Exchanges Under Section 1031* by Jeremiah M. Long and Mary B. Foster, Published by the Tomson/West Group, copyright 2005.

18. N.C. Gen. Stat. §93A-6(a)(11) and North Carolina Real Estate Commission Rule 21 NCAC 58A.0111.

19. *Mezzanotte v. Freeland*, 20 N.C. App. 11, 17, 200 S.E.2d 410, 414 (1973), *cert. denied* 284 N.C. 616, 201 S.E.2d 689 (1974). For a recent Georgia Court of Appeals case interpreting a "free look" provision, see *Sheridan v. Crown Capital Corporation*, 2001 WL 946488. In this case, the court found that the purchaser did not have an unlimited free look. Rather, the free look specified in the contract was for the purpose of determining whether the property would be satisfactory for the purchaser's use of it as a commercial shopping center development.

20. N.C.Gen.Stat. §22-2.

21. *Computer Decisions, Inc. v. Rouse Office Management of NC, Inc.*, 124 N.C. App. 383, 477 S.E.2d 262 (1996). Issue of whether an agreement meets the requirements of the Statute of Frauds and is valid. *Howlett v. CSB, LLC*, 164 N.C. App. 715, 596 S.E.2d 899 (2004).

22. See, for example, *National Advertising Co. v. NC Dept. Of Transportation*, 124 N.C. App. 620, 478 S.E.2d 248 (1996), where the plaintiff claimed, among other things, that it had a five year sign lease. The Court of Appeals held that plaintiff's failure to record his lease under N.C. Gen. Stat. §47-18 made it invalid against a subsequent purchaser of the property for value who recorded first. See *Chapel Hill Cinemas, Inc. v. Robbins*, 143 N.C. App. 571, 547 S.E.2d 462, *reversed* 354 N.C. 349, 554 S.E.2d 644 (2001), where the lessee lost a valuable right of first refusal contained in a lease because of failure to record. (The lessee prevailed in a suit for damages against the lessor who sold the property without honoring the right of first refusal.)

23. N.C.Gen.Stat. §47-118(c), §47-120.

24. N.C.Gen.Stat. §47-117 and §47-118.

25.   *Lowe's of Shelby, Inc. v. Hunt*, 30 N.C. App. 84, 226 S.E.2d 232 (1976).

26.   Even well drafted percentage rent provisions can require interpretation when unforeseen circumstances arise. In an Iowa Supreme Court decision, *Hartig Drug Company v. Hartig*, 602 N.W.2d 794 (1999), the Court held that a commercial tenant's gross sales did not include the total amount that the tenant received from lottery and stamp sales; instead, only the amount that the tenant received for its services in selling stamps and lottery tickets was to be included.

27.   *Estwin Corporation v. Prescription Center Pharmacy, Inc.,* 93 Nev. 251, 563 P.2d 78 (Supreme Court of Nevada, 1977).

28.   *English v. Harris Clay Co.*, 225 N.C. 467, 35 S.E.2d 329 (1945).

29.   Federal Comprehensive Environmental Response, Compensation and Liability Act of 1980, 42 U.S.C.A. §§ 9601 *et seq.* Other federal and state environmental laws may also be applicable. The coverage of environmental due diligence in this text constitutes only a brief summary. Compliance with environmental laws is both a legal matter and one left to environmental experts.

30.   Standards for Phase I and II ESAs are established by the American Society for Testing and Materials (ASTM).

31.   40 C.F.R. Part 312.

32.   *DiFrega v. Publiese*, 164 N.C. App. 499, 596 S.E.2d 456 (2004). In this case, the sublessee also lost a valuable option to purchase when the lessor terminated the head lease for breach and failure to cure without notice. *Gardner v. Ebenezer. LLC*, 190 N.C.App. 432, 660 S.E.2d 172 (2008), where the Court of Appeals affirmed the trial court decision that a tenant and a sublessee to a commercial lease forfeited their rights for failure to pay rent.

33.   North Carolina uses a "brightline" test instead of the "intention of the parties" test to determine whether a conveyance by a tenant of a leased premises is an assignment or a sublease. *Northside Station Assoc. v. Maddry*, 105 N.C. App. 384, 413 S.E.2d 319 (1992).

34.   *Atlantic and East Carolina Realty v. Southern Outdoor Advertising, Inc.*, 129 N.C. App. 612, 501 S.E.2d 87 (1998). Case involves issue of whether a sublease was properly renewed.

35.   *Lattimore v. Fisher's Food Shoppe, Inc.*, 313 N.C. 467, 329 S.E.2d 346 (1985).

36.   See, for example, *Gardner v. Ebenezer, LLC*, 190 N.C.App. 432, 660 S.E.2d 172 (2008), quoting as follows from *K & S Enter. v. Kennedy Office Supply Co., Inc.*, 135 N.C.App. 260, 520 S.E.2d 122 (1999): "[C]onstructive eviction takes place when a landlord's breach of duty under the lease renders the premises untenable. A tenant seeking to show constructive eviction has the burden of showing that he abandoned the premises within a reasonable time after the landlord's wrongful act."

20 | SELECTED LICENSE LAW CASES

To assist brokers in applying North Carolina Real Estate License Law and Commission Rules, the following summaries of actual disciplinary cases which the Commission has heard within the past decade are provided for discussion purposes. Brokers should review the brief factual description and then determine which subsections of G.S. 93A-6(a) and/or (b) and which Commission rules have been violated. Readers might find it helpful to have a copy of G.S. 93A-6 at hand, as well as the General Brokerage rules set forth in Chapter 58A.0100 of the Commission rules for ready reference as they assess each fact situation to determine the violations. Obviously, brokers are discouraged from emulating the behavior described below. The term "Respondent" refers to the broker against whom the complaint is filed, who is "responding to" the allegations of the complaint.

LICENSE LAW CASES

Case #1:

Broker was a broker-in-charge of her sole proprietorship. She entered into an Exclusive Right to Sell agreement with an owner of residential property in January. In July of the same year, several individuals became interested in the property and two different couples made offers on the property. Broker worked with both buyers as a seller's agent. One offer was a cash offer of $90,000 with a closing date of September 10 and the second offer was for $90,500 with a closing date of September 5. Seller thought the second offer was also a cash offer, but in fact it contained a financing contingency. Additionally, the second offer was not signed by the buyers. Broker used outdated REALTOR® forms to prepare both offers.

Seller accepted the second offer, based on Broker's advice and recommendation, and Broker deposited a $5000 earnest money deposit received from the buyers into her trust account. Problems arose and the second buyers were unable to complete the contract. Seller sought to enforce the contract, at which point it was learned that four different drafts of the purported agreement existed and the offer allegedly accepted by Seller was not signed by buyers. Amidst the confusion, Seller informed Broker, her agent, not to release the earnest money deposit, to which Seller felt she was entitled. Notwithstanding Seller's express instructions, Broker released the earnest money deposit to the buyers who lived outside of North Carolina.

What, if any, License Laws or Commission rules were violated?

Case #2:

A broker licensed in 1999 formed a limited liability company in 2000 and conducted her real estate brokerage business under her limited liability company between 2000 and 2003, but failed to obtain a firm broker license for her company. When she was contacted by the Commission, she immediately applied for and received a firm broker license for her limited liability company in February 2004.

What, if any, License Laws or Commission rules were violated?

Case #3:

Respondent was a licensed provisional broker who was employed by a real estate company under the supervision of a broker-in-charge. She represented a buyer who was purchasing a mobile home park. At the conclusion of the transaction, the provisional broker accepted a promissory note payable to her personally and secured by a deed of trust for her commission. Both the promissory note and deed of trust were recorded. The provisional broker ultimately agreed to assign the promissory note to the real estate company by whom she was employed.

What, if any, License Laws or Commission rules were violated?

Case #4:

Respondent was a licensed real estate broker, as well as a licensed residential appraiser. She notified the Commission in writing on August 19, 2003 that on May 28, 2003 she had been disciplined by the Appraisal Board for valuing a single family home at $327,000 in a subdivision in which the average values were $268,000. She had used comparables outside of the subdivision and had made a $50,000 adjustment to the subject property without any documentation or explanation. The Appraisal Board had issued a six month suspension which was stayed on condition that she complete certain educational courses with which she complied.

While the Commission was investigating the Appraisal Board action, it received a complaint filed by a husband and wife property owners. Broker, purportedly acting as a dual agent, had prepared an Offer to Purchase between an LLC and the husband and wife property owners which Offer was accepted and signed by both parties. Broker signed the Offer as escrow agent acknowledging receipt of a $500 earnest money deposit, which, in fact, was never paid. Broker failed to review the *Working with Real Estate Agents* brochure with either party, and while she did complete a Dual Agency Addendum with the LLC, she never had a listing agreement with the property owners nor a buyer agency agreement with the LLC. She later had the sellers sign a "Confirmation of Buyer Agency" claiming to act solely as a buyer agent. The transaction failed to close and when the sellers demanded the earnest money deposit, broker failed to advise them that it had never been paid. However when the sellers sued broker in Small Claims Court and obtained a judgment against her for the earnest money deposit and court costs, broker paid the judgment within one year of rendition.

What, if any, License Laws or Commission rules were violated?

Case #5:

Respondent is broker-in-charge of her own company, which she opened after being terminated from her former employer (not real estate related) due to downsizing. She was the only broker in her company. A former co-worker contacted broker and indicated that he was looking for a home and broker offered to assist him, to which he agreed. Buyer, through broker, made an offer to purchase a home in a subdivision marketed through a national builder on the builder's custom form. Broker's name never appeared in the offer to purchase or contract, although a registration slip maintained by the builder-seller identified broker as a "Realtor" and the buyer as the "client." By all accounts, broker had nothing else to do with the transaction after the offer was accepted and did not attend the closing, but received a commission check for approximately $4200.

After the closing, buyer approached broker to request reimbursement for a refrigerator he had purchased, maintaining that broker had promised to buy him a refrigerator as a housewarming gift. Broker denied the allegation and refused to compensate the buyer. A complaint ensued.

Upon inquiry, it appeared that broker had never reviewed the *"Working with Real Estate Agents"* brochure with the buyer nor had she entered into a written buyer agency agreement with the buyer. Broker initially maintained that she had presented a buyer agency agreement to buyer but that he had never signed or returned it. Buyer asserted that he had never been given any agency agreement and that if he had, he would have signed it, as he did not deny the agency relationship with broker. Broker next claimed that the buyer agency relationship was "understood" between she and the buyer, then later that she was a "referral broker" only and finally, that she was acting as a seller subagent. The closing coordinator for the builder-seller said that they require agents representing buyers to sign a registration form acknowledging that they are a buyer agent and that the builder-seller's company policy does not allow seller subagency. As to the issue of the refrigerator, broker denied making the promise, while buyer and one other witness maintained broker had promised to purchase a refrigerator for buyer.

What, if any, License Laws or Commission rules were violated?

Case #6:

Respondents are a husband and wife, both of whom are brokers who are employed by the same real estate company. They entered into an Exclusive Buyer Agency Agreement with an out-of-town couple who wished to purchase a three bedroom home, condominium or townhome to be used as a residence for their son who was attending college in that town, with the intent that the additional rooms would be rented to other college students. The buyer-couple specifically indicated that the residence must be in an area suitable for college students and at least 2 miles from campus so the students living there would qualify for parking passes. After several months of looking and rejection of an offer on a three bedroom unit, the buyers instructed the brokers to look for a four bedroom home to be used by their son and three roommates. Brokers found a four bedroom, two bath home listed with their company and obtained both the buyers' and sellers' written consent for the firm to act as a dual agent, utilizing a dual agency addendum which was appended to the appropriate underlying agency agreements. An offer was extended, negotiated and a contract created.

The buyer/dual agents clearly understood that the purchasers intended that the residence would be occupied by four unrelated persons (their son and three housemates) and assured the buyers that there would be no problem as other college students rented homes in the same area. The buyers entered into a buyer possession before closing agreement and the buyers' son and his roommates moved into the property one week prior to closing. Complaints from neighbors to the real estate agents, the police, and to the zoning authority commenced almost immediately, which complaints were communicated to the buyers by the respondents prior to closing. However, the buyer/dual agents also continued to assure the buyers that their son and his roommates could lawfully occupy the property, so the buyers closed on the property. Unfortunately, however, the County had an ordinance prohibiting occupancy of a residence by more than three unrelated people. The same day that the buyers closed on the property and the deed was recorded, a county zoning enforcement officer sent a complaint letter to the buyers by certified mail informing them of the occupancy limits. The buyers had to alter their original plans and incurred unforeseen costs to comply with the county zoning ordinance.

What, if any, License Laws or Commission rules were violated?

Case #7:

Respondent is an affiliated broker with a known real estate company/franchise. Broker began working with a prospective buyer in March and entered into a written buyer agency agreement with the buyer in mid-April and within days introduced her buyer-client to a builder in a new subdivision. The buyer and builder entered into a purchase agreement on April 17. The builder purchased the lot buyer desired from the developer of the subdivision on May 9 and began construction. The developer owns a corporation which held title to the real property and the developer's wife, a licensed broker, assisted him in marketing the subdivision. The buyer received a copy of a section of the neighborhood survey in April and asked her buyer agent what the lines behind the subject property were and her broker informed her that they were contour lines or power lines.

Buyer went to close on the purchase of the house and lot on August 24 at which time her closing attorney showed her a survey which indicated the rear portion of her lot was in a flood plain. He also provided buyer with a copy of a letter from the developer to the buyer's agent and the builder dated August 4 which stated that the developer would pay for engineered footings required for the foundation. Included with the developer's letter to the builder and buyer's agent was a copy of a FEMA letter stating that the property was not in a flood plain, but in the letter the developer offered to refund the buyer's money if she wished to terminate the contract or allow her to exchange building lots if she chose. The buyer agent admitted at this first closing that the date on the letter was incorrect and that she had received the letter in April. Buyer had no knowledge of this letter or its contents until the August 24 closing. At the attorney's suggestion, the closing was postponed to allow buyer to have a second survey performed. The second updated survey showed that the flood plain encroached on the rear of the property by a few feet. Buyer was reluctant to close on August 27, the rescheduled date, at which the buyer agent was not present at buyer's request, but did close due to builder's threats of legal action.

Buyer agent admitted that she became aware of the flood plain issue in April when the builder noticed it on a survey he had ordered. The buyer agent also had learned in April that the developer had filled the lot to alter the elevation and topography, and thus the flood plain boundary, prior to obtaining the letter from FEMA. Buyer agent admitted that she did not tell her buyer-client about the letter from the developer or about the flood plain situation. The developer contended that FEMA's determination was "the definitive word," notwithstanding the two contradictory surveys and the creek at the back of buyer's lot. The surveyor indicated that while the updated FEMA maps tended to show that the flood line may have shifted due to the fill of the property, he nonetheless continued to show the former 100-year flood line as referenced on the neighborhood plat maps recorded at the Register of Deeds.

Additionally, shortly after closing, buyer learned from neighbors circulating petitions that the owner of the property which bordered buyer's back yard had been attempting for years to persuade city council to allow him to rezone his property to develop a mobile home park. Buyer agent denied having any knowledge of this ongoing feud, although the developer and his broker-wife were aware of these efforts which repeatedly had been denied by the city council. A neighbor in the subdivision stated that most people traveling to or from the subdivision would not have been aware of the public hearing on the rezoning as only one notice had been posted on a seldom used road between the subdivision and adjoining tract, and that there was no media coverage because it was an old on-going issue and there had been little development in the area until recently.

What, if any, License Laws or Commission rules were violated?

Case #8:

The respondents in this case included a broker who was qualifying broker and broker-in-charge of his own company and who also was a licensed appraiser, and a provisional broker who worked for a different real estate company. The provisional broker received a call from her cousin who lived in Texas who wanted to know if the provisional broker was still involved in real estate. The cousin and his wife were interested in purchasing properties in North Carolina on behalf of various investors which properties were to used for group homes. The provisional broker's cousin came to North Carolina and both the cousin and provisional broker looked for properties which met the investors' specifications. They identified a suitable property which was listed at $348,400 and the provisional broker, through the real estate company with which she was affiliated, entered into a buyer agency agreement with her cousin, acting on behalf of the Texas investor group.

An offer was submitted to the seller for $450,000 with a modification on an addendum which stated: "Buyer will purchase property at sellers asking price of $348,400. Will need additional monetary allowances for improvements and upgrades to reflect pool allowance, wrought iron fence, window treatments and any other modifications to meet state requirements." The broker/appraiser appraised the property at the contract price, later explaining that he valued the property as if the improvements had already been made, based on the buyer's assurance that the improvements would be made after closing. Even if the improvements had been made, which they were not, it was questionable whether they would have increased the value of the property by $101,600, the difference between the contract price and sellers' list price.

It appeared from the settlement statement that the sale proceeds were distributed as follows: the sellers received their $348,400, the cousin was paid roughly $45,187 which was characterized as a seller paid item for a second mortgage (when in fact there was no second mortgage) and the remaining funds were used to pay the amounts due at closing from the borrower-buyers (who thus paid very little or nothing from their own funds).

What, if any, License Laws or Commission rules were violated?

Case #9:

Respondents herein include a licensed real estate broker who was serving as the bookkeeper for a duly licensed real estate corporation and the broker-in-charge who was also the vice-president of property management for the real estate company. Both the broker-bookkeeper and the broker-in-charge had check-writing authority on the company's operating account and both were required to co-sign all checks written to pay the firm's expenses. Both of these two brokers had the signature stamp of the other. During 2001 and 2002 the broker-in-charge used credit cards issued in her name to charge personal expenses such as toys, gifts, trips, and sundry merchandise. She then directed the bookkeeper to pay these credit cards from the company's operating account and both signed the checks. The bookkeeper was aware that many of the charges were personal, rather than business. The total of the unauthorized charges for the broker-in-charge's personal benefit was approximately $60,000.

The broker-bookkeeper also accepted a washer and dryer from the broker-in-charge which the broker-in-charge charged to her Lowes credit card, which was then paid from the company's operating account. The bookkeeper also knew that the broker-in-charge would sometimes cash finder fee checks received by the company for having placed tenants in certain rental properties and keep the money, or the broker-in-charge would substitute a finder's fee check in lieu of rent paid by a tenant in cash and pocket the cash. All of the foregoing acts were done without the company's knowledge or consent.

What, if any, License Laws or Commission rules were violated?

Case #10

The QB/BIC of a company listed a property in 2002 advertising it in the MLS as having 4 bedrooms. A couple, represented by a buyer agent affiliated with the listing company (i.e., dual agent) purchased it in March 2003 for $145,000.

The buyer-husband died in 2014; in 2015, the widow hired a listing company (not the 2003 listing company) to sell the property. The new listing broker checked the septic permit (from 1987) and discovered the system was only approved for a 2-bedroom house, not 4 bedrooms. Selling the property at the market value of a 2-bedroom house would not even pay off the outstanding mortgage. The widow was able to obtain a permit from the county to enlarge the system to accommodate a three bedroom house at a cost of roughly $1900 to have the septic tank pumped and the system expanded.

In their joint response, the QB/BIC and buyer/dual agent from the 2003 transaction denied making any statements concerning the septic system's capacity, other than listing it as 4 bedrooms, and argued that had the buyer-couple ordered a home inspection, they could have asked the inspector about the system's capacity.

What, if any, License Laws or Commission rules were violated?

Case #11

A company listed a property in 2008 advertising it as having 3 bedrooms, when in fact the septic permit limited a dwelling to 2 bedrooms. The property sold for $352,500. When the owner prepared to sell in 2011, s/he learned from the listing broker (different company) that the septic permit specified 2 bedrooms. To avoid a significant reduction in the property's value, the owner paid $10,775 to upgrade the septic system to support a 3-bedroom dwelling.

The owner contacted the 2008 listing company which replied, in essence, that the agents (acting as dual agents) had performed their duties and since the owner had multiple inspections, including a septic inspection, the brokers had no liability. The owner then filed a complaint with the Commission.

In their initial response, the 2008 BIC and broker-associate admitted that the listing broker did not pull the septic permit but instead relied on the tax records which indicated 3 bedrooms. They argued that there was no duty in 2007 to contact health departments or check septic permits, that it was not a willful misrepresentation, and that they had a right to rely on the tax records which have shown the property as 3 bedrooms since its construction in 1975.

The NCREC investigator provided the BIC with a copy of a 1993 *Bulletin* article regarding a broker's duty to discover and disclose matters affecting sewage disposal. The BIC reconsidered his position, settled the dispute with the property owner by paying for the septic system expansion, and conducted training for his associates emphasizing the importance of checking septic permits when listing any property.

What, if any, License Laws or Commission rules were violated?

Case #12

In 2009, a broker listed a one acre rectangular tract with a 2000SF office building located on a rural highway. The owner told the broker that the property had public water and sewer provided by a county-owned facility 100 yards down the road. The sign in front of the referenced facility read "Sanitary District Water Treatment Plant." The owner died in 2011 and the broker relisted the parcel for the estate, advertising it as being connected to public water and sewer based on the owner's earlier statement.

In 2013, prospective buyers discussed their plans for the property with the listing broker, who acted as a dual agent. The buyers explained that they wanted to build a second metal building on the tract for their appliance repair business and rent out the office space in the existing building. They also hoped to build a residence on the back portion of the lot. After a property inspection and boundary survey, the buyers closed on the parcel. While preparing to erect the metal building for their repair business, the buyers learned from a neighbor that they were building over the septic system for the office building. Upon further investigation, the buyers learned that:

- the septic system had failed and needed immediate replacement;
- the system was at capacity and could not be expanded;
- its capacity was barely sufficient to provide service for the appliance repair shop, thereby scuttling plans to rent the unused office space;
- there was no available public sewer service, as neither of the two closest public sewer authorities provided service to that area; and
- the county Sanitary District Water Treatment facility down the street only provided water.

The listing broker/dual agent admitted his misrepresentation. His errors and omissions insurance coverage paid approximately $28,000 in expenses the buyers incurred in replacing the septic system, relocating the second building, and related matters.

What, if any, License Laws or Commission rules were violated?

Case #13

This case involves two brokers affiliated with the same company. Broker #1 was the builder/owner of the property which he listed through Broker #2 and the real estate company where they both worked.

The listed property was located in a subdivision developed in the late 1980s/early 1990s in 4 sections. Of the approximately 100 homes in the subdivision, half were in Sections 1 and 2 with publicly dedicated streets that had been accepted for maintenance, and half were in Sections 3 and 4 with publicly dedicated streets that the developer intended to transfer to the NC Department of Transportation (NCDOT) upon reaching the required population density. However, when that time arrived, NCDOT wanted a culvert replaced before it would accept the streets. The developer did not have the $25,000 to replace the culvert, so he did nothing.

The developer (who lived on a publicly maintained street in Section 1) sold the unimproved subject lot to Broker #1 in 2008, at which time the population density had been met. Although the developer failed to provide him with a street disclosure statement, Broker #1 admitted that he knew the lot was on a private street. Broker #1 said he never asked the developer about the status of the transfer process because he did not feel it was necessary. Broker #1 then built a house on the lot and listed it with Broker #2, but did not tell her that the property was on a private street nor did the listing broker ask.

Broker #1 received and accepted an offer on March 21, 2009 through Broker #2 who was acting as a dual agent. Neither broker informed the buyer that the street had not been accepted for public maintenance; the appraisal report prepared for buyer's lender mistakenly indicated that the street was public. The transaction closed May 26, 2009, at which time the roads were in good condition.

Problems began in 2011/2012 when the buyer-owners saw a sign posted on a nearby street reading "State Maintenance Ends Here;" about this time, street repair issues began to arise. The developer refused to make any repairs, so in 2013 each property owner contributed $1,000 to repair the streets sufficiently to permit access by school buses and emergency vehicles. The buyer-owners, who were active military and had been transferred out of state, were under contract to sell the property in 2013, but their buyer's VA loan application was denied when the appraiser correctly reported that the property was on a private street.

As of 2013/2014, there were cracks and potholes throughout Sections 3 and 4 of the subdivision, with a 20 foot diameter crater at the entrance to the complaining party's cul-de-sac. At that time, the estimate to repair the streets sufficiently to allow acceptance by NCDOT was $100,000. There was neither an owners' association in this subdivision nor any road maintenance agreement.

Broker #2 admitted that she did not try to determine whether the streets were public or private because the property was in an established neighborhood, the roads were paved, and the plat map indicated the roads were built to state standards and would be dedicated to public use upon reaching a specified population density.

What, if any, License Laws or Commission rules were violated?

Case #14

A buyer represented by a buyer agent (and another broker assisting the buyer agent) contracted to purchase a house for roughly $200,000 in 2011. The listing agent (with a different company) stated in the MLS that the property had an oil-burning furnace. The buyer's home inspector reported that not only was the furnace in poor condition, but there also was an underground fuel storage tank. Based on the report, the buyer requested and the seller agreed to install a new HVAC system for approximately $5100 and the transaction closed.

At no time during the transaction did the buyer agent or broker assisting her counsel the buyer regarding potential issues with underground fuel storage tanks, so the buyer never raised the matter with the seller.

Four years later the new owner decides to sell and is told by her listing agent that the presence of an underground fuel storage tank must be disclosed to all prospective buyers and that a buyer's lender might require removal or at least soil testing. The owner accepted an offer to purchase, but the buyer's home inspection revealed that the underground storage tank (UST) was within inches of an enclosed porch the previous owner had added and the tank was leaking. The buyer's lender required removal of the UST and all contaminated soil. The buyers ultimately terminated the contract when the issue could not be resolved within an acceptable time frame.

After many estimates and advice from structural engineers and the EPA, the owner spent more than $13,000 to have an environmental firm close the UST in place (since it could not be removed easily) while monitoring the groundwater and recording soil samples. Of the $13,000+ total cost, the owner was eligible to be reimbursed roughly $7400 from the Department of Environmental Quality, leaving roughly $7750 out of pocket.

When contacted by the Commission, the BIC of the buyer agent at the time of the 2011 transaction submitted a written response to the Inquiry. He stated that he was not directly involved in the transaction, which had been handled by a broker not on provisional status, and that his company's policy as to USTs was the same in 2011 as in 2015, namely: "Get a licensed environmental company that deals with underground fuel tanks to advise the prospective buyer, and then read the report." The BIC acknowledged that the buyer agent should have educated the buyer about USTs and the company agreed to reimburse the owner all of her out-of-pocket expenses. The BIC also agreed to conduct training for his associated agents reminding them to disclose the risks of USTs.

The broker who served as the buyer agent allowed her license to expire June 30, 2015. She received two Letters of Inquiry, but failed to respond in writing to either. When contacted by phone, the broker-buyer agent stated that her job as a nurse was her top priority and that responding to letters from the Commission did not pay her bills. She said that the buyer was aware that there was an underground fuel storage tank and it was not the broker's job to inform the buyer of the possible risks or suggest an inspection or ask the seller to remove it. The buyer agent accepted no responsibility nor did she contribute to any financial settlement.

What, if any, License Laws or Commission rules were violated?

Case #15

A broker affiliated with a real estate company listed a bank-owned (REO) property for sale in November 2013, stating in the MLS that it had 4580 square feet of heated living area. The seller accepted a cash offer from a buyer who was interested in purchasing, rehabbing, and flipping the property. The transaction closed in January 2014. When the owner relisted the property for sale in April 2014, his listing agent measured the house using the Commission's *Square Footage Guidelines* and concluded that it only had 3702 square feet of heated living area (approximately a 24% difference), prompting the owner to file a complaint against the previous listing agent.

Upon inquiry, the listing agent (a full broker) admitted that he had used the county tax records to estimate the square footage until he could measure the house, but he claimed the listing went active before he had a chance to measure, and he was fielding multiple offers on the property. The response, prepared by the company's attorney, acknowledged that the firm's policy was to accurately report square footage, that this agent usually adhered to that policy, and that this was a lone oversight.

The Commission's investigator then reviewed the company's website and discovered 10 REO properties listed by the same broker. The MLS data sheets, listing history, and copies of the square footage measurements and calculations were requested for these transactions. The MLS data sheets and listing histories were provided, but no square footage calculations or measurements. The QB/BIC acknowledged that the company had no office policy concerning retention of square footage measurements and calculations.

What, if any, License Laws or Commission rules were violated?

Case #16

A broker who was the QB/BIC of her own company listed bank-owned properties for sale, entering the property information, including square footage, into the local Multiple Listing Service (MLS). The broker/company in one MLS listing stated the property contained 1,680 square feet of above grade living area, coincidently the same amount found in the local tax records. A buyer represented by a broker from another company saw the property and submitted an offer to purchase. The buyer agent asked the listing broker how she arrived at the 1680 square footage and the listing agent said that she measured the property. The buyer's broker then had a real estate broker and formerly licensed appraiser measure the property to confirm the accuracy of the square footage representation. The sketch by the former appraiser showed the property as having 1,188.96 square feet of living area.

When confronted with this information, the listing broker admitted that she took the information from the local tax records. The buyer's offer was withdrawn and the property remained on the market, but the listing broker made no correction to the square footage information in the MLS. The property later went under contract and was purchased by a different buyer represented by another broker. There was never any discussion about the square footage amount between the second buyer agent and the listing agent who never disclosed the former appraiser's measurements to the other broker or his buyer client.

The Commission sent Letters of Inquiry to the listing broker and her company asking her to provide measurements for the six property listings she had pending. The measurements received contained only a length, width, and the total amount for square footage of five properties that were the exact same figures as the local tax records.

What, if any, License Laws or Commission rules were violated?

Case #17:

The broker in this case had been licensed since the 1970s and was broker-in-charge of his sole proprietorship. In 1997, broker was contacted by an individual who wanted to purchase a home on the sound in the Topsail Beach area in the name of the individual's family corporation. Broker previously had listed and sold various lots for this person's family corporation. Broker undertook to act as a buyer agent, but did not enter into a written buyer agency agreement nor review the former desciption of agent duties and relationships with the buyer.

In attempting to locate a property for the buyer, broker reviewed the tax records and then contacted owners by telephone or mail to inquire whether they were interested in selling their property. Broker contacted one owner who lived in Sampson County and while she was not initially interested, broker persisted and assured her that the buyer would pay cash and that it would be a quick sale. Broker met with the property owner in July, 1997 and presented her with an Offer to Purchase, a dual agency addendum, and a draft settlement statement. The dual agency addendum and the offer identified the family corporation as the buyer. However, the family corporation's certificate of authority had been suspended by the Secretary of State in December 1994 for failure to file annual reports and it thus had no legal authority to transact business in North Carolina. Additionally, there was neither a listing agreement nor a buyer agency agreement. The addendum provided that seller would pay broker a commission equal to 8% of the sales price, but did not specify any date on which the agency relationship would terminate.

Broker determined the contract price for the property, $157,900.00, by adding his commission to the minimum amount seller said she must net from the property, even though the fair market value of the property was considerably higher than the contract price. Buyer submitted a $3,000 earnest money deposit with the offer which deposit was to be held by broker. Although broker had induced seller to sell by telling her that it would be a cash sale, the written Offer contained a financing contingency. When seller asked about the financing contingency, broker told her that it was merely a formality of completing the Offer to Purchase form. In fact, the buyer did not have the ability to purchase the property without obtaining a loan. In Paragraph 12 of the Offer regarding the Residential Property Disclosure Statement, broker wrote "does not apply, purchase in as is condition" which was initialed by both parties. Seller did intend to sell the property "as is" as it had sustained some flood damage from Hurricane Fran the preceding year. After both parties signed the Offer in July 1997, broker told seller that buyer needed access to the property to clean up the flood damage, obtain an inspection and prepare the property for an appraisal. Seller gave broker a key for the expressed purposes.

Several days later, seller and her son went to the property to remove some personal property and discovered that broker had given the key to buyer and allowed him unrestricted access. Seller found a workman rewiring the house at buyer's direction so buyer could have air conditioning and a dryer installed. Buyer arrived while seller was at the property and seller instructed buyer not to make any further modifications to the property prior to closing and seller immediately had the electricity turned off to prevent any further work without her permission. Seller also contacted broker, informed him of the encounter, and told him that buyer was not authorized to alter the property in any way prior to closing. Broker assured seller that the transaction would close and that even if it did not, the alterations already made would enhance the property.

In mid-August, broker visited the property and discovered that buyer had re-entered the property, reconnected the electricity, and was proceeding with major modifications including rewiring the house, adding a front porch, a closet, a bedroom, and a large red heart-shaped bath tub on the back deck. Buyer was living in the property, sleeping on a mattress on the floor of a room which he had redecorated entirely in red, and buyer's girlfriend and the workman also were living in the house. Broker did not tell seller about any of this.

Broker ordered an appraisal of the property which ascribed a value of $210,000.00. Broker then told seller that buyer wanted her to make certain repairs to the roof. Seller reminded broker that she was selling the property "as is," but went to inspect the roof herself, whereupon she discovered the buyer, his comrades and the various alterations, which at that point also included installing carpet without first cleaning the floors, thus trapping debris, as well as installing pilings for a pier or dock in the public waterway without the requisite permission. Seller again told broker that buyer was not to occupy the house or make any alterations prior to closing and broker again reassured seller that the transaction would close and that the alterations would enhance the property.

Buyer applied for a loan which was denied in part because buyer could not verify his income or produce income tax returns since he had not filed tax returns since 1973. Buyer applied to a second lender who would not lend to the corporation, but would consider a loan to the individual buyer, whereupon broker altered the contract by whiting out any reference to the corporation or the individual as president of the corporation, leaving only the individual as the buyer. Broker did not inform either party that he had altered the contract, did not obtain their consent, did not provide them with a copy of the altered contract and did not disclose to the lender that he unilaterally had made these changes.

On August 29, the projected closing date, broker and seller learned that buyer had been involuntarily committed to a mental institution by his adult children. The family removed the appliances and the red heart shaped bath tub which had been delivered to the property. On August 30, broker placed a "for sale" sign on the property holding himself out as seller's agent, and showed the property to two different parties who stopped by while broker was changing the locks to the property. Broker told seller of one party's interest in purchasing the property, as well as his own, and seller informed broker that the property no longer was for sale. On August 31, seller and her daughter visited the property and discovered broker's "for sale" sign. They also realized that broker had allowed buyer to continue to live there despite seller's directions to the contrary, and that a refrigerator, washer and telephone belonging to seller were missing. While at the property, buyer arrived and confessed to seller that he had a history of mental problems, that his financial affairs were now in his children's hands, and that he could not close. Buyer and seller agreed that their contract was terminated.

On September 4, seller spoke with buyer's adult daughter who apologized for her father's behavior and confirmed that her father did not have the funds to purchase the property. Seller then spoke with broker who said the loan package was ready and that seller would be required to honor the contract. Seller wrote broker a letter terminating the alleged dual agency relationship and informing him that he did not have any authority to represent her in any capacity. On September 5, without any authority from either buyer or seller, broker collected the loan package from the bank, which had issued a one month interim loan based on false information, and delivered it to the closing attorney without informing the bank or the closing attorney of buyer's institutionalization, lack of control over his finances, or the parties' agreement to terminate the contract. Since neither the title search, survey or termite inspection had been performed, the closing attorney called the seller to inquire about the closing, at which point seller related recent events and informed the attorney that the deal had been cancelled.

In October, 1997, with broker's assistance, buyer filed a lawsuit against seller for specific performance of the original contract (with the defunct corporation as buyer). In February 1998, seller learned that no permits had been obtained for any of the repairs or additions made by buyer, that virtually all of the alterations were in violation of the local building codes and that the estimate to correct the violations and restore the property was $15,169.

In March 1998, broker proposed to buyer that if buyer won the lawsuit for specific performance, broker would purchase the property from buyer by paying seller the monies due, plus giving buyer $6000. Buyer ultimately declined broker's offer and dismissed his lawsuit against seller, at which point seller dismissed all counterclaims against buyer.

In July 1998, broker refunded buyer's $3000 earnest money deposit to buyer, without first contacting seller or her attorney, even though seller had maintained that she was entitled to the earnest money deposit. In August 1998, broker, through his brother who is an attorney, sued seller claiming that she owed broker a commission in the amount of $12,600 plus interest and attorney fees, for having produced a ready, willing and able buyer. Having already incurred between $25,000 and $30,000 in expenses for repairs and defending lawsuits, seller chose to pay broker $3500 to settle the case.

While investigating seller's complaint in this case, the Commission also reviewed broker's trust accounts and discovered that the deposit tickets and bank statements for the rental trust account did not bear the words "trust account" or "escrow account," that parties were not identified on deposit tickets, that ledger sheets were not properly maintained and there was no running balance and the accounts were not reconciled monthly. The rental trust account had a $1,583 overage because broker was not disbursing management fees each month, plus broker was depositing monies from personally owned properties into his brokerage rental trust account. Broker's sales trust account was short $2008; broker did not properly maintain ledger sheets, did not have a running balance and did not reconcile the account monthly. Broker ultimately funded the shortage in his sales trust account to make it whole.

What, if any, License Laws or Commission rules were violated?

21 | BROKERAGE COMPENSATION ISSUES

A real estate broker's legal entitlement to compensation for brokerage services based on the broker's performance of services under agency contracts (employment contracts between a consumer and broker for the broker to provide brokerage services) is covered in depth in Chapter 9, as was the issue of prohibited "price fixing" under antitrust laws. This chapter focuses on practical aspects of compensating brokers for their services. While the law regarding who may or may not be paid for providing brokerage services is actually very simple, there are many issues related to paying brokers that frequently arise in practice. The Commission receives many questions from brokers asking whether they may pay another broker a commission or a referral fee, or whether they may pay a referral fee or provide a gift to an unlicensed acquaintance who routinely sends them clients/customers, or whether a broker's owner-client may pay a fee to the owner's neighbor for referring a renter for the owner's property, or whether an inactive broker may be paid a share of a commission for work performed while the broker's license was active. This chapter will address these and other matters related to payments for brokerage services.

We will begin with a review of the relevant statutes, then discuss the easiest category – that of persons who *cannot* be paid a brokerage fee – and then turn our attention to the broader category of brokerage activity, namely who *may* be paid a brokerage fee and under what, if any, conditions.

ACTIVE REAL ESTATE LICENSE REQUIRED FOR BROKERAGE COMPENSATION

The most basic requirement to lawfully receive compensation for providing a real estate brokerage service is to have an active real estate license. The **North Carolina Real Estate License Law** is found in **Chapter 93A** of the North Carolina General Statutes. The very first statutory provision (G.S. 93A-1) states:

> ...it shall be unlawful for any person, partnership, corporation, limited liability company, association, or other business entity in this State to act as a real estate broker, or directly or indirectly to engage or assume to engage in the business of real estate broker or to advertise or hold himself or herself or themselves out as engaging in or conducting such business without first obtaining a license issued by the North Carolina Real Estate Commission.... A license shall be obtained from the Commission even if the person, partnership, corporation, limited liability company, association, or business entity is licensed in another state and is affiliated or otherwise associated with a licensed real estate broker in this State.

What does it mean to "act as a real estate broker"? Paraphrased, the License Law in G.S. 93A-2(a) defines a "**real estate broker**" as a person or business entity that:

1) lists, sells, buys, auctions,* leases, rents, sells leases, or offers to do any of the foregoing, or otherwise negotiates the purchase, sale or exchange of real estate or improvements thereon,
2) for others,
3) *for compensation, valuable consideration, or the promise thereof.*

[* NOTE: The statute specifically excludes "a mere crier of sales" at a real estate auction from the real estate broker licensing requirement.]

G.S. 93A-8 states that anyone who violates any of the statutes in Chapter 93A is guilty of a Class 1 misdemeanor. Therefore, it is a criminal offense for anyone to provide brokerage services for others *for compensation in North Carolina unless they have an active NC broker license.*

North Carolina Real Estate Commission rules require that a real estate broker's license be "current" (renewal fees paid for current license period) and on "active" status at the time a brokerage service is provided in order to be entitled to receive compensation for such service.

GENERAL PROHIBITION AGAINST PAYING UNLICENSED PERSONS FOR BROKERAGE SERVICES

Based on the foregoing requirement, the GENERAL RULE OF LAW may be stated as:

No unlicensed person or entity (or broker with a license on "inactive" status) may be paid for engaging in any activity or conduct that is real estate brokerage. This is true regardless of whether the person making the payment is a real estate broker or an unlicensed person.

The first issue is whether the acts or services provided require a real estate license. If a license is required, then the person or entity must have an ***active*** *broker license throughout the period that services are rendered* to lawfully receive compensation for the services. Otherwise, *the person/entity **receiving*** the compensation is violating Real Estate License Law and committing a misdemeanor.

Thus, it is unlawful ***to compensate*** an unlicensed person or entity for performing brokerage services, as discussed below.

Payments by a Broker

Brokers are forbidden by statute from "**paying** a commission or valuable consideration to any person for acts or services performed in violation of this Chapter." [See G.S.93A-6(a)(9).] Real Estate Commission Rule A.0109(g) further reinforces this prohibition stating "... *a licensee shall not undertake in any manner, any arrangement, contract, plan or other course of conduct, to compensate or share compensation with unlicensed persons or entities for any acts performed in North Carolina for which licensure by the Commission is required.*" Thus, brokers are expressly forbidden from **sharing compensation with unlicensed persons** *for brokerage activity*. This prohibition includes *paying a fee for referring business to a broker, i.e., a "**referral fee**."* Violations may subject the broker to disciplinary action. (Note too that a *broker whose license is on inactive status should be treated the same as an unlicensed person*, as the inactively licensed broker may not legally engage in any brokerage activity. This will be discussed more fully later in these materials.)

Payments by an Unlicensed Person/Entity

It also violates the law for an *unlicensed person/entity* to **pay** another unlicensed person/entity for providing a brokerage service. Why? Because North Carolina *criminal statutes* state that it is illegal to pay someone else to commit an illegal act. **G.S. §14-2.6., Punishment for solicitation to commit a felony or misdemeanor**, reads in part:

> (b) Unless a different classification is expressly stated, a person who solicits another person to commit a misdemeanor is guilty of a Class 3 misdemeanor.

Thus, **it is also illegal for a person or entity who is NOT a licensed broker to compensate an unlicensed person or entity for brokerage activity.**

> *Example.* A seller's residence has been on the market for more than four months and the seller is getting desperate. The listing agent is aware that the seller has begun posting notices around the neighborhood and in area retail stores announcing that he will pay $3,000 to anyone who sends a buyer for his/her property. The listing agent should explain to the seller that it is illegal for the seller to offer consideration to an unlicensed non-party and for any unlicensed person to accept the seller's offer and receive the incentive for sending/referring a buyer to the property. Such an unlicensed payee violates License Law and could be charged with a misdemeanor for accepting the $3,000, and the payor commits a misdemeanor as well under G.S. 14-2.6.

EXCEPTIONS TO GENERAL PROHIBITION AGAINST COMPENSATING UNLICENSED PERSONS FOR BROKERAGE SERVICES

The two significant exceptions to the general rule against sharing compensation for brokerage services with unlicensed persons are discussed below.

Sharing Compensation with Parties to the Transaction

Brokers are sometimes surprised to learn that *there is no law or rule prohibiting a broker from sharing his/her brokerage fee with a* **party to the transaction** *in which the broker is involved.* Must a broker share his/her brokerage fee with an unlicensed party if the party requests it? **NO.** Must the party have a broker license in order to be paid? **NO.** Does it matter whether the broker sharing his/her brokerage fee is an agent of the property owner or a buyer/tenant agent? **NO.**

Why can brokers (or other persons, for that matter) *share a brokerage fee or give a rebate to a party to the transaction without breaking the law?* Remember that what requires a license is acting as a broker which, by definition, requires representing *others*. Parties are the principals in the transaction, i.e., buyer, seller, lessor, lessee, and are representing their own interests. Because they are not representing "others," they are not engaging in "acts which require a license." On the contrary, they are *principals in and parties to the transaction and attempt to promote only their own interests.*

Accordingly, a broker may share with or rebate to a party a portion of his/her brokerage fee. *However, any such sharing of a brokerage fee with a buyer* **must be disclosed to the buyer's lender and reflected on the settlement statement** *to avoid any possible charges of loan fraud.* The settlement statement should reflect all monies received or paid to anyone related to that transaction. Failure to list any payments or other consideration may constitute loan fraud, whether paid at closing or outside of closing. Thus:

- A **buyer's agent** may share a portion of his/her brokerage fee with his/her **buyer-client** *as long as the buyer's lender is aware of the arrangement and it is disclosed on the settlement statement.*

- A **seller's agent** may also share a portion of his/her brokerage fee with a **buyer-customer** *as long as the seller agrees, the buyer's lender is made aware of the arrangement, and it is disclosed on the settlement statement.* Of course, a listing agent is not required to share the commission with the buyer. The buyer may request it and the seller/listing agent either may agree or refuse. In any case, the listing agent must present the buyer's offer and communicate the buyer's request to his/her seller-client.

Note that a **seller's agent** may also reduce the amount of his/her brokerage fee to be paid by his/her **seller-client** to make a proposed sale acceptable to the seller. If the sale price and brokerage fee shown on the settlement statement are the true sale price and brokerage fee, then the seller's agent's brokerage fee concession to the seller does NOT need to be shown on the settlement statement. For example, assume a buyer offers $200,000 and the seller and listing agent agreed in the listing agreement to a 5% commission (which would be $10,000). If the seller is willing to accept the offer only if the listing agent will accept a 4% commission ($8,000), and the listing agent agrees, then the $2,000 brokerage fee concession would appear on the settlement statement as long as the settlement statement reflects the brokerage fee as $8,000. (It is highly recommended, however, that the agreement for a reduced commission be in writing to avoid any subsequent disputes. Also, if the reduced commission will reduce the amount of the commission paid to the selling agent, then the selling agent must also agree.)

Party Does Not Need a Real Estate License to Receive a Share of the Brokerage Fee. The fact that the party (seller, buyer, lessor, lessee) receiving the compensation does not have a real estate license is irrelevant. *Brokers may **not** tell a party that they are prohibited from sharing consideration with the party because the party does not have a real estate license because, in this instance, that would be untrue and thus a **misrepresentation*** (either willful or negligent).

Note: This is not intended to imply that brokers must or should share compensation or consideration with parties to the transaction. This is addressed because such requests from parties are not uncommon and brokers must understand that they *may* share consideration with *a party to the transaction* if they choose, even if the party is unlicensed. So, as with many rules, the general rule against brokers sharing brokerage compensation with unlicensed persons has one primary exception, namely, **brokers may share compensation with a PARTY TO THE TRANSACTION, as party-principals are not engaged in brokerage activity.**

Technically the party-principal is ***not*** receiving a "brokerage commission" as they are neither licensed nor acting as an agent; rather, they are receiving a gift or consideration or an unearned fee or whatever one might call it, but it is not "earned income." The broker who pays the consideration will clearly deduct it as a business expense, if it was included as part of the broker's gross income/revenue. The broker may well give the party a Form 1099 of some sort to evidence the miscellaneous or unearned income, depending on the amount.

Examples of Sharing Brokerage Fee with Parties/Principals

Example #1: A broker affiliated with a real estate company is approached by a buyer who wants to enter into a written exclusive buyer agency agreement for 45 days. The buyer is looking for a home in the $400,000-$450,000 range. The broker informs the buyer that the company expects to receive a commission equivalent to 3% of the purchase price of the home, but that the buyer will only be liable if the seller or listing agent will not cooperate. The buyer is willing to agree, but also wants the broker to agree to pay the buyer $1500 of any commission the broker receives.

A) Must the broker agree? **No.**

B) If the broker refuses, is it possible the buyer will leave and hire another broker to act as his buyer agent who is willing to share a portion of his commission? **Yes.**

C) May the broker tell the buyer that he would love to share with the buyer, but that he cannot because the buyer doesn't have a broker license? **No.** *Such a statement would be a "misrepresentation" (i.e., an untruth). The buyer does not need a license because he is not representing "others."*

D) May the broker tell the buyer that he would love to share a portion of his fee, but that his company's office policy or his broker-in-charge only permits associates to share with other duly licensed brokers? **Yes,** *if* in fact this is true!

E) May the broker agree to pay the buyer $1500 from the broker's fee if the broker is the selling agent and is paid by the listing agent/seller? **Yes,** *absolutely!* Where would this agreement be evidenced? In the written buyer agency agreement and the lender would be informed of the $1500 to be paid by the broker to the buyer at the time the buyer applies for a loan.

F) If the buyer agent agrees to pay the buyer-client, does s/he need the seller's permission? *Good question.* The answer is, *it depends.* If the broker is acting *only as a buyer agent, then no,* s/he does not need the seller's permission as the seller is not his/her client and is owed no fiduciary obligations. *However,* if the buyer agent has been transformed from a buyer agent into a dual agent (with proper consent of both seller and buyer) because it is an in-house listing, then the company has two principals, and the *seller principal has a right to know* that the broker is sharing some of its fee with the buyer client. Should the seller client care? Not really, as it does not change the amount the seller is contractually obligated to pay the brokerage company. It's just that the company or its affiliated agent has voluntarily agreed to share a portion of its/his fee with the buyer for whatever reasons.

Example #2: Listing company has an exclusive right to sell agreement with an owner. The owner has agreed to pay a commission equal to 6% of the purchase price and authorizes the listing company to share half of its fee with any buyer agent. The listing agent obtains an offer from an unrepresented buyer to pay $400,000.00 for the property, but the buyer has written into the "Other Conditions or Provisions" paragraph of the offer to purchase form the following language: "This offer is contingent on the buyer receiving $8,000 of the fee normally paid to the selling agent."

A) Could a broker acting as an agent include similar language about the brokerage fee in an offer to purchase? **No.** Rule A.0112(b) prohibits a broker from suggesting or including any language concerning his/her compensation or commission in an offer to purchase. Requests for compensation by a broker must be separate from the offer. However, this buyer is not a broker and is not bound by Commission rules, so s/he may include such language.

B) Must the listing agent show the offer to his/her seller-client? **Yes.** *Absolutely.* If the seller is inclined to accept the buyer's offer, *must the listing agent agree to pay $8,000 of his/her/its commission/fee to the unrepresented, unlicensed buyer?* Not exactly. This is where education and office policy enter. The listing agent should explain to the seller that the company and the seller already have a contract between them (i.e., the listing agreement) whereby the seller agreed to pay the company a certain fee, and the company in turn agreed to share a portion of that fee in certain specified situations — namely with a selling *broker* who is acting either as a buyer agent or as a seller's subagent, depending on what the seller authorized.

The listing agent is not compelled to share his/her compensation beyond those specified situations, so the seller can not *make* the listing agent share. However, the listing agent may agree to give a portion of his/her/its fee to the buyer as long as 1) the seller consents, 2) the amount is on the settlement statement, and 3) the buyer's lender is told at loan application. If the listing company is willing to share the $8,000 requested by the buyer, then the seller can accept that contract condition, but the listing company and seller should also agree in writing that $8,000 of the commission paid by the seller will be paid by the listing company to the buyer to avoid any subsequent misunderstanding about the matter. If the listing company is only willing to share $4,000 of its commission with the buyer, then the seller should counter in that amount to the buyer and, again, the listing company and seller should commit their agreement to writing.

C) Can the listing company tell the buyer it is prohibited from paying him/her because s/he does not have a license? **No.** No license is required because the buyer is a party and is not representing others. It is totally legal for anyone to pay the buyer, as long as payments are disclosed to any lenders involved and are reflected on the settlement statement.

D) May the listing company tell the buyer that it refuses to share a portion of the Company's brokerage fee with unlicensed parties to the transaction as a matter of policy? **Yes**, if in fact that is true. What if the Company refuses to share, but the seller wants to accept the buyer's offer anyway — is the Company obligated to pay $8,000 of its commission to the buyer under the terms of the sales contract? While it may depend on the wording, most likely not, because the Company is not a party to the sale/purchase contract and has not agreed to share its fee. The Company's obligation to share is governed by the terms of the listing agreement. The agent should caution the seller that if s/he accepts the offer as written by the buyer, the seller may be in a position where s/he owes the listing company the agreed listing commission *as well as being liable to the buyer* for the $8,000 payment under the contract.

Example #3: An apartment complex posts a huge notice outside its main drive declaring: "Free two months rent with one year lease!" Is this permissible? **Yes.** The apartment complex is offering a thing of value to persons who sign a new one-year lease and thus are parties to the lease transaction. This is completely legal.
Could the apartment complex legally distribute flyers to their current residents offering free rent for two months to anyone who sends new renters to the office? **No.** As discussed in the preceding section on prohibited payments to unlicensed persons, existing tenants would be breaking the law to accept two months free rent for having referred new tenants to the complex as the existing tenants are unlicensed persons who will not be parties to the new lease agreement, and the payor (apartment complex) has violated North Carolina criminal law by granting the free rent for a referral.

Payments to Travel Agents for Vacation Rentals

There is only one other exception to the general prohibition against brokers sharing their brokerage compensation with unlicensed persons. Besides parties to a transaction, the only other unlicensed persons with whom a **broker** may share consideration are *travel agents who refer tenants to a broker for vacation rentals only*. The Vacation Rental Act and implementing rules [Commission Rule 58A.0109(h)] were amended in 2002 to permit brokers to pay consideration (referral fees) to travel agents under certain specified conditions as described below.

Travel Agent Eligibility to Receive Referral Fees from Brokers

Brokers may pay "consideration" to travel agents (defined as a "person or entity ... primarily engaged in the business of acting as an intermediary between persons who purchase air, land, and ocean travel services and the providers of such services") *as long as*:
- the travel agent, as part of the regular course of her/his business, only "introduces" the tenant to the broker and "...does not otherwise engage in any activity which would require a real estate license;"
- the introduction by the travel agent is made in the normal course of the travel agent's business; and
- the travel agent does not solicit, handle or receive any monies in connection with the vacation rental.

Additional Requirements for Brokers Paying Referral Fees to Travel Agents

When undertaking to share consideration with a travel agent, brokers must:
- Prior to entering into a lease/rental agreement, provide the prospective tenant with a written statement advising the prospective tenant to rely only upon the written lease agreement and the broker's representations about the transaction;
- deal directly with the tenant after the "introduction" afforded by the travel agent;
- not pay the travel agent until after the conclusion of the tenancy; AND
- maintain records showing the vacation rental property, the tenant, the travel agent, the addresses of each, the dates of the tenancy, and the amount paid to the travel agent, which records must be kept for three years from the termination of the tenancy.

COMPENSATING AFFILIATED BROKERS

The next several pages will discuss the Commission's interpretation of the law and rules concerning compensating brokers for brokerage services, as well as compensating licensed and unlicensed assistants.

NOTE: While the Commission will entertain complaints concerning improper compensation of both brokers and unlicensed persons in violation of the License Law and Commission rules, it will not hear cases involving compensation *disputes under a brokerage cooperation agreement between brokers or firms.* **Rule A.0109(f)** states: "*The Commission shall not act as a board of arbitration and shall not compel parties to settle disputes concerning such matters as the rate of commissions, the division of commissions, pay of brokers, and similar matters.*" Available forums for compensation disputes include the applicable Board of REALTORS® for arbitration (which may be mandatory if both brokers are REALTOR® members) or the courts of law, most likely regular District Court, or, depending on the amount in dispute, Superior Court.

Broker Eligibility for Compensation

To receive compensation for brokerage services, the recipient must have a license that is **current** *(meaning renewal fee has been paid)* **and** *that is on* **active** *status. License pocket cards* only indicate that the broker has paid the necessary fee to *renew* his/her/its license; it *does not guarantee or certify that the license is on active status.* Commission **Rule A.0504(a)** states:

> ... the holder of a license on *active* status may engage in any activity requiring
> a real estate license and may be compensated for the provision of any lawful
> real estate brokerage service. The holder of a license on *inactive* status shall
> not engage in any activity requiring a real estate license, *including the referral
> for compensation of a prospective seller, buyer, landlord, or tenant to another real
> estate broker or any other party.* (Italics added.)

Current and Active License Status

Brokers NOT on Provisional Status. To have a current, active license, a broker NOT on provisional status (i.e., a "full" broker – one who has completed all required postlicensing education) must:

1. Pay the license renewal fee between May 15 and June 30 each year; AND
2. Complete eight (8) hours of continuing education (CE), including a mandatory Update course and one approved elective, prior to June 10 of each year.

NOTE: CE for most brokers (other than one who is a BIC or "BIC eligible") consists of the 4-hour mandatory *General Update Course* and a 4-hour approved elective course. If the broker is a BIC or BIC eligible, then s/he must take the *Broker-in-Charge Update (BICUP) course* each year beginning the first full *license year after* the license year in which s/he declared him/herself a broker-in-charge, *as well as* any approved four-hour elective course each year.

Maintaining an active license does not mean that the broker must be actively engaged in providing brokerage services; it merely means that the broker is eligible to engage in brokerage activity and may be paid for such activity, including referrals.

Provisional Brokers. Provisional brokers must also maintain a *current and active license* (timely renew his or her license and complete CE required to be on "active" status); **however, unlike a full**

broker, the provisional broker must satisfy two additional requirements below to have an "active" license:

1. be affiliated with a broker-in-charge; AND
2. complete a different thirty hours of postlicensing education by their license anniversary date in each of the first three years following initial licensure.

A provisional broker can pay the renewal fee each year and complete the required CE by June 10 of each year, but his/her license will still be on inactive status until such time as s/he becomese affiliated with a broker who is willing to act as the provisional broker's broker-in-charge. A provisional broker will be on inactive status whenever s/he lacks a broker-in-charge, even though s/he has completed all other requirements to maintain an active license. Note also that, unlike "full" brokers, provisional brokers can be on active status at the time of license renewal, but may become inactive during the license year because they fail to timely complete the required postlicensing education by the anniversary date of their license issuance.

Firms. The "current" and "active" license requirements also apply to business entities holding a **firm broker license**. *If a firm's license was expired or inactive during all or a portion of the time the brokerage services were performed by the firm's agents (as agents of either the owner or the buyer/tenant), then the firm may not be entitled to collect any brokerage commission for its services.* In that case, the individual agents involved in the transaction, who are entitled to compensation only by virtue of their affiliation with the firm, may not be able to collect any compensation. Their right to compensation depends on the firm's right to compensation.

Paying Provisional Brokers

G.S. 93A-6(a)(5) prohibits a *provisional broker* from "accepting a commission or valuable consideration as a real estate provisional broker for the performance of any of the acts specified in this Article ... *from any person except his or her broker-in-charge or licensed broker by whom he or she is employed.*" Thus, **all commissions, bonuses, incentives or other compensation paid to a provisional broker for real estate brokerage activity must flow through his or her broker-in-charge or employing broker-firm.** If a provisional broker accepts compensation for brokerage activities from any person other than his/her broker-in-charge or employing broker/firm, then the provisional broker is subject to disciplinary action.

Paying Brokers NOT on Provisional Status

There are no express statutory or rule restrictions as to paying non-provisional ("full") brokers. **In theory, a broker whose license is not on provisional status may receive commissions or other compensation for brokerage activities from anyone.** *However, if the broker transacts brokerage activities in association with and under the auspices of a brokerage firm, then most likely **the firm** owns the underlying agency agreement with the consumer, and thus any commissions arising from such transactions are due the brokerage firm.* It is then up to the brokerage firm to compensate the associated agent for his/her services pursuant to their underlying employment agreement. The concept that all brokerage compensation should flow through the company is reinforced by **G.S. 93A-6(a)(6)** which states that *a broker may not attempt to represent anyone outside of his/her employing brokerage company without the express knowledge and consent of all brokers-in-charge.* Thus, a broker should not be representing people "on the side" or receiving compensation, including referral fees, from brokerage activity outside of his/her employing firm unbeknownst to his/her broker-in-charge.

Company Policies Should Address Compensation of Affiliated Brokers. *Employing brokers and brokers-in-charge would be prudent to address the issue of affiliated broker compensation in their office policies and procedures manual.* If a company wants *all income* derived from the efforts of any of the company's affiliated agents, whether called a commission, a rebate, an incentive, a bonus, a referral fee, a prize or reward, to be paid first to the company and the company then decides the allocation, then the company needs a rule in its policy manual to that effect. Otherwise, there would be nothing which necessarily would prevent a full broker from attending a closing and directing the attorney to write the commission check to the company, but to issue the bonus amount directly to the selling broker. (Provisional brokers do not have this ability as *all* brokerage compensation must come through the company.)

Affiliated Broker is Agent of Firm. Every broker should understand that **when they are working as an affiliated agent with a company, the company is their principal, and they owe the company the same fiduciary obligations that they owe a client/principal**. Thus, it violates the duties of loyalty, obedience and disclosure of all information for any affiliated broker to accept compensation for any brokerage activity, including referrals, conducted outside of the company without the express knowledge and consent of the broker's broker-in-charge.

Paying Assistants

Payment to Actively Licensed Provisional Broker Assistant for Brokerage Activity. *The requirement that all brokerage compensation to provisional brokers be paid through the broker-in-charge applies equally to compensation paid **for brokerage activity** to an actively licensed provisional broker who is assisting any agent affiliated with the company.* The provisional broker assistant will only be on active status if s/he has a broker-in-charge. The broker (provisional or full) the assistant is helping is not acting as an independent broker, but rather is conducting his/her brokerage activity as an associated broker with a particular real estate company and is under the company's broker-in-charge at the office where they work. *The provisional broker assistant must be under the supervision of the Company's broker-in-charge at the office where he or she and the broker being assisted are employed, and payment to the actively licensed provisional broker assistant for brokerage services must be made directly by the broker-in-charge.* Obviously, the assistant's compensation for brokerage services is coming out of the compensation due the associate they are assisting, but it must be paid by the broker-in-charge. Again, this restriction applies only to *compensation due for brokerage activities* performed by an *actively licensed **provisional** broker-assistant.*

If the provisional broker assistant's broker-in-charge is at some other office, then the only services the assistant can provide at the office where he or she is working are clerical/administrative, as the assistant can only engage in brokerage activity out of the office where his/her broker-in-charge is located.

Payment to Actively Licensed Non-Provisional Broker Assistant for Brokerage Activity. If the assistant is a non-provisional ("full") broker, then he or she may be compensated by the broker he or she is assisting, the office's broker-in-charge or the employing firm, as dictated by company policy.

Payment to Assistants for Clerical/Administrative Functions. *Any broker or provisional broker may pay his/her assistant, licensed or unlicensed, directly **for clerical/administrative functions**.* **IMPORTANT NOTE:** Most assistants, licensed or unlicensed, are viewed by the IRS as W-2 employees when performing clerical or administrative tasks and someone should be withholding the appropriate FICA and taxes and sending it to the proper authorities. While the BIC may view the assistant as the associated broker's employee, the IRS may well view *the company* as the employer, because all the brokers at the office are working as agents of the company under the company's umbrella, which is why the company may be civilly liable for the conduct of its agents and support staff. Companies would be prudent to address the issue of ensuring proper tax withholding in its office policy manual.

Paying Brokers No Longer with Firm, Inactive Brokers or Former Brokers (License Expired)

When paying or sharing compensation, the **key question** is *whether all brokers (including any firms) were legally entitled to engage in brokerage activities throughout the period that services were rendered?* Did all the individual brokers who participated in the transaction have an active license while providing services? Were the firm real estate licenses of all companies involved in the transaction on active status throughout the transaction?

Basic Rule

If the licenses of the firm and the individual broker were on active status throughout the period during which services were rendered (properties viewed, offers negotiated, contracts signed, and post-contract issues addressed), *then the firm may be paid and the firm may in turn pay the individual broker, even if his/her license is inactive or expired at the time of payment.* As long as all licenses were active while services were provided and the fee earned, then the brokers may receive the fee. However, if the individual's license was not on active status when the services were provided, then neither the individual broker nor the firm may ever be paid. They all just did charity work.

Firm Entitled to the Commission

If brokerage services were provided through a licensed firm, *payment of the brokerage commission should always be made by the closing attorney* **to the firm** *that earned the commission,* not directly to any individual broker affiliated with the firm, even if the broker has a broker license or if the broker has left the firm. It is the **firm** that was the party to the agency agreement with the transaction principal (seller/lessor or buyer/tenant), not the individual broker. Accordingly, the firm is entitled to the compensation and it will then pay its current or formerly affiliated brokers according to the employment agreement with the broker.

If an **independent broker** (i.e., a broker acting independently and not affiliated with a firm) earned a commission, then the brokerage commission should be paid by the closing attorney directly to the broker, even if his/her license is inactive or expired at the time of payment.

When Broker Has Left Firm or Has Inactive/Expired License

If an individual broker (broker or provisional broker) held a current and active license throughout the period during which brokerage services were rendered through the broker's former firm, then the firm with which the broker was associated may legally pay the broker's commission share to the broker, **even though the broker is no longer associated with the firm and even if that individual's license is inactive or expired at the time of payment**. Payment to the individual will be dictated by the terms of the broker's employment agreement with the firm.

Understand that the Commission is *not* saying here that a firm *must* pay a former affiliated broker for brokerage services provided while with the firm – only that the firm *may* pay him/her if it chooses. Whether the firm must or should pay the individual will be governed by the company's office policies and procedures manual, and/or any employment contract with that individual broker (as well as principles of law or equity in the event of a legal dispute).

When Formerly Affiliated Provisional Broker Is Now with a New Firm

If the broker who earned a commission while working with a firm is a *provisional broker* who now works with another company, then the former broker-in-charge has a choice. S/he may pay the provisional broker directly since s/he was the provisional broker's broker-in-charge at the time the commission was earned, *or* the provisional broker's former broker-in-charge may pay the provisional broker's commission to his/her current broker-in-charge to pass on to the provisional broker. [If the provisional broker's license is inactive or expired at the time of payment, then clearly the former broker-in-charge would pay the provisional broker directly, as there is no current broker-in-charge.]

Miscellaneous Situations

Broker Working on a Pending Transaction After Leaving a Firm

Brokers-in-charge must be very careful in handling situations where a broker leaves a firm and associates with another firm, but has pending listing and/or sales transactions with the former firm. A **provisional broker** should not be allowed to continue working on a transaction once s/he has left the firm. Any other arrangement would be fraught with problems. A **non-provisional ("full") broker** *could* be lawfully associated with two firms with the express knowledge and consent of all brokers-in-charge, thereby allowing the broker to conclude any transactions still pending with the old company while beginning new transactions and consumer contacts with the new company. Brokers-in-charge who agree to such an arrangement should, however, consider potential liability issues for the broker's actions and, at a minimum, have everyone involved sign a written agreement describing the arrangement.

Individual Broker's License Expired or Inactive

*When a broker who is working on one or more transactions allows his/her license to expire or go inactive for failure to timely complete all required education, the broker must **immediately cease all work** on any transaction until the problem is remedied and the license reactivated!*

Example: Mary is a provisional broker working with Prime Realty with Ted as her broker-in-charge. She has a written buyer agency agreement with a buyer who makes an offer and goes under contract May 15, with a July 2 closing date. By the end of June, the deal is ready to close – no issues remain to be negotiated. On June 27, Mary realizes that she failed to take her Update course that year, so her license will be inactive as of July 1. May Mary still go to the July 2 closing just to make sure everything goes all right? **No.** Mary will not have an active license as of 12:01 a.m. July 1 and should not be permitted to engage in any conduct that requires a license thereafter until she has remedied any deficiencies.

A) May Ted go to the closing for Mary and pay Mary her commission split on July 3? Yes, even though Mary's license is still on inactive status. Her license was active until 11:59 p.m. on June 30 and she rendered all the services which earned the fee prior to that date. Thus, she may be paid her share of the commission.

B) What if Mary had done all her CE that year, but announced on June 27 that as of July 1 she had accepted employment with Rainmaker Realty. Could she still attend the July 2 closing? No, because she no longer is affiliated with Prime Realty and cannot be, since she is still on provisional status and may only have one broker-in-charge at a time. Could Ted go to the closing for her and then pay Mary her commission split? Yes. To whom should he pay the fee? While Commission rules would allow Ted to pay Mary directly (since he was her supervising broker-in-charge in the transaction which generated the compensation), the suggested course is that Ted call Mary's current broker-in-charge and ask to whom Ted should write the check.

*If a broker-in-charge allows an affiliated agent to continue working on a transaction or otherwise engage in brokerage activity after the agent's license has either expired or become inactive, then the firm jeopardizes its compensation by acting through someone who is not authorized to engage in brokerage services. **Both the firm and the agent may have forfeited any consideration to which each previously was entitled by rendering services when the agent's license was not properly on active status.***

One of the most painful (presumably) examples of this principle was an actual case several years ago when a real estate company agreed to surrender its claim to a selling side commission of nearly $550,000.00 because the provisional broker/salesperson who acted as the buyer agent over an eighteen month period in this commercial transaction had never had his license properly activated with the company. Thus, even though the company's license was active, because it provided its services through an agent who had never been on active status as an affiliated agent with the company at any time during the transaction, *both the company and the agent forfeited the selling commission.*

Firm's License Expired or Inactive

If a firm allows its license to become inactive or expire, it is not entitled to operate as a brokerage firm and loses its right to be compensated for any brokerage activity performed illegally while the firm license is inactive or expired. Even though the firm's individual "full" brokers may still have active licenses, they no longer are associated with the company because the company no longer has a license on active status — it may not have any license at all if it did not pay its renewal fee! Generally, this will occur on July 1. If the company corrects the problem *immediately*, as in a matter of days, *and* has kept its doors shut and did not engage in brokerage activity during the period when it did not have an active license, then it may salvage claims to compensation earned for services performed prior to the date of license expiration or inactivation.

Typically, however, it may take the company several weeks, and occasionally months, to realize that it has dropped the ball and does not have a license (failed to pay renewal fee) on active status (lack of qualifying broker with active license) and therefore is not authorized to engage in brokerage activity. If the company continues to provide services through its agents after its license expires or goes inactive, then both the company and its formerly associated brokers lose all claims to payment for post-deactivation services, as the brokers were acting as agents of a company which could not legally provide brokerage services. Such continued illegal activity may also impair or destroy claims for pre-deactivation services. Moreover, the firm violates the License Law by continuing to illegally engage in brokerage activity.

Paying Business Entities Created by Broker Associates for Compensation Purposes

Brokers-in-charge may encounter situations where associated non-provisional brokers create a business entity and want their brokerage compensation paid to their new entity, rather than having it paid directly to them as Form 1099 independent contractors. The *entity* created by the associated broker (most commonly a "Subchapter S" corporation or a limited liability company) *first must apply for* **and obtain** *a firm broker license* **before** *any compensation may be paid to the entity.* Otherwise, the broker-in-charge of the employing company is paying brokerage fees to an unlicensed entity, contrary to State law. Thus, a broker-in-charge's first question to the associate broker who wants his/her commissions paid to his/her entity should be: Where is your firm license? Until it is licensed, no fees earned from brokerage activity may be paid to the entity.

Every entity applying for a firm broker license must have a *qualifying broker*, namely, a principal in the entity (*officer* of a corporation, *manager* of a limited liability company) who possesses an *active broker's license* in good standing. A broker not on provisional status may wear all of the necessary hats; in other words, a broker can incorporate, own 100% of the shares of stock, name her/himself president and treasurer of the corporation, and be both qualifying broker and, if necessary, broker-in-charge, thereby fulfilling all License Law requirements (assuming s/he also has complied with all incorporation prerequisites imposed under North Carolina law). Similarly, a broker may form a one member limited liability company and be the sole manager of his/her limited liability company. This scenario partially inspired the creation of an exception, **Rule A.0110(d),** which currently reads:

> (d) A licensed real estate firm is not required to havde a broker-in-charge if it:
>
> (1) has been organized for the *sole purpose of receiving compensation* for brokerage services furnished by its qualifying broker through another firm or broker;
>
> (2) is treated for tax purposes as a Subchapter S corporation by the United States Internal Revenue Service;
>
> (3) has no principal or branch office; and
>
> (4) has *no licensed or unlicensed person* associated with it *other than its qualifying broker.*
>
> (Emphasis added.)

Example: Sam Producer conducts all of his brokerage activity as a non-provisional ("full") broker affiliated with XYZ Realty. Sam, on the advice of his CPA, decides to form either a corporation or a limited liability company (e.g., Producer Realty Inc/LLC) to allow commissions Sam earns through XYZ Realty to be paid to his business entity, rather than directly to Sam as an independent contractor. Once Sam has created his entity by registering it with the Secretary of State, Sam must next apply to the North Carolina Real Estate Commission for a firm broker license for Producer Realty Inc/LLC before his broker-in-charge at XYZ Realty may pay any of Sam's commissions to Producer Realty. As long as:

√ Sam formed Producer Realty for the sole purpose of receiving income that Sam earns elsewhere (at present, through XYZ Realty), and

√ Sam is eligible to be qualifying broker and is the only person in or associated with Producer Realty, and

√ the entity has no office (because Producer Realty is not engaging in brokerage under its umbrella – Sam is doing his brokerage under XYZ Realty's umbrella.), and

√ Producer Realty is taxed by the IRS as if it were a Subchapter S corporation, whether it is a corporation or a limited liability company .....

Then Sam will be qualifying broker for his company, but Producer Realty will not have any broker-in-charge, as it has no office, because it is not engaging in brokerage activities under its license. Producer Realty is a "shell" company – it exists solely to receive compensation earned elsewhere and no brokerage activities are conducted under its firm license.

Brokers-in-charge would do well to remember that they are *prohibited from paying any brokerage compensation to any unlicensed entity or person and are subject to disciplinary action if they do so.* Not only should brokers-in-charge request proof of licensure for any entities created by associated brokers for compensation (e.g., the firm's pocket card), but **when checking the broker's individual license renewal each year, they should also check to ensure that the broker renewed his/her "for compensation only" firm's license as well. If not, no further commissions or brokerage compensation should be paid to the entity until the broker reinstates the entity's license**.

Comments
- If the broker's entity *has **any other person** associated with it*, whether a shareholder or officer or member, licensed or unlicensed, or any affiliated broker paid on the entity's payroll, **or** if the broker conducts *any brokerage activity under the name of his/her entity* (as opposed to XYZ Realty), then the *Rule A.0110(d) exception will **not** apply* and the broker must name a broker-in-charge for his/her entity (which may be the broker him/herself, unless s/he already is a broker-in-charge elsewhere). **The A.0110(d) exception only applies when the broker's licensed entity exists solely to receive compensation that the broker earns elsewhere and no other person *is in or affiliated with the entity*.**
- Note that only limited liability companies and corporations which **meet all 4 requirements** of Rule A.0110(d) will be eligible for the broker-in-charge exemption. **Partnerships**, whether limited or general, by definition will be ineligible as there will be more than one person in the partnership.
- A **sole proprietorship** cannot avail itself of this Rule A.0110(d) exception, because the exception applies only to *licensed real estate firms*, and sole proprietorships are expressly excluded from the Rule A.0502 definition of business entity. Rule A.0110(a) provides the only exception as to when a sole proprietorship need not have a broker-in-charge.

SHARING COMPENSATION WITH NON-AFFILIATED BROKERS OR FIRMS

In addition to a broker or firm being able to share earned brokerage fees with affiliated or associated brokers, as discussed above, a broker or firm may also share compensation for brokerage services with other brokerage firms or other brokers NOT affiliated with the broker or firm. This section explores those situations when a broker or firm may share its compensation with non-affiliated brokers and brokerage firms.

Some might wish to draw a distinction between paying a **referral fee** to a non-affiliated broker versus **splitting a commission** with a non-affiliated broker as the selling or leasing agent. However, there really is no legal difference between referral fees and commission splits from the perspective of the License Law and Commission rules since they both constitute compensation for a brokerage service. The same legal principles apply, regardless of the amount or type of compensation being paid. Consequently, the discussions in this section regarding the sharing of brokerage compensation make no distinction between these types of compensation.

Current and Active License Required

Just as a broker or brokerage firm must have a current and active license to earn a brokerage commission from a client, and just as an affiliated broker must have a current and active license to be compensated, *any payment of a portion of a brokerage fee to a non-affiliated broker or firm must also be made only to a person/entity who held a current and active license at the time the brokerage service(s) was performed.* Brokers can search the Commission's website to determine the present status of a license; only the names of those individuals and companies that have an active license appear on the Commission's website. Thus, if a particular name can not be found, then that broker most likely does not have an active license at present. One can not search past license status on the website, but that information is available by obtaining the broker's license number and calling the Commission's Information Services section. One can call without the license number, but may need to know the proper name on record for the broker, since several brokers may have similar first and last names and the Commission does not show brokers by nickname.

Sharing Brokerage Fees Through Cooperative Listing Services

Most real estate sales transactions, especially residential sales, involve cooperation between non-affiliated brokers/firms. Brokers/firms earning brokerage fees are permitted to share or split earned brokerage fees with cooperating non-affiliated brokers/firms, but may not necessarily be required to share brokerage fees with every licensed cooperating broker/firm. *The sharing of brokerage fees among non-affiliated brokers/firms is determined by agreements between the affected brokers/firms regarding the sharing of such fees. The most common agreements for sharing fees are agreements among brokers who are members of a "cooperative listing service."*

A "cooperative listing service" is a membership organization formed by a group of brokers in a particular area for the purpose of cooperating with each other in the sale/lease of properties listed by member brokers. In North Carolina and elsewhere, the most well known cooperative listing services are those owned and operated by various local boards and associations of the National Association of REALTORS®, which are called a **"multiple listing service (MLS)**. These MLS organizations are separate and independent from each other listing service. *Only real estate companies who are members ("Participants") of a particular listing service may reasonably expect the listing company to compensate the selling company without specifically confirming in advance the selling company's entitlement prior to submitting an offer to the listing company.* This willingness to share compensation, if offered, is a benefit of membership, but *only extends to those **Participants** who have paid their dues to be a member of that particular listing service.*

Note that the REALTOR® Code of Ethics requires REALTOR® members to "cooperate" with *all other brokers*, not just other REALTOR® members. The ethical standard does not define "cooperation" other than to state that it "... does not include the obligation to share commissions, fees or to otherwise compensate another broker." "Cooperation" is defined in the REALTOR® Statement of Professional Standards #31 as an:

> ...obligation to share information on listed property and to make property available to other *brokers* for showing to prospective purchasers when it is in the best interest of the seller. An offer of cooperation does not necessarily include an offer to compensate a cooperating broker. Compensation in a

cooperative transaction results from either a blanket offer of subagency made through MLS or otherwise, or offers to compensate buyer agents, or, alternatively, individual offers made to subagents or to buyer agents, or other arrangements as negotiated between listing and cooperating brokers *prior* to the time an offer to purchase is produced. [Italics added.]

Understand as well that *the member/participant is the **real estate company** or entity or an owner thereof.* The agents associated with the company may be called "users" or "subscribers," depending on the listing service. Offers of compensation are made only as between the members/participants and the associated agents' rights to compensation depend on their employment agreement with the participant.

When placing a listing in a cooperative listing service, the listing firm typically indicates the percentage or amount of the listing firm's brokerage fee that the listing firm will share with a cooperating firm who procures a buyer or tenant.

Sharing Brokerage Fees Outside of Cooperative Listing Services

While the only brokers who may expect "automatic" cooperation that includes compensation are the companies who have joined a particular cooperative listing service, such companies are not prohibited from sharing compensation with actively licensed brokers who are not members of that listing service. However, *brokers who are not members of the same cooperative listing service as the listing broker, and thus not entitled to presumed cooperation, should confirm whether the listing company will share compensation with them and in what amount **before** extending an offer on behalf of any buyer/lessee.* Those who "assume" that the listing company will compensate them even though they are *not* members of that particular service may be sorely disappointed.

> **Example:** A broker is working with a buyer under a written buyer agency agreement which states that the broker anticipates receiving a commission equal to 2.5% of the purchase price, which the broker will first attempt to obtain from the seller or listing agent and the buyer will only be liable for the fee if neither the seller or listing agent will pay. The buyer's broker is not a member of any multiple listing service. The buyer ultimately finds a property on which he wishes to make an offer. The broker prepares an offer on his buyer's behalf, as well as a separate Request for Compensation for the broker's fee, and submits both simultaneously to the listing broker, who is a member of the local MLS. Two days later the buyer agent receives a fax of the offer that has been accepted and signed by the seller, as well as a note from the listing agent declining the buyer agent's request for compensation.
>
> A) Does the buyer agent have any claim against the listing company for compensation? Probably not, because the broker is not a member of the listing broker's MLS and thus is not entitled to the presumption of compensation available only to members. Because the broker failed to protect his own interests by determining the compensation issue *prior* to submitting the offer, he now has no claim against the listing company.
>
> B) Can the buyer now retract his offer? **No**, because it already has been accepted by the seller and that acceptance communicated to the buyer agent, thereby creating a

contract. The issue of the buyer agent's compensation was not (and should not be) one of the terms or conditions of the parties' contract to sell/purchase.

C)   How can the buyer agent be paid if the listing company refuses to share its brokerage fee? The only person to whom the buyer agent can turn for payment is the buyer, pursuant to the terms of the buyer agency agreement. However, the agent may have a rather unhappy client when the buyer is told that s/he now owes the agent x number of dollars (e.g., $5,000 on a $200,000 purchase) because the listing firm has refused to share. The buyer may well have offered less for the property had s/he known that s/he was responsible for his/her agent's fee.

D)   What if the buyer agent had requested compensation from the listing firm prior to submitting an offer and the listing firm had declined? The buyer agent should have shared this information with his buyer client and allowed the buyer to decide whether s/he still wanted to make an offer and if so, how much. No doubt the buyer's offer would be lower in this case, as the buyer's costs have increased because the buyer must now pay his/her own agent. The buyer agent may choose to attach a cover letter to his buyer's offer informing the seller and listing agent that one of the reasons his buyer's offer is lower than they might expect is because the listing company has refused to share compensation with the buyer agent.

Compensation Sharing Agreements "Should" Be Written

Fee-sharing arrangements between brokers should arise from an express or implied contract. Unless a broker has promised to pay a referral fee, there normally is no obligation. Most frequently the situation arises in "after-the-fact-referrals," i.e., those made to an agent *after* s/he already is working with the referred buyer, in which case the local agent generally can not be compelled to pay a referral fee. Understand, however, that *unlike agency agreements with consumers which **must** be in writing*, there is no requirement that cooperation or fee-sharing agreements **between brokers** must be in writing. The agreement may be oral, negotiated perhaps during a telephone conversation between the two brokers, but the problem will be proving what the terms of the agreement or understanding were if there is no written evidence of those terms and conditions. *A prudent agent will document any referral agreement or other fee sharing agreement through an exchange of letters or emails which set forth the terms of the brokers' understanding.* This will assist the payee later if s/he must sue the paying broker for breach of their agreement.

Maxwell v. Doyle

This principle is well illustrated in the case of *Maxwell v. Doyle, Inc.*, 164 NC App, 319, 595 SE2d 759, decided by the North Carolina Court of Appeals in May 2004.

Facts

The facts as recited in the Court's opinion were: Both Mr. Maxwell and Mr. Doyle were brokers practicing primarily commercial brokerage, the former in Cumberland County and the latter in Mecklenburg County and surrounds. Mr. Doyle had attempted over an extended period of time to persuade an owner of an apartment complex in Fayetteville to sell the property without much success. Doyle ultimately contacted Maxwell, who knew and had represented the complex owner, and told him that if Maxwell would open his past files to Doyle and help persuade the owner to list the property with Doyle, Doyle would split his commission equally with Maxwell.

Maxwell did as requested and arranged a meeting in September 2000 with the owner, Maxwell, and Doyle. Within two months of the initial meeting, unbeknownst to Maxwell, the owner entered into a listing and commission agreement with Doyle under which Doyle would receive a 2% commission upon the sale of the apartment complex. In late March/early April 2001, Maxwell learned while reading the local newspaper that the apartment complex had sold for $14,000,000.00. He contacted Doyle for his share of the $280,000 fee Doyle received. Doyle refused to pay Maxwell and Maxwell sued Doyle for the agreed fee. The trial court erroneously dismissed Maxwell's claim based on a procuring cause argument, and Maxwell appealed to the Court of Appeals, which reversed the trial court.

Court's Ruling

The Court of Appeals first noted that both parties devoted a large portion of their briefs arguing "procuring cause," which concept did not apply to the parties' dispute. Citing a 1968 North Carolina Supreme Court case, the Court of Appeals held that *the **procuring cause** doctrine applies to **disputes between property owners and brokers** concerning compensation, **not to** contractual compensation disputes between brokers.* Rather, "*a broker suing another broker for a division of a commission pursuant to an agreement between the brokers need not establish that he or she was a procuring cause of the sale. Instead, **the question is whether there was a breach of an enforceable contract between the brokers**.*" (Emphasis added.)

> "To be enforceable, the terms of a contract must be sufficiently definite and certain ...." and there must have been a meeting of the minds as to all essential terms. "Where a contract does not specify the time of performance ..., the law will prescribe that performance must be within a reasonable time ... taking into account the purposes the parties intended to accomplish."

Applying these legal principles to the case at bar, the Court of Appeals held that Maxwell had proved that there was a valid contract between he and Doyle, the terms of that contract, and a breach of that contract. The only issue was whether the sale of the apartment complex occurred within a reasonable time following the initial meeting and the parties' agreement, which issue was a question for the jury. Accordingly, the Court reversed the trial court's dismissal of Plaintiff's breach of contract claim and remanded the case back to the trial court for further proceedings. The parties ultimately settled the claim just prior to trial.

Listing Company Limitations on Sharing of Compensation

An interesting situation arises when a listing company wants to restrict the other brokers/firms with whom it will share earned brokerage fees. Typically, a listing company partially justifies the fee it is charging the property owner by explaining that the company anticipates sharing a portion of that fee with a broker who brings a buyer or tenant. The company seeks the owner's permission to share a stated portion of its total fee with a broker acting either as a buyer/tenant agent or as a subagent of the owner or according to the company's office policy (which most don't have so this rarely applies) and obtains its owner's written permission to share the firm's fee in the underlying listing/leasing agency agreement. These agency agreements usually give blanket permission to share with *any* duly licensed broker acting as a buyer agent or seller subagent, if applicable, not just with those brokers who are members of the listing company's MLS.

What if the listing company wants to impose the additional restriction that it will only share compensation with other members of its MLS? *In that case, the listing company should inform its property owners of this company policy during the initial listing solicitation, as it could influence who the owner hires. Failure to disclose the limitation up-front could also result in misrepresentation charges, as the company (assuming a standard NCAR agency agreement form is used) has told the owner that it will share a portion of its fee with **any** buyer agent or seller subagent, when in fact it will not.* If a company will not share with non-member brokers, or will share a lesser amount with non-member brokers, then the listing/leasing agency agreement should specify those conditions. For example, if the company will pay 50% of its agreed fee to any broker acting as a buyer agent who is a member of the applicable MLS, and will pay 40% to a buyer agent who is not a member of the MLS, this should be disclosed to the owner at the time of listing and should be stated in the listing agreement.

What happens if a listing broker reneges on a commission sharing agreement with a non-affiliated selling broker? What recourse does the selling broker have? See the below example.

> **Example:** Jane is a broker in Jacksonville and is working with a buyer as a buyer agent. She sees a property located in a nearby town advertised in her local MLS that meets many of her buyer's criteria. The offer of compensation in Jane's MLS is 2% of the purchase price to a buyer agent. She learns that the listing broker has offered 3% to a buyer agent through the MLS which serves the city where the property is located. Jane contacts the listing broker and asks whether he will agree to pay her a 3% commission if her buyer makes an acceptable offer. The broker agrees and he and Jane enter into a written agreement stipulating that the broker will pay Jane a 3% commission. Jane's buyer falls in love with the property and the parties successfully negotiate a contract. The morning of closing Jane receives a call from the broker informing her that he will only pay her a 2% commission, rather than 3%.
>
> Can/should Jane or her buyer client cancel the closing? No. The buyer has no legal grounds to withdraw from or cancel the transaction. The issue of Jane's compensation is not part of the Offer to Purchase and Contract nor should it be; thus, commission disputes are irrelevant to performance of the purchase contract. However, Jane's commission is the subject of a separate contract, signed by both the listing broker and Jane. Jane should bring that agreement to the closing and perhaps the broker can be persuaded to pay that which he agreed to pay. If not, Jane should take whatever check the closing attorney is authorized to issue, but not cash it if it is not for the full amount due until she first has consulted an attorney. Jane may need to sue the broker in Small Claim Court or District Court for the balance of any commission she claims is due.

Sharing Compensation with Foreign (Out-Of-State) Brokers

North Carolina brokers may compensate out-of-state persons or business entities who send them referrals or otherwise engage in brokerage services **outside of North Carolina involving a North Carolina property** *as long as* **the person or business entity possesses an active real estate license in the state from which it operates.** The two main criteria are that:

1) the foreign broker holds an active real estate license in the State from which s/he is conducting the brokerage activity;
    AND

2) at no time during the transaction does the foreign broker enter North Carolina to engage in any activity related to that transaction.

If these two criteria are satisfied, then a North Carolina broker may compensate a foreign broker, whether in the form of a referral fee or a commission split. The key to the out-of-state (foreign) broker's ability to be paid for brokering a deal where the property is located in North Carolina is that the broker must physically remain in the state where s/he is licensed and conduct all of his/her brokerage activity from that state and not enter North Carolina to engage in any activity related to the transaction, unless s/he is also licensed in North Carolina.

Examples Involving Foreign (Out-of-State) Brokers

Example #1: Barbara Broker works with Sunshine Realty, LLC in residential sales. She receives a telephone call from Betty, a broker in Iowa whom she met at a trade convention. Betty explains that one of her very best friends is moving to North Carolina and needs a competent buyer agent and that Betty of course thought of Barbara, so Betty asked that if she referred her friend to Barbara and the friend ultimately purchased a home using Barbara as her agent, would Barbara pay Betty a referral fee. May Barbara agree to pay Betty a referral fee of whatever amount/percent? **Yes,** *as long as*:

1) Barbara asks Betty whether her Iowa license is still active; if Barbara has any reason to suspect that Betty no longer has a license, she may wish to check with the Iowa Real Estate Commission.

2) Betty does not accompany her friend to North Carolina. If Betty comes to North Carolina and participates in the transaction in any way, even as a "friend," she will forfeit her referral fee because she is engaging in brokerage activity in North Carolina without a North Carolina license.

3) If Betty is a salesperson or broker affiliated with a real estate company in Iowa, Barbara should make the check payable to the company. If Betty is a broker who is not affiliated with any real estate company, Barbara may issue the check to Betty directly.

Note: It is NOT necessary that the amount of the referral fee appear on the settlement statement form. Indirectly it is already on the settlement statement as it is subsumed within Barbara's fee. It would only need to be separately identified on the settlement statement if Barbara was sharing part of her money with one of the parties, i.e., buyer or seller.

Example #2: What if the facts are basically the same as in Example #1, except Betty's "friend" turns out to be her 28- year old son who is purchasing his first home. Betty wants Barbara to pay her a referral fee, but candidly acknowledges that she plans to accompany her son to North Carolina so he can have the benefit of her sage maternal advice. May Barbara pay Betty a referral fee if Betty comes to North Carolina with her son and views various properties wearing "her mother hat"? **No.** Betty's toes are now in a state where she is not licensed specifically related to a transaction in which she is not a party. She can not receive any consideration. However, knowing that this is what Betty wanted to do, could Betty and Barbara have reached some other agreement? **Yes.** Barbara could pay Betty nothing, and instead agree to share with

Betty's son, as a party to the transaction, an amount similar to what she was going to pay Betty. The amount Barbara is sharing with the son must both be on the settlement statement and disclosed to the lender long before the closing.

Example #3: A North Carolina broker primarily handles listings and advertises her owners' properties on the internet. She receives a call from a broker in Idaho who has a buyer client who is interested in two of the broker's listings. The Idaho broker wants to know if his buyer makes offers which are acceptable to the broker's sellers, will she pay him a commission? May she? **Yes,** *as long as:* the broker is actively licensed in Idaho, engages in negotiations from Idaho, and does not come to North Carolina related to either of the two transactions. If all three conditions are fulfilled, the North Carolina broker may pay the Idaho broker the agreed commission. The buyer client obviously may come to North Carolina, but the Idaho broker who lacks a North Carolina license may not.

Example #4: A North Carolina broker is approached by a potential buyer from Florida who wants to see several of the company's listings. After reviewing the "Working with Real Estate Agents" brochure, the buyer chooses to have the broker act only as a seller agent and the necessary signatures are obtained on the bottom of the disclosure form evidencing seller agency. After viewing several properties, the buyer has narrowed it to three properties, at which point he mentions that he has a broker license in Florida and would the North Carolina broker be willing to pay him the selling side of the commission.

A) *Must the company agree to co-broke with the Florida broker-buyer?* **No**, in fact they are prohibited from "co-brokering," because the broker is physically in North Carolina and does not have a North Carolina license and thus cannot engage in brokerage in this state.

B) *May the company voluntarily agree to share consideration with the Florida broker?* **Yes**, because he also is a *party to the transaction* and does not need a license to lawfully receive consideration because he is not representing others. The amount of the consideration must be on the settlement statement form and disclosed to the buyer's lender.

C) *What if the Florida broker had called the North Carolina broker from Florida and negotiated payment of a referral fee or commission where the broker was in fact the buyer, as above?* While the Florida broker attempts to negotiate a fee legally by calling from a state where he is licensed, the North Carolina broker still should share any consideration with this prospective buyer under his buyer hat and not under his broker hat, particularly because any other foreign broker forfeits any agreed fee the moment s/he steps into North Carolina related to the transaction. Here, the broker will obviously enter the state because he is the party in the transaction, placing the conduct outside the definition of brokerage activity because the broker is not representing "others," which further supports sharing any consideration under his buyer hat, not his Florida broker hat.

Commercial Brokerage
*The laws and rules discussed above apply to all brokerage transactions in North Carolina, **including commercial transactions.*** Thus, a foreign broker who is physically present in North Carolina and acting as a broker (i.e., representing others) in a commercial transaction, but who lacks a North Carolina

license is *illegally engaged in brokerage activity* and is not entitled to receive any compensation or other consideration for his/her activity. Any broker who shares consideration with the foreign broker who has entered North Carolina to represent others in the sale or lease of commercial property has violated License Law [G.S. 93A-6(a)(9)] and Commission rules [Rule 58A.0109(g)], and will be subject to disciplinary action. The North Carolina broker, as well as any unlicensed person who pays the foreign broker who does not possess a North Carolina license, will also have committed a misdemeanor under North Carolina criminal law by violating G.S. 14-2.6. The foreign broker also will have committed a misdemeanor by violating G.S. 93A-1.

Limited Non-Resident Commercial License

It is exceedingly easy for a non-resident salesperson or broker licensed in any other State or territory of the United States to apply for and obtain a North Carolina limited non-resident commercial broker license that would allow the foreign broker to *legally* enter North Carolina, engage in a commercial transaction and be paid for that activity. The foreign broker will not be required to complete any North Carolina education nor to take the State licensing examination. Rather, the foreign broker must only complete and submit to the North Carolina Real Estate Commission an application for this limited non-resident commercial license (available on the Commission's website) with the requisite application fee (currently $100), a criminal background report, and a license history from the state or territory where s/he is licensed and, assuming there are no negative character issues, the Commission will issue a limited non-resident commercial license to the foreign broker.

This license must be obtained *before the foreign broker may physically enter North Carolina.* However, once issued, the license may be renewed each year by paying the applicable renewal fee (currently $45) and will allow the foreign broker to enter North Carolina whenever s/he wants in order to engage in *commercial transactions only.* In addition to the license, the foreign broker must also have a written Declaration of Affiliation with a North Carolina broker and a brokerage cooperation agreement *before the foreign broker physically enters North Carolina.* See G.S. 93A-9(b) and Commission Rules 58A.1801 through 58A.1810. *North Carolina brokers should be aware of this option and inform foreign brokers with whom they have contact of this possibility,* **rather than expose everyone to criminal conduct and risk the suspension or revocation of their license for illegally paying foreign brokers who are in North Carolina, but who lack a North Carolina broker license.**

THIRD PARTY PAYMENTS TO BROKERS

Real Estate Commission Rule A.0109, entitled "Brokerage Fees and Commissions" addresses a variety of payments to brokers by third parties, including:

- Kickbacks, rebates or referral fees to a broker for expenditures made by the broker in behalf of the broker's principal to a provider of goods and services;

- kickbacks, rebates or referral fees to a broker for recommending, procuring or arranging services for a party; and

- compensation, incentives or bonuses paid to a broker by his/her principal or any other party.

Kickback, Rebate, etc. to Broker for Expenditure Made by Broker In Behalf of Broker's Principal to Provider of Goods or Services

Paragraph (a) of Rule A.0109 reads as follows:

> (a) A broker shall not receive, either directly or indirectly, any commission, rebate or other valuable consideration of more than nominal value from a vendor or a supplier of goods and services for an expenditure made on behalf of the broker's principal in a real estate transaction without the written consent of the broker's principal.

This provision requires disclosure to and written consent from a broker's principal that the broker may receive some consideration "of more than nominal value" for having made an expenditure to a provider of goods or services in behalf of the principal. What is "nominal?" The last sentence of Rule A.0109(e) defines **"nominal value"** as meaning "*...of insignificant, token or merely symbolic worth.*" It means a pittance, a token. It is not dependent upon nor related to the value of the property, goods or services provided.

If the broker recommends to his/her *principal* a provider of goods or services and expends the principal's funds for the recommended goods or services, then the rule requires the broker to have his/her *principal's **written** consent* in order to receive consideration (a "kickback") from the provider. Requiring the principal's *written* consent is intended to clearly evidence the principal's awareness of his/her agent's potential financial interest or incentive in selecting the provider, as the agent owes all duties of loyalty, obedience and disclosure of all information to his/her principal of any factors that might influence the principal's decision. The principal has a right to know from whom his/her agent is receiving any consideration so the principal may assess any potential bias or self-interest the agent may have, contrary to the agent's duty to promote the principal's interests, which are paramount to the agent's interests.

> **Example:** A broker-property manager, as part of his/her management duties, engages a cleaning service to clean each managed property following each tenancy. The broker pays the cleaning service from rents collected on the managed properties prior to disbursing rents to the owners. The cleaning service then pays the broker each month a $10 kickback for each property cleaned. The broker must have written consent from each property owner to collect the payments from the cleaning service.

Kickback, Referral Fee, etc. to Broker for Recommending, Procuring or Arranging Services for a Party

Paragraph (b) of Rule A.0109 reads as follows:

> (b) A broker shall not receive, either directly or indirectly, any commission, rebate or other valuable consideration of more than nominal value for services which the broker recommends, procures, or arranges relating to a real estate transaction for a party, without full and timely disclosure to such party.

This provision requires disclosure by a broker to **any party** (not just the broker's principal) that the broker may receive some compensation from a provider of services that the broker recommends, procures or arranges relating to a transaction. Although written disclosure is not required, it is highly recommended.

Example: A buyer's agent recommends a painter to a buyer-client. The buyer follows the agent's recommendation and uses that painter. The painter subsequently pays the agent a $200 referral fee pursuant to a prior arrangement between the agent and painter. The agent must disclose to the buyer-client the referral fee arrangement at the time the recommendation is made to the buyer. The disclosure does not have to be in writing, but that is highly recommended.

Example: A broker specializes in vacation rentals at the beach, acting only as the owners' property manager. He typically suggests to tenants that they consider purchasing vacation rental insurance in case they are unable to fulfill their tenancy for whatever reason. He gives prospective tenants the names of three different insurers and tells the tenants to tell the insurers that he (the broker) recommended them. The insurers give the broker 5% of the insurance premium for every vacation tenant he sends who purchases a policy. The broker must at least orally inform every tenant that he may receive a referral fee if they purchase a policy from any of the insurers the broker recommends.

Note on RESPA Restrictions on Referral Fees and Kickbacks

While Rule A.0109 permits third party payments to brokers acting as agents as long as the proper disclosure and consent requirements have been satisfied, the rule expressly prohibits any payments which may violate either the Real Estate Settlement Procedures Act (RESPA) or any HUD rules or regulations issued pursuant to the Act. **RESPA basically prohibits payment of any referral fees between or among any "settlement service providers" other than real estate brokers. Settlement service providers is fairly broadly defined to include virtually anyone providing a service related to the transaction, e.g., home inspectors, appraisers, attorneys, lenders, mortgage brokers, surveyors, pest inspectors, etc.**

Note that brokers must *always* comply with Rule A.0109 as to both disclosure and consent *whenever they are acting as an agent in ANY transaction*, even if RESPA does not apply. For detailed coverage of RESPA disclosure requirements and prohibited practices, brokers are referred to Chapter 14.

Compensation, Incentives, Bonuses, etc. to Broker From Anyone Other Than Broker's Principal

Rule A.0109 was substantially revised effective October 1, 2008 by adding paragraphs (c), (d) and (e) reprinted below: *These provisions apply only in **sales** transactions, both residential and commercial.*

> (c) In a real estate sales transaction, a broker shall not receive any compensation, incentive, bonus, rebate, or other consideration of more than nominal value:
>
> (1) from his principal unless the compensation, incentive, bonus, rebate, or other consideration is provided for in a written agency contract prepared in conformity with the requirements of 21 NCAC 58A.0104.
>
> (2) from any other party or person unless the broker provides full and timely disclosure of the incentive, bonus, rebate, or other consideration, or the promise or expectation thereof to the broker's principal. The disclosure may be made orally, but must be confirmed in writing before the principal makes or accepts an offer to buy or sell.
>
> (d) Full disclosure shall include a description of the compensation, incentive, bonus, rebate, or other consideration including its value and the identity of the person or party by whom it will or may be paid. A disclosure is timely

when it is made in sufficient time to aid a reasonable person's decision-making. (e) Nothing in this rule shall be construed to require a broker to disclose to a person not his principal the compensation the broker expects to receive from his principal or to disclose to his principal the compensation the broker expects to receive from the broker's employing broker. For the purpose of this rule, nominal value means of insignificant, token, or merely symbolic worth.

Basic Tenets of Commission Rule A.0109(c), (d) and (e)

1. No broker may receive any compensation, consideration, bonus, incentive, or rebate of more than nominal value *from his/her principal* unless the amount of that compensation, incentive, bonus, rebate or other consideration is specified in the appropriate *written* agency agreement between the broker and his/her client as required by Rule A.0104.

2. No broker may receive *any* compensation, incentive, bonus, rebate or other consideration *from any party or person* **other than** *his/her principal* **unless** *the broker fully and timely discloses to his/her principal the amount of all compensation/consideration* the broker expects to receive from such other party or person. The disclosure must include a *description of the value* of the compensation, bonus, incentive, rebate or other consideration *and the identity of the person* or party by whom it may be paid. The disclosure may be oral while showing properties, but must be confirmed in writing *before the principal makes or accepts an offer to buy or sell.*

3. A broker is *NOT* required to disclose to someone who is *NOT* his principal the amount or form of compensation or consideration the broker may receive from his/her principal, nor must an individual broker disclose to his/her principal the amount of compensation the broker expects to receive from his/her employing broker (i.e., the Company).

4. A broker is obligated to disclose to his/her principal the value of any expected compensation/consideration whenever such consideration in any form is "of more than nominal value." **"Nominal value"** is defined as meaning "...**of insignificant, token or merely symbolic worth**."

Reasons for 2008 Rule Changes. *The primary motive underlying the adoption the 2008 changes to the compensation rule was to address a problem related to the widespread practice of residential developers and homebuilders offering incentives, bonuses or other rewards to real estate brokers who procure a buyer for the developers' or homebuilders' property. The problem was that brokers acting as a buyer's agent were not disclosing the receipt of such incentives (or possibility thereof) to their buyer-clients. Thus, buyer-clients frequently were unaware that their agent would receive extra compensation if the buyer purchased certain properties. Even if the buyer's agent did not steer his/her client to properties offering a sales incentive, the fact that additional compensation might be paid to the buyer's agent by the seller, whose interests are opposite those of the buyer, created a situation with an inherent conflict of interest. Paragraph (c)(2) is the rule provision that addresses this particular issue.*

The underpinnings for this rule arise from the agent's fiduciary duties of loyalty, obedience and disclosure of all information to his/her principal that may influence the principal's decision in any given transaction. In addition to these common law fiduciary duties, a broker is obligated under the

Real Estate License Law to avoid any misrepresentation *or omission* of a material fact. The payment of a special bonus to a broker by a seller may reasonably raise an issue as to the broker's loyalty to the broker's buyer-client. This could especially be the case if all or most of the properties selected by a broker for viewing by a buyer-client involve an incentive to be paid by the seller to the selling agent. The buyer-client must be provided in a timely manner information about any possible compensation that the broker might receive from the seller of a property being considered by the buyer-client. Under the law of agency, an agent must hold his/her principal's interests paramount to the agent's personal interests or possible pecuniary gain. An agent's primary purpose is to promote and fulfill the lawful objects of his/her principal. Additionally, the payment to a broker of compensation by a party whose interests are opposed to those of the broker's principal is certainly a material fact about which the broker's principal needs to be informed prior to making a decision in a transaction.

Note: Basic tenets #1 and #3 listed above are essentially self-explanatory and will not be discussed further here. The focus of this coverage will be on basic tenets #2 and #4 listed above, which are Rule provisions A.0109(c)(2) and (e).

Broker Acting as a Buyer's Agent

Oral Buyer Agency Agreement Situation. Where a broker is acting as a buyer's agent under an express oral buyer agency agreement, the broker should have already reached agreement with the buyer as to the broker's compensation. If a situation then arises where the buyer's agent may be eligible to receive an additional bonus or incentive from someone other than the broker's employing broker (e.g., from a seller-developer) in connection with the sale of a property the agent will be showing to the buyer-client, then the broker minimally must orally disclose to his/her buyer-client any such potential additional compensation. This may be expressed either as a dollar amount or a formula such as a percentage. Disclosure to the buyer is also required if the listing firm for a particular property is offering to compensate a buyer's agent for an amount that exceeds the amount of compensation to the buyer's agent that the agent and the buyer had previously agreed. Remember that the buyer agency agreement must be in writing no later than presentation of any offer.

Written Buyer Agency Agreement Situation. Where a broker is acting as a buyer's agent under a written buyer agency agreement, but the buyer agent is showing the buyer a property where the compensation, including any bonus or incentive, offered by the seller or listing company exceeds the amount stated in the buyer agency agreement, then the buyer's agent still must orally disclose to his/her buyer-client the amount the broker/company would receive over and above the amount stated in the buyer agency agreement if the buyer were to purchase that property.

The broker also must confirm the disclosure of the additional compensation in writing to his/her buyer prior to preparing an offer on that property for the buyer.

Timeliness of Disclosure. In order to assure that the disclosure of potential additional compensation is made to a buyer-client in a timely manner as required by the rule, the Commission strongly recommends that a *broker disclose potential additional compensation to a buyer-client prior to or at the time of showing the property* featuring an incentive or bonus to the selling agent upon sale of the property.

Meaning of "Nominal Value." The rule does not establish a fixed maximum amount for compensation that would still be considered "nominal" in value. Rather, the rule relies on the common meanings of "nominal" as provided in various dictionaries and states: "For the purpose of this rule, nominal value means of insignificant, token or merely symbolic worth." The Commission provides the following examples to illustrate compensation, incentives, etc. that it would consider to be of "nominal value:"

- Dinner Gift Certificate for $50
- Bottle of Wine – Value $25

Any promised or expected compensation of any type to a broker from a third party in connection with a transaction must be disclosed to the broker's principal unless the compensation is of nominal value.

Broker Working with Buyer as Seller's Agent or Subagent

As long as a broker working with a buyer as a seller agent or subagent otherwise complies with the agency disclosure and agreement rule, and both the broker and the buyer have a clear understanding that the broker is working with the buyer as a seller's agent or subagent and thus owes his/her loyalties to the seller, and not to the buyer, *the broker working as a seller's agent or subagent has no obligation under the revised rule to inform the buyer of the amount or value of any compensation (including any bonus or incentive) the broker might receive from the seller or listing company.*

Broker Acting as a Dual Agent

Acting as a dual agent does not relieve the agent working with the buyer of the duty under the rule to disclose potential additional compensation to the buyer-client. Technically, a company acting as a dual agent must disclose to *both* principals the total amount of compensation the company will receive in the transaction. Since in its capacity as listing agent, the firm's compensation is specifically set out in the listing contract, and the standard practice in residential transactions is for the listing firm to only receive compensation from the seller, it would be rare for there to be a need to disclose potential additional compensation to the seller-client. On the other hand, because the standard practice with buyer agency and dual agency is for the buyer's agent to be compensated by sharing in the fee paid by the seller to the listing firm, and because the buyer is not privy to the listing contract, the buyer-client in a dual agency situation is not aware of the amount of compensation being paid to the listing firm (which is also representing the buyer because of the dual agency). Moreover, as with the regular buyer agency situation, buyer-clients will likely not be aware of any potential incentives or bonuses being offered to the selling firm/agent (or listing firm/agent) by a seller company. Therefore, as a practical matter, the issue in dual agency situations is the same as in regular buyer agency situations – **the buyer-client must be advised in a timely manner of the full amount of compensation the firm will receive, including additional incentives, bonuses or any other potential additional compensation that might be paid by a seller either to the firm or to individual agent working with the buyer.**

Some practical issues have arisen in the application of this rule. For example, some firms as a matter of policy have in the past not made the amount of the total brokerage fees for listed properties available to all affiliated brokers in order to avoid the brokers being able to figure out the details of commission splits between the firm and affiliated brokers. Brokers affiliated with a firm may not have ready access to listing files containing such information. Also, many firms may not have the brokerage fee information in an internal computer database that is accessible to affiliated brokers, and the firm's full brokerage fee (as opposed to the amount the firm will share with a cooperating firm) probably is not shown in the MLS. Thus, some problems have arisen when individual agents working with a buyer in a dual agency (or designated agency) situation have not been able to readily determine the firm's expected compensation as to any given property.

> **Example:** Buyer agent makes appointments to show houses to her buyer-client on a Sunday. When the agent takes the buyer to see one of the scheduled showings, the buyer notices a house across the street listed by the buyer agent's own firm and wants to see it. The buyer agent

has had no opportunity to research this property in advance of showing and does not know what compensation her firm has contracted to receive from the seller. The MLS provides her with information about the amount or percentage of commission being offered to the buyer agent, but not the full commission. How does the buyer (now dual) agent satisfy her duty to timely disclose, at least orally, the firm's compensation (which generally should be prior to showing)? And, if upon showing the property, the buyer wants to make a written offer, how can the broker comply with the rule's requirement that she provide her client written confirmation of the firm's compensation prior to presenting an offer?

There are several avenues by which the company may facilitate brokers' compliance with the rule. One is to make compensation information available on a company database accessible only by the firm's own agents. The firm could impose other restrictions to limit access to "need-to-know" situations only. Some firms may do this already, but others may not because the expense of creating the necessary programs would be prohibitive and/or for other reasons which they deem undesirable. Another possibility is that company policy may require the broker to contact the listing agent for the information, and to require the listing agent to keep that information and make it available in this circumstance. If the listing agent cannot be reached, then the broker showing the firm's in-house listing should be directed to contact other identified associates of the firm who have access to the information (e.g., the broker-in-charge, managers, a duty agent at the office, etc.).

What happens if the foregoing strategies fail and the agent is unable to immediately determine the firm's compensation? Under these circumstances, the buyer/dual agent should make a good faith estimate of the firm's compensation based upon what he or she reasonably knows, or should know, about the firm's listing practices and the property in question, and then proceed with the showing. Thereafter, the agent should check with his or her firm as soon as possible to confirm the accuracy of her disclosure and to promptly correct any discrepancy, in order to satisfy the rule's requirement that disclosure be made in sufficient time to aid a reasonable person's decision-making.

But what if the buyer wants to make an offer immediately, before the agent has been able to verify the firm's commission? The rule requires the agent to confirm the firm's compensation before the principal makes an offer to buy or sell. However, with all disclosure requirements, the Real Estate Commission will look at all the facts and circumstances surrounding a particular transaction before making a decision as to whether a broker behaved inappropriately. Some of the factors that would be considered in connection with a complaint that a consumer was not given full and timely disclosure of the firm's compensation as required by the rule will include:

- whether the broker gave the consumer a good faith estimate and how close the estimate was to the actual compensation to be paid;
- whether the broker had any reason to suspect the compensation might be different than disclosed;
- whether the compensation received was more, or less, than disclosed;
- what systems were in place by the firm to make the information available;
- whether the broker utilized the firm's systems but, because of unusual circumstances, was unable to obtain the necessary information;
- whether the failure to disclose was exceptional, or was it the standard operating procedure of either the broker or the firm; and
- all other relevant facts and circumstances concerning the particular transaction.

The Commission generally will not impose discipline against a broker who has made an error acting in good faith, particularly when the broker has taken reasonable steps to obtain and disclose the correct information, and when any error that occurred was corrected without harm or significant risk to a member of the public.

Examples of Compensation, Incentives, etc. to a Broker from a Third Party That Must Be Disclosed Under Revised Rule 58A.0109:

As clearly stated in the rule and reiterated immediately above, anything of more than nominal value that is promised to a broker in connection with a transaction by a third party must be disclosed to the broker's principal.

Example #1

ABC Homebuilders offers to pay to any broker who procures a buyer for one of ABC's inventory homes a bonus in excess of commissions of $1,000 payable at closing. Broker X intends to show his/her buyer-client one or more of ABC's homes. Broker X is operating under a written buyer agency contract that says X will seek a 3% commission from the seller.

Broker X must disclose the promised $1,000 bonus to his/her buyer-client.

Example #2

ABC Homebuilders offers to pay to any broker who procures a buyer for one of its inventory homes between stated fixed beginning and ending dates a bonus payable at closing as follows: 1st Sale – $1,000; 2nd Sale – $2000; 3rd or subsequent sale – $3,000. This bonus is payable in addition to any commission the broker may be entitled to receive under a listing agreement with ABC or under a commission-sharing agreement with the listing firm. Broker X intends to show her buyer-client one or more of ABC's homes, has already procured one buyer during the eligibility period, and has other buyer-clients to whom she is showing ABC's homes. Broker X is operating under an oral buyer agency agreement with her client and has orally disclosed that she intends to seek a 2.4% commission from the seller.

Broker X must disclose the bonus program to her buyer client AND the fact that Broker X has already sold one of ABC's homes and that her bonus will be at least $2,000 if the buyer purchases one of ABC's homes within the bonus eligibility period.

Assume the promised bonus (in addition to any brokerage commission earned under a listing contract or a brokerage cooperation agreement) in the above example was 3% commission for the first sale, 4% commission for a second sale and 5% commission for a third or subsequent sale instead of a lower fixed dollar amount. Then, the Broker must disclose the promised commission percentages, that she has already sold one of ABC's homes, and that her bonus would be at least 4% commission if the buyer purchases one of ABC's homes within the incentive eligibility period.

Example #3

ABC Homebuilders promises to pay to any brokerage firm procuring five (5) or more buyers for ABC's houses during a stated period of time a bonus of $5,000. Broker X of XYZ Realty is planning to show a buyer-client of XYZ Realty some of ABC's houses. Broker X is operating under a written buyer agency contract that says X will seek a 3% commission from the seller.

Broker X must disclose to the buyer-client the fact that XYZ Realty, which, like Broker X, is the buyer's agent, may receive a $5,000 bonus if the firm procures five or more buyers during the incentive eligibility period.

Examples Relating to the Requirement for TIMELY Oral Disclosure of Compensation from a Third Party under Rule 58A.0109(c) and (d)

Example #4
A broker working with a buyer as the buyer's agent under a written buyer agency agreement prepares a list of possible properties listed for sale that may meet the buyer-client's needs and reviews these possible properties with the buyer-client. From the list, the buyer selects the properties s/he would like to see and the broker shows those properties to the buyer. At the time the broker presented the list to the buyer client, the broker knew that the sellers of two of the properties selected by the buyer were offering a bonus to the buyer agent who produced a purchaser for their properties. The broker said nothing to his buyer about the bonuses as he showed the buyer the properties. After seeing all of the properties, and revisiting a few, the buyer decided to make an offer on one of the two properties which were offering a bonus. At that time, the broker told his buyer client that the seller would pay the broker a $3,000 bonus over commissions. The broker confirmed this with a written statement to the buyer. By then, several of the other properties on the original list had sold to other buyers.

Even though the broker provides a written confirmation of the disclosure prior to the buyer making an offer, the oral disclosure is NOT timely because disclosure at this point in the transaction does not provide the buyer-client sufficient time to make a fully-informed decision as to which property is the most appropriate for him/her to purchase. Moreover, the broker should have informed the buyer about the bonus offered by the seller of the other property at the time of showing so the buyer could evaluate the properties in light of that information.

Suppose the broker in the above fact situation had sent this email message to his buyer client: "Jim, attached please find the showing appointments for next Saturday. Note that the sellers of the Oak Street and Second Avenue properties are offering a bonus to the buyer agent." Would this have made a difference? Yes and No. The disclosure is timely because it is made before any showings occurred. It afforded the buyer an opportunity to evaluate the properties and his broker's advice concerning them knowing that the advice he received might be colored by the prospect of the seller-paid bonus. The form of the disclosure – a written email – also satisfies the rule's requirement for written confirmation, as the disclosure could have been oral at this point, and need only be reduced to writing if the buyer chose to make an offer on one of the properties paying a bonus. The problem with the disclosure is not its timing or form, but its completeness, or lack thereof. The rule requires the broker to include the value of the incentive or bonus in the disclosure. Here the broker failed to describe either the dollar amount of the bonus or the formula by which the value of the offered bonus would be determined.

Example #5

A broker working with a buyer as the buyer's agent prepares a list of possible properties listed for sale that may meet the buyer-client's needs/desires. When reviewing information about these properties with the buyer-client to obtain the buyer-client's decision as to what properties will be shown, the broker discloses orally for each listing under consideration any possible commission, incentive, bonus, etc. the broker may receive if the buyer-client purchases that property.

This disclosure is timely because by making the disclosure at the time of presentation to the buyer of possible properties for showing and prior to the buyer's selection of properties to be shown, the broker has given the buyer the maximum possible time to consider how the issue of the broker's compensation might impact the buyer's decision as to which properties to view and consider for purchase.

Example of Disclosure Required When Company/Broker Acting as Dual Agent

Example #6

XYZ Realty represents a seller. In its listing agreement, the seller agrees to pay the Company a 5.5% commission and authorizes the Company to pay 2.5% to any buyer agent or seller sub-agent who brings a buyer. The listing agreement also specifies that the seller will pay any selling agent a $2,000 bonus above the commission split offered a selling agent, and that the seller authorizes the Company to act as a dual agent. An agent with XYZ Realty is working with a buyer as a buyer agent under an oral buyer agency agreement. The buyer agent told his buyer client initially that the broker expects to receive a commission from the listing company or seller equal to 3% of the sales price of any property on which the buyer makes an offer which is accepted by the seller. After showing the buyer several properties listed with other companies, the buyer now decides she wants to see XYZ's listing. Prior to showing the property, the buyer agent orally informs the buyer client that they are now in a dual agency situation, obtains the buyer's consent thereto, and also tells the buyer client that the seller of this property will pay a total commission of 5.5% of the contract price plus a $2,000 bonus to the Company which is acting as the agent for both parties. After viewing the property, the buyer decides she wants to make an offer on the property. What must the buyer agent do?

Because as yet there is no written agency agreement with the buyer, the buyer agent first must prepare and have the buyer client sign a written buyer agency agreement in which the buyer also authorizes the Company to act as a dual agent. Since the buyer agent already knows what compensation is being offered on this particular property, the agent should specify that the buyer authorizes the Company to receive a 5.5% commission plus a $2,000 bonus as its compensation, all paid by the seller, if the buyer's offer is accepted. The agent may indicate that the Company will not hold the buyer responsible for any sums not paid by the seller.

After obtaining the buyer's signature on the agency agreement, *the broker may prepare an* offer on behalf of the buyer. Had the buyer agency agreement already been in writing and authorized dual agency and had it specified a commission when showing the property of 3% paid by the seller, then the buyer agent would have been required to tell the buyer that the Company would receive a 5.5% total commission and a $2,000 bonus paid by the seller. *Prior to preparing the offer, the agent must also confirm in writing to the buyer the amount of the total commission and bonus the Company would receive from the seller.* Total commissions and bonuses or consideration to be paid to the Company by either the buyer or seller must be disclosed to each principal in a dual agency situation because there is no "split" – the Company receives all consideration (both the listing and selling sides) paid by either principal.

APPENDIX A
REAL ESTATE LICENSING IN NORTH CAROLINA

G.S. 93A-1 *prohibits any person or entity from engaging in any real estate brokerage activity in North Carolina without first obtaining a real estate license* from the North Carolina Real Estate Commission. G.S. 93A-4 of the License Law requires any person or business entity desiring to engage in real estate brokerage activities in North Carolina to apply in writing to the Commission for a real estate broker license in the form and manner prescribed by the Commission. The present license application fee for both individuals and business entities is $100.00. The same statute establishes certain other minimum qualifications and requirements for license applicants and confers on the Commission in subsection (d) "...the power and authority to make and enforce any and all reasonable rules and regulations connected with license application, examination, renewal, and reinstatement as shall be deemed necessary to administer and enforce the provisions of this Chapter."

As discussed at the outset of Chapter 21, real estate brokerage in North Carolina consists of: 1) the temporary or permanent transfer of an interest in real property, 2) for others, 3) for compensation or consideration. Before any person or entity physically in North Carolina may provide brokerage services to any consumer, that person or entity must first obtain a North Carolina broker license and the license must be on active status to engage in brokerage services.

INDIVIDUAL LICENSES

To qualify initially for licensure, a person generally must take a North Carolina 75-hour Prelicensing course offered by a Commission-approved real estate school. Prelicensing courses taken in other states may qualify if found to be substantially equivalent to the North Carolina course. Within three years of successfully completing the course by passing the end-of-course examination, the person must submit an application for licensure with the $100.00 application fee and a criminal background check. The applicant will then receive a notice of exam eligibility that allows the applicant to contact the Commission's examination provider, pay a testing fee, and schedule an appointment to take the state license examination by computer. The individual has 180 days within which to pass the state license examination, but each exam attempt requires a new fee.

The state license exam has two parts, a 100-question national section and a 40-question North Carolina specific section (referred to as the "state section"). An applicant must pass both sections within the 180 day window and must wait at least ten days before testing again. Upon passing both sections of the state license examination, and assuming there are no character issues that would prevent licensure, the individual will receive a broker license *on provisional status*, usually referred to as a provisional broker ("PB"). To remove provisional status, the individual must complete a total of 90 hours of Postlicensing education comprised of three 30-hour courses; *minimally*, one 30-hour course must be completed by license anniversary date in each of the first three years of licensure for the licensee to remain eligible for active status. Upon completing the third 30-hour class within the first three years of licensure, provisional status will be automatically removed and the individual will hold a non-provisional or "full" broker license.

To maintain a license on active status, *i.e.*, one that can be used, a full broker must only: 1) pay the license renewal fee between May 15 and June 30 of each year and 2) complete one of the Commission's Update courses (4 hours) and one approved elective course (4 hours) by June 10 every license year after first license renewal. A full broker who does these two things every year will have a license on active status, even though the broker may not be affiliated with either a company or a broker-in-charge. *The same is not true of provisional brokers*; in addition to timely renewing their license and completing eight hours of continuing education, provisional brokers must also complete not less than one 30-hour Postlicensing course by license anniversary date in each of the first three years of licensure *and* must always have a broker-in-charge. A provisional broker will be on inactive status, and thus unable to engage in brokerage, whenever s/he does not have a broker-in-charge or if s/he fails to timely complete any required education or pay the renewal fee.

An individual who has a license in another state or territory of the United States or Canada that has been on active status at some point within three years preceding North Carolina license application will only be required to sit for the state-specific section of the North Carolina state license examination. Any applicant licensed in another jurisdiction must submit a license history from all states where licensed (even if the licenses have *not* been on active status within three years preceding license application), in addition to the written application, $100 application fee, and criminal background report. For the most current information on how to obtain a North Carolina license and the distribution of questions by subject area on the state license examination, readers should either order or download the free publication, *Real Estate Licensing in North Carolina*, on the Commission's website.

REAL ESTATE COMPANIES

There are two primary types of real estate companies, namely, those that are sole proprietorships and those that are some form of business entity. The rule pertaining to firm licensing is **Rule 58A.0502, "Business Entities."** The first sentence of this rule expressly excludes sole proprietorships from the firm licensing requirement, because a sole proprietor has not created something other than him or herself.

SOLE PROPRIETORSHIP

A sole proprietorship is a *business owned by only one person who remains personally liable for all debts and obligations of the sole proprietorship.* A sole proprietor may be a one person company, or the sole proprietor may employ numerous affiliated licensees to work for him or her. For example, Mary Smith is a broker who does business as a sole proprietor under the name "Smith Real Estate Services." (Note: there is no "Inc." or "LLC" or other initials after the name of her company, because she has not created something other than herself.) Mary could also hire 50 brokers to work for Smith Real Estate Services without changing the fact that she is doing business as a sole proprietor. All monies received by Mary and her 50 brokers would be reported by Mary on Schedule C of her individual tax return, minus the commissions or other sums she pays her 50 brokers, her office staff, and overhead expenses for rent, utilities, advertising, etc.

Mary would not be *required* to register the name Smith Real Estate Services with any Register of Deeds, as it is *not* an assumed name, because it includes her surname, thus notifying the public who Smith Real Estate Services is. However, if she wishes to prevent anyone else in the counties where she does business from using the same name, she must register the name with at least one Register of Deeds in a county where she does business to protect use of that name. If Mary begins using a name for her sole proprietorship that does *not* include her surname, then she would be using an "assumed name" and would be required to register it with the Register of Deeds in a county where she does business. (See G.S. §66-71.4, *et. seq.*)

As long as Mary remains a sole proprietor, regardless of the number of agents, she would never need a firm real estate broker license. If, however, Mary ever creates an "entity" under which to conduct her brokerage, then, having created something other than herself, she would need to apply for and obtain a firm broker license for her entity *before* she could engage in real estate brokerage under her entity.

BUSINESS ENTITIES

All business entities have been required to have a real estate firm broker license since January 1, 1997. Prior thereto, only corporations were required to have a separate firm broker license. Under G.S. 55-1-40(9) (the Business Corporation Act) an **entity** "... includes ... corporation and foreign corporation; nonprofit corporation; professional corporation; profit and nonprofit unincorporated association; business trust, estate, partnership, trust, and two or more persons having a joint or common economic interest; and state, United States, and foreign government." Note that a "foreign" corporation merely is a corporation incorporated in a state other than North Carolina. It does not necessarily mean a non-U.S. corporation. Partnerships, limited liability partnerships, and limited liability companies also are business entities that must apply for a firm broker license. *For licensing purposes, a "business entity" is simply any being other than a broker operating in his or her individual capacity as a sole proprietor.*

If a person forms a corporation, a limited liability company, or a limited partnership, whether a domestic or foreign entity, they first must register the entity with the North Carolina Secretary of State's office and will be given a Secretary of State identification number (SOSID). Once created and authorized to do business here, the entity then must apply to the Real Estate Commission for a real estate firm broker license.

Required Application Information

Firm license applications (REC Form 1.72) and related relevant information may be downloaded from the Commission's website. The application fee for a firm license is $100. The entity must state its legal name, the name under which it will do business, if different from its legal name, the principal business address, the entity's Secretary of State Identification number, if applicable, or a description of the entity's organizational form if not required to register with the Secretary of State, the names of its principals and whether any principals affiliated with the entity have been convicted of any criminal offense or had a professional license denied, revoked or suspended.

Most importantly for firm licensure is that *one of the principals of the business entity must hold an active North Carolina broker license in good standing and serve as the* **qualifying broker** *of the entity.* Rule A.0502(e) further dictates who must be the **qualifying broker** for the three main business entities, namely: a **general partner** of a partnership; a **manager** of a limited liability company; and an **officer** of a corporation. For any other entity, the qualifying broker must be a principal, i.e., someone who owns at least a 10 percent interest in the entity or who is an officer, director, manager, member, partner, or comparable position, and who has an individual North Carolina broker license on active status. The rule allows a licensed business entity to serve as the qualifying broker of another business entity as long as the qualifying business entity's qualifying broker is a licensed natural person, who will be responsible for assuring the fulfillment of the qualifying broker's duties for both business entities. **Note:** a provisional broker may not serve as the qualifying broker of an entity.

Understand that the owners or principals of a business entity may be *unlicensed persons*, as long as at least *one of the principals holds a broker license on active status in good standing*. The qualifying broker must be either an officer, general partner, manager, or a bona fide principal with some ownership interest and genuine management authority in a business entity that is not a corporation, partnership, or limited liability company.

If a business entity fails to comply with other laws concerning its existence or authority to transact business in North Carolina, such as being dissolved or having its Certificate of Authority revoked by the Secretary of State for failing to file an annual report, then its firm real estate license shall be canceled immediately by the Commission.

Note that **a firm real estate license does <u>not</u> authorize unlicensed individuals within the business entity to engage in real estate *brokerage* activities**, even if the activity is in furtherance of the entity's business. (Rule 58A.0502(f).) *Any individual within the business entity who wishes to engage in **brokerage** activities must possess either an individual provisional broker or broker license on active status.* This includes owner-principals to employees, top to bottom, **all** are prohibited from engaging in brokerage activities, i.e., *transactions in which the entity functions in an agency capacity*, without first possessing an active North Carolina license. The unlicensed owners may receive the net profits generated by duly licensed individuals, but the unlicensed owners may not engage in brokerage activities themselves.

Creating an Entity

Corporations, limited liability companies, and limited partnerships (but not regular partnerships) are required to register with the Secretary of State before they may do business in North Carolina. Under G.S. §66-71.4, referenced in Rule A.0103(c), so long as the corporation, limited liability company or limited partnership does business under its legal name, i.e., the name it registered with the Secretary of State, then it does not need to register that name with the Register of Deeds in any county in which it maintains an office, even though that name may not include the surname of any principal. For example, Sally Jones creates a corporation called Carolina Sunshine Homes, Inc. under which to conduct her brokerage activity and registers that corporation with the Secretary of State. Even though Sally's surname does not appear in her corporation's name, she does not need to register the corporate name with any Register of Deeds as long as she does business under Carolina Sunshine Homes. The same would be true if Sally had formed a limited liability company or limited partnership and registered that entity with the Secretary of State. Having created the entity and having registered it with the Secretary of State, Sally then would have submitted a firm license application to the Commission for her entity and *once the firm broker license was issued*, she could commence brokerage activity under her entity.

No entity may engage in or receive compensation from brokerage activities until it has been issued a firm real estate broker license.

Subchapter S Corporations

Some individuals may elect to transform a sole proprietorship, partnership, joint venture, or other business entity into a corporate business entity, whether a Chapter C or Subchapter S, primarily for perceived tax and other financial advantages. A common method for individuals to accomplish this goal is the formation of a Subchapter S corporation. A Subchapter S corporation initially is incorporated like any other C corporation with the Secretary of State under Chapter 55 of the North Carolina General Statutes. Once the corporation is formed, it acquires its Subchapter S status by filing the appropriate documents with the Internal Revenue Service which grants or denies the tax filing status request. While most C corporations have multiple shareholders, many individual licensees simply incorporate themselves, naming themselves as the sole shareholder of what becomes a Subchapter S corporation. While brokers may establish a Subchapter S or any other entity, provisional brokers will find it more difficult to form an entity for just themselves because a provisional broker can not be the qualifying broker, and no firm license can be issued to an entity unless it has a qualifying broker.

Permissible Names of Entities

Commission rules impose certain restrictions regarding the name of an entity. Specifically, Rule A.0103(d) states:

> (d) A broker shall not include the name of a provisional broker or an unlicensed person in the legal or assumed name of a sole proprietorship, partnership, or business entity other than a corporation or limited liability company. No broker shall use a business name that includes the name of any current or former broker without the permission of that broker or that broker's authorized representative.

Assume that Sally forms a limited liability company with Martha Brown and Jackie Page, neither of whom are licensees. All three are members (owners) of the member-managed limited liability company, which they name Brown, Jones & Page, LLC and register it with the Secretary of State. Because the entity is a limited liability company, they may name it Brown, Jones & Page, as corporate and LLC names may contain the names of unlicensed persons or provisional brokers, but no other entity may at present. While Brown and Page may not engage in real estate brokerage themselves, since neither is individually licensed, they may be owners of the entity and share in the net proceeds generated by duly licensed individuals' activity who are employed by the limited liability company as associated brokers or provisional brokers.

If Brown, Jones and Page had formed a partnership, rather than a limited liability company, they would not be permitted for licensing purposes to include Brown and Page's names in the name of the partnership. If they called their partnership "Three Ladies Realty," they would first be required to register that name with the Register of Deeds in at least one county where they intend to do business, before they file for their firm license.

The firm broker license is issued in the legal name of the entity. Generally, the legal name of the entity is the name under which it registered with the Secretary of State. If it is not required to register with the Secretary of State, then its legal name is the name under which it does business, and if that name does not (or can not, because of Rule A.0103(d)) include the principals' surnames, then the entity's assumed name with proof of registration with at least one Register of Deeds should be submitted with the firm license application.

Permissible Entity Business Purposes

Generally, one may form an entity for multiple business purposes. In fact, the articles of some entities broadly state that the entity is formed for and may engage in any legally permissible business. Thus, one could form a corporation or a limited liability company or partnership or whatever under which to engage in real estate brokerage, home inspections, photography, and cosmetology. While the entity would need a firm real estate broker license and must employ individuals who are duly licensed to practice in each of the various occupations if required by other statutes or rules, the entity could receive revenue generated from each of its four different ventures. The exception is that there are certain services or occupations that have been designated by the General Assembly as "professional services" and are defined in G.S. §55B-2. If you form an entity for the purpose of providing one or more of the enumerated 22 professional services, then the entity must be a professional corporation, a professional limited liability company, a professional limited liability partnership, or in some instances, a professional association. The relevant point is that real estate brokerage is **not** one of the designated "professional services," and thus ***real estate brokerage may not be one of the business purposes of a professional corporation or professional limited liability company or other "professional" entity***.

For example, foresters, engineers and land surveyors, geologists, soil scientists, architects, and landscape architects are all designated "professional services." Thus, if one forms an entity to provide these services, it must be a professional entity. Because real estate brokerage is *not* among the services classified as "professional services," it may *not* be one of the business pursuits of a professional entity. If you are a registered forester and a real estate broker, or a licensed engineer and a real estate broker, you could not have one company that provides both services, as the forestry and engineering aspects must be a "professional" entity, whereas real estate brokerage can not be part of a "professional" entity. Thus, you must either form two separate entities, one being a professional entity and the other being a regular corporation or limited liability company or partnership or whatever, or you could engage in one service as a sole proprietor and form the appropriate entity for the other service. Also, professional entities generally may only be formed for one purpose and may not combine multiple professional services within one entity, subject to certain limited exceptions set out in G.S. §55B-14.

Note also that *an unlicensed entity may not receive compensation from brokerage activity*, even when the service is rendered by an employee who has an active broker license. For example, an engineering firm that is a professional corporation may employ an individual who has a broker license to identify property for rights of way or easements for the firm's customers to lease or purchase. However, if the interest in the property (i.e., the right of way or easement) passes directly from the property owner to the engineering firm's customer, then any compensation for finding the property and negotiating the easement or right-of-way must be paid directly to the broker-employee, presumably by either the property owner or the grantee of the right-of-way or easement. The compensation may *not* be paid to the engineering company and then to the employee because the engineering company does not have a firm broker license and as an unlicensed entity, it may not receive any compensation or consideration arising from brokerage activity (i.e., real estate for others for compensation/consideration). The additional complicating wrinkle is that because the engineering company is a professional corporation (because engineering is a "professional service"), it is not a candidate for a firm real estate broker license because real estate brokerage is not a professional service.

Licensees should be aware both of the restrictions arising from the "professional services" statutes as well as from Rule A.0103(c) and (d) regarding permissible names of entities if they wish to avoid delays in processing firm broker license applications. Licensees also should be familiar with the requirements of Rule A.0502, "Business Entities," as to what is required to obtain a firm real estate broker license and who may serve as qualifying broker. Frequently, the attorneys or tax advisors you consult to form the entity may not be aware of these restrictions, particularly those arising from Commission rules, as few attorneys or other non-licensees have cause to read these rules.

Failure to Renew Firm License

The qualifying broker of an entity has nine responsibilities enumerated in Rule A.0502(g). One of these duties is to renew the firm's broker license each year. *If the qualifying broker fails to renew the firm's license by midnight on June 30, then the firm's license will* **expire** *at 12:01 a.m. on July 1.* **ALL firm office locations must close and all associated agents must cease conducting brokerage activities as of July 1 as the firm no longer has a real estate license.** Notice of the firm's license expiration will be sent to the qualifying broker. In addition, when the firm's license expires, all provisional brokers affiliated with the firm will be made inactive because they no longer have an employing broker nor a supervising broker-in-charge because the company no longer has a real estate license and thus no offices. The licenses of brokers affiliated with the former firm will remain active, but their business address will be changed to their residence address on Commission records and they will be viewed as independent brokers/sole proprietors.

While the firm's license may be reinstated by paying the currently $90.00 reinstatement fee, **it will *not* automatically reinstate all offices and agents to their former positions**; rather, new Broker-in-Charge Declaration forms (REC Form 2.04) must be submitted to the Commission to re-establish each office, as well as license activation/affiliation forms (REC Form 2.08) for all previously affiliated provisional brokers, and full brokers to change their business address back to the firm's office address in Commission records.

Lack of Qualifying Broker

A similar result obtains if the qualifying broker fails to timely renew his or her broker license or fails to fulfill his or her continuing education requirements for the preceding year. The firm's license will be on *inactive* status and all brokerage activities must cease because the company lacks a qualifying broker, i.e., a principal who holds an *active* broker license. Again, all offices must close, all provisional brokers become inactive, and all associated brokers' business addresses are switched to their home addresses because the company's license is inactive. Forms 2.04 and 2.08 must be completed to redesignate the brokers-in-charge, reactivate all provisional brokers, and change the addresses of all associated brokers from their respective homes back to the office address, once either a new qualifying broker is designated or the former qualifying broker cures his or her individual license defect and reactivates his or her individual broker license. The same result occurs when the qualifying broker notifies the Commission that he or she is resigning as qualifying broker and the Commission does not receive notice of who the new qualifying broker is within ten days of the former qualifying broker's departure.

Change in Structure or Merger

If a business entity changes its form, the newly formed entity must obtain its own firm broker license, unless the existing entity converts or "morphs" as it were into a new entity and retains the same Secretary of State identification number, all of which is governed by statute. If the old business entity is dissolved, then its qualifying broker must surrender its firm license to the Commission. For example, if a partnership changes either to a limited liability company or a corporation, it must surrender the old partnership firm broker license and apply for a new firm license for the newly created entity, setting forth on the firm license application all the information required by Rule A.0502.

Similarly, where two firms **merge**, with one existing company absorbing the other, the qualifying broker of the firm that will no longer exist must surrender its firm license to the Commission with a written notification of the merger. If neither company will continue, but instead a new business entity is formed from the merger with a new qualifying broker, then the qualifying brokers of both original firms must surrender their respective firm licenses to the Commission and the new business entity must apply for a new firm broker license and comply with all Rule A.0502 requirements. Prudent planning would include obtaining the new entity's broker license *before* surrendering the existing entities' licenses to allow uninterrupted servicing of brokerage transactions.

Internal changes in a business entity's composition, e.g. changes in the officers of a corporation, members of a limited liability company, or general or limited partners in a partnership, that do not change the original named qualifying broker do not need to be reported to the Commission. *Only changes in the form of the business entity itself or in the qualifying broker must be reported in writing to the Commission.* Rule A.0502(g)(5) requires a qualifying broker to notify the Commission "...in writing of any change of his or her status as qualifying broker within ten days following the change....". Without a qualifying broker, a firm's license will be placed on inactive status and all brokerage activity must cease.

APPENDIX B
DEFINITIONS OF SELECTED REAL ESTATE TERMS

This Appendix contains real estate terms a licensee may encounter in their practice. Some of the terms defined in this Appendix do not appear in the text of this *Manual*, but are included for the sake of completeness and as a service to the reader.

Abstract of Title — A condensed, chronological history of the title to a particular piece of real estate consisting of a summary of the various documents that have been recorded in the office of the Register of Deeds and certain other public offices constituting the various links in the chain of title. An abstract of title also includes a statement of all liens, judgments, taxes, or encumbrances that affect particular property. An abstract of title is *not* what is provided to a purchaser of real property in North Carolina; rather, the attorney searching title prepares an Opinion of Title based upon his review of matters in the abstract and elsewhere.

Acceleration Clause — A clause in a mortgage note or contract stating that upon default in payment, the balance of the debt or obligation becomes immediately due and payable.

Acceptance — In contract law, a promise by the offeree to be bound by the terms of an offer. An acceptance must be absolutely identical with the terms of the offer and must be communicated to the offeror in the manner indicated or implied in the offer.

Accord and Satisfaction — A settlement or compromise of a dispute between parties to a contract with the rendering of some different performance by one of the parties which is accepted by the other.

Accretion — The gradual and imperceptible deposit of additional soil to land by natural causes, usually the flow of water. See *Alluvion*.

Accrued Interest — The amount of interest due for the period of time that has passed since interest was last paid.

Acknowledgment — The act of one who has signed a deed or other written instrument when he goes before a notary public or other competent officer and declares the instrument that he has executed to be his voluntary act and deed. An acknowledgment is sometimes referred to as the written certification of the notary public or other officer.

Acre — An area or tract of land equal to 160 square rods, or 4,840 square yards, or 43,560 square feet, or a tract that is 208.71 feet square.

Adjustable Rate Mortgage (**ARM**) — A mortgage loan involving a payment plan that allows the lender to periodically (e.g., annually) adjust the interest rate (and usually the monthly principal and interest payment as well) in accordance with certain designated factors or indices which normally reflect trends in general market interest rates. Also called *Variable Rate Mortgage (VRM)*.

Adjusted Basis — For income tax purposes, the original cost (adjusted purchase price) of a property, referred to as its "basis," less the amount of allowable depreciation taken, plus the cost of capital improvements. (Note: A depreciation deduction is not allowed for a personal residence.)

Administrator — A person appointed by the court to manage and settle the estate of a deceased person who died intestate, that is, died without leaving a will. (Technically, the term *administrator* is now obsolete and the term *personal representative* is the proper statutory title. The old terminology remains in popular use, however.)

Ad valorem — A Latin term meaning "according to its value." Unless exempt, all real and personal property in North Carolina is subject to ad valorem taxation.

Adverse Possession — A possession that is inconsistent with the right of possession and title of the true owner. Adverse possession is the actual, open, notorious, exclusive, continuous, and hostile occupation and possession of the land of another under a claim of right or under color of title. If adverse possession is maintained for the period prescribed by statute, a new title is created in the adverse possessor and the title of the record owner is extinguished. An unusual feature of regular adverse possession in North Carolina is that the claimant must have the conscious intent to appropriate the land of another; i.e., land cannot be acquired under the regular doctrine (as opposed to color of title) by mistake.

Aesthetic Zoning — Zoning laws designed to regulate the physical appearance of property. Such zoning might require, for example, that junkyards be screened from public view by a fence or shrub-line.

Affidavit — A statement or declaration reduced to writing, and sworn or affirmed to before some officer who has authority to administer oaths or affirmations.

Affidavit as to Mechanics' Liens — An affidavit provided by a seller to a buyer assuring the buyer that no work has been done on the subject property that might give rise to the filing of a mechanic's lien.

Affirmation — A solemn declaration in the nature of an oath made by persons who have religious scruples against taking oaths.

Agency — The contractual relationship between a principal and an agent, whereby the agent is authorized to represent and act on behalf of the principal in certain business transactions. See *Agent* and *Principal.*

Agent — A person who represents and acts on behalf of another person, called the principal, in dealing with a third party or parties pursuant to a contract of agency.

Agricultural Fixtures — An item of personal property placed on real property by a tenant farmer for agricultural purposes.

Air Rights — The right vested by a grant (deed, lease agreement, or other conveyance) of an estate in real property to build upon, occupy, or use, in the manner and degree permitted, all of any portion of space above the ground or any other stated elevation within vertical planes, the basis of which corresponds with the boundaries of the real estate described in the grant.

Alienation Clause — See *Due-on-Sale Clause.*

Alluvion — Soil deposited on existing land by accretion; increase in land on the shore or bank of a river due to change in flow of stream. See *Accretion.*

Amenities — The qualities and state of being pleasant and agreeable. In real estate, those qualities that attach to property in the form of benefits derived from ownership other than monetary. Satisfactions of possession and use arising from architectural excellence, scenic beauty, and social environment.

Americans with Disabilities Act (ADA) — A federal law requiring that most "commercial facilities" and "places of public accommodation be designed to assure adequate access for persons with disabilities. It also prohibits employment discrimination against the disabled.

Amortization — The process by which the principal and interest of a mortgage loan are systematically eliminated over the period of the loan.

Annexation — (a) The permanent attachment of an item of personal property to real property, thus creating a "fixture"; (b) The addition of real property to its corporate limits by a city or town.

Annual Percentage Rate (APR) — The relationship, expressed as a percentage, of the total finance charges associated with a loan to the amount of the loan. This rate must be disclosed by lenders to borrowers, under the Truth-in-Lending Act and implementing federal regulations.

Appeal/Property Tax Valuation — A system for the formal appeal and review of tax listings and valuations is established by the Machinery Act.

Appraisal — An estimate or opinion of quantity, quality, or value. As applied to real property, it is an opinion as to a property's value, marketability, usefulness, or suitability. Also, the process of deriving a conclusion as to value, and the report setting forth such conclusion. See *Valuation.*

Appreciation — An increased conversion value of property or mediums of exchange due to economic or related causes that may prove to be either temporary or permanent; generally, an appraisal term referring to the increase in value of property.

Appurtenance — That which belongs to something else. In real estate law, an appurtenance is a right, privilege, or improvement that passes as an incident to the land, such as a right of way.

Appurtenant Easement — An easement over one parcel, the servient estate, that benefits (is appurtenant to) another parcel, the dominant estate. According to property law, whoever owns the dominant estate has the right to use the easement over the servient estate. (See also *Easement.*)

Architectural Committee — A committee of a common interest community authorized to review and approve or disapprove requests by members for home construction and exterior improvements to existing structures. Examples include paint colors and fence design.

Asbestos — A substance once used extensively in building construction, including roofing and insulation. A serious environmental hazard that is subject to abatement under federal and state environmental laws.

Assessed Value — The official appraised value of property for *ad valorem* property tax purposes.

Assessment — (a) The process of determining real property value for the purpose of *ad valorem* taxation; (b) a charge to a homeowner by a homeowner's association.

Assignee — The person to whom an agreement or contract is assigned.

Assignment — The method or manner by which a right or a contract is transferred from one person to another.

Assignment of Lease — Transfer by a lessee (tenant) of all his interest under a lease for the entire balance of the term of the lease.

Assignment of Mortgage and Note — A transfer of the mortgage and promissory note by endorsing the note to an assignee. Lenders originating the mortgage loan often sell it on the secondary mortgage market to investors. Ownership of the mortgage automatically transfers with the note under the common law and modern law rule that "the mortgage follows the note."

Assignor — One who makes an assignment.

Assistance Animal — Under Fair Housing Act regulations, an animal that works, provides assistance, or performs tasks for the benefit of a disabled person, or that provides emotional support that alleviates one of the symptoms of the disability.

Assumption of Mortgage — The taking of title to property by a grantee, wherein the grantee assumes liability for payment of an existing indebtedness secured by a mortgage or deed of trust against the property. He becomes a co-guarantor for the payment of said mortgage or deed of trust indebtedness along with the original obligor (maker of the note) unless the latter is released from the debt obligation by the mortgagee (lender).

Auction -- The sale of goods or real estate by means of exchanges between an auctioneer and members of an audience, the exchanges consisting of a series of invitations for offers made by the auctioneer, offers by members of the audience, and the acceptance by the auctioneer of the highest and most favorable offer. Auctions are defined and regulated under Chapter 85B of the N.C. General Statutes.

Auctioneer — A person who conducts or offers to conduct auctions. In addition to calling bids, an auctioneer contracts for options, accepts consignments, advertises an auction, offers items or real property for sale at auction, accepts payment or disburses money for items or real property sold at auction, or otherwise solicits, arranges, sponsors, or manages an auction or holds himself or herself out as an auctioneer. Subject to limited exceptions, an auctioneer must be licensed under Chapter 85B of the N.C. General Statutes.

Auction Sale "With Reserve" — An auction sale in which the owner of the property being sold has reserved the right to reject bids for any reason or subject to specific guidelines (such as a minimum bid requirement).

Attachment of Property — A writ issued at the institution or during the progress of an action that commands the sheriff or other proper officer to take possession of the property, right, credit, or effects of the defendant in order to secure it for the purpose of satisfying the demands of the plaintiff in the action. An attachment is used principally against absconding, concealed, or fraudulent debtors.

Attorney at Law — A lawyer; a licensed attorney; an officer of the court who is employed by a party in a case to manage the cause of action for the party.

Attorney in Fact — One who is authorized to perform certain legal acts for another under a power of attorney; the power of attorney may be a general power or it may be limited to authorize the performance of a specific act or acts. See also *Power of Attorney*.

Avulsion — The removal of a considerable quantity of soil from the land of one person, and its deposit upon or annexation to the land of another, suddenly and by the perceptible action of water.

Backup Offer — An offer to purchase a parcel of real estate on which there already exists a valid sales contract. Acceptance of a backup offer by a seller must be made contingent upon failure by the purchaser under the first contract to honor that contract; otherwise, the seller may have serious legal problems.

Balloon Payment Loan — A loan payment plan that does not amortize principal or that only partially amortizes principal so that at the end of the loan period a large "balloon" principal payment will be due.

Banker's Year — A 360-day year utilized in one method of proration in which all months have 30 days.

Bare Assignment — An assignment in which the assignee agrees to abide by the important covenants in the lease (such as the payment of rent) only as long as the assignee remains in privity of estate with the lessor.

Basis — For income tax purposes, the original cost (adjusted purchase price) of a property.

Bench Marks — Identification symbols on stone, metal, or other durable matter permanently fixed in the ground from which differences of elevation are measured.

Beneficiary — A person for whose benefit property or funds are placed in trust, or the recipient of funds from an insurance fund or annuity contract. A beneficiary of a trust is frequently called a *cestui que trust* in North Carolina. The lender under a deed of trust is the beneficiary. See *Mortgagee*.

Benefitted Land — Land that is benefitted by an easement or covenant located on the burdened land of another. Under the law of easements, the benefitted land is sometimes called the "dominant estate."

Bequest — A transfer of personal property by will.

Bilateral Contract — A contract under which each party promises to perform a specified act in exchange for the other party's promise to perform a specified act. The exchange of promises forms the basis or consideration for the contract and binds both parties. Most contracts, including most real estate contracts, are bilateral contracts. An option to purchase is not a bilateral contract because only the owner has promised not to sell to anyone else during the option period, but the optionee has not promised to purchase.

Bill of Sale — A written instrument that evidences the transfer of right, title, and interest in personal property from one person to another.

Binder — An agreement, usually temporary, executed by a buyer and/or seller, normally in connection with the deposit of earnest money toward the purchase of real estate; generally intended only to temporarily "bind" the signatories until a formal contract can be drawn; not commonly used in real estate transactions in North Carolina. In insurance, a binder is a temporary agreement given to one having an insurable interest who desires insurance subject to the same conditions that will apply if and when a policy is issued.

Blanket Mortgage — A single mortgage that covers more than one parcel of real estate.

Blockbusting — Persuading or trying to persuade persons to sell or move out by creating or exploiting fears of racial change in a neighborhood. An illegal practice under the Federal Fair Housing Act of 1968 and the State Fair Housing Act. Also known as *panic peddling*.

Bona fide — Made in good faith; good, valid, without fraud.

Bond — Any obligation under seal. A real estate bond is a written obligation, usually issued on security of a mortgage or deed of trust.

Boundaries — The legal location of the precise lines and limits of a parcel of land.

Breach — The breaking of a law, or failure of a duty, either by omission or commission; the failure to perform, without legal excuse, any promise that forms a part or the whole of a contract.

Brokerage, Real Estate — The field of real estate business that involves the bringing together of parties for the purpose of selling, exchanging, leasing or renting property.

Broker Price Opinion (BPO) — Same thing as a *Comparative Market Analysis (CMA)* in North Carolina. Both terms are defined by N.C.G.S. §93A-82 as "…an estimate prepared by a licensed real estate broker that details the probable selling price or leasing price of a particular parcel of or interest in property…" Distinguish from *Appraisal.*

Broker, Real Estate — Any person, partnership, association, limited liability company, corporation or other business entity who, for compensation or valuable consideration, sells or offers for sale, buys or offers to buy, or negotiates the purchase or sale or exchange of real estate, or who leases or offers to lease, or rents or offers to rent, any real estate or the improvements thereon for others. A person or entity who is licensed as a real estate broker by the North Carolina Real Estate Commission.

Budget Mortgage — Any mortgage where the monthly payments are set up to include not only principal and interest, but also deposits to an escrow (reserve or impound) account maintained by the lender and used to pay property taxes and insurance charges when they become due. Most single-family residence mortgages are "budget" mortgages.

Buffer Zone — In land use planning and zoning, a strip of land that serves as an undeveloped space separating or surrounding an area designated for protection. Buffer zones may have an environmental purpose such as the protection of wetlands.

Building Code — Regulations established by state and by local governments setting forth the structural requirements for building.

Building Line — A line fixed at a certain distance from the front and/or sides of a lot, beyond which no building can project. See also *Setback.*

Bundle of Rights — A term commonly used to describe the various rights and privileges of an owner of real property.

Burdened Land — Land burdened by an easement or covenant benefitting another.

Buydown Mortgage — Any mortgage where the seller has paid a sum of money to the lender to either temporarily or permanently "buy down" the interest rate and/or monthly payments for the buyer-borrower. Often used by developers when selling new residential properties.

Buyer Agency Contract — A contract between a prospective buyer of real estate and a real estate agent authorizing the salesperson/broker/firm to act as the agent for the prospective buyer in locating a particular type of property for purchase.

Buyer Premium/Auction Sales — As a condition of being allowed to bid, a bidder at an auction agrees that the final sales price will be the high bid *plus* the buyer premium, which typically is a percentage of the high bid.

Call — Under a metes and bounds property description, a reference to a course, distance, or monument used in describing a boundary.

Cancellation — The discharge of a contractual obligation by marking the document "canceled," surrendering possession of it, or by destroying it.

Capital — Accumulated wealth; a portion of wealth set aside for the production of additional wealth; specifically, the funds belonging to the partners or shareholders of a business, invested with the expressed intention of the funds remaining permanently in the business.

Capital Assets — Assets that are permanent or have a long life expectancy (e.g., land, buildings, heavy equipment).

Capital Expenditures — Expenditures made for the acquisition of capital assets (assets that are permanent or have a long life expectancy) or for capital improvements (permanent or long-term improvements). See also *Capital Assets* and *Capital Improvements.*

Capital Gain/Loss — For income tax purposes, the profit/loss realized upon the sale of a capital asset; the difference between the "amount realized" (sale price less closing expenses) and the adjusted basis of real property.

Capital Improvement — Any structure erected on real property or any permanent or long-term improvement made to real property that adds to its value and useful life.

Capitalization — A process used by appraisers in connection with the income capitalization approach method of appraisal to convert a property's actual or projected net income into an estimate of property value. In its simplest form, known as "direct capitalization," this is accomplished by dividing net operating income by a "capitalization rate." See also *Direct Capitalization; Yield Capitalization; Income Capitalization Approach.*

Capitalization Rate — Any rate, expressed as a percentage, used in the process of "capitalization" of income in connection with the income capitalization approach method of appraisal to derive an estimate of value based on a property's income. See also *Capitalization; Income Capitalization Approach.*

Cash Flow (before Taxes) — The net income produced from an income-producing property after deducting operating expenses and debt service from gross income received. See also *Cash Flow (after Taxes).*

Cash Flow (after Taxes) — The net income produced from an income-producing property after deducting depreciation and income taxes from the "before tax cash flow." See also *Cash Flow (before Taxes).*

Cartway Proceeding — A statutory method under which an owner of landlocked property may be qualified to establish an access easement, known as a "cartway."

Caveat Emptor — A literal translation of this term is "let the buyer beware." Under this old legal doctrine, a buyer of real estate has the duty to inspect the property he is purchasing and will be held to have accepted any defects or conditions that are discoverable by a reasonably diligent inspection. Under a strict application of this doctrine, the buyer is considered to take the property "as is." This doctrine has been eroded somewhat by modern court decisions so that sellers of real estate today have a duty to avoid any intentional fraudulent acts, such as taking steps to hide a property defect about which the seller has knowledge. (See also *Implied Warranty of Fitness* dealing with the sale of new dwellings.) The doctrine has little, if any, application to actions of real estate agents, who have extensive duties to both buyers and sellers under various state real estate license laws.

CERCLA — The federal **Comprehensive Environmental Response, Compensation, and Liability Act** that addresses the liability, compensation, cleanup and emergency response to hazardous substances released into the environment. CERCLA authorizes both the federal and state governments to institute actions for the containment, cleanup, and removal of hazardous wastes on property.

Certificate of Reasonable Value (CRV) — A form on which the appraised value of a property that is to be security/collateral for a mortgage loan guaranteed by the Veterans Administration (VA) is reported.

Chain — Unit of land measurement; 66 feet.

Chain of Title — A history of conveyances and encumbrances affecting the title to particular real property.

Chattels — Items of movable *personal property,* such as animals, household furnishings, money, jewels, motor vehicles, and all other items that can be transferred from one place to another.

Civil Rights Act of 1866 — An act of Congress that generally prohibits racial discrimination and that has been interpreted to allow a citizen to sue for racial discrimination in the sale or rental of housing.

Clean Water Acts — Federal and state **Clean Water Acts** make the depositing of dredged or fill materials into wetlands and other waters of the United States or North Carolina illegal unless a permit is obtained in advance.

Clear Title —Title to property that is free and clear of all encumbrances or defects.

Closing — The process of consummating a sale or exchange of real estate, usually accomplished under the direction of a "settlement agent" who in North Carolina typically is an attorney. Closing involves the "settlement" of all legal and financial matters among the parties (seller, buyer and lender, if applicable), the execution of all required legal documents, the receipt of funds required, the recording of the deed (and deed of trust, if applicable) and the disbursement of funds.

Closing Statement — A detailed accounting of all receipts and disbursements in connection with a real estate sale that is provided to the seller and purchaser at the settlement meeting. Also called a "Settlement Statement".

Cloud on Title — An outstanding claim or encumbrance, which, if valid, would affect or impair the owner's title.

Cluster and Open Space Development — Forms of land development that encourage designs providing greater protection of open space and natural resources.

Coastal Area Management Act (CAMA) — North Carolina legislation passed in 1974 that regulates real estate development within coastal areas of environmental concern.

Coinsurance — A clause placed in most property insurance policies requiring the insured to share the loss with the insurer if the property is underinsured.

Collateral — Something of value which is pledged or provided as security to guarantee performance of a contractual obligation. The real estate which is mortgaged to secure the repayment of a debt evidenced by a promissory note.

Color of Title — An apparent title founded upon a written instrument, a deed, will, or judicial decree that purports to convey and apparently passes title to land but fails to do so, either because of a defect in its execution or a want of title in the person executing the instrument.

Commercial Real Estate Broker — A person engaged in a commercial real estate transaction as a broker as defined by N.C. Gen. Stat. § 44A-24.2(3).

Commercial Real Estate Broker Lien — A commercial broker's statutory lien on commercial real estate pursuant to the terms of Part 4, Chapter 44A of the North Carolina General Statutes.

Commingling — The illegal practice by a real estate broker of maintaining personal or business funds in the same account with trust funds held for others.

Commission, Brokerage — Compensation earned by a broker for the performance of specific duties in connection with the sale or lease of a property. The amount of payment may be specified as a fixed amount, but is usually stated as a percentage of another sum and usually is paid by the seller (if a sale is involved) or owner (if a lease is involved).

Commissioner's Deed — In certain court actions or special proceedings, a commissioner is appointed to sell real or personal property and is empowered to give a commissioner's deed to the purchaser. Specific statutory procedures must be carefully followed by the commissioner.

Commitment — A pledge, a promise, or a firm agreement. See also *Loan Commitment*.

Common Areas (Elements) — Those portions of a property owned or rented by multiple parties (such as a condominium complex, apartment complex, or shopping mall) that are designated or reserved for shared use by all the owners or tenants.

Common Interest Community — A real estate development in which the owners of individual lots or units have a legal obligation to financially support maintenance of common areas and other costs of operating the community. Includes condominium and townhouse communities and many subdivisions or other planned communities.

Common Law — A body of law that is based on custom and cases decided in the courts, as distinguished from codified or statutory law enacted by a legislative body.

Comparable — A term used to describe a recently sold property that has similar characteristics to a property that is the subject of a comparative market analysis, broker price opinion or appraisal being appraised (the "subject" property) and that is used for comparative purposes when estimating the probable selling or leasing price or value of the subject property.

Comparative Market Analysis (CMA) — Same thing as a *Broker Price Opinion (BPO)* in North Carolina. Both terms are defined by N.C.G.S. §93A-82 as "...an estimate prepared by a licensed real estate broker that details the probable selling price or leasing price of a particular parcel of or interest in property..." Distinguish from *Appraisal*.

Compensatory Damages — A measure of damages utilized to place the party injured by the contractual breach in the same position that he or she would have been in had the contract been performed; the intent is to make the injured party whole rather than to penalize the breaching party.

Compound Interest — Interest paid on the original principal of an indebtedness and also on the accrued and unpaid interest that has accumulated.

Concurrent Ownership — The ownership of the same parcel of property by two or more persons. Concurrent ownership is generally referred to as "cotenancy" or "coownership." The three principal types of concurrent ownership are *Joint Tenancy, Tenancy in Common,* and *Tenancy by the Entirety.*

Condemnation — The taking of private property for a public purpose with compensation to the owner, by the state, other body politic, or public service corporation authorized to exercise the power of eminent domain; also, a declaration that a structure is unfit for use. See also *Eminent Domain.*

Conditional Use Permit — In zoning law, a permit that is issued authorizing a certain use to be made of property only after certain stated prerequisites have been met.

Conditional Use Zoning -- The term *conditional use* is sometimes used interchangeably with *special use.* These zoning terms require that the development and use of property comply with specific conditions and standards.

Condominium — A legal arrangement under which a person owns one unit of a multiunit development, such as an apartment building, plus an undivided interest in common areas used by all unit owners, such as hallways and grounds.

Conner Act — The North Carolina recording act that requires all conveyances of real property, contracts to convey, and leases of land for more than three years to be recorded at the office of the Register of Deeds in order to be effective as against certain third parties. See *Recording.*

Consequential Damages — A form of special damages that may be obtained where the damages were foreseeable or within the contemplation of the breaching party at the time of the contract.

Conservation Easement — A land use planning tool that restricts the use of land for environmental purposes. While titled an "easement," this tool is in legal form more akin to a set of restrictive covenants.

Consideration — Something of value, usually money, that is the inducement for a contract. Any right, interest, property, benefit accruing to one party, or any forbearance, detriment, loss or responsibility given, suffered or undertaken, may constitute a consideration that will sustain a contract.

Construction Lien — See *Mechanic's Lien.*

Construction Loan — A short-term loan, usually made to builders and developers, that is used to finance the cost of construction and that usually is collateralized by a mortgage on the land.

Constructive Eviction — A situation which arises when a landlord, either by his affirmative act or by his failure to perform some required act, prevents a tenant from enjoying the use of a leased premises in the manner contracted for in a lease. In such situation, the tenant is said to be "constructively evicted" from the premises even though he has not actually been denied possession of the premises. See also *Eviction.*

Constructive Notice — Notice given by the public records. Persons with a duty to search are bound by whatever information they would find by a reasonable search of the public land records whether they in fact make the search.

Consumer Financial Protection Bureau (CFPB) — A federal agency created in 2010 by the Dodd-Frank Act to perform various consumer protection and financial regulatory functions previously performed by several different federal agencies.

Contingency Provision — A provision in an offer or contract that makes performance and consummation of the offer or contract dependent or contingent upon the occurrence of some act.

Contingent Offer — An offer containing a contingency provision.

Contract — A legally enforceable agreement between two or more competent parties, based on legal consideration, to do or to abstain from doing some act.

Contract for Deed (Residential Property) — Also known as land contracts or installment land contracts. *See "Contracts For Deed," and "Lease Option Contracts."* North Carolina General Statutes, Chapter 47H, regulates this alternative form of home financing to prevent consumer abuses.

Conventional Conforming Mortgage Loan — A mortgage loan, not insured or guaranteed under any government program, that is underwritten to certain specifications established by the Federal National Mortgage Association and the Federal Home Loan Mortgage Corporation that allow it to be easily sold in the secondary mortgage market.

Conventional Life Estate — A life estate arising by intentional act of the parties which is an express transfer of land "To A for life," the estate being for the duration of A's own life. Upon the death of the holder of the life estate, title to the property will pass in fee to the person or entity named in the instrument creating the life estate, or if no one is named, to the grantor or his/her heirs. See also *Life Estate.*

Conventional Mortgage Loan — A mortgage loan that is not insured or guaranteed under any government program.

Conveyance — A general term for any document that transfers title to real property. The word is also a verb describing the act of transferring title to real property.

Cooperative — A multiunit development in which a purchaser obtains a stock certificate representing part ownership of the building and a lease to a specific apartment or unit within the development.

Cooperative Listing Service — An arrangement among real estate brokers in a given area whereby information on a property listed for sale with any of the brokers is shared with all other participating brokers so that all participating brokers can assist in selling the property. The participating brokers agree to split any earned commissions on a co-brokered sale. See also *Multiple Listing Service.*

Corporation — A legal entity or "person" created by complying with applicable statutes. A corporation has with a legal existence, liability, and powers separate from its shareholders. In North Carolina, a business corporation is governed by the Business Corporation Act, Chapter 55 of the General Statutes.

Correction Deed — A type of deed often used to remedy defects in title to property. For example, a title examiner might discover that a deed in the chain of title has been improperly acknowledged. A correction deed, properly executed and acknowledged by the same grantors who executed the defective deed, might be required to clear the title defect.

Cost Approach — An appraisal method or procedure used to estimate the value, usually the market value, of an improved property by summation of the land value and the value of improvements, each of which has been estimated independently. The estimated value of the land, considered as though vacant, is added to the estimated replacement or reproduction cost of the improvements, less estimated depreciation, to derive an estimate of the property's market value.

Cotenant — Any one of two or more parties who share an undivided ownership interest in real property.

Counteroffer — Under contract law, an offer made in reply to a previous offer or a purported acceptance of a previous offer that includes different terms or conditions not included in the previous offer. A counteroffer terminates the earlier offer.

Course — The direction of a line as used in a metes and bounds description of land.

Covenant — An agreement between two or more persons entered into by deed or lease whereby one of the parties promises the performance of certain acts, or that a given state does or shall, or does not/or shall not, exist. Simply put, a covenant is a promise.

Covenant of Quiet Enjoyment — An implied covenant in every lease that the lessee's possession during the lease term will not be terminated or interfered with by the lessor, by a party whose claim stems from the lessor, or by a third party with superior title to that held by the lessor. If a lessee is deprived of or removed from possession of the leased premises due to any of these circumstances, the lessor is liable to the lessee for breach of the covenant.

Covenants of Title — A traditional method of title assurance by the use of covenants (promises) by which the grantor indemnifies the grantee against a total or partial failure of title. The traditional common law covenants of title in a warranty deed are the Covenant of Seisin and Right to Convey, Covenant Against Encumbrances, and, Covenant of Warranty and Quiet Enjoyment.

Credit — A sum entered in favor of either the seller or purchaser on a closing statement. A credit indicates an amount that a party is to receive or be reimbursed for at closing, as well as the amount of any loan or deposit which is to serve as part of the purchase price.

Creditor — The party to whom a debt is owed.

Curative Statute — A law, retrospective in effect, which is designed to remedy some legal defect in previous transactions; specifically, they aid the title assurance process by eliminating technical title defects.

Curtesy — A life estate given under the common law to a husband in the lands his deceased wife was seized of during their marriage. The current statute, N.C. Gen. Stat. §29-30, provides a statutory substitute for curtesy whereby a husband is entitled to a life estate in one-third in value of all real estate owned by his wife at any time during their marriage, in the event the husband elects not to take as his wife's devisee or heir.

Damages — The indemnity recoverable by a person who has sustained an injury, either to his person, his property, or his rights, through the act or default of another.

Debit — A charge against either the seller or purchaser on a closing statement. A debit indicates an amount due from or owed by a party at closing.

Debt Service — Periodic payments of principal and accrued interest made toward the liquidation (amortization) of a debt.

Debtor — The party who owes a debt.

Decedent — A deceased person.

Decree — A judgment of a court of equity.

Dedication — A form of transfer, either formal or informal, whereby an individual grants title of an interest in land for some public use and such grant is accepted by or on behalf of the public in some recognized legal manner.

Deed — A signed writing under which an interest in real property is transferred from a grantor to a grantee upon delivery of the writing to the grantee. To be recorded, the deed must be acknowledged.

Deed in Lieu of Foreclosure — A deed given by a mortgagor, who is in default under the terms of the mortgage, to the mortgagee in order to avoid foreclosure of the property. The courts frown on this type of deed because of the potential for undue influence by the mortgagee on the mortgagor in default.

Deed of Gift — The transfer of real property by a deed not supported by any consideration. A deed of gift is perfectly valid, but it must be recorded within two years or it will become void under North Carolina law.

Deed of Trust — A document in the nature of a mortgage that is widely used in North Carolina. Under a deed of trust, the borrower conveys the land to a third-party trustee to hold for the beneficiary (mortgage lender) to secure a debt, subject to the condition that the conveyance shall be void and terminated on payment of the debt at maturity. Most deeds of trust contain a power of sale giving the trustee the power to sell the land in case of default and to apply the sale proceeds toward payment of the debt. Also called a *Trust Deed.* See also *Mortgage.*

Default — Failure to comply with an agreement to meet an obligation when due.

Defendant — The party sued or called to answer in any lawsuit, legal action, or proceeding.

Defeasible Fee — A fee simple estate created in such a way that it will terminate on the occurrence of some contingent event that may or may not happen.

Deficiency Judgment — A judgment for the balance owing on a debt after the collateral given as security has been foreclosed on or attached and sold and applied toward payment of the indebtedness.

Degrees and Minutes — Units of measurement used to describe angular measurements in legal descriptions of land. There are 360 degrees in a full circle. Each degree contains 60 minutes, and each minute contains 60 seconds.

Demise — The conveyance of an estate for a certain period or for life, usually by a lease.

Depreciation — (a) In appraisals, a decrease in property value brought about by ordinary wear and tear (physical deterioration), functional or economic obsolescence, or any other cause; (b) For income tax purposes, a deduction from the income of eligible income-producing properties allowed for a presumed loss in value of property over its useful life.

Derivative Titles — Titles obtained by a person from a prior owner either by deed, will, or inheritance.

Descent — The transfer of property ownership to the heirs of a deceased person by operation of law where the property owner dies intestate (without a will).

Devise — Traditionally, a term referring to the transfer of *real property* by will. The term is now a generic one referring to the transfer of either real or personal property by will. See N.C. Gen. Stat. § 12-3(14).

Direct Capitalization — A method of estimating the present value of a property by dividing projected annual net operating income by a market-derived capitalization rate. (Value = Net Operating Income/Capitalization Rate). See also *Yield Capitalization, Capitalization, Capitalization Rate,* and *Income Capitalization Approach.*

Disability — See "handicap."

Discharge of a Contract — Performance under a valid and binding contract may be legally discharged by a number of events, including: full and complete performance, a substantial breach by one of the parties, impossibility of performance, and by operation of law.

Discount — With regard to loan origination, the amount withheld from the loan proceeds by the lender as a charge, in the nature of interest, to obtain a lower loan interest rate. With regard to the sale of mortgage loans in the secondary mortgage market, the amount by which the sale price of the note is less than the note's face value. In either case, the discount has the effect of increasing the "yield" on the loan.

Discounted Cash Flow Analysis — See *Yield Capitalization.*

Discount Points — A fee charged by a lender (usually paid by the borrower) to increase the yield on mortgage loans with below market interest rates. The fee is stated in terms of "points." See also *Discount* and *Points.*

Discrimination in Housing — Segregating, separating, excluding, or treating unequally any person because of race, color, religion, national origin, sex, handicap or familial status in the furnishing of housing or facilities or services related to obtaining or occupying housing. Largely prohibited by federal and state law.

Dispossess — To oust or deprive a person of possession and use of real property.

Distance — The length of a line as used in a metes and bounds description of land.

Distress and Distraint — The practice of seizing a tenant's personal property for non-payment of rent. It is against public policy, and a lease provision to permitting it is void.

Documentary Stamp — A revenue stamp on documents for payment of a tax. The stamps no longer are used, but the excise tax still is required on real property transfers. See *Excise Tax on Real Property Transfers.*

Dodd-Frank Wall Street Reform and Consumer Protection Act ("Dodd-Frank Act") — A comprehensive 2010 federal law that provides for major reforms in the financial regulatory system. The law created a new federal agency, the Bureau of Consumer Financial Protection (more commonly known as the Consumer Financial Protection Bureau) to take over the consumer protection and financial regulatory activities previously handled by several different federal agencies. See also *Consumer Financial Protection Bureau.*

Domicile — The place where a person has his true, fixed, and permanent home and principal establishment, and to which, whenever he is absent, he has the intention of returning.

Dominant Estate — A parcel of land that is benefitted by an easement on another parcel of land (the servient estate).

Dower — A life estate that existed at the common law whereby a widow was entitled to one-third of the lands that her deceased husband was seized of during their marriage. Under the current statute, N.C. Gen. Stat. §29-30, a widow still is entitled to a life estate in one-third in value of the real property owned by the husband during their marriage.

Dual Agency Agreement — An agreement between a real estate broker and two (or more) parties to a transaction authorizing the broker to act simultaneously as the agent of both parties in the transaction.

Dual Agent — An agent who represents both parties in a transaction. Both parties must be informed of and consent to the dual agency in writing.

Due Diligence — A term used to describe the process of a buyer investigating a property being purchased in a diligent manner, usually within a period of time (the "due diligence period") prescribed in a sales contract, to determine if the buyer is satisfied with the property and wishes to proceed with the purchase.

Due-on-Sale Clause — A provision in a mortgage or deed of trust or promissory note stating that the entire balance of the mortgage loan will become due if the borrower transfers the mortgaged property without the prior consent of the lender. Also called *Alienation Clause.*

Duplex — A single structure with two separate units designed for two-family occupancy.

Duress — The unlawful constraint or threatening of a person, whereby he is forced to perform some act or to sign an instrument against his will.

E-Marketing — The marketing of services and real estate on the Internet.

E-Sign — The common name for the *Electronic Records in Global and National Commerce Act*, 15 U.S.C. §§ 7001 *et seq.* This federal legislation validates electronic contracts and signatures in transactions in interstate commerce and provides that they will not be denied validity and enforceability solely because they are in electronic form. See also *UETA.*

Earnest Money — A sum paid by a prospective purchaser of real estate as evidence of good faith, usually paid to the broker at the time an offer is made.

Easement — A right to use the lands owned by another person for a special purpose, such as a right-of-way to go across the property of another.

Easement by Condemnation — An easement created in favor of a government agency or public authority that has exercised the power of eminent domain.

Easement by Dedication — An easement, usually for the benefit of the public, that may be created under a number of express and implied circumstances.

Easement by Express Grant or Reservation — An easement that is expressly granted or expressly reserved by the grantor in a deed.

Easement by Implication — An easement that is implied from prior circumstances. There is nothing in writing that expressly creates the easement.

Easement by Necessity — An easement that is impliedly created when a grantor of property landlocks the grantee.

Easement by Prescription — An easement that is created by operation of law because of the long-continued, adverse use by the party claiming the easement.

Easement in Gross — A general category of easements that refers to all easements that are for the personal benefit of a specified individual or entity rather than for the benefit of a parcel of land. An example is an easement held by a power company for its transmision lines. Distinguish from *Appurtenant Easement*.

Economic Life — The period over which an improvement on real property may be profitably utilized or the period over which the improvement will yield a return on the investment in the property.

Economic Obsolescence — Loss in value of property due to factors that impair the desirability or useful life which arise from economic forces, such as changes in optimum land use, legislative enactments that restrict or impair property rights, and changes in supply-demand relationships; a cause of depreciation in property value. Also called *External Obsolescence*.

Effective Age — In appraisal, the age assigned to a property at a given point in time based on its condition. The effective age may be more or less than the actual age.

Effective Gross Income — In an operating budget for an income-producing property, the gross (maximum possible) income less projected vacancy and rent collection losses.

Ejectment — A form of legal action taken by a landlord to evict a tenant and regain possession of real property.

Electronic Notarization Act (E-Notarization) — A North Carolina law authorizing and setting forth procedures for the electronic notarization of documents. See Chapter 10B, Article 2 of the N.C. General Statutes.

Electronic Notary (E-Notary) — A person authorized by North Carolina law to perform electronic notarial acts. See 18 North Carolina Administrative Code 07C.0101 — 0604.

Electronic Recording (E-Recording) — A system of recording documents by electronic means. The Secretary of State of North Carolina is responsible for adopting e-recording standards with an adequate information security system to ensure that electronic documents are accurate, authentic, adequately preserved, and resistant to tampering. *See "Uniform Real Property Recording Act (UPERA)."*

Electronic Records in Global and National Commerce Act — See *E-Sign*.

Emblements — Things that grow on the land and require annual planting and cultivation.

Eminent Domain — The superior right of every sovereign state to take private property for public use upon the payment of just compensation. This power often is conferred upon public service corporations that perform quasi-public functions, such as providing public utilities. In every case, the owner whose property is taken must be fairly compensated.

Encroachment — A building, part of a building, or other improvement that intrudes or trespasses upon the property of another.

Encumbrance — Any right to, or interest in, land, which diminishes the value of the estate although it does not prevent conveyance of the estate by the owner thereof. For instance, mortgages, unpaid taxes, and judgments are encumbrances known as "liens." Both restrictive covenants restricting the use of lands to certain purposes and easements are encumbrances, although they are not liens.

Environmental Protection Legislation — Federal and state legislation enacted to regulate land use for the purpose of protecting the environment.

Environmental Site Assessment (ESA) — An environmental assessment of real property conducted by a prospective lessee's experts as part of the lessee's due diligence requirement under environmental laws.

Equal Credit Opportunity Act (ECOA) — The federal law that prohibits lenders from discriminating in the extension of credit on the basis of age, race, color, religion, national origin, sex, or marital status.

Equitable Conversion — An equitable doctrine stating that, as soon as a valid sales contract has been entered into by a seller and buyer, the buyer is treated as having "equitable title" to the land (and thus owner of the land for certain purposes), and the seller as having bare "legal title" as security for the payment of the purchase money by the buyer.

Equitable Servitudes — See *Restrictive Covenant*.

Equitable Title — The interest in real property that is held by (a) the grantor (borrower) under a deed of trust, (b) the buyer under a valid "interim" real estate sales contract pending closing, and (c) the buyer under an installment land contract. See also *Equitable Conversion*. Distinguish from *Legal Title*. (Note: The owner of real estate that is not encumbered by a deed of trust and is not the subject of a real estate sales contract holds both legal and equitable title to the property.)

Equity — (a) The financial interest or value an owner has in real estate over and above the debts against it; (b) A system of jurisprudence or a body of doctrines and rules developed in England and followed in the United States, serving to supplement and remedy the limitations and the inflexibility of the common law.

Equity Line of Credit — A loan where the borrower uses the equity that has developed in the borrower's real property to secure a line of credit. The borrower then has the right to draw funds up to the agreed upon loan limit. This equity line of credit is secured by a mortgage on the borrower's property. If involving a borrower's home, it is often termed a "home equity line of credit" or "HELOC".

Equity Loan — A loan where the borrower uses his or her equity in real property to secure a loan. An equity loan is usually a loan secured by "second" mortgage. If involving a borrower's home, it is called a "home equity loan."

Equity of Redemption — The right of an original owner who has mortgaged his property by mortgage or deed of trust to reclaim and recover his title to real property, even after the mortgage debt is past due, by paying to the obligee the principal of the debt, accrued interest, and costs incurred up to the time of redemption. Also called *Right of Redemption*. See also *Statutory Redemption Period*.

Erosion — The wearing away of land through natural causes, such as running water or winds.

Escheat — The reverting of property to the State when there are no persons legally entitled to hold title or when heirs capable of inheriting the property are lacking.

Escrow — An arrangement by which one deposits a thing of value with a third person (called an escrow agent) who will make delivery to another person when specified conditions are fulfilled. For instance, a contract, deed, bond, or other written instrument may be deposited with a third person, by whom it is to be delivered to the grantee or promisee upon the performance of some act.

Escrow Account — (a) With regard to real estate brokerage, a special demand deposit account maintained by a broker at a federally insured depository institution lawfully doing business in North Carolina for the purpose of holding trust funds on behalf of the broker's principal or other parties to a transaction (see also *Trust Account);* (b) With regard to mortgage lending, a special account maintained by the lender or loan servicer to cover the payment of property taxes and insurance on the mortgaged property.

Estate — A term used to refer to the legal rights and interests one has in real property as an owner or tenant. An estate in real property is either a *freehold* or a *nonfreehold* estate.

Estate for Life — See *Life Estate.*

Estate for Years — A less than freehold (i.e., a nonfreehold) estate created by the leasing of property for any fixed, definite period of time, whether such period be one week, one month, one year, ten years, or any other definite period of time. Also called a *Tenancy for Years.*

Estate from Year to Year — A less than freehold (nonfreehold) estate created by the leasing of property for an indefinite period of time. Such estates, which are also called *estates from period to period or periodic tenancies,* may be from year to year, month to month, week to week, etc., depending on the period of time for which rent is regularly paid. Such an estate may also be created when a tenant for years holds over and pays rent for an additional term and the rent is accepted by the lessor-owner.

Estate at Sufferance — A less than freehold (nonfreehold) estate created when a tenant who has lawful possession of a property holds over without the consent of the owner; the lowest estate in property. Also called a *Tenancy at Sufferance.*

Estate at Will — A less than freehold (nonfreehold) estate created when a tenant occupies land with the consent of the owner, but without any agreement for a definite rental period or for the regular payment of rent. Also called a *Tenancy at Will.*

Estates Not of Inheritance — A freehold estate that extends only for the term of some person's life.

Estates of Inheritance — A freehold estate that may continue beyond the life of the holder and pass to his heirs upon his death.

Estovers — The right of a tenant to take wood from the landlord's property to use as fuel or to make necessary property repairs.

Ethics — The principles of conduct established for its members by a profession or professional organization.

Et ux — Abbreviation for *et uxor,* meaning "and wife."

Eviction — The process instituted to oust a person from possession of real estate. Also the ousting or deprivation of one from the possession of lands or tenements. See also *Constructive Eviction.*

Excise Tax on Real Property Transfers — A tax imposed on the transfer of real property that is based on the total sale price and is paid by the grantor.

Exclusive Agency Listing Contract — A contract in which a property owner appoints one real estate broker as the sole agent for the sale of a property for a designated period of time. Under such contract the owner, himself, may sell the property without any obligation to pay the agent a commission.

Exclusive Right to Sell Listing Contract — A contract between property owner and broker giving the broker the exclusive right to sell the property for a designated period of time. In such a contract, the owner binds himself to pay a full commission to the broker even if the owner sells the property himself. The broker has not only an "exclusive agency" to sell the property, but he also has an "exclusive right to sell," which gives the broker a right to collect his commission no matter who sells the property during the term of his agreement.

Execute — (a) To perform or carry out a contract: (b) To sign an instrument such as a contract or deed.

Executed Contract — A contract that has been fully performed by the parties. (Distinguish from *Executory Contract.*)

Execution — A judicial writ or process issued by the court to the sheriff directing him to sell property to satisfy a judgment debt.

Executor — A man designated by the maker of a will [the Testator (male) or Testatrix (female)] to carry out the execution of the terms of the will. See also *Executrix.*

Executor's Deed — A deed given by a deceased person's executor.

Executory Contract — A contract that has not yet been fully performed by the parties, such as a real estate sales contract prior to closing.

Executrix — A woman designated by the maker of a will to carry out the execution of the terms of the will. See also *Executor.*

Expansion of Leased Space — A provision in a commercial lease providing the lessee with the option to add space to the leased premises in the event space in the building becomes vacant.

Expedited Eviction for Criminal Activity — Article 7 of Chapter 42 of the N.C. General Statutes authorizes an expedited eviction procedure for specified criminal activity by a tenant, a member of the tenant's household, or a guest of a tenant.

Express Contract — A contract stated in words, either orally or in writing.

Express Easement — See *Easement by Express Grant or Reservation.*

Extender Clause — Also called *Override Clause.* See *Protection Agreement.*

External Obsolescence — See *Economic Obsolescence.*

Extraterritorial Zoning Jurisdiction — The statutory right of a local government to exercise zoning and planning powers beyond that governments borders.

Extrinsic Evidence/Property Descriptions — Evidence that can be used to clarify and make certain a legal description of land containing latent ambiguities. *See "latent ambiguity."*

Fair Housing Act of 1968 — A federal law which, as amended, prohibits discrimination on the basis of race, color, religion, sex, national origin, handicap or familial status with respect to all significant aspects of the sale or rental of housing and other related activities. See also *State Fair Housing Act.*

Familial Status — A technical legal term that basically means discrimination against families with children (individuals under the age of 18), but also encompasses more than the traditional family.

Federal Deposit Insurance Corporation (**FDIC**) — The independent federal agency that insures the deposits of eligible commercial banks and savings and loan associations.

Federal Home Loan Bank System — The federal agency that regulates many of the activities of federally char-tered (and some state-chartered) savings and loan associations, primarily through control of the reserve require-ments of these institutions.

Federal Home Loan Mortgage Corporation **(FHLMC or "Freddie Mac")** — A private corporation subject to the regulatory authority of the Department of Housing and Urban Development (HUD) that, along with "Fannie Mae," plays a critical role in maintaining the secondary mortgage market by purchasing mortgage loans from primary lenders and reselling them to investors in the form of securities.

Federal Home Loan Mortgage Disclosure Act **(HMDA)** — A law that assists the federal government in en-forcing the requirement that lending institutions not discriminate against minorities by redlining or similar practices. The Act requires lenders to prepare certain information about their loan practices and to make that information available for public inspection.

Federal Housing Administration **(FHA)** — An agency of the federal government, operating under the De-partment of Housing and Urban Development (HUD), that insures mortgage loans made by lenders to certain qualified borrowers.

Federal National Mortgage Association **(FNMA or "Fannie Mae")** — A private corporation subject to the regulatory authority of the Department of Housing and Urban Development (HUD) that plays a critical role in maintaining the secondary mortgage market by purchasing mortgage loans from primary lenders and reselling them to investors in the form of mortgage-backed securities.

Federal Reserve System — Commonly referred to as the "Fed," the nation's central banking system that, through various actions taken by its governing board, regulates the money supply and interest rates.

Federal Servicemembers Civil Relief Act (SCRA) — A federal law (50 U.S.C. App. §501-597b) allowing members of the military and their dependents to terminate residential leases when the servicemember entered into the lease: 1) before active duty military service; or 2) while on active duty and then received permanent change of station orders; or 3) while on active duty and then received orders to deploy in support of a military operation for more than 90 days.

Fee — When applied to real property, an inheritable estate in the property.

Fee Simple Absolute — The highest quality of estate that a person can have in real property. It is of a potentially infinite duration and is transferable, devisable, and inheritable.

Fee Simple Determinable — A fee estate in land that is of potentially infinite duration but that might termi-nate prematurely and automatically if a condition attached to the estate is breached.

Fee Simple on a Condition Subsequent — A fee estate in land that is of potentially infinite duration but that might terminate prematurely if a condition attached to the estate is breached. The chief distinction between this estate and the *fee simple determinable* is that forfeiture of the fee simple on a condition subsequent is *not* au-tomatic if the condition is breached; i.e., the party who imposed the condition on the estate must step forward and enforce it.

Fee Tail — This is an obsolete fee estate that is created by the language "to A and the heirs of his body." Whenever this language occurs, North Carolina law automatically converts the fee tail into a fee simple absolute.

FHA Mortgage Loan — A mortgage loan that is insured by the Federal Housing Administration.

Fiduciary — A relationship wherein one party imposes special trust and confidence in another party, usually involving the holding or managing of money or other property for another. An example is the relationship between a real estate broker and his principal. Also refers to the party in whom special trust and confidence is placed.

First Mortgage — A mortgage (or deed of trust in North Carolina) that has priority as a lien over all other mortgages (or deeds of trust), which are "second" or "junior" mortgages.

First Right of Refusal — See *Right of First Refusal.*

Fit Premises — What a landlord must provide a residential tenant in North Carolina under N.C. Gen. Stat. § 42-42. That statute requires the landlord to do a number of things including putting and keeping the premises in a fit and habitable condition. See also *Residential Rental Agreements Act.*

Fixed Rate-Level Payment Mortgage — A mortgage with a fixed interest rate and a constant monthly payment for the entire loan term.

Fixed Rental Lease — A lease calling for payment of a fixed amount of rent at regular intervals during the term of the lease. Also called a *flat lease.*

Fixture — An item of personal property, a chattel, affixed to a building or structure or land in such a manner that it becomes a part of the building, structure, or real estate to which it is affixed and annexed. Fixtures affixed to real estate become appurtenances of the real estate to which they are affixed and subject to the legal rules that apply to real estate, rather than the legal rules that apply to personal property. This means that a fixture automatically passes with the real estate unless the contract to convey provides otherwise.

Flat Fee — A brokerage fee arrangement in a listing contract whereby the broker is to receive a fixed sum upon sale of the property.

Flat Lease — See *Fixed Rental Lease.*

Flat Fee Listing — A brokerage fee arrangement in a listing contract that involves the payment of a fixed fee to a broker. The fee is not a percentage of the ultimate sales price and may not even be tied to whether or not the broker is successful in selling the listed property.

Flood Hazard Area — Real property located in designated *"flood hazard areas"* that is subject to special federal laws and regulations. Flood hazard areas are designated on maps issued by the Federal Emergency Management Agency. *See "Flood Insurance."*

Flood Insurance — Insurance that indemnifies a property owner from flood damage and is required in all flood hazard areas under the National Flood Insurance Program if a federally-related mortgage loan is being made on improved property or property on which improvements will be made.

Foreclosure — A legal remedy to enforce security rights in land under a mortgage or deed of trust. The lender or creditor may bring an action in court to foreclose a mortgage or deed of trust to compel a public sale of the property involved and to apply the sale proceeds to payment of the secured debt. A valid foreclosure terminates the debtor mortgagor's interest in the secured property and the proceeds of the foreclosure sale are applied to payment of his indebtedness.

Foreclosure by Judicial Action — A method of foreclosure common in other states, but rarely used in North Carolina, where the lender or creditor must actually file a foreclosure lawsuit and obtain a court order directing the public sale of the property. Almost all North Carolina foreclosures are by "power of sale."

Foreclosure by Power of Sale — Many mortgages and deeds of trust contain a "power of sale" clause that allows the lender or trustee to compel a foreclosure sale upon the debtor's default in payments without filing a formal lawsuit. After proper notice and a hearing before a clerk of court to confirm the mortgage is in default, the mortgaged property is sold at a public sale.

Forfeiture — A loss of anything of value due to failure to perform, such as under a lease or contract for the sale of property if there is such a provision in the lease or contract.

Fraud — Fraud covers a multitude of intentional and deceitful acts committed by one party to take unfair advantage of another. Traditional elements of fraud are: a false representation as to a material fact, made with knowledge of its falsity, made with an intent to deceive, and resulting in action by the victim in justifiable reliance on the misrepresentation.

Fraudulent Misrepresentation — With regard to real estate sales, the intentional misrepresentation of a material fact by a seller or his real estate agent to induce the purchase of property. The purchaser under these circumstances will be entitled to certain remedies including damages and possible rescission. See also *Fraud.*

Freehold — An interest (estate) in real estate of not less than a life estate; either a fee simple estate or a life estate.

Front Footage — A property measurement for sale or valuation purposes consisting of the number of feet of street or road frontage.

Fructus Industriales — Crops or vegetable products that are the result of annual labor and cultivation and treated as personal property for certain purposes.

Fructus Naturales — Plant life that is the natural and spontaneous growth of nature requiring no annual planting or cultivation and treated as real property as long as it remains unsevered.

FSBO — An abbreviation of the term "for sale by owner."

Full Assignment — An assignment in which the assignee expressly assumes responsibility for all covenants and provisions in the original lease for the rest of the term.

Full Performance — In contract law, the complete performance of the contract terms by each party. See also *Executed Contract.*

Full-Service Lease — A type of lease, commonly used with multi-tenant commercial property, where the lessees share overall operating expenses for the building and common areas.

Functional Obsolescence — Loss in value of property due to factors that impair the desirability of a property which arise from its being out of date with respect to design and style, capacity and utility in relation to site, lack of modern facilities, or the like; a cause of depreciation in property value.

Future Advances Mortgage — a security instrument placed on real property to secure both present funds given to the borrower at the time of the mortgage and future funds (future advances) that will or may be given to the borrower. Article 7, Chapter 45 of the North Carolina General Statutes sets forth requirements and guidelines for future advances mortgages.

Future Estate (or Future Interest) — An interest in land entitling its owner to possession of the land at a future date, as, for example, the interest that a remainderman holds during the life of a present life tenant.

General Agent — An agent who is authorized by his principal to perform a broad range of acts, usually all acts necessary in connection with a particular business or venture.

General Assembly — The legislative branch of North Carolina state government charged by the North Carolina Constitution with the responsibility of enacting the statutory law for the state.

General Contractor — The contractor in general control and supervision of the subcontractors in a construction project. Also called the *Prime Contractor.*

General Lien — A lien that attaches to any real or personal property owned by a person in the county in which the lien is filed. A properly filed judgment lien, for example, is a lien against all property owned by the defendant-debtor in the county in which the lien is filed. Compare *Specific Lien.*

General Warranty Deed — A deed whereby the grantor agrees to protect the grantee against the valid claims of all persons whomsoever with respect to the land conveyed.

G.I. Loan — A loan guaranteed by the Veterans Administration under the Servicemen's Readjustment Act of 1944, as amended. See also *VA Mortgage Loan.*

GPS Coordinates — Modern method of determining the location of objects and boundaries on land using satellites and latitude and longitude. According to www.gps.gov, "… the Global Positioning System (GPS) is a U.S.-owned utility that provides users with positioning, navigation, and timing (PNT) services."

Good Faith — The absence of bad faith or evil intent. An intention to deal honestly. Even though good faith is exercised by a real estate agent, the agent nonetheless may be liable for negligent misrepresentation or non-disclosure (omission).

Good Faith Estimates (GFE) — A document previously provided by the lender to a borrower under RESPA at the time of the loan application or within three days thereafter containing a good faith estimate of closing costs likely to be incurred by the borrower. Since October 3, 2015, borrowers have received the Loan Estimate in lieu of the GFE and early TIL statement.

Good Funds Settlement Act -- This North Carolina statute (Chapter 45A of the General Statutes) requires the settlement agent (closing attorney) to verify funds paid to the settlement agent for the transaction by the buyer, lender or other party and to record the deed and deed of trust prior to disbursing any funds. The funds paid to the settlement agent are acceptable if they have been irrevocably credited to the settlement agent's escrow account or if they were paid by certified check, cashier's check, teller's check, official bank check, check drawn on an attorney's trust account, check drawn on a real estate broker's trust account or certain other specified types of checks.

Government National Mortgage Association **(GNMA or "Ginnie Mae")** — A government organization under the jurisdiction of HUD that plays an important role in the secondary mortgage market by attracting capital into the real estate finance market through the sale of securities backed by pools of mortgages, the timely payment of which are guaranteed by GNMA.

Government Survey System — Also known as the *Rectangular Survey System,* this system of land description is used extensively in midwestern and western states.

Graduated Lease — A lease calling for systematic increases in rental at regular intervals over the lease term.

Graduated Payment Loan — A system of repayment of a mortgage loan whereby monthly payments start out at a lower amount at first and then increase at stated intervals.

Grant — A generic term applicable to all transfers of real property; a technical term used in deeds of conveyance of lands to denote a transfer.

Grantee — A person to whom real estate is conveyed; the buyer of real estate.

Grantor — A person who conveys real estate by deed; the seller of real estate. Also, the person who conveys legal title to a trustee under a deed of trust; the owner of property subject to a deed of trust.

Grantor and Grantee Index — The traditional official index of North Carolina public land records based on the names of persons or entities who transfer or acquire an interest in real property.

Grantee Index — An alphabetical index in the Register of Deeds Office of surnames and entities who acquired an interest in real property.

Grantor Index — An alphabetical index in the Register of Deeds Office of surnames and entities who have conveyed an interest in real property.

Gross Income — The total income from property before any expenses are deducted.

Gross Lease — A lease of property whereby the lessor is to pay all property charges resulting from ownership.

Gross Rent Multiplier — A figure, used in connection with the income approach method of appraisal, which represents the relationship between gross rental income and value; derived by dividing value (represented by sale price) by monthly or annual gross rental income.

Ground Lease — A lease of land only that involves the separation of ownership of the land from ownership of the buildings and improvements on the land.

Ground Rent — The rent or earnings paid for or attributable to the right of use and occupancy of a parcel of unimproved land; that portion of the total rental paid that is considered to represent a return upon the land only.

Habendum Clause — The "To Have and To Hold" clause in a deed that defines or limits the quantity of the estate granted.

Habitability — See *Implied Warranty of Habitability.*

Handicap — A physical or mental impairment which substantially limits one or more major life activities; a record of having such an impairment, or being regarded as having such an impairment.

Hazard Insurance Policy — A policy of insurance that provides coverage against specified perils that might physically damage property.

Heirs — The persons who inherit property of a decedent owner who dies without a valid will.

Hereditaments — Every sort of inheritable interest in property, tangible (corporeal) and intangible (incorporeal). Used generally in connection with real property, meaning land and all of its incidents and appurtenances.

Highest and Best Use — That legally permissible and economically feasible use of a property which, as of the date of appraisal, will support the highest present value for such property or which will produce the maximum net return on the property over the period encompassing the foreseeable useful life of the property, or a given period of time; also, the optimum use of a property.

Highway Access Controls — State or local laws restricting access to land abutting a public highway or street. Prospective purchasers of abutting land should investigate whether highway access controls affect the property.

Historic Preservation Zoning — Zoning for the purpose of preserving the historic character of buildings and neighborhoods.

Holding Period — The period during which a party owns a property.

Holdover Tenant — A tenant who remains in possession of leased property after the expiration date of the lease term.

Home Equity Line of Credit (HELOC) — See *Equity Line of Credit.*

Home Equity Loan — See *Equity Loan.*

Homeowner And Homebuyer Protection Act — North Carolina legislation (Article 6, Chapter 75 of the General Statutes) addressing "home foreclosure rescue scams." The Act prohibits purported foreclosure rescue practices in which a property owner, in hopes of avoiding a foreclosure process that has commenced, is induced to sell the mortgaged property for less than fifty percent of its fair market value. It also addresses abuses in alternative home financing transactions, including the use of contracts for deed and leases with options to purchase as financing devices.

Homeowners' Association — Also referred to as Owners' Association, Lot Owners' Association, the asociation that governs a planned community under the North Carolina Planned Community Act. See N.C. Gen. Stat. § 47F-1-103(3). Homeowners' associations enjoy significant statutory powers under N.C. Gen. Stat. § 47F-3-102.

Homeowners' Insurance Policy — A "package policy" of insurance designed to insure a homeowner's buildings against a number of perils including fire, lightning, windstorm, hail, etc. and to insure the homeowner against liability claims.

Homestead — Real property owned by a person under special legal restrictions and exemptions from claims of his creditors under the Constitution.

Home Warranty Policy — A private policy that may be purchased to cover specified construction defects, heating and cooling systems, and appliances often offered to purchasers by sellers.

Horticultural Land — Land that qualifies under North Carolina property tax laws to be taxed at present use value.

HUD — The U.S. Department of Housing and Urban Development.

HUD-1 Uniform Settlement Statement (**HUD-1 Form**) — A standardized settlement statement form previously required in all residential real estate closings subject to RESPA, but replaced in RESPA transactions with the Borrrowers' Closing Disclosure and the Sellers' Closing Disclosure, both of which are disclosures, rather than settlement statements. The former HUD-1 settlement statement may still be used by settlement agents in non-RESPA governed transactions.

Illegal Contract — A contract that is unenforceable because it violates the law.

Illegal Use — Use of real property that begins after enactment of a zoning ordinance that violates the ordinance.

Illusory Offer — Under contract law, an illusory offer is a statement that looks like an offer to purchase but is so conditioned and worded that the person making it has really made no legally binding promise at all.

Imminently Dangerous Condition — The N.C. Residential Rental Agreements Act requires that a landlord repair or remedy an imminent dangerous condition on the leased premises within a reasonable period of time based on the condition's severity. The Act provides a series of examples to define the term, including unsafe wiring, lack of potable water, broken windows, lack of operable locks, and rat infestation.

Implied Contract — A contract that is implied from the conduct of the parties. It is not the result of an express agreement between the parties.

Implied Easement — An easement created by implication, by operation of law, as a result of the circumstances of a conveyance. For example, a grantor who landlocks a grantee has created an implied easement known as an easement of necessity.

Implied Warranty or Covenant — A guaranty or assurance the law supplies in an agreement, even though the agreement itself does not express the guaranty or assurance.

Implied Warranty of Fitness (New Dwelling) — As an exception to the doctrine of *caveat emptor,* the North Carolina courts have recognized that in every contract for the sale of a recently completed dwelling (or one under construction), a builder-vendor is held to warrant to the initial vendee that, at the time of the passing of the deed (or the taking of possession by the initial vendee, whichever occurs first), the dwelling, together with all its fixtures, is: (1) sufficiently free from major structural defects; and (2) is constructed in a workmanlike manner.

Implied Warranty of Habitability — A theory of landlord and tenant law holding that a landlord renting or leasing residential property impliedly warrants to the tenant that the property is habitable and fit for the use intended. The North Carolina Residential Rental Agreements Act incorporates this concept into a statute. See also *Fit Premises* and *Residential Rental Agreements Act.*

Impossibility of Performance — In contract law, the defense of impossibility of performance will excuse a party to a contract from performing in some instances. The defense must be in the nature of the thing to be done and not the inability of the promisor to do it.

Improved Land (Lot) — Either land on which improvements, such as buildings, have been constructed or land which has been prepared (improved) for further development by grading, draining, installing utility connections, or similar actions.

Improvement — A valuable addition to land (or real property) or a change in its condition, amounting to more than mere repairs or replacement, that is intended to enhance its value, beauty, or utility or to adapt it for new or additional purposes.

Improvements on Land — Structures, of whatever nature, usually privately rather than publicly owned, erected on a site to enable its utilization (e.g., buildings, fences, driveways, retaining walls, etc.).

Improvements to Land — Usually relates to publicly-owned structures, such as curbs, sidewalks, street lighting systems, and sewers, constructed so as to enable the development of privately-owned land for utilization. Also includes any site enhancement, such as driveways, ditches for drainage, landscaping, etc.

In Arrears — A method of charging and paying interest on a loan where the interest owed for a particular period is charged and paid at the end of the period. Example: A mortgage payment due September 1 pays the interest for the month of August.

In rem — Literally means "against the thing." Thus, real property taxes are levied "in rem," *i.e.,* against the property.

Income — A stream of benefits generally measured in terms of money derived from labor, business, property, or capital.

Income Capitalization Approach — A set of methods or procedures used to estimate the value, usually present market value, of an income-producing property by capitalizing expected future benefits (cash flow and reversion) using an appropriate capitalization rate. See also *Capitalization, Capitalization Rate, Direct Capitalization* and *Yield Capitalization.*

Indenture — A formal, written instrument made between two or more persons with different interests. The word comes from the old practice of indenting or cutting the deed on the top or side in a wavy line.

Index, Grantor and Grantee — An indexing system used in Register of Deeds offices whereby records of documents affecting title to land are listed in both the grantor's and grantee's name.

Index Lease — A lease calling for periodic increases or decreases in rent based upon some reliable government or private index or standard.

Informal Reference — The description of real property in an informal but sufficiently adequate way so as to identify a parcel of land. Use of a street address, for example, is an example of an informal reference.

Injunction — A writ or court order to restrain one or more parties to a suit from doing an inequitable or unjust act in regard to the rights of some other party in the suit or proceeding.

Innocent Misrepresentation — A representation made by one believing it to be true, although it is in fact untrue. While an innocent misrepresentation is not fraud, it is not necessarily harmless, and it can constitute *negligent misrepresentation* or, in some cases, *willful misrepresentation,* especially if made by a real estate agent.

Installment Land Contract — The sale of real estate by the seller on the installment method with the vendee given possession and with the vendor retaining legal title until all payments have been made or until some other agreed upon time. Sometimes called a *Contract for Deed.*

Insurable Interest — A requirement in insurance law that the insured party have a legitimate financial interest in the subject of the insurance.

Interest — A sum of money paid for the use of another's money.

Intermediate Theory — A hybrid theory of mortgage law which strikes a middle position between the pure title and lien theories of mortgage law. In essence, a deed of trust is taken and is treated as a lien only, unless and until the borrower defaults on the payment terms, at which point title theory is followed and the deed of trust is viewed as conveying legal title to the mortgagee. See also *Lien Theory* and *Title Theory.*

Interpretation of Contract Rules — Rules developed by the courts concerning the interpretation and construction of written contracts. The purpose of these rules is to aid in determining by relatively uniform standards the intentions of parties from the words used in their contracts.

Interstate Land Sales Full Disclosure Act — Federal legislation enacted to prevent fraudulent and misleading practices in the interstate sale of subdivision lots.

Interval Ownership — See *Time Share*.

Intestate — A person who dies having made no will, or one whose will is defective.

Intestate Succession — The transfer of property governed by statute when a person dies without a valid will. Statutes dealing with "Intestate Succession," sometimes called "descent and distribution," specify who is entitled to the deceased owner's real and personal property.

Investment Real Estate — For income tax purposes, real estate that is used in a business or held for income-producing purposes.

Involuntary Alienation — A transfer of ownership of real property without the owner's consent, such as by lien foreclosure sale, adverse possession, escheat, or eminent domain (condemnation). Distinguish from *Voluntary Alienation*.

Joint Tenancy — Property held by two or more persons together with the right of survivorship.

Judgment — The decision or sentence of a court of law as the result of proceedings instituted therein for the redress of an injury. A properly docketed judgment declaring that one individual is indebted to another individual creates a lien on any real property owned by the judgment debtor.

Judgment Lien — A general lien on all real property owned or subsequently acquired by the judgment debtor in the county where the lien is filed (docketed). The lien lasts for ten years after docketing.

Junior Mortgage — A mortgage lower in lien priority than another mortgage.

Jurisdiction — The authority by which judicial officers have the power to hear and decide cases.

Laches — Delay or negligence in asserting one's rights.

Land — In a legal sense, the solid part of the surface of the earth, as distinguished from water; any ground, soil, or earth whatsoever, regarded as the subject of ownership; every thing annexed to it, whether by nature (e.g., trees), or by man (e.g., buildings, fences, etc.), and everything on or in it, such as minerals and running water.

Land Contract — See *Installment Land Contract*.

Landlord — One who rents or leases real estate to others; the lessor.

Land Use Controls — Public and private restrictions on the use of real property.

Late Payment Fee — The N.C. Residential Rental Agreement Act authorizes a landlord to charge a late payment fee when a tenant is five days or more late paying rent. Statutory limits exist for the maximum amount of a late payment fee, and other restrictions exist.

Latent Ambiguity — A condition that exists in a description of real property in a deed or contract that is insufficient in itself to identify a parcel of property, but that provides a reference to outside facts by which the land involved might be identified. Compare *Patent Ambiguity*.

Latent Defect — A property defect which is not discoverable by a reasonably diligent inspection; a hidden defect. Compare *Patent Defect*.

Lateral Support — The right of a land owner to have the sides of his land supported in its natural state by the lands of adjacent owners. See also *Subjacent Support*.

Lawful Objective/Contract Law — An essential element of every contract is that the purpose or objective of the agreement and the means of accomplishing it must be lawful.

Lead-Based Paint Disclosure — A disclosure required to be given to prospective tenants or home purchasers under the Residential Lead-Based Hazard Reduction Act of 1992. Legal requirements are imposed on "target housing" constructed prior to 1978.

Leaking Underground Storage Tank — An environmental hazard requiring site cleanup and remediation under federal and state law. Prospective purchasers should environmental due diligence if there is any evidence that this hazard may exist on the real property being considered for purchase.

Lease — A type of contract, written or oral, between the owner of real estate, the landlord, and another person, the tenant, covering the conditions upon which the tenant may possess, occupy, and use the real estate.

Lease Option Contracts/Residential Property -- Chapter 47G of the N.C. General Statutes regulates leases combined with options to purchase residential property, an alternative form of financing, for potential consumer abuses.

Leased Fee — The interest of a lessor in leased property that the lessor owns in fee.

Leasehold — The interest (estate) a lessee has in real estate by virtue of his lease. Also called a *nonfreehold estate*.

Legal Capacity — A requirement that in order for a contract to be enforceable the parties must have the legal capacity to enter into a contract (cannot be a minor, insane person, declared incompetent, or an intoxicated person).

Legal Description — A statement containing a designation by which land can be identified sufficiently to meet the requirements established by law.

Legal Title — The interest in real property that is held by (a) the trustee under a deed of trust, (b) the seller under a valid "interim" real estate sales contract, and (c) the seller under an installment land contract. See also *Equitable Conversion*. Distinguish from *Equitable Title*. (Note: The owner of real estate that is not encumbered by a deed of trust and is not the subject of a real estate sales contract holds both legal and equitable title to his property.)

Lender's (Mortgagee's) Policy of Title Insurance — This policy insures the security interest of the mortgagee (lender) in real property. It protects the lender against any defects in the title and against prior liens on the property. It is a policy of diminishing liability, with the liability of the title insurance company limited to the outstanding balance on the mortgage loan at any given time. A lender'spolicy affords little or no protection for the owner, as the liability of the title insurance company is only to protect the interest of the lender. *See "Owner's Policy of Title Insurance."*

Lessee — The person who leases property from another; a tenant.

Lessor — The owner who rents or leases property to a tenant or lessee; the landlord.

Letter of Intent to Lease — An document summarizing the key terms of a future lease. It is usually not a binding contract and serves as a helpful way to clarify terms the lessor and lessee will agree to if the lessor and lessee agree to a binding lease.

Leverage — The creation of a higher return on a cash investment in real estate by using borrowed money.

Liability Insurance — As related to real estate, insurance that indemnifies a property owner in the event he is found liable for damages to a third party who has been injured on the insured's property.

License — A privilege or right granted to an individual by the state to engage in a business or profession, e.g., as a real estate broker. In real property law, a license is an authority to go upon or to use another person's land or property without possessing any estate therein.

Lien — A charge, hold, or claim that one person has upon the property of another as a security for the payment of a debt.

Lien Agent — A title insurance company or title insurance agency desgnated by the owner of real property to receive claims of lien and perform other duties under the North Carolina Mechanic's Lien Law. See N.C.Gen. Stat. § 44A-11.1.

Lien Foreclosure Sale — The involuntary transfer of property to satisfy a tax obligation, judgment, or similar obligation that has been secured by a lien on the debtor's property.

Lien on Personal Property/Leases of Non-Residential Property — In leases of *non-residential* real property, a lessor has a right to a statutory lien on the lessee's personal property for certain breaches of the lease by the lessee. The lien is authorized by N.C.Gen.Stat. §44-2(e).

Lien Theory — The theory underlying the method of pledging real estate as collateral for a loan that usually provides for the borrower to hold both legal title and equitable title to the real property during the term of the loan and for the lender to hold a lien against the property until the loan is repaid. The legal instrument used to accomplish this is a mortgage. See also *Title Theory.*

Lien Waiver — A document signed by a contractor, subcontractor, laborer, or materialman waiving the right to a mechanic's lien claim on the property.

Life Estate — An estate or interest in real property that exists only for the life of a certain designated person. The "life tenant" has the exclusive right to possession, control, and use of the property during the term of the life estate. Upon the death of the person whose life is the "measuring life," title to the property automatically vests in the designated "remainderman." See also *Life Estate Pur Autre Vie, Life Tenant,* and *Remainder.*

Life Estate Pur Autre Vie — A life estate in property measured by the life of another person (i.e., a person other than the life tenant). If the holder of this type of life estate dies before the measuring life, the heirs of the life tenant inherit the property and will hold it until the measuring life dies.

Life of Loan Cap — A ceiling (maximum upper limit) the interest (note) rate on an adjustable rate mortgage cannot exceed over the life of the mortgage loan.

Life Tenant — A person who owns a life estate in land or other real property.

Like Kind Exchange — Under the Internal Revenue Code, the exchange of property held for productive use in a trade or business or for investment for other property of a like kind to be held either for productive use in a trade or business or for investment.

Limited Common Element — Specifically defined areas or features of a condominium development designated for the use of one or more unit owners, but fewer than all unit owners. Common examples include balconies, patio areas, and reserved parking spaces.

Limited Liability Company (LLC) — A statutorily created legal entity that is governed by an operating agreement and has protections from liability similar to a corporation. Effecdtive January 1, 2014, a substantially new North Carolina Limited Liability Company Act, Chapter 57D of the General Statutes, became effective.

Limited Liability Limited Partnership — A partnership formed by registration with the North Carolina Secretary of State governed by The North Carolina Revised Uniform Limited Partnership Act, Article 5, Chapter 59. Like the limited liability company, the limited liability limited partnership includes protetions from liability that were not possible with a traditional partnership.

Limited Partnership — A partnership where some of the partners have their liability limited to the amount of money that they have invested. The entity must comply with the North Carolina Uniform Limited Partnership Act.

Liquidated Damages — An amount of damages, specified in the contract, recoverable by either party in the event of breach of the contract.

Lis Pendens — A notice of pending litigation concerning real property that is filed in the public land records. Persons dealing with real property subject to a lis pendens take the property subject to the outcome of the litigation.

Listing Contract — A document in which a property owner contracts with a broker as agent to find a buyer for the owner's property; the document executed by an owner giving a broker authority to act as the owner's agent in the sale of the owner's property. Often referred to simply as a "listing."

Littoral Owner — A person who owns real property having at least one boundary on an ocean or lake. The owner's littoral rights include direct access to the ocean and a continuing right to abut the ocean.

Loan Commitment — A commitment by a lender to make a particular mortgage loan to a loan applicant under specified terms. The commitment, which may be either a "conditional" commitment or a "firm" commitment, is valid for only a specified period of time.

Loan Origination Fee — See *Origination Fee.*

Loan Originator — A person or entity that processes mortgage loan applications from consumers and initiates the loan process.

Loan-to-Value Ratio — The relationship between the amount of a loan and the appraised value of the property secured by the loan, usually expressed as a percentage.

Machinery Act — The North Carolina General Statutes that govern the *ad valorem* taxation of property.

Maintenance — The act of keeping, or the expenditures required to keep, a property in condition to perform adequately and efficiently the service for which it is used.

Mailbox Rule — A rule of law that states that once an offeree's written acceptance is mailed (placed in the control of the postal service and out of the control of the offeree), the offer is considered to be accepted as of the date and time of mailing, even though the acceptance is not actually received by the offeror until several days later. The offeror cannot withdraw or revoke his offer after an acceptance has been mailed and the offeree cannot withdraw or revoke his acceptance after it has been mailed.

Manufactured Home — For purposes of ad valorem taxation, "a structure, transportable in one or more sections, which, in the traveling mode, is eight feet or more in width or is 40 feet or more in length, or when erected on site, is 320 or more square feet, and which is built on a permanent chassis and designed to be used as a dwelling with or without a permanent foundation when connected to the required utilities, and includes the plumbing, heating, air conditioning and electrical systems contained therein." N.C.Gen.Stat. §143-143.9(6). Sometimes referred to as a mobile home.

Manufactured Home (Real Property) — A manufactured home as defined in N.C.Gen.Stat. § 143-143.9(7) constitutes "real property" if it is a residential structure and has the moving hitch, wheels, and axles removed and has been placed on a permanent foundation on land owned by the owner of the manufactured home. N.C.Gen. Stat. §105-273(13). Manufactured homes are federally regulated by the U.S. Department of Housing and Urban Development (Manufactured Housing Construction and Safety Code) 24 CFR 3280.

Marital Life Estate — A life estate arising by operation of law where a married person owning an inheritable estate dies and is survived by his or her spouse who, under certain conditions, could have a life estate in part or all of a deceased spouse's real property owned at any time during the marriage.

Marketable Title — A title that a reasonable purchaser, well informed as to the facts and their legal bearing, willing and anxious to perform his contract, would be willing and ought to accept in the exercise of that prudence that businesspeople ordinarily bring to bear in such transactions; such a title as a court would compel a purchaser to accept; a title free from any encumbrances or clouds.

Marketable Title Act — North Carolina legislation passed in order to enhance the marketability of title to real property by allowing the title examiner to determine the status of title by a search of the relatively recent public records only. The Act is located at Chapter 47-B of the General Statutes and is subject to numerous exceptions.

Market Data Approach — The obsolete term for an appraisal method or procedure used to estimate the market value of a property by comparison and analysis of the sale prices of other recently sold similar properties. See *Sales Comparison Approach.*

Market Price — The price actually paid for a property (i.e., the sale price). Distinguish from *Market Value.*

Market Rent — The rental income that a property most probably would command on the open market as indicated by current rentals being paid for comparable space.

Market Value — The most probable amount for which a property should sell in a competitive and open market under all conditions requisite to a fair sale, with the buyer and seller each acting prudently and knowledgeably, and with the sale not being affected by any undue stimulus. Distinguish from *Market Price.*

Mass Appraisal — A method of determining the assessed values for all parcels of land in a particular county or city without performing a separate appraisal for each parcel. Usually performed by county tax assessors to determine market values for *ad valorem* taxation purposes.

Material Fact — In its broadest sense, any fact of substance relating to a property or a real estate sales (or rental) transaction that might affect a prospective purchaser's (or tenant's) decision to buy (or rent) the property or an owner's decision to sell (or rent).

Mechanic's Lien (Materialman's and Laborer's Lien) — A type of lien created by statute that exists in favor of persons who have performed work or furnished materials in the erection or repair of a building or improvement on real property.

Meeting of Minds — Occurs when all parties mutually agree on and assent to all material terms of a contract. It is an essential element to form a valid contract.

Memorandum of Contract — A memorandum of a sales contract (including an option) or a lease that complies with statutory guidelines that can be recorded in lieu of the entire document. A duly recorded memorandum constitutes record notice to subsequent purchasers for value and lien creditors. See N.C. Gen.Stat. §§ 47-118, -119, -119.1, -120.

Merger — A doctrine of property law holding that if a person acquires all outstanding interests in a parcel of real estate, those interests combine into the greater estate. For example, if a person acquires both the life estate and remainder, that person has a fee simple absolute estate under the doctrine of merger.

Merger Clause/Contract Law — A provision in many standard form contracts to convey real estate stating that the contract contains the entire agreement of the parties and that there are no representations, inducements, or other provisions other than those included in writing in the contract.

Metes and Bounds — The term comes from the old English words "metes" meaning measurements, and "bounds" meaning boundaries. It is generally applied to any description of real estate that describes the boundaries by distance and angles.

Mill Rate — A method of calculating the property tax rate in some states. A "mill" is used to express the tax rate. A "mill" is 1/1000 of a dollar or 1/10 of one cent ($.001). A *mill rate* is described in terms of "mills per dollar" of assessed value.

Mineral Deed — A deed transferring mineral rights which have been severed from surface rights to a grantee. Mineral deeds must comply with the Statute of Frauds (N.C. Gen. Stat. §22-2).

Mineral Lease — A lease entitling the lessee to explore for minerals and mine them if they are discovered. Mineral leases of any duration must be in writing under the Statute of Frauds (N.C. Gen. Stat. §22-2).

Misrepresentation — A false representation, either willful or negligent, of a material fact to another party. See also *Fraudulent Misrepresentation, Willful Misrepresentation,* and *Negligent Misrepresentation.*

Mistake of Fact — A basis for avoiding performance of a contract when there is a *mutual* erroneous impression by the parties to the contract concerning some material fact.

Mistake of Law — An erroneous impression by one or both parties to a contract concerning the law governing their agreement. Mistake of law does *not* excuse performance of a contract.

Mixed Use Zoning District — A zoning district that allows a combination of different land uses subject to specific regulations.

Modular Home - A modular home is a dwelling consisting of a series of rooms or units (modules) constructed and inspected off-site in accordance with the North Carolina State Building Code and then transported to its ultimate site and assembled on a permanent foundation. Modular homes may consist of one or more stories.

Monument — A fixed object on the ground used to establish real estate boundaries in a metes and bounds property description. Includes both "natural" monuments (tree, river, etc.) and "artificial" monuments (those made by man, such as a stone marker or iron stake).

Mortgage — A pledge of real property as security for the payment of money, the fulfillment of some contract, or the performance of some act, such pledge to become void upon such payment, fulfillment, or performance. See also *Deed of Trust.*

Mortgage Banker — A mortgage company that extends a full line of mortgage lending services, including the making of mortgage loans of all types and the servicing of the loans during their term.

Mortgage Broker — An agent or broker of a lender who brings together the lender and the borrower and receives a fee for this service.

Mortgage Company — See *Mortgage Banker.*

Mortgage Insurance — See *Private Mortgage Insurance.*

Mortgage Note — A legal "I.O.U." evidencing indebtedness and coupled with a mortgage or deed of trust on the property of the debtor. See also *Note* and *Negotiable Promissory Note.*

Mortgagee — The person to whom a mortgage is executed; the lender who holds a lien on real property to secure the obligation owed to him; same as the beneficiary under a deed of trust. See also *Beneficiary.*

Mortgagor — The person who executes the mortgage; the borrower-owner who gives the mortgage to the mortgagee as security for the debt owed by the owner; same as the grantor under a deed of trust.

Multiple Listing Service — A local or regional cooperative listing arrangement operated by brokers who are members of a local board or association of the National Association of REALTORS®. See also *Cooperative Listing Service.*

Mutual Assent — Agreement on definite terms required of both parties before a contract can come into existence. Synonymous with "meeting of the minds."

Mutuality of Obligations — The concept that both parties to a contract are equally bound or not bound. For example, the N.C. Residential Rental Agreements Act specifies that the obligations of landlord and tenant are mutually dependent.

National Association of Real Estate Brokers **(NAREB)** — A professional trade association of African-American real estate brokers. Members are called "Realtists." See also *Realtist.*

National Association of REALTORS® **(NAR)** — A professional real estate trade association which is the country's largest and most influential real estate professional organization. Members are referred to as "REALTORS" or "REALTOR Associates." NAR functions through affiliate state organizations and local organizations often referred to as "boards". The most prominent activity of most local boards in North Carolina is the operation of area multiple listing services in which brokers who are members of the local board may participate. See also *REALTOR®.*

National Environmental Policy Act (NEPA) — A federal law mandating that all federal agencies fully weigh the environmental effects of federal programs and to give proper consideration to the environment prior to undertaking any major federal action that significantly affects the environment.

National Historic Preservation Act — Federal legislation protecting and providing some assistance for historic properties.

Natural Monument — Those monuments used in a metes and bounds property description which are a product of nature (e.g. tree, creek, etc..)

Navigable Water — A body of water suitable for the usual purpose of navigation by vessels or boats. Ownership of land under navigable water is in the State of North Carolina in trust for all of its citizens.

Negative Amortization — A term used to describe the situation when the principal balance of a loan is increased by adding unpaid, but accrued, interest to the outstanding loan balance.

Negligence — The failure to exercise that degree of reasonable care required under the circumstances existing at a given time; the failure to exercise that degree of care that would be expected of a reasonably prudent person under the same or similar conditions.

Negligent Misrepresentation — The unintentional misrepresentation of a material fact by a party where that party "should reasonably have known" the truth of the matter that was misrepresented.

Negligent Omission — The unintentional failure to disclose a material fact by a party where that party "should reasonably have known" of the fact that was not disclosed.

Negotiable Note — An unconditional promise to pay a sum of money "to order" or "to bearer" thereby making the note transferable. A negotiable note is assignable by the lender. In contrast, a nonnegotiable note is payable only to a named person.

Net Lease — A lease where, in addition to the rental stipulated, the lessee assumes payment of property charges such as taxes, insurance, and maintenance.

Net Listing — A brokerage fee arrangement in a listing contract whereby the seller will receive a fixed price for his property and the broker will receive any amount realized (i.e., the "net") in excess of that price.

Net Operating Income (**NOI**) — In an operating budget, the income projected for an income-producing property after deducting projected vacancy/rent collection losses and operating expenses from projected gross (maximum possible) income. In an income/expense statement, the income from a property after deducting operating expenses from gross income actually received.

Nonconforming Mortgage Loan — A mortgage loan that is not a government insured or guaranteed loan and that is not made in conformance with "Fannie Mae" and "Freddie Mac" underwriting guidelines. Distinguish from *Conventional Conforming Mortgage Loan.*

Nonconforming Use — A use of land that predates zoning, but is not in accordance with the uses prescribed for the area by the later zoning ordinance. Because it was there first, it may be continued, subject to certain limitations.

Nonfreehold — Any interest (estate) in real estate which is less than a "freehold" interest. Also called a *leasehold estate.*

Nonnegotiable Note — A promissory note that is payable only to a specific named party and may not be transferred to a third party.

Nonrecourse Note — A promissory note secured by a deed of trust on real estate where the borrower is not personally liable for payment of the debt. If the borrower defaults, the creditor may foreclose against the property, but will not be entitled to pursue any deficiency against the borrower.

North Carolina Condominium Act — Chapter 47C of the N.C. General Statutes governed all aspects of condominium creation, unit sales, and association management.

North Carolina Environmental Policy Act — Legislation requiring environmental impact statements of state agencies for certain projects.

North Carolina Planned Community Act — A law enacted in 1998 effective January 1, 1999 that significantly expands the authority of homeowner associations and makes the enforcement of covenants and restrictions significantly easier in developments that fit the definition of a "planned community" by allocating authority to make and enforce annual and special assessments to the homeowner association.

North Carolina Residential Mortgage Fraud Act — A criminal statute, Chapter 14, Article 20A of the North Carolina General Statutes, that describes certain acts performed in residential mortgage transactions as constituting fraud and makes a violation a criminal felony offense punishable by imprisonment, forfeiture of property and restitution.

Notarization — A certification by an authorized notary public to the effect that the signatures on a document are authentic. See also Acknowledgment.

Note — An instrument of credit given to attest a debt; a written promise to pay money which may or may not accompany a mortgage or other security agreement. Also called *Promissory Note.*

Novation — The substitution of a new contract for the former one. All obligations under the old contract are discharged and replaced by the terms of the new one.

Nuisance — The unreasonable use of private property in a manner that is hazardous or offensive to the property or health of neighboring property owners or the public in general.

Obligee — A person who is owed duties or obligations from an obligee under a contract.

Obligor — A person bound to perform duties or obligations owed to an obligee under a contract.

Obsolescence — As applied to real estate, it is the loss or impairment of value due to becoming outmoded and/ or less useful as a result of social or economic changes. See also *Economic Obsolescence* and *Functional Obsolescence.*

Occupancy Restrictions — Reasonable occupancy restrictions in rental housing are permissible under the Fair Housing Act. Unreasonable occupancy restrictions may constitute illegal discrimination based on familial status under the FHA.

Octennial Reappraisal — Real property subject to taxation in North Carolina must be reappraised on a staggered schedule every eight years. "Octennial" means occurring every eight years. Counties may adopt a more frequent reappraisal of four years.

Offer — A promise by one party to another party to perform a specified act provided that the other party promises to perform some specified act in return. An offer may be either an "offer to purchase" or an "offer to sell."

Offer to Purchase and Contract — The most commonly used type of contract for the sale of real property in North Carolina. A widely used standard contract form has been prepared jointly by the North Carolina Bar Association and the North Carolina Association of REALTORS®. Also called *sales* or *purchase contract*.

Offeree — The person receiving an offer; the person to whom the offer is extended.

Offeror — The person making an offer.

Oil and Gas Lease — A lease transferring the right to extract oil or gas from the real property of the lessor.

Omission — The willful or negligent failure to disclose a material fact to another party. See also *Willful Omission* and *Negligent Omission*.

Online Real Estate Data Bases — Real estate records available on searchable online data bases administered by the register of deeds office.

Open End Mortgage — A mortgage with an additional arrangement allowing the borrower to secure funds up to a certain amount in addition to the original amount borrowed.

Open Listing — A general listing given to a broker by an owner to sell his property. Such listing is not exclusive and may be given to a number of brokers at the same time. The owner is not precluded from selling the property during the term of the listing, and, if the owner procures a purchaser, he is under no obligation to pay any commission. Only the broker who produces a purchaser is entitled to receive compensation for effecting a sale under this type of listing. A sale by one broker terminates all other such listings.

Operating Budget — A detailed statement of projected income and expenses for a specified period of time.

Operating Expenses — All expenses or costs of operating a property except for debt service, capital expenditures, and depreciation.

Opinion of Title — An attorney's report on the status of title to real property based on his examination of the land records and other relevant public records.

Option — A privilege sold by a property owner (optionor) to another (optionee) giving to the optionee, in return for the payment of a consideration, a right to buy or not to buy a property within a specified period of time at a specified price. Also called an *option to purchase* or an *option contract*.

Option to Renew — In landlord-tenant law, the right given to tenants in some leases to renew the tenancy for an additional term.

Ordinance — A law passed by the governing body of a county or city acting under authority granted by the state legislature.

Ordinary Gain/Loss — For income tax purposes, any gain/loss that is not a capital gain/loss.

Original Titles — Titles not derived from a prior owner, but arising by operation of law independently of any prior owner as a result of occupancy by an adverse possessor for a specified length of time.

Origination Fee — A one-time fee charged to a borrower by a lender for making a mortgage loan. This fee usually is computed as a percentage of the loan amount. Also called *loan origination fee.*

Overimprovement — An improvement that is not the highest and best use for the site on which it is placed by reason of excess in size or cost.

Overlay Zoning District — In zoning practices, a district or zone that superimposes a certain zoning use over the existing traditional zoning map. A historic preservation zone, for example, might be superimposed over existing traditional zones.

Override Clause — See *Protection Agreement.*

Owner's Policy of Title Insurance — A policy in which a title company promises to indemnify the insured against loss or damage resulting from the title not being as described in the policy. Existing defects disclosed in the policy are not covered by the insurance. In addition, title insurance covers title defects that a search of the public records will not reveal. *Compare "Lender's Policy of Title Insurance."*

Package Insurance Policy — A generic term describing an insurance policy that insures against a number of perils, such as a homeowners' policy.

Package Mortgage — A mortgage or deed of trust on both real and personal property.

Panic Peddling — See *Blockbusting.*

Parcel — A part or portion of land or an estate; synonymous with the term "lot."

Parol — Oral, as distinguished from written.

Parcel Identifier Number (PIN) — A computerized system of indexing real property transactions in the Register of Deeds Office based on a track system of indexing. Each parcel of land is given a unique identifying number, and a title search will reveal every real property transaction dealing with that PIN.

Parol Evidence Rule — An evidentiary rule that states that earlier informal and tentative agreements and negotiations are no longer valid or binding once there is a final and complete written contract between the parties, nor can the terms or content of any such earlier negotiations or agreements be introduced into evidence.

Participation Mortgage — (a) A mortgage whereby the lender receives a portion of the income from the property or a partial equity interest in the property; (b) A mortgage loan made by two or more lenders.

Partition — A division of land among those who own it in undivided shares, such as tenants in common. A partition may be by a voluntary exchange of deeds or it may be ordered in a judicial proceeding.

Partition Deed — A deed executed by concurrent owners of property in order to convert their ownership into ownership in severalty.

Partnership — An association, regulated by the Uniform Partnership Act and the Revised Uniform Limited Partnership Act, of two or more persons to conduct business for a profit. There are three types of partnerships: general, limited and limited liability.

Party Wall — A wall that is erected upon and over a line separating two adjoining properties which the owners of the respective parcels have a common right to use.

Party Wall Agreement — A contract between adjoining property owners calling for the construction and joint use of a wall between two buildings used for the support of both.

Patent Ambiguity — A condition that exists in an attempted description of real estate in a deed, contract, or other document affecting title that is so absolutely uncertain that there is no way of determining where the property is. A document containing a patently ambiguous description is void. Compare *Latent Ambiguity*.

Patent Defect — An obvious property defect that should be discovered by a reasonably diligent inspection of the property. Compare *Latent Defect*.

Payment Cap — A limit on the amount the monthly payment on an adjustable rate mortgage can be increased when the interest rate is adjusted upward.

Percentage Lease — A lease of commercial property in which the rent is computed as a percentage of the receipts, either gross or net, from the business conducted by the lessee, sometimes with a guaranteed minimum rental.

Percolation Test — The old, now obsolete, term used to describe a soil suitability test to determine if soil will absorb and drain water sufficiently for use of a septic tank. The current official term used to describe this test is "soil suitability test."

Periodic Tenancy — See *Estate from Year to Year.*

Personal Property — Movable property that is not real property. The term "personal property" includes tangible property such as money, goods, chattels, and also intangible property such as debts and claims (choses in action). Unless exempt, personal property is subject to taxation in North Carolina.

Personal Representative — A person appointed to wind up the affairs of a decedent; if appointed by the court, an administrator, or, if named by a will, an executor or executrix.

Pest Inspection Report — See *Wood-Destroying Insect Inspection Report.*

Pet Fee — A reasonable, nonrefundable fee authorized by the NC Residential Rental Act that can be charged to tenants with pets, but may not be charged for service or assistance animals.

Physical Deterioration — Impairment of condition; one of the causes of depreciation, resulting from wear and tear, disintegration, use in service, action of the elements, and other causes.

Plaintiff — The complaining party in a legal action or lawsuit.

Planned Community — Real estate with respect to which any person, by virtue of that person's ownership of a lot, is expressly obligated by a declaration to pay real property taxes, insurance premiums, or other expenses to maintain, improve or benefit other lots or other real estate described in the declaration, but specifically excluding condominiums.

Planned Unit Development — A "PUD" is a special use permitted under a zoning ordinance that allows a developer to deviate from construction on standard lots and develop tracts with varying land uses and densities. A PUD often involves cluster housing with areas of open space.

Plat Book — A public record in the office of the Register of Deeds of various recorded plans of subdivisions of land into blocks and lots.

Plat (Map) — A duly approved and recorded map showing the division of land into blocks and lots. Reference to a specific lot by lot and plat book and page number is a valid legal description.

Point — A "point" is one percent of the amount of a mortgage loan. See also *Discount Points*.

Police Power — The authority of states, often delegated to local governments, to place restraints on the personal freedoms and property rights of individuals to promote public health, safety, morals, or general welfare. The best example of the exercise of such power is zoning ordinances.

Power of Attorney — An instrument authorizing a person to act as the attorney in fact of the person granting it; it may be a general power or may be limited to performance of a specific act or acts.

Predatory Lending — Loans made on significantly unfavorable terms to the borrower usually accompanied by lending practices that involve varying amounts of deception and outright fraud on the part of the lender or mortgage broker.

Preemptive Right — A provision giving a person the first right to purchase the property. Two examples of a preemptive right are the right of first refusal and the first opportunity to purchase. Preemptive rights are most commonly found in commercial leases.

Prepayment Penalty — Charge by lender when mortgage loan is paid before it is due. Such penalties are prohibited by law in North Carolina on home loans of $150,000 or less.

Prequalifying a Buyer — The process of making a nonbinding preliminary determination of a prospective buyer's qualifications with respect to a mortgage loan. Prequalification may be performed by a lender or a real estate agent.

Present Value — The present worth of money to be received at some future time.

Present Use Value — A method of land valuation for ad valorem property tax law purposes based on specified uses of real property, including the categories of agricultural land, forest land, horticultural land, and wildlife conservation land.

Preservation Easements — A landowner's agreement to restrict land for public policy purposes, including historic preservation, farmland preservation easements, and conservation easements. The agreement is enforced by a qualified conservation of preservation or a public agency.

Prima Facie — From Latin meaning "first view." In law, prima facie evidence is sufficient to establish a fact unless rebutted.

Primary Mortgage Market — The market in which mortgage loans are originated. This market consists of lenders (such as savings and loan associations, mortgage companies, and banks) that make mortgage loans directly to borrowers.

Principal — (a) One who appoints or hires an agent to act for and in his stead; the client of an agent; (b) A capital sum loaned with interest; the amount of a loan.

Private Mortgage Insurance (PMI) — Insurance that insures a mortgage lender (and subsequent purchaser of the mortgage note) against default by the borrower on a conventional mortgage loan.

Privity of Contract — A set of rights and duties between the parties to a lease arising because of the express contractual promises of the lease.

Privity of Estate — A set of rights and duties between the parties to a lease arising because of traditional property law rules.

Probate — The judicial process by which the validity of a will is formally determined.

Procuring Cause — A legal term referring to that cause which originates a series of events that lead directly to the accomplishment of a goal. In real estate brokerage, a test applied to determine whether a broker has earned his commission under a listing contract (except for an exclusive right-to-sell-listing) by procuring a purchaser who is ready, willing, and able to complete a sales transaction in accordance with terms acceptable to the seller. See also *Ready, Willing and Able.*

Profits á Prendre — The intangible property right to remove products of the land of another, such as the right to hunt or fish on the land of another.

Professional Engineer/Land Surveyor — An engineer or land surveyor duly licensed under the North Carolina Engineering and Land Surveying Act, Chapter 89C of the N.C. General Statutes.

Prohibited Practices — Under the Federal Fair Housing Act, illegal discriminatory practices include refusing to sell or rent, discriminating in housing terms, making housing unavailable for sale or rent, discriminatory advertising, engaging in blockbusting practices, denying equal access to a multiple listing service or other broker organization, discriminating in lending practices, and, discriminating in appraising real property, when based on a protected class. *See "Protected Classes."*

Promissory Note — See *Note.*

Property — The term describing the rights and interests a person has in lands, chattels, and other determinate things. "Property" encompasses a "bundle of rights," various interests created and protected by law, giving an individual exclusive rights to own, possess, use, enjoy, and dispose of determinate things.

Property Manager — A real estate broker who is employed by a real property owner to lease, maintain, and oversee operation of the real property as an agent of the owner.

Property Tax — A tax on real and personal property ownership based on the market value of the property; called an *ad valorem* property tax.

Proprietary Lease — A lease given by the corporation owning a cooperative apartment building to a tenant (who is also a stockholder in the corporation) giving the tenant the right to occupy a particular unit.

Proration — The division or distribution of money or monetary obligations between seller and buyer in a real estate closing transaction.

Prospectus — A printed advertisement for a new enterprise, such as a planned subdivision development or office complex.

Protected Classes — The following classes of persons expressly listed as protected under the Fair Housing Act: Race, Color, Religion, Sex, Handicap/Disability, Familial Status, and National Origin. Gay, lesbian, bisexual, or transgender (LGBT) persons are receiving increasing protection from discrimination under the FHA, but are not expressly listed as a protected class.

Protected Tenant — A residential tenant or household member who is the victim of domestic violence under Chapter 50B of the N.C. General Statutes or a victim of sexual assault or stalking under Chapter14 of the N.C. General Statutes.

Protecting Tenants at Foreclosure Act of 2009 — A federal law, Pub.L. 111-22, effective May 20, 2009, protecting certain tenants who live in foreclosed residential property.

Protection Agreement — A separate agreement or a provision within a listing agreement between an owner of real estate and a real estate broker which protects the broker in the event the owner subsequently sells to a buyer produced by the broker and tries to avoid paying the brokerage fee to the broker.

Protective Covenants — A term sometimes used to describe the covenants and restrictions of a common interest community. See *Restrictive Covenant.*

Provisional Broker — The term applied to the entry level licensing in North Carolina formerly known as "salesperson." The person is provisionally licensed as a broker pending completion of specified postlicensing courses. A provisional broker may only engage in brokerage activities under the supervision of a "broker-in-charge."

Public Housing Tenant — A tenant residing in government-subsidized housing, for example, "Section 8 housing." Public housing tenants enjoy additional rights, eviction procedures and remedies under the federal law.

Public Offering Statement — A disclosure statement prepared by a developer that contains all material facts about a property offered for sale and that must be provided to a prospective purchaser in accordance with applicable state or federal law. For example, prior to the offering of any interest in a North Carolina residential condominium unit to the public, a declarant must prepare a public offering statement pursuant to N.C. Gen. Stat. § 47C-4-102.

Public Trust Doctrine — A doctrine that requires the State to preserve certain real property, such as the tidelands and beds under navigable waters, for use by and in trust for the general public. Title to public trust property cannot be conveyed to private citizens.

Pur Autre Vie — The traditional common law term for a life estate measured by the life of a person other than the life tenant.

Purchase Contract — An offer to purchase that has been signed by all sellers and buyers and notice of the last offeree's acceptance has been communicated to the last offeror, thereby forming a binding contract. See also *Sales Contract.*

Purchase Money Mortgage (or Purchase Money Deed of Trust) — A mortgage (or deed of trust) given by a buyer to the seller to secure part or all of the purchase price of real estate. The significance of a purchase money mortgage is that, in the event of default and foreclosure of the mortgage, the seller will not be able to sue the buyer for a deficiency judgment under N.C. Gen. Stat. 45-21.38.

Qualifying a Buyer — The process of determining whether or not a buyer of real estate applying for a mortgage loan is qualified under the qualification standards for that loan. Qualification of a buyer-borrower is performed by the lender. See also *Prequalifying a Buyer.*

Quiet Enjoyment — The right of an owner of an interest in land, whether an owner or a tenant, to protection against disturbance or interference with his possession of the land. If a grantee's or lessee's possession is disturbed by one who has superior title to that of a grantor or lessor, the grantee or lessee may sue his grantor or lessor and recover for breach of the covenant of quiet enjoyment in the deed or lease by which the grantee or lessee took his interest.

Quiet Title — A court action brought to establish title and to remove a cloud on the title.

Quitclaim Deed — A deed given when the grantee already has, or claims, complete or partial title to the premises; a deed that transfers any interest the grantor may have in real property, but in which the grantor makes no guarantee as to the quality of the title he transfers.

Racial Steering — An illegal practice under the Federal Fair Housing Act of 1968 and the State Fair Housing Act by which patterns of racial segregation are preserved and encouraged by steering members of racial and ethnic groups to areas occupied primarily by members of their own racial or ethnic group. See also *Steering*.

Rate Cap — A limit on the amount of adjustment that can be made in the interest (note) rate on an adjustable rate mortgage at each rate adjustment date.

Rate Spread Home Loan — A home loan defined in N.C.Gen.Stat. § 24-1.1F(c) that carries interest rates or annual percentage rates at certain percentages above that charged from traditional loans. Lenders who make rate spread home loans are subject to the additional requirements designed to protect consumers.

Ready, Willing, and Able — A self-explanatory phrase referring to a prospective purchaser of real estate who is prepared to purchase a property on terms acceptable to the seller and is in a position, financially and otherwise, to complete the transaction. See also *Procuring Cause*.

Real Estate — See *Real Property*.

Real Estate Commission — The North Carolina state agency charged with the responsibility of administering and enforcing the Real Estate License Law (which includes the Time Share Act). See also *Real Estate License Law* and *Time Share Act*.

Real Estate Investment Trusts (**REITS**) — A legal entity formed by a group of investors who desire to pool their resources for the purpose of real estate investment.

Real Estate License Law — The law enacted by the General Assembly that governs the licensing of real estate brokers, establishes standards of conduct for such licensees, and provides for disciplinary action against licensees who violate its provisions. The enforcing agency is the North Carolina Real Estate Commission.

Real Estate Settlement Procedures Act (**RESPA**) — Consumer protection legislation enacted by Congress requiring lenders to provide borrowers with specified information in residential real estate loan transactions. RESPA also prohibits certain practices in residential real estate closings.

Real Property — Lands, tenements, and hereditaments; the earth's surface, the air above, the ground below and all improvements and appurtenances to the land; the rights, interests, and benefits (sometimes referred to as the "bundle of rights") inherent in the ownership of real property. Synonymous with the terms *real estate* and *realty*.

Realtist — A term used to designate a member of the National Association of Real Estate Brokers.

REALTOR — A coined word owned by the National Association of REALTORS® which is used to designate a member, usually a real estate agent, of that professional trade association. Should not be confused with "real estate agent" because many licensed brokers are not members of the National Association of REALTORS®; however, most licensed real estate agents who are active in the brokerage business on a full-time basis are probably members of this association. See also *National Association of REALTORS®*.

Realty — See *Real Property*.

Reasonable Accommodation — The Fair Housing Act not only prohibits discrimination against a disabled or handicapped tenant, but also requires that the landlord allow requests for reasonable accommodations or modifications necessary to enable the tenant to access and use the rental unit.

Reconciliation — The final step in the appraisal process; the process by which an appraiser reconciles the estimates of value derived through the sales comparison, cost, and income approaches to select a single conclusion of value.

Record Title — The ownership of real estate as shown by the instruments recorded in the office of the Register of Deeds along with records in certain other public offices.

Recordation — See *Recording*.

Recording — The filing or registering of documents affecting title to real estate (and certain other documents) in the proper books in the office of the Register of Deeds of the applicable county so that a public record will be made. Also called *recordation*.

Recording Act — The North Carolina statute, also known as the "Conner Act," is found at §47-18 of the N.C. General Statutes. It requires certain contracts, leases, and deeds to be recorded in order to provide public notice to subsequent persons who deal with the same property and to protect the person who records first.

Rectangular Survey System — See *Government Survey System*.

Redemption — The right that an owner-mortgagor, or one claiming under him, has after defaulting on the mortgage payments to recover back his title to the mortgaged property by paying the mortgage debt, plus interest and any costs accrued, prior to a valid foreclosure. The payment discharges the mortgage and places the title back as it was at the time the mortgage was executed. See also *Equity of Redemption* and *Statutory Redemption Period*.

Redlining — An illegal practice under the Federal Fair Housing Act of 1968 and the State Fair Housing Act by which lending institutions deny or discourage loan applications within a given ("redlined") area based on its racial composition.

Refinance — Paying off an existing mortgage loan with a new loan secured by the same real property. For example, refinancing is attractive to a borrower when a higher interest rate on the original loan can be replaced by new loan at a lower rate.

Reformation — The correction of a deed or other instrument by reason of a mutual mistake of the parties involved or because of mistake of one party caused by the fraud or inequitable conduct of the other party.

Relation Back Doctrine — In escrow closings, a doctrine that treats the deed as having been delivered for certain purposes when it was delivered by the seller into escrow; i.e., the delivery of the deed to the purchaser by the escrow agent "relates back" to the earlier delivery of the deed into escrow by the seller.

Release — The giving up or abandoning of a claim or right to the person against whom the claim exists or against whom the right is to be exercised or enforced.

Release of Contract — A form of discharge of all duties under a contract where each party releases the other from all contractual duties. A release of contract must comply with the requirements for a valid contract.

Reliction — Process of gradual exposure of land by permanent recession of a body of water.

Remainder — An estate in real property to take effect and be enjoyed after another estate has terminated, such as a life estate. The holder of this estate is someone other than the grantor of the life estate and is called the "remainderman."

Remedies for Breach of Contract — If a nonbreaching party elects to sue the breaching party for damages, the most common remedies are money damages, specific performance of the contract, and rescission of the contract. Recall, however, that under the Standard Form 2-T contract, a seller of residential property cannot sue a breaching buyer, but accepts instead the earnest money deposit as liquidated damages.

Renewal of Lease — Unless a lease agreement provides otherwise, a lease terminates automatically at the end of the term. A lease renewal provision allows a lessee the option of renewing, in effect extending, the lease term for an additional period of time.

Rent — Compensation, either in money, provisions, chattels, or labor, received by the owner of real estate from a tenant for his occupancy of the premises.

Rental Agent — A licensed real estate broker who acts on behalf of the property owner to duties related to the rental and management of real property.

Rental Management Company — A company that acts on behalf of the owner of rental property to administer, manage, and preserve the property for the owner's benefit.

Rental Value — The worth of the right to use and occupy property for a stated period; the amount of rent that a reasonable and prudent tenant would be warranted in paying and that a reasonable and prudent lessor would be justified in accepting, for a stated period of time, provided both parties were fully informed and acted voluntarily and intelligently. See also *Market Rent*.

Replacement Cost — The cost of replacing an improvement with another having the same or equal utility, using current standards of material and design, and based on current prices for labor and materials.

Reproduction Cost — The cost of creating an exact replica of an improvement, using the same or very similar materials, based on current prices for labor and materials.

Rescission of Contract — The abrogating or annulling of a contract; the revocation or repealing of a contract by mutual consent of the parties to the contract, or for other cause recognized by law.

Reservation — A right retained or reserved by an owner when he makes a grant of property either by deed or lease.

Residential Rental Agreements Act — A sweeping legislative reform affecting residential tenancies in North Carolina. (The Act begins at Section 42-38 of the North Carolina statutes.) It imposes numerous obligations on landlords and provides tenants with rights and remedies nonexistent under prior law.

Residuary Estate — That which remains of a testator's estate after deducting all devises, bequests, and debts of the decedent.

RESPA — See *Real Estate Settlement Procedures Act.*

Restrictive Covenant — A privately imposed limitation on the use of real property that is imposed by a landowner or developer and set forth in a deed or in a separately recorded declaration. Such covenants constitute an appurtenance to the real property and "run with the land." Also called "protective covenant."

Retaliatory Eviction — Under common law theory, a landlord can evict a tenant for any legal reason, including no reason at all. The doctrine of retaliatory eviction modifies this rule as a matter of public policy by holding that a landlord cannot evict a tenant in retaliation for the tenant's assertion of some legal right (e.g., reporting a building code violation) or engagement in a protected activity. N.C. Gen. Stat. §42-37 adopts this doctrine for residential tenancies.

Revenue Stamps — Obsolete term, as stamps are no longer used. See *Excise Tax on Real Property Transfers.*

Reverse Annuity Mortgage — Instead of a payment plan whereby the debtor finances the purchase of real estate, a reverse annuity mortgage involves payments from the financial institution to a mortgagor who uses the substantial equity in his property as security. Eventually, this type of loan has to be repaid or refinanced.

Reversion — The residual of an estate left to a grantor, to commence possession after the termination of some particular estate granted out by him; the return of land to the grantor and his heirs after the grant is over. In appraising, the anticipated net profit a property owner will receive upon the future sale of his property.

Right of First Opportunity To Purchase — An owner of property is not bound to sell under this agreement; rather, the owner promises that, if he or she ever decides to sell the property, the owner will notify the holder of the right of first opportunity to purchase and offer to sell the property for a designated price. If the holder opts not to purchase, the owner is free to sell to a third person within a specified period of time. If the owner does not sell to a third person, the right of first opportunity to purchase remains valid and the owner cannot sell without once again offering the property for sale to the holder of the right. The holder of this right is most often a lessee.

Right of First Refusal — An owner of property does not bind himself to sell under this agreement; rather, he promises another that, if he decides to sell at some future time, the promisee will receive the first chance to buy or the opportunity to match offers to purchase from third parties. Often included as a provision in leases.

Right of Redemption — See *Equity of Redemption.*

Right of Survivorship — The right of surviving co-tenants to automatically acquire the interest of a deceased co-tenant where two or more were joint or concurrent owners of certain interests in real estate; the most important and distinguishing feature of tenancy by the entirety (spousal ownership) in North Carolina; also present in a joint tenancy, but subject to destruction by a transfer of any individual co-owner's interest.

Right of Way — A right whereby the owner of land has given to another the right to pass over his land, to construct a roadway or use as a roadway, a specific part of his land without actually transferring ownership of the land. A right-of-way also may be a right of one to construct over the land of the owner telephone, telegraph, or electric power lines, or to place underground water mains, gas mains, sewer mains and the like in the lands of the owner. See also *Easement*.

Riparian Owner — One who owns lands bordering upon a river or water course. A riparian owner has peculiar "riparian rights" to water that is on, under, or adjacent to his land.

Riparian Rights — Rights to use water enjoyed by riparian owners.

Risk of Loss — The allocation of loss between seller and purchaser due to damage or destruction of property during the interim period between the signing of a valid real estate sale contract and the closing date. Risk of loss can be specified by contractual agreement. Where the contract is silent, one must refer to the Uniform Vendor and Purchaser Risk Act or the common law.

Rod — A measure of length containing 5 1/2 yards or 16 1/2 feet; also the corresponding square measure.

Run With The Land — A property law term used to describe the rule that a properly created covenant or restriction attaches to the land and benefits or burdens subsequent owners.

Rural Development Loan — A mortgage loan made or guaranteed by the Rural Housing Services Agency of the U. S. Department of Agriculture for low-to moderate-income individuals or families purchasing, repairing or rehabilitating a primary residence in a rural area as defined by agency regulations.

Sale Leaseback — This is a real estate financing technique whereby the seller conveys title to a buyer-investor and at the same time leases the property back under a long-term net lease.

Sales Comparison Approach — An appraisal method or procedure used to estimate the market value of a property by comparison and analysis of the sale prices of other recently sold similar properties. Formerly called *Market Data Approach*.

Sales Contract — An agreement of sale. See also *Purchase Contract*.

Salesperson, Real Estate — The term formerly used to designate a salesperson license. A person employed by a real estate broker to perform, under the broker's supervision, any act authorized to be performed by a broker; one who was formerly licensed as a real estate salesperson by the North Carolina Real Estate Commission. This license category was essentially the same as the current North Carolina license category of "broker on provisional status."

Satisfaction of Mortgage — An instrument or notation on an instrument acknowledging payment of an indebtedness secured by a mortgage.

Scenic Corridor Zones — The designation of a portion of a landowner's real property as subject to development restrictions for the purpose of preserving the natural state of the land.

School of Government — The University of North Carolina School of Government is the leading source of practical articles on all aspects of state and local government, including land use planning and property taxation. The School's webpage is *www.sog.unc.edu.*

Seal — A particular sign or word impressed on a document, made to attest in the most formal manner the execution (signing) of an instrument. Originally, a formal stamp or wax seal impressed at the end of a deed or other important instrument, made to attest in the most form manner the execution (signing) of the document. In most modern documents executed under seal, the formal seal has been replaced by the word " Seal" printed after the signature line.

Secondary Mortgage Market — The term used to describe the "market" wherein various institutions and investors purchase for investment purposes existing mortgages originated by "primary" lenders, thereby creating additional capital with which lenders may originate more new mortgage loans.

Second Mortgage — A junior mortgage that is second in lien priority to a previous first mortgage.

Section 8 Housing — A shorthand term for Section 8 of the Federal Housing Act of 1937 that authorizes payment of rental housing assistance to private landlords who rent to low income tenants. Section 8 Housing may involve some or all rental units in an apartment building.

Section 1031 Exchanges — Section 1031 of the Internal Revenue Code allows property owners to defer taxes on the sale of investment property if they use the proceeds of the sale to purchase like-kind investment property within a specified period of time. See *Like Kind Exchange.*

Security Agreement — An agreement by which a person, usually a lender or seller, takes a security interest in personal property as collateral for a debt. (Examples: agreements in the nature of chattel mortgages or conditional sales contracts.)

Security Deposit — Money or things of value received by or for a property owner to insure payment of rent and/or satisfactory condition of the rented premises upon termination of the written or oral lease.

Security Interest — An interest in property that secures payment or performance of an obligation.

Sedimentation Pollution Control Act — North Carolina legislation requiring a statewide program to control soil erosion and sedimentation.

Seisin — The possession of real estate with the intent on the part of the possessor to claim a freehold estate in the land, either a fee simple or life estate.

Self-Dealing — Improper conduct by a broker who, while employed by a principal, deals with the property for the broker's personal interest or benefit without full disclosure to and consent by the principal. An example of self-dealing is the selling of a property to a broker's relative without disclosure and consent of the principal.

Self-Help Eviction — Occurs when a landlord unlawfully evicts a tenant without complying with the required legal process.

Self-Storage Facility — A facility in which real property is designated and used for the purpose of renting individual storage space to renters who have access to the space to store and remove personal property. *See Article 4, Chapter 44A of the N.C. General Statutes.*

Seller Financing — The financing of the sale of real property by the seller by either taking back a mortgage and note from the buyer or by the contract for deed (installment land contract) method, or other financing techniques.

Senior Mortgage — A mortgage on real property that is higher in priority that any other mortgage; usually the same as the "first mortgage."

Service Animal — Under the Americans with Disabilities Act, a service animal is a dog individually trained to do work or perform tasks for a disabled person. (Miniature horses also qualify in some instances.) Under the ADA, service animals must be allowed to accompany disabled persons in all areas where members of the public are normally allowed to go. The ADA definition of "service animal" is more narrow that the Fair Housing Act definition of "assistance animal."

Servient Estate — A parcel of land that is burdened by an easement for the benefit of another parcel of land (the dominant estate).

Setback — The distance from a curb or other established line within which no buildings may be erected. A "setback ordinance" prohibits erection of buildings or structures beyond defined setback lines.

Settlement — See *Closing.*

Severalty Ownership — Sole ownership where real property is owned by only one person. There is no one else who can sever the individual's ownership interest in the real property.

Severance Damage — The impairment in value caused by separation; commonly, the damage resulting from the taking of a fraction of the whole property, reflected in a lowered utility and value in the land remaining.

Sexual Harassment — The unsolicited overt requests or demands for sexual acts when (i) submission to such conduct is made a term of the execution or continuation of the lease agreement, or (ii) submission to or rejection of such conduct by an individual is used to determine whether rights under the lease are accorded.

Shared Appreciation Loan — A mortgage loan plan that requires the borrower to pay to the lender a share of the appreciated value of the property after a certain period of time. In return, the borrower obtains a lower interest rate.

Sheriff's Deed — A deed given by a sheriff conveying title to real property pursuant to an execution sale to satisfy a judgment against a judgment debtor who is a property owner.

Short Sale — A sale of mortgaged real property where the proceeds from the sale are insufficient to fully pay the outstanding balance on the seller's existing mortgage loan.

Simple Interest — Interest computed based on the remaining principal balance of a loan. Previously earned but unpaid interest is not included in the computation. Most mortgage loans are simple interest loans.

Small Claim Action — The procedure by which a complaint for summary ejectment is brought and by which most tenants are evicted.

Smoke and Carbon Monoxide Alarms — Safety requirements of the N.C. Residential Rental Agreements Act. Landlords are required to provide an operable smoke alarm in each residential unit and one operable carbon monoxide alarm per rental unit per level. Other statutory requirements detail the duties of both c

Soil Suitability Test — The test to determine if soil will absorb and drain water sufficiently for use of a septic tank. Former term used to describe this test in North Carolina is "percolation test," or "perc test," which is officially obsolete, but still commonly encountered in practice.

Special Agent — An agent who is authorized to perform a specified act or series of specified acts in accordance with detailed instructions. A real estate sales agent is usually a special agent.

Special Assessment — A legal charge against real estate by a public authority to pay the cost of public improvements, such as for the opening, grading, and guttering of streets, the construction of sidewalks and sewers, the installation of street lighting, and the like.

Special Purpose Deeds — Specialized forms of deeds used in connection with specific fact situations, court proceedings, or matters requiring a deed from a person acting in an official capacity.

Special Use Permit — A zoning procedure that allows a property owner to make a certain use of the property if certain stated conditions are met. It is sometimes called a *conditional use permit.*

Special Warranty Deed — A deed in which the grantor warrants and guarantees to his grantee that the title he conveys is free from defects or encumbrances that have arisen since the grantor acquired title; a warranty only against defects or encumbrances that have occurred "by, through, or under the grantor."

Specific Lien — A lien filed against a particular parcel of property. Compare *General Lien.*

Specific Performance — A remedy in a court of equity whereby the defendant may be compelled to do whatever he has agreed to do in a contract executed by him. Because all land is considered unique, this remedy often is applied in real estate law to enable a buyer to force a defaulting seller to transfer the specific real estate that is the subject of a sales contract rather than be compensated in money damages for the seller's breach.

Spot Zoning — The singling out of a parcel of land for either special or more restrictive treatment inconsistent with the zone in which the parcel is located. Spot zoning may or may not be legal in North Carolina, depending upon whether the use in question was shown to have a reasonable basis.

State Fair Housing Act — The law enacted by the North Carolina General Assembly that prohibits discrimination based on race, color, religion, sex, national origin, handicap or familial status in the sale, rental, or financing of housing. See also *Fair Housing Act of* 1968.

Statute — A law established by act of the legislative power; an act of the legislature; the written will of the legislature solemnly expressed according to the forms necessary to constitute it the law of the state of North Carolina.

Statute of Frauds — State law that provides that certain contracts, including contracts for the sale of real estate, must be in writing in order to be enforceable at law.

Statute of Limitations — Statutes declaring that no lawsuit shall be maintained on certain expressed causes of action unless they are initiated/filed within a specified period after the right accrued.

Statutory Duties/Residential Rentals — Duties of both landlord and tenant specified in detail under the N.C. Residential Rental Agreements. Act is a two-way street that places specific obligations and duties on tenants as well as on landlords.

Statutory Redemption Period — The statutory equivalent to the debtor's equity of redemption, the statutory redemption period is a grace period granted to a defaulting mortgagor to recover his title to the mortgaged property, even though the debt is past due, by paying to the obligee the principal, accrued interest and costs incurred up to the time of foreclosure sale or upset bid periods, as the case may be.

Steering — The illegal practice of guiding prospective real estate buyers or renters of a fair housing protected class to areas occupied mainly by members of the prospect's protected class and away from areas occupied by others not in the prospect's protected class.

Strict Foreclosure — A common law method of foreclosure not available to a mortgage lender in North Carolina in which the mortgaged real property vests in the mortgagee if the mortgage fails to cure a default. Strict foreclosure is a possible remedy in some contract for deed (land contract) transactions.

Subagent — An agent of an agent; one employed or authorized by an agent to perform part or all of the agent's duties on behalf of the agent in a real estate sales transaction.

Subcontractor — A contractor who contracts with a general or prime contractor to perform labor at or furnish materials to a construction site. A subcontractor is entitled to obtain a statutory lien against the real property if he has not been paid for his services.

Subdivision — (a) All divisions of a tract or parcel of land into two or more lots, building sites, or other divisions for the purpose of sale or building development (whether immediate or future) and includes all division of land involving the dedication of a new street or a change in existing streets. (b) A cluster of homes developed as a planned community.

Subdivision Plat — A map of a subdivision. (In some instances, various public officials must review it and give their approval before it can be accepted for recordation by the Register of Deeds.)

Subjacent Support — The right of a land owner to have his land supported from below when another owns or has the right to mine the land's subsurface. See also *Lateral Support*.

Subject — With regard to an appraisal, comparative market analysis, or broker price opinion the property for which an estimate of value or probable selling or leasing price is sought.

Subject to Mortgage — A term or phrase referring to the taking of title to mortgaged property by a grantee-purchaser, wherein he is not responsible to the holder of the promissory note for the payment of any portion of the amount due. In the event of foreclosure, the most that he can lose is his equity in the property. The original maker of the note (i.e., the seller-grantor) is not released from his responsibility.

Sublease — An agreement whereby a person who has leased land from the owner rents out all or a portion of the premises for a period ending prior to the expiration of the original lease.

Sublessee — A tenant who rents property from the original tenant (sublessor) under a sublease, or separate rental agreement apart from the original lease between the sublessor and the landlord.

Sublessor — The lessee under the original lease with a property owner who sublets (subleases) to another party, known as the sublessee, under a document separate from the original lease.

Subordination — A mortgagee, lessee, lien holder, or owner of some other right in real property may alter the relative priority of his or her interest by an agreement to relinquish that interest to benefit another. For example, a "first" mortgage can be subordinated to a "second" mortgage, in which case the relative priorities between the two are reversed.

Subordinated Ground Lease — A ground lease in which the lessor has agreed to subordinate his title in the land to a mortgage or deed of trust subsequently executed by the ground lessee.

Subprime Loan — A "nonconforming" mortgage loan that is not made in conformance with "Fannie Mae" and "Freddie Mac" underwriting guidelines, that is typically made to a borrower with a poor credit history and/or limited assets and that usually involves a considerably higher credit risk for lenders (as well as investors who may purchase such a loan through the secondary mortgage market) than is the case with a "conventional conforming" loan or a loan insured or guaranteed by a government agency.

Subsequent Modifications/Contract — An agreement by both contracting parties modifying the terms of their original understanding. Since both parties are in agreement, a subsequent modification can be accomplished even though the original contract states that it cannot be thereafter altered or modified.

Subsurface Rights — A landowner's right of ownership to minerals and water beneath the surface of land. The rights to these materials can be conveyed separately without conveying full ownership of the land.

Surety — One who guarantees the performance of another.

Surrender — A voluntary termination of a lease by agreement of the landlord and tenant prior to the normal expiration date.

Survey — The process by which the quantity and boundaries of a piece of land are ascertained; the statement of the courses, distances, and quantity of land is also called a survey. A survey also may include grades, contours, structures, or other physical features affecting the land.

Surveyor's Compass — A compass used in describing metes and bounds descriptions by reference to directions given in terms of deviation from north and south.

Survivorship — The distinguishing feature of a tenancy by the entirety, by which, on the death of one spouse, the surviving spouse automatically acquires full ownership by operation of law.

Syndication — A group of investors who combine to pursue a specific goal of investment in real estate.

Takeout Commitment — A commitment by a lender to grant a "takeout" or long term loan to a developer when construction of a project is completed.

Takeout Loan — A long-term ("permanent") loan promised by a lender to a developer upon completion of construction to replace an interim construction loan.

Tax — A charge or burden, usually pecuniary, laid upon persons or property for public purposes; a forced contribution of wealth to meet the public needs of a government.

Tax Deed — A deed given where property has been purchased at public sale because of the owner's nonpayment of taxes.

Tax Lien — A statutory lien against the property of a party who has failed to pay his taxes. Tax liens may be specific liens against specific property, as with property tax or special assessment liens, or may be general liens against all property of the defaulting taxpayer, as with federal or state income tax liens.

Tax Rate — The amount of tax imposed on personal or corporate income, capital gains, gifts, sales, etc.

Tax Sale — A sale of property for nonpayment of taxes assessed against it.

Tax Value/Property Tax — The assessed value of property established for *ad valorem* tax purposes is often referred to as the "tax value."

Taxing Unit/Property Tax — Cities and counties authorized to collect property taxes.

Tenancy at Will — See *Estate at Will.*

Tenancy by the Entirety — A form of joint tenancy held only by husbands and wives in which each spouse (tenant) holds an equal, undivided interest in the whole property. The most important characteristic of a tenancy by the entirety is the right of survivorship which exists in behalf of each tenant (spouse); upon the death of one spouse, the surviving spouse automatically acquires ownership in severalty of the entire property without the need for probate.

Tenancy for Years — See *Estate for Years.*

Tenancy in Common — A form of concurrent ownership of real property by two or more persons. Each tenant in common is the owner of an undivided, fractional interest in the whole property. The estate or interests of tenants in common need not be identical or equal; upon the death of a tenant in common his undivided interest descends to his heirs and there is no right of survivorship in the other co-tenants.

Tenancy in Severalty Ownership — Property owned by one person alone. See also *Severalty Ownership.*

Tenancy of Sufferance — See *Estate at Sufferance.*

Tenant — Technically, one who holds any estate in property, whether freehold or less than freehold. In a popular sense and as most commonly used, a "tenant" is one who, under a lease, has the temporary use and occupation of lands or tenements that belong to another; a *lessee.*

Tenant Security Deposit — See *Security Deposit.*

Tenant Security Deposit Act — Residential tenants are entitled to certain protections with respect to security deposits under this Act (N.C. Gen. Stat. Sections 42-50 through 42-55). These protections include limitations on the amount of the security deposit, standards regarding refund, and other requirements with which a landlord must comply.

Tenements — A common law term that signifies anything that was the subject of tenure at common law and includes "lands" as well as certain intangible rights, such as easements, issuing out of or annexed to lands.

Termination of Contract Offers — An offer made under contract law terminates in a number of ways, including receipt of a counteroffer or conditional acceptance of the offer, or rejection of the offer.

Termite Inspection Report — See *Wood-Destroying Insect Inspection Report.*

Term Loan — A loan, often used for construction financing, that involves no amortization of principal. Interest is paid on the full principal sum during the entire loan period, and principal is payable in full at the end of the loan period.

Testate — The condition of one who leaves a valid will at his death.

Timber Deed — A deed that conveys the right to harvest standing timber.

Time Is of the Essence — A phrase meaning that time is of crucial and vital importance and that failure to meet time deadlines will be considered a failure to perform the contract.

Time Share — Under the North Carolina Time Share Act, a time share is "....a right to occupy a unit or any of several units during five or more separated time periods over a period of at least five years, including renewal options, whether or not coupled with a freehold estate or an estate for years in a time share project or a specified portion thereof." A time share includes a vacation lease, prepaid hotel reservation, club membership, limited partnership, vacation bond or a plan where the right to use a unit for periods of time is awarded on the basis of points, vouchers, split, divided or floating use.

Time Share Act — The North Carolina law that governs the registration of time share projects, the licensing of time share salespersons, establishes standards of conduct for time share developers and salespersons, provides for certain consumer rights, and provides for disciplinary action against developers and salespersons who violate its provisions. See N.C. Gen. Stat. §93A-39 through §93A-59. The enforcing agency is the North Carolina Real Estate Commission. See also *Time Share.*

Timesharing — A concept utilized chiefly in resort developments whereby a purchaser receives ownership of or the right to use a physical area for a limited segment of time each year. See also *Time Share.*

Title — In relation to real estate, title is the sum, the union of, all elements and facts on which ownership is founded, or by which ownership is proved.

Title Assurance — The various ways by which purchasers, lenders, and others dealing with real property ascertain whether a seller or owner has title, determine the quality of title, and protect title.

Title Examination — A search conducted by a licensed attorney to ascertain the status of title to real property; accomplished by searching the public records.

Title Insurance — A policy of insurance whereby a title insurance company agrees to indemnify the holder of an interest in real property for any loss sustained as a result of defects in the title. Policies of title insurance frequently except from their coverage and do not insure against certain types of defects, restrictions, liens, and encumbrances.

Title Theory — The theory underlying the method of pledging real estate as collateral for a loan that provides for the borrower to convey legal title to real property to a trustee to hold for the benefit of the lender until the loan is paid. The borrower holds equitable title to the property. The legal instrument used to accomplish the transfer of legal title is a "deed of trust." See also *Lien Theory* and *Intermediate Theory.*

Torrens System — A rarely used system of land registration authorized by the North Carolina General Statutes, Chapter 43.

Tort — A wrongful act, injury, or violation of legal right to the person or property of another.

Total Circumstances Test — Legal test to determine whether items of personal property affixed to real property are fixtures and thus a part of the real estate; the factors to be examined are the intention of the annexor, character of the annexation, adaptability of item to use of the land, and relationship of annexor to the real property.

Townhouse — A unit in a non-vertically attached, multi-unit complex where the owner of the unit owns in severalty both the unit (including the entire physical structure) and the land on which the unit rests. The common areas are owned by the unit owners' association. A secondary meaning refers to a style of construction, that being a multi-level unit in a multi-unit residential complex, as distinguished from a single-level ("garden") style of unit in such complexes. Compare *Condominium.*

Trade Fixture — A fixture attached to realty by a tenant under a commercial lease to further his business. In most cases, trade fixtures are removable by the tenant at the end of his lease. See also *Fixture.*

Transfer Fee Covenants — A fee or charge payable upon the transfer of an interest in real property imposed by a covenant. With a few exceptions, private transfer fees are prohibited. N.C.Gen.Stat. §§ 39A-1, 39A-2, & 39A-3.

Trust — A relationship under which one person {called the trustee) holds legal title to property for the benefit of another person (called the *cestui que trust* or "trust beneficiary").

Trust Account — A demand deposit account maintained by a broker at a federally insured depository institution lawfully doing business in North Carolina for the purpose of holding trust funds received on behalf of or from the broker's principal or other persons. Also called an *escrow account*.

Trust Funds — Funds of others which are received by or entrusted to a real estate agent in connection with a real estate transaction (e.g., earnest money, down payments, tenant security deposits, and rents).

Trustee — A person in whom some estate, interest, or power in or affecting property of any description is vested for the benefit of another.

Trustee's Deed — A conveyance of property by a trustee under a deed of trust who has completed foreclosure proceedings.

Truth-in-Lending Act — A federal law which requires lenders or "arrangers of credit" to disclose various information concerning the cost of credit to borrowers or customers in connection with consumer loans, including real estate loans that are not made for business, commercial or agricultural purposes.

Unapproved Subdivision — A subdivision developed without proper subdivision approval.

Underimprovement — An improvement that is not the highest and best use for the site on which it is placed due to deficient size or cost.

Underwriting — With regard to mortgage lending, the process of analyzing the risk associated with a particular loan or type of loan. With regard to insurance, the process of analyzing and rating the risk associated with a particular policy or type of insurance.

Undivided Ownership — Ownership of a fractional interest (such as one-third, one-quarter, or one-half) in specific property by sharing possession of the whole (undivided) property with one or more other owners. For example, tenants in common have undivided ownership in North Carolina. If Erin and Tracy own equal interests in a tract of land as tenants in common, each owns an undivided one-half share in the whole tract.

Undue Influence — The improper influence over the mind and will of another to such an extent that the grantor does not act freely in signing the deed, but signs it because of a third person who is exerting excessive influence.

Unfair or Deceptive Trade Practices Act — Under N.C. Gen. Stat. §75-1.1, certain unfair or deceptive practices in a trade or business are prohibited. Prohibitions include the rendering of a misleading opinion or false inducement, failure to disclose a material fact, engaging in misleading advertising, and misrepresenting the nature or extent of a guarantee or warranty. Real estate brokers and salespersons are subject to the provisions of this statute.

Unified Development Ordinance — A comprehensive document that combines multiple ordinances, regulations, and standards relating to and regulating land development.

Uniform Commercial Code — A set of uniform laws adopted in almost all of the United States governing dealings in commercial matters. Matters relating to banking transactions, sales of goods, and numerous other commercial topics are covered. Real estate brokers will cross paths most frequently with the U.C.C. in the area of security agreements affecting fixtures.

Uniform Electronic Transactions Act (**UETA**) — The common name for the Uniform Electronic Transactions Act, located at Article 40, Chapter 66 of the North Carolina General Statutes. This legislation validates electronic contracts, other documents and signatures and provides that they will not be denied validity and enforceability solely because they are in electronic form. See also *E-Sign.*

Uniform Property Electronic Recording Act (URPERA) — Legislation authorizing the electronic recording of documents.

Uniform Residential Appraisal Report (**URAR**) — A widely used standardized form for presenting an appraisal of residential property. The form was created jointly by the Federal National Mortgage Corporation and the Federal Home Loan Mortgage Corporation and is now used additionally by the U.S. Department of Housing and Urban Development, the Veterans Administration, and the Farmers Home Administration.

Uniform Vendor and Purchaser Risk Act — A statute adopted in North Carolina (N.C. Gen. Stat. §39-39) that allocates the risk of loss between seller and buyer under an executory sales contract where the contract is silent on the subject. If, for example, the building should be destroyed by fire prior to the closing date, this statute would govern in the absence of a contractual provision on the subject.

Unilateral Contract — A contract under which one party promises to perform a specified act without receiving in return any express promise of performance by the other party; a contract whereby Party X promises to perform (e.g., pay some valuable consideration) upon the performance of some act by Party Y; in such case, Party X is obligated to perform (pay) only if Party Y actually performs the act called for in the contract, and Party Y has no obligation to perform.

Unilateral Rent Withholding — The N.C. Residential Rental Agreement Act provides that *a tenant may not unilaterally withhold rent prior to a court's determination that they have a right to do so.* A residential tenant's failure to pay rent because of inability to do so does not constitute unilateral rent withholding under the Act.

Unimproved Land — Land that is vacant or lacking improvements; undeveloped land.

Unit Ownership — A legal term used to describe ownership in a condominium unit.

Unity of Person — The requirement that only a husband and wife can hold property as tenants by the entirety, based on the fiction that they are one person.

Unity of Possession — An incident of all forms of concurrent ownership that gives each cotenant the equal right to possess the entire property.

Universal Agent — An agent who is authorized to transact all of the principal's business of every kind.

Upfitting Improvements — The providing of improvements to a commercial property by the lessor at the lessor's expense, usually at the request of a planned new tenant.

Upset Bid Period — A period often days that runs from the day of a foreclosure by sale of a deed of trust during which an upset bidder can submit a higher bid than the high bid received at the sale. See N.C. Gen. Stat. § 45-21.27 (2001).

Useful Life — See *Economic Life.*

Usury — The lending, or practice of lending, money at a rate of interest above the maximum legal rate prescribed by North Carolina law.

Vacancy and Collection Loss — The loss in potential rental income due to vacancies and the inability to collect rent due from tenants.

Vacation Leases or Licenses — A form of time share whereby resort property is leased (or obtained under a license) for a limited segment of time during each year and for the duration of a certain number of years. See also *Time Share.*

Vacation Rental Act — An act that governs all major aspects of the vacation rental business. The requirements of the Act are located in Chapter 42A of the N.C. General Statutes.

Vacation Rental — Under the Vacation Rental Act, "the rental of residential property for vacation, leisure, or recreation purposes for fewer than 90 days by a person who has a place of permanent residence to which he or she intends to return."

Valid — Having force, or binding force; legally sufficient and authorized by law.

Valuation — An estimate or opinion of value, normally market value. Also, the process of deriving a conclusion as to value. See also *Appraisal.*

Value — The quantity of one commodity that can be obtained in exchange for another ("value-in-exchange"); also, the utility or usefulness of a commodity ("value-in-use"). As applied to property, the present worth, usually expressed in terms of money, of all rights to future benefits arising from ownership.

VA Mortgage Loan — A mortgage loan guaranteed by the Veterans Administration.

Variable Rate Mortgage — A mortgage loan under which the lender may increase or decrease the interest rate periodically during the life of the loan in accordance with certain predetermined factors or indices. Also called *Adjustable Rate Mortgage.*

Variance — An exception to a zoning ordinance which may be granted by the governmental zoning authority authorizing a property use which is prohibited under the zoning ordinance.

Vendee — A purchaser; a buyer; the person to whom a thing is rendered or sold.

Vendor — A seller; the person who disposes of a thing for a consideration.

Veterans Administration (**VA**) — The federal agency that administers a wide range of programs, including housing programs, for the benefit of military veterans.

Victim Protection Laws — North Carolina laws providing special protection to a "protected tenant." *See "Protected Tenant."*

Visible Easements Doctrine — A doctrine stating that a purchaser of real estate takes title subject to certain visible easements even though the written sales contract and deed do not except the visible easement from the warranties of title.

Void — That which is unenforceable; having nor force or effect.

Void Contract — An agreement that is treated as a complete nullity by the law.

Voidable — That which is capable of being adjudged void, but is not void unless action is taken to make it so.

Voidable Contract — A contract with a defect that can be raised by one of the parties in order to avoid performance. If the defect is not raised, the contract is valid and enforceable.

Voluntary Alienation — A voluntary transfer of ownership of real property to another, usually by deed. Distinguish from *Involuntary Alienation.*

Waiver — A legal term signifying that a party has given up legal rights he would otherwise have; the renunciation, or surrender of some claim, right, or privilege.

Warranty Deed — A deed that transfers ownership of real property and in which the grantor guarantees that his title is free and clear of all encumbrances. Term normally used to refer to a *General Warranty Deed.*

Waste — A destruction or material alteration or deterioration of the land or buildings thereon done or permitted by any person in rightful possession to the lasting injury of the interest of the owner of the fee simple title, reversioner, or remainderman.

Wastewater Systems — State statutes and regulations that prove standards and rules for the treatment and disposal of wastewater. Buildings with water-using fixtures must discharge all wastewater directly to an approved wastewater system.

Water Rights — Property rights incident to the ownership of land whereby one is entitled to rights to a supply of water. See also *Riparian Rights.*

Waterway Vegetation Buffer Zones — Laws, regulations and zoning ordinances that require a buffer zone of undisturbed vegetation along some river basins and coastal waterways.

Will — A written document which, when properly executed, signed, and witnessed, is effective at the death of the maker to dispose of his property according to the terms of the document.

Willful Misrepresentation — (a) The intentional misrepresentation of a material fact by a party with "actual knowledge" of the truth of the matter being misrepresented; (b) The misrepresentation of a material fact by a party who does *not* have actual knowledge of the fact being represented, but who acts "without regard for the actual truth of the matter."

Willful Omission — The intentional failure to disclose a material fact about which a party has actual knowledge.

With Recourse Note — The most common promissory note in which the signer of the note is personally liable for repayment of the loan. Compare with a Nonrecourse Note under which the borrower is not personally liable for the underlying debt.

Wood-Destroying Insect Inspection Report — A report provided by a licensed pest control operator indicating that an improved property has been inspected and reporting any visible evidence of infestation and structural damage by various wood-destroying insects (including termites), as well as conditions conducive to such pests. Sometimes referred to by the old term "termite inspection report" or by the term "pest inspection report."

Wraparound Mortgage — A second junior mortgage in which the secured indebtedness (face amount of second mortgage note) is the sum of the new financing desired plus the principal balance due on the first mortgage. Such a second mortgage is thus said to "wrap around" the first mortgage. The mortgagee under the second (wraparound) mortgage may be either the first mortgage lender-mortgagee or a third party lender (usually the latter). In any event, the mortgagor under the first mortgage remains liable for the debt secured by that mortgage, even if the new second mortgagee makes the payments on the first mortgage out of the payments received on the second (wraparound) mortgage.

Yield — The return or profit on an investment. When expressed as a percentage of the amount invested, the yield is the "rate of return."

Yield Capitalization — A collective term used to describe various methods of estimating the present value of a property by discounting future benefits (cash flows plus reversion) to the property using an appropriate yield rate. Also known as "discounted cash flow analysis" or "annuity capitalization". See also *Direct Capitalization, Capitalization, Capitalization Rate,* and *Income Capitalization Approach.*

Yield Spread Premium — A fee, usually expressed as a percentage of the loan amount, paid to a mortgage broker by a lender when the mortgage broker places a loan with the lender at an "above-market" interest rate and charges the borrower either no origination fee or a lower-than-normal origination fee. The loan's higher interest rate will produce an increased yield to the lender and investor, thereby enabling the lender to compensate the mortgage broker for the loss of income from origination fees not paid upfront by the borrower.

Zoning — A process that allocates and prescribes permitted uses of land in various areas of a city or county by dividing the land within a particular governmental entity into districts or "zones" and then specifying what uses of the land are permitted and which ones are prohibited in each zone.

Zoning Map — An official map of a city or county displaying the various zoning districts.

Zoning Ordinance — A local ordinance exercising the police power of a municipal corporation or county that divides land into use classifications by zone or area and also usually regulates lot size and the placement, bulk, and height of structures.

APPENDIX C
FAIR HOUSING AND LICENSE LAW
CASE STUDIES RESULTS

FAIR HOUSING CASE STUDIES

Presented below are the analyses and query answers for each of the ten Fair Housing case studies in Chapter 18.

Case Study 1. Post-traumatic stress disorder is clearly a disability under the Fair Housing Act. The assumption in this case study is that the unit owner has substantiated the psychiatric disability and that the presence of a trained dog will not constitute and undue burden on the condominium association and other unit owners. The prior condominium board exception for a seeing-eye dog is irrelevant to this case study. The unit owner must prevail on the legitimacy of his or her disability and the need for a service dog. Will the "no-pets" policy become meaningless? This assumes that frivolous or weak claims for psychiatric service dogs (or cats) will have to be accommodated. That is not required under the Act. The Fair Housing Act's prohibition of discrimination against persons with disabilities is clearly not limited to physical disabilities. The correct answer is A.

Case Study 2. A person claiming failure of a landlord to reasonably accommodate is required by law to substantiate the existence of a handicap or disability as a prerequisite to receiving a reasonable accommodation under the Fair Housing Act. While a state-issued automobile handicap sticker or placard is some evidence of a handicap or disability, it is reasonable to request direct information from the tenant's doctor. There is also evidence of abuse and misuse of these stickers or placards by at least some users. The provision of other handicap parking space areas by the landlord is some evidence of the reasonable accommodation of all handicapped tenants and guest, but would not be conclusive if the tenant had a handicap or disability requiring a reserved parking space very close to the tenant's apartment. The correct answer is C.

Case Study 3. The tenant is clearly entitled to widen the doorways at the tenant's expense. A more challenging issue is whether the tenant must then pay to narrow the doorways at the end of the tenancy. HUD regulation, 24 C.F.R. § 100.203(a) reads in part: "the landlord may, *where it is reasonable to do so*, condition permission for a modification on the renter agreeing to restore the interior of the premises to the condition that existed before the modification ..." (*Emphasis added*) Example (2) following this section of the federal regulations provides, in part: "Further, the landlord may *not*, in usual circumstances, condition permission for the modification on the applicant paying for the doorway to be narrowed at the end of the lease because a wider doorway will not interfere with the landlord's or the next tenant's use and enjoyment of the premises." The modification of the doorways is at the tenant's, not the landlord's, expense. The temporary nature of the child's disability is irrelevant in this example. The correct answer is A.

Case Study 4. HUD regulation, 24 C.F.R. § 100.20(b) notes that the protections against discrimination based on "familial status" apply to any person who is pregnant. An occupancy limit prohibiting one infant in an efficiency apartment is per se unreasonable. Pregnancy is not a handicap or disability. The correct answer is B.

Case Study 5. HUD regulation, 24 C.F.R. § 100.50(b)(4) lists the following as a prohibited practice: "(4) Make, print or publish, or cause to be made, printed or published, any notice, statement or advertisement with respect to the sale or rental of a dwelling that indicates any preference, limitation or discrimination because of race, color, religion, sex, handicap, familial status, or national origin, or an intention to make any such preference, limitation or discrimination." The owner-occupied exemption under the Act does not permit discriminatory advertising. While perhaps a close question, the Craigslist posting, taken as a whole, sends a subtle but clear message that certain applicants for the unit may be excluded from consideration. A combination of the word "mature" with a requirement of pictures of any children sends a screening message. Actual subject intent to discriminate is not necessary. Rental to a Caucasian man is not proof of a violation of the Act; rather, it is the discriminatory posting that provides reasonable cause to believe that illegal discrimination has occurred. The correct answer is B.

Case Study 6. The sale of a single family home is exempt from coverage under the Fair Housing Act (except for the prohibition against discriminatory advertising), but the exemption does not apply unless the house is being sold "without the use of a real estate broker, agent or provisional broker." HUD regulation 24 C.F.R. § 100.10(c)(1)(ii). The correct answer is D.

Case Study 7. HUD regulation 24 C.F.R. § 100.65(b)(3) lists the following prohibited act: "(3) Failing to process an offer for the sale or rental of a dwelling ..." The broker's failure to process the offer of the African American couple the same way that any offer would be processed provides reasonable cause to believe that the Act has been violated. The fact that, by happenstance, the seller then received a higher offer is irrelevant. The Act has been violated by the broker. The correct answer is A.

Case Study 8. HUD regulation, 24 C.F.R. § 100.50(b)(4) lists the following as a prohibited practice: "(4) Make, print or publish, or cause to be made, printed or published, any notice, statement or advertisement with respect to the sale or rental of a dwelling that indicates any preference, limitation or discrimination because of race, color, religion, sex, handicap, familial status, or national origin, or an intention to make any such preference, limitation or discrimination." Indications of a preference or discrimination are not limited to the direct, obvious publications or notices; indeed, that would be extremely rare. There is no requirement under the Act that the complainant prove a subjective intent or motive to discriminate. It is the publication itself that violates the Act. The correct answer is A.

Case Study 9. There is no discrimination based on familial status (families with children), because the students are adults. The Fair Housing Act does not have a category of protected groups based on age. While Answer C might provide a business justification for the owner's dislike of college student renters, the correct answer is D. There is no "college students" category of protected persons under the Act.

Case Study 10. Is there reasonable cause to believe that the Fair Housing Act has been violated? More statistical proof would be needed to verify whether African Americans as a group are being discriminated against on a disparate impact theory. The fact that some African American couples receive loans does not preclude the likely possibility that the couple in this question were discriminated against because of race. An intent to discriminate is not necessary. The correct answer is B.

LICENSE LAW CASE STUDIES RESULTS

Shown below are the subsections of G.S. 93A-6 and the Commission rules which were violated in each of the cases summarized in Chapter 20, as well as the resulting initial disciplinary action. Note that more than one act may have violated a particular subsection of G.S. 93A-6, but the subsection will only be listed once. For example, each of two or three different things a broker did may constitute incompetent or unworthy conduct of a broker under G.S. 93A-6(a)(8), but the subsection will only be listed once below.

Case #1: G.S. 93A-6(a)(8), (10), and (13); Commission Rules A.0106, A.0107, and A.0111. Reprimand.

Case #2: G.S. 93A-6(a)(15) and 93A-1; Commission Rule A.0502. Suspended suspension for one year, reduced to reprimand if conditions satisfied.

Case #3: G.S. 93A-6(a)(1), (5) and (15); Commission Rule A.0506. Suspension, stayed subject to conditions; one year probation.

Case #4: G.S. 93A-6(a)(8), (15) and (b)(5); Commission Rules A.0104 and A.0113. One year suspension, 6 months active, balance could be stayed subject to conditions.

Case #5: G.S. 93A-6(a)(1), (3), (8), (10), and (15); Commission Rule A.0104(a), (c) and (f). 90 day suspension, 30 active, balance stayed subject to conditions; 1 year probation.

Case #6: G.S. 93A-6(a)(1). Reprimand as to both brokers.

Case #7: G.S. 93A-6(a)(1). 60 day suspension, subject to conditions.

Case #8: Provisional broker: G.S. 93A-6(a)(1), (8), (10), and (14). Broker/Appraiser: G.S. 93A-6(a)(1), (8) and (10). Broker/Appraiser's Real Estate Company: G.S. 93A-6(a)(1), (8) and (10). Licenses revoked for all three.

Case #9: As to broker-bookkeeper: G.S. 93A-6(a)(15) and Commission Rule A.0107(j). Permanently revoked. As to broker-in-charge: G.S. 93A-6(a)(1), (3), (7), (8), (10) and (15); Commission Rule A.0107(j). Revoked.

Case #10 *Listing company and listing broker:* both <u>reprimanded</u>. <u>Dismissed</u> as to buyer/dual agent.

Case #11 *BIC:* Reprimand, but <u>dismissed</u> if offers training session for associates re: pulling septic permits for listings. BIC held the required training so the <u>case was dismissed as to all agents and the company</u> and no names were published in the *Bulletin*. Why might this outcome have been different than that in Cases #10 where names were published in the *Bulletin*?

Case #12 *Listing Broker/dual agent:* 6 month suspension, stayed and converted to <u>6 month probation</u> if completes 1 required CE course by certain date. *Listing Company:* Closed.

Case #13 *Broker #1:* 3 month suspension, reduced to <u>reprimand</u> if takes specified CE by certain date. *Broker #2 and Listing Company:* Close and warn to discover and disclose material facts.

Case #14 *BIC and Company:* closed, but warned to educate associates regarding the need to disclose the potential risks and costs of USTs. *Broker/buyer agent:* <u>revoked</u>; cannot apply to reinstate prior to March 2017

Case #15 *Listing Broker:* 3 month active suspension, reduced to <u>reprimand</u> if completes 2 specified CE courses prior to certain date. *BIC & Listing Company:* Closed and warned to keep required transaction records.

Case #16 *QB/BIC and her Company:* both individual and firm licenses were permanently revoked. [Note: the QB/BIC failed to appear and defend herself at the hearing called by the Commission, despite notice of the hearing.]

Case #17: G.S. 93A-6(a)(1), (2), (3), (7), (8), (10), (12), (13) and (15); Commission Rules A.0104(a) and (b), A.0105(c)(2), A.0106, A.0107(d), (e), (f), and (g), A.0108, and A.0110(a)(3), (4) and (5). Revoked.

Index